Irene C. Fountas

Gay Su Pinnell

Guiding Readers and Writers

[Grades 3–6]

TEACHING

COMPREHENSION,

GENRE, AND

CONTENT LITERACY

HEINEMANN
Portsmouth, NH

We dedicate this book to our dear friend and mentor,
Martha L. King, whose foundational work in language
and literacy has made a profound difference in the
education of teachers and children.

Heinemann
A division of Reed Elsevier Inc.
361 Hanover Street
Portsmouth, NH 03801–3912
www.heinemann.com

Offices and agents throughout the world

© 2001 by Irene C. Fountas and Gay Su Pinnell.

The author and publisher wish to thank those who have generously given permission to reprint borrowed material:

"Shells" reprinted with the permission of Simon & Schuster Books for Young Readers, an imprint of Simon & Schuster Children's Publishing Division, from *Every Living Thing* by Cynthia Rylant. Copyright © 1985 by Cynthia Rylant.

Richard C. Anderson, P.T. Wilson, and L.G. Fielding, "Growth in Reading and How Children Spend Their Time Outside of School," 1988. *Reading Research Quarterly*, 23(3), pp. 285-303. Reprinted by permission of International Reading Association and Richard C. Anderson.

Excerpt from *Guests* by Michael Dorris. Copyright © 1994 by the estate of Michael Dorris. Reprinted by permission of Hyperion Books for Children.

Pages from "Keeping a River Healthy" by Barbara Keeler and Kathy Goldner in "Images: Take Care of Yourself"

from *Health Literacy* by Alvermann, et al. Copyright © 1995 by D.C. Heath & Company. Reprinted by permission of Houghton Mifflin Company. All rights reserved.

"Fog" from *Chicago Poems* by Carl Sandburg, copyright 1916 by Holt, Rinehart, and Winston, and renewed 1944 by Carl Sandburg. Printed by permission of Harcourt, Inc.

Page from "Red Alert," used with permission from *TIME for Kids* magazine, copyright © 2000, 2001.

Excerpt from *Nettie's Trip South* by Ann Turner reprinted with the permission of Simon & Schuster Books for Young Readers, an imprint of Simon & Schuster Children's Publishing Division. Text copyright © 1987 by Ann Turner. Also reprinted by permission of Curtis Brown, Ltd.

"Insects" written by Bettina Bird and Joan Short, from Mondo's BOOKSHOP Literacy Program. Text copyright © 1988 by Bettina Bird and Joan Short, reprinted by permission of Mondo Publishing, 980 Avenue of the Americas, New York, NY 10018. All rights reserved.

Library of Congress Cataloging-in-Publication Data is on file with the Library of Congress

ISBN 0-325-00310-6

Editor: Lois Bridges
Production: Michael Cirone
Interior design: Jeff Wincapaw
Cover design: Cat & Mouse Design/Catherine Hawkes
Manufacturing: Louise Richardson
Photography: Mark Morelli
Composition: Uppercase Production & Design

Printed in the United States of America on acid-free paper

09 08 07 06 05 ML 11 12 13 14 15

CONTENTS

ACKNOWLEDGMENTS

Over the years we have been privileged to work with remarkable teachers who have shown us how to make reading and writing interesting and joyful for students in elementary classrooms. Our first acknowledgment must be of the work of these dedicated teachers, in many schools, cities, and states, who have generously shared their practice with us. They created communities of learning within their classrooms and schools and invited us to join their exciting endeavors. In addition, the work that many teams of teachers contributed to our study groups has informed this book: you will find evidence of their implementation of the theoretical and practical aspects of the language and literacy framework throughout *Guiding Readers and Writers*.

We are extremely grateful to Carol Won and Rebecca Goodman, who graciously volunteered to implement the language and literacy framework over the past several years. They allowed us to observe, study, and photograph in their classrooms, and engaged in continuous reflective analysis of teaching and learning. They were an important part of our informal studies several years ago and then became part of the first Literacy Collaborative training group. We also thank their many students who shared their work with us. Special thanks to Erica Jones, Kelsey McLaughlin, Jackson Tucker, Mikala Caraminas, David Tannenwald, Nicole Williamson, Persephone Vogt, Michael Galluzzo, Kim Galluzzo, and Michael DeIorio. We also wish to acknowledge Bunny Meyer, principal, who values the partnership between universities and schools and who has always welcomed observation and inquiry.

We thank several dedicated teachers who were part of our early study groups: Barbara Butterworth, Mark Canner, Candace Chick, Joan Dabrowski, Caitlin Florschultz, Marcella Herrera, Alex Lelchook, Chris Monks, Norma Sokolowsky, Susan Sullivan, and Kristen Thomas. In addition, we acknowledge the first training class for the Intermediate Literacy Collaborative at Lesley University, including Donna-Jean Wosencroft, Pam Thayer, Raymond Plank, Denise Morgan, Debbie Gailey-Aiken, Barbara Evans, Maria Cordon, and Candace Chick, who put the framework into practice in their classrooms and offered valuable feedback.

We thank Salli Oddi and her staff at Cover to Cover bookstore in Columbus, Ohio, for sharing their wealth of knowledge of children's literature. We also thank Maureen Brown-Yoder for sharing her knowledge of technology.

Our dear friend and colleague Mary Ellen Giacobbe has reviewed our manuscript and offered valuable feedback. We thank her for her passion and respect for children and teachers, and for all that she continually teaches us about literacy learning. She is one of the pioneers on whose work we have built.

We also express appreciation to many other great thinkers who have informed teachers and researchers about the value and processes of writing. The work of these scholars has made concepts like minilessons, writing workshop, reading workshop, and writer's notebook part of the public exchange in the teaching of literacy. Nancie Atwell's brilliant work in reading and writing workshop has provided the foundation for many of the ideas expressed in this book, and we are grateful for her generosity, her collegiality, and her model of reflective teaching. We have learned much from the pioneering work of Donald Murray, Donald Graves, Lucy Calkins, and Shelley Harwayne. Ralph Fletcher, whose rich descriptions of a writer's notebook have given teachers and children new ways of thinking about themselves as writers, has provided ideas that are seminal to our framework. Georgia Heard, author and educator, has changed the conversation about poetry in elementary classrooms; her ideas have been essential to our work.

Producing any book requires a great deal of time and effort, as well as contributions from many professionals; we found *Guiding Readers and Writers* an especially challenging project. We offer sincere thanks to our colleagues at Heinemann for their understanding, support, and problem-solving throughout the process. We know that our editor, Lois Bridges, worked long hours, as she often answered our e-mails at 4:00 A.M. We value not only her expertise as a talented writer and meticulous editor, but her willingness to share her thoughts and perspectives honestly; we thank her for being our editor and friend. Thanks also to Alan Huisman, who added his care and thoughtfulness to a complex editing process. Leigh Peake and Mike Gibbons offered continuous encouragement, leadership, and valuable critical feedback throughout many phases of the production of this book and we thank them for their belief in our work and their vision for how we can best share it with others. Renée Le Verrier, Karen Chabot, and Lisa Fowler also provided important and valued assistance.

Finally, we are greatly indebted to Michael Cirone, who brought his special artistry to the layout and design of the volume and has been such a patient, wonderful colleague in this venture. Michael has truly made this book a personal project; we appreciate his sense of excellence and his constant, sincere interest and support, as well as his "can do" approach to the solving of any problem, great or small, no matter what day of the week or time of day.

We are grateful to the following funders for generously supporting Lesley University's literacy programs in the Boston Public Schools: The Carol and Howard Anderson Family Fund at The Boston Foundation, the Boston Annenberg Challenge, the Boston Annenberg Challenge Fund for Nonprofits, The Boston Foundation, the Virginia Wellington Cabot Foundation, Fleet National Bank Charitable Trusts, Harcourt General Charitable Foundation, John Hancock Financial, the Hilde L. Mosse Foundation, Say Yes to Education Foundation, the State Street Foundation, the Massachusetts Department of Education, and the U.S. Department of Education. Partnering with the Boston Public Schools and other regional schools around early literacy proved invaluable in helping us articulate the need for developing more effective techniques for literacy instruction in the intermediate grades.

We also thank Anthony Bryk, Sharon Greenberg, and the team at the Center for School Improvement of the University of Chicago, who have supported our efforts to investigate teaching, learning, and the education of teachers. Carol Lyons' work in this area has been especially informative, and we thank her as well.

The Ohio Department of Education, especially Nancy Ann Eberhart, has been supportive of our work over the last two decades; this foundational work in early literacy made the present volume possible. We also thank the John D. and Catherine T. MacArthur Foundation and the Charles A. Dana Foundation for their support of our research in early literacy. Finally, we thank Ohio State's Campus Partners and their Urban Systemic Initiative for supporting the OSU team's present work in Ohio.

We thank Jennifer Gleason for her leadership, energy, organization, and sense of excellence in assisting the Heinemann team in every detail of this production. We thank Jennifer Winkler and Heather Kroll for their enthusiastic teamwork. We also wish to express appreciation for the positive, spirited team at Lesley University, including Jan Rossi, Jennifer Warner, Pat Mullaney, Karen Travelo, Jennifer Rassler, Julie Skogsberg, Jessica Howard, Natalia Zuazo, Wendy Darcy, and Nora Menzi.

At Ohio State, Polly Taylor continually provides her valuable and always willing assistance in dozens of ways. We especially appreciate her work on the manuscript as well as her expertise in tracking down books and other missing items. We extend our special gratitude to Sharon Freeman, who contributed her administrative talent, delightful humor, and good ideas to the project.

We express appreciation to our families for their continual support and encouragement, especially Elfrieda Pinnell and Catherine Fountas. As always, we thank Ron Melhado and Ron Heath for patience and love during the long hours devoted to writing this book.

Many important people in our lives have contributed to our learning. We thank Martha King for what she taught us about language and literacy. We thank Charlotte Huck for her leadership in children's literature, as well as her focus on the joy of reading. We also thank Janet Hickman and Susan Hepler (and Barbara Kiefer, who joined them in recent years), coauthors of a wonderful children's literature reference from which we have learned so much. And we acknowledge with thanks Evelyn Freeman, who has helped us learn more about informational texts.

We also wish to acknowledge our colleagues in our work in Reading Recovery and Literacy Collaborative. Their desire to learn inspires us; their joy in what they do makes our professional lives richer. Diane DeFord's work with study groups of researchers and teachers interested in the intermediate grades has greatly enriched the collaborative OSU/Lesley project. At OSU we thank Joan Wiley, Pat Scharer, Emily Rodgers, Meredith Peoples, Andrea McCarrier, Jonda McNair, Linda Mudre, Justina Henry, Sharon Gibson, Peg Gwyther, Susan Fullerton, Paige Furgerson, Mary Fried, Rose Mary Estice, and Lisa Brandt. To Jane Williams we express grateful thanks for her painstaking and diligent attention to evaluation data from our school projects. At Lesley University, we thank Joanne Bartlam, Jill Lazarus Eurich, Doreen Fay, Eva Konstantellou, Diane Powell, Sandra Lowry, Patti Starnes. We highly value the learning community that has convened around the work we share in common.

Finally, we are grateful for Susan Hundley, our dear friend and colleague for fourteen years. Sue worked with us in Reading Recovery and the Literacy Collaborative, and was much admired and loved for her keen intelligence, her love of children and teachers, her good sense, and her serenity. Sue was a gifted teacher and a meticulous researcher. She exemplified the qualities of a lifelong learner. We miss her calm spirit and good judgment. She has left us the legacy of her teaching.

INTRODUCTION

The elementary school classroom is a laboratory in which students learn about themselves, about others, and about the world beyond the classroom door. Here they develop attitudes and habits about literacy and learning that will last a lifetime. In the upper elementary grades, students move from childhood to adolescence. As they continue to learn about reading and writing, they broaden and deepen their ability to use literacy as a multifaceted tool for learning. They discover their voices as writers and refine their instincts as readers.

Upper elementary students experience both the frustration and the joy of their evolving journey into full-fledged adult literacy. Our work, then, is challenging. In their primary years some students enjoyed a strong launch into literacy. Others did not. Some are confident; others are less so. But all intermediate students are entering a time of great change, physically, intellectually, and emotionally. From kindergarten through grade 6, they move from their first, tentative experiences with print to rapid, silent reading of long, complex texts that engage, inform, and inspire. What's more, they move from creating a few triumphant letters on paper to writing pages-long texts that serve a wide range of purposes. They expand their ability to express themselves in both oral and written language, and they learn to work independently and with others for longer periods of time.

In every grade-level cohort, there is great diversity among the students. The range of reading ability, for example, tends to become wider in each successive grade. Students' varied experiences and their diversity contribute to the learning environment we create in the classroom. The more they know, the faster they learn more, so students with good literary backgrounds may race ahead of others.

Our work presents significant challenges. Upper elementary teachers are likely to ask themselves: *How can I create a community of learners within this classroom? How can I recognize the individual strengths of this group of diverse learners and create a curriculum that provides a chance for every student to learn? How can I assure that all students achieve expected standards for performance in reading and writing?* We address these challenges in this book.

Our goal was to write a book about teaching reading in upper elementary classrooms, but we quickly abandoned that idea. The interconnectedness of reading and writing is profound and inescapable. We couldn't address reading without discussing writing as well, because literacy doesn't unfold that way in the classroom—or shouldn't. Fragmenting these complex literacy processes interferes with the greatest goal of literacy education—the construction of meaning from and through text. Using reading and writing together in harmonious concert enables learners to draw on these complementary processes at the same time they work to construct meaning. As we schedule the activities that take place in the classroom—a practical consideration that we address in detail—we also need to plan how writing and reading work together there.

Throughout this book, you will hear the voices of teachers and students. In fact, we begin with Erica's

Day, a snapshot of life and literacy learning in a fourth-grade classroom. The first section of the book presents the basic structure of the language/literacy program in the upper elementary grades. We introduce a broad language/literacy framework that encompasses the building of community through language, word study, reading, writing, and the visual and performing arts. The framework unfolds as three "blocks," which we interpret as conceptual units as well as time segments within the school day.

Section 1 introduces (1) the design of the language/word study block, including phonics, spelling, and a wide range of language and literacy activities that promote students' construction of shared meaning and knowledge about texts; (2) the reading workshop design, showcasing independent reading, guided reading, and literature study; and (3) the writing workshop design, featuring independent and guided writing, as well as investigations (i.e., student research) in which students read and write across genres and content areas. Section 1 also explains how to create the social and physical environment that fosters literacy learning in intermediate classrooms. Finally, we discuss the management of time, resources, and people, all practical considerations for teachers in upper elementary grades.

Sections 2, 3, and 4 provide the detail necessary to help teachers implement the three components of the reading workshop. These sections include chapters on the structure of independent reading and guided reading, and ways of engaging students in literature study. We describe how to use exciting techniques like a reader's notebook and include suggestions for effective minilessons on management, strategies and skills, and literary analysis. We also outline twenty minilessons to help you get started. Through these three powerful instructional settings, your students reap the benefits of extensive and varied daily reading. They enjoy independence and self-reflection; at the same time, you have the opportunity to provide direct instruction and encouragement.

Section 5 explores the complex processes related to reading, a fascinating but difficult topic. We invite you to look analytically at texts and what they require of readers. We also invite you to consider the nature of reading with understanding. Comprehension is not a *product* of reading. It is inseparable from the *process* of reading. Although we focus on comprehension separately in order to explain and discuss it, we cannot truly separate understanding from reading. Reading *is* comprehension. We describe twelve interconnected systems of strategies that work together in complex ways during the reading process.

The final section explores writing/reading connections in greater depth. This section includes a range of instructional contexts, all of which connect learning via writing and reading. For example, as students read and write poetry, they experience language in its most concise, precise form. They learn about composing powerful messages, selecting just the right words, and paying careful attention to layout and design. We also present a wide range of tools that support students' discussion and understanding of texts. Additionally, we offer strategies to help students learn the "genre" of testing and ways to perform successfully the reading and writing that tests require.

At the end of each section, you'll notice a recurring feature entitled *Struggling Readers and Writers: Teaching That Makes a Difference.* As the range and diversity of students widens in the upper elementary grades, inevitably some students will find many aspects of reading and writing difficult. We know from long experience that where we choose to invest our instructional time is a difficult decision. Students who need extra help need extra time, which is not always available. In these features, we provide specific suggestions for efficiently and effectively teaching readers and writers who need extra help in order to succeed. In writing these section *addenda*, we have chosen not to explore the numerous reasons students might be low achievers. We assume the point of view of the teacher, who is simply faced with helping these students succeed every day in the classroom.

Effective teaching in the intermediate grades begins with what we know about learners and their literacy journey. Year by year, students come to understanding more—and more difficult—concepts. They discover themselves as readers and writers who have preferences and make thoughtful and analytic decisions. Perhaps most important, they begin to understand and embrace the pervasive role literacy plays in their lives. Our goal is not only to help students learn to read and write but to introduce them to the success and joy inherent in the lives of those who do.

OPENING:
ERICA'S DAY

This book describes a comprehensive language and literacy framework designed to support young readers and writers like Erica, a student in Carol's fourth grade classroom. Join us as we accompany Carol and Erica through a day of intensive and engaging work, and you'll see how the framework plays out in the real world of teaching and learning. The three interrelated blocks—reading workshop, writing workshop, and language-word study—offer both Erica and Carol many opportunities to interact and learn from each other. Erica refines and expands her knowledge and ability to use oral and written language, while Carol makes moment-to-moment instructional decisions that enable her to offer maximum support to Erica (and her other students) in their learning.

Equally important, the classroom is inviting and organized. Everything has its place, so it's easy for the students to find the tools and supplies they need. Carol, Erica, and her classmates are free to go about the joyful business of learning and using literacy as a community of readers and writers.

The Classroom

Walking with Erica into her classroom, the first thing you notice is a small table by the door where students "check in." Inside a binder, Erica's teacher, Carol, has tucked a class list with the dates of the current week written across the top. Here, students sign their name and check off one of three options for each piece of yesterday's homework: (1) the homework is completed, and they remembered to bring it to school; (2) the

Carol's Classroom

Personal Book Boxes

Book Baskets

homework is completed, but left at home; or (3) the homework is not finished but will be by the date they specify.

The next thing you realize is that the walls are alive and brimming with students' work and a range of charts that summarize aspects of learning. One long wall chart, which stretches from ceiling to floor, is enti-tled "Books We've Shared" and lists all the books that Carol has read to the students or that they have enjoyed as a group so far this year. Carol has also posted the charts she developed in her minilessons on reading and writing. Several of these charts showcase word study principles and include examples of words that illustrate these principles.

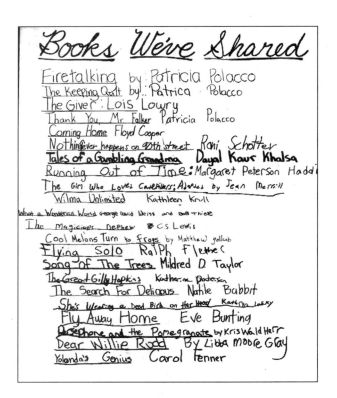

Books We've Shared

Book Recommendations Rack

The inviting physical organization of the classroom is immediately apparent. Student desks are clustered in groups of four, five, or six, fostering collaboration and a sense of community spirit. Work tables are available for ongoing projects. Materials are stored in attractive baskets that line the shelves and cupboards.

Near the windows, on several long shelves, is a copious collection of books in colorful baskets with clear labels. They are organized by author, genre, type of award, series, or topic. Among the authors you recognize are Judy Blume, Cynthia Voigt, Gary Paulsen, Avi, and Karen Hesse. There are baskets devoted to mysteries, biographies, diaries and journals, Holocaust books, animal books, and family stories. The tops of the bookshelves are used to display books that Carol has read to the students or that they are using for literature discussion.

You also notice a number of cardboard boxes, or "magazine files," with students' names on them. Each student has a personal box in which to keep books they are reading, a writer's notebook, a writing folder, and a reader's notebook.

In addition to her colorful book baskets, Carol has four baskets labeled "Monday Notebooks," "Tuesday Notebooks," "Wednesday Notebooks," and "Thursday Notebooks." On the assigned day, the students place their notebooks into the appropriate basket with their completed responses. Carol reads and responds to one set each night.

A child-designed sign enthusiastically proclaiming "Must Reads" perches atop a revolving rack. Each child, as well as Carol and the student teacher, has a section on the rack with his or her name on it; each section holds one or two books. Inside the front cover of each book they recommend, the students clip an index card on which they write why they like the book and why they think others will enjoy it.

In one corner is a large rug where the class settles in for all-group minilesson and sharing sessions, interactive read-alouds, shared reading and writing, and literature discussions. Here Carol has assembled a variety of materials to which she can turn as needed to highlight her lessons. She has easy access to an easel stocked with chart paper and markers. Next to the easel, she's placed a white dry erase board and markers. On a small cart, she stores a tray of magnetic letters, a small white board and markers, highlighter tape, scissors, a glue stick, index cards, and stick-on notes. There is a low chair next to the easel within reach of hooks on which Carol hangs her clipboards containing notes and student records. Near the walls on the edges of the meeting area are large cushions on which children can nestle while they read or listen to and participate in group meetings.

There isn't a large "teacher's desk" in this classroom. Instead, Carol relies on a series of "offices on wheels," carts loaded with movable baskets, which are parked in key areas of the classroom. Behind one of the work tables are shelves that house multiple copies of several sets of leveled books. This is where Carol meets with small groups for reading and writing instruction.

At the end of the room opposite this table are several chairs and two small tables with lamps. Small groups of students meet here to read and discuss their books. Baskets of dictionaries, thesauruses, and rhyming dictionaries; trays of magnetic letters; and a basket of word-sorting materials line a series of shelves labeled "Word Study Materials."

Poetry has a place of honor in Carol's classroom. She has assembled several baskets of poetry anthologies. And, each child has constructed his own personal poetry anthology. The pages display their favorite poems, personally illustrated, as well as poems they have written. The books are bound with tagboard and plastic spiral coil. (Most of the covers have been elaborately and imaginatively decorated.)

Another area of the classroom is labeled "Tools for Writing." Here you see two computers, several kinds and sizes of paper, a stapler and staple remover, stick-on notes, tape, boxes of markers and colored pencils, date stamps, a box of clipboards, and various other useful writing tools.

Elsewhere, math manipulatives (pattern pieces, Cuisenaire rods, Dienes blocks, cubes, rulers, measuring tapes) are housed in one bookcase; another holds magnifying glasses, a few microscopes, and eye droppers. In this "science and math" area, Carol has placed reference books as well as books focusing on the current topic of study.

Carol's classroom is orderly and inviting; it has a workshop quality, typical of a laboratory for learning. It is obvious that Carol is highly organized. She has worked hard to create a pleasant and stimulating environment in which students can easily access the tools, materials, and books they need to support their learning. This classroom is designed for all who work there.

8:30 to 8:45 ARRIVAL

Erica's Day

Erica enters the room and checks in, indicating that she has returned her homework completed. Next, she takes out her writer's notebook and adds more ideas to her list of special times she has enjoyed with her sister. Earlier she has drawn a picture of her sister as a baby and then as a young child.

Erica's Entry and Sign-in

Carol, A Professional Teacher in Action

As the children arrive, Carol confers with individual students who are reading independently or writing in their writer's notebook. Carol's beliefs about learning and teaching, coupled with her thoughtful organization and planning, enable her to make use of every minute of the school day; for example, she believes that her students:

- develop their literacy both at school and at home; accordingly, she assigns meaningful homework.
- should keep track of their own work and take responsibility for routines like attendance.
- should start work the moment they set foot in the classroom. The arrival period signals the serious start of a new school day.
- can generate their own topics for writing. Students keep an ongoing notebook of resources where they record ideas for future writing in a variety of forms.
- enjoy having choices; when they arrive in the morning, they choose whether to read or write in their notebook.

Working Independently

8:45 to 9:45 WRITING WORKSHOP

Erica

After all the students have arrived, Carol calls Erica and her classmates to the meeting area, greets them, provides two writers talks, and teaches a minilesson on how author Jacqueline Briggs Martin and illustrator Mary Azarian shared information about William Bentley in their book *Snowflake Bentley* (1998). The book is the life story of a scientist. At this point in the year, the students in the class are learning how to write about people's lives, so Carol invites them to analyze the ways that Martin and Azarian made the story of William Bentley's life interesting to readers: in narrative, in side bars with factual information, and in photographs. Each student is working on a picture biography of a person whose life has made a difference for others. Erica's choice is Amelia Earhart; she works on her biography during independent writing. She has gathered magazine articles and books and has taken notes in her writer's notebook. She and her classmates work without talking to one another; the room is completely quiet except for some whispering as Carol holds individual conferences or works quietly with a small guided writing group.

At one point in the period, Carol confers with Erica about whether to organize Earhart's biography chronologically or to start with the mysterious disappearance of the aviator. Carol uses a sheet on her clipboard to take notes on their discussion. At the end of the hour, Carol asks a few students to tell about one way they are making their biographies interesting to their readers.

Carol

Carol begins the Writing Workshop with a "writer talk" on Cynthia Rylant. She gives a minilesson, confers individually with three students, conducts one guided writing group, and facilitates a large group share. Carol's beliefs shape her Writing Workshop; she:

- believes that students need a full hour to write and work on their writing projects independently.
- values quality literature, recognizing that students apply what they learn in reading to their own writing.
- believes that picture books offer intermediate readers and writers sophisticated ways of looking at the craft of writing.
- chooses *Snowflake Bentley* as a strong example of how an author and illustrator can present information in varied ways. She believes that examples engage students in ways lecture or discussion alone can't equal.

8:45 to 9:45 WRITING WORKSHOP (continued)

Erica in Writing Workshop

Carol (continued)

- uses group discussion to bring examples to explicit attention; she models her analysis to show students how to analyze texts themselves.
- believes that a quiet atmosphere enables students to think effectively and concentrate fully on their writing.
- conducts frequent conferences with her students as a way to address their particular needs.
- keeps records of instructional conversations to inform her teaching.
- views sharing as another way to reinforce learning and extend a student's understanding.
- recognizes the relationship between reading and writing. What students learn as readers helps them as writers and vice versa.

9:45 to 10:45 READING WORKSHOP

Erica

After writing workshop, Erica and her classmates assemble on the rug for reading workshop. They listen to two "book talks" Carol gives on biographies. Erica jots down the title of the Willa Cather biography in the "Reading Interests" section of her reading journal.

In Carol's minilesson, she explains that every time you read, you make your own unique connections. You have your own way of experiencing a book. She asks the students to mark with stick-on notes one or two places that make them think of something in their own lives.

Erica goes to her desk and finishes writing in her reader's notebook, proofreads her letter to her teacher (required once each week), and places it in a basket labeled "Wednesday Notebooks."

*A Reading
Workshop*

Carol

Carol begins Reading Workshop with two "book talks," one on *Jesse Owens: Olympic Hero* (Sabin 1986) the other on *Writer of the Plains: A Story About Willa Cather* (Steissguth 1997). Carol then leads a minilesson, meets with one guided reading group, and confers with four students to address individual reading needs. At the end of the session she gathers the group for a quick sharing. Carol's beliefs shape the Reading Workshop; she believes that her students:

■ need a full hour to participate in reading instruction, engage in meaningful reading, and share for further reinforcement and feedback.

■ will engage with books that interest them as she highlights the books she loves and conveys her own enthusiasm.

■ should develop the habit of listing in their notebooks the books they want to read.

9:45 to 10:45 READING WORKSHOP (continued)

Erica (continued)

Then, for the rest of the hour, she continues reading *A Time of Angels*, by Karen Hesse. Hesse is one of Erica's favorite authors. She marks a place in her book that reminds her of a time when she was worried and sad (when her grandmother was ill). She works independently and silently, retrieving her morning snack from her backpack, and eating while she reads.

The room is completely quiet except for the low voices of individual conferences and the murmur of Carol's meeting with a guided reading group.

At group time, Erica shares with her partner the part of the text that she had marked with a sticky note.

Erica's Letter

> 11/8
>
> Dear Ms Won,
> The questions that you asked me in the journal really made me think. Yes I'm enjoying the Karen Hesse's books because her writing is fiction but it sounds real. Her books are all so different except for the feelings part. They all have worried, sad, and a waiting feeling. I am getting used to her writing style. My friend, Hannah is like Hannah in the book A Time of Angels because they have the same name. They both have brown hair, the both are Jewish, they have only younger siblings. If I were in Hannah's shoes I would deffenatly not have a boyfriend. I think I'd be myself better than being her because I wouldn't have to get a very bad disese and also take care of an older man as well. I have a question. Have you ever read Island of the Blue Dolphins by Scott O'Dell? If you had please tell me about it as I am thinking about reading them next.
>
> Love,
> Erica

Carol's Letter

> 11/9
> Dear Erica,
> I'm sorry I haven't written back in a long time. I never like it when I get sick! Your letters make me think a lot too. I really like your observation about Karen Hesse as an author and how you noticed that her books are pretty different except they tend to have similar feelings in them (worried, sad, waiting). These can be pretty serious feelings. Why do you think Karen Hesse focuses on feelings like these? Also, I'm wondering how it is that she is able to write different and separate stories but show the same feelings at the same time. Also, is there some overall message or lesson she is trying to send about feelings like these? Island of the Blue Dolphins is a genre called survival stories. This means the central character is in a situation where she/he needs to do certain things to try to stay alive. Scott O'Dell has written other survival stories. If this sounds interesting to you, you may want to try it! Let me know what you decide.
>
> Love,
> Ms Won

Carol (continued)

- ■ should develop the habit of recording in their notebooks the books they want to read.
- ■ must connect their reading to their own lives and be ready to talk about these connections as they read.
- ■ think deeply about their reading when they read silently in a calm atmosphere.
- ■ benefit from her frequent contact; therefore, she systematically replies to a different set of notebooks each day/evening thus avoiding a backlog of work.
- ■ may enjoy their morning snack when they wish.
- ■ can learn from one another as they weave a rich conversation around the books they read.

10:45 to 11:15 LANGUAGE/WORD STUDY

Forming Plurals

Erica

Erica joins the group on the rug and listens to Carol read more about Alvin Ailey. Erica has read many other picture-book biographies and listens intently, occasionally making a comment.

Erica also takes part in a word study minilesson on forming plurals during which Carol uses a chart on which is written:

1. Plurals made by adding *s*.
2. Plurals made by adding *es*.
3. Plurals made by changing the spelling.
4. Plurals that end in *y* (changing *y* to *i* and adding *es*, *flies*).
5. Plurals that end in an *f* (changing *f* to *v* and adding *es*).

Carol reviews the first four principles and teaches the fifth, a new principle. Students add words to the chart, which they worked on in previous lessons.

Carol

Carol reads aloud a biography, *Alvin Ailey* (Pinkney, 1995). She follows the read aloud with word study. Carol believes that her students:

■ gain greater access to texts when they hear those read aloud that they can not yet read for themselves.

■ should think about and share comments, insights, and predictions during read-alouds.

■ will learn how to write and illustrate a biography as they examine published biographies that demonstrate the possibilities in content and form.

■ need powerful, explicit demonstrations of how words work. She plans minilessons based on student needs and grade-four curriculum goals. From the students' writing, she determines they are learning about plurals but need wider knowledge of different patterns; therefore, she explicitly teaches a new principle on forming plurals.

10:45 to 11:15 LANGUAGE/WORD STUDY (continued)

Erica (continued)

Erica contributes a plural form to the chart. She then chooses five words that illustrate principles for forming plurals. These are her "core words" for her weekly spelling list. In addition, she selects five "personal words" from her "Words to Learn" list in her writing folder. She writes them on a card and then forms the words three times each with magnetic letters, each time checking the letters from left to right against the word card. Finally she places her spelling card in the library pocket on the board marked "Word Study."

Working with Magnetic Letters

Carol (continued)

- can use the interactive wall charts as handy references for their own reading and writing.
- should learn sets of useful principles to increase their spelling ability; Carol views systematic word study as essential.
- have particular spelling needs; their daily writing provides evidence of what they know and what they need to learn.
- will learn more about the sequence of letters in words by constructing them several times with plastic letters.
- should make choices and learn how to assess some of their own needs.
- should maintain and record their own weekly spelling list.

11:15 to 12:00 SPECIAL AREA (ART CLASS)

Erica

Erica and her classmates go to art class. Erica is learning about how different artists have painted flowers; she works on her own flower painting.

Carol

While her students attend art class, Carol begins responding to journals in the "Wednesday" basket. She writes a response to Erica since she believes that a conversation "reader to reader" is a meaningful way for students to enjoy and expand their reading.

12:00 to 12:45 LUNCH

Erica

Erica eats her lunch and spends the remainder of the time with her friends on the playground.

Carol

Carol takes a break to enjoy lunch with her colleagues.

In Playground

12:45 to 1:30 MATHEMATICS

Erica

Erica learns about estimating and works with a small group to estimate and test volume.

Carol

■ Carol teaches a mathematics minilesson; she believes in direct demonstration, small-group work, and hands-on experiences to extend concepts. Carol knows her students will understand mathematical equations better if they have experienced concepts firsthand.

1:30 to 2:15 SCIENCE

Erica

In science, Erica and her classmates study the properties of matter, solids, liquids, and gases. She performs an experiment with her partner.

Carol

Carol provides short demonstrations that require students to observe and discuss what they notice. Carol recognizes that as her students assume the role of scientists and participate in the scientific method, they develop their understanding of scientific principles.

In Science Class

2:15 to 3:00 SOCIAL STUDIES

Erica

In social studies, Erica and her classmates are investigating immigration. Several of the books on their "Books We've Shared" list were stories of immigrants—for example, *Peppe the Lamplighter* (Bartone, 1993), and *Journey to Ellis Island* (Bierman, McGraw, and Hefner, 1998). After Carol has reminded the students to think about some of the books they have read about immigrants, Erica writes a paragraph in her writer's notebook about how she might feel when moving to another country. The students then watch a short film about Ellis Island, and Erica talks with her partner about three things she learned from the film that she didn't know before.

Carol

Carol guides students as they write in their writer's notebooks, shows a short film, and helps them consolidate their new learning through discussion. She believes that her students:

- learn about a topic through talking, reading, writing, and viewing.
- will find learning more memorable as it relates to their own lives and enables them to find connections among texts.
- develop their literacy as they use reading and writing to investigate content area topics.

3:00 DISMISSAL

Erica

Erica's homework for the evening is to read her book *A Time of Angels* for 30 minutes and to write in her writer's notebook for 15 minutes.

Carol

Carol prepares a minilesson for the next day's independent reading and writing. She also plans for two guided reading groups.

A Foundation for Lifelong Reading and Writing

Carol's exemplary classroom supports her students as they develop language and literacy attitudes and skills that will serve them well over the course of their lives. Carol has provided the opportunity for Erica and the other readers to:

- Read often.
- Make their own choices.
- Recommend books to others.
- Talk with others about what they read.
- Get to know authors, illustrators, and styles.
- Read a wide variety of materials.
- Develop personal preferences as a reader and become conscious of those preferences.
- Reflect on their reading.
- Think critically about what they read.
- See themselves as readers.
- Develop competence as readers through instruction.
- Develop confidence as readers through successful daily reading experiences.

Carol has designed opportunities for Erica and the other writers to:

- Write often.
- See themselves as writers.
- Learn how to use writing as a tool for reflecting and learning.
- Learn how to write in different genres.
- Write to share experiences and feelings.
- Notice authors' technique or craft.
- Listen to others respond to their writing.
- Draw upon literary experiences as a resource for their writing.
- Develop favorite topics.
- Develop particular topics and a variety of genres.
- Develop competence as writers through instruction.
- Develop confidence as writers through successful daily writing experiences.

Clearly, Erica and her classmates are members of what Smith (1988) calls "the literacy club." Erica sees herself as a reader and a writer who engages with other readers and writers in a literate community.

In her classroom, Carol has created an environment within which writing and reading are accessible to every student. The level of text, the highly organized environment, and the instructional support Carol provides enable her students to experience success every day. Carol communicates respect for her students by creating a peaceful and productive atmosphere in which they can manage their own routines. In *Rethinking Our Classrooms* (1994), Bigelow, Christensen, Karp, Miner, and Peterson (eds.) describe the importance of designing our literacy teaching around the students who live in our classrooms:

> Curriculum should be rooted in children's needs and experiences. Whether we're teaching science, mathematics, English or social studies, ultimately, the class has to be about our students' lives as well as about a particular subject. Students should probe the ways their lives connect to the broader society and are often limited by that society. (p. 4)

The classroom we have described is a community within which learners support and cooperate with one another. Accessibility to knowledge and a supportive community are as "basic" as the skills of reading and writing. The schedule for teaching and learning is rigorous; students are productive. For example, in language arts during this one day Erica has:

- Generated ideas for writing and written them in her writer's notebook.
- Written a reading response in her journal.
- Participated in three specific lessons, one on the characteristics of biography, one on text interpretation, and one on principles for making words plural.
- Written part of a biography of Amelia Earhart, which required background research.
- Conferred with her teacher about the organization of her biography.
- Become familiar with two more biographies that might interest her.

- Read independently from a book of her choice.
- Listened to a biography read aloud and discussed it with her teacher and classmates.
- Selected spelling words to learn, five of which were related to principles for making words plural and five of which were personal, and studied them by first writing them with magnetic letters.

In addition Erica has shared her ideas and her work with a supportive group of fellow learners. She has received constructive feedback and guidance from her teacher on an important piece of writing that she has been working on for several days.

Carol has also been busy: teaching three mini-lessons, conferring with eight students individually, teaching two guided reading groups, reading aloud, giving book talks and writer's talks, and generally managing the class' workload. But Carol also made time to respond to every student's ideas. Her program is designed to balance direct teaching and experiential learning. It is efficient in that it involves both whole-group and small-group teaching, but leaves room to adjust to the individual differences that characterize the intermediate classroom. During the course of a week in Carol's classroom, all students participate in instruction that is tailored to their particular needs, including:

- Reading a book of their choice with Carol's guidance so that the selected book provides the right amount of challenge and support.
- Participating in small-group instruction geared to what they need to know next.
- Writing a reading response, to which Carol will respond.
- Sharing stories and informational pieces that Carol reads aloud.
- Selecting and working on their own spelling words, both personal words that they want to learn and words that illustrate important principles.
- Writing their own pieces with Carol's guidance.

A Foundation for Social Justice

We believe that teaching in the intermediate classroom also provides the foundation for creating a just society. Students who live in a respectful community and whose daily experiences communicate respect for all others are better equipped to create the kind of society that we will need in the future. In *Rethinking Our Classrooms*, Bigelow *et al.* (1994) offer an analysis of the interlocking components that together form a "social justice classroom" and, not surprisingly, reflect an effective learning environment. In social justice classrooms teaching begins with the students and recognizes their strengths, needs, and experiences; what's more, students:

- are encouraged to think, to offer criticism, and to question.
- are actively involved in their own learning, both mentally and physically.
- feel important and cared for; their opinions and their work are treated as significant.
- learn to trust and care for one another.
- are exposed to and draw inspiration from heroes who have struggled against the odds and promoted social justice.
- encounter high expectations for academic achievement.
- see themselves as truth tellers and change makers, who act on their ideas.
- play a role in helping their peers learn—and their teachers.
- are sensitive to diversity of culture and race.
- are committed to combating racism and ethnic discrimination and to creating an equal society.

Both academic rigor and social justice are possible in the design of a quality literacy curriculum for the intermediate grades. We hope this short visit to Carol's classroom will help you think about the literacy practices we describe throughout this book.

SECTION 1

Breakthrough to Literacy: Powerful Teaching for All Students

We describe a comprehensive language and literacy framework that serves as a conceptual tool for organizing instruction. Chapter 1 outlines the framework's overarching goal—to assure that all students in upper elementary grades become lifelong readers and writers. In Chapter 2, we describe three instructional blocks—language/word study, reading, and writing—that provide guidelines for arranging schedules and integrating the components of the framework. Chapters 3, 4, and 5 serve as introductions to the three blocks, explaining their designs, their instructional procedures, materials, and management. Finally, we provide suggestions for organizing and managing time and resources. The ideas we introduce in this section are explored in greater depth throughout the book.

## CHAPTER ONE

BECOMING LIFELONG READERS AND WRITERS: THE GOAL OF THE INTERMEDIATE LITERACY PROGRAM

The longer I write and read, the more I learn; writing and reading are lifelong apprenticeships . . .

—DONALD M. MURRAY

The first years of school establish the essential foundation of literacy that enables all future literacy achievement. In the intermediate grades, students use this foundation to develop a full, rich, wide-ranging facility. They assume the roles of readers and writers that will serve them throughout their lifetime.

As teachers, we see our intermediate students as they are, but we also have a vision for what they can become. Our high expectations foster their self-confidence, encourage their success, and enable them to achieve high goals.

Becoming Readers and Writers

What does it mean to become a reader? a writer? In our work with students, we try to help them become readers and writers in the fullest sense. We want them not only to learn to read and write but also to learn the many purposes of reading and writing. We want literacy to become an integral part of their lives.

Reading
Learning to read in the fullest sense means developing decoding skills, but much more. It means becoming readers who:

■ Read voluntarily and often.
■ Read a wide variety of materials.

■ Have confidence in themselves as readers.
■ Present themselves as readers to others.
■ Read to become informed on a wide range of topics.
■ Read to improve their lives.
■ Read to have satisfying and rewarding vicarious experiences.
■ Read to expand their world beyond the here and now.
■ Collect books and refer to favorites again and again.
■ Recommend books to others.
■ Talk with others about what they read.
■ Know authors and illustrators, genres, and styles.
■ Develop preferences and constantly expand them.
■ Reflect on their reading.
■ Make connections between and among the things they have read.
■ Think critically about what they read.

Readers do not read only when they are required to do so. Readers find time to read and find ways of acquiring good material. Research documents the benefits of wide reading. A study of fourth graders (Pinnell, Pikulski & Wixon 1995) revealed that students who read fluently and who reported reading at home also scored higher on standardized reading achievement tests. Students in the higher achievement groups were reading many more words per day, more minutes per day, and more hours per week than the students in the lower achievement groups, who spent very little time reading very few words. In general, those who read more, and with more purpose and satisfaction, succeed more all the way around.

Writing

In our society, more people see themselves as readers than as writers. Perhaps you feel quite comfortable describing yourself as a "reader" but do not believe you are a "writer." Learning to write in the fullest sense means more than developing composing and spelling skills. It means becoming writers who:

- Write voluntarily and often.
- Write in a wide variety of genres.
- Have confidence in themselves as writers.
- Present themselves as writers to others.
- Use writing as a tool for thinking.
- Write to communicate on personal and professional levels.
- Write to share experiences or information with others.
- Are sensitive to other writers, noticing techniques and styles.
- Invite comments on, responses to, and critiques of their writing.
- Draw on literary knowledge as a resource for their writing.
- Use organized sets of information as a resource for their writing.
- Explore favorite topics and genres.

Atwell (1985), as a teacher, regards her role as a teacher as helping students approach written language as "insiders" who have their own intentions (topics, purposes), use "insider" language (draft, edit), and ask for advice that they may choose to accept or reject. She cautions that it takes time to do the thinking, writing, and talking that will welcome students into this insider role. A "writing program" is really a way of life:

Writing workshop is perpetual—day in, year out—like breathing, but sometimes much, much harder. We're constantly gathering ideas for writing, planning, writing, conferring, and seeing our writing get things done for us in our real worlds. (p. 150)

This is our goal for our students: to engage in a literate life from childhood through adolescence and adulthood.

The Intermediate Grades: A Time of Change

In the intermediate grades, students move from childhood to adolescence. As teachers, we encourage them to find their voices as writers and refine their tastes as readers. Some of these students will develop confidence, skill, and style as writers and find it easy to express themselves; others will complete writing assignments with little interest or confidence. Some will enjoy reading and do it voluntarily; others will read only when required. Continuous good teaching can make the critical difference.

Effective literacy programs foster active, responsible learning. They help students begin to use literacy as a tool that gives them the power to find the information they need, to express their opinions, to take positions. Active learners have their own goals and are engaged over time. They recognize the teacher's requirements but also recognize that fulfilling these requirements will help them achieve their goals.

Diverse Interests and Needs

In every grade, we find great diversity among students—physically, intellectually, and emotionally. Indeed, the range of reading ability tends to become wider at each successive grade level as a result of the students' varied experiences. Their literacy backgrounds reflect their homes and communities as well as their previous years of schooling. As intermediate-grade teachers we appreciate this rich diversity; it enhances the literary culture that we create in our classrooms. At the same time, we recognize the challenges of teaching students who, each year, are experiencing life-changing transitions.

Effective teaching in the intermediate grades begins with what we know about learners and their literacy journeys. By the time students enter third grade, they have developed expectations for texts. They have broadened their world through reading and technology. They have developed tastes and interests as readers as well as confidence as readers and writers.

Far more than primary children, intermediate students can be independent, manage their own learning, and follow their own interests. They may have resonated to a particular author's style; they may have found themselves in books, recognizing their own feelings, fears, and emotions. As writers, they have begun to develop voice. They know more about the possibilities for writing. Certainly, they have become much more social. Intermediate students make connections among areas of learning. They use literacy in many ways to try to make sense of their world. Their peers are rapidly becoming more interesting—and probably more influential—than the adults in their lives.

Students in the intermediate grades are also undergoing some important cognitive changes. George and Lawrence (1982) have identified six dimensions of cognitive development that begin in the primary years and continue into adolescence. Students change:

1. From concrete to more abstract ways of thinking.
2. From an egocentric perspective to a social perspective.
3. From narrowly defined ideas about time and space to broader ideas.
4. From simplistic views of human motivation to a more complex understanding of people.
5. From reliance on simple maxims or guidelines to an internalized philosophy of morality.
6. From simple concepts to higher-order conceptualizing.

Year by year, as students learn through experiences, they can understand increasingly complex ideas. Reading and writing are part of that growth.

Broadening Writing Abilities

Intermediate students who have experienced a rich primary writing program already see themselves as writers. Although they are just starting to develop a writing process, they have produced many pieces of writing; some have been edited and published. They have explored a range of topics, appropriate to their own experience and knowledge. By the end of third grade, they can write many words automatically and have become composers who can think about their ideas while "encoding" written language. They no longer have to attend so closely to the act of writing. Handwriting has become automatic, and they can write many words quickly without even thinking about the

spelling, although they are still developing their knowledge of spelling principles and how words "work." And while they may still wrestle with more complex sentences, basic punctuation is in place.

Dimensions of Change

Some intermediate students struggle with basic writing skills and require special attention, but most are on the verge of greatly broadening their writing abilities in several dimensions (see Britton et al. 1975).

SKILLS

Intermediate learners are still developing basic writing skills, including spelling and punctuation. They use more multisyllable words and become more careful with word choice. As they write longer and more complex pieces, they encounter more demanding uses of punctuation. They begin to look at paragraphing and the need to create sections or chapters. Conventions such as capitalization and grammatical forms become automatic.

Intermediate students are also becoming more sophisticated in planning and organizing the texts they want to write. They vary sentence structure, learning to write in first, second, or third person and to use present, past, and future tenses with accuracy. They are becoming familiar with literary techniques such as figurative language, foreshadowing, and point of view.

FUNCTION

Increasingly, intermediate students learn to write for their own purposes. They broaden their ability to distinguish the three functions of mature writing:

1. *Transactional writing* is language to accomplish tasks and to inform, advise, or instruct others. Intermediate students learn to explain and explore ideas, transact business, record and synthesize information, persuade others to adopt a certain point of view, and express theories. They center much of their writing on the content areas, including reports that emphasize accurate and specific references.
2. *Expressive writing* is language "close to the self" (p. 90). Students write with a free flow of ideas that is relatively unstructured. They may "think aloud," as in writing a diary or journal; or they may write personal letters or e-mail as part of ongoing

communication. They are writing for themselves or for a known individual or group.

3. *Poetic writing* involves using written language as art. The writer may express feelings (as in expressive writing), but the feelings are arranged and ordered into a pattern that is pleasing in itself. Poetic writing includes poetry, of course, but also other writing that has a poetic dimension, such as short stories, novels, poetic essays. The difference between poetic and transactional writing is similar to the difference between a painting and a map (p. 90). The poetic writing pleases and satisfies the writer, and, as a result, the reader. It stands alone and does not become dated information. Poetic writing need not be accurate; in fact, it may involve fantasy and imagination.

Mature writers blend these functions as they set about creating their unique pieces of writing, but the full repertoire is in place. As intermediate-grade teachers, we want to create a rich and lively curriculum that inspires students to use all functions of written language.

AUDIENCE
In the intermediate grades, students learn to write for many different audiences. In general, they move from audiences "close at hand" on the following continuum to those farther distant:

- *Self.* A child writes for himself and only he can truly understand it.
- *Teacher.* A student writes to the teacher as a trusted adult (as in notebook entries) or as an evaluator (for a graded paper). The student may write to demonstrate particular skills.
- *Wider Known Audience.* The student writes to communicate with or inform a variety of readers he knows. He may adopt the role of the expert or serve as a member of a collaborative group. The writing must be clear enough to communicate to a wide range of readers, but the writer has good insights as to their knowledge and interests.
- *Wider Unknown Audience.* The student writes for a public that he can only imagine. The student's published work may go to a well-defined though unknown audience or to an unspecified audience. The writing is expected to exist beyond the present and to inform or entertain others who encounter it.

TOPIC OR SUBJECT
We all write best about what we know, and students in the intermediate grades have access to an expanding range of topics and subjects. It is still necessary, however, to involve students in concrete experiences before expecting them to write about their knowledge. Intermediate students who have explored a wide range of texts can write informational pieces on many topics. Also, as they learn about other times and places, they can begin to create fiction that transcends the present time and settings they have personally experienced.

FORM OR GENRE
One of the critical skills writers develop is the ability to determine the appropriate form, or genre, within which to place their ideas. Most intermediate writers are well on their way to producing narrative texts with a beginning, a series of events, and an end. They may organize longer narratives into chapters, and use dialogue to reveal characters and make texts more interesting. They are also experienced notebook or diary writers.

In the intermediate grades, students greatly expand their knowledge of the characteristics of genres and their ability to produce them in writing. They read material in many genres and often "borrow" the style or structure of favorite writers to produce their own pieces. They can recognize the difference between narrative and expository writing, and create a table of contents, headings, diagrams, definitions of terms, and an index. In a rich writing program students may create:

- *Functional writing,* such as lists, memos, notebook or diary entries, business letters, notes, records and observations (as of experiments), advertisements, brochures, recipes, instructions, invitations, map legends and directions, and forms or questionnaires with directions for filling them in. Functional writing helps students recognize that writing is a tool that is deeply interwoven with life in our society.
- *Narrative writing,* such as memoir, fantasy, science fiction, mystery, traditional tales, legends or myths, realistic fiction, and historical fiction. Writing narratives may lead students back into literature to study the writer's craft, or, conversely, it may lead to reading and studying informational texts for details about a place or time in order to understand the story better.

■ *Informational writing*, such as biographies of others and autobiographies of themselves, descriptions, summaries of information, interpretations of data, and reports. Informational writing may require research, experimentation, or scientific investigation. Students may also need to study informational texts to discover ways to organize information and present it clearly.

■ *Poetic writing*, in which students represent their thoughts, feelings, and experiences in highly structured and patterned language. Here they consider the sound of language and the images evoked by their choice of words; they use the poetic devices such as metaphor, simile, rhyme, and onomatopoeia.

Shifts Over the Elementary Grades in Writing

Figure 1–1 is a picture of how writing ability shifts over the course of the elementary grades. The entry-level skills on this chart may well exist in your classroom, and special segments at the end of each section provide specific suggestions for working with these students. Our primary interest, however, centers on grades 3 through 6 (the shaded area on the chart).

The goal of any writing program is to help all students make consistent progress. To that end, it is important that we as teachers:

■ Allow time for writing every day.

■ Provide minilessons that offer specific instruction on all aspects of writing.

■ Confer with students, offering assistance specific to their work.

■ Give feedback on writing.

■ Help students set goals and assess their own progress.

■ Expose students to different genres.

■ Support membership in a writing community that accepts an individual's present abilities and communicates high expectations for improvement.

A writer is not created from a few experiences. Almost all professional writers attribute their finely honed skills to hard work over many years. The same is true for our intermediate students. While they may develop basic writing skills in the primary grades, this is only the beginning of their developmental journey as competent writers.

Broadening Reading Abilities

The span of learning that takes place during the elementary years is amazing. Typically, children enter kindergarten with rather vague notions of what reading and writing are all about. During the next seven years, they progress from a rudimentary understanding to essentially an adult level of literacy. By the time students leave the sixth grade, they can read just about anything they have the background to understand; the experiences and the meaning they bring to reading are the key to their ongoing development.

Over Time

Figure 1–2 displays reading-development characteristics along a continuum. Information on emergent and early readers is included because (1) some students in intermediate classrooms will no doubt be reading at these levels and (2) it's helpful for any teacher to understand the full continuum of student development. As with writing, we would not expect all students to exhibit grade-level expectations. What's more, no one reader will exhibit all of the characteristics at any particular level. Certain readers may possess excellent word-solving skills, for example, while their awareness of text organization—in either fiction or nonfiction—is just developing. Other students may read voraciously in one or two genres but either are unwilling or lack the confidence to read more widely.

Providing the learning environment and the teaching that intermediate students need to move along this continuum from transitional to advanced levels is a challenge. The goal is to achieve consistent progress by knowing where to meet them as readers and knowing where to take them next. Students need time, materials, and explicit teaching. Progress to advanced levels will not be possible unless we are serious about providing extended periods of time for reading every day. As teachers we need appropriate books and other reading materials that will offer challenge and support to our developing students.

With content area learning becoming so important in the intermediate grades, it may seem difficult to find the time to teach reading this intently—and even students at self-extending and advanced levels need instruction. Remember that your teaching of reading may be coordinated with work in content areas. After all, students need to read widely, and some of that

Emergent Writers	Early Writers	Transitional Writers	Self-Extending Writers	Advanced Writers
❖ Write name left to right. ❖ Write alphabet letters with increasingly accurate letter formation. ❖ Hear and represent some consonant sounds at beginning and ends of words. ❖ Use some letter names in the construction of words. ❖ Sometimes use spaces to separate words or attempted words. ❖ Label drawings. ❖ Establish a relationship between print and pictures. ❖ Remember message represented with letters or words. ❖ Write many words phonetically ❖ Write a few easy words accurately. ❖ Communicate meaning in drawings.	❖ Write known words fluently. ❖ Write left to right across several lines. ❖ Write 20 to 30 words correctly. ❖ Use letter-sound and visual information to spell words. ❖ Approximate spelling of words, usually with consonant framework and easy-to-hear vowel sounds. ❖ Form almost all letters accurately. ❖ Compose 2 or 3 sentences about a single idea. ❖ Begin to notice the author's craft and use techniques in their own writing. ❖ Write about familiar topics and ideas. ❖ Remember messages while spelling words. ❖ Consistently use spacing. ❖ Relate drawings and writing to create a meaningful text. ❖ Reread their writing.	❖ Spell many words conventionally and make near-accurate attempts at many more. ❖ Work on writing over several days to produce longer, more complex texts. ❖ Produce pieces of writing that have dialogue, beginnings, and endings. ❖ Develop ideas to some degree. ❖ Employ a flexible range of strategies to spell words. ❖ Consciously work on their own spelling and writing skills. ❖ Write in a few different genres. ❖ Demonstrate ability to think about ideas while "encoding" written language. ❖ Use basic punctuation and capitalization skills. ❖ Continue to incorporate new understanding about how authors use language to communicate meaning.	❖ Spell most words quickly without conscious attention to the process. ❖ Proofread to locate their own errors, recognize accurate parts of words, and use references or apply principles to correct words. ❖ Have ways to expand their writing vocabularies. ❖ Understand ways to organize informational writing such as compare/contrast, description, temporal sequence, cause/effect. ❖ Develop a topic and extend a text over many pages. ❖ Develop pieces of writing that have "voice." ❖ Use what they know from reading texts to develop their writing. ❖ Recognize and use many aspects of the writer's craft to improve the quality of their writing. ❖ Write for many different purposes. ❖ Show a growing sense of the audience for their writing. ❖ Critique own writing and offer suggestions to other writers.	❖ Understand the linguistic and social functions of conventional spelling and produce products that are carefully edited. ❖ Write almost all words quickly, accurately, and fluently. ❖ Use dictionary, thesaurus, computer spell check and other text resources; understand organization plans for these resources. ❖ Control a large body of known words that constantly expands. ❖ Demonstrate a large speaking and listening vocabulary as well as knowledge of vocabulary that is used often in written pieces. ❖ Notice many aspects of the writer's craft in texts that they read and apply their knowledge to their own writing. ❖ Critically analyze their own writing and that of others. ❖ Write for a variety of functions—narrative, expressive, informative, and poetic. ❖ Write in various persons and tenses. ❖ Write for different audiences, from known to unknown. ❖ Write about a wide range of topics beyond the present time, known settings, and personal experiences.
Texts: Simple labels and sentences with approximated spelling.	*Texts: One or more sentences around a single idea on a few pages; some conventionally spelled words.*	*Texts: Longer texts with several ideas; mostly conventional spelling and punctuation; simple sentence structure.*	*Texts: A variety of genres; conventional use of spelling and punctuation; more complex sentence structure; development of ideas in fiction and nonfiction, use of a variety of ways to organize nonfiction.*	*Texts: A variety of long and short compositions; wide variety of purpose and genre; literary quality in fiction and poetry; variety of ways to organize informational text.*
Approximate Grades: K–1	1–2	2–3	3–4	4–6

Figure 1–1. Building an Effective Writing Process Over Time

Building an Effective Reading Process Over Time

Emergent Readers [Levels A–B]	Early Readers [Levels B–H]	Transitional Readers [Levels H–M]	Self-Extending Readers [Levels M–R]	Advanced Readers [Levels R–Y]
❖ Become aware of print.	❖ Know names of most alphabet letters and many letter-sound relationships.	❖ Read silently most of the time.	❖ Read silently; read fluently when reading aloud.	❖ Read silently; read fluently when reading aloud.
❖ Read orally, matching word by word.	❖ Use letter-sound information along with meaning and language to solve words.	❖ Have a large core of known words that are recognized automatically.	❖ Use all sources of information flexibly in a smoothly orchestrated way.	❖ Effectively use their understandings of how words work; employ a wide range of word solving strategies, including analogy to known words, word roots, base words, and affixes.
❖ Use meaning and language in simple texts.	❖ Read without pointing.	❖ Use multiple sources of information while reading for meaning.	❖ Sustain reading over texts with many pages, that require reading over several days or weeks.	❖ Acquire new vocabulary through reading.
❖ Hear sounds in words.	❖ Read orally and begin to read silently.	❖ Integrate sources of information such as letter-sound relationships, meaning, and language structure.	❖ Enjoy illustrations and gain additional meaning from them as they interpret texts.	❖ Use reading as a tool for learning in content areas.
❖ Recognize name and some letters.	❖ Read fluently with phrasing on easy texts; use the punctuation.	❖ Consistently check to be sure all sources of information fit.	❖ Interpret and use information from a wide variety of visual aids in expository texts.	❖ Constantly develop new strategies and new knowledge of texts as they encounter greater variety.
❖ Use information from pictures.	❖ Recognize most easy, high frequency words.	❖ Do not rely on illustrations but notice them to gain additional meaning.	❖ Analyze words in flexible ways and make excellent attempts at new, multisyllable words.	❖ Develop favorite topics and authors that form the basis of life-long reading preferences.
❖ Connect words with names.	❖ Check to be sure reading makes sense, sounds right, looks right.	❖ Understand, interpret, and use illustrations in informational text.	❖ Have systems for learning more about the reading process as they read so that they build skills simply by encountering many different kinds of texts with a variety of new words.	❖ Actively work to connect texts for greater understanding and finer interpretations of texts.
❖ Notice and use spaces between words.	❖ Check one source of information against another to solve problems.	❖ Know how to read differently in some different genres.	❖ Are in a continuous process of building background knowledge and realize that they need to bring their knowledge to their reading.	❖ Consistently go beyond the text read to form their own interpretations and apply understandings in other areas.
❖ Read orally.	❖ Use information from pictures as added information while reading print.	❖ Have flexible ways of problem-solving words, including analysis of letter-sound relationships and visual patterns.	❖ Become absorbed in books.	❖ Sustain interest and understanding over long texts and read over extended periods of time.
❖ Match one spoken word to one printed word while reading 1 or 2 lines of text.		❖ Read with phrasing and fluency at appropriate levels.	❖ Begin to identify with characters in books and see themselves in the events of the stories.	❖ Notice and comment on aspects of the writer's craft.
❖ Use spaces and some visual information to check on reading.			❖ Connect texts with previous texts read.	❖ Read to explore themselves as well as philosophical and social issues.
❖ Know names of some alphabet letters.				
❖ Know some letter-sound relationships.				
❖ Read left to right.				
❖ Recognize a few high frequency words.				
Texts: Simple stories with 1–2 lines.	*Texts:* Longer books with high frequency words and supportive illustrations.	*Texts:* Texts with many lines of print; books organized into short chapters; more difficult picture books; wider variety of genre.	*Texts:* Wide reading of a variety of long and short texts; variety of genre.	*Texts:* Wide reading of a variety of genre and for a range of purposes.

reading (as well as writing) can and should be on topics that are appropriate for content area study.

Broadening Appreciation for Reading

Teachers often bemoan the fact that their students can read but *don't*. Perhaps they are not experiencing the satisfaction reading can bring. As teachers, we need to help students explore the rich ways in which reading can fill their lives. If we reflect on ourselves as readers, we will discover all the reasons that guide our intermediate students' reading as well.

Carlson (1974) has described the stages, or levels, of appreciation through which avid readers progress (see Figure 1–3). These stages are not discrete periods but represent the full spectrum of satisfaction that emerges as readers deepen their experience:

1. *Reading for enjoyment.* At this stage young readers "lose themselves" in books. They no longer have to attend to the "skills" of beginning reading and find themselves completely absorbed; they are not conscious of reading as an act but are simply enjoying a story or satisfying their curiosity about the topic they are exploring.
2. *Reading for vicarious experiences.* Here readers still lose themselves in books, but they want to know how other people feel and live; they want to experience events and places that are distant from their own here and now.
3. *Reading to find yourself.* Young adolescents, in particular, are grappling with the problems of growing up and experiencing so many sudden changes. They select characters they read about as models and appropriate these characters' ways of dealing with things.
4. *Reading to understand issues.* Students' interests expand as they use literature to understand philosophical and social issues such as poverty, war, racism, and religious differences.

5. *Reading for aesthetic appreciation.* Mature readers are drawn to literature as works of art. They read for the inherent aesthetic experience, to enjoy the exceptional language and refined nuances of the writer's craft.

Some intermediate students are still learning to enjoy stories, but most are reading for enjoyment, for vicarious experiences, and to find themselves. Our reading/writing program must offer them the support, teaching, and materials they need to make continuous progress. Satisfaction and enjoyment must be present at every point along the continuum.

An important prerequisite for providing engaging instruction is to find out more about your students as readers and writers, to investigate their reading and writing habits, interests, and attitudes. One way to do this is to ask students to respond to a reading interview in writing (Atwell 2000; Goodman, Watson, Burke 1996) (included in Appendix 46) or to ask them some or all of these survey-type questions in an interview. The written questionnaire is easily administered and provides a great deal of information quickly. The oral interview will provide more and different kinds of data because you can explore their thoughts and opinions.

Another way to get interesting information about reading is described below:

1. Collect samples of different kinds of written materials. For example:

   ■ Novels at different levels of difficulty.
   ■ Magazine articles from several different sources (e.g., *Sports Illustrated, TV Guide, Time for Kids, Images, Muse, Cobblestone, Scholastic News, Cicada*).
   ■ Textbooks.
   ■ Poems.

Expanding Appreciation for Reading

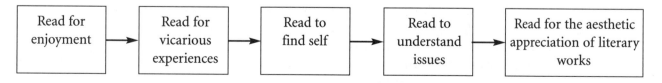

Figure 1–3. *Expanding Appreciation for Reading*

- Informational books.
- "How-to" guides of any kind.

2. Conduct a one-on-one student interview.
   - Ask the student what he is reading and how, what, and why he is reading it.
   - Ask the student to look at the materials on the table and to identify:
     the kinds of materials she most likes to read;
     the kinds of materials she least likes to read;
     the kinds of materials that are difficult or easy for her to read.

Connecting Reading and Writing

Reading and writing are separate but intimately related processes. Mature readers and writers are constantly making connections between reading and writing. Smith (1988, 25) calls this stance "reading like a writer to write like a writer." He maintains that when writers read, they notice aspects of text that then become possibilities for their own writing. In addition to enjoying a book, writers develop insights into the craft that produced the book. They notice interesting words or ways language is put together to communicate feelings or help the reader form images. When writers write, they remember their reading and use in their own writing what they have noticed about other texts. Readers and writers are always centering their attention on texts.

Beginners in the primary grades are learning what readers and writers do. They are developing those basic skills and strategies that allow them to engage in the acts of reading and writing. We should not forget, however, that while the focus may be on learning to read or write, the goal of the individual reader or writer is always the same—to enjoy, understand, and interpret text. Even young readers and writers are establishing important concepts about how authors and illustrators construct meaning. They learn how authors and illustrators organize ideas and use language. They learn how authors and illustrators use detail to arouse feelings, create characters, or build suspense. They learn that illustrations extend and enhance the meaning of the text and therefore need to be placed near the text to which they relate.

Much of this learning for very young children takes place while the teacher reads aloud to them; nevertheless, if quality literature is used even in the simple texts they read for themselves, there is much to notice about the craft of writing. Eckhoff (1983) found that young children's writing clearly reflected the features and style of the texts they were reading in the instructional context.

In the intermediate grades, students learn more about the processes of reading and writing and use the skills and strategies of readers and writers in a wide range of learning contexts. If their literacy program has provided the opportunity, these students have acquired a rich background of texts that they can, to a large extent, remember. They draw on these textual resources as writers, beginning to attend to the ways in which different authors and illustrators construct meaning. In turn, their growing awareness enriches their ability to develop and communicate ideas in writing.

Chew (1985) has provided an interesting summary of the parallel processes that exist in reading and writing. He says:

> [T]he reader is a mental writer, one who summarizes, gains information, and readjusts. As readers read they adjust the information base from which they operate and change their predictions of what is yet to come. (p. 170)

Figure 1–4 summarizes the important parallels between reading and writing. You will notice the many similarities though there are also important differences.

Reading and writing may be taught as separate subjects, but the connections across these two parallel processes must be made explicit. For example, a minilesson on some aspect of text—using language to create images, effective titles—might serve both for reading and writing. Connections between reading and writing are enhanced by the conversation that surrounds reading and writing in the intermediate classroom. When students discuss their writing with the teacher and with one another, they can use the text they have read as resources for just about any aspect of writing—from words to organization. When students talk about the books they are reading, they become aware of texts in ways that make features more accessible to them as writers. The teacher's presence is the key to creating these complex interrelationships.

How Reading and Writing Are Alike	
Writing	**Reading**
❖ Before and during writing, writers often talk, discuss, brainstorm, reflect, gather information, make lists, etc.	❖ Before and during reading, readers talk, make predictions, skim outlines or headings, and raise questions.
❖ Writers bring shape to the written piece as they draft and revise it.	❖ Readers do not change the print but they revise their thoughts, predictions, and concepts as they read.
❖ Writers learn to look at their work, rereading for needed changes.	❖ Readers learn to reevaluate their understandings about a written piece, often reading a text again.
❖ Writers share their work informally through discussion and more formally through publication.	❖ Readers share their understandings with others through verbal, written, or artistic responses.
❖ Writers appreciate the work of other writers.	❖ Readers appreciate the insights and understandings of others.
❖ Writers compose whole pieces of text.	❖ Readers draw understandings across whole texts.
❖ Writers bring their own meanings to the texts they compose; they express their ideas and feelings in written language.	❖ The meaning that readers derive from texts varies with their experiential background; in other words, they bring meaning to the text.
❖ Drafts reveal writers' attempts to apply their knowledge in new ways.	❖ Partially correct responses reveal readers' attempts to use information to solve words.

Figure 1–4. How Reading and Writing Are Alike

Suggestions for Professional Development

The ultimate goal of the literacy program is to enable students to learn how satisfying reading and writing are and to establish lifelong reading and writing habits. Teachers who themselves engage in reading and writing, and who examine their habits and attitudes as readers and writers, can best help students experience the power of their own literacy.

1. Take a piece of paper and write responses to the questions on the survey "Looking at Yourself as a Reader and a Writer" (Figure 1–5). Bring your responses to a meeting with a group of colleagues. If you can, also bring copies of the books you thought about as you filled in the survey and pieces of writing you are working on or have completed. (You may decide to have two meetings—one on reading and one on writing. If so, save responses from the first session to make connections between the two processes.)

2. Discuss your reading and writing responses. Ask a recorder to write on chart paper all the characteristics of reading and writing brought up by your group. This list will serve as a summary of what mature readers and writers do.

3. Compare your list with the lists at the beginning of this chapter and add ideas if appropriate.

4. Discuss the characteristics of readers and writers that you and your colleagues exhibit in connection with your students:

   ■ What experiences helped you create your habits and attitudes, likes and dislikes as readers and as writers?

   ■ How do you see some of the characteristics of readers and writers reflected in the students you teach? (You may want to respond to this question in grade-level pairs.)

   ■ What classroom experiences support students as they develop mature reading and writing habits, attitudes, and interests?

Looking at Yourself as a Reader and a Writer

Reading	Writing
1. Are you a reader?	1. Are you a writer?
2. Do you read for pleasure?	2. How do you feel about your writing?
3. When, what, and how?	3. What types of writing do you do?
4. How do you feel about yourself as a reader?	4. How often do you write?
5. What do you like most about reading?	5. Do you write for pleasure? When, what, and why?
6 What do you like least about reading?	6. Do you write for communication? When, what, and why?
7. What do you find easy to read?	7. Do you write to assist your learning? When, what, and why?
8. What do you find difficult to read?	
9. Who are your favorite authors? poets?	8. How do you select topics for your writing?
10. What types (genres) of books do you like to read?	9. Who are the audiences for your writing?
11. What aspects of these books are particularly interesting to or enjoyable for you?	10. What is the best part of writing for you?
12. What is the last book you read that you really enjoyed?	11. What is the most difficult part of writing for you?
13. What are you reading now?	12. How do you get feedback for your writing?
14. How do you find the books you read?	13. What is your most recent piece of writing?
15. How do you go about making your choices?	14. How much writing have you done in the past year?
16. How often do you read?	15. What "writers" do you know that help you think about your own writing?
17. How many books would you estimate you have read in the last year?	16. Bring a piece of writing that you have done. Be prepared to talk about why you wrote it and how you feel about it.
18. When do you find time to read?	
19. What different kinds of material do you read?	
20. What do you do following the reading of a book?	
21. Bring a favorite book and tell why you like it.	

Figure 1–5. Looking at Yourself as a Reader and a Writer

ACHIEVING LITERACY WITH A THREE-BLOCK FRAMEWORK: LANGUAGE & WORD STUDY, READING, AND WRITING

It's my job to surround (kids) with the best models; authors to whom they can apprentice them-selves, books they can lose themselves in, characters who tell them they're not alone, words that make them think and feel and learn.

— LINDA RIEF

Effective instruction in language, literature, and the content areas begins with thoughtful, artful organization and planning. A prevailing issue in intermediate-grade teaching is using time effectively so that students not only expand their reading and writing capabilities but also develop in-depth knowledge in the content areas. A three-block framework is an effective tool for designing and managing the instructional program in grades 3 through 6. The level of activity, the content, and the materials will vary greatly by teacher and by grade level, but the essential elements of the framework remain constant:

1. *Language.* Reading and writing are language based. Using language orally—discussing, sharing opinions, questioning, criticizing, describing, and performing—is the precursor to sharing your thinking in writing. Teachers must ask students to do their best thinking, to share it orally, and to find many different ways to share it in writing.
2. *Literacy.* Although we realize there are many kinds of literacy (artistic and technological, for example), our focus here is reading and writing. There are powerful and complementary interrelationships between reading and writing: we cannot talk about one without the other. When students are learning how to think about text as readers, they are also learning how to notice and use the craft of writing. When students are learning how to compose and construct writing, they are also developing key understandings about text that will help them develop greater insights as readers.

3. *Literature.* Throughout this book, we talk about the value of literature. Students in the intermediate grades flourish as they learn about and read quality fiction, nonfiction, and poetry. Each instructional context provides a different way in to this invaluable resource, from highly supported, teacher-guided analysis to independent reading to discussing literature orally and in writing.
4. *Content.* Learning in the content areas is woven throughout all three blocks of the framework. Students read and write about topics related to science, social studies, mathematics, health, communication, etc. The range of study for intermediate students is broad; they continuously increase their knowledge through experience, discussion, and reading in multiple genres, and they organize and communicate their knowledge through a variety of presentational formats. In the process, they expand their vocabulary and learn new ways of organizing written text. Infusing the language arts curriculum with rich content in many genres increases the sophistication of the language students use and expands their interests and knowledge.

This three-block structured framework will help you conceptualize the language arts curriculum, think about students' literacy learning, plan and organize instruction, and provide a high level of productivity and engagement. The framework is flexible. There are many possibilities for variation—in the content studied, the texts, the configurations of students (individuals, small groups, the whole class), and the daily time frames.

Why Use a Framework?

When you approach the intermediate reading and writing curriculum in a highly organized way, your students understand how the classroom functions, know what is expected of them, and accomplish more in the short school day. A structured framework has several advantages.

A Common Language and Vision

Using this structured framework across the intermediate grades will facilitate grade-level discussions and planning as well as planning across the grades. As you and your colleagues meet regularly to talk and plan, the framework will help you focus on a common set of practices and bring coherence to the intermediate program. Using a common language, including common definitions for such instructional settings as "writing workshop" and "guided reading," allows you to help one another. It makes it easier to articulate the curriculum across the grade levels, so that learning builds on previous learning.

This common language also helps students. Moving from one grade to another is a significant change, but meeting familiar structures, described in ways students understand, makes the transition smoother. Students know what is expected of them in terms of routine and responsibility; they can focus on continually expanding their skills.

Efficient Allocation of Instructional Time

A structured framework makes it easier to handle time. You, your students, and your colleagues know, for example, that there is a specific time period for reading instruction and a routine that must be followed. Schoolwide schedules are easier to plan and can accommodate the maximum amount of learning. Because the framework actively fosters instruction in reading and writing in combination with content-area study, two or even three curriculum goals may be addressed within the same instructional period. We have allocated between thirty and sixty minutes for language and word study, an hour for reading, and an hour for writing. You can schedule one continuous block of three hours, or three one-hour sessions at various points in the day. The important thing is that you and your students consistently make connections across the three blocks. Many elementary schools have instituted "departmentalized"

instruction as early as third grade level. We urge teachers and administrators to reconsider this policy since:

- There is no research to support this practice.
- Learners need teachers who know them fully and who can help them make connections across reading, writing, and content areas.

If you are in a school where there is departmentalization, work for a full hour of reading instruction and integrate writing with content areas and language arts. In addition, schedule many regular meetings with colleagues to discuss individual students and gain a full picture of progress. At this point, you may believe that devoting up to three hours to the language arts is impossible, but Chapter 6 shows you ways teachers have created schedules that work.

Routines for Independent Learning

If your students are constantly depending on you to tell them what to do, they will not develop the independence and self-direction that learners need. When your language and literacy program rests on a predictable structure, students can be more independent. Predictability and organization help your students deal with the daily ebb and flow; they can plan ahead with confidence, because they will have clear expectations for what they will accomplish on any given day. They will encounter a particular topic through reading, writing, and language/word study activities with an appropriate focus.

Making Connections

The framework also helps you recognize and plan for the relationships between and among different components of the curriculum. For example, what students are reading about can contribute to their writing or to their study of words. The content areas and literature are integrated; students read and write about the central, compelling aspects of their learning.

Let's look now at the way a typical school day unfolds around the three-block framework.

Community Meeting

The day typically begins with a whole-group community meeting, held before you move your students into language and word study. The purpose is to build the collaboration and cooperation necessary for learning throughout the day.

Group Planning

It is essential that you and your students outline and negotiate common goals and concerns. We can't stress enough how important it is for intermediate learners to take an active role in planning and evaluating their learning; they are not passive recipients. The group planning session, which typically occurs near the beginning of the day, brings the community together. You might review the daily schedule, determine the shared goals for the day, discuss current issues and topics, make announcements, or offer reminders.

The meeting is brief and efficient, not long or complicated. As a rule, it shouldn't last more than five to eight minutes. (Find other, more efficient ways to check off completed homework and take lunch count.)

Block 1: Language & Word Study

The focus of the first block is on developing children's language and word study knowledge and skills. Students investigate the nature of language as they explore high-quality literature, poetry, and informational texts. Later we discuss getting a poetry anthology started in the first few weeks of school. So the powerful language of poetic text becomes an integral part of reading, writing, and oral language from the start. After several weeks of poetry enjoyment and study in the language/word study block, the poetry work becomes part of a poetry workshop that takes the place of reading and/or writing workshop every week or every other week.

These components are discussed in greater detail in Chapter 3, "Investigating and Using Language," Chapter 22, "Teaching for Word-Solving," and Chapter 24, "Creating the Poetry Workshop." Of course, you won't select all these components every day. You'll use them over the course of a week (or several weeks) to achieve particular teaching goals.

Shared Language/Literacy

The block begins with a community meeting. Here you present a brief, focused experience intended to expand students' language and/or literacy skills. In the process, your students will become more sophisticated about the "do's" and "don'ts" of group interaction. Here are several examples.

- Ask students, in groups of three, to talk about a topic for three minutes. Then, as a class, have them share the key ideas that surfaced.
- Build vocabulary by reading a paragraph that features one or more new words and then talk about what the words mean.
- Provide a short handwriting lesson and ask students to practice letter formation.
- Give students a topic, ask them to write three or four sentences in their writer's notebook, and then share their writing with one another.
- Each day ask a different student to talk about something in the news, or have partners talk about a news item. (Assign this the day before so the students can prepare.)
- Provide short editing lessons by projecting a page of text on the overhead projector and have the students decide what to change.

Language/Word Study (30–60 minutes)

Shared Language/Literacy

Options:

- ❖ Interactive Edit
- ❖ Interactive Vocabulary
- ❖ Handwriting Minilesson
- ❖ Test Reading/Writing
- ❖ Current Events
- ❖ Modeled or Shared Reading/Writing
- ❖ Readers' Theatre/Process Drama
- ❖ Choral Reading
- ❖ Poetry Share/Response
- ❖ Word Study
- ❖ Interactive Read Aloud

Figure 2–1. Block 1: Language & Word Study

■ Each day read or have a different student read or recite a poem to the group. (Again, be sure there is a schedule of who reads when.) Invite comments on "What the poem says to you" or "What you notice about the way the author wrote the poem."

Shared interactive language/literacy is also an appropriate time for helping students learn clear and flexible ways of displaying their language and literacy knowledge. For example, everyone might work together on the different kinds of questions found on standardized tests—open-ended, multiple choice, and so on—and discuss strategies for evaluating and checking the answers. (We will discuss these kinds of activities more extensively in Chapter 28.)

Interactive Edit

An interactive edit is a brief activity (typically no more than five minutes long) focusing on conventions. There are several ways to involve the group in cooperative editing. For example, you can dictate one or two sentences that present challenges related to capitalization, punctuation, grammar, spelling, word choice, whatever. (Have one child write it correctly on the easel for all to see while the rest use their clipboards.) Or you can display the sentences on a chart or on an overhead projector. Then have students copy the sentences, editing individually or with a partner. Afterward, talk about the reasons for using the various conventions. (This is a good way to bring dictionaries, style guides, and similar references to their attention.)

Figure 2–2. Teacher and Students in Group Meeting

Handwriting

A five-minute minilesson once a week on letter formation will improve the legibility of student work. Make sure you include guided practice. One student can work on a chalkboard or flipchart while the others work on their own.

Word Study

A minilesson on a strategy or principle related to the ongoing word study described in Chapter 23 (see also Pinnell and Fountas 1998) helps students become better word users. The lesson can focus on the spelling of a specific word, sophisticated phonics principles, or on the development of vocabulary. Or you can ask student partners to complete structured activities that help them learn how words work.

Modeled/Shared Reading/Writing

You will want to model reading or writing or share the task of reading and writing to help your students expand their literacy understanding. In modeled reading, you read a text to students, engaging them by showing your thinking along the way. In shared reading, you and your students all have a copy of the same text (if the piece is relatively long) or the text is projected on the overhead or copied onto chart paper (if it's short). The students follow along while you read the text aloud, perhaps inviting them to join you or take over from time to time. This is an excellent way for the whole class to study the same text with your support. In modeled writing you demonstrate the writing of a text. During shared writing, you and your students work together first to discuss and then to compose a common text related to an experience they have had or something that they are studying. You are the scribe, using an easel, the chalkboard, or an overhead projector.

Interactive Read-Aloud

Reading aloud to students allows them to experience a variety of quality texts in different genres. In the typical read-aloud, the teacher reads and the students listen, period. In an interactive read-aloud, you pause at significant points, ask your students for comments, and invite brief discussion. Be sure to share your own thinking to demonstrate how experienced readers engage with and think about texts as they read. Do not

---

Reading Workshop (60 minutes)
❖ Independent Reading
❖ Guided Reading
❖ Literature Study

Figure 2–3. Block 2: Reading Workshop

stop too frequently or for too long or it will disrupt the flow.

These are only a sample of the shared language and literacy tasks you might choose. We will discuss several other interactive language and literacy options later in this book. You will want to design your block to include the options your students need.

Block 2: Reading Workshop

In a typical reading workshop, the teacher gives a mini-lesson, students read individually, and then everyone gathers as a group to share thoughts and opinions. Our version (see Figure 2–3) includes independent reading, which is certainly important, but we expand the idea to incorporate two other reading contexts—guided reading and literature study. All three components are described in Chapter 4, and each is covered in detail in its own section.

You will want to focus on reading for one hour a day five days a week—four if five is not possible—so that students do not lose their momentum. And it's always a good idea to encourage your students to read at home each night for thirty minutes as well.

Think about your own reading. What happens if you read a chapter or two of a book on Thursday and don't pick it up again until Monday? You probably have to work to recapture your sense of what the book is about. It's the same with students. If they're only reading now and then, they tend to lose interest and begin to see reading simply as another tedious assignment. Your teaching also loses momentum when there are long gaps between periods set aside for reading. The continuity is disrupted, and students forget the

kinds of strategies and skills you are trying to build day after day. Students who have the chance tomorrow to apply what they have learned today form stronger learning patterns.

Then, too, it is harder to establish routines when you do something occasionally rather than daily. Established routines help build community and security. When students read every day, they are continually learning new things that they can share with partners, small groups, or the whole class.

Independent Reading

In independent reading, students read individually and silently, typically selecting their own texts, sometimes with teacher guidance. When you implement independent reading for the first time, you will want to present several minilessons on how to select books. An organized book collection also helps students select appropriate books. While the students are reading, you will be able to hold one-on-one conferences. At the end of the period, you will want to conduct some sharing and evaluation.

Guided Reading

Guided reading is small-group instruction for students who read the same text. The group is homogeneous: the students read at about the same level, demonstrate similar reading behaviors, and share similar instructional needs. These small groups (anywhere from three to eight students) are temporary; they change as you assess your students' growth and needs. In the small group, you introduce a text that you have selected, and the students read it silently and independently. Students usually read silently, though you might ask individual students to read orally at regular intervals and talk with them individually about the book. You also explicitly teach effective strategies for processing a variety of fiction and nonfiction texts. You select teaching points based on the reader's needs and may assign oral and/or written responses and extensions. You might also engage the students in a minute or two of word work.

Literature Study

In literature study, you work with small heterogeneous groups of students who are interested in certain topics, authors, genres, or specific books. Together, you decide on a text, assign reading/writing tasks, and agree on meeting times. Students talk in depth about what they have read (or, occasionally, what you have read to them). You are generally present for the discussion, although the students may take turns facilitating it. In consultation with the group, you sometimes structure written responses or brief sharing projects.

Purposes

With all three elements of reading workshop, students read for an extended period during the one-hour block. In all three contexts, constructing meaning is the overall goal. You want to help readers make personal and textual connections at the same time they are learning from and about reading. But each approach has a different format, different roles for the teacher and students, and different primary purposes. The three contexts contribute in different ways to the development of readers and look different when they are implemented.

In independent reading, you want to help individuals become readers who like to read, develop their own tastes and interests, and consistently learn about their world and about themselves through their reading. Your overarching instructional goal is clear: to help individual students engage in all aspects of what readers do, from choosing books to reflecting on what they've read. Independent reading is an authentic context in which students develop the skills, habits, and processes of accomplished readers by doing everything good readers do. In guided reading, your goal is to help readers develop more effective and efficient processing systems and to expand their reading power to more and more difficult texts. In literature study your focus is on helping students develop a deeper appreciation for and understanding of literature.

Teacher and Student Roles

Your role in all three contexts is critical, but you will provide explicit teaching in different ways and at different times:

■ In independent reading, you present minilessons on everything from how to select a book to how to figure out unfamiliar words. You also have individual conferences with students "reader to reader" to discuss their reading, and guide the sharing in group meeting.

■ In guided reading, you select and introduce a text, observe and sometimes listen to individual students while they read, and teach specific focused skills after the reading. You might engage the students in extending their understanding, or in a minute or two of word work.

■ In literature study, you present book talks that engage the students' interest, demonstrate routines that make for good group discussions, summarize the points students have made, make learning visible during or at the end of the discussion, and introduce structures (oral, written, or pictorial) for responding to literature.

Students also have important roles and responsibilities in all three contexts, and these also vary according to the focus and format:

■ In independent reading, students are responsible for selecting their own books and using time efficiently for silent reading. They prepare written responses and should be ready to discuss their reading with others. They keep records of their reading and develop habits and attitudes of a reader.

■ In guided reading, students actively apply the new skills they are learning; they become more aware of themselves as readers and sometimes read orally, reflecting on and evaluating their reading performance. Before and after reading they raise issues and questions, offer examples from their own experience, and connect what they have read to other texts.

■ In literature study, students select the text or topic in conjunction with the teacher and other group members, attend the meeting at the proper time and place, and prepare for the discussion by reading and organizing their thoughts in advance. During the

---

Writing Workshop
(60 minutes)

❖ Independent Writing
❖ Guided Writing
❖ Investigations

Figure 2–4. Block 3: Writing Workshop

Figure 2–5. Independent Writing

must develop a "routine" for writing; it is a daily activity, not a series of isolated assignments.

When we set aside sustained time for writing, we communicate to students that we value it. In school, writing is one of the most necessary—and most evaluated—skills. We will not develop writers if we ask students to write only when we can "fit it in." And if we only assign writing as homework, students won't receive expert help or benefit from peer support and interaction. When we develop a community of writers, students have the chance to give help and receive help from others.

meeting, they take turns talking, following the rules of conversation, and may serve as facilitator at times. They may also work cooperatively with others on a longer project related to the literature they are studying.

Block 3: Writing Workshop

In writing workshop students learn what it means to be a writer—how writers think, plan, compose, revise, and share their work. A typical writing workshop (Atwell 1999) begins with a minilesson after which students write on their own while the teacher confers with writers, followed by sharing. Our concept of a writing workshop is somewhat broader, including three contexts for learning (see Figure 2–4). Each component is explained in detail in Chapter 5. The three contexts make it possible to offer students more instruction and guidance in specific aspects of writing, and they also allow students to write across the broad range of topics included in the content curriculum.

Daily writing is as necessary as daily reading. Focus on writing an hour a day five days a week—four if five is not possible. It is difficult for inexperienced writers to conceptualize and finish a piece that is left unattended for many days. Also, students build momentum and skill if they write consistently over time. They need to be able to use the feedback they get in conferences and sharing sessions while it is fresh. Finally, students

Independent Writing

Students work silently and individually on their own writing. You provide a daily minilesson based on the needs of the writers. Students write and sketch, sometimes using writer's notebooks, at other times drafting, revising, editing, or publishing a piece of work. Usually students select their own writing topics; occasionally they are assigned. The teacher confers with individual students, and the session is usually followed by sharing and evaluation.

Guided Writing

Small temporary groups of students meet to discuss aspects of writing and learn more about the writer's craft and conventions. These groups consist of students who have similar needs at a particular time and to whom you teach explicit strategies and skills. The groupings are usually short term, as you re-form groups based on what you are learning as you read their writing.

Investigations

Students work independently or with partners on long-term projects. Investigations are an ideal setting in which to integrate the content areas. Using reading, writing, and a variety of media resources, including technology, students explore topics in depth. An investigation often culminates in an oral presentation, performance, or display that includes written material. The teacher provides guidelines, a structure, and a time line for the projects, as well as explicit instruction as appropriate.

Teacher and Student Roles

In all three writing workshop contexts, you provide explicit instruction as well as guidance while students write.

In independent writing, you provide a minilesson for the entire class based on your observations of students' writing. The minilesson is followed by conferences with individual students that center on those aspects of writing they want help with and need to learn. The writing conference is usually a time to check whether students are applying the new understandings developed in the minilesson. It's also an opportunity to document specific writing behaviors that will require future minilessons.

In guided writing you identify small groups of students who need to work at a particular aspect of writing. You might meet with a group for several days in a row until new understandings become part of their writing. Or you might meet with the group over several weeks of more in-depth study (when introducing a new genre, for example).

Your role in investigations is more multifaceted, since it is connected to the whole range of instruction you provide for students in the content areas. You may assign a topic and guide students in investigating a specific aspect of it. You may stimulate interest in a topic through conversation, reading aloud, drama, demonstrations, or field trips. You may provide some print and nonprint resources and teach students how to locate others. You provide minilessons as needed on whatever students need to learn. Examples include:

1. How to conduct a good interview.
2. How to use the Internet.
3. How to find specific information in reference books.
4. How to formulate good questions.
5. How to plan the steps of an experiment.
6. How to locate print and nonprint resources.
7. How to use a table of contents, index, or glossary.
8. How to use the library.
9. How to take notes or use writing in other ways to support investigation.
10. How to organize different kinds of information.

Investigations offer students the opportunity to use everything they know about reading and writing, and to explore the many "ways of knowing" (Gardner 1993; Campbell, Campbell, and Dickinson 1998). They approach these investigations much as a scientist would, so their learning is invigorating and authentic. And they explore many different ways of summarizing and representing their findings: artistic, scientific, mathematical. Students come to understand the language arts as communication tools. Your role in guiding the entire process is essential.

The students' role in writing workshop includes working on their own pieces of writing during independent and guided writing and integrating research and content area study as they work on investigations. They also evaluate their own work and assist their peers.

Oral, Visual, and Technological Communication

We refer to a *language and literacy* framework because helping students learn language is a crucial aspect of teaching in the intermediate grades. We are always helping students develop, refine, and reshape their language. They are learning much more than new vocabulary: they are learning unique ways to put words together in clear and effective syntactic structures. They are learning the subtle nuances of what words mean in context. They achieve this through conversation, presentation, performance, and visual representation (see Figure 2–6). Students learn language, they learn about language, and they learn through language (Halliday 1975).

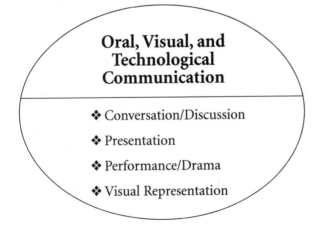

Figure 2–6. *Oral, Visual, and Technological Communication*

In our complex society, language is constantly changing. New words are coined every day to keep up with the new technology and new events and customs: *cyberspace, hypertext, web access.* Old words take on new meanings. For example, what do you think about when you hear words like *surfing, grazing,* or *wrap?* Ten years ago we might have thought of young people riding ocean waves, cows eating in a field, or a coat. But your intermediate students will think about checking out web sites, changing TV channels in rapid succession, or a new kind of sandwich. Language changes, and students continue to learn new language by hearing it, using it, and reading it. McWhorter (2000) holds that the changing nature of language is much more pervasive than the "slang" expressions that pop up and as quickly disappear. He says, "there is no society on earth where people could manage a conversation with their ancestors from a thousand years back or more" (p. 2).

We want our intermediate students constantly to broaden and polish their communication skills. In this age of technology the opportunities for, and the requirements of, communication are increasing dramatically: it is no longer a simple matter of writing or talking. Conversation in the business world, for example, is interwoven with visual images, sounds, and many kinds of print. Speakers use a number of media to communicate information to audiences, and that information serves a variety of purposes—to persuade, to inform, to challenge, to inspire. Even less formal gatherings, however, involve visual and technological communication.

Communication on the Internet is an entirely new genre of writing/talking, one that requires a different way of organizing and producing words. The originator is thinking in many dimensions and producing information that can be used by the recipient in flexible ways.

Our framework represents students' integration of reading, writing, talking, technology, and the visual arts as ways to represent, apply, and communicate what they have learned. With sufficient technology and teacher training, intermediate students can make PowerPoint presentations on their science experiment, their history investigation, their analysis of a novel or an illustrated poem. They can communicate instantly with people in different states, different countries, or different continents as they do their research.

The Importance of Oral Language

Four decades of research has established oral language as the foundation of reading and writing development, especially for intermediate students, who are expanding their use of literacy as a tool for learning.

The texts intermediate students encounter include sophisticated ideas expressed in complex language. As students read, they use what they already know about language to construct meaning. At the same time, they learn more about language. The more they know about language, the richer the experience they bring to reading. In language-centered classrooms, teachers value talk and its role in learning. "Language-centered," however, doesn't mean talk alone; it involves the juxtaposition of talk in conjunction with new, challenging learning experiences and texts. In other words, students are always talking about something: substantive, stimulating content and the exciting learning it inspires.

Learning New Language

We learn new language in several ways:

- *Conversation.* We talk with more expert others who provide new language models and interact with us in a way that inspires us to try something new.
- *Experience.* We experience something new and stretch to use new language to describe our experience to others. By talking with others about a challenging learning experience—performing a scientific experiment, solving a problem, looking at a painting, going to a play, taking a trip to a new place—we are moved to try new ways of expression as well as new words, phrases, or idioms.
- *Text.* We expand our control over written language when we encounter new texts. Written language is different from oral language in its structure and even its vocabulary. Our students' written-language abilities will not expand unless they are exposed to text, whether through reading or listening.

Connecting Oral, Visual, Technological, and Written Communication

Students not only learn through oral and visual communication but also express and display their learning through these means—and, in the process, they learn more. Figure 2–7 depicts our language and literacy framework in a nutshell.

Language and Literacy Framework
for Literature and the Content Areas

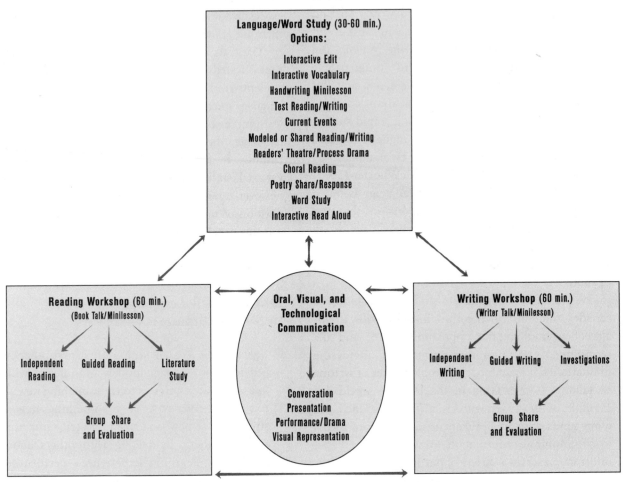

Figure 2–7. Language and Literacy Framework for Literature and the Content Areas (3–6)

At the center of our language and literacy framework, connecting reading, writing, and word study, is oral, visual, and technological communication. Students converse, present, perform, and draw, using oral language as they do so. Oral language is linked to specific work in reading and writing and supports the development of these sophisticated skills. It is also a way to internalize, summarize, and display knowledge. Students express meaning in many different ways within the language and literacy framework, and use technology to communicate their language in a variety of forms.

CONVERSATION

As students investigate topics and explore literature, they engage in conversations with others (Wilkinson 1970, 1971, 1975). Through focused conversation, they learn how to:

- Listen actively.
- Speak directly to others, articulating clearly.
- Arrange the participants so all can see and hear one another.
- Take turns, being courteous to others.
- Respond to and build on others' statements.
- Stay on the topic.
- Share information effectively.
- Consider an audience.
- Ask for information and incorporate it into later statements.
- Summarize and extend the group conversation.
- Check whether others understand and are following the conversation.

PRESENTATION

In making presentations, students use oral language

and tools such as illustrations, charts, diagrams, and artifacts to communicate meaning to an audience. In the process, they learn how to:

- Select interesting findings to incorporate in their presentation.
- Arrange ideas in an interesting and informative sequence.
- Consider appropriate places for visual or other kinds of enhancements.
- Introduce and summarize the topic.
- Engage the audience.
- Learn how posture, tone of voice, and gesture contribute to the effectiveness of a presentation.
- Maintain a lively pace.
- Select precise words that convey meaning to an audience, elaborating where needed.
- Answer questions about the presentation.
- Evaluate their own presentations.
- Evaluate and provide feedback on presentations by their peers.

PERFORMANCE/DRAMA

Through both improvised and more formal, memorized performances, sometimes incorporating art and music, students can explore the nature of story, learn about life, and empathize with other people. Dramatic performances enable students to enjoy literature and poetry in an active, participatory way. The language continues to "live" in their minds and is a resource for their own writing as they try out new ways of using written language.

Students can also use drama to imagine an experience (Heathcote 1983; Heathcote and Herbert 1985; Wilhelm, Edmiston, and Beane 1998). Guided by the teacher, the students interconnect inquiry and learning with being and doing. Events, materials, and new ideas are introduced to the community. For example, a class of students might imagine themselves as a group of pioneers heading West, encountering and solving various problems over a period of several weeks. They "step into the roles" as a way of making the thinking and experiences of others come alive. Both within and outside the roles, they gather the information they need—researching how many miles a day the wagon train could travel, for example. This process is particularly useful for exploring social studies and literature.

VISUAL REPRESENTATION

Visual representation is an integral part of communication. Readers may draw, sketch, or print as a way of sharing their response to a text with others. Writers might draw or sketch an idea before they attempt to put it into words.

Sketching and drawing also play an important role in inquiry. Scientists prepare diagrams or charts; biologists and botanists record their observations via sketches, drawings, photographs, and videotapes. As students strive to communicate with an audience, they can use whatever visual representations best embody the meaning they wish to convey.

Content of the Language and Literacy Framework

Schools are places where students engage with others in learning activities that broaden their understanding of literature and the physical and social world. Students learn about literacy as they use reading and writing to explore the world around them. As teachers, we continually ask, "What is worthwhile for children to learn?"

The Negotiated Curriculum

The goals we want all students to achieve are the map for designing curriculum. They help us plan content area study as well as reading workshop, writing workshop, and oral, visual, and technological communication. When designing your curriculum, you start with your state or district goals and requirements, but add to and adjust them in relation to your own interest and expertise, and student/family interest and expertise. The creation of curriculum is thus a negotiated rather than prescribed process, as shown in Figure 2–8. It includes all these components.

The Content of the Curriculum

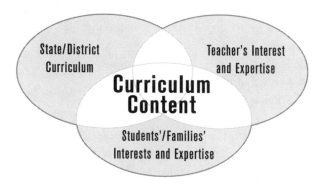

Figure 2–8. The Content of the Curriculum

You can contribute to the curriculum by using your own special interests and areas of expertise. For example, Petra, an avid gardener, helped her fourth graders examine different types of plant life. They planted a flower garden in one area of the school lawn and used it to study the characteristics of growing plants and their needs.

Your students also have a real contribution to make. When children are interested in a topic, they are much more motivated to investigate, read, and write about it. Family members or other people in the community can provide interesting perspectives and information as well. The most productive plan is to match your overall goals with the resources and people who can provide the corresponding information and to search for ways to match specific student interests with the larger concepts you want your curriculum to develop. For example, if one of your students is interested in flying, you might incorporate the history of flight into his study of the early twentieth century and persuade a parent who is a pilot to give an interview about what the job entails.

Range of the Curriculum

The language arts help us unite a broad range of curriculum. The literature we study should invoke the breadth of literary experience, including:

- Expository books, fiction, and poetry.
- Classics as well as contemporary works.
- Books that represent a range of cultures and languages, including works written by members of those cultural and linguistic groups (for example, *A Summer Life,* by Gary Soto, 1990).
- A wide range of genres, including articles and essays as well as books.

Students also need to read, write, talk, and learn about a wide range of subjects, including:

- Social studies.
- Mathematics.
- Science and health.

By investigating the content areas in connection with a wide range of reading, you are able to connect the elements of the language and literacy framework in a way that brings seamless learning to your students.

For example, the following shows how Norma's American Revolution emphasis played out in her fifth-grade classroom:

- Norma read aloud several picture books that made the times and events come alive.
- One literature study group was reading *Jump Ship to Freedom* (Collier and Collier 1987) while another was reading *Charley Skedaddle* (Beatty 1989).
- Norma filled a book basket with biographies about figures from the American Revolution and gave a book talk about them during independent reading.
- Norma and her students together compiled a list of possible topics the students could choose to investigate.

A note of caution: don't attempt to connect everything all the time. If you contrive connections where none exist, you'll end up with an artificial curriculum. Not all elements of the language and literacy framework will relate to every area of study. We also caution that reading and writing about science should not take the place of the process skills of the discipline such as hypothesizing, experimenting, observing, and so on.

Variety in Learning Resources

The world is filled with a wealth of print and nonprint resources that are highly effective in helping students expand their knowledge. Books, magazines, and newspapers are just some of them. Just think, for example, what students can learn from:

- Maps and globes, both current and historical.
- Photographs, audiotapes, and videotapes.
- Artifacts and objects.
- Original documents such as deeds and wills.
- Letters written in particular periods of history.

We will explore a great variety of print and nonprint resources for students to use in learning in Chapter 25.

Planning for the Three Blocks

You will want to plan for the language/word study, reading and writing workshop blocks across a week to be sure you are providing for well-sequenced, cohesive teaching and learning. We have provided two forms of a three block planning grid that we have found useful

(Appendix 1 and 2). You can copy and place them in a 3-ring binder to plan for and keep records of your teaching.

Organizing for Teaching and Record Keeping

We have found that three separate three-ring binders with various labeled sections help us organize effectively. In a Language/Word Study binder you can keep sections on the various options you use in the block—a list of the interactive edits, your word study minilesson plans, a list of the read-alouds, your test reading and writing minilessons, assessment records, etc. In the Reading Workshop binder you will want to keep lists of your minilessons, sample charts, reproducible forms for the journals, conference records, guided reading observations, book graphs, assessment records, and lists of book clubs. You may want a section in this binder for poetry workshop. We will describe each of these later in the book.

In the Writing Workshop binder you will want to keep lists of minilessons, conference records, writing assessments, lists of research projects, and other useful resources. The key is to organize each binder in a way that enables you to plan and keep records efficiently.

Conclusion

The language and literacy framework for literature and the content areas is a conceptual tool. The purpose of a framework is to make your teaching more powerful and easier to plan. It enables you to think about organizing time and content in effective, productive ways. The flexibility of the framework lies in the three blocks of time. You can move from one block to another in sequence or address each during nonadjacent periods of the day. Either way, the connections and support they offer remain, because students are reading, writing, discussing, and investigating exciting, invigorating topics.

Suggestions for Professional Development

1. With your grade-level colleagues, design a daily schedule that includes two-and-a-half to three hours of language and literacy teaching:

   ■ If you encounter problems, think "outside the box:" integrate subjects previously taught separately, rearrange your planning periods, reexamine how you incorporate special areas like music and art.

   ■ If you have departmentalization and cannot change it, work on a plan for allocating time for reading, writing, and word study, and for regular communication with other teachers so you can make connections over content areas.

   ■ Compare the time you have allocated for reading with the time you have set aside for writing. Writing is often shortchanged.

   ■ Talk about ways to incorporate more social studies and science into your literacy blocks.

   ■ Discuss ways to be more efficient. Could the first fifteen minutes of the day become part of the independent reading block?

   ■ Try out the schedule for one month and then revise it based on your experience.

2. Reevaluate the existing organizational structures in your classroom. Can some of these be changed? Can you find ways to incorporate some of them into the language and literacy framework?

3. With a group of colleagues, discuss changes you plan to make in terms of time, instructional approaches, classroom structure, or content.

## CHAPTER THREE

INVESTIGATING AND USING LANGUAGE: THE LANGUAGE AND WORD STUDY DESIGN

Words are all we have.
— SAMUEL BECKETT

Extending and refining our students' ability to use language is the primary goal of our language/literacy program. We want them to become proficient talkers, readers, and writers who use language to represent the world to themselves and to both known and distant audiences. In the thirty-to-sixty-minute language/word study block, your goal is to:

■ Create a community of learners within your class-room by giving students opportunities to talk, learn, and plan together.
■ Expose students to rich literary language and engaging content.
■ Present minilessons that help students learn about language and about the meaning and structure of words.
■ Provide a foundation for independent work on phonics, spelling, and vocabulary.

The instructional options for the Language/Word Study Block are listed in Figure 3–1. As you can see, the activities related to language learning vary broadly, from very explicit, focused lessons on aspects of word structure or meaning to reciting poetry aloud.

Reading comprehension and skillful writing are language processes. We want students to know about words and their meanings, but they also need to understand the way words are combined into sentences, paragraphs, and complete texts. Bringing students together as a community lets you augment their reading experiences with:

■ Direct teaching about how words look, sound, and mean.
■ Opportunities to encounter and notice words in meaningful contexts.
■ Opportunities to apply what they know about words as they read and write for real purposes.

Learning About Words

To comprehend written text, we must know what words—basic language units—mean. As adult readers, we can:

■ Quickly recognize most of the words we encounter.
■ Use letters, letter clusters, and word parts to decode words while reading for meaning.
■ Appreciate both literal and connotative meaning.
■ Use the information in a text to understand words in context.
■ Solve unfamiliar words.

As writers, we have a similar constellation of strategies. We:

■ Rapidly and unconsciously apply the movements (writing or typing) related to forming most words.
■ Construct words using letters, letter clusters, and word parts while composing and revising written text.
■ Select words for their precise literal and connotative meaning.
■ Spell words while writing to communicate.

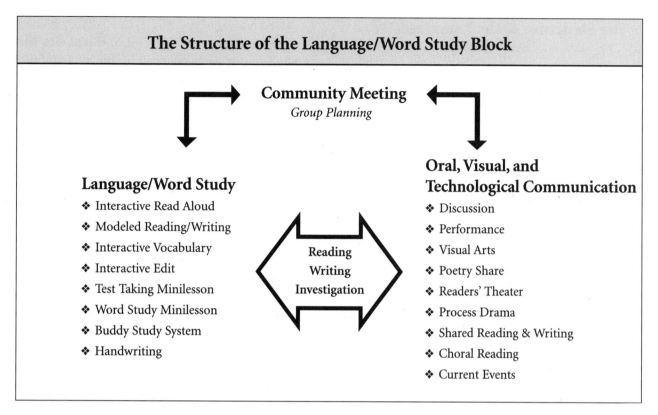

Figure 3–1. Structure of the Language/Word Study Block

Word solving in reading and writing is a complex process that involves decoding as well as taking in many layers of word meaning. Consider a word like *immolate,* for example.

> The fighters believed that the ultimate goal of the plan was to *immolate* individuals who spoke up for freedom.

You might notice that the ending of the word, *-ate,* indicates that the word is a verb, and the syntax of the sentence would confirm that. On the other hand, you could be thinking about the prefix, *-im,* which sometimes indicates negation of the quality (adjective) that follows, as in *immodest.* You might connect the word *immolate* with other words like *immoral* and *imminent,* which would not fit within the syntax; or you could come up with *imitate* or *ameliorate,* both of which would fit. In fact, if you are worried about pronunciation, *imitate* would be helpful in determining the syllable to stress—again, related to the fact that the word is a verb.

You may have an underlying sense that to *immolate* means to do something bad, but the context of the sentence does not really help you. If the sentence had said "the fighters *feared* that...," you would have more confirmation for your hunch. Connecting with a "like sounding" word like *emulate* (to imitate or surpass) would definitely lead you astray. If you look up the word and find that it means *to sacrifice or destroy,* the meaning of the sentence becomes much clearer. If you study words, you might even know that this word comes from Latin and means literally "to sprinkle a victim with *meal* prior to a sacrifice." Once you know the word's origin, you are unlikely to forget its meaning in the future! In your word solving, you would select the most helpful connections and discard the rest. Word solving would be rapid and largely unconscious.

In word solving we seldom go to a dictionary and look up a definition. Your connections between words are efficient and useful. The most important aspect of word solving is that we *learn more while doing it.* We not only decode and interpret the meaning of words but also develop strategies for understanding and remembering. We expand our power over language and increase our vocabulary.

The Structure of the Language/Word Study Block

Although the language/word study block can take place any time, most teachers prefer to schedule it first thing in the morning: exploring interesting new ideas in a community context sets the tone for the day.

Your work during the language/word study block is a springboard for students to engage in independent work on spelling, word study, reading, or writing:

■ What they learn in a spelling or phonics minilesson, for example, will be applied in reading and writing.

■ Books that you read aloud to students create a foundation of texts on which you can base reading and writing minilessons. Students can also talk about them in literature discussion.

■ Minilessons on language will be connected to students' work in reading and writing workshop.

The classroom is a microcosm in which students not only acquire information and skills but try themselves out as communicators—that is, language users. The classroom community provides:

■ A supportive audience for whom students can practice presentation skills.

■ Partners with whom students can undertake the shared reading of poems, plays, and other materials.

■ Opportunities to develop a set of shared texts that students can use as examples for further learning.

■ A place to raise questions and express opinions.

Managing Space and Time

You will want to create a comfortable area where students can meet together for word study and vocabulary, minilessons, reading aloud, and language work. (Chapter 6 discusses classroom organization in detail.) It is very important for all students to be able to see and hear one another. Some teachers prefer a circle of chairs, a combination of floor cushions and chairs, or students seated in a circle on a rug. Whatever your arrangement, you will need an easel on which to write and/or display materials. (If you wish to use a chart in connection with one of these activities you might want to have it prepared before school starts for the day.)

To plan your instruction during this block you need to think about how you use time within it over the course of a week or several weeks. Word study focuses on helping students learn about language and use it effectively in different contexts. Students can engage in a variety of shared language and literacy activities, either daily or on particular days. The extent to which you use any of these activities depends on the amount of time you have available. Since these language activities are very quick, sometimes taking only a couple of minutes, you may be able to introduce

Planning for the Language/Word Study Block				
Monday	**Tuesday**	**Wednesday**	**Thursday**	**Friday**
Interactive Read Aloud	Interactive Read Aloud	Shared Reading	Interactive Read Aloud	Readers' Theater
Interactive Edit	Poetry Reading	Current Events (2 students)	Interactive Vocabulary	Handwriting
Word Study: Making Connections	*Word Study:* Test	*Word Study:* Minilesson and Choose Spelling Words	*Word Study:* Look, Say, Cover Write, Check	*Word Study:* Buddy Check

Figure 3–2. Planning for Instruction in the Language/Word Study Block

several each day. A sample weeklong plan is shown in Figure 3–2.

Interactive Read-Aloud

Reading aloud to students is of great instructional value throughout the elementary school years (Huck, Hepler & Hickman 1993). We use the term *interactive* in connection with reading aloud to children to emphasize the active learning that goes on. Students do not simply listen passively and silently. Listening is an active process; with carefully selected texts and good reading, you involve students deeply in following engaging stories, getting to know unforgettable characters, or thinking about intriguing new information.

Interactive read-aloud is an excellent opportunity for students to discuss high-quality fiction, nonfiction, and poetry. Picture books are a favorite. Generally, teachers tend to read wonderful chapter books like *Maniac McGee* (Spinelli 1990) or *Tuck Everlasting* (Babbit 1975). Certainly, you will want to read good chapter books; but you can vary and enrich students' exposure to texts by also reading nonfiction books and articles, short stories, and poetry. Principles for selecting books to read aloud are listed in Figure 3–3 and an extensive list of picture books to use with intermediate students is in Appendix 56.

Reading aloud fluently and expressively communicates enthusiasm for reading and helps students realize its value. The current popularity of books on tape is proof that all of us enjoy the freedom of listening to a story when it is well read. Invite your students to read poetry aloud during the language/word study block. They can select and practice the poems and "sign up" to present them; each week, two or three students read poetry to the class.

We use the term "interactive" to characterize the teacher and students having a conversation as they process the text together (Barrentine 1998). Some general suggestions for making interactive read-aloud sessions enjoyable and interactive are:

■ Read the book first yourself so that you will be familiar with the content and can guide students' discussion.

Ten Suggestions for Selecting Books to Read Aloud

1. Use interest inventories, records of students' book choices, and your observations to determine the topics and kinds of texts that will interest and engage students.

2. Consider students' experiences in selecting texts that they can connect to their own lives and background knowledge.

3. Select texts that will engage students and are a little above the reading levels that most students can easily read independently.

4. Select texts that have themes, topics, and characters that lend themselves to meaningful discussion.

5. For picture books, select those that have artistic quality that students can look at and appreciate.

6. Keep a record of your read-aloud selections so that you can assure variety across the year.

7. Select books that will introduce students to new genres, new authors and illustrators, and styles of writing.

8. Select texts that you love yourself, so that your enthusiasm will be communicated to the students.

9. Select shorter texts when appropriate so that you can increase variety and engage students.

10. Select poetry that will support students' understanding of imagery, rhyme, rhythm, and figurative language.

Figure 3–3. Selecting Books to Read Aloud

- Be sure students are seated comfortably and can hear easily. If illustrations are integral to the text, be sure students can see them.
- Establish a purpose for reading: tell students why you selected the book and what you think they will find interesting. Familiarize them with the author, genre, and illustrator.
- Ask students to make predictions about the text based on the cover, illustrations, or setting.
- Divide a longer text into logical sections.
- Find a few places to pause and invite students to comment, react, or interpret the text.
- Encourage students to connect the text with their own lives and experiences and to make predictions.
- Utilize illustrations to help students attend to new aspects of meaning.
- Connect the topic, theme, characters, setting, or author to other texts the students have read, and invite them to make their own connections.
- Keep a list of books you have read aloud and post it in the classroom so that you and your students can easily remember them when making connections.
- Place books you have read aloud in a special basket or tub, or display them along the bookcase so that students can find and reread them.
- Pause at selected points for quality interaction but not so frequently that the text is disjointed. Keep it an enjoyable, well-paced experience.

Reading to students helps expand vocabulary by presenting words in context. As you read, you can demonstrate ways to derive word meanings from context by "thinking aloud." In the group discussion after the reading, help students focus on new words, new meanings for words, or connotations for words (for example, what made a character sound sarcastic?). The time for students to engage in further thinking or quick writing is after the reading of the text or a unified section of a long text, so as not to ruin the flow or enjoyment of staying connected to the meaning.

Interactive Vocabulary

Interactive vocabulary study focuses on word meanings. Using a chart or the chalkboard, you can conduct a short activity (five or ten minutes) that gets students thinking about the meanings of words. For example, when John noticed a number of words of French origin in the texts

---

Words That Come from the French Language

croissant

chalet

hors d'oeuvres

bouquet

parquet

quiche

ballet

Figure 3–4. Words That Come from the French Language

his students were reading, he and his students made the chart in Figure 3–4. The chart was then displayed in the room, and more words were added over the next few weeks. Later, students categorized the words and noticed that many referred to food or the arts.

Chapter 22 provides detailed information on vocabulary development and suggestions for a number of ways you can make word study active. Many of the tools discussed in Chapter 26 are also useful for vocabulary study. The particular activities you use will emerge naturally from your observations of your students' reading and writing: the errors they are making will help you decide what they "nearly know" or need to know next. Below are some specific suggestions to help you get started (vocabulary development programs contain many other ideas).

- Put two or three sentences on a chart and ask students to think of alternative words that would make the sentences more interesting. Model some possibilities for them, discussing why they are good choices and how to apply this knowledge to their own writing.
- Take two or three sentences out of a piece of literature that you have read aloud, that students have read, or that is in the classroom library. Select a word that students might not know but could figure out from the context (*belligerent,* for example). Ask students to talk about what the word means within the context of the text and help them learn how to use context to discover meaning.

■ Demonstrate word analogies and help students generate their own (for example, *hungry* is to *ravenous* as *happy* is to *delighted*).

■ Write two or three sentences on a chart and ask students to think of synonyms for nouns, verbs, adjectives, or adverbs in the sentence.

■ Start a list of related words and ask students to come up with words to add to the list (for example, *fancy, decorated, elegant, deluxe, fine, custom, elaborate*).

■ Write a word on chart paper and show students how to add prefixes and suffixes to change the meaning *(connect, disconnect, reconnect, connection, connector, disconnection)*; then invite students to come up with their own examples.

■ Provide a Greek or Latin root and ask students to come up with other words that contain it *(form [shape]: formula, reform, format, perform, free form, platform)*.

Figure 3–5. *Teacher and Class Working on Greek and Latin Word Roots*

Interactive vocabulary, with its focus on a lively discussion about one or two examples rather than a laborious drill, is a way to help students examine word meaning in different ways and learn how to be more precise in their word choice.

Interactive Edit

In an interactive edit, you explicitly demonstrate the process of editing (and, in so doing, teach important editing conventions) using two to three sentences, a short paragraph, or a short letter that has several errors in it. (Ideally, the errors should be ones you notice students are making in their independent writing.) You can also refer to the minilesson list in Chapter 5 for ideas for interactive edit.

As with interactive vocabulary study, it will save time if you already have the sentence on chart paper or the chalkboard. That way, students can copy it quickly, editing it. Teach students the standard editing symbols so that they can interpret editorial suggestions from you and act as an editor for others.

Test Taking

Performing on standardized tests requires special skills. You have to analyze the required task and understand what constitutes a "good performance." You have to provide the answers you know and make good guesses for those you don't. You have to work quickly and continuously evaluate your performance.

Even students who have good reading and writing skills can misunderstand reading and writing tests. For example, students who have done a great deal of "retelling" as a way of showing that they comprehend texts probably think that providing as many details as possible represents good performance. When asked to write a *summary* statement, they may not understand that they should select only important details.

Also, the vocabulary of test instructions may present difficulties. For example, we once discovered that many students did not know what was meant by the word *selection* in the question "What word in the selection means the same as _____?" They spent precious time trying to figure it out.

During the language/word study block you might plan to spend a few minutes on activities that will help students become more sophisticated in taking reading and writing tests. You can teach the structure of multiple-choice and short-answer questions. You can have them talk about what the questions really mean and evaluate answers.

It is important that work on test reading and writing be quick and lively. Long periods of drill will only decrease the time spent on the reading and writing that will help them develop the foundation

Week of _11/6_

Word Study Minilesson Plan

Spelling principle, pattern or strategy Some suffixes sound alike but are spelled differently
Most of the time, add suffix "able" to a base word.
If there is a root, use the suffix "ible"

Sample List:

predictable	possible
workable	horrible
comfortable	portable
favorable	visible
reasonable	incredible
affordable	edible
expandable	audible

Comments/Evaluation:
- made list of those that didn't fit
- next time work on more words -
those that drop e or
retain e before suffix.

Figure 3–6. Word Study Lesson Plan

they need. The bottom line is that students must be able to read and comprehend texts and to write with clarity if they are to perform well on tests. An interactive language activity can help them show what they know, but it cannot take the place of sound, basic instruction in reading and writing.

Word Study

During word study, students actively learn the rules and principles of phonics and spelling. We propose a systematic approach that includes:

- Presenting a minilesson on an aspect of phonics or spelling.
- Asking students to apply the minilesson by manipulating letters or words.
- Sharing and discussing words and how they work.
- Introducing a systematic way of studying spelling words.

Plan your word study program in a five day cycle. Typically, you will focus on a particular spelling pattern, rule, or concept each cycle.

The form in Figure 3–6 illustrates how to write the principle for your minilesson in one or two simple, very clear sentences. Writing this clear statement is excellent preparation for teaching the minilesson. If you can't write the principle in one or two sentences, then you may be combining too many complex ideas. A minilesson is meant to be highly focused.

In the next section of the form, write examples of words that will illustrate the principle you are teaching. Of course, you will invite students to come up with examples, but you also need to have some good ones ready. The bottom of the form is for any special notes to help you teach or evaluate the lesson. These forms can be saved from year to year and used for reference. (A reproducible form is provided in Appendix 3.)

MINILESSON

A minilesson is a brief, clear demonstration of a principle, pattern, or rule that students need to learn. The principle or rule may be stated directly or inferred from examples. In general, a minilesson does not allow for a long discovery period, although students should be encouraged to discover more on their own. You may

demonstrate how the concept works if it is something very new, but you should encourage students to come up with their own examples as much as possible. Any charts developed during the minilesson will usually remain displayed as a reference that can be used during instruction across the language/literacy framework.

The list of minilessons in Chapter 22 shows the variety that is possible. Published spelling and phonics programs will give you ideas as well. Your best guide for which minilessons to use is your assessment of your students' writing and reading abilities (see Chapter 28).

Chapter 8 explains how to select minilessons and make them effective. You can also use any of the procedures listed under active word study as part of a minilesson. The important thing to remember is that a minilesson is only the beginning of a process in which the students actively explore words in some way.

APPLICATION

The minilesson is followed by an activity in which students make their own discoveries relative to the particular principle. For example:

- Forming words with magnetic letters to illustrate spelling patterns or word parts.
- Word sorting, to illustrate spelling principles and connect words by their meaning or how they sound or look.
- Searching for words in various categories.

Figure 3–7. Erica Working on Plurals

Be sure to demonstrate explicitly what you want students to do. Application activities will not take a great deal of time if your materials are well organized and at hand. For example, cards for word sorting can be placed in labeled envelopes or margarine tubs (and if students work in pairs, you will need only one set for every two students). If you use magnetic letters, you will need about three sets of lowercase letters for each group of 4 or 5 students, or about 15 sets for an average class.

Older students can keep word study notebooks and record their discoveries there. These notebooks may have sections for spelling, vocabulary, and similar areas that serve as a record of students' word learning throughout the year.

SHARING

Conduct a brief group session at the end of the language/word study block so that students can share what they have learned. (If the students have word study notebooks, invite them to bring them to the session.) There won't be enough time for everyone to contribute, but a few students can quickly tell what they discovered.

INTEGRATING A SYSTEM FOR SPELLING INSTRUCTION

A systematic approach to spelling instruction should be part of your word study program. An effective one is something we call "buddy study" (see Figure 3–8), in which students learn spelling principles and effective techniques for studying and connecting words. Buddy study is based on a five-day cycle; some teachers begin on Monday, but those who want learning to span the weekend choose some other day. We find it best to begin the cycle on Tuesday, Wednesday, or Thursday. Characteristics of buddy study are described in Figure 3–8. (See also Pinnell and Fountas 1998.)

AN EFFICIENT MINILESSON

The process begins with a minilesson (the word study minilesson for that day) on some aspect of spelling.

SELECTING WORDS

Students are expected to choose a total of six to ten words per week (a relatively small number) that illus-

---

The Buddy Study Cycle

❖ **Minilessson.** The teacher provides a minlesson that focuses on what students need to know.

❖ **Day One.** *Choose, Write, Build.* Students select words from the minilesson examples and also from their "words to learn" charts. These charts are formed from writing conferences, in which they have added words that they want to learn plus words that the teacher has put on the list. Another source for the "words to learn" chart is the highlighted list of 500 high frequency words and spelling demons as well as Latin and Greek roots and other categorized lists with special features. Students can set a goal of knowing all of these words by the end of elementary school. The selected words are written on a small card that is checked and initialed by the teacher. With magnetic letters, they build each word three times, mixing up the letters between each attempt.

❖ **Day Two.** *Look, Say, Cover, Write, Check.* Students use a folder with three or four flaps cut so that columns of words can be hidden or revealed. The student writes the words accurately in the first column. Then, for each word, the student covers the word, says it, visualizes it, writes it in the second column, checks the word, and then writes it again in the third column, repeating the sequence each time.

❖ **Day Three.** *Buddy Check.* Spelling buddies, who are matched by spelling development, give each other a test and check it. Students learn how to self-correct and develop strategies for tricky words.

❖ **Day Four.** *Making Connections.* Students write connections for each one of their spelling words. They connect words by the way they sound (phonetic connections; beginning, ending sounds, rhymes, homonyms), look (visual patterns), and mean (synonyms).

❖ **Day Five.** *Buddy Test.* Buddies give each other a test in the word study notebook, which is checked by the teacher.

Figure 3–8. *Buddy Study Cycle*

trate an important spelling principle. They use three basic sources: (1) the spelling minilesson, which always includes several examples; (2) their "words to learn" list, which includes words from their own writing; and (3) a list of the 500 most frequently used words, which they keep in their folders and highlight as they learn them. They write the words on index cards, which you check and initial for accuracy in the upper right corner.

LEARNING AND USING EFFECTIVE WORD STUDY TECHNIQUES

On the first three days of the cycle, students learn three effective ways to study the words they've chosen.

1. Forming them with magnetic letters, working from left to right, and then checking them against the accurately transcribed words on their cards. *Forming the words as a concrete visual helps students notice details and patterns.*
2. Using the "look, say, cover, write, check" procedure. They look at the details of the word, say the word out loud, cover it up, visualize the word, write it, and then check the spelling from left to right. *This routine fosters conscious attention to the parts of words that are unusual or tricky.*
3. Taking a trial spelling test on the week's words. They check this test themselves, *again noticing parts of words that are hard to remember.*

Systematically implementing these study techniques is highly effective. Most students know how to spell almost all of their words by the third day of the cycle.

MAKING CONNECTIONS

On the fourth day, students make connections between their words and other words. They connect words in many different ways. For example, take the word *stationery*:

- Sounds like *state, vacation, bakery.*
- Starts like *Stacey, stallion, statue.*
- Has an ending sound like *very, berry, merry, marry.*
- Means the same as letter paper, note paper.
- Has an *er* like *paper, mother, matter.*

And don't forget the magic of homonyms! You'll want to point out that *stationery* has an oral twin—

stationary—that's spelled differently and means something different, too. Your students might also enjoy exploring the difference between homophones and homographs. The important aspect of making connections is the student's ability to associate likenesses in words and to write the part of the word that has the same feature correctly.

DOCUMENTING LEARNING

On the fifth day, students are tested to document their learning and provide evidence for evaluation. The connections they have made with other words may also be evaluated. Often the work is sent home to show parents what their children have been learning.

Oral and Visual Communication

In a world in which broad-based, multimedia communication is increasingly important, students need to practice arguing, documenting, persuading, and informing in increasingly sophisticated ways. The language and word study block, as well as the other two blocks should include many activities that incorporate oral, visual, and technological communication. (Since reports, presentations, and dramatizations take more time, you will occasionally also set aside special times in the school day for these activities.) Here are five such contexts:

Discussion/Conversation

There is no substitute for dynamic classroom conversation. It takes place during literature discussion, investigations, and sharing sessions. Conversation is a hallmark of the language/word study block. For example, students can discuss:

- Concepts, themes, and characters in the texts that they hear read aloud.
- The meanings of words and how they have learned about them.
- Connections they make between words.
- Ways in which the classroom can function better as a community.
- Issues triggered by presentations or current events.

You need to monitor the discussion carefully and encourage students to evaluate how things went: did everyone get a turn? did they listen actively? did speakers consider listeners' backgrounds? Learning to take part in group discussions effectively is an essential life skill.

Performance/Dramatization

Students enjoy performing for one another, and the experience can give them confidence as well as boost their language prowess. Here are several ways you can promote performance during the language/word study block.

POETRY

Students can read aloud poems that they have rehearsed or recite them from memory. In many classrooms, this is a regular activity; two or three students sign up to read or recite a poem every week. The poem is a published one or one they have written.

READERS' THEATER

In readers' theater, two or more people read a piece of writing aloud, usually assuming the roles of the characters. The piece may be performed in any appropriate way. You may alter the text slightly to make the performance smoother, as long as you remain true to the writing. There are any number of techniques you can employ:

- Have a narrator read the neutral and descriptive parts.
- Assign individual students to read the dialogue of specific characters.
- Let everyone read certain sections in unison.
- Give special passages special emphasis (loud, soft, fast, slow, just boy voices, just girl voices), depending on their meaning.

In readers' theater, the voice alone conveys the meaning—the story isn't "acted out." Even though nothing has to be memorized, students still need time to rehearse. Readers' theater presentations often emerge from literature study or the poetry workshop.

PROCESS DRAMA

Through drama, students are able to experience worlds other than their own and explore concepts and language in new ways. "Process" drama is not the performance of a play for an audience; rather students assume identities as a means toward empathy and understanding. The situation may be based on a

problem or issue students have encountered in real life, in content area study (history or social studies, for example), or in literature. The teacher or leader creates a frame or dramatic context that the students then explore by taking on roles (Edmiston 1993; Heathcote 1983, 1985; Rogers & O'Neill 1993).

Sometimes, exploring these situations requires research, both reading and writing. For example, inspired by their investigation of endangered species, students might portray a group of scientists searching to find ways to protect a particular habitat within their own state. Or, after reading several Civil War novels, they might dramatize a story about a group of slaves escaping along the underground railroad.

Process drama evolves over time. It may be short and self-contained—the impersonations lasting only a day or two—or may extend over several weeks. It involves pretense and role playing, but there are parameters within which students have to work. The dramatizations must be carried out in realistic ways: for example, slaves cannot suddenly time travel and escape by automobile! Scientists wishing to persuade policy makers to protect a particular environment must know the kinds of plants and animals that live in it and how their well-being is being threatened. Problems cannot have simplistic and unrealistic solutions.

As always, you will want to guide students to reflect on their work. When it is taken seriously, process drama has enormous potential for furthering students' language learning. Edmiston (1992) and Booth (1994) are two excellent resources for working with drama.

SHARED READING

Shared reading was developed for young children who are just beginning to learn to read (Holdaway 1979). In this technique, children read a familiar text in unison and at the same time look at an enlarged copy of the text, either on chart paper or in a big book. By reading it again and again, with great enthusiasm, children soon "learn" the text and become more familiar with the details of print.

Shared reading is valuable for older students as well, letting them read texts that may be beyond their current ability individually. You can also use the selection to teach word analysis, punctuation, and the like. Again, the students read the text in unison, either following along on an enlarged displayed copy or in

Current Events Schedule

Monday	Tuesday	Wednesday	Thursday	Friday
Marva	Jill	Boca	Julie	Matthew
Sarah	Shana	Lara	Antonio	Darla
Peter	George	Sam	Raheen	Onella
Larry	Naheen	Erica	Donald	Peter
Mark	Charles	Paul		

Figure 3–9. Current Events Schedule

their personal copies. Typically, shared reading is best suited for short, dramatic stories or poems. Through shared reading, students internalize new language and learn to enjoy the way words sound. They also develop the confidence to go on to other kinds of performance such as readers' theater, choral reading, and recitation.

CHORAL READING

Choral reading is the rehearsed recitation of prose or poetry by a group of voices. Students learn to read together, using intonation, rhythm, and pace to convey the meaning of the piece, which occasionally is memorized.

For example, recently a group of fourth graders read "The Bat," a poem by Douglas Florian (*Mammalibilia* 1994). The poem begins by describing the way the bat sleeps; in the succeeding lines, the bat wakes up and flies off into the night; finally the bat goes back to sleep. On the very last line, separated by a space from the others, are the words "upside down," written in inverted print. These fourth graders read the poem in unison, beginning softly and gently, becoming louder and faster in the middle, and dying away to very hushed voices at the end, taking a very definite pause before saying "upside down." It was an effective, amusing, and expressive interpretation that made use of volume, tempo, and emphasis.

Current Events Writing Guidelines

- ❖ Three paragraphs (at least).
- ❖ Includes opinion and explains why you feel that way.
- ❖ Each paragraph at least three sentences long.
- ❖ Give examples and/or make comparisons.
- ❖ 5 Ws (who?, what?, when?, where?, why?).
- ❖ Use a variety of words.
- ❖ Include interesting facts to connect to your opinion.
- ❖ Summarize effectively.
- ❖ Use your own words.
- ❖ Write clearly and neatly.
- ❖ Include supporting facts and details.
- ❖ Indent for paragraphs.
- ❖ Good punctuation, grammar, and complete sentences.

Figure 3–10. Current Events Writing Guidelines

Audience Standards

- ❖ Pay attention to the presenter.
- ❖ Raise hand when others are talking.
- ❖ Raise hand quietly.
- ❖ Stay still.
- ❖ Respectfully state disagreement.
- ❖ Respectfully correct misinformation.
- ❖ Raise thoughtful questions and comments.
- ❖ Raise hand to comment at least one time a week.

Figure 3–11. Current Events Audience Participation Standards

Presentation Standards

- ❖ Speak with a clear voice and no mumbling.
- ❖ Speak at a good pace.
- ❖ Speak so the audience can hear you.
- ❖ Pause a little after each sentence.
- ❖ Hold the paper down so the audience can see your face.
- ❖ Be serious at appropriate times.
- ❖ Be still when you are reading.
- ❖ Always speak with feeling.
- ❖ Respond to audience respectfully.

Figure 3-12. Current Events Presentation Standards

For choral reading, each student needs his own copy of the piece so that key words can be underlined and other cues and directions written in. Pick your choral reading material from pieces your students have particularly enjoyed in read-alouds, literature study, or poetry workshop. You might teach students how to create scripts for choral reading with poems of their own. You will want to decide how the text will be read—in unison, a line-a-child, in cumulative voices—as well as how much.

CURRENT EVENTS

Talking about current events builds students' interest in the world around them. Many public issues of the day are understandable to and relevant for students in grades three through six. Here are only a few examples:

- ▪ Caring for the environment.
- ▪ Scientific discoveries.
- ▪ Health concerns and treatment breakthroughs.
- ▪ Matters relevant to local education.
- ▪ Elections.

Taking part in a brief discussion of current events every week will help get students into the habit of noticing, finding out about, and becoming involved in the issues that affect them.

Rebecca, a teacher who devotes sixty minutes to language/word study in her classroom every day,

emphasizes current events. She has several students talk about them each week (see the schedule in Figure 3–9). The presentations arise from their independent writing assignments that they prepare as homework. She and her students have developed guidelines for writing about current events (see Figure 3–10), as well as standards for participating as a listener (Figure 3–11) and as a presenter (Figure 3–12). Students are well aware of the criteria and can evaluate themselves.

Variety in the Language/ Word Study Block

Teaching is always a matter of balancing established routines with variety. Obviously you have many more instructional options than you can accomplish during any one language/word study block. It's important, however, to establish the routine of a community meeting early in the year, letting your students know where to sit and teaching them how to interact. Begin by reading aloud and presenting a minilesson. Gradually add other options as you have time to teach students how to participate in them.

It is not efficient to teach everything through discovery; some things are best taught directly. In the language/word study block, you need to identify areas of learning you can teach efficiently by way of short, direct lessons that will encourage students to engage in further discovery on their own. The texts you read to them are also rich resources that support further learning.

The range of learning opportunities within the language/word study block is very broad. Since most activities are short and focused, you can include much more instruction than you might think at first glance. Work during the block often involves the entire class, although there are plenty of ways to invite students to work as partners or in small groups. The entire session should be lively, as you and your students construct meaning together.

You can make language/word study especially effective by taking into account your students' backgrounds. The more they bring to the discussions and the more they connect their own lives to what you read or teach them, the more effective the language/word study block will be. It is here that you establish the sense of community that flows through the entire framework.

Conclusion

As we strive to introduce our students to the magic inherent in the masterful use of language, we want to draw from a wide range of resources—beautiful literature, finely crafted news articles, poems that trip lightly on the tongue. Word study invites students to enjoy language on many levels. At the same time they investigate the particulars of language—the sounds, letters, and words that language comprises—they also develop a global appreciation of language's majesty. Our overarching goal, of course, is to help our students develop as nimble, creative communicators who can use language in masterful ways for many purposes.

Suggestions for Professional Development

1. Bring to a meeting with your intermediate-grade colleagues your grade-level goals, district curriculum guides, and any published materials that you have found useful.
2. Using this chapter, generate a list of options for the language/word study block.
3. Identify important concepts and principles you can teach in the language/word study block. Discuss understandings that can be taught quickly and those that will require many connections across the reading and writing blocks.
4. Design a weekly schedule for the language/word study block that includes what you need to emphasize for your students at this time.
5. Discuss how you will teach routines and how your schedule will vary through the year.

## CHAPTER FOUR

BECOMING JOYFUL READERS: THE READING WORKSHOP

Reading is the sole means by which we slip, involuntarily, often helplessly, into another's skin, another's voice, another's soul.

— JOYCE CAROL OATES

A reading workshop has come to be thought of as an organized set of language and literacy experiences (typically, a minilesson, individual reading, conferring, and sharing) designed to help students become more effective readers. Our definition is broader and includes three different kinds of reading, and response (see Figure 4–1):

■ *Independent reading,* in which individual students read a text, usually of their own choosing. Over time, students read and respond to a variety of texts independently. You provide minilessons, guide text

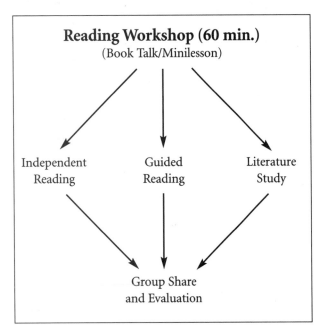

Reading Workshop (60 min.)
(Book Talk/Minilesson)

Independent Reading   Guided Reading   Literature Study

Group Share and Evaluation

Figure 4–1. Reading Workshop Block

selection, confer with individual students, and facilitate a shared discussion to extend students' understanding and enjoyment.

■ *Guided reading,* in which a small group of students with similar reading strategies work with you to learn more about reading. You select a text at an appropriate level, introduce it, and provide supportive teaching that helps the group understand what reading is and how it works.

■ *Literature study,* in which a group of readers discuss various aspects of a text or a set of related texts and sometimes work on projects to extend and share their learning. You show students how to analyze and discuss texts with one another in order to create shared meanings that are more refined and complex than they would discover on their own.

These three reading contexts are related and may take place simultaneously within the classroom.

The Origin of Reading Workshop

Reading workshop grew out of any number of individual approaches to teaching reading over the years. The concept of a systematic and easily implemented active approach to independent reading was introduced by Atwell (1987, 1998) and has been developed by several other theorists and practitioners (Hagerty 1994; Hindley 1998; Hansen 1987; Harwayne 2000). Atwell's pioneering work offered an alternative to the tradition of "assigning" reading. Her reading workshop invited students to become more actively involved in their own learning and, in the process, to learn more about how to read various kinds of texts. This workshop approach appealed to students in ways that traditional assignments did not, and it offered teachers a chance to delve into students' perspectives and offer systematic teaching when appropriate. Atwell writes:

> In establishing the structure of the reading workshop and organizing who would do what, when, and where, I looked to writing workshop for parallels. Writers had time in class to write, choices of topics and genres, access to materials, opportunities for peers to respond to their writing, and instruction and demonstrations from me in minilessons and conferences. I began to push the parallels across the curriculum, beginning with the right to choose one's own books. (1998, 35–36)

Expanding the Reading Workshop

Although independent reading is productive, intermediate students also benefit from other kinds of instruction. They need further opportunities and further instructional support to develop their reading skills. Many needs that are evident across the group can be addressed in whole- or small-group instruction.

Thus, we have expanded the reading workshop to encompass not only the independent reading that Atwell describes, but also small-group guided reading and literature study. All three contexts provide active learning and help students become more competent readers. Integrating all three approaches provides variety in the reading program and also allows for more explicit teaching to help students develop a range of effective strategies.

Instruction also must be efficient. Both guided reading and literature study help you make the best use of your teaching day. There is simply not enough time to teach every student individually, and small-group instruction is a flexible option.

Guided reading is built around small homogeneous groups. In your regular conferences with individuals, you gain important information about their unique strengths and needs. You observe patterns across the

group that you can use to cluster students who have similar learning needs. You then teach important concepts and principles to these homogeneous groups of readers and select texts that offer appropriate supports and challenges.

Literature study, built around small heterogeneous groups, also provides more powerful and significant learning than does working alone. With your guidance, students thoughtfully and thoroughly analyze a text together, learning more about the meaning of texts than they could on their own. The small-group context offers both specific teaching and expanded thinking and support.

Why Call It a Workshop?

We like using *workshop* to describe these three reading contexts because it suggests a group of people actively engaged in purposeful tasks. Activity is exactly what we wish to stress. Students learn by doing. Students learn to read by reading rather than simply hearing *about* reading:

> Not many years ago I began to play the cello. Most people would say that what I am doing is "learning to play" the cello. But these words carry into our minds the strange idea that there exists two very different processes: (1) learning to play the cello, and (2) playing the cello. They imply that I will do the first until I have completed it, at which point I will stop the first process and begin the second. In short, I will go on "learning to play" until I have "learned to play" and then I will begin to play. Of course, this is nonsense. We learn to do something by doing it. There is no other way. (Holt 132)

A reading workshop is a laboratory in which individual students are busily engaged in reading that reflects real life; that is, they are reading in ways that match what readers do all their lives. In the reading workshop, students:

■ Learn how to work together.
■ Set goals and evaluate their own accomplishments.
■ Engage in meaningful communication about what they read.
■ Take responsibility for their own learning and

supporting the learning of each other.

■ Work at their own pace but are expected to accomplish a series of tasks.

■ Make choices and carry out assignments.

Characteristics of the Reading Workshop

The reading workshop, as broadly defined, has some important characteristics that contribute to its effective use (see Figure 4–2):

1. *Readers learn how to work together as a community, supporting one another as well as pursuing individual goals.* They meet in guided reading groups to explore a common text at an appropriate level for learning more about reading. They meet in literature study groups to explore literary elements and analyze a common text or several related texts. In this context, they can share their perspectives and learn about others' views. In the sharing sessions that follow independent reading, they communicate with each other about what they are learning. Every learner has an equal voice, and passion, caring, and respect are highly valued. Collaboration is characteristic of the workshop setting, not only cooperation among students but between adults and students. Students help one another learn and share their successes.

2. *Readers talk, read, and write about things in which they are genuinely interested.* Students usually select texts for independent reading that they want or need to explore. You may occasionally assign a text, but always with the reader's interests and strengths

in mind. All reading is extended through talk, and much is extended through various kinds of writing. The social nature of the workshop helps students better understand what they are learning. This talking, reading, and writing provides multiple sources of information and exposes students to a variety of perspectives.

3. *Readers are actively engaged in reading.* Most of the instructional time is dedicated to reading continuous text—books, stories, and informational pieces rather than lists of words, multiple-choice questions, pieces of textbooks, or short paragraphs followed by questions. Students are active agents in their own learning; you provide the materials, information, and experiences that enable them to develop systems for learning more.

4. *The reading workshop is designed to build on each student's strengths and meet his needs.* You can adjust the balance of individual, small-group, and large-group activities to provide the amount of teaching and the level of support that individual students need. For example, some students will need guided reading just about every day. Other students need more time to read independently, exploring the range of texts and topics that engage them. The lively conversations in literature study groups stretch even the less capable readers to absorb books they might not be able to tackle on their own. Informed by your assessment records and sensitive observations of your students, you know how to challenge and lift each one's learning.

5. *Readers take responsibility for their learning.* Although you provide much explicit instruction during reading workshop, students have important roles as well. With your guidance, they learn to set their own goals. They evaluate their own procedures, accomplishments, and progress as readers. They also enjoy making important contributions to the group that will help others learn.

6. *The reading workshop is rigorous and challenging, with clear expectations for students' accomplishments.* In literature study, students are expected to read and reflect on a selection and share their insights with classmates. In guided reading, they read a text that offers challenges in comprehension, text organization, or word solving. Your support enables them to solve problems in reading a text that requires more of them. Students keep records of and monitor their

---

Esssential Characteristics of the Reading Workshop

❖ A community of learners.

❖ Genuine talk, reading, and writing.

❖ Individual strengths and needs.

❖ Individual and group responsibility.

❖ High expectations for achievement.

❖ High level of engagement.

Figure 4–2. Essential Characteristics of Reading Workshop

independent reading, documenting their accomplishments as readers. All three contexts are organized around routines and support structures that bring intention and rigor to the process.

The Advantages of Reading Workshop

Implementing a reading workshop produces multifaceted results, all of which reflect the kind of reading ability that lifelong readers exhibit and therefore contribute to the quality of life.

IT BUILDS AN EFFECTIVE READING PROCESS

In reading workshop, students read a variety of increasingly challenging texts that require them to use strategies in different ways. Literature study helps students learn to extend the meaning of texts and make connections among and between texts. In both independent reading and guided reading, teacher support helps students enjoy reading and learn more about themselves as readers at the same time. You don't first learn about reading and then read. You learn how to read as you read.

IT INCREASES THE AMOUNT STUDENTS READ

In the reading workshop setting, students receive the support and guidance they need to do a great deal of reading over the course of a school year. The amount of reading matters. We want our intermediate students to "put on miles" as readers—to read thousands of words, embedded in meaningful texts, every day. Their attention is seldom on words alone—it's on the meaning and the interesting aspects of the texts—but they solve words every time they read.

Research indicates that how much students read is important. Anderson, Wilson, and Fielding (1988) asked 155 fifth-grade students to note every day how many minutes they spent on a variety of activities outside of school, over periods ranging from eight to

twenty-six weeks. These researchers also gathered information about the students' reading achievement from second through fifth grade. The results (see Figure 4–3) were startling. "Among all the ways children spent their time, reading books was the best predictor of several measures of reading achievement, including gains in reading achievement between second and fifth

What Matters: Variation in Amount of Independent Reading				
Percentile Rank	Minutes Per Day		Words Read Per Year	
	Books	Text	Books	Text
98	65.0	76.3	4,358,000	4,733,000
90	21.2	33.4	1,823,000	2,357,000
80	14.2	24.6	1,146,000	1,697,000
70	9.6	16.9	622,000	1,168,000
60	6.5	13.1	432,000	722,000
50	4.6	9.2	282,000	601,000
40	3.2	6.2	200,000	421,000
30	1.8	4.3	106,000	251,000
20	0.7	2.4	21,000	134,000
10	.1	1.0	8000	51,000
2	0	0	0	8,000

Anderson, Richard C.
Wilson, P.T.
Fielding, L.G
Growth in Reading and How Children Spend Their Time Outside of School, 1988, Reading Research Quarterly, #23, pp. 285-303

Figure 4–3.   *Good and Poor Readers*

grade. However, on most days most children did little or no book reading [outside of school]" (285).

During the reading workshop, whatever the particular instructional contexts of any given day, the student spends almost a full hour processing text. On average, over time, a student spends about thirty-five to forty-five minutes reading texts and fifteen to twenty-five minutes either discussing or writing about texts. It is obvious that time is a precious commodity in the intermediate classroom; reading workshop makes it possible to use time efficiently and intensively to assure maximum student engagement.

IT INCREASES OWNERSHIP OF AND COMMITMENT TO READING

In reading workshop, students often select their own books, although you may also recommend and assign books. Choice is important to readers' enjoyment. In their independent reading, students usually select their own texts, with your guidance, thus increasing their commitment to the texts and their ownership of the process. Choice helps students become more aware of themselves as readers and develop their own interests and tastes. They learn how to select wisely and to monitor the breadth of their choices so that they begin to control their own development as readers.

In the other two contexts, guided reading and literature study, you either select books for children or guide their choices carefully. To do this, you need to know the readers and know how to engage them. In this way, students encounter texts they might not have selected on their own and learn about new genres, new authors, and new styles of writing.

It Broadens Readers' Literary Experiences

The *kinds* of reading students do also matters. You play an important role in helping students make good choices, not only to increase the amount and quality of what they read but also to help them gain breadth as readers. One of the purposes of guided reading in the intermediate grades is to introduce students to new genres and to the various ways in which fiction and nonfiction writers present information. You will want to include explicit examples of how to notice and use the structure of texts. Literature study invites students to analyze the features of a rich variety of texts. Guided reading and literature study nourish independent reading because students become acquainted with books different from those they would choose on their own and develop confidence in their ability to read different kinds of books.

As part of independent reading, students should be encouraged to evaluate their own lists of books and topics and think about how they might increase their breadth as readers. Here's how one teacher encouraged a reader to expand his choices:

TEACHER: What do you notice about your list?
STUDENT: I read mostly books about dinosaurs.
TEACHER: What do you think about that?
STUDENT: I'm really interested in reading about dinosaurs.
TEACHER: Yes, you are. Remember how I explained that one of the ways you can become a better reader is to read different

kinds of books this year? What might you do to be sure you are also reading other kinds of books?
STUDENT: I could read books about other things, like space, or I could read fiction books sometimes.
TEACHER: Did you like *Henry Huggins* (Cleary 1985) when I read it to the class?
STUDENT: Yes, I read it myself too.
TEACHER: Beverly Cleary has written a lot of books, and they are in that basket over there. You might want to look at them to see if there's one you would like to read.

It Develops Responsibility for Reading

Through independent reading, students become reflective and skillful planners of their reading "diet." They keep their own records, evaluating the number as well as the kinds of books they have read. They also evaluate the quality of their written responses. They even record potential titles and topics or genres of interest in anticipation of future reading. What an exciting change from quickly scanning a shelf because they have to "pick a book."

Students also learn to respect others' learning. They learn to care for books not because they belong to the teacher but so their classmates can read them. They learn the value of quiet work not because the teacher requires it but because their peers are reading and concentrating. Their actions have community value that transcends simply doing what they are told.

In literature study, students must be prepared to work with their group. Their contributions are important because they extend the learning of their peers. In guided reading, students read the assigned selection and complete any related tasks, such as writing about the text or analyzing it in some way. Readers must "keep on schedule" so that the group can have productive meetings to discuss the text and to continue reading it at a good pace. They also need to apply what you teach them in minilessons—for example, to notice how an author uses time in a story, to predict how a character might be feeling, or to look at prefixes.

It Encourages Personal Connections

Reading workshop enables students to bring their own experiences and interests to the act of reading. In guided reading, you prompt them to share things in their background that relate to the text you have chosen for the group to read. In independent reading, even though students make their own choices and read at their own pace, you talk with them about their reading afterward, bringing out and reinforcing the personal connections they have made.

IT TEACHES COLLABORATION

Readers learn how to talk with one another about their reading, sharing what they think things mean and helping others see things in a new way. In guided reading and literature study, there is a clear expectation that readers will be prepared and

Figure 4–4. Independent Reading

contribute to the discussion so that everyone can learn more and enjoy the experience. Students also have opportunities to talk about and recommend the books they read independently. They learn to be considerate of others, sharing space and materials.

The Reading Workshop Block and How to Use It

The three components of reading workshop are summarized in Figure 4–5. The reading block is meant to be flexible, to allow you to make decisions based on what students need to learn. For example, you might put more emphasis on independent reading at the beginning of the year. Your goal is to engage the students with "just right" books that will keep them on task and productive for the hour while you pull together small groups for guided reading and literature study.

Independent Reading

The reading workshop usually begins with a whole-group meeting that includes a few book talks and a minilesson. In a book talk you present a new book or point out books that will interest particular members of the class or provide opportunities for them to learn, providing just enough information to whet their

appetites. A minilesson is a short focused lesson on something most of your readers need help learning. Occasionally, the minilesson may need to be longer because of the particular content you plan to address.

Following the book talks and minilesson, students read independently for about forty minutes, usually a text they've chosen but sometimes one you've assigned. They read silently, without talking, in a comfortable place. The room is very quiet; you circulate, talking quietly with individual students and taking notes that will inform your teaching, enable you to create effective reading groups, and help you document progress.

Periodically, you ask students to respond in writing to what they've read. The response is usually shared with the whole group, occasionally with small groups or a partner. As a group, students evaluate their individual work and their ability to work together.

Unlike "free reading" or "sustained silent reading," independent reading is framed by instruction; you actively teach during this time rather than read your own book. The teaching happens in the minilesson, in the instructional conversations you have with individual readers, and in the sharing and feedback that takes place at the end. Independent reading also provides an opportunity for you to assess and document the reading progress of individual students.

Comparison of Reading Workshop Elements

Across all three elements, students are developing reading strategies, learning new vocabulary, reading with fluency, analyzing texts, making personal and textual connections, and building background knowledge.

	Independent Reading	Guided Reading	Literature Study
Description	Students independently read a variety of texts and prepare periodic written responses. The teacher provides daily minilessons and confers with individuals to support and assess reading as well as teach to individual needs. The reading is usually followed by a form of sharing and evaluation.	The teacher pulls together small temporary groups to explicitly teach effective reading strategies for processing a variety of fiction and informational texts. The teacher introduces the text and readers read it independently. The teacher selects teaching points based on readers' needs and sometimes assigns oral and/or written response tasks. Word work may follow.	The teacher and students set up assigned reading/writing tasks and agree on meeting times. Students engage in in-depth discussion about a text they have read or heard. The teacher is generally with the group for discussion, though the students take turns facilitating. The teacher, in consultation with the group, devises written responses or projects.
Primary Focus	To develop individual readers' tastes and interests and broaden their experience with a variety of texts. To enjoy personal reading.	To develop an effective processing system for reading increasingly challenging texts.	To develop a deeper appreciation and understanding of literary texts and to develop personal response.
Format	Individual	Small temporary homogenous group	Small heterogeneous group or whole class
Teacher	Provides explicit teaching through ❖ book talks ❖ minilessons ❖ conferring ❖ sharing Selects book.	Provides explicit teaching through ❖ introduction of text ❖ observing/conferring with students during reading ❖ teaching points after reading ❖ word work	Provides explicit teaching through ❖ routines for discussion ❖ demonstration ❖ summarizing ❖ devising written or artistic responses
Students	Read silently during designated time. Provide written response as assigned. Discuss/share the book with teacher and others.	Listen to/participate in introduction. Read designated text or part of text silently. Read orally with teacher occasionally. Become more aware of own reading process and participate actively in instruction after reading.	Collaborate on decisions about texts and meeting times. Read the text prior to meeting. Engage in group discussion following guidelines for turn taking, etc. Take turns facilitating the group. Provide written or artistic response. Participate in longer projects related to literature.

Figure 4–5. Reading Workshop Elements

Figure 4–6. Students in a Guided Reading Group

You base your specific teaching during guided reading on your observations of your students' reading behavior over time, always thinking about what students need to know. For example, you might show them how to break up multisyllable words or how to use spelling patterns. Or you might explain how to use the organization of the text to support comprehension, or how to interpret diagrams. You can also assign oral and/or written responses—for example, *represent the text structure using graphic organizers; sketch a scene from the story; talk with a partner about what the text means; write your thoughts about the text in a journal.*

Guided Reading

Reading instruction must be specific to students' needs. Reading is complex, and the demands on the reader increase as texts become more varied and difficult. Even intermediate students who have developed an effective reading process still have much to learn. In guided reading, you pull together small temporary groups of students who have similar learning needs. In these small groups, you can explicitly teach effective strategies for processing text. Guided reading groups allow you to introduce students to a wide variety of texts, fiction as well as exposition, short as well as long.

In guided reading you select a text that offers opportunities for the students in a group to learn more about reading. After your introduction, each student in the group processes a unified portion of the text independently, reading silently. The text can be any kind of material that students need to learn how to read; often, you will use short (i.e., capable of being read in one or two sittings) stories or articles on various content area topics. The students can apply the skills they acquire while working on these shorter pieces to the longer texts they read independently and for literature study. Sometimes students will read longer novels or informational texts for guided reading, meeting daily to be introduced to a new section and to discuss what they read. While students in the group read silently, you can ask one of them to read aloud as you take observational notes, confer with other readers in the classroom, or even get another group started.

Literature Study

Here, students talk with one another about various kinds of literature. Other terms for literature study include *book club, literature circle, literature discussion group,* and *response group.* Unlike guided reading groups, which are based on common instructional needs, literature study groups are heterogeneous. Students do not have to be able to read the book for themselves; they can experience it in a variety of ways (listening to the book on tape, having it read to them by you in class or by an adult at home) and still participate in the discussion. Sometimes each person in a group may read a different book on the same theme or by the same author, or with the same text structure.

The purpose of literature study is to enable readers to develop a deeper understanding of the things they read. The meaning they construct as they listen to one another's interpretations is greater than any of them could construct alone. Literature study also helps students become more aware of the inner workings of texts—how plots unfold and how characters develop. They appreciate the skill involved and enjoy reading more. Most important, literature study helps students connect complex concepts and ideas to their own lives and encourages them to become lifelong readers.

In collaboration with your students, set up assigned reading/writing tasks and agree on meeting times. Obviously, the particular text being read will determine the direction the discussion will take. For example, students may explore flashbacks or foreshadowing.

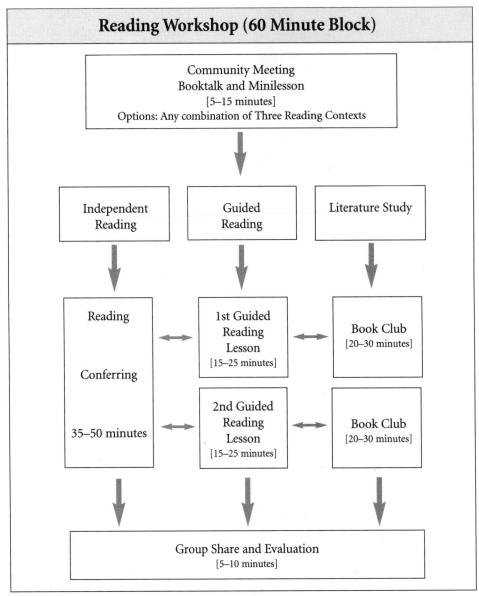

Reading Workshop (60 Minute Block)

Community Meeting
Booktalk and Minilesson
[5–15 minutes]
Options: Any combination of Three Reading Contexts

Independent Reading

Guided Reading

Literature Study

Reading

Conferring

35–50 minutes

1st Guided Reading Lesson
[15–25 minutes]

Book Club
[20–30 minutes]

2nd Guided Reading Lesson
[15–25 minutes]

Book Club
[20–30 minutes]

Group Share and Evaluation
[5–10 minutes]

Figure 4–7. Reading Workshop (60 Minute Block)

Managing Time and Activity in Reading Workshop

Students need to spend an entire hour in reading workshop. The time allocated for each component will vary day by day. Not every student will have time to participate in all three components each day; however, with few exceptions, each student will read independently every day and participate in guided reading and literature study as you arrange it. Some days a student may spend the core of the hour solely on independent reading, but the book may be one assigned from his guided reading group or one in preparation for a literature study meeting. Figure 4–7 is an outline for implementing the three components of reading workshop.

The block begins with a whole-class meeting.

They may connect the text to others they have read, talking about similarities in theme, ideas, or structure. They may explore how it feels to grow up, fight with a friend, experience the death of a parent. In any case, the learning will always be both literary and personal.

You will generally attend each literature study group meeting; although students can be productive on their own, when they have learned to work together effectively, they will learn more when you are there. Once students learn the routines, they can take turns facilitating the group; you are there as their guide. In consultation with the group, you may also devise and assign written responses or a culminating project.

First, you usually give one or more book talks to interest your readers in a variety of high-quality fiction, or nonfiction, books they might not choose on their own. You follow this with a specific minilesson that will help students as readers.

Then, students go to their seats or another comfortable spot and begin reading independently and/or writing about their reading in reader's notebooks. The atmosphere of the room is calm and peaceful; some teachers play soft classical music. While everyone is reading (or writing) silently, you continue teaching, choosing from the following options or creating your own combination:

- Confer quietly with individual students.
- Confer with some individuals and then teach a guided reading group.
- Teach one guided reading group and facilitate one literature study group.
- Teach two guided reading groups.
- Facilitate two literature study groups.
- Facilitate one or two literature study groups while one group of experienced students conduct their own literature study.
- Invite several literature study groups to discuss their books while you move from group to group.

For readers who struggle, you will want to support them in special ways to be sure they are productive during their independent reading time. The following are suggestions:

1. Help them choose their independent reading books initially.
2. Confer with them before they begin their independent reading.
3. Let them listen to their independent reading book on tape as they follow along in their own copy.
4. Have them read the first half of a book in a guided reading group, then let them read the rest independently.
5. Have them take part in more frequent guided reading meetings.

At the end of the reading workshop block, call the children together for another group meeting. You may want to invite them to share something about their reading and to evaluate their work during this class period.

At the end of reading workshop, students will have listened to your book talk(s), participated in a minilesson to expand their knowledge of principles related to literature or the reading process, read for an extended period of time independently, and responded to their reading in some form of writing or through discussion and sharing. In addition, over the course of the week, students will have conferred individually with you and participated in guided reading groups and/or literature study meetings. Through class discussion, they will have made connections between the books they have read and content area study, language study, or literature study. Reading workshop places priority on reading supported by skilled instruction. With thoughtful organization and comfortable, efficient routines in place, reading workshop makes a significant contribution to students' literacy learning every day.

Suggestions for Professional Development

1. Meet with a group of colleagues. Look at your existing program and analyze how much time students spend:
   - Reading independently.
   - Discussing their reading.
   - In whole-group reading (shared reading).
   - In small-group reading (guided reading).
   - Learning about reading through minilessons.
2. Discuss ways to increase the time that students spend reading extended text. Use Figure 4–5 as a resource.
3. Look at your own schedule and identify a consistent fifty- to sixty-minute period during which you can initiate independent reading. Begin by asking students to silently read books of their own choosing. This routine will form a foundation for fully implementing independent reading, the first step in implementing reading workshop.

CHAPTER FIVE

DEVELOPING ACCOMPLISHED WRITERS: THE WRITING WORKSHOP

Once we understand what great writers do we need to find ways of building classroom structures to contain that doing.

— RANDY BOMER

For more than two decades, writing workshop has been a remarkably effective structure for supporting developing student writers. It is commonly thought of as a portion of the school day during which students write independently on topics they choose themselves. We define writing workshop as an interrelated combination of writing experiences that occur during the writing block of the language/literacy framework (see Figure 5–1). It encompasses focused writing—both assigned and self-selected—in a variety of genres and content areas, including longer research projects. It also includes providing specific writing instruction to small groups of students.

Writing workshop provides the instructional support students need to become effective writers who can:

■ Conceptualize a message, story, or topic and express it in a more or less complete form of writing.
■ Use language with clarity and voice to communicate meaning.
■ Think about the reader (audience) while writing.
■ Organize a written text in a variety of ways to fit purpose, topic, and audience.
■ Demonstrate a command of spelling, punctuation, word usage, and sentence structure.
■ Rethink, revise, and edit their writing.

The purpose of the writing workshop is to give students opportunities to write within the school day and to provide appropriate, intensive, targeted instruction to the whole group, small groups, and individuals.

Three Instructional Contexts

The term *workshop*, applied to both reading and writing, implies activity and interaction. Our writing workshop plays out in three contexts (see Figure 5–1):

■ In *independent writing*, students work individually and silently on their own writing. The basic structure for independent writing is shown in Figure 5–2. Often, you or a student offer a "writer's talk," a brief look at an aspect of a professional writer's life or craft as reflected in her or his work (see Chapter 25). You then present a daily minilesson (within an appropriate course of study) based on the needs of the writers, after which you may do a status of the class to record what everyone is working on. Students write or sketch, sometimes using a writer's notebook, at other times drafting, revising, editing, or publishing a writing project. While writing topics are typically chosen by the students, they may be assigned. You confer with individual students to support and address their needs. Later you may decide to teach students to have peer conferences and they may sign up to confer with each other. The session is followed by a large group sharing and evaluation.

■ In *guided writing*, you pull together small temporary groups of writers and teach the craft, strategies, and skills those writers need at that particular time. (The students who do not need this instruction will not be wasting their time.) Group work may focus on developing specific writing skills and strategies (forming paragraphs, for example), on using writing

Comparison of Writing Workshop Elements

Across the three elements, students develop writing strategies, learn about the writer's craft, and use writing as a tool for learning and communication. They practice writing in different genres and apply conventions to communicate information clearly to a variety of audiences.

	Independent Writing	Guided Writing	Investigations
Description	The teacher begins with a "writer talk," and then provides a daily mini-lesson based on the needs of writers. Students engage in the writing process, sometimes using a writer's notebook and at other times drafting, revising, editing, or publishing a piece of work. Students sometimes use sketching as a way of capturing meaning in visual images. Topics are self-selected or, at times, assigned. The teacher confers with individuals to support and address needs. Students may have conferences with peers. The session is usually followed by group sharing and evaluation.	The teacher pulls together small, temporary groups of writers to provide explicit teaching based on the writers' needs at a particular point in time. Sometimes the teacher has noticed students' needs and forms the groups; at other times, students request group help with some aspect of writing. Topics also may be scheduled and students sign up for groups. The teacher explicitly and efficiently works with students to teach the writer's craft, strategies, and skills.	Using reading, writing, and a variety of media resources including technology, students explore topics in-depth. They use research skills to examine works of literature, study authors, or work in a content area (can be integrated with math, science, or social studies). The result is often an oral presentation, performance or display, related to the research. The teacher provides guidelines, a structure, and a time-line for the projects, as well as explicit instruction as appropriate.
Focus	❖ To help students understand what writers do and how they make a place for writing in their lives. ❖ To develop an understanding of the writing process. ❖ To develop writing skills and strategies. ❖ To develop skills related to clear written communication. ❖ To learn how to write in different genres. ❖ To use viewing and sketching as ways of developing and communicating meaning. ❖ To use technology to produce writing.	❖ To develop an understanding of the writing process. ❖ To develop writing skills and strategies. ❖ To develop skills related to clear written communication. ❖ To learn how to write in different genres. ❖ To use viewing and sketching as ways of developing and communicating meaning. ❖ To use technology to produce writing.	❖ To learn how to use oral language, reading, and writing, with the support of technology, as tools for inquiry. ❖ To make connections between reading and writing. ❖ To use various formats for writing. ❖ To explore written language in relation to other forms for expressing meaning. ❖ To use written language to display knowledge gained through inquiry. ❖ To use technology for publication.
Format	Individual	Homogeneous—small temporary group based on student needs or interests	Heterogeneous—individual, partner, small or large group.

Figure 5–1. Writing Workshop Elements

The Basic Structure for Independent Writing	
Writer's Talk [optional]	1–2 minutes
Minilesson	5–15 minutes
Status of the class [optional]	2 minutes
Writing [notebook or project] Conferring	30–45 minutes
Group Share and Evaluation	5–10 minutes

Figure 5–2.   The Basic Structure for Independent Writing

as a tool for inquiry, on learning to write in different genres, or on using technology to publish writing. The areas you focus on in guided writing are exactly the same as those in independent writing, except that you are working with a small group instead of with individuals. The groups may be convened either by you or by students who have determined on their own that they need help in a certain area or genre and have requested to be part of a group.

- In *investigations,* students explore a piece of literature or a content-area topic in depth, using reading, writing, and a variety of media resources, including technology. They may work individually, in pairs, or in a small group. The investigation often culminates in an oral presentation, performance, or display. You provide guidelines, a structure, and a timeline for the projects, as well as explicit instruction as appropriate. (Since investigation is a broad concept that bridges literature and the content areas, we describe this element in greater depth in Chapter 25.)

The Writing Process

Understanding the writing process lies at the foundation of any writing workshop. The writing process has been outlined by experts (Graves 1983, 1994; Calkins 1991; Harwayne 2000; Murray 1993; and Atwell 1985, 1999) who arrived at their judgments and descriptions by looking at themselves as writers, by talking with

writers and by observing what they do. As Murray (1993) describes the writing process, it is "the way many writers work most of the time; it is a method of writing from which you can depart when the writing is going well, to which you can return when it is not."

At any point in the writing process, you may confer with others. You may discuss your ideas with friends before you commit to a plan for writing, and that discussion may help you identify stories or topics that interest you as a writer. You may write pieces of text and ask others to react to them. You may have someone look at your first draft and offer suggestions for organizing your ideas or revising your language. You continually refine your writing through successive drafts and informal consultations. Publication requires formal consultation about conventions and format. Many of us ask someone else to proofread our work so that new eyes search the material for errors. In the classroom students rely on two kinds of conferring: (1) with the teacher and (2) with peers.

As illustrated in Figure 5–3, the writing process begins long before the writer sits down at the computer or with paper and pen. Wide exploration takes place before writing, while writing, and right up to publication. Exploration is vital to developing purpose, finding and focusing a topic, deciding the genre (or form) to use, calling up models of language from life experiences and reading—just about everything related to creating a written text. The process is a recursive one. You may be revising while drafting, or even while pub-

The Writing Process

Explore

* ❖ Notice events, people, objects in the world around you.
* ❖ Probe experiences for ideas.
* ❖ Record thoughts, observations through writing and sketching.
* ❖ Read, listen, and engage in exploratory research.
* ❖ Reflect to shape thoughts.
* ❖ Discover interest, focus, and purpose.

Draft

* ❖ Commit to a writing project—tentative audience and genre.
* ❖ Tentatively plan writing.
* ❖ Write discovery draft (Draft #1) and successive drafts to final draft.
* ❖ Revise, select from, or expand discovery draft.
* ❖ Focus on voice.
* ❖ Develop ideas and attend to text organization.
* ❖ Attend to sentence variety and word choice.
* ❖ Work on beginnings, details, language flow, and endings.

Edit

* ❖ Proofread and edit for conventions—grammar, spelling, capitalization, punctuation.
* ❖ Complete final copy.

Publish

* ❖ Conduct final, formal editing.
* ❖ Produce published piece with final layout, illustrations, graphics (as appropriate).

Figure 5–3. The Writing Process

lishing. You may be editing as you draft or publish. It is not a lockstep process as writers move back and forth on the journey to a final draft or published project (Murray 1993).

TERRITORIES

Your writing interests have been described as "territories" (Murray 1993; Atwell 1999). You could think of your writing interests as a collection of terrains that are related to your experiences, your passions, and/or what you know or want to share.

Writers explore the same territories again and again, a process that is evident when you look at the work of a single author. Madeleine L'Engle explores imaginary worlds, high level technology, and the struggle between good and evil. Patricia Polacco writes about family and friends and her cultural heritage. Patricia MacLachlan writes about the feeling and beauty of the prairie, her childhood home. As Isaac Bashevis Singer has said, "In all my writing I tell the story of my life, over and over again."

Learning How to Be a Writer in Writing Workshop

Writing workshop creates a space within the school day when students do what professional writers do—write. Writing workshop has several practical advantages:

- *Frequency.* In the daily writing workshop, students develop a rhythm for writing. Writing is not something you "hurry up and do" just before a project needs to be handed in. As a writer, you keep your writing in mind day after day, knowing that you will work on it at regularly scheduled times. The hours of practice bring increased proficiency.
- *A writing community.* The workshop enables students to experience living in a writing community. They learn what it means to consider the writing of others and to provide thoughtful comments and support. They learn that writing is not simply an assignment for a grade. They learn that writers teach one another.
- *Demonstrations by authors and illustrators.* Writing workshop takes place within a broad language and literacy curriculum that includes the study of quality literature. Students discover the craft of writing by analyzing and discussing what good writers do. As you read aloud to students, you expose them to the organizational structures and language that good writers use. Through minilessons based on books your students have read or you have read to them, you teach specific elements of the writer's craft. Biographies, autobiographies, and memoirs of authors provide important insights that may help young writers improve their skills.
- *Predictability.* The writing workshop is highly predictable. Students understand how the routines work, how supplies are organized, and how time is arranged. The structure makes it possible for you and your students to focus on the process of writing and to engage in learning conversations. Except for the soft murmuring of conferences and group work, the work is silent.
- *Purpose.* In the writing workshop, students learn that writing must have a purpose, that it is not simply an assignment to complete. They explore a rich range of such purposes—for example, telling a story, arguing, persuading, describing. They produce final drafts that are shared within the group; other projects, particularly long-term investigations of literature and content-area topics, are published.
- *Revision, editing, proofreading, and publishing.* Students are expected to revise and proofread their work. They learn that conventions are important. They value spelling and correct use of punctuation. They also carefully consider word choice and sentence structure so that their work achieves coherence and clarity. They give a final check, or proofread finished work and may publish the project.
- *Expectations.* Expectations for students during writing workshop are high. They write or engage in conferences or group work during the entire period. They also generate ideas for their own work and support the work of others. You stipulate the requirements for specific projects. For example, final drafts must use conventional margins, best spelling, and best punctuation. In other words, writers show all they know in a final draft, though it may not be entirely correct.

Roles in Writing Workshop

	Independent Writing	Guided Writing	Investigations
Teacher	Provides explicit teaching through ❖ writer's talk ❖ minilesson ❖ conferring ❖ sharing	Provides explicit teaching through ❖ lessons focused on the specific needs of individuals ❖ conferring with individuals within a small group	Provides explicit teaching through ❖ sparking student interest ❖ providing guidelines, structure, and timelines for projects ❖ presenting minilessons on inquiry tools ❖ suggesting resources ❖ providing materials and experiences related to the topic ❖ providing instruction in content areas
Students	❖ Explore what writers or illustrators do through studying authors or illustrators ❖ Participate in large group minilesson and apply new knowledge to individual writing ❖ Select topic ❖ Write during designated time ❖ Confer with teacher and other writers ❖ Share writing to solicit feedback ❖ Use feedback in revision and editing ❖ Use references and resources ❖ Publish writing as appropriate	❖ Participate in group lesson ❖ Apply new knowledge to individual pieces of writing ❖ Select topic ❖ Write during designated time ❖ Confer with teacher and other writers ❖ Share writing to solicit feedback ❖ Use feedback in revision and editing ❖ Use references and resources ❖ Publish writing as appropriate	❖ Formulate questions ❖ Gather print and nonprint resources ❖ Select and use various writing formats as tools for investigation ❖ Work cooperatively with other students in inquiry ❖ Create a variety of written and visual products to display and communicate findings ❖ Use technology as a tool for investigation

Figure 5–4.   Roles in the Writing Workshop

The Writing Workshop Block and How to Use It

The structure of the writing workshop block helps you organize activity and use time within the language/literacy framework. Once students become familiar with independent writing, guided writing, and investigations, you can vary the time you devote to these instructional contexts.

Teacher and Student Roles

Roles and responsibilities during writing workshop are clearly defined (see Figure 5–4).

TEACHER

After giving a brief writer's talk to introduce the class to a writer they may not know, teach the whole group directly via short, focused minilessons on a given aspect of writing. For example, the purpose of a minilesson may be to:

■ Spark student interest in topics or content areas.

■ Provide examples of writing that will help them learn more about the process.

■ Offer specific teaching relative to language, word choice, or conventions.

■ Show how to refine writing—for example, how to use details, how to present ideas in clear language, how to begin or end a piece.

■ Demonstrate the use of tools for inquiry.

■ Share nonfiction texts as a motivation for students to find their own topics to investigate.

■ Share examples of writing in different genres or in different content areas.

■ Discuss how writers work and how they make writing a part of their lives.

■ Provide a close look at one aspect of the writing life—what writers say about their writing, what influences them, how they find topics, how they make writing a part of their day-to-day lives. (As an alternative, you can share insights about yourself as a writer or positive insights about members of the class.)

Your minilessons are related to your observations of students' writing, as well as to the aspects of the writer's craft you want your students to learn. Through examples of picture books and other published works, you are showing writers the "possibilities" for their work. A series of minilessons is an integral part of your curriculum.

During writing you confer regularly with individual students about their work and provide guidance and feedback. Conferences may be held at any point in the writing process—from beginning exploration to publication. (Sometimes students may ask for a conference at a particular point in a writing project.) These discussions are informed by your observation of individual writing behavior as well as your analysis of the written products. It is important for students to "codirect" the conference. Teach students to analyze and evaluate their own writing projects and to initiate questions about their own writing.

Also, pull together guided writing groups for lessons based on particular interests or needs or work with small groups on research projects. This is an opportunity to teach more efficiently a topic you would otherwise address in an individual conference. The group lesson may involve direct teaching, discussing and analyzing examples, or sharing students' work.

STUDENTS

In independent writing, students write; they explore topics, draft, revise, edit, and publish. They are always working in their writer's notebooks or on a writing project. The expectation is that they are always writing or working on something directly related to writing. Usually they write independently, but they may also participate in small guided writing groups. They are expected to use a writer's notebook to gather and record ideas, sketch images, and organize information; use references and resources; edit their work for the accurate use of conventions; and learn to use technology for various purposes, including research and preparing writing for publication. They are also expected to confer with the teacher and with peers and to give and use feedback for revision.

Managing Time and Activity in the Writing Workshop

Students need to spend an hour each day in writing workshop, but the amount of time devoted to the various instructional contexts within the block (see Figure 5–5) will vary by student and by day.

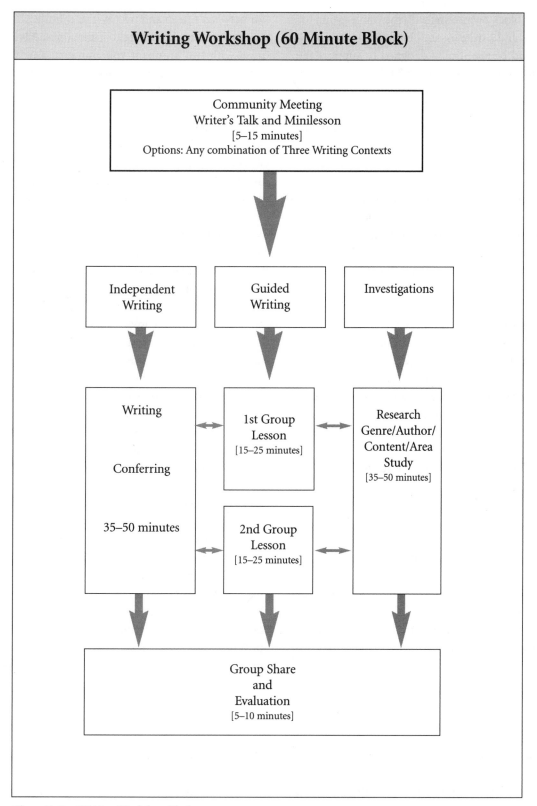

Figure 5–5. Writing Workshop Block

Begin the block by meeting with the whole group for a writer's talk and a minilesson. This meeting should be kept short and be specifically designed to support the learning that is needed by most of the writers in the class. Occasionally, for particular reasons, you may have longer lessons, but the idea is to focus students' attention on some aspect of writing that they can immediately apply as they get involved in their own work.

As Atwell (1999) suggests, during the minilesson older students (grades five and six) can take notes in a spiral notebook that becomes their own "writing/reading handbook." The table of contents should identify the various topics so that the notebook becomes an effective resource when the student is writing. This notebook can replace the large wall charts used for reference in the earlier grades.

INDEPENDENT WRITING

Following the writer's talk and minilesson, students work independently for thirty-five to fifty minutes on their writer's notebook or a writing project. Some students work independently for the entire period; others have conferences with you or one of their peers. Conferences:

- Help students decide what they want to say.
- Provide feedback.
- Help writers clarify meaning.
- Teach skills.
- Reinforce writers' strengths.
- Give writers new ways of thinking.

Take notes during conferences to inform your future teaching as well as to document students' progress. The length of a conference may vary from "checking in" for a minute or two, to having a five- to eight-minute conversation. When you leave the conference, the writer should feel he has learned something helpful to him as a writer.

GUIDED WRITING

Pull guided writing groups together several times a week as needed based on your ongoing review of students' writing folders and notebooks. These groups are flexible: their size and content will vary from day to day. A student who participates in a group will work individually for most of the period, moving into the group

for between fifteen and twenty-five minutes. In general, during the one hour block of time, you have time to meet with two groups if you eliminate any individual conferences; alternatively, you can meet with one group and conduct several individual conferences as well.

INVESTIGATIONS

An investigation is an in-depth study. The writing that students do as part of an investigation becomes their independent writing for the time the investigation is in progress. Alternatively, the work may take place during social studies or science times.

Tools like the writer's notebook can be used to record ideas or make drawings or diagrams. The notebook contains the seeds of ideas, but as students move deeper into the research, they will need to create files for organizing information.

The topic of an investigation may require a few days to research or take as long as a month and culminate in a report or presentation. Students typically work on the investigation for the entire period—individually, with a partner, or in cooperative learning groups. You may confer with groups, structuring your time as you do with guided writing groups. A conference may be as simple as checking on the group's progress, but it may also involve showing students particular resources or research techniques or helping them organize their information.

Every student, or just one or two groups, may be working on investigations. For example, on a given day some students may be writing individually, others may be working with you in guided writing, and still others may be working on an inquiry project. Over time, however, as small groups form and re-form, all students eventually participate in an investigation. You provide guidelines, a structure, and a timeline for the projects, as well as explicit instruction as appropriate.

SHARING AND EVALUATION

At the end of the writing workshop, bring students together for a five-to-ten-minute group share and evaluation. You might use a "writer's chair," which a writer sits in to read her piece to other students and invites comment or feedback (see Figure 5–6). Sometimes, the writer asks for specific help: "I need help with my lead," or "Listen to my description of this character." In a typical group share everyone gets a quick turn in a "read-around," or "go-around." For example, if the day's minilesson focused on titles, everyone might read her title, or if the lesson were on strong leads, each student reads her lead sentence. Sometimes you can have partner or triad shares, in which two or three students share with one another. Whatever form sharing takes, the object is to give the writer another set of ears and more to think about.

Creating an Environment to Support Good Writing

Young writers need the same support structures that professional writers need, including a quiet place to work and the necessary supplies. Writing is thinking. A peaceful environment is essential for students to do their best thinking and writing. No one can do her best thinking in a den of noise.

Figure 5–6.   *"Writer's Chair"*

Teach students to write in silence and to move around only if they need supplies or are using references or other resources. Except for minilessons, conferences, small-group guided writing, and sharing, they shouldn't be talking with one another about their writing. When you confer with students, whisper. Model the voice level that is acceptable in those settings.

Materials

It is important to have a good supply of basic writing materials in one very well organized place and to teach students how to use them. Introduce materials in minilessons so that students understand how they are to be used and know how to get them and put them back. Also, introduce the basic habits of conservation and have your students practice them. Basic writing supplies include:

- Special draft paper with places for initials, date, writing project #, draft # and page # (see Appendix 8)
- Special pastel final draft paper (see Appendix 9)
- Small sheets of paper
- Large sheets of paper
- Various colors and sizes of construction paper
- Computer paper
- Scratch paper
- Note pads

- List pads
- Stationery
- Different kinds of cover papers
- Stapler and stapler remover
- White cover-up tape
- Index cards
- Markers
- Colored pencils
- Regular envelopes
- Manila envelopes
- Cardboard
- Date stamp
- Paper clips
- Scissors
- Measuring tapes and rulers
- Labels
- Charts
- Telephone message pad.

Students can be helped by the paper they are given to write on. For example, one teacher designed a sheet of lined paper for drafts that at the top has spaces for the student's initials, the date, the writing project number, the draft number, and the page number. Students write on every other line. Another type of paper copied on a pastel color is provided for final drafts. Students realize that this final draft is a special copy, distinguished from the draft work they have been doing. (Reproducible forms are provided in Appendix 8 and 9). All writing projects during the year are numbered consecutively. The discovery draft of each project is draft 1, and the others are numbered 2 through as many as there are.

Students also enjoy variety in the paper they can use to publish their pieces. For example, you might offer stationery for letters, paper with different line widths, different-color paper, special paper for covers. Try to increase the variety of papers and utensils students have to choose from.

Writing Folders

Every student needs a writing folder in which to keep the current writing project. Finished projects are kept in separate hanging files in a central area, in a square plastic crate (like a milk crate). Type the students' names on protruding plastic tabs so they can find their files easily. Teach students to clip their drafts together—discovery draft on the bottom, successive drafts in ascending order, final draft on top—and place the entire packet in the hanging file. That way, you and your students will have an orderly, ongoing, easily available record of their writing, and the only work in each child's writing folder will be the current project. (A hint from Mary Ellen Giacobbe: if you use folders with gussets, important resources can be included in the center of the folder as well.)

We have designed five forms to place in the gusset of the writing folder.

■ *Record of Writing Projects.* A record of every writing project (see Figure 5–7; a reproducible version is provided in Appendix 5). The student indicates the writing project number, title, type of writing (genre), status, and date she completed the project.

■ *What I Learned About Being a Writer.* A record that indicates what students have learned from each writing project (see Figure 5–8; a reproducible version is provided in Appendix 6). After completing each project, students are expected to reflect on their writing experience and think about what they learned about the writer's craft and the use of conventions.

■ *Types of Writing.* A list of the different kinds of writing that students have completed over the year. Students list the type of writing and date each time they complete a writing project. (See reproducible version in Appendix 7.)

■ *Word List.* A list of 500 frequently encountered words, with "spelling demons" in bold (see Appendix 4). Students should gain full control of these words by the end of elementary school. As students proofread their pieces, they can refer to this list of words as a quick reference. Teach students to proofread carefully, notice words they aren't sure of, and check their thinking against this list.

■ *Words to Learn.* A blank form for students and teachers to list words the writer needs to learn how to spell. (See Pinnell and Fountas 1998.)

Mary Ellen Giacobbe suggests using four different-color writing folders and assigning a specific color to a quarter of the class. The colors have no relation to students' ability or progress. They simply allow a more systematic approach to examining the folders: you can look at the yellow folders on Monday, the blue folders on Tuesday, etc. Your review might be anything from a quick check to be sure that students are making progress to a more careful perusal that will help you plan writing conferences or guided writing groups. Other teachers prefer to use a specific-color folder for each area: red for writing, blue for reading records, yellow for mathematics, etc.

Rather than storing all these folders in the same crate, you may want to collect four or five crates, put the crates in different parts of the classroom, and place five students' folders (five folders of five different colors if you use a different folder for every subject) in each crate. Then when you ask students to get their red writing folders, for example, five students will go to each crate, and the entire class won't be trying to get their folders out of the same box.

Text Resources

You will need a good supply of the standard references and resources—dictionaries and thesauruses, for example—that support students in their writing. A wide range of informational texts will also help students. For younger students, post the wall charts that are produced during minilessons on conventions (for example, a chart explaining how contractions work); these charts are useful references. Teach students to go to the charts whenever they need help remembering conventions. Also make charts that help them understand the writer's craft (for example, a chart explaining how to create a good lead for a story). These charts can be beneficial all the way through elementary school, but as students become

Record of Writing Projects				
Project #	Title	Type of Writing	Status (D#__, FD, P)	Date Completed
1	Remembering Grandma	memoir	P	9/29
2	Lost	memoir	P	10/9
3	Found	memoir	P	10/18
4	Smoke out	news article	FD	10/27
5	Dear Marty	letter	P	11/7
6	Nothing But The Truth	book review	P	11/18
7	Tornadoes	report	P	12/15
8	Sun Dance	poem	FD	12/22

Figure 5–7. Record of Writing Projects

more sophisticated, you will want them to use dictionaries and thesauruses to improve their word skills. As we discussed earlier, older students can take notes on minilessons in a reference notebook, complete with a table of contents that they construct.

A writing resource that has a big payoff for students is a wide array of wonderful picture books. Appendix 56 is a bibliography of picture books appropriate for older students. These texts are cohesive and coherent works of art. The written text is complex; most of the books either are appropriate for intermediate students to read themselves or can be read aloud to them. They have the advantage of brevity (most can be read in one sitting), but they also enable students to take a close look at genre, the relationship between illustrations and text, the author's purpose and voice, and many other aspects of the craft of writing. Some of these picture books can become mentor texts (Anderson 2000) that you refer to again and again to help students understand the process of writing in different genres.

What I Learned About Being a Writer	
Project # 1	I learned how to write small by thinking about what really matters, to figure out what I really want to say. I can tell in fewer words and be more clear, also I learned how to revise by crossing out and using spider legs.
Project # 2	I learned that strong words instead of a group of words gets to my point. Cutting up the text to change order is an easy way for writers to move ideas around.
Project # 3	I can write about topics I care about many different times like other writers do. I learned that sometimes writers keep revisiting topics in different ways. Showing not telling makes my writing stronger.
Project # 4	Writers of news articles use words that stir the readers emotions. Crossing out information that doesn't matter to the reader helps a writer be more clear to my readers.
Project #	
Project #	

Figure 5–8.   *What I Learned About Being a Writer*

The Last Princess: The Story of Princess Kaiulani of Hawaii (Stanley 1999), for example, is a well-written biography that chronicles the life of Princess Kaiulani, the last heir of the royal Hawaiian family during the period of transition to U.S. government. The text is illustrated with captioned paintings and historical photographs. The writer uses a narrative style that engages the reader and captures the life of the princess; at the same time, a great deal of objective information gets through. From biographies like *The Last Princess*, students can learn how to write their own biographies.

Expectations

Part of creating a supportive writing environment is providing clear expectations. Discuss your expectations with your students and be sure that they understand them.

Expectations for Writing

1. Gather ideas and information in your notebook in school and out of school.
2. Try writing in different genres.
3. Complete a minimum of one final draft almost every week.
4. Publish one writing project every two to three weeks.

Figure 5–9. Expectations for Writing

The sample expectations listed in Figure 5–9 clearly communicate that students will be recording information in their writer's notebooks all year and using that information to fuel a number of specific projects.

A typical homework assignment is to require students to write or sketch in their notebooks for fifteen to thirty minutes each evening, Monday through Friday. This constant effort is not graded, other than to verify that substantive entries are made each evening.

Another expectation for students is to try writing in different genres. The Record of Writing Projects will document students' exploration of genres. In conferences with students, help them analyze the different kinds of writing they have completed and encourage them to vary their repertoires. This is not a matter of assigning a letter or a memoir. As students develop topics, they need to consider which genre will help them express what they have to say most clearly. In general, however, students should consciously work to experience and practice a wide range of genres.

Inviting Students into the Writing Process

The purpose of the writing workshop is to teach students to explore ideas, select topics, create, revise and edit drafts, and publish writing projects. As they engage in the process with numerous short pieces they increase their "writing power."

Getting Started

Sometimes the hardest part of writing is getting started. Some suggestions to help your students do so are

provided in Figure 5–10. Keeping a writer's notebook enables them to collect new material, or "seeds," for writing projects (Fletcher 1998). The notebook is a good place for them to write freely about any topic and is a powerful tool for helping them define and elaborate on their own writing territories.

Drafting and Revising

A "discovery draft" involves getting down on paper everything you know about a topic. The emphasis here is not on form, conventions, or organization but on the generation of ideas. With an idea in mind, the writer writes around a topic, discovering what is important and searching for the genre that will work best. In a sense, all drafts are "discovery" drafts, because with each draft, students learn more about the topic and what they really want to say. They also discover things about themselves as writers. Drafts are subject to revision, which involves paying attention to the content of the piece. Students often write several drafts, strengthening the project each time until the final draft.

Revision means going back to a written work and looking at it with new eyes, literally to "re-see." You will want your students to think about revision not as fixing something up but as re-creating it. For example, in revising a text, you look to see that:

■ The ideas flow in logical sequence.
■ Your voice comes through.

Getting Started

1. Have a quiet atmosphere.
2. Get the right supplies and equipment.
3. Take time to think.
4. Look through your writer's notebook.
5. Talk with others about topics.
6. Avoid distractions.
7. Get lots of ideas.
8. Do some planning.
9. Think of a working title.

Figure 5–10. Getting Started

Revising My Writing Project

_____ Do I have a good beginning?

_____ Do I have a good ending?

_____ Have I written about the topic in an interesting way?

_____ Have I selected an appropriate genre for the project?

_____ Are there some repetitious parts that I could leave out?

_____ Are there any sentences that don't make sense?

_____ Could I combine any of the sentences?

_____ Have I made good word choices? (strong, descriptive, precise, lively, interesting)

_____ Did I stay on the topic?

_____ Do the sentences flow well?

_____ Are the sentences interesting and varied?

_____ Are important details included?

_____ Does the writing make sense?

_____ Is the writing well organized?

_____ Is this my best work?

Figure 5–11.   _Revising My Writing_

■ Word choice strengthens meaning (for example, you want to use precise nouns, strong verbs and adjectives).

■ The piece is focused rather than rambling.

■ Irrelevant details or information are deleted.

■ There are smooth, appropriate transitions that give your sentences a flow.

■ Beginnings and endings are strong.

■ Information is organized so readers will understand.

■ Metaphor and simile are used accurately and effectively.

■ Dialogue sounds natural and reveals characters' feelings and thoughts.

Revision is a complex process. It is not copying over a draft to correct errors. There are skills students must learn to be able to see what they can change about their writing. They cannot understand the concept of revision until you have demonstrated the process directly. Revision is an ongoing process that involves thinking about language use, organization, and audience. Figure 5–11 is a list of questions related to revision that Jackie developed to assist writers in checking for revision.

Editing

It is important to distinguish between revising and editing. Editing refers to the changes and corrections a writer makes so that her work conforms with conventions. Standard punctuation and word usage were established for good reason: they make the writing more intelligible to the reader.

Conventions actually arose out of necessity and are deeply rooted in history. In the early days of written language, only a few people, in very specific positions, used reading and writing. Several different spellings of a given word were permissible. As the literate population grew, however, there was more need for standardization. Now, standard usage is essential.

One of the problems with many elementary school students is that they are so concerned with "getting it right" that they lose their creativity and flexibility. For example, a student may write the word _green_ rather than _emerald_ or _verdant_ simply because she knows how to spell _green_. You do not want that to happen, so there will be times when you set aside editing to work on revising content, on adding sparkle to your students' writing. Not for one moment, however, are we suggesting that conventions are unimportant. Unless the writer uses standard spelling, punctuation, and grammar, even the best ideas are masked from the reader.

Editing My Writing

_____ Have I read over my work?

_____ Are the words spelled correctly?

_____ Is the punctuation correctly used?

_____ Have I used correct spelling?

_____ Have I used correct grammar?

_____ Does each sentence give a complete thought (if prose)?

_____ Have I used capitals when needed?

_____ Have I organized my writing into paragraphs (if prose)?

_____ Have I organized my writing into large sections like chapters?

_____ Do I need to use chapters, side headings, or other features to show the organization of the information?

_____ Do I need a table of contents, glossary or other aid?

_____ Do my illustrations and graphic features match the written text?

Figure 5–12. Editing My Writing

Students can learn much from the editing process if the goal is to teach them about writing conventions rather than simply to fix a piece of writing. When you teach your students to edit, you may want to focus on:

■ Sentence fragments.
■ Punctuation, capitalization.
■ Spelling.
■ Paragraphing, indentation.
■ Handwriting.

You should also teach your students standard revising and editing conventions:

■ Put three lines under a letter to indicate a capital is needed.
■ Circle words to check for spelling.
■ Use a caret (∧) to indicate where to insert words, phrases, or sentences.
■ Cross out rather than erase words, phrases, or sentences you want to delete.
■ Use "spider legs" to add text (a strip of paper that you tape or glue onto the side of the page and fold in).
■ Cut up the text and tape it back together in a different order.
■ Use a box and arrows to show where to move or insert text.

■ Use white correction tape to cover over text and write something different.
■ You may also want to teach students to use one color pen for revising and a different color to edit so the improvements can be seen clearly.

You might want to make a chart of revising and editing symbols (see Appendix 10, Revising and Editing Tools) that writers will find useful. It is important however that you have taught each tool on the list as a separate minilesson.

You may also want to establish additional editing procedures of your own. Whatever editing marks and conventions you decide on, they should be taught through minilessons that include clear demonstrations, and students should be expected to use them in the designated way. You may want to develop a checklist like the one in Figure 5–12 to guide your students in looking at their work.

Teaching students to revise and edit their work can be the focus of minilessons, individual conferences, and guided writing lessons. Your first goal will be to get students writing freely in their notebooks so that they build up a store of recollections and observations from which they can draw for their discovery drafts. Once they have gotten their thinking down on paper, they can take on revising and then editing. Use judgment and care as to the amount of revision you will require for any one piece of writing. Learning a few new things from each writing project will suffice; too many lessons connected to one piece of writing can be overwhelming.

Establish procedures in your class that will help students systematically edit their work. Students should first edit their own writing. Checklists can be helpful provided students understand the concepts and criteria, and the process is not made too tedious. Students should be using what they know when they edit, not guessing at concepts and rules that they have not yet learned.

Peer editing can also be helpful; here students share their learning and experience with one another. They can use the same checklists. Finally, students should ask for a conference with you before writing a final draft, and you should edit a piece before it is published.

Ask students to place their final drafts in the editor's box. You will want to photocopy the project and then make your edits. Make it clear that students are expected to use their own editing skills before relying on yours. Your editorial review is meant to provide feedback that will help the student turn the writing into a publishable piece.

Remember that the goal of each writing project is not to create a perfect piece of writing. Students are learning how to reflect on their writing and to revise and edit; the process is as important as the product. Too much editing can discourage students. Focus on revision and editing that relates to what they need to learn next about the writing process; then move on to other pieces of writing. They will learn a few new things about the writing process each time.

Publishing

If the writing is to be published (which doesn't necessarily mean printed for wide distribution), students must produce a final copy after formal editing and proofreading. This process should be applied to any project (a report, for example) that will be read and evaluated by others. Published means "going public." Think about the variety of ways a writer makes a piece public—framing it, making a picture book, sending the letter, submitting a poem to a contest, giving it as a gift. Show students how to think about the text as a whole and evaluate how it communicates meaning and information through the use of conventions and visual elements such as layout and illustrations.

Minilessons

Minilessons are an efficient way to communicate specific information to the whole class. The characteristics of minilessons are similar whatever the subject.

What Is a Minilesson?

A minilesson is a short lesson focused on a specific principle or procedure (Calkins 1986, 1994). In a minilesson you teach students something important about writing and demonstrate an aspect of the writing process; however, minilessons are not all "telling." Effective minilessons are interactive, with students contributing ideas and examples. Three basic kinds of minilessons are essential to the writing workshop:

- *Management* minilessons help students learn the routines and procedures of writing workshop.
- *Strategy and skill* minilessons help students learn how to use the conventional rules for written language accurately and effectively.
- *Craft* minilessons show students how writers work.

Genre minilessons that show how content and purpose affect the form a writer chooses are a form of crafting.

Chapter 8 includes some general guidelines for effective reading minilessons. The guidelines for writing minilessons are essentially the same. They need to focus on a single aspect of writing, include clear, powerful examples, and invite students to participate by providing additional examples. And the learning they provide needs to be reinforced through application in individual, small-group, and whole-class work as well as in conferences and group share.

What Minilessons Should I Teach?

There are three basic sources for writing minilessons, and it's important to consider all of them.

CHARACTERISTICS OF GOOD WRITING

You need to have a comprehensive understanding of what makes good writing and what your students will need to know how to do as writers. Certainly, this includes the conventions of written language, the elements of the writer's craft, and effective management procedures. Deepening your own knowledge of how writers work will add to your minilessons in a very rich way. Over time, as you become more and more familiar with good writers and good writing, you will store up a wealth of examples that will become the basis for minilessons. Picture books will be one valuable source.

STUDENT WRITING

Just as you observe your students as they read, you will gain a great deal from observing students as they write. As you examine students' written products (in various stages of development), you will notice what they understand and need to understand about writing. The notes that you take during writing conferences are other important sources for minilessons. Periodically, examine conference records, looking for patterns that will help you decide what most of the group members need to know next about writing. (See Appendix 12, Conference Record Form.)

You may want to set up a schedule to ensure that you systematically review your students' writing. Some teachers ask students to turn in their writer's notebook, or their current draft on a particular day, each week or every two weeks. Others review all their students' writing folders every week, a few each day. However you go about it, the patterns you find as you examine your students' writing will help you plan conferences as well as minilessons.

When you begin the year, you will want several kinds of writing samples from your students in order to get information about where to start. Some teachers also find it helpful to conduct writing interviews (also see Atwell 1998; Rhodes and Shanklin 1993). A sample writing interview is included in Appendix 47. The writing interview provides important insights about how students see themselves as writers and gives you a point of departure.

CURRICULUM GUIDES

Every district has curriculum guides that describe the course of study. Chances are, these guides will closely dovetail with what you know about the writing process. You will want to consult these guides for a general "roadmap" against which you can check your planning of minilessons. You will also want to consult your state curriculum frameworks.

Management Minilessons

Management minilessons acquaint students with the procedures for the writing workshop and promote

order and efficiency in the classroom. They also help students learn about the rigor and organization it takes to become a good writer. Some examples of management minilessons are listed in Figure 5–13.

It's a good idea to introduce Guidelines for Writing Workshop (see Figure 5–14). The list of guidelines will be more meaningful if introduced *after* students have learned each of the procedures on the list. You will want to adjust them to fit the procedures you set in your class.

Even if most of your students come into your class with considerable experience in writing workshop, they will need brief, clear demonstrations of how it works in your classroom. It is well worth taking the time to be sure that students understand exactly what is expected of them and also that they can use routine procedures effectively. The more your students know, the less time you will have to spend explaining things to them, doing things for them, or reprimanding them.

Conventions Minilessons

Minilessons on *conventions* help students gradually increase their control of the more "mechanical" aspects of writing—the rules that have been established to standardize written communication. Some examples of lessons on writing conventions are included in Figure 5–15.

You want students to learn how punctuation can help them communicate meaning in a clear way. To that end, Carol gave her students a minilesson on quotation marks. She asked them to look at examples of texts on an overhead projector and come up with ways that quotation marks were used. They generated the list shown in Figure 5–16, which then served as a guide for their writing.

You also want students to become aware of word usage and sentence structure, those features of written language that make a text cohesive and coherent. For example, pronouns, which refer to people, animals, or things mentioned elsewhere in a text, must have clear antecedents; verbs need to agree with their subjects; sentences must flow logically from one to the next; and so on. You want your students to select precise words and to use verb forms, prefixes, and suffixes correctly.

Standard spelling is an essential skill; all words in published pieces need to be spelled conventionally. Students will be working on spelling daily in the Language/Word Study Block (see Chapter 3). There

Minilessons on the Management of Writing Workshop

Managing Time, Materials, and Equipment

❖ Schedule for writing workshop

❖ Basic writing materials and how to use them

❖ Using stapler, staple remover, hole punch

❖ Different ways to bind a book

❖ Using space for writing, conferring, and sharing

❖ Using different kinds of paper

❖ Using draft paper

❖ Using final draft paper

❖ Parts of the writing folder—*Record of Writing, What I Learned, Types of Writing, 500 Frequently Encountered Words, Words to Learn*

❖ Using the *Types of Writing* form

❖ Using the *Record of Writing* form

❖ Using the *What I Learned About Being a Writer* form

❖ How to use the frequently encountered word list

❖ What is the writer's notebook?

❖ Choosing a writer's notebook

❖ Using the hanging file to store finished writing projects—how to keep papers in order in the hanging file

❖ Learning the system for using the computers and printers

❖ How to use word processing on the computer

❖ Learning to use computer software (PowerPoint, Excel, graphics packages, programs for using digital cameras)

❖ Using AlphaSmart to prepare drafts

❖ References and resources that writers use (dictionaries, thesauruses, all kinds of books)

❖ Using the Internet

❖ Authors' websites

Managing Community Cooperation and Interaction

❖ Voice levels during conferences and group work

❖ The reasons for silent writing

❖ Self-evaluation of work

❖ Procedures for sharing work

❖ How to whisper

❖ Places for peer conferences

❖ Records and reporting for peer conferences

❖ Working according to the guidelines of writing workshop

❖ Procedures for editing—self-edit, peer-edit, teacher-edit

Managing Independent Work

❖ Expectations for writing

❖ Status of the class chart/survey

❖ How to get started in the writer's notebook

❖ Sketching in the writer's notebook

❖ The system for revising and editing a draft

❖ Using a revising checklist

❖ Procedures for turning in drafts for teacher's editing

❖ Reasons for writing conferences

❖ Structure/goals of peer conferences

❖ How to request a final draft conference with the teacher

❖ Options for publication

❖ Submitting your writing for publication

❖ Using draft paper: skip lines when drafting to permit editing and revision

❖ Using final draft paper

❖ Labeling drafts

Figure 5–13. Lessons on Management

Guidelines for Writing Workshop

1. You must always be writing or sketching in your writer's notebook or working on a writing project.

2. Put the date in the margin each day as you start writing.

3. You need to work silently so that everyone can do their best thinking.

4. Use a soft voice when conferring with the teacher.

5. When using draft paper, write on every other line and cross out when you make mistakes.

6. Request a teacher conference when you are ready for your final draft.

7. When using final draft paper, use your best handwriting and write on every line.

8. When you complete a writing project, record the information on your Record of Writing. Then record what you learned about being a writer.

9. After you finish a final draft, put your drafts in numerical order. Then staple them together with the final draft on top, and place your project in the hanging file.

10. Place your final draft in the editor's basket when you want the teacher to edit your project for publication.

Figure 5–14.   Guidelines for Writing Workshop

you will present minilessons that introduce students to important principles about how words work, and students will participate in a systematic study of words, as in "buddy study," which is described in Chapter 4 (also see Pinnell and Fountas 1999).

Make connections between students' word study, interactive edit, and the writing they do for themselves. Editing can be very productive in this regard, as students put into practice the principles they have been exploring through word study. You may occasionally want to present a spelling minilesson at the beginning of independent writing. If you teach in a departmentalized school and have discrete periods for reading and language arts, you may not have a language/word study block. In that case, you may need to work on spelling more often as part of the writing period.

The array of conventions that students must acquire is overwhelming until you realize that they will be writing every day; there is much opportunity to practice. It is important, however, to raise their consciousness about conventions so that they actively work to improve their writing. Minilessons are effective tools by which to accomplish this.

Craft Minilessons

Craft minilessons help students improve the quality of their writing over time by learning what makes good writing. Students may think that writing is simply a matter of correct spelling and being neat. Your goal in writing workshop is to help them understand that they can intentionally improve their writing by incorporating literary elements. This kind of writing is different from writing in a notebook or writing a formulaic paragraph or report. It requires that students learn how texts are crafted or shaped including how authors engage readers, and then begin a writing project with the full intention of achieving those qualities themselves. Examples of craft minilessons are provided in Figure 5–17. Remember that each concept on this long list is a complex idea that will require time and practice to learn. You will want to teach the same topic several times if needed.

Let's examine a few craft minilessons as they played out in the classroom. In one, Carol worked with her students to help them understand the concept of "show, don't tell," which means that instead of simply telling, the writer provides descriptive detail to illustrate an idea, thus leaving the reader to infer meaning and in the process making the writing more engaging. For the initial minilesson, Carol pointed out several examples of "show, don't tell" from two books she had read to the class—*Tales of a Gambling Grandma* (Khalsa 1986) and *Wilma Unlimited* (Krull 1996). The two lead sentences were written on chart paper (see Figure 5–18). She then asked students to read each quote and talk about what it really meant. They discussed how the writer had provided details that helped them visualize the meaning. They listed the things they had inferred from the description on the chart.

The concept of "show, don't tell" became part of the literary conversation for the rest of the week, as students discussed the idea again in relation to the books they were reading in guided reading and literature study and hearing in interactive read aloud. Carol also

Minilessons on the Conventions of Writing

Lessons on Spelling[1]

* Frequently encountered words (*and, the, is*)
* Spelling demons
* Adding *s* and *es* to form plurals (*cats, makes, lunches*)
* Forming plurals by changing *f* to *v* and adding *es* (*knife, knives*)
* Forming plurals by changing *y* to *i* and adding *es* (*party, parties*)
* Forming plurals by changing the spelling of the word (*mouse, mice*)
* Words that can be either single or plural (*sheep*)
* Vowel combinations and vowels with *r* (*house, horse*)
* Words with silent *e* (*flake, strike*)
* Contractions (*won't, wouldn't, shouldn't, haven't*)
* Compound words (*fairgrounds, foreword*)
* Affixes: inflectional endings, prefixes, suffixes (*prewar, portable*)
* Synonyms and antonyms (*green, emerald, jade, olive; inside, outside*)
* Homonyms (*break, brake*)
* Possessives (*child's, their, his*)
* Clipped words (*automobile, auto; bicycle, bike; telephone, phone*)
* Abbreviations (*Mrs., St., Ave.*)
* Syllabication (*for-es-try; cen-ten-ni-al*)
* Greek and Latin word roots (*helio, helium; phob, phobia*)
* "Hink Pinks" (words that rhyme and have meaning like *sad dad* or *weird beard*)
* Onomatopoetic words (words from sound, like *plop, splash, zing*)
* Portmanteau words (abbreviated like *breakfast + lunch = brunch*)
* *Qu* rule (always put a *u* after *q*)
* Syllable rule (every syllable has a vowel)
* Two sounds of *c* and *g* (soft *c* or *g* usually followed by *i, y,* or *e* (*city, cent, gem*)
* *Ei* or *ie* rule (when word ends in silent *e*, drop *e* when adding ending beginning with a vowel as in *like, liking*)
* Adding endings (double the final consonant of a word that ends with a single vowel and conso-nant before adding a suffix that begins with a vowel, as in *stop, stopping*)
* Adding endings to words that end in *y* (change *y* to *i* when adding an ending to a word that ends with *y*, unless the ending is *ing*, as in *carry* and *carries*

Lessons on Paragraphing

* What is a paragraph?
* Recognizing paragraphs in texts
* Using indentation to signal paragraphs
* How to write a paragraph
* How to divide text into paragraphs
* Important ideas and details in paragraphs
* Beginning and ending paragraphs

Lessons on Grammar

* What is a sentence?
* Making verb tense agree in a sentence
* Subject and verb agreement
* Keeping pronouns consistent with point of view (*I, you, he, she*)

Lessons on Punctuation

* How to use periods
* How to use commas
* How to use quotation marks
* How to use semicolons
* How to use apostrophes to indicate possession
* How to use apostrophes in contractions
* How to use colons
* How to use hyphens
* How to use dashes
* How to use parentheses
* How to use ellipses

Lessons on the Use of Capital Letters

* Using capitals at the beginning of sentences
* Using capitals to indicate proper names and the names of places

1 See Pinnell and Fountas, 1999, *Word Matters: Teaching Phonics and Spelling in the Reading/Writing Classroom*.

Figure 5–15. Lessons on Conventions

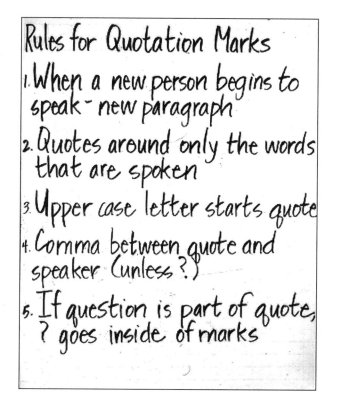

Figure 5–16. Rules for Quotation Marks

highlighted examples of how an author shows without telling in another story she read aloud. Students looked at their own writing projects to find examples of telling and then considered revisions that would show the reader without telling. As students became more sophisticated in recognizing this literary characteristic and incorporating it into their own writing, this concept would be explored and referred to again and again in minilessons, conferences, and conversations over the course of the year

Another craft minilesson focused on creating strong leads for writing. Rebecca began the session by placing two strong leads, both drawn from books that children knew on chart paper (see Figure 5–19). During the lesson students talked about what made these leading words interesting, came up with more examples, and began a chart on which they could record leads that were particularly good (see Figure 5–20). Over the next few days, students looked for interesting leads, added them to the chart, and discussed their efforts to create good leads for their own writing projects.

Enrique shared a story and listed some alternative leads (see Figure 5–20), asking students to choose which they liked best and give reasons for their choices.

Students generated alternative leads for their own projects and discussed them with a partner. The ideas also came up whenever the teacher read aloud to the group or facilitated literature study and guided reading. By the end of the week, students were aware of the importance of the leading sentence or paragraph of a text and knew that they were expected to craft their own leads carefully.

Another important type of craft minilesson is a variety of genre lessons. That content and purpose affect the form a writer chooses is important for students to learn. By the variety of the works you read aloud to your students, you demonstrate how writers work in different genres. Do not expect students to write in a genre unless they have heard many examples read aloud. Writing in different genres is related to literature study, but you will also want to provide specific instruction. Students need to study the characteristics of a genre before they are expected to write in it.

The key to teaching students to write in different genres is to:

■ Examine the characteristics of the genre.
■ Read aloud examples to students and help them generate charts that list the characteristics.
■ Through discussion, help them understand the different aspects of genre.
■ Ask them to examine their writer's notebook for ideas that might fit the genre you are studying. They should be able to find seeds of ideas, but if they can't, help them do some quick-writes on different topics.
■ Ask students to write in particular genres.
■ Have sharing sessions so that students can help one another with their writing.
■ Refer to the chart describing the genre.

Writing in a particular genre requires an internalized sense of the related structure. It is not a matter of hearing just one example or being given just one lesson. Students need to examine a large number of examples. They need to analyze and talk about the characteristics and then discuss their own attempts to write in the genre. The same will be true of teaching different formats such as letter, picture book, and advertisement. The learning takes place over time and is reinforced in many different contexts.

Notice how Persephone uses the conventions of expository writing in the draft of her project. (See

Minilessons: The Writer's Craft

Finding Something to Write About
- ❖ Your life and experiences are important
- ❖ Telling stories about your life
- ❖ Making a topics list
- ❖ Finding your own territories for writing—subjects, genres, audiences
- ❖ Noticing your world—sketching
- ❖ Collecting ideas

Learning from Writers/Illustrators
- ❖ Noticing what writers and illustrators do
- ❖ What makes writing good?
- ❖ How authors choose topics
- ❖ Writers have territories
- ❖ How illustrations and text go together
- ❖ Role of illustrations/different mediums
- ❖ What writers say about their writing
- ❖ Why writers write
- ❖ How writers engage in the writing process
- ❖ How writers use a writer's notebook
- ❖ How writers make their work believable

Using a Writer's Notebook
- ❖ Ideas for a writer's notebook
- ❖ Getting ideas down fast
- ❖ Writing and sketching quickly
- ❖ Jotting down possible genres to develop the ideas in your notebook
- ❖ Noticing entries that can be expanded or show something about writing (from teacher's or students' notebooks)
- ❖ Expanding ideas in the writer's notebook (leaving space to add more)

Developing a Sense of Audience
- ❖ Writing for known audiences: self, friends, relatives, teacher, partners, other adults
- ❖ Writing for unknown audiences: letter to political leader or editor, newspaper or journal article
- ❖ Writing for publication to wider known audience: school newsletter

Learning about Perspective
- ❖ Stories are told from a point of view
- ❖ How to tell the point of view
- ❖ How to change point of view: older/younger; different physical vantage point; participant to observer; participating to reflecting back in time

Learning about Purpose
- ❖ Why do people write?
- ❖ Writing to express personal opinions
- ❖ Writing to express feelings
- ❖ Writing to describe beauty
- ❖ Using writing to get something done
- ❖ Using writing to persuade
- ❖ Using writing to inform or explain
- ❖ Using writing to engage readers in an experience

Crafting the Writing Project
- ❖ Drafting—getting thinking down
- ❖ Writing small: five minutes vs. one week
- ❖ Eliminating unnecessary information
- ❖ Details in story
- ❖ Sequencing ideas
- ❖ Developing a good lead
- ❖ Drafting alternative leads and choosing the best
- ❖ Developing good endings
- ❖ Showing rather than telling
- ❖ Showing the reader the setting or background information
- ❖ Choosing a good title
- ❖ Making transitions—time, setting, points of view
- ❖ Using strong nouns and verbs
- ❖ Developing a character
- ❖ Describing action and events
- ❖ Describing people
- ❖ Taking different points of view
- ❖ Putting voice into your writing
- ❖ Writing epilogues and prologues

Figure 5–17. Lessons on Craft

Minilessons: The Writer's Craft (continued)

Revising

- ❖ Revising versus copying: purposes of revision
- ❖ Using tools for revision/editing (carets, crossing out, spider legs, cut and paste)
- ❖ Using a red pen to make revisions
- ❖ Ways to add information
- ❖ Adding details to make the writing more interesting or authentic
- ❖ Recognizing when there are too many details
- ❖ Eliminating words you don't need
- ❖ Making decisions about word choice

Editing

- ❖ Using a green pen to make edits
- ❖ Editing for word choice
- ❖ Checking grammar
- ❖ Proofreading a draft
- ❖ When a draft is ready for editing
- ❖ Checking spelling

Final Draft

- ❖ Planning the layout of the final draft
- ❖ Using final draft paper
- ❖ Proofreading your final draft
- ❖ Filing your final draft

Publishing

- ❖ Using different types of paper
- ❖ Creating a title
- ❖ Creating a title page
- ❖ Creating a table of contents
- ❖ Writing "About the Author"
- ❖ Writing the dedication
- ❖ Creating a glossary
- ❖ Illustrating the borders of the final draft
- ❖ Using call outs and labels
- ❖ Publishing on the computer
- ❖ Making a frame for your writing
- ❖ Art techniques for publishing
- ❖ Binding a book
- ❖ Sending your writing to magazines, contests

Integrating Research Skills

- ❖ Taking notes
- ❖ Organizing information for writing informational pieces
- ❖ Creating sections with headings
- ❖ Using description to provide information
- ❖ How to compare and contrast
- ❖ How to describe something in time sequence
- ❖ Using primary sources
- ❖ Using secondary resources
- ❖ Conducting interviews

Writing in Different Genres

- ❖ What is a genre?
- ❖ Writing a memoir
- ❖ Writing a letter (e-mail, personal, business, "thank you," invitation)
- ❖ Writing about sports
- ❖ Writing an adventure story
- ❖ Writing realistic fiction
- ❖ Writing a mystery (fiction)
- ❖ Writing a true mystery
- ❖ Writing scary stories (fiction and nonfiction)
- ❖ Writing tall tales
- ❖ Writing humor
- ❖ Writing comics
- ❖ Writing fables
- ❖ Writing scientifically based fantasy
- ❖ Writing biography
- ❖ Writing autobiography
- ❖ Writing a science report
- ❖ Writing a social studies report
- ❖ Writing a diary or journal
- ❖ Writing about current events
- ❖ Writing a news report/article
- ❖ Writing a book review
- ❖ Writing an advertisement/commercial
- ❖ Writing a short story
- ❖ Writing interview questions/report of an interview
- ❖ Writing an essay
- ❖ Writing an opinion/editorial

Figure 5–17. Lessons on Craft (continued)

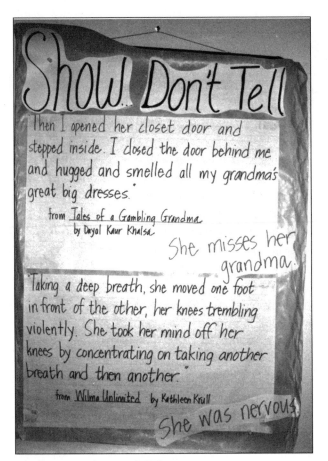

Figure 5–18.   Show Don't Tell

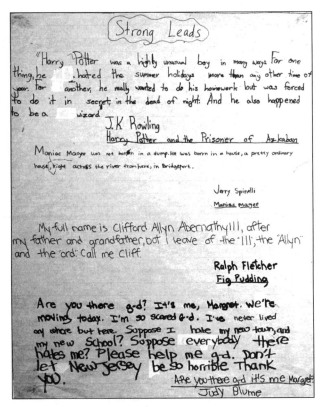

Figure 5–19a.   Strong Leads

Figure 5–21.) Her class listened to and discussed several examples of "how-to" texts, talked about the important characteristics, and wrote and illustrated their own. Through the study of how other writers construct texts effectively, writers learn to write their own.

A "Map" for Writing Across the Year

The lists in Figures 5–13, 5–15, and 5–17 represent a series of minilessons and discussions that might take place over the years from third to sixth grade. Some concepts are simpler than others, but within each are levels of complexity. Students begin to understand a concept, and then, over time, that understanding and the skill with which they use the concept deepens. If students have been richly exposed to literature in the primary grades, they will have internalized important concepts related to literary features and organization of texts, word choice, and connections between text and illustrations. If they have not had a great deal of experience, it is even more necessary to establish a rich base

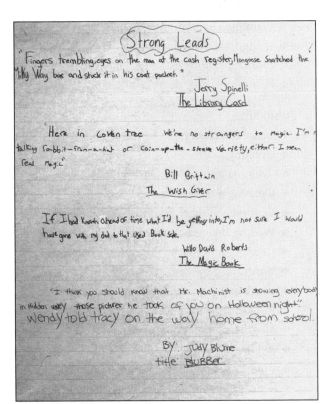

Figure 5–19b.   Strong Leads

by reading texts aloud and maintaining a good classroom library.

Even if students have heard many stories, they may not have consciously attended to literary features in a way that will allow them to apply these features to their own writing. Students are expected to master a wide range of writing competency by the time they leave elementary school. Many teachers find it helpful to develop a broad "map" for connected, focused attention to writing skills over the year (see Figure 5–22).

The teacher who prepared Figure 5–22 has chosen an overall focus on genres for this year. She has also indicated a general progression, having the students first get started with poetry reading and response in their personal poetry anthologies, and also has gotten them started writing in their writer's notebook. Then they move on to write on topics of their own choosing (this they will continue to do throughout the year). Over the course of the year, they explore memoir, letter writing, biography, the short story, the book review, the news article, and a history report. These genres are connected. For example, a memoir is a memory of an autobiographical moment in time. Wonderful picture books show students how people remember recent

---

Alternative Leads for Discussion

1. Painting is a wonderful talent.
2. Why do you think red and yellow make orange?
3. Today on a cold fall day, I have to paint a bright warm bird.
4. My babysitter, a tall curly-haired woman, reminded me that it was 4:15.
5. Painting is a wonderful talent. My babysitter, a tall blonde woman, reminded me that today was Wednesday, 4:15 already.

Figure 5–20. Alternative Leads

moments or those in the more distant past. Students then write their own memoirs and examine biographies (accounts others have written of people's lives), factual histories, and historical fiction. You will want to meet at your grade level and across grade levels to "map" or plan for writing in various genres so your students will have a range of learning opportunities.

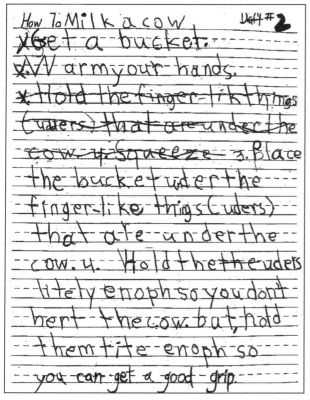

Figure 5–21. How to Milk a Cow

Map of Writing Projects Across the School Year

	Sept.	Oct.	Nov.	Dec.	Jan.	Feb.	March	April	May	June
Week 1	X	Writer's Notebook / Memoir FD	Writer's Notebook / News Article ★	Writer's Notebook / Investigation	Writer's Notebook / Memoir FD	Writer's Notebook / Biography ★	Writer's Notebook / Essay ★	Writer's Notebook / Choice FD	Writer's Notebook / Investigation	Writer's Notebook / Choice FD
Week 2	Writer's Notebook / Poetry Anthology¹	Writer's Notebook / Memoir ★	Writer's Notebook / Opinion/Editorial FD	Writer's Notebook / Investigation	Writer's Notebook / Choice ★	Writer's Notebook / Choice FD	Writer's Notebook / Choice FD	Writer's Notebook / Choice ★	Writer's Notebook / Investigation★	Writer's Notebook / Choice ★
Week 3	Writer's Notebook / Poetry Anthology¹	Writer's Notebook / Memoir FD	Writer's Notebook / Book Review ★	Writer's Notebook / Investigation★	Writer's Notebook / Biography	X	Writer's Notebook / Short Fiction	X	Writer's Notebook / Choice FD	X
Week 4	Writer's Notebook / Poetry Anthology¹	Writer's Notebook / News Article FD	Writer's Notebook / Book Review ★	X	Writer's Notebook / Biography	Writer's Notebook / Essay FD	Writer's Notebook / Short Fiction ★	Writer's Notebook / Investigation	Writer's Notebook / Choice ★	X

X = Vacation week
FD = Final Draft
★ = Publish a Project

1 = Poetry Anthology is part of getting started in Language/Word Study block. Then it moves to Poetry Workshop (see Chapter 24).

Figure 5–22. A Map for Writing Across the Year

Keeping Your Writing Rubric in Mind While Planning Minilessons

If you use rubrics (see Chapter 28) to assess students' writing progress, be sure to teach minilessons that develop the qualities of good writing. Our lists of minilessons incorporate the items on the sample rubric we provide, which parallel the elements of the writing process. In this case, it is a good idea to "teach to the test." If your district uses writing rubrics, we encourage you to keep them in your planning book or post them in the classroom. That way, you can always keep these rubrics in mind while planning your minilessons, and compare them with your students' current writing skills.

Writing and Conferring

The structure of independent writing is similar to independent reading and similar principles apply to conferences. Except for small-group work and conferences with you or their peers, students work on their writing projects in silence.

Managing Writing Workshop: Conferences and Status of the Class

You need a systematic way to manage conferences and to teach students how to monitor their own progress as well. Figure 5–23 illustrates an effective way Carol has developed to involve students in the process. (The original is about the size of a three-foot-by-six-foot bulletin board. It should be large enough so that the teacher and students can see it easily from at least halfway across the room.) Each column is headed by one of the aspects of any given writing project. The columns and topics are added as writers learn about the process. Students' names are on cards that they decorate. The back of each card has a Velcro dot so that it can be attached in any column. Stick-on notes might be an alternative. Students move their names along the chart as they progress through a writing project: exploring ideas in the writer's notebook or through research, writing a discovery draft, revising, editing, and producing a final draft or publishing a piece. At a glance, you can see what each student is working on that day.

You will be conferring with students throughout the process, but "conference" has been written in the fifth column for a reason. After editing and before preparing the final draft, students are expected to place their names on the chart requesting a conference with their teacher or place their project in a final-conference basket. This process ensures that students have engaged in some revising and editing to your satisfaction before preparing their final drafts. Some teachers design the system so that students are required to have a peer conference before the teacher conference that precedes the final draft. You may simply want to have the students put their draft in a final-conference basket. You can confer with the writer, read the writing, or write a stick-on note indicating that the writer has revised and edited adequately and can move on to the final draft. (If the project will be published, students place their final drafts in the editor's box. The teacher photocopies the project, edits it, and returns it to the writer to publish it.)

Keep your own record of conferences so you are sure you meet with each student regularly. These records also provide valuable information for planning minilessons. A simple conference record form is included in Appendix 12 or you can use a class list with five boxes and days of the week across the top. It shows at a glance whether each student has had a conference with you. Simply check the day you confer and write any comments. You might want to number the first two or three students you want to see after reviewing their writing folders. You may want to place an asterisk by comments that have implications for minilessons or place your minilesson notes at the bottom of the form. Experiment until you find the format that works for you.

Teacher Conferences

Experts advise taking the time to make conferences effective rather than just going through the motions. Hurried sessions, while a long line of students waits, may mean you are using the conference to deliver too much of your instruction (Calkins 1991). A literate classroom environment, with rich text resources, writing demonstrations, real reasons to write, and peer conferences, also supports students in their writing. You can alternate longer conferences with quick, efficient ones so that you have ample time to learn about students and their writing.

Calkins suggests that the conferences in which teachers learn the most are also those in which students talk the most: listening is the key. Conferences should be *conversational*, with the writer doing at least

Writing Projects

Explore	Discovery Draft	Revise	Edit	Final Draft Conference:	Final Draft	Publish
❖ Plant seeds ❖ Gather thinking ❖ Grow ideas ❖ Quick writes ❖ Sketches ❖ Big ideas ❖ List, notes, webs ❖ Graphic organizers ❖ Research ❖ Photographs	❖ Get down all your thinking ❖ Write quickly	Big Revision ❖ Purpose ❖ Genre ❖ Focus/Heart of piece ❖ Point of view ❖ Tone ❖ Pace Further Revision ❖ Leads ❖ Endings ❖ Word Choice ❖ Adding Detail ❖ Trainsitions ❖ Informing the reader about characters	Mechanics/Conventions— ❖ Grammar ❖ Spelling ❖ Punctuation ❖ Capitalization	❖ Best thinking ❖ Best revising ❖ Best editing Then— ❖ Request teacher conference or put in basket for teacher review before final draft	❖ Best work ❖ Best handwriting or typing	❖ Final teacher-edit ❖ Special paper/format ❖ Computer printed or very best handwriting Options ❖ artwork ❖ author's page ❖ dedication ❖ photos, etc. ❖ diagrams, charts, glossary, etc. ❖ special features
Dante	Chris	Mike	Jonda	Cory	Eduardo	Niko
Ellin	Shadé	Janitra	Kerry	Marva	Ashley	John
Jana	Mary	Lynn	Shawn		Leah	
Mikala	Joaquim	Tessiea	Michael		Elizabeth	
Edward	Dana					
	Theodore					

as much talking as the teacher. Some purposes of writing conferences are to:

■ Give the writer an audience.
■ Help students discover and focus topics for writing.
■ Identify instructional needs as a basis for planning mini-lessons.
■ Help students extend their writing strategies.
■ Listen to students talk about their writing.
■ Evaluate students' progress in writing.

Writing conferences may involve:
❖ Listening to students read the writing aloud.
❖ Helping the writer get to what really matters.
❖ Finding out what kind of help the writer wants.
❖ Talking with students about specific aspects of his/her writing.
❖ Finding the "gems" in a student's writing and showing them.
❖ Reinforcing the writer's strengths.
❖ Asking the writer what help is needed with this piece of writing.
❖ Showing the writer how to do something.
❖ Reviewing the writer's notebook or completed drafts.
❖ Setting writing goals.
❖ Sharing another piece of writing as a model..

Figure 5–24. Writing Conferences

Another key to an effective conference is to have as your goal *teaching the writer,* not refining or fixing the particular piece being discussed. Students should walk away knowing more about how to *write,* not just improve a particular project.

What you and a student do in a conference will vary, as will its length, depending on the particular student's needs (see Figure 5–24). On your conference record form, you'll want to keep a record of the conversations you have with writers so you can reflect and build on them. You will also want to make notes next to each student's name on the form as you look over their writing projects, indicating any areas you want to be sure to address in the conference. Figure 5–25 is a sample conference record form on which a teacher kept track of minilessons, the day she conferred with a student, and any comments she wanted to remember. Your previous conference notes will help you recall what the student needs to learn or discover how much progress the student has made during a given period. (See Appendix 12 for reproducible version.)

If you are new to holding conferences with students, it helps to have in mind some opening comments as well as some questions and comments that will encourage discussion (Anderson 2000). Figure 5–26 lists some suggestions, as well as some examples of student language. You will find more information on language for conferring in Chapter 8. Teach students that in order to participate in a writing conference effectively they need to:

■ Read the writing and think about the conference beforehand.
■ Be prepared with questions on parts they want to talk about.
■ Be prepared to read aloud the lead or a favorite part.
■ Be prepared to tell how the listener can be helpful.

A writing conference is a personal connection between you and your students. On the surface, they look like conversations, but as Anderson (2000) says, you have the "architecture" of the conference in mind. You want your conferences to move the student forward as a writer. You may focus briefly on any technical detail you need to, but your goal is to ensure that students learn something they can apply to their writing in the future. You will also gather important information for future minilessons.

Peer Conferences

After students have learned to participate productively in teacher conferences, you might want to teach them to confer with their peers. Be sure the structure for these conferences is understood, however. If peer conferences are disorganized, or if students use them to give each other poor advice, they are not only a waste of time but detrimental. We believe that peers act as good listeners to each other; however we have not found that many peers are able to give a "lift" to the writer in a conference the way a teacher does. If you choose to set up peer conferring, be sure to provide many supportive lessons on conferring.

Conference Record Form

Week of ___10/9___

Name	M	T	W	TH	F	Comments
Barbara	✓					working on focus — 5 minutes of skating draft #2
Chuck		✓				needs to get more thinking down, brainstormed to expand in writer's notebook
Dina			✓			rereading and expanding family entry in notebook
Elizabeth	✓					revised lead, showed independence in looking at picture books for inspiration
Enrique			✓			needs to be group member for editing focus on whether words look right
Gabriella			✓			publishing on computer, involved with art work and author's page on memoir
George		✓				writing a persuasive letter, focus on strong verbs, paragraphs
John				✓		word choice change look good, noticing use of words in other texts
Kayla	✓					wandering around on topic, need to make focus decision
Leo			✓			absent two days, switched from narrative to poem on star
Mikala		✓				selected portion of discovery draft, clear focus on the five minutes before the hurricane
Nick				* ✓		get to him first to get started, end of session check in — 3 paragraphs
Shayla	✓					wonderful use of language finally a meaningful topic
Steven S.					✓	voice strong — letter?
Steven T.		✓				listen to read — notice how language sounds — corrected in but on own
Susan					✓	ready to publish "Stories"
Ursula					✓	back to notebook to expand

Minilessons:
review getting small
notebook — artifacts
using spider legs
getting sentence variety

Figure 5–25. Conference Record Form

Group Share and Evaluation

It's important for students to come together and share what they have written. A wall chart like the one in Figure 5–23 will help you structure group sharing, because it shows so clearly where students are in their writing projects. Of course, not every student can share every day. You may invite particular students to share on the spot or set up a daily schedule. Sharing in pairs or trios guarantees that everyone gets feedback.

Getting Started with a Writing Workshop

Figure 5–27 sets forth some detailed suggestions for getting a writing workshop started. The first weeks of school are critical: it is then that your students must develop productive habits as writers. Over the first weeks, the plan in Figure 5–27 provides for:

- Building a rich resource of texts that students know and share.
- Establishing the schedule and routines for writing workshop.
- Getting students started in their writer's notebooks, a resource from which they can draw for their own pieces.
- Learning possibilities for work in their writer's notebooks: revise and edit it; complete a final draft; and publish a project.
- Beginning to vary writing by discovering different genres.

You will notice that the first few weeks involve getting started in the writer's notebook. You will want to spend several weeks showing the students how to gather lots of "stuff" that will serve as seeds for writing. They will do a lot of writing, become fluent, and discover their writing lives. They will learn how other writers use notebooks.

Next you will want to take them from their notebook to one discovery draft, providing several minilessons on revision based on what you learn about them as writers by reading their drafts and planning minilessons that will be most helpful to the particular group of writers. This will include tools for revising and editing (Figure 5–27).

Then you will want to teach them how to edit their

Language to Use in Writing Conferences

Teacher

- ❖ How is your writing going?
- ❖ How can I help you with your writing?
- ❖ What are you working on next in your writing?
- ❖ What did you decide to write about?
- ❖ How did you go about choosing this topic?
- ❖ Where are you in writing your draft?
- ❖ What do you think about this piece of writing?
- ❖ What have you learned about your topic that you want to say?
- ❖ Tell me more about . . .
- ❖ Read the part that you like best.
- ❖ Read your lead/ending aloud.
- ❖ What do you want to do next in your writing?
- ❖ Do you have any questions about your writing?
- ❖ I noticed that you . . . How/why did you do that?
- ❖ What is the best part of your writing so far?
- ❖ If you wanted to add to your writing, how would you do that?
- ❖ Is there a part where more information is needed?
- ❖ I noticed you used this word [   ]. How did you go about choosing it?
- ❖ Is there any part of your writing that is confusing?
- ❖ What would you like to do with this piece of writing when it is finished?
- ❖ Have you varied the way your sentences begin?

Student

- ❖ My writing is about . . .
- ❖ I am working on . . .
- ❖ I chose this topic because . . .
- ❖ This is my [discovery draft, draft #2, #3, etc.].
- ❖ I need [kind of help] to revise my draft.
- ❖ I am concerned about . . .
- ❖ I conferred with [peer] and found out that . . .
- ❖ I want to publish this piece because . . .

Figure 5–26. Language to Use in Writing Conferences

Getting Started with Independent Writing

Minilesson	Key Concepts	Learning Outcomes	Resources
Choosing and Using a Writer's Notebook	❖ Writers use a special notebook for gathering ideas. ❖ Writers collect ideas and information from their world.	❖ Students choose a writer's notebook and may decorate the cover.	❖ Teacher's Writer's Notebook ❖ Personal blank book for students ❖ Materials for decorating cover
Learning How Other Writers Use Their Notebooks	❖ Many writers use notebooks to record thoughts about their worlds. ❖ Writers use their notebooks in many different ways.	❖ Students learn a variety of ways other writers use notebooks.	❖ Resources from the bibliography of memoirs and writer biographies in Appendix 55—Sources for Writer's Talks
Gathering Seeds in Your Writer's Notebook (Writing and Sketching) **Sample Minilessons** ❖ Draw a self-portrait. ❖ Write about your name and how you got it. ❖ Write memories related to favorite object(s). ❖ Write about a special person. ❖ List favorite foods, movies, books, quotes. ❖ Collect strong story leads. ❖ Make a map of your bedroom, house, neighborhood. ❖ Write about a special time (five minutes) in your life. ❖ Sketch an observation in your yard, neighborhood. ❖ Respond to a poem or story telling how it speaks to you. ❖ List places you love. ❖ Make a web of vacation and special moments. ❖ Glue in a photo and write about it. ❖ Glue in newspaper or magazine headline and tell why you chose it. ❖ Glue in a letter from a special person.	❖ Writers collect and explore ideas in their writer's notebooks.	❖ Students use their notebooks to collect information and ideas by writing, sketching, and glueing in artifacts. ❖ Students date each entry when they begin to write or sketch.	❖ Writer's Notebook ❖ Artifacts ❖ Colored pencils ❖ Glue stick ❖ Clipboards

Figure 5–27. Getting Started with Independent Writing   **82**

Getting Started with Independent Writing (continued)

Minilesson	Key Concepts	Learning Outcomes	Resources
Sketching in your Notebook	❖ Artists use sketching to capture their world.	❖ Students learn basic tips on sketching from an artist. ❖ Students use sketching as a tool for conveying their thinking.	❖ Writer's notebook ❖ Colored pencils
Collecting and Recording Examples of Powerful Language	❖ Writers collect powerful words, phrases, snippets of dialogue in their notebooks.	❖ Students become more aware of rich language to use in their writing.	❖ Writer's notebook ❖ Resources such as nonfiction, picture books, articles, poetry ❖ Spoken and written words to collect in their writer's notebooks ❖ Column 1 (Explore) on Writing Project Chart
Rereading Your Writer's Notebook to Choose a Seed	❖ Writers reread their notebooks to expand entries and to select topics to develop into writing projects.	❖ Students reread, add to, and select entries to explore. ❖ Students use stick-on notes to mark possible seeds. ❖ Students use their notebooks as a resource for writing discovery drafts.	❖ Writer's notebook ❖ Stick-on notes
Writing a Discovery Draft on Draft Paper	❖ Writers get down their ideas and information to explore a topic.	❖ Students write a discovery draft to explore a topic. ❖ Students learn that through a discovery draft they can explore a topic, focus and genre.	❖ Draft Paper (Appendix 8)
Procedures for Writing a Draft	❖ Writers have a process for using draft paper effectively.	❖ Students learn to date their writing, label it, skip lines, and cross out instead of erasing as they are writing on draft paper.	❖ Draft Paper (Appendix 8) ❖ Column 2 (Discovery Draft) on Writing Project Chart
Organizing Your Writing Work	❖ Writers use a writing folder to organize work in progress.	❖ Students learn how to keep drafts of their current writing project in sequential order in their writing folder.	❖ Writing folder with gussets for resource material and pockets for current draft

Figure 5–27. Getting Started with Independent Writing (continued)

Getting Started with Independent Writing (continued)

Minilesson	Key Concepts	Learning Outcomes	Resources
Revising Your Writing **Sample Minilessons:** ❖ Writing about what you know ❖ Writing small: getting a focus ❖ Choosing a genre ❖ Writing with voice ❖ Writing for different audiences ❖ Mentor texts: picture books as examples of craft ❖ Eliminating unnecessary information ❖ Showing not telling ❖ Adding sentence variety ❖ Tools for revising and editing	❖ Writers "re-see," or revise their writing by making changes. ❖ Writers use a variety of strategies to refine a draft. ❖ Writers reread a project to be sure it conveys the intended meaning.	❖ Students learn to reread and "refine" their writing through successive drafts. ❖ Students use tools for revising to make changing the text easy.	❖ Drafts of writing project ❖ Charts from revising minilessons ❖ Column 3 (Revise) on Writing Projects chart
Editing Your Writing **Sample Minilessons** ❖ Rules for punctuation e.g. at end of sentence, quotation marks ❖ Rules for capitalization e.g. in titles ❖ Grammar rules e.g. tense agreement ❖ Starting a new paragraph	❖ Writers use a variety of editing tools to improve spelling, grammar, capitalization and punctuation. ❖ Writers sometimes use a list to remind them about the kinds of conventions to check before completing a project.	❖ Students use a variety of editing tools to show all they know as writers. ❖ Students refer to an editing list to check the conventions of their writing project.	❖ Edit list ❖ Reference Charts from minilessons ❖ Column 4 (Edit) on Writing Projects Chart
Conferring	❖ Writers have the opportunity to confer with others to get response, feedback, and suggestions while they are working on a writing project.	❖ Students learn how to engage in a conference to get feedback on their writing.	❖ Clipboard ❖ Teacher Conference ❖ Conference Record Form (Appendix 12) ❖ Column 5 (Final Draft Conference) on Writing Projects Chart
Checking the Spelling of High-Frequency Words	❖ Writers use lists, dictionaries, and other reference tools to check spelling.	❖ Students use resources to correct their spelling.	❖ Writing Folder Insert: Word List

Figure 5–27. Getting Started with Independent Writing (continued)

Getting Started with Independent Writing (continued)

Minilesson	Key Concepts	Learning Outcomes	Resources
Writing a Final Draft	❖ Writers sometimes use special paper for a final draft. ❖ Writers show all that they know about writing in their final draft.	❖ Students use final draft paper to create a complete, legible draft. ❖ Students place their writing projects in the editor's basket for a final edit prior to publication.	❖ Final Draft paper
Publishing A Writing Project **Publishing minilessons:** Options: ❖ Dedication page ❖ About the author ❖ Table of contents ❖ Types of illustrations ❖ Captions ❖ Diagrams, charts ❖ Glossary, index	❖ Writers publish some projects ❖ Writers publish projects or make them "public" so others can enjoy and learn from their work. ❖ Editors make final corrections on a writer's project.	❖ Students publish writing projects at regular intervals. ❖ Students share the published writing projects with the "public" by displaying, reading in the author's chair, distributing copies, placing on a bulletin board, submitting to a publication, entering a contest, etc.	❖ Editor's Basket ❖ Computer paper, special pens, pencils, and art materials ❖ Column 7 (Publish) on Writing Projects Chart
Keeping a Record of Writing Projects	❖ Writers sometimes keep records of their writing. ❖ Records of writing help writers evaluate the frequency and breadth of their work.	❖ Students keep records of drafts of completed writing projects. ❖ Students evaluate their writing for productivity and variety.	❖ Writing Folder Insert: Record of Writing
Recording What I Learned	❖ Writers sometimes analyze and summarize their new insights about writing.	❖ Students reflect on completed writing projects to discover what they learned about being a writer.	❖ Writing Folder Insert: What I Learned About Being a Writer
Using the Writing Projects Chart	❖ Writers understand that work on a project goes through many stages that are recursive in nature. ❖ Writers learn that they can indicate what aspect of a project they are focused on.	❖ Students learn that each component is not discrete but overlaps with other steps and may be revisited until completion. ❖ Students have an overview of the writing process from exploration in a writer's notebook through published project. ❖ Students learn how to place their names on the chart to indicate what they are writing on or to request a final draft conference.	❖ Complete Writing Projects Chart ❖ Stick-on names

Figure 5–27. Getting Started with Independent Writing (continued)

Getting Started with Independent Writing (continued)			
Minilesson	**Key Concepts**	**Learning Outcomes**	**Resources**
Storing Projects in the Hanging File	❖ Writers have a system for organizing their work so they can obtain it when needed or review what is accomplished.	❖ Students organize their final drafts and published writing projects in their hanging folders. ❖ Students arrange and staple the final draft on top followed by numbered drafts and place it in the hanging file.	❖ Students' hanging folders ❖ Crates or file cabinet ❖ Stapler
Types of Writing	❖ Writers learn more about writing by trying different genres. ❖ Writers can keep a record of the types of writing they have done.	❖ Students learn how to keep a record of the different types of writing projects they have completed. ❖ Students learn to evaluate the breadth of their writing.	❖ Writing Folder Insert: Types of Writing (Appendix 7)

Figure 5–27. Getting Started with Independent Writing (continued)

project and request a final draft conference by placing their names in the correct column. Following the final draft conference, the writer copies or types the project as a "final draft."

On the first cycle you will want to have every writer publish a project. Teach some simple ways to publish, and edit the projects students place in the editor's basket. It's a good idea to photocopy the writing first and make your marks on the photocopy. The student then publishes the project in some form. A good idea is to create one bulletin board or wall space with some colored paper, bordered by a curly ribbon. Invite students to post their first published project and have a celebration.

We suggest taking the whole group of writers from notebook to published project at the start, adding each column of the Writing Projects Chart (Figure 5–23) when it has been taught and understood. Otherwise the full chart is overwhelming. Following the publication of one writing project by each student, they can move back to the beginning, all working at different aspects of the process at their own pace.

The chart we provide for getting started will most likely encompass about the first six to eight weeks of

the workshop. We believe this foundation will prove important to later productivity and independence.

Becoming a writer is not accomplished within a given time nor at a particular stage in life. Students' knowledge about the many kinds of literature builds slowly over time but accelerates with the opportunity to experience, enjoy, and produce pieces for themselves.

Conclusion

Writing workshop follows a predictable schedule and routine that supports developing writers. Students are able to anticipate when they will write and the sorts of support available to them through conferences, minilessons, and guided writing. In a very real sense, they are able to think about their writing even when they are not directly participating in writing workshop. This continual thinking about writing may be the hallmark of the writer's life. Independent writing, guided writing, and investigations all work together to provide various levels of support and to introduce student writers to the various aspects of writing and the many ways in which writing can inspire and inform their lives.

The essential characteristics of the writing workshop are identical to those we outlined for reading workshop:

- It is a community of learners who support one another throughout the writing process. Students are part of a group of peers who see themselves as writers because they are treated as serious writers by others.
- It involves genuine talk, reading, and writing. Students are reading and writing for real purposes; collaboration and honest, considerate feedback are highly valued.
- It recognizes individual strengths and needs; effort and improvement are noted.
- There is both individual and group responsibility; students help one another improve their writing.
- Expectations for achievement are high.

As they examine their writing, students have the pleasure of reflecting on their developing skills as writers and researchers and realizing the extent of their learning.

Suggestions for Professional Development

1. Map your curriculum for the year.
   a. Bring the following documents to a meeting with colleagues across grade levels:

- Any records you have of students' writing—samples, checklists, anecdotal notes, notes on conferences.
- The school district curriculum outlining expectations for writing competency or national standards (*Performance Standards:* Volume 1, *Elementary School,* National Center on Education and the Economy and the University of Pittsburgh. 1999).
- "Practice texts" for the state proficiency exam or any important test.

   b. Discuss the expectations of students regarding writing. Think about:
- Conventions.
- Craft.
- Genres.

   c. Have teachers in each grade level map the kinds of minilessons and genres that will be essential. Then share the maps and revise them.
   d. By consensus, create a cross-grade-level map for grades three through six.
2. Have follow-up meetings each month to share and discuss the minilessons and assignments that you have presented. Talk about:
- What your students have learned.
- How samples of your students' writing show what they have learned.
- What they need to know next (or still need to know about the particular aspect of writing or the genre you have explored).
3. Give one another suggestions and advice. Revise the cross-grade-level plan as needed.

## CHAPTER SIX

MAKING IT WORK:
ORGANIZING AND MANAGING TIME, SPACE, AND RESOURCES

We put our trust in creating calm, joyful settings with simple, clear routines.

— SHELLEY HARWAYNE

Good management is part of effective teaching and a vital part of students' learning. Just as you establish a curriculum for literacy, you teach students how to manage their time and behavior in the classroom. They learn such "skills for living" as planning, managing time, evaluating, and problem solving. Self-management, so essential for a quality life, is not inborn or intuitive. Self-management is learned and can be taught.

Building a Community in the Classroom

One aspect of self-management is the ability to cooperate. In the classroom, you have the opportunity to teach your students how to work and collaborate with others. Students learn best if they are part of a community in which all members take responsibility for their own learning and also for one another's learning. Creating that learning community takes time and organization, but the payoff is great. Students not only develop their reading and writing competency, they also develop their ability to function as part of a group, to negotiate with others for space and materials, to collaborate in accomplishing tasks, to evaluate their own learning and their contributions to the learning of others, and to see different perspectives. A learning community is based on a number of principles:

■ All members are trusted with rights and responsibilities.

■ All members take responsibility for their own learning and for helping others learn.

■ All members take responsibility for managing time and activity productively.

■ All members learn self-management as part of the curriculum delivered by the teacher.

■ All members understand that keeping materials in order helps everyone learn.

The curriculum for creating a learning community is delivered in the way the classroom is organized, in the consistent expectations for individual, small-group, and whole-class operations, and in the climate you and the students establish and maintain. It boils down to two big ideas:

1. To the extent the classroom is a place in which students encounter respect and inclusion, they will value others.
2. To the extent the classroom is an organized and orderly place, students will value organization and order.

Almost all of us, both at home and at work, long to be organized; fortunately, there are thousands of ways to get organized. The best classroom management systems, however, are closely related to the learning that you want to achieve. If the system is built *with* your students around the way they need to work together, it will be sustainable.

Your classroom is a place in which twenty-five-plus students are living together for about six hours a day for an entire school year. The effectiveness of your instruction depends on developing, in your classroom, a community of readers, writers, and learners. In this chapter we address two aspects of the environment for learning:

1. Physical environment—how the space and materials are organized.
2. Social environment—how the people behave in the environment.

Both the physical and the social environment are critical concepts in helping you manage learning effectively, and the two are inextricably interrelated. You can prepare most of the physical environment before the students enter, but their cooperation is important in maintaining it. You can teach students important social skills that will support their cooperation, but the convenience, accessibility, and order of the environment must be in place; students should not have to compete for supplies or space.

Physical Environment

Your classroom should convey a warm, welcoming ambiance in which students feel they belong. Creating an inviting classroom means reflecting comfort and productivity throughout the daily routine. Your physical environment should be comfortable for all students, who will vary in both height and size. It should also accommodate both large- and small-group activity as well as the individual's need for quiet, solitary activity. You'll want to address both *ownership* and *independence*, two key concepts that permeate your classroom life:

■ You can set up the classroom before students arrive, but as the year progresses, you will find that some reorganization and problem-solving are necessary. Involve students regularly in considering the organization of space and materials in the classroom, so that they fully understand the importance of the environment in which they work.

■ Space and materials must be organized for optimal student independence. Students must know where to work for various purposes and where to find and put away the materials they need.

Books

One of the challenges in establishing a balanced literacy program is assembling and maintaining an adequate and well-organized supply of books. The classroom collection includes all the books that are housed there—either permanently or temporarily. The collection is carefully structured and its importance must not be minimized, since for most students it represents their primary literacy resource for the year.

Assembling a Varied Collection

The classroom collection of texts will include:

1. Books for literature study—either read by the teacher or read by students.
2. Poetry anthologies of various types—theme, poet, etc. (See Appendix 57.)
3. Picture books that offer students the opportunity to experience a piece of work with aesthetic unity—text, illustrations, layout. (See Appendix 56.)
4. Books for reference and information, such as dictionaries, atlases, and thesauruses.
5. Books categorized by topic, author, and genre.
6. Books that are part of a series, such as *Dear America,* or the *Little House* books.
7. Books introduced in book talks that are available for independent reading.
8. Books recommended by the students in the class.
9. Books that have received awards—Caldecott, Newbery, Coretta Scott King, and others.
10. Leveled books for guided reading.
11. Collections of short stories.
12. Journals, magazines, newspapers.

A richly varied classroom collection will enable your students not only to expand their reading abilities but also to expand their world. You will need a large collection of paperback books. In addition, we recommend a substantial number of beautifully illustrated picture books. (See Selected Picture Books—Fiction and Nonfiction in Appendix 56). These books not only explore complex topics in interesting ways, they attract students and engage their attention. They also trigger an aesthetic response to their coherent integration of illustration, text, and layout. The classroom library also includes a sufficient number of journals and magazines,

Figure 6–1. Student-Published Biographies

across the tops of shelves so that readers are attracted by the cover illustrations. Plate stands are a nifty device for holding books upright.

You can make your classroom especially appealing by using attractive colored baskets or book boxes, all the same size, to hold your books. In the accompanying photographs, you can see the variety in the collection as well as the way the teacher has organized and labeled books and other materials. These labels not only serve an organizational function, they *teach* students how to think about books:

such as *Time for Kids, Ranger Rick, Muse, Cricket, Cicada,* and *Images.* (See Appendix 58 for an extensive list of magazine resources). You might also consider a spot for the daily newspaper and current magazines.

Displaying Books

You'll want to arrange your classroom books to invite readers. Consider displaying picture books face front

1. The author—to think about characteristics of a writer's/poet's style, choice of topic, and background.
2. The topic—to explore a variety of informational sources or fictional/poetic treatments of a subject.
3. The genre—to connect examples of a particular type of text, noting their similarities and variations.

Figure 6–2. Classroom Collection

4. The theme—to connect books and poetry by big ideas relative to the human condition.

5. A series—to notice that a group of books have the same characters, sometimes telling about their lives over long periods of time.

6. Special features—to help students think critically about why some books deserve special attention, such as awards, and learn to use recommendations for their selections.

The collection of books expands students' literary experiences as well as supports research and inquiry.

Leveled Books

You will also have a substantial collection of leveled books for students to use in guided reading. (See Chapter 23.)

You might consider a few baskets of single copies of leveled books in your library for students who need some guidance in selecting. Leveled books have been organized and categorized according to characteristics that make them easier or harder to read. The continuum, or gradient, of difficulty is designated by the letters of the alphabet (A–Z). These rankings are only approximate, because each student responds slightly differently to any book.

Leveled books are useful for guided reading with temporary homogeneous groups (see Chapter 14 and the leveled book list in Appendix 61). You can store leveled texts in shoeboxes, magazine boxes, baskets, pots, or tubs on a bookshelf, indicating levels by letter or a designated color. Teach students how to select books they can read independently and use the levels as a rough guide when they need help.

We suggest that you keep your leveled texts for guided reading in an area to which only you have access. For the guided reading collection, you will need multiple copies of leveled texts. You will also want a good collection of "short reads," which would include articles and short stories. There are many good collections of short stories in the leveled book list in Appendix 61. If you find good articles that are useful in illustrating aspects of texts to students, you may want to save them in folders in a file crate; that way, you can use them year after year. As long as they do not become out of date, they can generate interest in successive groups of students.

Your guided reading books may be stored in a school book-room that you create in cooperation with col-

leagues. The school book-room houses multiple copies of leveled texts across grade levels for teachers to use as they need them. It works best when you and your colleagues have established a procedure for checking out and returning the collections. You might visit the book room with a book basket and select multiple copies to use with your groups for the next two (or three or four) weeks. In this way, the guided reading collection moves into a particular classroom and then moves out again. (Single-copy books that students may read independently and at home, however, remain in the classroom library permanently; students read them at their discretion and recommend them to one another.)

Working Areas

As a classroom teacher you have limited space within which to organize the materials and activities essential for instruction. Your organization of space and materials contributes to the ambiance of the classroom. Think about how order and beauty contribute to a feeling of calm and confidence in any environment. This principle is equally true of your classroom. Figure 6–3 shows how space has been organized in one classroom.

You will also need to consider the movement patterns in the classroom. Inefficiency and conflict arise when students have to wait in line and compete with each other to get at supplies or to enter an area. Students need to be able to move from one area to another without crowding. In the plan illustrated here, the teacher knows that students will need to move to the meeting area as a group. Notice that there are several ways to get there. Supply areas are also situated so that several students can use them at the same time.

ENTRANCE/EXIT

A cleverly designed classroom entrance helps students begin and end the day efficiently. Near the entrance, place a table with trays or boxes in which students can leave homework and other materials and you, in turn, can leave notices for them to pick up and take home. They can sign in or out and check off records such as lunch count (see Erica's Day). Using the entrance in this way will save a great deal of time and ensure that routines work more efficiently. Of course, the procedures you implement must suit your particular situation.

The entrance-area feature works most smoothly when students enter the classroom at staggered inter-

Figure 6–3. The Classroom

vals, perhaps during the fifteen-minute period when buses arrive. If your students enter all at once in a line, you will not want them to wait while every student turns in homework or signs in on the lunch count sheet. Instead, instruct them to hang up coats first and/or sit down with book boxes, turning in homework and signing in during the first five or ten minutes of the day. If you have a large class, you can increase the efficiency of such systems by having separate trays and sign in sheets, coded by color, for groups of five students.

COMMUNITY MEETING AREA

Establish a meeting place where you can work comfortably with the entire class. The meeting area might be an open space where students can sit in a circle on cushions or a carpet or sit in a circle of chairs. It might also be an area in which chairs can be placed in tiers. Typically, there is a low seat for you so that you can be part of the meeting and work with students on their level rather than stand above them. The meeting area also has one or two easels and/or a white board and dry erase markers so that you can make charts or visually illustrate principles

during minilessons. Since you will be presenting book talks in the meeting area, you will want to be able to display books on a chalk tray or other suitable place.

Whatever the meeting arrangement you provide, explicitly teach students how to organize and use it so that when you announce a group meeting, they know exactly what to do.

SMALL-GROUP MEETING AREAS

Create one or two areas where you can meet with small groups of four to eight students for literature study, guided reading, guided writing, or any other purpose. You may prefer a centrally located table so that you can scan the room at the same time you are working with a group. It's best to have at least two small-group areas. That way, you can convene one group and then convene another a bit later while the first one is still working. A corner of the room might be a good location for the second area.

CONFERRING AREAS

In addition, examine your room for potential conference areas where you can work with individuals and students can work with one another. Reading and writing workshop are times when students work silently and individually. You move around the room, speaking very softly with individual students at their own desks, but you may also want a space designated for partner or small group conferring or book clubs. This space may be anywhere in the room as long as it does not disturb others. Many teachers designate conference areas (such as two corners of the room) so that students can also work cooperatively with one another. Students understand that if they need to talk with another student during silent working times, they go to the conference area and speak in a soft voice as they work together.

A LIBRARY

Provide a library area that houses the bulk of the classroom collection of books (although there should be books in all parts of the room). Display the books attractively, and have several comfortable chairs and cushions where students can read. Reading lamps and plants add to the atmosphere. Make sure books are labeled and organized for easy and informed access.

Figure 6-4 shows a system Rebecca and her students developed for taking turns reading on the couch

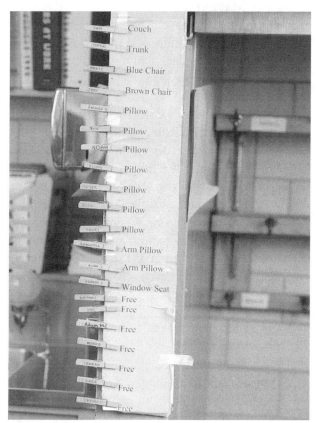

Figure 6–4. Turn-Taking System

and cushions. They clip clothespins with students' names on the four cushions and two couch seats, rotating them daily; that way every student enjoys a comfortable, relaxed read at least once a week.

WRITING SUPPLY AREA

Although students will do most of their writing in their individual space, they will need an area where writing materials are organized and easily accessible. Some essential supplies are:

- Various sizes and kinds of writing paper.
- White correction tape.
- Pens, pencils, colored pencils, markers.
- Staplers and staple removers.
- Correction fluid.
- Dictionaries and thesauruses.
- Letter stamps (for titles).
- Scissors.
- Glue and glue sticks.
- Tape.
- Rulers.

Students should be able to find writing supplies in clearly labeled containers. Some classrooms provide small keyboards (such as AlphaSmart) for students to use at their desks; these also are stored in the writing area.

Near the writing area, you will want to have a storage place for art supplies. For example, students often use watercolors, colored pencils, markers of various kinds, and different kinds of paper as part of their published written work and their poetry work.

TECHNOLOGY

Most classrooms today have computers for students' use. Locate computers in an area where students can work at them individually or with partners. Create an established routine for computer use. Teachers sometimes use a rotation schedule that is coordinated with students' projects or assigned work. You can also use a sign-up system. The kinds of software or special programs that you have selected will, of course, affect the way computers are used in your classroom.

Increasingly, commercial compact disks provide information for students in the content areas; for example, you can find encyclopedias of plants and animals, maps, historical documents, and photographs, as well as software programs for analyzing statistics and

Figure 6–5. Individual Storage Boxes

creating graphs and charts. Store all of this software in the technology area but label it clearly so that students can easily locate what they need when they are doing research in the content areas.

SOCIAL STUDIES AREA

You will need a space to display maps, photographs, or charts of various kinds. Based on your social studies curriculum, you may want to collect artifacts—for example, a globe, models, documents, pieces of art or clothing—and books. Relevant software will be housed in the computer area. These materials can be neatly stored in plastic boxes until needed. These kinds of materials are perfect for those hard-to-access storage spaces, leaving accessible space for materials that students need constantly.

MATHEMATICS AND SCIENCE AREA

In your science area, gather magnifying glasses, thermometers, microscopes, measuring devices, and other equipment useful for students to perform their own investigations in your science area. For mathematics, a wide range of "hands-on" materials, such as cubes and blocks, Dienes blocks, Unifix cubes, Cuisenaire rods, tangrams, and graphic drawing tools, are must-haves.

As in social studies, you will have artifacts that you may want to display at certain times (for example, bones, rocks). You'll need a backdrop for display as well as a table top for display and/or work. If your school has a central storage area, you can store artifacts

out of the way until they are needed. Or, simply borrow artifacts, invite your students to bring items from home to share, display temporarily, and then return.

WORD STUDY AREA

In the word study area, store the students' word study notebooks, letter cluster and word tiles, magnetic letters, electronic spellers, thesauruses, and dictionaries. Gather enough reference materials to use in both the word study and writing areas. (Technology assistance related to word study should be clearly labeled and stored in the technology area.) Create a wall display for the buddy study schedule and for the interactive wall charts that you and your students use or create during minilessons.

POETRY AREA

Here you'll want to create an attractive display of students' poetry anthologies (see Chapter 25) as well as an excellent collection of published poetry books and anthologies. You may also enjoy displaying student art related to poetry projects as well as charts you and your students created in poetry workshop.

INDIVIDUAL WORK AND STORAGE SPACE FOR LITERACY MATERIALS

Students will need to have a "home" space where they can sit and work. This individual space may be a desk or assigned seat at a table. If your students have individual desks with storage space, they can keep their personal supplies and textbooks in their desks. If not, you'll want to create an individual storage system. Cardboard or plastic magazine files stored on a shelf serve this purpose well because materials are upright and in clear view through the cut side. They are also sturdy and can be reused from year to year. Type students' names on address labels and label each file box; at the start of a new school year, you can easily replace the labels for your new class. As an alternative, collect cereal boxes of the same size and cut them in the same shape as magazine files. The students have individual storage boxes (see Figure 6–5) that contain:

- Their reader's notebooks.
- Their writing folders.
- Their writer's notebooks.
- The books they are reading.

Some reasons for providing individual storage space in a convenient public area are:

■ The materials are visible and accessible.

■ They are easier to keep in order and are not so easy to misplace or lose.

■ You can conveniently examine students' work because it is in one place and in order.

■ Students' work does not get crumpled.

■ The system shows high value for students' work.

As with every other system in the orderly classroom, keeping materials in these individual boxes saves time and also *teaches* students how to care for and keep up with their work-in-progress. You will be very grateful that you no longer have to urge students to go through messy desks looking for things.

General Suggestions for Storage

The more you can organize materials and make them accessible to students, the easier your classroom management will be. (In a similar vein, have you seen the pegboard that has the shapes of tools outlined on it? There's no doubt what belongs where!) For your classroom:

■ Place each type of material in a separate container that is appropriate in size and shape.

■ Label every container, as well as each space in which containers are stored.

■ Don't depend on students to arrange materials on shelves. Have a designated and labeled space for everything.

■ Eliminate materials that are not essential. An easy test is whether you have used the materials within the last year. If you haven't, get rid of them! Accumulating materials year after year clutters your classroom and interferes with smart management.

Displays and References

It is not necessary or even advisable to display commercially produced materials. Avoid large calendars, commercial posters with trite messages or slogans that your students do not "own," anything that serves primarily as decoration. Save your precious display space for items that foster your students' learning or their feelings of belonging in your classroom: examples of students' art and group projects, charts created from minilessons, and the guidelines that you and your students create for their daily routines. Your classroom should reflect the learning that goes with it. For example, you might want to display:

■ Guidelines for selecting books.

■ Guidelines for literature study groups.

■ Guidelines for selecting topics for writing.

■ Suggested topics for reading response journals.

■ Lists of genres for reference.

■ Daily and weekly schedules.

■ Guides for buddy study and other work schedules.

■ Published poetry and other writing.

And don't forget to look for extra display space, such as the backs of bookcases, the sides of file cabinets, under the windows and chalkboards, and both sides of flip charts.

Social Environment

The atmosphere or "ambiance" of the classroom is all important. We stress in this book that social interaction is critical for students' learning, but that does not mean that the classroom is noisy or disorderly—quite the opposite. Create a vision for yourself of a productive work environment in which:

■ Students read and write silently.

■ Students know where materials are and know how to use them and put them away.

■ Conversations in small-group work and individual conferences are conducted in very soft voices or whispers.

■ Community meetings are conducted in an orderly way: each student can hear and see others, and there are routines for taking turns.

■ Students know the schedule for group and individual work and follow it in a timely way.

■ All members of the class listen to one another in a respectful way.

A quiet, peaceful environment is essential for students to do their best work. Accordingly, students must learn to be sensitive to their own voice levels. Ideally, with their teacher's help, students become aware of their voice levels in kindergarten and revisit the topic in each grade thereafter. Work with your grade-level colleagues to develop a simple but important "curriculum" for teaching students how to talk in a small room that houses between twenty and thirty students all working and often talking. Students new to your school may enter your classroom not knowing how to modulate their voices. They either don't talk at all or talk loudly. One voice is not a problem, but twenty-five voices can create a terrible distraction that interferes with students' concentration and raises the stress level in the room. Teach students how to be conscious of their own voice levels; they should view it as one of their responsibilities as members of your classroom community.

As part of their discussion about how they are going to work together, Carol and her students address voice levels. They have developed the chart in Figure 6–6 to illustrate how their voices help create a harmonious learning atmosphere in the classroom and help them remember appropriate voice levels at various times during the day.

Cooperation

Good classrooms are based on the principle of cooperation. The atmosphere you want to create is one of people working together with common purposes. The more your classroom functions as a harmonious community, the easier it will be to manage. Typically, cooperation is a skill that must be learned. Just consider the underlying concepts. People who work cooperatively together:

■ Listen to one another.
■ Share the components of tasks (tasks are analyzed and subtasks conceived and allocated).
■ Consider one another's perspectives (their conversation elicits different points of view).
■ Invest in mutual ventures (they share goals and purposes).
■ Share in accomplishments (they recognize that a variety of contributions are essential).

As we consider the great accomplishments of our society, we realize that they are the result not of competition but of cooperation. Teaching cooperation is one of our most important instructional goals.

Mutual Respect

In a good classroom, everyone counts and everyone deserves respect. The curriculum is not focused on competition and comparison but on cooperation. If you teach your students to show appreciation for their classmates' contributions, they in turn will realize that their own contributions are valued. The entire curriculum should be organized around student success. The good teacher does not expect students to struggle through books that are too hard for them but she does provide challenge. The comprehension of difficult concepts and texts is supported by teacher-student and student-student talk and cooperative inquiry. There is a balance between student choice and teacher guidance, so that they are not left to flounder on their own.

Inclusion

Inclusion means that every member of the class has a place and a role. Everyone belongs. No one struggles for attention or for a voice. Every student activity is governed by the principle that *all of us are responsible for seeing that everyone gets a turn*. In literature study, for example, teach your students to evaluate their discussions both for quality and fair turn taking by asking, "Has everyone had something to say?" Or, "Alice, you haven't talked yet. Would you like to add something?" These conversational routines not only help your classroom work go more smoothly, they add immeasurably to students' interpersonal skills.

Inclusion extends to every aspect of classroom life,

THE VOLUME OF YOUR VOICE SHOULD BE...									
1	2	3	4	5	6	7	8	9	10
Independent work time Hallways		Conference	Snacktime Partner work Group work		Book clubs Whole class discussion				Outside recess
SILENT		SOFT WHISPERS	QUIET VOICE		REGULAR VOICE				LOUD VOICE

Figure 6–6. The Volume of Your Voice Should Be

and it refers to *all* students, including those who are different in any way. For many students, school is one of the few places in which they can learn to include others and appreciate differences, ignoring racial, economic, religious, or cultural categories. Difference is valued, not viewed as an obstacle. Students who encounter people different from themselves are fortunate because they develop a wider range of communication skills and, as a result, heightened social awareness, sensitivity and even compassion for all people. Interacting around the texts they read and write enables students to see and know one another in new and varied ways and appreciate the logic and insights of multiple perspectives.

Managing Time

The first challenge in establishing the language/literacy framework is to find three blocks of time for language/word study, reading, and writing. Review the way your school day is structured, identify chunks that provide forty-five minutes to one hour of uninterrupted time, and prepare a workable schedule. One hour each works best for reading and writing workshop; somewhere between thirty and sixty minutes is feasible for language and word study (if you can allocate an hour here as well, the learning will be greater). Remember that when students are writing and reading, you can integrate science and social studies content.

 Pacing and efficiency are related to effective instruction. General principles for using time include:

- Establish a productive and easy-to-accomplish task that students perform every morning as they enter the classroom.
- Find ways to take care of routine business efficiently.
- Vary the schedule across the week.
- Post the schedule each morning and briefly review it with students.
- Establish routines that will save time—for example, using notebooks for reading workshop, writers' notebooks and folders for writing workshop, and designated boxes to collect assignments.

Community Meeting
The community meeting, as part of the language/word study block, is your chance to set the scene for the day, teach routines, and establish the rationales for them.

You can help students learn how to help one another and to value the richness of language, culture, and ethnicity that may exist within the group. An orderly, cooperative classroom does not happen overnight. It is a product of demonstration, explicit teaching, and practice. While the community meeting is valuable, it should not be long and drawn out; nor should it be a "lecture." As is true for other aspects of instruction, the community meeting should be brisk and focused. Reserve the community meeting to present minilessons on pertinent topics, discuss topics of shared interest, review classroom procedures, and evaluate work.

Creating a Weekly Schedule
Figure 6–7 is a sample daily schedule used successfully by some intermediate teachers. Students come into the classroom and immediately begin reading independently or writing in their writer's notebooks. One teacher we know has the daily newspaper delivered through a "newspapers for schools" program. Her students begin each day by reading from the newspaper. Another option is to use a weekly newspaper, or a journal or magazine. The important thing is to have a consistent activity for students as they arrive. Often, students do not enter the classroom all at once; bus schedules always vary slightly, and we need to use those first moments of the day productively.

 By 8:30 the official day begins. All students are present and have segued into the reading workshop. The block begins with the teacher giving a few book talks to help students add to their "reading interests" list and providing a minilesson. Students then read books of their own choosing and/or write in their reader's notebooks. During this period, the teacher works with individuals in conferring or small groups of children in guided reading or literature study. The classroom is quiet; students are reading silently and the teacher is talking quietly with individuals or small groups. Finally the group gathers for sharing.

 Writing workshop begins at 9:30, with a minilesson on some aspect of writing. Students make entries in their writer's notebooks and/or continue working on their projects. The teacher confers with individuals and/or brings together four or five students for some focused work in a guided writing group. At the end of the writing workshop period students convene to share their writing and evaluate their work time.

Sample Daily Schedule 1: 8:15 – 2:45					
Time	Monday	Tuesday	Wednesday	Thursday	Friday
Arrival Time 8:15-8:30	Independent Reading/ Writer's Notebook	Independent Reading/ Writer's Notebook	Independent Reading/ Writer's Notebook	Independent Reading/ Writer's Notebook	Independent Reading/ Writer's Notebook
8:30-9:30	Reading Workshop*	Reading Workshop*	Poetry Workshop	Reading Workshop*	Reading Workshop
9:30-10:30	Writing Workshop*	Writing Workshop*		Writing Workshop*	Writing Workshop
10:30-11:15	Special	Special	Special	Special	Special
11:15-11:45	Language/ Word Study	Language/ Word Study	Language/ Word Study	Language/ Word Study	Language/ Word Study
11:45-12:30	Lunch/Recess	Lunch/Recess	Lunch/Recess	Lunch/Recess	Lunch/Recess
12:30-1:25	Math	Math	Math	Math	Math
1:25-2:05	Science	Science Workshop	Science	Social Studies Workshop	Science
2:05-2:45	Social Studies		Social Studies		Social Studies

*Reading and writing workshop often include social studies and science reading and writing.

Figure 6–7. Sample Daily Schedule 1

In this schedule, on Wednesdays the reading and writing workshops are merged into a poetry workshop. In this two-hour period you would read poetry to your students and invite them to read poetry, listen to poems, respond to poems through talk, art and writing, select poems, write their own poems, and perform selected pieces (see Chapter 25).

Notice that special instruction occurs in a regular time period, which allows each day to be highly predictable. To accomplish this regularity, you will need to work with colleagues across the grade levels, but it's possible to design a schedule that includes art, music, library, and physical education while still accommodating the three learning-blocks approach.

The period before lunch, 11:15–11:45, is set aside for language and word study. As described in Chapter 3, a variety of shared language and literacy tasks take place during this time. It may include time for a minilesson and individual or partner work with words. In this

classroom, students use buddy study, which involves a different word study activity each day for five days (see Chapter 23). In a five day cycle the students:

- Select words, write them on cards, and build them with magnetic letters.
- Use the "look, say, cover, write, check" procedure to study words.
- Have a "buddy check" and practice words.
- Make connections between words, considering how they look, sound, and what they mean.
- Take a weekly test that is graded by the teacher.

Other scheduled activities also differ by day. On Monday, Wednesday, and Friday, students share current events. On Tuesday and Thursday, students sign up to read poems to the group. Each day also features an interactive edit or interactive vocabulary activity.

After lunch is devoted to math, from 12:30 to 1:25,

Sample Daily Schedule 2: 8:30 – 2:45					
Time	**Monday**	**Tuesday**	**Wednesday**	**Thursday**	**Friday**
8:30–9:25	Reading Workshop*	Reading Workshop*	Reading Workshop*/ Poetry Workshop***	Reading Workshop*	Reading Workshop*
9:25–10:00	Language/ Word Study	Language/ Word Study	Language/ Word Study	Language/ Word Study	Language/ Word Study
10:00–11:00	Writing Workshop*	Writing Workshop*	Writing Workshop*/ Poetry Workshop***	Writing Workshop*	Writing Workshop*
11:00–12:00	Math	Math	Math	Math	Math
12:00–12:45	Lunch/Recess	Lunch/Recess	Lunch/Recess	Lunch/Recess	Lunch/Recess
12:45–1:30	Special	Special	Special	Special	Special
1:30–2:45**	Science/Social Studies Workshop*	Science/Social Studies Workshop*	Science/Social Studies Workshop*	Science/Social Studies Workshop*	Science/Social Studies Workshop*

*Reading and writing workshop often include social studies and science reading and writing.
**Option—Alternate full week of science and full week of social studies workshop or divide time evenly.
***Each week, either the reading or writing workshop time on Wednesday becomes a poetry workshop.

Figure 6–8. Sample Daily Schedule 2

and to science and social studies. On Monday, Wednesday, and Friday, science and social studies have forty minute periods. On Tuesdays and Thursdays, however, the time is opened up to provide for a much longer period (one hour and twenty minutes) so that "hands on" science experiments, as well as social studies workshops, are possible.

Because of the wide variations in the way schools operate, it is impossible to recommend one schedule that will work for every teacher. Designing your schedule is a problem-solving process. Figure 6–8 is an alternative schedule. In this schedule, students come into the room and immediately begin reading workshop. They have a minilesson, and then read independently while the teacher confers with individuals and also meets with small groups. After fifty-five minutes, the group assembles as a community to share and begin the language/word study block..

At 10:00, the writing workshop begins. Again, the teacher confers with individuals or meets with small groups and facilitates a group share. This activity is followed by math, from 11:00 to 12:00. Lunch/recess is followed by physical education, music, art, or other special areas, giving the teacher a one-and-a-half-hour planning or meeting time. The day ends with a science and social studies workshop that follows the same minilesson, work time, and sharing structure.

Schedule 3 accounts for more variation in special instruction. During the arrival time, students come into the classroom, and either read independently or work on word study with a partner. From 8:55 to 9:40 (a shorter time than on Schedule 1) students participate in reading workshop (poetry workshop on Fridays; but, of course, poetry workshop can be any day of the week). Language/word study alternates with writing workshop in the 10:25–11:10 time slot, followed by math. Notice that math is scheduled five days a week but occurs at a different time on Thursday. Science/social studies gets six periods a week, 1:35 to 2:20 every day and 12:00 to 12:45 on Tuesday. The challenge in this schedule is the very short reading and writing workshop. Even though this schedule includes more daily variations, it still provides a predictable routine over the course of the week.

Sample Daily Schedule 3: 8:40 – 2:20					
Time	**Monday**	**Tuesday**	**Wednesday**	**Thursday**	**Friday**
Arrival 8:40–8:55	Independent Reading	Word Study [Independent]	Independent Reading	Independent Reading	Independent Reading
8:55–9:40	Reading Workshop*	Special	Reading Workshop*	Reading Workshop*	Poetry Workshop
9:40–10:25	Writing Workshop*	Reading Workshop*	Writing Workshop*	Special	
10:25–11:10	Language/ Word Study	Writing Workshop*	Language/ Word Study	Writing Workshop*	Language/ Word Study
11:10–11:55	Math	Math	Math	Language/ Word Study	Math
12:00–12:45	Special	Science/ Social Studies	Special	Math	Special
12:50–1:35	Lunch/Recess	Lunch/Recess	Lunch/Recess	Lunch/Recess	Lunch/Recess
1:35–2:20	Science/ Social Studies	Science/ Social Studies	Science/ Social Studies	Science/ Social Studies	Science/ Social Studies
*Independent reading, reading workshop. and writing workshop often include social studies and science reading and writing.					

Figure 6–9. Sample Daily Schedule 3

Some steps in planning are:

- Create a grid of time blocks that match your school day, from the time students enter your classroom until the time they leave.
- Slot in special areas and other "unchangeable" events (as you work with your colleagues, try to introduce more strategic options).
- Find a place for language/word study, reading workshop, and writing workshop.
- Find a place for content areas—math, science, and social studies.
- Print your daily schedule on chart paper or on a board (this can be a single schedule if every day is the same; otherwise you'll need one for each day of the week).
- Plan how you will discuss this schedule with your students.

Time Management

Organizing time is related to organizing space and materials. You will be amazed at how much time you can save if you have taught students how to use materi-als and manage their own learning activities. Recognize these bottom-line factors:

- Time is limited by rigid parameters.
- There are more demands on your time than you can accommodate.
- Priorities must be established or time becomes fragmented.
- Every moment you save by establishing routines, you will realize in instruction.

It will help to stop periodically and analyze your use of time. Consider:

- What do you need more time for?
- What is taking too much time?
- What kind of routine procedure could replace time currently spent on something other than reading and writing, math and content study?

You will want to establish the schedule at a highly conscious level for both you and your students. Posting the schedule in the room will help everyone become aware of the need to "stick to it." You may even want to set a timer to help you and your students adjust your internal clocks to the way you have organized the day. Being aware of time has an impact on productivity; it is possible to internalize a pace for the day so tasks are accomplished within the time they should be. You may also find opportunities to layer time: that is, to do two things at once. For example, many teachers observe and/or teach individual students while everyone is entering the room and settling down to independent reading.

When the inevitable interruptions occur (unexpected assemblies, for example), reallocate your schedule: measure each task against its value to productive reading and writing.

A Week of Literacy Learning

You are the only decision maker who can create a workable schedule for your class. The school schedule has a definite impact, although you will be surprised at the changes you can make if you work closely with the principal and your colleagues. In fact, the school schedule (at least between the time students arrive and the time they leave) is one of the few areas over which a school staff can exercise control. By working together, you can rearrange many options.

It sometimes helps to think of your schedule from the perspective of the student, a perspective taken in the opening of this book, "Erica's Day." In all three of the sample schedules we have outlined here, an individual student's week includes:

- At least four hours of reading fiction and nonfiction texts.
- Writing or reading poetry for a minimum of one hour.
- Two or three 20-or-30-minute reading groups with teacher instruction.
- Writing for at least four hours—to include personal narratives as well as content area writing.
- Special instruction in physical education and the arts.
- Between five and six hours of content area study in math, science, and social studies.
- Between two and three hours of language/word study.

Just making a schedule will not guarantee the instructional time described above. Sticking to a schedule requires diligence as well as educating students to the task. Working alone, you cannot achieve the kind of efficiency you need. Students must understand the importance of using time effectively. The most powerful way to teach the value of time is to demonstrate it by modeling.

- Establish a schedule and stick to it day after day. Don't allow deviations until the value of time has been firmly established.
- Create time consciousness by setting a timer for important activities or appointing a student as a timekeeper who will remind the group.
- Let students help you evaluate the use of time each day until good habits are established.

Records of Reading and Writing

Once you have established your daily schedule, you need to start monitoring what individual students are doing within these blocks. It helps to have simple grids on which to keep a quick-reference record of students' learning. Figure 6–10 is an example of a form that helps you analyze students' participation in reading workshop. The keyed activities are independent reading, guided reading, literature study, reading conference (individual meeting with a student), poetry reading, poetry writing, and poetry conference. Analyzing this class record form, we see how often students participated in guided reading. Some but not all students participate in literature study. All students read independently every day and read and write poetry on Friday. The teacher's activity in reading workshop for the week (shown in the final row) included:

- Five minilessons.
- Two guided reading groups that met two times.
- One guided reading group that met twice.
- One literature study group that met twice.
- Fourteen individual reading conferences.

The chart in Figure 6–11 shows an example of students' participation in writing activities during a week of writing workshop. The teacher's activity for the week in writing workshop included:

- Five minilessons.
- Four guided writing groups.

Record of Reading **Week of:** _____ 3/14 _____					
Name	**Monday**	**Tuesday**	**Wednesday**	**Thursday**	**Friday**
1. Josh	IR/RC	IR	IR	IR/GR	PR & PW
2. Halema	IR/RC	IR/LS	IR	IR/LS	PR & PW/PC
3. Ray	IR	IR/LS	IR	IR/LS	PR & PW
4. Jerri	IR/GR	IR/GR	IR	IR/RC	PR & PW
5. Christi	IR/RC	IR/RC	IR/GR	IR	PR & PW
6. Stephanie	IR	IR/LS	IR/RC	IR/LS	PR & PW/PC
7. Madeleine	IR	IR/GR	IR	IR/GR	PR & PW/PC
8. Shelley	IR	IR/GR	IR/RC	IR/GR	PR & PW/PC
9. Rakime	IR/RC	IR	IR	IR	PR & PW
10. John	IR	IR/GR	IR/RC	IR/GR	PR & PW
11. Shana	IR/GR	IR	IR/GR	IR/RC	PR & PW
12. Mara	IR	IR/LS	IR	IR/LS	PR & PW
13. Johnathan	IR/GR	IR	IR/GR	IR	PR & PW/PC
14. Gareth	IR/GR	IR	IR/GR	IR/RC	PR & PW
15. Michael M.	IR/GR	IR	IR	IR/RC	PR & PW
16. Michael T.	IR	IR/LS	IR	IR/LS	PR & PW
17. Tyrone	IR	IR/GR	IR/RC	IR/GR	PR & PW
18. Tessie	IR	IR/GR	IR	IR/GR	PR & PW
19. Phillip	IR/GR	IR	IR/GR	IR	PR & PW
20. Susan	IR/GR	IR/LS	IR	IR/LS	PR & PW
21. Katherine	IR	IR	IR/RC	IR	PR & PW
22. T.J.	IR/GR	IR	IR/GR	IR	PR & PW
23. Jared	IR	IR/GR	IR	IR/GR	PR & PW/PC
24. Delight	IR/GR	IR	IR/GR	IR	PR & PW
25. LaDonna	IR/GR	IR	IR/GR	IR	PR & PW
Teacher	2 GR 4 RC	1 LS 1 GR 2 RC	2GR 4 RC	1 GR 1 LS 4 RC	6 PC

Key: IR=Independent Reading; GR=Guided Reading; LS=Literature Study; RC=Reading Conference; PR=Poetry Reading; PW=Poetry Writing; PC=Poetry Conference (includes both reading and writing).

Figure 6–10. Record of Reading

- Two meetings to support students' research.
- Twenty-three individual writing conferences.

Creating ways to see your and your students' activities at a glance will help you plan and manage your time.

Making and Enforcing Rules That Work

Sometimes, rules are a way to bring order to a classroom. In our experience, rules are not the answer unless they are part of the bigger picture. Think of rules as "standard operating procedures" or "agreements." They are descriptions of the way people agree to work together in a classroom. They are based not on your "authority" as the teacher but on the social conventions essential for a productive, harmonious classroom that enable students to do their best work and allow others to do their best.

There are two ways to look at "discipline." One definition is submission to authority; the other focuses on learning how to care for one's environment, oneself, and others. Self-discipline is learned; therefore, it can be taught. It is a legitimate and important part of the upper elementary grade curriculum. "In a learner-centered classroom . . . we strive to help our students create an internal focus of control, to take the initiative, think for themselves, and assume responsibility for their own learning and behavior" (Bridges 1995, p. 26).

State those rules that are essential for your group of twenty-five-plus students to share materials and to work individually and in small groups. Here are some suggestions for making "good" rules or guidelines:

- Work with your students to determine those rules that are truly key and necessary.
- Think of a rule as a behavior you can teach and your students will learn.
- Demonstrate the behavior the rule represents; in other words, think of each rule as a lesson plan that you state in specific, understandable language.
- Work to state the guideline or rule in a positive way; that is, state *what to do* rather than *what not to do*.
- Make sure the rules are achievable by your group of students.

- Help students think through the use of space and materials in the classroom and determine the kinds of agreement necessary for everyone to accomplish good work.
- Once rules are agreed upon, write them in a clear way on chart paper. There should not be so many rules that no one can remember them. Have students paraphrase and generate examples for the rules. Everyone should know explicitly what the rule "looks like" in action. Teach it explicitly; act it out as a demonstration. If appropriate, have students act it out so that you are sure that they know what it means.
- Avoid highly abstract or "fuzzy" rules that mean a different thing to each person—for example, "behave appropriately." Students will test vague rules in order to create an operational definition to their liking.
- Once you have identified and taught a rule, expect students to conform without exception. That means, enforce the rule every time it is challenged until your students have learned the expected behavior and it has become habitual. Remind the students of the rule with explicit reteaching if necessary. Consistency is absolutely essential.
- It is not necessary to create elaborate "bargains" with students by specifying punishments for the breaking of each rule. Approaching rule making and enforcement as a class problem is more productive. Your students should understand the reason for the rule because they worked together to create it and, accordingly, they should recognize that it is everyone's responsibility to make sure everyone follows the rule.

The process of creating and enforcing productive rules is ongoing. Rules and punishment can never "fix" a chaotic environment; they simply force students to test you constantly to see what behavior you will or will not accept. The worst mistake you can make is to be rigid at one time and to relax at another. The rules must be closely related to the goals of classroom instruction, which include creating a learning community. A highly organized environment, within which students are explicitly shown how to behave, is the foundation for self-disciplined behavior. In this case, rule making is simply a matter of codifying the most important agreements about working together.

Record of Writing Week of: 3/14					
Name	Monday	Tuesday	Wednesday	Thursday	Friday
1. Josh	IW/WC	IW	IW	IW/GW	PR & PW
2. Halema	IW/WC	IW/GW	IW	IW	PR & PW/PC
3. Ray	IW	IW	IW	I/WC	PR & PW
4. Jerri	IW	IW	IW/WC	IW/GW	PR & PW
5. Christi	IW	IW/GW	IW/WC	IW	PR & PW
6. Stephanie	IW/GW	IW	IW/WC	IW	PR & PW/PC
7. Madeleine	IW/WC	IW	IW	IW	PR & PW/PC
8. Shelley	IW/WC	IW	IW/GW	IW	PR & PW/PC
9. Rakime	IW	IW/WC	IW	IW	PR & PW
10. John	IW	IW	IW/WC	IW/GW	PR & PW
11. Shana	IW	IW/GW	IW/WC	IW	PR & PW
12. Mara	IW	IW	IW/GW	IW/WC	PR & PW
13. Johnathan	IW	IW	IW	I/WC	PR & PW/PC
14. Gareth	IW/WC	IW	IW	IW/GW	PR & PW
15. Michael M.	IW	IW/WC	IW	IW	PR & PW
16. Michael T.	IW	IW	IW/GW	IW/WC	PR & PW
17. Tyrone	IW/GW	IW	IW/WC	IW	PR & PW
18. Tessie	IW	IW/WC	IW	IW	PR & PW
19. Phillip	IW	IW/GW	IW	IW/WC	PR & PW
20. Susan	IW	IW/GW	IW/WC	IW	PR & PW
21. Katherine	IW/WC	IW	IW	IW	PR & PW
22. T.J.	IW/GW	IW	IW	IW	PR & PW
23. Jared	IW	IW/WC	IW	IW	PR & PW/PC
24. Delight	IW	IW/WC	IW	IW	PR & PW
25. LaDonna	IW	IW/GW	IW	IW	PR & PW
Teacher	1 GW 6 WC	1 GW 5 WC	1 GW 7 WC	1 GW 5 WC	6 PC

Key: IW=Independent Writing; GW=Guided Writing; I=Investigations; WC=Writing Conference; PR=Poetry Reading; PC=Poetry Conference (includes reading and writing).

Figure 6–11. Record of Writing

Getting Started With the Language/Literacy Framework

Establishing an organized, productive climate for language and literacy learning happens step by step. It helps if you accept that students will not necessarily enter your classroom door equipped to work independently in an organized educational environment. You will need to teach most students the ropes. Some general suggestions for organizing materials are listed in Figure 6–12. Most of the items on this list are tasks you complete *before* school starts or during a break. Once you have established a good foundation of organized materials, you can begin teaching students how to use the environment. Every moment invested in teaching routines will save hours of instructional time later.

Figure 6–13 provides suggestions for the first five weeks of implementing the language and literacy framework. This schedule assumes that students are relatively inexperienced in using reading and writing workshop. If your colleagues at the previous grade levels have been implementing the language and literacy framework, the start-up will be faster. In general, you should first establish routines for independent reading and independent writing and also for gathering the evidence needed to plan minilessons in reading, writing, and word study. You can vary this depending on your students' experience and needs. Some routines may take longer to teach and others may take less time. Reteach routines as often as necessary to establish them. Go slowly, relinquishing control only when you are sure students can succeed in their independent work.

Teaching Students to Care

In Chapter 1 we describe the creation of a classroom community as one that reflects the lives of students in the curriculum. The way in which a classroom is organized and operated *teaches* students every day what life in that classroom should be like.

The language and literacy framework works best in a classroom where the teacher and students value a sense of community and work together to create the kind of place where all are valued and have the opportunity to

---

Suggestions for Organizing and Using Space and Materials—First Five Weeks

❖ Be sure that there is an individual place for each student to sit and store materials.

❖ Be sure there is a good meeting place that will accommodate all students on either the floor or in chairs.

❖ Have wall space for posting: schedule, guidelines for a reading workshop, etc.

❖ Have the book collection well organized and categorized by topic, author.

❖ Have books and all materials well labeled so that students can return them.

❖ Preselect books to help students start independent reading; offer choices within limits.

❖ Preselect a good collection of read-aloud books that are appealing; go with picture books of high interest (see bibliography, Appendix 56).

❖ Have a special place to store books you have read aloud so that students can reread them easily.

❖ Create a well-organized writing center so that supplies are available and labeled.

❖ Have student notebooks or folders prepared for writing, reading, math, social studies, word study.

❖ Have reader's notebooks prepared for each student.

❖ Create baskets or boxes for notebook return; post schedule for M, T, W, Th students.

Figure 6–12. Suggestions for Organizing and Using Space and Material

Getting Started with the Language/Literacy Framework

Week	Suggestions
1	*Community Meeting/Language and Word Study* ❖ Share schedule for the day (on chart)—Week 1. ❖ Work mostly with the whole group. ❖ Familiarize students with the major areas of the room, especially organization of books and writing supplies. ❖ Begin to read aloud books that you can use later in minilessons. ❖ Practice using parts of the room—coming to meeting, etc. ❖ Practice getting books and materials and putting them back. ❖ Introduce routines related to attendance, homework, and other business. ❖ Conduct spelling tests to determine what students know about words. ❖ Observe students' writing to determine what they know and need to know. ❖ Read and invite response to poetry. *Writing* ❖ Start a self-portrait anthology. ❖ Conduct writing interview. ❖ Introduce writing area materials and show students how to select and use them. ❖ Teach students how writers use a writer's notebook. ❖ *Writing Minilessons:* Using a Writer's Notebook, Collecting Ideas. *Reading* ❖ Conduct reading interviews. ❖ Give book talks to raise students' interest in authors, titles, topics, and genres. ❖ Get independent reading underway with book selection and silent reading time. ❖ Practice using parts of the room and routines for reading time; give explicit directions and observe progress. ❖ *Reading Minilessons*: Selecting Books, Ways to Choose Books, Making Good Book Choices, Thinking about Your Reading, How to Buzz
2	*Community Meeting/Language and Word Study* ❖ Share schedule for the day (on chart)—Week 2. ❖ Work mostly with the whole group. ❖ Give book talks. ❖ Continue reading aloud picture books and poetry. ❖ Engage students in poetry anthology work. ❖ Begin weekly shared literacy tasks such as current events, interactive edit, interactive vocabulary, or handwriting. ❖ Provide language/word study minilessons based on spelling tests, reading and writing observations [whole group]. *Writing* ❖ Give writer talks. ❖ Continue minilessons on gathering seeds in the writer's notebook. ❖ Begin to teach guidelines for working together in a writing workshop. ❖ Writing minilessons. *Reading* ❖ Listen to students' reading to assess for grouping. ❖ Confer with individuals about reading choices. ❖ Begin teaching students to discuss literature in the whole group [from read aloud book]. ❖ Get students talking about their thinking related to books they are reading. ❖ Teach students to use sections of reader's notebooks. ❖ Begin to list guidelines for working together in a reading workshop. ❖ *Reading Minilessons*: Abandoning Books, Fiction and Nonfiction, Kinds of Fiction, Keeping Records of Reading, Working Together
3	*Community Meeting/Language and Word Study* ❖ Share permanent daily schedule; explain how the schedule will work; review each day. ❖ Continue to work with the whole group and confer with individuals. ❖ Continue reading aloud and conducting shared literacy tasks. ❖ Present language/word study minilessons based on spelling tests, reading and writing observations [whole group]. ❖ Have students apply techniques presented in minilessons. ❖ Continue work in poetry anthology.

Figure 6–13.   Getting Started with the Language/Literacy Framework

Getting Started with the Language/Literacy Framework (continued)

Week	Suggestions
3 (cont.)	*Writing* ❖ Consider getting students started on a discovery draft. ❖ Introduce the use of draft paper. ❖ Introduce writing folder for storing drafts. ❖ Confer with individuals. ❖ Continue writing projects chart. *Reading* ❖ Complete guidelines for working together in a reading workshop and post in classroom. ❖ Demonstrate writing letters in reader's notebooks. ❖ Explain M,T,W,Th schedule for notebooks. ❖ Have students write one letter and write a response to each of them. ❖ Listen to students' reading to assess for grouping. ❖ *Reading Minilessons:* Writing Letters, Schedule for Letters, Proofreading, Topics for Reader's Notebook, Using Stick-on Notes.
4	*Community Meeting/Language and Word Study* ❖ Review daily schedule each day; reflect on schedule at end of day or language/literacy block. ❖ Move poetry anthology work to poetry workshop. ❖ Continue reading aloud. ❖ Involve students in evaluating the day; use guidelines for working together. ❖ Continue language/word study minilessons with application. ❖ Introduce buddy study [same words for entire class]. ❖ Add elements of language/word study block: e.g., current events. *Writing* ❖ Present revision minilessons based on students' discovery drafts. ❖ Introduce final draft paper. ❖ Use Writing Projects Chart to guide writers toward publication of one project. ❖ Confer with individuals. *Reading* ❖ Listen to student's reading to assess for grouping. ❖ Reflect on M,T,W,Th schedule for notebooks and how it's working; share something from notebooks. ❖ *Reading Minilessons:* List of Reading Interests, Writing Book Recommendations, Checking for Understanding, Solving Words, Reading Punctuation
5	*Community Meeting/Language and Word Study* ❖ Review daily schedule each day. ❖ Continue working with the whole group and conferring with individuals. ❖ Continue reading aloud and other shared language/literacy activities. ❖ Involve students in evaluating the day; use guidelines for working together. ❖ Continue language/word study minilessons with application. ❖ Use buddy study system (begin student selection of words). *Writing* ❖ Present minilessons based on writer's notebook and other aspects of the process. ❖ Have students complete writing projects using the Writing Projects Chart. ❖ Confer with individuals. ❖ Bring one small group together for guided writing. *Reading* ❖ Begin with small reading groups at the students' instructional level. ❖ Confer with individuals. ❖ Plan minilessons based on observation of students' reading. ❖ *Reading Minilessons:* Focus on strategies based on observations of students' reading.

Figure 6–13. Getting Started with the Language/Literacy Framework (continued)

produce their best work. The classroom is, in fact, a laboratory for social justice. It is not only multicultural; it is also antiracist. That means students need to care about themselves, about others, and about the world in which they live. They adopt a critical attitude toward texts that they encounter in print and in all forms of media because they see themselves as part of building a just and equitable society. In *Teaching Children to Care,* Charney (1992) presents the compelling argument that we need to teach self-control and caring in the same way we teach academic subjects. Caring, she says, is not a "soft" or one-dimensional concept:

> . . . the word "care" has some interesting and varied connotations. It can mean "to take care"—to trouble oneself, give thought, forethought, painstaking attentions. Or it may mean "to care for"—to provide for, to look after, show regard. It can also refer to worry, as in "having cares" or "cares and woes." Thus, caring is a burden, a commitment, hard work. When we teach children to care, we ask them to accept this burden, to commit themselves to the hard work of caring. (p. 15)

We agree that caring has all of those implications and must be part of the curriculum throughout the elementary school. Additionally, students *care* for supplies and others' needs. They *care about* others' opinions and their opportunity to learn. We are asking students to take on increasing responsibility. One is responsible for oneself, for others, and for the environment that everyone shares.

The chart in Figure 6–14 reflects the thinking that Susan Sullivan and her students in Room 16 did over time. They set some goals (for example, "A Helping Classroom," "A Clean Classroom," "A Respectful Classroom"). They also made statements that indicated what it would "look like" when the goal was achieved. Not all of these statements are measurable or observable, but they are evidence that these students have developed workable definitions of some important concepts.

Don't forget to praise students for their development of social living skills. Their insights and behavior deserve recognition just as much as their academic accomplishments do. When you have a list of specific behaviors that

are expected, and students have contributed to and developed ownership for those behaviors, you can return to the list for collaborative evaluation of how learning is going in the classroom. Your examples of how students have helped one another or improved the environment will help them see how their positive actions are valued and contribute to the whole. Every student can contribute to the social capital of the classroom.

Suggestions for Professional Development

1. Take a practical approach to organizing your classroom for learning. Working individually or with grade-level colleagues:

   ▪ Take stock of the existing learning environment. Make a quick drawing of the classroom as it is currently set up, labeling supply and meeting areas. Analyze the arrangement for potential problems in traffic patterns or in students' access to supplies. Adjust the diagram to reflect a more workable arrangement.

   ▪ Look at how you are currently storing materials and books and consider alternatives. Instead of placing books in a bookshelf with spines out, display them in baskets or tubs so that that covers show. Acquire storage containers that will allow you to categorize books as well as writing materials, word study materials, other materials.

   ▪ Make a list of the activities that you want to use for classroom instruction. Working on one activity at a time, establish the kind of storage system you need (for example, folders in crates). Prepare the necessary materials as well as the storage system needed and find a place in the classroom for them. Plan a minilesson to teach your students how to use the system.

2. Invite a group of colleagues to visit your classroom after school and offer suggestions for improving the physical environment.

   ▪ Ask colleagues to look at the classroom and tell you what the physical environment "teaches." For example,

Room 16	
Goals	**Ways to Achieve Our Goal**
We are working toward a	*You will see us*
❖ Helping Classroom	❖ Give hints. ❖ Tell the teacher if someone is nervous. ❖ Help friends talk to a person who hurt them or made them feel bad.
❖ Quiet Classroom	❖ Use the quiet sign. ❖ Listen. ❖ Work quietly. ❖ Stop working when asked to.
❖ Peaceful Classroom	❖ Be calm. ❖ Work out our problems with kind words. ❖ Be quiet. ❖ Talk about problems.
❖ Clean Classroom	❖ Put things away. ❖ Keep materials organized. ❖ Pick up after snack, lunch, and work. ❖ Throw away trash. ❖ Wash tables.
❖ Respectful Classroom	❖ Not throw things. ❖ Take care of things (like put tops on markers). ❖ Do nice things for each other. ❖ Tell someone if we leave the room. ❖ Listen carefully to each other. ❖ Pay attention. ❖ Be quiet so others can learn. ❖ Not be a bully.
❖ Learning Classroom	❖ Get smart. ❖ Achieve. ❖ Get a good education. ❖ Try hard. ❖ Always do our best. ❖ Amaze you with our effort.

Figure 6–14. Room 16

■ What aspects of your classroom make students feel welcome?

■ How would students in the room know what to do, where to work, and how to get supplies?

■ What could students learn from the labeling of books and materials?

■ What operating procedures are evident simply by looking at the physical environment?

3. Compare your colleagues' responses with what you want to happen in your classroom and make notes for how you can make the environment more explicit. Then, walk your colleagues through your schedule [posted on a chart] and explain the way students move around the classroom and use materials. Invite suggestions for making your classroom work more efficiently.

4. Have a meeting with your students about the way your classroom is organized and operates. Explain the importance of using time and materials efficiently. Ask them to generate a list of suggestions. Then, bring the list to a meeting of grade-level colleagues. Together, analyze the lists, asking:

■ What do students understand about working together in the classroom?

■ What suggestions are workable and would increase students' ownership of the classroom environment?

■ What teaching is necessary to help students understand how to use the classroom environment?

STRUGGLING READERS AND WRITERS: TEACHING THAT MAKES A DIFFERENCE

Designing a quality literacy program begins with a commitment to serve *all* students. It is our responsibility to educate every child in our classroom and enable each one to achieve her or his full potential. We do our best to develop lesson plans that serve students with wide range of ability, but for many different reasons, some students require extra help in reading and writing.

Learning Challenges

Inevitably, if we teach long enough, we will meet students who "fail" or "struggle" or are "at risk." Some of these students have never learned to read except in a rudimentary way, and they get lost in the academic system. Others have learned to read but do just enough of it to get by; reading is a school requirement, not a lifelong passion. Still others have acquired "learned helplessness"; they stop trying and depend on teachers either to exempt them from the work or to do it for them. Finally, some students have not been able to learn the "language of instruction." They are not less intelligent or less creative than other students; they simply do not understand what their teacher is asking of them. In school, all of these students find themselves in situations where they cannot succeed. But when students do not achieve, it is the school that has failed them.

Students may possess knowledge that we fail to recognize. Their diverse personal experiences have almost certainly taught them a great deal, but it may not be knowledge that enables them to address school tasks. It

falls to us to find ways to make school relevant for all our students. Whenever possible, bring students' own life experiences into your classroom; help them make connections between the texts they read and their own lives; encourage them to write about what they know. Learn as much as you can about their cultures, their families, and the school community. This knowledge speaks volumes about your caring.

Students who need more help may struggle with decoding, comprehension, and many other literacy tasks. They may not be motivated to read or write. They may suffer from poor motor coordination or problems with visual perception. Emotional difficulties may interfere with their concentration and comprehension. What's more, they may lack the language experience and knowledge needed to meet the complex challenges of the upper elementary curriculum.

It is not our purpose here to delve into the possible causes of these difficulties. We do, however, want to help you find ways to teach and nurture these students.

Principles for Working With Struggling Readers and Writers

Readers who need extra help are *not identical* to one another. In fact, they are widely diverse. It is not possible to find *the* magic technique, program, or set of materials that works for everyone. Instead, we offer guiding principles that will help you adjust your materials and teaching for individual learners. These principles are based on what research tells us about struggling readers and writers:

1. ***Learn what students can do and build on their strengths.*** Instead of targeting weaknesses, find out what your students control or partially control. Teach them to use what they know and work from there. A deficit model focuses on what students do *not* know while a *difference* model meets students where they are and moves them forward.

2. ***Have high expectations for student performance.*** The first step with struggling readers is to assign tasks they can accomplish; just as important, however, is to expect them to perform. Research shows that in effective educational programs, teachers believe all students can learn. They don't give up: they find ways to reach and teach every student.

3. ***Promote high levels of student engagement.*** Adjust your classroom procedures and the instruction you provide so you engage your low-achieving students. Pitching your teaching to ensure success increases engagement. Asking students to sit front and center (as opposed to on the edges in the back) also helps ensure they will see, hear, and participate.

4. ***Increase the number of high-quality texts that students know.*** The more texts students encounter, the greater the background they can bring to understanding the new texts they read. Reading to students is one way to increase their knowledge of texts; it increases their vocabulary and helps them internalize the language structures that expand their abilities as readers and writers.

5. ***Increase the time students spend reading.*** Struggling readers *need to read more.* They need to read more words, more stories, more essays, more books, more of anything and everything. Often, because they struggle, these students read *less.* We need to give these students every opportunity to practice reading.

6. ***Increase the time students spend writing and the kinds of things they write.*** Struggling writers *need to write more,* and you can help by removing barriers to writing. Invite them to talk about their writing before they sit down to write. "Free them up" to produce a lot of rough drafts. Suggest they use computers to make writing and revising easier, and help them with editing.

7. ***Teach students to use effective strategies in their reading and writing.*** Most of these students have learned and used ineffective strategies for many years. Demonstrate effective strategies for them, and provide extra support to help them eliminate ineffective strategies and adopt the new effective ones.

8. ***Provide explicit instruction.*** Explicit demonstration is helpful to all students, but you might spend a few extra minutes helping struggling students through a "dry run."

9. ***Monitor the pace of your teaching, but don't "slow down."*** Ask questions they can answer quickly; get them writing fluently in their notebooks.

10. ***Be sure that tasks are within students' control.*** In reading, writing, word study, and the content areas, present students with tasks *they can do* with your support. That includes reading texts that offer only a few challenges and writing about topics that they know and understand.

11. ***Make your directions clear, and don't be afraid to repeat them when you need to.*** Make sure low-achieving students understand the nature of the tasks you ask of them; demonstrate and repeat when necessary. If a task is especially complex, invite students to practice the directions or ask them to repeat them aloud.

12. ***Be sure students understand the rationale of each assignment.*** It is most harmful to struggling readers and writers to complete an assignment without understanding why. This practice tends to create passive rather than active learners. Explain the goal of each assignment and how it will help them.

13. ***Invite students to make choices.*** Struggling students need to learn how to make good choices in the books they read, the topics they write about, or the poetry they choose to read aloud. Also, they will be more invested in material they've chosen themselves.

14. ***Provide predictability and routine.*** The language/literacy framework provides the kind of predictable routines that make learning possible. Struggling readers and writers may waste precious time because they do not understand the routines. Take extra time to walk students through the procedures of each new task and provide support until they know how things go.

15. ***Set short-term goals for students, check in with them often, and reward success.*** Struggling readers/writers typically need more support and guidance.

They may need frequent conferences with you; they may need help breaking down long, complex tasks into smaller steps; they may need more monitoring; and they may need explicit praise for their accomplishments.

16. ***Provide extra support to help students perform well in front of the class.*** Students who need extra help may experience anxiety when they have to share or perform in front of their classmates. Set aside extra time to help them practice so that they can participate fully in the life of the classroom.

17. ***Help students get started.*** Working with individuals or a small group, guide students through the beginning of an assignment. Help them begin their notebook responses, for example, or listen to them read the first page or two of a story.

18. ***Make sure students participate in heterogeneous groups.*** Be conscious of including students of varied achievement levels in investigation groups, literature study groups, choral reading groups, and so forth.

19. ***Use technology to support students.*** CD-ROMS and books on tape can help students who struggle with reading. An AlphaSmart keyboard frees them from tedious handwriting.

20. ***Highlight and applaud their work.*** Don't praise students for poor work but offer encouragement for diligence, productivity, and products that show clear improvement.

Using Extra Support Effectively

Make sure the support staff or volunteers who provide extra help for struggling readers and writers work closely with you, so that your most vulnerable students do not receive mixed messages. To that end, it's best that support teachers work in your classroom with you. That way, students experience the routines of your language and literacy framework, and less time is lost in coming and going. Volunteers can listen to students read or provide an appreciative audience for their writing projects, writer's talks, book talks, and other kinds of sharing. With some training, they can work with students on some of the routines related to word study or guided reading. Finally, they can read to students those texts students are eager to know but cannot read with ease themselves.

Working With Colleagues

While it's possible to address the problems of low-achieving students in significant ways in your own classroom, you will be more effective in your efforts if you join forces with your colleagues across grade levels and work collaboratively to create a school-wide program of support. Strong programs begin with clear goals, early intervention, and differentiated instruction in every grade. A team approach is always best for students who need extra support and guidance.

S E C T I O N   2

Independent Reading

Independent reading enables students to clock up mileage as readers, expand their reading powers, and fulfill the essential goal of daily reading. Four chapters describe independent reading. Chapter 7 presents the structure of teaching in independent reading; Chapters 8 and 9 focus on minilesson and conferences; and Chapter 10 explains in detail the best use of reader's notebooks. We emphasize the routine structures that support independent reading as well as learning experiences such as book talks that inspire growing readers. We also present twenty days of lessons to launch and support effective teaching in a reading workshop.

## CHAPTER SEVEN

ENCOURAGING
INDEPENDENT READING

*In books I have traveled, not only to other worlds, but into my own.
I learned who I was and who I wanted to be, what I might aspire
to, and what I might dare to dream about my world and myself.*

— ANNA QUINDLEN

ndependent reading, as we use the term, is a systematic way of supporting and guiding students as they read on their own. In independent reading, students silently read books of their own choosing while you confer with individuals; they also respond to their reading in a notebook approximately once each week. Independent reading is generally framed by two learning experiences: a book talk and a minilesson before, and group sharing and evaluation after. Later on you will also work with small groups and book clubs during this time.

Independent Reading Versus
Sustained Silent Reading

Perhaps the best way to understand independent reading is to compare it with sustained silent reading. Independent reading is a much more organized and supportive approach than simply giving students "free time" to choose books and read. It also differs from the commonly used structures for silent reading known as Uninterrupted Sustained Silent Reading (USSR) and Drop Everything and Read (DEAR). As Figure 7–1 shows, there are evident differences on three fronts: the purposes, the roles of students and teachers, and the way each reading experience is implemented.

Both sustained silent reading and independent reading are designed to help students increase the time they spend reading and give them continued opportunities to expand and practice reading strategies. Additionally, independent reading provides the oppor-

tunity for you to provide explicit instruction to increase reading competence and encourages students to monitor their own reading through record keeping.

In both sustained silent reading and independent reading students usually select their own texts with some teacher guidance, but in independent reading you are actively guiding the selection through book talks and minilessons. You also teach students to keep their own records and reflect on their independent reading (see Figure 7–1)—the topics, genres, and difficulty of the texts they read, as well as on how many books they are reading and how long it takes to read each one.

Roles

In sustained silent reading students are expected to read continuously through the period, and some teachers may have them note the titles and pages read. Teachers read their own books at the same time students are reading to serve as a model. (In some schools, everyone, including the administrative staff, stops what she or he is doing and reads.) In independent reading students read continuously, but they also participate in short instructional conferences with the teacher and write in their reader's notebooks, capturing their thoughts about what they read.

In independent reading you play a major instructional role *and* serve as a model. There are many ways to help students know you are a reader without sacrificing highly productive instruction. For example, you can share your reading passion through:

■ Your conversation about books you have read.

Comparison of Sustained Silent Reading and Independent Reading

	Sustained Silent Reading	Independent Reading
Purpose	❖ To increase the time students read. ❖ To increase the amount of reading that students do. ❖ To enable students to practice their reading.	❖ To increase the time students read. ❖ To enable students to practice their reading. ❖ To improve reading competence through instruction. ❖ To enable students to manage and keep records of their reading.
Text	❖ Student selects text with some teacher guidance.	❖ Student selects "just-right" text with some teacher guidance.
Time	❖ Any time during the school day. ❖ Usually from 15 to 30 minutes.	❖ During reading workshop—a regular block of time during the school day. ❖ Usually from 50 to 60 minutes.
Initiation of Activity	❖ At a signal, students begin to read and continue until they receive the signal to stop.	❖ Teacher provides a book talk and minilesson. ❖ Students gather books and notebooks.
Role of Students	❖ Read continuously.	❖ Read continuously. ❖ Keep their own records. ❖ Reflect on their reading. ❖ Confer with the teacher about their reading. ❖ Think about and write responses to their reading.
Role of Teacher	❖ Read as a model for students. ❖ Monitor student behavior.	❖ Provide a short book talk. ❖ Provide instruction in the form of a minilesson. ❖ Confer with individual students on a regular basis. ❖ Respond in letter form to each reader. ❖ Observe student's reading behaviors and keep records. ❖ Reinforce and extend students' learning through group sharing. ❖ Help students evaluate during group sharing. ❖ Use observation to inform teaching of minilessons, guided reading lessons, and literature study. ❖ Work with small groups of students in guided reading or literature study.
Closing of Activity	❖ At a signal, students put their books away.	❖ The group meets for sharing and evaluation.

Figure 7–1. Comparison of Sustained Silent Reading and Independent Reading

- The examples you use in your minilessons.
- The books talks you give.
- The written reading responses that you model for students.
- The enthusiastic way you talk about books in the classroom.
- The excitement you show, in general, about books.

We believe in modeling, but modeling happens in a variety of ways. Besides, time is of the essence! We have so many students to teach, our instructional day is so crowded, and we must make the best use of every minute of our time. There is no need to sit before a class reading silently to show that reading is valuable, and we know of no research that supports this action.

Management

The two kinds of reading are also managed differently. Silent reading usually begins with a prearranged signal, at which time students take out their books and read them until they receive the signal to stop. Reading sessions typically last fifteen minutes but may run as long as thirty minutes. Independent reading, as a component of the reading workshop block, may involve students in reading texts for thirty to fifty minutes every day.

You may begin the reading block with a book talk to promote new books and attract students to new titles. Then you provide a lesson on some aspect of reading. You design the minilesson based on your observation of your students' reading behavior during guided reading and individual conferences.

Prerequisites for Implementing Independent Reading

Effective implementation of independent reading requires several essential components:

1. A sufficient and varied supply of books at appropriate reading levels.
2. An organized, attractive, comfortable environment for reading.
3. Information about students as readers.
4. Building on background knowledge created from hearing and talking about books read aloud.

Books

We want our students to encounter a range of quality books. Accordingly, we need to fill our shelves with fiction, nonfiction, and poetry at various levels of reading difficulty so that students can immerse themselves in books they understand and enjoy. This collection of books usually stays in the classroom all year. Some teachers start with tested favorites and then add to the collection regularly, introducing new books with book talks. Thus the library keeps growing and changing day by day.

There must be enough books to match the reading levels of all the students in the class. The collection should include books that are known favorites of students at the particular grade level and should feature popular authors and topics as well as a variety of genres. You want these books to be inviting to students and to offer them variety.

An Orderly, Supportive Environment for Reading

Book talk, the minilesson, group share, and evaluation take place in the meeting area, which we describe in Chapter 6. Students' reader's notebooks are kept in a specific place from which it is easy for students to retrieve and return them. It is important to organize your classroom library so that books are accessible and well organized. Group books in labeled baskets, plastic tubs, or bins, so that students can select and return them easily.

The atmosphere of the room during independent reading is quiet and peaceful. Teach students to read silently and to walk about only if they are selecting or returning books. Help them understand that except for the minilesson and sharing, they do not talk with one another about their reading. The only sounds you'll hear are the whispers of an individual conference or the low voices of a guided reading or literature study group. The group conversations take place in a corner, away from the students who are reading silently.

Information About Readers

In Chapter 28 we discuss ways to use assessment to inform your daily instruction. You can gather needed information by observing students informally, making anecdotal notes, and employing systematic assessment measures. For example, you can use benchmark texts or a Reading Inventory to find out how students are taking apart words or acquiring reading vocabulary. You can also highlight and discuss new words in the books students are reading independently. As you watch them during independent reading or discussion groups and review their reader's notebooks, you can make hypotheses about how well students understand the meaning of different kinds of texts. For example, you may discover that certain students need to understand the principles of biography or attend to the way an author shows the sequence of events. You can provide minilessons based on the patterns of need you observe and reinforce the concepts in conferences and group share.

One way to find out more about students' reading interests and their independent reading perspectives is simply to ask them questions about themselves as readers. Sample questions are provided in Figure 7–2; these questions are repeated in a reproducible reading questionnaire in Appendix 46. You can adapt this interview to suit your own interests and purposes by adding or deleting questions. You can interview students orally or give them a questionnaire to complete in writing at school or at home with the assistance of family members. You will not only acquire a great deal of information to make your teaching more effective but also demonstrate to students that:

- You value their independent reading experiences, attitudes, and goals.
- They have important responsibilities in thinking about their own independent reading.

Background Knowledge

Students' knowledge of texts helps them learn more as they read. By reading aloud to your students every day, you will enrich their background knowledge. From kindergarten on up, every teacher who reads aloud to her students contributes to the resources they will be able to draw on in the future. These experiences form shared literary knowledge and can be used as examples in minilessons in independent reading and in independent writing. As a result, students gain a heightened awareness of the writer's craft and the way texts "work."

For example, Stephanie, a fourth-grade teacher, had read *Peppe the Lamplighter* (Bartone 1999) aloud to her students. *Peppe* is a poignant story about a

---

Reading Interview

1. Do you like to read? Why or why not?

2. About how many books did you read last year?

3. Do you read at home? How much and how often do you read at home?

4. Where do you get books to read at home?

5. What books have you read recently?

6. What is your favorite book? What made it your favorite?

7. How do you choose books to read?

8. Who are some of your favorite authors? Why are they your favorites?

9. What topics or subjects interest you?

10. What is your favorite kind of book? What other kinds of books do you like to read?

11. What are the titles of some books that you want to read?

12. What kinds of books are easy for you to read? What kinds of books are hard for you to read?

13. How can I help you become a better reader?

14. Is there anything else you want me to know about you as a reader?

Figure 7–2. Reading Interview

---

young boy who comes to the United States with his family to pursue the American dream. Stephanie wanted to illustrate how an author uses figurative language to describe the characters and communicate inner feelings, so she referred to *Peppe* in her minilesson. To show how writers use simile and metaphor, she pointed out how the author said, "his face was cold like stone" to describe the father's reaction to something Peppe said. The students quickly made the connection because the story was part of their shared literacy experience. They could then watch for examples of figurative language in the books they were reading independently and contribute these examples to the later group discussion.

Independent Reading 60-minute Block	
Time 5 to 15 minutes	Book Talk [optional] Minilesson Status of the Class [optional]
30 to 45 minutes	Individual Reading Conferring Written Response
5 to 10 minutes	Group Share and Evaluation

Figure 7–3. Independent Reading

A Basic Structure for Independent Reading

The basic structure for independent reading (see Figure 7–3), which you will adapt daily to fit your own needs and challenges, includes:

1. Book talk (optional).
2. Minilesson.
3. Status of the class (optional).
4. Individual reading, conferring, and written response.
5. Group share and evaluation.

You will want to begin independent reading by bringing students together in a community meeting that usually involves the entire class. You might choose to start with a book talk on one or two books and then present a minilesson. After the minilesson, students begin to read while you confer with individuals. At the end of independent reading, you will usually bring the group together again for a group share and evaluation.

Another option for this beginning meeting is called "status of the class" (Atwell 1998). You ask each student to state briefly what he or she will be doing during independent reading and note the responses on a class list, thus creating a record of how each student plans to spend her time. A more informal way to gather this information is to walk around the room at the begin-

ning of independent reading, glance over students' shoulders to see what they are reading or writing, and make a note of the title and page on your clipboard.

Book Talks

Talking about books is a way to spark students' interest and introduce them to new texts they might otherwise miss. When you are selecting books to talk about, consider:

- New books by authors whom the students love.
- Another book by an author whose book you've read aloud.
- "Best-selling" titles that are popular with the age group.
- Books on issues or topics that interest the students.
- Books that introduce a new author, genre, or illustrator.

Think of a book talk as a brief commercial for a book. You might prepare for your book talk by jotting a few notes on a sticky note to remind you of the essential points you want to make. Remember, commercials are short, punchy advertisements. You want to whet the students' appetites. A book talk will take only one or two minutes. A good book talk might involve:

- Talking about the title and the author.
- Showing the cover and some of the illustrations.

- Reading aloud the lead or a particularly interesting or exciting part of the book.
- Connecting the book to the students' lives.
- Posing questions.
- Giving a brief synopsis of the book.
- Connecting the book to other books the students like.
- Telling a little about the plot or about one character.
- Sharing your own response to the book.

The following are two book talks Rebecca gave to her fifth graders on books she thought would interest them.

This book is called *Taking Sides* and it's by Gary Soto (teacher is holding book up). It's about Link, a middle school boy who plays basketball. He's a little older than you are. He speaks Spanish and comes from a neighborhood, first of all, where a lot of kids speak Spanish. He plays for a basketball team and has lots of friends in his neighborhood. But he moves out of the city neighborhood to a suburb. The kids in his new neighborhood don't speak Spanish. He joins the basketball team in his new middle school and what happens is his new middle school plays his old middle school in basketball. It was hard for Link to go from his old neighborhood to his new neighborhood and what's really hard about it is when his new basketball team has to play his old basketball team. His first neighborhood is where his real friends are and that's the neighborhood he feels he relates

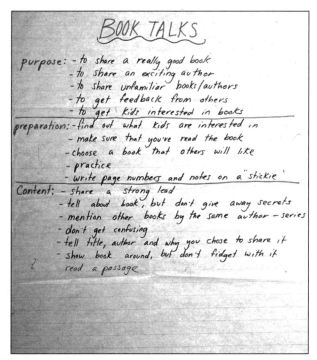

Figure 7–5.   Teacher's Chart on Giving a Book Talk.

to more, but he didn't have a choice about moving to his new neighborhood. He has to go through a lot of suffering inside when the time comes for the day of the big game and he thinks his old friends might think he's a traitor for playing on the new team. I decided to give this book talk today because lots of kids in our class like to read books about sports and you might be the kind of kid who likes to read about basketball.

When I was in school I always liked to read about friendship and about things kids were going through at my same age. Judy Blume has written many books about friendship. You may have read *Superfudge* or *Tales of a Fourth Grade Nothing*. Well Judy Blume has written this book, *Blubber*, that I remember reading when I was in fifth grade. It's the story of a fifth grade class and there's a girl in the class who ends up doing her animal report on whales. Kids start to make fun of her because she chooses to do her report on whales and because of the way she looks. The story deals with bullying and teasing and with kids being strong leaders and sticking up for kids who are being made fun of. So if you like

---

How to Give a Book Talk

- ❖ Look at everyone.
- ❖ Speak loudly so all can hear.
- ❖ Talk about the characters, the problem in the story, or some interesting information.
- ❖ Read a small part of the book to interest the readers.
- ❖ Get the readers interested in the book.

Figure 7–4.   How to Give a Book Talk

books about kids in fifth grade who keep going through the same kinds of things you're going through, you'll enjoy reading *Blubber.*

You can also have your students present book talks, once you have presented several minilessons on how to give one effectively. Figures 7–4 and 7–5 are examples of charts a teacher made to go with her minilesson on giving effective book talks. Rebecca also had her students keep a running list of the book talks they wanted to give (see Figure 7–6) and used it to schedule student book talks throughout the year.

Minilessons

Independent reading almost always involves a minilesson. This explicit teaching, designed to help students work more productively during independent reading, provides very specific instruction regarding effective reading strategies and skills or focuses students' attention on elements of literature.

Usually the point of a minilesson can be summed up in one or two sentences: "Looking at the cover and reading some of the pages will help you determine whether a book is right for you," or "When you come to a word you don't know, look for a part you know that can help you." As you deliver a minilesson, you will usually:

- Introduce a concept.
- Give one or more clear examples.
- Ask the students to generate additional examples.
- Remind students of what they have learned and how they will apply it in their own independent reading.

After presenting a minilesson, you will reinforce the new learning in conferences and in group share.

As part of the minilesson, you typically create a chart that illustrates the principle you just introduced and provides examples. Hang the chart up in your classroom so that your students can refer to it whenever they need to.

Several groups of teachers who are experienced in providing minilessons generated this list of elements common to good minilessons. Effective minilessons:

- May involve using the overhead projector or chart paper.

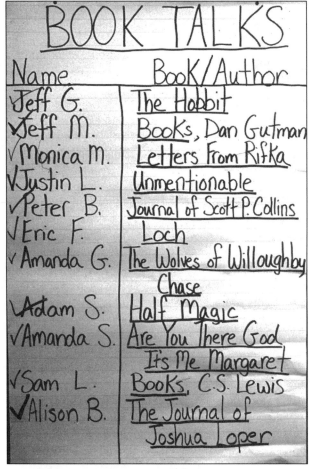

Figure 7–6. List of Student-Prepared Book Talks

- Are quick and appropriately paced.
- Can often be summarized in one or two clear sentences.
- Are brief, concise, and to the point.
- Focus on one procedure, skill, or understanding.
- Are well prepared and based on observed student needs.
- Involve the students in contributing and applying the understanding.
- Incorporate models produced by the teacher or by students or taken from quality literature.
- Employ selective reading of texts.
- Are part of a sequence of topics that build understandings over time.
- Involve revisiting topics for sharing, emphasis, and further understanding.
- Engage students from the beginning and involve active student participation.
- Use high-quality resources and powerful examples.

- Focus on topics that students and teachers think are important.
- Make connections between reading and writing.
- Don't include too much information in any one lesson.
- Use varied ways of presenting information and varied materials.
- Develop community through conversation and sharing.

Status of the Class

You may find it helpful to have each child quickly indicate what she will be working on during independent reading. Atwell (1998) calls this process taking "status of the class." For example, as the student announces the title of the book she is reading and states what page she is on, or reports that she will be writing in her response journal, you can jot this information on a class list. You can update the list daily or weekly to keep track of student accomplishments. As we mentioned, another way to record the status of the class is to take a quick walk around the room as students begin reading, noting what children are working on on a class list.

Some teachers find a record like this unnecessary because they regularly confer with children and get the same information. Also, you may find that the students' reading lists, which indicate the title and date of finished books, provide enough accountability.

Reading and Conferring

During independent reading, students are nestled in comfortable places reading or writing thoughtful written response letters in their notebooks. While the children are reading, you have the opportunity to confer with individuals. To confer means to have a genuine conversation with the reader about how the reading is going. The conference enables you to understand each student's reading process. What's more, it is a time when you can provide powerful, customized instruction that will help the individual student refine and extend her reading competence.

A reading conference is not an interrogation. The questions you ask need to be genuine questions. You are treating the student as a reader. An onlooker would probably observe two people engaged in lively conversation about a book, one perhaps showing the other a particularly intriguing twist in the plot or a uniquely moving paragraph.

You'll want to have a clipboard or notebook with a class list whenever you hold individual conferences with students during independent reading. You can make quick notes on the class list and/or refer to previous notes to guide your interactions during the conference. (See Conference Record Form in Appendix 12.)

You can pull up a chair and sit next to the reader or call the reader to sit with you at a table or desk tucked in a corner, away from the hubbub of classroom activity. "Leaning over" the reader gets in the way of a good conversation; sit next to the reader so that you are face to face, on the same level. Talk in whispers or very low voices so that you will not disturb other readers and will model the quiet atmosphere that you want to preserve.

The amount of time you spend with an individual reader varies. It might be as brief as one or two minutes, or a more involved six- to eight-minute session. Sometimes you will listen to a student read a portion of the text aloud. Consider asking the reader how you can be helpful; however, from your general conversation with the reader, you'll also determine one or two pointers that you can teach on the spot. We are describing valuable, powerful teaching. One explicit point directed to an individual student can contribute profoundly to the student's success as a reader. The following is an excerpt from a conference:

(Mrs. Bishins pulls up a chair and sits next to Dana who is reading *The Great Gilly Hopkins*)

MRS. BISHINS: How's this book going for you?

DANA: I'm really liking it because I like the way Katherine Paterson gives her characters interesting personalities. Gilly makes me laugh and feel sad at the same time. Sometimes I just can't believe the things she does.

MRS. BISHINS: Yes Gilly is quite a character. You are noticing *how* the author writes or the author's "craft." What is it about the way that Paterson writes that makes us feel so connected to her characters?

You might also want to reinforce the concept or principle you taught in the minilesson at the beginning of the independent reading period. Or you might have recorded on your class list aspects of reading that you want to help an individual student with. In essence, you are relating to the student as another reader, making specific teaching points, summarizing what you have taught her, and making notes on your class list that will guide your next instructional encounter with her.

Group Share and Evaluation

During group share and evaluation, the community of readers usually gathers in the meeting area to discuss their reading. Often, group share is related to the mini-lesson. At other times, you may simply ask pairs or threesomes to talk about some particular aspect of their reading or their journal responses at their seats. Make sure sharing sessions are varied and involve as many of your students as possible. Group share reinforces students' reading and extends their thinking as they bene-fit from the thoughts and ideas of others. It is a time both to summarize and to extend children's learning.

During this time, students also evaluate both their individual work and how the group worked together. Sometimes they solve problems or set goals for the next session. The ultimate goal of the group evaluation is for the students, as a community of readers, to sup-port one another's work. They share responsibility; it is not just the teacher's.

There are many ways you can vary how students share with the group. For example, you can invite students to:

- Talk about their reactions to their reading.
- Read parts of a book.
- Write something before they come to the group.
- Share responses from their notebooks.
- Share lists from their journals, such as interest lists.
- Mark places in their book with sticky notes before they attend the group meeting so they can quickly find the spots in the text they want to share.

Sometimes individuals share with the whole group; sometimes they share in pairs, threesomes, or small groups. The following list includes a variety of exam-ples we have observed in classrooms. They will help you think about the range of ways students can talk with one another as readers and writers.

- "Today, you learned how to record the kind of book—or genre—that you are reading on your reading list. Starting with Jaquita, share the title of your book and its genre so we can find out how many different kinds of books our class is reading. If you had trouble labeling your book, we'll all think together about what genre it might be."

- "Today we talked about how an author gets readers interested in the first few lines—or the 'lead'—of a story. If you are reading fiction, read the first line of your book. Let's go around the circle, starting with Jeremy. Say the title and author and read the first line of your book."

- "We've been talking about how you can make con-nections between the book you are reading and other books you know. Starting with Sarah on my left, talk in threes about how the book you are read-ing is like another book you know. I'll give you three minutes to talk with one another and then I'll ask a few of you to share with the group."

- "Today we talked about how authors choose titles for books. Starting with Alicia, share the title of your book and tell us what made it a good title for the book you are reading."

- "We've talked about several books that have sequels or prequels. If you are reading a book that has a sequel or prequel, tell us how the sequel or prequel relates to the one you're reading."

- "We've been studying how illustrators support and extend our understanding and enjoyment of books. If you're reading a book with illustrations, share one illustration with the group and tell us why you think this illustration is important."

- "Today we're going to have share at your tables. We have been learning about major and minor charac-ters. At your table, take turns talking about who is the most important character in your book and why. Then tell who is the least important character. What makes him or her a minor character?"

- "On our chart we listed many ways in which an author makes characters believable. I asked you to write down two ways your author made a character believable in the story you are reading. Share the notes you made in your group of three."

- "We've been talking about how authors evoke feel-ings about characters. Share with a partner your feelings about one of the characters in your book. How did the author get you to feel this way?"

- "Stories have a problem and a resolution. If you have recently finished your book, share the problem in your story and talk about how it was resolved. Tell us if that resolution was a satisfying ending for you."

- "Characters are important in stories because they learn and change. We have talked about how authors show us that characters are changing. At your tables, with a partner, talk about how one character in your book changed and what caused that character to change."

- "Time is sometimes a significant part of a story. Who is reading a story in which time is important? What made time important in your book?"

- "An important part of understanding your reading is figuring out what the author is trying to say to you as a reader. What is the author's message? In groups of three, briefly share the main message in your book."

- "We talked earlier about point of view. A story is usually told from one person's point of view, although sometimes a story has multiple points of view. (Judy Blume's *The Pain and the Great One* has two, for example.) The person whose point of view it is is the narrator of the story. I'd like everyone to briefly share who is the narrator of your book."

- "Authors use their own knowledge and experiences when they write their books. Sometimes they also do research to help them get the information right. This is true whether the author is writing fiction or nonfiction. Where do you think the author of your book got her information or ideas? Share at your table."

- "One of the reasons we like to read is that we meet characters who remind us of ourselves or people that we know. The author describes what the character says or does, how the character looks, and what others say about the character. These descriptions might remind you of someone in your own life. Share with a partner a character who inspires you to think of someone you know."

- "In groups of three, read the most interesting part of your notebook entry today."

- "I asked you to mark a place in your book where you were reminded of something or someone in your life. Talk with two other students about what you marked."

- "We have been reading informational books and talking about the importance of accurate information. What did you discover about your author's

background? How did that influence your opinion of your book's accuracy? Share around the circle, beginning with Josiah."

- "You marked two places to share: (1) a part where the character's talk reveals something about him or her, and (2) a part where the author reveals what the character is thinking. Share the two parts with your partner."

- "We have been learning different ways to figure out unfamiliar or new words. Today I asked you to put one or two sticky notes in places where you figured out a new word. Beginning with Sandy, share one word you solved and tell how you figured it out. I'll write your words on the chart."

- "Read to your partner the paragraph in your book that you prepared to read aloud. Ask your partner to comment on your phrasing and smoothness."

- "I asked you to take a few minutes to look over your reading list and think about the books you have read this year. How often did you complete a book? Were most of them easy, just right, or challenging? Then you wrote a paragraph about what you learned about yourself as a reader by examining your list. Read your paragraph to a partner."

- "Tell us why you believe your classmates would enjoy books by the author you're reading. Let's go around the circle so that we can learn about a number of authors."

Summary of Teacher and Student Roles in Independent Reading

The way we have structured independent reading, there are clearly defined roles for teachers and students. Figure 7–7 summarizes teacher and student roles in all components of independent reading.

Teacher's Role

Your role involves organization and routines; it also involves genuine, informed inquiry into students' learning and skillful conversations that support their learning. You are always trying to extend students' understanding as readers, sometimes through direct teaching and sometimes by supporting and extending their thinking. Remember that you are also another reader in a community of readers with a responsibility

Roles in Independent Reading		
Component	**Students**	**Teacher**
Minilesson	❖ Listen to and participate in the lesson. ❖ Offer comments, examples, or pose questions. ❖ Listen carefully for directions. ❖ Remember directions while reading and/or writing in reader's notebook.	❖ Select topic for minilesson based on observation of student needs, interests, and consideration of curriculum goals. ❖ Provide brief, engaging minilesson that focuses on one topic that will help the readers. ❖ Provide management minilessons that are essential for students to learn the routines and procedures of independent reading. ❖ Provide minilessons to help students learn effective reading strategies and skills. ❖ Provide minilessons to help students analyze literary works. ❖ Provide powerful examples from texts students know. ❖ Use visual aides such as charts or projected transparencies. ❖ Be clear and explicit in teaching and provide a summary of the lesson. ❖ Remind students to use what they have learned in minilessons as they do their independent reading.
Reading	❖ Select a book for independent reading ❖ Read silently without talking with others. ❖ Write responses in a notebook on various aspects of the text as directed by the teacher. ❖ Keep records of their reading.	❖ Provide minilessons on book selection and assist individual readers in selecting books. ❖ Monitor and analyze students' records of reading.
Conferring	❖ Confer with the teacher about some aspect of reading. ❖ Sometimes read aloud for the teacher's observation. ❖ Share reader's notebook with the teacher and talk about it.	❖ Have genuine conversations with students about all aspects of the texts they are reading. ❖ Assist individuals with performing the routines of independent reading. ❖ Teach individuals effective reading strategies and skills. ❖ Sample students' oral reading often, making notes on behaviors. ❖ Promote students' oral reading with fluency and phrasing. ❖ Sometimes discuss students' reader's notebook.
Group Sharing and Evaluation	❖ Share thinking with pairs, in threesomes, or with the whole group. ❖ Reflect on and/or extend application of the day's minilesson. ❖ Evaluate how personal reading is going, what was learned, and how the group is working together.	❖ Invite students to share their thinking. ❖ Vary the sharing activities to include pair and threesome sharing as well as the whole group. ❖ Reinforce the concept from the minilesson by asking for examples. ❖ Ask the class to share and evaluate how their personal reading is going. ❖ Ask the class to summarize what they have learned. ❖ Ask the class to evaluate how the group is working together during independent reading.
Options:		
Book Talk	❖ Listen for books that might be interesting ❖ Learn how to give a good book talk.	❖ Provide one or more good talks to interest children in a new book. ❖ Give a brief book description that has the qualities of a TV commercial—short, engaging, clever, and varied.
Status of the Class	❖ Inform the teacher of personal reading progress—book title, page, and any other information asked. ❖ Inform the teacher of progress on writing weekly reader's notebook entries. ❖ Have goals in mind for the day's work.	❖ In the large meeting or by walking around the room, quickly gather and record information on students' personal reading progress—book title and page number. ❖ Gather and record information on students' progress in writing responses in notebooks. ❖ Reinforce goals for the day's work.

Figure 7–7. Roles in Independent Reading

to participate as a member. You may not be able to read all the books your students are reading, but becoming familiar with the literature that interests your students will help you provide effective lessons.

Students' Role

Students, too, have specific tasks and responsibilities. They are responsible for carrying out the assigned activities, and they are expected to think about texts and to contribute to the learning of others. The routine tasks and responsibilities make the whole system work because once those are in place, you can focus your conversations on what students want to learn.

A Balance of Structure and Individual Choice

Independent reading involves structure and routines. It begins with a minilesson and ends with group sharing and evaluation; oral language is the foundation of learning in this dynamic instructional process. You and your students will develop systematic ways of monitoring reading progress and assuring quality time for daily reading. Students gradually learn to take ownership for their own reading development. You provide support and guidance, along with direction. Independent read-

ing also offers a way of combining reading and writing instruction, since some student responses can and should be in writing.

Suggestions for Professional Development

1. Work with your grade-level colleagues to create classroom collections to support independent reading.
2. Select two books that will expand your students' reading power. Prepare two book talks and share them with your colleagues. Talk about why these book talks will interest the particular students you teach.
3. Prepare two minilessons based on your assessment of your students. Share these minilessons with your grade-level colleagues.
4. State each important principle readers need to learn in one clear statement that can become the basis for a minilesson. Talk about how these minilessons will help your students become better readers.
5. Share two ways you had students share to assure variety.

## CHAPTER EIGHT

PLANNING EFFECTIVE MINILESSONS AND CONFERENCES

Minilessons are the ritual that brings us together as a community of readers and writers at the start of each workshop, when we come in from the rest of our lives—from lunch or the playground—and put on the cloaks of writers and readers.
— NANCIE ATWELL

Minilessons are a powerful, efficient way to deliver instruction to students in a reading workshop. By taking a closer look at how they work, we can make them exceptional.

Kinds of Minilessons

Various experts have categorized minilessons in different ways (Atwell 1987; Hindley 1996). We find three of these categories particularly useful:

1. Lessons on management.
2. Lessons on strategies and skills.
3. Lessons on literary analysis.

Minilessons on Management

Minilessons that help students manage independent reading and their responses to what they read are especially important at the beginning of the school year. Once students have established the routines and procedures of using materials and working together, management minilessons should still be presented as needed. In general, these minilessons help students take responsibility for their own learning and help them respect the learning of others.

Some examples of management minilessons are listed in Figure 8–1. Minilessons like these teach students how to manage the time they spend reading and how to use materials effectively, making it possible for them to focus on productive work.

In the minilesson in Figure 8–3, which Carol presented during the first week of school, she introduced her fourth graders to the classroom book collection and talked about how to select and return books. Notice that Carol made eight clear points. Remember, too, that a minilesson should be brief. Carol's took approximately five minutes, and that included interaction with the children. The points were clear, and Carol demonstrated exactly what she expected students to do.

In a management minilesson, you're not just telling students what to do; you're providing explicit teaching that will help students internalize the key point. Carol showed students what was expected and invited them to ask questions and discuss the proposed actions. An effective minilesson features a clear summary at the end, often repeating the point that you want students to take away with them, ready to act on it when appropriate.

In this case, Carol did not need to make a chart because there was a clear label on every basket. Often, however, you will make a chart of the one key point and the related management tasks to help students remember them. Figure 8–4 shows an example of such a chart.

Minilessons on Strategies and Skills

Strategies are "in-the-head" processes that readers employ as they construct meaning from print. Readers have a wide range of strategies they use to access different kinds of information. For example, as you read any text, you are constantly matching up text with what you already know about a topic, and you resolve the differences between them. You might consciously or

Minilessons on Management

Managing Community Interaction

❖ Respecting the learning of others

❖ Discussing a book in pairs or threesomes

❖ Sharing a book in a small group

Managing Materials

❖ Selecting and returning books

❖ Caring for books

❖ Becoming familiar with books in the classroom collection

❖ Caring for your reader's notebook

Managing Independent Reading

❖ Choosing easy, "just-right" or challenging books

❖ Recording the difficulty level of your books

❖ Keeping a reading list

❖ Keeping a list of reading interests

❖ Abandoning books

❖ Working according to guidelines for independent reading

❖ Learning the expectations for reading

❖ Using routines for independent reading

❖ Writing a letter in your notebook

❖ Reading letters in your notebook

❖ Writing book recommendations

❖ Writing book critiques or reviews

❖ Preparing for and giving a book talk

❖ Sharing information about authors

Figure 8–1. Management Minilessons

unconsciously revise your current notions as you understand an idea from a new perspective.

Typically, we view skills as the more mechanical aspects of reading: recognizing words, monitoring for accuracy, using the punctuation, and so on. In the past, some educators believed that they could teach reading skills simply by having students complete numerous exercises on worksheets. While a well-designed worksheet can help children engage in thoughtful reading work, especially if they complete the worksheet with a partner, as teachers of reading we want to be sure that our intermediate students develop effective strategies and skills day after day as they read texts. We can accomplish this goal best by providing texts that require readers to use strategies and skills in new ways along with specific instruction to help them do so.

Minilessons on strategies and skills are designed to help students improve their reading by becoming aware of information in a text and learning how to understand and use that information. A strategy/skill

Figure 8–2. Books from Carol's Classroom

minilesson focuses on one clear concept that will help students read more effectively. Usually, you will illustrate the concept with one or more clear examples and invite the students to participate. Whenever possible, use your students' successful examples to highlight your teaching point. Watch for strong student examples while you are observing your students' reading or examining their response journals. Some examples of

A Management Minilesson/Introducing the Book Collection

Carol begins: "You're going to get to read lots of wonderful books in fourth grade. I've organized them in a way that will help you find books you will enjoy. Let's take a look at the different baskets of books in our classroom. What do you notice?"

Several students read some of the labels on the baskets.

Carol mentions names of authors, showing sample titles. "You'll notice we have books by Cynthia Rylant, Jerry Spinelli, and Mildred Taylor. Have you read books by these authors?"

Several students say they have.

"If you want to read more books by a particular author, just find the author's name on the outside of the basket." Carol demonstrates finding a book by Johanna Hurwitz and putting it back in the correctly labeled basket.

Carol shows the second row of baskets, saying, "Some of our books are organized by the type of book. You can see that there are some mysteries in here. If you like to read mysteries, you can look in these baskets. Where would you go to find folktales?"

"Some of our books are organized by subject or topic. Can you see where you might go to find books about the Holocaust?" A student points to the basket labeled *Nonfiction: Holocaust.* "If you are interested in a particular topic, you might like to select a book about it."

Children point out baskets holding books about animals, the Civil War, families, and sports.

"In these baskets we have books that won special recognition for the way they were written, the Newbery Medal. We'll be learning about award-winning books this year. You might like to try some of these."

Carol then points out that still other books are organized by level of difficulty. "Sometimes you will want to find books that are just right for you. Some baskets have letters that help you know which books are a little easier or harder to read. The level-M books will be a little easier than the level-N books, and the level-O books will be a little harder to read. If you are having trouble finding books that are just right for you, I can help you find a level that's just right for you. We'll also be using some of these books in our group reading, so that will help you find books that are just right for you."

"When you choose a book from a basket, you can keep it in your book box while you are reading it. Be sure you remember the basket you take it from so you can put it back when you have finished it. For example, if you are reading a book by Roald Dahl, you would need to put it back in the Roald Dahl basket. If you choose a book with a letter level on it, just look in the inside cover. You'll see the letter written in pencil there and you can put it back in the right basket."

We will all get to share these wonderful books in our classroom this year. If we are responsible about selecting and returning them to the baskets, we will always be able to find the books we want to read.

Point #1: The books are organized to help you find books you want to read.

Point #2: Some books are organized by the author's name.

Point #3: Some books are organized by genre or type.

Point #4: Some books are organized by topics.

Point #5: Some books are award winners.

Point #6: Some books are organized by level of difficulty.

Point #7: (Summary) We are all responsible for taking care of our book collection.

Figure 8–3. Minilesson on Management

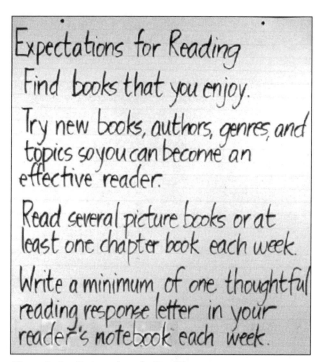

Figure 8–4. Expectations for Reading

use your students' successful examples to highlight your teaching point. Watch for strong student examples while you are observing your students' reading or examining their response journals. Some examples of minilessons designed to help students develop reading strategies and skills are listed in Figure 8–5.

Increasingly, teachers and students are faced with standardized reading tests, which test a range of highly specific skills. Accordingly, in Chapter 28, we describe many minilessons that are directly related to "test reading"—that is, the kind of skills that students need to be able to demonstrate on commonly used tests of reading proficiency in the intermediate grades. Regardless of any personal feelings about standardized tests and their role in education, given the importance that is often attached to these tests, it is wise to address them directly and provide your students with the test-taking strategies they need to succeed.

Figure 8–6 is a minilesson Paul presented to his third graders on using what a text says to make predictions and inferences and draw conclusions, along with a brief analysis of the essential points. (Again, notice that teachers do not make many key points in any one minilesson.) Paul's students had discussed *Stay Away from Simon!* (Carrick 1985) in literature study, so it was part of their shared literary experience. The book, set in the 1800s, centers on the theme of accepting a child who is different from others. Paul had written two quotes from the book on a chart in preparation for the lesson.

Minilessons That Promote Literary Analysis

Minilessons on literary analysis are designed to help students become familiar with the techniques and devices authors use to create works of literature. They also help students understand different genres and the characteristics and value of each. One of the goals of the language/literacy curriculum in the intermediate grades is to help students read more deeply. We want them to develop an extensive repertoire of texts that they enjoy, recognize, and understand. This is the time to open the world of literature to them in ways that will engage them for the rest of their lives.

In the intermediate grades, students encounter books and authors that they may remember all their lives—*Anne of Green Gables*, the Laura Ingalls Wilder series, *Little Women*—because these characters and plots capture their imagination. When students read books that engage them, they are also more willing to speculate about "how the author did it." Minilessons that promote literary analysis draw students' attention to the ways authors use language to communicate the "author's craft." Reading and understanding such "classics" as those by Jane Austen, Charles Dickens, or Edgar Allen Poe are easier if you already understand something about how settings help create the story's mood, how stories are organized, and how characters' thoughts and attributes are revealed in subtle ways.

Literary minilessons are of unique value because while they build students' understanding of and ability to analyze literary texts, they also help students learn how they can improve and extend their own writing. Some examples of minilessons to promote literary analysis are listed in Figure 8–7.

Figure 8–8 is a literary minilesson on how authors' reveal the characters in their stories. In this minilesson, Peter was working with a group of sixth graders who were reading *P.S. Longer Letter Later* (Danziger and Martin 1999). The characters and events of the story are revealed in a series of letters between Tara*Starr and Elizabeth, best friends who have very different personalities and live in separate cities. Here is a sample of Tara's writing:

I need more first-day details. . . . So what did you wear? I want to know. I wore my black leggings, my

Minilessons on Reading Strategies and Skills

Word Solving
- Building a sight vocabulary
- Using context to figure out new words and their meaning
- Using letter-sound relationships (individual letters, letter clusters, onset/rime, syllables)
- Recognizing and using base words
- Recognizing and using prefixes
- Recognizing and using suffixes
- Recognizing and using inflectional endings
- Finding known word parts
- Recognizing contractions
- Recognizing compound words
- Recognizing plurals
- Identifying and using Greek and Latin roots as clues to word meaning
- Using what you know about a word to figure out a new word
- Using letter-sound relationships to analyze a word
- Using syllables to take apart a word

Using Visual or Print Features
- Recognizing and using the punctuation, including commas, parentheses, ellipses, dashes, etc.
- Recognizing and using different kinds of print (italics, bold, etc.)

Processing Fluency
- Reading with phrasing
- Reading with intonation
- Adjusting reading speed
- Reading orally in an effective way
- Knowing what to do when what you read doesn't sound right
- Knowing what to do when what you read doesn't look right

Comprehending Strategies
- Attending to the important ideas in a text
- Identifying a sequence of events
- Selecting important events in a story
- Summarizing a text
- Creating sensory images from words
- Making and confirming predictions
- Locating evidence to support thinking
- Extending the meaning of a text
- Using language structures to anticipate text
- Finding important information in a text
- Summarizing the important information
- Summarizing as distinguished from retelling a text
- Integrating new information from reading
- Thinking beyond a text
- Skimming a text to pick up information
- Making a distinction between retelling the story and sharing your thinking about the story
- Reading assigned and unassigned dialogue
- Noticing the format for paragraphs and punctuation of dialogue

Characteristics of Texts
- Identifying the organization of ideas in narratives
- Identifying the organization of ideas in expository texts
- Identifying the organization of ideas in poetry
- Identifying the characteristics of a genre
- Using an index
- Using a glossary
- Using graphic aids (captions, diagrams, tables, charts)
- Using organizational aids such as a table of contents
- Comparing texts in different ways
- Making connections with your personal experiences
- Making connections with your previous knowledge
- Making connections between this text and other texts
- Comparing this text and other texts with similar topics, plots, or characters
- Self-monitoring as a reader
- Evaluating your reading

Personal Response
- Writing a quality response to a book
- Generating topics for a written response
- Evaluating your own written response
- Proofreading a written response
- Responding to an assigned topic for writing about reading

Figure 8–5. Minilessons on Strategies and Skills

A Strategies and Skills Minilesson on Predicting and Inferring

Paul began by saying: "When you are reading, you are always thinking about what you read. You make predictions and you come to conclusions. For example, you think about how people feel or whether people are good or bad. The information the author gives you leads you to expect certain actions or to have particular feelings."

Point #1: There is evidence in the text that leads readers to make predictions or conclusions.

"A lot of the time, the author doesn't just tell you how people in the books feel but shows you with the words he uses. The author uses words to help readers feel some of the same feelings, and that makes the writing more interesting. It helps you know more about who the characters are and you understand the story better. It may help you create pictures or images in your mind. You understand more than the exact words of the story."

Point #2: As readers we sometimes need to go beyond the exact words of the text to make interpretations.

"We've talked about the story *Stay Away from Simon*. In that story, Lucy was afraid of Simon. What did the author say that makes us think she was afraid? This is called finding evidence for your thinking. Here's an example (Paul reads from the chart):

Carol Carrick didn't exactly say Lucy was afraid of Simon. Here are some of the words she said: "Lucy felt a twist of fear. She stopped and turned. It was Simon. Was he following them?" (p. 31).

Several children said the words made them feel a little bit afraid. Paul offered another piece of evidence from the text: "Lucy did not feel relieved by the sly smile he gave her. To her, it had the same sweetness as the one the wolf must have given Red Riding Hood" (pp. 31–2).

Point #3: Examples from stories we have shared illustrate how we support our thinking with evidence from the text.

After discussing these two examples with the children, Paul asks them to come up with a prediction or conclusion from what they are reading today, decide what evidence in the text supports their thinking, and to mark the place with sticky notes for later sharing.

Finally Paul sums up the lesson: "As you are reading and thinking, notice the words the author uses to make you think or feel the way you do. In other words, find the evidence for your thinking."

Point #4: (Summary) You can find evidence in the text to support your thinking about a story.

Figure 8–6. Excerpt from a Minilesson on Strategies and Skills

long black T-shirt (sloganless), my red Doc Martens, and around my head I wore one of Barb's glitter scarves. (You know . . . the one she had on at "Back to School Night," when all of the teachers thought she was my older sister . . . not my mother.) By the way, I've made a slight change in my name. At first, I thought about starting out anew with a name like Mary or Sarah or Jane. Then I would change my look and my goals . . . but that didn't seem right, so instead of Tara-Starr Lane . . . my new name is Tara*Starr Lane. . . . Isn't that much more exciting looking? I have to go now. Barb and Luke are going to be home from work in about a half an hour and I've got to set the table. (What wonderful meal has Jeannemarie prepared for your family

Minilessons to Promote Literary Analysis

Genre/Author Study

❖ Getting to know different types of texts (genres), including:

Fiction	*Nonfiction*	*Poetry*
Folktales	Biography	Traditional rhymes (nursery)
Fairy tales	Autobiography	Sonnet
Myths	Diary/journal	Lyrical poetry
Legends	Informational books	Ballad
Tall tales	Directions	Limericks
Fables	Essays	Haiku
Fiction	Experiments	Epics
Fantasy	Interviews	Free verse
Realistic fiction	Letters	Couplets
Science fiction	Newspapers	
Historical fiction	Recipes	
Horror stories		
Mysteries		
Humor		
Riddles		
Jokes		
Humorous tales		

❖ Recognizing the typical elements of the story, including setting, characters, problems, events, resolutions

❖ Learning about particular authors

❖ Learning about particular illustrators

Features of Literary Texts

❖ Reading dedications in books

❖ Evaluating book titles

❖ Noticing and analyzing illustrations, including placement and artist's styles

❖ Noticing features of the text format and how format is related to meaning

❖ Appreciating the design of cover and end papers

Literary Elements

❖ Connecting prologues and epilogues

❖ Understanding the role of illustrations in a text

❖ Identifying major and minor characters

❖ Recognizing why characters are important in the story

Figure 8–7. Minilessons to Promote Literary Analysis

Minilessons to Promote Literary Analysis (continued)

❖ Identifying how the author makes the characters believable

❖ Identifying how authors reveal characters through what they say, how they look, what they do, and what others say about them

❖ Identifying the problem or plot

❖ Identifying the setting and its significance in a story

❖ Recognizing conflict in stories: person vs person, person vs nature, person vs self

❖ Recognizing how authors capture the reader's interest in the first few lines (the lead)

❖ Analyzing how authors conclude stories

❖ Analyzing the author's use of language to give readers images

❖ Noticing the language of the text; for example, whether it flows smoothly or is strong

❖ Identifying what characters say and what they think and distinguishing between the two

❖ Understanding how a literary work is organized, including devices such as flashbacks

❖ Analyzing how characters change

❖ Noticing how the author used time in the story

❖ Identifying the message or theme in a book

❖ Analyzing the author's perspective—from whose point of view was the story told or information given?

❖ Analyzing how authors use first (I), second (you), and third (he, she, they) person and how it affects you as a reader

❖ Determining the accuracy of information in nonfiction texts

❖ Understanding authors—how they get ideas and how they connect writing to their own lives

Connecting Books

❖ Learning about books in a series

❖ Learning about books with sequels and prequels

❖ Reading books that focus on the same major characters but are not sequels

❖ Relating books with the same or similar settings

❖ Connecting characters with others you have read about who are similar or opposite characters

❖ Connecting characters with others you have read about who have had similar problems to overcome

Personal Response

❖ Thinking about how stories make you feel (mood)

❖ Identifying how you as a reader feel about how characters behave

❖ Thinking about how characters remind us of people in our lives

❖ Thinking about how the text makes us think of our own lives.

Figure 8–7. Minilessons to Promote Literary Analysis (continued)

A Literary Minilesson

Peter: "Characters are the most important part of our fiction reading. Authors have many interesting ways to help us learn about the characters in the book."

"One of the books we've shared is *P.S. Longer Letter Later,* by Danziger and Martin. The story in this book is told entirely through the letters that Elizabeth and Tara*Starr write to each other. We learned a lot about them just through the way each character talked in her letter to the other."

Peter places Tara*Starr's letter on the overhead and invites the class to list what they can tell about this character from her letter. They say:

*Tara*Starr is kind of crazy.*

She wears loud clothes.

She calls her parents by their first names.

Probably her parents dressed funny too.

Her feelings are right out there.

She writes fast without checking her punctuation.

She seems to talk fast too.

Her family just eats McDonald's food.

She's creative and kind of showy.

She's lonely.

Peter asks whether the group has learned anything about Elizabeth from Tara*Starr's letter. They said:

She's rich.

She has a cook.

She eats fancy food.

She's very organized.

Peter shows the group how they learned something about Tara*Starr by how she talked, or in this case, wrote; how she dressed; her family circumstances. They even learned a little about Elizabeth from how Tara*Starr wrote to her. They could infer this from the writing style and the descriptions in her letter.

Then Peter elicits the same kinds of analyses for Elizabeth's letter, asking questions that correspond to the categories in Point #2.

Peter concludes: "Today, if you are reading a fiction piece, place two or three stick-on notes where the author is revealing the character by what the character says or does. Be prepared to share your best example and to tell how the author is revealing something important about this character."

> **Point #1:**
> Authors have many ways of revealing characters.

> **Point #2:**
> Characters are revealed by what they think or say, how they look, what they do, and what others say about them.

> **Point #3:**
> Knowing how authors reveal characters will help you understand more about your books.

Figure 8–8. Literary Minilesson

tonight? Her herbed chicken? Her caramelized carrots? Her chocolate parfait? Our dinner will be hamburgers, french fries, and beverages supplied by McDonald's and delivered by Luke, and cake prepared by Sara Lee.) (pp. 6, 7)

The following is an excerpt from Elizabeth's response:

Now I've read your letter for the 11th time and I'm going to answer all your questions in the order you asked them.

1. On the first day of school, I wore jeans, loafers, and a white blouse. Plus, Mom helped me French-braid my hair and lent me her gold hoop earrings.
2. Yes, Tara*Starr is much more exciting than Tara-Starr. I love it. What can you do for Elizabeth? Maybe I need a change too.
3. For dinner after the first day of school Jeannemarie made pork chops, string beans, and a salad. And she made crème brûlèe for dessert.

Deciding What to Teach

Select topics for reading minilessons that address the needs of the majority of students in your classroom. Think about what will be helpful to most readers based on your observations of their reading. Any problem you detect in the development of reading strategies and skills, understanding of the author's craft, or ability to manage becomes a minilesson. Use the following sources of information to help you design your minilessons:

■ *Look for patterns in your conference records.* In conferences you not only find out more about your students' responses, understandings, and interests, you sometimes listen to them read aloud. You note their phrasing and fluency, the speed with which they read, their word-solving strategies, and their ability to navigate the punctuation.

■ *Observe students while they share.* When students share their reactions, discoveries, and understandings with you and their classmates, they reveal what they are noticing about and taking from texts. You might observe, for example, that students under-

stand description but take some metaphorical expressions literally. You can then construct a minilesson on how writers use comparisons to help readers better understand events or characters.

■ *Attend to students' written responses for evidence of their understanding.* Examine your students' reading lists in their reader's notebook and note their interests and the range of genres they have read. If you notice a pattern of problems, you can create an appropriate minilesson. For example, if students aren't varying the kinds of reading they are doing, you can plan a minilesson on choosing books from different genres. If you notice that notebook entries are more like retellings, you might plan a minilesson that invites shared thinking about the content of notebook entries and shows students how to summarize without using all details.

■ *Look for significant reading behavior during guided reading lessons.* You will also be getting important information from your guided reading lessons, as we discuss in Chapter 11 and 12. As you introduce texts, observe readers as they process text, and engage them in discussion or word work, you gain important information about their reading needs.

■ *Look for significant reading behaviors during literature study.* Your observations of students as they discuss the literature they are reading in their study groups will provide information about their growing ability to analyze literary works. You can then use this information to plan for minilessons, as we describe in Chapter 8.

■ *Find out student interests and goals.* Wanting to read is a critical element in intermediate-grade children's success as students. To persist in reading and to truly understand texts, students must find them of personal value and/or be able to relate them to their own lives. We are drawn to fiction because it engages our hearts and minds and often addresses challenges we are facing in our own lives. Nonfiction, on the other hand, offers facts and information that satisfy our curiosity and our desire to know and understand the various dimensions of our infinitely complex and subtle world. Your knowledge of students' interests will help you select examples that are powerful for them. If children are interested in reading a certain genre, you will want to plan a minilesson on that genre. The same is true for an author they like. Often, you can use one genre or author as a springboard to introduce them to a new genre or author. Thinking about what interests your students as a way to expand their horizons means responding to them as people and as readers. We often share books or films with friends because we know their interests or we want to share new experiences with them; the same is true for our students.

■ *Use curriculum guides and state standards as a resource.* Your curricular grade-level goals are another source of information for your minilessons. Analyze the suggested skills and areas of knowledge specified in the guides you use, whether provided by your district, part of a publisher's program, or generated by you and your colleagues. Always remember, however, that the real curriculum depends on the particular students you teach. Think about what they already know and use that as your basis for showing them what they need to know next. Every need you derive from observation becomes the topic for a minilesson. Your students' needs within the context of your curricular goals determine the immediate priorities of your teaching.

Reading and Conferring

Following the minilessons, students begin independent silent reading, during which time you have the opportunity to work with individual readers. There is no right or wrong way to have a conference; you will find your own style. Conferences are not scripted—and can't be, because the shape of the conversation arises from the sharing that you and your students do with each other. Each child and each book is different. Your goal is to have a few enjoyable and productive minutes with each reader, getting to know the reader and reinforcing or expanding the reader's knowledge.

Although we cannot provide a prescription for an effective conference, we do have some suggestions. When you confer with a student, pull up a chair and sit next to him. It helps a great deal to be at the same height as the student rather than leaning down and hovering over him. And always ask yourself how you would want to have a conversation with someone about what you have read. The more *genuine* the conference, the more effective. The purposes of conferences are to:

■ Engage in meaningful interaction that supports the reader's ability to process a text with understanding and fluency.

■ Teach the reader, not the text—that is, your focus is on helping this student learn more about being a reader, not simply helping him read *this* book.
■ Become a set of ears, a guide, a sounding board.
■ Help the student solve problems.

The Teacher's Role

Your role in the conference is to help the reader with any problems he may be having, but the conference also gives you important information about the reader. With this information you can judge whether text levels are appropriate, arrange groupings, and plan minilessons. If you confer with many students over several weeks, you will gain information that will allow you to pull together small groups of students for specific instruction in guided reading. You are also getting feedback on the effectiveness of your minilessons.

Let's look at an example. Kara had asked her students to notice how writers sometimes use examples to help readers understand the story and also to make it more interesting. Aaron was reading *No Copycats Allowed!* (Graves 1998). In this book a little girl goes to a new school and experiences all the insecurities that can entail. In trying to make friends, she copies their actions, their goals, and even the spelling of their names.

In a conference Aaron and Kara talked about what it feels like to be a "new kid" and want to belong. He remarked that the character Gabrielle was even spelling her name differently to be like her friends. When Kara asked Aaron whether the author had used language in any special way to help readers know how Gabrielle felt, he identified this passage: "Gabrielle felt icky, as if the Cocoa Crunchies she had had for breakfast were exploding inside her stomach." Kara agreed that this was an excellent description for *icky*, and asked Aaron whether he thought the Crunchies were actually exploding. He said he knew they weren't, but it helped to understand the feeling to think about them that way and sometimes it really did feel that way. Aaron also asked Kara to explain the expression "bread and butter," which was used by Gabrielle's father to describe his trumpet (which he played to make a living).

As you can see, there is "give and take" in a reading conference. Teachers learn to use the meeting as a resource to help them understand their students better and learn more. There are also different kinds of conferences. One might simply be a brief check-in with reader to see whether he has selected a book that is right for him or to remind him of something that you talked about yesterday. Another might be much longer. In an in-depth conference you might:

■ Listen to the student read aloud.
■ Discuss something in the story.
■ Ask the student if there's something he didn't understand.
■ Refer to the minilesson. For example, if you had presented a minilesson on different types of books or genres, you might have a brief conversation on the type of book.
■ Discuss the content of a book.
■ Discuss the writer's craft.
■ Review the student's list of books read or his list of reading interests.
■ Together, set some goals.
■ Discuss letters written in reader's notebooks, commenting on recent letters the student has written or even working a bit on a letter the student is writing, with the goal of achieving clear expression.

Figure 8–9 lists some helpful language to use in conferences. The best "openers," of course, will arise from your own relationships with students. Over time, you will get to know their interests and their tastes as readers. You will share many conversations about books as, together, you recall books that the student has read and enjoyed or compare characters. Often, a conference will begin spontaneously, because a student will be eager to tell you what he thinks or what connections the book is evoking. You should feel really good when the student jumps right in with a comment or question.

Scheduling and Record Keeping

Mark on your conference record sheet (see Appendix 12) students you know you want to confer with in depth and students you want to check in with briefly at the start of the hour. Have a place in your classroom where students can sign up if they want to request a conference. Write down on the conference record sheet what you want to remember about the reader and what you want to help the reader think about next. You might also indicate that you need to present a minilesson on a particular topic. Keep short but pertinent notes to inform your teaching and assessment of a reader. You might want to place your conference record sheets in a binder at the end of the week so that you can look back and use the information for evaluation purposes.

Teacher and Student Talk

A good conference is balanced. It is not a time for you to tell the student everything that you want him to know about the book, but you certainly will want to ask pertinent questions and teach anything you think is essential. Two principles apply:

■ You must be a good listener, tuning in to what the reader is saying and thinking, identifying how you can be helpful.
■ The student should talk at least as much as you do, perhaps more. When the student does most of the talking, you have served him well.

Incorporating State Goals and Curriculum Frameworks into Your Teaching

Many states have standards or expectations for students at each grade level. In addition, many states have proficiency tests. Examine the state frameworks and the test guides to be sure you know what is expected. Again, you will need to match these guidelines with the students you teach. If the concepts or areas of knowledge are either too difficult or too easy for your students, your minilessons will be ineffective. Also remember that you do not have to incorporate all the test-taking skills or specified standards for achievement into your reading minilessons. You will be working toward competence in many other contexts:

■ In guided reading groups as you discuss books and connect reading and writing.
■ In literature study as students analyze texts, compare texts, and write about their discoveries.
■ In reading aloud interactively as you involve students in thinking about and discussing a text they all have shared.
■ In writing workshop, as students write for many purposes and in many different genres.

Placing Minilessons Within the Larger Literacy Framework

Minilessons are one way to teach the entire group directly, and that teaching will be reinforced throughout

Helpful Language for Conferences

Opening the Conversation

❖ How's your reading going?

❖ What are you thinking about your book?

❖ Where are you in your reading?

❖ Is this a good book choice for you?

❖ How are you enjoying this author?

❖ Talk to me about your reading.

❖ That is a [book, author] I love.

❖ That's a book I want to read.

Sampling the Student's Oral Reading

❖ Read a part you really liked.

❖ Read from where you are.

❖ Listen to your reading. How does it sound?

❖ Read your notebook letter so far.

Encouraging Monitoring and Reflection

❖ How well are you understanding your book?

❖ Do you have any questions for me?

❖ Are there any confusing parts?

❖ Is this book "just right" for you?

❖ How are you doing with the variety of books you are reading?

❖ How can I help?

❖ What can I help you think about?

❖ What's going well in your reading? What can I help you do better?

❖ What goals do you have for your reading?

❖ What do you think about your reading list so far?

❖ How are you doing with your notebook writing?

❖ Choose the best journal letter you've written so far. Why is it your best?

Encouraging Connections

❖ How is this book like [another book read]?

❖ When I read this book I ....

❖ This book reminded me of [another text, characters, place, plot].

❖ Did you notice that this author ...

Encouraging Critical Reading

❖ Would you recommend this book to other students?

❖ What's the best part of your reading so far?

❖ What do you think about the author's writing?

❖ How does this book compare with this author's other books?

Extending the Student's Reading Interests

❖ I suggest this [title, author, genre] because I think you would like it.

❖ What are you thinking about reading next?

Extending Problem-Solving Strategies

❖ Let me show you a way to figure out that word.

❖ In today's minilesson, we.... Have you tried that strategy? Or have you been thinking about that?

❖ How are you doing with what you just learned in the minilesson?

❖ What problems have you encountered that I can help you with?

Figure 8–9. Helpful Language for Conferences

the day in settings such as writing workshop, literature study, reading aloud interactively, and guided reading. As you meet with individual students during reading and writing conferences, you can discuss the concept again and, if needed, provide more teaching. Your minilessons help students become better readers each day.

Making Minilessons Powerful

In summary, here are four general guidelines for minilessons in a reading workshop:

1. Introduce the concept with clear, concrete examples.
2. Provide opportunity for student interaction.
3. Immediately ask readers to apply their learning to one or two new examples.
4. Reinforce and extend the learning in conferences, sharing sessions, and subsequent minilessons.

The first guideline is the most powerful and perhaps the most difficult. State the central understanding of the lesson in one clear sentence, such as "Readers need to choose just-right books" or "Readers notice when their reading doesn't make sense" or "Readers think about how the author organizes the information." When you use one key sentence, you help students return to their reading with that one essential understanding. Open the lesson with the sentence, sum up with the sentence, and write it on a chart with one or more examples for reference. If the point is clearly stated and well selected in terms of what readers need to know next, they can make significant daily changes in their reading behavior and ability.

In the real world of the classroom, it is obvious that not every student learns from every lesson. You want the minilesson to reach a large majority of your students, but you have the chance to fill any gaps in your follow-up. Sometimes you may need to reteach the lesson to most of the group; other times you will carefully reinforce the point with individuals or in small groups during guiding reading, perhaps by demonstrating it again.

Concentrating on one or two teaching points in each minilesson accomplishes two essential goals: (1) your students absorb the new information, understanding and acting on the lesson, and (2) you can easily determine that they have done so.

Suggestions for Professional Development

1. Bring records of your observations of students' reading behavior (from individual reading inventories or notes) as well as your school, district, or state reading curriculum to a meeting with your grade-level colleagues. Look at the documents together and generate a list of appropriate minilessons under each of the following categories: management, strategies and skills, and literacy.
2. Encourage each teacher to choose one minilesson from each category. For each of the three, teachers should generate *one clear point* for their students, either orally or in writing.
3. Invite colleagues to provide feedback to one another on the points they generate. Then, plan the minilessons by talking through each of them, again providing feedback.
4. Try out one of the minilessons in your classroom and schedule a follow-up meeting to discuss the results, asking:

   ▩ Was my initial point clear?
   ▩ How many points did I make in my lesson?
   ▩ What was the evidence (from follow-up observation) that my students understood my point?
   ▩ To what degree did I follow up on the minilesson in conferences, while reading aloud, and so forth?
   ▩ To what degree do I need to reteach the point of the minilesson?

## CHAPTER NINE

GETTING STARTED: THE FIRST 20 DAYS OF INDEPENDENT READING

The only joy in the world is to begin.
— CESARE PAVESE

More than anything else, establishing routines and procedures for managing independent reading will get your reading workshop off to a good start. Best of all, a tight, thoughtful organization will enable your students to read for a substantial period of time every day. Early in the year, you will want to present any number of minilessons on managing reading and writing, but once students have established the routines, you will rarely need to revisit these lessons.

For your students, a successful experience with independent reading begins with knowing the basics: how to use the book collection, choose books, and record their reading. Also, you will want to establish independent reading as a quiet, productive time; insist on silence from the start. When students are engrossed in their independent reading, you can more easily confer with individuals or work with small groups in guided reading and literature study.

During the first month of reading workshop, you have two critical goals:

1. Help your students think of themselves as readers by reading books that they enjoy and have them participate in all the choices and decisions readers make.
2. Establish the roles and routines of the reading workshop.

In this chapter we share classroom vignettes in which teachers achieve these early goals. They are not meant as scripts to follow but as a vision of what the first few weeks of independent reading can look like.

Figure 9–1 itemizes minilessons for the first twenty days of independent reading. Each minilesson is described in more detail in this chapter. After you have taught these minilessons several times, you will develop your own style and language. You will also determine the sequence of lessons that fits your particular students. For example, you may need to spend more than one session on a particular lesson or prioritize lessons that your students need before others. Figure 9–1 is just one sample sequence and selection.

It works best to be specific; use clear statements and clear demonstrations of procedures. Also, you want your lesson to be short and to the point, so it helps to think ahead about what you will say. We provide suggestions for language, particularly opening statements, that teachers have found helpful in communicating clearly with students. These examples appear in italics. Some of our example minilessons include specific classroom dialogue, presented as a script. Our comments are woven throughout the examples and appear in regular type.

You will notice that each minilesson has an opening statement and a demonstration or example. Lessons build on each other; points are repeated; charts are posted in the room and referred to again and again. The first day's lesson will be a little longer than usual because you want to help students learn two critical routines—caring for books and reading silently.

Independent Reading: The First Twenty Days of Teaching

Minilesson (M,S,L¹)	Key Concepts	Learning Outcomes	Resources Needed
Day 1 (M) Selecting Books and Enjoying Silent Reading	❖ We have specific ways to select and return books in our classroom so that we all can find and use them easily. ❖ We read silently and do not talk with others so we can do our best thinking while reading.	❖ Students learn how to maintain the organized classroom book collection. ❖ The routines of silent individual reading are established.	Organized classroom book collection. Chart—*Reading Is Thinking*
Day 2 (M) How Readers Choose Books	❖ Readers choose books in many different ways.	❖ Students use several different kinds of information to help them choose books. ❖ Students think carefully about book choice.	Chart—*Ways to Choose Books*
Day 3 (S) Making Good Book Choices	❖ Books can be easy, just-right, or challenging for a reader. ❖ Readers should choose just-right books most of the time.	❖ Readers have criteria to judge whether a book is just right for independent reading.	Chart—*Easy, Just-Right, Challenging*
Day 4 (S) Thinking and Talking About Your Reading	❖ Readers are always thinking about what they understand and about how they feel about what they understood. ❖ Readers can talk about their thinking.	❖ Readers are aware of their thinking and remember it in order to share with other readers. ❖ Readers talk with each other about their thinking.	Chart—*Reading Is Thinking* Example Stick-on Notes
Day 5 (M) How to Buzz with Each Other	❖ We can do our best talking about reading when we "buzz" well with a partner or in small groups.	❖ Students learn how to listen to each other and share effectively as partners or in small groups.	Chart—*How to Buzz Effectively*
Day 6 (M) Abandoning Books	❖ Sometime readers abandon a book for specific reasons.	❖ Students learn that, after a good try, they may have a reason to abandon a book.	Chart—*Why Readers Abandon Books*
Day 7 (L) Distinguishing Between Fiction and Nonfiction	❖ There are two types of books: fiction and nonfiction.	❖ Students are able to distinguish between two types of books as a foundation for learning about genre.	Chart—*Books We've Shared* Examples of books that have been read aloud

¹ M=Management Minilesson   L=Literary Analysis Minilesson
S=Strategies and Skills Minilesson

Figure 9–1. Independent Reading: The First 20 Days of Teaching

Independent Reading: The First Twenty Days of Teaching (continued)

Minilesson (M,S,L)	Key Concepts	Learning Outcomes	Resources Needed
Day 8 (L) Different Kinds of Fiction Different Kinds of Nonfiction	❖ There are many different kinds of fiction. ❖ There are many different kinds of nonfiction.	❖ Each genre has specific characteristics. Students learn to categorize types of fiction and types of nonfiction so that they can vary their reading.	Chart—*Books We've Shared* Chart—*Fiction* Chart—*Nonfiction*
Day 9 (M) Keeping a Record of Your Reading	❖ Readers keep a list of books they've read so that they can evaluate the breadth of their reading.	❖ Students will begin to use section one in their reader's notebook. ❖ Students begin to record books they have read using specific procedures.	Chart—Enlarged journal page Reader's Notebook
Day 10 (M) Guidelines for Reading Workshop	❖ As readers and writers, we follow specific guidelines to work together and help one another do our best learning.	❖ Students learn to use section three in their reader's notebook. ❖ Students are aware of and follow specific guidelines for independent reading.	Chart—*Guidelines Reading Workshop* Reader's Notebook
Day 11 (S) Writing Responses to Your Reading	❖ Readers can share their thinking about reading by writing a letter in a reader's notebook.	❖ Students learn to follow procedures for writing letters in reader's notebook.	Personal letter from teacher on chart paper Reader's Notebook
Day 12 (M) Writing Letters in Your Reader's Notebook Each Week	❖ Use the teacher's letter as a guide to writing your letter in your reader's notebook. ❖ Readers write one letter each week and place it in the *Completed Letters* basket.	❖ Students learn to respond to the teacher's letter as part of their letter writing in notebooks. ❖ Students follow procedures for the weekly letter.	Reader's Notebook with typed teacher letter glued in Chart—*Day Letter Is Due* "Completed letters" basket
Day 13 (S) Proofreading Your Letter	❖ The letters you write in your notebook will be your best work if you proofread them using guidelines.	❖ Students learn to use guidelines to proofread letters they write in their notebooks.	Chart—*Proofreading Your Letter* Reader's Notebook
Day 14 (S) Topics for Your Reader's Notebook	❖ There are many different kinds of thinking that you can write about in your reader's notebook.	❖ Students learn that there are a variety of topics that they can write about in their letters. ❖ Students learn to refer to a chart to help themselves.	Chart—*Topics You Can Write About in Your Reader's Notebook* Reader's Notebook

Figure 9–1. Independent Reading: The First 20 Days of Teaching (continued)

Independent Reading: The First Twenty Days of Teaching (continued)

Minilesson (M,S,L)	Key Concepts	Learning Outcomes	Resources Needed
Day 15 (M) Using Stick-on Notes to Prepare for Journal Writing	❖ Quick notes can help you remember your thinking when you are ready to write your letters and when you confer with the teacher.	❖ Students learn a process to help them remember their thinking so that they can write about it and talk about it.	Stick-on notes
Day 16 (M) Creating a List of Your Reading Interests	❖ Keeping a list of your reading interests will help you find books that you enjoy.	❖ Students learn to record their reading interests in section two of the reader's notebook and use that information to guide their choices.	Enlarged print version of *Reading Interests* Reader's Notebook
Day 17 (M) How to Write Book Recommendations	❖ Readers choose books by listening to the recommendations of others. ❖ You can recommend books to others.	❖ Students learn to evaluate books. ❖ Students learn how to write a brief book recommendation. ❖ The class builds a collection of recommended books.	Special place in classroom for recommended books Index cards Examples of book recommendations
Day 18 (S) Checking for Understanding as You Read	❖ Readers notice when the text doesn't make sense to them. ❖ Readers have different ways to figure out the author's meaning.	❖ Students learn to check on their understandings as they read. ❖ Students learn ways to make sure they understand as they read.	Chart—*How to Be Sure You Understand the Author's Message*
Day 19 (S) Solving Unknown Words	❖ Readers have a variety of ways to solve unknown words.	❖ Students learn a variety of ways to solve words.	Chart—*Ways Readers Solve Words*
Day 20 (S) Using Punctuation to Understand	❖ Readers use punctuation to understand the author's message.	❖ Students learn how the punctuation helps them understand the author's message.	Chart—paragraph from a book [*Russell Sprouts* used as example in text]

Figure 9–1. Independent Reading: The First 20 Days of Teaching (continued)

Day 1—Management Minilesson: Selecting Books and Enjoying Silent Reading

Part 1

This year you will get to read many wonderful books in our classroom and at home. I'd like to introduce you to our classroom collection of books. Let's talk about how we can choose, read, and return them in a way that lets us all find and use them easily.

Share the way books are organized; point out books categorized by author, by genre, by topic, by series, by illustrator, by format, by award winners, or by any other category you've established. Show students the place where each category of books is kept. Then show students how to take books out and return them to each basket.

We will all get to share these wonderful books in our classroom this year. If we are responsible for selecting and returning them to the baskets, we will always be able to find the books we want to read.

Part 2

Write "Reading Is Thinking" on a chart.

Today you are going to have a good block of time to enjoy your reading. Reading is thinking, and you can do your best thinking when it is quiet. When we do our independent reading, you will need to read silently without talking to the person next to you or to anyone else. The room is completely quiet so that you and your classmates can do your best thinking. When I am talking to a reader, I will be sure to whisper. So will the reader I'm talking with, so that we will not interrupt anyone's thinking. When we gather for our group meeting later we can talk about how well we did at keeping the room completely quiet so we could all do our best reading.

Day 2—Management Minilesson: How Readers Choose Books

Each of you has chosen a book to read from our classroom collection. We choose books to read in many different ways and for many different purposes. For example, I love to read mysteries, and so I often look for that type of book. What do you think about when you choose a book to read?

Write student responses on a chart. In Kristen's classroom, the students came up with the list in Figure 9–2.

Today we have listed many of the different ways you might choose books to read. I'll leave this list of ways readers choose books on the wall because you may think of other ways you choose books to read and we can add them. Now you can find a comfortable seat and enjoy your book. Remember, reading is thinking—so you will need to read silently. Do not talk, so that your classmates can do their best thinking. When you return, we'll quickly share how you chose the book you are now reading.

Day 3—Strategies and Skills Minilesson: Making Good Book Choices

One of the most important goals of early minilessons is getting your students reading "just right" books that they enjoy. As you teach the minilesson, create a chart with three categories, indicating the characteristics of *easy*, *just-right*, or *challenging* under each.

Today we are going to talk about how readers choose "easy," "just right," or "challenging" books to read. I'll make some notes on this chart to help you. Remember each kind of book we talk about.

Sometimes, easy books are fun to read. They're the kinds of books you read when you want to relax. You might pick a favorite picture book you've heard read aloud or a book that you have read before and enjoyed or a new book that won't take a lot of effort for you to read and understand. You can read the book easily and understand it very well. I'll write E on the chart to indicate "easy."

Just-right books are those that you understand well and can enjoy. You read the book smoothly and have only a few places where you need to slow down to figure out a word or think more about the meaning. These are the books that will help you become a better reader each time you read. Most of the time you should read just-right books. I'll write JR, for "just right," on the chart.

Challenging books are very difficult for you to read. You have trouble reading many of the words and don't understand most of what you are reading. These are books that are too difficult for you to enjoy right now, but you may find you will enjoy them later. Challenging books are not usually good choices for right now. I'll write C on the chart to stand for "challenging." There may be some times when you would choose a challenging book, such as when you needed to find some facts on a particular topic, but most of the time, you would save challenging books until they are "just right" for you.

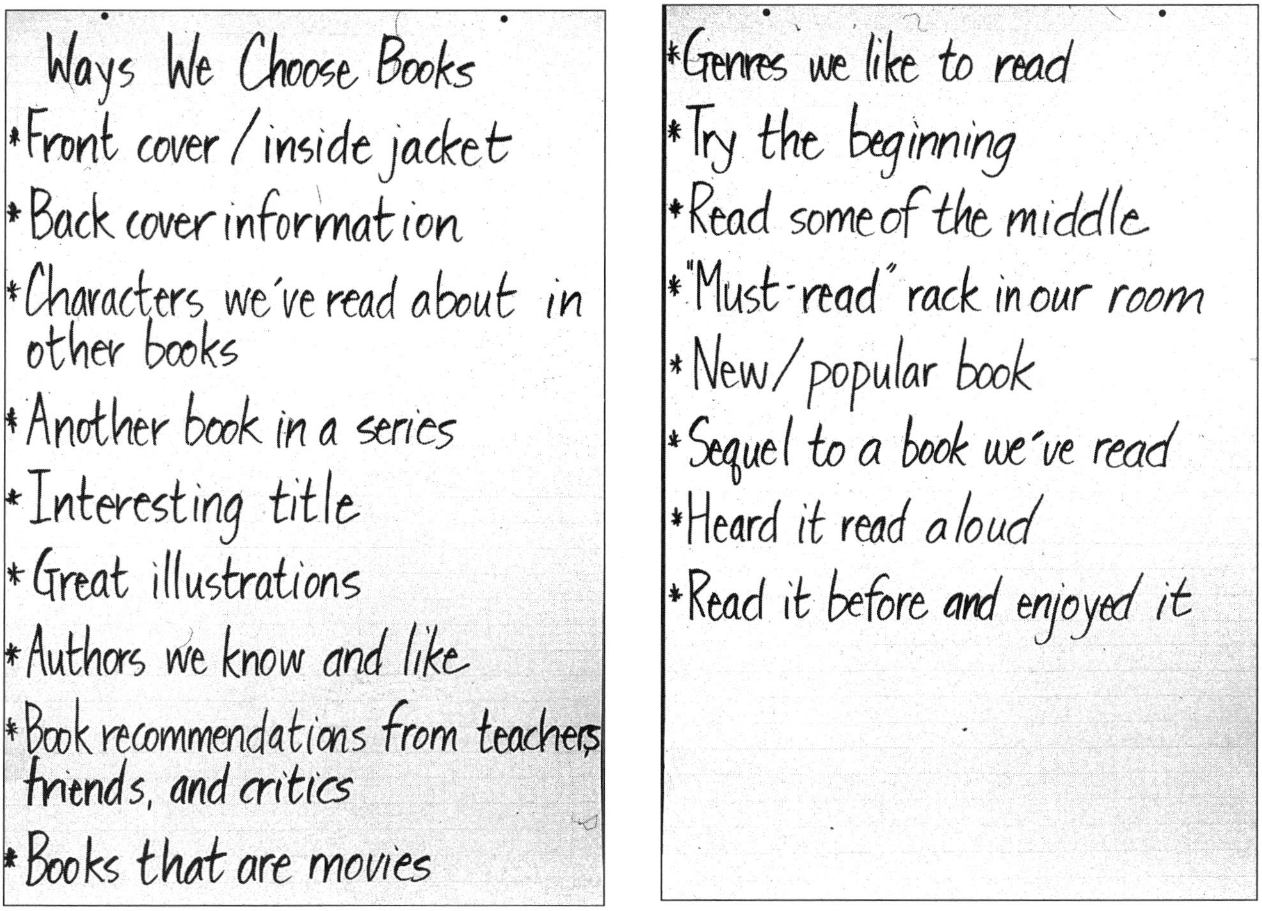

Ways We Choose Books
* Front cover / inside jacket
* Back cover information
* Characters we've read about in other books
* Another book in a series
* Interesting title
* Great illustrations
* Authors we know and like
* Book recommendations from teachers, friends, and critics
* Books that are movies

* Genres we like to read
* Try the beginning
* Read some of the middle
* "Must-read" rack in our room
* New / popular book
* Sequel to a book we've read
* Heard it read aloud
* Read it before and enjoyed it

Figure 9–2.   Ways We Choose Books

When you are reading today, think about whether the book you are reading is easy, just right, or challenging for you. When you return to the group, be prepared to share the category that best describes your choice. Yesterday you did a wonderful job reading silently so everyone could do his best thinking. Let's do the same today.

Day 4—Strategies and Skills Minilesson: Thinking and Talking About Your Reading

When I read I am always thinking about what the author is saying and how I feel. For example, when I read The Winter Room, *by Gary Paulsen, I was thinking about visiting my uncle's farm when I was a child. My aunt baked bread just like Eldon's mother did, and I could almost smell it. I felt that everything on the farm was old and well used. I liked the description of the names carved on the beds—names they didn't even know because the*

beds were so old. I wondered what the author was suggesting when he wrote: "I don't know what he meant exactly, but many questions I ask Father are answered that way, with words around the edges."

You will be thinking as you read your book today. You may be thinking about what you like or don't like, things the book reminds you of in your life or in other books, or questions you have. You might be making predictions, noticing something about the author's language or style, or thinking about how a character reminds you of someone in your life. I'll write some of the thinking we talked about on this chart to remind you. We can add more later.

Take a moment to list the kinds of thinking on the "Reading is Thinking" chart that you started on the first day. List topics such as how the book reminds you of another book, or something that confuses you.

Today while you are reading, mark two places in your book where you might share some of what you were thinking about as you read. Use stick-on notes to help you remember the place so we can share our thoughts when we gather in our group. We might want to add more kinds of thinking to our list.

Following the reading time, invite students to talk together about the thinking they did about their reading. Explain that they can talk about what they are thinking about their reading.

Day 5—Management Minilesson: How to Buzz With Each Other

Yesterday we talked about how readers think while they read, and you shared the thinking you were doing as you read. When we talk with a partner or in a small group, we are going to refer to our talking with each other as a "buzz." Let's talk a little bit about how we can buzz with each other well so we can do our best talking and learning. I'll write our thoughts on this chart.

Elicit the students' suggestions, shaping them to create a simple, clear set of guidelines. Marcella created the chart shown in Figure 9–3 with her students.

When we are finished reading today, we will buzz in threes about what is capturing our interest in the books we

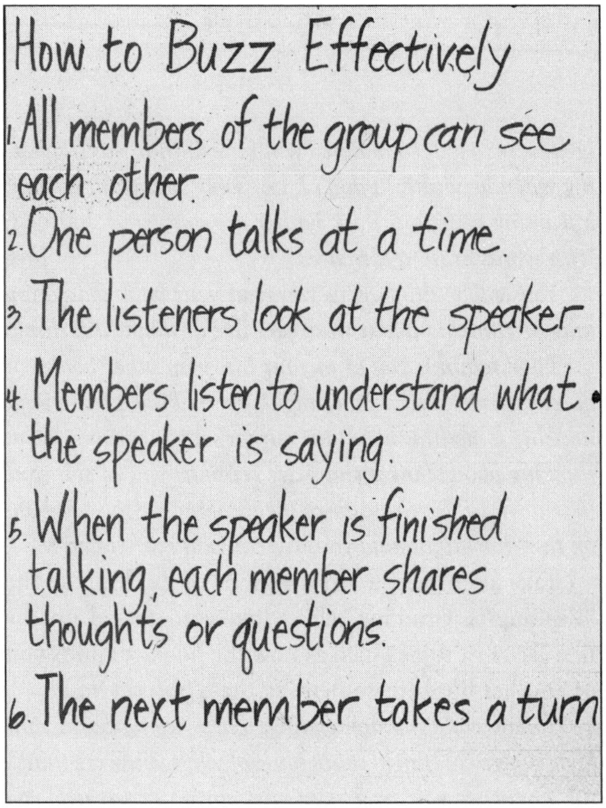

Figure 9–3. How to Buzz Effectively

are reading. Then we will use our chart to evaluate how well our buzz sessions are going.

Day 6—Management Minilesson: Abandoning Books

Once in a while readers choose a book to read and even after they have given it a good chance, they find that they are not enjoying it. They're not interested in reading it anymore, and they want to stop. They may decide to read it later. When a reader stops reading a book, it's called "abandoning the book." Today let's talk about why readers might abandon books.

As students give different reasons readers abandon books, create a chart. One class made the chart shown in Figure 9–4.

Are any of you reading a book that you are really not interested in? Of course, it's important to give a book a chance before you decide to abandon it, but readers do abandon books sometimes. If you're considering abandoning your book, why is that? Have you given it a good chance? When we gather to share today, we'll check in with one another to see whether any readers abandoned the books they were reading so far this year and they can explain why.

Day 7—Literary Analysis Minilesson: Distinguishing Between Fiction and Nonfiction

If this subject is too basic for your students, skip it and go on to Day 8.

There are just so many different kinds of books to read. We have read many kinds of books together. Let's look at the list of books we've read aloud together so far this year.

Refer to your list of books on the chart headed "Books We've Shared." You'll update this list every time you read a book aloud to the students.

We read some fiction books like Pink and Say, *by Patricia Polacco,* The Rough-Faced Girl, Fig Pudding, Sadako, Spider Boy, *and* Baseball Saved Us. *Fiction books are not true stories, though the ideas may have come from experiences that really happened. We've also read some information books, such as* Amistad: A Long Road to Freedom, Alvin Ailey, Safari, *and parts of* The Snake Book. *All of these books are nonfiction. That*

Why Readers Abandon Books
* Too easy
* Too difficult
* Boring - not interesting and not going anywhere
* Not interested in the genre now
* Too long before the action begins
* Disappointing sequel
* Expected something different from this author
* Don't like the characters
* Found I didn't like this point of view
* Too sad
* Too scary
* Too confusing
* Found another book of interest
* Plot is confusing
* Print is too hard to read
* Too similar to another book
* Not good for now but might go back to it

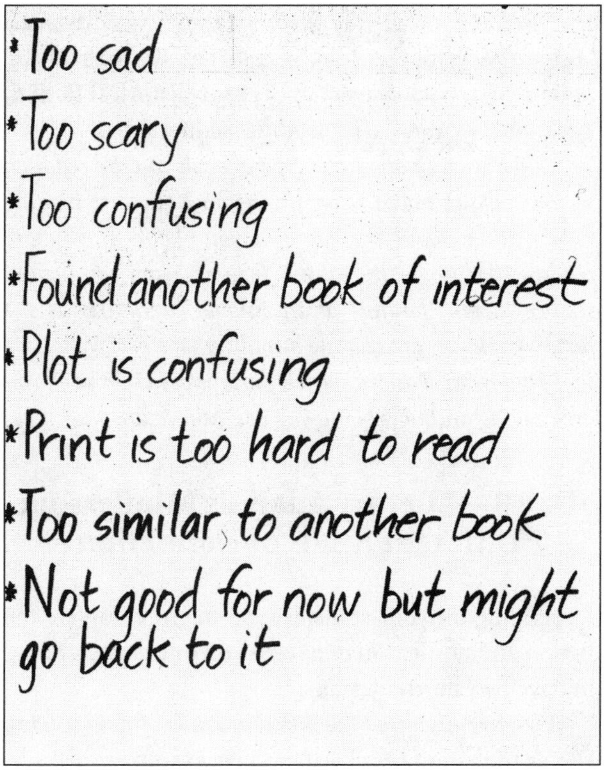

Figure 9–4. Why Readers Abandon Books

means they are not fiction. In other words, they are true stories and should contain accurate information.

Today, think about the kind of book you are reading. Is it fiction or nonfiction? When we share today, be prepared to tell whether the book you are reading is fiction or nonfiction and how you know what type of book it is.

Make a chart that says fiction texts are basically not true. Nonfiction texts contain accurate, truthful information. Put one or two examples of each.

Day 8—Literary Analysis Minilesson: Different Kinds of Fiction

This minilesson is for readers who already understand the categories of fiction and nonfiction. If your students are not ready for this lesson, skip to Day 9.

We have discussed the difference between fiction and nonfiction. Today let's look at the different kinds of fiction books we have read together.

Point to the list and the labels for each book.

Pink and Say *is a fictional story that takes place during the Civil War. The author tells a story that seems real and took place in the past or in history, so it is called "historical fiction." Often, an author tells a fiction story using actual people or events of the past. But some of the story came from the imagination. Are there any others we've read together that are historical fiction?*

Spider Boy *is a story about a boy and his adventures that could be happening today. It seems real, so it is called "realistic fiction."*

Fiction books that tell about supernatural events are called "science fiction." They are a kind of fantasy based on science. Books like Charlotte's Web *that contain unrealistic elements are called "fantasy." Books like* The Rough-Faced Girl *are traditional stories or stories that were passed down orally throughout history. They include folktales, fairy tales, myths, and legends. Both fairy tales and folktales are traditional tales, but fairy tales have magic in them. Folktales are just old stories that people tell, and sometimes they have a lesson in them. Have we read any other folktales or fairy tales? So the old stories that are passed on from generation to generation are called traditional stories.*

Discuss and label all the books on the list headed "Books We've Shared" with the letters RF for realistic fiction, SF for science fiction, HF for historical fiction, F for fantasy, and TL for traditional literature.

When we talk about the type of book you are reading, we are talking about its genre. Before you start reading today, think about the genre of your book. If you are reading fiction, is it realistic fiction, historical fiction, science fiction, fantasy, or traditional literature? Is the fiction book you are reading a traditional story? When we share today, we'll ask you to tell the type of fiction book you are reading and to explain why you believe it is that type.

Day 8—Literary Analysis Minilesson: Different Kinds of Nonfiction

Depending on your students, you might complete the fiction and nonfiction minilesson on one day or choose to have two shorter lessons.

We have discussed the different kinds of fiction texts. (Refer to yesterday's chart and give examples of traditional literature (folktales, fables, myths, legends, fairy tales) and fantasy, science fiction, realistic fiction, and historical fiction—to review those categories.)

Today we are going to talk about different kinds of nonfiction texts or texts that give accurate, truthful information. There are two types of nonfiction texts. The first is Informational (Write an **I** next to an informational book on the Books We've Shared chart.) *Informational texts are those that give us information about history, science, language, or other subjects. The second is biography.* (Write a **B** next to titles of biographies on the Books We've Shared chart.) *Biography texts tell about people's lives. If a person is telling a story about his/her life, it is called autobiography. If an author tells about some memories or certain experiences in his/her life, it is called a memoir.*

Before you start reading today, think about whether you are reading an informational book or biography. We will talk about the nonfiction books people are reading at group share.

Day 9—Management Minilesson: Keeping a Record of Your Reading

You have been doing lots of wonderful reading and thinking about your books. Readers sometimes keep a list of books they've read so they can look back at their reading. Today I am going to give you a very special notebook that

Figure 9–5. Example of a Reader's Notebook (Heinemann, 2000)

is just for you to help you remember the books you have read. You will be using your reader's notebook to help with your reading. In one part there is a place for you to record the titles you are reading.

Hold up a *reader's notebook* (see Figure 9–5).

Your notebook will have four sections. The first section is called "Reading List."

Point to the section label on the large-print copy of the Reading List form you have prepared and posted on chart paper. (See the reproducible version in Appendix 13.)

This is a page on which you can keep a record of the books you have read.

Continue talking about and demonstrating how students will use their notebook. Here is a detailed description of a part of one teacher's minilesson:

TEACHER: Nicola, what book are you reading right now?

NICOLA: *The View from Saturday.*

TEACHER: On Nicola's reading list, when she starts to read a new book, she writes the number 1 for the first book she is reading. *[Writes 1 in the column on the chart.]* Under

"Title," she copies the title, explaining that she is putting capital letters where they belong. *[Copies the title.]* Nicola, who is the author of your book?

NICOLA: E. L. Konigsburg.

TEACHER: Nicola will write the author's name in the "Author" column, spelling it correctly because she is copying it from the book. The next column says "Genre." You have learned how to think about the genre, or type, of the book you are reading. Nicola, what is the genre of your book? Explain how you decided its type.

NICOLA: *The View from Saturday* is a fictional story that could take place today, so we would call it realistic fiction.

TEACHER: When Nicola finishes her book and is sure this is the genre, she will write RF for *realistic fiction* in the column labeled "Genre," and write the date she completed the book. *[Writes RF in the genre column.]* I'll write tomorrow's date just for this example. [Writes date.] In addition, Nicola will fill in the last column with an E, JR, or C to tell whether the book was easy, just right, or challenging for her. Nicola, since you have read most of your book already, can you tell us whether it is easy, just right, or challenging for you?

NICOLA: Just right.

TEACHER: So I'll write JR in the column to show it is a just-right book for her. Usually you will fill that in when you have completed reading the book. *[Summarizing.]* The directions for filling out your reading list are at the top of the page in your journal if you forget. Let me read them to you. *[Reads the three sentences at the top of the reading list.]* Today, list the number 1 and write the title and author of the book you are reading. Each time you start a new book you will list it. When you finish the book, fill in the genre, date, and difficulty level. If you have already finished some books this year, just fill in the information on the list and then write the one you are reading now. I'll put this chart on the wall with Nicola's book listed as an example of how to record your books on

your list. Remember, your journal will be a special book for you this year, and you will want to take very good care of it. Your name is on the front, and you will want to keep it in your book box so you can find it when you need it. When we gather for group share today, bring your reading journal so partners can check each other's reading list to be sure we've all started to use it correctly.

Day 10—Management Minilesson: Guidelines for Working Together

Note: You may want to teach the minilesson earlier, e.g. on Day 7. The reason we place it here is because now the students understand what each one means (except for writing).

As readers and writers we need to work together in our classroom, helping each other do our best learning. We have been talking about some of the ways we can help each other as readers and writers. On this chart are the ideas or guidelines for our workshop that we have already talked about and one that we will talk about soon.

You have already written the guidelines in large print on chart paper (see Figure 9–6) and glued them on the inside back cover of the reader's notebook.

Here is an excerpt from Michael's lesson on working together:

MICHAEL: Samantha, read our first guideline.

SAMANTHA *[reading]:* You must always be reading a book or writing your thoughts about your reading.

MICHAEL: You have been very good at focusing on your reading and soon you will learn how to write in your reader's notebook. Louis, read number 2.

LOUIS *[reading]:* You need to be working silently to enable you and your peers to do your best thinking.

MICHAEL: How well do you think we've been helping each other do our best thinking?

CLASS: Good. We're helping each other.

MICHAEL: I agree. We've all been able to do our best work. Number 3 says, "When conferring with the teacher, use a soft voice." This is another way we can help each other do our

Guidelines for Reading Workshop

1. You must always be reading a book or writing your thoughts about your reading.

2. You need to work silently to enable you and your peers to do your best thinking.

3. Use a soft voice when conferring with a teacher.

4. Select books you think you'll enjoy and abandon books that aren't working for you after you've given them a good chance.

5. List the book information when you begin and record the date when you finish.

6. Always do your best work.

Figure 9–6. Guidelines for Reading Workshop

best thinking. Marion, read number 4.

MARION [reading]: Select books you think you'll enjoy and abandon books that aren't working for you after you've given them a good chance.

MICHAEL: Yes, we all want to enjoy the books we are reading. Matthew, read number 5.

MATTHEW [reading]: List the book information when you begin and record the date when you finish.

MICHAEL: You have all learned how to record your information. And number 6 says, "Always do your best work." These guidelines are written on our chart, and they are also glued into the inside back cover of your notebook to remind you. If we all observe these guidelines, we can do our best work. Any questions? It's time to start reading.

Day 11—Strategies and Skills Minilesson: Writing Responses to Your Reading

Together we have shared our thinking by talking about books I have read aloud to you. You have been doing good thinking and talking about the books you have chosen to read. You have talked about your thinking with a partner and in groups. Now instead of only talking about your thinking, you're going to put your thinking on paper. When you write about your thinking, you can remember it and share it with others who read it.

In our class this year, you're going to share your thinking by writing your thoughts in a letter to me in your reader's notebooks. Each week you are going to write one letter to me, sharing what you are thinking about the book you are reading. I will read your letter and write a letter back to you. I have written a letter to you today to share my thinking about a book I'm reading.

Read the letter, which you have already written on chart paper. See the one in Figure 9–7 for an example, and adjust your own letter to the background and knowledge of your students.

What do you notice about the letter I wrote?

The following dialogue took place in Carol's classroom after she had shown her students the letter she had written:

JACKIE: You told how you were thinking of your family and other people.

MIKE: You told what you noticed about the way the author used words.

SARA: And you told about the kinds of books you like to read.

CAROL: That's a good description of my thinking. You described the content, the information about my thinking I gave my readers in my letter. Now let's talk about how the letter was written. What do you notice about its form?

NICOLA: You wrote the date in the upper right corner.

CAROL: Yes, so you will know when I wrote it. The month begins with a capital letter and is followed by a comma.

BRIANA: You wrote it like a letter, with "Dear Class," and signed your letter "Love, Ms. Won."

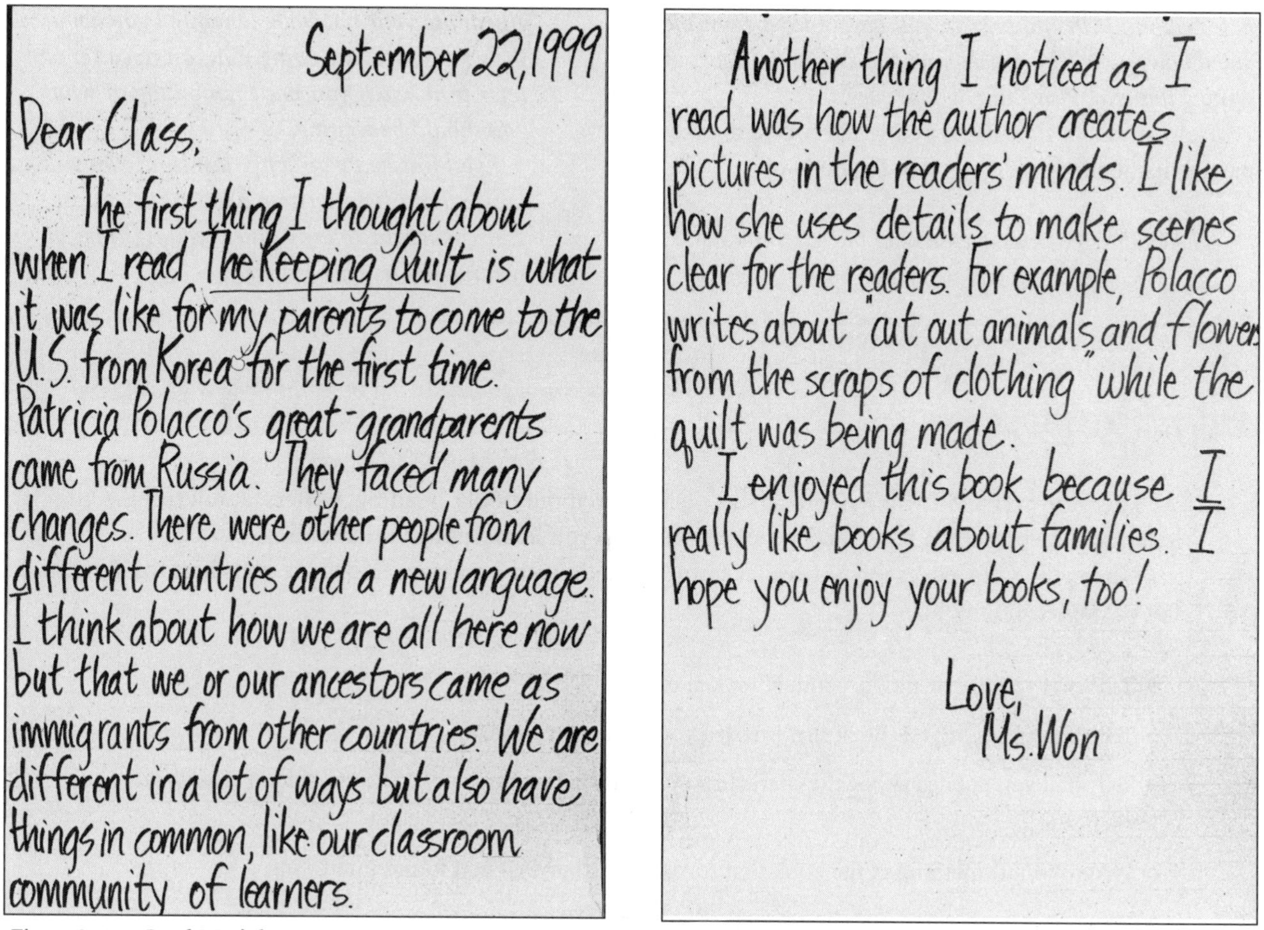

September 22, 1999

Dear Class,

The first thing I thought about when I read The Keeping Quilt is what it was like for my parents to come to the U.S. from Korea for the first time. Patricia Polacco's great-grandparents came from Russia. They faced many changes. There were other people from different countries and a new language. I think about how we are all here now but that we or our ancestors came as immigrants from other countries. We are different in a lot of ways but also have things in common, like our classroom community of learners.

Another thing I noticed as I read was how the author creates pictures in the readers' minds. I like how she uses details to make scenes clear for the readers. For example, Polacco writes about "cut out animals and flowers from the scraps of clothing" while the quilt was being made.

I enjoyed this book because I really like books about families. I hope you enjoy your books, too!

Love,
Ms. Won

Figure 9–7. Carol Won's letter

CAROL: Yes, you noticed the letter has an opening—a greeting to the person or persons receiving the letter—that starts on the left, begins with a capital letter, and is followed by a comma. You noticed the closing starts halfway across the page with a capital letter. It is also followed by a comma, and the name of the writer is directly below it. This is the conventional form of a personal letter. That means it's how readers will understand it is a friendly letter.

This is how you will write your letter each week—you will write your best thinking in the form of a personal letter. Our letters will be like a conversation between two readers. Any questions about the form? Okay, today I'd like each of you to return to your seat and write a letter about your thoughts on the book you are reading. Address it to me. Start your letter on the first clean page in your notebook section marked "Responses." *[Holds up a notebook.]* Today in group share, you will be sharing the letter you wrote about your book with a partner, and then I will read them and write a letter to you. Now go to your seats and begin your letter. You should try to finish it today. At the end of reading time, you'll put your notebook in the basket marked "Completed Letters."

Day 12—Management Minilesson: Writing Letters in Your Reader's Notebook Each Week

Please bring your reader's notebook to our group meeting. Yesterday we talked about how each week you will be writing a letter about the book you are reading or have just finished. I've asked [Name] and [Name] to read their letters to the group. [The students read their letters.] In your reader's notebook inside the front cover, you have a letter from me about how you will be sharing your thinking about books in writing this year. Please turn to that page.

Help students find the typed letter you've already pasted inside the front cover (see Figure 9–8).

TEACHER: *[Name], please read the letter aloud.*
[The student reads the letter.] *This letter is*

glued into your notebook to remind you about the writing you are doing. You can reread it or refer to it when you need reminding of what you should be writing.

If you finished your letter last time, you will notice that I have written a letter back to you. You can begin today's quiet reading time by reading my letter. Next week, when you write

---

Date

Dear _____,

This year, you and I will write letters to each other about books, reading, writers, and writing. Our letters will help us learn together. The letters will help you learn more about reading.

When you write letters in your reader's notebook, do your best work and share your best thinking. For example, you might:

❖ Tell what you like or dislike about a book and why.

❖ Tell about parts of your book that puzzled you or made you ask questions.

❖ Tell what you noticed about the characters, such as what made them act as they did or how they changed.

❖ Write about something in the book that surprised you or that you found interesting.

❖ Write your predictions and about whether your predictions were right.

❖ Ask for help in figuring out the meaning of your book.

❖ Tell about the connections that you made while reading the book. Tell how it reminds you of yourself, of people you know, or of something that happened in your life. It might remind you of other books, especially the characters, the events, or the setting.

❖ Write about the author's style and how it makes you feel.

❖ Write about the language the author used and why you think the author wrote this way.

❖ Write about the author's craft—what was effective about the way the author wrote.

Write a letter to me once each week. The completed letter is due on the day indicated on the notebook list. Use a letter form and include the title and author of your book. It is important that your letters are neat and easy to read so I can understand what you are thinking. Read through your letter to make sure that it says all you want it to say before you place it in the basket.

When I read your notebook, I will learn from you, and we will learn together about books. What fun we will have getting to know each other and books!

Eager to read your letter,

Figure 9–8. Example of a Letter

to me, you will want to review the letter to be sure you respond to what I wrote. If you did not finish your letter yesterday, you will need to do that first today and put your notebook in the "Completed Letters" basket.

This time you all wrote your letters on the same day so you could learn how to do it. From now on, you will have one week to finish your letter, and you can choose the day you want to write it. You will have an assigned day that your letter must be finished and put in the "Completed Letters" basket. Look at this chart to see what day your finished letter is due.

Review the chart called "Letters Due" with students (see Figure 9–9).

This means that on Monday, some of you need to turn in finished letters; Tuesday, some others; Wednesday, the next group of names; and Thursday, the last group. This will help me read some of your notebooks each day and do my best to get them back to you the next day. You will have five school days to write your letter, but on the day it is due you'll know it must be completed and put in the basket. It is important that you make sure to start your letter by the day before it is due. That means that Monday people need to be sure to start a letter on Friday and Tuesday people need to start by Monday. Now it's time for reading.

Initially, on the day before a group of letters is due, remind those students that they'll need to write their letters that day if they haven't done it on their own yet. For example, on Tuesday, speak with the students whose letters are due on Wednesday so they can finish them in class. As students become more familiar with the process, they should not need reminders.

Day 13—Strategies and Skills Minilesson: Proofreading Your Letter

Your letters to me have been very interesting. I am enjoying our written conversations about the books you are reading. You are asking good questions, sharing what surprises you, and writing about how your book reminds you of something in your life or of other books. Today we're going to talk briefly about how you read over—or proofread—your letter to be sure it is your best work. To make sure your letter is your best work, what are a few things you need to check for? I'll write them on this chart.

Write the students' responses on a chart headed "Proofreading Your Letter" (see Figure 9–10).

Here is one class's conversation about proofreading:

TEACHER: It will be important to begin by rereading your letter to be sure it will make sense to the reader and that you have responded to what I wrote.

TESSA: Be sure you write the date.

IVAN: Be sure you can read it.

TEACHER: Yes, you need to be sure your reader can easily read your handwriting. You can choose to print or write in cursive, but be sure your writing is very clear and well formed. Anything else?

DIANE: Check for the opening and closing, and be sure they start with capitals.

SARAH: Do your best spelling and check punctuation.

TEACHER: Yes, that's important, too. Layla, please read all the reminders we have on our chart.

[*Layla reads them*] Today, begin by proofreading your last letter;

Letters Due			
MONDAY	TUESDAY	WEDNESDAY	THURSDAY
Maia	Ronny	Jennifer	John
Peter	Edward	Lara	Natalie
Lorinda	Erica	Pedro	José
Sam	Manessa	Ramir	Miguel
Gabriel	Rahim	Robert	Vladmir
Elijah	Jenny	Michael	Marinda
		Tessie	

Figure 9–9. "Letters Due" Chart

check for all the points we talked about. Every time you write a new letter you need to refer to the proofreading chart and check to be sure you have done your best work before placing your notebook in the basket.

Day 14—Strategies and Skills Minilesson: Topics for Your Reading Journal

Your writing is your thinking. In your letters to me, you have been telling about your thinking. Today we are going to make a list of all the different kinds of writing about books you have done and can tell about in your notebook letters. What are some of the topics you can write about in your notebook? I'll write them on this chart.

Create a chart similar to the one shown in Figure 9–11.

This is a very good list. I'm sure we will have many more to add as we continue to write about books we are reading. Let's place our list on the wall and you can suggest others to add as you think of them. If you are having difficulty thinking about what you want to share in your letter, this list may help you. We'll see if you have any more today at our group share. It's time to get started with your reading.

Proofreading Your Letter
1. Reread your letter to be sure it makes sense.
2. Be sure you have responded to what the teacher or a peer wrote to you
3. Write the date.
4. Check the opening and closing.
5. Check your spelling, capitalization, and punctuation.

Figure 9–10. Proofreading your Notebook

Day 15—Management Minilesson: Using Stick-on Notes to Prepare for Letter Writing

We have been talking about all the different ways we think about what we are reading and how we share our thinking in our notebooks. As you read this week, stop one or two times to make some quick notes about your thinking on stick-on notes, and place them on the pages in your book that prompted you to have these thoughts. When you are ready to write your letter, you can use your notes about the marked places to help you remember the parts you want to write about. When I confer with you, you can share some of the places you marked and explain why you chose them. This may help you write letters that show lots of good thinking about your reading.

Caution: You will not want to overdo the use of stick-on notes because it will interrupt the reading process. (See Chapter 4.) Some children will not need the support of stick-on notes.

Day 16—Management Minilesson: Creating a List of Your Reading Interests

Please bring your reader's notebook to the group meeting today. An important part of being a reader is finding books you really enjoy. In your reader's notebook is a section called "Reading Interests." This is a place for you to make lists of topics, genres, authors, and titles that you want to read. Let's look at this chart, which is like the page in your notebook.

Point to the large version of the "Reading Interests" form that you have posted on a chart. (See Appendix 14 for reproducible version.)

In the first part you can keep a list of topics or subjects you want to read about such as basketball, space, the Holocaust, or camping. [Write these topics in column one.] In column two, you can list genres or types of books you are interested in. What genres interest you?

Here is an excerpt from the lesson:

GARY: I'm interested in science fiction.
TEACHER: I list science fiction in the genre section. *[Writes it on the chart.]* Talk with your partner about authors you want to read. *[Students share with each other.]* Now let's list some of the authors that you shared. I'll write them on the chart in the third section.

156

Topics for Your Reader's Notebook
- What the book is about
- How the book reminds you of another book
- How the book makes you feel
- How the author describes things
- Whether you like the book or not and why
- Why you think the author wrote the book
- Why you chose the book
- How you feel about the author's writing
- Whether or not you would recommend the book to another reader
- Why you abandoned a book
- What you predict will happen
- What you would change about the book
- Examples of stereotype or bias
- What you found interesting
- What you are wondering about
- Whether the book is easy, just right, or challenging and how you can tell
- About the genre
- What you think is the author's message
- What books you look forward to reading
- What you don't understand or questions you have
- How you feel about a character
- What you notice about the author's style/language
- Something about the author and what it has to do with the story
- What was funny to you
- What you like/dislike about the setting
- How the setting affects the characters
- About good word choices/special language
- What you think about the author's lead
- How the author captured your interest

Figure 9–11. *Things You Can Write About in Your Reader's Notebook*

CAROLYN: Avi.

PAUL: Paulsen.

[Teacher writes author names on the chart.]

TEACHER: The last section of the page is for listing titles you want to read. You might list titles from our book talks or titles recommended by friends. What is a title you are interested in reading?

ROYI: *Winter Room.*

MARA: *Shiloh.*

TEACHER: If it is a title you want to read, write the title, author if you know it. *[Lists* Winter Room *and* Shiloh.*]* After you read the book, you can place a checkmark next to it.

Today when you return to your seat, write at least one item on each list to get you started on collecting information on books you want to read. When we share later, you will quickly tell about some of the items you put on your list today.

Day 17—Management Minilesson: How to Write Book Recommendations

One way readers find good books to read is by listening to the recommendations of others. See the revolving rack over there? That's where we'll display the books that we believe are so good we don't want our classmates to miss them! We'll call these books "Must-Reads."

If you read a book that you believe should be on the Must-Read rack, take one of these index cards and note the following information.

Write a book recommendation on a book you have

shared as a class to create a clear example together. Then review with students the guidelines on the chart headed "Book Recommendations" (see Figure 9–12).

Your recommendations should sound like a short commercial telling the good things about the book. Let's look at a couple of Must-Read recommendations written by others.

Project a transparency of a book recommendation such as Figure 9–13.

[Name], please read this recommendation aloud.

After the student reads the example out loud, discuss with the class how the person making the recommendation gave just enough information to entice other readers. Discuss the strengths and weaknesses. Then share a second recommendation (see Figure 9–14).

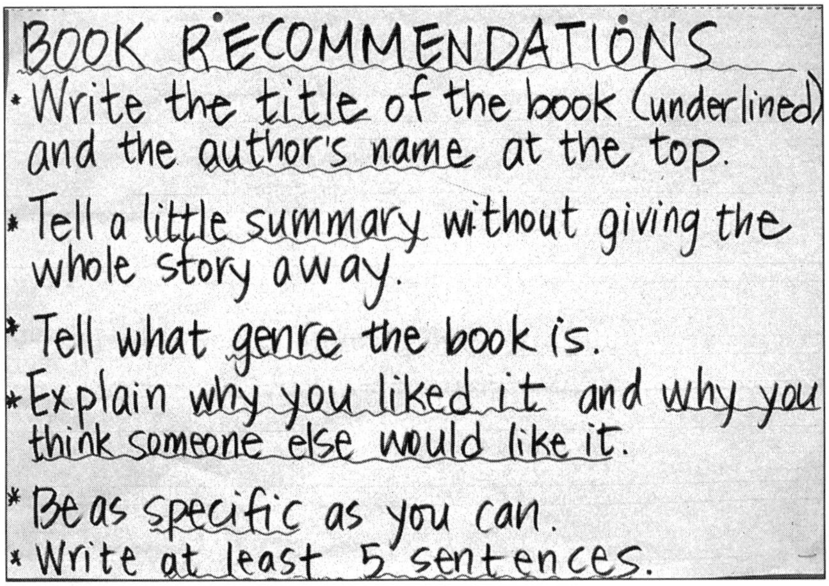

BOOK RECOMMENDATIONS

* Write the title of the book (underlined) and the author's name at the top.
* Tell a little summary without giving the whole story away.
* Tell what genre the book is.
* Explain why you liked it and why you think someone else would like it.
* Be as specific as you can.
* Write at least 5 sentences.

Figure 9–12. Book Recommendations

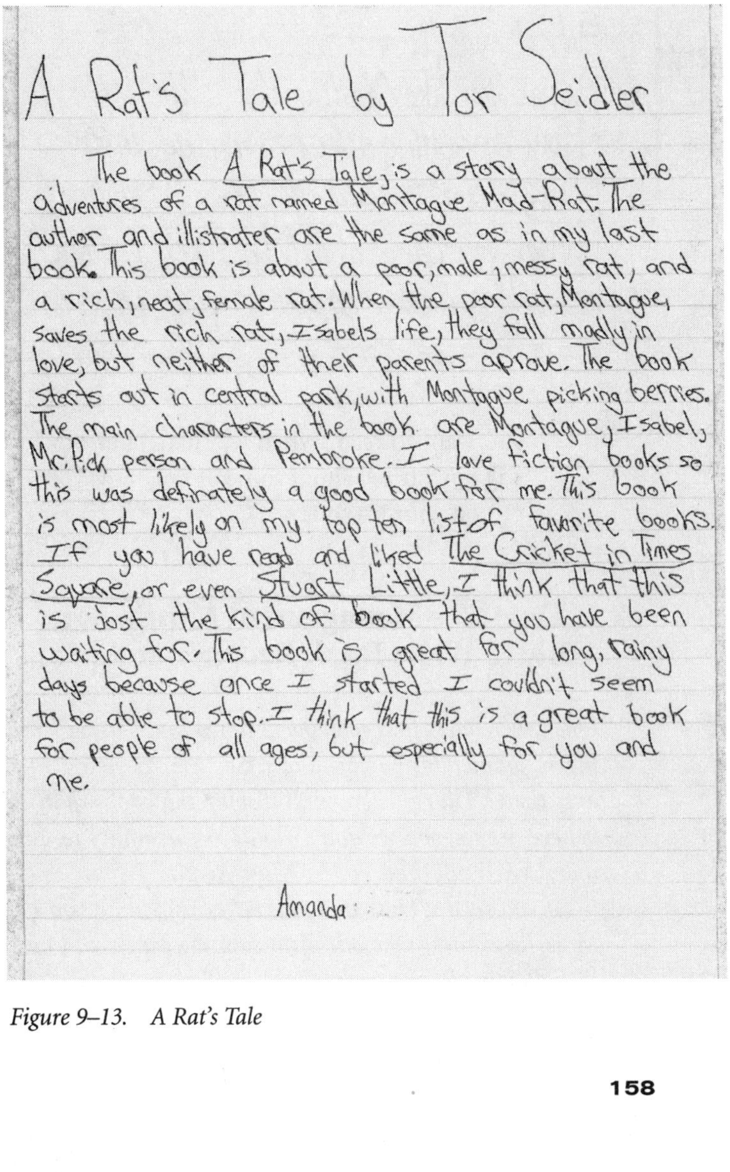

A Rat's Tale by Tor Seidler

The book A Rat's Tale, is a story about the adventures of a rat named Montague Mad-Rat. The author and illistrater are the same as in my last book. This book is about a poor, male, messy rat, and a rich, neat, female rat. When the poor rat, Montague, saves the rich rat, Isabels life, they fall madly in love, but neither of their parents aprove. The book starts out in central park, with Montague picking berries. The main characters in the book are Montague, Isabel, Mr. Rich person and Pembroke. I love fiction books so this was definately a good book for me. This book is most likely on my top ten list of favorite books. If you have read and liked The Cricket in Times Square, or even Stuart Little, I think that this is just the kind of book that you have been waiting for. This book is great for long, rainy days because once I started I couldn't seem to be able to stop. I think that this is a great book for people of all ages, but especially for you and me.

Amanda

Figure 9–13. A Rat's Tale

[Name], please read the recommendation for The Wainscott Weasel *aloud.*

Discuss with students the features of the recommendations and refer to the Book Recommendations chart.

Today, I'd like each of you to think of one of the best books you've ever read. Write a book recommendation on a white index card following the directions on our chart. Bring your recommendation to the group share. Use the same proofreading list you use to check your notebook entries to be sure it's your best work.

Whenever you find a book that you would recommend to others in the class, take an index card, write your recommendation, and clip it to the inside cover of the book. Then put it on the revolving rack. The rack will be a good place for us all to look for books that our friends and teachers have recommended.

You might also invite the student teacher, custodian, cafeteria personnel, and librarian to make book recommendations of titles they enjoyed as elementary students.

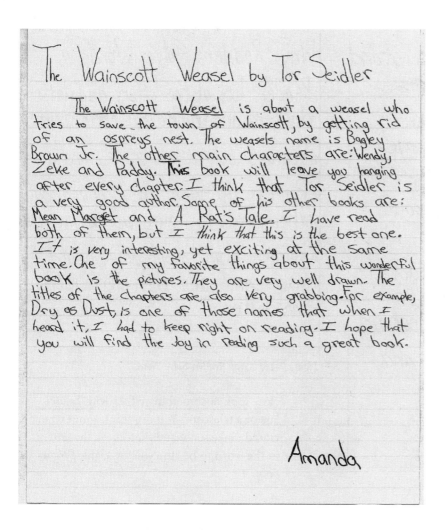

The Wainscott Weasel by Tor Seidler

The Wainscott Weasel is about a weasel who tries to save the town of Wainscott, by getting rid of an ospreys nest. The weasels name is Bagley Brown Jr. The other main characters are: Wendy, Zeke and Paddy. This book will leave you hanging after every chapter. I think that Tor Seidler is a very good author. Some of his other books are: Mean Margret and A Rat's Tale. I have read both of them, but I think that this is the best one. It is very interesting, yet exciting at the same time. One of my favorite things about this wonderful book is the pictures. They are very well drawn. The titles of the chapters are also very grabbing. For example, Dry as Dust, is one of those names that when I heard it, I had to keep right on reading. I hope that you will find the Joy in reading such a great book.

Amanda

Figure 9–14. The Wainscott Weasel

Sometimes you stop and think about what you know so far and that helps. You might think about what you already know about where the story takes place or the time in history. Or you might think about what you know from other books by the same author.

LINDA: I go back and read the paragraph again.

TEACHER: If you have tried all of these ways of figuring out the meaning and you still don't understand it, you can ask for help in our reading conference or when we are meeting in groups. You can also ask for help in your letter to me in your notebook. This chart will remind you that you need to notice when something doesn't make sense and that good readers have lots of ways to solve the problem.

Day 18—Strategies and Skills Minilesson: Checking for Understanding as You Read

When readers read, they notice when something doesn't make sense and they take some action to resolve the problem.

When you are reading your book and something doesn't make sense, what do you do? I'll write your ideas on this chart.

Write student responses on a chart like the one shown in Figure 9–15.

Here is one group's discussion on this topic:

GARY: I stop and think about it.

ANNE: I keep on reading and figure it out.

TEACHER: *[Writes these ideas on the chart.]*

Review the chart with your students.

Day 19—Strategies and Skills Minilesson: Solving Unknown Words

When readers come to words they don't know, they have lots of ways to figure them out. You know some ways to figure out words. Let's list them.

Create a list with your students like the one shown in Figure 9–16, which was based on the following dialogue:

KARA: I sound it out.

BRIAN: The letters and sounds go together in a word and you can tell what it is.

TEACHER: Yes, readers think about the sounds that go with the letters and sometimes the clusters of letters like *br* or *sh*. *[Writes point 1 on the chart.]* Sometimes you take a word

How to Be Sure You Understand the Author's Message

Readers notice when something doesn't make sense. They have different ways to solve the problem.

1. Readers stop and think about what they know.

2. Readers go back and reread the sentence or the paragraph to clarify the author's meaning.

3. Readers continue reading and look for more information.

4. Readers ask for help with understanding.

Figure 9–15.   How to Be Sure You Understand
             the Author's Message

Ways Readers Solve Words

1. Readers look at the letters and letter clusters and think about their sounds.

2. Readers look at parts of words.

3. Readers use what they know about other words to figure out new words.

4. Readers think about what would make sense and then check with the letters.

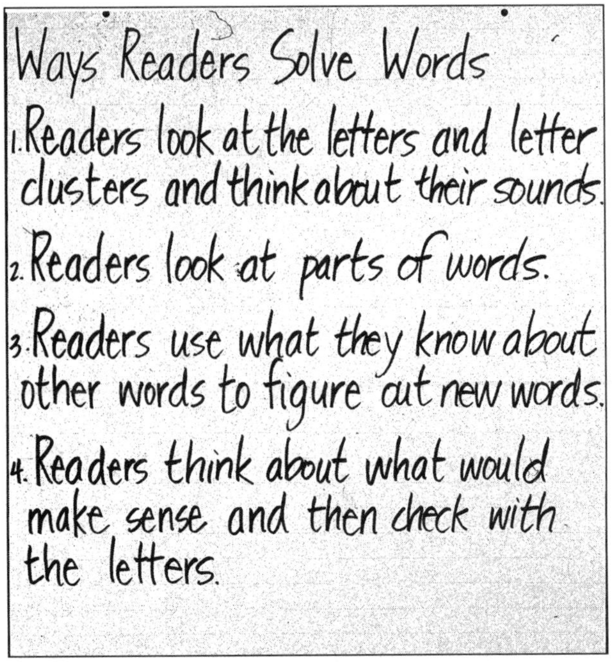

Figure 9–16.   Way Readers Solve Words

close look at something either with binoculars or a telescope. You can think about what would make sense and then check the letters in the word to be sure you are right. *[Writes point 4.]*

Day 20—Strategies and Skills Minilesson: Using Punctuation to Help You Understand

Readers use the punctuation to understand the author's message. When you read, the punctuation marks help you in lots of ways.

The following dialogue is one class's conversation about punctuation:

TEACHER: For example, the period lets you know when one thought ends. What does your voice do when you reach a period?

MARY: It goes down.

TEACHER: Yes, your voice drops. What do you do when you see a comma?

MARY: You pause a little.

TEACHER: So marks like that help us sound good when we read aloud, and we are thinking about them when we read silently. They

apart, noticing the parts. For example, if you are trying to figure out the word *candle,* you might divide it into *can,* which you know. You'd also know the *dle* ending and that would help you solve the word. How can we write that here?

TARA: Readers look at parts.

TEACHER: *[Writes point 2.]* You also use what you know about other words to figure out new words. For example, Brian was trying to figure out the word *telescope* when he was reading *Arthur Rocks with Binky* [Brown 1998]. He noticed that the first part of the word was like *tell* and like *telephone.* Then he thought about the letters and sounds and quickly solved the rest of the word. *[Writes point 3 on the chart.]*

KARA: I think about what would make sense.

TEACHER: Yes, Brian knew *telescope* would make sense because they were trying to get a

remind us to pause a little. Look at this paragraph. *[Points to the paragraph in Figure 9–17 from* Russell Sprouts, *which she has rewritten on a chart.]* Mary, read the second sentence that begins with *But.*

MARY *[reading]*: But instead, Mr. Michaels said the bad word.

TEACHER: Listen to the way Mary took a short breath after the word *instead.* That helped us understand the sentence. We've talked about quotation marks, or talking marks. They help us know when the characters are talking. Can you find a place in this paragraph where someone is talking?

KEN: Yes, Mr. Michaels is talking. He says, "Schmatz!"

TEACHER: You notice that in this sentence there are talking marks before and after the word *Schmatz,* showing us that this is what the character says. Did you notice how Ken read *Schmatz?*

DINA: He was excited.

Teacher: Ken, how did you know to read it that way?

KEN: Because there's an exclamation point.

TEACHER: You're right. Exclamation points also help us understand the author's meaning. He wanted Mr. Michaels to sound irritated because Russell had soaked his pants leg. What Mr. Michaels said is inside the quotation—or talking—marks. It has its own ending punctuation, the exclamation point. What characters say is usually set off by quotation marks and has its own ending punctuation. Let's read this paragraph out loud together and observe all the punctuation. *[The students do so.]* Remember to notice and think about the punctuation while you read because it will help you understand what the author is trying to say. Have a paragraph from the book you are reading ready to share with a partner during group share later. You will read your paragraph to each other, observing the punctuation marks.

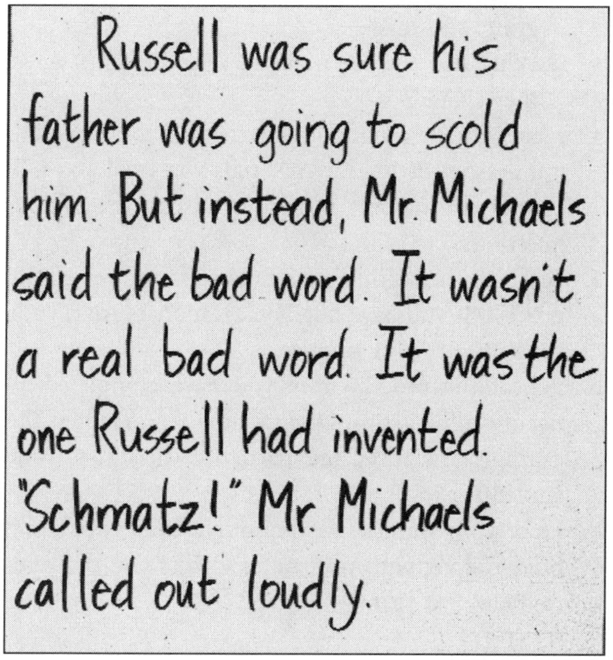

Implementing Independent Reading: The First Twenty Days

We have described one way of getting started with minilessons for independent reading and provided examples to show you how you might begin. Of course, the examples will not fit your students perfectly, and you may want to vary the sequence and/or the lessons. The important thing is to meet the unique needs of your own students.

Fine-Tuning Lessons for Your Students

You will want to think about what your students already know. Take your cues from your particular students and prioritize the kinds of lessons they need. Some of these lessons may be too simple for your students; on the other hand, you may need to repeat others. Many of them you will revisit several times across the year, such as topics for letters in notebooks. Some may be very effective with most of the students, but a small group may need reteaching in a guided reading or literature study group. Individuals may need reteaching or reinforcement in a conference setting.

Resources You Will Need

Consider the resources you will need (see the far right column of Figure 9–1). In general, the materials and

Russell was sure his father was going to scold him. But instead, Mr. Michaels said the bad word. It wasn't a real bad word. It was the one Russell had invented. "Schmatz!" Mr. Michaels called out loudly.

Figure 9–17. Russell Sprouts

resources needed for independent reading are simple and easy to use. For example, a list of all the books you have read aloud together as a class will help you create minilessons on book genres. In fact, the shared experiences with books and reading may lie at the heart of many of the minilessons you provide.

You will need to have a highly organized and well labeled classroom collection of books that matches your students' reading levels. See Chapter 23 for suggestions on acquiring books and Chapter 6 for suggestions on organizing them. Charts and notebooks are also must-have materials. See Chapter 10 for detailed descriptions of reader's notebooks and Appendix 16 for notebook page reproducibles. The notebooks will enable your students to reflect day by day on a quality body of work. What's more, the notebooks provide you and your students' families with visible evidence of their progress as well as insights into the breadth of their reading and the ways in which their interests change.

Early Minilessons as a Foundation

The minilessons we've featured are designed to establish independent reading as a quiet, structured, productive time in your classroom. While the first lessons focus mainly on routines, students are also reading a great deal and, in the process, becoming more aware of the essential elements of their reading. This system helps readers assume responsibility for their own learning. Everything they do in independent reading, even if it is a routine procedure, highlights aspects of reading that will support them as lifelong readers. For example, as they write their lists of reading interests, they learn that the book choices they make are not random but are governed by their unique interests. As readers, they learn to monitor their interests over time and note how they change. Accordingly, when we offer them a chance to select a book, we expect they'll choose a book that matches their interests.

Reading a book is not simply a task to get through; reading means thinking about and reveling in what you read. Thinking includes awareness of yourself as a reader so that you become the director and manager of your learning. This move toward independence is crit-

ical for intermediate students as, increasingly, they need to work as self-managed learners who can use literacy as a tool, fully realizing its rewards—both utilitarian and aesthetic.

Suggestions for Professional Development

1. Over the course of these twenty days, meet frequently with your grade-level colleagues to support one another in launching your workshops.
2. Follow a reflective process of implementing minilessons, gathering information about their effectiveness, and discussing them with colleagues.
3. Try out the first few minilessons. After each minilesson, make notes using these guiding questions:
   - What went well?
   - Were there any surprises?
   - What would you have done differently?
   - Would you have changed any of your language to be more clear?
   - How effectively did students follow up the minilesson by engaging in the behavior you wanted?
   - How effective was your chart? Did you refer to it again during the day or on subsequent days?
   - Were there opportunities to reinforce the points made in the minilessons or in conferences? in group sessions?
   - What did you learn about your students when they shared?
4. Meet with your grade-level colleagues to discuss the minilessons. Bring the materials you used and talk about your students' responses. Discuss the guiding questions.
5. Teach the next group of minilessons and repeat the process. If you have notebook responses from your students, bring in samples.
6. Repeat the process until you have completed all twenty minilessons. Discuss how you adapted the examples to meet the particular needs of your students.
7. Place your minilessons in your reading workshop binder along with your notes so that you can refer to them next year.

## CHAPTER TEN

WRITING TO EXPLORE MEANING: READER'S NOTEBOOK

The more passion you have about something, the more likely it will translate into a passion in the student. Everyone develops a passion because someone shared a passion when that person was young.

—KATHERINE PATERSON

The goal of all reading is the construction of meaning. Scholars who have examined reading in depth maintain that meaning is tied to the reader's personal response to the text. In Chapter 18, we describe how the reader accesses three primary funds of knowledge: personal, world, and literary. While a writer creates a text with a particular meaning in mind, the meaning that readers derive is highly influenced by their funds of knowledge. No two individuals are exactly alike; we all create our own interpretations of texts, our own images, and our own subtle meanings. In general, it's a fallacy to believe that we can uncover one correct meaning of a text. On the other hand, readers can share their unique, personal meanings through conversations "reader to reader" about a text.

Clearly, readers actively *respond* as they read. *Response* refers to the thinking that individuals do as they approach a text, while they are reading it, and after they have finished. It includes their feelings, their emotions, their memories, and the connections they make to their funds of knowledge. As readers, sometimes we remember characters in books as if they were childhood friends or people we actually knew.

Writing letters in a reader's notebook is one way to increase the depth of reader response. Practical and easy to use, they build students' awareness of reading's many dimensions. Notebooks are also a way for teachers systematically to assess students' responses to the texts they are reading independently. Although we briefly explore response theory here, we revisit it in greater depth in Chapter 18.

Response Theory

Rosenblatt's (1938, 1978, 1983) theory of reading response has widely influenced educators' thinking about the reading process. Rosenblatt sees reading as a *transaction* between the reader and the text. The text conveys meaning as expressed by the author, but during reading the author's meaning connects or *transacts* with the reader's. According to Rosenblatt, the *stance* we take toward the text—our purpose for reading—influences how we focus our attention. For example, we might read a text primarily to gain information; Rosenblatt calls this an *efferent* stance. Picture examining a text for information; our attention is directed in specific ways and our goal is to increase our knowledge.

On the other hand, consider those books we read for pleasure. When we "live through a book" we take an *aesthetic* stance. We "get lost" in the book as we enjoy its language, picture the faraway places vividly described, share the feelings of the characters, experience suspense, even visualize ourselves as part of the story. In this case, our attention is directed toward the more personal aspects of the text—the associations, feelings, and ideas aroused in our own head. The notebook entry in Figure 10–1 illustrates an aesthetic response to a text. Notice how Erica shares her feelings about what happened in the text and how her teacher supports it.

Any text can be read with an efferent or aesthetic stance or some combination of the two, but with a given text, readers tend toward one end of the continuum or the other. Your goal in reading workshop—through independent reading, guided reading, and

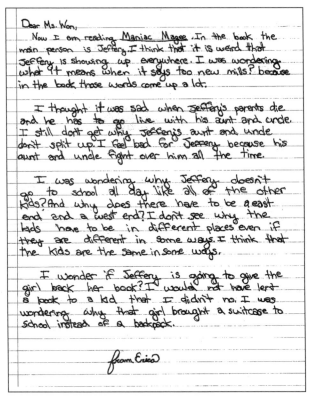

Figure 10–1. Example from a Reader's Notebook of an Aesthetic Response to a Text and Teacher Reply

literature study—is to foster students' responses to reading so they are active constructors of their own meaning and vary their styles and stances according to purpose. You will find evidence of their response to reading in their talk, in their writing, and in various forms of artistic expression such as drawing, painting, and drama.

As you work with student reader's notebooks, keep in mind these key principles:

- A response to reading is not a test of knowledge; rather, it is a thoughtful, critical reflection on a text.
- Readers read from the unique perspective of their own experience, drawing from their personal, world, and literary funds of knowledge. Therefore, different readers approach and read the same text differently.
- For any given text, no single meaning exists.
- Readers may vary their stance toward a text as they read.
- Students' responses provide you with a window on the thinking they did as they read.

- As students share their responses with others, they deepen their understanding.
- When readers talk about their responses, they expand their reading power.

Talking About Reading

The reader's first response is "in the head," but talking enables the reader to put thoughts into words. When we value our students' oral responses to reading, they become more conscious of their own thinking as meaningful and important. Talk invites students to think about their learning. Students develop a deeper understanding of meaning because they are contributing to one another's understanding. Through talk, they learn to:

- Interpret a text, recognizing that there is no one right way.

- Support their thinking about texts.
- Express their thinking so that they—and their peers—can consider their ideas.
- Reflect on their own reading.

Talking about reading is an invaluable exercise. Chances are you develop your own response to reading through your conversations with others. You may talk about novels you have read and discuss daily newspaper and journal articles. Even when you discuss a TV newscast or a sitcom, you are responding to written language you have heard read aloud by a news reporter or dramatized by actors. We talk with each other to sort out what we don't understand, to get more information, to gather different perspectives, or to express emotions. Talk expands our understanding and helps us clarify our own feelings; it is a tool for learning.

As a teacher, you will want to be sure that students have many opportunities to talk about their reading before they attempt to put their thoughts in writing. Their talk about reading reflects their thinking about their reading. You will plan lessons to help students learn to talk about their reading as a first step toward writing meaningful responses.

Sketching or Drawing About Reading

Readers can also share their thinking about reading through the images they construct. Giving students opportunities to draw or sketch in response to the texts they read may lead to fresh insights and deeper connections. In her work with adolescents, Rief found "Those students who normally do not experience success through the written word often meet their goals through spoken or visual representations of all they know and think." She advocates letting students observe and view, interpret and represent their work with more than words (Rief 1999).

Writing About Reading

Traditionally, teachers have assigned book reports as a way to encourage a response to reading. Often students regard book reports as a task by which they are to *prove* they have read a book. It's no surprise, then, that book reports have become ends in themselves and that many of them are full of tortuous details with little personal response to or interpretation of the text. And it's quite possible for students to produce an adequate book

report after reading only part of the book or none of it. Thus, the book report doesn't necessarily help students become better readers.

We view writing about reading as a tool for reflection and as a way to share and explain one's personal reactions, questions, and interpretations of texts. The writing may range from very brief notes to longer, more polished essays. When students write entries in their notebooks, they may give a brief summary; nonetheless, the goal is not to summarize or retell the story in order to prove they've read it but to uncover the meaning of the text and their response to that meaning.

There are many different ways for students to write about their reading, including:

- A comment on stick-on notes.
- A paragraph or page of written reflection.
- A letter to the teacher.
- A letter or an e-mail to another person.
- A web, chart, or list.

Over time, as students record their thoughts, questions, and reflections in a reader's notebook, they learn more about what readers do when they actively respond to a text. The whole process is surrounded by meaningful talk. The writing emerges from discussions, and students often use their reader's notebook entries as a springboard for discussion.

Response as Inquiry

While we create unique meanings that stem from our individual experiences, we also possess *socially shared* meanings, born of common experiences and communications with others. These socially shared meanings are important in every individual's learning. Human beings learn through inquiry and investigation. We actively seek answers to questions and revise our current knowledge. Inquiry arises from and contributes to the socially shared meanings that exist within any group (Vygotsky 1986; Bakhtin 1981). New learning rests on the combination of individual and shared meanings. Many instructional contexts within the language arts framework promote interaction and the construction of shared meanings. Reader's notebooks are one opportunity for you and your students to engage in inquiry through dialogue.

Lindfors (1999) has described two different approaches to inquiry: (1) *information seeking,* which means clarifying, explaining, or confirming; and (2) *wondering,* which means reflecting, exploring, or considering possibilities. As students write in their notebooks and you respond, you can demonstrate both forms of inquiry. The emphasis here, however, is on wondering. As a teacher, you can demonstrate the process of inquiry and help students consistently expand their curiosity and reflective powers.

Below are some excerpts from Emily's letters and corresponding responses from Carol Won, her teacher. Notice how Emily's thinking evolves and how Carol supports her in the process of wondering. (Emily's spelling and punctuation are largely conventional, but she does make some errors. We have standardized all spelling and punctuation.)

9/29

Dear Ms. Won,

I just started reading *The Helen Keller Story,* by Catherine Owen Peare. In Helen's second winter she gets a horrible fever and she becomes blind and deaf. And because she is so young, she couldn't speak either. Soon she becomes out of control. They go to Boston, then Washington, DC. They get in touch with Mr. Anagnos and eventually he sends them a twenty-year-old Anne Sullivan.

I think it is so, so, so horrible about what happened to Helen. Helen is extremely lucky that she is getting her wish. She is learning how to talk! I think her mom and dad shouldn't have given in every time she did something. She is getting spoiled. She is lucky she has a great teacher who helps her learn.

From Emily

9/30

Dear Emily,

I agree with you that it's horrible what happened to Helen Keller when she was so young. It is hard to imagine something like that when you haven't gone through it yourself. I imagine also how difficult it must have been for her parents. Why do you think they tended to

spoil her so much? There must have been so much to think about and so many decisions to make.

I also agree that she was very fortunate to get all that support in order to learn. It makes me think of people who don't have that kind of support for whatever reason—maybe they cannot find it. I think you are right to make this observation that she was fortunate and we shouldn't take this for granted.

Love, Ms. Won

In the first paragraph, Emily gives a brief synopsis of the book; in the second paragraph she expresses her own feelings and offers opinions. She comments on characters' actions and draws conclusions. Carol responds by recognizing Emily's feelings and by empathizing with the characters herself. She prompts Emily to interpret the characters' actions instead of merely judging them. Carol also raises a larger issue by connecting Helen's story to a contemporary issue. She provides a model for "wondering" about situations *like* Helen's.

10/24

Dear Ms. Won,

I am reading another Helen Keller story, by Lorena A. Hickok. I think the interesting thing about people who write about the same subject is that they are unique. They are all the same in a way but sometimes they don't start in the same place or end in the same place. But they usually have the same middle. (At least that's what I found in this book.)

I can't really tell a big summary because it is closely related to the other Helen Keller book I read. But I can tell that everyone who writes about Helen Keller is trying to say that Helen Keller is a remarkable person and tried to do anything she could to try to help people who were just like her and try to make them feel better. But she didn't start out that way. If Anne Sullivan wasn't there to help there would be a big problem, because the parents weren't great role models to her because mostly all that they did was spoil her and let her do whatever she wanted and someone had to stop her somehow or she would be taking things from other peoples' plates. And she just would be doing a lot of things she shouldn't have been doing. But Anne Sullivan made it clear that you can't do that!

From Emily

10/24

Dear Emily,

I think it's interesting what you wrote about how authors can be writing about the same subject (like a person's life) but it seems different because of where they end and start their stories. I hadn't thought of it that way, but I think you're right.

So what you're learning from reading these Helen Keller books is that she was remarkable and wanted to help others? What lesson do you learn from this? Why do you think biographies are written about certain people?

I agree that Anne Sullivan played an important role in Helen's life. What do you think would have happened if Anne hadn't been a part of Helen's life?

Love, Ms. Won

Emily's 10/24 entry shows her ability to connect and compare texts, which Carol encourages in her response. Emily is noticing aspects of the writer's craft through her comparisons. She also recognizes that her audience doesn't need details from the story; is more inclined to make conclusions about Helen's life; and infers that Anne's role was critical to Helen's success. Carol invites Emily to take her thinking to a higher level by considering what can be learned from studying lives like Helen Keller's. She helps Emily get to the real-life issues and also to think about aspects of the genre of biography.

11/8

Dear Ms. Won,

I am not sure what would have happened if Anne Sullivan wasn't a part of Helen's life. But I know this story wouldn't be the way it is, because Anne Sullivan is the big role model of all of Helen Keller's life. Without her, Helen Keller wouldn't have learned all the wonderful things she did! I also think the reason they write about special people in biographies is because Helen Keller learned how to talk and Lorena A.

Hickok just wanted people to know that it is possible to talk when you are deaf and blind.

Love, Emily

11/8

Dear Emily,

Why would Lorena A. Hickok just want people to know that it's possible to talk when you are deaf and blind?? What's the bigger picture here, Emily?

Love, Ms. Won

11/15

Dear Ms. Won,

I think the bigger picture is that everyone can learn no matter what disabilities you have. We can all learn but in different ways. Other people write biographies so that you can know about other people's lives and what they accomplished.

I am reading *Danny, the Champion of the World,* by Roald Dahl. Mr. Canner read most of it to us last year for read-aloud, but he never finished it; I want to know what is going to happen past the point he read last year. Danny is the main character in the story. He is very brave. He knows how to drive a little bit and is very smart. After Danny's father goes poaching he falls into a pit. He doesn't know what to do because he was supposed to come home 4! hours ago. Danny *drives* the baby Austin [the car] to Hazell's wood to get his father. Is the rope going to get him out before sunrise and before the keepers come?

Sincerely, Emily
P.S. Why do authors write only about specifics?

11/16

Dear Emily,

I agree with you about the bigger picture in terms of the biography about Helen Keller. I think reading a story like that *does* send a message about how everyone learns in different ways and that everyone can learn. Do you think that there are other biographies that have "bigger pictures" too? And what do you think about biographies in general? Do you think that you could come up with an even bigger picture that could apply to any biography that you read?

Danny (in Roald Dahl's book) *does* seem interesting. What makes him brave? Does the book say that "Danny is brave," or are there things that he does and says that lead you to believe he is? You know how you can just realize some things about a character because you are thinking about him/her?

Love, Ms. Won

P.S. I'm not sure I understand your P.S. question—could you please clarify in your next letter?

11/21

Dear Ms. Won,

I am reading *The Gypsy Game,* the sequel to *The Egypt Game.* They decide to be Gypsies because a lot of people really know about Egypt so it wouldn't be fun anymore. So they call it Gypsy camp. Toby (the boy) is the Gypsy and wants to be part of Gypsy camp, but Melanie, April, Marshall, and Christine don't know if they should invite him or not.

I think the kids in the Egypt game and starting the Gypsy game are made to be very imaginative kids. They really don't let anything really bother them at all! They try to make others really fun. Is there a sequel? What would it be if there was? If there is or was, I would read it!

I'm sorry I didn't finish writing my question. My question was how do authors choose people to be in biographies. How do they find them?

From Emily

P.S. Is there a sequel? Is one getting published?

11/21

Dear Emily,

Thanks for clarifying that question. I think it's a good one and an important one to ask. It seems you could write a biography about anyone, really. Why do authors of biographies choose certain people and not others? What do you think?

By the way you write about the kids in these books, it sounds as if you admire them. Is this true? How do you know they are imaginative? What things would bother you? What are

some specific examples of these things that you are talking about?

I think that as readers, it's important for us not only to make conclusions about characters but also to apply what we realize to our own lives. We should ask, "What does this have to do with me?" This extends and S-T-R-E-T-C-H-E-S our thinking. What do you think?

As for another sequel, I'm not sure. These are pretty recently published books, but you could find out by writing to the publisher. Let me know if you are interested.

Love, Ms. W.

12/1

Dear Ms. Won,

Yes I think I might admire them. They think up awesome things, and I wonder how they think of their ideas. The reason I think they are imaginative is that they think about a different way to play, not just a board game or house. They find a way to play that feels real to them. Does the professor know they are in his back yard?

I'm not sure that I agree with the idea that you can have a biography on anybody, because if you could write a biography on anyone, it even could be me! Don't you have to have something about you to be in a biography?

Love, Emily

P.S. I will write to the publisher.

12/1

Dear Emily,

I think it's very interesting what you've said about biographies. I think I partially agree with you and disagree at the same time. I definitely think biographies are usually written about people who are famous or in the news a lot for whatever reason, but I don't think it *has* to be that way. Why do you think biographies are written? And what do you mean, you'd have to have something about you? Why do people read someone's biography and what do you think they get out of it? Why couldn't you write one about yourself?

Love, Ms. Won

P.S. Do you do what the kids in *The Egypt Game* do in terms of trying to think of things in different imaginative ways?

As we follow the interchange between Emily and her teacher, we can identify several important ways in which Emily is extending her thinking:

■ She is learning to connect texts with big ideas; that is, she is searching for the "lesson" or the main ideas to be gained from reading about people like Helen Keller.
■ She is exploring a network of questions about biographies, such as:
    1. What do people gain from reading biographies? What do they learn from them?
    2. How do biographers select their subjects?
    3. What is important to learn from studying people's lives?
    4. How do writers make biographies unique even though they are writing about a person who has had many other biographers?
■ She is becoming more aware of her own feelings and her ability to empathize with characters.
■ She is learning that characters have reasons for behaving as they do and that, as a reader, it is valuable to think about those motives.
■ She is refining her interests and tastes as a reader.
■ She is monitoring her own comprehension of the text by asking questions as she goes along.
■ She is making connections between texts and drawing observations across texts.

Carol treats Emily as a reader. Every comment she makes recognizes Emily as another literate person. Sometimes Carol shares her own thinking about literacy. Often she asks Emily questions, but notice that these questions probe for information that Carol really wants to know. Her questions are not a "test" of whether Emily remembers details from the story.

When Emily is confused, Carol provides information. She tells Emily when she agrees or disagrees, and she asks for clarification or more information when needed. Through the written conversation, Carol supports, encourages, affirms, shares, and questions in such a way that with each subsequent letter, Emily goes a little further in her exploration of a topic or idea.

Finally, Carol demonstrates genuine curiosity—the act of wondering—which teaches Emily how to become an inquirer into texts on her own. The goal of the reader's notebook is much greater than simply increasing the quantity of students' independent

reading (although it is obvious that Emily is reading about a book a week), and it is much greater even than developing reading skill. The goal is to develop students as lifelong readers who engage in inquiry as they encounter texts.

Using Reader's Notebooks in a Reading Workshop

The conversational writing in a reader's notebook is quite different from a book report. The reader's notebook contains an active dialogue in which the reader communicates thoughts and feelings about the books he is reading. The emphasis is on the intersection of thinking, talking, and writing throughout the reading of a text. The notebook is a storehouse of thoughts about reading, a place to record these thoughts so that one can return to, review, and reflect on them.

What Is a Reader's Notebook?

A reader's notebook is a notebook or folder of bound pages in which students write about their reading. You regularly assign writing or drawing activities for them to complete in their notebooks. The reader's notebook is used throughout the academic year and the assignments are completed in school. Students write in longhand and make hand-drawn charts or quick sketches, or use computer software to complete their written or graphic responses. All messages are written in the notebook (or glued in, if produced on a computer) as a continual record of one reader's reading responses through the year.

Students may divide their notebooks into different sections for different information. For example, students may keep a list of books they are currently reading in one section, a list of books they are interested in reading in another section, their letters about their reading in still another, and their writing related to book club meetings in another.

What Are the Purposes of Reader's Notebooks?

When children write, they can discover more about what they think and feel about a text. The reader's notebook is a way to catalog those thoughts and feelings. Not only are students learning through writing, but their writing is constantly available for reflection and sharing.

Reader's notebooks are not just about keeping students accountable for what they read, although they do provide an ongoing record. Their primary use is to help individuals become better readers by:

■ Engaging in critical thinking and learning about how to interpret a text.
■ Connecting reading and writing.
■ Developing flexibility in responding and going beyond simple retelling or answering questions.
■ Using the notebook to promote and support discussion.
■ Formulating thoughtful and personal responses to what they read.
■ Responding and reflecting continually during the reading of a text.
■ Engaging in meaningful independent work while the teacher works with groups of students.
■ Collecting, examining, and using interesting words and language patterns.
■ Examining the writer's craft and recording the techniques they notice for later discussion and use in their own writing.
■ Sketching or drawing to express their understanding in images as a support for discussion or writing.

When and Where Do Students Write in Their Notebooks?

How often students write in their notebooks varies. Some teachers ask students to write for a few minutes every day. We have found that expecting students to write one thoughtful response once a week works very well. They might write their response in a letter form all at one time or over the course of two or three days, spending part of their time on reading and part of their time on writing on any given day. They can choose which days they want to write, as long as the letter is completed the day before it is due.

Students share their thinking through letters as they are reading a text or at the completion of the text. A flexible schedule allows students to add to the response whenever ideas occur to them. During the independent reading time, students spend most of their time reading and some of their time writing.

Writing in the reader's notebook is not a homework assignment. If we value writing in school, we want to be sure that there is time for it in school. We have found that when students take their reader's note-

books home and forget them, problems are created.

Can Students Use Computers to Write Their Reader's Notebooks?

Certainly. If enough computer work stations are available in the classroom, students can compose their letters and their reading interest lists on the computer, and teachers can respond by computer. This can make it much easier for teachers to provide timely and thoughtful responses. We do recommend that the computer time be organized efficiently—for example, if time is limited, students might outline a few ideas on stick-on notes before sitting down at the computer.

There are a couple of potential drawbacks to using computers, which must be addressed:

■ If responses are recorded on the computer only, it may not be easy to browse through previous responses and refer to interest lists. This concern can be dealt with if you and the students print hard copies of your entries and glue them into a notebook so that the volume becomes a complete and permanent record of your conversation.
■ If computer time is limited, students will not have access to their notebooks whenever they are ready to write down their thinking. Using a combination of handwritten responses and glued-in typed responses takes care of this problem.

What Do Students Write in Their Notebooks?

Students usually write a letter to the teacher and sometimes to each other. Each produces a thoughtful response in which thinking is shared about books they are reading or have completed.

CONTENT OF RESPONSES

Since students choose how to frame their responses to a book and write without an assigned topic, the letters they write cover a wide variety of topics. We examined a large number of student entries from grades 3 through 6 for the range of thinking evidenced, which went far beyond retelling the story. Instead of just recounting information about the text, the students revealed active engagement with the text and shared their thinking as they:

- Recapped the story and summarized the plot.
- Stated the author's purpose.
- Elaborated on an opinion.
- Expressed an interest in the topic.
- Made connections with the characters.
- Showed empathy with the characters.
- Appreciated the richness of the author's choice of words.
- Noticed the size of the print and other elements of the text layout.
- Made predictions about the story.
- Requested information about books by the same author.
- Reflected on their writing in relation to the author's.
- Noticed and commented on illustrations and details.
- Referred to a previous entry.
- Gave an example from the text.
- Quoted passages from the text.
- Made connections between the author's life and the book.
- Generalized on the theme.
- Questioned the author's purpose for writing.
- Commented on the author's use of language.
- Commented on the mood of the story.
- Related the story to their own lives.
- Posed questions to resolve meaning.
- Showed personal reactions to the story.
- Compared books by the same author.
- Wrote in stream of consciousness.
- Showed pride in their writing.
- Reacted to characters.
- Compared the world of the characters to their world.
- Made connections to other books and movies.
- Explained their struggle with a text.
- Wondered why an author made a particular decision about some aspect of the story.
- Commented on how the character changed.
- Commented on the author's style or craft.
- Gave reasons for abandoning the story.
- Reflected on themselves as readers.
- Critiqued authors and shared what they would do differently.
- Recommended books and authors.
- Explored bigger issues beyond the text.
- Connected themes in books.
- Discussed genre.

A letter in a reader's notebook is the reader's thinking on paper. Most of the time, students choose what they want to say but occasionally, you may assign a focus. For example, if you have presented a minilesson on how authors reveal characters in their stories, you might ask students to include in the weekly letter at least one paragraph about that in relation to the story they are reading. Or, if you have been showing students how to notice the author's use of metaphor, you might ask them to look for metaphors while they are reading and devote one paragraph in the letter to this literary technique.

For example, Carol asked her students to set some goals for their reading and to write about those goals in their weekly letter. Here is Emily's response:

Dear Ms. Won,

My goal is to think more about what I'm reading and to think about the feelings of the characters in the story. The reason I've decided to make the goal is because the book that I am reading is called *Hide and Seek*. It's about the Holocaust. This book has really made me think about the feelings of the characters, especially because it is true. I still don't understand why the Jews and other religions were separated because of their religion. This book is really making me think and I want to keep it up.

What I am going to do to keep my goal is after a few chapters I'm going to explain to myself what happened and make a picture in my mind.

From Emily

Dear Emily,

It's clear to me that you are going to take this goal very seriously and work hard and think hard to get better in the way you describe in your letter. It's interesting that you began thinking about this because of a particular book you read. I think the Holocaust is a very powerful subject for a book and can help us to think more. Let me know if you'd like to do more reading about the Holocaust and we can look for books together.

Love, Ms. Won

Assigning a focused response is appropriate when you connect it to the teaching you do in a minilesson.

In Chapter 17, we describe focused response to literature in greater detail and provide an extensive list of guiding questions to support higher-level thinking about texts.

FORM OF RESPONSES

The students' written responses are first drafts, and we do not ask them to revise or copy over their entries. We do, however, expect them to strive to produce clear, legible text that reflects their current knowledge of grammar, spelling, and punctuation. In a minilesson, we show them how to note the date and use other letter conventions (see Chapter 9).

You may also want to present minilessons that introduce students to alternative responses. For example, if you provide a minilesson on how to write a book review, you might ask your students to write a book review in their notebooks that week. Or, if they have been working on perspective, you might ask them to write from the perspective of a character in their book. An alternative response like this is a variation from the weekly letter that asks students to think about text in specific ways.

LENGTH OF RESPONSES

Entries may vary in length, although about one page seems appropriate for most third- through sixth-grade students. Less experienced students might write slightly less than a page. Older students might write longer entries. Students should understand that length is not synonymous with the quality of the response. You will want to teach them what comprises a thoughtful response and provide examples of detailed entries that reflect lucid, analytical thinking.

When Do I Respond to Student Letters?

You will want to respond to the letters on the same day they are completed. If we require students to turn in their writing on a certain day, we need to value their sense of commitment and achievement by providing immediate feedback. It takes about five minutes to write a thoughtful response to each reader. If you have a class of twenty-five students, you might respond to five each day. Some teachers spend thirty minutes after school writing responses; others spend fifteen minutes before school and fifteen minutes after. Others manage to write a few responses during short periods of free time during the school day. You should always try to get

the letters written at school, but be aware that sometimes you'll have to carry them home. In unusual situations when there simply is no time for a prompt response, explain the delay.

Should Students Write Responses to Each Other?

In most cases, the teacher is the primary audience and writes back to the student. Sometimes it is also appropriate for students to respond to each other. They enjoy conversing about books with each other. In addition, students may sometimes share their letters to the teacher with other students. Generally, though, your response is essential, because:

- You give every reader an opportunity for a personal interaction with you.
- You provide a model for reflecting on reading, which enables the students to understand what constitutes a quality response as they strive to meet your criteria.
- You reinforce and expand your students' understanding.
- You direct students' thinking to more effective or useful ways to reflect on the text.
- You provide positive reinforcement for students' valuable thinking, thus encouraging more of it.
- You learn more about the readers—the kinds of books they like and what they are thinking about those books.
- You gain information from which to plan for minilessons.
- You learn more about your students' writing skills so that you can address their needs in your writing program.
- You get to know your students in more personal ways.
- You can make recommendations to readers about books and authors.
- You give students "a lift"—that is, you help them understand something in a way they did not understand before.
- You get important feedback on your teaching.
- You delight your students!

Students love reading personal letters from their teachers.

If you do invite students to respond to each other, you will want to teach them how to respond well by

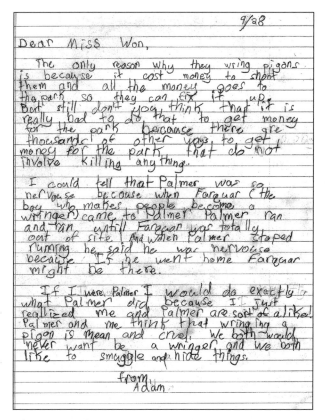

Figure 10–2. *Letter*

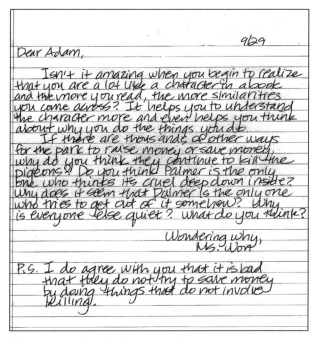

Figure 10–3. *Teacher Response to Letter*

providing several minilessons on writing a quality response to someone's letter. Just as they learn to write quality responses to you, they can learn how to write quality responses to each other. While they enjoy writing to each other about their reading, they may be less careful about writing conventions. Thus, you will want to read their peer-to-peer letters so you can assess the quality of their responses, check their use of conventions, and examine the information they reveal about students' reading and writing.

What Should I Write?

The use of letters enables you to bring your own rich and varied experiences as a reader to your work with intermediate students. You approach this interchange as a friend would talk with another friend about beloved books. You value the students' thinking as you would a conversation with another literate person, reacting genuinely as a reader as you discuss reading, writing, books, and authors. You ask genuine questions and share your own opinions as a reader.

Of course, conversation between adults and conversation between you and your students are inher-

ently different. You are responsible for helping these young readers develop their reading comprehension and interpretation. You reinforce good thinking, extend perspectives, and offer challenges and suggestions. It is not your role to test readers or pepper them with comprehension questions. Your questions should be authentic. If you find your students' writing confusing or illegible, say so, and offer them real reasons to improve. In the examples shown in Figures 10–2 through 10–5, notice the variety of responses and the ways in which the teacher accomplishes the goals we have described.

Here are some suggestions for providing effective, high-quality responses to your students' letters in their notebooks:

- Read the students' letters carefully so that you can respond precisely to their thoughts and questions. Do not correct the students' writing in the notebook; use the inaccuracies to inform your minilessons, and model correct spelling and form in your own writing.
- Structure your message so that it connects directly with the students' message in some way. You can acknowledge their thinking or feelings, agree or disagree with them, or share similar feelings.

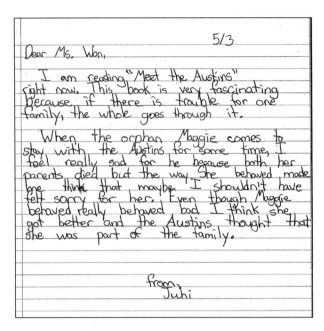

Figure 10–4. Letter

■ Extend the readers' thinking by providing more information or clarifying facts.

■ Pose questions that prompt further thinking on the part of readers.

■ Share your own reading experiences and your thoughts about yourself as a reader or writer.

■ Share your own preferences and interests as a reader—authors, books, and genres you like.

■ Make recommendations to readers about titles, genres, or authors that they might like to read next.

■ Pose questions about things that you do not understand in the notebook entry.

■ Inform students when they have not provided enough information for you to understand what they are trying to say.

■ Inform students if their entry is unclear or illegible. You may request that they rewrite it so that you can read, understand, and respond to it.

■ Show that you value your students' thinking, reminding them that there is no single interpretation of a book. Encourage a variety of interpretations.

■ Refer one reader to another to converse about the same book or to compare books by the same author or books with similar themes. They might share notebook entries or simply talk about their books.

Is it Important for Me to Have Read the Book the Student Is Reading?

In general, teachers should read as many books as possible as a way to understand the texts that interest students—or might interest them—as well as the various dimensions of reading that students need to learn. Indeed, reading good intermediate-level books is a highly enjoyable and relaxing experience: carry one or two with you for those moments when you have some time to spare. Also, it's nice to spend part of your evening, weekend, or vacation with an intermediate-level book. Over time, you will certainly develop a broad knowledge of the books that are available to students in your school.

In any given year, however, it is probably impossible for you to read all the books your students are reading. Nevertheless, you can enjoy a genuine conversation with a student, just as you can with an adult, without having read the student's particular book. Our universal human experience lets you easily connect the student's book with other books you have read. Indeed, you may find a student's response so interesting that he will persuade you to read his book!

The Organization of the Reader's Notebook

A reader's notebook generally features five sections:

1. The Reading List.
2. The Reading Interests List.
3. Books to Read List.
4. The Letters.
5. Guided Reading/Book Club (writing about reading).

Assembling the Notebook

We use a spiral-bound notebook of lined paper (see Figure 9–5). You can use a standard-size 8½"-by-11" notebook, but we prefer one that is 8" by 10" because it is more compact, looks more like a special notebook, and fits easily into students' book boxes. The notebook should have a stiff tagboard cover rather than a plain paper one. A spiral-bound notebook works better than a stapled notebook because pages tend to rip from stapled books. A spiral-bound notebook also works better than a three-ring binder because binders are typi-

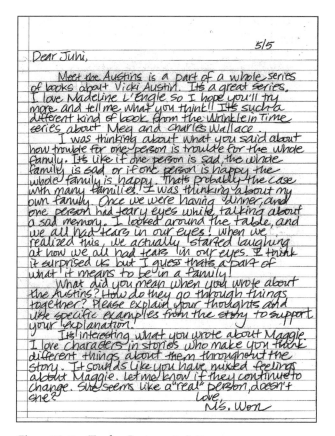

Dear Juhi,

Meet the Austins is a part of a whole series of books about Vicki Austin. It's a great series. I love Madeline L'Engle so I hope you'll try more and tell me what you think! It's such a different kind of book from the Wrinkle in Time series about Meg and Charles Wallace.

I was thinking about what you said about how trouble for one person is trouble for the whole family. It's like if one person is sad, the whole family is sad or if one person is happy the whole family is happy. That's probably the case with many families. I was thinking about my own family. Once we were having dinner, and one person had teary eyes while talking about a sad memory. I looked around the table, and we all had tears in our eyes! When we realized this, we actually started laughing at how we all had tears in our eyes. I think it surprised us but I guess that's a part of what it means to be in a family.

What did you mean when you wrote about the Austins? How do they go through things together? Please explain your thoughts and use specific examples from the story to support your explanation.

It's interesting what you wrote about Maggie. I love characters in stories who make you think different things about them throughout the story. It sounds like you have mixed feelings about Maggie. Let me know if they continue to change. She seems like a "real" person, doesn't she?

Love,
Ms. Won

Dear Ms. Won,

When I talked about the Austins and when I said that I thought they went through things together, I meant that if one person in the family was sad, then the whole family was sad, and if one person in the family was happy, then the whole family was happy. Also if one person is in trouble the whole family tries to help them to get out of trouble. Like when Maggie gets in trouble for losing Rob all the kids try to help her to find him, so that she doesn't get into deep trouble. Sometimes at the dinner table (in my family) (just like you) my brother or the rest of my family say something sad about something and then we would find out that we are all crying and tears are streaming down our cheeks. We would all start laughing really loudly.

I think you are right that Maggie is a "real" person. She keeps on changing throughout the book sometimes she is nice and sometimes she can get very unpleasant. I don't think anybody can be (in their whole lifetime) just only sweet or just only unpleasant. We keep on changing. This author is a very good author. I like the way she writes about her characters like ~~what~~ what they say or what they do. I plan to read the series with Vicky Austin in it.

From,
Juhi

Figure 10–5. Teacher Response to Letter

cally quite bulky. Also, with three-ring binders, students may need to punch holes in the paper, which slows the process, and papers may fall or tear out. Finally, binders can be noisy and disruptive as students click and unclick them to insert or move pages.

Some teachers prefer to give students a notebook that is already organized and ready to use, with every section in place and tabs attached. You will want to place five different colored plastic, flag-type tabs across the top of the pages to create five different sections of the notebook. The tabs are available in office supply stores. It's helpful to glue a copy of the Guidelines for Reading Workshop inside the back cover of the notebook (see Chapter 9). Appendix 16 contains a reproducible copy.

You will also want to glue the Reading List form onto the first page of the first section of the notebook (see Appendix 13 for a reproducible version). Leave about ten blank pages so readers can continue the list throughout the year.

After the ten blank pages, glue in the Reading

Interests form (see Appendix 14 for a reproducible version). Three or four blank pages should follow so readers can continue the list throughout the year.

The introductory letter that you write to students explaining how to use the notebook should be glued inside the front cover or on the opening page of the response section.

The professional look of a well-designed notebook influences students' thinking: they take it seriously from the beginning. If you assemble the notebooks with the help of small groups of students, supervise them step by step. The notebook's polished appearance emphasizes that it is a valued, organized, and standardized piece of work.

Reading List

The reading list (see Chapter 10 and Appendix 13) documents the amount and kind of reading that students do and is an invaluable resource for both you and your students. Parents will also find it interesting and rewarding to see a complete list of books their children have read throughout the year.

EXPECTATIONS FOR READING

Students will read between thirty and forty-five minutes a day in reading workshop, and they will spend time reading at home. This comes to about five hours of reading each week. The expectations you establish with your students regarding the approximate number of books they should read during a time period will vary depending on their grade level and the size of the books they are reading. Setting expectations will keep students on track and encourage them not to waste time between books. Also, keeping a list of books to read next helps students find another book quickly.

In general, we expect fourth- through sixth-grade students to read about one chapter book per week, or about 40 books per year. Most third graders will read shorter books and may be able to read two or three in a week. These books vary considerably in length, so you will need to show children in a concrete way what you expect regarding the quantity of reading they do. Remember, too, that they will place books on the list that they have read in small-group instruction, guided reading, and literature study.

Some students may need minilessons that help them grasp two essential concepts: (1) how much to read, and (2) at what pace to read. In other words, you want your students to read at a comfortable pace that allows for reflection and understanding. They need to savor the full act of reading rather than simply race through as many books as possible. Notice that we have not asked students to indicate the *number* of pages for each book. We would not want the pages read to be the focus, nor would we want competition as to quantity.

You will also need to establish the variety of reading you expect. Some teachers set yearly expectations for the number of books their students should read in each genre, negotiating the number of informational biographies, historical fiction, realistic fiction, fantasy, science fiction, or traditional titles they will read each quarter.

USES FOR THE READING LIST

Students use the reading list to keep a record of the books and other materials they read. Figure 10–6 is Dana's reading list. It is immediately evident that Dana has read a great many books, most of which were "just right" (as indicated by JR in the right-hand column). She read forty-one books for the year, which is almost one book for each week of school. She abandoned only

two during the year. Her list reflects great variety, including:

- Short story collections, such as *Throwing Shadows* (Konigsburg 1979) and *Altogether One at a Time* (Konigsburg 1971) .
- Realistic fiction that focuses on everyday problems, such as *Meet the Austins* (L'Engle 1960) and *The Summer of the Swans* (Byars 1996).
- Fantasy, such as *The Wish Giver* (Brittan 1970) and *The Search for Delicious* (Babbit 1969).
- Biography, such as *The Helen Keller Story* (Peare 1959) and *The Story of Clara Barton* (Woodworth 1997).
- Historical fiction, such as *Anna Is Still Here* (Vos 1995), *Letters from Rifka* (Hesse 1992)
- Humor, such as *Danny, the Champion of the World* (Dahl 1998) and *Absolutely Normal Chaos* (Creech 1997).
- Animal stories, such as *Stay! Keeper's Story* (Lowry 1997).

Through her reading, Dana is exploring important themes such as death—*Meet the Austins* (L'Engle 1960), *A Ring of Endless Light* (L'Engle 1980), *Bridge to Terabithia* (Patterson 1977), *Anne Frank: The Diary of a Young Girl* (1993). She is trying to understand historical events like the Holocaust. She enjoys animal stories, especially those that present unique ideas or perspectives. She is interested in adolescent topics such as love, dating, and popularity. She often selects more than one book by the same author, so she is developing a list of favorite writers. She likes sequels. She tends to select female authors and books with strong female characters.

Dana is reading historical fiction, but it tends to be on one topic. As her teacher, you might suggest ways for Dana to broaden her reading and ask her whether she would like to read more poetry or informational titles. You can also ask students to confer with each other so they can learn to take responsibility for increasing their own breadth as readers. If this is an issue for several children, you can provide a minilesson on how to examine the list of books and increase the number of authors, topics, or genres.

Reading Interests List

Readers also keep a list of what they want to read. One part of the form is a list of topics, genres, and authors

Reading List

Select a book to read. Enter the title and author on your reading list. When you have completed it, write the genre, and the date. If you abandoned it, write an (A) and the date you abandoned it in the date column. Note whether the book was easy (E), just right (JR) or a challenging (C) book for you.

#	Title	Author	Genre	Date Completed	E JR, C
1	Bridge to Terabithia	Katherine Paterson	RF	9/18	JR
2	Heidi	Joann Spyri	RF	9/21	JR
3	Search For Delicious	Natalie Babbitt	F	9/24	JR
4	Helen Keller Story	Catherine Pearce	B	10/2	C
5	The Little Prince	Saint-Exupery	F	(A) 10/4	—
6	Summer of the Swans	Betsy Byars	RF	10/9	JR
7	Mrs. Frisby and the Rats of Nimh	Robert C. O'Brien	F	10/4	JR
8	Pigs might Fly	Dick King Smith	F	10/22	JR
9	Story of Helen Keller	Lorena Hickock	B	10/29	JR
10	Who Put the Hair in My Toothbrush	Jerry Spinelli	RF	(A) 10/31	—
11	Story of Clara Barton	Oliver Price	B	11/4	JR
12	A Night without stars	James Howe	RF	11/8	JR
13	Danny the Champion of the world	Roald Dahl	RF	11/10	JR

#	Title	Author	Genre	Date Completed	E JR, C
14	The Gypsy Game	Zilpa Keatley Snyder	RF	11/14	JR
15	Absolutely Normal Chaos	Sharon Creech	RF	11/19	JR
16	Throwing Shadows	E.L. Konigsburg	RF	11/27	JR
17	Altogether One At a Time	E.L. Konigsburg	RF	11/29	E
18	Hide and Seek	Ida Vos	HF	12/1	C
19	Anna is still Here	Ida Vos	HF	12/8	C
20	I Have Lived a Thousand Years	Bitton-Jackson	HF	12/14	C
21	Missing May	Cynthia Rylant	RF	12/22	JR
22	Meet the Austins	Madeline L'Engle	RF	1/4	C
23	The Big Lie	Isabella Lettner	RF	1/9	JR
24	A Ring in Endless Light	Madeline L'Engle	RF	1/12	JR
25	Bad Girls	Cynthia Voigt	RF	1/15	JR
26	Bad Badder Baddest	Cynthia Voigt	RF	1/19	JR
27	Stay! Keepers Story	Lowry	F	1/21	JR

Figure 10–6. Reading List

they want to read. There is also a place to list titles they want to read. They check titles off as they read them (see Figure 10–7 for an example). When students are interested in a book on which you have given a book talk, they typically add it to their reading interests list.

By examining children's reading interests lists, you discover their favorite titles, genres, topics, and authors. You also learn what book talks you might present as well as what books you should feature in your classroom. Reading interests lists show you not only what individuals want to read but reading patterns across age and grade. This helps you select titles and numbers of copies for your classroom library; you'll want to purchase multiple copies of the "hot," popular titles. (You might also share what you've learned with your school librarian.)

Peter's reading interests list (Figure 10–7) indicates that he is noticing authors like Dick King Smith, Scott O'Dell, Roald Dahl, and Avi, all of whom he mentions more than once. Peter is interested in reading realistic fiction, fantasy, and science fiction. He is also interested in reading about space and planets, indicated not

#	Title	Author	Genre	Date Completed	E JR, C
28	Not Just Anybody's Family	Betsy Byars	RF	1/28	JR
29	Tangerine	Edward Bloor	RF	3/4	C
30	Four Perfect Pebbles	Lila Perl Marion Lazin	I	2/8	JR
31	Memories of Anne Frank	Alison Leslie Gold	HF	2/11	JR
32	The Wish Giver	Bill Brittan	RF	3/24	JR
33	Snake Scientist	Sy Montgomery	I	3/30	C
34	On My Honor	Marion Bauer	RF	4/5	JR
35	Spider Boy	Ralph Fletcher	RF	4/12	JR
36	Number the Stars	Lois Lowry	HF	4/19	JR
37	Wilma Rudolph Run for Glory	Linda Jacobs	B	4/26	JR
38	The Year of the Boar and Jackie Robinson	Bette Bao Lord	RF	5/3	JR
39	Letters from Rifka	Karen Hesse	HF	5/12	C
40	Wilma Rudolph Olympic Champion	Victoria Sherrow	I	5/19	JR
41	Holes	Louis Sachar	RF	5/27	JR

only by his topics list but by some of the specific entries on his title-and-author list. He has listed books by Seymour Simon and Joanna Cole and wants to find out about the human body. Informational books on science intrigue him as does realistic fiction, especially survival stories like those by Gary Paulsen.

Responses

This section includes students' written responses, often in the form of letters to you. You write an introductory letter, giving students directions for sharing their thinking in their reader's notebooks (see the example in Chapter 10). This letter models the form of the letter, including date, salutation, body, and closing. It helps students

understand the purpose of the reader's notebook and how you will interact with them in the notebook. The letter also provides some directions for what they can write about in the notebook and communicates clear expectations for writing the letter and turning it in on the date it is due. The letter is positive and motivating.

Classroom Example

The following example of a fourth grader's entry and his teacher's response is typical in terms of length and complexity, assuming you are continually *teaching* students how to write quality responses.

10/15
Dear Ms. Won,

I have done a lot of thinking about this book called *The Music of Dolphins*, by Karen Hesse. It's about a girl who used to live with the dolphins and has been taken away by doctors. She has to learn English and do human ways, something that she never knew. I want to know if Mila [the girl's name] gets to go back to the ocean and play with the dolphins.

I like this book because it's like a fiction autobiography. It's weird because in the beginning of the book the letters start big and bold and then they get smaller and smaller.

I have a question for you if you have read the book. Do you know why Shay always locks herself up? I mean, who wouldn't enjoy playing and listening to music?

Sincerely,
Jerrod

10/15
Dear Jerrod,

I think it's fascinating to think about people who are taken out of or leave the environment they are used to and go to an unfamiliar environment. It seems that would be a hard thing to do. Well, actually, I know it is difficult sometimes, because I've moved before, although my situation is different because I don't feel as though I was forced and also I felt safe because my whole family was with me. I wonder what it must be like for Mila. What do you think?

Reading Interests

Topics That Interest Me	Genre/Types of Books That Interest Me	Authors that interest Me
space	Realistic fiction	Smith
planets	Fantasy	O'Dell
human body	Science fiction	Dahl
science		Avi
survival		Paulsen
funny books		Cole

Books to Read

Title	Author	Check When Completed
Hatchet	Gary Paulsen	
Pigs Might Fly	Dick King Smith	✓
Island of the Blue Dolphins	Scott O'Dell	✓
Charlie and the Chocolate Factory	Ronald Dahl	
What Do Fish Have to Do With Anything?	Avi	✓
The Black Pearl	Scott O'Dell	
Mr. Ape	Dick King Smith	
James and the Giant Peach	Ronald Dahl	
S. O. R. Losers	Avi	✓

Title	Author	Check When Completed
Comets, Meteors, +Asteroids	Seymour Simon	
The Heart: Our Circulatory System	Seymour Simon	✓
The Magic School Bus Inside the Human Body	Joanna Cole	

Figure 10– 7. Reading Interests

This is interesting because we can tie it to our social studies unit about moving. We can begin thinking about why people leave a place, why people go to other places, and what the adjustment is like for them.

Why do you think the size of print changes? What do you think that means? I think you ask a good question when you ask about Shay. I agree with you about enjoying music. Why do you think Shay acts that way?

Love,

Ms. Won

Notice that the notebook entries are a conversation between two readers who are sharing genuine thoughts and questions. As in a true conversation, they are responding specifically to what they read in the other's entry. "Through the conversational turns of the discussion, they deepen their own understandings and others' and come to know the text in new ways. . . . In the process, there is not mere understanding of the information provided, but interpretation that creates shared meaning and new understandings" (Pinnell 2000). Active listening is especially important in the process of inquiry.

In this example (an open response), Jerrod selects the aspects of the text he is thinking about. What students as readers select to share offers a window on their thinking. Often their notebook responses reflect thinking beyond a literal recall of the text. Indeed, we've found that student reader's notebooks almost without fail reveal deeper analytical thinking and a more sophisticated synthesis of ideas than students produce when they are asked to answer a list of comprehension questions.

Jerrod considers the genre of the book ("fiction autobiography"). He notices aspects of the print format and searches for the meaning or symbolism they imply. He delves into character motivation and considers potential endings. Jerrod's response moves quickly from a brief statement about the book to a profound understanding of how authors use literary devices to create subtle, complex meanings and develop full-bodied characters.

He is not trying to prove to Carol that he has read the book; rather, he is engaged in a sophisticated literary conversation with her. He's eager to share his thoughts about various aspects of the book and looks forward to receiving Carol's response. Clearly, Jerrod grasps the literal meaning of the text (the main idea and the girl's name, for example), but he is also involved as a true reader grappling with the nuances of meaning within and beyond the text. As he reads, he asks searching questions that lead him ever deeper into a complete engagement with the text.

Using the Reader's Notebook

Every section of the notebook requires explicit teaching. You don't simply hand out the notebooks on the first day of school. First you introduce your students to reading response by having them talk about their books. As they learn to discuss their books with one another, sharing their thoughts and feelings orally, they come to understand what it means to build a relationship with a book—and how one can share that relationship with others through conversation. Eventually, students learn that they can enjoy an equally stimulating written conversation about their reading with their teacher through their reader's notebooks. Remember the guidelines and each of the forms are meant to lead students toward a more thoughtful response. If students are not using the notebook correctly or as fully as you envision, you will want to provide additional instruction.

In her classroom, Carol has clearly established the routines for using the reader's notebook, and her students practice the routines daily. In particular, they:

- Keep their reader's notebooks in their book boxes.
- Write in their reader's notebooks during independent reading.
- Complete their responses in class, not as homework assignments.
- Write in their reader's notebooks during book talks to record titles of books they want to read.
- Bring their notebooks to the minilesson if they know Carol is going to ask them to write or sketch in them.
- Bring their notebooks with them when they share so that they can use them as a basis for discussion.
- Produce one thoughtful reader's notebook response each week.
- Turn in the reader's notebook to Carol on the assigned day. (Carol reminds the group the day

before the notebook is due, although the reminders eventually become unnecessary.)

■ Proofread their responses before turning them in.

■ Write a letter to Carol, unless she has asked for a different format for a particular purpose.

■ Frame their own response and address those topics that capture their attention unless Carol has given them a focus for a particular response.

■ Write, on average, a page, although the length may vary.

■ Receive a prompt response from Carol, who writes back to a quarter of the students each day (Monday through Thursday).

■ Expand their understandings by extending and refining their own responses as they reflect on the model Carol sets in her response.

■ Discuss their entries in individual conferences with Carol, who helps them think more deeply about what they are writing.

Teaching Students to Write Quality Responses

It is necessary to *teach* students how to write quality responses in their notebooks. Remember that talk supports their thinking. For this reason, we do not recommend starting the notebooks until you have implemented reading workshop for several days, each time sharing oral responses to text. Then explain to students that they have been "talking with each other about their thinking." Now they are going to write it down so they can look back and share it with others in different ways. (See the discussion on getting started, in Chapter 9, for descriptions of appropriate minilessons.)

Here are some additional details that will help you teach students about using their notebooks:

■ Start with a common text, one students have talked about previously as a class, such as a book that you have read aloud to the group. Talk about what they might write in a letter to you about the book. Have each student write a letter responding to the book and then share and compare responses. Show some responses to the group as a whole and talk about how each reader shared thinking.

■ Have students use stick-on notes at two or three points in their reading—places where they have questions or thoughts about the text. They can use those stick-on notes to write their first letters. The notes will help them remember their thinking along the way.

■ Write a letter to the class about a book you are reading. (We presented an example of one teacher's letter in Chapter 9. In the minilesson, the teacher engaged the students in a conversation about the content and form of the letter she wrote to them.) Rebecca, a fifth-grade teacher, provided an excellent example for her students to discuss, which is shown in Figure 10–8.

■ Teach students to use highlighting pens to identify questions in your letter that they will need to answer in their letters to you.

Even after students have become accustomed to writing letters in their reader's notebooks, you may want to revisit the activity through a minilesson to encourage more thoughtful responses or a variety of kinds of thinking. You can make charts, for example, that list topics or ideas for writing (see Chapter 9). You will need to present many minilessons on the quality of response and on different ways of responding to develop and refine the way students think about text across the school year.

Assessing Student Responses

As you work with students you will continually assess their responses. We have described the valuable information that notebooks provide about students' understanding of text and their use of writing conventions—information you can use to plan your minilessons. You will also want to add to your store of information about each student and about the group as a whole, so that you can provide good individual instruction in conferences and assess the effects of your reading/literature program. Many teachers find that when students start discussing literature with one another in Book Club (see chapters 15 and 16), notebook entries tend to improve. It makes sense that providing numerous opportunities to talk about books will contribute to students' ability to write about books.

Independent reading, in connection with written responses, contributes to overall achievement in reading, which can be measured in many ways. It is difficult to assign a letter grade to specific entries in reader's notebooks. One important aspect is the completion of the task, but there are many qualitative

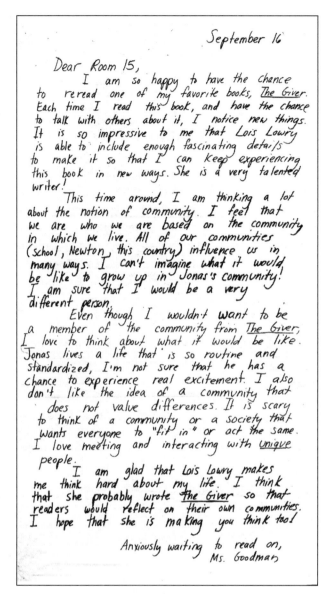

Figure 10–8. Rebecca's Letter

September 16

Dear Room 15,
 I am so happy to have the chance to reread one of my favorite books, <u>The Giver</u>. Each time I read this book, and have the chance to talk with others about it, I notice new things. It is so impressive to me that Lois Lowry is able to include enough fascinating details to make it so that I can keep experiencing this book in new ways. She is a very talented writer!
 This time around, I am thinking a lot about the notion of community. I feel that we are who we are based on the community in which we live. All of our communities (school, Newton, this country) influence us in many ways. I can't imagine what it would be like to grow up in Jonas's community! I am sure that I would be a very different person.
 Even though I wouldn't want to be a member of the community from <u>The Giver</u>, I love to think about what it would be like. Jonas lives a life that is so routine and standardized, I'm not sure that he has a chance to experience real excitement. I also don't like the idea of a community that does not value differences. It is scary to think of a community or a society that wants everyone to "fit in" or act the same. I love meeting and interacting with <u>unique</u> people.
 I am glad that Lois Lowry makes me think hard about my life. I think that she probably wrote <u>The Giver</u> so that readers would reflect on their own communities. I hope that she is making you think too!

Anxiously waiting to read on,
Ms. Goodman

dimensions. Below are some areas to consider in assessing students' reading responses.

Voice

Analyze the responses to determine whether students are developing voice as writers. Voice is the "personality" that resonates from the page—the unique ways in which a writer expresses himself in words so that you can "hear" him. Voice infuses life into the writing. It may involve unique expressions as well as personal reflections. Ask, *To what degree is this writer's response interesting and uniquely his?*

Clarity of Expression

Clarity of expression refers to the way the writer uses language effectively to communicate ideas. Clear writing is logically developed and features a smooth progression of ideas; furthermore, lucid sentences showcase the point so readers can easily discern the writer's intended message. Words have been carefully chosen to illuminate each thought, and the entire piece is effective, convincing, and a pleasure to read. Ask, *To what degree does the writer use language to communicate ideas clearly?*

Evidence of Understanding

When writing about texts they are reading, students demonstrate through their examples and comments that they understand the main ideas of the text. They make inferences and provide evidence from the text to support their points. They are able to summarize concisely and accurately, but they also go beyond the text to think of more possibilities. They make connections between the text and their own lives. In other words, they continually add to their understanding of "big ideas" from the information and human stories they read about. They are able to return to texts to find support for their thinking, and they also make connections between and among texts that they read, as well as connections to themselves and to the world. Ask, *To what degree does the writer demonstrate understanding (including providing evidence and making connections)?*

Awareness of Characteristics of Genre

Writers who are thinking about the texts they read notice characteristics of their structure and organization. They may note, for example, that biographies tend to have certain characteristics in common. They may already be aware of broad categories like fiction and nonfiction and gradually begin to differentiate among genres within the two areas as they gain more reading experience. The act of writing about how texts are similar or different focuses readers' attention on structure and genre; they become aware of their own tastes. Ask, *To what degree does the writer show he is aware of the characteristics and structure of different kinds of texts?*

Use of Conventions

Conventions refer to the standardized spelling, grammar, punctuation, capitalization, and organization that bring clarity to the piece and help the reader. While you will not be correcting students' notebook entries, you will want to keep notes or records on their use of conventions. You should see steady improvement because students are learning about writing conventions in language/word study and in writing workshop. They will also learn about conventions as they converse with you in their notebooks, and should apply what they know every time they write. Remind students that you expect them to "show what they know" when they write to you about their reading. Ask, *To what degree does the student use conventions (spelling, grammar, punctuation, and capitalization) in a standard way?*

Awareness of Self as a Reader/Writer

A principle goal of independent reading is to help students become lifelong readers, so you will want to assess your students' enjoyment and awareness of themselves as readers and writers. Look for evidence that your students are revealing genuine, honest feelings about the texts they read. As you respond to entries over time, you should note that students are developing opinions and refining their "reading tastes"; that is, they know what kinds of books they like and they have opinions about what makes a book "good." They discover favorite authors, topics, and genres. They search for books that meet their needs in terms of learning about the world and about themselves. They do not view independent reading as just a chore to get through, but as a time to relish a great book. They are particular as readers. They know why they may abandon books, and they know how to recommend books to others. Ask, *To what degree is the student gaining awareness of himself as a reader and writer?*

A Rubric for Thinking About Students' Responses

The rubric in Figure 10–9 incorporates the thinking we have described above. You may want to use this rubric as a basis for discussion with your colleagues. We recommend using the rubric in conjunction with several notebook entries by a student rather than a single entry. In fact, you might read through a student's entries over several weeks or even months so that you can determine whether he is developing according to all the rubric's dimensions. Or you may select one dimension of the rubric as a priority, examine all your students' notebooks to see how they measure up against that particular dimension, and emphasize that dimension in additional minilessons if necessary. The rubric is simply a tool for thinking about the quality of response.

Reader's Notebooks—An Integral Part of the Reading Program

Once established, reader's notebooks are easy to use and will encourage students to take responsibility for some of their own reading development. For you, they are an easy-to-manage, personal connection with each student. Perhaps most important, they prompt students to think deeply about themselves as readers and the remarkable experiences they enjoy as they immerse themselves in reading.

Suggestions for Professional Development

1. Meet with your colleagues across grade levels to discuss student response letters. After establishing the definition and characteristics, consider the two student/teacher entries provided in Figures 10–10 and 10–11.
2. As a group, look at each student response in terms of the rubric presented in the last section of this chapter:
   - To what degree is this writer's response interesting and uniquely his?
   - To what degree does the writer use language to communicate ideas clearly?
   - To what degree does the writer show evidence of understanding (including providing evidence and making connections)?
   - To what degree does the writer show he is aware of the characteristics and structure of different kinds of texts?
   - To what degree does the writer use conventions (spelling, grammar, punctuation, and organization) in a standard way?
   - To what degree is the student gaining awareness of himself as a reader and writer?
3. Then, talk about how the teacher's response was designed to help the student grow along one or more of the dimensions indicated by the questions.

Qualities of a Reading Response

Quality	4	3	2	1
Demonstration of Text Understanding (including providing evidence and making connections)	shows multi-dimensional understanding of text	shows adequate understanding of text	shows some understanding of text	shows no understanding of text
Quality	**4**	**3**	**2**	**1**
Voice/Personality	uniquely expressed and interesting to read	contains few interesting parts	mostly dull	trite/empty
Quality	**4**	**3**	**2**	**1**
Clarity of Expression	uses language very effectively to communicate ideas	uses language adequately to communicate ideas	shows some difficulty using language to communicate ideas	is unable to use language effectively to communicate ideas
Quality	**4**	**3**	**2**	**1**
Use of Conventions (spelling, grammar, capitalization, punctuation)	uses conventions accurately so response is easily understood	uses adequate conventions so response is mostly understood	uses a few conventions so parts of response are understood	uses almost no conventions so writing is difficult to read and understand
Quality	**4**	**3**	**2**	**1**
Awareness of Self as a Reader and Writer	shows high level of awareness of self as a reader and/or writer	shows adequate awareness of self as a reader and/or writer	shows little awareness of self as a reader and/or writer	shows no awareness of self as a reader and/or writer

Figure 10–9. Rubric for Responses

Dear Ms. Won,

In Jonas's Life it's more like a dream. Everybody is living a life with no misery, no war. There are no choices at all and they don't have to pay for anything.

I made a slight mistake on his job. The Giver gives Jonas the memories so Jonas can be the next Giver.

Everything that is wierd to them is regular for us. And everything that's wierd to us is regular to them. For example, Snow is incredible to them. It's suprising to us that they don't have to pay for anything. They do this because they don't want anyone to make the wrong choices. I think that they are not people but a different kind of species. They are brainwashed and they have no feeling.

I feel bad for them and mad at them because they don't know the real pleasure of life.

love,
Jon

10/14

Dear Jon,

I think its interesting the way you describe Jonas' life as a "dream." I wonder who else would describe it this way. What I mean is, it seems that different people would describe a dream in different ways.

I agree with you that there are different aspects of this world Jonas lives in that I would consider wonderful like how there's no war or sickness. But its also interesting to look at the "price" that is paid in order to live in such an organized society. That is, I don't think I would want everyone and every family to be the same. What do you think?

You bring up another good point in your comments about how people from two differing societies view the other society. Things seem weird to us, but is it because they are really "weird" or merely because we don't see them and are not used to these things because they are not a part of our society?

What do you think about the brain-washing? I mean, how does this happen to people?

Love,
Ms. Won

D.S. What a great journal entry you wrote, packed with thoughts and feelings!

Figure 10–10. Student Response and Teacher Reply

4. Have students write response letters to a book you have read aloud to them (see suggestions in this chapter).

5. Bring three letters, along with a copy of the book, to a professional development session. Take one letter from a high-achieving student, one from an average-achieving student, and one from a student having difficulty in reading and/or writing.

6. Make copies for everyone in the group so that you can look at the responses together.

7. Using the five questions posed for assessment of student responses (see above), discuss these notebook entries.

8. Look at the letters of the high-achieving students and talk about what you are seeing in their responses across the dimensions. Discuss how you can demonstrate some of these qualities to your entire class in an interactive read-aloud as well as by writing a letter together.

9. Select one dimension and think about how you can help students improve their responses through several minilessons and/or conferences.

Dear Rita,   5/2

Have I told you? I love Ramona. She was my favorite character when I was growing up. I read the Ramona books over and over again because I liked them so much and because I was comfortable with the books. Actually, I became comfortable with Ramona – as if she were a real person whom I knew well and loved. She was a real person to me. I liked how the books were, just specific events in Ramona's life and how she dealt with things. I, too, found her to be very funny sometimes – silly almost. Also, I felt like she did things that I did or at least thought about doing. In one book, she gets into trouble for pulling out all the tissue from a tissue box.

How do you feel about Ramona? What have you learned about who she is? Sometimes I think about how there are times when she is very insecure and other times when she seems more sure of herself. I think about how I am like her. I just liked that the books told me a lot Ramona's personal thoughts and feelings, and this made me feel that if I could meet her, she'd understand me. I think we'd be great friends.

How do you see Ramona? What about any of the other characters?

Love,
Ms. Won

P.S. Please answer all of my questions.

Figure 10–11.   Teacher Response and Student Reply

Dear Ms. Won,
I will try to answer all your questains in this Jurnal Entery.

The first quastain you asked me is if you told me you love Ramona books in some other entery.

The second quastain you asked me is how I feel about Ramona. I feel like she's a real person I know because in the Ramona books Beverly Cleary describes Ramona a lot!

The third quastin you asked me was what have I learned about who she is. I have learned that she sometimes wants to do something that she knows her mom woun't be to happy about and she thinks she will do it a little bit but then gets caried away with whatever she is doing. Like for example when she squized tooth past. She thougt she would squize just 1 little squize but then she got caried away and squized the whole toob.

The 4th quastain you asked me was how I see Ramona. I think that she is a very funny charecter. I think she sometimes wants to do something but she knows that it is bad to do but she does it anyway. She is just like me.

The last quastain you asked me was what I thought about the other characters in the book. I really like Beezus too. She is funny in ways she thinks she isn't. Once Beezus and her mother had a big hair argument. Beezus wanted something her parents couldn't afford. The argument was sort of funny!

I finished the book and now I'm reading another Romona book called Romona Forever. It is a great book too. It has one part that is very similar to what I did when I was little. There was a 3-way mirror, and Ramona danced in front of it. The same thing happened to me when I saw a 3-way mirror in a store and I just started to hop around in front of it. It was pretty fun!

Have you ever danced in front of a 3-way mirror? Have you read Romona Forever? Do you like the book Romona Forever?

from Rita

P.S. Can you please answer all my Q's?

STRUGGLING READERS AND WRITERS: TEACHING THAT MAKES A DIFFERENCE

Students who wrestle with reading may find it difficult to:

- Select appropriate books for independent reading.
- Become engaged in reading books for themselves.
- Sustain their reading independently.
- Respond in writing to the texts they are reading.

You can assist struggling readers by providing extra support in the right areas; indeed, the investment of only a little time adds up to big payoff.

1. *Make sure you have an extensive, varied collection of books at levels suitable for the readers who need more help.* A diverse collection—both in subject matter and in the degree of challenge—offers more possibilities for engaging students.
2. *Provide book talks that cater to students who are reading on the easier levels.* Book talks take only a minute or two and may focus on any text that is interesting, not just on "grade level" material. When you showcase a book as the subject of a book talk, it's clear you think highly of the book. Many students will add it to their lists.
3. *Help students craft book talks for one another.* Help them perform well by preparing and practicing the talk with you or another adult before giving it to the class.
4. *Attend carefully to your reading interviews with struggling readers.* Help students select books that are both interesting to them and instructionally appropriate.

5. *Check in with your struggling readers at the beginning of every reading workshop.* Be sure they have the right materials and are getting started either with reading their books or writing their response letters.
6. *Seat struggling readers next to classmates who serve as good role models.* Pair less capable readers with peers who are enthusiastic about reading and eagerly attend to reading their chosen books and writing in their journals.
7. *Help students who need extra help find books that are easier to read.* By reading lots of books that are relatively easy, readers will improve their reading ability.
8. *Confer with struggling readers more frequently than with other students.* While it is not always necessary to have a long conference, regularity is essential.
9. *Observe your students' oral reading frequently.* When you confer with them, ask your struggling readers to read a section of their text aloud to you (choose a part that they have already read silently). Notice their word-solving strategies and take notes that will enable you to work effectively with them in guided reading.
10. *Talk about the books with your students.* Your real conversations with your struggling readers will help them solidify their understanding and will help you determine what meanings they are bringing to the activity as well as what they are constructing from their reading. These notes will help you work effectively with them in guided reading.
11. *List books in the Reading Interest section of their reader's notebooks that are appropriate for your struggling readers.* In this way, they will always have books in mind to read.

12. ***Make available an AlphaSmart or computer for students who struggle with writing.*** Encourage them to type their responses to their books and then glue them in their reader's notebooks.

13. ***Take extra care in answering struggling readers' reader's notebooks.*** Reinforce their good thinking about texts and suggest further reading you know they can handle and will enjoy. Ask genuine questions that stimulate students to respond. Share your own reading attitudes and experiences so that the students can connect with you as another engaged reader.

14. ***Coordinate with parents.*** Help them understand the importance of quiet, uninterrupted reading. Parents may think of "homework" as filling out worksheets or answering questions at the back of a textbook. Be sure they understand that thirty minutes of independent silent reading is homework.

15. ***Check in with students regularly on their home reading.*** As they arrive in the morning, ask your students how their reading went and talk for a minute about noteworthy details from their reading. These quick check-ins provide your struggling readers with much-needed encouragement and enable you to discreetly monitor their home reading.

S E C T I O N   3

Guided Reading

Guided reading is an instructional setting that enables you to work with a small group of students to help them learn effective strategies for processing text with understanding. The chapters in this section define and describe the structure of guided reading in the upper elementary grades. Four chapters explain planning for guided reading, dynamic grouping for effective teaching, and selecting and introducing leveled texts. Careful text selection is facilitated by a gradient to organize texts in order of difficulty. We describe characteristics of texts related to difficulty and factors to consider in both selection and introduction. We also discuss how to organize texts for easy, practical classroom and school use.

## CHAPTER ELEVEN

UNDERSTANDING GUIDED READING

The aim of guided reading is to develop independent readers who question, consider alternatives, and make informed choices as they seek meaning.

—MARGARET MOONEY

Reading instruction is a routine part of the day for children in the primary grades. Each day they receive explicit teaching that improves their "processing power." Students in third, fourth, fifth, and sixth grade (and beyond) still have much to learn about reading challenging texts. Becoming literate is best understood as a continuum. Even as adults, we learn new skills that enable us to navigate a new array of texts—the Internet, e-books, our cell phone instruction booklet. Learning how to read and using reading to learn are inseparable.

Many children enter third grade with good decoding strategies. They can read with general accuracy just about anything you put in front of them. (This is not true for struggling readers, of course, and special segments at the end of each section of this book provide specific suggestions for working with these students.) But in our work with teachers and children, we have learned to distinguish between simply reproducing the words of a text, or "calling words," and truly "reading" it with understanding.

What does it mean to "read" a text? In reading we may:

- Identify and understand the important information.
- Connect personally with such things as setting, characters, and plot.
- React to the text emotionally, perhaps experiencing humor, loneliness, hope, terror, or grief.
- Derive the author's precise meaning even when it's subtle or ironic.

- Reproduce the author's intended syntax and phrasing when reading aloud.
- Incorporate the meaning of the text into our own knowledge of the world.
- Make inferences beyond the text.

A reader who is simply calling words will probably engage in few, if any, of these cognitive and affective experiences. The word-caller who reads without understanding *is* missing the point: reading *is* understanding. Meaning is being built from the moment a reader picks up a text and anticipates reading it. Then, while reading, the reader continually draws in meaningful information, synthesizes and organizes it, and responds to what she understands. And the meaning remains present long afterward as the reader reflects on the text, remembers it, and connects it to other texts. As Mooney (1995) writes:

> . . . there's a difference between merely reading and being an avid, lifelong reader, and between "reading anything" and being able to pursue an interest, solve a problem or satisfy a need or desire through selecting and delving into the printed word. (p. 75)

Even after they have acquired the "basics," elementary school students have much to learn if they are to become *readers*. They begin their literacy journey in the primary grades. Those who have rich literacy experiences there understand from the beginning that reading is supposed to make sense. They can recognize many frequently encountered words in print, and they possess good word-solving skills. But they still need instruction in how to process a variety of increasingly challenging texts.

What children know when they enter third grade depends on their past experiences. Many children have read widely and recognize different types of books. Others have had more limited experiences. Intermediate-grade teachers recognize that there will be wide differences in the support students need to construct meaning from text and go beyond it. These different levels of support can be provided through guided reading.

Rationale for Guided Reading

Considering the complexity of the reading process, students need ongoing instruction even after they understand the essence of reading. They must adjust their strategies as they read for different purposes or encounter new genres. They need to learn how to organize their knowledge in order to summarize or draw inferences from increasingly difficult texts. We cannot expect them to expand their reading abilities on their own, even if they are given time to read. Explicit instruction is essential for most students and will make reading more powerful for all students.

The purpose of guided reading is to meet the varying instructional needs of all the students in your class, enabling them to greatly expand their reading powers. During guided reading, they read a book you have specifically selected to provide a moderate amount of challenge, and you support them in tackling the necessary problem solving to overcome the difficulties they may encounter. Mooney (1990) has described the element of challenge as "manageable" for readers (p. 45). The teacher's role is to "help children learn how to overcome these difficulties, without taking away the privilege of setting up their own dialogue with the author on the first reading of the text" (p. 46).

Through guided reading you can demonstrate how a reader constructs meaning from text, makes personal connections with text, and goes beyond text. You can provide specific support for readers as they delve into texts for themselves, meeting challenges by using a range of skills. The students are engrossed in reading. Because you have carefully selected a text that is just right for their developmental ability, they feel in control. Students enjoy reading because they are successful, and, in the process, they learn and practice the kinds of strategies good readers use.

The Role of Guided Reading Within the Language/Literacy Program

Guided reading is only one part of the literacy program, but it is a critical part. We have described the language and literacy framework as consisting of three blocks: language/word study, reading workshop, and writing workshop. Within the reading workshop block are three interrelated contexts for teaching reading:

1. Independent reading.
2. Guided reading.
3. Literature study.

As we discussed in Chapter 2, each context has particular purposes. Guided reading gives students the opportunity to read at the right instructional level. Moreover, it introduces students to new books that offer a moderate challenge. As students read, they learn more about the reading process.

In guided reading, you bring together groups of students who are similar in their reading behavior, their text-processing needs, and their reading strengths. Your instruction, then, is specific and focused, finely tuned to the needs and challenges of the particular group of students with whom you are working.

Working in "The Learning Zone"

Guided reading allows you to help students move forward in their reading development. Through specific teaching and careful text selection, you make it possible for students to learn more than they could learn on their own. The Russian psychologist Lev Vygotsky (see *Mind in Society* 1978) has presented educators with a compelling theoretical idea. Vygotsky maintains that with the support of another, more experienced person,

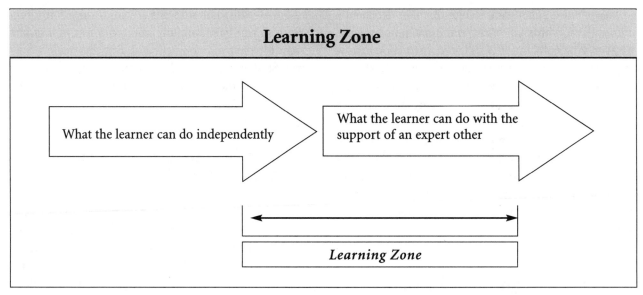

Figure 11–1. Learning Zone

the learner is able to do more than he could on his own. Whatever the task, the learner is supported as he attempts it with assistance from his more capable partner. Gradually, the learner takes over the task and becomes expert, but meanwhile his teacher, parent, or other learning partner works to extend the learner's knowledge and skills even further.

Vygotsky used the term "zone of proximal development" to describe the experience of a learner who works successfully with the support of another and extends his knowledge in the process. Some educators refer to this heightened learning experience as "the learning zone" (see Figure 11–1). You create a learning zone for your students when you carefully select and introduce a text, support and interact briefly with them during reading, and teach with clarity after reading.

You are making it possible for students not only to read a more difficult text but also to reflect on the text, understand it, and use it as a way of learning more about reading. In the Vygotskyian sense, guided reading makes it possible to teach at the cutting edge of students' understanding. Your support is light. You do not take the problem solving away from the student; instead, your teaching helps students read more productively and more intensively.

Most students in the intermediate grades have full control of basic reading strategies. Guided by their teachers, they have learned how print works, how to read and understand shorter texts, and how to vary their reading according to the type of book they encounter. But there is still much to learn. Like primary students, intermediate students need our support to work in "the learning zone." The understandings and strategies they are developing are more complex. As they read silently, they do not display the overt behavior that helps us know what is going on in their head. Much of their processing is—and should be—automatic and unconscious. Do these characteristics make it harder to help them work in the learning zone? We say no, because intermediate students are better able to talk and write about their reading. They can attend to details within text and, with teacher support, be more aware of what they do as readers.

With each guided reading lesson, you are using a "zoom lens" to provide very specific and focused instruction to small groups of students. Through your instruction, you address your students' needs at one particular point on the developmental continuum in order to expand and refine their reading ability. Without teaching "at the point of need," many students will not progress. When you provide small-group guided instruction that enables children to discover how to think about a text, they will be able to use their reading competency in all other classroom reading—independent reading, literature study, and the content areas. They will develop effective reading processes they can apply across the curriculum.

Overview of Guided Reading

Guided reading is a *teaching* approach designed to help individual students learn how to process a variety of increasingly challenging texts with understanding and fluency. Guided reading occurs in a small-group context because the small group allows for interactions among readers that benefit them all. The teacher selects and introduces texts to readers, sometimes supports them while reading the text, engages the readers in a discussion, and makes teaching points after the reading. Sometimes, after reading a text, the teacher extends the meaning of the text through writing, text analysis, or another learning experience. The lesson also may include work with words based on the specific needs of the group.

A Guided Reading Lesson: Fiction

Let's take a look at Marcella as she gives a guided reading lesson to a small group of her students during reading workshop. Four students have gathered at a horseshoe-shape table at one corner of the classroom. The other students are reading independently or writing in their reader's notebooks. Because students are working individually and silently, no voices are heard except for those of Marcella and her small group.

At the beginning of the year, these four students were reading books like the Poppleton series (Rylant) and the Mr. Putter and Tabby series (Rylant). Marcella was teaching them about stories with multiple episodes. They were required to sustain their reading, keeping track of the meaning, over several days. They moved from reading these easy chapter books to books like *Keep the Lights Burning Abbie* (Roop 1987) and the M&M series (Ross). They also discovered the mystery genre as they read the Nate the Great series (Sharmat 2000).

What is Guided Reading?

Guided reading is a teaching approach designed to help individual students learn how to process a variety of increasingly challenging texts with understanding and fluency.

Figure 11–2. What is Guided Reading?

Over a three-day period, the group had completed *Cam Jansen and the Mystery of the Stolen Diamonds* (Adler 1997). Listening to their discussions, Marcella knew these students were able to follow the story line and to compare the book with other Cam Jansen books they had already read. They knew the characteristics of a mystery and could quickly list the clues Cam and his friends found. The book's vocabulary was minimally challenging.

Today, Marcella has selected *Arthur's Mystery Envelope* (Brown 1997), a book she believes offers a moderate challenge for these students. For example:

- The word *mystery* is used in a different way than in the Cam Jansen series. In *Arthur's Mystery Envelope*, there is no mystery to solve; the term refers to the fact that Arthur doesn't know what's in the envelope.
- Periodically in the text, Arthur reveals his imaginative thinking. He moves into a fantasy world that is connected to the present but full of exaggerated events and people. The transition from realism to fantasy is signaled by type set in italics; the reader must understand the switch in order to understand Arthur.
- The vocabulary related to new concepts may be challenging. The letter is "private and confidential," and Arthur's mother is an "accountant."
- The text is slightly more complex than the chapter books the students have read previously.

Introducing the Text to Students

As Marcella prepared to introduce the text to her students, she thought about the challenges this new book presented. (Chapter 12 has a detailed discussion on how to prepare introductions.) This is how her introduction played out (The comments that appear in bold explain the underlying purpose of her actions and interactions.):

Introduces title and author.

MARCELLA: Today we're going to begin reading another book that has several chapters that tell the longer story. It's called *Arthur's Mystery Envelope,* and it is written by Marc Brown.
LESLIE: Oh, Arthur!
JOHN: He's on TV.

Confirms students' previous knowledge.

MARCELLA: You recognize the character Arthur, the aardvark, and you must know some of the other characters in the story as well. In this story, Arthur has a problem.

Invites students to recall previously read texts.

MARCELLA: We've been reading stories that are mysteries, like Cam Jansen. In those stories, the characters looked for clues to solve a mystery.

Provides information.

MARCELLA: In this story, the word *mystery* is used in a different way. The "mystery envelope" just means that Arthur doesn't know what is in that envelope and he's very worried about it. Do you see the envelope on the front cover?
CAROLE: It says *private.*

Probes for knowledge of word meaning.

MARCELLA: You're right. What does *private* mean?
CAROLE: It means it's just yours and nobody else should look at it.

Provides information about word meaning.

MARCELLA: Yes, and there's another word on that envelope that also means no one else should look at it. The word is *confidential. [She says it normally as a whole word and then says it again, emphasizing the syllables.]* Say confidential. *[Students repeat the word.]* This envelope is private and confidential, and the school principal has asked Arthur to take it home and give it to his mother.

Prompts students to interpret illustrations; emphasizes feelings.

MARCELLA: Look at the picture on page 4. *[Children turn to page 4.]* Notice Arthur's face. The principal is calling him to the office through that speaker up on the wall.
JEFF: He looks scared.

Defines the problem or plot of the story.

MARCELLA: He sure does. That's the problem in this story. Arthur is very worried that the envelope might have some bad news in it, because the principal told him to deliver the sealed envelope to his mom.
LESLIE: Maybe he misbehaved in school and has to stay late.
JOHN: Maybe it's his report card and it's bad.
MARCELLA: Well, it's a mystery to him because he doesn't know what's in there, and he can't open it because it's private and confidential.

Invites personal response.

MARCELLA: Have you ever had something you worried about like Arthur is worrying about the mystery envelope?
CAROLE: I was worried when I broke my mom's glass box and I didn't want my sister to tell her.
MARCELLA: Did you tell your mom?
CAROLE: Yes.
MARCELLA: I bet you felt better when you finally told her.
CAROLE: Yes, she just said that accidents happen and to be more careful.

Draws attention to illustrations to foreshadow a literary device.

MARCELLA: Let me tell you something else about Arthur. He is very imaginative; he's always making things up in his head, especially when he's worried or scared. Look at the picture on page 12. There's a picture of Arthur and the bubble shows what he is thinking or dreaming. *[Students turn to page 12.]*

JEFF: He's locked up in jail.

CAROLE: He's doing papers and his friends are outside.

Elaborates on the meaning of the text.

MARCELLA: Arthur is imagining that he didn't do well on his test and that's what the principal said in the mystery envelope. He thinks that he'll have to go to summer school instead of playing with his friends. There's the envelope right there and it's making him think of those things.

LESLIE: My brother had to go to summer school.

Explains how print and language signal the use of a literary device to reveal the character's inner thoughts.

MARCELLA: That's what Arthur is imagining. Turn back to page 11. Find the part where the print looks different from the rest of the book. When the print is slanted like that, it is called italic print. In this book, Marc Brown has used italic print to show us when Arthur is thinking and imagining something. It says, "He saw himself chained to the wall of a dark dungeon." Was he really in a dungeon?

JOHN: No, he was just thinking that he might have to be indoors and he would think it's like jail.

Draws attention to an important character.

MARCELLA: I guess he would feel like that if all his friends were playing and he couldn't. Now in this book, Arthur has some good friends who help him, but he also has a little sister who teas-

es him all the time. Look at her picture on page 22. *[Students turn to page 22.]*

JEFF: That's D.W. She always is a pest on the TV show.

MARCELLA: She and Arthur are always bickering with each other, and it doesn't help that she teases him about the envelope.

Draws attention to an important character and introduces new vocabulary; encourages students to say the new word.

MARCELLA: Now, look at the picture on page 27. *[Students turn to page 27.]* There's Arthur's mother and there's her briefcase. She's an *accountant.* Say that word.

STUDENTS: *Accountant.*

Provides important information.

MARCELLA: An accountant helps people keep their accounts; that means to keep records of their money. One of the most important things they do is help people fill out their forms for taxes every year. Arthur's mother is really busy and he's hoping that she won't notice the envelope.

In this book, as Arthur thinks more and more about the envelope, he gets more and more worried about what his parents will say when they open it. He imagines that the envelope is getting bigger and bigger.

Promotes active reading of the text; focuses attention.

MARCELLA: Today I'd like you to read the first three chapters—to page 18. In this part of the story, Arthur is going to get some advice from his friends about how to handle the envelope. As you read, decide which friend you think gives Arthur the best advice, and mark the place in the book where you determine this with a stick-on note. If you finish reading before others, take a card from the middle of the table and write your predictions about what is going to happen to Arthur.

Reading the Text

At the reading table, the five students read the chapters silently. While they read, Marcella confers briefly with each reader. When she touches a reader's hand, that reader begins to read out loud until Marcella moves on to another student. She takes notes on how the student is processing the text and occasionally helps an individual reader problem solve or exchanges a quick comment about the story. Here are several interactions Marcella had with individual readers.

MARCELLA AND LESLIE

On page 10, the text is:

> She looked surprised. "Really?"
> Everyone else nodded.
> "Well, still . . ." Francine tapped the envelope.
> "The proof is right here."

LESLIE *[reading]:* "Well, still Francine tapped the envelope." *[She does not pause to acknowledge the ellipses.]*

Explains and demonstrates how punctuation is used to convey the author's meaning.

MARCELLA: Leslie, let me show you something about the print. Do you see those three little dots? They mean that Francine was talking slowly and paused there. Like this. *[She reads the text, acknowledging the ellipses.]* She's showing that even though Arthur got one question right on the test, she is not convinced that he passed it. You read it that way. *[Leslie reads, pausing at the ellipses.]* Those little dots help you know how to read it so that you can understand what the character really meant. Those dots are called ellipses. They mean a little longer pause than a comma.

MARCELLA AND JOHN

On page 16, the text is:

> "Not interesting," said Muffy. "Risky. You need to get it as far away from your house as possible. Buy it a first-class ticket to Alaska or Timbuktu."
> "I don't have that kind of money," said Arthur.

JOHN: *[Reads the text fluently and laughs.]*

Recognizes the student's enjoyment of the text and comments on meaning.

MARCELLA: I think Arthur thinks that's a serious suggestion, don't you? *[They laugh.]* Nice reading.

Discussing and Revisiting the Text

At the end of the lesson each student reads the part of the text where he or she feels a friend gave the best advice. After a brief discussion, the group agrees that Francine gave the best advice.

CAROLE: Because if he gets rid of it, then he'll be in even more trouble.

Invites students to revisit the text to find evidence for their thinking and reinforces their judgment.

MARCELLA: Does everyone agree?
JOHN: He should give it to his mom, and then he'll just be in trouble for what's in the envelope.

Teaching for Processing Strategies

MARCELLA: I want to show you something interesting about the punctuation in this book. Turn to page 15. Find the place where it says, "The Brain was staring hard at Arthur's envelope." There are three little dots after the next thing he says.
CAROLE: What are they called?
MARCELLA: They are called ellipses. You know what you do when you come to a comma.
JOHN AND SEVERAL OTHERS: Stop and take a breath.
MARCELLA: Yes, that's right. When you see ellipses like these three little dots, you read slower and take a little longer pause than a comma. Listen. *[Reads to demonstrate.]* How did that sound?
JOHN: Like he was thinking.
LESLIE: Like he wasn't sure what to do.
JEFF: Like he slowed down but wasn't really finished with what he wanted to say.
MARCELLA: Yes, authors use that punctuation to help readers know how the characters sound.

Turn back to page 10, where Francine is talking at the bottom. Jeff, read what Francine says and notice the ellipses. [*Jeff reads, pausing appropriately.*]

MARCELLA: How did that sound?

LESLIE: Like she wasn't sure or she didn't agree with them.

Explains and demonstrates how punctuation is used to convey the author's meaning.

MARCELLA: The punctuation helped you understand how Francine was talking.

Extending Understanding

A guided reading lesson is also your opportunity to introduce your students to story elements and literary devices: plot, characters, setting, metaphor, symbolism, and the like. In the examples that follow, note how Marcella directs her students' attention to the elements present even in a simple story like *Arthur's Mystery Envelope*. Understanding how these elements and devices work to create a complex story line with believable characters enhances students' enjoyment of the story.

MARCELLA: Remember when we talked about how in a chapter book each chapter tells a part of the story? Together, the chapters in order tell the whole story of the book. [*She turns to a blank story map on chart paper clipped to the easel. She's already written the title and author's name on it—see Figure 11–3. A blank reproducible can be found in Appendix 24.*]

Reinforces understanding of story elements— setting.

MARCELLA: We've talked about the parts of stories. Let's take a look at the first three story parts on our map. What is the setting for this story?

JEFF: They were at school.

CAROLE: And he's going home.

MARCELLA: The story starts at Arthur's school and we read to the part where he goes home, so I'll write *school and home* for setting.

Reinforces understanding of story elements— characters.

MARCELLA: Who are the characters we've met so far?

JOHN: Arthur.

JEFF: The principal.

[*Marcella writes* Arthur *and* Mr. Haney *on the chart. Other students look through the chapters they read to notice names of characters.*]

CAROLE: His friends Buster and Binky.

JEFF: The Brain.

LESLIE: Francine, Muffy, and Prunella.

[*Marcella writes the characters' names as the children think of them. They mention everyone except Arthur's family.*]

Reinforces understanding of story elements— plot.

MARCELLA: What was the problem?

JEFF: He has to go to the principal's office and he gets this envelope that's private and confidential and he doesn't want to take it home.

MARCELLA: What does Arthur think might be in the envelope?

JOHN: His test.

CAROLE: Or a note that he has to go to summer school because he failed the test.

[*Marcella writes the problem on the chart.*]

MARCELLA: What are the important events that have taken place so far, after he got the envelope?

LESLIE: His friends wanted to help him get rid of the envelope.

JOHN: He imagined he was in a dungeon.

MARCELLA: The author is showing us Arthur's imagination so that we know he is worried in this book. It's helping us know how he feels.

Reinforces understanding of story elements— events.

MARCELLA: For events, we just want to know what happened, so I'll write a sentence here about his friends making those suggestions and we'll see what happens next tomorrow.

Story Map

Title: Arthur's Mystery Envelope
Author: Marc Brown

Setting:
School and Home

Characters:

Arthur	Prunella	Pal, the dog
D.W.	Muffy	Mrs. Reed
Buster	The Brain	Mr. Reed
Binky	Mr. Haney	
Francine		

Problem:

Mr. Haney, the principal, gave Arthur a sealed envelope to take to his mom. Arthur thinks the envelope has bad news about his school work.

Events:
Friends suggest ways to get rid of the envelope.
The envelope falls in the trash before Arthur's mother sees it.
D.W. teases Arthur about the envelope.
Arthur worries about the envelope all night and has bad dreams.
His conscience bothers him because he didn't tell his mother about the envelope.

Resolution/Conclusion:
Arthur gives the envelope to Mom, who opens it. Mr. Haney's tax papers were in it. Arthur learns that putting off something doesn't make it get any better and sometimes it makes it worse.

Figure 11–3. Story Map for Arthur's Mystery Envelope

Word Work

Guided reading lessons are also the perfect opportunity to discuss and demonstrate effective word-solving strategies that are needed by a particular group of readers. Using a white board, Marcella writes the following words, one at a time: *absent, contest, insect, paper, plastic, subtract, surprise, fantastic, invention, vacation,* and *wonderful.* Spending one to two minutes, she invites the students to look at the parts of each word to solve it. After working with each word, she erases it and writes a new one.

MARCELLA: We've been working on longer words. It helps to look at the parts of longer words. [*Writes* absent.] What is this word?

STUDENTS: *Absent.*

MARCELLA: What is the first part?

STUDENTS: *Ab.*

MARCELLA: And the last part?

STUDENTS: *sent.*

[*Marcella continues through the list of words, writing them and asking students to identify them quickly. They do not always identify the first and last parts of words. When she gets to the three-syllable word* fantastic, *she writes* fan.]

MARCELLA: This is the first part of the word.

LESLIE: *Fan.*

[*Marcella writes* tas.]

LESLIE: *Fantas . . . tic, fantastic.*

MARCELLA: Yes, *fantastic* has three parts—*fan . . . tas . . . tic.*

Helps students become more flexible in solving two- and three-syllable words.

Marcella continues through the three-syllable words, writing each part of the word. Students quickly find that they can identify most words from the first or second part and can then check their accuracy by looking at the whole word. They suggest two or three other three-part words, which Marcella writes down as well.

Summary of the Sample Guided Reading Lesson

In the above example of a guided reading lesson, Marcella was not simply teaching her students to read *Arthur's Mystery Envelope.* This particular text provided new opportunities for students to become better readers. By asking her students to read it, and guiding them through the reading, Marcella was teaching them *how*

to process a text so that they would be able to apply these strategies to any text.

Before the group began reading, Marcella carefully introduced the text to support their subsequent comprehension of this longer chapter book. Because she made the meaning and language of the story available to her students, they could turn their attention to aspects of print that contributed to text meaning, such as italicized print and ellipses. Against a backdrop of highly accurate reading, each student solved some unknown words that presented a new challenge. Word solving did not detract from their understanding of or focus on what the story meant. They already knew most of the words in the story, and they had effective strategies for solving unfamiliar ones. Students were reading silently most of the time, except for brief periods when Marcella listened to them read out loud. Her interactions with students at those times gave her an idea of how they were processing the text.

After reading, Marcella facilitated the students' discussion of the text and encouraged them to revisit it to substantiate their arguments. She extended their understanding of the text structure through a story map, which they finished over the three days they spent reading the eight chapters of the book.

Finally, she introduced two minutes of quick word work designed to help the children become more flexible in looking at words with two and three parts. Though she doesn't use word work every day, she often spends a minute or two focusing on word-solving strategies that match the demands of the texts the children will be reading. The words are not from a particular text but illustrate principles that will help them in all the reading they do.

Over the next two days, the students finished the book. The first lesson was the longest; since Marcella had introduced the whole text on day 1, the next two lessons were shorter. The introduction on day 2 was a brief reminder about the story, along with the suggestion to think about the events as they read Chapters 4, 5, and 6. In this section of the book, Arthur's relationship with his sister is prominent, and the children briefly discussed problems related to siblings, comparing their own experiences with Arthur's. They talked more about Arthur's problem and what he should do.

On day 3, Marcella began by reminding students what the italicized print signaled—that Arthur was dreaming or imagining. Students finished the book and completed the story map (see Figure 11–4). Jeff said that this story wasn't really a mystery like Cam Jansen's mystery, a comment that led the students to discuss the different meanings of *mystery*. Another discussion addressed the fact that Arthur's mother was an accountant, and the students surmised why "tax time" was such a busy period for her. At the end of their third session, Marcella showed them several other books in the Arthur series and placed the books in a basket from which they could be picked for independent reading.

The purpose of guided reading is to teach individuals to read increasingly difficult texts with understanding and fluency. First and foremost, these students read *Arthur's Mystery Envelope* with understanding and enjoyment. But they also learned more about the reading process:

■ They increased their reading power, learning how to process a longer text, for example by remembering events and details from one reading to the next and recalling and altering their interpretations as they read more.

■ They learned important processing strategies—such as using punctuation to access the author's meaning and syntax, solving words while holding

meaning, and sustaining fluency—that they can use to process other texts.

■ They learned about the ellipsis and how to use it to help them construct meaning.

■ They strengthened their ability to think about the whole story while reading segments of it over a number of days.

■ They sustained interest in and awareness of characters and plot over several days.

■ They formed opinions about the story and made predictions.

■ They used a story map to think about the cohesiveness of a longer story and how it all fits together and develops.

■ They added the words *confidential, accountant,* and *tax return* to their vocabulary.

■ They learned how to read actively by attending to important information.

A Sample Guided Reading Lesson: Nonfiction

Ben was working with a group of students to help them develop their ability to read expository texts. After searching for a short, interesting text that would illus-

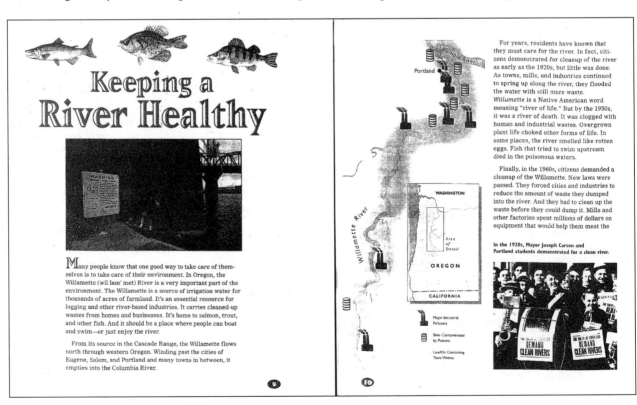

Figure 11–4. *"Keeping a River Healthy"*

trate some of the ways readers derive information from nonfiction, he selected an article titled "Keeping a River Healthy" (Keeler and Goldner 1995). The page size is 8½" by 11", and there are illustrations on every page (see Figure 11–4). The piece is well documented. For example, the authors cite details about how the river was polluted, and they make a striking comparison when they report that the river, Willamette (a Native American word for "river of life"), is called a "river of death" that smells like rotten eggs.

The article begins with a big idea: "Many people know that one good way to take care of themselves is to take care of their environment." The writers then use the Willamette river as an example, telling the story in chronological order. The layout switches from one to two columns. Most sentences range from ten to fourteen words, although a few are longer. Each paragraph begins with a sentence that communicates a clear main idea that the authors then develop.

The authors detail important historical events and identify environmental advocacy groups. Students can imagine their own role in environmental actions because the authors highlight a group of middle school students, depicted in many photographs, who have become involved and are using the wetlands as a laboratory for learning. The middle schoolers' decision to take action offers potential for discussion. The vocabulary of the article includes technical words like *irrigation, slough,* and *dissolved.* The authors use hyphenated words such as *clean-up* and *fast-moving* and compound words such as *outfall* and *runoff,* for which students can predict meaning. The authors also use dashes for emphasis within sentences. Students need to understand concepts like *the source of a river, pollution,* and *public health,* but many technical terms have explicit or implied definitions within the text.

The graphic design of the article includes a map of the river (with an inset showing a larger geographic area on a smaller scale), modern photographs, and a photo from the 1920s; these illustrations add considerably to the meaning of the text. For example, people are shown holding a sign warning of combined sewer outfall. Reading the captions to the pictures will add to the students' ability to understand what's happening in them. In addition there is an inset, which is related to the article but which can stand alone, entitled "Water and Your Health." The voice of the inset is slightly different from the article in that it uses the imperative case.

Introducing the Text to Students

In preparing his introduction, Ben considered the text's characteristics, selecting aspects to call to the students' attention. His goal was to help students learn how to process this particular text without taking away some of their own discoveries. This is part of the conversation:

Introduces genre, title, and author.

BEN: Today we're going to read an informational article called "Keeping a River Healthy," by Barbara Keeler and Katy Goldner.

Encourages students to use their background knowledge.

BEN: You know what we mean when we say a person is healthy. How could a river be healthy or unhealthy?

DESIREE: If it's dirty, it's kind of like it's sick.

PHILLIP: If it has chemicals, like the Charles River sometimes.

ALAN: There's pollution in it because people dump things in there that they shouldn't.

BARBARA: Or the water gets very low and you can see it's murky and you know that it's polluted.

Draws attention to photograph in contrast to topic.

BEN: Open to page 9, and look at the picture of a river in the northwest part of the United States in a state called Oregon. How does it look in the picture?

ALAN: Clean and fresh. Like you could swim in it.

NIKKI: But it's really not clean because look at what it says there. It used to be dirty.

PHILLIP: How can it be dirty when it's blue? The Charles River looks dirty because it's brown, and my dad says it's polluted.

ALAN: Water is blue because of the sky. It's like a mirror, but it still could be dirty with chemicals or something.

BARBARA: Or, like, the stuff from the sewer. Some water even smells bad.

Provides information, foreshadows content, and introduces one of the main ideas of the article.

BEN: In this article you're going to learn that this used to be a very dirty river and it got cleaned up. You're also going to learn that cleaning up a river is just like cleaning your room; it has to be done over and over to keep it clean. *[Students laugh.]* In this article the river was cleaned up twenty years ago, but now it needs another clean-up because there are new sources of pollution.

Invites students to use background knowledge to predict the information they will find.

BEN: What information would you expect the authors to give you about keeping a river healthy?

DESIREE: All the things that pollute it and make it not healthy.

ALAN: What problems are caused by dirty rivers . . . why we need to clean them up.

BEN: In this article the authors will give you many different sources of pollution, and you'll be thinking about why it's important to clean up rivers.

NIKKI: What people did to clean up the river.

Confirms students' responses and introduces another big idea.

BEN: Yes, in this article, you'll learn about all the different people who were concerned and did something about the river. It even includes a teacher and her students because they were concerned.

Asks for summary.

BEN: So what's the problem going to be in this article?

SEVERAL STUDENTS: Pollution. A dirty river.

Focuses attention on the important information in the text and suggests a purpose for reading.

BEN: And you're going to read about all of the ways people have tried to find solutions to the problem. Remember how we have been talking about how authors give information on how to pronounce names? If you look on page 9 you'll find the name of the river and how to pronounce it.

Draws attention to something they can use to figure out pronunciation (an aspect of word solving).

BEN: Use the information in the parentheses to pronounce the river's name. *[Several students try using the pronunciation guide.]*

Prompts them to search for important information and notice metaphor.

BEN: You notice how the accent is on the second syllable of the word *[wil lam' met]*. That's a Native American word. You'll read what it means and see whether that's a good name for it. Turn to the next page. What do you notice?

BARBARA: A map.

BEN: Yes, it's a map of the river that shows how it flows from its source in the Cascade Mountains to Portland, Oregon. This map has symbols on it that represent three sources of pollution and a key that tells you what they stand for. What are some of them?

ALAN *[reading]:* Major industrial polluters.

Brings out important vocabulary; teaches students to use graphic features to access information.

BEN: What does *industrial* mean?

ALAN: Factories and stuff.

BARBARA *[reading]:* Sites Contaminated by Poisons.

BEN: . . . and *contaminated* means . . .

BARBARA: It's poison.

DESIREE: It's polluted.

PHILLIP *[reading]:* Landfills containing toxic wastes.

BEN: *Toxic* also means *poison*. People were dumping poisonous things into low parts of the land.

Generalizes information on graphic features.

BEN: Many times maps have symbols that help you understand what's going on at the places shown on the map, and the key will also help you. You might also notice the smaller map in the top corner of the river map. It shows three states and the entire river.
NIKKI: Oregon is north of California.
BEN: I can see you know how to read maps. What about the photograph on that page?
NIKKI: Is it a band?

Teaches students how to access information in pictures.

BEN: You'll find that you need to read the captions for pictures in this article to get more information. They give you more information than the picture alone. Read the caption to yourself.
ALAN: They're demanding a clean river.
NIKKI: It was in 1920.
BEN: Look at page 11. When there is more than one picture there will be clue words to tell you where to look. Do you see where it says *above?* That means to look at the picture that is right above the caption. Do you see where it says *right* on the third line?
[*Students find* above *and* right.] That means to look at the picture to the right of the caption.

Generalizes information.

BEN: You should look for those clue words when you're reading captions under pictures so you are sure you are looking at the right one.

Teaches students how to use text layout in connection with the author's purpose for writing.

BEN: Look at page 12. There is a green box there with print on it. It's not part of the article but provides related information about water and your health. The authors offer some good advice there for us as readers. You can read the material in that box any time—before you read the article, after you finish, or sometime in the middle of reading it.

Helps students attend to word solving—how a word looks and what it means.

BEN: Look at the first paragraph in the second column, where the authors mention that the River Watch managers are really worried about the Columbia slough in North Portland. The word *slough* ends just like the word *rough.* The authors help us understand what a slough is by giving us more information in parentheses. Read the definition of *slough* and see if it fits with what you know.

Tells them to search for important information while reading and summarize it afterwards.

BEN: I'm going to ask you as you are reading to notice all of the actions that people took to solve the problem and to write a list of them in your writer's notebook.

Reading the Text

After Ben has introduced the article, the students read the article silently and make lists in their notebook while Ben works with another group. Ben meets with them again about fifteen minutes later.

Discussing and Revisiting the Text

Students share their lists of actions described in the article and discover they have identified quite a few. As they share their actions, Ben quickly writes them on a piece of chart paper so that everyone can see (see Figure 11–5).

The students are particularly interested in the work of the group of middle school students cited in the article. Two of Ben's students say they want to find out about pollution in their own city and later do some research on the Internet. The discussion turns to why it is important to take care of the environment in general. Students mention several school projects that have occurred within the year connected with "Save Our Earth," a campaign for taking care of our earth.

The students then take turns directing the others to places in the article that they found interesting or places where they learned something new. They have a productive discussion about pollution and wonder what they can do to make a difference in the environment.

Teaching for Processing Strategies

Ben reminds them that they have learned some ways to think about reading articles that they can use while reading other articles.

Reinforces new processing strategies that they can use in reading other expository texts.

For example, they have learned about:

■ Reading the captions along with the pictures.
■ Using the information in charts and maps.
■ Noticing symbols and what they mean.
■ Reading insets or boxed features.

Encourages students to think beyond the text.

Ben asks the students why they think the authors wrote this article. Students believe the authors have written the article to persuade adults and kids that they must:

■ Keep working at keeping a river clean.
■ Clean up the environment; this helps keep everyone healthy, so it's everyone's job.
■ Do something about the environment if they are interested in making a healthier world.
■ Make a difference by working together.

Summary of the Sample Guided Reading Lesson

In this lesson Ben provided an introduction to the text, the students read the text individually, the group discussed what they had read, and Ben taught for processing strategies. (Ben didn't extend the meaning of the text or do word work, because he decided these actions weren't needed by the students.) The students, motivated by what they had read and talked about, initiated further reading and inquiry.

The introduction to this lesson took about five minutes; students read for about fifteen minutes; and when Ben returned to the group, he worked with them an additional five minutes. So, in about twenty-five minutes Ben helped his students learn some important aspects of processing expository texts. Using a text that offered appropriate conceptual and reading challenges, Ben helped these students use their background knowledge to access information. They learned how to

---

What We Can Do to Keep a River Healthy

1. Don't let factories dump waste in it.

2. Test the water often.

3. Look at the fish to see if they are poisoned or deformed.

4. Educate people to know how important clean water is.

5. Don't use weed killer or other chemicals.

6. Recycle bottles and cans.

7. Write letters about it.

8. Warn people about the danger of pollution.

9. Keep working at it all the time.

Figure 11–5. Completed List of Actions

use graphic features such as maps, symbols, and legends and text features such as insets and photo captions. They were able to relate the topic to themselves and the world. They practiced using a pronunciation guide. They attended to the organization of ideas in the piece, relating the problem the authors described and the solutions that arose. The students enjoyed reading an interesting article and increased their reading power. Equally important, they became interested in further reading and inquiry and were able to use reading and writing for real purposes.

We trust that these classroom vignettes have given you a conceptual—and concrete—understanding of guided reading in action. As you have seen, it is a highly focused instructional segment in which students and teacher zero in on key aspects of the text, always with an eye toward creating, extending, and refining meaning. Within the comfortable, familiar routine of the guided reading lesson, you help your students mentally and emotionally "lock in" on the text. In this way, they develop a fluid, flexible reading process that they can alter and adapt as the challenges of each reading experience demand. The next chapter is a step-by-step guide to implementing an effective guided reading lesson, focusing on the all-important introduction.

Suggestions for Professional Development

1. To begin exploring how guided reading lessons can work in your classroom, meet with your colleagues in grade-level teams.

2. Before the session, ask each team to select a chapter book (fiction) and a short informational text (an article or part of a longer text) that would be about right for the average students in their classes. All members of the team should receive a copy and then read the book and the informational text.

3. At the session, taking one book or informational text at a time, generate a list of the learning opportunities in the particular text. What demands does the text place on the readers? What will you have to teach them how to do? You can also use the sample lessons in this chapter as models.

4. Compare the fiction and nonfiction texts. What are the differences in the demands these texts make on readers? What are the differences in opportunities to learn?

## CHAPTER TWELVE

PLANNING FOR GUIDED READING

In any guided reading session, the teacher needs to know what knowledge and understanding each child will bring to the reading and what supports or assistance will be necessary to ensure that the students can read the text successfully.

— MARGARET MOONEY

Frank Smith (1979) maintains that individuals learn to read by reading—and we agree. But there is no guarantee that a student will develop effective reading strategies simply by choosing and reading any book or being assigned to read a section and answer questions. Smith also says the teacher must create conditions that support the child in this process. The careful selection of "just right" texts together with your skillful introduction of the texts provides ideal conditions for your students as they develop their reading skills.

With the assistance of a more "expert other," students do learn to read by reading. Careful planning and thoughtful organization enable you to focus your teaching energies on the guided reading lesson and serve as your students' expert guide. There are a number of materials you will want to have at hand for the guided reading lesson and a series of steps to take before, during, and after the lesson.

Basic Materials

Most teachers use a round or horseshoe-shape table to meet with guided reading groups. You will need an easel, a small whiteboard, dry-erase markers, and an eraser, all close to the reading table. You should be able to reach for an item without getting up or stealing precious time from your teaching. (One teacher we know parks a small cart next to the guided reading table to store supplies such as magnetic letters, stick-on notes, pens, pencils, markers, and book sets.) You will also want to have a clipboard on which you can place your record-keeping forms.

The easel is handy for writing words during word analysis. You can also jot down what you want the students to do after they finish reading the assigned text. This procedure will serve as a helpful reminder and is also useful for creating large graphic organizers such as story maps or character webs with the group as a whole.

Students bring their copies of the book to the guiding reading lesson. They also often bring their reader's notebooks in case you ask them to do some writing in connection with reading in the last section.

Figure 12–1. Guided Reading Group

Summary of Steps Leading Up To and Following the Lesson

Before the guided reading lesson you should:

1. Think about the last reading lesson in which you observed the students. Refer to your notes. Consider whether you are going to make any grouping changes.
2. Select a book or other text that you think will build on the readers' processing strengths and meet their processing needs.
3. Read the book with your readers in mind.
4. Plan your introduction, writing a few sentences or making notes on what you want to communicate or features you want to emphasize. You may want to place stick-on notes on the cover and in the book.
5. Make sure your record-keeping system is ready and all materials are organized and available.

At the end of a guided reading lesson, you should:

1. Think once again about whether your grouping is appropriate for all the students.
2. Consider what you learned from observing the students read the text and how that will influence which book you select next or your next lesson using this book.
3. Make some quick notes on what students need to learn how to do next and the possible texts you can use to accomplish that goal. In other words, how can they improve their processing strategies?
4. Reflect on the effectiveness of your teaching. What did the students learn how to do today as readers that they didn't know how to do before?
5. Be sure to leave your materials in good order for the next group or the next day. It's best to organize as you go rather than leave a disorganized pile of books for the end of a busy day.

You have a very limited time for guided reading, so it is important to be well organized and efficient about your preparation. Planning becomes easier and more efficient once you are familiar with the books and know more about your readers.

Lesson Frequency

Create a system whereby you will meet regularly with all students. Lower-achieving students need more guidance and more supported instruction; therefore, consider meeting with them almost every day. Higher-achieving students will not require a group meeting every day and can do more on their own after a quick check-in with you. Still, higher-achieving students also deserve regular small-group teaching that helps them refine and extend their comprehending strategies.

Experience suggests it is better to work with a group over several consecutive days rather than every second or third day. We encourage you to design your reading block in weeklong chunks, delineating the times you can meet with guided reading groups. That will give you an estimate of how many groups per week are feasible.

Number of Texts

Some readers are able to read more than one book at a time with no problems. They can switch from one book to another for different purposes and to suit different moods without confusion or loss of interest. Readers who can manage this variety can read one book for independent reading and start a new book for guided reading during the same day. You will want to exercise caution, however, with immature readers who may require more structure and focus.

One way to help such readers is to use short texts in guided reading, so that they finish the text in one or two lessons. That way, it becomes an interesting addition to their independent reading but doesn't detract from it. If you are going to use a longer text for guided reading with these students, let them know in advance; they may want to make an extra effort to bring their independent reading books to completion at school or take them home for evening reading. Then you can start them in a new book in guided reading that they read as part of the group. The text used in guided reading may be assigned eventually to independent reading. The goal is to minimize the number of books a student is reading at one time.

Classroom Management

It takes good management skills to implement small-group reading instruction in a class of twenty-five to thirty students. A good management system is a prerequisite for guided reading.

What Is the Rest of the Class Doing?

Working with small groups always gives rise to the question: *What are the other students doing?* Reading workshop also provides for ongoing independent work on the part of your students. As we explain in Chapter 4, students are engaged in productive activity, including:

- Reading self-selected or assigned texts independently.
- Writing in reader's notebooks.
- Reading texts for literature study.
- Completing assigned tasks related to guided reading instruction.

Teaching the Routines

It is possible to have good management and ineffective teaching, but it is not possible to have poor management and effective teaching. You will want to teach the routines of reading workshop—to include independent and guided reading—just as you would teach anything else—with demonstration, practice, and feedback—until students know them very well and can operate within them effectively.

Designing Guided Reading

Every guided reading lesson is different because each group of readers has different strengths and needs. Furthermore, the text used differs from lesson to lesson and offers an additional set of unique challenges. Nevertheless, we recommend that your guided reading lessons adhere to the basic design set down in Figure 12–2, which supports both the development of student reading strategies and effective teaching interactions. The advantages of this lesson structure are that it:

- Allows for better planning and efficiency.
- Helps students know what to expect because they internalize a way of working together and can focus their attention on the text.

A Framework for Guided Reading Lessons

- ❖ Selecting the Text
- ❖ Introducing the Text
- ❖ Reading the Text
- ❖ Discussing and Revisiting the Text
- ❖ Teaching for Processing Strategies
- ❖ Extending the Meaning of the Text (optional)
- ❖ Word Work (optional)

Figure 12–2. A Framework for Guided Reading Lessons

- Provides for different kinds of learning in different ways; each element has a function related to students' ability to construct meaning.

These components work together to form a unified whole and create a solid base from which to build comprehension. You teach actively and intensively within every component of the guided reading lesson.

Selecting the Text

You will select particular texts for specific groups on the basis of a combination of three kinds of knowledge:

1. Detailed information about the readers in the group.
2. Familiarity with the available texts.
3. Knowledge of the reading process and the general principles of reading development.

Regular consultation of your notes on student behavior and your records of student reading will help you to get an idea of the kinds of strategies students are using. With students' strengths and needs in mind, select a text from your collection of books categorized by level of difficulty (see Chapter 14). If you are working with students with low English skills, be especially careful to assess the text in terms of accessibility of its language structure. Plan an introduction so that it supports and develops the reader's language knowledge. Since the goal of guided reading is to provide opportunities for students to learn, the text should be slightly more difficult than one students can read independently. Your introduction will support their new learning.

Text selection is a complex process and you'll get better at it as you read books yourself and use them with different learners. (Text selection is discussed in greater detail in Chapter 14.)

Introducing the Text

RATIONALE

The introduction is a guide to the reader who will be processing the text. Rogoff (1990) has described "guided participation" as providing supportive structures for the novice. By demonstrating and communicating needed information, you remove some of the complexity of the task, thus enabling the reader to take on new challenges. Guided participation also involves tacit communication and the transfer of responsibility to the novices over time. Students will need introductions to new and challenging texts; they can read other texts independently, questioning and guiding their reading on their own. The "scaffold" provided by the text introduction will support effective processing of the text.

PLANNING THE INTRODUCTION

First and foremost, emphasize that reading is understanding. When you introduce a text to a group of students you might:

- Help them connect the text to their own lives, to their knowledge of the world, or to their literary experience.
- Demonstrate the kinds of questions readers ask about a text.
- Prompt them to think about the author's style.
- Help them recall what they already know about a topic (for an informational text) or the setting or plot (for a narrative text).
- Help them discover and internalize literary language patterns they might not use in everyday speech.
- Reveal the structure of the whole text—how the author has organized the information.
- Stimulate their interest in the text so they want to read it.
- Bring to their attention conventions of print such as punctuation, titles and subtitles, or chapter headings.
- Show them how to use text layout (side headings, for

example) to help them search for information.
- Teach them to use the table of contents, indices, appendices, and other reference sections of texts.
- Highlight the genre and help them predict the characteristics of the text they are reading based on past experience.
- Encourage them to look at the cover of the book and generate expectations of the text.
- Prompt them to examine and interpret illustrations, charts, graphs, maps, and other visual aids and discuss how they communicate the meaning of the text.
- Pay special attention to vocabulary and language structures that will be needed for English learners.

PLANNING FOR THE APPROPRIATE LEVEL OF SUPPORT

While all introductions are fairly brief, they range from a rich discussion that gives students a great deal of information to a few focused comments that will guide their reading. The length and content of the introduction will depend on the complexity of the text and these particular readers' background knowledge, experience with text features, understanding of genre, and reading skills.

It is a misunderstanding to assume that students reading at lower levels need richer introductions and students at higher levels need less support. The introduction is always planned in relation to the challenges and learning opportunities this particular text offers to these particular readers. Advanced readers who are introduced to *Out of the Dust* (Hesse 1999), for example, might need a very supportive introduction to understand the setting, the period of history, the phenomenon of blowing dust, and the layout of print on the page. Another group of readers being introduced to *Ginger Brown: Too Many Houses* (Wyeth 1996) may need only a brief discussion before they begin reading this straightforward story.

Figure 12–3 depicts a "sliding scale" to apply every time you plan the introduction of a text to a group of students (Fountas and Pinnell 1996). What the students bring to the text has an inverse relationship to the level and kind of support you provide in the introduction. The introduction is really a way of teaching children how to think for themselves as readers. After all, eventually as mature readers, they will need to discover and introduce texts for and to themselves.

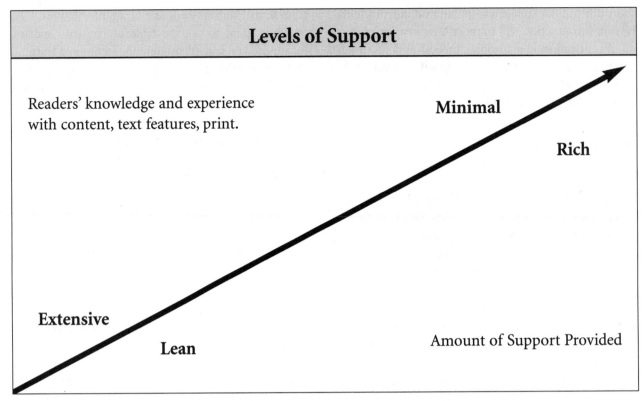

Figure 12–3. *Levels of Support*

Reading the Text

Following the introduction, each student silently reads the entire text or a unified portion of it. Guided reading differs from traditional group instruction in which "round robin reading"—students taking turns reading aloud—holds center stage. Guided reading also differs from shared reading, in which students read in chorus or follow along as the teacher reads.

In guided reading, students are expected to embrace the role of reader independently. All students work individually, reading silently. They know that they must actively use the processing strategies they control to solve problems while reading. Anticipating the discussion they will have with their friends after the reading, they may focus on particular aspects of the text. To provide evidence for their thinking or to identify and remember their questions, they may write things down on stick-on notes. Be careful not to require constant interruption of the flow of reading, however.

Your role during the reading is multifaceted and involves making moment-by-moment decisions. While the students are reading, you might want to

sample their oral reading by moving around and asking individual readers to make their voices audible as they continue reading. Some readers in the group may need a little more attention than others. You can take a moment to reinforce something new a reader is doing or shift her away from unproductive behavior. We emphasize that the interaction must be brief. If it takes too long, you will interrupt the reader's construction of meaning and cause her to fall behind the others in completing the assigned section of the book. Note the need that will take time to consider and address it at the end of the reading or you can attend to the need in your next lesson.

You may interact briefly with all members of the group or work a little longer with some students, making a point to listen to the others the next day. Alternately, you may decide to allow students to read entirely on their own while you work with another group or confer with other students in the class, returning to the original group once they have finished their silent reading.

Your observations during guided reading are valu-

Guided Reading Observations

Guided Reading Observations

Peter	Lanisha
¹⁰/₁₅ What's Cooking Jenny Archer (m)	¹⁰/₁₅ What's Cooking Jenny Archer (m)
p. 35 - Noticed use of italics and stressed with voice. Generally fluent, phrased oral reading.	p. 34 - Said Jenny is trying to please too many people and you can't please everyone. Noted - A Deli is more expencive than a store - using prior knowledge to predict.
¹⁰/₁₆ p. 41-42 Said that you have to use all ingredients or cookies will not turn out right - use of prior knowledge to predict.	¹⁰/₁₆ p. 50 Said Jenny is always getting into a mess because she gets ideas but doesn't always read directions and think about it - connections to the character in general.
Maria	**Redo**
¹⁰/₁₅ What's Cooking Jenny Archer (m)	¹⁰/₁₅ What's Cooking Jenny Archer (m)
p. 36 Thought 50¢ was a lot for one cookie - did not notice italics but did use emphasis after talking about it.	p. 37 Oral reading slow - not noticing punctuation.
¹⁰/₁₆ Worked on wrap, wrapped, and unwrap. Able to summarize Jenny's problem as not satisfying customers and having lunch cost too much.	¹⁰/₁₆ p. 52 Predicts Jenny's parents aren't going to let her do it. (Inferred from their asking what if someone got sick.) Worked out customers.
Luke	**Matt**
¹⁰/₁₅ What's Cooking Jenny Archer (m)	¹⁰/₁₅ What's Cooking Jenny Archer (m)
p. 35-36 Oral reading accurate but little phrasing. Noticed punctuation. Pointed out italics.	p. 38 Oral reading largely fluent - using punctuation. Notice and used italics.
p. 49 ¹⁰/₁₆ Said - You get ideas from TV that are good but don't always work. Jenny took 1 idea but it led to others. Notice she set temperature too high so cookies burned.	¹⁰/₁₆ p. 46 Noticed that author makes it sound like people are really talking. Noticed Sometimes author uses italics and sometimes all capitals like a title. What's the difference?

Figure 12–4. Guided Reading Observations

able; they help you make powerful teaching points after the lesson and prepare for the next lesson. The notes you make during your observations reveal students' strengths. (Figure 12–4 shows one teacher's notes over several days of guided reading lessons. A reproducible form is included in Appendix 48. An alternative form is presented in Appendix 49.) Photocopy the form before adding students' names and keep a supply on hand. You can write the students' names in the narrow boxes on the sheet. A neat trick is to place blank stick-on notes in the larger boxes and write your comments on the notes, later moving the stick-on notes to a card in the students' literacy record folder.

Discussing and Revisiting the Text

After the reading, talk with students about the meaning of the text, inviting them to make connections. They may revisit the text to search for more information or find evidence to support their thinking. The activities that follow reading draw attention back to the text and build on the learning that took place earlier in the lesson.

Inviting your students to talk about their personal response to a text is a key aspect of the guided reading lesson. In the example in Chapter 11, as children were reading *Arthur's Mystery Envelope* (Brown 1997), they placed stick-on notes on a part of the text they would share with others. These notes were a stimulus for discussion. Sometimes you might ask students to make a few notes when they finish reading and then share their thinking with the group in the discussion.

Through the discussion, you help students:

- Summarize and synthesize information.
- Communicate their ideas to others.
- Make inferences and hypotheses related to the text.
- Express the connections they are making between the text and their own lives.
- Evaluate the text in light of their knowledge and experience.
- Benefit from the interpretations and understanding of others.
- Confirm and extend their understanding.
- Consult with others as they resolve dilemmas.
- Relate the text to other texts they have read.
- Think critically about the text—the facts or the language.

- Search the text for information to support or disprove their thinking.
- Converse with one another about character development.

Developing students' knowledge of vocabulary is always a good reason to revisit a text. Examining words in a text your students have just read makes it easier to explore the meaning of the words and to determine how they fit into the larger meaning of the piece. Students will discover new meanings for words they already know; they can also pick up on the subtle shadings of meanings—the connotations of words—as they are used in different contexts. (See Chapter 22 for a discussion of vocabulary.) You may want to revisit the text with students for other reasons as well, such as to clarify meaning, search for themes, or notice the author's use of language. Remind your students to provide evidence from the text to back up their conclusions about a book.

Teaching for Processing Strategies

You will also want to highlight one or two important processing strategies. We have already specified that this teaching should be brief and explicit. It is effective because it follows so closely their successful reading of a text and helps them see how to problem-solve by flexibly using sources of information.

Your teaching examples arise from your observation of students' reading behavior as well as ongoing assessment of their needs. You know what your students can do as readers, and you also keep in mind the processing strategies they need to develop or refine and extend (see Chapters 20 and 21). For example, if you want students to be able to use word parts and base words to solve words while reading for meaning, you might have them turn to a part in the text where word solving is necessary, then work through a short, explicit example on a white dry-erase board or an easel. In a clear and concise way, demonstrate the word-solving behavior. Then ask the students to go back to the text to see whether the word makes sense in the story.

You might think of this kind of teaching as a very quick minilesson related to the text and to the problem-solving actions that you want students to learn. The purpose of this teaching is not to enable students to read the particular text but to *develop strategies they can apply to all reading.*

Extending the Meaning of the Text (Optional)

Sometimes you may want to ask students to write about the text or do some other activity designed to extend their understanding. An extension activity is an optional component but sometimes can be an important one.

You may extend meaning by asking students to compare and contrast:

- Different authors' treatment of the same topic.
- Different books by the same author.
- Different biographies of the same individual.
- Similar concepts across fiction and nonfiction texts.

Or you may ask them to analyze characters or explore concepts from different perspectives. You can incorporate art by asking students to sketch their response. Sometimes students role-play how the characters would talk and behave in different situations. Some teachers use graphic organizers to help students learn how to analyze the structure or some other aspect of the text. In the example lesson in Chapter 11, after the students read *Arthur's Mystery Envelope,* they used a graphic organizer (on a large piece of chart paper) to specify setting, characters, plot or problem, events, and resolution. They were learning how to discern the structure in a longer narrative. (Chapter 26 further describes the use of graphic organizers as a tool for extending children's understanding of a text. A variety of reproducible graphic organizers are included in Appendices 24–30.)

Often, further reading or data gathering on a topic is a way to help students extend their understanding. Reading leads to more reading when students are pursuing a topic that interests them. For example, reading a book may send students to the Internet to discover books by the same author or to research history and geography related to the setting for a story. One group of students who read *Snowflake Bentley* (Martin 1998) used the Internet to look up the central character. They found that he was, indeed, a real person, and they located a number of other biographies written about him. In this way, students come to appreciate reading as a tool for learning.

Remember that you don't need to plan for an extension activity after every book. Most often it is best simply to go on to another book that offers new learning opportunities. As adults, we seldom "extend" books beyond talking about them with our friends. Occasionally, when we are very interested, we might read up on a topic or use the Internet for further research. We might seek out other books by a new author whom we enjoy. When you help students extend the meaning of a text, you are not only teaching them to think in different ways about a text; you are also building the kind of reader who understands that reflecting on a text and connecting it with his life in some way are key aspects of reading.

Word Work (Optional)

One important aspect of being an effective reader is the ability to solve words rapidly and easily while reading continuous text. Word work is a one- or two-minute optional component of a guided reading lesson. You ask the students to play with words or help them discover how words work by writing several examples on a chart, chalkboard, or dry-erase board. You can also use word parts on magnetic strips or have students write words. For students who are having difficulty learning about print, it is sometimes helpful to use multicolored individual magnetic letters that can be manipulated for kinesthetic stimulation.

During word work, students are analyzing individual words in isolation, using only visual information. You don't want to emphasize word work in isolation, but a very brief amount of time spent paying close attention to the structure of words helps students become more aware of letter patterns and word parts. They learn how to recognize parts and patterns; they learn how to be flexible in using print information while reading text.

It makes sense to perform this word analysis at the end of a guided reading lesson, because students in the group have similar needs and are meeting similar challenges in the texts they are reading. In addition, you can engage their attention more effectively in the small group. Word work is a good way to focus their attention; it is also an excellent way to involve them more intensely in the overarching word study you may be doing with the entire class. For example, if you are working on prefixes with your whole class, you might focus the small group on prefixes as well, thus giving them an instructional boost.

Not all students will need word work as part of the guided reading lesson. Notice how quickly and easily students are able to take words apart while reading text and how flexible they are in applying a variety of word-solving strategies. Observe how they attend to parts of words. If students are easily meeting the word-solving requirements of texts at a particular level, they probably will not need this word work.

Seeing the Lesson as a Whole

The components of guided reading lessons give you a structure that will help you plan and manage them. However, comprehending the text is the unifying goal for all these components. All teaching in a guided reading lesson is directed toward helping children develop a system of strategies they can use to construct meaning while reading. Comprehending is the purpose of making connections, word solving, using prior knowledge, and all other processing strategies you help students use (see Chapter 19).

In addition to developing students' reading strategies, we need to consider their attitudes. Reading must be a satisfying experience; our guarantee that it will be so begins with finding engaging material for our students to read successfully. While students are learning about reading, they are also developing lifelong habits as readers. Tedious drill will make students drop the reading habit as soon as they leave school.

The guided reading lesson is designed to be fast-paced and productive. Move smoothly from one lesson component to another, keeping the strand of the lesson going. Children need to feel their growing competence; they need to understand what it is they are doing and how it is helping them. Don't be afraid to confirm what students are learning. Give them positive feedback. Acknowledge their achievements.

The essential elements of guided reading can be examined from both the student's and the teacher's points of view. Figure 12–5 provides a summary of what happens before, during, and after reading of the text in a guided reading lesson.

Self-Assessment for Teaching Guided Reading

You will also want to think about your progress in implementing guided reading over time. A self-assessment inventory, outlining eight dimensions of guided reading, is included in Appendix 50. This instrument

will help you think about where you are in the process and what resources and support you might need.

Guided reading is a superb instructional context for introducing small groups of students to a wide range of reading strategies. When you work with twenty-five or thirty students at a time, it is impossible to select texts that will fit them all. For some, the text will be so difficult that they cannot possibly learn anything positive about reading as they struggle simply to "get through it". For others, the text will be so easy it won't offer the appropriately stimulating reading challenge necessary for learning. Selecting and introducing texts for a particular group of students who share similar developmental needs at a point in time creates a context that supports learning.

Students' reading achievement is largely determined by their individual efforts and by effective teaching that expands their capacity to learn more. It is our role to provide the guided reading instruction that keeps them engaged. Engagement begins and ends with successful reading experiences and a profound enjoyment of reading.

Suggestions for Professional Development

1. Meet with your colleagues in grade-level teams to prepare a guided reading lesson for a fiction and a short informational text you have selected previously.
2. With your students in mind, think through the shape of a guided reading lesson for each text. Consider:
   - What will you address in the introduction?
   - How will you invite students to access background information?
   - What text organization characteristics will you point out to students?
   - Which concepts/vocabulary will you cover in advance, and which will you leave for students to discover?
   - *For the fiction book,* how will you break up the reading? What are the natural dividing points?
   - *For the nonfiction text,* how does the author organize and present ideas?
3. Determine some possible discussion points to introduce when you revisit the text after reading. Consider:

The Essential Elements of Guided Reading

	Teacher Role	Student Role
Before the Reading	❖ Select texts that will provide opportunities for students to expand their processing strategies. ❖ Prepare an introduction to the text that will help readers access and use all sources of information in a fluent processing system. ❖ Introduce the whole text or unified sections of the text, keeping in mind the demands of the text and the knowledge, experience, and skills of the readers. ❖ Leave some opportunities for students to independently solve problems while reading (moderate amount of challenge).	❖ Engage in a conversation about the text. ❖ Understand the purpose for reading the text ❖ Access background knowledge (personal, literary, world) as they prepare to read a new text. ❖ Raise questions about the text. ❖ Build expectations for the text. ❖ Notice information in the text. ❖ Make connections between the new text and others they have read.
During the Reading	❖ May listen to individuals read a segment orally. ❖ Interact with individuals to assist with problem solving at difficulty. ❖ Interact with individuals to reinforce ongoing construction of meaning. ❖ Observe reading behaviors and make notes about the strategy use of individual readers.	❖ Read the whole text or a unified part to themselves (silently). ❖ Use background knowledge and strategies effectively to construct meaning. ❖ Think about what they understand and questions that they have about the text.
After the Reading	❖ Talk about the text with the students and encourage them to talk with/to each other. ❖ Invite personal response. ❖ Return to the text for one or two teaching opportunities such as finding evidence or discussing problem-solving. ❖ Assess students' understanding of what they read. ❖ Invite students to ask questions to expand their understanding. ❖ Sometimes engage the students in writing—personal responses, comments, questions, or other forms to extend understanding. ❖ Sometimes engage students in two minutes of isolated work with words to increase flexibility and speed in word solving.	❖ Talk with each other and the teacher about the text. ❖ Think about what they understand and questions the text raises. ❖ Check predictions and react personally to the text. ❖ Raise questions or make comments to clarify confusion and expand understanding. ❖ Express personal, text-related, and world-related connections. ❖ Revisit the text at points of problem solving as guided by the teacher. ❖ Revisit the text to provide evidence for thinking. ❖ Sometimes engage in revisiting or responding to the text through talk, writing, or visual arts. ❖ Sometimes engage in taking words apart and discovering how words work.

Figure 12–5. The Essential Elements of Guided Reading

■ How can you help students relate ideas in the text to their personal, world, and literary knowledge?

■ How can you help students summarize and synthesize information from the text?

■ How can you help students think *about* the text?

■ How can you help students think *beyond* the text?

4. Summarize what you have learned in this meeting that will change your teaching in guided reading.

5. After you have been using guided reading for a few weeks, bring a group of intermediate teachers together to discuss the self-assessment instrument in Appendix 50. Invite each member of the group to review the first four items on the inventory and indicate his or her progress toward implementing guided reading.

6. Set goals for the next couple of weeks. Brainstorm ways that you can help one another achieve your goals.

7. Ask members of the group who are providing guided reading lessons to observe and help one another develop the lesson framework. Meet again to share your experiences and set new goals.

8. Continue your self-evaluation, working toward smooth management of the guided reading lesson.

## CHAPTER THIRTEEN

DYNAMIC GROUPING FOR EFFECTIVE TEACHING IN GUIDED READING

A teacher cannot establish her reading groups at the beginning of the year and keep them intact throughout the year. If she does, she is not addressing individual differences, and not responding to differential rates of progress or allowing for different paths to the same goal. Somehow her practices are locking children into fixed rates of progress.

— JEANNE OLSHESKE

In the upper elementary grades, relationships with peers are increasingly important. Both inside and outside the classroom, intermediate students are experiencing an intense discovery of self, a discovery that is continually shaped and defined as they develop relationships with others their own age. Furthermore, they are growing more independent and need opportunities to work alone and cooperatively with their peers. While guided reading offers optimum teaching opportunities, it also recognizes your students' emotional and social needs for both independent and cooperative learning. Thoughtful grouping for maximum learning is a cornerstone of guided reading. Dynamic grouping for effectiveness, efficiency, and social learning is a central feature of guided reading.

Forming Groups for Guided Reading

Guided reading usually involves small groups of students who are at a similar place in their reading development. These students demonstrate similar learning needs and process text at about the same level. At times, you may group students of mixed abilities who share a common learning need, such as how to read charts and tables in informational texts. Research demonstrates that when students work together in mixed groups, they make significant learning gains (Johnson et al. 1981; Slavin 1983a, 1983b).

While guided reading groups may come together to serve a variety of purposes, all are temporary and *dynamic.* You bring students together for an instructional purpose because they share common needs at a particular time.

You will also need to consider the size of your class and the number of students you can have in each group. Most teachers find that five or six students is an ideal group size.

Rationale for Groups

There are several compelling reasons for bringing students together in groups based on their learning needs at a particular time. Guided reading is only a small part of our students' day, but with teaching that is effective, efficient, and socially supportive, it is an opportunity to accelerate their learning.

EFFECTIVENESS

Small-group instruction is effective because teaching is focused precisely on what the students need to learn next to move forward. Ongoing observation of your students, combined with systematic assessment, enables you to draw together groups of students who fit a particular instructional profile.

Your goal, as you strive to provide the most effective instruction possible, is to match the difficulty of the material with the student's current abilities (Graves and Graves 1994; Lapp, Flood, and Farnan 1996); material should provide a challenge that is "just right" for your students. Extensive research shows that a text's difficulty level is a critical factor in helping early elementary readers (New Standards Primary Literacy Committee 1999; Snow, Burns, and Griffin 1998). The National Committee on the Prevention of Reading Difficulties reports, "Fluency should be promoted through practice with a wide variety of well-written and engaging texts at the child's own comfortable reading level" (Snow, Burns, and Griffin 1998). The committee describes three levels: reading that is independent, frustrating, or instructional for individual students. Our goal in guiding reading is to work with students at their instructional level—that is, with books that are within the student's control but offer a moderate amount of challenge (Mooney 1990). Ideally, students should be able to read with more than 90 percent accuracy. Guided reading with appropriate texts helps individual students build the reading strategies they need to read new books on their own. (We discuss text selection in more detail in Chapter 14.) With texts that are too difficult, students can't learn how to read better.

EFFICIENCY

Class size prevents us from individually reaching every student every day. While we may grab a few minutes here or there to confer with students about their independent reading or writing, learning effective reading strategies demands a substantial amount of time and necessitates that we teach our students in groups.

As you observe and confer with students in your classroom, you will discover learning needs and patterns across the group. You will notice that several students may share similar learning challenges, and that a particular level of text seems just right for them. Working with a small group enables you to provide fifteen to twenty minutes of high-quality, intensive instruction that is appropriate for every member of the group. And your students receive direct instructional time with you, which ultimately has a great impact on their independent reading. Gradually, as students gain control, you can lift the level of text. More challenging texts foster more learning opportunities.

Needs-based grouping gives your teaching maximum impact. For example:

- *Working for phrasing and fluency.* If you notice that some students in your class are not reading with appropriate phrasing and fluency, even though they are reading texts independently, you can pull them together for a brief time, select a text that is just right (instructional) for them all, demonstrate phrasing, and teach them to listen to their reading.

- *Solving multisyllable words.* If some of the students in your class are struggling to solve multisyllable words during the reading of continuous text, you can bring them together, introduce a book that is at the instructional level for them, and then demonstrate how to take a word apart, solve it, and check the meaning in the context of the piece.

- *Introducing new genres.* If a number of students with mixed abilities share an interest in biographies, you can bring them together and introduce the genre with a biography that is easy enough for *all* of them to handle. After they have learned more about reading the genre, they can choose to read biographies at different reading levels.

- *Learning how to read new kinds of texts.* If you want to introduce a new kind of text, such as magazines or newspapers, you can pull together small groups and teach them how to tackle the unique reading challenges inherent to this print medium, such as what they need to know about reading the different sections and features. You will need to choose a text that will be accessible to all.

- *Connecting personally with reading.* If you notice from reader's notebooks that some students are not connecting personally with their books, you can bring those students together and engage them in a conversation that helps them consider how their reading relates to their own lives. In this way they will learn to make richer, more personal interpretations of their reading.

- *Learning how to read tests.* If a group of students did poorly on a particular area of the state reading test, you can pull them together to help them develop the kind of skills they need to conquer standardized tests, such as how to interpret comprehension questions; how to skim short paragraphs; and how to ascertain, within a time limit, the goal of each particular section of the test.

- *Learning how to read and study textbooks.* If your students seem to be struggling with social studies, science, and math textbooks, which offer unique reading challenges even when the vocabulary and conceptual challenges are appropriate for the grade level, you can work with them in small groups. Small groups provide an ideal setting to teach students how to access textbook information: how to skim for information, taking in heads and subheads; how to read charts and tables; how to absorb photograph captions; and how to use footnotes, reference lists, indices, and bibliographies.

■ *Thinking deeply about reading.* Sometimes even strong readers can benefit from lessons on thinking more deeply about what they read. Bring them together and challenge their thinking in ways that will lead them to deeper, more thoughtful reading.

SOCIAL SUPPORT

Grouping also fosters communication and encourages students to help one another. In a guided reading group, while each student reads independently, peer-teacher discussions extend and refine comprehension. Vygotsky (1978) stressed the social nature of learning and, indeed, meanings are socially constructed. The more you talk about what you understand and listen to others' interpretations, the more you get out of an experience.

In the guided reading group, the student is supported by you (an expert literacy user!) and his peers. Interactions between students "may facilitate the course of development by exposing a child to other points of view and to conflicting ideas which may encourage him to re-think or review his ideas" (Wood 1988, 17). Social interaction plays an important role in learning; indeed, the knowledge of text that a student derives may be the product of "joint construction" involving the teacher and the student's peers.

Forming and re-forming groups is a way to create a sense of community in the classroom. In the comfort and support of a small group, students learn how to work with others, how to attend to shared information, and how to ask questions or ask for help. Besides, reading is more enjoyable when students can share the experience.

Small-group work is particularly important for students who have difficulty learning to read. Frequently, they are lost during whole-group instruction, becoming passive and disengaged as they struggle to read one text after another—often without ever making sense of them. These students will not develop as effective readers unless the reading is brought to a level that will enable them to process text. In guided reading, the text is "just right," and they gain additional support through their discussions with their peers. You can tailor instruction to meet your students' needs—making it as explicit as necessary to help them learn what they need to know.

In a large-scale review of schools that were most effective in raising student achievement, Hill and Crevola (1997) found three factors related to high achievement:

1. Strong student engagement.
2. High expectations for student performance.
3. Teaching that meets the needs of the students.

In our view, the third factor is the key to achieving the first two. Focused teaching in small groups makes it possible to provide appropriate instruction even for a diverse class of learners and, accordingly, bolsters expectations for success as well as students' self-confidence.

Grouping—A Dynamic Process

Guided reading groups are temporary, an important difference from traditional grouping practice. Dynamic groups avoid the traditional problems of grouping, because teachers change the composition of groups regularly to accommodate the different learning paths of readers.

In the last two decades, grouping nearly disappeared from elementary schools, a change that was made with good intentions. We'll summarize some of the reasons. In the past, groups were pervasive and based solely on "ability." Students moved through fixed sequences of text materials, with firmly established and tested prerequisite skills that made it practically impossible to alter the composition of the reading groups.

Students from minority groups were more likely to be assigned to the low groups, as were students who had not had preschool experience (Eder 1983; Good and Marshall 1984; Sorenson and Hallinan 1986). Sadly, because of the inflexibility of the groups and the fact that they didn't recognize or honor developmental differences and changes over time, placement was practically a life sentence. In other words, once in the low group, always in the low group (Hiebert 1983; Good and Marshall 1984).

Students in low-achievement groups typically received lower-quality instruction than their higher-achievement peers (Allington 1983; Allington and McGill-Franzen 1989). Perhaps most troubling of all was the damage to self-esteem that students in lower groups suffered (Filby, Barnett, and Bossart 1982). These students often felt "dumb" and less capable than their peers who were sailing along in the high-achieving reading groups.

Rigid systems that perpetuate static groups are replete with problems, but teaching the class as a whole group with a single text also has serious drawbacks. For example, whole class instruction tends to marginalize those students who need more interaction and closer contact with the teacher and a text they can read successfully. In whole-class instruction, it is easy for some students to "tune out" or avoid taking risks. In small groups, students find it easier to participate in discussions that support the development of deeper understanding.

Grouping that is flexible and varied allows students to support one another as readers and to feel part of a community of readers. So the answer is not to prohibit groups but to design the kinds of groups we use very carefully and thoughtfully. Within the comprehensive language and literacy framework, groups are formed and re-formed for many different purposes.

The gradient text levels for the intermediate grades (see Chapter 14) are much broader than those defined for younger elementary students. Within levels, there is a wide variety of texts. You might have two groups reading at the same *level* but with different emphases or needs. So, based on what you know about the particular readers, you could be selecting informational texts for one group and helping the other group learn about story structure in novels.

In general, you will follow these steps as you decide how to group students for maximum instructional benefit:

1. Work consistently with students who read at the same instructional level, gradually increasing the level of text difficulty through supportive instruction. You can focus best on needs when they read just-right texts on a regular basis. Conduct ongoing assessment. If most members of a group move faster than one or two or if one or two surge ahead, change the makeup of the group.
2. Convene a small, needs-based group for a concept that some students need to learn and are ready to learn. *If the concept is one students can explore across several different levels of text, the group can be heterogeneous. If the concept is characteristic of a particular level of text or genre of text, the group should be homogenous.*
3. Use a minilesson with the whole group, followed by application, to help the class learn a concept that all students need and are ready to learn.

Figure 13–1 is a portrait of a fourth-grade class over an eight-week period, charting the grouping shifts the teacher made for a variety of instructional reasons. The teacher met daily with two or three level-based groups, ranging originally from L through P.

During the eight-week period, the teacher raised the text difficulty level to N for Noah, Risa, Michael, Maria, and Edward and eventually moved Risa to a group reading at level O. When Risa moved to level O, the teacher moved Ray to level N so that he would have more practice reading different types of books and could improve his fluency. Kimarie was moved to a group reading at level Q. This group read varied texts in level Q throughout the eight-week period. Nicholas and Aneeca advanced to a group reading at level Q and then on to R. At the same time, Serena was shifted back to the Q group to gain more experience at that level.

During the eight weeks, the teacher also created several needs-based groups that met for focused study. These groups were based on her observation of students' reading and writing behaviors. The amount of time devoted to the topic varied by group:

- She asked Lisa, Michael, Edward, Noah, Gabriel, and Tamala to meet with her for about fifteen minutes a day for three days so she could provide explicit instruction on how to read textbooks.
- She noticed that Edward, Rebecca, Matthew, and Kyle tended to give somewhat superficial summaries of books and articles. She met twice with them to discuss thinking beyond the text.
- Pierre, Kyle, Kalina, Stephani, and Ray were unfamiliar with the genre of science fiction and tended not to select it for independent reading. She selected a collection of science fiction short stories and provided guided reading to this group of students for two days. They read two of the stories and were then given the choice of finishing that book or selecting another science fiction book.
- Another needs group—Dahli, Matthew, Ray, Pierre, Justina, and Jason—participated for several days in lessons designed to help them learn how to to skim and scan texts. These students did not have a common text; each practiced the skill on the information books they were using for independent reading as well as on a textbook, and they discussed what they had learned from the process.

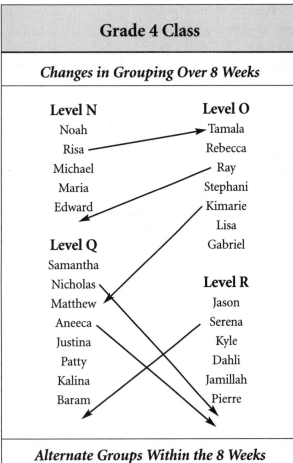

Grade 4 Class

Changes in Grouping Over 8 Weeks

Level N
Noah
Risa
Michael
Maria
Edward

Level O
Tamala
Rebecca
Ray
Stephani
Kimarie
Lisa
Gabriel

Level Q
Samantha
Nicholas
Matthew
Aneeca
Justina
Patty
Kalina
Baram

Level R
Jason
Serena
Kyle
Dahli
Jamillah
Pierre

Alternate Groups Within the 8 Weeks

Facilitate Textbook Reading
Lisa
Michael
Noah
Gabriel
Tamala

Build Thinking Beyond the Text
Edward
Rebecca
Matthew
Kyle

Introduce New Genre: Science Fiction
Pierre
Kyle
Kalina
Stephani
Ray

Teach How to Skim and Scan Text
Dahli
Matthew
Ray
Pierre
Justina
Jason

Figure 13–1. Grade 4 Class

Notice that all of the students in the class participated in level-based guided reading groups; not all students participated in the needs/interest-based groups; and some students participated in more than one needs/interest-based group.

You do not want to establish permanent groups or give them names because you want a very flexible system that will allow you to teach with maximum efficiency. If you work with a needs-based group on "reading the punctuation," for example, you will want to disband that group after a few sessions.

Using Assessment Data for Dynamic Grouping

When grouping students and matching books to their reading ability, it is always wise to rely on several sources of assessment information. No one measure can give you a complete picture of student progress. Think what you can learn from the following:

■ Listening to a student read one hundred to two hundred words of a text will enable you to determine accuracy, fluency, and error behavior. It will give you a picture of the student's problem-solving actions.

■ Examining students' response journals will help you recognize the kinds of things students are taking from the books they read independently—what they understand.

■ Reviewing students' writing will give you a notion of the kinds of language structures and text structures they control as well as their knowledge of spelling patterns in words.

■ Taking notes as students respond during book discussion will help you hypothesize about the depth of their comprehension and surmise their ability to summarize and infer from text.

■ Using a set of benchmark readings (short pieces representative of levels of text difficulty) will provide you with a more formal way of assessing students' ability to read accurately, read with phrasing and fluency, find key information in the text, and interpret the text (see Chapter 14).

■ Informal reading inventories can indicate an approximate ability level as well as the rate of reading, how the student solves problems while reading text, and the degree of comprehension.

■ Discussion of texts before and after will give you important information about the students' level of understanding.

Examining several kinds of assessment tasks, as well as observing the student closely as she participates in guided reading, will help you monitor your groupings. If a student seems to struggle with the text day after day, you will need to do some closer observation. The level may be too difficult or the student may need some instruction on how to read the particular kind of text. Students who finish before everyone else and remember, understand, and interpret the text may need more challenge. Grouping is a dynamic process that you must always examine critically. The reading records you keep enable you to make informed decisions about effective grouping.

The following factors enable dynamic, rather than static, grouping. In particular, you:

■ Select books for your students based on their reading abilities and needs rather than following a prescriptively defined list of ordered books. It is unlikely that any two students will read the same series of books in the same order over the school year. As a result, you have eliminated the practice where lower-level students "follow" the higher-level ones through a series.

■ Involve students in many different kinds of groups—some based on instructional needs and some based on interest or content studies.

■ Use both heterogeneous and homogeneous groups.

■ Consider the role of genre as a factor in students' reading abilities. For example, they may be able to read higher-level novels easily but need more instruction with information texts at the same level.

■ Make sure that students are reading at their instructional level and making maximum use of the reading workshop. Students are protected from struggling or waiting for your help because they are reading at a level that fosters learning; furthermore, they are receiving frequent guided reading lessons that make independent reading more productive.

■ Avoid "round robin" reading in which everyone takes turns reading aloud. This awkward process—agonizing for both the highly capable students who must wait for their slower peers and the less experienced students who are embarrassed to read in front of their peers—slows down instruction and gives grouping a bad name. Instead, make sure that each student reads the whole text or a unified part of the text silently and independently.

■ Integrate guided reading, independent reading, and

literature study. Students begin reading a text in guided reading and move to independent reading or literature study. Students are learning how to do something they can apply in other contexts. This interrelationship helps to move a guided reading group along, so that it is not bogged down in a very long book for a long time. Using short pieces and changing what students read allows for more flexible grouping. Groups can change regularly as students plunge into new books.

In sum, your attention to this cornerstone of guided reading—dynamic grouping—will ensure that your students get the most out of their instructional time with you.

Suggestions for Professional Development

1. Meet with a group of grade level colleagues interested in forming groups for differentiated instruction. Discuss the process of forming groups for guided reading instruction and look at several texts that are officially designated as "grade level" in your school. If there are no such texts, look at the chart aligning grade levels and the levels on the gradient of text in this book (Chapter 14). Select several "grade level" texts using the book list.

2. As a group, decide on one or two texts to use as a beginning assessment. You may want to select only one text, or you may want both a narrative and an information selection.

3. Select a segment of the text (or the whole text if it is short) for students to read. You may want to devise some standardized procedure, for example, providing a very brief (2–3 sentence) introduction and/or reading the first page of the text to the student. Decide on a uniform part of the text for students to read (about 250 words but also a meaningful piece of text). Type out the selected section of text, triple spaced so that you can record student errors above the words; leave a blank column on the right side so that you can make more notes.

4. Then, have all the students in the class read the selection individually while being observed by the teacher, who is taking notes. (You can try this exer-

cise with a smaller group of students if you wish.) After oral reading, the teacher engages the student in a conversation designed to explore the extent to which the student understood the text.

5. Reflect on the students' reading.
   - *Use a rough rubric to assess accuracy:* 1 = Below 90%; 2 = 90% to 95%; 3 = 96% to 100%.
   - *Use a rough rubric as a beginning assessment of comprehension:* 1 = demonstrated little or no understanding; 2 = understood the text at a literal level and remembered important details; or 3 = understood the text at a deep level, making inferences where appropriate.
   - *Use a rough rubric as a beginning assessment of fluency:* 1 = for the most part, slow, halting, word-by-word reading; 2 = a combination of word-by-word reading and fluent, phrasing at some appropriate places; 3 = mostly fluent, phrased reading, slowing down for some problem-solving but speeding up again.

6. Meet again as a group with your class records of reading behavior. Bring your conference records, your records of reading errors and other behaviors, and the results of your rubric assessments. Talk about:
   - *The kinds of errors students made.* What do they indicate about the level of their understanding? About their word solving abilities?

- *The accuracy of students' reading.* For which students was the text easy? Hard? Just right?
- *Students' understanding of the text.* Which students understood the text at a deeper level? For which students was it difficult?
- *Students' reading fluency.* Which students read the grade level text(s) fluently? Which students exhibited slow, word-by-word reading?

7. Using the combination of factors you have uncovered, group students into three, four, or five groups, including:
   - Those who are clearly above grade level and will need more challenging texts.
   - Those for whom the "grade level" text is just about right.
   - Those who need easier texts to help them build a reading process.

8. This beginning assessment will give you a start on grouping, but you will fine tune the procedures as you work with students over the next few weeks and also as you read and understand other chapters in this book.

9. Select texts that you think fit your groups and try them out the following week. You may want to start with the "grade level" readers; it will probably take more searching to find appropriate texts for the other groups.

## CHAPTER FOURTEEN

SELECTING, INTRODUCING, AND USING LEVELED TEXTS

If a group of competent eleven-year-olds must read a text containing new concepts and vocabulary, they may learn a great deal more if their teachers take time to introduce this new text to them than if they are left to struggle through it on their own.

— MARIE CLAY

The most important decisions in guided reading center on selecting and introducing texts to readers. For the reader to use processing strategies to construct meaning, the text must be accessible, comprehendible, and offer the student opportunities to *problem-solve and learn.*

Selecting Texts: An Overview

The first consideration in selecting a text for your students is choosing something that they will enjoy and/or find interesting or helpful. Think about your own reading. You read some texts for pure enjoyment, others for specific information. In either case, your reading is purposeful. You have a reason to read your chosen text even though you may find some parts puzzling or difficult. We rightly laugh at the thought of reading a book solely to practice becoming a better reader—reading is not like practicing a golf swing.

When you select books for students, remember that the purpose for reading cannot be simply to learn more about reading. Upper elementary students require (and deserve!) a better reason than that. In fact, a focus of guided reading is helping students read for many different purposes, not just to get through a book because it is assigned or to read the book because they need to "practice" reading. Text selection is critical to engaging students in purposeful reading.

The text you choose, then, must engage readers and at the same time provide opportunities to extend their reading ability. You must simultaneously consider:

- Readers' present strategies.
- Readers' interests and background knowledge.
- Text complexity in relation to readers' current skills.
- The language of the text in relation to readers' experience.
- The content of the text in relation to readers' background knowledge.
- The appropriateness of the content to the age group.
- The representation of gender, racial, ethnic, and socioeconomic groups in positive ways.
- Your own assessment of the learning opportunities inherent in a text and their match to your instructional goals.
- The quality of the text: language, illustrations, layout, writing style.

Keeping the Readers in Mind

In Figure 14–1 we list a few of the factors to consider in selecting texts with readers in mind. The better you know your readers, the easier it is to predict their interactions with potential texts and the more effectively you can plan your introductions. There are many different assessment approaches, depending on what you want to know. Chapter 28 describes ways of assessing students' reading competency; also consider using the reading questionnaire provided in Chapter 2.

Using Leveled Texts

Reading is a "self-extending" process. As we apply strategies to meet challenges to our comprehension and fluency, we extend and refine our ability to read. However,

Knowing Readers: A Foundation for Selecting and Introducing Texts

Questions about readers:	Sources of information:
❖ What topics or content areas do students know a lot about? ❖ In what topics or content areas will they need more support in reading? ❖ What topics or content areas especially interest the readers? ❖ What experiences have students had to widen their worlds?	❖ Administer content questionnaire or interview. ❖ Examine the content curriculum adopted by the school. ❖ Look at choices for study in content areas. ❖ Have students brainstorm a list of topics they would like to read about. ❖ Hold conversations with students.
❖ What is the quantity/quality of students' reading vocabulary? ❖ What kinds of words do students solve quickly, with understanding, while reading text? What kinds of words cause difficulty in decoding or understanding? ❖ How fluently do students read? ❖ To what extent do students notice and use punctuation? ❖ What kinds of language structures are easy for students to process and what kinds of structures are difficult?	❖ Observe the students' speaking vocabulary in informal conversation and discussion. ❖ Look at their writing to see the words they use. ❖ Observe students' oral reading using informal reading inventories or other procedures. ❖ Observe oral reading using a rubric to assess overall fluency and phrasing as it develops over time. ❖ Observe oral reading, noting students' phrasing in relation to the punctuation.
❖ What kinds of personal experiences do students bring to their reading? ❖ What kinds of settings or plots will students find easy to understand? What will they find harder to understand? ❖ What kinds of characters will students feel empathy for or identify with? ❖ What kinds of characters will they find hard to understand or remove from themselves?	❖ Encourage personal writing and look at it for information about students' lives. ❖ Make visits to homes. ❖ Confer with parents. ❖ Get to know the community where students live. ❖ Observe students as they discuss characters, settings, and events in books they read or you read to them. ❖ Read students' reader's notebooks.
❖ What literary knowledge do the students have? ❖ What is the extent of students' experience reading different genres? ❖ What genres have they read successfully? What genres do they avoid? ❖ What kinds of texts do students find easy to interpret and extend? ❖ What kinds of texts do they find difficult to interpret and extend?	❖ Examine and analyze students' records of independent reading. ❖ Interview students about books they have read. ❖ Assess their ability to identify with characters. ❖ Interview students while sampling oral reading. ❖ Analyze students' writing about texts. ❖ Have conversations with students after reading.
❖ What books and others texts have students read previously? ❖ What kinds of connections do they tend to make as they read texts—personal/emotional, literary?	❖ Examine records of students' independent reading. ❖ Keep a list of books that you have read aloud or previous teachers have read to students.

Figure 14–1. Knowing Readers

if we are working with texts that are within our control. If the text is too hard, the process breaks down, and comprehension is lost. The struggling reader cannot perform effectively, and learning is short-circuited. To provide effective guided reading lessons, teachers must select texts that present only a few challenges in terms of word solving, concepts and ideas, and language.

Most students cannot improve their reading ability independently—they need to be taught. Through guided reading lessons and conferences, you interact with them in ways that support efficient processing. But you cannot provide good teaching if the text you use is inappropriate. If the text is too easy, students do not face enough challenges to learn; if it is too hard, no amount of good teaching will help.

This chapter explains the gradient text levels for intermediate students, describes how to match books with readers, and discusses how to use the book list in Appendix 61. The book list in the Appendix of this book provides a sampling of over 1000 books from early grade two level through grade six. The companion volume to this one, *Leveled Books for Readers, Grades 3–6*, contains detailed information about how to analyze texts yourself and position them within the gradient. It also provides an extensive book list of several thousand titles, grouped by level and genre. (*Matching Books to Readers: Using Leveled Books in Guided Reading* is an extensive list of leveled books for students in kindergarten through grade three.)

What Is a Gradient of Text?

A gradient of text is an ordering of books according to a specific set of characteristics. Gradient means ascending or descending in a uniform or consistent way, so the levels of a gradient are defined in relation to each other. As you go up the gradient of text, the texts get harder; conversely, as you go down, they get easier. At each level of the gradient, there is a cluster of characteristics that helps you think about the texts at that level and how they support and challenge readers.

Some Clarifications about Text Gradients

The gradient is not a precise sequence through which all students move as they progress in their reading development. It is a collection of books arranged by category and level of difficulty from which you can

select texts that are suitable for groups and individuals.

Individual students cannot be categorized as, for example, "level M readers." Their background knowledge varies widely according to the experiences they have had at home, in the community, and in school. Their reading ability develops along many dimensions. As they gain reading experience, for example, they learn how texts are organized; they also develop content knowledge as part of their experiences and study. All of this knowledge has an impact on the level of text a student can read, and it does so in a differential way. There is probably a range of levels any given student will feel comfortable reading, based on his general understanding of vocabulary, experience in reading texts with different structures, experience in reading different genres, and interests.

At bottom, no matter how interested students are in the topic, the text must be accessible to them. An engaging plot or attractive character may help, but students must be able to read the words and understand the text. Conversely, no matter how well they are able to read a text, it must be relevant or interesting. When you evaluate texts you need to be aware of these limitations and make cautious selections. Test your decisions against students' reading behavior (as you sample oral reading), their conversation about texts, and their journal writing.

Another caution: you certainly do not want to require students to read all the books at one level before going to the next. Nor would you want to alter a group's reading level on the basis of one text that causes them particular difficulties. You are looking for broad patterns of reading behavior in your students as they change over time; you are looking for clusters of characteristics in texts that match readers' growing ability. The gradient is a rough guide to help teachers match books to their readers.

Determining Text Difficulty

Readability literally means how easy or hard the book is for a reader or for a group of readers of a certain age or at a grade level. A term that we like very much is *manageability,* which refers to the individual's ability to read the words, access the language, use the organizational features to get information, and construct meaning from the text. Our gradient was created by looking at a large variety of texts and trying them out with readers at different levels. As shown in Figure 14–2, a complex range of factors are related to the level of difficulty of a text.

Book and Print Features

Book and print features can either support the reader or make a text more difficult. They include characteristics such as size and clarity of print as well as layout. The placement of print in space (sections, chapters, paragraphs, for example) guides readers to the underlying organization of the text and is sometimes a new learning challenge for developing readers. Length, too, is sometimes a consideration. Short texts may be packed with hard vocabulary and difficult concepts, but we recognize that, in general, longer texts require of readers more stamina and greater capacity to remember details. Illustrations and graphic features aid readers by providing information that supports and extends the meaning of a text; readers need to learn how to use and interpret photographs, drawings, charts, maps, and diagrams.

Vocabulary

The words in the text reflect the difficulty of the topic. In general, the harder the words, the harder the text; multisyllable words add to difficulty. An analysis of the difficulty of words has limited value, however, because the words must be appropriate to carry the conceptual load of the topic; simply substituting simpler words will not necessarily make a difficult concept easy.

Sentence Complexity

Longer sentences with embedded clauses are, in general, more difficult to read than shorter sentences. Readers must learn how to use punctuation and cue words, such as *therefore* or *when,* to access the underlying meaning of the sentence. Here, too, assessment of complexity is not always straightforward. The style makes the piece interesting. It's part of the literary quality. Some textbooks, in an attempt to make material more accessible for students, use artificially shortened sentences that are hard to read and do not convey concepts well. Some authors vary sentence length as part of literary style.

Text Structure

Text structure refers to the way information is organized and presented in a text. For fiction, the levels of difficulty range from simple narratives organized chronologically to complex plots that may involve stories within stories. For nonfiction, many different patterns, such as compare/contrast, temporal sequence, description, cause/effect, or problem/solution, must be internalized by readers so that they can understand how to get information. Structure must be logical and visible to the reader.

Content

We have talked extensively in this book about the relationship between students' background knowledge and their ability to read and comprehend texts (Adams and Bruce 1982). Background knowledge includes vocabulary but goes well beyond words to the relationship between ideas and organizational structures in informational texts (see Chapter 23) and to concepts related to the setting and plot in works of fiction. We can present a general description of the level and accessibility of text content, but you will always want to consider the particular knowledge levels of your own students in gauging the difficulty of content. Certain content areas may also have specialized graphic features such as maps or diagrams that require readers' interpretation.

Language and Literary Features

Manageability is related to the complexity and sophistication of the language in the text. Features such as figurative language tend to make a text more difficult to read and comprehend. For a metaphor, a simile, or onomatopoetic language to make sense to students, they must understand it. Dialogue, usually present in fiction, can be assigned or unassigned. Often readers have to read through a long series of speeches, keeping track of the speakers by whose turn it is or their characteristic ways of talking. In terms of language and literary features, readability is related to students' previous experience with texts, both from hearing them read and reading them for themselves.

Themes and Ideas

A text may be readable for your upper elementary students because they can decode the words and understand the ideas, but it may still not be suitable if the

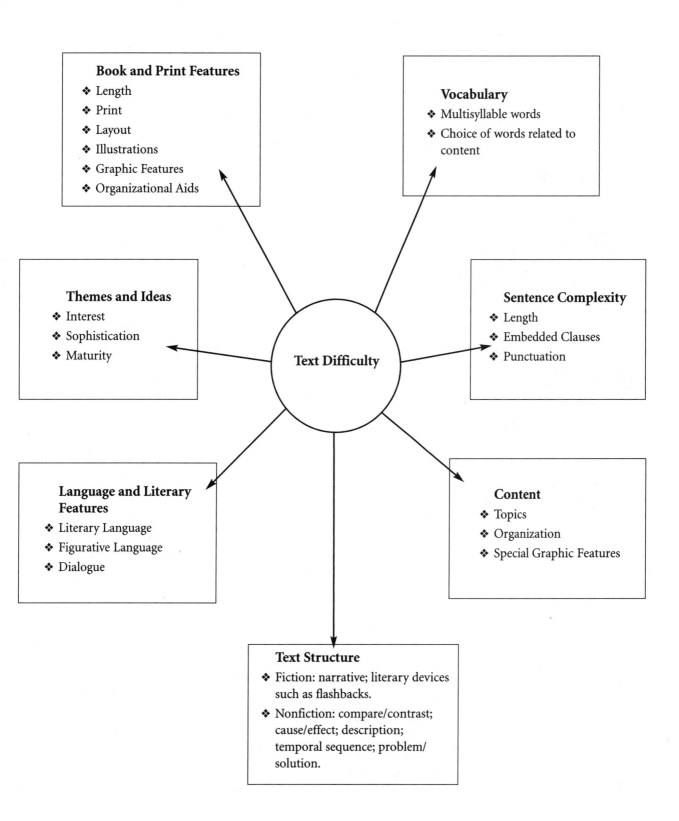

Figure 14–2. Factors Related to Text Difficulty

themes are too sophisticated or the content immature for students of their age level. Books with particularly mature themes, such as violence and sexuality, must be placed at higher levels of the gradient. You will want to analyze carefully how these themes are handled.

Creating a Gradient of Text

To create a graded collection of books, you evaluate texts against the characteristics established for each level as you consider your students' knowledge. A quality literacy program requires thinking about what makes texts difficult in relation to your students and recommending appropriate texts for their use. A gradient of text makes it easier for you to select books for readers that meet their needs and allow them to rely on their strengths as readers.

Creating a gradient of text requires attention to a range of factors that research indicates contribute to the reading difficulty of a text. It means classifying books along a continuum based on the combination of variables that support and confirm readers' strategic actions and offer problem-solving opportunities that extend the reading process.

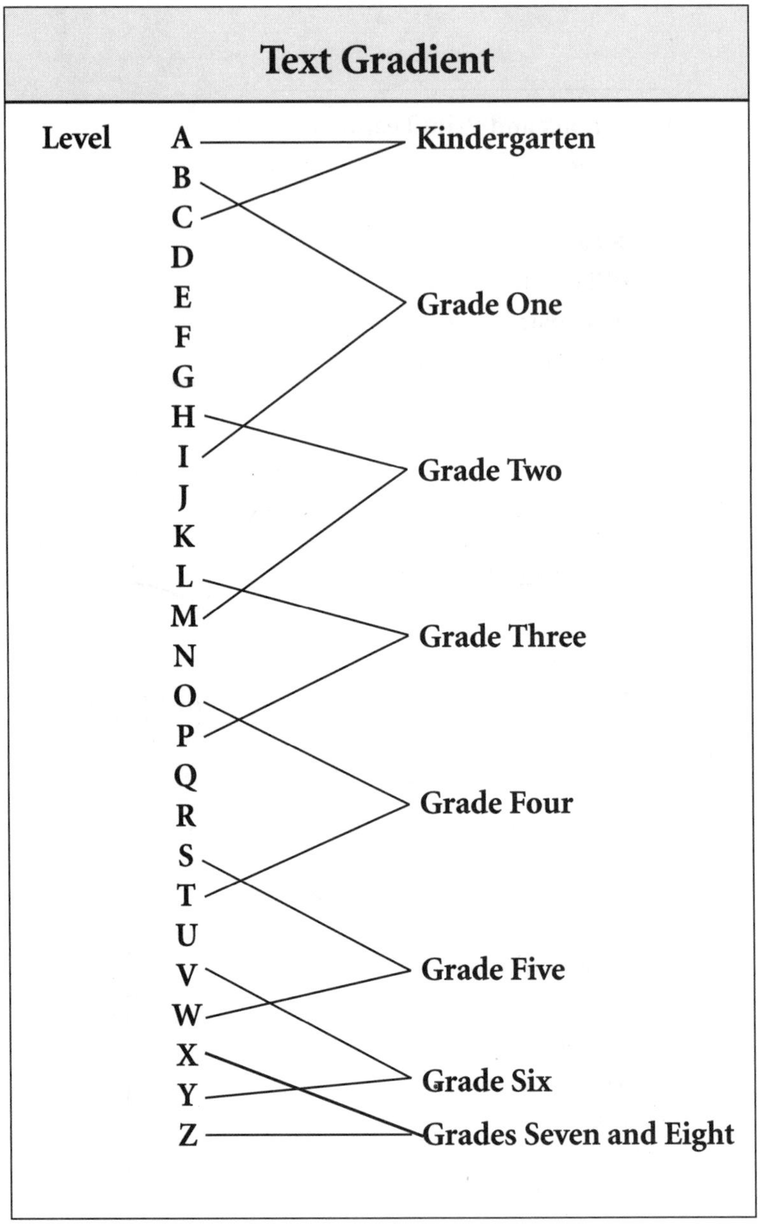

Figure 14–3. Text Gradient

The Leveled Collection

The leveled collection consists of books grouped by difficulty. Books at a particular level are similar to one another in terms of difficulty. The level is described by a cluster of characteristics; no text will have every characteristic listed for the level. To estimate the level of a text, you find the cluster of characteristics that most closely represents that text and then study your students' responses to the text over time. In this way you discover more about the text and can determine whether the level designation is reliable or needs to be adjusted.

Characteristics of Texts Along the Gradient

We have organized these texts from easier to harder in the order of the alphabet. Each level is labeled with a letter from A to Z. Remember that the level designation is only an approximation; within each level, some books will be easier and some harder.

Figure 14–3 shows the entire gradient of text from kindergarten through grade 6. Levels are related to approximate grades, but it is more important to see the gradient as a continuum of progress for your readers. The central goal is to determine the level that is appropriate for students to read independently and for instruction. In this book, "grade level" means the kinds of texts that students at that grade are *typically* reading. If your students fall below the levels associated with a certain grade, they will require extra instruction or intervention to help them extend their reading ability, but they will need to begin at the levels that are right for them. *There is no way for a student to reach grade level without starting the teaching where the student is.* Notice that there is no rigid division between grade levels. We also recognize that "grade level" may vary according to the school, district, or region.

Grade-Level Designations

We include approximate grade-level ranges because they will help you determine whether your students are reading within average ranges. Responsible and competent teaching begins with recognizing acceptable student achievement and knowing when you need to intervene. If you have readers who are working well below grade level, you will want to choose texts from the lower levels. Search for content that is appropriate for them, however. Students in upper elementary grades do not want to read "baby" material even if the level is right for them. Check informational texts as well as fiction—the goal is find material all students will love to read. Then assure daily reading and intensive instruction.

The leveled book list helps you select texts for students that are "just right" for instructional purposes. It can also help you evaluate texts, so that you can identify texts that are suitable for students' independent reading as well as for instructional purposes (those that offer a small challenge or reflect a new text feature that students are not familiar with).

The Demands of the Text on Readers

Every text demands that the reader use a combination of strategies to solve words and construct meaning. At *every level* of this gradient, texts demand that readers:

1. Recognize frequently encountered words quickly and automatically.
2. Use multiple sources of information in an integrated way while reading for meaning.
3. Read orally at a good pace, with appropriate phrasing, slowing down to problem-solve and speeding up again.
4. Read silently when reading independently.
5. Use a range of strategies to problem-solve new words, particularly multisyllable words.
6. Self-correct errors that result in loss of meaning.
7. Make inferences to understand what is implied but not stated.
8. Work to understand characters.
9. Recognize important elements of setting.
10. Predict and analyze the plot.
11. Sustain attention to meaning, memory, and interpretation over several days of reading.
12. Bring background knowledge to bear in understanding concepts and topics.
13. Predict events, outcomes, and problem resolutions while reading sections of text.
14. Determine the perspective from which narrative texts are told.
15. Understand the organizational structures used to present information.
16. Revise interpretations as new information becomes available.
17. Recognize relevant aspects of the writer's craft.
18. Think critically about the concepts and ideas in the text.

This long list is only a sampling of what readers do during the act of processing text with understanding. Readers meet the demands of texts by engaging numerous strategies simultaneously. Reading texts that are easy for you makes fewer demands on the processing system.

You select books from a level on the gradient that is just challenging enough to require your students to use their strategies to problem-solve. The more they read, the better readers they become and the challenges of the texts at that particular level decrease. Then you once again select books from a slightly more challenging level, and your students again are exposed to a more complex constellation of strategies. In a way, the gradient of text is a ladder readers climb as they learn to apply their strategies to increasingly demanding texts.

Balancing Readability and Theme

The further up the gradient, the more complex are the characteristics. You may find a range of easier-to-harder to read texts at the upper level of gradients, but the content may influence the level. A text that is easy to decode but features demanding ideas, language, and concepts that may challenge students' understanding will appear at the upper level of the gradient. *The Midwife's Apprentice* (Cushman 1995), in which a young girl who has been deserted is found by a midwife and eventually takes on the profession, is one such example.

How to Use the Book List

The book list included in Appendix 61 is a sampling of fiction and nonfiction books at each level. The list is presented alphabetically by title, and we indicate the level, genre, author or series, and publisher/distributor for each book. You can look up individual titles of books that you may have in your classroom. A much more extensive list is included in *Leveled Books for Readers, Grades 3–6*, which is available from Heinemann. If a book you want to use is not included on this list, look at its characteristics in relation to other examples on the list. Above all, make text evaluation and selection your own. The more you know about texts and their characteristics, the more effective you become at selecting and introducing texts to students.

Introducing Texts

In guided reading, students read the text for themselves with the support of your strong introduction, which is the key to students' understanding and successful problem solving on a challenging new text. A text introduction is an easy, conversational exchange that makes a text accessible to readers. When you introduce a text, you:

- Engage the attention of the students and draw them into the activity.
- Help them explore and access their knowledge.
- Help them attend to critical features of the text.
- Anticipate the features that may be difficult.
- Make problem solving easier for them.

The introduction guides readers to reconstruct the author's text. It is a teaching exchange that is built on readers' needs.

How to Introduce Texts

Each text introduction is unique to the readers and to the text. There are several important steps to follow in preparing text introductions.

THINK ABOUT THE TEXT IN RELATION TO THE READERS.

First, read the text carefully, paying attention to factors that will affect readers' ability to process the text and learn from it. In this chapter we have included a detailed list of text features to consider in analyzing texts; that list will also help you plan your introduction. In particular:

- *Analyze book and print features, such as length, print size, layout, punctuation, and illustrations.* Can the text be read in one session? If not, how will you break it up? Will print size be a factor? Books with print in a small font place more words on a page and require more of the reader. Will students need help understanding features of layout, such as columns, insets, or side headings? Does the text contain punctuation that students do not yet understand and need to learn? What is the role of illustrations? Will you want to discuss the illustrations with your students as a way to help them build their background knowledge?

- *Evaluate the content, themes, and ideas in the text.* Are your students familiar with the subject matter or does it represent new topics or content? Does technical vocabulary pose a potential problem? Is the theme appropriate for the age level and experience of your students? Will they find it interesting? Can they identify with it? Do they have the sophistication to understand it? Can your students access the big ideas of the text or are ideas so complex that students will need your support to understand them?

- *Think about the structure of the text.* For narrative texts, think about the predictability of the story. Does it proceed chronologically or are there twists and turns and literary devices such as a "story within a story"? How easy will it be for your students to understand the setting or to follow the development of a character? Will you need to provide background knowledge or show your students how a particular character changes? How complex is the plot? Does the author skip time periods or place characters in very complex situations? Is the episodic structure straightforward and easy to follow?

In expository texts, is the information presented in a straightforward manner or are students asked to read multiple opinions and decide for themselves? Must they interpret charts and diagrams in order to understand the text? Does the author use organizational patterns such as chronological development or does he rely on more complex categories to organize and present information? How close is the information to students' own background of knowledge?

■ *Consider the language and literary features of the text.* Is the story told as a simple narrative from one point of view, or does the author present multiple perspectives? Must students infer or analyze in order to understand the text? Is the text written in simple sentences or are they long and complex? Is the text divided into paragraphs, chapters, and sections? Does the writer use literary devices such as metaphor, simile, onomatopoeia, and poetic language that students might find difficult to understand? Is the vocabulary used in the text accessible to students? Will they be able to understand most of the words? Do the writer's words suggest multiple connotations that students might not catch? How many and what kind of words are in the text? Will large numbers of multisyllable words frustrate students?

PLAN THE INTRODUCTION.

We have said that introductions cannot be scripted. So, what *can* you plan? You can think about how the book works. Write down some quick notes on a planning sheet or on a stick-on note placed on the cover of the book. The notes will remind you of the important ideas you want to be sure to mention. They will help you keep the introduction focused on what is important. Notes might include:

■ One or two sentences about the main ideas or themes of the book.

■ Page numbers of illustrations that you can use to discuss concepts. (If a book has no page numbers, take a pen and quickly number them, because you will need to refer students to specific pages.)

■ Vocabulary that you want to use in conversation and/or explicitly define as you provide the introduction.

■ Words that might be difficult for readers to solve that you might want to call attention to in the text or write on the board.

■ Information about the author, illustrator, or genre.

■ Processing strategies that you want to reinforce.

■ Something special about the text features or layout.

■ Unusual language structures that you want to make accessible to readers.

■ The number of pages you want the students to read in this time period.

■ What you want the readers to do when they finish the assigned reading.

In your planning, give special thought to students who are learning English. They may need more support when reading a new text. Are there words or language structures that will be important for them to hear and/or say prior to reading the text? Many of these students are learning aspects of the English language along with their literacy. You will need to make accessible the language they are about to read.

Of course, you will not highlight all of these features in any one introduction. With the readers and the text in mind, you select from the list of possibilities. The fact that you have thought it through and have notes will help you introduce the text quickly and efficiently. A long, meandering discussion will tire students out before they even begin to read. A strong introduction is a lively discussion that moves right into enjoyable reading.

DECIDE HOW STUDENTS WILL READ THE TEXT.

There are many alternatives here. The one you choose will depend on your readers' experience, their ability to read longer texts, and their need for support in reading the particular text. There may also be important text features to consider, such as whether there are chapters or sections or harder and easier parts. Here are some ways in which you might proceed, and you will think of others:

1. Introduce the text and then ask students to read the whole text to the end. This alternative will work best with short texts.
2. Introduce the whole text and ask students to read the first section. Provide a short introduction to each of the remaining sections as students read them. A section can be a unified section of the text or a group of chapters.
3. Introduce the first section and ask students to read it; then introduce the second section and have students read it and any remaining sections. Your guid-

231

ance for the first two sections will be enough support for them to read the rest independently.

4. Introduce the first section of a long text. Continue to introduce a new section each day for four or five days. Students read and discuss their reading on the same day.

5. Introduce the first section of the text. Ask students to read the first section and then discuss it. Direct students to read several more sections independently. Bring them back together to introduce the last part of the text. After they've read it, discuss the whole text.

The important thing is to introduce the text in the context of teaching students to be better readers. You decide when an introduction will be helpful to the readers and how much introduction they will need.

DECIDE WHAT YOU WANT STUDENTS TO ATTEND TO AS THEY READ.

It is also important to ask yourself, *How will I be sure these readers pay attention to important aspects of the text?* On occasion you may want to focus attention with a light overlay, giving students aspects to notice as they read. Be cautious however because you don't want to artifically narrow the reader's processing the whole meaning of a text. On occasion, you may want them to read the text more than once, each time with different aspects to notice. Sometimes the light overlay helps them to be more active readers because they are thinking of something specific as they read, but they will need to attend to the whole meaning along with attention to the particular aspect. Overall, the overlay will prompt them to raise questions in their mind that:

- Open up the text and get them thinking.
- Call up background knowledge.
- Help them understand how the text is organized.
- Help them search for evidence to support their thinking.

It's a good idea to write the specific directions on the easel or board. This ensures that you have clearly conceptualized what you want them to do and that students have it clearly in mind while reading. Remember that attention to one aspect of a text should only be in relation to the whole meaning.

PLAN WHAT STUDENTS WILL DO WHEN THEY FINISH READING.

Always give students directions for what to do. Usually you will want them to complete their reading and any related work at the table. Generally they stay well-focused and you are ready to engage them in after-reading discussion. You may want them to return to their seats to complete the assigned reading and any writing or other extension that goes with it. Afterward, they can go on to other work prior to a discussion. If there are great differences in the rates at which students are finishing the text, you may need to work with one or two students on fluency or check to see whether the text level is appropriate.

Reflecting on Text Selection and Introduction

As you proceed through the guided reading lesson, simultaneously reflect on your introduction and text selection. You will get immediate feedback on the teaching in the introduction as you observe and support the students' processing of the text. By sampling the oral reading of several students and interacting with them briefly, you'll notice how they are using the information you previously provided. Students may be having difficulties in places where more introductory support would have enabled them to solve problems. They may have questions about what they do not understand. You can judge whether the text was too hard or too easy and how well the introduction mediated the text for the students.

We do not mean to imply that students should have *no* difficulties processing the text. In fact, if they read perfectly and fluently, there probably were too few opportunities for new learning. Either the text was too easy or your introduction was too supportive—perhaps both. You want to observe evidence that students are understanding what they are reading and using problem-solving strategies in a flexible way.

Another piece of evidence is any writing that students produce after they have read the text. You can check the writing to see how well you were able to focus their attention, and you can look for any confusion that the writing may reveal. As you examine the writing, you can assess how deeply students are thinking about the text or how well they understood the information and ideas.

After the students read, you will be talking with them about the text. What they say is a key to what they have understood. This discussion also helps you evaluate your introduction. As students chat about the book, you can determine whether they searched for and answered the questions you raised in the introduction or whether they found new information based on your prompts.

Examples of Text Introductions

Let's now examine several introductions to three different books that represent a variety of text levels and genres. We have not specified grade levels here because any one of these levels could be used to meet the diverse needs of students in a number of grades.

Introduction to Meet M & M, Level K

Francine introduced a simple chapter book, *Meet M & M* (Ross 1980), a straightforward story about two girls who are friends (see Figure 14-4). She selected the level K book for the students because its content is so familiar. All students understand friendship, a topic close to the readers' own lives.

Francine believed the book would provide just the right amount of challenge for the group. While the vocabulary is generally simple, a few multisyllable words provide more challenge. The text has supportive features, including a readable font size, open spacing between words and between lines, and an appealing layout. Every sentence starts on a new line. However, the text also includes a list that places each new item on its own line, which might be a challenge to some readers. There are a number of illustrations to keep images alive for the reader and add interest. The story is humorous and entertaining.

Francine also hoped that as students read this chapter book they would become interested in reading more books in the series, which would help students extend their reading "mileage" by reading quite a bit of easy material.

Francine began by introducing the title, characters, and setting and connecting the text to students' own experience. Throughout the introduction, it was evident that students were thinking of their own relationships with family members and friends. Francine used the illustrations in the text to help them understand the setting (an apartment building) as a key to the plot and the problem resolution. She also made sure they understood the simile "stick like glue."

The words *shaggy* and *crabby* offered an opportunity to call students' attention to patterns within words and to link words. In this way, Francine showed students how to apply their knowledge of letter patterns while solving words within a text. Students saw the word *shaggy* used in a new way. The idea that people might "look shaggy together" is a whimsical way of illustrating just how much the two girls liked each other.

Francine predicted that the sentence structure of the long list, divided by commas, was likely to be a challenge for students. She drew it to their attention and asked one student to demonstrate how to read it. She also pointed out how the illustrations could be helpful. Finally, she turned over the reading to the readers. Francine wanted the students to enjoy and understand the story and perhaps become interested in reading more books in the series. She predicted that this would be an easy story to read; however, students were expected to sustain their reading over a text of forty-one pages, which would provide good reading practice.

Introduction to Wolves, Level N

Alice selected *Wolves* (Wilde 1999), a level N book, to help students learn more about reading informational books. Information is packed into this twenty-three-page book. The beautiful photographs of wolves are a big plus. Alice knew that the photographs and the topic would be interesting to these students. The book has a table of contents and an index. Each one of the seven sections presents a different set of understandings about wolves. The book can be read from beginning to end, as these students did, but it could also be used as a reference book, with students allowed to skip around searching for different facts about wolves.

She began the introduction by foreshadowing the purpose for reading *Wolves*. Her students were searching for and using information centered on one topic. She reminded them that it's important to think about the author of informational texts as a way to evaluate the information you are gaining. She provided background information on the author/photographer and also engaged the readers by telling a bit of a dramatic story. She encouraged the students to make personal and literary connections with the text. Throughout the

Introduction to Meet *M & M*

Introduces title, characters, and setting.

Teacher: *Meet M & M*, Mandy and Mimi. They're very good friends and neighbors. Though they're not twins, they look a lot like each other and they pretend to be twins. Look at them on the cover.

Kaya: My cousins are twins but they're grown up.

Recognizes students' personal experience.
Probes for background knowledge.

Teacher: So you know a lot about twins. What are some of the things twins do together?

Kaya: They dress alike and they go everywhere together.

Provides more information.
Probes personal experience.

Teacher: Well Mandy and Mimi do some of those things because they do look alike. They aren't really twins but they are very good friends. On the cover it shows Mimi holding her dog Maxi and there's Mandy. Do any of you have a friend you like to do everything with?

Eddie: We play football and sometimes we wear baseball caps the same.

Denise: My friend lives in the next apartment and we call each other on the phone.

Calls attention to illustrations to understand setting and plot.

Teacher: Look at the dedication page—it's the fourth page in. There's Mimi in apartment 3B looking down at Mandy in apartment 2B. Turn to page 9. You see two pictures there showing you some things they like to do.

Mike: Play dress up.

Eddie: And take a bath!

Supports students' understanding of literary language (simile).

Teacher: On page 8 the writer says the girls "stick together" like glue. What does she mean by that?

Mike: They just do everything together and they're always with each other so nobody can even tell them apart.

Kaya: It's like when you glue something it sticks tight and you can't pull it apart and they're like that. They're always together. If one does something the other one always wants to do it.

Defines vocabulary.
Supports students' understanding of language use.

Teacher: They even grew their hair alike. They both have bangs. That's hair that comes down across your forehead and is cut straight across.

Denise: Like mine?

Teacher: Yes, a little bit. The bangs can be cut evenly but if you let them grow a lot they might look uneven. Mandy lives in apartment 2B and Mimi lives in 3B. Find a word on page 8 that begins with *sh* like *she*. [Students search and find *shaggy*.]

Teacher: Look at the parts of the word and read it.

Mike: Sh-shag-y-shaggy.

Teacher: That was good figuring out. You noticed that it ends like *happy* . They grew out their bangs so they would look alike. The author says they looked *shaggy* together. [She writes *shaggy* on the chart.]

Kaya: They need barrettes.

Values student input.

Teacher: Yes, barrettes would help if your hair is kind of shaggy.

Figure 14–4. Introduction to Meet M & M

Introduction to Meet *M & M* (continued)

Explains the plot.

Teacher: You know, sometimes even good friends can have arguments, and that's just what happens in this story. Mandy and Mimi have a really bad day. They argue about everything and then they aren't friends anymore.

George: I sometimes have fights with my brother and we don't let each other come in the bedroom.

Calls attention to a pattern within a word.
Makes connection between words.
Supports the meaning of a word.

Teacher: That's the kind of thing that happens here, George. Now look at page 14. Find the word that starts with the consonant cluster, *cr*.

Students: *Cr-crabby!*

Eddie: My mom says "don't be so crabby."

Teacher: [Writes *crabby* below *shaggy* on the easel.] The word is *crabby* and it means grouchy and hard to get along with. I bet your mom says that when you're being grouchy, Eddie. Both of these words have two consonants in the middle and they end like *happy*.

Foreshadows resolution of problem.
Invites personal response from students.

Teacher: The rest of this book is about all the things they do when they are mad at each other. For example, they set up lemonade stands and they both try to get the most customers by offering extra things. It doesn't feel very good when you are mad at someone.

Denise: When I'm mad at my sister I still like her.

Kaya: I don't like getting in fights with my friend.

Eddie: You don't have anything to do if you're fighting with people and they won't come over. You just have to do everything by yourself.

Kaya: And then you make up and you can do things together again.

Shows students how illustrations can help them.
Draws attention to punctuation.
Provides demonstration of how to read a particular sentence structure.

Teacher: Go to page 36. On that page you're going to read a long list of things that they send to each other while they trying to make up. All of the things in the pictures—see the hairbrush, and the puzzle? The things in the list are separated by commas. Remember that you pause and take a breath when you come to a comma. Kaya, read all the things they sent. Remember to take a breath when you see a comma.

Kaya: [reading] "They sent small pictures, racing cars, one hairbrush, crackers in a plastic bag, comic books, a puzzle with only two pieces missing, and a million notes."

Passes control to the readers.

Teacher: Good, she read each item all at once and paused between them, didn't she? Now I'd like you to read the whole book silently to yourself. I will come around and listen to each of you.

Figure 14–4. Introduction to Meet M & M *(continued)*

Introduction to *Wolves*

Introduces author and title.
Explains the genre and its characteristics.
Provides background on author.

Teacher: Today we are going to learn interesting things about wolves. The author of this book, *Wolves*, is Buck Wilde. Remember how we've been talking about informational books and how important it is to think about how the author got the information and whether the book is accurate? This book has photographs of real wolves in this book that the author took himself.

Buck Wilde is a photographer who decided to write this book because many years ago he saw a wolf when he was taking a picture of a deer in the woods. He was so frightened he curled up in a hollow tree; after some time he fell asleep. When he woke up he saw seven wolves staring at him with their amber eyes—a golden yellow. He thought they were cruel animals and they gave him the shivers.

Lara: Did they want to eat him?

Peter: If I saw seven wolves staring at me, I'd be scared too.

Elaborates background information.
Encourages text-to-text connections.

Teacher: Well, the wolves went away and Buck began photographing and studying wolves. In this book Buck shares what he has learned, along with the beautiful photographs he took. He shows us that wolves are curious, not cruel animals as they are portrayed in many stories we read.

Sasha: Like the *Three Little Pigs*!

Gabe: And *Red Riding Hood*.

Confirms students' text-to-text connections.

Teacher: You're right. In most folk tales wolves are cruel characters. In old days, there were many wolves and people were afraid of them.

Rhonda: They look cuddly like dogs. They remind me of my aunt's German shepherd.

Demonstrates how to use text features.
Communicates the value of previewing the information in the book.
Links to students' input.

Teacher: Rhonda, you'll find out why they remind you of dogs in this book. Turn to the table of contents. There are several sections of information in this book. Take a quick look at the kinds of information the author will give us in his description.

Peter: He wrote about pups. They must be like dogs.

Gabe: Maybe they are related.

Provides background information on concepts and vocabulary.

Teacher: Turn to page 7. This section of the book gives you information about different kinds of wolves that live in different habitats. See the picture on page 6. Those are called gray wolves, but really they can be black or white.

Rhonda: There's a coyote.

Teacher: Yes, a coyote looks a lot like a wolf but is a different animal. The black wolf is a timber wolf who lives in the subarctic region. That's below the arctic circle.

Rhonda: Does he live in the forest, because that's what *timber* means?

Teacher: That would be a good thing to find out. It makes sense. Turn to page 8. There's the tundra wolf, who is white. The tundra wolf lives inside the arctic circle where it's very, very cold and the only thing that grows is thick grass called *tundra*.

Figure 14–5. Introduction to Wolves

Introduction to *Wolves* (continued)

Demonstrates how to use text features to get information.
Reminds students of purpose of index and table of contents.

Teacher: You have some hunches, and this author will help you know. Flip to the final page. This book has another feature to help readers. It's an index. What information does the index give you?

Lara: It tells you the pages to find out more about wolves.

Teacher: Yes, it does tell you where to find out more but how does it differ from the table of contents?

Peter: I think it tells more exact information like coyotes or arctic wolf or timber wolf.

Lara: There is more detail.

Prompts students to examine a specific example

Teacher: Notice that the index tells the reader where to find information about the alpha male or female.

Peter: Yes, it's on page 15 and 16.

Explains the meaning of vocabulary in the text.

Teacher: Alpha is the Greek name for the letter A. See the word beta? It's the Greek letter for B.

Rhonda: So there's an *A* and a *B*. Probably he is the leader and the B follows.

Draws students' attention to other text features.

Teacher: You'll find that out when you read those pages. Move your eye down the list. What do you notice?

Gabe: The list is in ABC order.

Lara: That's different from the table of contents.

Teacher: That's an important difference. Not only does the index give more detail but it tells topics in the book in alphabetical order to help you find information quickly.

Expands the meaning of a word they know.

Teacher: There are some longer words that you read in this book. Find the word *communication*. There are four places in this book where you will read about communication by wolves. What do you think it means for wolves to communicate.

Gabe: Maybe they bark at each other like dogs.

Lara: They kind of howl, don't they? Real scary. They might run together and just see each other.

Teacher: Go to page 18 and find out what the author means by *communication*.
[Students turn to page 18 and skim it silently.]

Peter: They howl and bark.

Lara: They talk to each other by howling. They lower their heads too.

Teacher: Yes, they howl and bark. The book also says they make *gestures*. That's what Lara was talking about when she said they lower their heads. Find the word *gestures*.

Lara: It starts with *g* but sounds like *j*.

Teacher: Yes, it starts with *g* that sounds like *j*. When we make *gestures* to each other, we may use our hands or arms like this [demonstrates]. When wolves make gestures, what do they do?

Gabe: Move around, wag their tail.

Peter: It says that they tuck their tails between their legs. I've seen my dog do that when he's done something bad.

Focuses the reading.
Reminds students' to use word-solving strategies.

Teacher: You'll find out more about wolf communication in this book. You're going to read the whole book. You'll find that the author tells you a lot about how wolves live together and help each other. After you read, write down three ways that wolves help each other to survive and we'll share what we've found out. Do you remember what to do when you come to a long word that you are not sure that you know?

Rhonda: Look for a part you know.

Lara: Cover up part of it and say the part you know and think about what it could be.

Teacher: Yes, that will help you try the word.

Figure 14–5. Introduction to Wolves *(continued)*

introduction, she supported and supplemented students' background knowledge to help them understand the text better. She used words like *timber, tundra, subarctic,* and *arctic,* suggesting their meaning. She also drew students' attention to text features such as the table of contents and index. The students had used these features before, but Alice decided a quick refresher course was in order.

Alice focused her students' reading by asking them to write three things that wolves did to help each other survive. This question focused students on the text, provided a starting point for a discussion of what they learned from the text, and established a foundation for a more sympathetic view of wolves as an endangered species.

Finally, Alice prompted them to remember what they knew about solving multisyllable words. They had been learning strategies for taking multisyllable words apart. This text offered some challenges, such as *rendezvous, territory, communication, descendants, ancestors,* and *settlements,* as well as a hyphenated word: *well-developed.* Except for reviewing the meaning of *communication* in relation to wolves, Alice did not preview these words but returned to some of the tricky ones after the reading to make connections to the word study.

Introduction to Yang the Youngest and His Terrible Ear, *Level P*

Jerry introduced *Yang the Youngest and His Terrible Ear* (Namioka 1992), a level P fiction book. He selected this book because it is realistic fiction that is humorous and still deals with significant issues to which students can relate. The text offers several reading challenges: to understand a cultural conflict; to identify with any youngster's need to please his family; and to recognize that the need to be accepted is a basic human value. Jerry's students are learning to read longer texts and to think about literary language; the text involves foreshadowing and the use of literary elements. It also offers opportunities to look at diverse perspectives. Jerry believed this book would expand the students' vocabulary and help them extend their ability to read more literary texts at this level.

Jerry began with an overview of the setting, theme, and characters. Students need to understand that Yang and his family have recently moved from China to the United States, so Yang is learning lots of new things, such as baseball. Yang wants to fit into his new home by spending time with his friends, but his family also expects that every family member will become a musician. Jerry explained the title, defining what an "ear" for music means. He also modeled reflecting on the story and interpreting Yingtao's feelings. He expanded on the setting and the geographical background of the story, inviting students to think how different China and Seattle, Washington might be. This contrast would later serve as a foundation for comparing the Yang and Conner families.

Jerry drew attention to the cover illustration and asked students to predict Yingtao's feelings from the drawing. He also gave some background on the author and encouraged them to reflect on the author's experiences and point of view. He identified the genre of the text as fiction even though it is realistic and based on true experiences. As they began reading the first two chapters, Jerry asked students to place stick-on notes where they found evidence of the differences between Chinese and American people, so they could make a chart together later.

Introduction to Insects, *Level U*

Stephanie introduced *Insects* (Bird and Short 1997), a level U informational book.

Stephanie likes using this book with her students because its features are similar to the students' science textbook. The information is:

- Presented in a succinct and organized way. Every paragraph presents a new set of facts about insects.
- Set in a structure that is strictly informational; facts are clear and straightforward.
- Presented in numerous technical words, labeled photographs, diagrams with labels, charts, drawings, and timelines.
- Structured into three levels introduced by headings and subheadings. (The book is divided into sections on four different topics.)
- Enhanced by a pronunciation guide and an index.

Stephanie also liked the interesting photographs, often presented alongside scientific diagrams of the same insect or body part.

After asking students to predict what kind of information the authors might be revealing about insects in this book, Stephanie asked them to look at the table of contents. She pointed out that the letters in bold print represented the main ideas or important kinds of information in the text. The book had four main sections, each focusing on a kind of information about insects. She also pointed out that the text had a pronunciation guide and an index. She asked them to turn to page 5 and think of the different ways that authors of informational texts provide information. The students mentioned pictures and the teacher summarized by saying that they would find information in pictures, drawings, diagrams, and charts. She drew their attention to the directional labels under pictures that are necessary to read if you want to know which picture matches the label; each student read one.

Stephanie then spent time helping students understand how information in the text is organized. (See Figure 14–7.) She directed their attention to major headings and subheadings, asking them to notice the size and type (upper case or upper and lower case) of print. After she had walked them through one section with subheads, she asked them to test the next section by seeing if it followed the same pattern. She was helping them learn about categories and subcategories and the textual features that signal them. Finally, she asked them to make an information web to show what they had learned in the section when they finished reading. These students were learning skills related to outlining. They were learning how to think about the relationship between ideas.

Introduction to Lyddie, *Level U*

Karyn introduced a historical novel, *Lyddie* (Paterson 1991). She chose it because it offers a compelling story as well as a portrait of heroism. Additionally it dovetailed with a study of the industrial revolution that was part of the students' course of study. Although it is not necessary to organize books in "themes," when possible, Karyn tries to link texts to inquiry in social studies in order to make better use of instructional time. She knew that students the previous year had studied the underground railroad as well. She also knew that some of these readers had previously found Paterson's work interesting and that stories about female heroines appealed to them. She wanted to introduce Katherine Paterson as an author to other members of the group.

She planned to teach them about character development by asking them to chart the events in the story and consider how they affected the character. She wanted them to notice how Lyddie responded to the events in her life, how they encouraged her to become more determined than ever to overcome obstacles. Lyddie is a positive character who exhibits self-determination, dignity, and integrity. As readers relate to the early events of the story, they'll discover that Lyddie behaves with courage that carries her through to the final outcome. Karyn also wanted her students to become more aware of the literary elements. For example, a bear and the concept of slavery are used throughout and have multiple meanings.

Karyn began by introducing the title and author and prompting students to share some of the other books they had read. That reminded them of some of the characteristics of Paterson's books. She drew attention to the main character, mentioning the cover illustration, and invited students to speculate about what this young girl might be like. She asked them to identify the genre and discuss its characteristics. She foreshadowed the use of metaphor by explicitly explaining the bear symbol and alerting them to the fact that Lyddie would meet a runaway slave.

Karyn did not have to provide a lot of background knowledge, but she did elaborate on the reward for a runaway slave so that students would know how tempting it might be to Lyddie and could better draw conclusions about her character. She quickly read some of the unusual language of the story so that students could get a feel for the sound of the characters' talking. She focused the reading by asking students to place a stick-on note on any part of the story they would like to read aloud or talk about. Rather than specifying page numbers for the first part of their reading, she asked them to read to a certain part of the story, leaving it to them to monitor themselves by being aware when they reached it.

We have also provided a summary of Karyn's discussion with the students in the second session. Lyddie is a fairly long text with lots of words on each page. Instead of working in detail on the background of the mill town, Lowell, Karyn waited until her second session with the readers, when she explained more about the working conditions in the factories. First, she asked for personal responses; it is obvious that the students

Introduction to *Yang the Youngest and His Terrible Ear*

Introduces the setting, theme, and characters.

Teacher: This is a story about a Chinese boy named Yingtao who moves with his family from China to America. On top of having to learn many new things about his new country, Yingtao has two big problems. Everybody in Yingtao's family is a talented musician—except Yingtao. He cannot play the violin very well at all. Yingtao's family is having an important recital to get more music lesson business for his father. Yingtao is afraid he will ruin the recital with his terrible violin playing. When he meets a new American friend named Matthew, Yingtao discovers that he wants to play baseball, not the violin. But he is too afraid to tell his parents this. Together, Yingtao and Matthew try to come up with a plan that would save the Yang family's recital and allow Yingtao to play baseball.

Introduces and expands upon the title.
Explains vocabulary.

Teacher: This story has an unusual title, *Yang the Youngest and His Terrible Ear*. Let's think about what this title may mean and why the author chose it. What do you think "Yang the Youngest" may mean?

Alex: He is the youngest kid in the family.

Teacher: Yes. And since their family name is Yang, he is Yang the Youngest. Now, what about the "Terrible Ear" part?

Emily: If you're good at music, you have an ear for it, so if you're really bad at singing or playing an instrument, you could have a terrible ear.

Teacher: That's right. It means you can't hear the differences in pitch, or how the notes change, so you're always off-key. Yingtao's terrible ear makes him unable to hear the note changes, so his violin screeches. Meanwhile, everybody else in the family has great ears, so they play beautifully and think Yingtao just isn't trying hard enough.

Provides a model of reflecting on the story.

Teacher: Can you imagine how Yingtao feels, being yelled at and told to try harder when he really is trying his best? Wouldn't that be terrible?

Peter: He's probably embarrassed because he can't play good.

Alex: It's not fair to tell him to try harder when he is doing his best!

Jen: He probably feels left out in the family because he's the only bad musician.

Expands upon the setting and geographical background of the story.

Teacher: Who remembers where the Yang family is from?

Emily: China.

Teacher: Now, see if you can find China on the globe.

Emily: Right here. [pointing correctly].

Teacher: Well, when the Yangs moved to America, they came to Seattle. Which state is that in?

Peter: Seattle, Washington.

Teacher: Right. Can you find Seattle?

Jake: Here it is, in the corner.

Teacher: Let's trace how the Yang family traveled over to America.
[Students trace path with fingers on the globe.]

Jake: Wow! They had to go over to the other side of the world!

Teacher: That's right. It's a long distance, and the two countries are very different.

Figure 14–6. Introduction to Yang the Youngest

Introduction to *Yang the Youngest and His Terrible Ear* (continued)

Predicts theme of story from cover illustration.

Teacher: Now, thinking about what we've talked about, take a look at the cover of the book. Why do you think the illustrator chose this picture for the book's cover?

Jake: That's the boy it's about. He's looking at the violin that he's bad at and doesn't like. He has a baseball in his hand because that's what he likes better.

Emily: He looks a little sad, like he doesn't know what to do.

Alex: Yeah, he's confused about it.

Emily: Look. There's a little Chinese design on the top, because he's from China.

Peter: And the words look like Chinese writing too.

Encourages students to reflect on author's experiences and point of view, as related to the text.
Promotes reading-writing connection.

Teacher: You're right, and you'll notice that you learn much about the Chinese culture when you read this story. The author is from China, herself. She moved to America when she was a child, just like Yingtao. Her family was very musical, just like the Yangs and she also had a terrible ear for pitch. She now lives in Seattle, Washington, which is where this story takes place. So, when you read about how a Chinese family lives and the pain Yingtao goes through, a lot of the information may be based on her own experiences. Do you ever do this when you're writing a story?

Jake: Yeah, I add information about things I know a lot about.

Jen: I sometimes make a story about something that really happened to me and just change the details around.

Alex: Me too. But sometimes, it's just all from my imagination.

Calls students' attention to genre of the text.

Teacher: Lensey Namioka does a little bit of both. The story is based upon true experiences of a woman from the Chinese culture, so the information is realistic and the story could really happen. But, to make it an interesting story, she had to use her imagination to add many other things to it. We call this "realistic fiction" because the story is realistic, but it is still a fictional, made-up story.

Focuses students' reading to search for important information that will help in understanding the characters and plot.

Teacher: You've noticed how far the distance is from China to Seattle. As you read this story, you'll find that even though Yingtao and Matthew are good friends, there are a lot of differences between their families. As you read, try to notice some of those differences and put a sticky note on one of them to share.

Figure 14–6. Introduction to Yang the Youngest *(continued)*

THE BODY OF AN ADULT INSECT AND HOW IT WORKS

THE HEAD

On the head of an adult insect are the eyes, the antennae (feelers) and the mouth parts.

Eyes

Most adult insects have two large compound eyes, one on each side of the head. Each compound eye is made up of many tiny six-sided lenses that fit perfectly together. Each lens takes in a very small section of what the insect is looking at, and together these sections provide a total picture.

As well as compound eyes, many insects (such as dragonflies, grasshoppers, bees and cicadas) have three simple eyes on top of their heads. These eyes are called *ocelli*. They can distinguish only light and shade. Insects do not have eyelids so their eyes are always open.

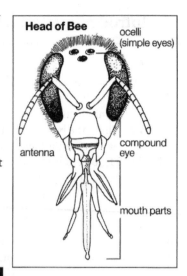

Head of Bee

ocelli (simple eyes)

antenna

compound eye

mouth parts

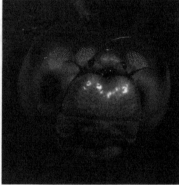

Far left: Compound eyes of a robber fly. The six-sided lenses fit together like the cells of a honeycomb
Left: Compound eyes and the three ocelli of a dragonfly. Each compound eye may have as many as 30,000 lenses. The ocelli form a triangle between the two compound eyes

Figure 14–7. Page 9 of Text, Insects

were becoming involved in the book. She prompted them to think about a significant event when Lyddie gives the runaway slave her money. She drew them into a brief comparison of Lyddie's own life with that of a slave. These inferences would be valuable to students as they studied conditions of working in the industrial revolution. Finally, she asked students to share what they noticed in the text. Notice that the second session was much shorter than the initial introduction and that students were doing much more of the talking.

The Role of Text Introductions in Supporting and Extending Learning

The text you select and the way in which you introduce it provide a special kind of support, enabling students to work at the edge of their learning. Human beings extend their skills by performing at increasingly higher levels. In the case of reading, new texts present new demands.

The reader encounters a new text element such as a new way of learning how characters feel or think, new vocabulary, new literary devices such as foreshadowing, new ways of interpreting charts or graphs, or new punctuation or organizational features. At first the reader may need help noticing the new feature or characteristic and understanding what it means, but before long, if the reader has more opportunities, he will have internalized this knowledge and be able to use it automatically. The text presents new opportunities to learn; the introduction mediates the text so that the reader can take advantage of the new learning and work in his "learning zone" (Vygotsky 1978).

Introduction to *Insects*

Introduces title and genre.
Connects to textbooks.
Probes readers' interests.

Teacher: I have an informational book for you today called *Insects*. You'll see that it's very much like a chapter in your science textbook and I'm going to help you think about how to read and understand all the information. Do you like insects?

Several students: No! (laughing)

Teacher: Are there any insects that are friendly to you? Like a ladybug or a butterfly?

Emily: My sister loves spiders.

Introduces authors.
Invites students to predict information.

Teacher: We're going to learn a bit about insects today. The name of this book is *Insects* by Bettina Bird and Joan Short. The authors of this book have written it to give readers lots of information about insects. What kinds of information do you think the authors will give you?

Hannah: What certain insects eat?

Jeffrey: Names of insects.

Hannah: Where they live.

Emily: The parts of their bodies.

Teacher: That would be interesting.

Emily: How they move.

Probes students' interests.

Teacher: Any other things you would be interested in as a reader? Something you would like to know?

Royi: How they fly, Or, *if* they fly.

Probes students' current understandings.

Teacher: Maybe not all insects fly...What do you think that might be related to—whether they fly or not?

Royi: Whether they have wings.

Teacher: So it really does have to do with their bodies, doesn't it? So you have some good questions.

Draws students' attention to and defines print feature—contents.

Teacher: Open up past the title page and let's take a look at some ways the authors have organized this book so that it is easy for you to understand it. The contents tells us all the different kinds of information we can find in this book.

Draws students' attention to print features that signal important information.

Teacher: Do you see the dark black print? Those are the big ideas—the titles of chapters. What are the main ideas the authors have chosen to tell us about?

Hannah: [reading] Main features common to insects. The life histories of insects. Insect behavior. Insects as survivors. Life history chart. Pro...pro.... What's that word?

Teacher: Pronunciation.

Hannah: Pronunciation guide and index.

Teacher: The pronunciation guide tells you how to pronounce or say some tricky scientific words.

Reviews organization of the text.
Draws attention to text features.

Teacher: So there are four sections of information and there's a life history chart, a pronunciation guide and an index.

Repeats definition of genre.
Directs students' attention to sources of information—words, illustrations, diagrams, section head.
Teaches how to use text feature—labels for photographs.

Teacher: Turn to page 5, the introduction. This is an information book. It's not made up; it is a factual text.

Figure 14–8. Introduction to Insects

Introduction to *Insects* (continued)

One of the ways that the authors have given us information is through the words and another way is…

Emily: Through the pictures.

Teacher: Yes, so we see some real photographs. One of the things we have to do in information books is notice the photographs and read the information connected to them. The author is giving us directions about which picture is which. On the left is..

Jeffrey: Silk moth.

Teacher: Above is, Emily?

Emily: Cicada.

Teacher: And below, Hannah?

Hannah: Wasp!

Teacher: And bottom?

Jeffrey: Jewel beetle.

Teacher: So if we read this little information by the photographs, it tells us where to look, doesn't it? Another way they've given us information is through diagrams. Turn to page 7 and you'll see a diagram. It's a drawing that has some labels. So the first section is called MAIN FEATURES COMMON TO INSECTS and that's what we're going to learn today through diagrams, photographs, and words.

Teaches how to recognize categories of information—larger sections and subsections designated by headings at each level of information. (See Figure 14–7.)

Teacher: I want to show you something the author did. Do you see how the title of this section is all in capital letters?

Students; Yes.

Teacher: Now turn the page. Look at page 9. There's another title all in capital letters but the letters are smaller. That means that the section is divided into smaller sections. The whole section 1 is called MAIN FEATURES COMMON TO INSECTS and this part of the section is called THE BODY OF AN ADULT INSECT AND HOW IT WORKS. Then it's divided into even smaller sections, like this one, THE HEAD, which is smaller and in italics. And under that is a smaller heading, and this time it's not in capitals.

Teacher: Why do you think the authors decided to put the print that way?

Royi: Because first of all the big heading is about the body of the adult insect and how it works. Then they just show a part of the body, the head, and then a part of the head, the eyes.

Teacher: Let's turn the page and see if you are right.

Royi: Antennae, mouth parts.

Teacher: You're on the right track. And then what do we see next? The thorax.

Teacher: Is that a big head or a little head? Does it go under the head? Or is it a new idea?

Royi: A new idea.

Teacher: How can you tell?

Royi: Because it's in all capitals.

Teacher: So let's look at the thorax, that's a body part, and see if there are any other little heads under it.

Hannah: Legs and feet. Wings.

Uses advance organizer to help students understand text organization.

Teacher: I'd like you to read about the main features common to insects. This whole section will help you learn more about the bodies of insects through the words, the pictures and the diagrams. When you finish, I want you to make a web about the body. Remember how you put the big idea in the middle and then body and head. [She starts the chart for the students, placing the word *insects* in the middle of the web and branching off with the word *body*. Coming out from body, she illustrates writing *head*. You can get started now. Enjoy your reading.

Figure 14–8. Introduction to Insects *(continued)*

Introduction to *Lyddie*

(SESSION ONE)

Introduces author and prompts for connecting the texts to other texts.

Teacher: I've selected a book called *Lyddie* for you to begin reading today. It's by Katherine Paterson. I know that Rebecca has read some of her books.

Rebecca: I've read *Jacob Have I Loved*. It was really good.

Sue: I've read that too and another one about Gilly.

Teacher: *The Great Gilly Hopkins*. And, *Bridge to Terabithia*. Have any of you read that? (Several students nod.)

Raises expectations about author's purpose and style.

Teacher: Katherine Paterson is a good writer. Lots of her characters are girls about your age. You know that the characters in her books always have problems to overcome.

Draws attention to main character and encourages interpretation.
Draws attention to setting and establishes plot.
Draws attention to characteristics of genre.

Teacher: This story is fiction, but it is about the real problems that girls and women had in the 1800s. Lyddie is very poor. Her father leaves and her mother can't take care of the family, so Lyddie has to go to work in a tavern for 50 cents a week. She is always hungry and works hard but she is always trying to make things better for herself. Lyddie lived in the 1800s. So what kind of book is this?

Anna: Historical fiction. It's set back in history but it isn't necessarily true. But some of the things are true—like maybe there will be events like wars.

Teacher: The name of this book is the name of the character and we know that characters are what makes stories interesting. The picture on the cover is already giving us some information about Lyddie.

Sue: She looks old fashioned.

Anna: What is that in her hand?

Teacher: There is a loom behind her and she's holding one of the tools in her hand. In this book, Lyddie works in a factory where they weave cloth.

Anna: How old is she?

Teacher: She's 13 years old when the story starts

Anna: She looks either serious or kind of angry.

Sue: Sad.

Rebecca: Mean or strong.

Teacher: I think Lyddie was all of those things during the time of this story. She has to be very strong and determined to overcome her problems. She is on her own and has to make her own living in a very hard way. She is always trying to make her life better.

Explains literary device (metaphor) and relates to main character.

Teacher: Turn to the table of contents. The first chapter is called The Bear. And that bear is important because Lyddie and her family just barely escape from the bear. Lyddie is really brave at that time, and after that, when she is afraid of something, she always thinks about "staring down the bear." She had stared straight into the bear's eyes while all of the family escaped up a ladder and then she climbed the ladder fast and pulled it up after her.

Sue: She must have kind of hypnotized him.

Rebecca: She *is* brave.

Elaborates on the plot by talking about a significant event.
Prompts students to access background information.

Teacher: Another thing that happens in the story is that she meets a runaway slave. It's the first black person

Figure 14–9. Introduction to Lyddie

Introduction to *Lyddie* (continued)

she has ever met. You know in the 1800s, many black people were slaves in the South. If they could escape and go North…

Rebecca: To Canada with the underground railroad.

Sue: They could be free, and people helped them.

Rebecca: Yes, we studied Harriet Tubman. And some people in churches had stations on the underground railroad.

Teacher: Well, in this story some people called Quakers were helping slaves. You know that in those days people who turned in runaway slaves got a $100 reward, and that was a lot of money then. You'll get to see what Lyddie does when she meets Ezekial Abernathy.

Draws attention to unusual language in the story.

Elaborates plot.

Teacher: Some of the language of this book is very different from the way we speak today. Listen to these examples. [reads] "You want I should go with you as far as the village?" "She minded mightily being beholden."

Rebecca: It sounds old fashioned and like she's not educated.

Teacher: You'll also find that Lyddie has a lot of trouble writing. She doesn't know how to spell words very well, but that's another thing she really works on.

Turns the task over to readers.

Focuses reading.

Teacher: Today I want you to read to the part where Lyddie meets Ezekial Abernathy and find out why he is so important to her. Place a sticky note on any part of the story that you want to talk about or that you have questions about.

(SESSION TWO)

Invites personal response.

Prompts personal connections.

Teacher: How do you like the book, *Lyddie*?

Anna: It's good. But it's sad where her mother is sick and she just loses her whole family.

Sue: It's bad that she doesn't have any money and has to work so hard for the mean woman.

Rebecca: I read the part where her mother wrote her. Her mother doesn't know how to spell very well either.

Sue: I guess in those days lots of people didn't write very much and she didn't go to school either.

Rebecca: Some people were kind to her though, her neighbors and Luke.

Teacher: Yes, they were the Quakers.

Rebecca: They were the ones hiding the slave. What was his name?

Anna: Ezekial.

Prompts to summarize part of the story.

Teacher: Why was he important to her?

Anna: She hadn't ever seen a black person before so that was something unusual. And, at first she was tempted. She could get with the $100 reward for turning in a slave, but after she got to know him, she couldn't do it. And she gave him her money so he could get away.

Repeats student's interpretation.

Teacher: She was sorry that he had been a slave and she wanted him to be free?

Rebecca: Yes, and she feels kind of like a slave too.

Figure 14–9. Introduction to Lyddie *(continued)*

Introduction to *Lyddie* (continued)

Prompts for inference.

Teacher: What makes you say that?

Rebecca: Well, she has to work so hard and she doesn't have the freedom to do what she wants.

Sue: And she can't be with her family and the mean woman treats her like a slave.

Summarizes a main idea of the text.
Invites students to share personal responses.

Teacher: This whole book is about Lyddie making choices about her own life. Did you mark any places to go back to?

Sue: I marked the part about being a slave.

Teacher: Take us to that part and read it. *One student read the part about staring down the bear. Another read the part about the frog in the butter churn, and they discussed why that was an important metaphor.*

Summarizes a main idea about the character.
Provides background information.
Focuses readers on character development.

Teacher: You're getting to know some of the reasons that she is so determined to be strong. This time, read to the end of Chapter 9 and you'll see that she goes to work in the mill. The mill is in Lowell, Massachusetts. Girls went there to work so that they could help their families, but the work was very hard. They had to work six days a week for 13 hours a day. The rooms were dark and the air was filled with lint. That's like fuzz from the cloth they were weaving. That lint was very unhealthy and got in their lungs and made some of them sick, but in those days they didn't really have health standards.

As you read, mark any places that you want to talk about. Be thinking how Lyddie is changing in the story, and look for some evidence to share about that. Put a sticker to mark two places that show Lyddie is changing.

Figure 14–9. Introduction to Lyddie *(continued)*

Suggestions for Professional Development

1. Convene a group of your grade-level colleagues to discuss text introductions. Have each person bring a copy of something his or her students will be reading during the following week: a short story, an article, a section of a textbook or novel.

2. Begin by looking at two of the introductions in this chapter. There should be at least one close to the level you want. Analyze the introductions using the following questions:

▪ How did the teacher create a framework of meaning for the text?

▪ What was the structure or genre of the text? Was it made clear to readers?

▪ How did the teacher engage the interests, knowledge, or experiences of the readers?

▪ Did the teacher provide critical new information or concepts?

▪ Did the teacher address any specific language structures or vocabulary?

▪ Were there particular words that the readers were asked to notice?

▪ Were there particular aspects of the format or print that required attention?

▪ Were there any other special features that readers would need to be familiar with in order to process the text with a high level of understanding?

▪ What else did you notice about how the teacher made the new text accessible to the readers?

▪ What did the readers learn how to do that will help them process not only this text but other texts better?

3. Now look at the texts that you plan to introduce to a group of readers. Working in teams, analyze the demands of the text and then plan the introduction.

4. Take the text back to your classroom and introduce it to a small group of students. If possible, either videotape or audiotape your introduction.

5. Meet again and apply the previous questions to your own introductions as you try to improve them. Provide suggestions for colleagues and try it again.

You will find that as you work with analyzing and introducing texts, the process will get easier.

6. Look again at the Self Assessment for Guided Reading, Appendix 50, this time concentrating on items 5 (text selection), 6 (text variation), and 7 (text introduction). Over the next few weeks, apply this self-assessment guide to your work with one guided reading group.

7. Meet again to discuss what you have learned.

STRUGGLING READERS AND WRITERS: TEACHING THAT MAKES A DIFFERENCE

Guided reading offers many advantages as you work with students who need extra help. First, you are providing explicit instruction and support that directly address their needs and they are reading texts that present only a few challenges. Students are asked to "stretch" themselves on decoding, vocabulary, and comprehension, but the task is manageable within teaching and their current abilities. Your support makes it possible for them to learn from their reading just as your stronger readers are doing.

Guided reading also makes it possible for struggling readers to read more, because they can read with high accuracy and reasonable fluency. Finally, guided reading allows you to spend extra time working on word analysis teaching principles that the rest of the class may already know but struggling readers need to address.

In guided reading, students are grouped because they have similar behaviors and read about the same level of text. Chances are, you will have a small group of struggling students who are quite varied in their abilities. You can group them together as long as you select texts carefully, emphasizing easier rather than harder ones. Grouping students at the lowest end of the achievement continuum together is essential so that you can offer maximum support and observe them closely. Be sure, however, that they read the text independently, so that they can build strategies and stamina as readers.

You will also need to teach students to listen and interact during the text introduction and the discussion after the reading. They may not understand the importance of asking questions and listening carefully.

Demonstrate how the introduction can help them think about the story. You may also need to spend more time discussing the text afterward to be sure that all students benefit from the conversation.

Here are specific suggestions for working in guided reading with readers who need extra help:

1. **Involve them in guided reading every day.** The students at the lower end of the achievement continuum are the ones least likely to gain from independent work; they need the most instruction. Carefully selecting texts for them and providing supportive instruction will enable them gradually to tackle more difficult texts.

2. **Provide appropriate levels of text for them to read.** Students can not use effective reading strategies when the texts are too difficult. Use the text gradient to find books that students can read and, at the same time, find interesting.

3. **Guide them to search for information in the text.** As students raise questions during discussion, they may need to confirm their hypotheses with information from the text. For fiction texts, they may have difficulty recalling specific character descriptions or details of action or setting. Teach them how to search for information in the text to find answers to their questions.

4. **Emphasize fluency in reading so that language can power the reading process.** Many struggling readers read slowly. They have been reading too difficult texts for so long that the only logical solution is to read slowly. Reading slowly interferes with comprehension, however; the slower you read, the harder it is to think of the text as conveying meaning. As these

students read texts at the appropriate level, you may need to teach fluency. Activities like shared reading, choral reading, readers theater, poetry sharing, and books on tape support fluency.

5. ***Give them opportunities to discuss their reading.*** Oral language supports and extends students' understanding of what they read. More than other students, struggling readers need time to talk before reading, while reading, and after reading. The greater their struggle, the more essential the conversation.

6. ***Have them write in connection with reading.*** Writing is the ideal activity to extend their understanding of what they read; and they learn more about writing at the same time.

7. ***Provide opportunities for silent reading.*** Silent reading is faster than oral reading. It is also easier to comprehend when reading silently. Most of your students read silently most of the time; this should also be true of your struggling readers. If students are reading at an appropriate level of difficulty, they will be able to read silently. You do not need to hear every word a student reads but can sample oral reading.

8. ***Provide a few minutes of word work at the end of the guided reading lesson.*** Using magnetic letters, dry-erase boards, or markers and paper, quickly explore principles that will help struggling readers understand how words work (for example, changing letter clusters with the same rime to make new words). Show them the principle; then have them apply the principle to several examples. Make this work gamelike; vary instruction to increase readers' flexibility.

9. ***Be sure that they spend their time reading text.*** Struggling readers especially need to spend their time actually reading rather than doing all of the extraneous activities that seem to surround reading. Filling out worksheets will not help these students read better; there is not a shred of evidence that such activity fosters achievement.

10. ***Introduce them to series books in guided reading lessons.*** Almost all students in the intermediate grades love series books; they are especially good for students who need extra help because they provide extra practice on easy material. Once they have read one or two books in a series, it is easy to read more.

SECTION 4

Literature Study

Students in the upper elementary grades need and deserve a rich, joyful experience with quality literature. In Chapter 15 we describe the elements of literature study, including teacher and student roles before, during and after literature discussion. Chapter 16 provides specific suggestions for forming groups, guiding student choices, and establishing and teaching routines for literature discussion. In our rush to help students perform on texts, it is easy to forget our primary goal is to open the doors of literature to foster a lifelong love of reading. In Chapter 17 we discuss the unique meanings each individual brings to a work of literature and the ways in which we can encourage increasingly sophisticated responses.

## CHAPTER FIFTEEN

DISCOVERING LITERATURE STUDY: THE ESSENTIAL ELEMENTS

By supporting tolerance of the opinions and interpretations of others, by recognizing that interpretations will vary, and by learning to cope with ambiguity, teachers help children stretch the boundaries of their own knowing.
— MARYANN EEDS AND RALPH PETERSON

Literature study is the third element in the reading block of the language/literacy framework, and an integral part of all three blocks. Literature study brings students together for an in-depth discussion of a work of fiction or nonfiction. The discussion emerges from the students' own personal responses to the text and may focus on any aspect—characters, events, genre, or author's writing style and literary techniques. Students share their questions, their insights, and their emotional responses.

As they participate in literature study, students develop new understandings as readers. By sharing meanings and listening to multiple perspectives, they come to understand texts in a deeper, more fully developed way than they can on their own. Through literature study, students also begin to improve their own writing. Analyzing an author's style and technique often prompts students to reexamine their own writing and develop their self-expression.

What Is Literature Study?

Literature study is known by many other names, including *literature circles, literature clubs, lit clubs, book clubs,* and *readers' circles.* You may want to adopt one of these "user friendly" labels. We like the word *study* because it conveys precisely what takes place: a focused examination of a text. Whatever the label, it refers to an instructional approach that involves these key elements:

1. Reading and thinking about works of literature.
2. Collaborating with others to reflect on, analyze, and criticize literature.
3. Developing and sharing aesthetic responses to literature.
4. Extending understandings through talk and/or writing.

Specific Purposes of Literature Study

As part of a broad framework of reading and writing experiences, literature study is specifically designed to:

- Increase students' enjoyment of reading.
- Make students aware of the value of their personal responses to what they read.
- Engage students in meaningful literary discussion.
- Provide rich experiences with a range of genres representing many periods and cultures.
- Expand students' literacy and background knowledge.
- Build students' knowledge of authors and illustrators.
- Deepen students' understanding of the qualities that make well-crafted literature.
- Demonstrate new ways of interpreting and analyzing text.
- Foster critical thinking.

These purposes are achieved through a range of classroom learning activities.

A Basic Sequence for Literature Study

While informal talk about books is important, literature study is an instructional approach to help readers achieve a broader understanding of texts than they can accomplish by reading alone. Here is a brief description of the basic sequence of activities for literature study (see Figure 15–1):

A Basic Sequence for Literature Study

Self-select

Form Group

Make Schedule

Read, Think, and Note

Discuss

Response or Project

Figure 15–1. A Basic Sequence

1. Usually, students *select for themselves* the books they read for literature study, although you guide the process. You structure learning by collecting books, introducing them, and inviting students to make choices from a limited selection. As students become more sophisticated in their awareness of text, they may suggest choices for literature study.

2. Students work in *small heterogeneous groups organized by the books chosen.* Generally, all of the students in the group read the same book, but they can also read different books by the same author or illustrator or different books on the same topic or theme.

3. The students and you set up a *schedule for meeting and discussing the book.* You also agree on how much will be read by the meeting date.

4. As students *read or reread the book,* they may mark, note, draw, or write in preparation for the discussion.

5. The group *meets to discuss the book.* While you play an important role, it is important that students learn to listen to and address one another. In general, you demonstrate and promote effective discussion techniques. You may intervene to point out information or new language that students have neglected or to nudge students forward in their thinking. By observing the group, you gather valuable information on what students are comprehending and learning about texts.

6. Following the discussion, students may share their new understanding of the book with classmates through a *response or a cooperative project.*

How Literature Study Contributes to Students' Learning

Specifically, literature study contributes to students' learning in five major areas:

1. *Expanding reading comprehension strategies.* Students develop and use a range of comprehension strategies. They make connections between the literature they read and their own personal knowledge, world knowledge, and text knowledge. They use what they know to make inferences from the text as well as to summarize, synthesize, analyze, and criticize.

2. *Learning to think critically.* Guided by their own interpretations as well as yours and their peers', students learn to make decisions about the relevant information in texts. They also consider and explore a variety of perspectives.

3. *Appreciating the aesthetic qualities of literature.* Learning early to enjoy and respond to superlative literature helps students develop an artistic appreciation that we hope will connect them to great writing throughout their lives. In addition, they develop an emotional—even compassionate—response to the human problems and issues reflected in literature. And they learn to appreciate the way writers use language to evoke emotions and create images that "show" rather than "tell" about life. Finally, as they immerse themselves in the intellectual and emotional intensity of literature study, they learn to form sensory images that move their comprehension beyond words.

4. *Developing communication skills.* Students develop their ability as communicators. They learn to listen to others and express complex opinions. They learn to sustain a discussion by building on the ideas of others. They consider more than one side of an issue, and they find ways to agree and disagree with others.

5. *Extending writing skills.* Students learn to make rich connections between the texts they read and their own writing. They discern the qualities of powerful models and analyze them in ways that help them

use language creatively to express ideas, support an argument, and organize facts to reveal a larger meaning.

Organizational Structures for Literature Study

You can engage students in thoughtful discussion of literature in a variety of ways. In the language/word study block you foster high-level thinking about texts as you read aloud a text to your group. You can also engage your students in shared reading of a text. For example, you read aloud a book such as *Bridge to Terabithia* (Paterson 1977) with each student having a copy of the book. All students can enjoy the experience and discuss its content regardless of their reading level.

Alternatively, you can assign or give a choice of texts for students to choose and read independently. Follow this with small group meetings to discuss the text. As you meet with one literature study group during the reading workshop, the other children are reading independently or writing in their response journals.

An Example of Literature Study

All of Sarah's third graders were reading stories about families. Students could choose from the following titles, all available as paperbacks:

- *Always Grandma* (Neison 1988).
- *Annie and the Old One* (Miles 1985).
- *Tales of a Gambling Grandma* (Khalsa 1986).
- *Abuela's Weave* (Castañeda 1993)
- *Grandma According to Me* (Magneson 1994).

One Monday, Sarah gave a very short introduction to each book, telling the title and the author, giving a brief description of what the story was about, and mentioning which titles were a bit more difficult than others. Then she let the students browse through the books briefly. Next, Sarah gave each student a list of the five titles and asked them to indicate their choices in priority order from 1 through 5. Students knew they were expected to choose a text they could read, although they also had the option of asking a parent to read the book aloud to them.

Sarah sorted the slips, listed which students would be reading which book, and posted the list with dates for each group meeting. The group of five students who chose *Tales of a Gambling Grandma* began to read their book during independent reading. They had two days to finish the book. Sarah asked them to mark one place in the text and one illustration that they would like to talk about with the group. She wanted them to come to the meeting prepared to tell why they chose the illustration or segment and to read the segment aloud.

These students had been taking part in literature study since the beginning of the year. Sarah had acquainted them with lively discussion about books through her interactive read-alouds. She had also taught the routines of small-group discussion, so when they came together for their meeting, they were ready. Taking turns, students shared the illustrations and sections of text they had chosen. Here are parts of the conversation that took place about the illustrations:

DERRICK: I'll start with my picture choice on page 12. I like this where they go to the amusement park. I chose it because I like roller coasters and I'd like to have a grandmother or someone who likes to go to places like that. On the other page is a show with a hippo, but I don't know where they would have something like that.

RASHI: I think it's a long time ago, and they maybe used to have stage shows with animals.

RHONDA: She's really old, but she still likes to go places and do things with the little girl.

. . .

LAQUITA: I picked this picture—turn to page 4— where she is gambling in the window and it looks very mysterious. I like the big bridge in the background, too.

RHONDA: It looks kind of like gangsters.

DERRICK: That's what it was really, with Dutch somebody. But Grandma is really kind of like a gangster, because she's gambling.

RHONDA: But she's not really like a bad gangster, because she doesn't kill people and stuff.

DERRICK: I don't understand that. Wasn't gambling against the law?

RHONDA: I noticed the car is really old and that means that it was a long time ago. Back then maybe gambling was against the law.

. . .

BEN: I picked page 18 where all the old ladies are sitting under the umbrella and doing their gambling and the clothes are hung out on the line like my grandmother used to do.

RASHI: I picked the next page where Grandma is in the train taking a bath in orange juice with those guys pouring it in. That couldn't really happen.

LOQUITA: No, she wouldn't take a bath with two guys standing there.

RHONDA: And orange juice would cost too much.

LAQUITA: And it would be really sticky.

SARAH: But why do you think she told the little girl that story?

RASHI: I think the author meant that she liked everything to be exciting and she wanted to tell a story the girl would like.

LAQUITA: I agree with Rashi; she wanted to tell a good story.

RHONDA: Me, too. That's like in the picture where the soldiers are in the kitchen. There wouldn't really be soldiers in the kitchen, but it was just a way of telling the little girl something.

SARAH: Remember that the author is someone who is remembering something that happened when she was really a little girl, and she's writing it almost like a little girl would say it.

RASHI: Maybe the little girl just kind of remembered it that way!

DERRICK: We don't know, because the book doesn't tell, but since it couldn't really be true, it has to be one or the other—that she told a story or the girl didn't remember it right.

SARAH: Or maybe it's a little bit of both. You know how in a memoir, we were talking about how people remember things in different ways.

The group then discussed their text selections. One of the students read the following paragraphs aloud, which show how the little girl felt after the grandmother died.

And I said what I had heard other people say sometimes: "Oh, I'm sorry to hear that." And I went upstairs to my grandma's room.

I opened the drawer of her treasures and made sure that everything was there: the pennies, the bottle of cologne, the snapshot, her hairpins and false teeth, and the little bag with the ring.

Then I opened her closet door and stepped inside. I closed the door behind me and hugged and smelled all my grandma's great big dresses. (30)

The students discussed how objects can remind us of people who have gone away or died, and they shared a few personal examples. They also revisited a couple of Grandma's lessons—such as never going into the woods alone or keeping plenty of borscht in the refrigerator.

As Sarah supported this discussion, the group began to consider the text as a memoir. On the last page, the text says that although the ring wasn't made out of gold and diamonds it was even more precious. The students noted that the dedication—to "all the Khalsa children"— was noted by students as suggesting the story is authentic. In the course of the discussion, students expanded their understanding of realistic fiction and memoir. A few times Sarah intervened to redirect their attention or to pose a question that got them to think about a literary element in a new way.

Tales of a Gambling Grandma is a wonderful example of a text with many layers of meaning. The illustrations go beyond the text to provide a great deal of additional information, such as visual clues to the historical period, the humor, and the mood of the story. The students' discussion clearly showed their awareness of the illustrations.

Essential Elements of Literature Study

The essential elements of literature study can be examined from both the students' and teacher's point of view. There are a number of stages, including what happens before, during, and after a literature study session (see Figure 15–2).

The Students' Role
Students have an active and important role in literature study. While you guide the process, students are expected to take highly responsible roles at every phase.

BEFORE THE DISCUSSION
Students are expected to make thoughtful book choices that show a commitment to reading. In addition, they commit to meeting with others, noting the time and the sections they have agreed to read. Students also prepare by reading and completing any task that you have assigned or that the group has agreed on.

DURING THE DISCUSSION
The roles students play during the literature discussion are complex, but you can teach students these roles over

Essential Elements of Literature Study

	Before	During	After
Students	❖ choose a book ❖ note meeting time ❖ note sections to be read ❖ understand task ❖ prepare by reading and completing any assigned task	❖ try to understand others ❖ make personal connections ❖ share their thinking ❖ actively participate ❖ give others opportunities to participate ❖ provide evidence from the text or illustrations ❖ stay focused on the text ❖ relate text to other texts ❖ relate text to the world and others ❖ add to one another's responses ❖ share agreement or disagreement ❖ pose real questions ❖ provide a different interpretation	❖ evaluate their participation ❖ evaluate the quality of the discussion ❖ make a plan for next steps ❖ plan and carry out projects (optional)
Teacher	❖ establishes and teaches routines ❖ gathers book choices ❖ sets meeting time ❖ decides on sections to be read (with students) ❖ may assign task	❖ facilitates, coaches, reinforces ❖ redirects discussion ❖ demonstrates thinking ❖ interjects and summarizes ❖ restates or gets children to restate ❖ encourages students to extend responses ❖ adds new information ❖ moves discussion forward	❖ gets students to evaluate discussion ❖ invites comments, questions, opinions ❖ plans next steps (more discussion, writing project, more reading or rereading)

Figure 15–2. Essential Elements of Literature Study

time as you provide demonstrations and guide the process. Students are expected to participate actively and to share their thinking, which may include providing evidence from the text or illustrations to substantiate personal connections; relating the text to other texts; or relating the text to their knowledge of the world. They are responsible for posing real questions and valuing interpretations other than their own.

In addition to speaking up, students are expected to collaborate by listening to others, giving others opportunities to participate, adding to one another's responses, and sharing agreement or disagreement. Together, students take the responsibility for keeping the discussion focused on the text. They also take turns courteously.

AFTER THE DISCUSSION

After the discussion, students evaluate the meeting, reflecting on the quality of their participation and making a plan for next steps. Students may work together to create a project to share the meaning they gained from the text. (Projects are described in the next chapter.) Typically they involve some kind of presentation that combines visual or performing arts with text. Students may, for example, create a group art project or role-play characters in a way that represents the meaning either directly or symbolically.

The Role of the Teacher

Your role is multifaceted and involves a balance between demonstrating, directing, supporting, redirecting, and observing while students work independently. Your goal is for students to take over the conversation.

As students are learning to participate in literature study, you establish and teach the routines you want them to use. Over time, they will need less teaching, but every time you introduce a new way of interacting or a new expectation for the kind of discussion students will take part in, you will need to show them explicitly what you want them to do.

Your other instructional roles include gathering book selections and guiding student choice. Pull together collections that represent topics, genres, and authors at levels that will be accessible to most readers. The selected books must support student understanding and wide-ranging intellectual discussion—the sort of high-energy thinking and talking that reflects your goal.

Carefully guide the number of meetings, the sections to be read, and the time allotted for reading between meetings. You may also assign tasks that will support students' thinking and ensure a quality discussion. In the process, you teach students to manage their own learning, but you continue to stay involved as both monitor and encourager.

DURING THE DISCUSSION

During the discussion you facilitate and redirect the conversation as needed, helping students understand that while there are no right or wrong answers, they need to support their thinking with evidence from the text, their personal experience, or background knowledge. After establishing routines and demonstrating what students need to do, you continue to have an important role in supporting students. As students take the task into their own hands, coach them carefully, helping them interact with each other in ways that extend thinking. Reinforce the ongoing discussion and get students to extend their responses. You may restate a comment or ask the student to restate it for clarity. If students need more information, you may offer it in a way that helps them synthesize new ideas. Redirect the discussion if it wanders off topic or nudge the discussion forward if it gets bogged down.

AFTER THE DISCUSSION

You also have an important teaching and facilitating role after the discussion. Teach students to evaluate their participation and the success of the discussion; help them to identify the characteristics of a quality conversation. Invite comments, questions, and opinions in a way that helps students reflect on the discussion which will help them consider their own thinking and synthesize knowledge. Finally, work with them to plan the next steps, which might involve more discussion, writing, projects, or more reading or rereading of the same text.

Literature Study As an Essential Part of the Reading Workshop

Learning about literature takes place across the language and literacy framework. Ideally, students have studied a range of literature from the time they entered kindergarten. Reading aloud is an important way to introduce students to a wide range of literature and support them in thinking about text. Independent reading provides opportunities for readers to gain mileage as they read texts they've chosen themselves. Guided reading provides efficient, organized instruction to help students develop the strategies they need to read texts with understanding. In literature study, students use their comprehending strategies to investigate the meaning of texts in a deep, intensive way. Through literature study, they learn how to explain their ideas in public, the goal being to gain greater meaning than they can on their own. Each context is an important dimension in building a strong reading processing system.

Theoretical Underpinnings of Literature Study

Response to Literature

Throughout this book, we reiterate how important it is for students to make connections between the texts they read and their own lives, their background knowledge, and their literary knowledge. As readers, we each understand and respond to a text differently based on what we know and feel from our past experiences. The theories of reader response discussed below are meant to help you realize the importance of teaching students to bring their own ideas to reading.

READING AS A TRANSACTION

Where does meaning reside? Is it in the text or in the reader? Reader response theory suggests that meaning is a synthesis both of the reader's knowledge and of the information in the text, and that meaning consists not just of factual information but of emotion and visual images. Louise Rosenblatt argued that reading is transactional—that is, meaning is a result of the interaction of the reader and the text:

> A text is merely ink on paper until the reader (if only the author) evokes meaning from it. (1983, 25)

When students encounter their first stories, they react in terms of their own experiences. Our reaction to stories as adults is quite similar. The qualitative difference is that we have accumulated and synthesized a lot more information through travel, study, and, of course, reading. We've learned about beauty, love, and grief. We bring what we are to our literary transactions. How wonderful that in the early 1800s Jane Austen could create upper-class English characters who still appeal so thoroughly to readers in the second millennium! That's the conversation of reading. Across time, space, and culture, each of us responds in a different way to the same book and constructs a different meaning that reflects our own personality, experiences, and values.

STANCE TOWARD READING

Response to literature is further affected by purpose for reading. Rosenblatt (1978) distinguished between readers who seek information and assume an "efferent" stance during reading and those who seek an emotional, pleasurable experience and assume an "aesthetic" stance. If you read with an efferent stance, you search texts like a newspaper article, a historical account, or a biography for meaning, using logic and rationality. On the other hand, if you read with an aesthetic stance, you seek an emotional response. You might be enraptured with the poignant feelings that a poem provokes or enter into a story so thoroughly that you feel you are *with* the characters, crying and laughing (at least inwardly) with them.

It might seem that an efferent stance is reserved for nonfiction while an aesthetic stance serves fictional texts. This is generally true, but the lines are blurred. For example, you might experience a visceral reaction to a brutal story you read in a newspaper, becoming distraught and angry. On the other hand, you might gain a wealth of factual knowledge from reading fiction that depicts cultures different from your own, such as *The God of Small Things*, by Arundhati Roy, a luminous account of the lives of East Indian twins. Many people, when they travel, read novels written by local authors. Not only do they enjoy the literature, but they learn something about the area and its people.

A quality piece of literature often transcends "type" and reflects layers of meaning. And, of course, when you travel to distant lands you well may remember texts you have read throughout your life that gave you a picture that you now may or may not find to be accurate. Response incorporates all of the reactions readers make to many texts in many ways.

MAKING RESPONSE PUBLIC

In literature study, readers share their responses with others and, in the process, they refine and expand them. In other words, they make them public in some way, which may involve speech, writing, art, or drama. Langer (1995) has described the interplay of reading, writing, and discussion as students move from personal to public ways of sharing their understandings. She says this interplay is characteristic of an "envisionment" classroom, one that is based on the dynamic and changing nature of individuals' understandings. "Envisionment" here refers to "the world of understanding a person has at any point in time" (Langer 1995, 9), including all of the books, texts, films, dramas, music, art, and travel that person has experienced. It includes all the connections among and between understandings that the individual currently has.

Learning and Development

Reading and talking about literature helps students develop more sophisticated levels of thinking. Supported by a "more expert other," learners can perceive more than they can see when they're working alone. In the case of literature study, you are supporting students in a way that allows them to go further than they would by simply reading books on their own.

The sophisticated ways of thinking, sometimes called "higher-order thinking," that human beings are capable of doing are made possible through the use of symbols. Through these higher mental functions, individuals understand and regulate their environment; they also consciously realize that they are thinking. Higher mental actions are learned via social interactions and are mediated by signs and symbols. Language is our primary tool for organizing thinking, developing memory, attending to and using information, and making connections (Vygotsky 1978; Wertsch 1985). In literature study, students are able to use language as well as visual images as tools in constructing their thinking. You provide demonstrations of talk and then support students as they engage in a wide range of ways to share meaning. In other words, you *teach* them how to use language for:

- Inferring meaning from text and expressing inferences to others.
- Providing evidence to back up inferences.

- Drawing conclusions and commenting on the thoughts of others.
- Eliciting the perspectives of others.
- Synthesizing information and making clear statements to reflect thinking.
- Asking questions about aspects of text such as character development, plot structure, and so forth.
- Forming opinions about texts and expressing those opinions to others.

You are guiding the process, but the learners are constructing their own understandings. According to Wood (1998), this process of constructing understanding is essential if we expect students to internalize the operations and perform them on their own. Some of these processes represent the highest forms of comprehension. They go far beyond repeating what is in a text or answering a series of so-called comprehension questions.

In guided literature study, students are *acting* on text, reflecting on these acts, and capturing them in language that is part of an ongoing interplay. In the process they are interacting with the culture in exactly the way young people have always done—by using the available cultural tools in the company of a more mature, experienced person who can guide, refine, and extend the process. This "apprenticeship" model of learning fosters the development of internal mental processes; thus learning "leads" development. In other words, we are not waiting for students to develop higher levels of thinking before inviting them to participate in a literature study; rather, we are showing them the way through this supported engagement with literature (Vygotsky 1978).

The Social Construction of Meaning

Meaning is constructed in a social context. While we possess our own unique meanings born of our individual experiences, we also embrace the socially shared meanings that arise through communication and our common human experience (Vygotsky 1986; Bakhtin 1981).

We learn by using the various forms of language— oral and written. In our literate culture, higher-order thinking is highly dependent on literacy. So, as they use language, students enjoy the opportunity both to create a meaningful response and to share it publicly, and in doing so, to refine and elevate this meaning.

Reading is a broad community; written language is composed and published in a variety of ways. Readers have access to this community, with all its diversity of forms and ideas. They can enter the conversation at any time and bring it into their oral discourse.

The Construction of Meaning Through Inquiry

Students who are engaged in literature study are *inquiring* into meaning. That is, they are engaged in the act of *wondering* about something and searching for the answers, an act that may be partial or complete but typically sparks more wondering. Inquiry arises from and contributes to socially shared meanings (Vygotsky 1986; Bakhtin 1981). Inquiry rests on the combination of individual and shared meanings because using language for inquiry involves making connections with others in an attempt to build understanding, or *to learn*. Lindfors (1999) describes two broadly defined types of inquiry:

1. *Information seeking*, which involves seeking clarification, explanation, justification, or confirmation.
2. *Wondering*, which involves others in reflecting, predicting, exploring, and considering possibilities.

These understandings help us think about how we interact with students as well as how we teach them to interact with one another. According to Lindfors (1999), information seeking is text-bound and seeks closure.

For example, the group of students who read *Tales of a Gambling Grandma* (Khalsa 1986) could probably repeat the details of the story, such as:

■ Grandma came from Russia.
■ She knew how to gamble and liked to do things with the little girl.
■ She got old and died.

They might learn the meaning of words like *borscht* and *luxurious,* and they might even learn about Grandma's rules. Yet with all that knowledge, would students have truly comprehended *Tales of a Gambling Grandma*? We would probably say no, because we would be searching for evidence that they understood this text at a deeper level. We would want them to recognize the special nature of the relationship, the

poignant quality of the writing, the significance of the items that Grandma left behind, and how those items evoked vivid memories replete with sensory images for the little girl. We would want them to reflect on, recall, and relive similar experiences of their own. We'd want them to know, in the deepest sense, why the fake ring was irreplaceable. These understandings arise from inquiring into text.

Inquiry means active investigation on the part of learners, and we believe the study of literature is framed as inquiry. Barnes (1992) speaks of students "making sense of a poem by talking their way into it" (25). As students discuss books they are reading, what they say may sound like simple conversation, but the stance is one of inquiry. As Lindfors (1999) notes, "They turn toward one another and toward their topics in uncertainty and invitation" (118). Through the conversational turns of the discussion, they deepen their own and others' understandings and come to know the text in new ways.

Listening, too, is important in inquiry. As teachers we model listening and actively teach students to listen to one another. In dialogue, partners acutely tune into each other, seeking responses of a particular kind and being aware of what is being sought. The surprises they provide for each other are incorporated as ideas to wonder about, and in the process shared meanings are created.

Often the language is not precise. Barnes (1992) describes "groping towards a meaning" (28). One idea builds on another as students think aloud; literature study provides the time for this exploration. We may teach students the routines and precise language that enable them to begin, but learning literary dialogue is not the same as perfecting a skill. The routines of that dialogue are just a beginning to help students become inquirers who support one another in the process of wondering.

Summary

Literature study is an introduction to the pleasures of the intellectual life. Through this carefully structured and teacher-supported instructional experience, your students learn how to value their own ideas, form their own opinions, and share them in such a way that others can follow their thinking. What's more, they learn how to build on others' ideas, thus participating in a full-blown intellectual conversation about a literary work. As they share, they learn to use the analytical power of their mind in ways that will serve them well across all their future endeavors, enriching their lives immeasurably.

Suggestions for Professional Development

1. Treat yourselves and your colleagues to a discussion of literature. The following are eleven titles you might be able to find in your library:
   - *Pink and Say* (Polacco 1994)
   - *Star of Fear, Star of Hope* (Hoestlandt 1995)
   - *The Wall* (Bunting 1992)
   - *Fly Away Home* (Bunting 1993)
   - *Nettie's Trip South* (Turner 1987)
   - *The Faithful Elephants* (Tsuchiya 1992)
   - *On the Bus with Rosa Parks* (Dove 1999)
   - *A Boy Called Slow: The True Story of Sitting Bull* (Bruchal 1995)
   - *More than Anything Else* (Bradley 1995)
   - *The Lotus Seed* (Garland 1993)
   - *How to Get Famous in Brooklyn* (Hest 1995)
2. If you cannot find any of these titles, ask your librarian to recommend picture books that showcase significant issues. If you have more time, you may substitute any chapter book that explores issues of interest to you and your group.
3. Read the book before you come to the session or at the beginning of the session. However, it is essential that each of you has time to read (and perhaps reread) the book carefully and thoughtfully rather than hurriedly. Ask everyone to mark two places in the book to share some thoughts about. If the illustrations are a key part of the communication of meaning, also ask everyone to share something about the illustrations.

4. Appoint two members of the groups as "process observers." The observers' role is to list the different kinds of talk the group is having about books, such as:
   - Making connections to your own lives or bringing background knowledge to bear on your interpretations.
   - Making connections to other texts.
   - Discussing the authors' language.
   - Reacting to a character.
   - Noticing and interpreting the illustrations.
   - Making inferences.
   - Generating new understandings.
   - Analyzing the text as a piece of literature.
5. Establish some simple ground rules:
   - One person shares her thoughts and asks others to react or add to the discussion.
   - Everyone is responsible for ensuring that each person in the group has a chance to talk.
   - Each participant should identify the page in the text that she is discussing.
   - Everyone is responsible for ensuring that the talk stays focused on the book or topic rather than wandering away.
   - At the end of the discussion, the group evaluates the session: Did everyone have an opportunity to participate? Did the talk stayed focused on the book? Was the talk enjoyable? What might you like to change for the next time?
6. After the evaluation, ask the observers to share the lists they made of the different sorts of talk.
   - Discuss the kind of thinking your talk represents.
   - Talk about how—without any particular focus—the discussion was filled with a range of interesting ideas and a great variety of ways of using language.
   - Relate what you have learned to your work with intermediate students.

PUTTING LITERATURE STUDY IN ACTION

Just as I need to garden, to dig my hands into soil and draw substance from the earth, I need to read and draw substance from words.
— KAREN SMITH

Literature study enables students to help one another learn. Our goal is always student independence. We want individual students to take responsibility, manage themselves as learners, complete tasks, and discover how to learn on their own. At the same time, we recognize that learning is interdependent. Accordingly, we want our students to participate in learning groups in which they can contribute to the learning of others. When students work in groups they doubly benefit: they gain the support they need to learn, and they begin to offer support to others and provide leadership.

The key characteristics of literature study are summarized in Figure 16–1. The process is characterized by cooperation, respect, and inquiry. The goal is active participation that results in increased comprehension. Reaching this goal requires good teaching decisions related to each of the following:

1. Selecting texts.
2. Forming groups.
3. Establishing routines.
4. Facilitating discussion.
5. Varying the organizational models or designs for sessions.

Selecting Texts for Literature Study

You will want to select a great variety of high-quality texts specifically for literature discussion (see Figure 16–2). We recommend that you identify between thirty and fifty titles that you believe will spark energetic discussion. You will need several copies of each of these books. Some schools solve the multiple-copy problem by pooling the titles in a central book room; however, each classroom still needs its own quality library. You can:

- Use book clubs to obtain inexpensive or free books.
- Get duplicate copies from the library.
- Ask students to bring in copies of books they might have to make enough for a group.
- Borrow from other teachers to make a set.
- Pool books with your grade-level colleagues.
- Work with teachers in the grade below and the grade above to share books at different times of the year.
- Submit grant proposals to buy books.
- Search for books at garage sales.

In Section 3 of this book, we discuss the range of texts that will form the classroom collection as well as the shared collection in the book room. A section of the school book-room should be devoted to books especially suitable for literature study.

Developmentally Appropriate Content

Students in the intermediate grades are developing both physically and emotionally. They enjoy and respond to books that echo their own complex intellectual and emotional processes. They like characters who reflect their own mental attributes and experience problems to which they can relate (Huck, Hepler, and

---

Key Characteristics of Literature Study

- ❖ The students or the teacher select the reading material.
- ❖ Students read the same or different books.
- ❖ Small, temporary heterogeneous groups are formed.
- ❖ Group meetings are scheduled and reading tasks are sometimes assigned.
- ❖ Students sometimes draw or write before, during, or after reading the text.
- ❖ Students often meet several times to discuss the same book.
- ❖ The teacher and students generate discussion.
- ❖ The teacher sometimes demonstrates, clarifies, gives information, or guides, showing ways of thinking about or responding to a text.
- ❖ The teacher may move the group forward.
- ❖ Discussion may lead to further reading or writing or projects for sharing.

Figure 16–1. Key Characteristics of Literature Study

Hickman 1993; Tucker 1981). Most students like stories about young people who are slightly older than they are but who experience problems that interest them.

Students between the ages of eight and ten are typically interested in friends, neighborhoods, humor, and adventure. They are still dealing with fairly straightforward plots. They can understand characters who have both "good" and "bad" traits. They are beginning to understand that perspectives may vary and that some situations are not exactly as they seem. Their interests run toward the type of realism shown in series such as the *Ramona* or *Julian* books. At this age, students can understand more sophisticated literary aspects of texts that are *read aloud to them* in the classroom.

Students between the ages of nine and twelve can typically tackle more sophisticated plots and more complicated literary devices, such as stories within stories. They can read and enjoy stories that take place in the distant past or the far future, feature characters who speak in dialects, or focus on characters from other cultures. Intermediate students are particularly engaged by stories that portray characters who are growing up, meeting challenges, and enjoying adventures. They are capable of exploring and recognizing perspectives and life styles different from their own. They can also tackle challenging themes such as death, aging, prejudice, or poverty. Before age nine, there is little difference in

Texts for Literature Study

Texts for Literature Study should:

- ❖ Be developmentally appropriate.
- ❖ "Teach" and "stretch."
- ❖ Include layers of meaning.
- ❖ Exemplify worthwhile issues.
- ❖ Reflect a variety of perspectives.
- ❖ Represent our diverse world.
- ❖ Encompass a variety of authors/illustrators.
- ❖ Encompass a variety of genres.
- ❖ Encompass a variety of formats.
- ❖ Encompass a range of levels.
- ❖ Exemplify special features.

Figure 16–2. Texts for Literature Study

boys' and girls' preferences, but between ages ten and eighteen, preference tends to diverge by gender. Both boys and girls enjoy mystery, humor, adventure, and animals, but boys tend to like action, adventure, and sports stories while girls tend to prefer fantasy and stories about people and relationships.

Students who have read a variety of books and stories may develop more mature, wide-ranging preferences. You will also encounter students in your class who can read very well. Still, you should not assume that just because students can read the words in a particular book it is appropriate material for them. Students will get more meaning from a text that is appropriate for their overall psychological and cognitive development. For example, a fifth or sixth grader might find it easy to read *Animal Farm* (Orwell 1996), *The Outsiders* (Hinton 1997), *The Contender* (Lipsyte 1967), or *The Cage* (Sender 1980); however, the mature themes and sophisticated concepts might short-circuit full comprehension. If they read these books when they are bit older, they will comprehend them better. Of course, there are always exceptions to any discussion of "ages, stages, and preferences," but you will want to structure your classroom collection around those books your students will find most meaningful.

The Ability to "Teach" and "Stretch"

Select texts for literature study that offer students opportunities to learn more about how books work (Meek 1988). If books are within the students' control but offer new features for them to notice and use in their search for meaning, simply reading the text will, in a sense, "teach" them. In addition, texts that offer new ways of using language or ideas to puzzle over will "stretch" children because they will need to expand beyond their present abilities. Literature study is a scaffold that makes the task easier.

Layers of Meaning

High-quality texts can be understood in many different ways. The books you select for literature study should be rich enough to be read and reread, enabling students to discover new meanings each time they read them. For example, students can read *Tuck Everlasting* (Babbit 1975) the first time just to enjoy the adventure story. Then, in literature study, you can ask them to reread the text (or portions of it) to understand the significance of symbols, such as the circle. You want to select texts that can withstand deeper analysis. Students will discover different aspects of literary works simply by reading and rereading these texts and discussing them with others.

It is essential to use well-crafted texts that offer the reader different levels of analysis. As Peterson (1990)

has said, "Teachers of literature want children to be more than plot readers" (26). You also want your students to become analyzers of texts.

Worthwhile Issues

Literature is a window to life. Literature study brings students together to talk about texts, and that discussion inevitably leads to talking about people's lives. The issues embedded in the books students read shape the discussion. Since time for literature study is hard to come by, it is essential that we search for books with worthwhile issues. In other words, we want students to learn to care about what matters. Books like *Lyddie* (Paterson 1995), *Number the Stars* (Lowry 1989), *Nothing But the Truth* (Avi 1991), and *Stay Away from Simon* (Carrick 1989) raise important questions for young readers and address a number of key issues:

- Taking responsibility
- Being your own person.
- Working for goals.
- Fighting against oppression.
- Appreciating differences.
- Looking below the surface.
- Thinking critically.

A Variety of Perspectives

Students in the upper elementary grades are beginning to form their own opinions. Now is the time to help them understand something important about life—that every topic fosters a range of perspectives. While it is important for students to know what they think, it is equally important for them to understand the perspectives of others. The literature study group provides a context for students to do just that. The books you select should offer opportunities for different interpretations. Readers will learn that there is no single right or wrong answer; issues can be examined from a variety of perspectives. Different students can find points of agreement and disagreement as they work through their analysis.

Students can also learn about perspectives in other ways. As they develop sophisticated reading strategies, they will encounter texts that challenge their thinking and points of view. This experience provides much for students to discuss. Two stories suitable for literature study provide the Japanese perspective on World War II. *Shin's Tricycle* (Kodama 1995) tells the story of the bombing of Hiroshima. A young child is killed while riding his tricycle, which then becomes a museum piece to remind people of the pain and destruction innocent people endure during war. *The Faithful Elephants* (Tsuchiya 1988), told from the perspective of a Japanese zookeeper, graphically illustrates how in every war helpless, innocent people and creatures suffer. There are still other books that reveal a variety of perspectives through plot and character development. For example, *The Pain and the Great One* (Blume 1984) is narrated by two separate characters, the older sister and the younger brother.

As students work with a variety of perspectives, they learn to search for answers to their own dilemmas. As they read and analyze a text, they sort out the similarities to and the mismatches with their own background knowledge and experience. This process is much more engaging and meaningful than searching for the answers to someone else's comprehension questions.

A Representation of Our Diverse World

Books that you use in literature discussion should represent the lives of all children and help students expand their knowledge of the diversity in the world in which they live. Implementing literature study means looking carefully at the balance of books that you provide for students. You want to guide their selections so that they read about people like themselves but also read about others who look different, speak differently, or have different lives.

It is important that the texts you select portray culture accurately. You want texts that give students an opportunity to learn about people from other groups but also to be critical. The ability to look for stereotypes, either by *omission or caricature,* is a critical strategy we want all students to develop.

Be sure that the collection is *inclusive.* Reading books that leave out certain groups sends a message. The availability of good books across the cultural spectrum was a problem in the past, but today there is a wide variety of books that spotlight diversity within an excellent, well-written story.

Students not only need to see people from their own cultures reflected in stories; they also need to see people like themselves as authors. In addition, we want students to read views of a culture written by its members. Including such works in your literature collection sends positive messages to all students.

You can check on the diversity of your entire reading program (which includes reading aloud, independent reading, guided reading, and literature study) by examining students' lists of the books they've read. You'll want to ensure that literature of diversity is included within each of the four reading contexts as well as (for the individual student) across the reading program as a whole.

A Variety of Authors/Illustrators

Diversity also impacts writing and illustration styles. Some writers are best known for their superb use of descriptive language; others are famous for portraying galloping good adventure; still others are known for weaving fantastic worlds or creating wildly humorous plots. Within the world of children's literature, such variety gives students maximum opportunity to observe how writers and illustrators construct and convey meaning in different ways. Through richly diverse reading, they learn to recognize styles and internalize models while at the same time refining their own tastes as readers.

A Variety of Genres

The variety of genres that students need to read in the intermediate grades is described in Chapter 23. By examining students' reading records, you can determine the kinds of texts they are choosing for themselves. One of the goals of literature study is to help students learn to recognize a genre by its characteristics; a broader goal is to help them learn *how to read* many genres.

Your selections for literature study should take into account those genres with which students are less familiar. The idea is to choose texts that are in line with students' interests and reading abilities but that stretch them in terms of reading and understanding different genres. The collection should include a variety of expository and narrative texts, such as folktales, biographies, diaries, historical fiction, and realistic fiction. Information texts provide a rich discussion of facts and ideas.

A Variety of Formats

In addition to variety in genres, look for books in a variety of lengths and formats. For example, consider including picture books like *Molly Bannaky* (McGill 1999), a nonfiction text, that present true historical characters in an artistic and interesting way. You'll also want collections of well-crafted short stories like *A View from Saturday* (Konigsburg 1996) or *Baseball in April* (Soto 1991). Additionally, collect a range of short chapter books and longer chapter books.

A Range of Levels

Every group of students represents a range of reading levels. The books you provide for literature study must be within a range that ensures that students *can* read and understand them. If they are constantly struggling to read difficult books, they will not be enthusiastic about discussing them with others. You can occasionally pair less capable readers with more capable or older readers, which makes even challenging books available to all students, but overall you do not want these students always to be dependent on others. It is important to have texts that are geared to the ability levels of all the readers in the classroom.

Using assessment tools and observation, keep an ongoing record of the approximate level of text appropriate for each student. Remember that as students encounter new genres or new text features, they may need easier examples at first. If your school has a central book collection that is leveled (as described in Chapter 14 and also in Pinnell and Fountas, 1999, 2001), you can compare your literature selections with the levels appropriate for students' needs. Remember that some literary texts have unique features. When you want students to attend to such features, level may not be the most important consideration. A book can be easy to read, but filled with worthwhile issues for discussion.

Special Features

As you read children's literature, you will find many quality examples of books you want your students to learn to appreciate. There are books with beautiful illustrations, for example, that provide a way to help students become more sophisticated viewers. Artists like Faith Ringgold, Ed Young, Gerald McDermott, and Aliki provide visually striking and meaningful images. Many books showcase special artistic features such as illuminated letters, borders, interesting dedications, or special formats. The picture book *Imagine That!* (Wilson 2000), for example, depicts the life of a one-hundred-year-old woman. In the text a grandmother is telling her young granddaughter stories about her life. Around the edges, you see a time line arranged by

decade. Next to each decade is a wealth of information related to specific topics, such as the role of women. The grandmother's simple story touches on each topic as it affected her life. The illustrations are a potpourri of images connected to the topics across the decades. All of these features sensitize students to the cohesive nature of a text—how all features work together to convey a meaning larger than any one aspect. They learn to notice and appreciate the aesthetic whole of literature as it conveys meaning to readers.

Your literature selections should also celebrate the writers of children's books who use language in ways comparable to any great artist. Writers like L'Engle and Babbit take readers to different worlds that are full of adventure, symbolism, and universal truths. Avi, Hesse, and Paterson craft stories in a way that makes characters seem as real as people we know. You will want to include books in the collection that showcase exemplary literary craft. Powerful examples help students recognize style and learn to talk about authors and illustrators in a literate way.

Forming Groups for Literature Study

Groups for literature study are heterogeneous and are usually based on the books students have chosen to read. The ideal size for groups is five or six students, although as many as eight might participate in an interest group. The groups must function as collaborative learning groups, in which students are invested in the outcomes. When you provide choice to students, they tend to take more ownership of the tasks at hand.

Considerations in Forming Groups

In forming groups, it is important to consider students':

- *Reading abilities,* including the level of text they find comfortable to read. Your observations in independent and guided reading, as well as your regular assessments, will enable you to make this determination.
- *Reading interests.* These should be evident in the reader's notebooks that students keep, the notes you have taken during informal consultation, and interest interviews.
- *Previous reading experience,* including other titles the students may have read. Again, you can find this information in their reader's notebooks.

There are a few other factors you should keep in mind as well. Be sure to mix boys and girls, and monitor the groups to confirm that the students within them are working productively together.

Guiding Student Choices

Students join groups based on the book they have chosen. Initially, they may not know how to choose well, so you will want to teach them how to think about selecting a book that works best for them. You can make book selection the topic of minilessons that show students how to:

- Listen to a book talk and match characteristics of the book to their interests.
- Examine book covers, cover copy, and illustrations.
- Sample a bit of the text to get a feel for the language and the author's style.
- Think about the topic, considering their interests and previous knowledge.
- Think about how the book matches their own reading background and experience and whether they would need to listen to an audiotape or have another person read it to them.
- Consider whether the book will offer challenges or opportunities to expand their knowledge or skill.

Selecting a book is a complex task, but one that is well worth learning. As adults, we regularly select books that offer opportunities to relax and enjoy ourselves, to learn more about living, or to increase our knowledge of the world. While we don't specifically choose books to increase our reading skills, we may challenge ourselves to get to know a new author. Students, too, might want to learn to read a new author or genre or increase the variety of their reading. Generally, however, they select books just as we do: they choose one that looks interesting.

You will work with students to help them choose books that, for the most part, they can read for themselves. Remember, however, that there are other ways to support students' reading if they choose difficult books. Often, students can discuss a piece of literature intelligently even if it is beyond their specific reading level. One way to help them is to provide other ways for them to access the difficult book. Many books are available on audiotape; students may also ask their parents,

another student, or a volunteer to read the book to them. These students simply need to experience the book; they don't have be able to read it for themselves in order to benefit from the shared meanings created through the discussion. Indeed, the support of the rich discussion often helps them eventually read the book on their own.

Variations in Forming Groups

There is no single best way to form groups for literature study. You have a range of alternatives, and your decisions will depend on:

- The students' familiarity with the routines for literature study.
- Your goal for the particular kind of literature study.

In some cases, you might want to create the group yourself. Draw on the knowledge that you've gathered through assessment and observation, and base your grouping decisions on the opportunities you want to offer particular students.

Remember that it's important to give students some choice. Provide several selections from which students can choose, and introduce these choices with brief book talks (see Chapter 7). Let students browse for a limited time, ask them to indicate preferences, and form the groups based on this information. There are many ways to solicit children's choices:

- Post a sign-up sheet with a fixed number of lines for each group. When the lines are filled for one group, students select from the remaining groups.
- Give children a list of titles and invite them to indicate their first three choices or rank their choices in priority order. Form the groups yourself using the data.

Establishing Routines for Literature Study

In order for literature study to be valuable and productive, students must understand that the routines are not simply your rules but agreements that enable them to work together in the classroom. In particular, students must learn:

1. *To be prepared.* Students need to read the section of the text to be discussed and complete any assigned task. They need to understand that being prepared is essential if they are going to be able to contribute to the group.

2. *To sit where they can see everyone.* A circular arrangement works best, because every member of the group can see every other member. Students can sit on the floor or on a rug, but sitting in a circle of chairs, preferably in a quiet corner of your classroom, works best.

3. *To share leadership roles.* You will demonstrate how to facilitate a group before students take over the role. There are several ways to lead a literature study group. One student may be responsible for calling on others for the entire group meeting, with the role of group leader rotated during subsequent meetings. Alternately, the student who is sharing his question or comment calls on others while that point is being discussed. The next student to bring up a question or comment leads the discussion on that point. Finally, in some groups there is no leader. Students simply have a conversation without a facilitator.

4. *That only one person can speak at a time and that there are established procedures for getting a turn.* Literature study is an ideal setting for students to learn the skills of turn taking. There is no single right way to establish these routines. In some groups, students raise hands and are called on by the leader. In other classrooms, students wait until someone has finished talking to say something; the discussion follows the general rules for polite conversation. A third alternative is to teach students to signal that they have something to say. For example, they could make a fist and extend two fingers if they want to contribute to the idea being discussed at the moment or extend the thumb if they have a new idea to raise. The leader calls first on the students with two fingers extended and then on the students with thumbs extended (see Jewell and Pratt 1999).

5. *To take responsibility for ensuring that every person has a chance to talk.* If one member notices that another has not had an opportunity to talk, it is his responsibility to call it to the attention of the group.

6. *To keep the conversation focused and move it forward when appropriate.* Group members are encouraged to monitor the discussion to make sure they don't stray from the topic. If that happens, a comment like "I think we are getting off the topic" helps the group stay on track and encourages individuals to monitor their own contributions to be sure they are adding to the meanings the group is building. Of course, when students first begin literature study, you will monitor their comments and intervene to help them stay focused. Students will gradually take over the role.

7. *To evaluate the discussion and agree on any next steps.* At the end of the discussion, the group participates in a very brief evaluation of how well the members engaged in the process. They also decide how and when to meet again if there is more to discuss. Then they agree on a focus for the next discussion or when to work on a group project to share with the class.

Suggestions for Teaching Routines

Unless students have participated extensively in literature study over their years in your school, you will need to teach explicitly each routine related to effective participation. Even if literature study is widely used, you will still want to show students how it works in your classroom. Here are some suggestions for teaching routines:

■ Early in the process, facilitate the discussion yourself so that students can see what the role requires. Gradually invite students to take over this role.

■ Work with one group at a time over several days to learn and practice routines.

■ Place one group in a circle while the rest of the students form a larger circle outside the group. In this "fishbowl" format, students can observe what is going on in the literature discussion. Afterward the whole class can talk about what made the discussion effective. Make sure all students have read or listened to the book that the inner group is discussing so they can determine whether the discussion was truly successful and will find the observation more interesting and beneficial.

■ With small groups or the whole group, ask students to evaluate the effectiveness of their discussion. You might generate a list of criteria with the students.

Teaching Students to Evaluate Literature Study

Evaluation should take place regularly even after students have learned the routines, because you want them to be reminded of the process. A good evaluation not only focuses on the technical points, such as taking turns and being courteous, but it addresses the ways in which students are contributing to the group. Students should remember to evaluate both how much they learned and how much they contributed to the learning of others. They should see themselves as part of a group of people who are supporting one another's learning. Figure 16–3 is an evaluation chart one class developed over time.

Facilitating Discussion

Even after students have learned the basic routines for literature study and can evaluate their participation, you will continue to play a critical role in students' learning. Literature study is not simply an activity you assign; it is an intensive instructional context. Students are taking the lead because of your teaching and support. You are not always present in the group, but you have taught them how to talk with one another and to evaluate. You also monitor via brief observations or by talking with them afterward.

Level of Teacher Support

You have choices about the level of support you provide: it depends on the students' experience and reading levels as well as the type of text they are discussing. After the initial stages of literature study, you can choose any level of participation (see Figure 16–4). The four main levels of support include:

1. *Facilitator.* You perform all of the functions of the leader, calling on students and ensuring that the conversation stays on track and moves forward.
2. *Participant.* You are part of the group and enter into the discussion to about the same extent as the students. You may use your own comments to model effective group behavior or effective ways of communicating ideas. You may also redirect the group, remind the group to stay on track, or make sure that all members have an equal chance to speak.
3. *Occasional guide.* You enter the discussion only occasionally for specific purposes, which are usually directed toward helping students expand ideas or keeping the group focused. Usually, you sit outside the circle so that your presence does not dominate the group.
4. *Rotating observer.* You move about the room, working with other literature study groups or working with students in other ways. Occasionally, you stop by the group to observe, but you do not usually intervene.

These roles are not discrete categories. Think of these levels as a continuum that helps in your decision making. At any point, with any group, you might use any one of the roles. You may even find yourself shifting from one role to another as you work with a group in a single session or in subsequent sessions. For example, you may act as a participant the first time a group meets but become an occasional observer the next time.

Evaluation of Literature Discussion

❖ Everyone got a chance to talk.

❖ People spoke clearly.

❖ People looked at the speaker.

❖ People used signals to get a turn.

❖ The group worked as a team; no one said, "Hurry up."

❖ People in the group were polite and kind to one another.

❖ People commented on one another's thinking.

❖ People were reminded to show evidence for the points they made.

❖ Group members went to the text to show what they meant.

❖ People stayed on the topic.

❖ The leader did a good job being patient.

❖ People in the group referred to illustrations.

❖ Group members gave details in their answers to questions.

Figure 16–3. Evaluation of Literature Discussion

The Role of the Teacher

As students encounter challenging ideas in texts, they learn to talk in new ways. Again, your role is to model specific procedural routines such as taking turns, making sure everyone has a chance to talk, and moving on when a topic is exhausted. Additionally, you will demonstrate new ways of talking; redirect the group's attention; and "lift their learning" so that students go beyond the present understandings and oral language skills of individuals and the group as a whole.

The following actions will help you meet these goals:

1. *Provide positive comments that affirm students' responses.* Suggested language includes:
   > That was good thinking.
   > I like the way you backed up your thinking with your own experiences.
   > That was a nice connection you made to another book you read.
   > I like the way you are listening to each other.
   > I like the way you added to ____'s comments.
   > You're really thinking.
   > You've got some good ideas.

2. *Restate students' ideas in a way that helps them clarify meaning.* Suggested language includes:
   > Do you mean _____?
   > Could it be _____?
   > Maybe _____ is trying to say that _____?

3. *Encourage students to provide evidence.* Suggested language includes:
   > What makes you think that?
   > Can you provide some details?
   > What part of the story led you to that conclusion?
   > I like the way you are providing details to support your thinking.
   > I can see why you think that because you are providing evidence.

4. *Guide students to elaborate and extend their thinking.* Suggested language includes:
   > Can you say more about that?
   > Please be more specific.
   > Can anyone add to ____'s comment/description/idea?
   > What else does that make you think of?

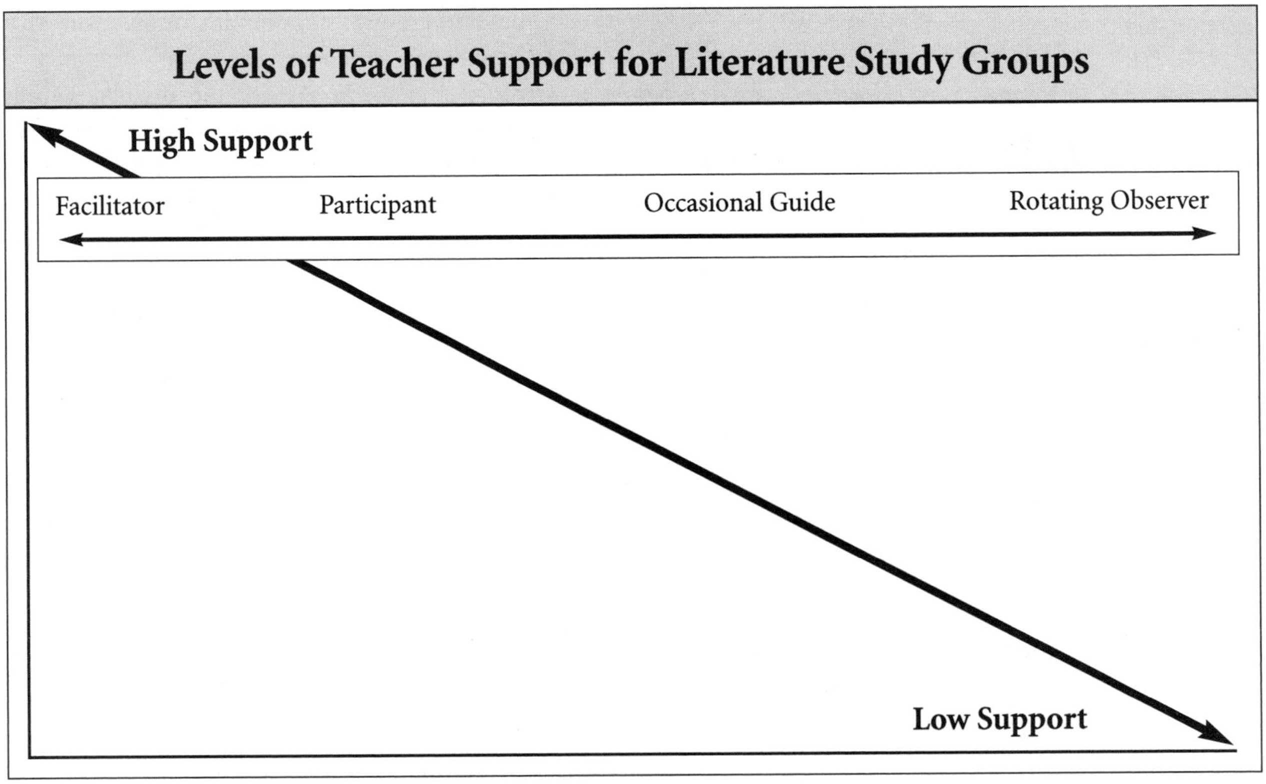

Figure 16–4. *Levels of Teacher Support*

5. *Encourage making connections.* Suggested language includes:

> What does that remind you of?
> I like the way you are connecting _____.
> Can anyone think of a connection here?
> That makes me think of _____.

6. *Encourage inferring, summarizing, and synthesizing.* Suggested language includes:

> Why do you think _____?
> What is the author trying to say?
> What was that all about?
> What's the big idea?
> Some of the important ideas to remember here are _____.
> What did you learn that was new?
> How have your ideas changed?

7. *Promote analyzing and criticizing texts.* Suggested language includes:

> What type [genre] of text is this?
> How is this text like [examples of books from different genres]?
> What's the problem in this story?
> How did the character(s) change?
> How important is the setting to the plot of the story?
> How did the author make you interested in the story?
> Do you think the characters/events are believable? Why or why not?
> What do you notice about the author's writing?

Making Changes Over Time

Establishing routines takes place over time. Furthermore, as students continue to engage in literature study, the quality of their discussions improves, and they need skills that go beyond the basic routines. In the following progression, we've assumed that the students in your class have little experience with literature study. In schools where teachers have been working on literature study for some time, the differences throughout the year may not be as evident because students will begin at a more independent level.

1. At the beginning of the school year, initiate literature study by reading aloud interactively. Read literature selections to students so you can engage the whole class in discussion and model some of the techniques that you want them to use. You will find the lists of picture books that we provide especially useful. Invite students to write or sketch responses.

2. Later in the fall, read literature selections aloud and ask students to respond in their writer's notebooks, choosing either writing or sketching. Then ask students to discuss the selection in small groups. Work with one group at a time over successive days or during independent reading. Facilitate the group yourself, gradually moving from facilitator to a participant role. Teach students to evaluate their participation.

3. In early winter, form small literature discussion groups based on books the students choose. Ask students to write or sketch in reader's notebooks to record and elaborate on their thoughts. Meet with students in small groups and provide support as facilitator, participant, or occasional guide, depending on the text and on student progress. Emphasize the importance of routines and of developing ways of using language. Remind students that they need to back up their statements with evidence. Ask for details. Students should continue to evaluate their participation.

4. In late winter, continue to meet with students in small groups. Your role may still range from facilitator to occasional guide. Students should respond in their notebooks as part of a regular routine. Demonstrate and encourage ways of thinking related to strategies for comprehending. Continue evaluating discussions; encourage students to judge their contributions for clarity and depth.

5. In early spring, have students continue to meet in small groups, varying the structure for different purposes. Encourage them to use the "book club" section in their reader's notebooks to record thoughts and questions for sharing. Assign group projects that invite sharing and the synthesis of ideas. Continue evaluation, focusing on the strategies you are developing. Participate in their literature discussions as an occasional guide or observer.

Models for Organizing Group Discussion

After literature study has been introduced and students are developing a basic sense of the routines, you can organize your instruction using a variety of group processes. We describe eight organizational models here, but the possibilities are endless.

Model 1: Whole Group, Same Text (see Figure 16–5)

Read the story or informational piece to the students or ask them to read it for themselves. The entire class listens to or reads the same text. Ask students to respond by writing or sketching in the book club section of their reader's notebooks. You can guide the response by asking them to focus on various aspects of text or you can leave it open. Then form groups of four, five, or six students, which meet simultaneously. You take the role of rotating observer.

Model 2: Small Group, Same Text (see Figure 16–6)

Have students select a text from the choices given. Students who selected the same text form a group and make a schedule to meet. Then, they read the text or designated amounts of text, making notes or marking sections according to your guidance. They meet in a circle for discussion. From their discussion, they formulate a group response that they share with the other students in the classroom. This project may involve drama, music, oral presentation, readers theater, or technology.

Model 3: Small Group, Same or Different Text (see Figure 16–7)

Students select a text from the choices given. Students in each group may read the same book or different books. Students read the book they've chosen. They meet in small groups to share and discuss their books. Then they engage in responding in their notebooks after the discussion. Afterward the whole class shares what they learned in their small groups.

Model 4: Small Group, Text Sets (see Figure 16–8).

You provide brief book talks on books organized into sets. Sets of books may be the same genre, written by the same author, have the same topic or theme, or have similar characters. Students have the opportunity to browse through the books and make selections. Then they read the books and meet with a small group of stu-

dents who selected the same text. Group members discuss the book and then generate a group project (as in Model 2) to share what they learned with the class.

Model 5: Small Group, Partners (see Figure 16–9)

Students select a book from the choices given, or all students may read the same book. They discuss the book first with a partner and then in a small group.

Model 6: Whole Group, Individual Follow-Up (see Figure 16–10)

All students in the class listen to (or read) one text. The text may be:

- A version of a traditional tale.
- A book on a particular theme or topic.
- An example of a genre.
- An example of a particular structure or literary technique (such as a cumulative tale or flashback).
- A book by a particular author or illustrator.

Then students each select another version of the story, another example of the text type, or another book by the same author/illustrator. After reading, students respond by writing or sketching in their response journal. Then students meet in small groups to discuss the texts they chose.

Model 7: Whole Group, Small-Group Follow-Up (see Figure 16–11)

All students read (or hear read aloud) the same text. (The type of text may vary, as in Model 6.) You then give book talks on the books students may choose. (The selections follow the kinds of variations described in Model 6.) After reading, students meet in small groups to discuss their texts.

Model 8: Whole Class and Small Group, Same Book, Issues (see Figure 16–12)

You select a book for the whole class that you think will generate an awareness of social issues, such as *The Watsons Go to Birmingham* (Curtis 1973). Either read the book aloud to students or have them all read it for themselves. After the reading, work with the whole class to generate a list of issues exemplified in the book and, by consensus, select one issue to discuss. Then divide

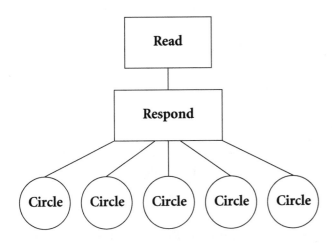

Figure 16–5. *Model 1: Whole Group, Same Text*

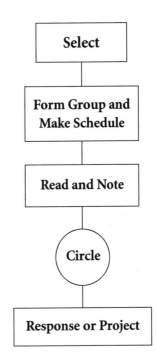

Figure 16–6. *Model 2: Small Group, Same Text*

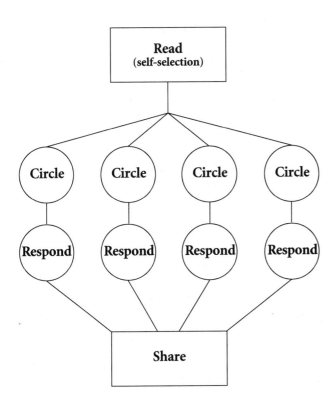

Figure 16–7. *Model 3: Small Group, Same or Different Text*

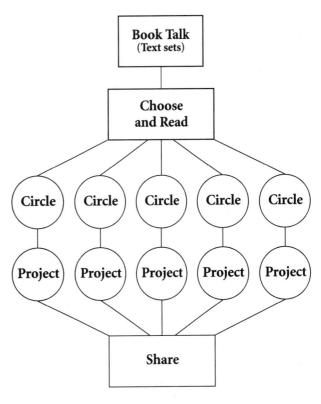

Figure 16–8. *Model 4: Small Group, Text Sets*

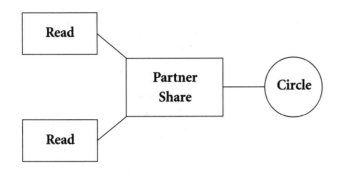

Figure 16–9.   Model 5: Small Group, Partners

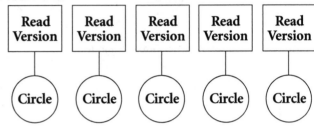

Figure 16–10.   Model 6: Whole Group, Individual Follow-up

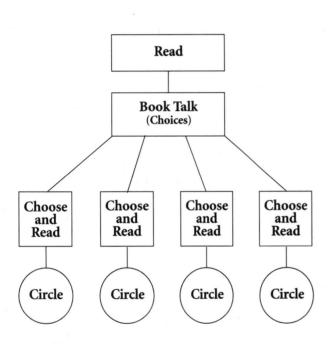

Figure 16–11.   Model 7: Whole Group, Small Group Follow-up

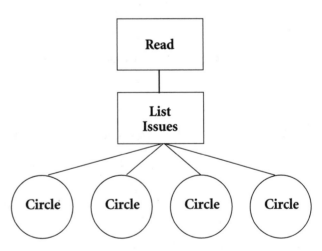

Figure 16–12.   Model 8: Whole Class and Small Group, Same Book, Issues

students into small groups to talk about the issue. Alternatively, have the students each select one of the issues from the list and form different groups to discusses each issue.

Variations of the Models

Once you have explored some of these models and students are familiar with some of the routines, you can:

- Combine models to create different configurations.
- Alter models to accommodate shorter or longer periods of time.
- Focus on theme, topic, issues, author, writing styles, language, or other aspects of text.
- Use the same procedure for two related texts and then compare them.
- Let students decide how they will work together to discuss a text or texts.

These organized ways of responding provide structures that support students' discussion about the texts they read.

Summary

The procedures related to implementing literature study in the classroom require making complex decisions. It is essential to collect and select high-quality texts that provide a network of support through variety and example. You will also need to think carefully about how to group students, keeping in mind that literature study is intended to involve students in heterogeneous groups. A key to success is teaching routines. So that students can work toward independence, you vary your own role to provide the right amount of support at a particular time. The different models for organizing and varying groups will keep the routines of literature study fresh and interesting, a key factor in engaging students. Above all, this framework of routines will free students to improve their ability to consider and reflect on texts.

Suggestions for Professional Development

1. Meet with your colleagues across grade levels to build book collections for literature study. You will want not only to build the classroom collections carefully but also to look across the grades to get an overview of the variety of texts students are experiencing.

   - Hold a meeting of the upper elementary teachers who want to get started with literature study. If possible, include the school librarian and/or reading resource teacher in this discussion.
   - Ask each participant to bring ten books that would work well for literature study at a particular grade level. Try for variety—fiction and nonfiction, picture books, short stories, and chapter books.
   - Share books and talk about why each is particularly good for literature study. You may want to exchange some books and do some reading over the next couple of weeks. Then meet again to talk about the collection.
   - Consider the books as a whole set and evaluate the collection in light of Figure 16–2, Texts for Literature Study. Across the grade levels, do you have texts that represent every category? What about within grade levels? If you could expand classroom collections, grade-level collections, or the whole collection, what would you need?
   - Have every grade level create a plan for at least fifty titles that would be excellent choices for literature study. (More than fifty titles will give students more choice.) The plan should specify type of text as well as genre.
   - As a whole group, make a plan for acquiring more texts for literature study and begin to think about how you will organize a school resource to support classroom collections.

2. Once you have begun literature study and taught students the basic routines, meet with colleagues to discuss the models for organizing instruction.

■ As a group, select one of the models to try out in your classroom. Set another meeting to discuss the results. If you are just beginning literature study, choose one of the simpler models.

■ Try out the model in your classroom. You will be using different books, but the structure will be the same.

■ Meet with colleagues to share your results. What went well? What problems did you encounter? What did students learn? What was the evidence of learning?

■ Select another model and repeat the process or have each person select a different model.

■ Meet to share and analyze the results.

## CHAPTER SEVENTEEN

RESPONDING TO LITERATURE: MULTIPLE PATHS TO DEEPER MEANING

A novel or poem or play remains merely inkspots on paper until a reader transforms them into a set of meaningful symbols. The literary work exists in the live circuit set up between the readers and text.

— LOUISE ROSENBLATT

Literature illuminates our students' lives, enabling them to transcend the boundaries of their own world and gain a deeper understanding of what it means to be human. Literature invites students to live vicariously, to experience lives that may be far removed from their own. Through literature, students may:

1. Understand the great events of history from the personal view of imaginary characters or the real people who lived them.
2. Learn what life might have been like in other times.
3. Empathize with characters who experience tragedy, adventure, and political struggle.
4. Learn about people in places far distant from their own communities.
5. Develop the shared meanings of their own and other cultures.
6. Be inspired to reach their hopes and visions of the future.
7. Find escape from everyday problems.
8. Enjoy humor, drama, and mystery.

Literature invites aesthetic response as it offers access to our greatest thinkers across time and culture. Elementary school is typically the time when students either embrace reading as a profound aspect of their lives or reject it. Students need the chance to discover themselves in literature—to realize and learn from their own experience reflected in the pages of a book. Without this personal, even visceral, experience with literature, they are unlikely to embrace it as something

of value. Even if they succeed in developing reading competence, they are unlikely to create a cherished place for literature in their lives.

While we believe strongly in helping students become competent readers who can use a range of comprehension strategies, we always keep in mind why we are doing it. The bottom line is developing passionate readers—students who not only can but do read, with a spirited enthusiasm that opens wide the doors of literature and yields the riches of both fiction and nonfiction texts.

Literature study brings together three elements:

1. *Shared experience.* Students enjoy a common experience from which they can learn and construct understanding together.
2. *Rich text.* The text provides students with opportunities to form interpretations across layers of meaning.
3. *Personal response.* Each child's unique response to a text is important to the discussion. Readers learn to value their own responses to text, share them with others, and expand their understanding.

What Is Response?

Response is the sum total of what you are thinking while you read and when you reflect on what you've read. When you read, your eye gathers information from print and your brain acts on this information in complex ways. Let's say you are reading *Snow Falling on*

Cedars (Guterson 1995), the story of a Japanese-American couple, their young daughter Hat Suy, and the citizens of a small Pacific Northwest fishing town. The words and sentences carry you into the narrative, as do your actions as a reader. Sustaining strategies move you along, but you generally remain unaware of them. In other words, you take the following actions but do not think about them:

1. Recognize words and/or take them apart to solve them.
2. Put words together into phrases.
3. Monitor, check, and repair your reading as needed.
4. Integrate language systems to help you anticipate the text.
5. Gather important information as you read along the lines of print.

As these internal processes operate, you make the connections you need to understand and build meaning. In your mind, you respond to the experiences you have with the text.

As you read *Snow Falling on Cedars*, the pull of the narrative may cause you to "live through" the experiences of the women as they journey to Manzanar, a Japanese internment camp, and struggle with their first weeks there. At other points in the book you may step back to notice the writer's style. The words and phrases become visible again, as if you suddenly notice a pane of glass in a window while you are admiring the view beyond. You find yourself examining language in an analytic or critical way.

Your reading experience also depends on whether or not you previously knew about Manzanar. Even if you did, this fact alone would not have evoked the emotional response sparked by this tightly written drama. As these Japanese Americans are torn from their homes, stripped of their rights as American citizens, and forced to live behind the barbed wire of the internment camp, the spare description communicates a powerful depth of emotion. Your response is more an *aesthetic* stance (which involves emotion and literary appreciation) than an *efferent* one (which involves seeking information) (Rosenblatt 1978).

This story might prompt you to search for more information about the difficulties that Japanese-American citizens faced during World War II. Biographies, histories, or other novels might provide

resources. Here, too, the words and language become transparent, letting you see through to what they mean. Your attention is on what you are learning; you are trying to determine how the information fits with what you already know and what is new. You might scan a text to locate information, perhaps noticing headings or other signals that show how the text is organized. In that case, aspects of print become visible again.

Readers are always engaged in response, because they are always thinking. You might decide you can't get into a book, or you might have such a profound literary experience that the book becomes a lifelong reference point. You may always recall certain aspects of the text—a character or setting—as you experience your own life and read other texts. Response resides in the individual and is internal. What you *say* or *do* is evidence that response is taking place.

Multiple Paths to Meaning

While talk is always central, there are four paths to meaning:

- *Talking:* Using oral language to describe and/or analyze response.
- *Writing:* Capturing thinking in writing (e.g., keeping dialogue or reader's notebooks, jotting down thoughts and ideas, taking notes, or writing letters).
- *Reading:* Doing more reading about the topic or the author.
- *Visual and performing arts:* Responding through sketching, drawing, mapping, and charting, or through movement and dance or music and drama.

You'll want to direct your students so that they have access along all these paths. All four processes mediate, extend, and refine the meaning of the text your students are reading, and all four establish a foundation for literary analysis and critique.

Students frequently use more than one mode of expression as they explore the meaning of their text in greater depth. Increasingly, students may rely on technology to capture their thoughts. For example, one group of students instigated an e-mail conversation while they were reading *Flying Solo* (Fletcher 1998), a book in which a sixth-grade class takes charge of their own school day when a substitute teacher fails to show

Mediating Text in Literature Study	
Open ←	→ **Directed**
Talking: ❖ Talk about the book. ❖ Have an open conversation about anything that anyone in the group suggests.	*Talking:* ❖ Have a specific focus for the talk. ❖ Have students look for something in particular to bring to the discussion. ❖ Ask students to write or sketch first to bring focus to the discussion. ❖ Use graphic organizers as a tool for focusing the discussion. ❖ Remind students to come with questions. ❖ Engage students in process drama framed in a certain way.
Writing: ❖ Have students make notes on anything of interest on bookmarks or stick-on notes. ❖ Write in reader's notebooks—unstructured response.	*Writing:* ❖ Decide on very specific elements or issues to focus writing on. (You may want to let students decide.) ❖ Use graphic organizers as a tool for writing analytically about some aspect of text. ❖ Have students write in response to specific questions.
Reading: ❖ Encourage students to select from books that are related in some way—theme, topic, issue, author. ❖ Suggest through book talks texts that are connected.	*Reading:* ❖ Follow the reading of a text with another that is connected and that the whole group will read and discuss. ❖ Follow the reading of a text with individual selections assigned to small groups or individual readers. ❖ Select texts as part of a planned sequence of study—author, theme, genre, etc.
Using the Arts: ❖ Encourage students to express meaning through the arts.	*Using the Arts:* ❖ Demonstrate and/or work with students to plan different uses of the arts—drawing, music, movement, drama.

Figure 17–1. Mediating Text in Literature Study

up. The story is told from the perspective of different students in the class and delineates their response to such issues as lying, responsibility, conflict, even death. This group of readers' electronic discussion, identified by the subject line "solo," entailed deep reflection. Individuals agreed and disagreed about issues, and they enjoyed a lively exchange about what children can and can't say when adults are present.

Your teaching should include each of the four modes for expressing response. Depending on your purpose, you can choose to have your students engage in "open" response or more "directed" response, as indicated in Figure 17–1. For example, the discussion may simply be an open conversation in which you and your students report whatever you found interesting about a book. Or it might be very focused. You may ask students to search for a particular point to bring to the discussion, or to do some writing or sketching that will focus the discussion in a particular way. Similarly, you may direct students to come to the group with questions, or you may even use graphic organizers as a way of stimulating and focusing discussion (see Chapter 26).

Talking

The Centrality of Talk

Our primary means of expression, of course, is oral language. Conversation is the easiest, most natural way to share meaning, and throughout our reading lives we may talk frequently with our friends and family members about the books we are enjoying. Even if your students explore and mediate their response by writing, by reading additional books, or through the visual and performing arts, most often they will begin with an oral discussion.

Conversation is central to both communication and learning. Wilkinson even coined the term "oracy" to stress the importance of language skills (1965, 1970, 1971, 1975). Language use is related to intellectual and social development as well as to personal and aesthetic need. "Language is used to express identity, enable cooperation, and confer freedom on those who have access to and control over a wide repertoire of language strategies" (Raban 1999, p. 101). Most important, language is a tool for learning (MacLure 1988; Marland 1977; Corson 1988).

Your Role in Supporting Conversation

You play a key role not only in deciding the structure for your literature discussions but also in guiding the process so that students extend their ability to express meaning to others. After students have learned how to engage in a quality literature discussion, they can talk on their own, but we believe that the teacher's presence (at least for a significant part of the time) is essential to lift the level of discussion and, ultimately, foster the learning available through the discussion.

Basic Guidelines on Teaching Students to Discuss Literature

To ensure that effective conversation can take place, you will need to teach students "ground rules" that groups simply must follow. At the beginning of the year, students need to learn basic group interaction skills such as how to get the discussion started and keep it going. Be sure to teach them the basics of active listening: to look at the speaker, listen courteously, and build on one another's ideas. Students must always show respect and never laugh at someone else's comment. The cardinal rule is simple: all ideas are valued.

Other rules apply as well. Your students will need to learn how to signal when they want a turn to talk; they also need to be aware when a few students are monopolizing the discussion. You may have to teach them how to sit in a circle, facing the speaker, with hands quiet. Students should not flip books or journals around, which detracts from the learning of others. These "nuts and bolts" skills of interaction will benefit students in other areas of the curriculum as well.

During the first few months of literature study, encourage students to analyze the behaviors that make for good discussion. Susan, a fourth-grade teacher, decided to conduct a "fishbowl" to teach her students how to engage in literature discussion. She met with a small group of students while the rest of the class observed from an outer circle. The small group discussed the story as Susan facilitated.

Afterward, the whole class talked about what had made the discussion work well, and they started a working list of the characteristics that make a good discussion (see Figure 17–2). They returned to this list periodically over the next few days and finally created a summary chart that listed their ten most important

Ways to Have a Good Discussion
1. Be prepared.
2. Sit so everyone can see each other.
3. Get started right away.
4. Look at the person who is talking.
5. Listen to understand.
6. Ask questions to understand better.
7. Speak clearly but not too loud.
8. Wait for the speaker to finish.
9. Signal when you want a turn.
10. Be sure everyone gets a turn.
11. Build on each other's ideas.
12. Respect each other's ideas.
13. Stay on the topic.
14. Provide evidence for your thinking.

Figure 17–2. Ways to Have a Good Discussion

ideas. Susan displayed the chart in the literature discussion area, and students used it throughout the year for a quick evaluation and reflection on their discussions.

Teaching Thoughtful Student Response

Thoughtful response to reading is learned behavior; it is not "inborn" or "intuitive." While some students may be more attuned to literature response than others, these differences are mainly due to their previous experiences in reading and the support they have had in sharing meaning with others. The teacher's role is to help students deepen response and extend their ability to share response (Jewell and Pratt 1999).

TEACH STUDENTS TO VALUE PERSONAL RESPONSE.

Students can begin to understand reader response and realize that their own thinking is of paramount importance in their ability to understand and enjoy literature. They can learn that:

■ Readers are always thinking and responding.
■ Everything you think or feel is part of your personal response to literature.

■ Through talking, writing, reading, and the arts, you can share your responses with others.
■ Sharing responses with others is a good way to learn and to grow in your enjoyment of reading.
■ When you are talking about your personal responses to literature, there are no right answers. Everyone's point of view is valuable and contributes to the learning of others.

TEACH STUDENTS TO SUPPORT RESPONSE WITH EVIDENCE.

You can also demonstrate to students how to elaborate on their responses to communicate meaning more clearly and how to back up their responses with evidence from the text or from their own background knowledge. Let them know that as long as they can back up their thinking, responses are acceptable. Finding evidence strengthens the coherence of their arguments, and they also learn more about the text in the process. Over time, teach students to:

■ Provide facts or information from specific pages of the text to support statements.
■ Read passages from the text to support statements.
■ Retell a part of the text for the specific purpose of providing evidence.
■ Call on background knowledge or personal experience to support statements.
■ Tell "why" or use "because" statements to support their responses.
■ Provide details and examples to help others understand.

TEACH STUDENTS TO LISTEN CAREFULLY TO AND CONSIDER THOUGHTFULLY OTHERS' RESPONSES.

Help students recognize that they can react to others' responses in a variety of ways. Specifically, they can:

■ Agree or disagree.
■ Ask for clarification.
■ Expand on an idea.
■ Repeat or paraphrase to verify their understanding.
■ Call for evidence.

Doing these things, they not only understand other perspectives better, but they rethink their own responses.

The Language of Response

- ❖ I agree because . . .
- ❖ I disagree because . . .
- ❖ I also noticed . . .
- ❖ I'd like to add that . . .
- ❖ I didn't understand . . .
- ❖ Say more about what you mean.
- ❖ I don't understand what you mean.
- ❖ Can you show where that is in the text/illustration?
- ❖ What is your evidence?
- ❖ Why do you think that?
- ❖ I think the author meant . . .
- ❖ How do you know that?
- ❖ We're getting far away from the text.
- ❖ What does the author say that makes you think that?

Figure 17–3.   The Language of Response

Approaches to Teaching Response

There are a number of ways you can teach students to respond thoughtfully:

- *Model response.* Explain your own responses to literature, providing evidence. Use the language of response when reacting to student comments (see Figure 17–3).
- *Demonstrate and tell.* Show students what it means to provide evidence or to listen and summarize what others are saying.
- *Facilitate effective response.* Ask questions like *Can you take us to the place in the text that makes you think that?* Lead the students to elaborate and provide evidence for their statements.
- *Reinforce effective response techniques* by providing specific praise. Throughout the discussion, respond with phrases like *Sarah, that was a good challenge you raised.*
- *Take notes while observing* a discussion and point out what students did and what worked. Use statements like *You did a good job adding to one another's comments.*

- *Use a "fishbowl" technique* like Susan tried with her fourth graders. Afterward, discuss what language was effective in keeping the discussion going and exploring the ideas in depth. Ask students to identify effective discussion techniques and create a chart to remind them.
- *Ask one student in the group to jot down effective language* and share it with the group afterward.

Reading Aloud Interactively: A Bridge to Literature Discussion

Reading to students is a great way to teach them how to think and talk about fiction and nonfiction texts. Ideally, students will have been discussing the literature they've heard read aloud since kindergarten. If not, it is high time to start. When you read aloud interactively:

- The entire class becomes a community of readers and learns how to respect and support one another in a discussion.
- The text is available to all students, because you have read it to them with appropriate expression.
- You can usually read the text in one sitting, so that discussion can begin immediately.
- If you read a picture book, the meaning of the text is conveyed not only through the written words but also through the illustrations.
- You can select relatively short texts that provide multiple layers of meaning.
- You can demonstrate and model response to literature as well as engage students in expressing their own responses.

Reading aloud interactively serves a dual purpose—it not only provides a context for helping students learn how to discuss literature but also is a source of examples for minilessons in independent reading and writing. Let's look at how Leah accomplished these two goals.

Leah planned to read aloud a work of historical fiction called *Nettie's Trip South* (Turner 1987) to her grade five students. The story takes the form of a letter that ten-year-old Nettie writes to her friend Addie in 1859. As the letter begins, Nettie has just returned from a trip to the American South with her older brother, a newspaper reporter, and her sister. The story, based on the real diary of the author's great-grandmother, is full of contrasts: Nettie's luxurious life and the life of slaves; the warm, sweet smell of Southern cedars and the odor coming from the slave quarters. Nettie first tells Addie that what she remembers most is seeing the slaves. She then recounts the journey in chronological order, beginning with the excitement she felt getting ready to leave, acquiring new furs, traveling by train. Nettie describes her reaction to slavery in the powerful language of poetry with the language of the text laid out as follows across five pages with charcoal illustrations.

> Addie, I can't get this out of my thoughts:
> If we slipped into a black skin
> like a tight coat,
> everything would change.
> No one would call us by our last names,
> for we would not have them.
> Addie and Nettie we'd be,
> until we were worn out and died.
> When someone called, we'd jump!
> We could not read in the apple tree
> with the sun coming through the leaves,
> for no one would teach us to read
> and no one would give us a book.
> And Addie, at any time we could be sold
> by a fat man in a white hat
> in a tight white suit
> and we'd have to go, just like that.

Nettie finishes her letter by saying, "I have bad dreams at night."

Before Leah began reading the *Nettie's Trip South,* she provided some background information, explaining that Nettie was traveling to the South with her older brother Lockwood and her sister Julia. She also told them that the story is set right before the Civil War, before slaves were freed. She explained that Nettie lived in New York and had never seen the South or slavery. She read the first page of Nettie's letter to Addie—spare, terse comments—with a serious tone. Then she asked students what they were thinking. Here's what they said:

SARA: She sounds like something really bad happened on the trip.

JOAQUIM: There was a lot of stuff that happened that it's hard to write about.

DANIEL: Maybe she wishes she didn't go?

Leah told the students that Nettie was now going to start telling her story from the beginning of the trip. She read on as Nettie told of the train ride and of keeping her worries to herself about slaves being three fifths of a person, as described in the Constitution. After that section, Laura asked, "What does that mean? Three fifths of a person?" Leah then explained the compromise that had been made to allow owners to have a three-fifths vote for each slave. Spontaneous conversation followed:

SARA: It's not fair for the slave owner to vote for the slaves. And that's just ridiculous for someone to be three fifths, like just a little more than half.

DAVID: The slaves were free after the war, but they didn't even really get to vote then because people kept them from it. They had to fight for it.

LAURA: I'd be thinking that too—that they would be all there—like a ghost or something.

LEAH: Nettie was trying to make sense of it like you are, but these were ideas that were hard to understand.

Leah read on to the end of the book, and there was a brief silence after she finished. She asked the students to talk in pairs about what they were taking from the story. She directed them to focus their discussion on two questions she had written on chart paper:

■ What are you thinking about?
■ What do you want to know more about?

At the end of the session, Leah quickly added the students' questions to the chart paper.

The next day, Leah prepared to read *Nettie's Trip South* to the class again. She said, "When I finish the story this time, be ready to share something new that you thought about." After she read the story the second time, the students shared their responses as a group. Here is an excerpt from the discussion:

SARA: I noticed that the pictures are all gray and black-and-white and they don't show anything really happy. They are old-fashioned and seem sad.

LAURA: I noticed the pictures too. That's probably because Nettie is so sad and the slaves are sad because they can't be free and are sold away even if they don't want to be.

ENRIQUE: She said it would be like a "tight black coat." I thought that was a really good way to say that, and then she told all the things they would have to do.

INGRID: The people in the North are rich but they don't have slaves and there are rich people in the South but the slaves are really poor and they aren't taken care of. They are just owned by people. Like at the one place they were grown up but when somebody said to jump, they just had to jump, but I don't know why.

DALIE: Maybe Nettie will be a person who fights against slavery.

LEAH: What did the author say that makes you predict that?

DALIE: Because she can't forget it. She has bad dreams. Sometimes I think about bad things like my parents' divorce or something and then I dream at night about it.

MARIAH: She was probably never the same afterwards. Sometimes when you have a bad experience you learn from it and you are different. Like after my dog died I was really sad and every time I see a dog I think about my dog.

LEAH: You know, this was a real story. The author's great-grandmother, Henrietta, wrote a diary and Nettie's letter is based on it. That makes it really special.

DALIA: Maybe that's why the letter sounds like it really happened. It didn't just go on and on. There were lots of things she didn't tell about the trip—like what she ate and stuff—but she just talked about what was important.

ENRIQUE: I wonder how much she changed the diary.

Leah returned to the list of questions the group had composed the day before. She and the students discovered that some had been answered on the second reading; others would require more reading and discussion. In groups of three, they each shared a question they still had and helped one another search for answers to the questions.

In this example, Leah was modeling authentic response to a text. She was teaching her students to talk with one another about their response to reading. She encouraged them to discuss their questions rather than simply ask them. With your direction, reading aloud can provide a firm foundation for discussions that take place in small groups.

Our understanding of reader response reminds us that reading is not simply a matter of "getting the author's meaning"; reading is always a matter of interpretation. Reader response lies at the heart of comprehension (Langer 1990). The text, of course, is the focal point of the response because it guides thinking and forms the basis for the reader's search for meaning. In *Nettie's Trip South,* the students were living "in the text" as they worked to figure out the unfolding events and Nettie's experiences.

Writing: Exploring Meaning Through a Reader's Notebook

The writing students do in a response journal is another path to meaning. (Reader's notebooks are discussed in Chapter 10.) In our literacy program students write a letter to their teacher once each week sharing responses to a text they are reading. The final section of the reading response journal is titled Book Club. This section is reserved for any kind of written preparation or reflection that the students will use in literature study. Students can make notes, lists, webs, or complete "free writes" (quick stream-of-consciousness writing) in preparation for or after literature discussion. Other writing, sketching, and diagrams (such as character webs) also fall into this category. For example, students might:

- Make statements about what they know, want to know, or have learned.
- Compose a poem about the book or on a topic related to the book.
- Sketch in preparation for discussion.
- Design a chart or diagram.
- Jot down notes about the text.

Sometimes students need a little more support to focus their notebook entries. You can provide a selection of leading sentences to help initiate students' thinking. These leads help students adopt more complex analytical behavior. Some examples of sentence leads are provided in Figure 17–4.

Sentence Leads for Reader's Notebooks

This [character, place, event] reminds me of .... because ....
I like/dislike this book because ....
I like/dislike this part of the book because ....
This situation reminds me of something that happened in my own life. (Tell the story and talk about the connections.)
The character I [like best, admire, dislike the most] is .... because ....
I like this part of the story because ....
The setting of this story is important because ....
This book makes me think about [an important social issue, a problem, and so on]
A question that I have about this book is .... because ....
When I read this book I felt ....
If I were this character, I would ....
[Character] reminds me of [myself, a friend, a family member] because ....
If I could talk to one of the book's characters I would (ask or say) ....
I predict that .... because ....
This [phrase, sentence, paragraph] is an example of good writing.
This [person, place, time] reminds me of ....
I admire [character] because ....
I didn't understand the part of the story when ....
This book reminds me of another book I have read.
The most exciting part of the book was ....
The big ideas in this book were ....
Some important details I noticed were .... They were important because ....
My favorite part of the book was ....
I think the author wrote this book to ....
I found this book hard to follow when ....
The author got me interested when ....
The book is really about ....
After the book ends, I predict ....
I am like or different from [character] ....
I learned ....
This books makes me want to [action, further reading].
After reading the first [paragraph, page, chapter] of this book, I felt ....
The title of this book says to me ....
If I could be any character in this book, I would be .... because ....
What I want to remember about this book is ....
I'd like to read another book by this author because ....
The most important [word, phrase, idea, illustration] in this book is ....
My feelings about [the book, characters] changed when ....
This book was an effective piece of writing because ....
As compared to other books [by this author, on the same topic], I think this book is ....
I thought this book was [realistic, unrealistic] because ....
I question the accuracy of ....
The genre of this book is .... because it has [characteristics].
I [agreed/disagreed] with the author about ....
I think the illustrations ....
I noticed that the author ....
If I were the author, I would have changed the part of the story when ....
The author is qualified to write this book because ....
To summarize the text, I would say ....
This book helped me to ....

Figure 17–4. Sentence Leads for Reading Response

The primary advantage to including both independent reading responses and literature study responses in one notebook is that a body of work representing the students' thinking about text accumulates over time. We have found that when students are participating in literature study, their weekly letters often become much more thoughtful because they have had so much practice discussing texts in interesting ways. In literature study, you model different ways to talk about and write about your thinking; these models are examples students can apply to their own oral and written responses.

Reading: Mediating Meaning Through an Author Study

We carry within us a collection of all the texts we've ever read—the sum total of our literary experience—which mediates our reading of all future texts. There are times when you'll want to select supplementary reading to expand and refine your students' response to a particular text. An author study (Jenkins 1999) is one simple method for extending students' literacy and literary understanding through additional reading. For example, if your students enjoyed Ralph Fletcher's *Fig Pudding* (1995), they may enjoy learning that Fletcher grew up in a family of eight. Introduce them to *Relatively Speaking: Poems About Family* (1999), a book about Fletcher's experiences as a boy, so they can discover firsthand how authors draw from their real-life experiences to create their stories. For an in-depth author study, pull together a text set of Fletcher's books:

Flying Solo (1998)
I Am Wings: Poems About Love (1994)
Ordinary Things: Poems from a Walk in Early Spring (1997)
Spider Boy (1998)
Twilight Comes Twice (1997)
Grandpa Never Lies (2000)
Tommy Trouble and the Magic Marble (2000)
Water Planet (1991)

As your students pair up or work in small groups to read Fletcher's body of work, they will respond aesthetically, critically, and biographically, extending their literary understanding of how authors work to create

vivid characters, captivating plots, and stirring settings. Your students may even enjoy the opportunity to hone their own writing by reading Fletcher's writing tips for kids:

Breathing in, Breathing Out: Keeping a Writer's Notebook (1996)
Live Writing: Breathing Life into Your Words (1999)
A Writer's Notebook: Unlocking the Writer Within You (1996)

The students' lively discussions and reading of Fletcher's other books will necessarily alter their original interpretation of *Fig Pudding* (Fletcher 1995). After you've completed the author study, invite your students to reread *Fig Pudding*. Ask them to discuss how the author study has changed their original perceptions and understandings of *Fig Pudding* and of Ralph Fletcher as an accomplished children's author.

The Visual and Performing Arts: Exploring Meaning Through Process Drama

In process drama the teacher and students take on the roles of characters from their literature study and enter into an imagined world that is strongly guided by their interpretation of a text. Process drama plunges students into an aesthetic experience "because it places the reader in the story—as if it is happening now" (Edmiston 1997, p. 89).

Students use the text as the basis for the dramatic exploration, and they draw on their own life experiences or their previous reading experiences. In a sense, drama brings the act of ongoing construction of meaning into full view. As your students take on roles, they begin to respond, react, and think like a character in the text. In so doing, they are "acting out" their comprehension. The world they construct is a combination of their understanding of the text and their own perspectives and ideas. Booth (1985) says:

> Story drama occurs when the teacher uses the issues, times, characters, mood, conflict, or spirit of a story as a beginning for dramatic exploration . . . of the meanings of the story. (p. 196)

Drama may be used at any point during the literature study. Students may read a chunk of text and then break from their reading to act out their assumed roles. After the drama, they return to their reading. Or they may engage in dramatic exploration after they've read the entire text.

In process drama, you take one or more roles yourself in order to help students get organized, introduce the techniques they will be using, and show them the range of possible interactions with characters. You may take on roles spontaneously to grab students' attention, provide new information, or introduce interesting questions.

Process drama may extend over days or weeks and may involve research. For example, you might ask your students to dig for details about a particular book setting or investigate which tools and resources the characters in a specific story might have used. Drama is a highly dynamic, artistic response that brings together reading, writing, and language. Students may read related material; write notes, diaries, advertisements, or newspapers; and spend fruitful time discussing, planning, and organizing their dramatic response.

Shared Meaning: More Ways to Foster Reader Response Through Talk, Writing, Reading, and the Arts

As you explore reader response with your students, you'll discover that more often than not they take multiple paths to meaning. In other words, talk, writing, reading, and the arts come together in almost every learning experience. As you prompt reader response, you'll rely on techniques that range from promoting "open" or "directed" approaches along the continuum (see Figure 17–2). As you adapt the following examples, you'll discover that you can generate many alternative designs.

Thinkmark

Thinkmarks (Figure 17–5) are a tool for students to make quick comments, write questions, or note an interesting phrase or sentence, and mark the appropriate spot in the book. Students then bring the thinkmarks to a group discussion. Reproduce the form in Appendix 15 on white tag or card stock, cut the thinkmarks apart, and keep a box handy for your students to use.

Short-Writes Before, During, or After Reading

Ask students to write a sentence or paragraph at intervals while reading a text. Using stick-on notes, note paper, or their reader's notebooks, students write about what they are thinking, feeling, or visualizing in response to their reading. They can also note personal connections they are making. During the discussion, invite students to take turns reading their notes while other students respond.

Letters Related to the Text

Encourage students to write a letter to a character in the text, to the subject of a biography, or to the author of an informational text. Have students share their letters and explain why they wrote them.

Story Map

A story map (Appendix 24) depicts the major characters (or subject) and events in a text and typically indicates some kind of movement (e.g., from beginning to end or through periods of history). Show students how to create these visual "models" of the story or informational text. They can draw the model on large sheets of chart paper or butcher paper, or they can create a more elaborate mural. Story maps can spark many valuable discussions as students plan the project and explain it to others. The story map generally combines reading, writing, talking, and the arts.

Webs

Webs consist of a central idea with branches (and subbranches) reaching out to subsidiary ideas. Students can create a web that shows character or setting features, historical places, related vocabulary words, or any other textual feature. Have students discuss their webs, noting why some ideas are subordinated under others.

Time Lines

Traditionally, students create a time line to highlight the major events in the life of a subject who is profiled in a biography. While this technique is particularly useful for nonfiction, it can also be used to help students understand the structure of fiction. For example, after students read *Tuck Everlasting* (Babbitt 1975), they might create a time line that demonstrates how the story unfolds over four seasons.

Written Conversation

Invite pairs of students to chat about something they've read in writing, on paper or via e-mail. They can enjoy an open discussion of a story or an informational book, or you can help focus their conversation through a series of questions (Short and Harste 1995).

Graphic Organizers

As you consider different processes to support response, you can also refer to the graphic organizers provided in Chapter 26. Tools like "sketch to stretch," KWL, or comparison charts can benefit students' discussion of response to literature.

Sharing Meaning Through Extensions

Frequently, students share their understanding of a text through an extended project that may involve several modes of expression: poetry, art, drama, movement, music, and writing. Possible extension projects include:

- Role play or drama.
- Readers theatre.
- A "jackdaw" (a collection of documents and artifacts related to a period of history or to a text, including letters, photographs, deeds, and wills).
- PowerPoint presentations.
- A pamphlet that presents information in a concise and attractive way, including sketches, quotes, and diagrams.

Extension projects have two primary goals:

1. To give students an opportunity to show the audience what they have learned.
2. To include information from the text for the benefit of others' learning.

As students create these projects, they must revisit the text and analyze and transform ideas into new media. Projects work best when students:

Thinkmark	Page 25
Name Natalia Title Fantastic Mr. Fox Author Roald Dahl	The Beans don't give up, and have gone to all lengths to catch the Fox, meanwhile have affected the lives of other animals that live underground.
Page 8 Foxes are seen as witty, clever and steal food to survive.	Page 53 Would I steal something to help my family? How would I act if something was stolen from me?
Page 9 The Bean Brothers want revenge on the Fox and will do anything to get the Fox as well. They want to protect what is theirs.	Page 59 "Two wrongs don't make a right." Something my mother always said.
Page 12 Fox uses his senses to save both himself and his family.	Page 74 It is always good to help others when they need it. It makes you feel good. Always share!

Figure 17–5. Thinkmark

- Are highly engaged in a text over time.
- Have learned a great deal through discussion and analysis.
- Know how to use the different modes of expression that are available to them.
- Select their own format in which to present their knowledge.

Extension projects typically involve groups of students working in cooperative groups or pairs, although students may work individually. The learning benefits to students are evident as they discuss and plan the project and present it to the entire class, rather than just to the teacher. At times, other classes, the principal, or parents may be involved.

Projects need not necessarily be lengthy. Here are some examples of projects that are effective but don't take much time:

- A quick skit after reading *The Watsons Go to Birmingham, 1963* (Curtis 1995), a book about ten-year-old Kenny and his family, who travel to the South during one of the darkest moments in American history.
- A painting after reading *Number the Stars* (Lowry 1989), a book about ten-year-old Ann Marie, who saves the life of her best friend, Ellen Rosen, during the Holocaust.
- A pamphlet that showcases poems and illustrations after reading *Go Free or Die: A Story About Harriet Tubman* (Ferris 1988), a biography of the former slave who risked her life to help hundreds of slaves follow the underground railroad in the 1800s.
- A debate in which students take on character roles that reveal different perspectives.
- An experiment described in *What's the Big Idea, Ben Franklin?* (Fritz 1976), a biography that highlighted Franklin's ingenuity.
- A performance of a poem by Eloise Greenfield.
- A role play in which students take the role of one of the family members in *Fig Pudding* (Fletcher 1995), the story of a family of six children.

Careful planning, specific time limits, and definite deadlines are all essential for a successful presentation. Additionally, students need to practice their presentations so they are brisk and polished and keep the audience engaged. The ultimate goal of the project, of course, is to spur the members of the audience to read the text.

Once students have presented their projects, they need to evaluate the quality of their work and examine how well they worked together. You can provide students with a short evaluation form that contains the following questions:

- How well did you work together on your project?
- To what extent did you go beyond the text to create greater meaning?
- How would you judge the quality of your presentation?

You may want to work with the students over time to create some criteria that will help them evaluate their extension projects.

It is certainly not necessary to have students engage in extension projects for every work of literature they read and discuss. Most of the time, you will use simpler reader responses: quick-writes, sketching, and discussion. We caution against letting students spend undue time on lengthy and elaborate presentations. The key is for them to spend most of the time reading. On the other hand, when a truly engaging text warrants this extra involvement, an extension project takes response public.

Helping Students Learn to Analyze and Criticize Texts

Literature study is an ideal setting for helping students learn about the writer's craft. You can also help them realize the need to use critical thinking as they approach fiction or nonfiction texts. With your guidance, students can recognize how to bring their own ideas and background knowledge to bear in the analysis.

Demonstrating Analysis and Criticism

As you've seen in this chapter, there are many ways to promote analysis and criticism of texts. For example, after reading *Nettie's Trip South* (Turner 1987) you could talk to students about your own response to Nettie's description of the South, noting how the author uses the sense of smell to symbolize the character's growing feelings of horror. You could describe how the language of the text becomes angrier, providing examples of what you mean, and inviting students to share what they noticed about language. Together, you might create a group chart of the phrases or sentences that created vivid images in your mind.

With an informational text, you might demonstrate how to use side headings to find information or to predict the kind of information the sidebars showcase. You can also demonstrate how to interpret graphic features of text. Students might make a chart listing important information provided by the author as well as where to find it. You can use any of the graphic organizers or other tools provided in Chapter 26 to demonstrate processes to students. They can also use these tools as individuals, with partners, or in small groups; but we stress that these processes are best used to support discussion.

As you'll discover, analysis and criticism are complex processes. For most of us, these strategies took years to develop; in fact, as adults we are still developing our critical powers. Wolf, Huck, and King (1967, 4), who conducted an in-depth study of critical reading, see reading and critical thinking as two interrelated processes that cannot be separated. Readers use critical thinking to evaluate ideas that are presented in printed form. "Critical reading does not begin after the author's ideas have been grasped, but is an ongoing part of the process of securing meaning. Evaluation occurs at every stage of reading as the reader selects suitable information and rejects the unsuitable, interprets a descriptive phrase, recognizes the techniques of persuasion, or analyzes plot development." (Wolf, Huck, and King 1967) They determined that elementary school children can be taught to read critically, and further, that literary analysis supports the development of critical reading skills. Teach students different ways to analyze and criticize texts, gradually increasing the level of complexity. For example, students who know how to identify and talk about the main character in a simple novel may be ready to examine a character in a book that features a story told by different characters from different perspectives or a story that plays with time. Students who know how to use side headings in a text organized into topical sections may be ready to try one that integrates chronological order as well as topics. Continue to support and challenge students with more difficult tasks over time.

Questions That Prompt Student Response

Once students understand the way you are helping them analyze or criticize a text, you can use questions to focus their written or oral response. For example, you may rely on questions to prompt student response in journal entries. It is important to remember, though, that *questions alone will not ensure that students are able to develop and use complex strategies for analyzing and criticizing texts.*

The best questions to focus response are "open-ended"; they can have more than one answer and are designed to elicit divergent responses. Open-ended questions:

- Promote an understanding of different perspectives.
- Help students understand that there is no single correct answer but that all answers should be backed by evidence from the text.
- Guide students to think more analytically or critically about text.

Questions are influential in focusing students' responses in different ways. For example, questions can:

- Prompt students to recall prior knowledge or the connections to their lives.
- Elicit emotional or aesthetic response.
- Encourage students to recall and/or summarize information.
- Prompt students to make inferences or go beyond the text.
- Encourage students to synthesize information to create new knowledge.
- Help students explore the deeper meanings of texts.

At different points in time, you might select questions from any of these categories.

While it might be essential for students to recall information from a text, developing response requires that they go beyond literal meaning. For example, suppose your students are reading *Nettie's Trip South* (Turner 1987). You can ask questions regarding what they know about the year 1859 or what issues led to the Civil War, and you will elicit valuable information. Students may summarize Nettie's experiences and construct a chronology of the book. They might compare the book with what they know about the time period and the historical settings—both the North and South. But when they are finished, will they have comprehended the book? We recommend that students do more "wondering" and consider additional possibilities. For example, students might describe how they feel as the story moves from Nettie's initial excitement to the accumulating sorrow she feels at every new experience with the slaves in the South. Here are some sample questions that would encourage students to wonder:

- What kind of person was Nettie? How was she different from her brother? (These questions prompt students to search for evidence to make inferences about her character.)
- While Nettie was physically sick at the slave auction, I wonder if she was sick in another way—perhaps in her spirit. Why did she have those bad dreams?
- The sweet smell of cedars was really a contrast, wasn't it? To what?
- How might this trip have affected the rest of Nettie's life?

A text like this one has many layers of meaning. Understanding it goes well beyond simply reading and recalling events.

The sections below discuss examples of questions that elicit personal connections to life experiences, other texts, and background knowledge or that encourage students to make inferences, summarize, synthesize, and respond analytically and critically. You will generate specific questions that relate to each particular genre you are exploring with your students. We suggest parameters for generating these questions in Chapters 17 and 23.

QUESTIONS TO PROMPT RESPONSE TO FICTION TEXTS

Figure 17–6 lists some questions that focus students' attention on aspects of fiction. The goal of all reading is to enjoy the text and form new understandings about oneself and one's world. These questions invite students to make personal connections but also to think about elements such as characters, plot, theme, perspective, and language. As students focus their response journal entries and their discussions more closely on these literary elements, they will increase their analytic thinking. By stepping back and looking at a story, students can understand it more deeply and can understand more about its characteristics, its relationship to other stories, and its literary value. As readers internalize these questions over time, they begin to develop new ways of thinking about texts.

QUESTIONS TO SUPPORT COMPREHENSION OF INFORMATIONAL TEXTS

Figure 17–7 lists some questions that focus students' attention on aspects of nonfiction texts. You'll want to invite your students to examine how the authors of nonfiction texts select and organize content to make it available to the reader. Additionally, students should consider the accuracy and authenticity of the text. The questions also prompt them to notice features of the author's style, such as how the author used facts or details to provide evidence or used language to make the topic interesting. Questions can also direct students' attention to the information they acquire from illustrations, charts, drawings, diagrams, maps, and other visual or graphic features.

QUESTIONS TO SUPPORT COMPREHENSION OF BIOGRAPHY

Since biography is commonly read and discussed in upper elementary grades, we include questions specific to this genre. Biography is a bridge between fiction and nonfiction. The text is informational, but it is often structured as a narrative. Upper elementary students enjoy reading biography because:

- Information is presented in narrative form.
- The subjects are individuals whom students typically admire and find fascinating.

Figure 17–8 lists questions to guide students' understanding. Many of them prompt students to think and talk about the subject's life. For example, how did the time or geographical location influence the individual? What challenges did he or she face? You can also ask them to notice how the author organized the biography. At what point in the individual's life does the text begin? Often, especially in biographies for children, the writer provides details or dialogue to make it more interesting. Readers will need to think about whether the dialogue is supported by fact.

They should also think about the "bigger message" of a biography. What can they learn from studying the life of this individual? Why is this person important, and what difference did he or she make? The goal of reading biography is not only to learn more about the individuals who have played an important role in history or current affairs, but also to synthesize the information with our own knowledge. A biography should contribute to the students' view of the world and, perhaps, inspire them. Your questions can prompt discussion that supports the process.

Conversation, Not Interrogation

While thoughtful questioning is an effective strategy, it can be overdone. Questioning is best when it fosters students' own thinking. We don't want our students simply to scramble for the answer they think the teacher wants. Our goal as questioners is to prompt discussion that creates a greater understanding than a single reader can derive from a text.

Your questions should not overwhelm the students' responses. When you step back and reflect on your lessons, you do not want them to look or sound like inter-

Questions to Support Comprehension of Fiction

Personal and Textual Connections
❖ How does the story make you feel?
❖ Have you ever had similar experiences?
❖ Does the book remind you of another book?
❖ Do any of the characters remind you of someone in your life?
❖ How is this story like any other story you know?
❖ How are the characters, setting, and problems like those in other stories you have read?
❖ How are the characters, setting, and problems connected to your life?
❖ Were you reminded of anything in your own life?
❖ What does this story make you think or wonder about?
❖ What surprised you?

Setting
❖ Where and when does the story take place?
❖ Where else could the story take place?
❖ Could the setting be a real place that exists in our time?
❖ Is the place important to the story? How?
❖ What words did the author use to describe the place?
❖ What can you hear, see, feel, or smell as you read?
❖ How important is the place or time to the story?
❖ How much time passes in the story?
❖ In another time or place, how would the story change?
❖ How did the author control the passing of time?
❖ How is the setting like another place you know?
❖ Does the season or the time affect the characters or the plot of the story?

Characters
❖ Are there any powerful characters in the story? What makes them that way?
❖ Who is the most interesting character? Why?
❖ Who is the most important character? Why?
❖ What character is the fairest? Why?
❖ Who is the bravest character? Why?
❖ Which character taught you the most?
❖ Who else could be in the story?
❖ What choices did a character have?
❖ How does the author/illustrator reveal the character? (Look at what the character does, thinks, or says; or what others say *about* the character.)
❖ How does one of the characters change? Why?
❖ Which characters change and which don't? How is character change important in the story?
❖ Who is a character that plays a small role? Why is this character necessary in the story?
❖ What did you learn from one character in the story?
❖ How did characters feel about one another? Why?
❖ Are the characters believable? Why or why not?

Figure 17–6. Questions to Support Comprehension of Fiction

Questions to Support Comprehension of Fiction (continued)

Plot

❖ How did the author begin the story to engage the reader?

❖ What is the story problem? How do you think it will be solved?

❖ What challenges do the characters encounter and how do they deal with them?

❖ What choices did the characters have?

❖ How does a character's actions affect other people in the story?

❖ What was the most important part of the story?

❖ How would you describe the story shape? (linear, triangular, circular; for example, home-adventure-home)

❖ What is the high point of the story?

❖ What are the important events in the story?

❖ What is the order of events in the story? (for example, series of sequential events, letter or diary, record, flashback)

❖ Could the order of events be changed or could any of the events be left out?

❖ Were you able to predict the story ending?

❖ How did the story end?

❖ If you were the author, would you have ended it in any different way? How?

❖ What clues did the author give to allow the reader to predict the ending?

❖ What lesson does this story teach about life?

❖ What do you think will happen next in the story?

❖ What do you think will happen next for the characters after the story ends?

❖ Do you think the story really could have happened?

❖ How does the author provide information or details to make the story seem realistic?

❖ How does the author help you feel that you are really there [in both realistic stories and fantasy]?

❖ How was the story resolved?

❖ What two or three sentences summarize the whole story?

❖ Make a sketch or picture of an event in the book.

❖ What are the most important events of the story?

❖ Do you have any unanswered questions about the story?

Theme

❖ What is the author's message?

❖ What is the story really about?

❖ Do you think the title is appropriate for the story?

❖ What does the story mean to you?

❖ Why did the author write this story?

❖ What is the author really trying to say?

Perspective

❖ Who tells the story? Is this the best person to tell it? Why?

❖ Whose point of view is used in the story?

❖ What other voices could tell the story?

❖ How would the story be different if told through another character's eyes?

Figure 17–6. Questions to Support Comprehension of Fiction (continued)

Questions to Support Comprehension of Fiction (continued)

Language

❖ What are some interesting words, phrases, or sentences?

❖ Are there words that were used to create a feeling or picture in your mind?

❖ Where did the author describe something well?

❖ What images did the writing evoke? How did the author use language to evoke images?

❖ What were some of the strongest words the author used?

❖ How did the author begin/end the story?

❖ Was any of the language especially interesting, vivid, or surprising?

Illustrations

❖ What do the illustrations add to the story?

❖ How important are the illustrations?

❖ What is the role of illustrations in conveying the meaning of the story?

❖ What is your favorite illustration? Why did you choose it?

❖ Could you picture what was happening when there was no illustration?

Author/Illustrator

❖ Would you read other books by this author? Why or why not?

❖ Have you read other books by this illustrator? How is this text similar to or different from others the artist has illustrated?

❖ What other books does this book make you want to read?

❖ Why do you think this particular author wrote this book?

❖ What did the author have to know to write this book?

❖ What did the author do to interest the reader or pull the reader into the text?

❖ Did the author keep you interested? How or why?

❖ How is this book like other books by this author?

❖ Why do you think the author began/ended the story this way?

❖ Why did the author choose the title? Would you choose the same one?

❖ What do you notice about the writing—the way the author wrote?

Genre

❖ What is the genre? How did you know?

❖ Is this text a good example of this genre? Why?

❖ How is this book like other books you've read in this genre?

❖ What do you find difficult about reading books in this genre?

Figure 17–6. Questions to Support Comprehension of Fiction (continued)

rogations: teacher question, student answer, teacher question, student answer, and so on. Your goal, is to ask questions and make comments that spark discussion *among* the students. You want them to ask questions—to generate an intellectual excitement that pushes the conversation into new territory. The questions are merely a light scaffold that helps students examine texts in new ways.

If you find your discussions seems more like interrogations, you might:

■ Evaluate your questions to be sure they are genuine.

■ Think about the number of questions you are asking; one or two well-selected questions that open up the discussion or shed new light on the text are sufficient.

■ Intersperse questions with comments that model open-ended response so that students can "piggyback" on your comments (e.g., *I wonder . . . , I was thinking about . . . , If . . .*).

Questions to Support Comprehension of Nonfiction

Personal and Textual Connections
❖ What do you already know about this topic?
❖ How does this [book, article, topic] remind you of other texts you have read?
❖ What have you experienced in your life that helps you understand this topic?
❖ Does this text provide useful information for you personally?
❖ What is your interest in this topic?
❖ What experiences or life circumstances led you to read about this topic?
❖ How does the information in this text fit with what you already know?

Content
❖ Why is this topic important [socially, scientifically, and practically]?
❖ What perspective does the author take on this topic?
❖ What part of the topic has the author chosen to present in the text?
❖ What are some of the most important words related to the topic, and what do they mean?
❖ What are some of the most important ideas related to this topic?
❖ Were there parts of the book you didn't understand? What puzzled you? What questions do you still have?
❖ Is the topic covered adequately?
❖ Are different viewpoints presented on the topic?
❖ Does the author explain how facts were arrived at?
❖ What did you learn about this topic?
❖ What does this text make you want to learn more about?

Accuracy and Authenticity
❖ Is the information up-to-date?
❖ Is sufficient evidence provided to support what the author says?
❖ How has the author established the authenticity of the text?
❖ Are the illustrations authentic?
❖ Are the facts and information in this text consistent with other sources?
❖ Is all important information included? Was important information missing?
❖ Does the author make a clear distinction between fact and opinion?
❖ Has the author presented information to accurately represent people and places—without stereotypes or omissions?
❖ Has the author been fair?
❖ Do facts and information support the author's general statements?
❖ Did the author present an objective point of view?
❖ Is there any information that could be misleading?
❖ Have any groups been omitted from the [history, record of scientific progress]?

Style
❖ How has the author made this topic readable?
❖ How has the author made this topic interesting?
❖ How has the author made it easy for you to find information?

Text Structure/Organization
❖ What are the ways the author presents information on this topic?

Figure 17–7. Questions to Support Comprehension of Nonfiction

Questions to Support Comprehension of Nonfiction (continued)

Text Structure/Organization
- ❖ What are the ways the author presents information on this topic?
- ❖ How is information organized [by topic, in time, by contrasting ideas, etc.]?
- ❖ Is the information presented clearly?

Text Features/Illustrations/Format
- ❖ What does the title tell you about this text?
- ❖ How do headings and subheadings help you find information in this text?
- ❖ What information is provided through illustrations [drawings, diagrams, maps, charts, etc.]?
- ❖ Does the text have reference aides such as table of contents, index, bibliography, glossary, and appendices? Are they easy to use? How are they helping you?
- ❖ Are the illustrations clear and understandable? Are they easy to interpret?
- ❖ Are the illustrations explained by labels, legends, and captions when needed?
- ❖ Does the total format of the text help you understand the topic better?

Author
- ❖ What qualifications does the author have to write this text?
- ❖ How does the author use experiences and/or knowledge to do a good job of providing information?
- ❖ What is the author's perspective or stance toward the topic?
- ❖ What has the author said that makes you question the accuracy of the information?

Figure 17–7. Questions to Support Comprehension of Nonfiction (continued)

Questions to Support Comprehension of Biography

Note: Many questions suitable for discussion of narrative texts and informational texts are also appropriate for biography. The follow questions are specific to biography.

Personal and Textual Connections
- ❖ What do you already know about the subject of this biography?
- ❖ What does the story of this person's life make you think or wonder about?
- ❖ What surprised you about this person?
- ❖ How does this person's life story remind you of your own life or the lives of people you know?
- ❖ What do you know about the period of history in which this person lived?
- ❖ Does this person's life remind you of other biographies you have read or of fiction texts?
- ❖ How is the person in the biography like people you know?
- ❖ How are this person's problems like the problems of people in other biographies or fiction books you have read?

Setting
- ❖ How important is the setting [place, time in history, and other events taking place at the time] to the subject's life or accomplishments?
- ❖ How does the author include details that help you understand the subject?

Figure 17–8. Questions to Support Comprehension of Biography

Questions to Support Comprehension of Biography (continued)

❖ Does the setting change over the person's life?

❖ Is the information about the setting authentic and consistent with history?

❖ How did the author write about the setting to make it authentic?

Structure or Organization

❖ At what point in the person's life did the author begin the biography?

❖ How did the author organize the telling of the events of the person's life (chronological, under topics, etc.)?

❖ How did the author use dialogue, flashbacks, foreshadowing, and other ways of organizing text to make this person's life interesting?

❖ If dialogue is invented to make the text interesting, how well does it work?

❖ How did the author use anecdotes, original documents, eyewitness accounts, and interviews to make the person's life interesting?

❖ Are the events depicted for the subject's life believable and consistent with other information about the time period?

Events

❖ What were the important events in the subject's life?

❖ What were the challenges faced by the person?

❖ What were the important actions the person took?

❖ How did the subject's actions affect others?

Author

❖ Why did this author choose this subject?

❖ How did the author go about getting to know the subject?

❖ What research or other action did the author take to make the biography authentic?

❖ What did the author have to know to write this biography?

Theme

❖ What was the author trying to say by writing about this person?

❖ Why did the author think this subject was important?

❖ What was the most important thing about the subject of this biography?

❖ Are different points of view on the times or events presented in an objective way?

❖ What insights does the book provide into today's problems and issues?

Subject

❖ What does the character look like?

❖ What kind of person is the subject?

❖ Is the subject living now or did the subject live in past history?

❖ How does what the subject says inform you?

❖ What do others say about the subject?

❖ Does the subject change over the biography? How and why?

❖ How do the subject's actions reflect the times in which he or she lived?

Figure 17–8. Questions to Support Comprehension of Biography (continued)

Our goal in encouraging reader response is to help our students increase their ability to frame questions, express their opinions, and generate new knowledge and ideas. In the process, they discover both the intellectual and emotional pleasure inherent in literature as well as the joy of sharing this pleasure with others.

Summary

Anais Nin once wrote, "We write to taste life twice." So it is with response to literature. We partake of the pleasures of a good book once again when we revisit the text in conversation with friends or as we find new mediums—music, art, drama, and the like—to represent our experience with the book. Indeed, not only do we "taste" the book twice, but our initial experience is deepened, expanded, and refined as we return to the text—perhaps again and again—and push our understanding in new ways each time. It is this deepening and stretching of reading that characterizes both reader response and the passionate reader. It's one we want our students to relish as well.

Suggestions for Professional Development

1. Work with a group of colleagues to analyze a literature discussion that you conduct with your students.
2. Select a fiction text for a group of students in your class.
3. Videotape or audiotape the session. Then view or listen to the tape and reflect on what you see or hear.

4. Use the chart in Figure 17–2 to evaluate the general character of the students' discussion. How well do they understand the routines and expectations? To what extent are they talking to and listening to one another as well as building on one another's responses? In addition, ask:

- How did you build on students' responses?
- Were there places where the discussion wandered or went off topic? How did you/could you guide it back?
- What kinds of questions did you ask?
- Did your questions or comments assist students in clarifying their responses?
- Were there other questions that you wish you had asked?
- Did you balance questions and comments so that the discussion was a real conversation?
- What did the students learn from this discussion? How will they be better readers as a result of the discussion? How did their understanding of the text change?

5. Bring your tape and your reactions to it to a meeting with colleagues and share the insights you gained. (Or have one participant bring a videotape for everyone to analyze and discuss.)
6. Repeat the process using a nonfiction text.
7. Follow this experience with an in-depth look at the questions that are appropriate to different kinds of texts. Bring some high-quality fiction and nonfiction texts to a session. Using the questions in Figures 17–6, 17–7, and 17–8, select two or three questions that you think would be most appropriate for each text.

STRUGGLING READERS AND WRITERS TEACHING THAT MAKES A DIFFERENCE

Reading and discussing literature is a powerful way to help your struggling readers and writers internalize literary language as well as expand their vocabulary. Also, as students discover the structure and language of texts, they learn how to apply such features in their own writing. Literature study increases students' enjoyment of reading and the extension projects in which they participate with more able students may expand their understanding of texts. Literature study also helps students learn about different genres.

Literature study is a freeing experience for low-achieving students because it is not so concerned with "answers." In literature study we are concerned with students' response to literature. As they make connections between literature and their own lives, students learn the value of reading and are persuaded that their own thinking about literature is important. Therefore, with low-achieving students:

Take every opportunity to involve them in literature discussion with higher-achieving students. Through literature study, low-achieving students have the opportunity to discuss books within a mixed group. They learn from others' comments and also expand their ways of using language.

Teach them explicitly how to listen and use language as they discuss literature with other students. You may even meet with some students briefly to rehearse some of the comments they want to make. Act as a coach during literature study to prompt and remind them how to engage in the discussion. Learning the language of discussion offers powerful advantages for low-achieving students.

Provide alternative ways for them to access the texts that they need for literature study. Students can talk about a text without reading it themselves; in other words, look for books on tape. You can make your own tapes of books you feel are especially important. Or students can discuss picture books that you read aloud to them. Also consider partner reading and inviting older students to read to younger students.

Use graphic organizers to help them analyze literary texts. Students who need more support will benefit from charts that highlight relationships between ideas. Such displays make it easier to see relationships between characters, the sequence of events within the plot, and comparisons of various kinds. It is especially important for low-achieving students to use these graphic organizers in an active and interactive way. You can work with them in a small group to create a chart or diagram on the easel.

Direct their attention to the features of nonfiction text and teach them how to take information from them. Low-achieving students may need special help to use the features of nonfiction texts. Select exemplary texts to read aloud to students and demonstrate how to derive information from graphic features.

Guide their text selection. It is important that students find the texts used for literature study interesting and relevant. And if they are to read the texts themselves, the books must offer manageable concepts and vocabulary. To this end, help your students make the best choices for literature study.

Communicate to all students that there are a wide range of good books worthy of literature study. When students are looking for books to discuss as literature, they should focus on texts that evolve around big ideas, memorable characters, interesting plots, high-quality illustrations, and interesting information. You can find high-quality texts across a wide range of reading levels. When introducing books to students that they might want to discuss, always include books that will be within the reading abilities of your lower-achieving readers.

Encourage them to read series books. Students may be introduced to series books in guided reading and can discuss them in literature study. Series books will help your lower-achieving students clock reading mileage. The books have interesting characters and they are usually pitched at about the same reading level. As students read them, they gain and apply knowledge of writer's style, plot, and typical vocabulary; with each book they read, reading becomes easier. Thus, students gain momentum as they read through hundreds of pages in a series.

SECTION 5

Comprehension and Word Analysis

Reading for meaning is our goal every time we read. While reading, we engage in a complex process that involves the orchestration of multiple strategies. In Chapter 18 we explore the reading process, describing both oral and silent reading. In Chapter 19 we describe processes and behaviors related to comprehension and explain how best to support students in constructing meaning. In Chapters 20 and 21 we discuss twelve strategy systems for sustaining the reading process, making connections, and expanding meaning. In Chapter 22 we explore the key roles of phonics, spelling, and vocabulary in literacy development, discussing a range of word-solving strategies and outlining effective vocabulary and spelling instruction.

## CHAPTER EIGHTEEN

UNDERSTANDING THE READING PROCESS

I regard meaning as the 'given' in all reading—the source of anticipation, the guide to being on track, and the outcome and reward of the effort.

— MARIE CLAY

Reading is a complex, multifaceted process that begins and ends with meaning. In response to the demands of a text, the reader draws on both cognitive and linguistic strategies as well as a range of information—inside and outside the text—to process continuous print with understanding. The reading process is constructed as younger children learn to read with understanding the continuous print in extended stories with little picture support and develops over time as students have opportunities to learn how to process increasingly challenging texts. Students read texts that not only increase in difficulty but also offer varied structures, organization, and subject matter.

The demands of text require ever expanding processing systems. As summarized in Figure 18–1, effective readers:

- Maintain a consistent focus on constructing meaning while problem-solving words.
- Monitor understanding and print.
- Use language structure and meaning to anticipate the text.
- Process the print with fluency, noticing and using punctuation and phrasing.
- Vary the rate of reading according to the demands of the text and the purpose for reading.
- Use multiple sources of information while reading, including background knowledge, personal experience, literary experience, visual information, and language.
- Have questions in mind before, during, and after reading.

- Recognize and attend to important ideas.
- Form sensory images as part of understanding the meaning and connotations of the text.
- Recognize a large body of words automatically while reading for meaning.
- Solve words using a variety of strategies while reading for meaning.
- Extend the meaning of text through inferences and information synthesis.
- Integrate into their understanding the information gained from reading.

Reading for meaning—*comprehending*—is the goal of every reading episode as well as of our teaching. We want students not only to understand what they read but also to enjoy texts, interpret them, and apply their learning from reading to other areas.

Reading, then, is the process of constructing meaning from print. The reader brings understandings to the text, reads the words of the text as continuous language, synthesizes information from the text, and integrates it with existing understandings.

Let's try an experiment related to background knowledge. Read the following description and try to determine what is being discussed:

The procedure is actually quite simple. First you arrange things into different groups. Of course one pile may be sufficient depending on how much there is to do. If you have to go somewhere else due to lack of facilities that is the next step, otherwise you are pretty well set. It is important

An effective reader:

- ❖ Maintains focus on meaning.
- ❖ Checks on understanding and print.
- ❖ Uses language structures to anticipate text.
- ❖ Processes print with fluency.
- ❖ Varies the rate of reading.
- ❖ Uses many different sources of information together.
- ❖ Has questions in mind.
- ❖ Attends to important ideas.
- ❖ Recognizes many words automatically.
- ❖ Uses a variety of strategies for solving words while reading for meaning.
- ❖ Extends the meaning of texts using synthesizing and inferencing skills.
- ❖ Integrates information.

Figure 18–1. An Effective Reader

not to overdo things. That is, it is better to do too few things at once than too many. In the short run this may not seem important but complications can easily arise. A mistake can be expensive as well. At first the whole procedure will seem complicated. Soon however, it will become just another facet of life. It is difficult to foresee any end to the necessity for this task in the immediate future, but then one never can tell. After the procedure is completed one arranges the materials into different groups again. Then they can be put into their appropriate places. Eventually they will be used once more and the whole cycle will then be repeated. However, that is a part of life. (Bransford and McCarrell 1974, p. 132)

If you have not seen this piece of writing before, you may be having a little trouble determining the topic of the paragraph. You can read all the words and discern the sentence structure and punctuation. You can even read the paragraph fluently, with expression. But answering a test question about it might be difficult. If you *have* seen the piece of writing before, or if something

triggered a connection or two, you know that the topic is "doing the laundry." You were able to bring your existing knowledge to bear as you read the words of the piece, and you constructed meaning effectively and efficiently.

During the intermediate grades, students continue to learn "how" to read because they are exposed to a wide range of texts and use literacy for many purposes. They exponentially expand their reading abilities. For most, this period represents the critical time during which they learn to value reading as a tool of inquiry, to enjoy reading and fully value the contribution it can make to their lives, and to become part of a community of readers who share books with one another. Survey research indicates that children who are avid readers in fourth grade have a high chance of remaining avid readers throughout their lives; sadly, the opposite is also true.

As teachers, we need to understand the complexities of the reading process. Students build these processes over time as the demands of the texts they are reading require different ways of operating on and using information. The process involves bringing personal knowledge, gained from experience, to the text and, at the same time, selecting and synthesizing information from the text in order to construct a unique set of meanings while reading. The reader accesses the author's meaning but also *adds* to that meaning through personal interpretation.

Oral and Silent Reading

The reading we do in life is almost always silent. That is also true of the reading students do in intermediate-grade classrooms. Silent reading is faster, and most people can concentrate better on the meaning when they read silently. Some research indicates that even in groups, students are more attentive when they read silently than when they read orally. They also participate better in discussion after silent reading; that is, they are able to remember and retrieve information from the text.

Students read silently during independent reading as well as most of the time in guided reading. There are, however, some good reasons for including oral reading within the reading workshop. While cautioning *against* "round robin" reading, Opitz and Rasinski (1998) argue that reading has a social dimension and is meant to be shared in many ways. For example, when teachers read aloud to students, they demonstrate what it means to enjoy literacy and model important uses of literacy. When teachers read aloud, students are able to enjoy literacy with others. In sum, oral reading in the classroom enables students to:

- Share information with others.
- Access texts that may be more difficult than they can read for themselves and thus build their knowledge of text structure and expand their listening vocabulary.
- Develop fluency and expressive reading.
- Attend more closely to aspects of print such as punctuation and other typographical cues that convey meaning.
- Reread, which leads to interpretation and deeper comprehension.
- Benefit from more practice with the syntax and meaning, which is particularly helpful for English learners.

Assessing students' reading abilities includes both silent and oral reading. To determine what things students have derived from a text through silent reading, invite them to discuss the book or perform a range of tasks after their reading. You can also sample their oral reading to determine how they use decoding skills, employ phrasing, notice punctuation, and use expression appropriate to conveying meaning as they proceed through the text. Oral reading is included in the IRA/NCTE English language arts standards (International Reading Association 1996). It is also specified as one of the four expectations for performance in *Performance Standards: Volume 1—Elementary School, English Language Arts,* published by the National Center on Education and the Economy (1998):

> The student reads aloud, accurately (in the range of 85–90%), familiar material of the quality and complexity illustrated in the sample reading list, and in a way that makes meaning clear to listeners by:
> - self-correcting when subsequent reading indicates an earlier miscue;
> - using a range of cueing systems, e.g. phonics

and context clues, to determine pronunciation and meanings;
> - reading with a rhythm, flow, and meter that sounds like everyday speech (p. 22).

Additionally, the New Standards group recommends that students read aloud to peers or younger children, participate in readers' theater productions, and record reading on audiotape or videotape.

Sources of Information Available to the Reader

Readers use a network of strategies or strategic actions to sustain their reading, the goal of which is the construction of meaning. They use information to:

1. Monitor or "check on" their reading.
2. Search for and use information.
3. Correct their reading.

Strategies are in-the-head actions taken by readers to help them read accurately with understanding. We cannot see these strategies, but we know they are being used because the reader is processing and comprehending text. We observe the reader's *behavior* as evidence of strategies. For more advanced readers, these subtle signals are often not visible, but we may gain insights into the reader's comprehension through their overt behavior— when they talk, draw, or write about the text, for example. We may also sample oral reading periodically for further evidence that the reader is using strategies.

The sources of information on which readers draw (see Figure 18–2) are located in the text and also outside the text. For example, readers possess funds of knowledge about the world and about language that they access as they read. They also access information in the language and illustrations of the text. The categories of information we have defined for young readers are equally valid for advanced readers, although the understandings implied by the categories become much more complex.

Meaning

Readers use meaning to monitor and correct their reading. For beginning readers, using meaning is related to

Sources of Information That Readers Use

Meaning The semantic or meaning system of language Imagery or visual meaning	❖ Meaning from words ❖ Meaning across a text ❖ Meaning across varieties of text (genre) ❖ Personal sets of knowledge: life experience, literary background, and world knowledge
Language Structure The syntactic system of language—the patterns or rules by which words are put together in meaningful phrases and sentences	❖ Sentence structure ❖ Inflectional endings, such as *ing* and *ed* ❖ Phrase units
Phonological and Visual Information The sound system of language—the phonemes in words (what you hear) The orthographic system of language—the letters and letter clusters that make up spelling patterns (what you see)	❖ Sounds in words ❖ Distinctive features of letters ❖ Patterns of letters in words—simple to complex ❖ Punctuation

Figure 18–2. Sources of Information that Readers Use

whether the text makes sense to them and matches what they see in the illustrations. Meaning is, in a sense, straightforward because the texts are simple and clear and they deal with mostly familiar topics. For more advanced readers, meaning becomes much more complex. Let's consider the various ways to think about meaning.

CONSTRUCTING MEANING FROM WORDS

Words have meaning and that meaning changes in relation to the other words that surround them. We often talk about the "vocabulary" in a text and whether or not students know the definitions of words; however, even vocabulary is not a simple concept. As Weaver (1994) has said, "We are able to grasp the meanings of individual words only when we see how they interrelate with each other" (p. 18). The sentences in which words are embedded let us know their meaning and their pronunciation. For example:

Three boys were *present* at the game.
I received a *present* for my birthday.

Harry had to *present* his case.

The spelling of words is also related to meaning:

The *bare* walls were covered with slime.
He could hardly *bear* the tension in the room.
He turned and saw an enormous *bear* crashing through the woods.

Meaning is related to sentence structure and to the content under discussion. For example, the words home and run mean one thing separately, but when they are used together, they mean something quite different. And words may be used metaphorically. You might read about a character who makes a "home run" (meaning she has "met with success") even though she's not playing baseball. Words also have multiple connotations or shades of meaning. An evil character who smirks, "Hello, my little dears," is not exchanging a loving greeting. And the remark "Isn't she a sweetheart?" in reference to a vexing character is ironic.

CONSTRUCTING MEANING ACROSS A TEXT

It is not enough for a reader to grasp the meaning of individual words, even words situated in phrases and sentences. To comprehend, a reader must continually construct meaning while processing an extended text. Readers keep the meaning of the whole text in mind, and this process varies with the kinds of texts they read.

Some texts, to be fully understood, must be read from the beginning. Narratives, biographies, and other texts are constructed so that the reader can accumulate meaning. Readers learn early in the text what the characters are like and how the setting is related to the plot. That information helps them interpret later events, lets them be surprised or pleased with the outcome. Some texts, mainly informational texts, can be read by skipping to the points of interest, but the reader is always aware that if meaning is not clear, he may have to consult other parts of the text. Good readers do not continue to read very long if they are not constructing meaning while processing the print; they search, go back, and consult other sources. In some cases, they abandon the book.

CONSTRUCTING MEANING ACROSS A VARIETY OF TEXTS

Genres are a system for classifying types of texts. A genre is a "family" of written texts that have similar characteristics. We realize that we have an internal sense of these characteristics when we recognize a biography, a memoir, or a folk tale without being told the genre.

Particular genres share common features such as types of characters, settings, actions, typical language, and overall form or structure (how the ideas are organized and presented). Narrative genres tell stories. Expository genres primarily communicate information. And poetic genres express imagery, feelings, or other meaning through a combination of the sound and rhythm of language and the way the print is organized on the page. Often, a piece of literature will contain aspects of two or more genres; the boundaries are not clear. For example, a piece of historical fiction might tell a story but also provide background information about the time period in which it is set; it might also include documents like land deeds, proclamations, or letters.

Many specific genres are included within each of these three major categories. For example, historical fiction, fantasies, and realistic fiction are all forms of narrative. Essays and articles are usually expository. Some informational texts—biographies, for example—even though they present facts, are like narratives in their organization because they tell a story. Ballads and epics are narrative poems; other poetic genres include sonnets, lyrics, blank verse, and so on.

Readers learn that genres are organized in different ways; knowledge of text organization contributes to, and in most texts is essential to, readers' ability to construct meaning. As adults we are unaware of our sense of the underlying structural characteristics of genre, but we continually use the information it provides.

Consider what we encounter as we read a biography. The biography opens at a particular point in time—the person's birth; some moment within his life; or his death. As readers, we know that a biography will recount and illuminate the events of a person's life and that by the end of the book we will know and understand these events. As readers, we organize these events in our head and also, perhaps, associate with each the influences on the character or the emotions he felt. We step into the person's life and search for details that provide clues to a multitude of understandings. We also know that the text is true or represents the biographer's interpretation of the truth. In order to check the accuracy of the text, we draw on what we already know about the person and the times in which he lived. We may connect the text with other biographies or histories we have read to form a fuller picture of the time period and, again, derive a more accurate portrait of the individual. All of these acts of reading are instantly available to us because we know the genre of biography.

CONSTRUCTING AND REVISING PERSONAL SETS OF KNOWLEDGE

Personal experience also figures into the construction of meaning. If you have visited a particular place and then later read a historical novel set in that place, you bring more, or at least different, meanings to your reading of the story. So readers access the author's meaning, but they go further to construct their own unique understandings. In a sense, every reader of a text gains a different set of meanings because of his unique connections with knowledge and the world (both factual and experiential), the personal emotions or memories that might arise, and the sum total of experiences drawn from reading other texts.

Readers use three categories of background knowledge (Figure 18–3):

■ *Life experience*—our personal experiences as we grow up in our families and communities. For example, a student who has experienced the death of a friend or family member brings a different set of meanings to the reading of *A Taste of Blackberries* (Smith 1973) or *Bridge to Terabithia* (Paterson 1977) than a student who has not. One of the values of wide reading is that it allows students to extend their life experiences vicariously. Skilled readers become adept at making connections between their personal lives and the texts they read, even as they read about people in other times or in distant places. In quality narrative texts, the universal human experience transcends time and place. Students also make connections between phenomena they observe firsthand or through technology as they interpret informational texts. Our life experiences enable us to infer from texts, to extend beyond the meaning, and apply the understandings in new and novel ways.

■ *Literary background*—our experience with texts over time. While reading, we actively connect with other texts. Additionally, we draw on our generalized expectations about texts as a support for constructing meaning. For example, to understand the significance of *Tuck Everlasting* (Babbit 1975), which involves many traditional symbols and literary devices, readers are assisted by their mental storehouse of other folk and fairy tales they may have read. As readers accumulate a repertoire of texts, they grow to have expectations for particular authors; they become familiar with styles and types of plots. Children who have had experience with picture books even learn to study the art in texts and develop specific expectations for particular illustrators. Some readers carry this sense of visual meaning into adulthood, as they learn to associate meaning and text interpretation with illustrations. Through wide reading, along with teacher guidance, readers also learn about and internalize the characteristics of the different genres. They develop expectations for the structure and language of mysteries, fantasies, biographies, diaries, joke books, science fiction thrillers, historical accounts, and others. These understandings about how the text is organized make it easier for readers to access and construct meanings.

■ *World knowledge*—the understandings we have about the world and about others. This knowledge is built through direct experiences, such as traveling, as well as through reading and/or studying in the content areas. The more we know, the easier it is to comprehend both narrative and expository texts. Understanding the goals and events of the civil rights movement helps readers comprehend *The Watsons Go to Birmingham–1963* (Curtis 1995), a fictional account of an African-American family, in 1963, traveling to visit relatives in Alabama at the time several children were killed in an African-American church. This body of knowledge would be equally helpful in reading *Martin Luther King, Jr.: A Man Who Changed Things* (Greene 1989). World knowledge is continually revised through experience and reading. The student who reads both books will gain immeasurably—both in general knowledge about how the world works as well as in his more complete and refined knowledge of the civil rights movement.

Language Structure

Readers use language as a source of information in reading. Language has three major systems:

Constructing Meaning from Sets of Knowledge

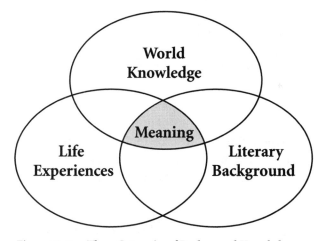

Figure 18–3. Three Categories of Background Knowledge

- The *semantic system* refers to the meaning of language—the words and parts of words that convey meaning as well as the way sentences, paragraphs, and whole texts are interpreted by listeners and readers. We've discussed the strong role meaning has in the reading process. Readers draw on a network of understandings available in the semantic system.
- The *syntactic system* refers to the patterns of rules by which words are put together in meaningful phrases and sentences.
- The *phonological system* refers to the sounds of the language—how the sounds we make are related to meaningful units. Sounds by themselves mean nothing, but when these sounds come together in specific ways, they form words and parts of words that mean something.

Young readers use their knowledge of how language should "sound." We are not talking here about phonology but about the way words are put together. Readers use their knowledge of the rules of syntax (the "grammar" of language) as a way to monitor reading. For example, a child who reads "Mary ran off to see her friends" as "Mary ran of to see her friends" should stop, realizing that the reading didn't "sound right." It didn't sound as English should sound.

The words in the sentence help the reader reduce alternatives or possibilities for what subsequent words would be. Language knowledge also helps the reader constantly monitor what is read. The structure of the sentence helps readers read inflectional endings such as *ed* or *ing* or various verb tenses with accuracy, since their use is related to the syntactic structure. For example, when you read "She was running and suddenly tripped over an exposed root," the word *was* helps you predict the *ing* ending as well as the *ed* ending.

Advanced readers are always using their awareness of syntax to monitor or check on their reading. Sophisticated readers, when reading aloud, will even rework the syntax while they read to make it "sound right" if they miss a cue earlier in the sentence. Advanced readers recognize the phrase units of written language and they attempt to reproduce the author's meaning by using the phrasing. People who read aloud as a profession work on interpretation of text through intonation, rise and fall of voice, and breaks in the reading related to the syntax. If you do not read the phrases right, you may lose the meaning of the sentence, and

that applies to both oral and silent reading. A belabored reading—when the reader bogs down and processes the text one word at a time—is less understandable. Consider this quote from *Harry Potter and the Prisoner of Azkaban* (Rowling 1999):

> Deciding that he'd worry about the Hogsmeade form when he woke up, Harry got back into bed and reached up to cross off another day on the chart he'd made for himself, counting down the days left until his return to Hogwarts. Then he took off his glasses and lay down, eyes open, facing his three birthday cards.
>
> Extremely unusual though he was, at that moment Harry Potter felt just like everyone else—glad, for the first time in his life, that it was his birthday. (p. 15)

Read these paragraphs aloud to yourself, highlighting each phrase. There are several different ways of breaking the quote into phrases. Here is our analysis:

> Deciding that he'd worry about the Hogsmeade
>   form when he woke up,
> Harry got back into bed
> and reached up
> to cross off another day
> on the chart he'd made for himself,
> counting down the days left
> until his return to Hogwarts.
> Then he took off his glasses and lay down,
> eyes open,
> facing his three birthday cards.
> Extremely unusual though he was,
> at that moment
> Harry Potter felt just like everyone else
> —glad,
> for the first time in his life,
> that it was his birthday.

Phrasing makes a difference. For example, saying "Extremely unusual [pause] though he was," would make "though he was" seem an aside, or parenthetical expression. Reading it all at once conveys the appropriate meaning. When students are reading written language, they use everything they know about spoken language as an aid to comprehension as well as to help them read the text accurately.

Phonological and Visual Information

The phonological system of the language has to do with the way listeners construct meaning from the streams of sounds that are produced by talkers. The sounds of language are called "phonemes." Phonemes are categories of sounds that can be heard separately. For example, *eight* has two phonemes, /a/ and /t/. Young children gradually become aware of the sequences of sounds in words. This information is useful for beginning readers because they can then attach the sounds to the symbols or groups of symbols. They also learn to hear the "parts" in words—the syllables. This ability to hear the breaks in words is related to word analysis. For example, a reader or writer might approach a multisyllable word by first thinking about the breaks, analyzing each part, and finally synthesizing the information.

Visual information is what you *see* when you read. The relationships between the phonological system and the print help the reader solve words. The phonemes are mapped onto the graphemes, which are letters or letter clusters that represent sounds. When we read, understandings related to all language systems—meaning, syntax, and phonology—are connected with the written symbols that make up print. To make those connections, we have to be able to perceive the features of print. In fact, young children must learn to "look at print." Perceiving the letters is not an easy task, because there are very small differences between them. This feature makes our writing system efficient. We can make 26 letters with just a few lines, circles, and curves, and we can write the 500,000 to 600,000 words in the English language with just those 26 letters (54 if we count upper and lower case and the typeset *a* and *g*). But the young reader must learn to perceive those small differences, the "distinctive features" that distinguish one letter from another, before he can attach a sound to it. For example, the sound of *a* as in *ate* may be connected to *a* but also to patterns of letter clusters, including: *a-consonant-e; eigh; ay, ey, ea,* and even *et.* During their first years of reading and writing, children build categories of visual patterns that are linked to sounds, and they use this knowledge in connection with meaning and language structure to solve words while reading for meaning.

Advanced readers also use phonological and visual information as they work to solve complex, multisyllable words. Word solving becomes more and more sophisticated, so that it can take place rapidly and usu-ally without conscious thought. Advanced word solvers become adept at breaking down words and using phoneme-grapheme relationships. For example, if you were trying to read the word *cacophony*, you might break it into these parts: *ca co phon y.* Competent fourth-grade readers can *decode* (say the words in) most texts, even advanced ones. The key is whether they can connect meaning and syntax with their decoding skills so that comprehension occurs consistently.

What other kinds of phonological and visual information do advanced readers use? For one thing, the phonological features of a word are simply more available to the reader if he has a large listening/speaking vocabulary. Advanced readers have had time to learn more words, especially if they have heard written language read aloud and engaged in wide reading themselves. When they see a word in print, they make more connections.

In addition, advanced readers attend to a wide variety of visual features of text. We have mentioned the visual patterns of letters in words. But the punctuation is also an important piece of visual information that assists the reader in accessing the phrases of a text. Look again at the example above from *Harry Potter*. What is the role of commas, periods, and the dash in producing an accurate, phrased, fluent reading of the piece? Think about the role of question marks, quotation marks, exclamation marks, parentheses, italics, bold, ellipses, and other marks in everything you read. Layout of text, too, is a visual feature that assists (and sometimes interferes with) reading. The layout of text signals the genre and helps the reader form expectations. For example, think about how paragraphing and side headings help you know how to search for information in expository texts. Advanced readers who have experienced a wide repertoire of texts adjust automatically to the signals sent by these visual features. Weaker readers may find the variety of visual features confusing.

Complex Systems of Strategies for Processing Texts

Readers access meaning, syntax, and phonological/visual information by employing a range of *strategies*. We cannot observe these strategies directly; we must infer them from our students' reading behavior.

Teachers help readers develop and use these in-the-head strategic actions by demonstrating effective ways of working with print and by prompting and reminding students to adopt them. (Examples of supportive teaching actions are described in Chapter 21.)

These *cognitive actions* are what readers do in order to understand text, but they are abstract notions. They occur simultaneously and rapidly, in a coordinated way, whenever readers read. Readers cannot necessarily be aware of and talk about strategies while they are reading, because the very act of thinking about strategies, prompted by talking about them, subtly alters the way the brain is working at the time. Imagine a piano player who is thinking about the movement of his fingers and how they strike the keys rather than feeling and interpreting the piece. It is necessary to learn fingering movements, but playing music eventually requires automatic control of the basic physical strategies.

It is also true that reading is probably far more complex and involves many more strategies than we can mention here. Our categories represent hypotheses, but they are based on observations of behavior. The inner workings of the brain remain largely a mystery, but the deeper we delve into the process and the greater the detail in which we describe behavior, the more refined and complete our hypotheses will be. It helps to think of two broad areas of strategies that work together to help the reader process a text for meaning (see Figure 18–4).

One system of strategies makes it possible for readers to *sustain* their reading of a text by adjusting their rate and style. These strategies keep the momentum of the text going: the reader solves words while extracting meaning from print, uses "repair" strategies that monitor and correct reading, and maintains fluency and expressiveness by processing language and noticing punctuation and other typographical features.

Readers also have a system of strategies for *expanding* their understanding of the concepts and ideas presented in a text. As part of expanding meaning, readers also employ a system of strategies for *making*

connections while reading. These connections help them understand the text in light of their personal experience and their world experience, including content they have learned. They constantly match up and compare their own experiences with what is happening in the text. They compare their current understandings with the information in the text and perhaps revise their sets of knowledge. Readers also make connections between texts they have previously read (or heard read) and the text being read. Readers who have a broad background of experience with text know how information is typically organized in different kinds of texts.

These systems for expanding meaning work for both fiction and nonfiction texts, although the process is somewhat different for each. In fiction texts, readers continually summarize so as to remember the gist of the story, important details, events, actions of characters, and visual images. They make inferences about the motives, thoughts, and feelings of characters or about the meaning of particular events or aspects of settings;

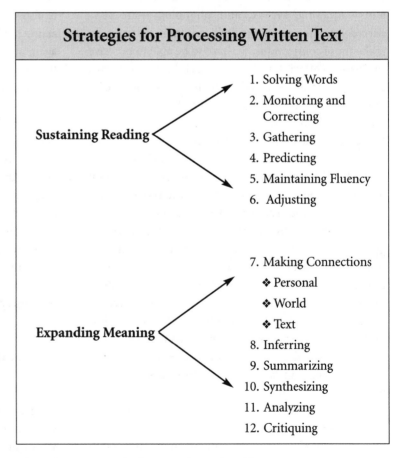

Figure 18–4. Strategies for Processing Written Text

they synthesize information, thinking about the meaning of the whole story or an important part of it; and they may even criticize aspects of the plot, the actions of characters, or the way the writer presents information.

For nonfiction texts, readers also summarize information so that they are deriving information as they go. They put ideas together to make inferences and draw conclusions, and they also synthesize ideas and concepts by integrating information with what they already know. They may criticize what they read, asking whether the text is accurate or presents information fairly.

You may feel that these strategies overlap, and they do. All of these cognitive actions (and probably more that we have not yet conceptualized) are rapid, complex, and interrelated. Our goal as teachers is to become better at hypothesizing what the reader is doing so that we can support ongoing development. Naming and talking about in-the-head strategies helps us to increase our awareness.

Strategies for Sustaining Reading

Readers have strategies, largely unconscious, that allow them to move through a text, picking up essential information in a smooth and fluent way. They use meaning, language, and visual information "on the run" as their eyes move across the print.

By second or third grade, most students have developed a reading process but are still refining their strategies as they encounter more difficult and varied texts. The basic, interrelated strategy systems for sustaining reading include ways to solve words, check on and correct reading, maintain fluency, anticipate and locate information, and vary reading (see Figure 18–5). We are largely unaware of these sustaining strategies because we use them automatically.

SOLVING WORDS

Word solving involves taking action to read a particular word while keeping the overall meaning of the text in mind. Readers employ a wide range of word-solving strategies, and in so doing, they access meaning, syntax, and visual information. Knowing the meaning of words and accumulating meaning from the text helps the reader to narrow the possibilities in the process of word-solving; the same is true of syntactic information. This attention to meaning and syntax is used in combination with the analytic skills by which readers access visual information. Good word solvers:

- Use the meaning and language of the text along with the print information.
- Attend to the visual features needed to solve the word quickly.
- Recognize most words instantly.
- Use letters and letter clusters at the beginning, middle, and end of words.
- Draw from their knowledge of words they can read to solve unfamiliar words.
- Use base words to analyze longer, unfamiliar words.
- Use parts within wholes of written language.
- Analyze words from left to right, using letters and letter clusters.
- Combine strategies in a flexible way.
- Monitor their reading to be sure it "looks right"— that it fits with the visual information in the print.

MONITORING AND CORRECTING

Students use strategies to access meaning, syntax, and visual information to monitor understanding and accuracy in reading. Most important, students need to know whether what they are reading makes sense. They bring their prior knowledge to the reading. For developing readers, just thinking about whether the reading makes sense means constantly monitoring the language of the text.

For advanced readers, the process becomes more complex. It might entail drawing on literary knowledge to determine whether a plot is probable or a character believable. It might mean matching the text information with what is already known about the period of history in which the text is set to determine the authenticity of the piece and understand it more fully. Readers might surmise whether a text reflects a particular author's style or revel in the clever way an author has mixed two genres. In reading fantasy, advanced readers might examine the techniques the writer uses to create an imaginary world and compare the techniques to those of other fantasy writers. Monitoring understanding centers on an active engagement with the author of the text while continually asking, *How does my understanding fit with what I am reading?*

When meaning "breaks down," good readers know it. They rely on a variety of strategies to correct the situation. They may recognize that something doesn't fit, but they continue reading, hoping to obtain additional information that will help them overcome their temporary breakdown. The point is, they are aware of the

Systems of Strategies for Processing Texts

Strategic Actions for Sustaining Reading

	Definition	Readers need to:	Teachers help readers learn how to:
Solving Words	To use problem solving strategies to recognize, decode, and/or understand the meaning of words.	Use a range of problem-solving strategies to take words apart and understand word meaning while reading continuous written text.	❖ Recognize known words. ❖ Use letters and letter clusters at the beginning, middle, and end of words. ❖ Use syllables to break up words for analysis. ❖ Use parts and base words within wholes of written language. ❖ Analyze words from left to right, using letters and letter clusters. ❖ Use known words, word parts, and base words in solving new words. ❖ Use meaningful parts of words (e.g., roots) to solve words. ❖ Use letter/sound relationships and visual information in connection with meaning and language knowledge. ❖ Combine word-solving strategies in flexible ways. ❖ Use language and text meaning to gain individual word meaning.
Monitoring and Correcting	To check on and regulate performance.	Check on whether their reading sounds right, looks right, and makes sense.	❖ Notice when they do not understand. ❖ Search for and use information that will increase understanding. ❖ Notice mismatches between their responses and the print. ❖ Self-correct when essential for understanding or oral reading performance. ❖ Use multiple sources of information to check on and correct reading.
Gathering	To pick up, accumulate, or bring together.	Search for, identify and select different sources of information from the text.	❖ Search for, identify, pick up and put together all sources of information from the text. ❖ Locate and use the important language, ideas and their organization as presented in a text. ❖ Grasp the literal meaning of the text. ❖ Recognize and use print features (punctuation, italics, headings, etc.) and graphic features (diagrams, photographs, illustrations) to assist in identifying information. ❖ Recognize and use organizational features (index, glossary, table of contents) to identify information.

Figure 18–5. Strategic Actions for Sustaining Reading

Strategic Actions for Sustaining Reading (continued)

	Definition	Readers need to:	Teachers help readers learn how to:
Predicting	To say in advance what one believes will happen.	Anticipate what will follow while reading continuous text.	❖ Use knowledge of language syntax to narrow possibilities and reduce the conceptual load on decoding words. ❖ Use language redundancy for efficient word reading. ❖ Use knowledge of characters, plot, setting, or theme to predict what will happen next in a text. ❖ Generate expectations based on genre, author, or topic. ❖ Predict kinds of information available given the topic or the organization of the text.
Maintaining Fluency	To read easily and smoothly.	Integrate sources of information in a smoothly operating process that results in smooth, phrased, and expressive reading.	❖ Use knowledge of language to keep reading moving forward. ❖ Maintain a good rate while reading, slowing down to problem solve and speeding up again. ❖ Use rapid automatic word recognition and word-solving skills. ❖ Change voice tone and use pausing to create phrase units that convey meaning. ❖ Read punctuation and phrase units to reflect the intended meaning of the text.
Adjusting	To adapt as needed to fit the circumstances and surroundings.	Read in different ways as appropriate to purpose and type of text.	❖ Vary rate and intonation as appropriate to text, audience, and purpose. ❖ Vary speed to provide for the amount of problem solving needed. ❖ Adjust reading for different genres and different purposes.

Figure 18–5. Strategic Actions for Sustaining Reading (continued)

misfit and are searching for answers. Sometimes the answer is provided later in the text and sometimes it isn't. Readers may stop and think, search back in the text, discuss the problem with someone, or use reference tools. Readers know how to "sort" the information in the story, focusing on the key details that will enable them to interpret the story. Skillful readers do what is most efficient and leads to satisfactory understanding.

The reader also monitors accuracy by using a wide range of word-solving skills related to visual and phonological information. Advanced readers know a large number of words that they recognize quickly and automatically. We are not consciously aware of this quick word recognition, but we consciously attend to a word that is unfamiliar, is used in a slightly unfamiliar form, or doesn't seem to fit the sentence's meaning or

313

syntax. When reading aloud, we might also stop if we are not sure how to pronounce a word.

What's significant about the monitoring strategies is that students are able to monitor themselves. They know when they have departed from the accuracy of the text, at least when that departure creates a breakdown in meaning. They know not only that they have made errors but also how to correct errors. Sometimes, students correct themselves mentally while reading aloud, noting the error but not overtly changing it. This monitoring and correcting system relies on the same set of strategies that readers use for word solving. In addition, readers notice and use punctuation to monitor and correct their reading. For example, a reader might encounter a long sentence and lose the meaning by the end of it. A quick look back, however, might reveal punctuation patterns that aid understanding.

This process is most evident when individuals read aloud; they may read the words accurately but then go back to change the emphasis. For example, Devon was reading *Arthur Rocks with Binky* (Brown 1998). The text says: "If you say so. But right now I'm in the middle of the show. Can you wait for the commercial?" (p. 22).

He read the first two sentences as if they were "If you say, 'So but right now I'm in the middle of the show,'" ignoring the period after *so*. At that point, he returned to the beginning of the line and read the expression "If you say so" as a unit, letting his voice drop to indicate a period and then resuming reading as if the speaker were continuing. He was indicating both an awareness of punctuation (the period) as well as an awareness of a larger unit of meaning ("if you say so").

GATHERING INFORMATION

As they read, readers use strategies to interpret texts and to connect them with prior knowledge. To make these inferences and interpretations, they need information. They use strategies to search constantly for important information. The skilled reader easily derives information from the text; and indeed, it is this recognizing and locating information that makes strategies such as inferring possible. The reader grasps the literal meaning of the text and is able to follow important events and characters. In nonfiction text, the reader selects important facts and begins to summarize or weave them together.

To help them gather information, readers continually ask themselves questions that they want answered from the reading. These questions are seldom explicit; rather, they are implied by the readers' searching behavior. Readers find ideas to wonder about, which makes reading more purposeful and efficient. Questioning signifies an active reader—one who is having a conversation with the author about the topic.

Readers know how to gather information from both narrative and expository texts. In each of these text groups, the type of information being sought is different. Readers have strategies for approaching each type of text, and those strategies are critical to making meaning successfully. Research indicates that good readers use knowledge of text structure in this process (Beck, Omanson, and McKeown 1982; Englert and Hiebert 1984). Meaning is inherent in the text and readers constantly look for it. They might, for example, look for the details that are most important in making judgments about a character, in interpreting an event, in answering questions that arise in the mind of the reader or in the minds of characters. Informational texts pose particular problems for some students, who collect a great deal of information but have difficulty in sorting out the larger concepts.

Literary knowledge is particularly helpful to students in finding and using information. A reader who can access knowledge of how different texts are organized has a better idea of how and where to look for the information he needs. He knows, for example, that aspects of setting are usually described at the beginning of the piece or at the beginning of a new section. He knows to pay attention to ways that characters reveal themselves (through their own thoughts and through the perspectives of others, for example) and knows how to relate those revelations to aspects of plot. Advanced readers often also know how particular authors reveal important information: for example, through symbolism, description of artifacts, or conversation among characters. In regard to expository texts, a reader knows that the author presents information in different ways. For example, in an expository essay, the reader may find charts, diagrams, maps, legends, and photograph captions. The graphic information must be integrated with the body of the text in the construction of meaning.

Readers also find themselves looking for further visual information. The example of Devon's reading illustrates a search for information about phrases defined by punctuation. Sometimes the information needed is in a word and the reader is required to use word-solving skills to sample more visual information, to look at prefixes or endings, or to use any kind of visual information that will help determine the precise meaning of the text. For example, it makes a difference whether a character is *obvious* or *oblivious*; one would want to do a precise reading, which might not be available simply by sampling visual information in relation to contextual information.

PREDICTING

We can think of the act of predicting in several ways, each one related to sources of information. Knowledge of language helps propel the reading forward. Clay (1991) refers to a "feed forward" system that powers the reading process. Meaning and syntax work together to help the reader anticipate and predict in a way that makes processing the information more efficient. Good readers attend to visual information but benefit from the redundancy of language. For example, think how plurality is signaled in the sentence "The three runners wound their way downhill, the sounds of their feet echoing tiredly up the steep canyon walls": the words *three, their* (twice), and *feet*, and the *s* at the end of *runners, sounds*, and *walls*. The reader has more signals than he needs to capture the idea that there is more than one runner. Visual images are also signaled by more than one word: *wound, downhill, echoing, steep,* and *canyon walls* all help convey a picture of the setting. Readers' knowledge of syntactic and semantic systems make it easier to check on their reading and to reduce alternatives.

Good readers continually search and access information that enables them to build meaning before they read a text, while they are reading it, and as they reflect on it after reading. They simultaneously access world knowledge, literary knowledge, and personal knowledge; and they use this information to construct meaning of words (and often, their pronunciation), sentences, paragraphs, pages, chapters, and whole texts of all kinds. Both world and personal knowledge are concept storehouses that students bring to the texts they are reading.

Students bring their understandings about texts, authors, and illustrators to every new textual experience. When they search to understand characters, for example, and anticipate their actions, thoughts, and feelings, they activate knowledge from literature they have read or heard read. They use what they know about text structure to help them find information and understand how a story or expository essay or poem works. This background knowledge of the kinds of syntactic patterns that are found in different genres of written texts helps them anticipate the language of the particular text they are reading.

Students may be highly aware of prior knowledge and literary knowledge when they read series books, like Beverly Cleary's *Beezus and Ramona* books, *Amelia Bedelia* (Parish), or *Harry Potter* (J.K. Rowling). Their reading is shaped by their expectations:

■ They already know most of the people in the book.
■ They know where they live and what their lives are like.
■ They remember their past mistakes and funny events of the past.
■ They have an idea how they will react in new problem situations.

Many children have grown up knowing the characters in *Little Women* (Alcott) or *Little House on the Prairie* (Ingalls Wilder) almost as if they were friends or family members. Reading series books helps students develop the strategies related to anticipating and predicting while reading.

MAINTAINING FLUENCY

A range of strategies work together to help the reader sustain fluency and momentum, especially when reading longer texts. Fluency is rapid reading phrased so that the reader reproduces the author's intended syntax (grammatical structures) while constructing meaning. Successful readers read fluently. When they read aloud, they sound like good readers because their voices rise and fall, they use appropriate pitch, stress words effectively to convey meaning, and pause appropriately. When they read silently, they process the print at a good rate, moving forward with momentum, gathering meaning, again seemingly without effort.

Fluency may involve:

■ Using the "feed forward" mechanisms of meaning and syntax to anticipate the text.
■ Reading at a good rate of speed.
■ Recognizing words rapidly and automatically.
■ Decoding words rapidly and apparently effortlessly.
■ Attending to language and noticing punctuation to produce accurate phrasing.

■ Changing pitch or voice to reflect punctuation.

■ Slowing down to problem-solve when needed but speeding up again for reading that is mostly smooth and expressive.

Fluency results from a complex interrelationship of processes that is more than the sum of these component parts. Accuracy is important but is not enough to produce fluent reading. Fluent readers use language syntax, phrasing, and expression in a way that is related to meaning and goes far beyond simply being able to read words.

Fluency relates significantly to comprehension. Results of the NAEP Integrated Reading Performance Record assessment for fourth graders suggest that there is a high correlation between accuracy, rate, fluency, and scores on comprehension (Pinnell et al. 1995). The fluent reader is not only fast but flexible; maximum attention is given to meaning and phrasing because of the interrelation of the processes above.

ADJUSTING READING

Reading varies according to your purpose and the text. Consider *why* you are reading something. You may:

■ Read slowly, searching for and remembering important information.

■ Scan for the information you need, ignoring everything else.

■ Reread parts of a text to be sure you understand it.

■ "Get lost" in the text, focusing so strongly on the story that you read it avidly, rapidly, with personal and emotional responses.

■ Read and make notes to use later in conversation or in a presentation.

■ Read slowly, savoring the language.

■ Practice reading, trying out different emphases, for later performance.

■ Search back and forth to determine how a text is organized.

■ Engage with a difficult text on an interesting topic, understanding that more problem solving will be required.

■ Read sections of a text in between taking action of some kind (for example, following directions on setting up a computer).

These are only a few of the ways that competent readers vary speed and style to suit particular purposes. As students learn to read, they also learn how to vary reading. The implication here is that classroom programs must provide the variety needed for readers to learn to make these adjustments. Students need opportunities to read for many different purposes. They need to read texts on a variety of topics and from a range of genres.

Strategies for Expanding Meaning

Strategies for connecting, summarizing, inferring, synthesizing, analyzing, and critiquing add considerably to the power of the reader. These strategies are often unconscious acts; however, they usually also involve conscious attention to aspects of text. (See Figure 18–6.)

MAKING CONNECTIONS

Readers constantly search for connections between what they already know and what they encounter in a text. They may connect a text to something they have experienced in their personal lives or to the "world" knowledge that they have developed over time—both in and out of school. Literary experiences figure strongly in a reader's ability to make connections between texts as they start to recognize similar language, ways of organizing, types of characters, or settings.

In a sense, each reading of a book is unique because readers rely on strategies for connecting the text with their own life experiences. Active readers use strategies for connecting the text to what they know and feel. While we recognize the universals of human experience, no two people live the *same* lives and, therefore, no two people can interpret a text exactly the same way. Visual images drawn from the text, for example, are highly personal.

The emotions evoked by the events of the text are linked with emotions experienced in real life or while reading other texts. *Pinballs* (Byars 1977) is a poignant story about orphans. A child who has grown up with one or no parents will interpret the book differently than a child who has grown up in a two-parent home. In *Yang the Youngest and His Terrible Ear* (Namioka 1994), a young Asian boy is growing up in a musical family but would rather play baseball. Students who have experienced the weight of stereotypes or unrealistic family expectations will bring different feelings and meanings to the book than students who are reading more objectively. Our response to texts is really about ourselves; reading helps us plumb our own feelings, emotions, and dreams, and all of these come into play when we connect with texts.

Systems of Strategies for Processing Texts

Strategic Actions for Expanding Meaning

	Definition	*Readers need to:*	*Teachers help readers learn how to:*
Connecting	To show or think of how two or more things as related. To relate one aspect to another.	Search for and use connections to the funds of knowledge that they have gained from personal, world, and text experiences.	❖ Understand/develop purposes for reading texts. ❖ Connect knowledge of topic, plot, characters, or setting to personal experiences and their knowledge of the world and other texts. ❖ Bring background knowledge to their reading of a text. ❖ Interpret texts using personal experience and background of world knowledge. ❖ Make connections between and among texts they have read, seeing similarities and differences.
Inferring	To arrive at a decision or opinion by reasoning from known facts or evidence.	Go beyond the literal meaning of a text to derive what is not there but is implied.	❖ Construct theories that explain how characters behave or plot unfolds. ❖ Have empathy for fictional or historical characters. ❖ Use background knowledge and information from the text to form tentative theories as to the significance of the events. ❖ Create sensory images related to character, plot, setting, theme, or topic. ❖ Understand what is not stated but is implied in the text.
Summarizing	To present the substance or general idea in brief form.	Put together important information while reading.	❖ Relate important ideas, events, details, or other information related to comprehending the whole text. ❖ Continually organize information extracted from print. ❖ Distinguish between summarizing important information and remembering/retelling all the details of a text. ❖ Select important information after reading and bring together in a concise report.
Synthesizing	To bring together parts or elements to form a whole.	Put together information from the text and from personal, world, and literary knowledge to create new understandings.	❖ Relate important ideas to each other. ❖ Deepen understanding of an idea, concept, or topic by integrating new knowledge with prior knowledge. ❖ Expand personal understandings by incorporating the "lived through" experiences from texts.

Figure 18–6. Strategic Actions for Expanding Meaning

Strategic Actions for Expanding Meaning (continued)

	Definition	Readers need to:	Teachers help readers learn how to:
Analyzing	To separate and break up a whole into its parts to find out their nature, proportion, function, interrelationship, or properties.	Closely examine elements of a text to achieve greater understanding of how it is crafted or constructed.	❖ Recognize plot development based on knowledge of text structure. ❖ Recognize and use text characteristics related to genre. ❖ Discover the underlying organization of a text related to topic, genre, or theme. ❖ Recognize the author's use of language to communicate meaning and emotions in various ways. ❖ Analyze elements of a fiction or nonfiction text to gain an understanding of how the author communicated meaning. ❖ Analyze illustrations or other graphic features as to how they evoke aesthetic responses and communicate meaning. ❖ Recognize and use graphic features of texts (such as maps and charts) to increase understanding. ❖ Recognize and use literary features of texts to expand understanding. ❖ Analyze the whole text to determine how illustrations, text, and format communicate meaning in an integrated way.
Critiquing	To make judgements through analyzing the qualities and evaluating them.	Judge or evaluate a text based on personal, world, or text knowledge.	❖ Assess whether a text is consistent with what is known through life experiences. ❖ Judge whether a text is authentic in terms of plot or setting. ❖ Evaluate the writer's craft in light of appropriateness of genre, use of language, or other criteria. ❖ Judge the accuracy of information. ❖ Judge the qualifications of the writer to produce an authentic fiction or nonfiction text. ❖ Examine and discover bias in texts. ❖ Appreciate the aesthetic qualities of a text.

Figure 18–6. Strategic Actions for Expanding Meaning (continued)

Strategies for making connections help the reader in a wide variety of ways, including connecting to other books:

▪ In the same series.
▪ In the same genre.
▪ By the same author or illustrator.
▪ In the same setting or historical period.
▪ About the same character or similar characters.
▪ About the same culture/ethnic group.
▪ On the same topic or theme.
▪ On the same social issue.
▪ About children in the same age group.

Many young readers deliberately seek these connections as they devour books about horses, heroes, baseball, the Holocaust, or biographies of young girls in various periods of history. These strategies for making connections are related to strategies for predicting, but they are slightly different. Strategies for making connections refer to the reader's continual building of networks of connections in the head while reading and remembering texts.

It is readers' ability to go far beyond the particular text they are reading—to extend the meaning of texts—that:

- Deepens comprehension.
- Changes the reader in some permanent way.
- Adds to readers' understanding of life and the world.
- Motivates readers to engage with other texts.
- Expands the reader's language system—both oral and written.
- Promotes enjoyment.

INFERRING

Readers infer from the text during and after reading. Making an inference means to induce or hypothesize, to make conclusions based on information from the text. Inferring means going beyond the words of the text to make a judgment about what is not there but is implied. Readers make inferences about how characters feel even though the author may not have explicitly written about the characters' feelings. They make judgments about the significance of events and how those events reflect turning points in the plot without an explicit explanation from the author. They make judgments about the true or deeper meaning of the text— what it symbolizes or what the underlying message might be. Skillful readers often reflect on what the author is really trying to say.

SUMMARIZING

Readers constantly extract information from a text and accumulate that extracted information in summary form. Summarizing does not mean simply that readers can "sum up" a text afterward, although that is part of the skill. It means that readers are remembering the text in "put together" ways so that they can engage in ongoing interpretation. It is summarizing as you read,

putting together what you have read so far as you continue to process the text.

SYNTHESIZING

Readers also synthesize information from the text. They reconfigure it so that they can add it to and integrate it with their own stores of knowledge—personal, world, and literary. They address such questions as:

- What does the information in this text mean to me?
- What information is useful to me and how does it fit (or not fit) with what I already know?
- What am I taking away with me?

A reader who is expanding meaning by synthesizing is bringing together information derived from the text with background knowledge to develop a whole that is greater than the parts. The understandings that arise from synthesizing are new.

ANALYZING

Readers who find reading pleasurable are often motivated to examine elements of a text closely to understand better how it is constructed. Your memories of analyzing texts are probably connected to a literature course in which you "picked apart" great literary works or poems. Depending on the text and the method of instruction, you may or may not have enjoyed this process. What we are talking about here is helping upper elementary students discover how writers create the works that evoke such meanings in us when we read them. Analyzing can help us understand how a text "works" and can boost comprehension in many ways.

We want our students to discover how texts are organized to provide important information and to understand how language is used to convey meaning. Readers who recognize a particular genre (fantasy, for example) can use the features of that genre to support their understanding. If you read *Harry Potter* and recognize it as a fantasy, you know the events do not have to be "real" but must fit together in some other coherent way. You are on the lookout for humorous parts and are always ready for magic. The same is true of a mystery; you know that you should be searching for clues and noticing details. At the same time, you are watching for understanding that can be applied in the real world.

Supported analysis can help young readers develop and deepen their comprehension strategies. They learn to recognize plot and character development, and they can make their understandings explicit through talk, writing, or drawing. They analyze the writer's craft and develop new ways of using and understanding language. They may analyze texts as coherent wholes, pointing out the significant ways that the text, illustrations, and format work together to communicate a meaning that has greater significance than the elements or parts. This kind of analysis goes well beyond simply understanding and interpreting a text. It builds insight into the way texts are constructed.

CRITIQUING

Readers use strategies to reflect on their reading and evaluate it. In a sense, readers are always making judgments while they are reading a text. Sometimes those judgments are the difference between keeping on with or abandoning the text. A reader makes judgments about whether the text is interesting to him, whether he finds the characters or events engaging, whether the characters seem real, or whether the events or characters seem believable. To hold the reader, a novel must draw him into another world so that he is absorbed.

Readers are always monitoring and judging whether they are engaged. An informational piece must offer new information or a new angle on the facts in order to capture reader interest. After reading, individuals typically reflect in an evaluative, critical way on what they have just read. Indeed, if we decide the piece was truly worthwhile, we may choose to share it with others.

Readers summarize and synthesize information so that they can integrate it with their own stores of knowledge; however, as teachers, we want our students to be selective about what they choose to embrace and integrate. For example, even if our students thoroughly enjoy the story *The Indian in the Cupboard* (Banks 1981), in which a young boy finds a Native American toy "action figure" fully alive in an old cupboard, we want them to notice and be critical of the inherent stereotypes. We also want them to think about how women are portrayed in many books—often not as strong characters but dependent on others and overly concerned with appearance. The point is not to be suspicious or highly critical of every selection but to be ever thoughtful and alert about what to accept and what to question during and after reading.

Being critical means thoughtfully considering both the strengths and challenges of every aspect of the text. After reading *Sarah, Plain and Tall* (MacLachlan 1985), a touching, poignant story set in the early 1900s about a woman who becomes a "mail order" bride and leaves her home by the sea to take care of two motherless children, readers might consider how Sarah grew to love the children more than the sea. What's more, being critical means using the information embedded in texts to help you think about social issues and human problems. For example, reading books like *My Brother Sam Is Dead* (Collier and Collier 1974) or *The Faithful Elephants* (Suchiya 1988) might help a student think critically about the consequences of war. Readers are asking: What do I think about this text? Was it true? Was it effective? What made it effective [or not]? Did I like this author and would others? Did the author express meanings, even covert meanings, with which I disagree? From whose perspective was it told? Is there part of the story that is not told?

INTERRELATED SYSTEMS OF STRATEGIES

These sets of strategic actions are not discrete entities. The reading process is highly complex, and cognitive operations cannot be compartmentalized. We have attempted to identify important processes and critical aspects of this highly complex thinking process. Readers employ these strategic actions in a fluid way before, during, and after reading. Some strategic actions are more important before reading, some are more important during reading, and some are more important after reading; nevertheless, they all work together for the full construction of meaning.

Suggestions for Professional Development

Select a text from your grade-level collection that you would expect to use for guided reading, one that would be appropriate for almost all your students at some time during the year.

Photocopy a section of the text (about two pages, or between 300 and 500 words) and ask your grade-level colleagues to work with you to analyze what this text requires of readers. Give participants a copy of the text and ask them to address these questions:

1. What information do readers need to bring to the text in order to read it with understanding? Consider personal knowledge, world knowledge, and literary knowledge.
2. As readers process the text, what new information will they gain? What meanings will they construct? How will these meanings be integrated with their existing knowledge?
   - Are there places in the text that are likely to lead to confusion? What strategies will readers need to resolve the confusion?
   - What word-solving challenges will this text offer? Does it contain words that students know but must understand in new ways (word connotations) in order to comprehend the text? Are there multisyllable words that students will need to break apart and relate to other words or parts of words that they know?

- Are there language structures in the text that students may never have heard before?
- Are there any challenges in terms of text organization or format? Does the print layout assist readers or offer challenge?

3. Now take the text and mark phrase units with slashes (see our analysis of *Harry Potter* in this chapter). You will probably need to read the selection aloud to do this. Share your insights regarding the phrasing. There is no single way to pick out phrase units. There will be much agreement, however, and you may find some subtle differences in meaning with the different interpretations. Some phrase units will be marked by punctuation, and some will not. Discuss how phrasing and punctuation are related to comprehension.
4. As a follow up to the session, ask each participant to invite a student to read the selection and tape-record the reading. Listen to the recordings in another session and analyze the students' phrasing and the difficulties they encounter.

## CHAPTER NINETEEN

TEACHING FOR COMPREHENDING WRITTEN TEXT: ACROSS THE LANGUAGE AND LITERACY FRAMEWORK

Reading words without understanding is a string of meaningless noise.
— DON HOLDAWAY

The Statue of Liberty stands as a profound symbol of hope, beckoning all those who have immigrated to our shores in search of a better life. We may marvel at its impressive size and the monumental engineering effort it represents. We may be touched by the story of school children saving their pennies to support it. But the important thing about the Statue of Liberty is what it stands for and how that makes us feel.

When you visit the Statue of Liberty, you may recall stories from your family history, handed down from generation to generation, and realize that your own relatives saw it as they arrived in North America. Your experience may help you understand and empathize with new immigrants. Or you might relive a childhood trip to the statue or think about postcards from a favorite aunt who visited the statue years ago. Or you might recall books you have read in which the statue appears, remembering characters that seem as real as people you've known.

Experiences are more meaningful if we share them with friends or family members. We talk together about our interpretations, connections, and hypotheses. We share interesting tidbits and big ideas. People who have shared an experience can remember it together and discuss it in ways that expand their understanding of the experience. Their shared meanings ultimately transcend their individual understandings.

The nature of thinking means that we are never alone—we carry with us all the meanings we have previously created with others through our common life experiences and our common encounters with books, films, music, and art. Certainly, we are always making connections with those texts we have previously experienced; we use them as companions in making mean-

ing. As the poet Tennyson said, "I am a part of all that I have met." The greater our life experiences—the broader our knowledge of the world—the richer the meanings we take from every subsequent experience.

Our Statue of Liberty metaphor is meant to convey one explicit understanding: *the important thing about reading is comprehension*. Reading is the construction of meaning. Without understanding, there is no reading. Everything about reading is directed toward making meanings that are infused with active curiosity, emotion, and satisfaction. When we read, we pick up information and our minds work continuously to:

■ Connect that information to what we already know.
■ Remember what is important.
■ Adjust our funds of knowledge to incorporate new ideas or interpret them in a different way.
■ Read "between the lines" to get at deeper meaning.
■ Evaluate information and ideas.

As our eyes rapidly scan print to access visual information, our brains engage in fast, complex operations. When we try to describe these operations, we're often left with lists of behaviors that often sound like "steps". Yet there is nothing linear about reading.

Let's compare reading to swimming: as you swim, you simultaneously move all parts of your body in an orchestrated and streamlined way. You know when to glide and when to kick forward, when to breathe and close your air passages. Your mind and body feel the water's buoyancy and motion, and adjust. You know whether you are taking in enough air or staying warm enough.

Clearly, swimming is not linear. You don't first kick your legs and then remember to breathe. You must do everything at once in a coordinated way. You cannot even learn swimming motions one at a time, because all are necessary to move through the water. If you do nothing but move your arms, you may sink; a beginner must experience the buoyancy of water in connection with breathing and moving her body.

Reading is a hundred times more complicated than swimming. The brain is far more complex than we can describe; it cannot be neatly divided. A strategy is not an isolated process. It is a network of in-the-head operations that work together to achieve a goal that is related to wholeness of meaning for the reader. Teacher support can help readers continually refine and develop these networks.

Readers in the upper elementary grades are still expanding and fine-tuning their own constructions of the reading process. Since reading *is* comprehension, our overarching teaching goal is to help our students develop a wide range of comprehending strategies. To help us talk and think about these strategies we have categorized them into two sets of systems: one for sustaining the reading process and one for expanding meaning (see Chapter 18). Teachers can support a reader's development of comprehending strategies across the language and literacy framework and especially in the reading workshop. However, elements of the entire framework ground and extend meaning for the readers.

The Centrality of Comprehension

Comprehension is central to every aspect of schooling. As teachers, our attention is divided as we:

- Watch for evidence that students understand.
- Adjust our teaching when we see behavior indicating understanding has been lost.
- Demonstrate ways of getting to the meaning of text and going beyond it.
- Prompt students to make connections and inferences while reading.
- Ask students to reflect on their reading and extend meaning.

There is no one way to teach for comprehension. Note that we tend to insert the preposition *for* to

remind us that comprehension takes place in the brain of the reader. We can bring an effective technique (for example, noticing an author's ability to evoke images) to students' attention, but we cannot give it to them directly. They must construct a network of techniques for themselves. This is why as teachers we consistently attend to comprehension across many instructional contexts.

A powerful strategy such as connecting a text to one's personal experience cannot be taught in one minilesson, reinforced, and then considered "covered." Whenever we address comprehension, we risk simplifying a complex process. We do not propose a "comprehension curriculum" that is delivered in a linear way, because we need to work on all aspects of a complex process at the same time. We are required to work "on all fronts" to keep the process working well. There is, however, a great deal we can do to support and extend students' comprehending strategies through effective teaching.

Comprehension is not something that happens *after* reading. Comprehension is the thinking we do before, during, *and* after reading. In the past, many publishers and teachers have erroneously thought that "teaching comprehension" hinged on the retelling of a story or on the list of questions to ask after students had read a text or part of one. In fact, those questions only *tested* comprehension and didn't do a very good job of that.

There is nothing wrong with asking questions when you really want to know what your students are thinking. However, asking a series of "comprehension questions" (an interrogation!) serves no purpose. After you read a book like *Fortune's Rocks*, by Anita Shreve (1999), you long for a conversation with a friend who has read the book too. Your friend might begin by asking you what you enjoyed most about the book, and you may respond emotionally, explaining how and why the book hit home for you. You might discuss the technical aspects of the author's writing style and the fact that the point of view constantly shifts. You might share other written accounts of strong women caught in the restrictive conventions of their times or caught up in passions they cannot control and do not understand.

While you'd enjoy the natural give and take of a true conversation, at no time would either you or your friend lapse into an "instructional inquisition"—asking one question after another—to test the other's comprehension. Indeed, we chuckle at the very thought.

Retelling is commonly used as a tool for assessment and/or a regular part of instruction. You will want to be careful not to overuse this technique. If retelling means students simply repeat everything they can remember after reading a text, then the task is one of memory. Students can learn to do it well, but it is time-consuming and may become a formulaic exercise that does not involve summarizing and synthesizing information.

After all, remembering everything in the story or informational piece is not the critical act of comprehension. The reader must select important information, weave it together, and integrate it with background knowledge. (In some contexts, however, retellings are scored lower if the reader adds related information from his own experience!) Reading is about *responding* to reading. We would not want our students to read solely for the purpose of delivering a verbatim account of their texts.

Comprehension is integral to reading; indeed, understanding should occur before, during, and after reading. Readers employ strategies for making meaning from the time they consider reading a text to long after they have read it, often encountering new experiences or acquiring new information that provides deeper insight. For example, you may have read *The Diary of Anne Frank* (1952) as a child. As you watch a documentary on the Holocaust or read *Shindler's List* (Keneally 1993), you may recall reading Anne's diary and realize anew what courage it took for those Dutch citizens to hide the Frank family. Your new understanding will be enhanced by your childhood familiarity with Anne and her story, and, in turn, your understanding of *The Dairy of Anne Frank* will change.

How Comprehension Works

To illustrate how the systems of comprehension strategies work together, we invite you to think about your own reading of "Shells," a short story by Cynthia Rylant (*Every Living Thing* 1985). (This book of short stories is ideal for guided reading. Each story stands alone and is rich with meaning. Upper elementary students relate to the topics and bring meaning to them.) Read the story, which is reprinted in Figure 19–1, now.

Your Response Before Reading "Shells"

Most likely, our description of the author, title, and genre set up immediate expectations. For example:

■ If you have read other stories by Cynthia Rylant, you may have expected an air of poignancy, a reflective mood, or an exploration of something sad or nostalgic. You may have expected a story about human relationships, or one that reflects an appreciation of life, of nature, or of family.

■ Knowing that you would be reading fiction may also have created expectations. You knew that the piece could be realistic or a fantasy; it might be sad or humorous. Since the genre was a short story, you knew the plot would move quickly and that both characters and setting would be presented immediately. Character change would occur rapidly and might be tied to one culminating event. After all, a short story is only a few pages; you expected that the problem would be resolved quickly.

■ The title may have suggested that the setting would be a beach town, or that the story might relate to a visit to the sea. You may have recalled your own experiences searching for shells on beaches.

Any and all of these expectations are evidence that you were activating prior knowledge by making connections with your own personal experiences, with your knowledge of the world, and with your previous reading of texts.

Your Response While Reading "Shells"

The moment you started to read, you probably changed some of your expectations. You knew from the first sentence that this story is about relationships. The setting is delineated quickly: Michael, a fourteen-year-old whose parents have died, is living with his aunt in a complex for wealthy older people who are afraid of the world and have little trust. Perhaps you drew on your own experience with fourteen-year-olds to try to understand Michael, and you may also have considered what a challenge living with a troubled teenager would be for a single woman. Moreover, you quickly realized that Detroit is nowhere near the sea. Would Michael and his aunt visit the sea? What else could the title mean?

Moving through the text, you learned more about the characters. You saw several sides of Esther—she is

Shells
by Cynthia Rylant

"You *hate* living here."

Michael looked at the woman speaking to him.

"No, Aunt Esther. I don't." He said it dully, sliding his milk glass back and forth on the table. "I don't hate it here."

Esther removed the last pan from the dishwasher and hung it above the oven.

"You hate it here," she said, "and you hate me."

"I don't!" Michael yelled. "It's not *you*."

The woman turned to face him in the kitchen.

"Don't yell at me!" she yelled. "I'll not have it in my home. I can't make you happy, Michael. You just refuse to be happy here. And you punish me every day for it."

"*Punish* you?" Michael gawked at her. I don't punish you! I don't care about you! I don't care what you eat or how you dress or where you go or what you think. Can't you just leave me alone?"

He slammed down the glass, scraped his chair back from the table and ran out the door.

"Michael!" yelled Esther.

They had been living together, the two of them, for six months. Michael's parents had died and only Esther could take him in—or, only she had offered to. Michael's other relatives could not imagine dealing with a fourteen-year-old boy. They wanted peaceful lives.

Esther lived in a condominium in a wealthy section of Detroit. Most of the area's residents were older (like her) and afraid of the world they lived in (like her). They stayed indoors much of the time. They trusted few people.

Esther liked living alone. She had never married or had children. She had never lived anywhere but Detroit. She liked her condominium.

But she was fiercely loyal to her family, and when her only sister had died, Esther insisted that she be allowed to care for Michael. And Michael, afraid of going anywhere else, had accepted.

Oh, he was lonely. Even six months after their deaths, he still expected to see his parents—sitting on the couch as he walked into Esther's living room, waiting for the bathroom as he came out of the shower, coming in the door late at night. He still smelled his father's Old Spice somewhere, his mother's talc.

Sometimes he was so sure one of them was somewhere around him that he thought he was going crazy. His heart hurt him. He wondered if he would ever get better.

And though he denied it, he did hate Esther. She was so different from his mother and father. Prejudiced—she admired only those who were white and Presbyterian. Selfish—she wouldn't allow him to use her phone.

Complaining—she always had a headache or a backache or a stomachache.

He didn't want to, but he hated her. And he didn't know what to do except lie about it.

Michael hadn't made any friends at his new school, and his teachers barely noticed him. He came home alone every day and usually found Esther on the phone. She kept in close touch with several other women in nearby condominiums.

Esther told her friends that she didn't understand Michael. She said she knew he must grieve for his parents, but why punish her? She said she thought she might send him away if he couldn't be nicer. She said she didn't deserve this.

But when Michael came in the door, she always quickly changed the subject.

One day Michael came home with a hermit crab. He had gone into a pet store, looking for some small living thing, and hermit crabs were selling for just a few dollars. He bought one and a bowl.

Esther, for a change, was not on the phone when he arrived home. She was having tea and a crescent roll and seemed cheerful. Michael wanted badly to show someone what he had bought. So he showed her.

Esther surprised him. She picked up the shell and poked the long shiny nail of her little finger at the crab's claws.

"Where is he?" she asked.

Michael showed her the crab's eyes peering through the small opening of the shell.

"Well, for heaven's sake, come out of there!" she said to the crab, and she turned the shell upside down and shook it.

"Aunt Esther!" Michael grabbed for the shell.

"All right, all right." She turned it right side up. "Well," she said, "what does he do?"

Michael grinned and shrugged his shoulders.

"I don't know," he answered. "Just grows, I guess."

His aunt looked at him.

"An attraction to a crab is something I cannot identify with. However, it's fine with me if you keep him, as long as I can be assured that he won't grow out of that bowl." She gave him a hard stare.

"He won't," Michael answered. "I promise."

The hermit crab moved into the condominium. Michael named him Sluggo and kept the bowl beside his bed. Michael had to watch the bowl for very long periods of time to catch Sluggo with his head poking out of his shell, moving around. Bedtime seemed to be Sluggo's liveliest part of the day, and Michael found it easy to lie and watch the busy crab as sleep slowly came on.

One day Michael arrived home to find Esther sitting on

Figure 19–1. "Shells"

Shells (continued)

the edge of his bed, looking at the bowl. Esther usually did not intrude in Michael's room, and seeing her there disturbed him. But he stood at the doorway and said nothing.

Esther seemed perfectly comfortable, although she looked over at him with a frown on her face.

"I think he needs a companion," she said.

"What?" Michael's eyebrows went up as his jaw dropped down.

Esther sniffed.

"I think Sluggo needs a girl friend." She stood up. "Where is that pet store?"

Michael took her. In the store was a huge tank of hermit crabs.

"Oh my!" Esther grabbed the rim of the tank and craned her neck over the side. "Look at them!"

Michael was looking more at his Aunt Esther than at the crabs. He couldn't believe it.

"Oh, look at those shells. You say they grow out of them? We must stock up with several sizes. See the pink in that one? Michael, look! He's got his little head out!"

Esther was so dramatic—leaning into the tank, her bangle bracelets clanking, earrings swinging, red pumps clicking on the linoleum—that she attracted the attention of everyone in the store. Michael pretended not to know her well.

He and Esther returned to the condominium with a thirty-gallon tank and twenty hermit crabs.

Michael figured he'd have a heart attack before he got the heavy tank into their living room. He figured he'd die and Aunt Esther would inherit twenty-one hermit crabs and funeral expenses.

But he made it. Esther carried the box of crabs.

"Won't Sluggo be surprised?" she asked happily. "Oh, I do hope we'll be able to tell him apart from the rest. He's their founding father!"

Michael, in a stupor over his Aunt Esther and the phenomenon of twenty-one hermit crabs, wiped out the tank, arranged it with gravel and sticks (as well as the plastic scuba diver Aunt Esther insisted on buying) and assisted her in loading it up, one by one, with the new residents. The crabs were as overwhelmed as Michael. Not one showed its face.

Before moving Sluggo from his bowl, Aunt Esther marked his shell with some red fingernail polish so that she could distinguish him from the rest. Then she flopped down on the couch next to Michael.

"Oh, what would your mother *think*, Michael, if she could see this mess we've gotten ourselves into!"

She looked at Michael with a broad smile, but it quickly disappeared. The boy's eyes were full of pain.

"Oh my," she whispered. "I'm sorry."

Michael turned his head away.

Aunt Esther, who had not embraced anyone in years, gently put her arm about his shoulders.

"I am so sorry Michael. Oh, you must hate me."

Michael sensed a familiar smell then. His mother's talc. He looked at his aunt.

"No, Aunt Esther." He shook his head solemnly. "I don't hate you."

Esther's mouth trembled and her bangles clanked as she patted his arm. She took a deep, strong breath.

"Well, let's look in on our friend Sluggo," she said.

They leaned their heads over the tank and found him. The crab, finished with the old home that no longer fit, was coming out of his shell.

Figure 19–1. "Shells" (continued)

fiercely loyal to her family, prejudiced and afraid, selfish and complaining, gregarious with her women friends. You learned about Michael, too—he is lonely and grief stricken, trying to make the best of a situation and failing. With this initial knowledge, you were ready for the events of the story to unfold.

You learned quickly that "shells" had something to do with the hermit crab; perhaps you drew on your background knowledge of these animals. Meanwhile, you continued to amass information about Michael and Esther; in fact, her personality emerges in a surprising way. You probably didn't picture her at first as "dramatic—leaning into the tank, bangle bracelets clanking, earrings swinging, red pumps clicking on the linoleum." As a reader, you were surprised along with Michael, and you recognized the significance of the scent of his mother's talc. It may not have been until the final paragraph that you truly understood the double significance of the title.

Your Response After Reading "Shells"

After the reading, you probably reflected for a few moments on the whole story. The significance of the last paragraph may have helped you understand the first part of the story in a deeper way. You may even have turned back to search the text for significant language, but chances are you simply thought about it. Your sympathy for both Michael and Esther deepened; life has offered them hard choices and one choice is to grow. The old "shells" no longer fit; along with Sluggo the crab, both have to "come out" and create a new life. Looking back on the story, you probably saw that both Michael and Esther have the inner strength to do so.

Discussing "Shells" with a friend, you may talk about the personal experiences the text brought to mind. You may discuss your own thinking process and how your expectations changed as you read the story. You may even discuss hermit crabs, although this is not the main point of the story. You will be led through a range of interconnected topics, because conversation extends meaning.

"Shells" is the final story in the book. If you have read one or more of the earlier stories, you will discover additional layers of meaning, and have larger themes to share. Each story focuses on the connection between people and nature; each has value for life.

Applying Systems of Strategies to Your Reading of "Shells"

In this short experience, you undoubtedly employed the full range of reading strategies we have outlined in Chapter 18. Did you use them one at a time? Were you even conscious of using them? Probably not, and that is exactly as it should be. The emphasis is on smooth, coordinated processing rather than laborious, conscious implementation of individual actions. However, we offer some possible examples to illustrate the process.

STRATEGIES FOR SUSTAINING READING

As you read the story, you rapidly solved words and constantly checked on your understanding. Probably you read quite fluently, your attention on the meaning of the story. You may have varied your reading slightly, lingering over the description of Esther or other detail-laden information. You may even have stopped and looked back to check a detail you thought was important. For example, how did Michael's parents die? You never found out, but you probably inferred that it was an accident of some kind. At the end, you may have decided it wasn't important to the overall meaning of the story.

STRATEGIES FOR EXPANDING MEANING

Chances are, your real pleasure came as you expanded the meaning. As you read, you constantly made connections between your own life and experiences and those in the text. You used your background and knowledge. You thought about the characters and

interpreted their actions in the light of your own knowledge of people from personal experiences, film, or other books. You were constantly remembering and summarizing information. Previously gained information accumulated and helped you understand new information. You constantly made inferences about:

■ How the characters felt or what motivated them.
■ The history of both Michael and Esther.
■ What caused the characters to change and open up to each other.
■ The significance of the hermit crab and the connection to the people in the story.
■ The layers of meaning related to the word *shells*.

You probably synthesized information from the story to gain a larger meaning, one that you could apply to your own life or to the lives of people you know. In addition, you may have been critical in your thinking about the meaning of the story or the writing. For example, you may have changed your judgment of the characters constantly as the story progressed. You may have reached the conclusion that even though Michael's story was tragic, his presence in his aunt's house was the best thing that could have happened to her. You may have felt that the author really should have given more information—such as how Michael's parents died or what kind of kid he was before the tragedy. Or you may have simply felt that "Shells" was a perfect short story, one that touched your heart and made you think about life. All of those sentiments involve evaluation or criticism.

Paying Conscious Attention to Reading

Text introductions and prompts help students notice more as they read, which gives them a richer experience. Your job is to bring your students' conscious attention to aspects of text that will help them access more of their own thinking or become more analytic. In the process, they will learn more about how to be a reader.

In teaching for comprehending strategies, we encourage a "light" rather than "heavy" approach. We want to enrich students' reading experience, not interfere with it. Examining what readers actually do when they read guides our thinking and helps root our teaching in effective practice.

Thinking While Reading

All the time you are reading, you are actively responding and thinking. These thoughts are fleeting, elusive, and largely unstated. You are not wholly conscious of your thinking while reading, although when talking with someone afterward, you may suddenly express something you thought about or an emotion you felt while reading. You feel shadows of questions arising in your mind as you anticipate what might happen next or find something puzzling. Sometimes your thoughts are evaluations; sometimes they involve sensory imagery; sometimes they evoke sadness, empathy, or fear. Skim the range of thoughts listed in Figure 19–2 and consider how they reflect experiences you've had while reading.

When we are immersed in a particularly captivating novel, we may become so lost in the story we feel as though we are thinking the thoughts of the character and experiencing the events ourselves. When the characters are surprised, we are caught off guard, and when they experience tragedy, we are despondent. As we read *Fried Green Tomatoes at the Whistle Stop Café* (Flagg 1992) or *Cold Sassy Tree* (Burns 1984) on an airplane, we may start to cry or burst out laughing. Coming to consciousness, we glance around furtively, concerned our fellow passengers will think us mad.

Every reader constantly experiences a stream of unique thoughts, images, and emotions. We become aware of our own thinking processes only when our minds wander briefly. Perhaps we are distracted by a problem or find ourselves remembering a list of things to do. Suddenly, we realize that our eyes have been moving over print, but our thinking is elsewhere. Either we stop reading and focus on our problem, or we firmly put our problem aside, turn back a few pages, and begin where we first wandered away. Perhaps this kind of brief experience is the only way we can grasp what it's like for one of our students to read through a piece of text, saying the words but not understanding. Comprehension requires active thinking, and without comprehension, reading is pointless. Indeed, reading without understanding is not even reading in the true sense of the word.

We read to think. We seek the experience again and again because it takes us out of the everyday world, activates our emotions, creates sensory images, satisfies curiosity, or tells us what we need and want to know. Readers read for pure pleasure as well as for specific purposes. When was the last time you picked up a book because you wanted to identify three metaphors or do a character web?! We crave reading for what happens *while* we read. But that doesn't mean we are averse to expanding our reading potential by engaging in opportunities to think in new ways about texts.

Mediated Thinking: The Role of Attention

Before you read, you may have expectations based on the theme, author, setting, or topic. Let's say your friend advises, "You have to read *The Divine Secrets of the Ya Ya Sisterhood* [Wells 1996]. It reminded me of my mother!" Your reading will be slightly but inevitably altered. It will be mediated by a light overlay of intention that makes you more conscious of the connections to your friend and her mother or even to your own mother. To mediate means to "go between" two elements (such as between sides in labor relations). Your friend has entered "between" you and the text in a way that affects (and in this case enhances) your understanding. At other times, mediation can detract from your reading experience, such as when you watch a film version before reading a book.

A friend might persuade you to read *84 Charing Cross Road* (Hanff 1970) and mention the format of letters. In this situation, you would be more likely to notice the text structure.

Suppose you belong to a book club that has agreed to discuss Jane Smiley's *A Thousand Acres* (1996). As you read in preparation for the meeting, you probably experience the same range of responses as any general reader, such as connecting the characters' relationships to your own family or recalling what you know about Midwestern farms. But with the book club meeting on your mind, you are probably more conscious of searching for something to share with the other members, such as an intriguing idea or colorful language. You may be more aware of your own questions: "I'm trying to picture what they mean by all that pipe underground and what it does." Likewise, you may be more consciously critical of the plot: "I think this is unrealistic." You might place some stick-on notes on specific pages in the book so you can find your exam-

Thoughts That Might Come to Mind While Reading

Examples of thoughts:	System of Strategies:
❖ That word looks familiar. ❖ What does that word mean? ❖ How do you say that word? ❖ I think the word is _____ or means _____	Solving words
❖ I'm confused. ❖ That's not right. ❖ Oh, that's what it means. ❖ I get this. ❖ I don't get this.	Monitoring/Correcting
❖ I see that. ❖ That's important. ❖ I didn't know that. ❖ That's interesting.	Gathering
❖ I wonder if . . . ❖ Oh, no! ❖ I want to know . . . ❖ What is going to happen? ❖ I know what's going to happen.	Predicting
❖ This is easy reading.	Maintaining Fluency
❖ I need to look for [information]. ❖ How would this sound to the listener?	Adjusting
❖ That reminds me of [people, places, and other books]. ❖ I'd like to do [see] that. ❖ I know somebody like that. ❖ I've felt like that before. ❖ I've seen [heard, smelled] that. ❖ I've felt what it's like. ❖ This story is like [another text]. ❖ I've read something like this before. ❖ That's so funny. ❖ This is like . . .	Making Connections

Figure 19–2. Thoughts That Might Come to Mind While Reading

Thoughts That Might Come to Mind While Reading (continued)

Examples of thoughts:	System of Strategies:
❖ Why did [character] do that? ❖ How sad . . . or wonderful! ❖ I think he'll turn out to be . . . ❖ She must feel . . . ❖ I'd feel . . . I felt just like that. ❖ I can just picture [hear, feel, smell] that. ❖ Laughing, crying, shuddering . . .	Inferring
❖ I get it. ❖ I'm confused. ❖ The important things I learned are . . . ❖ What's the point here? ❖ Let me think about what I now understand.	Summarizing
❖ I understand this in a new way. ❖ These ideas are really interesting. ❖ That must be one of the reasons it [historical or political event] happened. ❖ I see the [historical event] more clearly after reading this. ❖ Now, I understand [group] better.	Synthesizing
❖ Her characters are so well developed. ❖ What a complex plot! ❖ That's the style of this writer. ❖ What makes everyone like this book? ❖ I'm figuring out the mystery. ❖ I like the way this author makes you feel as if you are there. ❖ The use of language is skillful.	Analyzing
❖ This is unlikely. ❖ People wouldn't act that way. ❖ I don't believe this. ❖ What wonderful language! ❖ Should I keep reading this? ❖ That's not the way a fantasy is supposed to work. ❖ This biography is not authentic. ❖ Some important information is missing here. ❖ This shows the attitude of the author. ❖ This is wonderful writing.	Critiquing

Figure 19–2. Thoughts That Might Come to Mind While Reading (continued)

ples quickly, or you might jot comments in the margins or note pages you want to reread inside the back cover. Your heightened consciousness provides an "active thinking" overlay that adds to the reading experience rather than interfering with its quality.

Another example: You are reading a book on teaching because you plan to lead a discussion group in your next professional development seminar. Now, your reading process is drastically altered. When you read for information that you plan to share, the overlay is heavier; your attention is highly focused. You search for the important information, make notes in margins, highlight quotes, and place stick-on notes on pages. You may reread or repeat ideas to yourself. You may even think how you will rephrase ideas or compose arguments to help others see your own point of view.

A final example: Your family is taking the trip of a lifetime—a trip to Africa. You gather materials, first to organize and plan your trip, and then to enhance your enjoyment. On the plane, you take out a book that you've saved for this occasion, *The Poisonwood Bible* (Kingsolver 1998) and settle down to read. You connect this segment of African history to places you're planning to visit. You read about the terrain and visualize the locale. You make a note about a side trip you'd like to take. Periodically, you poke the nearest family member, saying, "Listen to this!" while you read aloud your latest discovery.

If the experiences that surround reading are meaningful and supportive, most readers find that these "overlays" enhance the process. They don't just read differently, they read with greater breadth and scope. They experience the text in a more pleasurable and meaningful way, and they may even begin to change their reading tastes and abilities. Oprah Winfrey's Book Club, for example, has prompted people to interact in social ways around books that they might not otherwise have read. They discover new authors and learn to appreciate their writing styles, or they begin to understand issues in new ways, which opens the door to reading about new themes or topics. Sometimes they even find books that may change their lives in profound ways. Providing such "overlays" is integral to teaching intermediate students.

We are not suggesting that your students' experiences will occur as easily and naturally as the adult experiences we've described. In the classroom, you are *intentionally* providing direction for reading. Your responsibility is to guide and expand your students' ability to comprehend a wide range of texts. Your overlays will be deliberate and carefully planned. The underlying purposes of learning more about content, learning more about text, and learning more about reading are always there.

On the other hand, your ultimate goal is to enable your students to seek experiences just like the adult experiences we've described. The balance in instruction is to prompt and encourage the focused thinking that enhances reading without destroying the quality of the experience for students. You want them to delve deeper into texts and get excited about them. When guidance becomes too heavy-handed, the quality of the experience may be lost.

We mediate students' thinking any time we interact with them. For example, we might:

- Give a book talk that prompts students to connect a book to their own experiences or engages them in topics of interest (see Chapter 7).
- Engage in oral or written dialogue with students about their reading to foster ongoing thinking about responses and connections (see Chapter 8).
- Introduce a book to a small group in a way that prompts them to connect the book to other texts or notice aspects of the writer's style (see Chapters 12, 14).
- Ask students to discuss aspects of text structure, language, plot, or character as they reflect on a text they have read (see Chapter 16).
- Ask students to revisit a text to provide evidence or justify their thinking (see Chapters 12, 16).

All of these experiences happen before or after the act of reading, but they influence the readers' thinking during reading.

Thinking About Reading

Thinking *about* reading is different from thinking *while* reading, even mediated thinking. In thinking *about* reading, you are conscious of connections, questions, and responses. You may even consciously try to apply specific strategies to understand text in a deeper way. In thinking about reading, you are really *thinking about thinking*, an act called *metacognition*, which literally means "big thinking." You are consciously examining and monitoring your own brain's processing.

Metacognition has been the subject of much study as researchers have attempted to describe ways educators can actually "teach" students to become more effective or "strategic" thinkers (Palinscar and Brown 1984; Paris, Lipson, and Wixson 1983). The idea is that students can become more effective readers by engaging in conscious acts such as questioning, visualizing, and gathering or synthesizing information. In reciprocal teaching, for example, students are taught to rephrase information and ideas in several ways so they can consciously learn to internalize new ideas for themselves. The goal is for these overt acts to become automatic, simply a part of the individual's way of thinking.

As adults, we seldom focus directly on our own thinking processes, but if we did, it might look something like this:

- You read *Tuesdays with Morrie* (Albom 1997) and then say, "Isn't it amazing how I could almost hear Morrie's voice—the cadence of it and the tenor of it—it's as if I were re-creating his talk in my head!"
- You go to see the newest film version of *Little Women* (Alcott 1994) and then remark, "I read that book many times when I was young, and I always pictured Jo as tall and dashing. Winona Ryder was all wrong for the part!"
- You pause while reading *Beach Music* (Conroy 1995) and think, "I went to that part of the country last year. I could almost smell the salt air as I read this book."

In these instances, you are reflecting on your own thinking processes, and you hypothesize about what's happening in your brain. It would be unusual, though, for you to say, "Wow, that visualizing was a very good thing for my brain to do. I think I'll do more visualizing when I read the next book." You might *do* it, and reflect on it, but it's quite another thing to give it a label and *plan* to do it. In other words, readers don't pick up a book with the intention of directing their brains to visualize or infer from the text.

How Do We Help Our Students?

How much to focus students' reading requires careful thought. We have the difficult task of helping readers expand their systems of strategies while maintaining an authentic reading experience. Do we simply encourage students to read and bring their own meanings to text? Do we guide and support the reading so they will think in new ways? Do we teach students techniques for analyzing their own cognitive actions? One instructional approach to developing reading comprehension is to help readers think *about* their reading strategies *while* reading.

Students benefit as they become more aware of themselves as readers, and we can prompt them to take conscious action. For example, we might say, "As you are reading, think about what you already know about this time in history. Find some places in the text where the author has woven in historical facts. Later we'll discuss how this technique adds to the story. We'll also check whether the facts are accurate or whether the author has altered them somewhat to fit the story."

The reader who is following these directions will consciously attend to a feature of historical fiction. In the process, she will learn something about:

- Gathering important information.
- Making connections with world knowledge.
- Critiquing the information in a text.

The direction we give must fit with what is appropriate to do in this particular text and what is appropriate to enhance the experience of *these* particular readers at *this point in their development.*

Teaching for Strategies Across the Literacy Framework

If comprehension is central to reading and writing, then students will be in a position to use comprehending strategies almost every moment they spend participating in the three components of the language arts framework. Comprehension is built primarily through the three types of reading in the reading workshop (see Chapters 7 through 17) but also through writing and language/word study.

Reading Aloud Interactively

Reading aloud certainly doesn't stop when children enter the upper elementary grades. In fact, it's *just as important* because through it you can create shared literary experiences as a foundation for learning how to comprehend texts.

As part of the language and word study block of the literacy framework, you can read aloud short stories and informational pieces. You can also use beautifully illustrated picture books with complex themes that students will enjoy hearing and discussing. Picture books are a very good way to help students understand the characteristics of genres that are new for them.

Let's look at how one teacher has used reading aloud to help her students develop their comprehension strategies. Marilyn selected *Peppe the Lamplighter* (Bartone 1993) to help her students learn more about historical fiction. Peppe is the oldest child and the only boy in a family of Italian immigrants who live in the late 1800s. He has three sisters. His father wants him to become someone very important in this new country; his expectations are high. Peppe, though, wants to get a job that will contribute to the family resources, so he becomes an assistant lamplighter. Every night, Peppe goes through the streets, lighting the gaslights so people walking or riding in carriages can see their way. The illustrations show what American cities were like before electric streetlights and store lights, flashing traffic lights, and fluorescent signs. On each page, luminous gaslights glow through the darkness.

When Peppe becomes a lamplighter's assistant, his father cannot hide his disappointment. Like many immigrants, he struggled to come to the United States and achieve the American dream—if not for himself, for his children. Being a lamplighter is simply not important enough, and he refuses to speak to Peppe. The boy becomes discouraged, and one day he decides not to light the lamps. That same day, one of Peppe's little sisters gets lost while trying to find her way home through the dark streets. No one can even look for her without lights to guide their way. Peppe's father, frantic about the child, finds the boy and asks him to light the lamps. By the end of the story, everyone realizes how all work, done well, is important and honorable.

After Marilyn read this story to her fourth graders, they explored various concepts in a free-ranging discussion. They approached the text in many ways, and the particular strategy the readers probably used is highlighted in parentheses after each of their comments:

- Peppe was trying to make his father proud of him. (Identifying information)

- Peppe's family came to America from Italy. (Identifying information)

- The word *immigrant* means someone who is a citizen of one country but moves to another country to live. (Word solving)

- The word *lamplighter* is a compound word that means "a person who lights lamps," but it must be something special in this story. (Word solving)

- It is sometimes hard to meet our parents' expectations. (Connecting to personal experience)

- In the 1800s, people didn't have electricity; they used candles, fireplaces, and gaslights. (Connecting to world experience/content knowledge)

- The lamplighter performed an important function that no longer exists today because we have electricity. (Connecting to world experience/content knowledge)

- Peppe was responsible; he wanted to help the family. (Inferring)

- Peppe's father at first didn't like the lamplighter job but then he changed his mind. (Summarizing)

- In stories of long ago, authors use details that help the reader understand life in the historical past. (Connecting to literary knowledge—genre)

- We could find out whether this author was accurate about the job of the lamplighter. (Critiquing)

- The events in this story seemed to fit together; they didn't have electricity or automobiles, or any of the things we have now to make our lives easier. (Critiquing)

- While it is understandable that parents want their children to have a better life than they did, it's also hard for children to do just what their parents want them to do. (Synthesizing)

- Many immigrants from many countries come here to fulfill their dreams of a better life. (Synthesizing)

- We could find out about immigrants who come to our neighborhood or school. (Connecting to personal experience)

Independent Reading

Often, teachers ask students to mark places in the text or take a few notes during or after independent reading. This light guidance raises students' conscious attention to content and prompts them to use comprehending strategies without unduly distorting the reading process.

In Chapter 8 we outline a minilesson that focuses students' reading and reminds them to activate strategies during independent reading. For such a minilesson you and your students can revisit a brief part of a text you have previously read aloud or you can simply say something like, "Remember how the author of _____ did _____" and move from that shared meaning to focus on some aspect of the reading process.

Let's look at Marilyn's minilesson, which took place several days after the oral reading and discussion of *Peppe the Lamplighter*. Her goal was to help students become more active in making connections while reading. She summarized her point in one sentence: "Readers make different kinds of connections as they read books to understand them better." On an easel, she placed a chart with three columns. As the students made comments, she recorded their observations under one of the three headings: Connections to Our Lives, Connections to Other Books, and Connections to What We Know About the World (see Figure 19–3). Here are some excerpts from the minilesson:

MARILYN: Do you remember when we read *Peppe the Lamplighter*? We talked about the little boy's experiences and how they may have reminded you of something in your life. We also talked about how the story reminded us of other books we've read about young children coming to America, such as *Lily's Crossing*. We made lots of connections with our own lives, with what we knew about other people and places, and with other books. What were some of the things *Peppe the Lamplighter* reminded you of?

CLORINDA: It reminded me of the story of Booker T. Washington and how there was a light on every page and how Booker had a hope or dream and also *More Than Anything Else*.

MARILYN: What did the light make us think about?

FRANCISCO: It was like hope, a symbol of hope.

MARILYN: So *Peppe the Lamplighter* reminded you of a character and illustrations in another book. I'm going to write that connection here *[she writes on the chart]*. What were some other connections we made?

MARQUITA: It reminded me that my friend Habib came here from Syria.

JULIUS: And my grandmother came from Cuba.

CHERYL: It made us think of our social studies book when they talked about immigration and

Ways We Made Connections While Reading *Peppe the Lamplighter*

Connections to our lives.	Connections to other books.	Connections to what we know about the world.
Friends who came from other countries	*Lily's Crossing* (Giff 1994)—about immigrants	What we knew about the Statue of Liberty
Relatives who came from other countries	*More than Anything Else* (Bradby 1995)—illustrations are symbols of hope	What we knew about immigrants from different countries
How parents have expectations of children		What we knew about times with no electricity
Relationships with brothers and sisters and how they help you	Light on every page—symbol is often used in books	What we knew about living in apartments in cities
How families help each other	Similar character—Booker T. Washington	What we knew about people from Italy or "little Italy" in our city
Being respectful to your father		

Figure 19–3. Making Connections

all the different countries that Americans have come from.

FARAD: There was also the book about the Statue of Liberty; the immigrants that came to New York saw that first.

* * *

MARILYN [summarizing]: There were three different ways that you made connections. Let's look at the headings on the chart. This book reminded us of our own lives—for example, our relatives who came to America from other countries. We make connections with our own lives as we read. It also reminded us of what we knew about the world—people, places, and things. For example, you remembered some ideas about how people had to live without electricity, and you also made connections to what you had learned in social studies about immigrants. We make connections with things we know about the world while we read. You also made connections to other books you had read. We thought of books like *More Than Anything Else*, which had illustrations using light as a symbol of hope—just like in *Peppe the Lamplighter*. That was really good thinking. We can make connections to other books while we are reading. So when you are reading your books today, mark one place that reminds you of something in your own life, something you know about the world, or some other book you have read. Your connections can be in any of these three categories. When we share the connections we've made, we'll see the different kinds of connections readers make.

Conferring

After the minilesson, students dispersed to read their own books independently, and Marilyn conferred with several students. Here is an excerpt from a conference between Marilyn and Diana, who was reading *Sadako and a Thousand Paper Cranes* (Coerr 1999):

MARILYN: What is this book making you think about?

DIANA: It makes me think about how war hurts children. It reminds me of *The Faithful Elephants* [Tsuchiya 1988], because in that story the elephants starve when no one can feed them. The elephants never did anything wrong, but they died just the same. So I felt kind of sad and kind of angry. I'm wondering if Sadako is going to die or get well.

MARILYN: Both of those stories took place a long time ago, didn't they?

DIANA: Yes, is it the same war that Rose Blanche was in?

MARILYN: Yes, they were both girls in that same war, but they lived in different parts of the world. The war was called World War II because it was the second big war that involved many countries in the world.

In this short interchange, Diana revealed personal connections to *Sadako and a Thousand Paper Cranes*. A young girl herself, she was relating to the girls in the story (personal connections). She made connections to what she knew about war (world knowledge) and to the theme of two other books (literary knowledge).

Sharing

When the students came back at the end of reading workshop, Marilyn facilitated a "read around." In turn, children quickly shared one place in their book that reminded them of their own lives, of other books, or of what they knew about the world. She summarized by saying, "Readers make different kinds of connections as they read books to understand them better. So when you are reading, you'll want to be thinking about things the book reminds you of. In your journal letter this week, be sure to write at least one paragraph about a connection you made while reading your book."

Guided Reading

Guided reading is designed to teach for comprehending of texts. It is an ideal structure because:

■ Students are grouped because they have similar characteristics and similar needs. They read texts that are about the same level and the same complexity. Their experience with various kinds of texts is comparable, and they are at about the same level in their word-solving ability. Given those characteristics, you can select a text that is appropriate for the group, one that will provide the challenges they need in order to learn. Reading expands in response

335

to the demands of varied texts.

■ All students in the group are reading the same text. Your introduction can focus and mediate their reading so they notice new aspects of text, thus expanding their processing powers.

■ Students in the group will build shared meanings. As they discuss the text, they can share their ideas and support one another in a way that expands meaning and creates richer interpretations.

■ Since students will have read, discussed, and often responded in writing to the same text, they will have shared memories that they can access and discuss in relation to new texts. (Remember, though, that group membership shifts and changes, so not all members in the group will necessarily have previously read the same texts.)

In a guided reading lesson, you actively work to help students notice and use the information they will need to comprehend different kinds of texts. Guiding them through the reading of several texts will show them how to use the same strategies in their independent reading.

Let's look at an example. Jan has chosen an article titled "Red Alert" (see Figure 19–4) from *Time for Kids,* a journal that provides "short reads" that can be used to illustrate aspects of the reading process. The article is about two volcanoes, one in Argentina and one in Guatemala and has a rich variety of text and graphics to support Jan's goal of showing that authors provide information through words, pictures, and other graphic features:

■ The title and subtitle capture attention, communicate danger, and provide information as to why this is an important story (it affects thousands of people on opposite sides of the world).

■ There are dramatic photographs with captions underneath identifying where the picture was taken and what is happening.

■ A cut-away drawing shows how a volcano works, requiring readers to match the information in the caption with the parts of the drawing and to expand

Figure 19–4. Page of "Red Alert"

their vocabularies (*magna,* for example).

■ The map showing the "ring of fire" that rims the Pacific Ocean explains why two volcanoes so far apart might have erupted at the same time.

■ The text begins with a description of one volcano followed by a heading signaling a description of another danger spot.

Here is an excerpt from Jan's introduction:

JAN: We've talked about volcanoes before, and today I have an interesting article for you about some volcanoes that have erupted recently. What do you know about volcanoes?

ROYCE: They're mountains that have liquid rock down deep in them, and it explodes out the top.

JAN: Yes, there's a lot of pressure down deep under the earth and it's very hot.

CAROLYN: It's molten; it's so hot that it melts the rock like ice melts.

ROYCE: The molten rock is lava that flows down and when it gets cool it's rock again.

JAN: Well, this article is about two volcanoes that occurred about the same time at two different parts of the world. Read the title.

ALL STUDENTS: "Red Alert!"

JAN: Do you think that's a good title?

ROYCE: It sounds dangerous.

LAKISHA: And the volcano is red with fire.

JAN: So it is a good title. Listen as I read the first sentence of the article.

[She does so.] Does that lead sentence get you interested in the article?

LAKISHA: It sounds like it's really dangerous.

TJ: Next to the title it says that thousands of people were in danger.

JAN: Yes, look at the bold print. It's exactly what TJ is saying. There are two volcanoes in two different parts of the world that have put thousands of people in danger.

LAKISHA: Why are there two at once?

JAN: That's a good question. Let's look at the map at the bottom. What do you see that you recognize?

TJ: There's North America. We live on the East Coast.

CAROL: There's the Pacific Ocean.

JAN: Right. And across the Pacific Ocean you see Asia, a big continent where China is. This whole area around the Pacific Ocean is called the "ring of fire" because there are so many volcanoes. How has the writer shown the "ring of fire" on the map?

CAROL: It's bright like fire. Is there molten lava all under the ocean?

JAN: Surrounding the Pacific Ocean and under it there are places that have very hot rock. The pressure builds up and causes strings of volcanoes. They don't all happen at once, but over the years, there are lots of them. Read what it says under the map. *[Students do so.]* So one way you can learn about volcanoes in this article is to look at the map and use the information there. Now look over at the drawing in the box at the bottom right. The writer is providing information in still another way. Talk

about what you see there.

JOY: It looks like half a mountain.

ROYCE: Is it like a diagram? It's not a photograph.

JAN: It is like a drawing and kind of like a diagram. It is showing the mountain sliced open so you can visualize what the inside is like. Look at some of the labels on the drawing. Do you see the *crust?* That represents the crust of the earth, far below the ocean.

JOY: The water's on top and then there's land below and that's the crust? I thought there was sand under there.

JAN: There might be sand, but below it is a hard surface. The hard surface sometimes moves and changes, and when it does, it builds up pressure that makes the hot air and hot rock explode all the way out of the top of the mountain. See where it says *molten rock?* The writer is showing you where it is and how it can spew out the top. Have you ever seen a teakettle when the water boils? The steam comes out the spout and it's really hot!

CAROL: Ours whistles.

JAN: The teakettle whistles because the hot steam expands and builds pressure so the air rushes out. In the case of the volcano, it's huge—as big as a mountain—and steam and hot gases and molten rock come out. Can you see how it is very dangerous?

CAROL: It could kill people and burn them up and their houses.

JAN: That's right. This article is about two of those volcanoes. Look at the print. You'll start reading about the first volcano, which is in Argentina. Do you see a heading in red about halfway through the article? That tells you when you will begin reading about the second volcano, which is in Guatemala. Now read the article, and don't forget to take information from the title, the map, *and* the drawing. There are some really good photographs, too, at the top of the page. We've talked before about how important it is to read the information under the photographs.

In this introduction, Jan invites students to make connections to prior knowledge, and she also directs their attention to the various ways that the writer conveyed information. In later discussions, they summarized information from the article, drawing from the different sources provided—map, drawing, headings, and text. They synthesized information by writing what they now knew about volcanoes, incorporating new learning. In other words, they came out with a deeper understanding of why volcanoes occur, and also where they are likely to occur and why. They learned more about how to process an expository text. They had a direct demonstration of why it is important to look at the graphic information and integrate it with the text information.

Literature Study

The opportunity to study and talk about literary aspects of a text supports students' development of processing strategies. You may read aloud to students for literature study, or they may read texts on their own to discuss with peers. You teach students how to talk about the texts they have read, and you may guide the discussion at times, but the goal is for students to talk with one another. In the process, they share meanings and understand texts in greater depth.

A group of students in Karen's class was reading *Sarah, Plain and Tall* (MacLachlan 1985). Karen initiated the discussion by reading aloud the first few pages and briefly noting the setting for the story—the widespread prairie of waving grass with no trees. Students talked about how lonely it must have been sometimes, especially for children with no mother. The concept of a "mail order bride" was interesting to them, and they talked about what they could tell about Sarah just from her letter.

The students had previously discussed how chapter titles can give hints about what might happen next. Since *Sarah, Plain and Tall* has chapter numbers but no chapter titles, Jan suggested they could think of an appropriate title for each chapter as they read. She asked them to read the book over the next week, stop at the end of each chapter, think about the most important idea in the chapter, and write a title. When they met again to discuss the book, students shared their ideas for titles. Their consensus is shown on the table of contents in Figure 19–5.

Karen's direction is deceivingly simple: in order to create a good title for a piece of writing, an article, a chapter, or a book, students must summarize and syn-

thesize the most important information, asking:

- What is really important here?
- What's the big idea?
- What is the writer trying to help the reader understand?

Students then have to narrow this information to a few words—words that should also engage the readers and make them want to continue reading. Moreover, the words should help the reader understand and/or predict important ideas. This exercise helps students use the strategies of summarizing and synthesizing information. In this case it also sparked a rich conversation about the book.

Writing Workshop

As students explore a range of texts, they learn to think about how writers communicate meaning to readers. As they learn more about an author's craft, or the way authors communicate meaning, they are able to think about themselves as writers and how they will use various techniques as writers. For example, if they have thought about how an author presented content in different ways—a photograph, a diagram, a heading—they can consider those options as writers. If they noticed how an author used symbolism (the light in *Peppe the Lamplighter,* for example), they can incorporate symbolism in their own writing. They are learning how to incorporate the techniques of writing in their own pieces.

Our Table of Contents for *Sarah, Plain and Tall*

1. A Letter from Sarah
2. Sarah's Coming
3. Sarah's Arrival
4. Getting to Know Sarah
5. Our Dune
6. Having Fun
7. Sarah Feels Better
8. The Squall
9. A New Start

Figure 19–5. Our Table of Contents for Sarah, Plain and Tall

Suggestions for Professional Development

1. With a group of your colleagues, examine picture books that can be used to demonstrate a range of comprehending strategies.

2. Have each person bring a book that would be appropriate to read aloud to a group of students in upper elementary grades. (Alternative: Collect four or five of the picture books recommended in Appendix 56.)

3. Spend some time reading the books in preparation for discussion.

4. For each book, think about the opportunities the text provides for helping students learn to think in different ways as readers. For example:

   - At what places might you would stop and get students to think as readers in ways they can take to their own reading?

   - What literary aspects would be important to notice (e.g., use of metaphor, symbolism, character development, important details)?

   - What can students learn about taking information from various sources—text, graphics, illustrations?

   - Are there historical notes or information about the author that will help students be critical about the text's authenticity or gain insight into why the author wrote the book?

   - Are there literary techniques used by the author that students could incorporate into their own writing?

   Discuss how you can use these picture books to demonstrate many of the comprehending strategies.

5. Get a copy of *Every Living Thing* (Rylant 1984). Read some of the stories and reflect on your own reading, as modeled in this chapter. Make charts categorizing some of the groups' thinking on reading.

## CHAPTER TWENTY

TEACHING FOR SUSTAINING STRATEGIES IN GUIDED READING

*Fluent reading is the product of a complex combination
of knowledge, skills, and understandings.*
— NEW ZEALAND MINISTRY OF EDUCATION

Your students expand their reading systems with every text they read—whether they are searching the Internet for their favorite BMX website or reading Shel Silverstein poems to a younger sibling. Writing also contributes to their understanding of how words work, how sentences are formed, and how texts are constructed. Within the literacy framework, guided reading plays a central role in showing students how to use strategies in increasingly sophisticated ways.

By the time they enter third grade, most students have developed an early reading process, which expands as they read increasingly complex texts. But two challenges exist at every grade:

1. Some students will work on very basic reading skills such as word analysis and comprehending simple texts.
2. All students need instructional support so they can expand their competence across a greater variety of increasingly challenging texts.

In the upper elementary grades, it is important for students to have regular time with you to learn how to become more effective readers. Guided reading is the best setting to accomplish your goal. Students can take what they learn in guided reading to their independent reading, literature study, and content area reading.

Your goal in guided reading is to strengthen students' processing power across increasingly challenging texts. Let's look at a guided reading lesson to learn how you can support the readers' network of developing strategies.

Teaching Within a Guided Reading Lesson

Rebecca is introducing *Guests* (Dorris 1994) to a group of five students. *Guests* is a historical novel about a Native American boy who is about twelve years old. Moss, so named because he clung so hard to his mother while a young child, is longing for and curious about his "time away," when he will go out on his own in the forest and come back with mature, manly insights. It's time for the harvest festival, which is important to Moss's family and to the whole community. Moss's father has invited some "guests," who the boy thinks will ruin the party. These guests are quite mysterious. They wear "thin cloth," bring no gifts, and do not appear to understand local customs. Dorris subtly communicates that Moss is a bit spoiled and that his father and grandfather are principled, strict, and loving. Moss and a girl named Trouble run away to the woods rather than help with the feast; in the process, Moss grows up and changes. Here is an example of Dorris's language:

> I wished they had never left wherever they came from before they got here. I wished they would return there again and forget the trail through the sea that they followed. I wished they would grow their own food, trap their own furs, keep their pots and thin cloth and hard-headed hammers. I wished for just one more right time before things began to change. (p.15)

While the author does not specifically say that the guests are Europeans, the reader makes that inference. It is obvious that this text can be read at many levels. "Things" changing can refer to Moss's own growing up, to the way life probably changed for his people as more and more Europeans came to the area, or to the simultaneous longing and fear experienced by preadolescents in the process of growing up.

Rebecca's goal for the lesson is to help students deepen their understanding of the writer's craft, specifically to notice how Dorris "shows without telling," requiring the reader to infer from the text and discern the figurative meaning of his metaphors. As students work to understand how texts are constructed, they increase their ability to transcend literal meaning and comprehend challenging texts. As an additional benefit, students may begin to use literary features such as "showing without telling" in their own writing.

Rebecca has two additional goals in mind. She wants students to gain more experience with the genre of historical fiction and to understand that their knowing facts about other cultures and times enhances their appreciation of this kind of text. Additionally, she plans to show them some of the print features Dorris uses to signal passage of time, dreams and thoughts (as opposed to dialogue), and emphasis or tone of voice.

Before the Reading

Rebecca begins by introducing the author, Michael Dorris, and asking students to discuss what they already know about the writer. Several students have read his *Morning Girl* (1992) and *Sees Behind Trees* (1999). She prompts them to make connections between this text and their knowledge about other texts by asking them to think about how Dorris uses descriptive language in his books. Students give examples of how Dorris uses details and personification in unique ways and helps readers see things in ways they might miss otherwise.

Rebecca then introduces the new book:

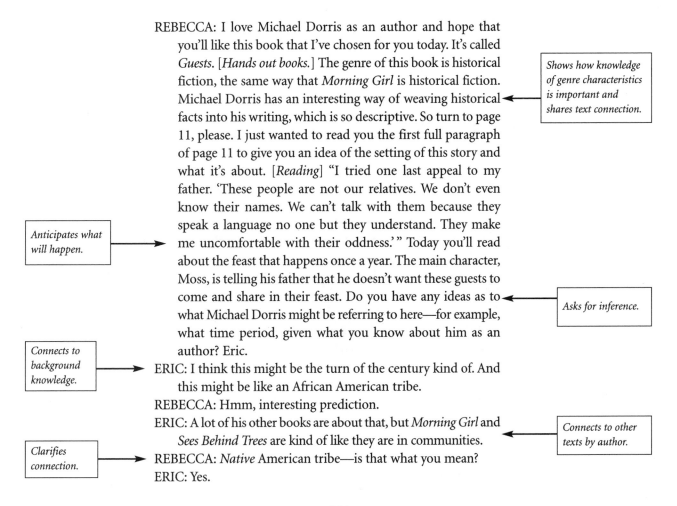

REBECCA: I love Michael Dorris as an author and hope that you'll like this book that I've chosen for you today. It's called *Guests*. [*Hands out books.*] The genre of this book is historical fiction, the same way that *Morning Girl* is historical fiction. Michael Dorris has an interesting way of weaving historical facts into his writing, which is so descriptive. So turn to page 11, please. I just wanted to read you the first full paragraph of page 11 to give you an idea of the setting of this story and what it's about. [*Reading*] "I tried one last appeal to my father. 'These people are not our relatives. We don't even know their names. We can't talk with them because they speak a language no one but they understand. They make me uncomfortable with their oddness.'" Today you'll read about the feast that happens once a year. The main character, Moss, is telling his father that he doesn't want these guests to come and share in their feast. Do you have any ideas as to what Michael Dorris might be referring to here—for example, what time period, given what you know about him as an author? Eric.

Shows how knowledge of genre characteristics is important and shares text connection.

Anticipates what will happen.

Asks for inference.

ERIC: I think this might be the turn of the century kind of. And this might be like an African American tribe.

Connects to background knowledge.

REBECCA: Hmm, interesting prediction.

ERIC: A lot of his other books are about that, but *Morning Girl* and *Sees Behind Trees* are kind of like they are in communities.

Connects to other texts by author.

REBECCA: *Native* American tribe—is that what you mean?

Clarifies connection.

ERIC: Yes.

REBECCA: Okay, yes, he does keep that as a theme in this book. Gayle?

GAYLE: And maybe also kind of like when Columbus came maybe, because he was talking about how they were speaking a language that no one could speak.

REBECCA: So, it's an important detail, isn't it, that they can't speak the language.

Connects to background knowledge.

GAYLE: They couldn't understand each other, so maybe they came from far away like Spain or England.

ALISON: Maybe Thanksgiving. He might be talking about the Pilgrims, because I just saw "the first Thanksgiving" on the back of Amanda's book.

Calls attention to setting.

REBECCA: So keep in mind everything that you've just mentioned here. As you read the first chapter, you'll have a better idea of where this is set. The name of the book is *Guests*, and that's what it's referring to.

Rebecca explains that in Dorris's books and in many Native American stories, people have names like Sees Behind Trees that tell something about the person. As she points out several of the names in *Guests*, she asks, "How can you make sure when you come across a word that is a name instead of just a word?" Amanda suggests looking for capital letters. Rebecca replies, "Yes, so pay careful attention to how he signifies a name by using a capital letter. It's kind of beautiful to think of how he is showing but not telling through the use of names. The main character, Moss, got his name because he liked to cling so closely to his mother. That's one of Michael Dorris's techniques."

Provides background.

Rebecca also points out that in between the different sections in *Guests*, the author uses three asterisks to signal a change. Students speculate that the asterisks might mean a change of setting or that time has gone by, and she confirms their thinking. The book also has some text set in italics.

Calls attention to important detail.

REBECCA: The author also uses italics a couple of times in the book. I was trying to think to myself why it is that authors use italics, and I came to the conclusion that it isn't just for one reason. What do you think, Amanda?

Calls attention to important information in print feature.

AMANDA: Maybe they want to say something with more exaggeration, like "And then we *went* home" [*she emphasizes* went].

REBECCA: I agree, maybe for emphasis. Alison?

ALISON: Like somebody's saying something important. Just say like the mayor came and said something important, he might put italics around what he said.

Connects to personal experience and other texts.

REBECCA: Yes, good. Something different?

ERIC: Sometimes if they're quoting someone in the book who is not right there in the setting—a character in the book is quoting someone who is not there—I think sometimes they do that.

Connects to world knowledge.

REBECCA: Okay, I think you've all given great examples. Amanda hit it on the head when she said, "For emphasis." The italics appear any time the author wants you to look twice or think that something a little different is going on. You'll notice that one time in this book, Moss, the main character, actually meets a porcupine. And he has dialogue with the porcupine, but you're not exactly sure whether the porcupine is actually talking or whether it might be in his imagination. So the author put the porcupine's words in italics.

Confirms student response. Provides information about text features and the plot of the story.

GAYLE: So you know that it's the porcupine talking.

REBECCA: Yes, and it's not like a real person talking. Also there's a couple of times when people tell Native American legends, and those stories are put in italics to set them apart from the rest of the story.

Provides more information about text features.

At the end of the introduction, Rebecca sets a task for the students to guide their reading:

REBECCA: As you read the book, I'd like you to spend some time thinking about the ways Michael Dorris uses his language and the way he uses that idea of "show, don't tell." You have some stick-on notes and pens. As you are reading, I want you to make notes to yourself of any places when you think, *Wow, this language is beautiful* or *Look at the way he paints this picture* or *Look at the way he makes me feel as if I'm actually there.* You can do this when you are reading at school and also at home. I found this middle paragraph on page 77 that I want to read to you. She reads a descriptive paragraph that begins with the phrase, "I heard home before I saw it . . ." The paragraph describes the sounds of the voices of family members, of wood being chopped, the vibrations of the earth and the footsteps of the people. The writer also describes the smells that Moss encountered as he entered the village. It's just one paragraph that I found in the book that really made me feel I could see what it was that Michael Dorris was seeing.

Directs attention to literary features.

Models task. Provides examples.

ALISON: When we have our stick-on notes we can write down page numbers that we might want to go over. Or talk about a word.

REBECCA: Sure, if you use page numbers, be sure to be specific enough; you might want to jot down a word or specify the paragraph so you will be able to find it later. The focus is language that really grabs you by "showing, not telling." You'll have about twenty minutes for reading, so get started.

Clarifies task.

During the Reading

As students read silently, Rebecca confers with individuals. During the conference the student:

■ Reads a short piece of the text aloud softly.
■ Offers examples of interesting language.
■ Asks questions.
■ Converses with Rebecca.

Here are two examples of conferences.

> AMANDA: [*Reading*] "Standing behind me, my father put his hand on my shoulder. His touch was light as a breeze that blows before rain, and I leaned back into it to feel it harder. Grandfather nodded, then gave the basket four shakes, one for each direction, causing the beads to leap and dance among themselves. He looked up at me, his face serious" [p. 4].
>
> REBECCA: I know you probably noticed how he showed how Moss felt about the father's touch—about it being light as a breeze. Isn't it amazing how he can make you feel it without too many descriptive words?
>
> AMANDA: It makes it sound beautiful.
>
> REBECCA: Yes, it's beautiful.

This interaction is brief and supportive. Rebecca is assured that Amanda is noticing the author's language, and they share a brief comment.

Next, Rebecca stops to talk with Eric:

> REBECCA: What have you been noticing?
>
> ERIC: Right there, that first sentence. [*Reading*] "'I know,' Cloud admitted. 'It's just that you . . . I . . . well, you can't . . . All I can say is, when it's your turn just open your mind and watch what you see.'" "'Open my mind and watch what I see.' I repeated Cloud's words slowly to prod him into continuing. Nobody would ever talk about their away time, yet mine was all I could think about [p. 6]."
>
> REBECCA: That's like another part back on the other page where his mind was sliding back and forth!
>
> ERIC: [*Continues reading*] "'I won't,' I promised him, then gave his own word back to him. 'Instead, I'll remember how this year never *properly* ended, how next year never *properly*

began, because we failed to *properly* celebrate the bridge between them.'
>
> "I shot a glance to gauge my father's reaction, but he had closed his eyes and made himself invisible to me. His mouth had become a thin straight line and his nostrils were wide.
>
> "I stepped close to him, stood on tiptoe. 'My mind won't change just because you ignore me,' I whispered directly into his ear.
>
> "He opened one eye. 'I might as well be talking with your grandfather.'
>
> "Grandfather was well known for being stubborn in his ideas. For instance, you couldn't convince him to cross a frozen river until he had found deer tracks on the center ice. You couldn't substitute a single word when repeating an old story. You had to go to sleep facing east so that you would be ready to greet the sun when it returned."
>
> REBECCA: He was like his grandfather!
>
> ERIC: Yes, like kind of stubborn, and he makes sure when they do something, they do it right. He's worried about the ice breaking so he's making sure that there are deer tracks in it. And he makes sure that when they sleep, they go to bed facing the east, so that they can wake up facing the sun.

From this interchange, Rebecca has ample evidence that Eric is making inferences from the text. On the surface, these dialogues look like a conversation. Rebecca is not asking a series of questions to test understanding; instead, she is inviting students to offer their own examples as guided by the task she has provided. She has directed the reading by setting the task.

After the Reading

After about twenty minutes, Rebecca reconvenes the group for a short discussion. First, she checks on their understanding. Then she invites them to share some of the language that they have found interesting. Both Amanda and Eric share language that they have also discussed in the conference.

> REBECCA: We're off to a nice start, I think. Before we even get into talking about the language, is there anything that you're not understanding?

Did everyone understand what a wampum belt is? [*Students nod.*] I'd like to have you share some interesting language and then explain why you like it or what it is that the author is showing by using that language that he couldn't have shown without using that language.

AMANDA: [*She reads the quotation she shared with Rebecca in their conference.*] I kind of like the beads leaping and dancing. They are bouncing around in the basket, but he makes them like they're dancing all together in one big group.

REBECCA: And that's what beads do when you shake them.

ERIC: [*Expanding on his thinking about the author's meaning*] I like page 6 at the beginning of the last paragraph, when it says, "Open my mind and watch what I see." I think that "open my mind and watch what I see" is really like saying that you give everything a chance. You shouldn't just say no or yes right away, but you should think about it first.

REBECCA: Hmm. Gayle, did you have that place marked too?

GAYLE: Yes.

REBECCA: Did you have anything to add to that?

GAYLE: Just like he was wondering what he was doing, and Cloud was telling him that he had to open up to whatever it was. Just by watching it, he can't understand it. He had to open his mind. He couldn't be thinking about grocery shopping or something. [*Everyone laughs.*]

REBECCA: That's a really nice way of saying it!

ALISON: On page 2, [*reading*] "The design held a story from long ago, a story that took place one way and no other. If the arrangement is confused, even a little bit, so is the story along with it." I think that's sort of like personification. The beads telling the story. Beads can't really talk.

REBECCA: Good. And Michael Dorris knows so much about Native American culture that this whole idea of having a belt that is made up of shells to tell a story—he can weave that into his writing and make it come alive. I found another example of a simile on page 4. [*She reads the passage about the boy's father touching his shoulder. Then she sets the scene for further reading: the students will finish this book as independent reading and come together again to discuss it.*] So we came up with all those beautiful examples of writing. As you keep reading, don't feel you have to write down something about each chapter; but the bits of the book or the paragraphs that really grab you the most, please write them down so that when we come together next week, we can share those and talk about them. Maybe we can share them with the rest of the class because we're always looking for examples of colorful, descriptive language, and this book is just so packed with that.

This lesson has a clear focus: Rebecca is helping her students notice how the author constructs language for particular purposes. The students are making personal and literary connections, but they use those connections to learn something about the way writers work. Rebecca's decisions and interactions mediate their reading in a way that helps them notice more and think more analytically about their reading without interfering with personal response and enjoyment. They are beginning to *analyze* a text in a way that will deepen their understanding.

Teaching for Strategies Using an Accessible Text

You do not select a text for the purpose of teaching a particular strategy. For example, you would not group texts as "texts to teach inferring" or "texts to teach summarizing." Readers use many strategies simultaneously while reading texts. You want to use high-quality, rich texts that offer students the opportunity to use a full range of comprehending strategies.

As you read a text in preparation for teaching, you decide what demands the text will make on the processing systems of the readers. As you teach, you are aware that students are using strategies simultaneously, and you are alert to ways to support the process.

From Unconscious to Conscious Acts in Reading

Light Attention				Heavy Attention
Open Response				Directed Response
❖ Experience and enjoy the book.	❖ Read the book and share something about it afterward. ❖ We'll talk about this book after we read it. ❖ Write a letter in your reader's notebook to share your thinking.	❖ As you read, be thinking about _____. ❖ Stop and think about _____ and mark one or two places. ❖ Mark one or two places you want to talk about.	❖ Stop at the end of each section and make notes on _____. ❖ Mark one or two places to show how the author _____. ❖ Highlight phrases and sentences where the author _____. ❖ Jot down phrases and sentences that show _____. ❖ Reread and mark places where the author _____. ❖ Include one paragraph in your letter that discusses _____.	❖ Place a code or mark on the text every place that _____. ❖ Think about all the things a writer does and mark examples throughout the text. ❖ Make marginal notes at places where you find _____ kind of information. ❖ Mark all the places in the text that show _____. ❖ Write a letter in your reader's notebook about _____. ❖ Take notes of new language and new words you find. ❖ Identify your thought processes and place marks in the text when you have them.

Figure 20–1. From Unconscious to Conscious Acts in Reading

Teach particular strategies through experiences with many different texts. One text offers many opportunities to learn; you must decide how to mediate the text to guide your students' learning experiences. Over time, you will build a repertoire of clear examples that lend themselves as teaching tools.

Undoubtedly you will use the same text to help students think about strategies in different ways. No text requires the reader to think only in one way. Remember, the purpose of guided reading is to help students:

- Extend the strategies they do control.
- Learn new processing strategies.

Mediating the Text

Given the complex systems of strategies we have described in Chapters 18 and 19, we would not expect any one lesson to focus on more than a few new ways of thinking. For example, Rebecca's students could easily make connections to other texts by Michael Dorris; they could bring background knowledge to the text; the concepts and the vocabulary were within their reach. Rebecca chose this accessible text to help her students think more analytically about the literary features that Dorris used and to help them make inferences. Her goal was not to solicit right or wrong answers but to invite

students to notice aspects of the writer's craft and to think deeply about the meaning.

Figure 20–1 presents a continuum from open to directed responses in reading. The continuum moves from simply experiencing and enjoying a text, an "open response," to systematically marking a text to record thoughts and responses, a highly "directed response." This directed approach is similar to "studying" the written material. When a reader encounters a text without mediation from a friend or a teacher, the response is open to any connection or thinking the reader might make. In a sense, it may be that no response to a text is truly "open," because we each connect our experiences so strongly; but the intentional teaching in guided reading definitely mediates students' responses. Just how much guidance you give is your decision.

Rebecca provided a "moderate" amount of mediation in her lesson. She asked students to be aware of a particular aspect of the text as they read, to stop and think about it, and to mark several places to share with the group. This kind of teaching is appropriate and very beneficial. As students become consciously aware of their insights and share them through discussion, they become better observers and interpreters of aspects of text (such as "showing rather than telling").

Nevertheless, such instruction can be overdone so that it interferes with students' understanding and enjoyment. The meaning a text offers the reader is an organic whole. Would any of us read very much if we always had to mark places in the text, make marginal notes, or "code" a text to identify thought processes? We must not train students to treat reading as a school exercise.

The idea is to teach *for* strategies in a way that reveals new aspects of reading and, ultimately, adds to students' enjoyment because they see so much more in their reading. As you make decisions about teaching, think carefully about what students can do and what will enhance their understanding. Then select a level of mediation that will nudge them gently toward deeper interpretation.

Level of Mediation

There are a range of options for helping students expand their comprehending strategies. Remember that students are reading

---

Level of Teacher Mediation

Show

❖ Demonstrate, explain behaviors related to the processing strategies.

Support

❖ Give readers opportunities to use the processing strategies with your support.

Prompt

❖ Call readers to action so that they use processing strategies for themselves.

Reinforce

❖ Acknowledge effective reading behaviors using specific description or praise.

Observe

❖ Notice behavioral evidence and infer readers' independent use of effective processing strategies.

Figure 20–2. Level of Teacher Support

silently most of the time and are in control of their own processing. We cannot tell exactly what they are doing when they are reading (and we don't need to).

When we talk about teaching *for* strategies rather than *teaching* strategies, we stress that comprehension takes place within the reader's head. We cannot directly teach students to understand, but we can engage in a range of options that help readers learn the processing strategies that are available. Figure 20–2 outlines five teaching options that range from providing very explicit and direct demonstrations to simple encouragement.

SHOW STUDENTS EFFECTIVE READING BEHAVIORS

The most direct approach is to demonstrate or explain behaviors related to a particular strategy. New behaviors always needs to be demonstrated, and many demonstrations are usually needed in connection with the complex strategies we are dealing with here. For example, if you want students to draw inferences from texts, you might take a section and "talk through" an inference you are making about a character or an event. You can also demonstrate how to select details with which to summarize a text, or how to make charts or diagrams to retrieve what you know about a topic prior to, during, and after reading. Students will need these demonstrations again and again, especially as they encounter new genres and increasingly challenging texts.

SUPPORT STUDENTS' EARLY ATTEMPTS AT EFFECTIVE READING BEHAVIORS

As soon as possible after demonstrating and explaining a behavior, you'll want to make it possible for students to use it for themselves. Select texts, during the reading of which, students will find it very easy to engage in the behaviors you want to support. Encourage and praise students for engaging in behaviors such as making inferences or analyzing. Make explicit to them what they have done and demonstrate again if necessary. The first chapters of *Guests* had plenty of opportunity for Rebecca's students to notice how writers can "show without telling."

PROMPT STUDENTS TO ENGAGE IN EFFECTIVE READING BEHAVIORS

Once readers understand helpful behaviors such as summarizing or making inferences, you can prompt them to use those strategies while reading. For example,

Rebecca prompted students to take an analytic stance toward the text. She had previously shown them how writers can "show without telling," a literary technique, which she demonstrated again. She asked students to note places where they found evidence of this technique. In doing so, she heightened their awareness before they began to read the text. During reading, she again prompted them to call up examples from their analysis of text. After reading, they shared those examples.

REINFORCE EFFECTIVE READING BEHAVIORS

Rebecca's conversations with students during and after reading helped them realize that what they noticed made them understand the story better and enjoy it more. She commented positively on what students noticed and encouraged them to search further. Another way to encourage and reinforce students' behavior is to enter into the activity with them, working alongside, listening intently, and responding to their ideas constructively.

OBSERVE STUDENTS USE OF EFFECTIVE READING BEHAVIORS

Finally, it is essential to observe students' reading behaviors consistently to gather evidence of their growing abilities. Observation is your most powerful tool, whether you are demonstrating for the students and engaging them in conversation or whether they are reading on their own.

In Chapter 28, we describe systematic ways of gathering information on students' reading ability; however, you will find that every moment you work with students, you are observing and noting important information. For example:

- *Listen to the questions they ask.* How are they directing their attention? What are they finding confusing? What insights are they revealing?
- *Notice their responses to your demonstrations and explanations.* Is there evidence that they understand your demonstration? Do they actively try to understand the new behavior?
- *Notice partially correct responses.* Are students showing that they are taking on the new behavior?
- *Listen to their conversations with one another.* Are they asking questions and searching for new understandings as they support one another?

■ *Observe them read silently.* Are they engaged? Do you notice any nonverbal reactions that indicate their enjoyment of or interest in the text?

■ *Observe them read orally.* What do their errors reveal about the information they are using (letter/sound relationships, language structure, meaning)? Is the reading fluent? Do they read in phrases that reflect the meaning?

■ *Read what they write in response to the texts.* Is there evidence that they are making connections to their personal lives, the world, or other texts? Are they analyzing the author's craft or critiquing the contents? Are they deriving meaning not directly stated in the text? Are they expressing new understandings?

As you decide whether to show, support, prompt, reinforce, or observe students, you will always be thinking about the range of strategies that you want them to acquire and use effectively while reading. Within a guided reading lesson, you can teach students strategies that sustain reading and expand meaning. You can apply these same teaching moves in conferences with individuals during reading workshop.

Teaching for Word-Solving Strategies

At bottom, students must be able to read the words of the text and know what they mean. Of course, comprehension involves thinking well beyond the word level, but words are the building blocks of meaning. For most students in the upper elementary grades, vocabulary is a larger issue than decoding. They can apply the general rules they need to "pronounce" a word, although that pronunciation may be halting or awkward and they may have only a vague idea of what the word means. You don't want them to proceed with partial or complete loss of meaning; you want students to use effective strategies to derive meaning from words.

Decoding

Many students in grades 3 through 6 are still learning how to take words apart, or "decode" them. Other students have good decoding skills but need more sophisticated analysis skills to be able to take apart complicated multisyllable words. Almost all students meet new challenges as they encounter the complex lan-

guage of more difficult texts. The most intimidating words have many syllables and unusual vowel or consonant patterns. The decoding load is made harder if students have never heard the word and/or do not know what the word means.

Teaching for word solving means helping students build strategies for approaching difficult words. Learning words in isolation by writing them or using them in a sentence is inefficient. Students need to employ more general strategies such as:

■ Noticing the parts of words.
■ Using letter-sound relationships in combination with predictions about meaning.
■ Connecting new words with known words.

It's not particularly useful to tell students to "look for the little words" within a multisyllable word. While students do notice words within words on occasion, the strategy can be overused. More important, it's often misleading. For example, it works to notice the word *base* in *basement* but not the word *sob* in *disobeyed*. It's much more productive for students to know a wide variety of word patterns and spellings to help them associate meaning.

As adults, we all employ such strategies, but most students will need many demonstrations in many contexts before they can apply them easily and flexibly across the texts that they read. While the primary focus of guided reading in upper elementary grades is the expansion of comprehending strategies, word solving is still a concern for teachers and should not be neglected.

Let's take an example. Most third graders enjoy reading *A Toad for Tuesday* (Erickson 1974), a whimsical story about two little toads, Morton and Warton, who live together in cozy domesticity. Morton is a good cook, and Warton is very tidy. Here is an example of the story's language:

> After finishing a huge supper they settled back to enjoy dessert. As Morton poured a cup of clover-blossom tea Warton said, "This is the finest beetle brittle I have ever eaten."
>
> "Thank you," Morton replied.
>
> Then Warton said, "I'll bet dear old Aunt Toolia would surely love some." (p. 9)

Warton's desire to take a journey leads him to rescue a mouse from a snowdrift and later be captured by a grumpy, sneaky owl who hunts in the daytime. The owl says he will eat Warton on Tuesday (the owl's birthday). During the five or so days before Tuesday, Warton and the owl have tea and talk, gradually becoming friends, although the toad becomes increasingly apprehensive as Tuesday draws near. The story ends in a dramatic rescue in which skiing mice deliver Warton from the owl's tree, after which all the mice in the vicinity band together to chase away a fox before he can kill the owl. This story is packed with interesting words like *flabbergasted, piercing, snarly, fascinated, gratitude,* and *salamander.* The characters are anthropomorphic, humorous, and engaging. The sixty-two-page book is not divided into chapters, and nearly every page features black-and-white line drawings.

When Diana introduced this book in a guided reading lesson, she recognized the opportunities for helping her third graders learn more about how words work. After she introduced students to the toad characters and the main plot, she had them turn pages as she engaged them in a conversation about the story. As she came to Aunt Toolia, she drew their attention to the print. Proper names are often difficult for students, but attempting to pronounce them offers opportunities to learn more about decoding:

> DIANA: Warton is going to give some of that delicious beetle brittle candy to his aunt. [*She writes* Aunt Toolia *on a small whiteboard with a dry-erase marker.*] Sometimes names are difficult, but if you look at Warton's aunt's name, you can find something that you know about the word.
> JERROLD: It has a *t* at the beginning.
> DIANA: Yes, but look further.
> ALICE: There's the word *too.*
> NYNA: It has *ia* at the end like *Julia.*
> DIANA: Yes, if you look at the first part of the word, you see *t, o, o,* like the word *too.* Add the *l* to that.
> NYNA: Tool. Toolia. That's a different name, but it's kind of like Julia.
> DIANA: He's going to see his Aunt Toolia. So when you see names, try to see whether there's something you know about them, just like you

would a word. You're also going to see some pretty long words in this story. [*She talks more about the story and invites some student comments. When she gets to page 14, she asks students to find* apologizing.]
> JERROLD: That's got four syllables.
> DIANA: Yes, and it's easier to figure it out if you break it up into syllables by saying and hearing it. It starts with *a* like *apart,* and then there are three more syllables. Read the word. [*Students read through the word.*]
> ALICE: It has *ing.*
> [*They finish discussing the story and then Diana makes one more point about the print.*]
> DIANA: This writer does one more thing that's interesting. Sometimes he puts together two words to show that they mean one thing. He puts a hyphen between the words to join them together—a mark like this [*demonstrating*]. Can you find an example on page 9?
> NYNA: Clover-b . . .
> JERROLD: It's clover-blossom? Clover-blossom tea?
> DIANA: Yes, that hyphen shows that the tea is the flavor of a blossom of clover. They go together. At first it looks like a long word, but you will find that you can divide it.

When Diana drew attention to the hyphenated word, she was not only teaching decoding strategies but also helping students with meaning.

Another opportunity to demonstrate word-solving strategies occurred when Steve was working with a group of students who were reading an editorial about a housing development. As part of their discussion after reading the piece, they had an opportunity to bring up words they found puzzling.

> WHITNEY: I have a question. What is *subdivision*?
> STEVE: Great! That's one of the words that can be broken down. [*Writes it on the whiteboard.*] What part do you see that you know?
> KAYLA: *Sub.*
> WHITNEY: *Division.*
> STEVE: So what does *division* mean?
> LARICE: You divide something up.

STEVE: If you subdivide something . . . does anyone know what that means?

WHITNEY: You take something away—subtract.

STEVE: If you divide something once, you've divided it. It you divide it again, you've subdivided it.

WHITNEY: Oh, like you have the big question and under it you have smaller questions.

STEVE: Right, like the submarine goes underwater . . . it's under it.

KAYLA: In subtract, something goes under.

STEVE: Yes, I see how you're thinking.

Students in this group were actually using their knowledge of the organization of ideas as a model for understanding the word *subdivision*. They were calling up mental images of outlines or mathematical problems. They were building networks of meaning around words and parts of words as well as learning a process for deriving the meaning of a multisyllable word.

EXPANDING VOCABULARY

Students in upper elementary grades continue to develop a reading vocabulary. The average student's reading vocabulary tends to grow by about three thousand to four thousand words each year (White, Graves, and Slater 1990). Even after the elementary years, students are still required to learn many new words. Nagy and Anderson (1984) have estimated that from fifth grade on, students probably encounter about ten thousand words a year that they have never seen in print. Experts recommend a combination of direct teaching of important words and concepts as well as instruction in learning words independently as they read (Graves and Graves 1994).

It is important for students to read texts that contain a large number of words they can read and understand or easily derive the meaning of from other information in the sentence or paragraph. Students also need to be challenged to develop strategies for acquiring new vocabulary. Knowing word meanings is especially important when reading in the content areas, since that's probably when words are most difficult. While comprehension involves far more than knowing the meaning of individual words, there is a high correlation between scores on vocabulary tests and scores on passage comprehension.

"Knowing" a word means that you know the literal meaning (the *denotation*). In addition, good readers:

- May know several different meanings for a word.
- Know that words with the same definitions can have subtle—sometimes emotionally connected—meanings to different people or groups of people (*connotations*).
- May connect word attributes to larger bodies of knowledge.

Most of the words in *A Toad for Tuesday* were accessible to Diana's group of students. While some words presented a decoding challenge, they were within students' listening vocabularies. Diana did call attention to the word *salamander*, in part because she thought some students might not know the meaning and also because this writer used the word in an unusual way: "He had also made ski poles to push with from porcupine quills and salamander leather" (p. 12).

SUPPORTING DECODING AND DERIVING MEANING

You can support students' decoding strategies in the following ways:

- Tell readers a word or the meaning of a word and point out important characteristics.
- Demonstrate analyzing word parts.
- Demonstrate using context to suggest a meaning for the word.
- Demonstrate how word parts are related to meaning.
- Prompt students to use a range of strategies to problem-solve.
- Reinforce effective problem solving.

As you confer with students, ask them to read aloud and prompt them to use the word-solving strategies you have been demonstrating. Some helpful prompts are listed in Figure 20–3. Your goal is to support students in applying what they know as they work to solve unfamiliar words. Make sure you use very clear language.

Prompts to Help Students Problem-Solve While Reading

Noticing and Correcting Errors

You noticed what was wrong.

Find the part that's not quite right.

Does that look right?

Where's the tricky part of the word?

What's wrong?

Why did you stop?

Do you think it looks like _____?

Were you right?

I like the way you worked on that word.

I like the way you worked that out.

It starts like that. Now check the last part.

Something wasn't quite right. Can you find your error?

You almost got that. See if you can find what is wrong.

You've got the first [last] part of the word right.

Try that again.

Try it another way.

Check the middle of the word.

You're nearly right. Try that again and think what
would look right.

Try that again and think what would sound right.

Try that again and think what would make sense.

That makes sense but does it look right?

That sounds right but does it look right?

That looks right but does it make sense?

Analyzing Words

Do you see a part that might help?

What do you know that might help?

Do you know a word like that?

Do you know a word that starts with those letters?

Do you know a word that ends with those letters?

Think of what the word could mean.

Is that word like another word you know?

Look for a part you know.

Say the first part, the next part … [letters and letter clusters]

Look at the middle of the word.

Look at the first syllable.

Notice the syllables.

Look at the root word [or base word].

Look at the prefix, the suffix.

Look at the ending of the word.

Cover the last part of the word.

Cover the first part of the word.

Deriving Word Meaning

Read the sentences [or paragraph]. What could that word
mean?

Is that word like any other words you know?

Think about the root word. It means …

Using Multiple Sources of Information

Think of what would make sense and check with the letters.

Sound the first part and think about what the word could be.

Predict what that word could mean. Would it fit the sentence
[paragraph, story]?

What can you do to help yourself?

What do you know that might help?

Do you know a word that would fit the meaning and looks
like [starts like, ends like] this word?

What could you try?

Read from the beginning and try that again.

Supporting Reading Fluency

How do you think your reading sounds?

Read the punctuation.

Make your voice go down when you see the period.

Make your voice go up when you see the question mark.

Take a short breath when you see the comma [or the dash].

Use emphasis when you see the exclamation point.

Make it sound like the characters are talking.

Set off the parentheses by stopping before and after them.

Read it like this [model phrase units].

Read this much all together [cover part of print to expose
the phrase unit].

Put your words together so it sounds like the way you talk.

Make your voice show what you think the author meant.

Figure 20–3. Prompts to Help Students Problem-Solve While Reading

Teaching for Monitoring and Correcting Strategies

Part of learning to solve words is learning to notice errors. Students must monitor their reading so that it is accurate and the meaning is clear. We're not talking here about slow, ponderous reading in which they pay attention to every word and correct every insignificant error. Many competent readers make errors, perhaps even note them at the time, but do not overtly correct them. During silent reading, readers stop and go back only when they lose meaning or encounter an unusual word that is puzzling. In general, though, high levels of accuracy are essential if the student is to apply higher-level comprehending strategies. In other words, the text must be accessible to the student. Problem solving related to gathering information, solving words, or deriving meaning must take place against a backdrop of accurate reading.

Even more important than accuracy is the student's ongoing awareness of whether he understands a text—whether it makes sense. The moment a reader loses the meaning, we want him to search for more information and problem-solve. In guided reading, you can:

■ Demonstrate how to notice errors.
■ Demonstrate how to confirm reading accuracy.
■ Prompt readers to notice errors and confirm accuracy.
■ Reinforce reading behaviors that indicate monitoring.

You are teaching for monitoring and correcting across the lesson, although the greatest opportunities will come during and after reading.

Before the reading, you introduce the text. The way you help students understand the text structure and meaning gives them something to "check against" as they are reading the story. For example, Diana's introduction to *A Toad for Tuesday* helped students understand that the characters were animals that had uniquely human personalities. She read a bit of the language so the students got an idea of Warton's way of thinking to himself and of the owl's personality.

As you listen to students read aloud, you can decide to intervene briefly, prompting and reinforcing the way they are noticing and repairing errors (see Figure 20–3). You may also decide simply to observe, gathering information that will inform your teaching. Remember that not all correcting will be observable even when

students are reading aloud. Students may note an error and, in the interest of efficiency, move on, or they may even change the subsequent syntax of the sentence to accommodate the error—a sure sign that they have noticed it and mentally corrected it. Effective readers *repair* the errors they make even if they do not explicitly *correct* them. If students are reading accurately, with understanding, you can assume that their monitoring and correcting systems are operating. The most efficient readers will probably reveal the least evidence of their sustaining strategies at work.

After reading, it may be appropriate to bring an explicit example to students' attention. Here are some ideas:

■ Ask students if they encountered tricky parts. Return to those parts and talk about how to search for the information they need.
■ Revisit a part of the text where you observed several students experiencing difficulty. Model ways of working to correct the error.
■ Identify a word, concept, or other aspect of text that offers an opportunity to illustrate how students can use their sense of meaning and visual aspects of text to monitor their reading. Walk through the process of noticing and using critical information.

Here's a classroom example. While reading the beginning biography *Laura Ingalls Wilder* (Blair 1981), the students in one of Lisa's guided-reading groups stumbled over the word *centennial* in the following passage:

> Soon it was 1876, America's centennial, which celebrated the first one hundred years after the country had fought for and won its independence. (p. 34)

The students had so much difficulty with the word in this rather long sentence that the process fell apart. They could not decode it, and they did not know what it meant. They tripped over the word but continued anyway. Here is how Lisa helped Jennie and David realize that learning about Laura meant checking on their own understanding of her world:

> LISA: You had a tricky word on page 34, didn't you? Let's find it.

353

DAVID: That one.

JENNIE: It's long but I don't know what it is.

LISA: Yes, I'd like you to clap it as I say it. *Cen-ten-ni-al: centennial.*

DAVID: There's four parts.

LISA: Now watch while I write it in parts. [*She writes the word on the whiteboard.*] Look at the first part.

JENNIE: It's like *cent*, like *one cent*.

LISA: It could be. The first syllable is *cen* [*points to it*], but if you look further, it does look like *cent*, which is like a penny. The next syllable is *ten*.

DAVID: Like the number *ten*.

LISA: Yes, this word is *centennial*. It does have something to do with numbers. It means the hundred-year birthday of a country. You may know a word that is a little like *centennial*. [*She writes* century *below* centennial.] A *century* is one hundred years. What parts are alike?

JENNIE: *Cent!* It's one hundred years old.

LISA: Yes, the Declaration of Independence was in 1776. One hundred years later, in 1876, it was like the country's one-hundredth birthday, the *centennial.* When you come to a word like that, you need to stop and think what it might mean based on connections you can make. If you can't figure it out, it's good to come back afterward like we just did. It helps you understand Laura's story because her family was having such a hard time while everyone else was celebrating.

Teaching for Information-Gathering Strategies

As students move through a text, they perceive and select the important information they will use as they apply higher-level comprehension strategies. To help students learn this process, you can:

■ Model noticing important information.
■ Ask students to locate important information and tell why it's important.
■ Make a list of the important information in the text.

In your introduction, you may communicate to students some of the important ideas they will encounter in the text, leaving others for their discovery. For example, as the group prepared to read *Laura Ingalls Wilder*, Lisa pointed out that it was important to notice every time Laura and her family had to move. She explained that while they experienced hard times, they also enjoyed new and exciting adventures. In *A Toad for Tuesday*, Diana helped students notice that the rescued mouse gave Warton a red scarf, along with a very specific warning. As students learn to gather information while reading, they increase their ability to make predictions.

Teaching for Predicting Strategies

Language and meaning together help readers predict what will come next. This sense of anticipation or expectation assists at both the word level and the meaning level. The reader is looking ahead to what *could be,* taking in the full range of possibilities. The syntactic patterns of the language reduce the alternatives, so the reader can use visual information efficiently. When students understand the structure of the text, they can select the information that is important and supports meaning.

The text introduction is the place to induce this anticipatory mind-set. During reading, you will want to observe students' behavior to determine whether they are using sources of information to propel their reading forward. When you and the students discuss a text after the reading, you can explore and expand their sense of anticipation.

Teaching for Phrasing and Fluency

Most of the time students will read silently, but fluency is still an issue and a goal of guided reading. We want students to be able to read with a rhythm, flow, and meter that sounds like everyday speech. A basic guide to promoting students' fluency is to select texts that are within their control: make sure that most words are in their reading vocabularies.

You can model fluent reading in your introduction as well as after students have read part of the text. Illustrate how to use phrasing and how to notice and use punctuation. After the reading, you may want students to read aloud brief parts of the text. Ask them to share a passage that highlights the writer's style or that contains an idea they found interesting or moving. This helps them practice fluency, because they will want what they read to be understood.

When students read aloud, they bring their own interpretations to the text as they reproduce the writer's emphasis, syntax, and tone. According to Marie Clay (1993):

> Fluent reading will arise from teacher attention to the role of oral language, and thinking and meaning, and increasing experience with the visual information in print, and practice in orchestrating complex processing on just-difficult enough texts. It is a matter of successful experience over a period of time moving up a gradient of difficulty of texts which can support fluent and successful reading. (p. 52)

As you confer with students while they are reading, you may want to prompt their oral reading in a way that increases their awareness of fluency. Some suggested prompts are presented in Figure 20–3.

Teachers are also concerned about students' rate of reading. A good rate for oral reading is about 100 to 150 words per minute; a good rate for silent reading is about 200 to 250 words per minute. Here are some ways to think about reading speed:

■ Rate of reading has a great deal to do with anticipating meaning. When students read quickly, they think about what might come next, and they confirm it using visual information. They don't just read words as isolated units. To build a good reading rate, students must understand what they are reading. The story introduction provides critical support to help students understand the language and the meaning of the text.

■ The ability to quickly recognize print information is another factor affecting the rate of reading. If a text has many words students do not know, their reading rate will slow down. Automatic, rapid word recognition allows students to think about the meaning, which in turn fosters fluency.

■ Most readers are more fluent (or decipher the

meaningful syntactic patterns better) on the second reading. Research by Samuels (1979) supports that when students read a passage aloud more than once, their reading is more free-flowing, largely accurate, and meaningfully phrased.

■ Shared reading, in which you and your students read together from a common text, supports fluency. (Many texts have songs, rhymes, or poems embedded in the text that are particularly appropriate for shared reading.)

Teaching for Adjusting Strategies

As readers, we approach different texts in different ways depending on our purpose; sometimes the structure of the text also influences how we read it. We may read some selections rapidly, perhaps even skimming over the print to pick up information. We may read other selections (or parts of texts) more slowly, pausing to think or make notes. When we read poetry, we may "hear" it in our head. These reading techniques may be part of your explicit teaching in guided reading. In the introduction, for example, you may instruct students to skim for some important information that is essential for them to understand while reading on their own. Before, during, or after reading, you may demonstrate reading to appreciate the language of the text or some other aspect such as humor. You may demonstrate slowing down to reflect on something in the text and then picking up speed again. You can highlight all these behaviors, making them observable to students so they can incorporate them into their own repertoire.

As students learn to think about the purpose for reading, they also learn to adjust their reading. In your introduction, make sure you make clear the relationship between purpose, text, rate, and method of reading. You may need to teach students to examine and think about what side headings mean in an informational text or to look at the legends under pictures. This kind of reading takes slightly more time than reading a narrative that flows from event to event. Remind students that if they need to remember details for later discussion, they may need to slow down in order to collect that information and relate it to what they already know. If they are reading to find a certain topic of interest and do not need to attend to other parts of the text, show them how to skim or scan the text to find where to focus.

Summary

The processing strategies support the operating system as students construct meaning with a text. You may want to photocopy Figure 20–3 and put it on a clipboard so that as you confer with students you can use language that enables them to learn how to problem-solve for themselves.

Suggestions for Professional Development

1. Work with a group of colleagues at your grade level or across grade levels.
2. Have each person audiotape a student reading about three hundred words of a text.
   - The text should be at an appropriate instructional level for the student.
   - Ask the student to read through the text silently before reading into the tape recorder.
   - Calculate an accuracy rate for the reading (percentage of words read correctly).

3. Bring photocopies of the text to a work session to share with colleagues. Take turns playing your audiotapes. Each time, consider the following questions:
   - What evidence is there that the student is solving words? How is the reader working on unfamiliar words? Is the reader stopping, saying the whole word, doing a sound analysis, or using parts of words? What is the reader paying attention to as a word solver?
   - What evidence is there that the reader is monitoring and correcting his reading?
   - Is the reading fluent? Is the reader using phrase units? Is the reader using the punctuation?
   - Does the reader slow down to problem-solve and then speed up again?
   - Does the text support the reader's use of sustaining strategies? Is it so difficult that the process breaks down in places?
   - What does this student's oral reading indicate that he needs to learn next?
4. After analyzing several readers, talk about the new insights you have about the reading process and how that will impact your work with individual students in guided reading.
5. Follow up this session by repeating the analysis with struggling readers. Make sure to select a text that is appropriate for their needs.

## CHAPTER TWENTY-ONE

TEACHING FOR CONNECTING AND EXPANDING STRATEGIES IN GUIDED READING

The gift of creative reading, like all natural gifts, must be nourished or it will atrophy. And you nourish it, in much the same way you nourish the gift of writing—you read, think, talk, look, listen, hate, fear, love, weep—and bring all of your life like a sieve to what you read. That which is not worthy of your gift will quickly pass through, but the gold remains.

—KATHERINE PATERSON

One of the key decisions you make as a teacher is whether and how much to influence students' reading. Too much interaction while students are reading can interrupt and fragment their processing and interfere with comprehension. Heavy-handed assignments that force students to take detailed notes or answer specific questions can have the same result. Yet you want to help readers move forward in their development of the comprehension strategies that are required for sophisticated academic and, ultimately, professional work.

Guided reading provides a context in which you can actively and intentionally support students' development of a wide range of connecting and expanding strategies. In the enjoyable and interactive process of guided reading, you can help students recognize the importance of making connections between their own background knowledge and the ideas they meet in a text. Through this experience, they begin to see how sharing these connections can enhance their appreciation of a text. Guided reading is also ideal for showing students ways of going beyond the meaning of any particular text to select what is important and draw inferences and conclusions. Students begin to see that analysis and criticism do not need to be dry academic exercises.

Teaching for Strategies That Expand Meaning

Reading comprehension involves using complex strategy systems to construct meaning. Strategies are both conscious and unconscious; they are used simultane-

ously; and they access, use, and modify the knowledge the reader already has. The prior knowledge that students bring to reading greatly influences comprehension. This prior knowledge is organized and stored in the brain, so that readers can, as needed, seek, select, and use information (Smith 1988). The storage and organization systems, sometimes called the "building blocks of cognition" have been described as "schemata" (Rumelhart 1982). According to Vacca and Vacca (1999, p. 16), these "schemata influence reading comprehension in three ways:

> First, schema provides a framework for learning that allows readers to *seek and select* information that is relevant to their purposes for reading…*to make inferences…anticipate content and make predictions* ….
> Second, schema helps readers *organize* text information … [to] *retain and remember…*
> And third, schema helps readers *elaborate* information.

The concept of a schematic structure helps us think about the reader's knowledge as an organized set of information (Anderson, Spiro, and Anderson 1977; Rumelhart 1977). A *schema* can be a diagram, an outline, or a mental image. Knowledge is organized in the mind according to a person's current understanding; these mental models are accessed when the reader makes connections, and they are modified as the reader takes on new knowledge. Visual or sensory images may be incorporated into the reader's schematic structures, and emotions may be connected with the ideas in the mental model.

As we read, the connections we make with our own sets of knowledge make it possible for us to engage in the higher-level comprehension strategies of connecting, inferring, summarizing, synthesizing, analyzing, and critiquing. This is not an exhaustive list, since what happens in the brain is complex; nor are these discrete categories. As we read, we are *simultaneously* summarizing information and forming inferences and synthesizing information so that we modify (if in very slight ways) our own stores of knowledge or mental models.

It is impossible to think of each of these strategies as the focus of a specific lesson. There is a difference between learning an *item of knowledge*, which is then stored in the memory, and in learning a *process*. An item of knowledge might be something like a letter, the name of a color, or the shape of an object. Items are useful because they can be added to the knowledge organized in our mental models. A process, on the other hand, is a series of complex actions. Learning a process involves *doing it* again and again in different ways, each time learning more about how to adjust, modify, and refine the series of actions.

Connecting

Readers bring information to their processing of the text, and these connections set the scene for higher-level comprehension. They draw on their personal experiences, their knowledge of the world, and their previous experiences with texts as a basis for connecting, inferring, summarizing, synthesizing, analyzing, and critiquing. If students approach the reading of each text as an isolated experience—one of processing words or trying to remember facts without making connections to other information—they will not be able to engage in these complex cognitive activities, all of which require the application of previous knowledge. You can help your students become active "connectors" by:

■ Sharing your own connections between your reading and your personal life, your knowledge of the world and content areas, and other texts with similar themes, settings, and characters or by the same author.

■ Showing them how to make their own connections between reading and self, the world, and other texts.

■ Prompting them to make these connections to their experience and other texts they have read and to recall background information.

■ Giving positive feedback when they share their experiences, bring background knowledge to bear while reading a text, or mention other texts that are similar to the one they are reading.

■ Observing students' conversations with one another and with you to determine the extent to which they are actively making connections.

MAKING PERSONAL CONNECTIONS

You can help students make personal connections before, during, and after reading. In your introduction, you can invite students to consider questions like these:

■ How are the events in or the subject matter of this text similar to your own life? Different from your own life?

■ How are the events in or the subject matter of this text similar to the life of people you know? Different from the life of people you know?

■ What does this book's [characters, setting, plot] remind you of?

For example, when Linda introduced *No Dogs Allowed* (Cutler 1992), students immediately "tuned in" to this funny story featuring a five-year-old (who thinks he's a dog) and his exasperated older brother. Linda invited students to look at the picture on page 13, showing the little boy sitting up like a dog and begging to a policeman. Mentioning that "sometimes little brothers or sisters can be weird," she invited students to share their own connections. Almost everyone had a little brother, sister, cousin, or younger family friend.

MAKING CONNECTIONS TO WORLD EXPERIENCE

The more the reader knows about a topic or the information in a text, the easier it is to comprehend that text. New information presented in context is easier to extract, and summarizing and synthesizing can take place. For example, readers who know something about what life was like on the prairie for pioneers, what work on a farm is like, or what it meant to travel in wagons instead of automobiles and trains will find *Laura Ingalls Wilder* easier to read and understand.

Your observations of students' behavior will help you determine what they already know so you can select texts that will expand that knowledge. You will want to show, support, prompt, and reinforce the process of bringing prior knowledge to the reading. In her introduction to *Laura Ingalls Wilder*, Lisa asked students to think about what they knew about pioneers and their lives. Some answers were:

- They traveled in covered wagons.
- They went west.
- They didn't go to school sometimes.
- They had a hard life.

From these responses Lisa knew that even though these students had as yet undertaken no formal study about pioneer life, they had enough information to be able to anticipate what Laura's life was like even before reading the book. She explained, "You know some things about pioneers, so you already know something about the life of Laura Ingalls Wilder. This is a biography of Laura. You'll find that the writer of this biography has mentioned some of the ideas you came up with." In this way, she signaled to students that it is important to think about what they know as they begin to read a text and while they are reading it.

Background knowledge is especially important when students encounter informational text. A text can never tell readers everything they must know for full understanding. Readers create meaning by bringing outside information to bear, connecting it with the information in the text, and inferring ideas from that connection.

For example, reading a book about whales should prompt students to recall "facts" they have learned, such as:

- Whales are mammals, but they live in the sea.
- A mammal is a warm-blooded animal.
- Whales aren't fish.
- Whales breathe air as we do.
- Whales bear their babies live.
- Whales are endangered.

They might also call up images of whales (for example, *Whales: Killer Whales, Blue Whales, and More*, Hodge 1997) they have seen in person or in films. With these facts and images in mind, they will be able to understand expanded concepts in the text, such as:

- The whale is the largest mammal.
- Whales breathe air through blowholes.
- There are two kinds of whales, baleen and toothed.

- Whales have been hunted until they are almost extinct.
- Whales eat plankton from the top of the sea.

As you work with students, you can help them make connections to background information by:

- Modeling your thinking about background information during the introduction.
- Eliciting information from the group and reminding students that they already know something about the topic that will help them as they read.
- Prompting students to recall what they already know while they are reading.
- After the reading, asking them to compare what they already knew with what they learned.

As students make connections, they expand the number of words they know or have seen; they also learn new words that they can connect with known words. For example, in a guided reading lesson, Rebecca and a group of students were examining the editorial page of a newspaper. She pointed out that editorials are opinions and described several kinds. One of the editorials in the paper that day was about the fact that people don't walk to school anymore. Here's part of their discussion:

REBECCA: Here's a word that you will see in this editorial that you might want to think about. It's *entrenched*. What do you think it might mean?

ANDREA: *Entrenched* . . . is that like . . . like bad habits you want to break?

REBECCA: Not necessarily, but from the context you were doing some good thinking; it does sound like it's related to a bad habit.

DAVID: Is it like a deep habit, maybe?

REBECCA: Yes. Why do you say that?

ERIC: It's like entrenched . . . maybe in your mind or something. It's kind of hard or something— it's really like you always do that or something.

REBECCA: What's a trench?

ANDREA: I agree with David about its being a deep habit, because when I think of *trenched*, I think of soaked up.

REBECCA: Oh, *drenched*—like *soaked*? Okay. You might have to dig a trench when it rains.

DAVID: It's like a deep, deep habit—you can't get away—it's very bad.

REBECCA: Exactly. So if something is entrenched in society or entrenched in our culture, it means that people are doing it and it's so deeply engrained, or entrenched, that they can't break out of it.

MAKING CONNECTIONS TO OTHER TEXTS

One of the wonderful things about reading is that readers constantly make connections between and among the texts they read. The more they read, the easier it is to understand how texts are organized and how writers use language to create characters, plot, and meaning. Furthermore, readers don't just make connections among texts they have read; they learn from texts they have heard read aloud or viewed as a film. Engaging with a text may involve making connections to:

- Content: I've read another book on this topic.
- Genre: This is a mystery like . . .
- Author: This author always . . .
- Illustrator: I recognize these pictures by . . .
- Setting: _____ took place in this same location.
- Characters: She reminds me of ___ in another book I read.
- Illustrations: These illustrations remind me of the ones in _____.
- Plot: This story is like _____.
- Structure: This story has a [literary device, such as flashback] just like _____.
- Theme: I'm learning the same lesson in this book as in _____.
- Language: This writer's language reminds me of _____'s.
- Tone: This book is [funny, sad, angry] just like _____.

Choose books for guided reading that will encourage readers to connect with other texts. For example, one of the reasons Lisa selected *Laura Ingalls Wilder* was that several students had read at least one of the *Little House* books. She knew they would be sure to make text-to-text connections between this biography and other books. Through their connections, the students:

- Realized why Laura Ingalls Wilder was important

enough to warrant a biography.
- Compared Laura's real life with the life she described in her books.
- Learned more about Laura's real family members.
- Found out that Laura was relatively old when she began to write and that she wrote many books.
- Added details of Laura's real life to what they knew from the books they'd read.
- Realized the authentic base of the Little House books.
- Began to understand the differences between biography and historical fiction.

INFERRING

Inferring involves going beyond the literal meaning of a text to derive what is not there but is implied. When you infer, you use the connections you have made and the information extracted from the text to form tentative theories and to create sensory images. "Visualizing" like this makes reading come alive. You think you actually know the characters—how they look or sound. You imagine a setting and feel you are there. You may feel empathy for characters, sadness at tragic events, or anger at injustice—all because you understand the text beyond the literal level.

Students learn to make inferences by reading meaningful texts that offer the opportunity for them to form such theories. When Rebecca asked her group to consider the meaning of the passage in *Guests* (Dorris 1994) that begins "These people are not our relatives . . . ," she provoked them to:

- Think about the author and other books he has written.
- Call up what they know about the time period in which Native Americans lived in villages such as the one described in the story.
- Consider who the "guests" might be who speak another language.

Rebecca wanted the students not only to make connections but to go beyond that to infer what was not stated—that Moss's family are Native Americans who are encountering strangers who do not know their culture. These inferences would help them make further inferences about the main character's feelings and understand why he acts as he does.

Another way to help students learn to make inferences is to model the process yourself. When Rebecca introduced the editorial about walking to school to her students, she presented several facts: "The editor is talking about the fact that not many children are walking to school. When my parents were young, most children walked to school, and when I was young most children walked to school. I think the writer is trying to say that, now, most children do not walk to school and that might be a problem. I'm relating this problem to his major point that kids don't get enough exercise today. So when you read what the writer says, you are always trying to think, *What does the writer really mean?*"

When you model your own inferences, you help students learn how to engage in the process. You may also want to suggest that they look for meanings the author suggests but does not state precisely. Some examples of questions that can foster inferences are:

- What did _____ make you think about?
- What do you think this character really meant by saying that?
- Why did this character [act, think, talk] that way?
- What's this story really about?
- What does this character want to do?
- What do you think this character might do?
- What is the author really trying to say?

Summarizing

Summarizing involves putting together information while reading. The reader identifies information, extracts it from print, and forms an ongoing summary of what it means. It is important for readers to remember important ideas, events, details, or other information. The organizing and reorganizing process not only supports memory but also helps readers sort ideas into useful categories that can be connected. Summarizing involves bringing the information together in concise form. Learning to summarize helps students add information to the stores of knowledge organized in their brain. It also helps them take information from the text and make it their own.

Most students need teacher support to learn sophisticated strategies for summarizing. You may need to model summarizing and involve students in a group discussion that leads to summary. For example, Diana met with a group of students to generate a summary

Figure 21–1. Our Summary of Dear Mr. Henshaw

on chart paper for *Dear Mr. Henshaw* (Cleary 1983). During the discussion, the students began by providing a lot of details about the main character:

- In second grade he wrote to the author.
- In fourth grade he made a diorama.
- He had to move to a new town in sixth grade.
- His dad drove a truck and took the dog with him.
- His teachers always wanted him to make a book report or do something about a book he had read.
- He always wrote to the author every year because he didn't want to read another book.

From these details, the students were able to put together concise statements that contained only the essential information, coming up with the summary shown in Figure 21–1. Diana helped these students distinguish between "retelling" a story (which is simply recounting as many details as you can) and "summarizing," which involves selecting information and creating a concise statement.

To help students learn to summarize, you can:

▪ Write a summary yourself of a text that students know or have read and ask students to analyze what makes it a summary.

▪ Begin the process with short texts that do not have too many details and are easier to summarize.

▪ Work together to create a group summary, selecting and deleting details.

▪ Record a retelling of a text on chart paper and turn it into a summary.

▪ Have students work in pairs to create alternative summaries of a text. Share them in the group and point out the summaries that are concise and include only the necessary details.

▪ Have each student write a summary and then share it with a partner.

▪ Ask students to summarize a text in their reader's notebook, and respond to this summary in the letter you write back.

▪ Encourage students to practice summarizing by making book talks to recommend books to their friends.

Remember that summarizing is an in-the-head strategy. The purpose is to help the reader comprehend the text. The current emphasis on proficiency tests—*write a summary* or *select a good summary* from alternatives or *annotate the text*—makes summarizing a required skill. The goal however is larger than passing the test. We want students to be able to abstract the important ideas and carry them forward as tools for thought.

Synthesizing

Synthesizing requires bringing together information from the text and from personal, world, and literary knowledge to create new understanding. Here, students are getting the "big picture"; the whole is greater than the parts.

While summarizing brings together information from the text, synthesizing involves taking that information and creating *newly organized and formed understandings* that are different from the text and also different from the reader's previous understandings. In synthesizing, readers see the relationships between ideas and expand their personal understanding. As with summarizing, you can model synthesizing by talking aloud about your own understanding and what you have learned from a text. Synthesizing lets readers recognize the "big ideas" in books and link them to themes of human life.

Kristen was working with students who were reading *Yang the Youngest and His Terrible Ear* (Namioka 1992; see Chapter 14). They had just finished reading the first two chapters of this story of Yingtao, whose family had just immigrated to the United States from China. Kristen asked the students what ideas this book helped them think about. Students came up with this list:

▪ People can be friends even though they are from different kinds of families.

▪ It's difficult sometimes to do what you want and still please your family.

▪ The differences between a Chinese family and an American family are interesting, not bad.

▪ Sometimes you want to be able to do something to fit into your family but you aren't good at it; you have to do what you are good at doing.

▪ It's hard to be a new person in a school, especially if you come from a background that is different from that of the other kids.

All of these ideas are themes running through the book. Themes connect the particular text with the human experience and help us modify our own thinking as we take on new information or have vicarious experiences. As students read this book, they learned a little bit more of what it is like to be an immigrant in a new country. They were not only synthesizing some new information about Chinese culture but also synthesizing ideas that are universal to all people, especially children their age. They were looking for the larger meanings that lie below the surface.

You can help students learn to synthesize across texts. While *Charlotte's Web* (White 1954) is a story about a spider and a pig, students may also realize that it is a story of friendship and interdependence among persons who have differences. If you encourage them to connect the story to stories like *Amos and Boris* (Steig 1971), a picture book about an unlikely friendship between a whale and a mouse, they will develop a fuller awareness of the theme.

You can use a book introduction to engage students in conversation that will foster synthesis and get them thinking about the big ideas. For example, when you introduce a story like *Yang the Youngest*, you might ask students to mark a place in the book that suggests the challenges a person who is new to this country might face. After they have read a section of the text, ask them to discuss what they have noticed, with the goal of revealing one of the overall themes. Well-written books such as *Yang the Youngest* will have several layers of meaning through which students can make connections. As they synthesize the information in light of their own experiences and background, they will begin to understand the text in a larger way.

As you help students synthesize, you want to encourage them to support their thinking with evidence from the text or other sources. For example, in the discussion of *Yang the Youngest*, several students said that Yingtao and Matthew were becoming friends even though they were different. They supported their thinking with these details from the text:

- Matthew didn't have much money and didn't like to talk about it, but Yingtao made him feel okay because Chinese people don't mind talking about money.
- Matthew just laughed when he saw the fish in Yingtao's bathtub, but it wasn't a mean laugh.
- Matthew thought it was funny when Yingtao thought he wanted to take a bath because he asked where the bathroom was instead of where the toilet was.

As students synthesize ideas and information from text, they are constantly using the connections they make to their personal experience, world experience, and text experience. Some questions that prompt students to synthesize are:

- What is the author's message?
- What is the story really about?
- What message does this story teach about life?
- How has your understanding of the topic changed?
- What do you know about this topic after reading this material?
- What evidence supports your thinking about the big ideas?

Analyzing

In analyzing, readers take on the stance of examiner. They are not simply experiencing the text or gaining information from it but are:

- Standing back and looking carefully at the text.
- Determining how the text is organized—how it "works."
- Discovering how the literary elements of the text work together to convey meaning and emotion.
- Thinking about how writing, graphic features, illustrations, and format work together.

Through analyzing, readers gain a deeper understanding of a text by looking at the elements and how they fit together. In the process, they are learning about how writers craft a text.

In guided reading, you have the opportunity to teach readers to look at the elements of texts. In the introduction, during reading, and during discussion, you can engage students in analyzing the text (or parts of the text) from several points of view.

Guided reading also provides a good context for helping students learn to read a new genre and to identify characteristics of that genre:

- You have selected the text to be "readable" for the group.
- All students are reading the same text, so they will share meaning and can support one another's learning.
- You know the experiences students have had with texts in this genre (e.g., from hearing them read aloud in the classroom) and can help them make connections.

ANALYZING FICTION

In the introduction of a work of fiction, you can guide your students to focus on particular aspects of the text.

For example, you can ask students to:

▪ Identify the main character or characters.
▪ Show ways in which they used the descriptions of the characters to infer what the characters are thinking.
▪ Look for what characters say or think, their physical appearance, what they do, or what others say about them.
▪ Discover how the author reveals the setting.
▪ Search for the problem in the story and think about how the main character reacts.

As Rebecca's students were reading *Guests*, she encouraged them to look for language indicating how the writer was "showing" instead of "telling." Analyzing the writing was the main focus of the guided reading lesson; this direction required students to make inferences but also to enter into beginning literary analysis by noticing how the writer was using inference.

Analyzing Nonfiction

Students need to learn how nonfiction texts are organized in order to understand how to gather information. In your introductions, you can guide them to examine the structure of trade books, content area textbooks, newspaper articles, informational brochures, magazine articles, online material, and any other expository materials that students need to read.

As they read nonfiction, students need to notice how information is presented in ways other than continuous text. There might be diagrams, maps, charts, and photographs, each with explanatory material attached in the form of legends or labels. The text might be organized so that headings help the reader put together the information. Your introduction can guide students to be aware of important factors as they read, including:

▪ How the author has organized information and identified that organization by heads and subheads.
▪ The ways in which information is presented, such as chronologically, in categories, or in contrasting sets.
▪ How the author uses "signal" words and phrases, such as *first, second, next, finally*, or *on the one hand* and *on the other hand* to show passage of time or the relationship of ideas.
▪ How the causes or consequences of events are presented in the text.

▪ How the author compares one idea, place, species, and so on with another.

Marcella's fourth graders were about to start reading *Cesar Chavez: A Photo-Illustrated Biography* (Davis 1998). This short biography covers the subject's life, but it can be read in one sitting and provides information in a clear, understandable way. The volume contains ten one-page sections, each of which presents some important information about the farm labor leader. The back matter includes quotes by Chavez, important dates in his life, a glossary, recommendations for further reading and Internet sites, and an index. Marcella began by showing the children that the first section provided some important information about Cesar Chavez. She read the first paragraph and talked briefly about what was important about Chavez. She also showed students how they could derive information from the text:

MARCELLA: Look in the first paragraph where it says "a union called the *United Farm Workers*." What does it say next?

JOSEPHA: [*Reading*] "A union seeks fair treatment and better pay for workers."

MARCELLA: A union is a group of people. What do they want?

RAYMOND: Better pay and a better life.

HAROLD: They want to be treated fair.

MARCELLA: That's what Cesar Chavez and his union wanted. Sometimes in this book, you will find that a word will be defined for you right after it is used. Do you see how the word union is defined? Now read the next paragraph. [Students read the next paragraph to themselves.] Did you find that one of the words is explained?

RAYMOND: Yes, *violence*. It says, "Violence is the use of force."

MARCELLA: Yes, if you don't understand a word, look for help in the paragraph. Chavez's union wanted fairness but they didn't want violence, so they organized boycotts, and that will be defined for you in the book if you don't know what it is.

Next, Marcella showed the students how the text is organized into sections and told them that the heading of each section would give them an idea about the information they would find there. Also, she pointed out that there is a picture for each section and one sentence in bold at the bottom of the text page that contains an important fact drawn from the material on the page and related to the picture.

In later discussions of the text, students looked again at the statements in bold and the pictures. This information helped them make their own summary of the book. They also examined the quotes by Chavez, talking about what he might have meant and relating his words to his life. They looked at the time line of events in Chavez's life, thinking about their lives in relation to his. Marcella reminded them that this chart would be useful to return to as they looked at the lives of other historical characters. Marcella also created some prompts to help them summarize Cesar Chavez's most important accomplishment:

- What differences did Cesar Chavez make in peoples' lives?
- What problems did he try to overcome?
- How did he do it?
- What will we remember him for?

This simple biography taught students about an important figure in recent history, and it helped them learn how an informational text works. In this case, the content was highly factual, so it did not offer much insight into Chavez's personal dilemmas, conflicts, or emotions. As students read more complex biographies, you will want to teach them to raise questions such as:

- How did the person change in the course of her life?
- How did this person's personal life experiences and challenges contribute to her accomplishments?
- What problems and difficulties did she struggle with?
- What were the problems and difficulties of the times in which she lived?
- What have we learned from this person that we can apply to our own lives?
- What was the author's perspective on the subject of the biography? Can you tell where and how the author got her information?

Critiquing

We use critiquing here in the broadest sense of the word, which is evaluating against standards or criteria.

Critiquing involves judging or evaluating a text based on personal, world, or textual knowledge. As with analysis, the reader's connections form a basis for reading with a critical eye. For example, the more you know about a particular period in history, the more likely you are to be critical of (or delighted by) the way characters and setting are presented in a historical novel. If the characters behave in ways that are totally out of *sync* with what you know about prevailing values and attitudes of the period, you may question the authenticity of the story. If only one character violates those norms, that might be the theme of the story. If settings are described in ways that you know are inconsistent with a particular place at a particular time, you will be cautious about believing the account.

The key is to engage your students in the process, so they become thoughtful consumers of print. You don't want them to grow up thinking, *If it's in print, it must be true.* Much printed material is incorrect and/or biased, and right from the start young students need to begin detecting inaccuracies, inconsistencies, and prejudice in the material they read.

Criticizing may have either positive or negative outcomes. Students who learn to question the texts they read are engaging in critical reading, the highest form of comprehending. One of the first steps is to encourage students to ask questions: help them make questioning a habitual part of their reading. You can share your own questions and opinions about what the author says. You can model how you bring your own background knowledge to bear as you question what the author is saying.

This process can be particularly important as students read textbooks. In an effort to present a large amount of information, publishers sometimes leave out some seemingly "insignificant" material—such as the contributions of women and African Americans. Teach your students to notice what's missing, and help them find other resources that contain the information.

Here are some other suggestions for starting students on their way to becoming critical readers:

- In your introduction to a text, ask students to start thinking about some of the knowledge they already have about the topic, setting, or genre. Recalling what they know will give them criteria against which to evaluate the text.
- Before or after reading, discuss the author. Help stu-

dents form the habit of looking at the author's qualifications (particularly for informational books).

■ Ask students consciously to raise questions about the topic or setting while they are reading and to make notes to share with the group.

■ In discussions after the reading, invite students to compare their reactions and share their assessments of the authenticity of the text, the overall message, the perspective, the bias, or some other aspect.

■ Ask students to write their assessments of fiction and nonfiction texts from several points of view.

■ Focus students' attention on a particular aspect of the text that you want them to learn to criticize, such as use of description, character development, or plot sequence. Help them understand how this text measures up against criteria for quality within a genre.

You will want students to become critical readers of both fiction and nonfiction. Some questions you might encourage readers to ask about a nonfiction text are:

■ What is the perspective from which the history or biography is told? Are there other perspectives?

■ What information is left out of the text?

■ How accurate is the information in terms of the subject?

■ What is the source of the information? Is it reliable? Is it authentic?

■ How effective is the writer in conveying the information?

Some questions you might teach readers to ask about a fiction text are:

■ How believable is this story?

■ Are the details of the setting accurate?

■ Are the characters believable in the way they talk, feel, or act?

■ Do characters relate to one another in ways that make sense?

■ Does the plot proceed in a logical way to a conclusion?

■ How well does the author communicate the mood of the story and its effect on characters?

■ How effectively does the author communicate the theme of the story?

■ How effectively does the author use language to bring the reader into the story?

■ Is the author effective in engaging the reader's interest or creating empathy for characters?

An Example of Teaching for Expanding Strategies with Fiction

Abel's Island (Steig 1976) is a highly literary novel about a little mouse, Abel, who is blown away from his wife, Amanda, and is marooned on an island for a long time. Abel's personality is key to enjoying the story, so Emily wanted to be sure that her students appreciated how the author captured the tone of the story and established the main character. Here are the opening paragraphs:

> Early in August, 1907, the first year of their marriage, Abel and Amanda went to picnic in the woods some distance from the town where they lived. The sky was overcast, but Abel didn't think it would be so inconsiderate as to rain when he and his lovely wife were in the mood for an outing.
>
> They enjoyed a pleasant lunch in the sunless woods, sharing delicate sandwiches of pot cheese and watercress, along with hard-boiled quail egg, onions, olives, and black caviar. They toasted each other, and everything else, with a bright champagne which was kept cool in a bucket of ice. Then they played a jolly game of croquet, laughing without much reason, and they continued laughing as they relaxed on a carpet of moss. (p. 4)

After listening to Emily read the paragraphs, students generated these comments:

■ It's an old-fashioned story.

■ Abel and Amanda are very fancy.

■ They are very polite.

■ Abel talks about how it wouldn't be so "inconsiderate" as to rain.

■ Everything just goes their way.

■ They eat fancy things.

■ The writer gives a lot of details of their picnic.

Emily encouraged them to talk about why these details are important in how the writer sets the tone of the story. Students commented that:

- It's showing us that they are very polite and proper.
- The writer lists all those things they ate because he wants us to know that Abel is used to getting what he wants.
- Abel likes lots of good things.

Then, Emily asked students if they thought Steig does a good job of introducing Abel in the first two paragraphs. Student comments were:

- I think he did because he gave us the date, which is long ago, but also his language is old-fashioned. He used old-fashioned words like jolly. We don't talk like that.
- He was good because he had so many details of what they had to eat. Caviar—that costs a lot of money, so he was showing that they were kind of rich.
- He even showed that they had an ice bucket at a picnic. He was really saying that these are kind of particular people. Even though they're just mice, they're like people.

Emily pointed out that these animals did have human qualities and that Steig is really effective in making his animal characters seem like people. In his books, he introduces real-life issues by presenting these characters and describing their adventures. Thus Emily set the scene for the misadventures that befall this very particular mouse.

The students began by simply gathering information from the first two paragraphs, but they moved on to analyze the writer's style. This analysis formed the foundation for evaluating the effectiveness of the opening paragraphs of the book. Analysis and criticism go together because:

- Students need to analyze to be aware of the writer's craft.
- Students need to form their own opinions, to be aware of what makes quality, and to apply judgment while reading.

An Example of Teaching for Expanding Strategies with Nonfiction

A group of students had read the first twenty-one pages of *What's the Big Idea, Ben Franklin?* (Fritz 1976) and were discussing it with their teacher. Fritz reveals many details of Franklin's young life, and the volume is illustrated with pictures that not only give readers a picture of young Ben but also show some of the more ingenious ways he approached problem solving.

Janet asked, "What are some of the ways Jean Fritz lets you know what kind of person Benjamin Franklin was?" Some student responses were:

- She tells how he was the youngest son of the youngest son and so on and that made him special and he was smart.
- There are pictures of swimming, and she tells all the different ways he tried swimming, like using a kite to pull him across the pond, but it was funny that he didn't have his clothes.
- He did magic squares in math.

Janet then asked students whether they felt this book was helping them get a new picture of what Benjamin Franklin was like. Some comments were:

- Yes, because the way Jean Fritz tells interesting stories makes him seem more interesting than what I knew about him.
- The author is showing that he was really smart, not just saying he was smart. She gives examples of all the things he did that a smart person would do.

First Janet invites students to synthesize information from the text and take an analytic stance: what does the writer do? The second question moves them to a critical stance—that is, it prompts them to examine their own growing knowledge in relation to the writer's skill.

In a later discussion, after students had finished the book, they talked about what they had previously known about Benjamin Franklin and what new information the book gave them. They raised questions about facts that were presented in the book and checked those facts against other books about Franklin in the classroom library. Janet shared some information about Jean Fritz and how she does the research for her books, which provided support for the authenticity of *What's the Big Idea, Ben Franklin?* Students also examined the "notes" at the back of the text. They concluded:

■ It seems real because the author gives some more facts at the back that kind of explain things.

■ If you see a page number in the notes, you can go back to the page and read it again and think about it.

■ It's interesting that on page 8 she talks about Franklin's brothers but the note just says, "He also had 6 sisters." That's kind of insulting, isn't it? Like the sisters weren't even important enough to talk about. They weren't even as important as the four brothers who died young.

■ Maybe Fritz couldn't find out about the women because they weren't really important enough for people to keep records on. Like it says here that "no one knows who William Temple's mother was." She couldn't get every bit of information.

■ Maybe she should have said something in the notes about how they didn't know what happened to the sisters.

The notes in the book were a kind of cross-referencing system that supported students' thinking critically about the text.

If students can learn to be critical consumers of written text, they will be better citizens because they will be equipped to recognize social issues that arise, understand them, and address them in a thoughtful, informed way. Paulo Freire's work in Brazil (Freire 1973, 1998) was dedicated to teaching adults to read so they could use literacy as a tool for changing society. One of the purposes of education is to empower people to improve their own lives and the lives of others.

Literacy and Power

In a very real sense, reading is power. Being a lifelong reader means you can use literacy to fulfill purposes in your life. It's a key to success. Being able to summarize and synthesize information from print is basic to the kind of reading that is required in academic environments as well as on the job. Analytic skills are essential for looking "below the surface" to determine what a writer is trying to do. And critiquing skills are necessary for the reader to evaluate what the text is saying.

Without question, analysis and criticism play an important role in modern society. A collective gain comes from a literate citizenry composed of competent readers who also think critically about what they read. Being a "critical" citizen means questioning what one hears or reads and evaluating those texts for accuracy. It means evaluating political decisions for the impact on people and the environment.

Suggestions for Professional Development

1. Select a text for a guided reading lesson with a group of students in your class.

2. Plan your book introduction. Think about what you want to focus on as well as what you think students will notice.

3. Audio- or videotape your introduction and the discussion after students have read all or a section of the text.

4. Afterward, listen to the tape and make a list of the students' contributions to the introduction and to the concluding discussion.

5. Bring the book and your list of students' comments to a meeting with your colleagues.

6. Share the book that you introduced. Share and discuss the different kinds of thinking that students were doing during the introduction to the text.

7. Then share some of the comments students made after they read all or a section of the text.

8. Now look at the chart in Chapter 18 that represents expanding strategies.

9. As a group, look again at students' comments to find evidence for connecting, inferring, summarizing, synthesizing, analyzing, and critiquing.

## CHAPTER TWENTY-TWO

TEACHING FOR WORD-SOLVING: PHONICS, SPELLING, AND VOCABULARY

The best way to develop fast accurate perception of word features is to engage in meaningful reading and writing, and to have multiple opportunities to examine those same words out of context, in isolation, in all their glory.

—DONALD BEAR, MARCIA IVERNIZZI, SHANE TEMPLETON, FRANCINE JOHNSTON

The curriculum of the language/literacy framework immerses students in reading and writing continuous text. Every time they open a book, pick up a pen, or put their fingers to the keyboard, they develop their knowledge of words. Our goal is to teach students how to recognize and access the meaning of words that are embedded in text—the real test for a "word solver." Word study is not so much about learning individual words as it is about learning how written language is organized—how written language "works." There are many word-solving strategies you can teach students to help them learn important concepts related to decoding, spelling, and vocabulary. You can also support word solving during reading and writing.

Word solving in reading is a complex process that involves both decoding and deriving meaning; the two processes are inseparable. Decoding is part of the process of figuring out a new word that you meet in a text, but unless you also know the meaning of the word you haven't "solved" it; you don't have complete access to the meaning of the text. The same is true in writing. If you want to write a word that you don't usually use, you need to have strategies for approaching the task.

Let's take the word *inveigle*. You might meet *inveigle* in a text like this:

Her mind lurched to the cold realization that, after all, he had managed to inveigle her in the web of his lies.

First of all you would know that *inveigle* is not a good thing; the connotations are negative. You might notice the prefix *in* and the *le* ending. You know that it is a verb. Even without precise knowledge of the word, you would have some idea of the meaning. You might connect *inveigle* with the word *entangle* and think that's close but not quite right. If you are reading silently, you might briefly try a pronunciation but probably would not spend time checking its accuracy.

There are many words that all of us read without worrying about how to say them. We discover this fact rather suddenly when asked to read something aloud. If you had to read the text aloud, you would be focusing on the second syllable of *inveigle*, and you would probably connect it with *either, height, veer, involve, veil, eight*. You'd select the most helpful connections and ignore the others. The same would be true if you heard the word aloud and needed to write it. Most of this would happen with lightning speed and take place at an unconscious or implicit level.

In solving this problem, you would almost never go to a grammar book and look up a rule. In fact, stating a rule would be less likely to help you than the connections you have made between words. As a word-solver, you have categories in your head. As you meet unfamiliar words, you connect them to those categories. The "rules" are deep inside you. The goal in phonics, vocabulary, and spelling instruction is to help upper elementary students expand the categories by making connections among words and drawing out important principles that they know in a deep way.

We have said that readers and writers learn more while doing it. They not only decode and interpret the meaning of words but they develop strategies for

Strategies for Solving Words

By Sound (Phonemic Strategies)	You can read or write some words by thinking about the sounds. (*man, hot, bed, hit, cup*)
By Look (Visual Strategies)	You can read or write some words by thinking about the way they look. (*the, pie*)
By Meaning (Morphemic Strategies)	You can read or write some words by thinking about what they mean. (*suitcase, two/to/too*)
By Connections (Linking Strategies)	You can use what you know about a word to figure out a new word. (<u>tree</u>, <u>my</u>—*try; connect, connection*)
By Inquiry (Research Strategies)	You can use reference materials to learn more about words. (lists, dictionary, charts, computer programs)

Figure 22–1.   Strategies for Solving Words

remembering, understanding and learning. The very act of word solving expands students' power over language. They increase their reading and writing vocabularies.

In this chapter, we explore how you help students learn and apply word-solving strategies during the language/word study block and in guided reading and writing workshop. We will discuss effective strategies for rapidly identifying words, as well as for expanding vocabulary and spelling abilities.

Strategies for Word Solving

Solving words—taking words apart while reading for meaning and spelling words while writing to communicate—sustains reading and writing. Readers use a range of strategies to recognize, decode, and understand the meaning of words. Writers select words to convey precise meaning, and they use a range of strategies to spell them accurately.

Competent word solvers use information systematically. They know that word solving is not simply a matter of learning words and their definitions. Some broad strategies that readers and writers use to solve

words are listed in Figure 22–1.

Phonemic Strategies

Phonemic strategies are basic to word solving in both writing and reading. Decoding words requires a left-to-right analysis of letter-sound relationships, which young children learn as a beginning reading strategy. While we want readers to understand the basic principles underlying phonemic strategies, we recognize that there are limitations when readers and writers employ only phonemic strategies. In English, words like *hat* are regular, but a one-to-one correspondence does not exist for all words. For example, "sounding out" or phonetically spelling the word *inveigle* would take you only so far. Without making connections to other words and considering the context in which the word appears, you would be uncertain about the pronunciation, the spelling, and the meaning.

Efficient readers learn to use phonemic strategies in combination with other strategies. Most upper elementary students are so skilled at using letters and sounds that they sample information rapidly and automatically, leaving their attention free for more complex operations. Nevertheless, they will meet unfamiliar

370

words that require them to use decoding skills. In addition, you will have some students whose word-solving strategies are undeveloped and who use only the very simple letter-sound relationships.

Visual Strategies

Efficient readers and writers use the visual patterns that make up words. The letters in *freight*, for example, would make a strange-sounding word indeed if they were "sounded out" individually. In this case, the *fr* and *t* represent single sounds and the *eigh* represents the sound of long *a*. There are entire clusters of letters that represent sounds in words. Some letter sequences are complex and rarely used, such as those in the word *gracious*. Readers learn to recognize visual patterns as they see words thousands of times. Writers learn to use these letter-cluster patterns in the words they spell.

Morphemic Strategies

A *morpheme* is the smallest unit of meaning. A letter all by itself has no meaning (except as a one-letter word, like *I* or *a*). Clusters, or morphemes, that stand alone as words can be combined to make compound words (*anything, elsewhere*). Stand-alone morphemes can also be combined with morphemes that simply add meaning, like affixes (prefixes, suffixes) and inflectional endings (*ed, ing*).

Readers and writers use these building blocks as clues to the pronunciation and spelling of the word and as a way to discover its meaning. For example, if a reader knows the meaning of *deliver* and also knows how the suffix *able* changes meaning, the word *deliverable* is easier to understand and to spell.

Linking Strategies

Word solvers see the visual patterns of words (and smaller parts within words) and link them with sounds and meaning. They are always thinking about how words sound and look and what they mean; the process is facilitated by their ability to create categories that connect words. Skillful word solvers use the largest chunks of information they can and are constantly searching for connections. *Equivalent* can be linked to the words *equal* and *value*; the connection provides a clue to the meaning: "of equal value." *Equivocal*, on the other hand, means something that can have more than one interpretation (or "voice"); it can be linked to *equal* and *vocal*.

Searching for connections between words is not a simple matter of looking for "words within words." Words can be connected by how they *sound*, how they *look*, and what they *mean*. For example, consider the word *moat*:

- *Moat* sounds like *mood, mole, mote,* and *goat*. Any part of the word can be connected with other words. The simplest connection here is the first letter, but flexible word solvers can instantly make many connections by sound.
- *Moat* looks like *most, float, moan, moor, oak, moa, oar, soar, soap, coal, molar,* and *moot*. Of course, since sounds and letters are so clearly linked, most of these words also sound like *moat*, but words like *moa* (a large extinct bird), *moor,* and *most* have visual features in common with differences in sound.
- *Moat* means the same as *trench, canal, furrow, gutter, channel,* and *ditch*. These words come from a thesaurus, and they do have similar meanings, although none is a precise synonym for *moat*. If you look at the original meaning of *moat*, you see that it means a ditch or heap of earth. These ditches were used to surround a fortress or castle and were sometimes filled with water.

The connections your students make reveal how they are thinking about words, including whether they can consider any part of the word, look at it in different ways, or notice and connect different aspects of words. A good word solver will make many connections, ignoring the connections that don't help and using those that work.

Research Strategies

In the elementary grades, students form the learning habits that serve them for a lifetime. It is especially important that they develop the ability to:

- Write clearly and accurately and comprehend what they read.
- Proofread written work.
- Search for the precise meaning of words.
- Use references and resources to find out more about words.

A competent reader notices an unfamiliar word, examines its parts, makes connections, and forms guesses about the meaning and pronunciation. If it is important to the meaning of the text, the reader goes further—perhaps using a dictionary or thesaurus. Writers take a more proprietary stance toward words, collecting them, always expanding their vocabularies so they can express precise meanings. Writers love words, delighting in how they sound and go together.

Readers and writers become more independent as they use dictionaries, word lists, thesauruses, glossaries, and computer spell-checking software. However, your students will not begin using these resources overnight. You can introduce them to reference skills through mini-lessons and practice, but the central goal of the word study curriculum is to help your students develop a lively curiosity about words and an appreciation for choosing good words and spelling them correctly. Consulting references shouldn't be a chore but a pleasure.

Ways of Learning About Words Are Interconnected

The strategies readers and writers use to make sense of words are interrelated. Becoming literate means learning the "inner workings" of language, both oral and written. Although we separate processes and categories of understanding so we can plan instruction, we cannot forget that all learning is interconnected. Language processes overlap.

Word-learning strategies are not discrete entities engaged in as separate, linear, consecutive activities. From one millisecond to the next, our brains search in many places for the understanding we need. That is not surprising given research on how the brain works (Damasio 1999): it is not so much a computer, with separate files and linear processes, as it is a symphony. The interrelationship of the melodies and rhythms flow together in pleasing, orchestrated ways.

Phonics: Teaching Students Word-Solving Skills While Reading

Readers have a wide range of strategies for solving words while reading for meaning. We want our students to develop effective strategies for fluently and rapidly identifying words as well as for analyzing words using their component parts.

Word Analysis: Recognizing Whole Words

Competent readers automatically and rapidly recognize thousands of words by sight. In a text that is read with fluency and accuracy, the reader has only a few words to analyze; the rest are known. To read fluently with understanding, readers need instantly to recognize about 95 percent of the words in the text (Adams 1990). In the beginning stages of reading, children recognize certain words by sight, and these words help them figure out that letters and sounds are related (Ehri 1991). Visual word recognition continues to be very important for several reasons:

- Some words in English require visual recognition because of inconsistent letter-sound generalizations (e.g., *of, some, who, the*) (Vellutino and Denckla 1987, 1991).
- Rapid, automatic word recognition is related to competent, fluent reading with understanding (Juel 1988; Lesgold, Resnick, and Hammond 1985; Stanovich 1985; Juel, Griffith, and Gough 1986). According to Stanovich, "While it is possible for adequate word recognition skills to be accompanied by poor comprehension abilities, the converse virtually never occurs. It has never been empirically demonstrated, nor is it theoretically expected, that some instructional innovation could result in good reading comprehension without the presence of at least adequate word recognition" (p. 418).
- The more words an individual knows and recognizes, the easier it is to learn more. Juel (1988) found that children who had good word recognition ability read twice as many words in books as their peers who lacked competence in word recognition. It appears that students develop strategies for learning words. The more they know, the easier it is to learn more; they know *ways of learning words*.

Students who have developed ways of learning words do so constantly and effortlessly. Students who have learned fewer words may benefit from reading and writing the five hundred frequently encountered words, as well as from more specific work on phonics and word analysis.

Word Analysis: Using Word Patterns

To use phonemic strategies, students must be able to hear the sound breaks in words. They must also be able to separate words into component parts and relate those parts to letters and letter clusters. Vowels cause particular problems for students because they are influenced by the letters around them. For example, when the vowel is followed by *r*, the sound changes (*altar, father, urn, curator, whirl*), so it's useful for students to think about *vowel + r* as a "chunk" or cluster of language. Students who attempt to solve words by analyzing them one letter at a time are inefficient readers and writers.

You can teach students about the building blocks of language by showing them the patterns in words and helping them hear such patterns. Students can analyze words by looking at the *onset* (first part of the word) and the rime (last part). For example, the onset of *fish* is *f*, and the *rime* is *ish*. When the last parts of words are the same, the words *rhyme* (e.g., *f-ish, d-ish, w-ish*). When you put words with regular patterns together, you can see that the first-letter substitution makes the difference.

Phonogram patterns, which are rimes, are clusters of letters that remain consistent across words (*-act, fact, tact; -ain, pain, main; -each, reach, peach; -eft, left, theft*). Phonograms, sometimes called "word families," can be parts of multisyllable words (e.g., *rab-bit*). If students know how to use the thirty-seven most frequent phonograms in English, they can apply that knowledge to a large number of words that they want to spell. These frequently used phonograms, along with numerous examples, are listed in Pinnell and Fountas (1998).

Awareness of the sounds in words ideally develops during the years of early childhood as students experience and enjoy rhymes, songs, and poems. They grow more sensitive to the sounds in language so they can detect when words are alike at the beginning and end. If students have not learned to hear sounds in words, you can work with magnetic letters or cards to make words, and you can also match and sort words according to their phonetic features.

Word Analysis: Using Syllables to Take Words Apart

A word study program helps students break words into syllables and notice and connect words by these sound and letter patterns. A syllable is a word or word unit that contains a vowel. A syllable may be "open," with a consonant/vowel combination (such as *mo* in *motor*), or it may be "closed," with a consonant/vowel/consonant combination (such as *run*). Multisyllable words are especially challenging for students. They need to learn how to hear the syllable breaks so the word becomes easier to analyze. You can help students learn how to separate words by sharing some simple and useful principles:

- Words have parts that you can hear. It may be helpful for students to clap and count the syllables as they say a word.
- Some words have one part (syllable) and others have more than one part.
- Every syllable has a vowel sound.
- Words may be divided into syllables by separating the word between two consonants (*at-tic, col-lect, rep-tile, ran-dom*).
- Sometimes consonants are "blends," or *digraphs*, meaning that they always go together (*tr* in *trouble*; *ch* in *charity*). In this case, the two consonants always stay together in the syllable (*mul-ti-ply; flex-i-ble*).
- When you have a single consonant between two vowels, the consonant may go with one syllable or the next, depending (*re-pent, rap-id*).
- Syllables ending with a vowel (open syllables with single vowels) have long vowel sounds (*ro-bot, le-gal*).
- Syllables ending with a consonant (closed syllables with single vowels) have short vowel sounds (*run-ner, mas-ter*).
- Inflectional endings like *ing* and *es* are usually separate syllables.
- Prefixes and suffixes are usually separate syllables, with longer ones separated into two syllables (*re-turn, pro-logue, port-a-ble*).
- Prefixes and suffixes change the meaning of the word.
- When you add a prefix, the spelling of the root word doesn't change (*pre-view, re-read*).
- When a word ends in *le*, the consonant preceding it joins the cluster to make a syllable (*trou-ble, dou-ble*).
- If you search for and recognize clusters such as *-tion, -able, auto-*, and *con-* as syllables, you can determine how to start or end a word.

Ask students to find a few examples of each type to help them internalize the strategies.

Rules for Adding Inflectional Endings to Words
1. *Most words.* Simply add the ending to most root words. For example, *walk* becomes *walks, walked, walking.*
2. *Words ending in* e. When a word ends in silent *e,* drop the *e* when adding an ending that begins with a vowel (*come, coming*).
3. *Words ending in y.* Change the *y* to *i* when adding an ending unless the ending is *ing* (*carry, carried, carrying*).
4. *Words ending in a single vowel and a consonant.* Double the final consonant before adding an ending that begins with a vowel (*hop, hopping, hopped*).

Figure 22–2. Rules for Adding Inflectional Endings to Words

Word Analysis: Using Letters in Sequence

Students also need to be able to analyze words letter by letter if necessary. Occasionally, a completely unfamiliar word will not present recognizable parts or features. In that case, you attempt to read or spell the word phonologically. Using connections between sounds and letters or letter clusters, you analyze the word left to right. Readers need to learn how to use letter-by-letter analysis as an option when it's not possible to recognize and use larger parts of a word.

Spelling: Teaching Students to Construct Words While Writing to Communicate

Spelling ability develops over time and is directly related to the richness of students' experience with words. In the upper elementary grades, most students go from beginning-level spelling to something close to adult level. Some spellers may still be working to master challenges such as using long vowels with "silent" e, selecting the correct short vowel, building a collection of frequently encountered words, and working out the spelling of verb tenses and plurals. Others have moved on but are challenged by doubling consonants, selecting among homophones, writing words with affixes, and the notorious *schwa* sounds (the sound represented by the underlined vowel in: *agent, focus, collect, family, ago*). The schwa, evident in unstressed vowels, is difficult for even the most expert spellers.

Connections, Visual Patterns, and Structure

Help students by showing them how to connect words, such as *family* and *familiar.* You will also want to help students develop a sense of visual patterns and the structure of words, including:

- Complex contractions, which require an understanding of both visual patterns and the underlying principles for omitting letters and replacing them with an apostrophe.
- Compound words, which may be derived from the meaning of the combined words (*sideboard*), change the meaning of the combined words altogether (*butterfly*), or have metaphorical significance (*firestorm*).
- Affixes—prefixes, suffixes, and inflectional endings—that add meaning to a word or change the tense or part of speech. Help students understand the rules for adding inflectional endings to words (see Figure 22–2).
- Homonyms, which include homophones (words that sound the same but are spelled differently and have different meanings—*suite, sweet*) and homographs (words that sound the same and are spelled the same but have different meanings—baseball *bat,* mouse-eared *bat*).

Spelling Rules

Rules like those in Figure 22–2 are useful to know and refer to, but students will learn them more effectively if they have a chance to derive the rules themselves by exploring numerous examples. A few other more arbitrary spelling rules are highly consistent and truly useful:

- Always put a *u* after *q*.
- Every syllable has a vowel.
- The "soft" sound of *c* or *g* is usually followed by *i, y,* or *e* (*cinder, gym, gentle*).
- Write *i* before *e* except after *c* or when sounded like *a* as in *neighbor* or *weigh*.

Post these rules, with examples; discuss them with your students; and invite them to record these rules in their word study notebooks for future reference. Memorizing rules will not result in better spelling, and we strongly advise against tests that require students to write spelling rules. Finding words that fit (or don't fit) the rules and referring to them when appropriate can help students organize their knowledge and support better spelling. It is more important for students to categorize words and think of their own examples than it is to memorize and repeat rules.

Vocabulary: Learning the Meanings of Words

Good readers know the meaning of many words. Increasing vocabulary is, indeed, basic to education. That sounds like a simple idea until we consider the many ways there are to "know" a word, which range from seeing it as totally unfamiliar to placing it within a rich network of understanding that includes subtle shades of meaning, connotations, even historical origins or geographically specific meanings (Beck, Perfetti, McKeown 1982; Beck and McKeown 1991).

Words and the concepts they convey don't stand alone; they are bound by meaningful relationships with other words. We hypothesize about word meanings continuously as we read text. While we know some words well, we are just barely acquainted with others. The wonderful thing about reading is that we learn more about the meanings of words as we encounter them repeatedly in continuous text.

If you really know a word, you can:

- Read it in many different contexts, understanding the meaning each time.
- Use it in a decontextualized way, mapping out the different meanings that are possible given the context.
- Realize the connotations (implied meanings) that a word may have when used in a certain way (e.g., as part of irony or sarcasm).
- Use the word metaphorically if appropriate.

Understanding exists along a continuum of familiarity. If a text has many words we do not know, it becomes incomprehensible. We may manage to work through it (no doubt mispronouncing some words along the way), but meaning is lost. If at least the literal meaning of all the words in the text is known, then we will most likely comprehend it unless the writer is using metaphor in very subtle and complex ways. No doubt you've experienced having to reread a text several times even though you know what the individual words mean, as you attempt to discover hidden meanings or puzzle out the larger symbolism. Clearly, comprehending a text transcends the meaning of individual words; rich, connected text is important.

Vocabulary Challenges for Upper Elementary Students

Upper elementary students vary widely in the number of words they understand. Some students have had a wide variety of background experiences—such as visiting science centers and museums or traveling—as well as having books read to them. Others have not. When students have limited background experiences, it is especially important to provide rich experiences with words.

Even when elementary students have acquired large speaking vocabularies and their reading and writing vocabularies are growing rapidly, they still face challenges:

- Learning new words for concepts they already understand. For example, a student might know *large* but not *massive*, or *easy* but not *facile*.
- Realizing how context affects the meaning of words, either changing the meaning or conveying subtle shadings ("*cover* the charge," "*cover* up a mistake,"

"get the book in hard *cover*").

- Learning new meanings for words they already know and realizing that words are not one-dimensional but have multiple meanings (for example, a "shell" can be an animal's exterior, a person's reserved, shy nature, or something empty or hollow).
- Learning that words can be used figuratively ("a sweet breeze," "delicious words," "wolfed his food").
- Learning that words have connotations—feelings or associations connected to a word that are different from or in addition to the explicit meanings (for example, during World War II, in occupied France, the word "collaboration" which should be positive, took on negative tones).

You need to help students link this new learning with their prior knowledge as they meet new words many times in many contexts.

Learning Vocabulary from Reading

Students must know a huge number of words just to be able to read texts at progressive grade levels. It would be impossible to teach these words in vocabulary lessons. The development of vocabulary is such an enormous achievement that experts are not sure of the precise process involved. The average elementary school student probably learns about three thousand words a year (Nagy 1988). Fortunately, a great amount of word learning occurs as we read (Nagy and Herman 1987; Nagy 1988; Anderson and Herman 1987).

Students learn vocabulary constantly as they read and derive word meanings from context (Herman 1987; Jenkins, Stein, and Sysocki 1984). Some researchers have suggested that the answer may lie in sheer volume (Fielding, Wilson, and Anderson 1986): when students are reading grade-level texts under natural conditions, there is a one-in-twenty chance they will learn new vocabulary from meeting it in context. That percentage may seem quite low until you realize that the average fifth grader reading about twenty-five minutes a day will encounter about twenty thousand unfamiliar words, which could result in a net gain of about a thousand words. Within our language/literacy framework students will read about forty-five minutes a day in reading workshop and will also read at home; the advantages are obvious.

When students read a wide variety of texts within their range of control (independently or with teacher

support), they have the opportunity to integrate new words with their prior knowledge. They may meet words several times in different written contexts, and this repetition is helpful. Additionally, they encounter the words in meaningful contexts rather than simply working to memorize them. Fielding, Wilson, and Anderson (1986) maintain that the amount of free reading students do is the best predictor of vocabulary expansion. Even as adult readers, we may suddenly notice a known word being used in new ways.

Explicit Teaching of Vocabulary

Although students will indeed learn vocabulary from reading in context, we need to be aware that:

- Students who most need to expand their vocabulary are likely to be those who read the slowest (and therefore read less material). They are usually also the most reluctant to read.
- Students may be able to read but not know how to derive and connect meanings while reading.
- Meaning may not be clear from context in literary texts.
- Reading by itself will not provide the degree of vocabulary growth necessary.

Explicit instruction directed toward helping students *learn how to learn* words can greatly enhance the speed, quantity, and quality of vocabulary development.

Traditionally, teachers have taught vocabulary by asking students to look up words in dictionaries and write definitions. Research suggests that while it is important for students to learn word meanings, simply teaching definitions of new words will not, in itself, improve reading comprehension (Beck, McKeown, and Omanson 1987). Nagy (1988) cautions teachers to be "deeply distrustful" of definitions because they do not actually tell the reader how to use or understand the words in context. Even using words in sentences has limited value.

Nevertheless students benefit from direct vocabulary instruction. No method is consistently better than any other method. Instead, you should employ a variety of techniques to ensure that students have repeated exposures to words and to present opportunities for students to make connections between words and concepts (Beck and McKeown 1991; Stahl and Fairbanks 1986).

Making Word Study Active: Phonics, Spelling, and Vocabulary

Learning about words is not a simple matter of committing them to memory, like entering them into a computer. We do not file, label, search, and retrieve in neat, numerically based actions. Concepts intermingle; they flow and blend into one another. We learn about words by comparing, contrasting, and combining them. As teachers, we need to make word study active, so that students not only expand their knowledge of words but make the powerful connections they need to understand the internal structures of words as well as their shades of meaning.

As part of minilessons, you can create wall charts that illustrate principles and provide a place for students to list examples. These wall charts become ready references for the kinds of generalizations that students are exploring, and they illustrate the value of constantly searching for connections. As students become more sophisticated learners, you can have them keep their own word study notebooks, in which they write the rules and principles they are discovering in relation to sound and letter patterns, as well as examples to which they can refer. For example, notebooks can have sections for words that rhyme, homonyms, words with double consonants, words with inflectional endings, and words with affixes. Notebooks can also have a section for vocabulary. As students engage in active word study, they can record their discoveries in appropriate sections.

We also suggest an interactive vocabulary activity one or two times a week (see Chapter 3). This is a short, interactive lesson focused on developing word meanings. For example, you might write a paragraph on a chart or overhead and engage the students in figuring out the meaning of two or three words, highlighting various strategies. Or you might construct a "word web" with a Greek or Latin word root at the center. You might start with *cred*, meaning "believe" and write *incredible*, and other words that you and the students can connect. You may choose to write a few bland sentences and then together change a couple of words to make the sentences more interesting. The options are many, but the important point is to explore a variety of new words and strategies for building vocabulary.

More detailed direction for teaching phonics is provided in *Word Matters: Teaching Phonics and Spelling in the Reading/Writing Classroom* (Pinnell and Fountas

1998). Three other excellent resources are *Phonics They Use: Words for Reading and Writing* (Cunningham 1995); *Word Journeys: Assessment-guided Phonics, Spelling, and Vocabulary Instruction* (Ganske 2000); and *Words Their Way: Word Study for Phonics, Vocabulary, and Spelling Instruction* (Bear et al. 2000).

Making Words
We know that students learn a great deal about words by constructing them with magnetic letters or letter cards. For example, students can make words that:

- Start or end the same.
- Feature silent letters.
- Are contractions.
- Are compound words.
- Contain prefixes or suffixes.
- Are homonyms (homophones, homographs).
- Have the same root (Greek or Latin).
- Contain the same number of syllables.

As students become more sophisticated about language, they can research the historical origins of words, record interesting derivations in their word study notebooks, and complete assignments in which they connect words.

Word Sorting
In word sorting (see the directions in Figure 22–3), students compare and contrast words in order to discover essential features (Henderson 1990; Templeton and Bear 1992; Zutell 1996, 2000). They work with words printed on cards and sort them into categories, either "open" or "closed":

- *Open* categories are those students create themselves as they notice various features (e.g., consonants, vowels, endings or beginnings, and meaning).
- *Closed* categories are those you assign.

Word sorting helps students form hypotheses about the properties of written words and make connections between words.

Figure 22–4 delineates the kinds of word sorts as well as ways you can vary the task. You can ask students to:

1. Sort by sound, spelling patterns, or meaning.
2. Sort once for a particular purpose or take a set of words and sort in several ways.

Directions for Word Sorting

Definition: **Word sorting** is a way to help students compare and contrast words according to specific features. Word sorting will enable students to form hypotheses, concepts, and generalizations about the properties of written words as well as link new words to the familiar ones they can already spell.

1. Identify words that fit into the categories of features you want students to notice. Decide whether the sort will be *open* (they create categories by discovering shared features) or *closed* (they find specified features and sort into identified categories).

2. Write words on cards. You can keep them together with rubber bands and/or placed in envelopes so that students can take turns using them.

3. Students usually work with a partner (taking turns in each role) because it promotes discussion about the word:
   ❖ For *open sorts,* one partner may sort the words and other partner may guess the basis for the categories.
   ❖ For *closed sorts,* there are directions about the principle to use (such as first letter, last letter, vowel sound, etc.) and often there are key words. Students place the key words at the top of the column and lay words that fit into that category under each column.
   ❖ There is usually a column with a **?** for words that don't fit the categories. These words provide more topics for discussion.
   ❖ Sometimes one partner reads the words aloud without showing the print and the partner has to indicate where to place the word (or writes it). This is called an *auditory or blind sort.*
   ❖ Sometimes one partner reads the word and *shows* the word to the other, who indicates where to place it in the column. This is called a *visual sort.*
   ❖ A *meaning sort* or *concept sort* involves grouping words (or pictures) in categories related to their meaning (e.g., clothing, food, animals that swim and walk).
   ❖ In a *speed sort*, students are asked to work quickly to build processing skills.
   ❖ In *write to the sort*, the task is for students to *write* the words in the columns.
   ❖ In *multiple sorts*, students have a bank of words that they can sort in several different ways. They first sort them one way and then sort them another way.
   ❖ Students can use blank cards to add their own examples to the word sorts.

4. The partners check over the whole sort to be sure words are categorized as they want them to be. They discuss the words.

Figure 22–3. Directions for Word Sorting

Types of Sorts

Sound (Auditory) Sort: Words are categorized according to their sound features. [**SOUND**]

Spelling Sort: Words are sorted according to relationships between pronunciation, visual patterns, meaning units, and/or word origin and spelling. [**LOOK**]

Concept/Meaning Sort: Words are categorized according to properties that are independent of pronunciation or spelling. [**MEANING**]

↓

Characteristics of the Task

↓

Picture Sort: Children sort pictures or objects.

Letter Sort: Children sort letters made of a variety of different materials (for example, magnetic letters).

Word Sort: Words are written on cards for sorting.

Single Sort: Items are sorted once for a particular purpose.

Multiple Sort: A set of items is sorted several times for different purposes and in different categories.

Open Sort: Students choose categories for sorting and then organize items (or subsets of items) into columns based on categories. Others try to "solve" the sort by hypothesizing about features of categories.

Closed Sort: The teacher decides the categories and selects key words to head each category (with one marked ?). The sort is limited to a specific subset of known words.

↓

Varying the task

↓

Visual Sort
Students have the opportunity to look at the word, examine its features, and compare it with other words in various categories as they decide where to place it.

Blind Sort
Someone else (teacher or student) reads the word to the student and the student decides on placement in categories without seeing the word first. The student checks categorization after the word is placed.

Speed Sort
The student is asked to work quickly as well as accurately.

Write to the Sort
Students have key words available for reference. The words are read to them but they do not see them. They write words correctly in the appropriate category.

Figure 22–4. Word Sorting Chart

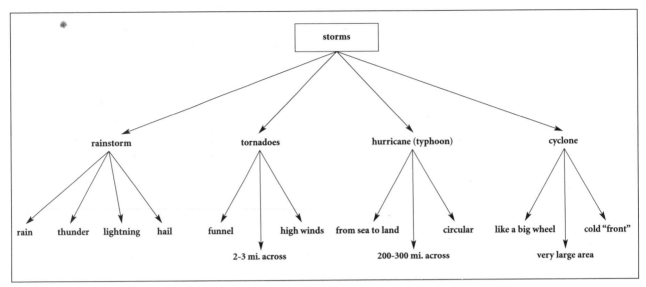

Figure 22–5. Storms

3. Sort by prearranged categories or by categories that the students create.

4. Look at the word and compare it visually with other words.

5. Listen to words read aloud and place them in categories without seeing them in writing.

6. Sort quickly.

The categories are endless. Sorting helps students realize how words are connected, attend to specific features of words, and move beyond simple letter-sound correspondence. The exponential effect on spelling can be startling, because students discover underlying spelling principles. Word sorting may be used in whole-class, small-group, or independent work. Make sure you explicitly demonstrate the routines to students and then observe and coach them before allowing them to word-sort independently.

Organizing and Representing Word Structure, Meanings, and Relationships

You can use many of the graphic organizers described in Chapter 26 to help students analyze word meanings and connect words based on those meanings. The real value of using these techniques are the conversations about words that take place around them. Working with the whole class or a small group, use a large chart or a transparency so that students can see how the words are treated in relation to one another. The following ideas involve creating diagrams:

■ Make a word web, placing a word in the center and branch out to synonyms, short definitions, or sentences from texts where students have encountered the word.

■ Make two columns and label them Is and Is Not. Select a word, and then write synonyms in the first column and antonyms in the second column.

■ Make a chart with two columns and choose a word that represents a concept. Have students write what they know about the word or what they predict it might mean in the first column. Then have students read material that provides more contextual information. Have them add what they have learned in the second column.

■ Have students separate words with affixes or compound words into smaller, meaningful parts, write the meaning of the parts, and then write the meaning of the whole word.

■ Place a word in the center of a web and ask students to answer the following questions on each of the surrounding "branches": What do I think this word means? What parts of this word do I know? Where would I probably find this word? Why is this word important?

Relationships among Word Meanings

boring →dull →unexciting →acceptable →interesting →pleasing →exciting→fascinating →compelling

Figure 22–6. Linear Chart

■ Use a mapping technique to explain hierarchical relationships and/or to relate information to a word (see Figure 22–5 for an example).

On a linear chart, or continuum, list words that demonstrate increments of meaning (see Figure 22–6 for an example).

Do some "wordstorming." Have students generate a large number of words on a given topic, and then ask them to sort the words into categories, placing labels on each (Allen 1999). As an alternative, have students generate words from a text they have just read or are reading. Then place the words into categories yourself, and ask students to identify and label the categories. The process of categorizing and labeling will help students see relationships between words.

Map multiple meanings by placing a word in the center of a piece of paper and branching to like meanings on one side and opposite meanings on the other side.

Analyzing Semantic Features

In our discussion of spelling, we stressed how important it is for students to connect words based on how they look and sound and what they mean. Vocabulary, too, is enhanced when readers and writers actively work to connect words with similar or opposite meanings. In semantic feature analysis, students make word grids that explicitly demonstrate how words are related to one another; in the process they improve both vocabulary and categorization skills. The idea is to help students analyze the similarities and differences among concepts that are related in some way.

Analyzing semantic features encourages students to draw on their background knowledge to understand the meaning of a new word or expand the meaning of a known word (Pittelman et al. 1991). This technique capitalizes on the way information is stored in the memory.

Through the oral language that surrounds seman-

Semantic Feature Analysis

1. Select a category of words and place at the top of a large chart, on which you have drawn the beginnings of a table or grid, with columns and rows.

2. In the first column, list several words in the category. Have students suggest more. For your first experience, don't have too many words.

3. At the head of each succeeding column, list traits or features shared by some of the words that you listed down the left column. You can suggest some features to get started, but have students add features that at least one of the words suggests.

4. One word at a time, place a + or – to indicate whether the word has the particular feature or characteristic. (You could also write *yes/no* or use other symbols.) If students are not sure whether the word has the feature, place a ? in the box.

5. Complete the grid, adding more words and features.

Figure 22–7.   Directions for Semantic Feature Analysis

Semantic Feature Analysis									
	historical	modern	made of metal	protects someone	hurts someone	a type of person	something soldiers wear		
armor	+	-	+	+	-	-	+		
shield	+	-	+	+	-	-	-		
weapon	+	+	+	?	+	-	-		
sword	+	-	+	?	+	-	?		
helmet	+	+	+	+	-	-	+		
cross-bow	+	-	?	?	+	-	-		
warrior	+	?	-	+	+	+	-		
champion	+	+	-	+	+	+	-		
army	+	+	-	+	+	+	-		
tunic	+	-	-	-	-	-	+		
bearers	+	-	-	-	-	+	-		

Figure 22–8.   Example of Semantic Feature Analysis

tic feature analysis, students are able to bring out their own examples and relate the concepts under discussion to their own experiences. General directions for semantic feature analysis are listed in Figure 22–7; an example is provided in Figure 22–8.

Teach students to use the technique by working through a number of grids together. You can demonstrate the process using concrete, easy-to-understand categories and suggesting words and features. Start with just a few. As students become more sophisticated, they can add many words and features.

Making the Most of Active Word Study
The strategies we've discussed here will be most useful if the activities:

- Are fun rather than tedious.
- Show students how much they already know about words.
- Do not interfere with time for reading and writing.
- Foster discussion and negotiation.

- Encourage students to bring their own background knowledge to the learning.
- Promote connections between active word study and understanding what one reads and writes.

Expanding Language Through Reading and Writing

Word study is highly effective, but what students learn must be put into action in reading and writing.

Learning About Words During Reading Workshop
In reading workshop—guided and independent reading and literature study—you want students not only to apply principles you have taught them but also to develop ways of learning words through the act of reading. Adults who have large vocabularies didn't learn those words through direct instruction or by looking

Prompts to Help Students Solve Words During Reading

To help the student solve words:

What could you try?

It starts like _____.

It ends like _____.

Look at the parts.

What do you know that might help?

Do you see a part that you know?

Do you see a part that can help you?

Do you know a word like that?

Do you know a word that ends with those letters?

What's that like?

Think of what the word means. Is it like another word you know?

What other word do you know like that?

What letter do you expect to see at the beginning [or end]?

Try the first part.

Think about what would make sense.

Think about what would sound right.

To help the student notice errors:

You noticed what was wrong.

Find the part that's not quite right.

Check to see if that looks right.

Where's the tricky part? [after an error]

Get a good look at the word.

There's a tricky word on this line.

What did you notice? [after hesitation or stop]

What's wrong?

Why did you stop?

Do you think it looks like [word]?

Think about how that word looks.

Something wasn't quite right.

Were you right?

To help the student notice errors and fix them:

That sounds right, but does it look right?

That makes sense, but does it look right?

I like the way you worked that out.

It starts like that. Now check the last part.

You made a mistake. Can you find it?

You almost got that. See if you can find what is wrong.

Try it.

You've got the first part [last part] right.

Try that again.

Try it another way.

You've almost got it.

Figure 22–9. Prompts to Help Students Solve Words

up definitions; there simply aren't enough days in a lifetime to support such strategies! Readers learn thousands of words because they encounter them over and over in texts, and they have built-in ways of relating them to known concepts and storing them in memory.

The best way to teach vocabulary is to discuss a text with students and weave in words that may be unfa-

miliar to them. Students will still need to solve these challenging words when they encounter them, but you will have laid the foundation for noticing, decoding, and understanding new words.

You may interact with individual students while they are reading and support their word solving in ways that help them learn *how* to solve words. Your

Principles for Teaching How Words Work

- ❖ You can add letters to the beginning of a word to make a new word (*h + and = hand*).

- ❖ You can add letters to the end of a word to make a new word (*sea + t = seat*).

- ❖ You can change the first letter of a word to make a new word (*car, tar*).

- ❖ You can change the last letter of a word to make a new word (*had, has*).

- ❖ You can use a word you know to solve a new word (*car, cart; part, party*).

- ❖ You can add endings to make new words (*book, books; read, reading*).

- ❖ You can change the beginning and ending letters of a word to make new words (*his, hit, sit*).

- ❖ You can change the middle letter or letters to make new words (*cat, cut; chair, cheer.*)

- ❖ You can add letters or letter clusters to make new words (*it, pit; pitch, pitcher*).

- ❖ You can use parts of words you know to figure out words you don't know (*tree + play = tray; she + make = shake*).

- ❖ You can show that some words sound the same and look different (*sail, sale*).

- ❖ You can show that some words look the same and sound different (*present, present*).

Figure 22–10. Principles for Demonstrating How Words Work

goal is to help them learn strategies they can use again and again while reading other texts. Students will read silently, but you can ask them to raise their voices briefly so that you can sample oral reading. Language teachers have found helpful to prompt students to solve words is included in Figure 22–9.

In discussions of their reading, students can bring up words they had difficulty decoding or did not understand. In your teaching after guided reading, you can explicitly demonstrate how to work with the words in the selection the group has just read.

If students need additional support in learning how words work, spend an extra minute or two at the end of each guided reading lesson working on words in a playful way. Use magnetic letters, whiteboard, or chart paper to teach students how to manipulate parts of words. Some principles for manipulating word parts are listed in Figure 22–10. Make it a game, inviting students to add, delete, and change word parts so they become very flexible in taking apart and constructing words.

Literature Study
Literature study is a rich source for learning about words, particularly since students may be talking about texts that are more complex (with more difficult words) than those they read for themselves. The discussion surrounding literature helps students build vocabulary, and you may teach some of these same words in minilessons. Students can also collect examples to record in their word study notebooks.

Learning About Words During Writing Workshop
Your word study program will bear fruit in your students' writing. Students' discovery drafts and edited projects should reflect their growing knowledge of words.

INDEPENDENT WRITING
In writing projects, students can make use of their growing knowledge of conventional spelling. They can also consciously work to vary their writing vocabulary.

Students do not have to edit or correct their writer's notebooks. Instead, they record their thoughts, reflections, and sketches for possible later use. As you look at their notebooks, however, you should be able to see evidence of growth in the number of words they spell quickly and accurately, as well as the new words they are selecting and trying out.

Your students' quick-writes also provide evidence of their learning. After they respond freely to a designated topic, you can examine their work to see the variety of words they have at their disposal in relation to a specific subject.

GUIDED WRITING

You bring students together for guided writing to provide some specific instruction. Often, this instruction will focus on the writer's craft, of which word choice is an important aspect. You can teach students about using words figuratively, as well as selecting words to convey the precise meaning they want. You can refer to language and word study minilessons as you help students with their specific writing problems.

INVESTIGATIONS

An investigation, which is connected to a content area of the curriculum, gives students a chance to encounter many new challenging words. As students engage in long-term research projects, they develop new concepts as well as acquire the new words to label those concepts.

Conclusion

There are any number of effective ways to direct students' attention to phonics, spelling, and vocabulary. All students need this kind of instruction. Good readers and writers can enhance their skills by learning how words are connected, and advanced readers and writers can continue to develop and expand their vocabularies. Most important, word study should be quick and interesting rather than tedious, and there should be consistent opportunities for students to apply their knowledge.

Suggestions for Professional Development

1. Connect word study with students' writing development by working with your grade-level colleagues to analyze students' writing. Select five students and bring in three writing samples from each of them. Select a range of students who are at the middle level of achievement in terms of using conventions of spelling and/or writing vocabulary.

2. Analyze the writing samples by:
   - Calculating the number and percent of words that are spelled conventionally.
   - Writing the errors in the first column of a table, what kinds of understanding students seem to be acting on in the second column, and what students need to know in the third column.
   - Noting the variety of the vocabulary students are using.

3. Compare your writing analysis with your district- or school-recommended spelling curriculum. Ask:
   - What do these students need to learn?
   - What kinds of minilessons would be appropriate?

4. Connect word study with students' reading by working with your grade-level colleagues to analyze texts. Collect three texts that are "on grade level" for your students. Select a section of each text— about 1,000 words—for analysis.

5. Select the vocabulary that will be new or challenging for most of your students.

6. Decide which words can be learned from context. For these words, discuss how you can show students how to derive meaning from context. Then discuss how can you use active word study activities to enhance understanding of words derived from context.

7. For words that will be difficult to derive from context, discuss ways to help students relate words to what they already know.

8. Working with your grade-level colleagues, select one active word study approach from this chapter (e.g., word sorting).

9. Design the activity to match your students' needs (perhaps using some of the information gained from activities described above).

10. Teach the routines of this activity to students and try it out in your classroom.

11. Meet again with colleagues to discuss the results. Ask:
    - What did students learn from the activity?
    - How was their behavior different from that in traditional word study/vocabulary instruction?
    - What did you do that made the activity successful for students?
    - What is the potential of the activity for future use?

STRUGGLING READERS AND WRITERS: TEACHING THAT MAKES A DIFFERENCE

When students are struggling with texts that are too difficult, it is next to impossible to employ strategies for understanding and extending texts. When you select appropriate texts for your students, carefully consider their background knowledge and the concepts they currently understand. Once you find texts that students can read, you still need to support their ability to construct meaning:

1. *Provide introductions that specifically link concepts in texts to students' background knowledge.* The more students can connect texts to their own lives, the easier it will be for them to construct meaning. As you discuss the books with them, help them see how their own knowledge enables them to interpret the text.

2. *When needed, build background knowledge before reading the text.* If you've selected appropriate texts, you won't need to provide extensive preparatory experiences, but you may need to provide extra support regarding concepts that are new to them. If the text is illustrated, draw your students' attention to the pictures and talk with students to build knowledge.

3. *Engage in rich conversations about texts before, during, and after reading.* One of the best ways to be sure your low-achieving students understand the texts they read is to talk with them. Model your own ideas about what texts mean and invite students to offer theirs.

In reciprocal teaching (Palinscar and Brown 1986), the teacher and students take turns being responsible for leading conversations about text. You explicitly coach your students in predicting, questioning, summarizing, and clarifying information; explain to them what they will be learning and practicing and why this learning is important; and model strategies such as asking questions. Gradually responsibility will transfer to students, and they will eventually take the principal role in discussions because you have given them the language structures they need. Reciprocal teaching provides *temporary* support. Students benefit from explicit demonstration of the language processes they need to employ.

You might also consider using cloze techniques to demonstrate effective reading processes. This involves deleting selected parts of a text, thus forcing students to attend to the information they need to solve these words. The cloze technique works as follows:

- *Cloze:* Take a passage of 250+ words and delete every fifth word. Be sure that the lines indicating a deleted word are exactly the same length. Ask students to predict the deleted words. Afterward, discuss the kinds of information they used to make their predictions. Reveal to them the words you actually deleted and discuss what additional information they might need to reinsert the deleted words accurately. You can make the task easier by deleting every tenth word.

- *Modified cloze:* Delete words using the same procedure, but make the line indicating the deleted word exactly the length of the word deleted. This will help students attend to the length of words.

■ *Modified cloze:* Delete words in the passage but retain the initial letter or clusters of letters. In this way, students become more conscious of how they attend to visual features of words in connection with meaning and language structure.

■ *Progressive exposure:* This technique involves projecting a transparency of one or two paragraphs. Show part of the text and have students read it up to that point. Encourage students to predict the next part of the text using the information at their disposal; then, expose a portion of the remaining text—the first letter or letters of a word or phrase. Work your way through the selection, thinking aloud about the processes you are using.

Paired reading is another effective strategy for troubled readers. The student chooses the text and sits next to an adult. Together, they read the text aloud at a rate that is comfortable for the younger reader. The adult may point a pencil or finger under the line of print to help the student keep his place. The reader signals the adult when he can read on without support, but the adult joins in again immediately as needed. If the reader comes to an unknown word, the adult supplies it right away. Doing this ten minutes a day enables low-achieving students to experience fluent reading. It's a perfect way for volunteers and parents to help (Topping and Lindsay 1992).

Since reading fluency is highly related to reading comprehension, help your students increase their fluency:

■ Echo your partner: you read a sentence or section of text first; the student follows closely—echoing your reading.

■ Read the entire section of text to the student; next the student reads it to you.

■ Ask the student read the passage silently before reading it aloud.

■ Have students read the text several times in a row, each time working on their fluency.

■ Engage students in choral reading, shared reading, and readers theatre.

■ Share poetry by reading it together a number of times.

■ Recast stories as scripts and invite students to perform them.

■ Invite students to tape-record passages of their reading.

Low-achieving students must learn a wide range of word-solving strategies that they can use in reading and in spelling. Word solving involves taking words apart and spelling them in addition to knowing their meaning. You may need to provide special instruction in word study for students who are at the extreme end of the achievement continuum:

■ *Teach students effective strategies for taking words apart.* Many students who are having difficulty in reading struggle at the word level. They use primitive, inefficient strategies to solve words. They need to approach words in playful ways to discover the inner workings of words. Opportunities for such play and exploration arise in guided reading and in word study.

■ *Teach students effective ways to spell words.* Struggling writers may believe they have to memorize each word to spell it accurately. Show them how to use spelling patterns; small-group experiences manipulating words may help.

■ *Work with students' writing to draw their attention to conventions.* When you confer with your students, help them understand why conventions are important. Teach them to edit their work to enhance meaning.

■ *Attend to one or two conventions at a time.* A student who is forced to examine and correct a large number of errors in one piece of writing may quickly become discouraged. Look at your assessment data to determine what students know and determine what they need to know next. Target one or two conventions in each lesson and teach them explicitly. Don't attempt to teach the universe of conventions through one piece of writing.

■ *Modify the number of words and guide selection of words that students are expected to learn to spell each week.* Work with students to help them choose the words that offer the biggest learning payoff. Struggling writers may have fewer words to learn than other students, but the words chosen should help them make important connections.

■ *Enrich their daily language experience with talk about words.* Engage students in rich conversations about words in which you place words into categories, notice visual features and spelling patterns, and discuss their meaning. Your at-risk students will require much more talk about words.

■ *Find ways to help students connect words.* The more connections you can help students make between words, the better they will understand spelling patterns and meaning. Work with high-risk students in small groups to show them explicitly how to make connections between words.

■ *Use tools to help students understand words.* You will enhance your students' vocabulary as you help them organize their information about words. In Chapter 26, we describe a number of tools that help students delve into the meaning of words. You can use these tools and others you devise to help students make explicit what they know about word meanings.

■ *Use games and puzzles to support word learning.* There are a wide variety of commercial products that support student learning of vocabulary, or you can devise some of your own. In addition, computer software may offer opportunities for students to work on vocabulary acquisition.

SECTION 6

The Reading and Writing Connection

The reciprocity across the complementary processes of reading and writing accelerate learning in both areas. In Chapter 23, we discuss the variety of genres that are essential for intermediate learners to understand as skillful readers and writers. Chapter 24 showcases poetry, a microcosm of complex and sophisticated language in which students can learn a great deal about reading and writing. Chapter 25 explores content literacy. As students investigate topics of interest, they not only develop research skills and content knowledge, but they learn how to write informational texts and present their findings. Chapter 26 offers a wide range of tools to help students construct visual models that help them explicitly recognize the structure of text as well as connections among words. Chapter 27 describes a "testing genre," and provides specific suggestions for helping students learn to perform on standardized tests and state proficiency tests. Assessment is basic to informed teaching, and we provide a survey of assessment techniques for both reading and writing in Chapter 28.

## CHAPTER TWENTY THREE

TEACHING GENRE AND CONTENT LITERACY: EXPLORING FICTION AND NONFICTION TEXTS

. . .trying to become a writer without having been a reader is like setting forth to sail across the ocean in a boat without sails.

- WILLIAM STYRON

The best classrooms are literacy havens where students flourish as readers, writers, and learners as they explore their physical and social worlds. Learning captures their curiosity and imagination and propels them into a lifelong love affair with it. We cannot predict with certainty what today's students in grades 3 through 6 will encounter in the twenty-first century, but we do know that their world will be driven by information and those who seek it. For these students, quality of life will depend on their ability to use a wide variety of texts—in both print and nonprint media. Their literacy experiences in the elementary grades will set the scene for their later performance.

As we look at written texts of various kinds, we must consider what we want our students to understand about them. Our goal is to help students:

- Develop an appreciation for and an understanding of a wide range of fiction and nonfiction texts.
- Broaden their world experience and increase their knowledge.
- Enrich their knowledge of language, including but not limited to vocabulary.
- Develop informed tastes as readers.
- Form their own opinions about authors and illustrators.
- Become critical of what they read.
- Learn how to select texts for themselves.
- Develop skills in using the library and in making their own collections of books.
- Learn to read differently for different purposes (for example, reading fiction from cover to cover but skimming nonfiction texts to find the desired information).

The Value of Knowing Texts

In order to help students grasp the structure of books and their complex ideas, you need to have read them yourself. An essential foundation for effective teaching in the upper elementary grades is familiarity with literary work that appeals to students at those ages. If you identify books that students especially like or authors that appeal to them, read those books yourself. You will not only add to your repertoire as a teacher but also understand your students' interests as readers and their personal tastes and goals.

Over time, you will become more and more knowledgeable about the texts that your students will enjoy. Make a point of building your knowledge: pack children's literature to read on trips; read books along with your students as you prepare for literature study; browse in your favorite children's bookstore, sampling those books that look most inviting; organize a lunchtime "children's book club" with your colleagues.

Plan your own reading to include nonfiction as well as fiction. Some of the older classics deserve rereading with a new eye. Read picture books, novels, short stories, poetry anthologies, magazines and journals, biographies, and informational books. The category of nonfiction, in particular, has grown from traditional "textbooks" to a wide variety of visually striking, appealing texts.

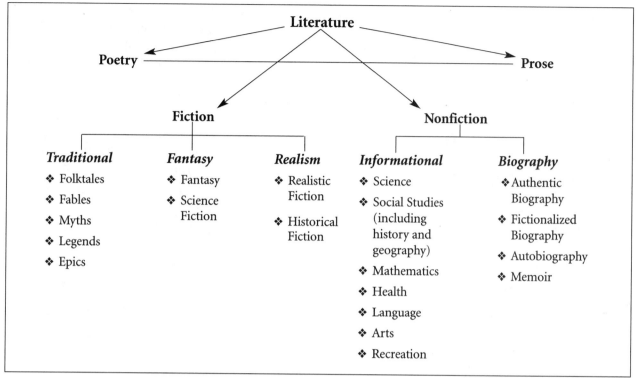

Figure 23–1. Types of Literature

Knowing texts means more than simply reading them. It's important to attend to both the author's and illustrator's craft. What makes the book enjoyable and understandable? How do the text and art come together to create a unified meaning? What is the potential of the text for generating student response? What is your own response?

To help you organize your books and plan for your teaching in the reading workshop, you need to classify texts by type, or genre. As students learn more about genre, they increase the breadth of their reading experience and look at texts in different ways. Within and across these genres, you also consider themes and the essential strategies students need to read effectively.

Categorizing Literature: Poetry and Prose

Literature can be divided into *poetry* or *prose*. Prose can then be divided into fiction or nonfiction, and those categories can be further divided by genre (see Figure 23–1).

Poetry is compact writing that is both imaginative and artistic. It uses language that is honed to communicate specific meanings by evoking sensory images and feelings and features figurative language, rhythm, and sound patterns. Poetry may involve rhythm or verse, but not everything that rhymes is poetry. Simple playground verses are most children's first encounter with poetic language. More sophisticated readers/listeners grow to appreciate poetry that reflects deeper meanings.

Poetry is distinct from prose because meanings are packed into a few words and lines. For people who appreciate poetry, reading a poem only once is unimaginable. When you find a poem that evokes feelings or images, you read it again and again, finding new meaning each time. One or two words open a universe of meaning.

Prose employs language in a more elaborated way. The writer of prose informs, shows, describes, and explains. Prose and poetry may achieve the same goal, but they accomplish it different ways.

Both poetry and prose encompass all types of literature, whether fiction or nonfiction. Poetry can tell of fantastic events; it can portray stark realism. All human emotions—humor, love, grief, and defeat—find expression in poetry. Chapter 24 discusses poetry as a special category of literature and describes how you can introduce your students to both reading and writing poetry.

Any piece of literature, whether poetry or prose, may fulfill any of literature's functions. We can divide literature several different ways (Tunnell and Jacobs 2000):

1. We can think about the *format*, which includes picture books, illustrated books, chapter books, short stories, plays, magazines, newspapers, and Internet materials (see Figure 23–2). Poetry and prose can appear in any of these forms, as can fiction and nonfiction.
2. We can think about the *content*, which may address social issues or subjects of study or interest.
3. We can think about categories, or *genres* (type or kind).

If students ask for "something to read about animals," you will need to think in terms of content divisions, but you can also look across the various formats in which reading materials are available. There are also times when students are eager to read material in a particular format—magazines or picture books, for example—but in any genre or on any topic.

Categorizing Books by Genre

Genre is a French word meaning type or kind. Genres are a classification system formed to provide a way of talking about the characteristics of texts. Figure 23–3 summarizes the important genres to include in a literature study curriculum. We have drawn most of the following material from Lukens (1999) and Huck, Hepler, Hickman and Kiefer (1997), and we recommend both books for further study.

As you sort books by genre, remember to be flexible; many texts share multiple characteristics. A piece of historical fiction like *Sadako and the Thousand Paper Cranes* (Mochizuki 1979) is also biographical because it is based on a real character. A work of fiction (fantasy) like *Charlotte's Web* (White 1952) includes sections that provide scientific information. An informational text might showcase stories, jokes, and tales that illustrate people's lives and values.

Many volumes being published now deliberately include multiple genres. In Chapter 16 we mentioned *Imagine That!* (Wilson 2000), is a work of fiction in which Auntie Violet, a one-hundred-year-old woman, reminisces about her life. Her reminiscences are not chronological; instead she jumps from topic to topic— home appliances, women's roles, clothing, air travel, and so forth. The borders of the book contain a decade-by-decade time line (which you'd typically expect to find in nonfiction) listing true facts and events that occurred during the one hundred years. The volume also has almost seven hundred small images connected to the time lines, including pictures of people like Amelia Earhart and Charles Lindbergh, fashions over the years, airplanes and rockets, telephones and computers. This book offers a wealth of information for students and will guide them to areas for further study.

We want our students to understand that we can connect texts by examining their characteristics. Knowing about genres:

■ Gives students language with which to talk about texts.
■ Helps them learn how information is organized and presented, a process that supports comprehension.
■ Helps them use what they know about the characteristics of texts to write in various genres.
■ Lets them anticipate the form texts in a particular genre will take.
■ Helps them identify the kinds of books they like and want to read more of.
■ Allows them to evaluate the breadth of their reading.

Formats of Fiction and Nonfiction Texts

❖ Picture Book

❖ Chapter Book

❖ Illustrated Chapter Book

❖ Short Story

❖ Play

❖ Short Text: Article, Essay, Pamphlet, Brochure, the Internet

Figure 23–2. Format of Fiction and Nonfiction Texts

Genre at a Glance		
Fiction		
Code	*Genre*	*Definition*
TL	Traditional Literature	Traditional literature originated in the stories passed down orally throughout history. It includes folktales, (including fairy tales), myths, legends, and epics.
F	Fantasy	Fantasy is fiction that contains unrealistic or unworldly elements. It includes modern fantasy (which has a known author) and science fiction.
SF	Science Fiction	Science fiction is a special division of fantasy that involves or is based on scientific principles.
RF	Realistic Fiction	Realistic fiction is drawn from the writer's imagination but is true to life. It often focuses on universal human problems.
HF	Historical Fiction	Historical fiction is drawn from the writer's imagination but is true to life in some period of the past.
Nonfiction		
Code	*Genre*	*Definition*
I	Informational	Informational texts provide ideas, facts, and principles that are related to the physical, biological, or social world.
B	Biography	A biography is an account of the life of an individual.
AB	Autobiography	An autobiography is an account of the life of an individual written by the subject.
M	Memoir	A memoir is the account of a personal or historical event.

Figure 23–3. Genre at a Glance

Fiction

Fiction is generally defined as a narrative that is imagined rather than real (compared with nonfiction, which is based on fact). Fiction is a large category that includes many kinds of literary work, including historical fiction, realistic stories, plays, fantasies, and folklore. A fictional text may be a novel, short story, or play. The purpose of fiction is to entertain and involve readers (or listeners) in stories of life. On occasion, the overriding purpose of fiction is to inform or persuade. Classic examples include Orwell's *Animal Farm* (1940), which exposed the dangers of totalitarianism, or *Uncle Tom's Cabin* (Stowe, 1861), which stimulated support for the abolition of slavery. High-quality works of fiction, however, are crafted primarily to engage and satisfy readers.

As you read a work of fiction you have certain expectations. For example, you may expect to encounter:

- *Characters*—either animals, people, or fantastic creations that will be confronted with challenges and, as a result, change as the story unfolds.
- A *problem* or conflict that creates tension and sparks a sequence of events that culminate in a solution.
- A *setting*—place and time—that influences the lives of the characters and the story line.

Your expectations become even more precise as you read specific genres within the broad category of fiction, such as fantasy or science fiction. Expectation helps you understand how the text "works" and is basic to comprehension of a text.

Types of Fiction

TRADITIONAL LITERATURE

Traditional literature arose from the oral tradition and gradually entered the world of writing. Traditional literature includes different kinds of folktales, stories that have been passed down from generation to generation. The characters are generally flat, the plots are simple, and good triumphs over evil. The study of folktales is a good way to help students become aware of other cultures. It's interesting that versions of the same tale often emerge in different parts of the world. For example, almost every region has a "Cinderella" story. Subtypes of traditional literature include:

- *Cumulative tales,* which involve telling a story again and again from the beginning with elements added each time (*The House That Jack Built*).
- *Pourquoi tales,* which provide explanations for natural phenomena (*Why the Sun and the Moon Live in the Sky*).
- *Beast tales,* stories about animals that have been human characteristics (*The Three Little Pigs*).
- *Noodlehead or numbskull tales,* humorous stories about people who bumble about *(The Sillies).*
- *Trickster tales,* which involve a clever character who outsmarts others, especially those more powerful (*Anansi*).
- *Realistic tales,* which may have grown out of actual events (*Zlateh the Goat*).

- *Fairytales,* which showcase magical characters and objects (*Snow White*).
- *Tall tales,* which exaggerate characteristics and accomplishments (*Johnny Appleseed*).
- *Fables,* stories that involve animals with human traits and always include a moral or lesson (*The Lion and the Mouse*).
- *Myths,* stories that answer questions about things that people cannot explain and may involve heroic quests (*Lord of the Sky: Zeus*).
- *Legends,* which portray a hero figure, supposedly based on a real person but often exaggerated (*John Henry*).
- *Epics,* extended stories of a hero's quest (*Jason and the Golden Fleece*).

FANTASY AND SCIENCE FICTION

Fantasy is fiction that contains unrealistic or unworldly elements, such as magic. Writers of fantasy make an unreal world seem believable; readers willingly suspend their disbelief, entering another world with characteristics that may be quite different from their own view of reality. In the process, they learn about truths that transcend everyday reality. The blending of fantastic and realistic detail is a hallmark of fantasy. While the events and setting are fantastic, the characters seem real.

Important elements of fantasy include:

- *Time and setting.* Fantasies may be set in the past, present, or distant future. The place where the story occurs may be enchanted.
- *Characters.* Fantasies may include people or animals with magical or supernatural powers. Sometimes the characters represent stereotypes of good and evil. They may be extraterrestrial beings.
- *Theme.* Fantasies usually communicate some universal truths, so that by reading about the fantastic world, readers gain insight into their own life and world.
- *Humor.* Fantasies are often humorous or entertaining.

Science fiction is a special type of fantasy. It involves and/or is based on scientific principles. Science fiction has the appearance of scientific probability because the stories are based on extensions of known technology. Through a typically fantastical array of adventures, usually set in the future or involving future technology, characters pursue truth and experience human problems.

REALISTIC FICTION AND HISTORICAL FICTION

Realistic fiction, a favorite with intermediate students, includes stories drawn from the writer's imagination but that could happen in real life. Students enjoy these books because they can identify with settings or problems not so different from their own.

Realistic fiction can inspire students by portraying characters in powerful roles who learn to solve their own problems. It can also open new worlds, showing readers the lives of people in other cultures and places.

A work of realistic fiction must be believable. Humor is often a characteristic of realistic fiction, but you will also find just about every problem known in today's society, including peer relationships, family dysfunction, issues related to growing up, cultural diversity, disability, and death. Students often select realistic fiction that centers on their personal interests—pets, horses, sports, journeys, survival, or adventure.

A mystery is a work of realistic fiction with particular structural features. The problem centers on a question that needs resolution, and the text contains clues.

Historical fiction is set in the past. Typically, the major characters are imaginary, but the writer uses historical details such as food, cooking, and transportation to substantiate the setting. Sometimes, real historical events and people enter the story. Historical fantasies combine elements of fantasy (through time travel) with historical events of history.

Literary Elements in Fiction

The literary elements that come into play when talking about fictional texts (see Figure 23–4) may be familiar to you from high school and college classes, but you may not have considered how you can use them to enhance your students' enjoyment of fiction (and your own for that matter). Analyzing these literary elements helps readers see so much more in a text, especially as they reflect on and discuss their analyses with others.

We want our students to read beyond the words and literal meaning, to be swept up in inferences that shape and drive their thinking. We want them to become aware of how the writer uses language, symbolism, or other literary devices to foreshadow events and outcomes. High-quality texts offer many levels of meaning. Peeling away the layers helps students think more deeply

---

Elements of Fiction

❖ Characters—people, animals or inanimate objects in a story [who].

❖ Plot—the interplay of action and tension in the story [what happens].

❖ Setting—time and place in which the story takes place [when and where].

❖ Theme—the story message or messages.

❖ Perspective—the point of view taken by the narrator of the story.

❖ Style and Language—how the author uses language to convey meaning.

❖ Illustrations—how meaning is communicated by the art that accompanies the text.

❖ Design—the entire visual presentation of the text.

Figure 23–4. Elements of Fiction

---

about issues and relationships. In this way, literary experience adds qualitatively to their life experiences.

SETTING

The *setting* is the time and place in which the story occurs. We learn about the setting through words and pictures. Setting is more important in some stories than in others. In *Hatchet* (Paulsen 1987), for example, the wilderness setting is integral to the story, in which a boy must survive on his own. Setting, however, can also be simply a backdrop for the events of the story. *Ginger Brown: Too Many Houses* (Wyeth 1996), a story about a little girl whose parents are getting divorced, could happen anywhere.

CHARACTERS

The *characters* are the people, animals, or inanimate objects that appear in a story. The writer reveals characters by showing what they do, what they say or think, and how they look. Characters are also revealed through their relationships with other characters, and through those characters' thoughts, dialogue, or actions.

In literary terms, character development refers to how

the author creates the characters and makes them believable and to the ways in which the characters change during the story. For example, in *The Secret Garden* (Burnett 1987), the two major characters, spoiled and selfish children, learn to think of others while restoring a garden with the help of a neighborhood boy.

A story usually has one or more main characters and a number of supporting characters. The main character is called the *protagonist*. Sometimes an *antagonist,* an opposing force, creates conflict or tension, which, typically, the protagonist must overcome.

The protagonist is well developed or "rounded" because her traits are fully described and her motives are understood. *Dynamic* characters are well-rounded characters that change. Characters who are not fully developed are *flat*. Flat characters are secondary to the main characters; they may play a pivotal role in the story, but their personalities do not develop beyond one or two dimensions. They seldom change, or the way they change is not the main point of the story.

We may find *rounded* characters profound because they are believable and memorable. For many readers, characters "make" the story; they come to life in ways that make us feel as though we know them. As you look at characters in the books you provide for students, make sure there are strong male and female images as well as representatives of our diverse society. Students need to read books about people like themselves, but they also need to meet characters from other social, cultural, and economic groups. We want students to encounter strong characters—across a diverse range—who will inspire them.

PLOT

The *plot* is what makes a story a story. It is a description of action—what happened, to whom, and why. The plot is the structure of the action: the episodes or events. If a book does not have a good plot, it will not hold readers' interests. Traditionally, stories have:

- A beginning that introduces the setting, characters, and problem.
- A series of events (called the rising action) in which the character takes action to solve the problem.
- A high point (called the climax) in which the tension is at its highest and the problem is about to be resolved.
- A resolution of the problem.

- A brief ending (the falling action, or denouement) that ties up loose ends and gives a sense of completeness.

There are many variations on this sequence. Not every one of the elements is always present. Plots can be simple or complex. Some plots end at the high point. Some stories focus on a series of everyday events; there may be tension over relationships or everyday problems, but the story does not proceed to a high level of tension or a clear climax.

Writers make different uses of time. The plot may move in chronological order, as tension and conflicts increase until the overall problem is resolved. Alternately, a plot may have episodes linked to each other by common characters or a unified theme. The writer may also use devices like flashback or flash-forward to relate past or future events that are relevant to understanding the present. Flashbacks, flash-forwards, and epilogues expand time, so that the story can encompass a wider span. Writers also use "stories within stories" to explain events. For example, in *Maniac Magee* (Spinelli 1991), the author provides a series of stories about the main character prior to the beginning of the action of the main plot.

Through the ordering of events, accompanied by conflict, the writer evokes response from readers. There are four basic patterns of conflict (Lukens 1999):

1. *Person against nature.* Tension comes from the character's battle against strong forces of nature. Examples include survival stories such as *Abel's Island* (Steig 1976), *Julie of the Wolves* (George 1972), and *The River* (Paulsen 1991).
2. *Person against person.* Tension comes through the conflict between the protagonist and the antagonist. The strain between the characters holds readers' interest. In *The Dark Is Rising* (Cooper 1999), the hero battles the forces of darkness as represented by evil characters. In fairy tales, a person-against-person struggle is often obvious and clearcut, as with *Cinderella* or *Little Red Riding Hood*. Person-against-person conflict may be resolved when good overcomes evil in some way—either vanquishing evil or changing evil to good.
3. *Person against society.* Tension comes from the main character's struggles against some societal factor that must be overcome. In *The Fighting Ground* (Avi 1984), Jonathan experiences what it is like to face

death in a war. In *Just Juice* (Hesse 1998), Juice struggles against the poverty and illiteracy that has kept her family disadvantaged.

4. *Person against self.* Tension is created as the protagonist faces internal conflict. The hero has two or more courses of action and must decide which course to take. In *Caddie Woodlawn* (Brink 1936), a young girl struggles with shaping her behavior to meet the demands of being female.

Complex stories will often have multiple plot lines; events occur simultaneously and there are many levels of conflict. In *Seedfolks* (Fleischman 1997), thirteen residents of an urban community are polarized by their own diversity. They struggle to find ways to overcome prejudice and become a community. Each tells his or her story, which involves internal conflicts as well as conflicts with others in the group. Turning a trash-filled vacant lot into a garden helps them work together, overcoming drug problems and ethnic barriers, still another pattern of conflict.

THEME

The *theme* is the big idea—what the story is primarily about. Most stories have several themes. A theme is a message that the author conveys about life. For example, in *The Tenth Good Thing About Barney* (Viorst 1976), the theme is coping with the death of a pet. In *Hatchet* (Paulsen 1987), the primary theme is survival. In *Baseball Saved Us* (Mochizuki 1993), a theme related to courage takes center stage.

The theme ties together the characters, the setting, and the plot. A theme may be explicitly stated; the most obvious example is a fable, in which a moral or lesson is always stated at the end. In *Miss Rumphius* (Cooney 1982), Great-Aunt Alice advises, "You must do something to make the world more beautiful" (p. 25).

Themes can also be implicit—unstated but understood. In *Jalapeno Bagels* (Wing 1996), Pablo helps his Mexican-American mother make empanadas and pan dulce; then he helps his Jewish father make bagels and challah. Finally he decides to take jalapeño bagels to school because they are a mixture of both his parents' cultural backgrounds. This story of everyday life carries the underlying message of cultural integration.

A theme will raise questions in the mind of a reader that may lead to a change in perspective or values. In complex stories, it becomes harder for readers to discern the theme. In one sense, the theme consists of the meanings the reader actually takes from the book. Beyond that, unifying truths are presented, and we need to help our students discover them. Writers do set parameters for meaning by the way they construct their plots and present their characters. In other words, there are limits to the meanings a reader can create from any one particular story.

We want our students to grow in their sophisticated ability to recognize the main theme or themes. In the different book lists provided in Appendix 61, you will find many different themes that will interest intermediate students. Certainly, you and your students will discover additional themes in every book you read together.

Works of fiction are open to interpretation; the reading experience is different for everyone. By making connections and sharing them with others, students can broaden their sense of the big ideas in the stories they read.

PERSPECTIVE

The *point of view*, or *perspective*, is the position the narrator takes. Stories may be told in the first person (using I) or the third person (he or she). Stories told in the third person may focus on one character, revealing her thoughts, feelings, and actions. The perspective can be biased toward a character or tend toward a more objective stance that allows readers to draw their own conclusions.

Style and Language

Style refers to how the author uses language to convey meaning. Style is not what is said, but how it is said. The author chooses words and arranges them in phrases, sentences, and paragraphs to tell the story.

Author Eve Bunting, for example, uses a straightforward, spare style that nevertheless evokes emotional response in the reader. She uses no extra words, does not describe what characters are thinking, or even give them names. Instead, she shows through their actions what they are feeling. In *The Wall* (1990), a father and son visit the Vietnam memorial. They look at the wall, search for the name of the child's grandfather, and talk briefly and quietly about death. The story ends like this:

> But I'd rather have my grandpa here, taking me to the river, telling me to button my jacket because it's cold.
> I'd rather have him here.

In this understated text, the wall and the tribute people pay to it serve as symbols of the futility of war.

Figurative Language

Authors may incorporate *figurative language* in their styles to better communicate meaning. Figurative language is a way to say a lot in a few words. Here are some common terms:

- A *simile* is a comparison using the words *like* or *as*. For example, "...into the feeling of fear and respect that Jiro had for Yoshida, there appeared a new strain—hatred. It was like a rivulet of hot, molten lava deep within a mountain" (*The Master Puppeteer*, Paterson 1976, p. 55).
- A *metaphor* is a direct comparison. For example, "Flames danced over the frozen ground and snapping sparks licked the darkness" (*Dreamstones*, Trottier 1976, p. 15).
- *Personification* is imbuing animals or inanimate objects with human characteristics. For example, in *Pigs Might Fly* (King-Smith 1980, p. 17) agitated mother sows sound the alarm: "For just as we say 'dirty as a pig' or 'fat as a pig,' so pigs repay the insult the other way around. And all along the row, from Mrs. Troughlicker to Mrs. Grubguzzle, the cry went up, 'Dirty fat man! Leave him alone!' while nine pairs of jaws chomped and nine pairs of eyes glittered."

Imagery

Writers use language to appeal to the senses—to help the reader imagine how something looks, smells, sounds, or feels. Creating "pictures with words" is the hallmark of the writer's style. Imagery enables the reader to "see" setting, characters, and actions. This description, from *The Cricket in Times Square* (Selden 1960), catapults us right into the action:

Above the cricket, towers that seemed like mountains of light rose up into the night sky. Even this late the neon signs were still blazing. Reds, blues, greens and yellows flashed down on him. And the air was full of the roar of traffic and the hum of human beings. It was as if Times Square were a kind of shell, with colors and noises breaking in great waves inside it. (p. 32)

Symbolism

Writers use *symbolism* to bring layers of meaning into play. A symbol has significance beyond itself; it has both a literal and a figurative meaning. Some symbols are universal—the dove, for example, is a widely recognized symbol of peace. In *Sadako and the Thousand Paper Cranes* (Coerr 1999) the crane is a symbol of hope. In the short story "Shells," from the collection *Every Living Thing* (Rylant 1985, pp. 73–81), the hermit crab, which sheds its shell as it grows, is a symbol for the people who change and grow.

Mood

The *mood* of the story is the emotional atmosphere that the writing evokes. It may be frantic, funny and exaggerated, as in *Maniac McGee* (Spinelli 2000), or droll, tongue-in-cheek as in *Ella Enchanted* (Levine 1997). In *Fly Away Home* (1991), Bunting creates a somber tone while Bauer, in *On My Honor* (1986), evokes anxiety and remorse.

Illustrations

Meaning is also communicated by the *illustrations* in the text. Art or photography may extend the meaning far beyond the words; illustrations also help set the mood. Line, color, and space define the artist's world. Drawings can be strong and powerful or light and delicate. The charcoal drawings in *Dakota Dugout* (Turner 1985) and the bold colors in McDermot's *Arrow to the Sun* (1974) communicate the central theme of the stories as well as mood and culture.

Illustrations may involve different media—woodcuts, collages, pen-and-ink drawings, charcoals, watercolors, oils, or acrylics. The art may be composed of photographs or involove three dimensional features. Look for art that is aesthetically pleasing and appropriate to the theme and mood of the story. Even though there is room for artistic license, accuracy and authenticity are also important features of illustrations. In picture books the illustrations and text work together to form a cohesive whole; neither stands alone. In some books, the illustrations carry a great deal of the meaning. For example, in *Arrow to the Sun*, the reader tracks meaning over several pages by looking at abstract drawings.

DESIGN

Closely related to the illustrations is the entire visual presentation of the book—the *design*. It includes elements such as:

- Size and shape.
- Type of print, font, and layout.
- Integration of illustrations and text.
- Quality of paper, binding.
- Cover design.
- End papers.

When we think about design we may consider durability and convenience, but the most important aspect of design is appeal to readers. The text may have special features such as border designs, foldouts, or illuminated letters. It is important that such features have an integral relationship to the topic, theme, or setting of the book.

BELIEVABILITY

Judging a work of fiction often comes down to *believability*. If anything in the text suddenly reminds us that the story or characters are not real, the story loses credibility and its power to move us. A sudden improbable coincidence that neatly wraps up the plot, the sentimental treatment of a character, characters who don't reflect realistic behavior for an age group or a culture, and events or artifacts that don't fit the time or setting substantially diminish the quality of a story.

The writer may have created a world of fantasy; but within this world, the events must fit together logically and the people must be motivated by needs and challenges that seem real. In *Tuck Everlasting* (1975), Babbit creates a situation in which drinking from a well allows people to live forever. The heroine, Winnie, considers a decision that readers can relate to—whether to live her natural life fully or drink from the well and extend her life eternally. The situation is fantasy, but within that structure, Winnie's dilemma is believable. The best fiction comes alive because the author draws the reader into a seemingly real world.

QUALITY

The *quality* of a text is related to the ways in which the elements work together. A compelling plot, well-devel-

oped characters, effective style and language, good use of illustrations, and believability are all related to the quality of a book. Judging quality is your responsibility as a teacher. As you select fiction texts for your students, you will want to consider the literary elements. Your selections must also encompass your students' interests and experiences.

Nonfiction

Nonfiction is intended to provide factual information through text and visual images. A nonfiction text, whether it is a picture book or a longer text, focuses on a particular topic. The line between fiction and nonfiction is a fine one. Works of fiction often do include factual information, but the heart of the story has been fashioned in the author's imagination. Nonfiction texts, on the other hand, must be documented; the information is verifiable from other sources. Accuracy is of supreme importance in works of nonfiction.

Informational Texts

Informational texts contain ideas, facts, and principles related to the physical, biological, or social world. Informational texts may take many different forms: picture books, photo essays; chapter books, articles and essays, letters, diaries and journals, observational notes, factual references (almanacs, books of statistics, books of world records), brochures and manuals. The primary purpose is to communicate information.

Information books cross all areas of study in which readers are interested—geology, sports, religion, space, technology, history, animals, cooking, and so on. In the past, much of the content curriculum was delivered through textbooks, but in recent years the quality of information books has improved, and the number of informational books published has greatly increased (Tunnell and Jacobs 1997). These books often include beautiful art and other graphic features. In addition they provide timely, well-written information by qualified experts.

In general, textbooks are not considered literature and would not be part of literature study. High-quality informational books and biographies, however, do have the qualities of literature, as well as special elements of their own. We consider them literature and a vital part of our literacy program.

High-quality informational texts are key to students' development of an important concept called *content literacy*. Content literacy involves the strategies required to read, comprehend, and write informational texts in a variety of subjects. Different styles and ways of organizing texts are used for different subjects. For example, a historical account of the Civil War is organized differently from a botanical guide to the different varieties of mountain wildflowers. The vocabulary of the two books differs, as does the ways in which the two authors use language.

Content literacy involves knowing what to expect—anticipating the kinds of organizational structures the reader might encounter. Content literacy also involves understanding the kinds of graphic features the reader needs to interpret, as well as vocabulary specific to the topic. The reader uses the text's organization, language, and visual features in a unified way to derive meaning. In other words students must learn how to read history, biology, environmental science, geographical descriptions, and other kinds of texts.

Learning how to read informational texts involves strategies such as gathering information, summarizing and synthesizing information, and making connections to prior knowledge. Readers of informational texts must analyze where information is located within the overall organizational framework. They must also be critical, asking such questions as "Is the information documented? Do the ideas fit together?"

Elements of Informational Texts

Three important elements are present in high-quality informational texts (see Figure 23–5).

Elements of Nonfiction

❖ Integrity

❖ Accuracy and Authenticity

❖ Style and Language

Figure 23–5. Elements of Nonfiction

INTEGRITY

The writers of high-quality informational texts are *honest* with readers, selecting important ideas and breaking them down into parts that can be understood, all the time making decisions about what to include and what to leave out. High-quality texts include essential information, the omission of which would lead to misconceptions or stereotyping. The authors reveal their sources, distinguish fact from opinion, and reveal their biases. They avoid attributing human qualities to entities that are not human. They present different perspectives as required, and they support their claims with evidence. In *Cowboys* (Sandler 2000), the writer presents a realistic picture of the life of cowboys, actively working to dispel the romantic myths that surround the job and lifestyle.

ACCURACY AND AUTHENTICITY

Informational books must be *accurate*. The author must either be personally or professionally qualified to write the book or have the manuscript checked by experts. Significant facts are included, the illustrations or other graphic aids are accurate, and summary statements are supported by details. Other sources can be used to confirm the statements in the text. *Galaxies* (Simon, 1988), for example, contains tightly woven, readable text alongside photographs taken through a telescope. The facts and definitions of technical terms can be checked against other sources. Simon has also written other informational texts, establishing his reputation for accuracy.

Unlike fiction, informational texts can become dated. Therefore, when we pick up an informational text, we want to consider when it was written. For example, a book about computers that was written in 1985 might be of historical interest, but it would not provide up-to-date information about topics such as the Internet.

STYLE AND LANGUAGE

Style and *language* are both important aspects of nonfiction. Style refers to how the writer makes the information interesting. The author's style must be clear in order to present information accurately, and it must consider the audience, providing definitions or illustrations of technical terms where necessary.

Through language, the author develops his style

and voice. It is important for the nonfiction writer to give the text personal "voice" without violating the integrity or authenticity of the text. In *Sketching Outdoors in Winter* (1988), Arnosky presents a series of sketches, with commentary and artistic advice. The personal comments are clearly indicated:

> When you spend a day outdoors sketching bird nests, you come home carrying little pieces of wherever you have been. Clinging to clothing are seeds, thorns, slivers of bark, broken brittle branch tips, and fragments of dead leaves—all picked up while you were climbing and crawling through thickets where birds have raised their young. (p. 16)

Structure of Informational Texts

The text's overall structure reveals how the writer has organized the content. Information may be presented in categories; simple ideas may be presented first so that more complex ideas can be built on them. There are many different ways to structure the information in a text, including:

- *Narrative.* An informational text can be organized much like a narrative, with a beginning, a series of events, and an ending. This kind of structure is easy for students to understand and is often used in nonfiction texts for younger children.
- *Sequential.* A number of informational texts lend themselves to organization using chronological order. These texts may have a narrative quality, but not necessarily. Directions are usually organized in a step-by-step chronological way. Narrative and chronological organizational patterns are like stories; they should be read from beginning to end in order to comprehend the ideas clearly.
- *Categorical.* Writers often present information around a topic by organizing ideas into categories. This makes it possible for readers to "dip into" the text. They can decide what they want to learn about the particular topic and focus on that particular section, an efficient way to read. Sometimes a writer will start with a single aspect of a topic and build ideas through successive sections, summarizing at the end. On the other hand, a writer may begin with a larger topic and break it down into sections.

Writers may go from simple to complex ideas, building one concept on another. Ideas may be so interdependent that the reader will find it necessary to start at the beginning of a text and read it through (or at least to search back in the text for needed background information). Often, though, the reader can assess his own background knowledge and skip sections as needed, even when the writer's ideas are interdependent.

Features of Informational Texts

Figure 23–6 lists four kinds of features that are typical of informational texts. All of these features help the reader locate information in the text.

Features of Informational Texts		
Print Features		
❖ font ❖ bold print ❖ colored print	❖ bullets ❖ titles ❖ headings ❖ subheadings	❖ italics ❖ labels ❖ captions
Graphic Aids		
❖ diagrams ❖ sketches ❖ graphs ❖ figures	❖ maps ❖ charts ❖ tables	❖ cross-sections ❖ timelines ❖ overlays
Organizational Aids		
❖ table of contents ❖ index	❖ glossary ❖ preface	❖ pronunciation guide ❖ appendix
Illustrations		
❖ colored photographs ❖ colored drawings ❖ black and white photos ❖ black and white drawings	❖ labeled drawings ❖ enlarged photographs ❖ acrylic, watercolor, oil paintings	

Figure 23–6. Features of Informational Texts

Patterns of Text Structure in Informational Texts

Text Pattern	Definition	Key Words	Examples
Description	Use language to help the reader form images or visualize processes	descriptive details—words like *on, over, beyond, within* descriptive adjectives	❖ *A Drop of Water*
Temporal Sequence	Present ideas or events in the order in which they happen	*first, second, before, after, finally, then, next, earlier, later, last*	❖ *Fire in the Forest* ❖ *Salmon Summer* ❖ *Look to the North: A Wolf Pup Diary*
Comparison/ Contrast	Discuss two ideas, events, or phenomena, showing how they are similar and different	*while, yet, but, rather, most, either, like* and *unlike, same, as opposed to, as well as, likewise, on the other hand, although, the same, similarly, opposites*	❖ *Wolf Pack: Tracking Wolves*
Cause and Effect	Provide explanations or reasons for phenomena	*because, since, thus, so that, if…then, therefore, nevertheless, due to, this led to, as a result, then…so, for this reason, on account of, consequently*	❖ *The Most Beautiful Roof in the World*
Problem/Solution	Identify problems and pose solutions	*propose, conclude, a solution, the problem* or *the question, research shows, the evidence is, a reason for*	❖ *Once a Wolf: How Wildlife Biologists Fought to Bring Back the Gray Wolf*

Figure 23–7. Patterns of Text Structure in Informational Texts

PRINT FEATURES

In informational texts, print features are important in guiding the reader through the patterns of organization. For example, chapter titles guide readers to the particular categories the writer has used to frame the book; they also outline the sequence. Titles, headings, and subheadings help readers find important information. Different kinds of information may appear in different-size fonts or may be emphasized by italics, bold print, bullets, or color. The labels or captions that accompany illustrations are another source of information.

ORGANIZATIONAL AIDS

Features such as a table of contents also help the reader find information in a text. Many informational texts include additional guides to organization, such as:

■ A table of contents provides an efficient way to find information contained in a broad topic.
■ An index that provides a quick way to find information on specific pages of the text.
■ A glossary to define technical terms.
■ A pronunciation guide to help readers say the words.

■ Appendices that offer additional information.

Learning to use these features will greatly benefit readers of informational texts.

GRAPHIC AIDS

Graphic aids include diagrams, sketches, maps, charts, graphs, tables, cross-sectional drawings or views, time lines, flowcharts and other figures. The graphic aids represent information in some specific way. Graphic aids may be used in connection with all the structural patterns listed below.

ILLUSTRATIONS

Illustrations for informational texts may include color or black-and-white photographs and drawings. Drawings or photographs may be labeled and are often accompanied by explanatory captions. Photographs expand the meaning of the text, and can be used to illustrate organizational patterns; for example photographs taken at different seasons can be used for comparison or to show sequence. It is especially important that illustrations in informational texts be accurate and authentic because they carry much of the meaning.

Structural Patterns and Language

Several types of structural patterns appear in informational texts (see Figure 23–7). Writers of information texts use these structures to arrange and connect ideas (Irwin and Baker 1989; Freeman and Person 1998). A writer typically employs several structural patterns in the same text, but on occasion an entire volume may be organized around one of these patterns.

DESCRIPTION

Description is widely used because it enables writers to help us visualize and understand phenomena. Typically, the writer of an informational text explains the characteristics of the subject or topic, emphasizing key concepts and using details to support the ideas. Let's look at this excerpt from *A Drop of Water* (Wick 1997) in which the author describes a close-up photograph of a soap bubble.

There are few objects you can make that have both the dazzling beauty and delicate precision of a soap bubble. Shown here at actual size, this bubble is a nearly perfect sphere. Its shimmering

liquid skin is five hundred times thinner than a human hair. (p 15)

Description involves language that helps the reader form images or visualize processes. We are likely to encounter words that describe relationships among phenomena, for example, *near, on, over, beyond, within, contiguous*. The writer uses descriptive adjectives to make images more vivid and provide details.

TEMPORAL SEQUENCE

The writer can organize ideas or events in the order in which they happen. In addition, the writer uses details to support the key events or understandings. In *Fire in the Forest* (Pringle 1995), the writer uses paintings and text to present the full cycle of a forest fire: from destructive inferno to renewal of the forest. Visually the reader is treated to beautiful images that move from mature forest through the cycle and back again. The text provides a range of information for each stage. The writer also relies heavily on description.

In *Salmon Summer* (MacMillan 1998) the writer provides details to describe the act of fishing:

Alex baits a hook with his salmon, attaches a heavy sinker, and hangs the line overboard. It drops to the bottom. He waits and feels with his fingers for a tug on the line. He feels a nibble. He pulls. Nothing. He feels another nibble and tugs hard. He's got it. The hook is set. Alex holds on and starts pulling it in. (p 26)

Here the writer is describing a sequence of actions but is also using descriptive language in a brisk, engaging way. Writers often rely on specific words to signal a temporal sequence—*first, next, before, after, finally*.

COMPARISON/CONTRAST

The writer compares two ideas, events, or phenomena, showing how they are similar and different. The writer states the issues or concepts being compared and explains them in enough detail to help the reader understand why the comparison is significant.

In *Wolf Pack: Tracking Wolves in the Wild* (Johnson and Aamodt 1985) the authors define wolves by comparing them to dogs. This text is organized categorically, a different topic presented in each chapter.

Within the text the writers use description as well as comparison/contrast to make points. Again, language signals the comparison— *while, yet, but, rather, most, either, like and unlike, same, as opposed to, as well as, likewise, on the other hand, although, the same, similarly.*

CAUSE AND EFFECT

Writers of informational texts also provide explanations for readers that include the reasons for various phenomena. Ideas are related because they represent causes and effects. In *Wolf Pack,* for example, the writers explain that wolves are carnivores and that they must search for prey to survive. Wolves work in packs or groups because it is essential for them to cooperate in order to survive. In *A Drop of Water*, the writer explains that water can be a gas. When it seems to disappear, it has evaporated, or turned into water vapor.

When the writer is using the cause/effect pattern you are likely to encounter these words: *because, since, thus, so that, if…then, therefore, nevertheless, this led to, as a result, then…so, for this reason, on account of.*

PROBLEM/SOLUTION

Writers of informational texts often identify problems and pose solutions. The problem should be clearly stated, including pertinent details, so that readers can understand the solution. It is also necessary to show the reader why the problem and solution are important.

This process inevitably includes an examination of cause and effect. For example, in *Wolf Pack,* the authors reveal the endangerment of wolves as a problem. They suggest that wolf endangerment stems from ranchers and local land owners who misunderstand the effort to reinstate wolves to their traditional environment as well as hunters who pursue wolves for their furs and to protect domestic animals. Legal protection and research, the authors suggest, are the answer.

Obviously, cause/effect and problem/solution are related structures. Question and answer patterns are also similar. You can explain causes without necessarily having a problem or a solution; but it would be hard to have a problem and solution without discussing cause and effect. The ideas are implied in the very act of solving a problem and arguing for your approach. Similar language is used to signal both processes, so the problem/solution structure would incorporate the same key words listed for cause and effect. In addition, you may see such words as *propose, conclude,* a *solution,* the *problem* or the *question, research shows, the evidence is.*

COMBINING TEXT STRUCTURE PATTERNS

A well-written text probably combines several of the patterns listed above. For example, in arguing to support saving the wolves, the writers use description, comparison/contrast, cause/effect, and problem/solution at various points in the text. In *Stones, Bones, and Petroglyphs: Digging into Southwest Archaeology* (Goodman 1998), the author combines an account of a group of eighth graders visiting Crow Canyon with information about ancient dwellings. The students' visit proceeds in chronological order and follows a narrative structure. Photographs support the narrative into which information is woven. Some of the pictures feature quotes from students as captions, which gives the piece a personal voice. It is suggested that a long drought (documented by tree rings) may have caused the ancient civilization to leave the area. Chronological order is also used to describe events in the life of the historic people; sequence describes processes, such as how to work at an archeological dig or steps in the scientific process. Description is used throughout to provide main ideas and details. Problem/solution is also involved as students explore the question, Why did they leave? The underlying message is that we can learn from the artifacts that ancient people have left behind.

When students recognize the ways that writers of informational text help them understand ideas, they not only comprehend at a higher level but also may learn how to use those structures in their own writing.

Biography

A biography is a factual work that describes the life of a real person, the subject. Biographies are based on known facts about the person and the time in which she lived. The subject must have accomplished something or be of interest in a way that makes the biography worthwhile. There are a number of variations:

- *Fictionalized biographies*—to add interest, the writer has invented some details and dialogue.
- *Biographical fiction*—the writer imagines a narrative based on a real person's achievement *Ben and Me* (Lawson 1939).
- An *autobiography* has been written by the subject.

An autobiography can never be fully objective because the person must talk from her own point of view. Examples are *Fire Talking* (Polacco 1994) and *But I'll Be Back Again* (Rylant 1989).

▪ A *memoir* is an account of a historical or personal event as recalled by the author. It is technically not autobiography, but it is related—the focus is on making clear one's own observations, memories, and feelings at a certain point in time. *Nettie's Trip South* (Turner 1987), which depicts a young Northern girl's first experience with slavery in the days just before the Civil War, is an example of a constructed memoir in that it is drawn from actual diaries and letters.

A *complete* biography shows an individual's life from beginning to end. A *partial* biography provides information on a segment or particularly important part of a person's life. A *collective* biography presents the lives of several people, usually connected by a common theme or characteristic. (For example, *Five Brave Explorers* [Hudson 1995] discusses five African-American adventurers.)

In high-quality biographies:

▪ The author knows the subject well either personally or through research.
▪ The life of the subject is presented in an interesting but authentic way.
▪ Facts are accurate and can be substantiated; they are based on primary data.

Elements of Biography

❖ Setting

❖ Characterization of subject

❖ Theme

❖ Accuracy

❖ Structure

❖ Illustrations

❖ Graphic Features

❖ Structural Patterns

❖ Organizational Features

Figure 23–8. Elements of Biography

▪ The subject comes to life through character development.
▪ The importance of setting is explained.

Structure of Biography

Biography is nonfiction, but it has many characteristics of fiction. For example, biographies are usually narratives because they do, in fact, tell a story about a person. The story may begin at any time in a subject's life, dealing with previous events retrospectively.

Literary Elements of Biography

Biographies blend fiction and nonfiction literary elements to some extent (see Figure 23–8). They have many of the features of fiction that appeal to students—a central character, events, tension, and problem resolution.

SETTING

Setting often influences the events in a person's life. You will want to note the place, the time in history, and other events that occurred during the subject's life. For example, the biography *Laura Ingalls Wilder* (Blair 1981) details Laura's farm life and experiences from her childhood on. The rural setting and the events of the period influenced her writing.

CHARACTERIZATION

Characterization, the representation of the subject's character and motives, is one of the most important aspects of biography. After all, the book is about an important person, and she should be presented in a compelling way. The writer should clearly show the subject's accomplishments and, so far as possible, make hypotheses (based on evidence) about the events and people who influenced the subject's actions and decisions. Seeing the social-political climate of the time through the subject's eyes helps students understand history and sociology.

THEME

The big ideas of biography or *themes* are the same as those of realistic and historical fiction. Students witness conflicts between people, internal conflicts, and the struggle against nature and society. People of achievement typically have shown courage in overcoming obstacles and have made contributions to society. For many readers, the impact of biography is even more powerful than fiction because the person and events are real.

ACCURACY

All biographies must be *accurate*. Information for biography is drawn from letters, documents, interviews, newspaper and magazine archives, reference books, and informational books. A book's foreword usually tells something about the writer's research. The degree to which a writer consulted original sources contributes to the authenticity of the biography. Whenever possible, the biographer should check one source against another.

When there are conflicting opinions on the part of reputable historians, the uncertainty should be acknowledged. Biographers are also responsible for selecting the information they include. Not all of the information on famous people would be interesting for elementary students to know; however, omissions should be made carefully after assessing whether the omission could lead to misconceptions.

STRUCTURAL PATTERNS

Biographies generally follow a temporal sequence, although there are variations. For example, a biographer can focus on a certain segment of a subject's life. In *Eleanor* (Cooney 1996), the author focuses on Eleanor Roosevelt's childhood and her schooling in France, which helped her grow from a shy child to an accomplished and educated woman. Her later life is summarized in an afterword. The biographer can begin at any point in the subject's life, using flashback or flashforward to fill in as necessary.

The biographer may also use comparisons between the subject's personality, capabilities, attitudes, or circumstances and those of other people. It is typical for the biographer to use description to help the subject seem real and important. Biographers also explain the subject's attitudes, motivations, and actions, the problems she faced, and the actions she took to solve them.

ILLUSTRATIONS AND GRAPHIC FEATURES

Typically, biographies are illustrated by authentic photographs or an artist's renderings of the subject and the places in which she lived, conveying a real sense of the times. Some biographies, such as *The Last Princess* (Stanley 1991), include both photographs and artistic renderings. *Bard of Avon: The Story of William Shakespeare* (Stanley and Vennema 1992) includes detailed paintings of the Globe Theatre and Elizabethan society in the 1500s. Like other informational texts, biographies can also include charts, maps, diagrams, or graphs—anything that has to do with the subject's life and work.

In general, biographies are like fiction—they are intended to be read from beginning to end. When students are researching a particular topic, however, they may search the text for specific information. Biographies may have chapter titles; like informational texts, they may also have headings and subheadings to help readers easily locate specific information.

ORGANIZATIONAL FEATURES

Biographies may have such organizational features as a table of contents, a glossary or pronunciation guide, or an index. They also generally have a bibliography of sources. This list of references helps establish authenticity and is valuable if students want to check the background sources or read further.

Analyzing Texts for Racism and Sexism

The world around us is full of messages. Your upper elementary students are beginning to define themselves by what they see and hear. The models and attitudes they encounter in the texts they read influence their perceptions of the roles and capabilities of less powerful groups. If books contain stereotypes and misconceptions, even subtle ones, then reading can distort rather than broaden students' perceptions. With your help, upper elementary students can learn to detect racism and sexism in both fiction and nonfiction.

The Council for Interracial Books for Children has provided some excellent guidelines for analyzing texts for racism and sexism (see Figure 23–9). While you will not want to apply the list rigidly or unthinkingly, eliminating a quality book that conforms in all but one of these aspects, you will want to eliminate books that are clearly unacceptable. Involving your students in recognizing racist and sexist language and content will sensitize them to these factors throughout their lives.

Implications for Teaching

It is important to have a classroom library that is categorized by genre as well as by the topics that interest students. This will enable students to find texts more easily. The categories will also help you monitor stu-

Analyzing Books for Racism and Sexism*	
What to do...	**What to ask...**
1. Look at the illustrations.	❖ Are there stereotypes or tokenism? ❖ How are minority roles depicted?
2. Examine the story line.	❖ Are white roles and ideas of success the only standard for success? ❖ How are problems of minorities presented and viewed? ❖ Are the causes of poverty and oppression explained? ❖ Is passive acceptance or active resistance encouraged? ❖ Could the same story be told if sex roles were reversed? ❖ Are the achievements of female characters based on initiative or superficial, stereotypic traits?
3. Look at the characters' lives.	❖ Do the lives of people of color represent stereotypes or contrast unfavorably with white norms? ❖ Are the lives of minorities represented in a simplistic way or do they offer genuine insights?
4. Analyze the relationships between people.	❖ Do whites have power and leadership, relegating people of color and females to subordinate roles? ❖ Are the family relationships presented in a stereotypic way? ❖ Is it recognized that societal conditions are among the reasons for family problems and separations?
5. Discover the role models and heroes.	❖ Are people of color depicted as "safe" heroes who avoid conflict with the establishment? ❖ Do minority heroes resemble white heroes ignoring other criteria? ❖ In whose interests does the hero work? ❖ Are there persons with which children of color can readily identify, with positive results? ❖ Does the story portray norms that are within the aspirations of children of color? ❖ Does the story portray norms that are within the reach of females who do not conform to stereotyped standards of beauty?
6. Consider the author or illustrator's background and perspective.	❖ Is the author or illustrator a member of the group being written about? ❖ If not, what qualifies the author or illustrator to present the subject? ❖ Does the author's perspective substantially weaken or strengthen the value of the work? ❖ Do omissions and distortions directly influence the overall message of the book?
7. Look at the language.	❖ Are there "loaded" words that have insulting overtones? ❖ Is there sexist language that excludes or diminishes women? ❖ How is the male pronoun used?
8. Use copyright dates as a warning to examine the book closely.	❖ Given the time of writing, indicated by publication, how likely is the book to be overtly racist or sexist?
	* Adapted from "10 Quick Ways to Analyze Children's Books for Racism and Sexism," Council on Interracial Books for Children.

Figure 23–9. Analyzing Books for Racism and Sexism

reading to ensure that they extend their reading abilities as well as their tastes. You can encourage your students to read about a variety of topics in a variety of genres by a variety of authors.

To help students develop responsibility for varying and broadening their own reading habits, you might want to establish expectations for each genre. Figure 23–10 sets out the minimum requirements one teacher sets for fourth graders. The forty titles are balanced across traditional literature, fiction, informational books, and biography, and there is still room for students to choose a few titles of whatever genre they wish. ("Short texts" such as articles or individual short stories read in guided reading are not included on this reading list, so the amount of reading, especially nonfiction, that the students do is higher. And if forty titles seem like a lot, remember that except for writing in reader's note-

Grade 4 Book Requirements Book Minimum: 40 Titles	
Traditional Literature	3
Realistic Fiction	6
Historical Fiction	6
Fantasy	1
Science Fiction	2
Informational	6
Biography	6
Choice	10

Figure 23–10.   Grade 4 Book Requirements

Coding Titles on the Reading List	
TL	Traditional Literature
RF	Realistic Fiction .
HF	Historical Fiction
F	Fantasy
SF	Science Fiction
I	Informational
B	Biography (includes Autobiography and Memoir)

Figure 23–11.   Coding titles on the Reading List

books and their book discussions, students are reading for the entire reading workshop.) On average, the students are reading one book per week, which includes the independent reading, guided reading, book club reading, and home reading they do. For efficiency, you may want to have students use standard codes (see Figure 23–11) as part of their reader's notebook book lists to keep track of the different genres they are reading.

Suggestions for Professional Development

1. Talk with your colleagues about the structural patterns found in expository texts—description, sequence, compare/contrast, cause/effect, and problem/resolution.
   - Then read "Knee Immobilizers" (Figure 23–12), a set of tongue-in-cheek paragraphs that demonstrate the various structural patterns. Identify which paragraph demonstrates which pattern.
   - Afterward, discuss your solution with the group.
   - How did you know which paragraph exemplified which pattern? What were the language clues that signaled patterns?
   - Finally, examine several informational picture books or short illustrated chapter books. Find examples of the different patterns in those books and share them. Remember that whole books will contain a variety of ideas organized in these ways.
2. Hold a meeting with all the teachers in your school to talk about racism and sexism in books.
   - Have each teacher bring two or three books from her classroom collection. The books should depict people of color.
   - Using Figure 23–9, analyze the texts for racial and sexist stereotypes.
   - Share your results and thinking.
3. Either by yourself or with a group of your grade-level colleagues, analyze the breadth of reading available to your students.
   - Organize the books in your classroom into genres using the "Genre at a Glance" list in Figure 23–3.
   - Does any genre predominate?
   - Are there enough texts in every genre?
   - What types of books should be added next to the classroom collection?
   - What additional kinds of organization would be helpful to you and your students?

Knee Immobilizers

A knee immobilizer has some key features. It is padded with foam to add comfort and a sleek look. It has three steel bars sewn in the inside to keep the leg straight. To keep it firm on legs of varying sizes, it has velcro straps.

What is a knee immobilizer?
It is a tool for keeping the leg straight so the shapely knee joint will not move and the muscles and ligaments around it can heal.

A knee immobilizer will make you miserable for a while, but it may improve the painful condition of your leg.

A knee immobilizer and a cast are designed to keep a leg in a straight line, preventing any movement. A knee immobilizer is lighter and soft, while a cast is hard and stiff. The weight of a knee immobilizer is more comfortable than that of the hard plaster cast. Both are designed to be used with crutches to keep the body weight off of one's leg.

A knee immobilizer can irritate your skin on a very hot day. To make it more comfortable, sprinkle a smooth, refreshing powder on your leg before putting the awful thing on your leg.

First, place the immobilizer flat on a surface. With the velcro on the outside, lay your leg in the center. Next, wrap the immobilizer around your leg. Finally, wrap the velcro as tight as you can. Now you can be miserable all day.

Figure 23–12. "Knee Immobilizers."

## CHAPTER TWENTY FOUR

CREATING THE POETRY WORKSHOP: READING, WRITING, AND THE ARTS

When we begin to speak in the language that is ours and tell our own stories and truths, we are surprised that this too is poetry.
-GEORGIA HEARD

Poetry was a means of communication long before people used written language. Even in later civilizations, where a few people could read or write, poems were created to communicate history and newsworthy events as well as to entertain and inspire. To this day, most poems are best enjoyed when read aloud because of their musical sound, rhythm, and language.

Why Poetry?

When you immerse your students in rich, lively poetry, you introduce them to intense, concise, skillfully crafted language. They learn how authors convey a maximum amount of thought and feeling in the fewest, carefully chosen words. In a way, everything they need to know about reading and writing exists within a poem. To appreciate poetry is to appreciate the art of language. In particular, poetry:

- Enables students to appreciate the sound and imagery of language.
- Invites students to understand and view themselves and their world in new ways.
- Enriches students' lives as they discover words, sound, and rhythm in unique, creative ways.
- Intrigues students as it offers puzzles within puzzles.
- Captures the essence of meaning in the sparest of language.

Poetry is invaluable for the quality it brings to all our lives. Additionally, for writers—including student writers!—it illuminates the art and mystery of language and meaning.

What Is Poetry?

You must experience poetry before you can even begin to think about what makes poetry: "There is an elusiveness about poetry that defies precise definition. It is not so much what it is that is important as how it makes us feel." (Huck, Hepler, and Hickman 1993, p. 452)

Poetry brings together sounds and words in unique, intriguing ways that may evoke intense imagery and profound meaning. The best poetry frequently contains an element of surprise. You encounter language that you want to read over and over, and when you do, you experience the poem anew each time. Your thoughts and emotions may be aroused by a single word.

Many people mistakenly believe that poetry must rhyme. Rhyme is only one of many poetic elements, and not all poetry rhymes. By teaching your students the elements of poetry, you help them understand how poets use language to evoke imagery and emotion. And when students experience these elements in poems they enjoy, they begin to use them in their own writing.

Meaning and Emotion

In poetry, ideas are communicated in novel ways. Consider the following:

THE FOG
The fog comes
on little cat feet.
It sits looking
over harbor and city
on silent haunches
and then moves on.
—*Carl Sandburg*

In Sandburg's poem, you feel the softness and quiet as the fog shrouds the city and harbor; you may see gray, dim light and feel the stillness and withdrawal. Sandburg helps us experience fog in new ways.

The language of poetry is magic; it compresses meaning in just a few words. This compact expression intensifies emotion; every word may convey a powerful message.

CONVERSATION

We stood in the doorway
opening up memories
like you'd open up
the little drawers
that go from floor
to ceiling down at Sampson's
General Store.

—Donald Graves

Figurative Language

Poets use language in ways that tantalize our senses—touch, sight, smell, hearing, or taste. Eve Merriam advises us to "lick the juice" of a poem; Sy Kahn observes that giraffes are "finger painted."

Figurative language links one thing with another in ways that help us compare them. A *metaphor* is a word or phrase denoting one kind of object or idea used in place of another to suggest comparison. A *simile* is a metaphor using *like* or *as*. Both elements also appear in prose, but poets use them more intensively, capturing emotion and meaning in clever twists of language.

Personification, in which the poet gives human characteristics to inanimate objects, animals, or concepts, is another literary device that helps us see in new ways. Emily Dickinson personifies death in these famous lines:

Because I could not stop for Death,
He kindly stopped for me . . .

Your students will love using figurative language to express their ideas in novel ways. After reading some of *Hailstones and Halibut Bones* (O'Neill 1961), an anthology of poems about color, Gabby wrote "Brown."

BROWN

Brown is oak
smooth as silk
and cinnamon on hot buttered muffins
the smell of bread baking
and creamy chocolate pie.

A statue
of an ancient God.
and fur
of a light brown dog.

She characterizes the color by comparing it to oak, but goes further to bring images of how "brown" would feel, taste, and smell. She shows that she has learned from O'Neill how to use figurative language to communicate the feeling of color.

Rhythm, or Cadence

Rhythm is the ordered application of stress from one syllable to the next. The rhythm of the poem may be *fast* or *slow*. Each style conveys specific meanings. For example:

■ A *fast* rhythm indicates action, excitement, tension, or suspense.
■ A *slow* rhythm suggests peacefulness, fullness, harmony, and comfort.

Rhythm in a poem is like the beat in music. Repetition of pattern adds to the rhythm. Often, a change in rhythm signals a change in action or a change in meaning. Remember that poetry is meant to be heard; meaning is conveyed by the way the reader uses the voice to convey strong and weak elements in the flow of sound and silence in speech. If you have heard enough poetry read aloud or recited, you can hear the rhythm in your head as you read.

Rhyme and Sound Patterns

Poems characteristically feature a repetition of sound, which carries the words along and gives pleasure to the listener. *Alliteration* repeats consonant sounds. In "Hoops," Robert Burleigh (1997) describes "the smooth, skaterly glide and sudden swerve." This language also demonstrates the use of rhythm. *Consonance* repeats the consonant sounds in the final position, such as a "tight, swift, fist."

Assonance is the repetition of vowel sounds. In "Shoes," Douglas Florian (1999) describes how an individual can "bruise" and "abuse shoes." *Onomatopoeia* is the use of words that imitate the sound of what they denote, such as buzz, slurp, or whiz. In "Cynthia in the Snow," Gwendolyn Brooks (1956) describes how snow "shushes" and "hushes" loudness.

Monica's poem reflects her awareness of how onomatopoetic words can add to her writing. Notice that she also slows the rhythm of the poem at the end by placing the last three words on separate lines.

SKIING

Down the mountain
Gliding, sliding
Swish, swoosh
Almost down
Turning right, turning left
Really close
Swish, swoosh
At
the
bottom.

Shape

Monica also uses line breaks to create the shape of the poem. Unlike prose, poems are laid out in lines, stanzas, and verses. The smallest unit is the line, which is placed within a stanza (a group of lines conveying an idea). In long poems, stanzas are grouped into verses.

In poetry, white space indicates that the writer wants the reader to pause or be silent for a second. Poets place line breaks strategically not only to shape the rhythm but also to represent meaning. Notice how Monica uses a line break to capture the change in the speed of skiing.

Some poems are actually laid out to look like the subject of the poem. The result may be a solid block of print that takes a particular shape, or lines that snake around, creating a picture. A good example is Brian's poem below.

Dainty as a feather Flies so heavenly Through the cooling air. Touch your heart. and The delicate Pattern of colors. Wings that light up your day

The Forms of Poetry

Poems may be fiction or nonfiction. They may showcase a particular setting, feature characters, convey a point of view, or employ a narrator. Poems often suggest a theme or message, and they typically adopt a special style or tone. What's more, poems highlight an unending array of topics: historical events, a moment in someone's life, current events, fantastic journeys. Poems can help us appreciate the wonders of nature or come to know a scientific fact in a deeper, more vivid way, thus extending the meaning of informational texts. (Scientists often use metaphors to communicate their discoveries.)

Clearly, the range of poetry within a classroom collection—and the range of poetry that students write—is varied and rich. A good resource on the great variety of poetic forms is *The Teachers and Writers Handbook of Poetic Forms* (Padgett 1987). Another is *Patterns of Poetry: An Encyclopedia of Forms* (Williams 1986). Here are the most familiar forms:

- *Free verse* is poetry that does not rhyme and has no regular rhythm. In free verse, the poet creates the rules, drawing on his intuitive sense of how the poem should look, sound, and express meaning.
- *Lyric* poetry is personal and descriptive; it helps the reader feel through the senses. Lyric poetry showcases melodic language that conveys a sense of song.
- *Narrative* poems tell a story or a sequence of events. The ballad, also a song, is a type of narrative. Very long narratives, called epics, were used in history to pass on stories about heroes and their heroic deeds.
- *Limericks* are humorous poems that are structured in five lines. The first and second lines rhyme, as do the third

and fourth. The fifth line yields a surprise ending or humorous statement and rhymes with the first two lines.

- A *cinquain* (also referred to as a five-line stanza) is a form of syllabic verse, which means that the form is built on the number of syllables. The five lines of the cinquain have, respectively, two, four, six, eight, and two syllables.

- *Concrete* poems dramatically represent meaning not only by the way words sound but how they look. The print of the poem itself takes shape as a collage or picture that conveys meaning. With the different fonts, typefaces, and other technologies available, the possibilities for concrete poems are endless.

- *Found* poems are pieces of writing that were not intended as poems but appear in the environment for us to discover (see Figure 24–1). From a few sentences in a text, Frieda created the poem by arranging the language in space. You can find "poems" in newspaper ads, on signs, or in the written and oral language your students use. The poem is in the reader or "finder."

- *Haiku* is a style of poetry that originated in Japan. It uses simple language, contains no rhyme, and rarely includes metaphor. A haiku has three lines. The first and third lines are the same length and the middle one is a little longer. Frequently, a haiku has a syllable structure of five, seven, and five. Monica's poem "Duckling" is an example of haiku.

HAIKU DUCKLING

Duckling in the pond
Paddling his little legs
Reaching for his home

- A *list* poem, also called a "catalogue" poem, may be rhymed or unrhymed, short or long. It may list objects, a series of events, specific characteristics, or any other set of items.

- To create *formula* poems, writers insert words into a preestablished structure. Formula poems give students a sense of accomplishment because they can create a poem quickly. There are many kinds of formula poems. A biopoem requires the writer to produce nine lines describing a character. In sequence, place the name of a character in capitals; four words that describe; a word or phrase that describes relationship; a line that starts with "who fears," and lists three items; one that starts with "who would like" followed by three items; "resident of" (place); and the last line giving the character's last name. Mia, Grade 6, wrote this biopoem about a character in Babbit's *Tuck Everlasting*.

Alvin Ailey, Dancer

They tried to follow
Alvin's moves,
But even Alvin didn't know
Which way
His body would reel him next.

Alvin's steps flowed
From one to another.
His loops
And spins
Just came to him,
The way daydreams do.

Whatever he's doing,
He's sure doing it fine.

From: Pinkney, Andrea Davis. 1993. *Alvin Ailey.* Il., Brain Pinkney. New York: Hyperion Paperbacks for Children. P. 15.

Figure 24–1. Found Poem

TUCK EVERLASTING
by Natalie Babbit

MAE
Loving, upset, eternal, kind
Mother of Jess and Miles
Lover of Tuck, Winnie, children
Who feels trapped within the world,
scared of living
afraid the secret may be discovered
Who fears the everlasting turn of the
ferris wheel,
being found out,
thought of others drinking the
magic spring water
Who would like to redo the scene of
drinking the magical water,
to have her turn to get off from
the ferris wheel,
to move along with the rest of the
world
Resident of Treegap
TUCK

The best way to expose students to new forms is to read examples to them. Only after you have experienced poetry can you begin to write it for yourself. Avoid beginning with formulaic poetry. A lasting love for reading and writing poetry will come from rich experiences with free verse prior to the study of other forms.

Poetry Workshop

Poetry is an essential, integral part of the language/literacy curriculum for intermediate learners. We do not view poetry as an "add-on" or as a single unit of study you might enjoy during "poetry month." We recommend that you incorporate a 90- or 120-minute poetry workshop (see Figure 24–2) into each week or at least twice a month. The poetry workshop can take the place of reading and/or writing workshop one time per week. It is also vital to include poetry sharing as a regular part of language/word study.

Making a poetry workshop part of your weekly routine clearly shows students how much you value poetry. It also enables them to develop momentum in their poetry learning and to build their understanding of poetry over time. A single "poetry unit" cannot accomplish this goal.

Poet Talk

We suggest beginning the workshop with a "poet talk." Take a minute or two to share an insight about a poet—what he says about his poetry, and the aspects of his life and work that are revealed in his poetry. (For example, Paul Fleischman, the author of *Joyful Noise: Poems for Two Voices* [1988], learned to play the recorder when he

was in high school and later played duets with a flute player. In the process, he discovered that two voices are better than one.) At first you model poet talks; over time, students begin to sign up to give them to each other. You will want to present some minilessons on what constitutes an effective talk.

The Place My Words Are Looking For (Janeczko 1990) and *An Introduction to Poetry* (Kennedy and Gioia 1998) are excellent sources for poets' thoughts about their lives and their work. You will also want to visit websites and other biographical texts (see Appendix 54).

Poetry Read Aloud and Poetry Minilesson

Even though you are providing specific instruction on the reading and writing of poetry, the most important aspect of the workshop is helping students experience and enjoy poetry. When you read new poems, avoid long introductions. Simply read the piece aloud without analyzing it or introducing vocabulary. Read it again, ask for comments, or invite partners to talk with each other. You can ruin poetry by focusing too much attention on what must be learned (Graves 1992).

Over time, as you and your students read poems daily, the class will develop a reservoir of personal favorites. These familiar poems can then serve as models for analyzing writing craft and mentoring students as they try their hand at writing poetry.

There are many variations in the poetry lesson. For example, you may want to take students outside to observe and sketch in response to a poem, invite them to listen for something specific (for example, the beautiful language of a poem), or ask them to respond to poetry in their writer's notebook. Potential poetry lessons are listed in Figure 24–3. Each of these lessons represents complex learning that takes place over time. Focus several lessons on each topic. Spend several days or a week establishing specific concepts, or cycle back to help students learn more.

Poetry Projects and Poetry Centers

For the bulk of the poetry workshop, students are:

- Reading and responding to poems from anthologies or picture books.
- Collecting poetry seeds in their writer's notebook.
- Drafting, revising, and editing their poems.
- Creating art to accompany their poems.

Structure of the Poetry Workshop
(90-120 minutes)

- ❖ Poet Talk
- ❖ Poetry Read Aloud and Poetry Minilesson
- ❖ Poetry Projects and Poetry Centers: Reading, Writing, Conferring
- ❖ Poetry Sharing

Figure 24–2. The Structure of Poetry Workshop

Poetry Minilessons

Enjoying and Responding to the Craft of Poetry
- ❖ Finding poems
- ❖ Searching for what a poem says to you
- ❖ Exploring the themes of a poem
- ❖ Listening for special language
- ❖ Finding special words or phrases
- ❖ Noticing the beginnings and endings of poems
- ❖ Creating images with words
- ❖ Noticing/using metaphor/simile
- ❖ Noticing/using personification
- ❖ Noticing/using repetition
- ❖ Noticing/using pattern
- ❖ Noticing/using rhyme
- ❖ Noticing/using alliteration
- ❖ Noticing/using assonance
- ❖ Noticing/using onomatopoeia
- ❖ Noticing/using consonance
- ❖ Noticing how a poet uses line breaks
- ❖ Noticing how a poet uses space
- ❖ Highlighting words, phrases, or lines you love

Reading Poems
- ❖ How to read poetry
- ❖ Making a poetry tape
- ❖ Memorizing a poem
- ❖ Exploring the variety of anthologies

Performing Poetry
- ❖ Choral reading
- ❖ Varying voices in choral reading
- ❖ Adding movement/sound effects to choral reading

Collecting Poems
- ❖ Selecting poems that tell about you (a self-portrait anthology) [Heard 1999]
- ❖ Making an anthology—nature, family/friendship, life experiences, particular theme or poet or type, etc.
- ❖ Choosing poem gifts
- ❖ Writing comments about poems
- ❖ Creating a theme section in the anthology
- ❖ Labeling and writing section introductions in the anthology
- ❖ Binding and publishing an anthology
- ❖ Designing and making anthology covers
- ❖ Creating a title for your anthology
- ❖ Writing a dedication for your anthology

Writing Poetry
- ❖ Making a read map for topics
- ❖ Using the writer's notebook for poetry
- ❖ Collecting seeds in the writer's notebook
- ❖ Finding topics for poetry
- ❖ Changing prose to poetry
- ❖ Turning a dull sentence into poetry
- ❖ Creating poems with magnetic poetry
- ❖ Using line breaks and white space
- ❖ Sketching your world
- ❖ Choosing the exact word
- ❖ Writing beginnings
- ❖ Writing endings
- ❖ Writing titles
- ❖ Revising for word choice
- ❖ Revising for rhythm
- ❖ Eliminating words
- ❖ Editing a poem
- ❖ Ways to publish a poem
- ❖ Writing poem gifts
- ❖ Writing free verse
- ❖ Writing haiku
- ❖ Writing narrative poems
- ❖ Writing cinquains
- ❖ Writing limericks
- ❖ Writing concrete (shape) poems
- ❖ Finding poems
- ❖ Editing prose to make poetry
- ❖ Using poetry formulas
- ❖ Borrowing a phrase or sentence from another poem for yours

The Writing Lives of Poets
- ❖ What poets say about writing
- ❖ How poets look at the world
- ❖ How poets find poetry
- ❖ How poets use language
- ❖ Finding information about poets
- ❖ How to give a poet talk

Forms of Poetry
- ❖ Free verse
- ❖ Lyric poetry
- ❖ Narrative poetry
- ❖ Limericks
- ❖ Cinquains
- ❖ Concrete poetry
- ❖ "Found" poems
- ❖ Haiku
- ❖ List poems
- ❖ Biopoems
- ❖ Formulaic poems

Figure 24–3. Poetry minilessons

■ Illustrating poems they have heard or read.
■ Working on their anthologies.
■ Engaging in poetry center activities.
■ Conferring with the teacher.

This period is a real workshop in which students are actively engaged in a wide range of exploration and production.

Students need opportunities to write poetry of their own. As your students gain experience, they will be able to distinguish one poetic form from another, analyze their characteristics, and try them out for themselves. An important part of the poetry workshop is a large block of time to engage in drafting, revising, and editing poems on a variety of topics and in a variety of forms. Ideally, each student will feature a few published pieces of poetry as part of his literacy portfolio (see Chapter 28).

The writing that students do in the writing workshop and poetry workshop is interconnected. In poetry workshop, they may continue a project they started in writing workshop. One helpful way to teach students how to write poetry is to show them how to take prose and create a poem from it. The Alvin Ailey poem (Figure 24–1) is a good example. Give them a descriptive paragraph from a published work of prose, and let them experiment with:

■ Taking it apart into words and phrases.
■ Arranging the words and phrases in a new form.
■ Deleting unnecessary words so that the essential words will be more powerful.
■ Punctuating the poem.
■ Reading it aloud to determine whether revisions are needed.
■ Adding some special feature, such as repetition.
■ Gluing it down and illustrating it.

This is a very concrete way for students to see how a poet carefully selects and arranges the language of a text. Beautiful information books are an excellent resource for material.

During workshop you will conduct individual conferences with your students, helping them reflect on their work and learn to revise it. Invite the student to read his poem aloud to you and/or read it aloud yourself. (You take a different stance toward a poem when you hear it read aloud.) If it feels cluttered or disjointed or has less interesting parts, you can help the student delete words that do not contribute and that may actually detract from the language and meaning of the poem. It is amazing what a difference eliminating nonessential words can make. You can also ask students to highlight words or language they really like in their own poems as well as words or language that is not interesting or is overused. They can then look for more interesting words.

You might also choose to work with small groups of students to provide specific help with the craft of poetry in a reading or writing context. You discuss their writing and help them find topics for poems, get started, or revise and publish poems.

You may also wish to set up one or two poetry centers for use during the workshop. A small group of students focuses on a particular task, such as listening to poems or finding poems. For a rich description, see *Awakening the Heart: Exploring Poetry in Elementary and Middle School* (Heard 1999) and *For the Good of the Earth and Sun* (Heard 1989). Both books are excellent tools for helping you think about a quality poetry program.

Examples of poetry centers include:

■ Amazing Language Center—students share words and language that fascinates. Establish a bulletin board where students can collect amazing words and phrases they find in the books you read to them as well as in the literature and poems they read themselves.
■ Listening Center—students hear poetry read aloud. You can use professional tapes from the library, read poems on tape, and teach students to make their own tapes.
■ Poetry Window— clipboards, pencils, paper, or other materials are placed by a classroom window, a portion of which has been outlined so that students can look through and describe and sketch what they see.
■ Illustration Center—students use a variety of art media to illustrate poems they have read and enjoyed. (Place these illustrated poems in a poetry notebook or display them on the wall.)

Poetry Sharing

To conclude the poetry workshop, convene students for sharing. Students can share finished poems or those in progress; they can share art work or written comments or perform poems; they can invite help from other students as they do during reading and writing workshop.

Getting Started with Poetry Workshop

In the first two or three weeks of the school year, we suggest that you spend fifteen or twenty minutes on poetry as part of the language/word study block. The purpose is to make poetry an integral, enjoyable part of literacy from the start by launching personal poetry anthologies. We will describe four phases for launching poetry workshop, each with a minilesson, activity, and two or three minutes of partner or group sharing. Later you will want to move this work into your weekly or bimonthly poetry workshop.

Phase One: Self-Portrait Poetry

In Phase One, begin a self-portrait section of a personal anthology (Heard 1999). An anthology might be made of about 30 white tag sheets bound with a plastic coil or a blank book for writing and sketching. A self-portrait poem is one you choose because it tells something about you or your life. You might begin by reading a poem that you chose and explain why you chose it. Place baskets of anthologies (see list in Appendix 57) in the center of the tables for students to explore. Have them choose poems that connect to their lives and copy them into their personal anthologies. Ask them to leave the first two pages blank. Be sure they copy the poem exactly as it is written, placing words the way the author placed them. Invite students to illustrate the poem chosen. Continue sharing poems that relate to your life. Each day invite comments on your poem and ask students to choose and illustrate new poems to copy in their personal anthologies.

Phase Two: Responding to Poems

After three or four days, move to Phase Two, reading poems you love and inviting response to two questions: 1) What does the poem say to you? 2) What do you notice about the way the author wrote the poem? Be sure to read the poem at least twice so students can notice more about the meaning and craft each time they hear it. List what they notice about the craft on chart paper. Give them a photocopy to glue into their anthologies. Invite them to write one or two sentence comments about why they like it.

Phase Three: Connect Your Own Poem

After a few days of reading wonderful poems and enabling students to hear and respond to poems, move to Phase Three. Invite students to choose a poem from the anthologies and comment on what the poem says to them. Ask them to share what they notice about the way the author wrote the poem. Now ask students to write a poem that links to their chosen one in some way—use of a technique such as repetition, same topic, a favorite phrase or line, same mood. Once again, invite them to illustrate the poem. The author's poem should be placed on the left and the student poem on the right, making a two-page spread.

Now that students have a good sense of what is in the anthology, it is time to invite them to give their anthology a title and decorate the cover. The first two blank pages allow room for students to write a dedication and create a table of contents.

Phase Four: Finding the Poetry in Your Life

For Phase Four, invite students to write and illustrate their own poems about anything that is meaningful to them. Many topics will emerge from their work in their writer's notebook. Another good source of topics for poetry is a heart map (Heard 1999). Students draw a heart, create sections and illustrate and label each section with topics that are important in their life, topics that "tug at their hearts." Students can glue the heart map inside the back cover of the anthology and these topics from the heart will make wonderful sources for poetry.

Students should work on draft paper, revising and editing their work to achieve a published poem to glue in the anthology. Once they understand how to write their own poetry, you will want to move all the poetry work into the weekly poetry workshop.

Creating a Culture of Poetry

In addition to the getting started phases and the weekly poetry workshop, there are many ways to teach students to value poetry every day. Give poetry a place of honor in your classroom. Post it on the wall, make anthologies readily available to students, and weave it naturally throughout your curriculum. As poetry becomes part of the physical and social environment, a culture of thoughtfulness and expressive language will flourish in your classroom.

Make Poetry Accessible

Georgia Heard speaks of a "living anthology," inviting us to consider poetry both inside and outside the classroom. She suggests creating collections of poems to brighten the walls, hallways, and out-of-the-way places. For example:

- A poem on a window might muse about views from windows.
- A poem on a door might play with language about possible mysteries behind closed doors.
- A poem on a drinking fountain might capture the delight of rushing water.

When the school is "peppered" with poems, students are on the lookout for places in which a poem might pop up unexpectedly. Each poem so encountered invites students to step out of the rush of routine life and see the world in surprising new ways.

Sometimes you might accompany these poems with illustrations. Invite students to illustrate poems and post the illustrated poems in unusual locations. In addition, try these tips for making poetry a living part of your classroom:

- Invite students to a select and tape a poem to their desks that they want to read over and over again. They might select a new poem every month.
- Provide baskets of poetry anthologies or audiotapes that students can enjoy in free time or as part of their work in the workshop.
- Frame students' published poems and display them on the classroom walls.
- Designate one wall in a centrally located corridor as your school "poetry gallery." Change the theme every month to feature nature poems, poems from different cultures, poems by a particular poet, and so forth. Invite students to add poems they have selected, copied, and illustrated, or poems they have written and illustrated themselves.
- Ask each class to post a special poem on the classroom door for others to enjoy as they walk by.

Support Poetry Experiences

Make sure you have many poetry resources so students can enjoy poetry daily. Provide labeled baskets or tubs with different kinds of poetry, including:

- Humorous poetry—rhymes, limericks, and funny narrative poems.

- Special types of poetry—poems for two voices, haiku, concrete (shape) poetry, and limericks.
- Poems written by students in the class.
- Picture book poems.
- Story poems.
- Poems on particular themes—e.g., animals, family.
- Poems by particular poets.

Many wonderful anthologies for upper elementary classrooms are listed in Appendix 57. Keep a variety in your classroom, including anthologies that contain:

- Poems about nature.
- Poems about animals.
- Poems about sports.
- Poems from particular cultures.
- Love poems.
- Poems for every letter of the alphabet.
- Bilingual collections.
- Nonfiction poems.
- Poems for two or four voices.
- Poems by famous poets.
- Concrete or shape poems.
- Poems about simple things.
- Haiku or other specialized poems.

In addition to anthologies there are many beautiful books that illustrate a single poem, such as Frost's "Stopping By the Woods on a Snowy Evening."

Build a quality collection of poetry over time. Read poems aloud to students, encourage them to read poetry together, and help them find poems to use as models for writing. As poetry plays a bigger role in your students' lives, you will notice that they select anthologies from the school or public library and find poetic texts more accessible and enjoyable.

Suggestions for Reading Poetry

Model the reading of poetry so students can learn to read it for themselves. The following tips will help you read poetry aloud successfully:

- Read it to yourself first and consider the meaning, language, rhythm, and other features of the poem that you will highlight for your listeners.
- Convey the meaning of the poem with your voice.

- Allow students to hear the poem first before they see it on a projected transparency or on paper.
- Tell them the title and the poet but avoid long, elaborate introductions.
- Read in a natural voice, letting your tone convey the mood.
- Don't emphasize the beat; let language provide the rhythm.
- Enunciate each word and syllable clearly because each word is important.
- Slow down from your normal pace of reading so listeners can savor the words.
- Use your voice as a tool; whisper or elongate words as appropriate.
- Read the poem several times.
- Encourage students to reflect on a poem, but invite a short discussion rather than a long analysis.
- Avoid activity extensions of every poem—a few quick comments, a partner share, or a quick sketch are efficient, enjoyable options.

Students who are immersed in the vibrant sounds of poetry will write better poetry themselves; what's more, they are more likely to develop a lifetime appreciation for poetry.

Encouraging Response to Poetry

If you have established a culture of poetry in your classroom, students will respond frequently and passionately, as revealed in both their nonverbal behavior and their spontaneous comments. You can encourage them to reflect on poems in many ways.

Discussion
Short discussions following a poem can be enjoyable. You will want to allow for open-ended response. This is not the time for a lengthy analysis, which is best done as a minilesson. Instead, you can ask:

- What does the poem say to you?
- How did the poem make you feel?
- What did the poem make you think about?
- What did you think about the poem?
- What did you notice?
- Were there any words or phrases you especially liked?
- Does the poem remind you of anything in your life?

- What do you think the poet was thinking?
- Who's talking in the poem?
- What did you notice about the way the author wrote the poem?

By using open-ended questions, you encourage students to express their response in words. You can also have students talk in pairs or small groups about poems, or jot down some thoughts or sketches in their writer's notebook before or after sharing.

Writer's Notebook
The writer's notebook is a good place in which to collect thoughts about poetry. Your students can sketch, make a list, or write freely to describe thoughts on a particular poem. They may also choose to copy or glue a poem or some lines from a poem in the notebook. They may write about those lines, or use them in their own writing projects in the future. Many students reserve a few pages for special words, phrases, or sentences they want to keep.

Memorizing Poems
After hearing a poem many times, students begin to internalize the language. You might ask them to memorize one or two poems each year and perform them for one another. After all, holding a poem close to your mind and heart is of value in and of itself. Additionally, memorizing poetry creates lasting internal resources. While students may not remember every line of every poem for the rest of their lives, as they grow and mature and take in broader slices of life, the lines of particular poems will reappear, yielding pleasure and joy. In a sense, "owning" a poem helps you step into the poet's shoes for a moment and understand the world through the poet's eyes.

Collecting and Sharing Poetry

Collecting poetry is putting together a treasure box. You may ask students to collect poems in a folder. Later in the year, students can take out their poems, sort them, glue them on paper, write an introduction to each group, and bind them, creating an organized anthology with section openers.

We strongly recommend that students glue poems into blank books or anthologies throughout the year. As we discussed earlier, students create art for each poem that is shared and sometimes write a few brief comments, sharing their thoughts about the piece. They might write a poem in response to one they heard, connecting it in some way. Students might collect poetry by a particular writer or on a particular theme in a section of the anthology and write an introduction about the poem or poems.

As an example, Rebecca's students made anthologies that combined poems they selected with poems they had written themselves. On the left side of a notebook, they glued and created an illustration for a published poem that the class had shared. On the right side, they glued a poem of their own that used the same technique, form, topic, language, or theme. After hearing Loyen Redhawk Gali's "My Hair Is Long," Whitney wrote a poem called "My Smile Is Big" that was linked to what she heard.

My Smile is Big
By Whitney

My skin is as brown as a tree's bark
As I sit in the shade
My eyes are as shiny as the stars
But as dark as the sky surrounding
My hands are as gentle as a cloud
In the blue sky
My legs are as long as two rulers
As I trace to make a straight line
My heart is as red as my blood
As it slithers through my body
My voice is as loud as thunder
But also as soft as rain
And my smile is as big as the universe

Students can share their poetry selections or poetry anthologies in many different ways. For example, groups of five or six can select poems by the same poet, read them aloud, and share research about the poet's writing style and life. Students can also find poems on the same topic or in the same form and read them aloud to one another. You will want to have a special place to display the anthologies and engage students in working on them throughout the year (Figure 24-4).

You can also integrate poetry with all content areas of the curriculum. If students are studying insects, for example, make poems about insects available for them to read. Help them understand the details about particular insects that inspired particular poems. As Chatton and Collins (1999) note, scientists and poets have much in common:

Scientists and writers are investigators. Both are involved in careful consideration of the world around them; both are explorers, observing and formulating ideas about what they see. Too often, though, our curriculum doesn't reflect linkages between subjects like science and writing, and we limit children by assigning certain types of writing to certain subjects. We ask children to write informatively for science lessons and creatively in language arts. However, if we look at books on science and nature for children, we discover that neither scientists nor writers have such constraints. Poets observe nature through the eyes of scientists, describing what they experience in careful sensory detail . . . scientists sometimes write poetically and humorously. (p.78)

Figure 24-4. A Display of Student Anthologies

Ask your students to consider what scientists and poets have in common, and encourage them to write poems as part of their science studies.

Performing Poetry

Many poets intend for their work to be read aloud and performed. Students can perform poetry for one another, other classes, or groups of younger students. A performance invites students to interpret and communicate poetic meaning using many symbol systems including art, dance, and music (Gardner 1983).

We have discussed memorizing poetry as a way to internalize language. The same is true of different kinds of performance, which may involve a single student, a small group, or the entire class. Students can memorize poetry or simply read it aloud. They can select published poems to share or poems they've written themselves.

The next time you invite your students to perform poetry you might suggest:

- Combining poetry with music. For example, some students played Asian music in the background while reading haiku. For a poem by Eloise Greenfield, some students used a "rap" beat with movement as they said the words.
- Adding art, such as watercolor prints, or creating props.
- Devising related sound effects, gestures, or body movement.
- Conducting a choral reading, varying lines with solo or multiple voices, high and low voices, or soft and loud voices.
- "Building up" the choral reading of a poem cumulatively, adding more voices as the stanzas continue.
- Reading in a "round," with each group starting and ending at different times.
- Reading in echoing voices.

A good resource for helping students learn to enjoy performing poetry is *Joyful Noise: Poems for Two Voices* (Fleischman 1988), a collection of poems about nature that have been arranged for two readers or two groups of readers. The words in the poems are arranged in two columns. At specific points, one or the other reader reads a line or phrase alone; later both may chime in together. Students enjoy the process enormously. After reading and performing poems in two voices, Peter wrote the poem "Seasons." Notice the solo lines (print on one side only) and the lines in which two voices are reading the same or different words (print on both sides).

SEASONS

Winter	Spring
Summer	Fall,
I love seasons	
I love them all.	I love them all.
Cold	
Hot	Hot
Warm and	Freezing
People smiling	And people sneezing
Winter	Spring
Summer	Fall,
I love seasons	
I love them all.	I love them all.

Conclusion

Poetry is a microcosm for learning. Through the precise, concise language of poetry, students learn a lot about reading and writing. They can explore word choice, leads, endings, sentence flow, development of topics and ideas, and text layout. As Eudora Welty said, "Poetry is the school I went to in order to learn to write prose." (Welty 1983). Even more important, they can learn what poetry is and what it means to them as literate human beings.

After many experiences with fine poetry, students in Carol's room captured their definition of poetry with the chart shown in Figure 24–5, constructed during her minilesson in the poetry workshop. These students are on their way to understanding the "inner workings" of poetry for themselves. They recognize poetry when they see it, whether it rhymes or not. All intermediate students deserve a deep, rich immersion in poetry as part of their literacy learning. By launching your own

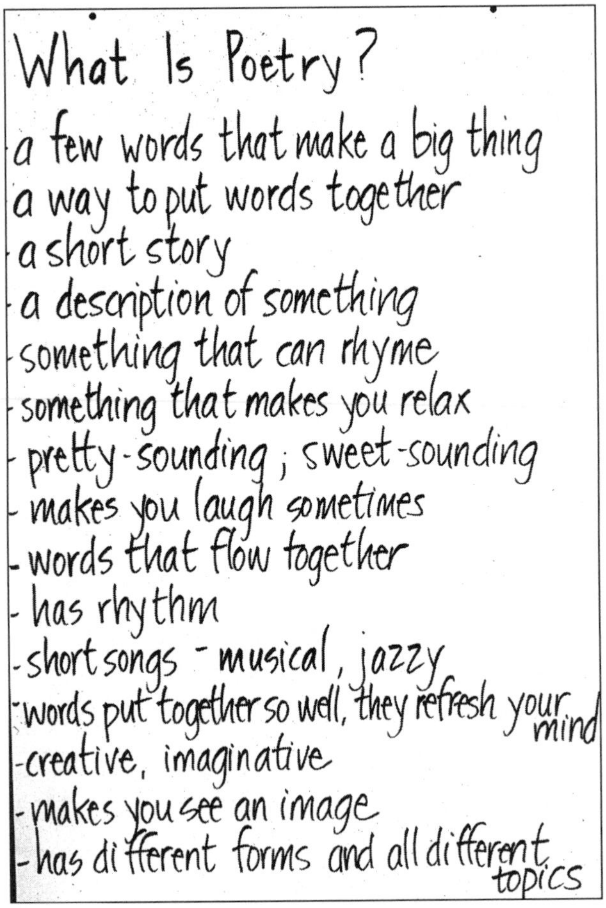

What Is Poetry?

- a few words that make a big thing
- a way to put words together
- a short story
- a description of something
- something that can rhyme
- something that makes you relax
- pretty-sounding; sweet-sounding
- makes you laugh sometimes
- words that flow together
- has rhythm
- short songs - musical, jazzy
- words put together so well, they refresh your mind
- creative, imaginative
- makes you see an image
- has different forms and all different topics

Figure 24–12. What Is Poetry?

poetry workshop for your students, you'll discover poetry as a treasure that brings light to language as well as to your teaching.

Suggestions for Professional Development

1. Collect poems you think your students will enjoy and read them aloud every day. Make sure to reread poems and talk about them briefly with students. Select different kinds of poems for variety so you learn what most appeals to your students.

2. Invite colleagues interested in poetry to a meeting. You should each bring a poem that tells something about yourself, an anthology of poems you have used with children, and a beautifully written paragraph from a piece of literature you have used with children.
   - ■ Begin by reading the poem that reflects yourself. Talk about why you selected it. Everyone takes a turn.
   - ■ Share the anthologies you use with children and tell why.
   - ■ With partners, take the paragraph and turn it into poetry. Write it on a chart and share your poems.

3. Try turning prose into poetry with a group of students in your class.
   - ■ Select a paragraph from a book you are reading to them and show them how to take it apart, delete words, and create a poem.
   - ■ Encourage students to do this for themselves.
   - ■ Discuss what you learned from this exercise.

4. Try another aspect of poetry workshop with your students.

## CHAPTER TWENTY FIVE

Exploring the Writer's Terrain: Writer Talks, Writer's Notebooks, and Investigations

Books wind into the heart... We read them when young, remember them when old. We read there of what has happened to ourselves... We owe everything to their authors.

—William Hazlitt

Don Murray (1968) and Nancie Atwell (1998) have both described the writer's interests as "territories" over which the mind may roam, lighting on interesting details, starting points, feelings, or ideas. Writers have many such territories—ideas that intrigue them, experiences they want to share, topics they want to explore in greater depth. And writers explore the same territories again and again, something that becomes evident when you look at the work of a single author. Madeleine L'Engle, for example, explores imaginary worlds, high-level technology, and the struggle between good and evil. Patricia Polacco writes about family, friends, and her cultural heritage. Patricia MacLachlan writes about the feeling and beauty of the prairie, her childhood home. As Isaac Bashevis Singer said, "In all my writing I tell the story of my life, over and over again" (Winokur 1986).

The writing terrain spreads out in many directions, real and imaginary, and encompasses in-depth intellectual investigations of biology, geology, history, anthropology, and the like. In our classrooms, reading and writing come together in writer talks, writer's notebooks, writing projects, and investigations to support the writer's journey.

Writer Talk

We learn about writing from writers—their lives and their craft. A writer talk is a glimpse into a writer's life that reveals details important to her work. You might also focus on an illustrator. Initially, you will present these talks; over time, students can be responsible for

doing the research and presenting the talks to one another. You will want to provide several minilessons on giving a writer's talk. The questions in Figure 25–1 may be helpful in directing your students' attention to useful insights.

Preparing a Writer Talk
What can you learn from the writer that helps you as a writer?
What did you learn about the writer that gives you a new understanding about how the writer writes?
What did you learn about the writer that gives you a new understanding about a particular book he wrote?

Figure 25–1. Preparing a Writer Talk

To begin a writer talk, take a few moments to read aloud a passage from an autobiography by a writer, a writer's biography, or memoir. An extensive bibliography of biographies, memoirs, and autobiographies for use in writer's talks is in Appendix 55. The list of author websites (Appendix 54) will also be useful. These excerpts should provide significant details that reveal how or why the person engages in writing, something about his craft, or something about a particular book he wrote. For example, Avi (1996) explains that he views stories as maps, similar to traditional oral literature that helped and inspired people to make their life journeys. He wants to create characters and situations that will help young people deal with the harsh realities of life. On the other hand, Cynthia Rylant (1989) notes, "I did not have a chance to know [my father] or to say goodbye to him, and that is all the loss I needed to become a writer." When Faith Ringgold was a little girl, her father used to take a mattress up to the roof and the family would have a picnic, play cards, and look at the sky. The tar floor of the roof was their "beach," and that inspired *Tar Beach*. (Ringgold, Freeman, Roucher 1996). These insights can motivate students as they consider ideas for their own writing, and they can teach students more about the start of the creative process as well. Figure 25–2 presents some great insights from authors about their lives. Use this list as a beginning and add more insights as you read widely.

As you share your writer talks with students, you can focus on:

■ Where the author gets ideas.
■ Something that influenced the writer in her work.
■ Advice from the writer on how to get started in writing.
■ Information about the use of a writer's notebook.
■ An anecdote from the writer's childhood.
■ Comments on the creative process.
■ Suggestions for revising and editing.
■ Insight about his books or illustrations.

To help students create their own writer talks:

■ Present quite a few talks when you first initiate writing workshop; these will serve as models.
■ Create a basket of biographies and autobiographies of writers (see Appendix 55 for a list).
■ Create a basket of audiotapes, interviews, or CDs by various authors.
■ Provide a list of writers' websites for students to use (see Appendix 54).
■ Teach minilessons on how to give a one-minute talk that peers will enjoy.
■ Create a sign-up sheet or rotation schedule whereby students will share their own writer talks.

As students search authors' websites, biographies, and interviews, they will come up with more ideas for writer talks. Sometimes writers will participate in live chats or will consent to interviews online. Save these conversations and search them for usable quotes.

Writer's Notebooks

The writer's notebook is a basic resource for students' independent writing. Don Murray (1996) describes his "daybooks" as notebooks filled with thoughts, ideas, observations, and things he wonders about, hopes for, or wants to know more about. Similarly, the writer's notebook is a place for students to collect observations, ideas, feelings, facts, lists—just about every kind of thought that can be recorded in writing. As Lois Lowry says, "Stories don't just appear out of nowhere. They need a ball that starts to roll." The writer's notebook is that ball: a place to preserve ideas so they will be available for future conversation and writing.

Fletcher (1993) has written extensively about his use of notebooks in the writing process.

Writers are like other people, except for at least one difference. Other people have daily thoughts and feelings, notice this sky or that smell, but they don't do much about it. All those thoughts, feelings, sensations, and opinions pass through them like the air they breathe.

Not writers. Writers react. And writers need a place to record those reactions.

That's what the writer's notebook is for. It gives you a place to write down what makes you angry or sad or amazed, to write down what you've noticed and what you want to forget, to record exactly what your grandmother whispered in your ear before she said goodbye for the last time.

A writer's notebook gives you a place to live like a writer, not just in school during writing time, but wherever you are, at any time of the day. (Fletcher 1996)

A writer's notebook is not limited to print. Students may include sketches, photos, diagrams, artifacts, or other visual representations—any kind of exploratory material that represents the writer's thinking and may feed the writing process. Figure 25–3 shows David's entry about a pet, which later became the basis for a longer piece called "When the Cage Comes Up."

Various writers have suggested ways they have used their notebooks (Murray 1968; Fletcher 1966; Harwayne 1992). The following list is a sample.

Learning About Writing from Writers

When Cynthia Rylant was a little girl her father died and her mother left her with her grandmother for four years. They lived in West Virginia and she has written many stories about that part of the country. She really did go to an outhouse and had no running water in the house. She really knew about ticks. *When I Was Young in the Mountains* was dedicated to her grandparents. (Rylant 1989)

Walking gives James Howe a chance to daydream. He thinks that reading and daydreaming are two of the most important things a writer does. And, he always carries a notebook with him. (Howe 1994)

James Howe says that Pink and Rex stories are really based on his own childhood, and some of the things in the stories like the spelling bee really happened. He says that Pinky is a lot like him. (Howe 1994)

Eve Bunting writes her stories out first in a notebook that she always carries with her. Everywhere she goes, she writes—even during traffic jams or on a floating chair in the swimming pool. (Bunting 1995)

When Eve Bunting saw the pictures of visitors to the Vietnam Veterans Memorial Wall in Washington, D.C., it made her cry. She even cried while she was writing her picture book, *The Wall,* and sometimes she even cries when she reads it. (Bunting 1995)

In *The Keeping Quilt,* Patricia Polacco tells about a real quilt that she uses. The story tells about her mother's people, who came with her from Russia. *Rechenka's Eggs* was also about her Ukrainian grandmother, who taught her how to decorate those beautiful Pysanky eggs. (Polacco 1994)

David McPhail has written lots of stories that he likes but no one else wants to publish them; he puts them in a drawer labeled STORIES NOT YET PUBLISHED. (McPhail 1996)

Joanna Cole had a science teacher who was not just like Mrs. Frizzle in *The Magic School Bus,* because she didn't do magic things. But she was really interested in science, did all kinds of experiments, and showed Joanna how interesting science could be. (Cole 1996)

When Jean Van Leeuwen writes a book about the past, she does a lot of research. She wants to know all the little details, like what kind of clothing people wore, how they cooked, and how they lived. She even learned how to spin flax and dye wool for a book she was writing. (Van Leeuwen 1998)

David Adler's 2 1/2 year old nephew came to visit him and asked question after question. When he left, David was exhausted but he kept thinking about all those questions and wrote them in his journal, along with the answers. That was the beginning of his first book, *A Little at a Time.* (Adler 1999)

David Adler once knew a boy with a photographic memory and that gave him the idea for Cam Jansen. (Adler 1999)

Thomas Locker lives beside the Hudson River. He says, "Living beside a great river is a wonder. Water is so powerful and crucial to life. It gave me the idea for a book about the water cycle." It took nearly two years to publish his book, *Water Dance.* (Locker 1999)

When Rafe Martin edits the stories he's written, he walks around the room reading them aloud to see how they sound. (Martin 1992)

When he writes books about space, Seymour Simon gets the most up-to-date information from space scientists around the world. (Simon 2000)

Figure 25–2. Writers on Writing

Learning About Writing from Writers (continued)

"People always ask 'Where do you get your ideas?' The answer is—from everywhere." (Yolen 1992)

George Ella Lyon's stories come from the stories that her family told around the table in the living room, when they sat on the porch, and when they rode in the car. (Lyon 1996)

George Ella Lyon went to Civil War battlefields to write *Cecil's Story* and *Here and Then* and inside a coal mine to write *Mama is a Miner*. She says, "I have to be willing to do whatever it takes to make the best story I can." (Lyon 1996)

When Lynne Cherry was eight years old, she wrote and illustrated a story about her cat Kitty. When she was grown up and had published several books, she showed her editor *Kitty's Adventures*. She redid the illustrations and the book was published. She says, "You see, the stories you write now could become published books some day." (Cherry 2000)

Lynne Cherry traveled to Brazil so that she could get the feel of the rainforest for her book *The Great Kapok Tree*. She wrote this book because she remembered a woods she had loved as a child. The woods was bulldozed and all of the animals lost their home. (Cherry 2000)

"If you want to write, make sure you have some free and quiet time each day. Pay attention to little things. Spend time outdoors. Listen to the sounds around you. Investigate." (Cherry 2000)

"Sometimes I try too hard to make a sentence perfect the first time, instead of writing a 'not so perfect' sentence and making it better later." (Pringle 1997)

The character of Henry came from Cynthia Rylant's own son Nate. She used to know a big dog named Mudge. (Rylant 1992)

Cynthia Rylant's grandmother still lives in the house she wrote about in *When I Was Young in the Mountains* and the relatives, from *The Relatives Came* still visit there. (Rylant 1992)

"Sometimes it seems as if a person from long ago steps out from a page and speaks to me. Then I know I have to write another book." (Fritz 1992)

Jean Fritz writes in longhand first so that she can cross out, rewrite, and cross out again. She says, "I can never seem to find the right words the first time." Then she types it up on the computer. (Fritz 1992)

When she goes on vacation, Jean Fritz puts the manuscript she's working on in the refrigerator so it will be safe. (Fritz 1992)

"People sometimes think that artists and writers just wait for inspiration. I have to work every day, and for long hours. Some days it seems all work and little inspiration, and I seem to cross out everything that I write." (Goble 1994)

"I often make a quick sketch rather than take a photograph, because to draw something makes you look at it closely." (Goble 1994)

Joseph Bruchac saves articles that interest him. Sometimes an article will be the start of a new book. (Bruchac 1999)

"Being a reader led me to writing." (Bruchac 1999)

Figure 25–2. Writers on Writing (continued)

new sneakers

grandpa better

turtle

dog

WISHES

bird

roller blade

camping

Dog
pet store/Debby's Petland
turtle
bird
cage
learning how to talk
broken cage
escaping

Figure 25–3. A Page of David's Notebook from which "When the Cage Comes Up" Was Generated

- Record their memories.
- Capture beautiful and/or interesting language or images.
- Freeze moments in time.
- List ideas.
- Store special documents such as letters, photos, clippings, or poems.
- Write a response to a piece of literature, a film, a current event, or a work of art.
- Note useful and/or interesting information.
- Record questions.
- Experiment with different forms of writing.
- Describe characters.
- Plot ideas.
- Write letters or notes to self and others.
- Record favorite poems or favorite book passages.
- Keep "top ten" lists (e.g., ten best books to take to camp or ten books guaranteed to make you laugh).
- Make drawings or sketches.
- Create webs of their ideas or concepts.
- List favorite foods, songs, things to do.

You can introduce the writer's notebook with mini-lessons that show students how important notebooks are to writers and how writers use them. One of the most powerful ways to motivate your students to do their best work is to share your own notebook with them.

During the first weeks of school, students can generate a great deal of material in their notebooks to use for later writing projects. It's important to talk with them about the kinds of writing they will be doing. One class created a list of purposes for the notebook (see Figure 25–4), which they hung on the wall as a reminder. Another class created a list of ideas for writer's notebooks (see Figure 25–5) and added to it over the year.

Once students appreciate how they can use their notebook, invite them to write an introduction to glue in the front. You can model this introduction by writing one of your own. The example in Figure 25–6 was written by a fifth-grade teacher who shared her notebook with students.

How and Why Writers Use Notebooks

- ❖ To enjoy writing.
- ❖ To remember all the things that you have read and seen and heard.
- ❖ To get things out of your head so that they don't get stuck up there.
- ❖ To keep memories.
- ❖ To remember moments.
- ❖ To remember days.
- ❖ Write when there's nothing else to do.
- ❖ Jot down something you read.
- ❖ Get stress off of your mind—"Tell it to your notebook."
- ❖ Write about what you think of someone's ideas.
- ❖ Work on writing and collect it.

"There always something to say. I just have to let the ideas come down from my head."

- ❖ Sit down and write every day!
- ❖ Don't stop!
- ❖ Keep on going!
- ❖ Never erase!

Figure 25–4. How and Why Writers Use Notebooks

Ideas for Writer's Notebooks

- ❖ Describe a photo, including its history.
- ❖ Revisit old stories.
- ❖ Try out new stories.
- ❖ Write a story based on observations.
- ❖ Wonder about something.
- ❖ Focus on small details.
- ❖ Make word lists
- ❖ Poems.
- ❖ Small quotes.
- ❖ Thoughts and feelings.
- ❖ Stories about friends and family.
- ❖ Quick drawings.
- ❖ Record the events of the day.
- ❖ Quick notes about the weather.
- ❖ Ideas for things to do.
- ❖ Tell family stories that are passed down.
- ❖ Short joke or story.
- ❖ Record your dreams.

Figure 25–5. Ideas for Writer's Notebooks

Your students can also use children's literature as a basis for some of their entries. As you introduce poems, stories, or sections of stories and read them aloud, students can jot down words, phrases, or sentences they want to remember. Appendix 59 lists a number of books that contain memorable language. As you discuss these beautiful texts, ask stu-

About My Writer's Notebook

My writer's notebook is filled with my thinking. Sometimes I share my thinking in words and other times in sketches. I share what is important to me, what I notice, what I hope, what I hear, what I think about, what I read, and what I learn. Sometimes I share a poem, a quote, favorite words, or photographs or other small items that help me remember special times. I fill this book with words and images that I want to hold on to forever.

Figure 25–6. About My Writer's Notebook

dents to reflect on how the content reminds them of their own lives or suggests possible writing topics.

Students are also motivated by stories in which the main character keeps a notebook or journal (some examples are listed in Figure 25–8). Some students enjoy keeping a notebook so much they adopt the practice for life.

Writing Projects

As we discussed in Chapter 5, a "writing project" involves selecting a topic, writing a discovery draft, and

Books with a Character Who Writes or Keeps a Notebook

- ❖ *A Rainbow for Robin* (Vance 1966)
- ❖ *The All New Amelia* (Moss 1999)
- ❖ *Amelia's Family Ties* (Moss 2000)
- ❖ *Amelia's Notebook* (Moss 1999)
- ❖ *Amelia Hits the Road* (Moss 1999)
- ❖ *Amelia Takes Command* (Moss 1999)
- ❖ *Anastasia Krupnik* (Lowry 1984)
- ❖ *Arthur for the Very First Time* (MacLachlan 1989)
- ❖ *Beans on the Roof* (Byars 1990)
- ❖ *Harriet the Spy* (Fitzhugh 1985)
- ❖ *Hey World, Here I Am* (Little 1990)
- ❖ *How To Grow Famous in Brooklyn* (Hest 1995)
- ❖ *I'm in Charge of Celebrations* (Baylor 1986)
- ❖ *Luv, Amelia Luv, Nadia* (Moss 1999)
- ❖ *Pageant* (Lasky 1986)
- ❖ *Poor Jenny, Bright as a Penny* (Murphy 1974)
- ❖ *Night Letters* (LoMonaco 1996)
- ❖ *Nobody is Perfick* (Waber 1991)
- ❖ *Mr. & Mrs. Thief* (Kojima 1980)
- ❖ *My Notebook* (*With Help from Amelia*) (Moss 1999)
- ❖ *Sister* (Greenfield 1992)
- ❖ *Summer Rules* (Lipsyte 1981)
- ❖ *The War With Grandpa* (Smith 1984)

Figure 25–7. Books with a Character Who Writes or Keeps a Notebook

revising and editing subsequent drafts through a final draft and/or publication (Calkins 1986, 1991, 1994; Harwayne 2000; Calkins and Harwayne 1987). Figure 25–8 shows fifth-grader David's published writing project, "When the Cage Comes Up," which was based on the notebook entry shown in Figure 25–3. David's skill as a writer is evident. He has created a dedication and an "about the author" section, his lead is engaging, and his voice shines throughout. Just look at his word choices:

- "Sipping a glass of iced tea."
- "She inquired."
- "He would be ecstatic."
- "Enhance his anxiousness."
- "Repeatedly ringing."
- "She replied."
- "A cross tone."
- "Was abruptly stopped."

David's teacher had summarized the writing process from the "seeds" to the "bloom" (Figure 25–9). She illustrated a seed, sprout, bud, and bloom. "When the Cage Comes Up" is the product of a beginning idea taken through the joys and challenges of the writing process. David explored his ideas in his writer's notebook, conferred with his peers and teacher, revised, and edited and published a memoir in picture book format. Along the way, he learned how to take an idea and turn it into a special piece of writing.

Investigations

Learning begins with asking questions—and asking questions within the supportive context of writer's workshop can lead to a full-blown student research project also known as an inquiry project or investigation. Investigations are particularly useful in developing content literacy and, as a result, they often spill over into the social studies or science block. Investigations provide a structure for students to use their reading, writing, oral, artistic, and technological skills across the curriculum. Investigations:

- Allow students to conceptualize, plan, and sustain work over time.
- Immerse students in the process of inquiry as they pursue topics of interest.
- Provide authentic research experiences that require skills in talking, reading, and writing.
- Present the opportunity to examine primary and secondary sources of information in a variety of ways.
- May be pursued for homework as well as incorporated into content area study.

Investigations might involve both "mini research projects," topics that students might investigate for a few days, and "maxi research projects," topics that involve more in-depth study that last several weeks. Long-term projects often result in oral presentations, displays, or performances that include a variety of media. Many projects result in a published product.

Topics for investigations will arise from explorations of the content curriculum, students' interests, and works of literature. Inquiry involves formulating questions and then using a variety of resources to investigate the questions, come to conclusions, and share results. Investigations may involve interviewing, using the Internet or computer software, planning and performing an experiment, viewing films, reading, taking notes, sketching, diagramming, and any other means of gathering the data needed to address a question or topic of study.

Through their investigation, students learn a wide range of invaluable skills that will serve them well in future school and life experiences. They learn "how to learn" about their world as well as how to solve the problems they might encounter. In addition to finding answers, they learn to find and pose questions, use resources, cooperate with one another, share information in clear oral or written language, and understand the different ways to communicate information, such as the visual arts or technology.

Selecting Topics

Students experience the joy and challenge of learning when we invite them to develop a passionate curiosity about a topic and then find answers to their own questions. Whenever possible, students should be allowed to "own" their research topics—to pursue subjects that arise out of their own sincere interests.

Many students need help identifying a topic of study. As you read aloud to your students, take them on field trips, show them films, or set up "hands on" experiments, you introduce them to new ideas and help them focus their interests. Students can use their writer's notebooks to record ideas that intrigue them, their ini-

When the Cage Comes Up

written by David Tannenwald
illustrated by Nicole Williamson

You know those action movies that end with breathtaking chases? This was just like that. You either win or you lose!!!

It all started one rainy day in second grade. You see my brother and I had been begging our parents for a pet for more than two months. My brother had his heart set on a turtle, but you could say my parents were terminally opposed to the idea. The kind of turtle my brother wanted carried diseases, which I guess is a logical reason, but all I wanted was a dog, one puppy. Apparently, that was too much to ask!

1

Anyway, when I got home that day I was fairly wet, and tired. As usual, I had beaten my brother home. My mom was looking through a pet store catalog and I was peeling a scrumptious naval orange while sipping a glass of iced tea when my mom stopped reading.

She inquired, "David, how would you like a bird for Hannukah?"

"I guess so-o," I said, "but I'd rather have a poodle, or a cocker spaniel."

"Anyway, what kind of bird would we be getting?" I asked.

"Well, there are a bunch of parakeets on sale and I've already cleared it with your father, so I was thinking," she began, when the doorbell cut her off.

2

Oh great, I thought, my brother is coming home. He would be ecstatic because I just wanted a pet. I mean anything, and the fact I was kind of opposed to the idea would only enhance his anxiousness, not that I had my hopes up about getting a dog, but majority rules, and being the youngest in my family I was a minority.

My mom interrupted my thoughts, asking me to open up the door for my brother who was now repeatedly ringing the doorbell and hollering in a continuous chorus,

"OPEN UP"
"OPEN UP"

3

Then I ran to the front door, unlocked it, and let him in. My brother pushed passed me, without even thinking of me.

"Nice to see you to, " I said sarcastically.

When my brother came into the kitchen, he noticed my mom, turned sweet and said, "Hi Mom."

"Hello," she replied.

"How are you today?" she asked.

"I'm fine," he answered, "but I got a plentiful supply of homework," he said in a cross tone.

After that my mother explained everything about the bird to my brother and he was ecstatic about it. Anyway, for the rest of the week, I was exasperated, irritated, and I was rankled.

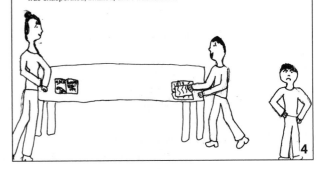

4

Figure 25–8. When the Cage Comes Up

Finally, on a bright Saturday morning, my dreams of a dog halted. Reality set in when I walked into the pet store. I was met by a strong aroma of droppings, and a piercing sound of barking and chirping. As we looked through the various parakeets I couldn't help getting excited.

When we found the one we wanted, a man reached into a very large cage. In the cage there were a few parakeets.

The one we had chosen was a bright turquoise blue like the sky on a bright summer day. He put his hands securely on the bird's wings (so it wouldn't fly away). Then he put it in a box and we went home. We named him Bluebird.

5

A few nights later the action started. You see we still didn't know how the bird cage worked, so we had to open a door which meant the bird could escape!!!!!!!!

6

Now I suppose you can guess what happened, the bird escaped!!!! My mom let out a high pitched screech, and the bird took off.

First into the hallway and then he went so fast down the stairs you'd think you were sitting in the first row of the Indy Five Hundred race track! He first went to a window and was abruptly stopped by the glass wall, just as Bluebird thought he had freedom. Looking a bit startled, Bluebird set off looking for escape. I was a little excited chasing the bird, but it felt like the movies!!

7

Bluebird eventually realized he could not escape so he went back to his cage. Bluebird is now three years old, and I still don't have a dog!!!

8

Figure 25–8.   When the Cage Comes Up

The Growth of a Writing Project

[seeds]_____Writer's Notebook: A place to plant seeds and grow ideas.
- ❖ Quick-writes
- ❖ Lists
- ❖ Topics

[sprouts]_____Discovery Draft: A place to grow stories.
- ❖ Get the whole story out.
- ❖ Write quickly.

[bud]_____Second/Final Draft: A place to feed and nourish stories.
- ❖ Make changes.
- ❖ Add details.
- ❖ Cross out.
- ❖ Edit.
- ❖ Very best handwriting.

[bloom]_____Published Piece: A place to display developed stories.
- ❖ Final changes.
- ❖ Teacher edit.
- ❖ Special paper/format.
- ❖ Typed or very best handwriting.

Figure 25–9. The Growth of a Writing Project

tial questions, and quick bits of information they think might lead to investigations. For example, they might:

- Note their observations during a class experiment or field trip.
- Make quick sketches or diagrams to help them remember processes.
- Write down interesting quotes from fiction or non-fiction texts.
- Note bibliographic information on authors.
- Jot down notes during interviews.
- List the structural characteristics of nonfiction texts.
- Glue in photos, pictures, or postcards.
- Summarize information drawn from the Internet.
- Record poems, rhymes, and sayings.
- List ideas for projects.
- Collect interesting information on a topic.

As you work with students in investigation, take the opportunity to share your own interests and passions for learning. Working alongside students, you can ask authentic questions and join them in searching for information and share with them what you learn.

Formulating Questions

Questions help focus and give direction to research. Through investigations you can show students the value of questions and their role in learning. You can also show them that real research involves using a variety of means to get information, not simply paraphrasing one or two sources.

Formulating questions is a complex task for any researcher. Chances are, your intermediate students are just learning to determine their own questions. You may help them in the following ways:

- Model asking questions as you read aloud to them.
- Encourage question posing during classroom discussions; pull out questions and list them as ideas for investigation.
- Help students structure questions around the words who, what, where, when, why, and how.
- Share books that show students how to pose questions e.g., *Once a Wolf* (Swinburne 1999), and *Stones, Bones, and Petroglyphs* (Goodman 1998).
- Examine current events to pique students' curiosity and suggest that they record questions in their writer's notebooks.
- Create a question web by placing the question in the center and the answers on the branches to illustrate that a question may have a range of answers (Harvey and Goudis 2000).
- Invite students to look through their writer's notebook to recall areas of curiosity and form questions.
- Use the KWL process to summarize what students already know, what they want to know, and what they want to learn (see Chapter 26 for details). Notice the understanding and questions Kristen Thomas's class posed prior to their class study and what they learned (see Figure 25–10).

Gathering and Using Resources

Researchers must know where to go to find information and what to do once they have found it. You will want to provide a wide array of resources for students to use in their research. Of course, the Internet now provides remarkable and easy access to vast storehouses of information that greatly expand students' research opportunities. You will need to use some caution around technology, however. Judging the readability and the validity of Internet materials is an imperfect process; in addition, it is easy for students to become distracted while "surfing" the net. Finally, some material on the Internet is inappropriate for elementary students, so plan to supervise closely. In any case, you will need many traditional resources as well. Be sure to include a CD-ROM encyclopedia such as *First Connections* (Golden Book Encyclopedia) for grades two or three, and the CD-ROM *World Book Encyclopedia* for grades two and above. Add some almanacs such as *World Almanac for Kids* or the *Real World Almanac*. Consider the New York Public Library's *Desk Reference on American History* and the one on science. Both are practical reference sources based on actual questions from the New York Public Library. You might want to create a research hotlist, a number of useful websites for quick student access such as www.howstuffworks.com or www.brainpop.com. A list of suggested resources for investigation is provided in Figure 25–11.

Research Tools

Researchers use specific tools in their investigations that you will want to make available in the classroom. The writer's notebook, of course, enables an ongoing record of developing ideas. Some teachers prefer that students keep separate notebooks (a bluebook, for example) for

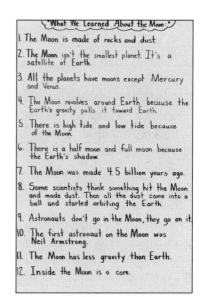

Figure 25–10. Learning About the Moon

Resources to Support Investigation

1. A wide variety of informational books—biographies; books on the social and physical sciences, mathematics, and recreation; diaries; journals

2. Reference books such as dictionaries, encyclopedias, thesauruses, books of quotations

3. Maps, globes, and atlases

4. Museum publications

5. Charts that illustrate processes—for example, diagrams of the human body, flow charts of the U.S. mail, etc.

6. Magazines and newspapers

7. Brochures from travel agencies and airlines

8. Travel guides

9. Catalogues of products and services

10. Almanacs and calendars

11. Equipment manuals

12. Reproductions of documents that reveal local history—old newspapers, deeds, maps, letters and other primary sources of information

13. Telephone books

14. Website addresses

15. Internet access

Figure 25–11.   Resources to Support Investigation

units of study, or they ask students to organize projects into file folders. Your students may also need:

- Baskets, boxes, large folders or manila envelopes to store information in one place.
- Index cards of various sizes to take notes and organize them.
- Planning tools such as calendars to set time lines for projects.
- Tape recorders, cameras, and video cameras to use to conduct interviews and add media as part of the final project presentation.
- Videocassettes, audiotapes, CD-ROMs, DVDs, and the equipment to play them.
- Scanners to incorporate art and graphics into written reports.
- Science/math equipment such as magnifying glasses, microscopes, beakers, thermometers, tape measures, yardsticks, rulers, and scales.
- Postal supplies, fax machines, and telephones to conduct inquiries.

- Highlighters and stick-on notes to identify information in texts.
- Clipboards to take observational notes in the field.
- White correction tape to edit and fix minor mistakes on visual displays.
- Drawing instruments to produce neat and accurate visuals.
- Chart paper, transparencies, and markers to illustrate processes.
- Computers, appropriate software, and access to the Internet to conduct online research.
- Copy machines to duplicate material for presentations.

Research Techniques

Students can obtain information from both primary and secondary sources. Traditionally, they have used secondary sources—encyclopedias, textbooks, informational books, and references. These sources provide key vocabulary, but research comes alive if students can also consult primary sources, including original documents (deeds, diaries, letters), and talk with people who have witnessed history or are part of current events.

Another primary source is the student's own observations. You will want students to develop a wide range of research techniques for accessing both primary and secondary sources of information. Techniques include:

- *Interviewing.* Students can conduct interviews with people who lived through interesting times or who have direct access to key information; interviews may be conducted by e-mail.
- *Creating and administering questionnaires.* Students can develop instruments to conduct surveys and gather information from larger groups.
- *Note taking.* Note taking is a skill that students can use while they are observing, interviewing, or reading in the area of interest. Teach students to take clear, succinct notes so they can decipher them later. Also teach them how to create headings for cards and take notes in categories.
- *Viewing or listening to CD-ROMs, videotapes, and audiotapes.* Often, you can find videotapes or audiotapes that feature interviews with people who had specific experiences or made discoveries. Documentaries are another source of key information, and CD-ROMs provide access to a wide range of primary sources.
- *Searching the Internet.* The Internet provides access to many sites on specific topics. Many authors, for example, have their own sites. As the teacher, you will want to carefully monitor students' use of the Internet, but it is a rich resource of information.
- *Going to museums or visiting their websites.* The originals of many historical documents are stored in museums, and you may be able to obtain photocopies. Students especially benefit from reading diaries and letters written by people who lived in earlier times. They may also have archives of photographs that help explain phenomena.
- *Conducting direct research.* The community in which students live is a natural laboratory for investigation. They can examine the history of the area, look at maps, and interview senior citizens and public officials. Your local courthouse has a wealth of legal documents available for public scrutiny. Street names alone tell a history that is well worth investigating, and museums house artifacts and documents of local interest.

Learning research skills can be as fascinating as solving a detective story. Students can use many different resources and employ a wide range of techniques to ferret out information that addresses their questions. In the process, they also develop high-level learning strategies.

Organizing Information

Eventually, students need to categorize their information so they can understand and present it. Teach students how to break down the topic or question into smaller categories and organize it into sections. Beginners (or advanced students dealing with complex subjects) will need to place information within the categories physically. To demonstrate this process you can work with chart paper and stick-on notes. For their personal projects, students can use note cards. Students can use the categories as guides as they establish sections, main headings, and side headings.

Presenting Information

Today's abundant media give students many ways to present research findings. Invite students to move beyond the written report as the primary way to demonstrate their knowledge. Depending on the sophistication of the equipment and software available in your classroom, students can combine text, graphics, videotapes, audiotapes, CD-ROMs and overhead transparencies.

Just like other aspects of investigation, you will need to teach students how to present their work. This might involve a variety of genre writing (a multi-genre report) and/or a variety of media. Be sure they experience the process themselves rather than rely on their parents' help at home. Creating a beautiful display is not the point; learning and displaying the information to teach others lies at the heart of the research.

Fifth-grade teacher Rebecca worked with her students to create a chart to guide quality projects (see Figure 25–12). She displayed the chart in the classroom so students could refer to it and evaluate their own displays before adding final touches.

An Example of a Content Area Investigation

Brad's investigation, "How Are Tornadoes Formed?", is an example of the kinds of learning inherent to the inquiry process. His final presentation included a number of visual aids. Brad organized his information on

Guidelines for Visual Display

1. You will need a poster board or display board that will stand up.

2. You may include:
   -pictures
   -time lines
   -maps
   -graphs
   -charts
   -audio or other technology

3. Use only your original writing.

4. Be sure that all written work is typed or written in your best handwriting.

5. Be sure the written work and the visual displays are neat.

6. You may use the computer for typing or to make graphs and charts.

7. Remember color and balance.
   -Make sure there are no large empty spaces.
   -Make sure the board does not have a cluttered look.
   -Make sure that written information and pictures go together.

8. Think about what your audience will see when they look at your display.
   -What will be interesting?
   -What will they learn?

Figure 25–12.   Guidelines for Visual Display

Figure 25–13.   How Are Tornadoes Formed?

storms in general using a mapping technique (see Figure 25–13), including facts that he thought would interest the group and that they could use to solidify their knowledge about various kinds of storms. Then, with a visual image of a tornado as background, he delineated the Fujita scale, which indicates the degree of damage done by a tornado, its strength, its description, and its wind speed. He provided photographs with captions, including a series of sequential pictures showing the stages in the formation of a tornado. His written text featured heads and subheads to organize and present the information. His presentation also had a bibliography and a list of websites where readers can find more information. Clearly, Brad has learned to consider his audience and to organize and present information in a coherent way.

The students in Brad's class worked on their projects during science period, in writing workshop, and at home. Here's how it worked:

■ Each student was expected to give a final oral presentation that included a display board and/or a scale model.

■ The class was broken up into study groups. Each student pursued her or his own questions, but the other members of the group helped the student researchers break the "big question" into smaller questions.

■ Each student wrote a proposal that included the big question, smaller questions, and plans for conducting the research and developing the display board/model.

■ The study groups used checklists similar to rubrics to guide the research projects and create the displays/models.

- Study groups, with teacher guidance, helped students choose headings for note cards so they could gather information in an organized way.
- Searching many and varied sources of information, students took notes over a two-week period and checked in with their groups to report progress.
- In their groups, they determined how best to sort the information into meaningful chunks.
- The teacher provided several minilessons on how to create a display that would present their understanding in a way that would engage and inform their peers. They talked about the text, the graphic features, and the design.
- Students mocked up the display board design at home and, as additional homework, wrote the text for the display.
- The students presented an oral demonstration or simulation that helped others understand their project.

The entire project took about five weeks to complete.

An Example of a Literature-Based Investigation

Rebecca had the students in her class investigate the genre of biography. She began working with them in guided reading to examine the characteristics of biography:

- What key information about the life of a person is essential to include in a biography?
- Why are biographies important?
- Why do we read biographies?

Students then discussed how researching and writing a biography could help them discover universal truths they could apply to their own lives. They chose subjects many of whom had accomplished great things but had not been recognized in traditional history books (see Figure 25–14). Rebecca expected each student to read three books on their subjects, take notes, and write a narrative report. With student input, Rebecca made a chart setting out possible note card headings (Figure 25–15) and created a checklist to help students monitor their progress (Figure 25–16). She placed a check when all students had completed that aspect.

As a final product of the investigation, the students each created a picture biography of their subject and read it to a group of younger students. Figure 25–17 shows the sample layout Rebecca designed to help her

Biography Topics

- ❖ Life is Beautiful—Robert Monty
- ❖ The Life and Death of Anne Frank
- ❖ The Jackie Robinson Story
- ❖ The New Moses Harriet
- ❖ Marcus Garvey: Jamaica's First National Hero
- ❖ Science and Art: Leonardo da Vinci
- ❖ The Wright Brothers: Above All
- ❖ Anne Sullivan: A Miracle Worker
- ❖ Wilma Rudolph: The Olympic Champion
- ❖ Martin Luther King Jr.—Man of Peace
- ❖ Helen Keller: From Darkness to Reality
- ❖ Dreams Can Come True: A Story About Georgia O'Keeffe
- ❖ The Legacy of Justice: Thurgood Marshall
- ❖ Jim Thorpe: Keeper of the Sports
- ❖ J.F.K
- ❖ Biography of Muhammad Ali
- ❖ Neil Armstrong: Man of the Moon
- ❖ The Man Behind $E = MC^2$—Albert Einstein

Figure 25–14. List of Biographical Subjects

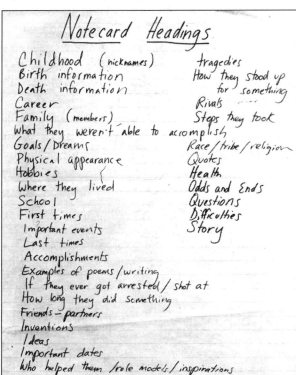

Figure 25–15. Note Card Headings

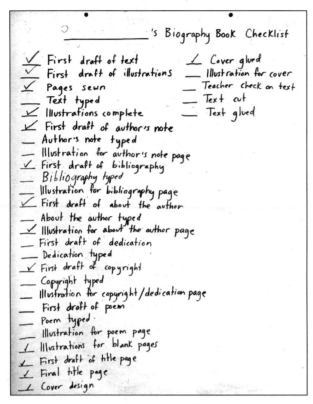

Figure 25–16. Biography Book Checklist

OUTLINE

Text	Picture
p.1 - birth - early school - childhood - family	picture of farm w/ family
p.2 story about the time he broke his leg	hospital
p.3	
p.4	
p.5	M.L.K. delivering speech
p.6	
p.7	
p.8	

Figure 25–17. Sample Layout of Biography Picture Book

students plan their picture book biographies. In her sample, she provided examples of what might go on pages 1 and 2, and allotted pages 3, 5, and 6 to pictures only. She crossed-out pages to indicate a full double-page illustration without text. Other pages feature a full page of text.

The "biography" investigation is an example of an in-depth study completed over several weeks. You can see how the students have engaged in authentic inquiry using the wide range of communication skills and resources learners need to use in their lives.

In this chapter we have explored a variety of ways students engage in using writing for a variety of purposes. Our goal is for students to see writing as a source of enjoyment and a tool for learning throughout their lives.

Suggestions for Professional Development

1. Meet with your colleagues to study writing by examining the life of a writer.

- Find a biography about a writer (preferably a writer of books that your students read) or use the Internet to find out something about a writer and share an interesting tidbit about the writer's life with your colleagues.
- Photocopy a page from the book that would be useful for a writer talk to give to your students.
- Talk with your colleagues about the writer's life experiences and how they might have influenced her writing.

2. Choose a special notebook that will become your own writer's notebook.

- For the first entry, create a list of writing "territories" for yourself.
- Next, sketch something that is very important to you. It might be a family member, a pet, an object, or a setting. You could also sketch an abstract symbol that represents something very significant to you. Write about your sketch.
- Using a new page, write about the origin of your name.
- Select a picture book that you would use with

students to stimulate their thinking about issues that would lead to writing. The picture book should provide an example of good writing. In your notebook, write what makes the writing in this book good.

3. Share and discuss each of the entries with your colleagues. Talk about the implications your writing experiences have for your own students.

4. Over the next few weeks, use your writer's notebook to explore for yourself what this consistent, daily collection of thoughts, ideas, and memories may offer the writers you teach.

5. As an alternative, meet with a supportive group of friends or colleagues—any grade level—to inquire into your own writing "territories."

   ▨ Select a writer's notebook and begin by writing something about your own name.

   ▨ Set a goal of writing for fifteen to thirty minutes every day. You can make lists, "free write" on any topic, collect memorable language, sketch, or do any other kind of writing (see the suggestions in this chapter for students).

   ▨ Meet regularly over lunch to share tidbits from your journal.

6. Try telling stories from your life and write snatches of them in your notebook. Paste in important letters, postcards, or memos and write why they are important.

7. When you have quite a bit of material in your notebook, show it to your students and share some of your writing. This is the best way to inspire them to write.

SUPPORTING READERS AND WRITERS: TOOLS THAT MAKE A DIFFERENCE IN COMPREHENDING AND CONSTRUCTING TEXTS

The critical aspect of writing is not writing, it is reading.

-AVI

Language is the superhighway to comprehension. It's the fastest, most powerful, and most reliable route to meaning. Therefore, supporting student discussions before and after reading keeps them focused on their thinking. Writing, too, supports thinking. Talking and writing are usually sufficient to help students develop comprehension strategies. At times, however, you may wish to introduce more structured ways of focusing their attention and illustrating the process of comprehension.

Teachers and researchers have created a variety of tools that can help students organize their thinking in relation to fiction and nonfiction texts. These tools help in two ways:

1. They enhance the ability to remember, which helps students share their ideas.
2. They provide a visual frame for organizing ideas, which helps students develop explicit understanding.

Still, tools like this are not meant to be used so frequently that they become "exercises." They should not take the place of reading and writing.

As you use these tools with students, be sure to reexamine their effectiveness over time. If the tools work, students eventually outgrow them and engage in powerful strategies without them. Treat them as scaffolds to be dismantled when you no longer need them.

These tools are particularly useful for students who struggle to understand the structure of expository material. Research indicates that instruction in text structure enables children to recall what they read and to write summaries (Armbruster, Anderson, and Ostertag 1987; Berkowitz 1986; Myer and Rice 1984; Stein and Glenn 1979; Taylor and Beach 1984). Furthermore, such instruction in a particular genre may help students make the genre part of their own writing repertoire and increase their sense of audience and purpose (Crowhurst 1991; Englert and Heibert 1984; Englert, Raphael, Anderson, Anthony, and Stevens 1991; Jones, Pierce, and Hunter 1988).

The tools presented here are an explicit way of making text structure, as well as other elements of informational and narrative text, visible. There are four things to remember as you use these tools to teach reading and writing:

1. *The tools are focused.* They are designed and used to teach a particular concept at a particular time.
2. *They are temporary.* Once the concept has been established, the tool is no longer needed.
3. *They are occasional.* Not every concept requires the use of explicit, structured tools.
4. *They are targeted.* The tools are selected for a particular group of students who require their support.

You can use most of these tools in various components of the language and literacy framework as well as in whole-class minilessons, in daily language/literacy activities, or as part of shared reading. Additionally, you can use them effectively with small groups in guided reading or literature study, or with individuals in conferences.

Graphic Organizers

A graphic organizer is a visual diagram that shows the relationships among a number of ideas. Use graphic organizers to help students see the important interrelationships in the information they are reading or to become aware of the way authors have structured a text. These insights help students with their own writing as well as reading. Using graphic organizers helps students:

■ See how ideas are organized or organize their own ideas.
■ Use a concrete representation to understand abstract ideas.
■ Arrange information so it is easier to recall.
■ Understand the hierarchy of ideas (from larger to smaller).
■ Understand the interrelationship of complex ideas.

As you are working with a group of students, you can create the graphic on an easel, the chalkboard, or a projected transparency. Discussing the information and ideas is the important link to understanding. You can stimulate discussion by inviting students to work with partners or in small groups to generate their information and then share with the whole class.

Appendices 17–43 contain perforated, reproducible versions of most of the graphic organizers discussed below, and you are free to make copies. Let students work in pairs or small groups; don't ask them to "fill out" these organizers individually as if they were forms. Discussing words and ideas supports learning; the graphic organizer is simply a structure that facilitates discussion.

Using Graphic Organizers to Understand Characters

Understanding a narrative text usually involves considering the characters and how they respond, develop, and change through the story.

CHARACTER WEB

Webbing is the most common graphic organizer. Webs have many uses, such as expanding word meaning or exploring a topic. Place the topic in the middle of the web and invite students to generate words, phrases, or sentences that describe that topic. Place the words or phrases on branches that connect to the center. You can then divide these branches to add more details. Figure 26–1 is an example of a web about Patricia MacLachlan's *Sarah, Plain and Tall.* (See reproducible in Appendix 17.)

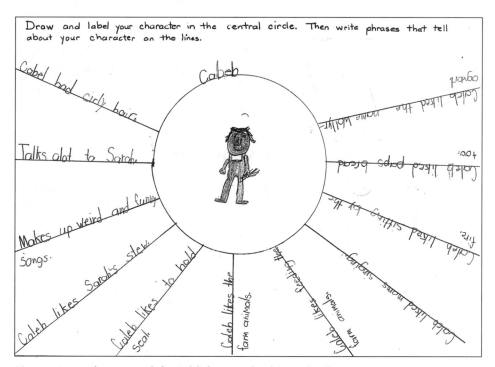

Figure 26–1. Character Web for Caleb from Sarah, Plain and Tall

CHARACTER COMPARISON

Making comparisons can help students understand individual characters and their relationships. You might use the relationship between ideas or a Venn diagram to show traits that two characters share as well as those that form a contrast. See Figure 26–2 for an example of a comparison between Matthew and Yingtao from Namioka's *Yang the Youngest and His Terrible Ear*. (See reproducible version in Appendix 18.)

CHARACTERS' RESPONSES TO STORY EVENTS

You can help students become more aware of the sequence of events in a story by selecting significant events and then citing evidence from the text that shows how a character reacts to them. Examples are shown in Figures 26–3 (Amber Brown's reactions in Danziger's *Amber Brown Wants Extra Credit*) and 26–4 (Leslie's death in Paterson's *Bridge to Terabithia*.) (See reproducible version in Appendix 19.)

CHARACTER CHART

A character chart helps students think flexibly about different attributes of a single character in a narrative text. The chart has three columns: Character (Name), Physical Appearance, and Personality Traits. Students add each character and fill it out. They can add more columns (Changes During the Story, for example) as they grow more sophisticated at analyzing characters. (See reproducible version in Appendix 20.)

CHARACTER SOCIOGRAM

A character sociogram helps students analyze the relationships among and between characters. A sociogram

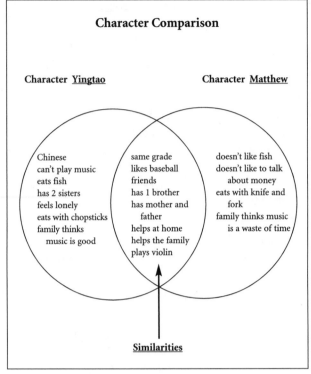

Figure 26–2. *Character Comparison*

has a weblike structure, with the central character's name in the circle, but arrows with comments are used to indicate the relationships between characters. The sociogram in Figure 26–5, for example, shows that:

- Shirley really cares for Emily, and Emily likes Shirley.
- Shirley is embarrassed around Mrs. Rappaport, who thinks Shirley is a good student.
- Shirley and Tommy like each other.
- Mother and Father and Shirley love one another.

Amber Brown Wants Extra Credit		
Page	**What happened**	**What Amber thinks or does**
6	Her mom wants her to meet her boyfriend.	She doesn't want to do it because of her dad.
12	Amber's mom starts to cry.	Amber says she will meet Max.
19	She goes to a pajama party.	She has fun.
30	Amber finds out Max is coming over.	She is scared and mad. She stomps her feet.

Figure 26–3. *Character Events/Response Chart*

- The clansmen miss Shirley, and she doesn't want to forget them.
- Shirley likes Jackie Robinson, but Jackie knows nothing about Shirley. (See reproducible version in Appendix 21.)

CHARACTER GRID

A character grid invites students to discuss comparisons. Make a grid with four columns and several rows. Place the character's name in the left margin beside the first row, and label the four columns Says/Thinks, Looks, Does, and Others Say/Think. Ask students to contribute words and phrases for each column. After you and your students have analyzed one character, you can add other characters row by row. The result is a snapshot of several characters compared across several attributes. (See reproducible in Appendix 22.)

CHARACTER-TRAIT-AND-EVIDENCE ANALYSIS

A character-trait-and-evidence analysis combines the web structure with the evidence required by some of the other graphic organizers. Students place the character's name in the center of the web and traits on the lines extending out from the center. Under each trait, students generate lists of evidence, complete with page number, to support their thinking about the character. Evidence may include what the character says, thinks, or does and what others say or think about the character. (See reproducible version in Appendix 23.)

Using Graphic Organizers to Understand Narrative Text Structure

Graphic organizers provide visual support for students who have difficulty remembering story events and understanding how a story is organized. You can use some of the basic models—Venn diagrams, grids, and webs—in this way.

STORY MAPS

A story map is a flowchart that shows the story's main elements as they follow one another to a resolution of the problem. You will remember the basic story map of

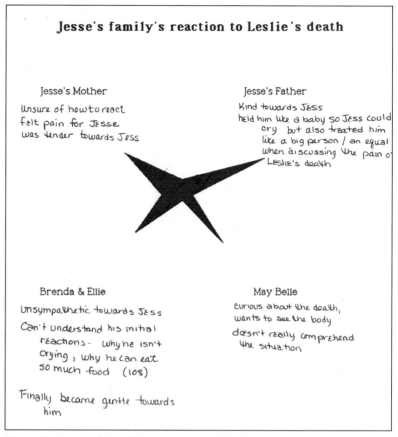

Figure 26–4. *Jesse's Family's Reaction to Leslie's Death*

Arthur's Mystery Envelope (Chapter 11 and Appendix 24 and 25). The story map in Figure 26–6 is actually a parallel map of a story from the point of view of the mouse Amos, and the whale Boris, from Steig's eloquent friendship story *Amos and Boris*. These organizers create an awareness of narrative structure, and they help students learn the special vocabulary that people use to discuss a story. Key elements include:

- Setting: When and where the story takes place.
- Characters: The people/animals that are important in the story.
- Problem: The problem or challenges faced by the main character in the story.
- Goal: What the main character wants to achieve, which may be overcoming the problem.
- Events: What happens in the story, including the climax when the problem is addressed and resolved.
- Resolution: How the problem is resolved.

If your students are not familiar with story mapping, you will want to teach it as a routine:

Character Sociogram

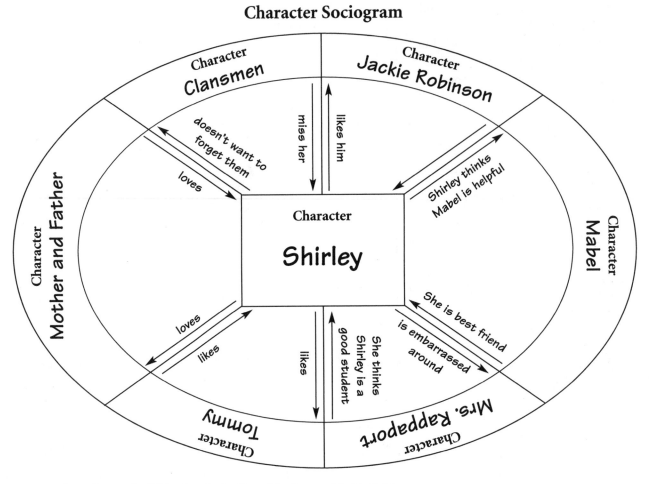

Figure 26–5. Sociogram for Shirley from In the Year of the Boar and Jackie Robinson

1. Draw a story map outline on a piece of chart paper or the chalkboard.
2. Discuss the sections of the map and tell students why you are using it.
3. Read a story aloud. You might consider rereading a story that students have heard before. Be sure that they are familiar with the material they will draw on the map.
4. Review the mapping steps, modeling the process. Discuss each element and invite students' input, but don't be afraid to show them what to do. Think aloud to demonstrate how to select the most important events (as opposed to minor details). They should learn to ask, "Is this detail important for understanding what happens in the story?"
5. After the story map is complete, hang it in the classroom as a reference.
6. Do several more story maps with students on familiar texts; they will gradually take on more of the task.

After students are familiar with the structure of a story map, they can use it in small groups, with a partner, or on their own. As students share and compare their story maps, you can promote a rich discussion around their comprehension of the story.

ESSENCE CHART AND CHAPTER GRID
A chapter grid helps students summarize the important information in each chapter of a narrative text. Make a large grid with boxes, one for each chapter of the book. As readers finish each chapter, have them write a summary of important information in the appropriate box using phrases or sentences. When completed, the grid is a well-organized summary of the entire book (see Figure 26–7 for an example). This form and an alternate version are reproducible in Appendix 26 and 27.

To teach this technique to students:

1. Begin working with a small group in guided reading. All students read the same book, appropriate for their level.

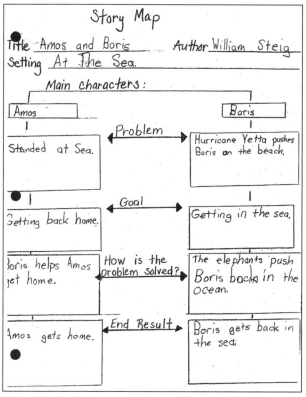

Figure 26–6. *Story Map for* Amos and Boris

2. After reading the first chapter, write the chapter title in the box and then demonstrate how to summarize the chapter in one or two sentences or a few key phrases. Show them how to select the most important information; you want them to learn how to ignore less important details.

3. Continue recording a summary statement after each chapter of the book.

After you have completed several chapter grids with students, they will know how to use this technique themselves.

You can use a variation of the chapter grid to create chapter titles for books that don't have them. Thinking of their own titles for a chapter—a short, catchy phrase that captures the most important events or feelings—helps students focus their attention on the vital information in the chapter.

STORY NOTES

With story notes, students briefly record the information they extract from the text on a table or grid that categorizes kinds of information. To get students started, think about the kinds of information you want them to notice, and then prepare a grid. Place the title of the selection at the top of the grid and then label boxes:

Setting, Character (use one box for each), Problem, Special Language, Interesting Parts. At the bottom, label a large box as Theme, or Story Message. (See reproducible in Appendix 28.)

You can vary the box labels according to the focus that students need. This organizer helps students improve their ability to notice important information or features of the text. The way ideas are organized visually will also support their thinking about the deeper meaning of the story.

IMPORTANT ELEMENTS CHART

Using a chart, students can record important evidence related to story elements such as setting, characters, and plot. To begin, place three boxes on the page. Then:

▪ In the first box, write the word Setting, followed by a sentence starter "The story takes place. . . ." Ask students to complete the sentence. When they are through, write Evidence below the sentence and ask them to add phrases that support their description of the setting.

▪ In the next box, write Character, followed by "An important character is. . . ." Again, have students complete the sentence and provide evidence. You may need to provide space for several characters and evidence.

▪ In the last box, write Plot, followed by "The problem begins when. . . ." Add subsequent sentence starters that begin "Then . . . ," "After that . . . ," and "Finally. . . ." Again, students complete the sentences and provide evidence.

This structure leads students through the process of identifying important story elements and justifying their thinking. Work with students in small groups before they try this on their own. (See reproducible in Appendix 29.)

BOOK-COMPARISON CHART

A book-comparison chart is created over time as students read a group of books that are related by theme, setting, or topic. To create a book comparison chart, create a table or area with six columns labeled Title, Major Characters, Setting, Problem, Solution, and Theme. (See reproducible in Appendix 30.)

After students read a book, they fill in a new line, noting each story element. After four or five books, students will discover patterns of similarities and differences across several texts.

Chapter Essence Chart

Name: __Jenny__   Date: __October 3__

Book Title: __Missing May__   Author: __Cynthia Rylant__

1 Summer, age 6, travels to Ob and May's trailer to live with them. She finally feels loved. Summer finally feels that she has come home.	**2** May dies when Summer is 12. Summer worries about how she and Ob will live without May. Ob feels May's spirit in the garden. Summer worries that Ob will die from missing May.	**3** Ob befriends Cletus, a kid who rides Summer's bus. Cletus says Summer thinks and acts like a tired old woman.
4 Ob tells Cletus that he felt May's spirit. Summer feels cut off from Ob when he tells Cletus about May's spirit visits.	**5** Ob, Cletus, and Summer try to get May's spirit to come to the garden. Ob tells stories of the sweet things May did for him and Summer. May doesn't come to them. Cletus tells Summer that she has a great imagination but she always fights it.	**6** Summer gets scared that Ob has given up on living. Ob tells Summer that he's worried that he won't be able to take care of her. All he does is miss May.
7 Cletus brings Ob and Summer a newspaper clipping about a woman Reverend who can speak to spirits. Ob decides they'll go find the Rev. Young to help them talk to May's spirit. Summer worries that Rev. Young is a fake.	**8** Ob and Summer go to Cletus' house to meet his parents. Summer realizes she and Cletus are different. Summer has always been afraid she'll loose everything, just like she lost her parents.	**9** They leave for Putnam County to find the Rev. Young. Summer feels peaceful on the drive. They drive through the capitol and Ob promises they can stop on the way back. Summer thinks that someday Cletus will do something important.
10 They get to Rev. Young's house but she died a few months ago. Her nephew gives them a pamphlet about the church. They leave and drive past the capitol without stopping. Summer is scared that Ob has given up. Ob then changes his mind and turns the car back towards the capitol.	**11** Ob decides to keep living, even though they didn't reach May's spirit. Summer thinks it's because he didn't want to leave and for her to hurt the way he hurts for May. They spend the afternoon at the capitol. Summer realizes that she'll never see May again.	**12** Summer and Cletus and Ob bring the whirligigs outside and put them in May's garden. Cletus reads from Rev. Young's church handouts. A big wind comes and sends the whirligigs spinning. The wind helps Ob and Summer stop missing May.

Figure 26–7. Chapter Grid for Missing May

COMPARISON GRID

Comparison grids also help students draw comparisons across texts. Students read a group of books related by genre, specific type of story within a genre, setting, theme, or topic. In the example in Figure 26–8, students are beginning to compare folktales—in this case, Cinderella stories by different authors and from different cultures. These students are not only comparing story elements pertinent to folklore, but they are incorporating a story map into their comparisons.

- To begin, label the lines in the left column of a grid as follows: Setting, Characters, Problem, Events, Solution (Ending), Magic [or any special feature of interest], Illustrations, Other. Across the top of the grid write Title and the name of the story or topic you want to analyze.
- At the top of the next few columns, write the names of the authors and/or titles of the selections you will compare.
- Write Similarities in the next column, followed by Differences. In these columns, have students place words that describe similarities and differences relative to each of the elements in the left column.
- Mark the final column Conclusions. In the Cinderella grid, for example, students might conclude that the three folktales they examined took place "long ago" or "far away" or had illustrations that reflected the culture.

You can teach students to use this kind of comparison chart by starting with a large piece of chart paper along a wall or bulletin board. You can fill out the chart rows after reading each version of a folktale. Later they will be able to use grids like this and work as partners or triads. This is also a useful response project or a follow up to book clubs. Working on a chart like this over time helps students make connections between and among texts across a number of categories and builds their consciousness of the characteristics of a particular genre. (See reproducible in Appendix 31.)

Using Graphic Organizers to Learn about Biographies

Biography combines elements of expository text with narrative elements. A biography is an informational text focused on a particular individual. Biographies can be organized in many different ways; the text can start at any point in an individual's life or it can focus on a particular period. While we present three examples of graphic organizers to use with biographies, you may also adapt some of the narrative text models.

BIOGRAPHICAL WEB

Using a web to analyze the subject of a biography helps students identify the person's important accomplishments (which typically spotlight the reason the biography is written in the first place). To create the web, write Biography: Significant Accomplishments at the top of the page with the person's name underneath. In the center box, write Summary Statement. Leave extra room in the box to write. Create branches to other boxes that are empty. Number these boxes, which students will fill with accomplishments. You can use the reproducible form in Appendix 32 or design your own to reflect the number of accomplishments you want students to identify.

Show your students this technique on a large chart before you expect them to try it on their own:

1. Work with a small group of students. Read a picture book biography aloud or ask them to read a biography themselves.
2. Invite students to discuss the subject's accomplishments.
3. Model selecting important accomplishments and/or guide students to select them.
4. Place each important accomplishment in a circle, using phrases.
5. Ask students to review the accomplishments and generate ideas for a summary statement.
6. Write one or more concise summary statements in the center circle.

IMPORTANT LIFE EVENTS

Identifying the most important things that happened to the subject helps students explore the influences of these experiences. Focusing on this information helps students discuss the relationship between life events and outcomes, a discussion that will lead them to make inferences and synthesize information.

Write the name of the biographical subject in the center of a circle divided into pie-shaped wedges. Follow the steps for making a biographical web. Instead of listing accomplishments, write phrases representing life events

Comparing Folklore

Title Cinderella	San Souci (Ojibwa)	Louie (Chinese)	Climo (Persian)	Similarities	Differences	Conclusions
Setting	A village beside a lake, deep in a forest of birch trees.	In the dim past of Southern China.	Persia, long ago when it was a land of princes and poets	All take place long ago	One story is in China, one in Persia, one in North America.	Folktales usually exist in the past.
Characters	Sootface, the middle and eldest sisters, their father the hunter, the Invisible Warrior, and the Invisible Warrior's sister.	Beautiful Yeh-Shen, Stepmother, Stepsister, King	Settareh, her stepsisters Leila and Nahid, Prince Mehrdad	Each story has evil sisters, stepmothers, or stepsisters. Cinderella is beautiful but unappreciated by her family. Indifferent fathers.		Cinderella remains kind and beautiful despite cruel or mean family.
Problem	Sisters make Sootface do all the chores and are unkind to her. Won't lend her clothes to wear to meet the Invisible Warrior.	Yeh-Shen had to do most unpleasant chores. Stepmother kills her pet.	Stepsisters are mean to her. Settareh is lonely. Father gives her money to buy new gown for Prince's party. She buys a clay pot that grants wishes instead.	Cinderella character is lonely, has to do many chores, treated poorly by her family, wants to find love.		Cinderella wants to change her life.
Events	Invisible Warrior says that the woman who can see him and tell what kind of bow he has will become his wife. All women in the village go to try and see him but none can. Sootface wears a birch bark dress and flowers and tries to see the Invisible Warrior.	Yeh-Shen goes to festival once, loses shoe, returns home. King is given slipper and searches for owner.	Settareh wishes for a gown to wear. Goes to party, loses anklet. Stableboy finds anklet, gives to the prince. Prince decides he will marry the woman who lost anklet. He searches for anklet's owner.	Magic gives Cinderella opportunity to go to meet the prince/king/warrior.	Ojibwa Cinderella does not lose a slipper or anklet to find the prince.	The Prince/King and Cinderella characters have problems but they find each other.

Figure 26–8. Comparing Folklore

Comparing Folklore (continued)

| Title
Cinderella | San Souci
(Ojibwa) | Louie
(Chinese) | Climo
(Persian) | Similarities | Differences | Conclusions |
|---|---|---|---|---|---|---|
| **Solution-Ending** | Sootface sees the Invisible Warrior and his bow made from a rainbow. Invisible Warrior names her Dawn-Light. They marry. Everyone is happy for them but the unkind sisters, who now have to do all the work by themselves. | Yeh-Shen takes slipper from King who follows her. When put on both slippers, rags become gown. Marries King. Stepmothers and stepsisters crushed to death by stone. | All the women in the city try to put the anklet on, but it only fits on Settareh. Prince and Settareh plan to wed. Stepsisters are jealous, wish pot will turn Settareh into a dove. Prince searches for her, discovers she is a dove sitting on his window sill. She changes back into a person. They marry, stepsisters hearts burst with jealousy. | All eventually marry the warrior/king/prince.

Sisters/stepsisters are jealous and unhappy. Cinderella marries. | Stepsisters in two stories die because of their jealousy/cruel actions. | The story ends happily for the good people. The bad sisters are punished. |
| **Magic** | Invisible Warrior can only be seen by certain people. | Bones of her dead fish give her dress and warn her not to lose her shoes. | Clay pot grants wishes, casts spells. Settareh turns into a dove. | Magic helps Cinderella in some way. | External magic helps Chinese/Persian Cinderella.

Internal magic helps Ojibwa Cinderella. | Magic is essential to story. |
| **Illustrations** | Realistic, earthiness, watercolor. | Soft, water color, pastel, elegant. | Vibrant, magical pictures. Colorful, intricate page borders. | All depict Cinderella as beautiful. | Illustrations show cultural differences. | Illustrations support story by showing beauty of Cinderella. |
| **Other** | | | | | | |

Figure 26–8. Comparing Folklore (continued)

in the wedges of the pie. Afterward, discuss the process with students. (See reproducible in Appendix 33.)

SUMMARY AND COMPARISON CHART

Students can make a comparison chart as they read several biographies. Make a grid or table with columns headed Book Title and Author, Famous Person, and Accomplishments. (See reproducible in Appendix 34.)

This activity prompts students to make summary statements for each subject's accomplishments. As they add biographies to the chart, they begin to synthesize their ideas about what kinds of accomplishments deserve the attention of biographers. They also examine concepts such as courage, persistence, talent, and commitment.

Using Graphic Organizers With Other Informational Texts

Graphic organizers are particularly useful for helping students understand the structure of expository texts, identify how information is organized, and see how ideas and facts are related. Typical text structures include cause and effect, classification, comparison and contrast, description/definition, sequence, and problem/solution. Question and answer may also be used.

IDEAS-DETAILS CHART

Preparing an "ideas-details" chart helps readers learn about description as an informational text structure. On the chart, they identify important ideas and provide supporting details. The chart features boxes down one side of the page for important ideas, identified by a phrase or sentence and a page number. On the right side, adjacent boxes provide details related to each important idea. (See reproducible in Appendix 35.) To get started:

1. Read an informational picture book to students or have a small group read one.
2. Show students how to identify several important ideas and enter them in the boxes on the left.
3. Then have students go back to the text to look for supportive details.
4 If too many details are suggested, show them how to select the most important ones.
5. After completing the chart, discuss the process.

INFORMATION WEB

Another tool for helping students learn about description and relate ideas and details is the information web

(see the example in Figure 26–9). Start with a concept in the center of a web and branch to several important ideas. For each important idea, branch out to provide details. The bird example shows all ideas and details listed with single words. You can also use phrases, but keep the identifiers concise. The information web is fast and efficient and can be used almost any time. When students understand the basic procedure, you can quickly draw the web on an easel or chalkboard with their input. This activity helps students learn how to organize ideas and description and summarize and synthesize ideas from text. You might start a web prior to reading a text and add to the web upon completion. (See reproducible in Appendix 36.)

SEQUENCE OF IMPORTANT EVENTS

Historical events are often presented in chronological order; directions occur in sequence; change follows a logical order; scientific observations are recorded in a precise order. Students need to understand a sequence of events and be able to distinguish important events from less important ones. A sequence-of-events chart supports their understanding of this kind of text structure. It is a simple series of boxes connected by arrows. Students place events or ideas into each box in order. (See reproducible in Appendix 37.)

CYCLE OF EVENTS

Natural processes often involve cycles of activity. For example, rainfall begins and ends with moisture in the atmosphere. The life cycle of butterflies and other insects begins and ends with eggs. A cycle-of-events diagram can support students' understanding of this circular process. It is a simple circle with arrows going around the circumference. Students place events around the circle in order. (See reproducible in Appendix 38.)

COMPARISON/CONTRAST CHARTS

A simple comparison/contrast chart can help students focus on informational elements that are different from one another. Draw a line across the top of a page and divide it into two columns to make a T. (See reproducible in Appendix 39.) At the top of each column, list one of the two items being compared. A comparison/contrast chart can be used in any content area. Comparing two things helps students focus on important information and understand text structure that depends on comparison to communicate meaning.

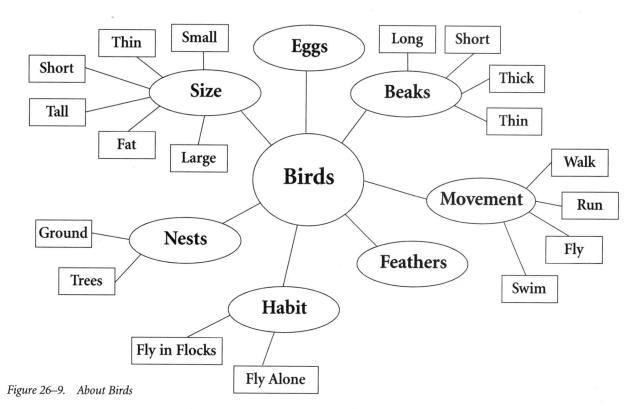

Figure 26–9. About Birds

An alternative form is the H chart. (See reproducible in Appendix 40.) This chart also has two columns headed by the two elements being compared. The two columns are joined by an open bar (as in an H) in which to place characteristics or ideas that are common to the two elements.

CAUSE-AND-EFFECT CHART

To understand reading in the content areas, students often must identify causes of events or phenomena. Understanding cause and effect is challenging to students because they must sort out important events and then analyze contributing events to make hypotheses about causes.

You can create a simple cause-and-effect diagram by placing boxes down the left side of a page or chart and insert arrows leading to another set of boxes on the right side. First, students generate the "effects," which might be outcomes, results, events, or scientific or social phenomena. They place these on the right side. Then they search the text for the likely causes of these outcomes and place identifying phrases or notes in the boxes on the left. (See reproducible in Appendix 41.)

A more complex variation involves placing a major event in a box in the middle of the chart or page. (See reproducible in Appendix 42.) Draw boxes labeled

Causes at the top of the page with arrows going to the "event" box. In these boxes, write phrases or words that indicate causes of the event. At the bottom of the page, draw boxes labeled Effect at the end of arrows leading from the "event" boxes. In these boxes, place words or phrases indicating the outcomes of the event.

SEMANTIC FEATURE ANALYSIS

Analyzing semantic features helps students compare features of words, understand word meanings more fully, and remember these meanings better (Baldwin, Ford, and Readance 1981; Johnson and Pearson 1984). In this organizer, a matrix visually represents the way words are related to each other (see Figure 26–10):

1. Select a topic from the content area curriculum or a work of literature.

2. Generate a list of key words or concepts that are familiar to the students and related to one another and the topic.

3. Create a grid or matrix. In the first column on the left, list the key words you have come up with. The headings of the remaining columns identify semantic features the words might share.

4. Each square of the matrix is an intersection in which to indicate whether and how the word is related to

the feature. For example, in the analysis of spiders shown in Figure 26–10, the different kinds of spiders share some features (they all have eight legs), but do not share other features (they are not all poisonous).

5. Indicate by marking in each square whether the key word on the left shares the attribute in the vertical column. You can select the marks during class discussion. You might use + and – signs or designate additional signs for partial agreement or uncertainty.

6. Have students explain their rationale for each designation. This discussion will help them deepen their understanding. If a particular text has been the source of the analysis, they may revisit the text or search for more information elsewhere.

7. As you study the topic again in the future, you can add terms or features to the matrix.
   (See reproducible in Appendix 43.)

Focus Questions

Focus questions give students something to think about as they read a text. Questions can be written on a chart or chalkboard or provided on a card or piece of paper. You may want to have students mark the text in some way, using stick-on notes or bookmarks, to help them remember the evidence they gathered in response to the focus questions. If students are permitted to write on the text, they can make marginal notes or use a highlighter. You can also give students one or two questions to think about after the reading. This task can result in talking, drawing, or writing.

Anticipation Guides

An anticipation guide (Herber 1978; Vacca and Vacca 1999) helps students activate their prior knowledge, focus their reading, and engage their interest. Some students have misconceptions that may interfere with their comprehension of the text. The statements on the anticipation guide confront their ideas and prompt them to read to find accurate information. After reading, they can discuss what their misconceptions were and how they have revised their thinking. Here's how it works:

1. Identify the concepts that students need to learn from reading.

2. Determine how their beliefs might be consistent

Spiders	have 8 legs	spin webs	poisonous	eat insects	harm people	eat animals	live in water	live in burrows
house	+	+	–	+	–	+	–	–
garden	+	+	–	+	–	+	–	–
chilean red leg	+	–	+	+	–	+	–	–
water	+	–	–	+	–	+	–	–
trapdoor	+	–	–	+	–	+	–	+
purse web	+	–	–	+	–	+	–	+
black widow	+	+	+	+	+	+	–	–
Australian funnel	+	+	+	+	+	+	–	–

Figure 26–10.   Analysis of Spiders

with or divergent from these concepts, including confusions or misconceptions that students might have.

3. Create a number of statements with which students might agree or disagree. The statements should be designed to uncover important misconceptions and to address major concepts. The complexity of the statements depends on the students' level of sophistication.

4. Ask students to work independently, placing an A or D in the column to indicate whether they agree or disagree with each statement.

5. Go over each statement, asking how many students agree or disagree with each.

6. Ask students to discuss their answers in partners, small groups, or the whole group. Students should have a chance to defend or justify opinions.

7. Have students read the selection, finding evidence related to the statements.

8. After they have finished, have them revisit their original responses and revise incorrect or partially correct

responses. For items that have still not been verified, ask students to identify the information they need.

9. Discuss what students have learned from using the anticipation guide.

A sample anticipation guide is shown in Figure 26–11. An organizer like this helps students:

- Active prior knowledge.
- Evaluate what they know.
- Think about what kind of information they might encounter in the text.
- Raise their consciousness regarding the purpose for reading.
- Predict and think about what they will learn.
- Raise their awareness of what they have learned from reading.

Quick-Write Prior to Reading

Prior to reading about a topic, students can list the related words and terms they know, write a paragraph discussing what they know about the topic, or make notes about it. These actions help them activate and summarize their knowledge and anticipate what they will read about. After reading, they can go back and add to this information, crossing out ideas that are not correct or do not apply to the topic and writing another paragraph that reflects the integration of their existing and new knowledge.

One, Two, Three

The "one, two, three" technique helps students consciously attend to what they are learning on subsequent readings of a text. We do not want students to go over and over the same material as if trying to memorize it; we want them to summarize what they know and add to their store of knowledge. This technique shows students the benefits of reading a text more than once to gain information or understand something difficult or technical; they begin to see that on each reading, their understanding expands.

Give students a sheet of paper with three columns, headed 1, 2, and 3 (see Figure 26–12). Then ask them to read an article or chapter and put it aside (they cannot

return to the text until they have filled in the first column). In column 1, they are to write everything they learned from the article. Have them repeat the process two more times, and then share the differences between what they learned on the first, second, and third readings. (See reproducible in Appendix 44.)

Know, Want to Know, and Learned (KWL)

KWL (Ogle 1987) is a technique that parallels the research process. It's designed to help students access prior knowledge, establish a purpose for reading, recognize what they want to know, and improve their ability to summarize and synthesize information. You can use KWL with the whole class or a small group, recording students' responses before and after reading on a projected transparency or an easel. Alternatively, students can use KWL in their reading journals, working individually, or with partners.

Have students head a sheet of paper with three columns, labeled What I Know, What I Want to Know, and What I Learned. (The language can vary as long as the concepts are the same.) Prior to reading, they generate ideas for the "know" and "want to know" columns.

Amazing Spiders
____ 1. Spiders are insects.
____ 2. Spiders have eight legs.
____ 3. There are more than 50 different kinds of spiders.
____ 4. All spiders are poisonous.
____ 5. Spiders can be as big as cats.
____ 6. Spiders' webs can be turned into cloth.
____ 7. Spiders catch their means in webs.
____ 8. Banana spiders eat bananas.
____ 9. Spiders don't have wings.
____10. Some spiders eat birds; some spiders eat mice.
____11. A spider makes a good pet.
____12. Spiders eat insects.
____13. Spiders are helpful to people.

Figure 26–11. Anticipation Guide for Spiders

Name/s   Josiah

One, Two, Three

1	2	3
• Water is wet. • Water flows to the lowest point. • Water is made of molecules. • Water forms drops. • Water clings to water like magnets. • Water molecules cling to things. • Bubbles have skin. • Ice is frozen water. • Snowflakes are water that is frozen. • Snowflakes are crystals. • Steam is water that has evaporated. • Water is dew. • Water is necessary for life.	• Bubbles are spheres with very thin skin. • When new drops go into water, they split up and become part of the water. • There can be frozen water, which is ice. A rock is frozen but it takes much more temperature to melt it. • When vapor meets something cold, it condenses and becomes water again. • Clouds have dust in them but rain doesn't taste dusty because particles are small. • Snowflakes are ice crystals. • Frost and dew are the same thing; it depends on the temperature.	• Water has something like an elastic skin. • Water in a glass has surface tension. • There can be a wave in a glass just like in the ocean. • Water goes up plant stems and and other tubes because of capillary attraction. • Water goes up plant stems because of adhesion. • Capillary attraction means that water gets into the tiniest crevices. • Soap helps water stretch it's surface tension without breaking. • Heat keeps the molecules of water moving so that they are always coming together. • The molecules of water vapor stick to cold surfaces.

Figure 26–12.   One, Two, Three Analysis

After reading, they address the last column. (See the example in Figure 26–13 and the reproducible in Appendix 45.) Some variations on the approach involve adding a Still Want to Know (S) column or columns headed What We Want to Know Now (N) and Where We Will Find It (F). You may also add a column labeled How We Learned (H), particularly if students are investigating the topic in several ways: it helps them become more aware of their own learning processes.

Students then read and stop at intervals to reconsider their original predictions. They cross out those that were not correct and confirm those that were correct with a checkmark. Then they make more predictions, which are again subsequently crossed out or confirmed. At the end, they can revisit all their predictions, noting those that were discounted and those that were accurate. As an alternative, you can help students revise predictions and/or expand them. This activity can also be the basis for writing a summary of the text.

Directed Reading Teaching Activity (DRTA)

The DRTA (Stauffer 1959) prompts students to predict what they will learn from reading a text. You invite students to make predictions, which are written on a chart.

Sketch to Stretch

"Sketch to stretch" (Short and Harste 1996) offers students an opportunity to generate more insights about a text by exploring a different medium—sketching.

(K)	(W)	(L)
The moon revolves around the earth.	What is the moon made of?	The moon is made of rocks and dust.
The moon has no gravity.	When was the moon made?	The moon revolves around the Earth because the Earth's gravity pulls it toward Earth.
If you go to the moon, you can see the Great Wall of China.	Why is the moon white?	The moon was made 4.5 billion years ago.
The moon rotates on its axis.	Why does the moon revolve around the Earth?	The first astronaut on the moon was Neil Armstrong.
The moon does not give off light.	Who was the first person on the moon?	There is high tide and low tide because of the moon.
You can walk on the moon.	Do other planets have a moon?	The moon is a satellite of earth.
The moon rotates very slowly.	Do scientists have another name for the moon?	All the planets have moons except Mercury and Venus.

KWL Chart   Name Gretchen

Figure 26–13.   KWL Analysis

Through this process, they also find new ways of talking about a text and new ways of sharing meaning with others. The idea is to expand understanding by taking what is learned in one system (language) and "recasting" it in another system, in this case drawing (variations could be devised using music, movement, and so forth).

Working in small groups, students read a selection or hear it read aloud. Then, thinking about what they read, they draw a sketch of "what this story means to me." The sketch should not be an exact depiction of the story; instead, encourage students to find a way to represent the personal meaning they derive from the text. Short and Harste suggest modeling this process by drawing a sketch yourself and talking about it; this helps students get started and recognize that there are many ways to express meaning.

After sketches are completed, students share their work with other group members, who generate ideas about what the drawing means. Finally the artists give

their comments about what they drew. In the process, students expand their own interpretations by hearing other points of views. This technique helps them realize the value of bringing their own experiences and knowledge to bear on the understanding of a text.

Reciprocal Teaching

Reciprocal teaching (Palinscar and Brown 1984) focuses on teaching strategies that will help students monitor and expand their own comprehension of texts, particularly in the content areas. The idea is to teach students explicit ways to summarize ideas, ask questions, provide clarifications, and make predictions. You model these four sophisticated language uses and then help your students practice them on their own. The process is "reciprocal" in that it is shared.

Students learn to make their language much more

precise as they use it for inquiry. The technique is particularly appropriate for readers whose decoding skills are adequate but who lag behind in comprehension. To begin, find text selections that provide opportunities for clarifying, questioning, summarizing, and predicting. Then demonstrate each step of the following process:

1. *Notice and clarify difficult vocabulary and concepts.* Demonstrate for students, explaining parts of the text they might find difficult. This process involves making sense of confusions that may serve as barriers to comprehension.

2. *Generate appropriate questions.* Show how to develop important questions about the material, including what you don't know, what you need to know, or what you would like to know.

3. *Summarize the selection.* Demonstrate how to identify and condense the most important points in the text.

4. *Make predictions about the selection.* Demonstrate how to make predictions using the information given in the text. You may also refer to the graphic features of the text or to text structure to predict what information may be provided next. Background knowledge also plays a role in making predictions.

After a few demonstrations, students can begin to take over the instructional responsibility. Form groups of students and have them work through the text a paragraph at a time, approaching each paragraph from four perspectives: clarifier (pointing out problems posed by vocabulary or text structure); questioner (generating questions based on what has been read); summarizer (giving a brief summary); or predictor (hypothesizing what will happen next). Students may each take one of these roles in turn, or a different student may assume all four roles for one paragraph. You provide guidance and feedback. You may make good use of this technique with guided reading groups that need this level of temporary support.

Assisted Reading

Assisted reading is a supportive "side-by-side" activity in which the teacher and student read aloud simultaneously from the same materials. Assisted reading has also been called the "neurological impress" method (Heckleman 1966). To begin:

1. Select a text that is an appropriate level for the child.
2. Read it to the child, sitting side by side so that attention is directed to the print.
3. Read the text fluently but go a little more slowly than you would normally proceed. Invite the student to read along with you, but do not stop for mistakes that the student makes. For students who need particular attention to print, you may want to slide a finger under the print while reading.
4. Keep going and read the entire text. Do not stop to discuss the story, answer questions, or solve words.
5. At first you may read slightly faster than the student, but as fluency increases, the two of you may read at the same rate. In this case, do not let the student stop to solve words but fill in any that he does not know right away.

This technique has been known to strengthen the student's memory. The student benefits by receiving immediate feedback on words that are not known or are only partially known. Students who read slowly are helped to process more text. The goal of assisted reading is fluent, silent reading.

Question/Answer Relationships (QARs)

A QAR (Figure 26–14) helps the reader search for and summarize information in the text as well as access and use background information (Raphael 1982; Raphael and Au 1996; Anthony and Raphael 1989). Students are prompted to ask the kinds of questions that will strengthen their control of text:

■ *Text-based* (in-the-text) questions are classified as "right there" questions (the answers are clearly stated in the text) and "think and search" questions (the answers are in the text but require the reader to think, search the text, and pull information together). An example of a right-there question is "Where did the boy live?" A think-and-search question might be "What activities did the boy engage in at camp?"

■ *Knowledge-based* (in-your-head) questions are classified as "author and you" questions (the answer is not directly in the text and so must be inferred) and "on your own" questions (the answers are based on the reader's background knowledge). An example of an author-and-you question is "Why was the character so angry?" An on-your-own question might be "How do you feel about the extinction of the animals in the rain forest?"

To use QARs effectively, students need to understand the questions and be able to skim and scan text for answers. To begin:

1. Make sure students understand the different types of questions included in the QAR. Talk about how the activity will help them summarize and recall background knowledge.
2. Model text-based and knowledge-based questions that might be asked before, during, and after reading.
3. Provide a number of demonstrations of how you answer each type of question while students follow in a text. Talk about why you chose a specific question-answer relationship to explore the text.
4. Provide time for guided practice over several days.
5. Have students take more and more of the responsibility with your support and feedback. Have students explain which question-answer relationship is best for answering the question and why.
6. Help students check their answers to see whether they make sense so they can determine how well they are using the strategy.
7. Encourage students to use the QAR technique independently in literature study or other group reading activities.

Readers Theater

In readers theater, you work cooperatively with students to develop a favorite text into a play that students perform (Sampson, Sampson, and Van Allen 1995; Wolf 1993; Young and Vardell 1993). The activity connects reading and writing. As students read a text several times, they increase fluency. Readers theater also gives them a chance to practice oral reading, develop positive attitudes toward reading, and examine the differences between two genres—narrative texts and plays. You may also use readers theater for informational text if the language is appropriately interesting. To begin:

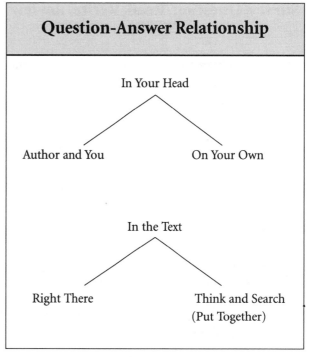

Figure 26–14. QAR Analysis

1. Help students select a text they will transform into a play.
2. Show students how to select key sections of the text to include.
3. Help students decide which parts should be turned into dialogue and which need to be recited by a narrator.
4. Demonstrate how to turn text into dialogue.
5. Work with students to revise parts of the script, including dialogue and narration.
6. Gather props as necessary.
7. Divide parts among students and practice reading. Students can create actions to enhance the performance. They do not need to memorize their lines; they simply read from the script.
8. Arrange for the students to perform the play for an audience.

It is important for students to prepare their own scripts rather than work from professionally prepared ones; the goal is to help them identify important information and rewrite it as a drama. As they practice reading with expression, they learn about interpretation and develop ownership of the presentation.

Survey, Question, Read, Recite, Review (SQ3R)

SQ3R is a traditional study method that helps students gain and remember information from expository material, which is a prerequisite to summarizing and synthesizing. The steps in SQ3R are:

1. *Survey:* Students preview the material to acquaint themselves with the overall organizational format. As you guide your students in previewing material, you can point out special features such as graphs, charts, legends under maps, and pictures. You can also point out the way titles, major headings, and subheadings give clues about the content.
2. *Question:* Students formulate questions based on the text's headings and subheadings. You may need to model the construction of questions related to text organization and then have students do it on their own.
3. *Read:* Students read the text and answer the questions they raised.
4. *Recite:* Students attempt to answer the questions without referring to the text. You can also prompt them to talk about the main ideas of the text.
5. *Review:* Students refer to the text again to get more information on the answers to the questions.

Cloze Procedure

In a cloze procedure, teachers guide students in reading text in which words have been omitted. This technique was first developed by Taylor (1953) (also see Gillet and Temple 1982; Weaver 1994; McCormick 1999). A cloze procedure helps students:

- Use context before and after missing words.
- Develop prediction skills.
- Understand the role of language structure in helping them read.
- Use a variety of sources of information to solve words.

Often students find that they need to read the entire paragraph in order to make a good prediction for the missing word. They learn to stop and review or to reread the text to gain more information. To begin:
1. Observe students to determine what sources of information they are using while reading and what they need to learn.
2. Select a piece of text that offers some challenge for students as well as opportunities for problem solving.
3. Write the text on an easel, individual sheets of paper, or a projected transparency.
4. Select nouns or verbs that you want students to problem-solve and delete them from the text.
5. Ask students to predict the words that have been deleted. You can focus their attention on what they need to learn by asking questions such as "What would make sense in this space?" (prompting them to use meaning) or "What would sound right in this space?" (prompting them to use language). You can promote visual analysis by providing part of the word and asking, "What would make sense in this space and starts like [or ends like] this?"
6. Help students predict the missing words. Write their answers in the blanks or on stick-on notes.
7. Reveal the words actually used in the passage and compare them with students' predictions. Talk about the similarities between students' predictions and the actual words; talk about differences in meaning and word structure.
8. Vary the procedure by deleting adjectives, adverbs, and so forth.

The original cloze procedure required the deletion of every fifth word, but teachers now adapt it to focus on word-solving techniques their students need to learn. For example, you can omit:

- Words that contain key concepts to encourage students to see how words can be predicted and/or understood from context.
- Inflectional endings of words *(ing, ed, s)* to draw students' attention to the relationship between language syntax and word endings.
- Function words *(for, of, to)*, to help readers notice how syntax and content are helpful in reading these words quickly.

A variety of materials are appropriate for cloze procedures, including songs, poems, stories, and informational texts. You will want to use caution in applying cloze procedures when working with students who are learning English as a second language; the syntax will not be readily available to them and the exercise may be confusing.

Note Taking

Writing is a tool for recording one's thinking. Many people find that taking notes helps them remember information they hear or read. Later, notes help them get back to the information, summarize it, or to use it in various ways, including synthesizing.

Guided reading and guided writing are good contexts for showing students how to take notes in a purposeful way. There are several places for students to take notes:

- In the margins of the text if permitted.
- On note cards or a notepad.
- On stick-on notes that can be placed on the specific page of a book or article.
- In the writer's notebook.

Marking

Marking and coding are tools for selecting information and making it easier to retrieve for discussion or to use as a reference. Students often need to return to specific parts of a text to:

- Justify their thinking.
- Provide details.
- Get more information about a particular idea.
- Talk about something they didn't understand.
- Share with others something they found interesting or understood in a special way.

Marking the text also mediates reading in particular ways. When students are looking for something specific, such as language that explains why characters act or think as they do, their awareness is heightened.

Students can mark texts in several ways. They can use bookmarks or stick-on notes to mark parts of the text quickly. If they can write on the text, they can highlight material using a colored marker or by circling, underlining, or placing brackets around it. Photocopy some texts so you can teach students how to underline and highlight. Short texts are ideal for this purpose.

Notebooks

The use of various types of journals enables students to write their way into thoughtful reflection. Ask your students to keep a "learning log" in which they write one-liners or short paragraphs to record their understandings prior to or following the study of a topic. They can also reflect on their own learning processes. A two-column notebook is another useful format: students record their understandings on the left and their feelings or questions about those understandings on the right. Many of these short writes can be completed in the writer's notebook.

Matching Tools to Readers' Needs

In this chapter we have described a variety of tools that can assist readers in discovering the ways texts provide information. You will find that as readers learn more about the organization of text, they make use of this knowledge as writers. When using these tools, it is important to keep the purpose in mind. Sometimes, simply talking about the text and finding organizational patterns within it is all that will be needed to help students learn about the structure of narrative and expository texts. The analytic tools we have presented here provide a way to look much more explicitly at aspects of text, but their use should be closely related to what students need to know next as they encounter texts of increasing difficulty. As you use these tools, you should see a diminishing need for them. For example, if students can quickly produce compare/contrast items or describe characters orally, there is no need to go through the entire exercise of doing charts. These tools should be used to help students move to new levels of understanding and gradually integrate this kind of analysis into their own repertoires of thinking about text.

Suggestions for Professional Development

1. Choose a nonfiction text and a fiction text to read aloud to your students. For each, choose one graphic organizer to support text analysis.
2. Over two days, read the texts and work with students to construct the appropriate information in the organizer.

3. Bring the two graphic organizers to a grade-level meeting with your colleagues and share your tools. Discuss the following:
   - In what ways did each tool support the students' comprehension?
   - What did the readers learn how to do for themselves?
   - What were new insights for you?
   - What would you have done differently? What priorities do you have next for the readers?

4. At the end of the meeting, choose another tool for supporting readers that you will all try with a small guided reading group. Have at least one person in the group videotape a lesson to bring to the next meeting for discussion.

5. At your next meeting, share and compare your experiences using the graphic tool.

6. Watch the videotape(s) and discuss the same questions.

UNDERSTANDING THE "TESTING GENRE": PREPARING STUDENTS FOR HIGH-QUALITY PERFORMANCE

It makes sense to us that the strategies needed in
test-taking would be better learned if they were part of daily curriculum.
—KATHE TAYLOR AND SHERRY WALTON

Being tested is part of being alive. Throughout history people have tested their skills against the forces of nature, in competition with other human beings, and against their own pain, fear, and fatigue. They cleared the land, sailed the seas, fought for food and freedom, and developed technology to expand their competitive edge. Survival depended on the ability to perform with a high amount of effort and concentration. Success often depends on knowledge and skills.

Students in school are tested continually, and their success is most often measured by their performance on paper-and-pencil tests. In addition to the standardized tests that have been used for decades, many states have instituted "high stakes" proficiency tests in grades 3 or 4, 9, and 12, the stakes being whether students will be permitted to move to the next grade or, in grade 12, to graduate.

Such consequences are extremely dangerous. Retention has been shown to have little benefit for those who must repeat the grade (Roderick 1994). Extra drill in summer school or after school can also drive students to give up and drop out. Once students drop out of school, it becomes even more difficult for them to achieve a quality life.

The stakes are also high for teachers because their performance is judged by how many students meet the criteria for success. The demand for accountability is intense and has the potential to reduce the language and literacy curriculum to a very narrow set of exercises. If we care about our students, we need to make sure test taking has positive outcomes.

While we cannot ignore tests, we cannot let them control our lives and the lives of our students. We need to find ways to cope with the demands of the testing environment and still help our students have happy, productive, and satisfying literacy experiences. To cope with testing demands:

1. Analyze the genuine underlying skills that students need in order to be able to perform well on comprehensive proficiency tests.
2. Create an ongoing curriculum to help students develop the genuine reading and writing abilities that will provide a foundation for good test performance (as well as all the benefits of a literate life).
3. Analyze the ways of reading, writing, and displaying knowledge that tests require.
4. Familiarize students with the ways to display knowledge and skills that will be expected of them in test performance.

Without the first two steps, the others are ineffective. Being a competent reader and writer is basic to performing well on tests.

At the same time, we need to give students specific guidance on how to use their abilities in the limited and high-pressure situations they face. To help students develop test-taking skills, we need to look at testing as a genre—a particular kind of reading and writing. We must analyze the demands of tests, determine how to embed test-taking skills within the activities of the language and literacy framework, and recognize how to help our students learn the specific responses they need to call into play while being tested.

Standards-Based Testing

Standards-based tests are meant to determine whether students can meet standards based on the skills required to survive and succeed in society. Policymakers have set these standards to help schools implement the kind of instruction that ensures students will achieve. Standards, benchmarks, and tests are interrelated.

Standards and Benchmarks

A standard is a model, principle, measure, or example used to compare items within the same classification to determine their quality. It is agreed upon and, in general, followed by the majority. We can also think of a standard as a "banner" or an "emblem" used as a symbol to rally support. Both of these definitions relate to standards in literacy education today. The idea is to create a common vision for levels of achievement that will ensure that our educational systems achieve their goal—helping every citizen use literacy effectively. Standards establish performance targets toward which schools and students can strive.

Ideally, standards are based on research that reveals what students who achieve success know and can do over time. Establishing standards is, in fact, an imperfect science. A general procedure is to build on the consensus of experts as they are published by professional organizations such as the International Reading Association or the National Council of Teachers of English. These professional groups—or "learned societies"—include researchers and other experts who "pool their wisdom." Experts make their best judgments about what research suggests students need to know at various stages of learning. The process is open to differences of opinion.

Standards are usually expressed as broad-based clusters or profiles of behaviors and competencies. Standards represent lofty goals. When a school, district, state, or nation adopts a standard, they commit to implementing a plan to achieve the criteria set forward for success. To that end, time and money are dedicated to implementing the plan; meeting the standards is the goal.

Benchmarks are specifically defined, measurable behaviors along a continuum of progress. Sometimes educators establish benchmarks as a way to assess whether students are making progress toward meeting the target performances defined by standards.

Benchmarks are milestones; they tell us whether students are learning at satisfactory rates and whether they need intervention, extra instruction, or differentiated instruction. In Chapter 28, we discuss establishing benchmarks along the continuum of leveled texts as one way of making sure that students' reading progress is on track. Benchmarks may be established in any area of knowledge.

Tests are designed to determine whether a student's performance meets specific standards. Testing is also an imperfect process. Standards are far reaching. They may describe a piece of work, a specific performance, conceptual understanding, skills and tools, or an accomplishment based on effort. Just consider the reading and writing standards published by the New Standards™ of the Center for Education and the Economy.[1] The reading standard requires students to "go deep" and make connections in some area that interests them. The intent is to encourage readers to pursue themes, authors, and genres of their choosing. The student reads and comprehends at least four books (or book equivalents) about one issue or subject, or four books by a single writer, or four books in one genre, and produces evidence of reading that:

- Makes and supports warranted and responsible assertions about the texts.
- Supports assertions with elaborated and convincing evidence.
- Draws the texts together to compare and contrast themes, characters, and ideas.
- Makes perceptive and well-developed connections.
- Evaluates writing strategies and elements of the author's craft. (Performance Standards, p. 22)

The standard captures the complexity of the ways readers make connections among texts. The specificity of the statement (e.g., four books) is meant to help educators assess students' performance. We cannot

---

[1] New Standards™ is a joint project of the Learning Research and Development Center (LRDC) at the University of Pittsburgh and the National Center on Education and the Economy (NCEE). It was founded by Lauren Resnick, director of LRDC, and Marc Tucker, president of NCEE, and is supported by a consortium of twenty-six state education departments and six additional school districts in other states. The standards above are from *Performance Standards: English Language Arts, Mathematics, Science, Applied Learning, Volume 1: Elementary School* (Washington, DC: National Center on Education and the Economy and the University of Pittsburgh, 1997).

imagine making a good assessment of students' performance relative to this standard without working with them over time, recording their reading habits, examining their writing in response to reading, and observing many of their conversations about books.

The writing standard is intended to ensure that students become familiar with report writing and to help them internalize criteria to review and revise their work. The student produces a report that:

- Engages the reader by establishing a context, creating a persona, and otherwise developing reader interest.
- Develops a controlling idea that conveys a perspective on the subject.
- Creates an organizing structure appropriate to a specific purpose, audience, and context.
- Includes appropriate facts and details.
- Excludes extraneous and inappropriate information.
- Uses a range of appropriate strategies, such as providing facts and details, describing or analyzing the subject, and narrating a relevant anecdote.
- Provides a sense of closure to the writing. (Performance Standards, p. 24)

As with the reading standard, we cannot imagine a real evaluation of students' writing against this standard without observing their investigations over time as they gather and categorize information about a topic, interact with others around the topic, consider different audiences and how to engage them, compose and revise the report, and present it orally or answer questions about it.

Measuring Performance

Can a test measure performance relative to a standard target? The obvious answer is no. By its very definition, *a* test can provide only partial information because:

- It is taken during a limited and defined period of time.
- The tasks are of necessity contrived rather than authentic.
- Students are required to work alone rather than with the support of others.
- Emotional factors may interfere.
- Students may or may not have the background experience required by a test that is designed to assess large populations.

These limitations mean that working toward achieving standards is a much bigger endeavor than working toward performance on proficiency tests. Again, developing a student's reading and writing is the key to student performance.

Tests as a Genre

It helps to think of testing as a genre—a type of discourse that is distinguishable by characteristics of form, style, and content. Students must learn how to understand and use these characteristics (Reardon 1990). Tests tend to follow this pattern:

- Typical "test vocabulary" includes words such as *selection, answer, what, which, why.*
- Selections are short; often they are excerpts from longer texts.
- Longer selections may feature one or two illustrations; many selections have no pictures.
- The text provides instructions about how to answer the questions, but the student must figure them out; they are not immediately evident. The puzzle of figuring out how to respond is part of the test.
- The selections on a test are not related to one another (as they would be in a cohesive informational text, a newspaper, or a novel).
- The text contains questions that must be answered.
- Questions may appear in several forms:
  1. Multiple choice: the student chooses the best among a limited number of answers.
  2. Short written responses: the student writes a concise, specific answer.
  3. Extended written responses: the student composes a longer, more complex answer.
- The print on the page is all the student has to answer the questions.
- On a writing test, students must address specific topics in a particular genre rather than choosing their own.
- Written responses are evaluated according to specific criteria.

Just as you teach students to read and understand biography or fantasy, you can teach them to read and respond to the genre of tests. Testing reflects a kind of reading and writing that is similar to the reading and writing that people do for authentic purposes. The major difference is that on tests readers are concerned about what the tester is looking for and about displaying their knowledge in a way that shows their competence.

Performing on Reading Tests

You can help your students perform at higher levels on reading proficiency tests in several ways:

- ▪ Ensuring that a range of authentic reading is occurring in your classroom.
- ▪ Providing as much literacy instruction as you possibly can.

- ▪ Embedding test-taking skills within every element of the language and literacy framework.
- ▪ Starting early to teach students the kinds of specific skills they will need to be successful test takers.

Differences Between Reading and Taking Tests

Figure 27–1 compares readers and test takers. Their purposes for reading texts are different, as are the time limits and text length. Readers read for a wide range of purposes, including pleasure and learning. They respond to the text emotionally and connect it to other texts. They remember important information, which they often discuss with others. They get to know characters and empathize with them; they connect the text to their own lives.

What Are the Connections Between Reading and Test Taking?

Readers
- ❖ Read for various purposes —enjoyment, getting information, etc.
- ❖ Process continuous text of various lengths.
- ❖ Actively search for and use a variety of informational sources—language, meaning, letter-sound relationships, visual information.
- ❖ Respond to the text in terms of feelings and connections with their lives.
- ❖ Remember details and make interpretations throughout the reading of a text.
- ❖ Connect texts to others they have read.
- ❖ Compare texts to others they have read.
- ❖ Construct, remember, and talk about the main idea and/or theme of a text after reading.
- ❖ Notice interesting words that extend meaning and start to use them in their own talk and writing.
- ❖ Get to know and empathize with characters and their problems.
- ❖ Use reading to understand life problems and situations and/or complex scientific or technical concepts.

Test Takers
- ❖ Read for the purpose of answering questions and/or performing in writing.
- ❖ Process a text of limited length within time limits.
- ❖ Display knowledge of text through writing.
- ❖ Identify and/or write down key information in texts.
- ❖ Identify and write about a sequence of actions in narrative text or descriptions of processes in informational texts.
- ❖ Identify or write interpretations of the text.
- ❖ Find or write key words from texts.
- ❖ Write or select statements that precisely summarize a text.
- ❖ Identify the difference between main and supporting ideas in an informational text.
- ❖ Identify words by their precise meanings within a text; evaluate the use of words in a text.
- ❖ Write about plot, problem, solution, or setting.
- ❖ Write or identify correct information from illustrations (diagrams, etc.).
- ❖ Write or choose among alternative endings, sequels, and problem solutions.
- ❖ Write about in list or text form the ways texts are similar and different.
- ❖ Use references and resources to help in understanding a text.

Figure 27-1. Readers and Test Takers

Some of those actions may also occur when readers take tests, but the similarities are limited. Test takers read to answer questions or to produce writing that displays their understanding of a text. They process a text within time limits, noting the information they need to answer questions or include in summary statements. They have to gather and select the right information and discard irrelevant details. They may have to choose among alternative endings or identify the correct information from illustrations. They need to show explicitly that they understand how items are similar and different. Test takers are reading in a particular context. They step back to use their reading and writing skills in ways that conform with expectations for certain kinds of texts at a particular time. Test takers are performing.

Familiarize your students with the test genre to help them understand the demands of tests. Students must be able to:

■ Locate information in or beyond the texts.
■ Understand what test questions require.
■ Process a variety of texts effectively so they learn the characteristics and demands of different texts.

Teaching Students to Take Reading Tests

Before you can teach students how to demonstrate understanding and skills under testing conditions, you must be sure they can actually read the material and have the basic knowledge they need to perform. You can't teach them "techniques" for answering questions if the text material is beyond their reading ability.

Anyone learning new skills needs to begin in familiar, comfortable territory with predictable outcomes. You don't give new drivers their first driving lesson in a downpour on a California freeway. Accordingly, teach test-taking techniques using material that students can read with only a little support.

MULTIPLE-CHOICE QUESTIONS

Students who look at tests as a kind of problem-solving activity know that answering multiple-choice questions is an exercise in itself. They recognize that the conditions of timed, multiple-choice tests are different from authentic reading and writing, and they can set about learning how to demonstrate their knowledge under the rules that exist in that setting.

The task in multiple-choice questions is usually to select the best answer from a limited number of choic-

es. It requires literal comprehension of a text as well as going beyond the text. Students need to gather information that may be explicitly stated or clearly implied, and they may need to make inferences. Questions are more difficult when:

■ There are two or more "right" answers but one is the best according to criteria that may not be explicitly stated.
■ Selecting among alternatives requires interpretation of the text.
■ Selecting among alternatives requires going back into the text to gather or compare information.
■ Selecting among alternatives requires paying extremely careful attention to the wording.

Language frequently used in multiple-choice questions is listed in Figure 27–2. If you look at the multiple-choice tests (or "practice" tests) your students are expected to read and understand, you will no doubt be able to add to this list. To plan minilessons to help students understand these questions, determine exactly what the language requires of the reader. Then, in five-to ten-minute minilessons, show students what the question requires and walk through several examples.

Use an easel and chart paper or a projected transparency to display the language and principles. *It is not wise to spend long periods drilling on many questions.* A quick referral to one example a day will be sufficient over time to help students figure out the testing puzzle. The language-word study block is an ideal time for this quick, interactive whole group work.

Figure 27–3 presents some general suggestions for helping students do their best on multiple-choice questions. Focus a minilesson on each of these procedures and circle back for another minilesson on the principle if needed. Have students spend time using a pencil or highlighter to identify important information. Ask them to cross out the wrong answers after they have discussed why they do not fit. This physical act rivets students' attention and keeps the focus on specifics rather than generalities.

Many students will not understand the process of test taking unless you walk them through it. Encourage them to:

■ Highlight important details in both questions and answers that can make a difference in which answer they select.

The Language and Demands of Multiple Choice Questions [and What It Means]	
Key Language	**Demands on the Reader/Test Taker**
Which sentence tells . . . ?	Keep a concept in mind while examining the precise language of several sentences. Select the sentence that answers the question or provides the necessary information.
Which sentence best tells . . . ?	Keep a concept in mind while examining the precise language of several sentences, more than one of which contains the answer. Select the sentence with the best language.
Choose the best answer.	Consider several answers, more than one of which may be right, and select the one that is most accurate or suitable. The choice may involve understanding word connotations or choosing whether details are necessary or superfluous.
Choose the sentence that tells about . . . ?	Match concepts with precision when selecting among alternative sentences.
This section is mostly about . . .	Determine the main idea of a sentence and then select the alternative that most closely matches that idea.
According to the selection . . .	Summarize information from the selection.
Who is telling the story?	Read a short or longer text and determine the narrator. The test taker must understand the difference between first and third person narrative.
The story is being told from the perspective of . . .	Read a short or longer text and determine the point of view. In a third person narrative, the test taker is required to identify the character whose thoughts, actions, and perspectives are described as central to the plot.
_____ says "_____". This means . . . **or** **In the selection, "_____" means . . .**	Read a word, phrase, sentence, paragraph, or section of text, interpret it, and choose among alternatives the best statement of meaning. One or more of the alternatives may be accurate, so the test taker may be required to distinguish among subtle differences. Knowledge of word connotations may be required.

Figure 27–2. The Language of Multiple Choice Questions

Doing Your Best on Multiple-Choice Questions

1. **Read the question and all answers carefully.**
   It's important to pay attention to the specific words in the question and the details in each possible answer.

2. **Select the answer carefully.**
   Read all the options carefully even if one initially seems correct. Cross out the ones you are sure are incorrect. Then focus on the ones that are left to make your choice.

3. **Use what you do know in the answers.**
   Even if you don't know very much about the question, focus on what you do know about a topic to make a reasonable choice.

4. **Do not always choose your first answer.**
   Often the authors of the test include frequently made wrong answers. Always check your response.

5. **Make good use of your pencil and highlighter.**
   Cross out answers you know are wrong so you have fewer to think about. Circle or highlight important information.

6. **Be careful of answers containing words like "always" or "never."**
   Unless specifically stated in the reading passage, absolute answers are rarely correct.

7. **When a question requires the "best" answer, realize it may not fit exactly.**
   It is simply better than the other answers.

8. **When asked to respond to the main idea, read the passage and determine the main idea for yourself.**
   Then see if any of the answers fit. Often, all the answers contain ideas from the passage.

9. **When you don't feel comfortable with any of the responses, make a guess.**
   You'll have some chance of getting a correct response if you have one answer instead of none.

10. **Spend a limited amount of time on each and go back if you have time.**
    It's important to finish the test, so large amounts of time spent on a few questions will not be helpful. If you are not sure of a response, mark your best response and circle the question number so you can go back if you have time.

Figure 27–3. Doing Your Best on Multiple Choice Questions

The Language and Demands of Short-Answer or Extended-Response Questions

Language	Demands on the Reader/Test Taker
Which sentence tells how…?	Identify a specific place in the text that provides information.
How do you know?	Identify evidence in the text or from your own knowledge or experiences to support your point.
Use the selection to explain why… **Why was [did]…? Use the story to explain your answer.**	Provide an explanation that is backed up by specific evidence from the text.
What does _____ mean? How do you know? Use the story to explain your answer.	Write the concise meaning of a word, phrase, or symbol; back up your answer with evidence from the text.
Retell the story.	Select important details and report them in order; the answer should provide enough information that someone who hasn't read the story can tell what happened.
This story is about…. **The most important ideas in this selection are….**	Select important details and provide a concise summary that includes only the main or important ideas.

Figure 27–4.   The Language of Short-Answer or Extended Response Questions

- Share their "first responses" with each other and critique them, noticing how the test makers may have tried to mislead them.
- Use a highlighter to search through the text for words like always and never and discuss why they are misleading.
- Line up answers in order of best to worst and discuss why each one falls where it does along this continuum.
- Brainstorm what they know as a group and discuss how they can use even partial knowledge to make a strong attempt at answering a question. (Model this process for them so they will know how to approach such a challenge when they take tests on their own.)

There are many resources for finding examples of multiple-choice questions. While test-practice workbooks and practice tests are useful, don't take too much of a "workbook" approach. In particular remember that:

- Explicitly teaching a limited number of examples is ultimately more powerful and helpful than hours of drill on vague workbook examples.
- Too much drill undermines the time for more meaningful curriculum, which deprives students of vital opportunities to build basic reading and writing strategies.
- Education is much more than test preparation; you want to communicate this important understanding to your students.
- Parents will appreciate the test preparation you do, but you want them to understand that your curriculum is much richer and broader than teaching to the test.

Doing Your Best on Short-Answer Questions

1. Read and be clear about the questions.
Read the question carefully, highlighting or underlining important words. Know what the question is.

2. Note important words or phrases.
In the margin or in blank space write key words or phrases you will want to use.

3. Organize in your head.
In your head, organize your answer. Be sure it is complete, logical, and detailed.

4. Write your response.
Using your margin notes, write your response.

5. Reread for sense and completeness.
Reread the question and your answer. Be sure your response makes sense and is complete.

Figure 27–5. Doing Your Best on Short-Answer Questions

SHORT-ANSWER QUESTIONS

Short-answer questions require students to compose concise responses that directly address the demands of the question. Therefore, it's critical that your students understand what the question is asking. Figure 27–4 contains examples of the language of short-answer questions, along with what is required of the test taker. (The same language is used for extended-response questions; the difference is the need to organize the more complex and elaborate response.)

You can use these question "stems" as a basis for minilessons and model responses or prompt the class to generate responses. You can also invite students to work in small groups and then compare their group responses as a class. They can compare their answers to the text, highlighting how they used evidence in the text to generate their answers. Help your students internalize criteria they can use to evaluate their own responses as they take tests alone.

Figure 27–5 offers some suggestions to help students do their best on short-answer questions. Teach students to highlight or circle important words that will help them understand the task required and to organize answers in a way that precisely addresses the questions.

Asking students to write appropriate test questions for a specific text also helps them comprehend the requirements of a test. Groups can write questions, trade them with another group, and then explain how the responses do or do not answer the questions. Designing their own questions leads students to the inner structure of the test and helps them analyze it from the point of view of the examiner.

EXTENDED-RESPONSE QUESTIONS

Extended responses require much more time and thought on the part of the test taker. It is critical that students learn how to organize their responses before writing the final text (see the suggestions in Figure 27–6). Students will need to read the selection carefully; show them how to highlight important ideas or make marginal notes. Many students will be distracted by details that are important but are not directly relevant to the question at hand. Organizing the final response will be easier if students look back at their notes and number them in a logical order.

Students also need to have some criteria in mind for evaluating their responses:

■ Is the response complete? Or is an important piece of information missing?

Doing Your Best on Extended-Response Questions

1. Read and be clear about the question.
Read the question carefully, highlighting or underlining important words. Know what the question is so you can be sure that what you write answers the specific question.

2. Note important ideas, phrases, words.
Use the margin or blank space to write notes as you read.

3. Reread to highlight and add to notes.
Reread or skim the passage to underline or highlight important parts that relate to the question. Add these to your notes.

4. Organize your notes by numbering.
Number your notes in a logical order so that they can be an outline of important ideas or words for your written response.

5. Write your response.
In your own words, write your response, giving the important ideas and details. Be sure you have answered the question.

6. Reread for sense and completeness.
Reread the question and your answer. Be sure your response makes sense and is complete.

Figure 27–6. Doing Your Best on Extended-Response Questions

■ Does the order of the sentences make sense?
■ Does the response answer the question? Is a response to any part of the question missing?

Teach students to reread their responses, making sure they make sense and answer the question in full.

Embedding Test Reading into Daily Reading Instruction

The activities described here are designed to teach students specific test-taking skills that can make a difference in their ability to understand what the test requires and to shape successful answers. These test-taking skills work very effectively when students are reading texts that are within their control. The real key to test performance is the high-quality reading instruction that students experience daily throughout their elementary years.

Reading in the Classroom and Reading Required by Tests

The reading workshop offers challenging and productive reading experiences that help students develop the very same strategies they will need to know to do well on tests. To some extent, reading is reading. Whatever the milieu, readers:

■ Adjust their reading to take into account characteristics of difference genres.
■ Gather information in a way appropriate to the way the text is organized.
■ Notice and use illustrations and graphic features that provide different kinds of information.
■ Solve words by decoding and/or understanding their meaning.

- Use background knowledge, summarize information, and keep facts and events in mind in order to synthesize information.
- Reread to be sure they understand.
- Make notes to organize their ideas.

At the same time, there are quite a few differences between classroom reading and test reading (see Figure 27–7). For example, in the reading workshop, students select texts that interest them and read them over time until they are finished; letters in their reader's notebooks represent their own thoughts and feelings about the texts they have selected; and they work collaboratively with others and benefit from the support and assistance of their peers. In contrast, on tests they read an assigned text, usually short, within a designated amount of time; write responses to specific prompts or questions; and work alone without talking. Although some tests do give students as much time as they need, and those with open-ended responses allow for some flexibility, most reading proficiency tests are highly restrictive.

Reading Workshop Activities to Support Students' Test-Taking Skills

As a natural part of reading workshop, you can involve students in specific activities that promote ongoing learning and help them perform better on tests. We caution you not to use these activities as exercises; they are effective to the extent that students encounter them repeatedly during their reading of a variety of texts. Some general activities are listed in Figure 27–8. These general approaches can be used for many different purposes as students read fiction and nonfiction. For example, just about every activity would support content area reading as well as a deeper understanding of fiction. See Chapter 26 for additional tools to support students' understanding and analysis of text.

Your goal is to prompt students continuously in a way that will help them understand the kind of thinking that helps them comprehend texts. To guide students to specific information, use statements like these:

- Give an example . . .
- Give three examples . . .
- Give an example from each selection . . .
- Give examples that show . . .
- Using examples from the text, explain . . .
- Describe and explain why . . .

- In the text, what is meant by . . .
- Use evidence from the text to support . . .
- Why do you think . . .
- Explain in your own words . . .
- Describe and use information from the story . . .
- Explain how the author . . .
- How can you tell . . .
- What is meant by . . .

Many reading proficiency tests make a distinction between assessing two learning outcomes:

1. Constructing meaning from texts.
2. Examining and extending the meaning of texts.

The goal is to help students understand the overall meaning of what is read and demonstrate that understanding.

Helping Students Construct Meaning

To support students in constructing meaning:

1. *Teach students to summarize the text.* Summarizing requires students to produce concise lists of major ideas and to discard unnecessary details. In summarizing, they need to know that they cannot add topics, ideas, or details from their own experience. They need to learn and use criteria for selecting the "best" summaries—those that have main ideas, important events, and reasons for characters' actions. In non-fiction texts, summaries should focus on major and supporting ideas and the relationships between or among them. By writing and evaluating their own summary statements, students will also develop criteria for selecting summary statements in multiple-choice items.
2. *Teach students to use graphic aids and illustrations.* Give explicit attention to how students can use graphic displays and illustrations to provide information. Often, students need demonstrations of how to connect the text information with these sources of additional information.
3. *Teach students to retell the text in writing.* To retell a narrative or informational text, students need to provide major points and supporting details in correct sequence and in their own words. Teach them how to reread and check for anything that the test

Reading Workshop		Reading Test
← Different	Same ↓	Different →

Reading Workshop

Students:

- Read books daily over indefinite time period.
- Read at own rate.
- Choose texts on basis of interest or with guidance of teacher.
- Usually read longer texts.
- Write their own responses according to factors they notice; sometimes write responses as assigned by teacher.
- Work with others.
- Talk with others.
- Get feedback from others.
- Request help if needed.
- Receive encouragement and suggestions to complete tasks.
- Use a dictionary or other resources.
- Recommend books to others.

Same

Students:

- Adjust to type of text (fiction vs. nonfiction).
- Decode words.
- Understand words.
- Use reading strategies.
- Note author's purpose.
- Think about author's message.
- Note how text is organized.
- Attend to the text type.
- Use context to understand unfamiliar words.
- Use background (prior) knowledge.
- Read to understand the author's precise message for comprehension.
- Collect important information.
- Predict what's going to happen.
- Keep the sequence of events in mind.
- Reread to understand or be sure the response is clear.
- Notice and use graphic features.
- Make notes or organize ideas on separate paper.
- Connect text to self, previous knowledge, and other texts.

Reading Test

Students:

- Are expected to read a designated amount of text within a specific time period (sometimes not timed).
- Read assigned texts.
- Usually read a paragraph or page instead of a longer text.
- May read a section of a longer text that they do not know.
- Write own response to specific questions or prompt (or choose best response).
- Underline, highlight or make notes in margins (if allowed).
- Work alone, without help.
- Monitor pace and productivity without teacher support.
- Evaluate and revise without assistance.
- Cannot use a dictionary or other resources.

Figure 27–7. Reading Workshop and Reading Tests

Suggestions for Embedding Test-Taking Skills in Reading Workshop

1. Involve children in reading and discussing a variety of fiction, poetry, and nonfiction.

2. Use a variety of graphic organizers to help students understand the structure of fiction and nonfiction texts.

3. Teach students to identify the genre and text structure in reading selections and to select a text structure for a written response (e.g., retell, summary, comparison/contrast).

4. Engage students in thinking about the text and talking about it in read aloud, literature study, guided reading, and independent reading.

5. Attend to students' reading level. *When they are beyond their appropriate level, they are not able to develop effective strategies.*

6. Provide numerous opportunities for rereading texts for different purposes (1-2-3 strategy).

7. Include numerous opportunities for pairs or triads to discuss and evaluate oral and written responses.

8. Consistently require students to provide evidence from the text to support their thinking.

9. Use the language (vocabulary and phrases) that are frequently used in tests as part of instructions for oral and written response to reading.

10. Teach students to distinguish when information comes directly from the text or requires thinking beyond the text.

11. Provide students with highlighters and teach them how to use them as a part of classroom instruction.

12. Teach students how to highlight key words and phrases in questions, directions, and reading selections.

13. Teach the children to organize their thoughts in writing quickly (phrases, lists, web diagrams) before writing their responses.

14. Provide numerous opportunities for timed short writing (e.g., one paragraph) and long (e.g., one page) written responses to reading. Have students talk about and evaluate their responses.

15. Teach students that when reading selections are preceded by a boxed headnote, the information is essential. Show them how to read headnotes and look at the examples carefully.

Figure 27–8. Suggestions for Embedding Test-Taking Skills in Reading Workshop

how to reread and check for anything that the test evaluators would interpret as copying. As with summarizing, they should not give new details, create new beginnings and endings, or offer opinions.

4. *Identify and interpret vocabulary (words, phrases, expressions) critical to the meaning of the text.* In guided reading and literature study, you can ask students to notice and identify key words that:

■ Reveal meaning.
■ Describe a character.
■ Tell about the setting.
■ Indicate cause and effect.
■ Summarize a story or an informational piece.
■ Discriminate between two interpretations of a fact or story.

They can also evaluate the ways in which words are used to communicate meaning in sentences, paragraphs, and stories and notice how they are used figuratively rather than literally.

HELPING STUDENTS EXPAND AND EXTEND MEANING

Many students find it more difficult to examine and extend meaning than to identify the literal meaning. The goal here is to help students move beyond the text to make inferences. To begin:

1. *Help students respond to the text.* As part of independent reading, have students routinely explore their responses to the text in writing. In addition, engage them in oral discussion throughout the reading workshop. Students need opportunities to state orally and in writing the explicit connections they make with their personal experiences, their feelings, and local, national, or world events. Given these connections, they need to provide their own opinions, backed up by a clear rationale; they also need to show that they understand a variety of perspectives in interpreting text.

2. *Help students make inferences from the text.* Show students how to grasp important ideas that are implied but not directly stated in the text. For fiction texts, they might predict what characters will do, interpret actions/motivations, and weigh alternative solutions given specific actions. For nonfiction texts,

students can interpret observational or other data as well as descriptions of processes and apply them.

3. *Help students compare texts.* Students are often expected to respond to a series of questions that require reading several different texts, sometimes of different genres. Because your students are reading many different texts in guided reading, literature study, and independent reading, you can easily guide them to compare and contrast those texts. They can compare characters' appearance, actions, motives, points of view, and so forth; plots or events; and settings. They can compare fiction, nonfiction, and poetic texts on the same topic or with the same setting (geographic or historical). Comparing texts helps them delve into the deeper meaning of complex concepts such as "heroism" or "voyages."

4. *Help students analyze the text.* In guided reading, literature study, and individual conferences, you can encourage students to articulate the characteristics of fiction and notice and connect action sequences; for nonfiction texts, they can identify particular structures—compare/contrast, problem/solution, description, and so on.

5. *Help students choose materials related to purposes.* As part of a reading test, students may be asked to identify reference materials or resources, either fiction or nonfiction, that would be appropriate sources for information. As part of content area reading, you will be teaching students to choose or identify reference resources to locate specific information. You can also help them develop these skills in writing workshop as they work on investigations. Guide them to choose appropriate resources and materials to solve problems and make decisions.

Performing on Writing Tests

Proficiency tests that include students' writing are a real testing breakthrough. These tests usually require students to respond to a prompt, and evaluators mark the writing based on the students' ability to compose and develop a topic. The rubric in Figure 27–9 is an example of the kinds of guides used to assess writing competency. Be sure to teach your students the important factors related to idea development and use of conventions that are spelled out in your state and district rubrics.

A Sample Rubric for Evaluating Writing

Development of Ideas/Topic

1	2	3	4	5	6
❖ Little topic/idea development. ❖ Few details, only slightly related to topic. ❖ No evidence of organizational structure. ❖ Little evidence of audience or purpose.	❖ Limited or weak topic development. ❖ Some extraneous or loosely related material. ❖ Organizational structure attempted but unclear.	❖ Topic development attempted and purposes addressed. ❖ Organizational structure reflects conventions such as beginning, middle, and end.	❖ Moderate topic/idea development. ❖ Evident organizational pattern; text arranged in logical order. ❖ Adequate supporting details.	❖ Full topic/idea development. ❖ Clear and/or subtle organization. ❖ Sufficient details to clearly communicate meaning. ❖ Appropriate use of language.	❖ Rich topic/idea development. ❖ Purpose and audience skillfully addressed. ❖ Ample supporting details. ❖ Organization integrally related to topic/ideas. ❖ Effective/rich use of language.

Conventions of Writing

1	2	3	4	5	6
❖ Limited or inappropriate vocabulary so meaning is not clear. ❖ Serious errors that interfere with communication. ❖ Gross errors in word usage and spelling, punctuation, and capitalization so that communication is impeded.	❖ Limited vocabulary. ❖ Word usage and spelling errors that interfere with communication. ❖ Knowledge of conventions such as punctuation and capitalization indicated but not consistent.	❖ Limited vocabulary but suited to topic. ❖ Word usage and spelling errors evident; some interference with communication. ❖ Awareness indicated of some common spelling patterns. ❖ Conventions related to capitalization and punctuation observed but not consistent.	❖ Generally good use of conventions such as grammar, usage, mechanics, and punctuation. ❖ A few errors which do not interfere with communication. ❖ Mostly simple sentences but evidence of ability to use complex sentences to relate ideas.	❖ Variety of simple and complex sentences. ❖ Consistent standard use of conventions such as grammar, usage, mechanics, and punctuation.	❖ Full and skillful control of sentence structure, grammar, and usage. ❖ Full control of mechanics. ❖ Wide use of punctuation in a way that enhances writing style and communicates rich meaning.

Figure 27–9. Sample Rubric

Embedding Test Writing into Daily Writing Instruction

Most writing standards provide that students will:

- Develop ideas and topics with logically related ideas and adequate supporting detail.
- Organize their writing with a clear structure that is related to meaning, topic, audience, and purpose.
- Select types of writing (genres) and styles of oral or written discourse for different purposes and audiences.
- Use tools such as note taking, summarizing, outlining, ordering, and questioning to develop their topics and ideas.
- Use research methods to gather information from different sources.
- Use knowledge of conventions for sentence structure, usage, punctuation, capitalization, and spelling to edit their writing.
- Develop and use criteria for assessing their compositions and research projects before presenting them to varied audiences.

All of these competencies are important to consider in classroom writing instruction, and they form the foundation of successful test performance.

Comparing Classroom Writing and Test Writing

In general, tests of writing require the same processes that writers use in the classroom. Figure 27–10 outlines the similarities and differences between the writing that students do in the classroom and the writing they are expected to do on tests.

Writing Workshop Activities to Support Students' Test-Taking Skills

Writing workshop is the best way to help students prepare for these tests. To begin, you may want to plan minilessons related to topic development and conventions (see Figure 27–11). You should also engage students in activities that specifically prepare them for the test situation. It is important to show students the criteria used to judge their work and have them apply it as they rewrite their pieces. Figure 27–12 is a checklist that can help students evaluate their own writing. You will want to create a checklist based on the criteria used to evaluate the writing on your tests.

Another way to help students use the evaluation criteria is to let them apply them to writing samples from former students. Ask students to work in groups to improve pieces you've kept from previous years (just be sure all the examples are anonymous). In the process, they will learn how to use the criteria to evaluate and revise their own work. Figure 27–13 contains suggestions for embedding test-writing skills in writing workshop.

Supporting Test-Taking Skills in Language and Word Study

The activities you do in language and word study also contribute substantially to students' ability to perform well on proficiency tests. During the language/word study block, you can present minilessons specific to performance on proficiency tests. You will also be presenting minilessons to help students learn how words sound and look and what they mean; tests are made up of words.

Just about everything that students are expected to do on tests can also be practiced in an authentic way when students respond to texts you have read aloud (for the most part, texts that are more difficult than they could read alone). In addition, interactive editing and interactive vocabulary sessions give students a chance to learn how to use conventions in their writing.

Using and Understanding Graphic Representations

Graphic representations—line graphs, bar graphs, pie charts, time lines, maps—provide important information in a highly organized way (Jones, Pierce, and Hunter 1988). When students construct these models for themselves, they learn how to interpret information from the graphics included in tests.

Chapter 26 describes a number of tools for helping students read and understand texts; among these tools are graphic organizers. A group of graphic organizers is also included in Appendix 17 through 45. You can use all of these graphic organizers to help students increase their understanding of texts and teach them how to create graphic organizers of their own.

Figure 27–14 is a graphic representation Peter and his students created to organize the information in *The*

Writing Workshop		Writing Test
Different ←	**Same** →	→ **Different**
Students:	*Students:*	*Students:*
❖ Keep a list of topics or short drafts that are the seeds for writing.	❖ Define a topic and organize ideas around it.	❖ Write in response to an assigned topic.
❖ Select topics according to interests.	❖ Provide supporting details.	❖ Write in a defined period of time.
❖ Write regularly, accommodating time to the demands of the topic and organizational plan.	❖ Organize the text with a logical structure that flows.	❖ Write to an assigned audience.
❖ Interact with others around the topic.	❖ Create a text with a sense of wholeness.	❖ Write for a predetermined purpose.
❖ Assist others in planning writing and receive assistance.	❖ Vary length and complexity of sentences.	❖ Respond to directions for the assigned piece as a genre.
❖ Ask for help when needed.	❖ Effectively use standard conventions—sentence structure, usage, paragraphing, punctuation, spelling, and capital letters.	
❖ Use references and resources, including technology.	❖ Select and use words effectively.	
❖ Write to a known or unknown audience that is clearly defined.		
❖ Sometimes write on a focused topic or in a particular genre.		
❖ Select a purpose and genre for writing.		

Figure 27–10. Writing Workshop and Writing Test

Minilessons to Support Student Performance on Writing Tests	
Idea/Topic Development	❖ Planning for Writing (jotting, note taking, webbing, listing, brainstorming) ❖ Organizing Ideas for Writing ❖ Topic Focus and Development ❖ Use of Details to Support Topic ❖ Use of Examples ❖ Writing with Clarity ❖ Writing with Voice ❖ Language and Word Choice ❖ Genre—Fiction ❖ Genre—Nonfiction (description, comparison/contrast, sequence, problem/solution) ❖ Providing Evidence to Support Thinking ❖ Writing for Different Purposes, Audiences
Conventions	❖ Sentence Structure (correctness and variety) ❖ Paragraphing ❖ Spelling (patterns, word roots, relationship to meaning) ❖ Grammar and Usage ❖ Capitalization ❖ Punctuation ❖ Reference Skills (dictionary, thesaurus, technology)
Evaluation	❖ Understanding the Criteria for Evaluating Writing ❖ Questions to Ask Yourself About Writing ❖ Rubric for Evaluating Idea/Topic Development ❖ Rubric for Evaluating Conventions

Figure 27–11. Minilessons to Teach Test Writing Skills

Great Fire (Murphy 1995), an illustrated history of the great Chicago fire. It uncovers both the primary and secondary causes of this great event.

Peter read sections of the book aloud over several days and encouraged students to think about cause and effect in relation to the fire.

■ Peter read the introduction to the book. He then invited students to contribute to a cause and effect chart.

■ They made hypotheses about the possible causes; inevitably, some students drew on the old song about the O'Leary's cow. They listed causes in a web formation, with arrows leading to the fire.

■ As Peter read sections, he invited students to add causes to the list. Soon, they had a much longer list. It was evident that there were multiple causes.

■ Some students began to notice that there were many factors that, while they didn't cause the fire, contributed to its spread. Peter helped them categorize the factors as primary and secondary causes.

■ Finally, the group created the graphic representation shown in Figure 27–14.

Once students have learned how to make graphic representations and have many possible structures in their heads, they can work in small groups or in pairs to create these mental models. Discussing and sharing the

Doing Your Best Writing	
Ideas	❖ Did you give the readers an indication of your purpose for writing?
	❖ Did you organize your ideas in a way that the reader can understand?
	❖ Are your ideas easy to understand?
	❖ Did you limit your information to the topic?
	❖ Did you give enough details to support your idea or topic?
	❖ Did you give examples to help readers understand your ideas or topic?
	❖ Is your writing interesting to the audience you have identified (or the test asks for)?
Conventions	❖ Are all your sentences complete?
	❖ Did you use correct punctuation in every sentence?
	❖ Did you use different kinds of sentences?
	❖ Did you choose your words carefully to be sure that readers know what you mean?
	❖ Is the spelling correct?
	❖ Did you use capitals when needed?
	❖ Did you use correct grammar?
	❖ Did you use paragraphs?

Figure 27–12. Doing Your Best Writing

models can lead to rich discussion. Some steps in the process are:

1. Examine the text, noting headings, illustrations, and other visual features. Read the introduction.
2. Make some hypotheses about the organization of the text and think about graphic models that might fit, for example "problem/solution" or sequence.
3. Have students examine their background knowledge to think about how the model should be organized.
4. Create a "draft" visual model that represents thinking. As they learn about the technique, you can help students to focus their attention on one or two characteristics of text that you want them to notice.
5. Read the text, stopping at various points to compare the new information to the draft graphic representation. Make notes or adjustments to the model.
6. After reading the entire text, reflect on overall understanding of the text. Look at the draft model and revise it. What was left out? How should the organization be changed?
7. Complete the graphic model.
8. Use the graphic representation as a basis for discussion, oral reporting, and writing summaries of the text.

It is important to explicitly demonstrate the process of using graphic organizers to students before you expect them to do it in partners or small groups. *For every kind of model, do it yourself as a demonstration while you let them in on the thinking you are doing before, during and after reading.* Reading aloud is an ideal context for demonstrating these techniques. This kind of organization will be quite helpful to students in extracting and

Suggestions for Embedding Test-Writing Skills in Writing Workshop

1. Make sure students write several times daily.

2. Give students regular opportunities to write to a prompt as well as to self-select topics.

3. Provide numerous opportunities for timed writing.

4. Have students revise papers within time limits.

5. Teach a variety of planning techniques such as note taking, listing, and webbing.

6. Teach revision and proofreading and give students opportunities to apply these skills in timed sessions.

7. Teach students to edit in a short daily interactive session.

8. Present focused minilessons on writing for different purposes and audiences as well as writing in different genres.

9. Help students learn how to write about their reading.

10. Teach students how to read the prompt and the questions to understand the writing task and select the organizational pattern (graphic organizer) that will best suit an effective written response.

11. Teach students to use highlighters to mark key words in the prompt and the questions as well as pertinent information in the reading passage that will be important to the written response.

12. Teach students how to use the scoring checklist for writing and use it regularly.

13. Engage students in partner or small-group oral presentations on a topic followed by group feedback. Their ability to plan and present information on a topic orally is the same process required on a written test.

14. Engage students in partner or small-group writing, revision, and proofreading sessions. Include group sharing and feedback.

Figure 27–13. Suggestions for Embedding Test-Writing Skills in Writing Workshop

evaluating information, interpreting the text in terms of underlying structures, and creating summaries.

The kind of thinking that goes into creating visual representations like this supports students' comprehension, which will help them when they decode and respond to test questions. It will also help them organize their written responses.

General Guidelines for Working Across the Language/Literacy Framework

There are some overarching guidelines for helping students perform well on tests that apply from kindergarten through fifth and sixth grade:

■ Engage your students in reading, enjoying, and studying a wide range of genres, which ensures that students do not meet totally unfamiliar text structures on proficiency tests.

■ Emphasize poetry. Often poetry is relegated to a single "unit." Within the language and literacy framework, students read and write poetry weekly so they know how to recognize the forms of poetry and derive meaning from them.

■ Match books to readers. We cannot expect students to apply high-level strategies such as gathering information, inferring, summarizing, synthesizing, analyzing, and critiquing texts unless they can read the material. When we ask students to meet rigorous criteria for constructing and extending the meaning

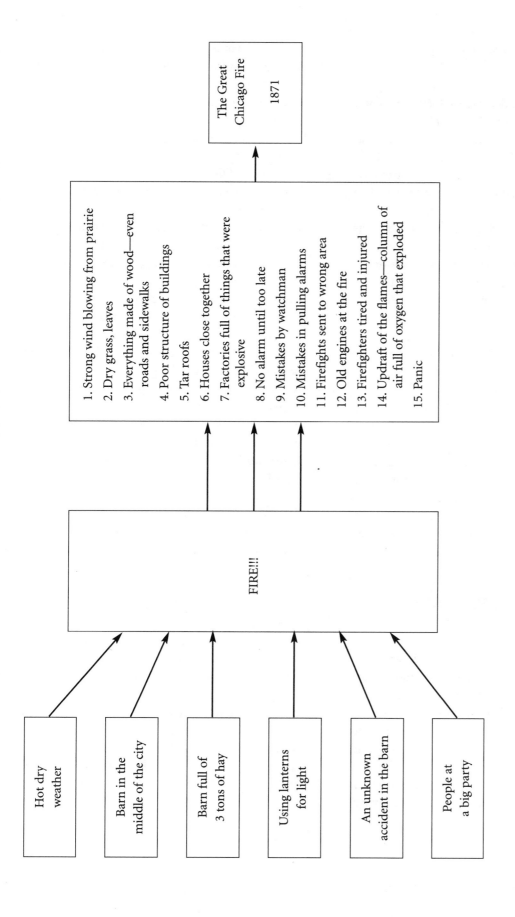

Figure 27–14. What Caused the Great Chicago Fire?

of texts, we must provide a learning arena that enables them to do so.

■ See that your students do a lot of reading and writing. Their success ultimately depends on their experience. If students have read carefully chosen texts and discussed them in the classroom, they will extend and refine the background they bring to the test. Similarly, the more they write and consider their writing in relation to well-grounded criteria, the better they will be able to perform on a timed writing test.

■ Prepare students for the language and expectations of the tests. In other words, let them in on the secrets. Teach them how to use the language of the test, such as *selection, evidence,* and *best tells.* Discuss how their responses to reading will be evaluated and allow them to participate in the process enough to be able to evaluate their own responses. Encourage students to consider how their writing will be evaluated so they can use these criteria daily.

In this chapter we have talked about test reading and test writing as a particular type of text with special demands of readers. Students need numerous opportunities to develop effective reading and writing skills; that is basic to a good education. When they have some specific instruction on the format and expectations of tests, they will have a better chance of successfully demonstrating their knowledge and skills in the highly demanding context of a standardized test.

Suggestions for Professional Development

1. Work with colleagues to conduct a thorough analysis of the demands of the tests your students are required to take. If you can, involve teachers from the primary grades. This information will be extremely helpful to them because you will want to develop "test taking" skills in an interesting and authentic way in the early grades.

2. Collect sample tests of various kinds from several grade levels. (Or, you can focus on one proficiency test.) Select typical items from each section of the test.

3. Working in small cross-grade-level groups or as a whole group, first answer the items for yourself (even if they are short/extended responses). Then analyze the knowledge base and processes that were required. What did you have to know as readers and writers? What thinking strategies were required to:

   ■ Understand the question?
   ■ Access information (in the text and from background) essential for the response?
   ■ Put the information into words or match it with words on multiple-choice questions?
   ■ Self-evaluate the answer for correctness, completeness, and clarity?

4. Keep a running list on chart paper of the kinds of questions you explore and what is required of readers. This list can then be reorganized as a developing "curriculum" for helping your students become more sophisticated in taking tests.

5. Compare the list of test-taking skills with your own language/literacy curriculum. Think about all the possible ways to embed practice on these skills in ongoing good instruction —through reading aloud, shared reading and writing, guided reading, and guided writing.

   ■ How can these skills be used in a way that is authentic?
   ■ How can these skills be fostered in a way that is interesting for students?
   ■ How can you help students see the purposes for these skills?

6. Use the list to plan some minilessons and practice sessions that are specifically designed to help students understand the genre of test taking.

7. Reorganize the list and copy it over so that the key ideas stand out clearly. You can place this list on the wall of your work room or meeting room and refer to it throughout the year. You'll find that you can add ideas to the chart as you work with students during assessment and as you have more experience with tests. You can also add a list of successful instructional techniques.

## CHAPTER TWENTY EIGHT

MAKING TEACHING DECISIONS USING CONTINUOUS ASSESSMENT

Teachers investigate learning, gathering evidence to illustrate not only that their students are learning, but what it is they are learning.

—KATHLEEN AND JIM STRICKLAND

Effective teaching begins with what we know about learners and their literacy. Because our continual observations of what students do as readers and writers provide the best evidence of learning. We need to collect, manage, summarize, communicate, and store this information. Standardized measures enter in, but we must focus on practical language/literacy assessment tools.

Assessment and Evaluation

Assessment and evaluation are related and complementary elements of the ongoing process of gathering and judging the evidence of students' learning. Although assessment and evaluation serve slightly different purposes within a quality language and literacy program, the two processes are inseparable.

Assessment

Assessment, which involves collecting information about or evidence of your students' learning, is a continual and integral part of quality teaching. In fact, teaching without continual assessment is akin to "teaching without the children."

As you gather evidence of students' learning, you continually summarize and reflect. Like researchers who make tentative hypotheses and revise them as they gather evidence, you build an ongoing picture of what students know so you can take them where they need to go next. These tentative judgments are based on several different kinds of evidence that you pull together informally as you teach. While you observe a student's reading, you notice his level of accuracy and reading fluency. You speak with him about the text, note how he talks with classmates about the text, and/or read something he has written about the text. Your analysis of multiple forms of this type of data informs your instruction every day, moment by moment.

Evaluation

At particular points in time, you "take stock" by pulling together your various data. You may examine the observational notes you've taken on your students' learning over time or administer some additional formal and systematic measures. The results will affect your daily teaching as well as your long-term plans for students' learning.

Evaluation means judging or placing a value on student performance: you create a picture of progress by comparing the characteristics of a student's performance with established criteria. As with assessment, *no single measure will give you all the answers you need*. It is also true that no one point in time provides a full picture; to evaluate students' progress with integrity, you need to identify starting points and notice steps along the way.

Balancing Instruction and Assessment

There's a delicate balance between assessment and instruction. You may feel as though you are doing so much testing you don't have time to teach—and your students don't have time to learn. In this period of intense accountability, we certainly recognize the challenge of juggling these dual demands.

Chapter 27 addresses student performance on standardized tests. When you consider other assessment measures, select those that are informative and can be embedded in instruction. Design a system that allows for easy, streamlined, and habitual record keeping to document students' progress in reading and writing.

Authentic Assessment

Designing a system that includes authentic assessment is one answer to the problem of balancing the time you spend teaching and testing. Authentic assessment involves students in activities that are the same or as close as possible to the "real life" tasks of readers and writers. Authentic assessment:

- Is continual.
- Informs teaching.
- Is integral to the curriculum.
- Is developmentally and culturally appropriate.
- Recognizes self-evaluation.
- Invites active collaboration. (Bridges 1995)

With authentic assessment you are not taking students' time away from reading and writing, because they continue to read and write while you collect data. Also, you are not losing instructional time because typically your instruction and assessment take place simultaneously. In independent reading, for example, you can listen to a student read aloud and then talk with him briefly about the text, pointing out something he didn't notice or showing him something about solving multisyllable words. You might record significant reading behavior, as well as the evidence of comprehension.

When you systematically observe students as they read and write every day, you are conducting authentic assessment. As noted in Chapter 27, you can even determine the underlying strategies that standardized proficiency tests require and find ways to help students use those strategies in more authentic ways during classroom instruction. By definition, classroom work is not totally authentic because the tasks are deliberately structured to help students learn more. You can, however, create a classroom environment that promotes authentic instruction. The same is true for assessment.

The Importance of an Integrated System for Assessment and Evaluation

When you create a system for assessment and evaluation, one process flows into another; one level is an integral part of the next. It is necessary to collect the data for ongoing assessment systematically so it can be summarized and used as part of your evaluation.

To streamline the process, collect only the assessment data that is truly useful, and keep only the data that you can summarize and use in evaluation. When you collect too much trivial information, the system becomes inefficient. Students' folders bulge but it's hard to find the information you need.

An efficient system also uses the same data at several levels. Some of the information you collect on individual performance can be compiled to help you plan for and evaluate class performance. You might note the level of texts that individual students can read and understand and thus create a profile of levels that members of your class are reading.

Also, some of the data that inform your teaching in the classroom can be used in schoolwide evaluation. Whenever possible, coordinate your assessment measures with colleagues to support the balance between assessment and instruction. For example, if you all agree that a certain reading level is the criterion for satisfactory performance at the end of the year, you can use classroom profiles to calculate how many students in your school can read at that level with accuracy, fluency, and understanding. Use that information when you are setting goals or analyzing the instructional program.

Figure 28–1 lists the purposes for evaluation at three levels: individual, classroom, and school. Think through your goals at each level. Data that can serve more than one level will help you streamline your work.

Involving Students in Assessment and Evaluation

By the time students enter third grade, they have built expectations for the demands of different types of texts. They have broadened their world through print and technology. They have developed their tastes, interests, and confidence as readers and writers. Intermediate students can work independently and manage their own learning. Accordingly, they can play a larger role in assessing their own progress—and it is essential that they do so.

Purposes for Evaluation at Three Levels

Individual	Class/Group	School
❖ Document individual students' progress over time. ❖ Make decisions about group placement and individual work with the student. ❖ Assign grades to selected performances. ❖ Report to parents on individual students' progress and achievements. ❖ Involve students in learning to assess their own progress and achievements.	❖ Document the progress of a group of students over a specific time period. ❖ Plan for instruction for the whole group, small groups, and individuals. ❖ Adjust the curriculum to meet the needs of the whole group and small groups. ❖ Help students become aware of criteria for good performance. ❖ Evaluate your teaching over a period of time by looking at specific student outcomes by group.	❖ Evaluate the effectiveness of the educational program in a school. ❖ Judge how well the program works for different groups of students (for example, economic, cultural, language and racial groups). ❖ Be accountable to district administrators and public officials. ❖ Indicate trends in achievement over time. ❖ Document educational improvement over time.

Figure 28–1. Purposes for Evaluation at Three Levels

One of the important goals of the intermediate-grade curriculum is self-evaluation. When students are part of the process, they are invested in success, inspired by their progress, and focused on their goals. They know what they have learned and where they need to go.

Acknowledging Cultural and Linguistic Diversity

Cultural and linguistic diversity is a strength of our society. However, while we recognize we must find ways to embrace and value diversity, our large-scale assessments are "standardized." The tests are meant to encourage teacher accountability and ensure success for all students, but they ignore individual strengths, the foundation for all future learning.

The language and format of many standardized techniques are culturally and linguistically biased (Figueroa 1989). Too often, students who do not speak English as a first language or who may simply misunderstand the testing format are inappropriately labeled "learning disabled." A disproportionate number of stu-

dents who are learning English as a second language are assigned to special education. To correct the bias in standardized tests, it is important to:

■ Work to understand what the test does and does not measure.

■ Analyze the demands of the test and consider those requirements in terms of your students' understanding.

■ Rely on multiple measures to ascertain exactly what your students know and can do.

■ Encourage ESL learners to use both their primary language and their target language as they interact with you around the assessment task.

■ Build "testlike" tasks into daily instruction, demonstrating, explaining, and discussing what students think they are meant to do.

■ Work cooperatively with parents to explain assessment.

■ In your assessment system include some measures that are congruent with your students' own culture, background, and/or language.

■ Be sure that assessment is continual and that you administer measures over time so your students' progress is revealed. (Cummins 1984)

Performance Assessment

Performance assessment means that you ask students to perform tasks, and then you compare their performance to specifically described standards of what students should know and how they should demonstrate their knowledge and skills. Additionally, you may have exemplars of student work against which you can measure your students' efforts (Falk 2000). An exemplar might be a sampling of written essays typical of each level or an audio- or videotape showing oral performances or visual arts.

Like criterion-referenced tests, performance assessments help you compare students' demonstrated competence with accepted levels, but the required tasks are generally closer to the real reading and writing students experience in the classroom. Sometimes you can implement performance assessment in a way that makes it quite unobtrusive, nearly invisible. Systematically collect samples of your students' ongoing writing and data from conferences or informal reading inventories. Then compare the samples to the standard criteria.

While good performance assessment guides you to examine aspects of process (such as reading behavior, accuracy, and level), the procedure focuses on a product. In addition to regular and systematic performance assessment, make sure you are also implementing more informal assessment (such as taking observational notes) that gives you insight into students' learning processes moment by moment, day by day.

Rubrics for Performance Assessment

A rubric is a scoring guide used to evaluate the quality of a student performance. Typically, rubrics list written criteria that describe the levels of proficiency on a task. The written descriptions define the task with great specificity and are a useful guide to proficiency. Rubrics may be holistic or segmented to measure components or traits of a process.

HOLISTIC SCORING
Holistic scales bring together identifiable characteristics of performance along a continuum from low to high

that typically spans four or five points. Performance, as a composite of characteristics, is described for each level of quality, from poor to excellent. The rater considers the cluster of characteristics for each level and matches the student's performance to the characteristics. Usually, an assessment team establishes exemplars that guide raters toward greater accuracy.

TRAIT ANALYSIS
Trait analysis allows you to compare students' performance along a continuum, but instead of using a single holistic rating, you look at individual, specific traits. For example, you might rate students' use of writing conventions along a continuum, from low to high, or you might rate the same writing sample for literary quality, organization, and content. The traits are defined by the rubric. Using rubrics in this way provides a rich, multidimensional view of reading and writing tasks. The rubric for written responses in Chapter 10 is one example.

Using Rubrics with Students

A rubric may be created for just about any kind of performance in which students engage. Some rubrics are for teacher use alone, but others are constructed with accessible language to help students understand the expectations for performance. Students can use rubrics to identify areas for improvement in self- or peer evaluations. The more they know about how rubrics work and what they mean, the better they will understand what constitutes a fine performance—and the greater their investment in producing winning results.

It is especially helpful if students help construct the rubrics. The process lets them analyze for themselves the criteria for good performance. They can help you construct rubrics for every kind of writing they do, thus "owning" these reminders of what they are striving for. Remind students that the language must be clear so they can understand exactly what is expected.

To assist students with their writing skills, Irene Hannigan and her colleagues developed rubrics with their students to establish the criteria for various types of writing. In helping their students develop the rubric shown in Figure 28–2, Irene and Linda Penniston followed these steps:

1. Students looked at a varied collection of reviews, which included professional book reviews, reviews from previous editions of a children's newspaper,

A Rubric for a Book Review

❖ 1	❖ 2	❖ 3	❖ 4
❖ No lead	❖ Dull lead "I read the book…"	❖ A good lead but nothing special	❖ Strong lead to capture reader's interest
❖ Main idea is often missing	❖ Main idea is hinted at but leaves the reader with questions	❖ Overview tells main idea of the book	❖ Overview clearly tells main idea of the book
❖ Few details	❖ Too many unimportant details. May be repetitious	❖ Important details are given for the most part	❖ Important details are given
❖ May fail to give opinion	❖ Minimal support for opinion ("I love the book because I love pandas.")	❖ Opinion is supported by a few reasons	❖ Opinion is supported by convincing reasons
❖ No conclusion	❖ Weak conclusion ("If you want to know what happens, read the book.")	❖ Has an ending sentence	❖ Has an effective conclusion
❖ Unconnected ideas	❖ Not clear how ideas are related; "jerky"	❖ Generally smooth connections between ideas	❖ Nice flow of ideas— one sentence leads to the next
❖ Mechanical errors seriously interfere with communication, lack of attention to spelling, punctuation, capitalization, and paragraphing	❖ Errors in spelling, punctuation, capitalization, paragraphing are distracting	❖ Reasonably competent spelling, punctuation, capitalization, paragraphing, and usage	❖ Correct spelling, punctuation, capitalization, and paragraphing

Figure 28–2. A Rubric for a Book Review

and reviews written by former students (with the names deleted).

2. Students listed the criteria for a good book review. As they considered the finished product, they listed the essentials of a strong review as well as the attributes that characterize the truly outstanding review.

3. They defined the specific traits that would be important to evaluate. The students agreed that a strong book review might score high on use of details, but low on another trait. They settled on seven traits in all.

4. They began to describe the levels of quality, one trait at a time. They articulated a description of quality for each trait from 1 (low) to 4 (high) and selected examples that fit each level. They continued to discuss what makes a book review "good" relative to a specific trait.

5. They tried the rubric with several more sample book reviews to see whether their definitions and examples were clear.
6. They revised their descriptions.
7. They used the rubric for self- and peer assessment. They also used the rubric to revise their book reviews.

Assessment and Evaluation of Reading

Because reading is a process rather than a product, we cannot truly assess students' reading ability unless we know something about how they are processing text and deriving meaning. For older students most of the processing is "underground." Students are reading silently, and we do not know precisely what is going on in their head. Our ways of measuring reading are limited to what we observe when students read aloud (which, admittedly, qualitatively alters the reader's processing of text), what they say or write after reading, and what they say or write about the way they read.

To think about reading assessment, we need to consider what we can assess. Five kinds of indicators serve as evidence of learning:

1. Fluent processing: the degree to which students read with accuracy, ease, and fluency.
2. Comprehension: the degree to which students understand the texts they read with accuracy, ease, and fluency.
3. Amounts, type, and quality of reading: the amount of reading students do as well as the range of genres they read.
4. Level of text: the level of difficulty at which students can read with accuracy, ease, and fluency.
5. Attitudes and interests: how students view themselves as readers and the extent to which they are positive about reading.
6. Response to literature: how students respond personally to texts they read.

Observing Processes

We learn about students' processing strategies by observing oral reading behavior. As you listen to students read, you record the rate of reading and the accuracy level; judge the fluency; and note behavior that indicates they are using meaning, language structure or syntax, and visual information. There are several ways to record this information for your analysis.

READING WORDS

While the best measure of students' ability is to observe them while reading continuous text, you can also learn much about their word-solving strategies by having them read individual words. Certainly students should be able to recognize frequently encountered words (Appendix 4) automatically and unconsciously. You can create your own informal assessments to detect whether students can recognize and/or pronounce words in isolation.

You can also create inventories that will provide information about their knowledge of vocabulary. To begin:

1. Create a list of words. Use a graded list (see Dale and O'Rourke 1976), take words from a basal series, or pull words from content areas.
2. Ask the student to read each word, use it in a sentence, explain the meaning, or provide a synonym or antonym. For a written test, you can have them match words with meanings, synonyms, or antonyms or provide multiple-choice answers.
3. Look at the results. What do students know about words? What kinds of connections do they make? What can you learn from partially correct responses? The answers will help you plan your word study program and inform your work with students in guided and independent reading.

Keep in mind that there are many ways of knowing words, and any test of words in isolation can only provide limited information.

INFORMAL READING INVENTORIES

An informal reading inventory helps you measure accuracy rate, reading rate, and fluency as students read orally. To begin, you ask students to read two or three selections at grade level, substituting harder or easier selections as their performances warrant. They may read one or two selections silently and one or two orally, or the first reading may be silent and the second oral. During oral reading, record their errors (deviations from print) and determine the percentage of words read accurately. Analyzing the errors lets you identify areas for teaching. Let's look at a few examples:

■ If a student reads *hurry* for *harassed* and continues without noticing or self-correcting, he has sampled visual information but not checked to be sure that the attempt made sense and sounded right. You may want to prompt him to notice and analyze more of the visual information as well as monitor his reading more closely using multiple kinds of information.

■ The text says, "I let them lift me, wash me, feed me; but my eyes stayed closed while I waited for the next unspeakable thing, not knowing what it would be, or how it would come, but certain that it would happen and that I would not be able to keep it away" (Lowry 1980, p. 180). The student reads, "I let them lift me, wash me, feed me; but my eyes stayed closed while I waited for the next *un*—the next *instead* thing, [pause] not knowing what it would be, or how it would come, but *certainly* it would *have, happen* and that I would not be able to keep it away." This student has missed only two words in the sentence (unspeakable and certainly), and has shown some evidence of processing by noticing the first part of *unspeakable* and making an attempt to solve it. The substitution, *instead,* does not really make sense, and the pause following that attempt may indicate he's aware that it doesn't. The student also made a first attempt at *happen,* producing a verb that partially fit visually and syntactically in the sentence. Noticing further visual information, however, he self-corrected. Be sure to note how your students use meaning to solve words. In addition, show them how to break longer, multisyllable words into their component parts, another valuable word-solving strategy.

Informal reading inventories are available commercially. You can also construct your own using any gradient of text, including the one presented in this book. Simply reproduce a page or pages of the text to be read. Enlarge the text to leave room for coding, or retype it, leaving spaces between lines. To use it, sit beside the reader and ask him to read it without assistance. Give him words only if you must or after you have given enough wait time. On your copy, code the reader's errors as he reads. We have shown an example of a coding system that is consistent with running record coding (Clay 1991). The coding system used in Figure 28–3 is one possibility, but you can easily devise your own. (If you are working with colleagues on a standard reading portfolio, make sure you all use the same codes.)

To determine accuracy, count the errors and subtract that number from the total number of words in the passage to arrive at the number of words read correctly. Divide the number of words read correctly by the number of words in the passage. The resulting percentage is the accuracy rate. To determine the reading rate, time the reading and divide the number of words in the passage by the time it took to read it (words per minute.) See Chapter 18 and later in this chapter for further discussion of rate. We describe assessment of fluency later in this chapter.

MISCUE ANALYSIS

Miscue analysis was devised by Kenneth Goodman (1982) and developed by other researchers (Goodman, Watson, and Burke 1987) as a professional development and assessment tool. It provides an in-depth analysis of a student's reading behavior and text processing, yielding specific information about that student's reading ability and also helps you to add to your own knowledge of the reading process.

After an introductory interview with the reader, you audiotape his oral reading and then ask him to close the book and retell the story. Later, you listen to the tape, note and record miscues, and then analyze them in detail. For each miscue, you think about (and code) whether it is:

■ Semantically acceptable (the word fits with the meaning).
■ Syntactically acceptable (the word is the same part of speech and/or the sentence has been transformed in some way to be syntactically correct).
■ Graphically similar (the word is visually or phonetically close to the accurate word).

This analysis helps you recognize the kinds of information the reader is using to process the text. It also allows you to look for patterns in the reading, such as how the reader is using visual information.

Miscue analysis allows you to trace a reader's progress over time so you can create a profile of growth. Miscue analysis is widely used in clinical settings where teachers are working with struggling readers. The more you know about what students are attending to as they read—and how they are specifically processing text—the more you can craft instruction that will help them improve. Retrospective miscue

Coding Reading Behaviors

Behavior	Code shown with error
Accurate Reading	✓ ✓ ✓ ✓ ✓ ✓ ✓ ✓ ✓ The giant's heavily loaded cart rumbled to a halt.
Substitution	✓ ✓ <u>heavy</u> ✓ ✓ ✓ ✓ ✓ ✓ The giant's heavily loaded cart rumbled to a halt.
Self-correction	✓ ✓ <u>heavy |SC</u> ✓ ✓ ✓ ✓ ✓ ✓ The giant's heavily loaded cart rumbled to a halt.
Repetition	✓ ✓ ✓ ✓ R ✓ ✓ ✓ ✓ ✓ ✓ The giant's heavily loaded cart rumbled to a halt.
Repetition with self-correction	✓ ✓ <u>heavy |R |SC</u> ✓ ✓ ✓ ✓ ✓ ✓ The giant's heavily loaded cart rumbled to a halt.
Omission	✓ ✓ ——— ✓ ✓ ✓ ✓ ✓ ✓ The giant's heavily loaded cart rumbled to a halt.
Insertion	✓ ✓ ✓ ✓<u>wood</u>✓ ✓ ✓ ✓ ✓ The giant's heavily loaded cart rumbled to a halt.
Long Pause	✓ ✓ ✓ # ✓ ✓ ✓ ✓ ✓ ✓ The giant's heavily loaded cart rumbled to a halt.
Told	✓ ✓ ——— T ✓ ✓ ✓ ✓ ✓ ✓ The giant's heavily |T loaded cart rumbled to a halt.

Figure 28–3. Coding Reading Behaviors

analysis is one way to encourage students to think about their own processing. Conduct the miscue analysis as usual, but then you discuss with the student whether the miscues made sense or should have been corrected. Some researchers have found that retrospective miscue analysis helps students, especially those who are having difficulties, understand themselves better as readers. It also makes reading less of a "mystery" (Strickland and Strickland 2000).

RUNNING RECORDS

The running record is a method designed by Marie Clay (1993) to analyze students' oral reading for processing strategies. A running record may be taken on any text the child is reading. Typically, the teacher uses a blank form and records reading by looking at the text and entering a √ for every word read accurately and codes for other miscues (see Figure 28–3). It is not necessary to tape the reading. Do the coding and analysis while the child reads. Later, reflect on the performance later and look for patterns in the codes.

Accuracy is one indicator of the difficulty of the text, and you calculate the accuracy rate as part of the running record. You also code and analyze reading behaviors to determine the likely sources of information from which students are drawing. The running record is a particularly powerful tool for recording the behavior of your struggling readers and helping you choose texts that will let them develop appropriate strategies.

CHECKLISTS

Checklists provide a frame of reference for the observational data you collect. List observable behaviors relative to various stages of development, and organize these into checklists to be used at specified points in time. Checklists may be specific to your instructional plans or can be used to determine student grades. In general, though, you should use them to refine your knowledge of a reader so you can determine the next teaching step.

(A caveat: checklists may constrain and limit your thinking about a student's behavior. If you use checklists, be sure to leave blank space on the form where you can capture your own insightful observations.) Also remember that often categories mean something different to each observer.

ASSESSMENT OF FLUENCY

Although we all think we know fluent oral reading when we hear it, there is no single acceptable definition of fluency in the research literature. Fluent reading no doubt involves rapidly and automatically recognizing or decoding words, but that is certainly not the whole story. Fluency also requires readers to use language systems; it is not necessarily "fast," although it should move along at a good pace. Fluency is evidence that the reader is accessing the deeper meaning of the text. It is associated with rate, accuracy, and scores on comprehension tests (Pinnell et al. 1995).

Figure 28–4 depicts a reliable scale for assessing

NAEP's Integrated Reading Performance Record **Oral Reading Fluency Scale[1]**	
Level 4	Reads primarily in large, meaningful phrase groups. Although some regressions, repetitions, and deviations from text may be present, these do not appear to detract from the overall structure of the story. Preservation of the author's syntax is consistent. Some or most of the story is read with expressive interpretation.
Level 3	Reads primarily in three- or four-word phrase groups. Some smaller groupings may be present. However, the majority of phrasing seems appropriate and preserves the syntax of the author. Little or no expressive interpretation is present.
Level 2	Reads primarily in two-word phrases with some three- or four-word groupings. Some word-by-word reading may be present. Word groupings may seem awkward and unrelated to larger context of sentence or passage.
Level 1	Reads primarily word by word. Occasional two-word or three-word phrases may occur—but these are infrequent and/or they do not preserve meaningful syntax.

Figure 28–4.   NAEP's Scale for Assessing Oral Reading Fluency

[1]Reprinted with permission from Pinnell, G.S., Pikulski, J.J., Wixson, K.K., Campbell, J.R., Gough, P.B., & Beatty, A.S. 1995. *Listening to Children Read Aloud: Data from NAEP's Integrated Reading Performance Record (IRPR) at Grade 4*. Report NO. 23-FR-04   Prepared by Educational Testing Service under contract with the National Center for Education Statistics, Office of Educational Research and Improvement, U.S. Department of Education. (p. 15) Permission: Education Information Branch, Office of Educational Research and Improvement, U.S. Department of Education, 555 New Jersey Avenue, NW, Washington, D.C. 20208-5641. 1-800-424-16167; IBSN: 0-88685-167-X; Educational Testing Service.

oral reading fluency. (Although it was constructed to use with fourth graders, it can be used in grades 3, 5, and 6 as well.) It was developed by a research team who listened to a large number of tapes of students reading with high accuracy. They identified several key elements of accurate oral reading:

1. Readers' phrasing, or grouping of words, as evident through intonation, stress, and pauses. Readers emphasize the beginnings and endings of phrases by rise and fall of pitch or by pausing.
2. Students adhere to the author's syntax or sentence structure, reflecting their comprehension.
3. Readers are expressive; their reading reflects feeling, anticipation, and character development.

Accuracy is not part of this fluency scale because the researchers were assessing the performance of students who were reading texts at an appropriate level (from 90 to 100 percent accuracy). We can judge whether a reader can read fluently only if the text is within the right range of difficulty. However, halting, slow reading, even at high levels of accuracy, is not good reading.

Perfect accuracy is not necessary. All readers, even the most fluent, make some errors as they read. Of course, readers who deviate significantly from the printed words will have difficulty making sense of their reading and will not read fluently. Similarly, readers who have to stop often to solve words will not score as high as readers who handle most of the words quickly and automatically, but speed is only considered as it contributes to the reader's ability to read in phrase units and reproduce the author's syntax.

You can use the fluency scale whenever you listen to a student reading aloud; just don't apply it if the material is too hard. The fluency scale can be a part of informal reading inventories as well as miscue analysis and running records. If students aren't reading with fluency, first check to be sure the concepts in the text are clear to them and that they can read with 90 to 100 percent accuracy. Find easier texts if needed.

Stilted reading often indicates that the student needs to work on fluency. Encourage students to read together, engage in shared reading of short texts or poems, or perform in readers theater. Model fluent reading and provide books on tape so students hear what fluent reading is supposed to sound like. You can also ask students to reflect on their own fluency, using a rubric that is written in words they understand.

While rate or *speed* of reading is seen as an important factor related to understanding and fluency, it is difficult to be specific about what a "good" reading rate really is. After all, speed varies greatly by the individual's purpose, the context for reading, and the difficulty of the material for a particular reader. While 206 words per minute has been reported as median performance for sixth graders, Pikulski (1988) found only 81 words per minute for oral reading and 116 words per minute for silent reading in a study of high-achieving sixth graders.

In a study of fourth graders' oral reading of narrative text, researchers (Pinnell, et al. 1995) found that 64 percent of the students read at 124 words per minute or slower; however, students who read at 130 words per minute or higher had the highest average proficiency scores on the NAEP Integrated Reading Performance. In Figure 28-5 we recommend general goals for reading rates both silent and oral, for students reading at instructional levels J through Y, or approximate grade levels of two through six.

Assessing Comprehension

Comprehension is the degree to which students understand the texts they can read with accuracy, ease, and fluency. There are a variety of ways to assess whether students understand what they read. One of the most important indicators is fluent reading. Day after day, gather evidence of their understanding by:

■ Observing how students talk with one another about texts.
■ Examining the kinds of questions they ask about texts.
■ Looking at what they write about texts.

Rate of Reading		
Current Instructional Level	**Oral Reading Rate**	**Silent Reading Rate**
Levels H–M	75–100	75–100
Levels L–P	100–124	115–140
Levels O–T	115–140	130–175
Levels S–W	125–150	160–200
Levels V–Y	135–170	185–225

Figure 28–5. General Goals for Rate of Reading

- Engaging them in analysis and critique of texts.
- Observing pitch, stress, pausing, phrasing, smoothness and rate.

Comprehension is best revealed in the conversations you have every day with students about what they read. Within the natural flow of a reading conference or a group conversation, you can ask questions, offer and elicit responses, and talk over the material. Analyze their responses to be sure they understand. Keep anecdotal records during reading conferences (as described in Chapter 8) as ongoing evidence.

You can also ask students whether they comprehended a text. Ask them to explain their understanding. If this is not a test and if you have won their trust, they will answer honestly and reveal what they found confusing. In addition to this informal assessment, there are several ways to collect additional information that shows comprehension.

Observing Think Alouds

This procedure requires students to stop at points in their reading and talk about what they are doing and understanding as readers. This technique offers you information about both processing and comprehension. Readers talk about skipping text, rereading, searching back in the text for information, predicting, and visualizing. They also report the feelings and understandings they experience as they read a particular text. Students may also sketch their understandings, or use cutouts of symbols to represent their understanding and thoughts, a process that may facilitate talk (Enciso 1990).

Prompting Retellings

Retelling is a standard part of miscue analysis, and is widely used to collect evidence of comprehension after reading. After the student finishes reading out loud, ask him to tell you about the text. You may also use questions to probe for information the reader understood but did not state. Record the retelling and analyze it with a rubric that assesses the extent to which the reader includes detail, demonstrates attention to sequence, and makes sense of the text in general. (You can create your own rubrics for assessing students' retellings. Collect multiple retelling samples, order them by the degree to which students demonstrate comprehension, and use them as exemplars for future retellings you conduct with other students.)

There are, however, many limitations to the information you get from retellings:

- The situation is artificial. Under normal circumstances, you would not have the reader repeat the story information unless you weren't paying attention. You will need to tell students that they are explicitly demonstrating (as in a test) what they understood and remember about the text.
- Retelling depends on memory. If they know they will need to "retell," students may read quite differently—paying less attention to the overarching concept, feelings, or the main idea, and focusing instead on details.
- Repeating the text verbatim is not the same as summarizing or synthesizing the text. To summarize and synthesize, you must select information and put it together in a logical way that stays true to the story.
- Retelling is a learned task. You can teach students to retell and it may not mean they understood the story.

If you keep these limitations in mind, retelling can be one way to gather data about the kind of information students have noticed while reading a text.

Consulting Reader's Notebooks

Using reader's notebooks, as described in Chapter 10, helps students reflect on their reading. At the same time, these notebooks provide evidence of how students have understood texts. Reader's notebooks are often the basis for students' talk with one another and the entire group, so they stimulate further discussion that provides more information on comprehension. The written responses provide rich evidence of understanding and response.

Administering Cloze Tests

The cloze procedure, as described in Chapter 26, is used to test students on the level of text they can read and understand. Take a passage (about three hundred words long) that is at a general reading level for students and systematically delete every fifth word. Replace the words with underlines that are all the same length so that the reader cannot use the length of the blank space to guess the deleted word. Ask students to read the passage orally as you write their guesses in the blank. Score the cloze test by determining the percentage of words guessed accurately. (Only an exact match counts as correct, but you will of course take note of synonyms as well as of the way their substitutions preserve the syntax of the passage.) A score of above 85 percent is an independent reading level; 50 to 84 percent is an instructional level; below 49 percent is a frustration level.

Assessing the Amount, Kind of, and Quality of Reading

READING LIST

As we described in Chapter 9, students use a reading list glued in their reader's notebooks to keep records of the books read. Scanning this list will provide good information about the quantity, breadth, and difficulty level of reading students do. Work with them to examine their choices as readers and develop a plan to expand their reading expertise. This list is a rich assessment tool.

Assessing the Level of Text Reading

RECORD OF BOOK READING PROGRESS

You will want to keep a record of the level of text that students can read. This of course will include how the reader's processing of increasingly challenging texts changes over time.

A simple way is to note the students' reading level at regular intervals (see Figure 28–6 and the reproducible form in Appendix 51). To begin, invite the student to read a text or a section of a text silently. You can use the book that the student is reading for guided or independent reading or a special set of books that you have designated for assessment (see the discussion on benchmark books, below). Ask the student to read the same selection orally, and note the errors, using the techniques described for informal reading inventories or running records. You can also note whether the student understood the text at a satisfactory level by using any of the techniques described for comprehension.

Record the student's instructional level with an open circle if the level is instructional or easy (90% or better). Place a filled-in circle if the text is providing difficulty (accuracy is below 90% and/or understanding and fluency is not adequate). The student's text level at the start of the school year can be determined by coding behavior on an informal reading inventory or benchmark books. This will be important for beginning guided reading groups. Throughout the year, you and your colleagues can decide what will be appropriate regular intervals for recording

text levels at your particular grade level. You can decide on formal assessment as just described, or you may decide to record the guided reading level from informal observation in guided reading groups as the measure for marking the record of book-reading progress. The form can be kept in your reading binder for ongoing documentation and passed to the next year's teacher in the student's literacy file. We provide an alternative form in *Leveled Books for Readers, Grades 3–6* (Pinnell and Fountas 2001).

As an example of ongoing documentation of the text level, see the record of book-reading progress in Figure 28–6. It tells us that Alicia began third grade reading at level K, which is slightly below grade level as defined by the standards adopted by the district. It also appears that level K was too difficult for her. During the year, Alicia took part in guided reading almost every day, and she read a large number of books. Her record shows steady progress, with leaps in level in December, February, and June. She finished the year at a satisfactory level for her grade.

CONFERENCES WITH BENCHMARK BOOKS

Another option for gathering a greater range of assessment information is to select short stories and other short texts such as informational books or picture books to use in conference-based assessment. Invite a student to have a pre-conference in which you introduce the text and give directions to the student to read it silently, to write a response as directed on the conference protocol, and then to have a short conference with you to discuss the reading and writing.

As a follow-up, have a conference with the student to discuss the text, review the written response and listen to the student read orally while you code the reading behavior for analysis. The discussion questions require the reader to provide information that can be found in the text (T) and to go beyond the text (BT). You have a typed passage of about 150–250 words on which you code the oral reading and analyze the processing strategies. The conference might also include a discussion of the written response and of general questions about the student's self-perception as a reader. (See conference protocol example in Figure 28-7.)

Some teachers standardize the text level assessment by establishing a set of "benchmark" texts. A benchmark text is stable for the level and highly reliable; that is, the passage will be appropriate for the large majority of the students who are demonstrating similar behaviors at a certain point in time. Accuracy is part of the picture. The

Record of Book Reading Progress

Name **Alicia**   Grades ✓ 3 ___ 4 ___ 5 ___ 6

Title of Text, Accuracy Rate, SC Rate (○ = above 90%; ● = below 90%)

Book Level	Nate the Great 80% Tardy Tortoise 1:8	Frog and Toad Are Friends 97% 1:2	Cam Jansen – Mystery Haunted 100% nil	Pinky and Rex Spelling Bee 96% 1:2	What's Cooking Jenny Archer 100% 1:1	Matt Christopher Man out at First 97% 1:2	Boundless Grace 94% 1:2	Shoeshine Girl 97% 1:2
Z								
Y								
X								
W								
V								
U								
T								
S								
R								
Q								
P								
O								
N								○
M					○	○	○	
L			○	○				
K	●	○						
J								
I								
H								
G								
F								
E								
D								
C								
B								
A								
DATE	9/13	10/20	12/9	1/12	2/28	3/21	5/18	6/1

Figure 28-6. Sample Record of Book-Reading Progress

tain point in time. Accuracy is part of the picture. The foundation of reading at any level or in any genre is being able to process the print with an acceptable level of accuracy. Accuracy seems to be a *contingent* factor, meaning that it is necessary *but not sufficient* for comprehension. We all know that sometimes students can say the words but not understand what they read; but they certainly can't understand if they can't read the words.

Establish your benchmarks by selecting three or four typical texts at each level on the gradient. (You might want to include both fiction and nonfiction.) Select passages that are about 250 words. (Short stories and short informational texts make effective benchmarks.) It is important not to cut off the text mid-sentence or at some place that will destroy the meaning, so you will want to be flexible here. It is the percentage that matters. Either photocopy the pages, or better, prepare forms that have the passages typed, with space between lines and space in the margins in which to write notes about fluency and indicate any other comments. Place the books in a sealable plastic bag and the conference protocols in a binder or a set of pocket folders and you are ready to gather a significant amount of information about the student as a reader.

Assessing Interests and Attitudes

Examining students' reading interests and attitudes is an important part of assessing their reading progress. We all have too many students who *can* read but *don't*. They read what they must to complete assignments but seldom choose to read anything extra. As a result, their reading is limited. These students will not build the text background they need to deeply comprehend complex texts.

Earlier, we discussed the use of reading and writing questionnaires to gather important information about your students as readers and writers You can use these forms as is, modify them, or use them as guides for face-to-face interviews. You may also interview or survey parents to gain more information about what the students are interested in and how they feel about reading.

Assessing Response to Literature

Response to literature is both emotional and intellectual. It typically includes feelings evoked by the text, interpretation of ideas, and empathic identification with characters and events. Personal response to literature is quite difficult to assess. You will need to look across these sources of information:

- Students' writing about reading in their response journals.
- Your observation of literature discussions.
- Your observation of text reading in guided reading groups.
- Conferences with students about books they are reading.
- Writing projects that incorporate literature.

Rely on procedures that you can use regularly and systematically, and plan your follow-up instruction as you evaluate what you find out.

Assessment and Evaluation in Writing

Assessment in writing generally focuses on the following key factors:

- Conventions of grammar, capitalization, punctuation and spelling.
- Spelling.
- Organization and development of ideas.
- The writer's craft—voice, word choice, use of language.
- The student's interests and attitudes toward writing.

Some ways to gather evidence about students' ability in these categories are rubrics, spelling tests, writing records, and writing checklists.

Rubrics

Rubrics are especially helpful in assessing students' writing. Generally, writing rubrics include two levels or kinds of assessment:

1. *Content,* which includes the organization of the text and aspects of the writer's craft.
2. *Conventions,* which include spelling, sentence structure, capitalization, punctuation, and the like.

Rubrics usually have a three-, four-, or five-point scale. At the classroom, school, and district levels, you can use one of many published rubrics, modify a rubric, or create your own to include the characteristics of writing you want to assess such as the book review rubric we described earlier. Work with colleagues to create your own rubrics based on your agreed-upon criteria for quality writing; this helps you develop

Conference Protocol Example

Conference Protocol: Level R: (Fiction)
Slower Than the Rest" from *Every Living Thing* by Cynthia Rylant

Text Introduction
This story is about Leo, a fifth grader, and Charlie, the turtle he finds. As you read, you will find that Leo and Charlie have some characteristics in common.

Instructions
Silently read the story *Slower Than the Rest* on pages 1–7. After you are finished, write a paragraph describing how Charlie helped Leo to change.

When we meet again, I will ask you to talk to me about what you wrote and to share your thinking about what you read. As we talk about this book, I may also have a few questions to ask you.

[When the student returns, have him/her read the response aloud and discuss it. Prompt the child to share his/her thinking further. During the discussion, place a (+) next to any of the questions listed below that the child answers while sharing his/her thinking. Ask any of the questions that have not been answered, and mark a (+) or (-) next to each one. Transfer this information to the data sheet.]

Discussion Questions [Answers]
[Accept reasonable answers that the student accurately supports with evidence from the text. Questions requiring more than one answer will be so noted.]

T1. How did Charlie become Leo's pet turtle?
  [Leo found Charlie on the highway on his way to church with his family.]

BT2. Describe how Charlie and Leo were alike.
  [People thought that they were both slow. They were both interested in the world.]

T3. What was Leo's class assigned to do for prevent Forest Fires Week at school?
  [They were assigned to write a report dealing with forests.]

BT4. Why did Leo keep Charlie's box closed tight on his way to school?
  [He didn't want other children to see Charlie before he gave his report. He wanted to keep Charlie safe.]

BT5. Why do you think Leo won the award for his report?
  [He shared a lot of important information. He explained how animals like turtles would not be able to escape a fire because they are slow. He explained things clearly and with the emotion that he felt. He made people "love turtles and hate forest fires."]

BT6. How do you think Leo changed form the beginning of the story to end?
  [Leo felt "slow" in the beginning and at the end he felt "fast." At the beginning, he believed that he was slow and couldn't succeed, but at the end, he had more self-confidence and believed that he was smart. He was happy at the end and unhappy at the very beginning.]

Figure 28–7. Conference Protocol Example

greater insights into the process of writing. Most important, internalize the characteristics of writing in each category so you not only use the rubric for assessment but teach toward it every day.

Many districts and states have instituted a "standardized" writing assessment. They design standard conditions under which students produce writing, and they use anonymous raters to evaluate the writing. The writing is often evaluated holistically, using broad categories. By prescribing the conditions of the task and conducting the assessment under standard conditions, a district can compare scores across classes and schools. A standardized writing assessment, however, cannot take the place of one you carry out in your own classroom.

Spelling Tests

Spelling tests provide a measure of a student's conventional spelling and are ubiquitous in elementary schools. Of course, spelling individual words correctly is not enough. The real measure is the students' accurate spelling in writing projects. Parents often expect spelling tests, and you may depend on these tests as one indicator grade in spelling and/or the language arts. The best spelling tests enable students to set and achieve meaningful goals and enable you to determine what your students need in the way of spelling instruction.

Frequently Used Words

An easy first action is to assess your students' knowledge of the five hundred frequently used words and spelling demons (Appendix 4). It is very important that students know these words so they can write them quickly and automatically by the end of fourth grade. In many schools, this list is first assessed (in a few spelling tests) in second or third grade; words students know are highlighted. The list is passed along in the students' folder from grade to grade. Students can use the list as a resource for placing words on their "Words to Learn" list, which is part of a "buddy study" system (see Chapter 3 and Pinnell and Fountas 1998).

Developmental Spelling Analysis

To plan your spelling instruction, it is necessary to learn what students know about words and how they work. The Developmental Spelling Assessment (DSA) (Ganske 2000) is designed to help teachers identify children's strengths and needs as spellers and to make hypotheses about their levels of development. Based on Henderson's

(1990) stages of spelling development, the DSA series includes a screening inventory and two feature inventories.

You use the screening inventory to identify a child's most likely stage of development. You dictate twenty words, grouped in sets of five, and the student writes them. The groups of words become increasingly more difficult and represent phases of development. Once screening is completed, you use the two feature inventories, which are parallel forms, to gather more information about what children specifically understand about words. These feature inventories are intended to be used flexibly; Ganske has outlined "brief" and more comprehensive alternatives. The main value of the DSA series is that it allows you to discover what kinds of spelling patterns students are aware of and can represent; you can use this information to plan minilessons as well as for ongoing assessment of progress.

Writing Records

As an integral part of your writing program, your students will do many kinds of writing that you can also use for assessment.

WRITER'S NOTEBOOK

Look at samples from writer's notebooks to determine how your students are collecting and expanding upon ideas, how they are using language, literary techniques, genres, and creative ideas and to trace how they develop their ideas into writing projects. The writer's notebook also provides a rough idea of the amount of writing that students are producing; indeed, how frequently and consistently they use their notebook is one factor to consider in grading.

WRITING PROJECTS

Students will store their final drafts in the hanging file together with drafts from previous stages. You can assess the quality of the final draft for content and conventions, but the evolution of students' writing—evident in their first and subsequent drafts—also offers rich assessment data. You will want to notice revision strategies and look particularly at the self-edited draft to discover what students know about spelling and other conventions.

Writing Checklists

As with reading, you can create and use writing checklists to guide your assessment of students' writing. Many districts use broad checklists as part of grading. You can use checklists to guide discussion during writing conferences and streamline your record keeping. You can also construct checklists that help you analyze the strengths of student writing.

Checklists may incorporate aspects similar to rubrics, but you use them in a different way. You can use a checklist to evaluate one piece of writing, simply marking off characteristics rather than rating the entire piece, or you can use the list to make general judgments about the writer's progress. The problem with using checklists is that they may limit your focus and the items on the checklist often mean something different to each person who uses it. A good checklist should help you think carefully about students' writing. Make sure you leave room for comments, and jot down observations the checklist doesn't include.

Amount and Type of Writing

The students' writing folders, as described in Chapter 5, contain a form that lists the writing projects students tackled throughout the year (Appendix 5) and a list of types of writing (Appendix 7). You can analyze the projects on this form to determine the amount and kind of writing each student has undertaken. As with reading, involve students in your analysis throughout the year so they become aware of their breadth as writers.

Examining the writing projects for your entire class over a given period will also provide valuable information about your writing program. You may find that students need more support to become interested in or learn how to write in a certain genre.

Student Reflection and Attitudes Toward Writing

Another form in the writing folder is used by students to note what they have learned from each piece they've written (Appendix 6). These documents also reveal the insights that guide their own lives as writers. The writing interview (Appendix 47) is yet another way to determine your students' ideas and attitudes toward writing.

The Literacy Portfolio

Portfolios are a popular way to present students' work over time so that progress is evident. Many of the assessments described in this chapter can be part of a writing

portfolio. The goal is to guide the process carefully so portfolios don't become unwieldy and time-consuming collections of "stuff" that no one examines or uses to inform teaching.

What Are Portfolios?

A portfolio, by definition, is a carefully selected sample of a student's work. Some schools create portfolio systems that span grade levels. One school, for example, has instituted a folder of "Best Literacy Works" that follows the student through each grade. Each year, the student adds one writing sample, a record of books read, and comments for his next teacher. Guidelines for selection and reflection are printed right on the folder. This record is compact and serves as a tangible record of progress that parents can keep when the student leaves the school.

You will want to consider several questions when using portfolios:

■ What do you select for the portfolio?
■ What do you pass on to the next teacher at the end of the year?
■ How do you involve students in constructing the

Reflections on Writing

I chose this piece because it will help me remember some very special memories. I think this piece showed very strong vocabulary and it was very neat (for me). It seems to have a certain flow to it so readers won't get bored.

This piece sounds as if I'm writing a mystery which is a new genre for me. I am beginning to write more interesting projects and vary the kinds of writing I do.

I feel I'm very good at writing though I have to learn more about writing in different genres. My biggest problem is neatness but besides that I'm very confident about my work.

David

Figure 28–8. David's Reflections

portfolio so they learn more about evaluating their own progress?

You will collect reading data and writing projects throughout the year. Many teachers keep all products for the year, selecting materials for the "pass on" portfolio in the spring. Others identify particular times when the portfolio is examined in conjunction with the child; some pieces are sent home and others remain in the portfolio. Some general considerations for the type of the information to include in the portfolio follow:

- Include a list of the books the student read and the writing projects he completed.
- Feature "best work" or a range of writing projects and poetry (e.g., several pieces that you and the student have selected for a particular reason).
- Document the level of texts the student read during the year as well as the range of genres he attempted.
- Illustrate the student's growth and progress through a thoughtful selection of writing samples.
- Include writing projects or investigations that demonstrate the student's ability to use knowledge in content areas.
- Encourage self-reflection by asking the student to write rationales for his portfolio selections: why he chose to include writing samples, how he chose books to read, and his reflections on his growth as a writer and reader. (See Figure 28–8 for an example.)
- Feature writing samples from all the genres the student studied and explored in his own writing.
- Weave in written evaluations by the student about his growth as a reader, writer, and learner.

Involving Students in Creating Portfolios

Some teachers have students create their own portfolios. The volume of work included is not large, but it includes reading and writing as well as self-reflection. The selection process prompts them to assess their work as they reflect on why they want to include (or not include) a given piece. If you go this route, you will want to help students establish appropriate selection criteria. Figure 28–9 is a sample list of components included in the portfolio that reflect the work completed in one classroom using the language and literacy framework.

Carol has her students include periodic reflections on their writing by completing the following questionnaire:

1. The most important thing in our classroom that I am trying to do well is . . .
2. This is important to me because . . .
3. Two things I have done well so far this year are . . .
4. One thing I need to work harder at is . . .
5. Something that I am proud of so far this year is . . .
6. One main goal for the rest of the year is . . .
7. This is what I will do to accomplish this goal: . . .

Her students also include a periodic questionnaire about reading. Figure 28–10 shows Ruth's reflections in December. Ruth is clearly thinking about the quantity and breadth of her reading. Her reading list (Figure 28–11), also included in the portfolio, had sixteen books on it at the end of the first quarter. She also included some copies of reading response entries she wanted to save.

Literacy Portfolio Components
A Sample Plan

Reading:

One reading journal entry and a paragraph describing what it shows about you as a reader.

Reading List with a paragraph describing what it shows about you as a reader.

Favorite poems (at least two) with a caption telling why you chose them.

Self-assessment: reading (Appendix 52)

Writing and Spelling:

One writing project (final draft or published) with a paragraph describing what it shows about you as a writer.

Writing List with a paragraph describing what it shows about you as a writer.

Your personal spelling list of words learned.

Self-assessment: writing (Appendix 53)

Figure 28–9. Literacy Portfolio Components: A Sample Plan

Name: __Ruth_____   Date: __12/7_____

READING

1. This is how I feel about reading so far this year: _I'm thinking more about_ what I'm reading. I like to read moe than before I came to forth gread in september. What's helping me to understand what I'm reading most of all is my Reading Jurnal. I like reading more because I've tryed to read a lot of good books and now I like to read more.

2. These are things that I'd like you to notice about the list of books I've read so far this year: _I want you to notice that I'm reading a lot of Animal Storys_ and a lot of Realistic fiction. I mostly read books that are Just Right but I sometimes stop and read an Easy book like Anita's notebook. I also want you to notice that I've read a lot of books in theese 3 months

3. These are the things that I'd like you to notice about the journal entries I chose: _I want you to notice how I wrote the part I liked in the_ story. I used deatales to make a sort of picture in your mind. I'm also writing questains for Ms. Won to answer in her next letter. I'm writing some of the things the character must of felt.

4. This is how I think I've improved as a reader so far this year: _I think I_ can read faster than last year. I also think I understand the book more.

5. This is my goal in reading for the rest of the year: _I want to be a_ faster reader because I won't have to waist any time looking and sounding out words.

Figure 28–10.   Reading Questionnaire—Ruth

Reading List

Select a book to read. Enter the title and author on your reading list. When you have completed it, write the genre, and the date. If you abandoned it, write an (A) and the date you abandoned it in the date column. Note whether the book was easy (E), just right (JR) or a challenging (C) book for you.

#	Title	Author	Genre	Date Completed	E JR, C
1	Flowers on the Wall	Miriam Nerlove	HF	9/8	E
2	Poppy	Avi	RF	9/12	JR
3	Poppy and Ray	Avi	RF	9/20	JR
4	Tom Babbet	Avi	RF	9/28	E
5	Ralph S. Mouse	Beverly Cleary	F	10/8	JR
6	Amelia's Notebook	Marissa Moss	RF	10/12	E
7	Amelia Writes Again	Marissa Moss	RF	10/14	E
8	Number the Stars	Lois Lowry	HF	10/19	C
9	The Haunted Clubhouse	Caroline Leavitt	RF	10/22	JR
10	Sadako and the Thousand Paper Cranes	Eleanor Coerr	HF	11/8	JR
11	Tom Sawyer	Mark Twain	RF	11/17	C
12	The Music of Dolphins	Karen Hesse	RF	11/23	C
13	Great Gilly Hopkins	Katherine Paterson	RF	11/27	JR
14	Ribsy	Beverly Cleary	RF	11/30	E
15	Ramona the Pest	Beverly Cleary	RF	12/6	E
16	Huckleberry Finn	Mark Twain	RF	12/9	C

Figure 28–11. Rita's Reading List, 9/8 to 12/9

By the end of the year, Ruth's reading list included thirty-nine books. Most books she read were realistic fiction, but she did read one fantasy (Alice in Wonderland, which she classified as "adventure"), and several works of historical fiction. She abandoned two of the books, but nevertheless documented a productive year of reading.

In their literacy portfolios, Carol's students also include selected writing projects and poems. Each piece of work included student writing supporting the selection.

These portfolios are not just methods of documenting and assessing; they are instructional tools that help students learn the kinds of goals they need to achieve in their literacy performance. Appendices 52 and 53 contains a self-assessment questionnaire for reading and writing that students, teachers, and parents will all find informative.

Portfolio assessment requires excellent organization and effort, and storing them may become a problem (most schools still use file folders and include hard copies of student work; they soon eat up lots of space). However, technology should soon make portfolios easier and less cumbersome—we already have the capability to scan student work onto an electronic file and store it on a CD. However, the goal is not to save more but to involve students in their own learning; even when archives can be computerized, examining hard copy is still advisable.

Grades and Reporting

Any discussion of assessment always leads to the issue of grading. Grading is a reality in most schools; parents and students both are concerned about grades. You need a sound basis for establishing the criteria for grades and ways to communicate clearly with parents.

Communicating Expectations

Be sure to communicate your explicit expectations to your students. They deserve to know the basis on which they will be graded. They need to know how many books you expect them to read, the number of writing projects they need to complete, and your general expectations for daily productivity.

Beyond quantity, they need a practical understanding of your expectations for quality. You can ask them to help you establish quality standards for every activity you grade in the classroom. For example, Chapter 25 includes a student-made list of characteristics of quality visual presentations that were posted in the classroom so students could refer to them continually. As you and your students create these guidelines, photocopy them and ask your students to glue them into their notebooks or folders for frequent, handy reference.

Grading

Grades can be based on a wide range of criteria, and you will want to establish those criteria as you begin the year. Identify the subjects in which you will need to award grades, and decide which assessment processes are essential for each. You may want to consider:

■ Consistent productivity (quantity).
■ Dependability in fulfilling assignments.

- The quality of students' work at regular intervals.
- Progress as an indication of effort and attention.

Help students understand how care in record keeping provides an important basis for grading. Grades are not based on single tests or measures; they reflect the accumulation of a student's work and effort. Students need to understand that working toward their goals is a daily process.

A good time to reinforce this concept is during the first parent-teacher-student conference. The more concrete examples of progress you provide, the more effective the conference will be. By sharing examples with parents and students, you can help them understand what the student has accomplished.

Assessment is a complex process that must be coordinated with your grading periods. Create a time line or map of the year so you can follow a schedule of continuous assessment that is systematic and efficient. This will also help you determine which assessments will form the basis for grades and which will be used for other purposes. As with any other classroom work, it is best to start with a simple plan that you can realistically accomplish; as you grow more skilled and organized, you can implement additional assessment techniques. You and your colleagues might want to create a grid of the different assessment tools used in daily classroom teaching, and in formal assessment throughout the year. A sample time line for a variety of informal and formal assessments across a school year is provided in Figure 28–12. (You will of course include district-required assessments, if any, in your schedule.)

Standardized Tests

The quality of most schools is measured by student performance on standardized tests. These published tests are created and tested by experts in psychometrics. Items are constructed to measure various aspects of reading and writing, such as word analysis or getting the main idea of a paragraph. The test is tried out on large, representative populations of students. Items are tested and those that discriminate between higher and lower performers are selected. A good test is considered to be one that separates the test takers into groups or categories along a continuum of achievement or that reveals whether or not students have met some criteria for success.

Standardized measures have been tested to determine whether they are reliable, which means that the results are consistent and dependable. If the test is given in the same way to the same group or type of group, the results will be consistent. Each test has also been checked for validity, which is the degree to which it measures what it is designed to measure. For example, if a test is designed to measure vocabulary, then those who score high on it would also demonstrate their vocabulary knowledge on other tests either at the same time or later.

It is obvious that a great deal of time and money are invested in creating and publishing a standardized test. Costs range from $5.00 to $10.00 per student. Typically, tests are shipped in sealed boxes, and you are required to administer them under prescribed conditions. Either they are scored at the district office or returned to the test publisher for machine scoring. Depending on the test or the company, it may take months to obtain the results; thus, standardized tests are used mainly to evaluate large groups of students. In many places, students take a standardized test every year or every other year.

Most standardized tests are beyond your direct control as a teacher, although many districts do involve teachers in test selection. It is extremely important, however, that you understand the different kinds of tests that are used as well as what they tell you about learners. Above all, it is important to have a logical, usable, and responsible assessment system for literacy in the elementary grades.

Norm-Referenced Tests

Norm-referenced tests are designed to compare students with one another: students' scores are distributed along a continuum. Picture a continuum divided into 100 segments called "percentiles." The first "percentile" is 1; the percentile at the top end is 99. The continuum may also be divided into "stanines," which involves dividing the scores into nine equal groups ranging from the lowest (stanine one) to the highest (stanine nine). The middle stanine (five) includes the scores of students who fall just on either side of the mean (average).

The majority of students make up the "average" group, with fewer students above and below average. When your students take a norm-referenced test, the number of items they get right is compared with the performance of a norm group. If a student's score is

Sample Timeline for Assessment: Grades 3 to 6										
Assessment	Sept.	Oct.	Nov.	Dec.	Jan.	Feb.	Mar.	Apr.	May	June
Reading and Writing Interview	X									
Conference Benchmark Assessment	X									
Record of Book Reading Progress	X	X	X	X	X	X	X	X	X	X
Reading List [ongoing]	X	X	X	X	X	X	X	X	X	X
Reader's Notebook [ongoing]	X	X	X	X	X	X	X	X	X	X
Record of Writing Projects [ongoing]	X	X	X	X	X	X	X	X	X	X
What I Learned as a Writer [ongoing]	X	X	X	X	X	X	X	X	X	X
Writing Assessment-Rubric	X						X			
Spelling Inventory	X								X	
Spelling Tests [weekly]	X	X	X	X	X	X	X	X	X	X
Spelling—Lists of Words Learned [ongoing]	X	X	X	X	X	X	X	X	X	X
Poetry Anthologies [ongoing]	X	X	X	X	X	X	X	X	X	X
Self-Assessment Questionnaire— Reading/Writing									X	
Literacy Portfolio				X					X	
Parent Interview	X						X			
Parent/Student/Teacher Conference		X				X				

Figure 28–12. Sample Timeline for Assessment

exactly the same as the average score of the norm group, then the student is "average," designated as at the 50th percentile. The student's score is also in the fifth stanine.

So what are you finding out when you look at your students' scores on norm-referenced tests? You literally know how they compare with the norm group. Therefore:

■ Find out about the norm group. Who are they? How do they compare or not compare with your students?

■ Realize that these tests are designed to distribute students along the continuum. By definition they place half the students below average and half above average, whatever their knowledge level. The test makers "update" these tests with new norm groups every few years.

A norm-referenced test usually provides very little useful data for daily teaching. It can confirm your own assessment of students' learning by placing their performance in a national context.

Criterion-Referenced Tests

Many of the new state proficiency tests are criterion-referenced measures. A standardized criterion-referenced test has the same qualities as a norm-referenced test—carefully tested and selected items, prescriptive directions for use, and data on reliability and validity. The information it provides about test takers, however, is quite different. A criterion for accepted achievement, mastery, or performance is established. There may be a single criterion against which performance is measured, or there may be levels (for example, from satisfactory to excellent), each with a separate criterion.

When your students take a criterion-referenced test, they are measured against the specified level of performance. They meet the criterion or not. If they do not, how far below the standard do their scores fall? Or they may meet the criterion on one part of the measure but not on another.

For these tests, you might ask:

■ What is the criterion level and what does it mean?

■ How is the specified criterion related to the reading and writing skills that students need?

■ What do my students need to know to meet the criterion?

■ Does the criterion really predict future performance?

Criterion-referenced tests provide some useful information but only in broad strokes. After getting the results of criterion-referenced tests, you will still need to sit down with your students and get some very specific assessment information in all your categories of interest.

Summary of Principles for Establishing a High Quality Assessment System

This chapter has described and provided examples of ways to establish a practical and informative assessment system. Undoubtedly, you will encounter other assessment requirements in your school or district; you will want to find measures that meet your needs and that you can implement routinely and systematically. That might mean starting with just a few procedures, working to establish them, and then adding more. As you establish your assessment design over time, keep in mind these key generalizations:

1. *Determine what students know and can do.* This is the main goal of assessment. Finding students' strengths is the first step in effective instruction. Assessment that reveals only failure will not inform teaching or improve education.

2. *Assess performance across the language and literacy framework.* You will want to gather numerous examples of student performance in several contexts so you can judge how your students use reading and writing for many purposes.

3. *Assess students' reading and writing of many types of texts.* As literate citizens, students must read, understand, and learn from a wide variety of fiction and nonfiction texts. How do they process a range of texts? What do they understand about the organization of different texts? You will also want to know what they understand about the topic or theme and whether they can think critically about the text.

4. *Gather data on what students do in the process of reading and writing as well as the products.* Observational data is a powerful indication of what your students know and can do. Scores on tests or levels of achievement are informative, but you also need to collect observational data as students read, write, and talk. Examining students' errors is especially helpful; look for patterns of errors in reading and writing and the problem-solving processes students use.

5. *Use multiple sources of information as a base for making educational decisions.* No one source of information can provide the basis for making decisions about individuals or about how you teach your class. With any measure, you need to keep in mind its limitations as well as its benefits.

6. *Connect assessment with an understanding of developmental patterns of learning as well as the complex processes of reading and writing.* In any given class, you will have a wide range of students. Understanding normal development of complex processes will help you determine where your students are in the development of reading and writing and what they need to learn next. Clearly, students' background knowledge and prior experience figure strongly.

7. *To the fullest extent possible, integrate assessment and teaching in a streamlined, manageable system.* Making assessment an integral part of your teaching ensures that you will collect more authentic indicators of students' learning and save valuable time.

8. *Teach students to reflect on and assess their own progress.* An important skill for students to develop during the elementary school years is the ability to assess their own progress. Becoming a lifelong learner involves self-awareness, self-direction, and responsibility.

9. *Report in specific and clear ways to parents and ask their perspectives.* Parents may value test scores, but they also appreciate specific examples that clearly show evidence of their child's progress. Performance samples, taken over time, can be helpful as vehicles for communication. Also, parents can provide valuable information about your students, and they will appreciate being included in their child's evaluation.

10. *Use evaluation data to look critically at the environment you have provided for students as well as the instruction.* The causes of achievement or failure are not located within students; they are in the personal experiences and opportunities they have as well as in the accumulation of educational experiences. Evaluation data is the most valuable tool you have to improve your own teaching as well as the quality of education in your school.

11. *Use standards to help you develop a high-quality assessment system.* Professional organizations, research laboratories or agencies, and state education authorities have created standards for student performance. These standards are a valuable resource as you work with colleagues to achieve your own vision of what students need to know and be able to do as readers and writers.

These summary statements are challenging, but if you can meet them or work toward them, you have a chance of using assessment in productive ways that will inform your teaching and help students. Education cannot exist without evaluation. We have to know the degree to which we are successfully serving students. The key to good assessment is to take charge of it yourself, so that the outcomes are positive.

Suggestions for Professional Development, Option 1

1. Gather a large number of assessment instruments. You can include standardized tests, content area and basal reading tests, writing rubrics, word tests, informal reading inventories, the fluency rubric mentioned in this chapter, and any other assessment procedures used in your district. Work in groups to look at the assessments. Ask:
   ▪ What does this instrument really measure?
   ▪ What will the results of this assessment tell me about students? What will the results not tell me?
   ▪ What expenditure of my time and effort will be required to administer/analyze this assessment procedure?
   ▪ How can this assessment inform my grading and reporting?
   ▪ How would this fit into my year of instruction?
2. Use this discussion to help you analyze the advantages and limitations of assessment procedures. Where you have choices, select the procedures that you want to use this year. Include required assessments as a "given."
3. Then create a time line for the year to guide your use of assessment procedures (see Figure 28–14 for an example). At the end of the year, evaluate the process.
   ▪ Were you able to use all of the procedures you planned?

- Which were most informative?
- Which should be eliminated?
- Which were easiest to use regularly as an integral part of instruction?
- Did you find that you were missing some important information? Do you need to add some kinds of assessment? How would you integrate additional assessment into your instruction?

Suggestions for Professional Development, Option 2

1. Work with colleagues from each grade level to create a writing rubric for assessment in your school. Work from the students' writing first. You may find that some sample writing rubrics (such as the one in Chapter 27) will be helpful later on.
2. Collect a large sample of students' writing papers. It does not matter whether they come from this year's class or even what time of year students produced them. Just be sure you have a range of development represented in the sample. You may even want to include some excellent pieces that have been published by elementary school students so you have a vision of top quality.
3. Arrange the pieces along a continuum. Discuss why certain pieces are more advanced than others.
4. Put together the pieces that are just about the same quality.
5. Decide what traits you are looking for in students' writing. You may want to stay with a holistic assessment. In that case you will be writing descriptions that include statements about conventions, text organization, writer's craft, and other aspects of writing. If you decide to use trait analysis, you will be dividing your scale. Sort the pieces of writing according to the specific trait being discussed (such as conventions). If you are new to rubrics, you may find it helpful to start with one aspect of writing.
6. Gradually work toward collapsing categories into four levels. You will have to create written descriptions for each level, so fewer are better than many.
7. Try out the scale using the papers you have and compare your ratings. Then, use the scale over several months with students in your school. Meet again to compare results. Ask:
   - Does the rubric capture improvement in students' writing?
   - Does the rubric show differences from third through sixth grade?
   - How can this rubric inform teaching?
   - How can we use this rubric to help students create their own?

STRUGGLING READERS AND WRITERS TEACHING THAT MAKES A DIFFERENCE

Writing and reading are complementary processes; progress in one assists progress in the other. Struggling readers and writers need more opportunities to make reading/writing connections, and they are less likely to make these connections on their own. Low-achieving students need to experience a wide range of genres:

1. *Be sure that the text examples for new genres are as simple and easy to understand as possible.* When they encounter a new genre, students need very clear examples and, in addition, require an explicit discussion of the text characteristics. They will need many examples in order to internalize the characteristics and organizational patterns of new genres, especially nonfiction.

2. *Read aloud to help students access texts.* As they hear a text read aloud, struggling readers can concentrate on the characteristics of the genre.

3. *Help students use text examples as they attempt to write in different genres.* Low-achieving students require many examples of a genre before they can write it for themselves. Teach them to use texts they hear read aloud or read themselves as examples.

4. *Use the writing of others to help students in their own writing.* The texts that students experience provide powerful models for them to use as they work on their own writing projects. During your writing conferences and guided writing sessions, explain how writers use and organize language to craft their texts.

The rich language of poetry is a delight to share with others; therefore, poetry is a wonderful way to engage readers who need more help:

1. *Read poetry aloud to students to help them access literary structure, language, and meaning.* Read poetry aloud to struggling readers frequently; invite them to join in after you have read it several times. Reading together supports their enjoyment of the text and gives them the opportunity to experience reading with appropriate pauses and emphasis.

2. *Involve students in the shared reading and performance of poetry.* Shared reading or the kinds of performance we have described in this section are ideal ways to engage students who need more help. By working in mixed groups during shared and choral reading, they greatly expand their knowledge of language.

3. *Help students write their own poetry based on entries in their writer's notebook.* You will need to work especially hard to find kernels of language in their writer's notebook that they can expand into poetry. This process illustrates better than any other the control that even your low-achieving students can achieve over language.

4. *Talk often with students about their writing of poetry.* Conferring with students about their writing will encourage them and show that you value their work. It will also motivate them to write more.

5. *Encourage students to display and illustrate their poetry.* It is especially important that low-achieving students produce writing they are proud of and others appreciate. Beautifully illustrated poetry, published in class books or displayed in the classroom, is one way to accomplish that goal.

Low-achieving students often stumble with content literacy because they experience "double jeopardy." First, they find reading itself difficult because they are still working to develop an effective reading process; therefore, they find it very difficult to use reading to gain information. Second, they probably don't have a lot of background knowledge to bring to informational texts. Because they have not been able to read as much as other students, they have not acquired as much information about the specific content area *or* about the way informational texts are organized.

It is important for students who need more support to engage in investigations. As they conduct their own research, they can follow their interests and develop their knowledge of informational texts. They may work in heterogeneous groups with other students and benefit from their collaboration with more successful students. They will also profit from the opportunity to make presentations to other students.

1. ***Use tools to help students understand the structure of informational texts.*** This section discusses a large number of tools that will reveal the internal structure of texts to students. These tools are useful in helping them understand how structures such as comparison/contrast and cause/effect are used in informational texts. Working on a chart with them or having them work in pairs (after experience with the tool) is a way to assure that they understand texts at a deeper level.

2. ***Use tools to help expand students' understanding of vocabulary in informational texts.*** Students who need extra help are likely to have trouble with the vocabulary in informational texts. They may need concrete experiences to understand content words, but it will also help to connect words through semantic mapping or other techniques.

3. ***Confer with students often during their investigations.*** Low-achieving students will need more monitoring, and you may need to provide more support and guidance.

4. ***Use reciprocal teaching to help students understand informational texts.*** Ask students to make predictions based on headings in the text and then read sections of the text, summarizing and noting information that requires clarification. Ask students to discuss their questions, summaries, and clarifications either orally or in writing. Reciprocal teaching is a temporary scaffold. Through reciprocal teaching, students gradually learn to take on strategies that help them process the text. You demonstrate; then students try it themselves.

5. ***Provide support for research.*** Struggling readers and writers may find it difficult to access the sources of information that other students are using in their investigations. You may need to supplement their work with simpler sources as well as information on audio- or videotape.

Standardized tests are most worrisome for students at the lower ends of the achievement continuum. For these students, no amount of drilling on test-taking skills will guarantee success. In fact, by spending an inordinate amount of time *preparing* for the test, you may actually interfere with time that students could use to build their reading and writing abilities. It is critical that these students have time for reading and writing so that they are developing the literacy foundation they need. Remember, if they know *how* to read and write, you can provide some intensive work just before the test to help them understand the particular challenges the tests represent:

1. ***Assess students' reading, writing, and spelling abilities frequently and analyze their strengths and needs.*** It is especially important to know what low-achieving students know, so that you can help them draw on their knowledge for the tests.

2. ***Build testlike exercises into guided reading and guided writing lessons.*** The test situation is an artificial one often surrounded by high pressure. Working daily with students in guided reading and writing, you can help them display their knowledge in ways that match the tests but in a much more supportive situation. Thus, students build their confidence.

3. ***Provide quick, intensive practice on testlike performance skills.*** As part of guided reading or guided writing, you can ask students to do quick readings of paragraphs and then answer questions orally or in writing. This helps familiarize students with the testing situation. Afterward, they can reflect on and evaluate their responses.

FINAL THOUGHTS

As you reach the end of this book, it is likely you will find that you have invested many hours as a reader. You may have been motivated to read other professional books and enticed to acquire and read some stirring books for children that were new to you. Perhaps, also, you have taken notes, jotting down ideas you want to remember and recording your own thoughts. You and your colleagues may have participated in professional development experiences and, in the process, discussed and debated your responses to the ideas in this book. You may have been inspired to start a writer's notebook, using its pages to sketch, or write a memoir, or you may have begun to create your own anthology of favorite poetry.

Our lives as readers and writers are foundational to our work with students. When we read and write ourselves, we are able to teach reading and writing "from the inside." Our own experiences give direction and depth to our teaching.

We encourage you to cherish and protect your life as a reader and writer. Take time to read for enjoyment as well as to search for practical and helpful information. Pack children's books in your travel bag or keep a stack next to your bed. Explore the role of writing in your life. You may find you enjoy capturing memories, hopes and dreams in a special notebook of your own. Your passion for literacy will guide and enrich your work with your intermediate students, enabling them, also, to experience the profound joys inherent in lifelong reading and writing.

I. C. F
G. S. P.

APPENDICES

The appendices to this book are designed to support work with students in the upper elementary grades. We include forms for language/word study, for reading and writing workshops, and for literary assessment. Additionally, we have listed the 500 most frequently used words, highlighting the spelling "demons" in bold. We also provide lists of websites, magazines for kids, and a variety of graphic organizers. We also provide lists of useful text resources for teaching reading and writing. Finally, we provide a book list of over 1000 books, organized by title and level for use in guided reading.

APPENDICES

ORGANIZING AND PLANNING

Three Block Planning

Week of _____

	Language/Word Study	Reading Workshop	Writing Workshop
M			
T			
W			
T			
F			

Three Block Planning

Week of _____

	Monday	Tuesday	Wednesday	Thursday	Friday
Language/Word Study					
Reading Workshop					
Writing Workshop					

Word Study Minilesson Plan

Spelling principle, pattern or strategy _____

_____

_____

_____

_____

Sample List: _____

_____

_____

_____

_____

_____

_____

_____

Comments/Evaluation: _____

_____

_____

_____

_____

_____

_____

_____

_____

_____

Five Hundred Plus High-Frequency Words

*(bold, italicized words are **Spelling Demons**)*

a	baby	but	*didn't*	fact
able	back	*buy*	died	family
about	bad	*by*	*different*	fare
above	ball		dinner	fast
across	be	call	do	father
add	*beautiful*	called	*does*	*favorite*
after	became	came	*doesn't*	*February*
again	*because*	can	dog	feel
against	become	*can't* (can not)	doing	feet
air	bed	*cannot*	done	fell
a lot	*been*	car	*don't*	few
all	*before*	care	door	*field*
all right	began	carry	down	fight
almost	begin	cat	draw	*finally*
along	*beginning*	catch	dream	find
already	behind	caught	dry	fine
also	being	certain	during	fire
although	*believe*	change		*first*
always	below	children	each	fish
am	best	city	early	five
among	better	class	earth	fix
an	between	clean	easy	follow
and	big	*close*	eat	food
animal	bike	*clothes*	*eighth*	for
another	black	cold	either	form
answer	boat	*come*	else	*forty*
any	body	*coming*	end	found
anyone	books	complete	*enough*	four
anything	boot	*could*	*especially*	free
are	both	couldn't	even	*friend*
around	box	country	ever	from
as	boy	cut	*every*	front
ask	bring		*everybody*	full
asked	broke	dad	*everyone*	fun
at	brother	dark	everything	funny
ate	brought	day	*except*	
away	build	deep	*excited*	game
a while	bus	did		gave

get	hit	large	men	or
getting	hold	last	*might*	order
girl	*hole*	later	mind	other
give	home	*laugh*	miss	*our*
go	hope	learn	mom	out
goes	hour	leave	money	outside
going	house	left	moon	over
gone	how	less	more	own
good	however	let	morning	
got	hurt	*let's*	most	page
grade		life	mother	paper
great	I	light	move	park
green	*I'd*	like	much	part
group	idea	line	must	party
grow	if	list	my	past
guess	*I'm*	little	*myself*	*people*
	important	live		perhaps
had	in	lived	name	person
half	inside	lives	near	pick
hand	instead	long	need	picture
happily	*into*	look	never	*piece*
happy	is	looking	*new*	place
hard	it	*loose*	next	plants
has	*it's* (it is)	*lose*	nice	play
have	*its*	lot	night	possible
having		lots	*no*	pretty
he	job	love	*none*	*probably*
head	jump	lunch	not	problem
hear	just		nothing	put
heard		mad	now	
heart	keep	made	number	rain
heavy	kept	main		ran
help	kids	make	of	read
her	killed	*making*	*off*	*ready*
here	kind	man	*often*	real
he's	*knew*	*many*	old	*really*
high	*know*	may	on	reason
hill		maybe	*once*	*receive*
him	lady	me	*one* (number)	red
his	land	mean	only	rest

ride
right
river
room
round
run
running

said
same
sat
saw
say
says
scared
school
sea
second
see
seen
separate
set
several
shall
she
ship
shoes
short
shot
show
shown
sick
side
simple
since
sister
sit

size
sky
sleep
small
snow
so
some
someone
something
sometimes
soon
sound
space
special
stand
start
started
state
stay
still
stood
stop
store
story
street
stuff
such
summer
sun
sure

take
talk
teach
teacher
tear
tell

ten
terrible
than
that
that's
the
their (belongs to)
them
themselves
then
there
these
they
they're (they are)
things
think
third
this
those
though
thought
three
threw
through
throw
time
tired
to
today
together
told
tonight
too
took
top
tree
tried

trouble
try
trying
Tuesday
turned
two

under
until
up
upon
us
use
used
usually

very

walk
want
wanted
was
wasn't
watch
water
way
we
wear (shirt)
weather (rain)
Wednesday
week
well
went
we're (we are)
were
what
when

where
whether
which
while
who
whole
why
will
win
winter
wish
with
without
woke
women
won
won't
work
world
would
wouldn't
write
writing
wrote

yard
year
yes
you
your
you're (you are)

Record of Writing Projects

Project #	Title	Type of Writing	Status (D#___, FD, P)	Date Completed

Project #	Title	Type of Writing	Status (D#___, FD, P)	Date Completed

What I Learned About Being a Writer

Project #	
Project #	
Project #	
Project #	
Project #	
Project #	

Project #	
Project #	
Project #	
Project #	
Project #	
Project #	

Types of Writing

Keep a list of the different types of writing you do. Each time you complete a writing project (final draft or published), write the month and day (e.g. 9/20). You will need to list the types on the left.

Type	Dates

Initials _____ Date _____ Writing Project _____ Draft _____ Page ____

-
-
-
-
-
-
-
-
-
-
-
-
-

_____

_____

_____

_____

_____

_____

_____

_____

_____

_____

_____

_____

_____

_____

_____

_____

_____

_____

_____

_____

_____

_____

_____

_____

_____

_____

_____

_____

_____

Initials _____ **Date** _____ **Writing Project** _____ **Final Draft   Page** _____

Tools for Revising and Editing

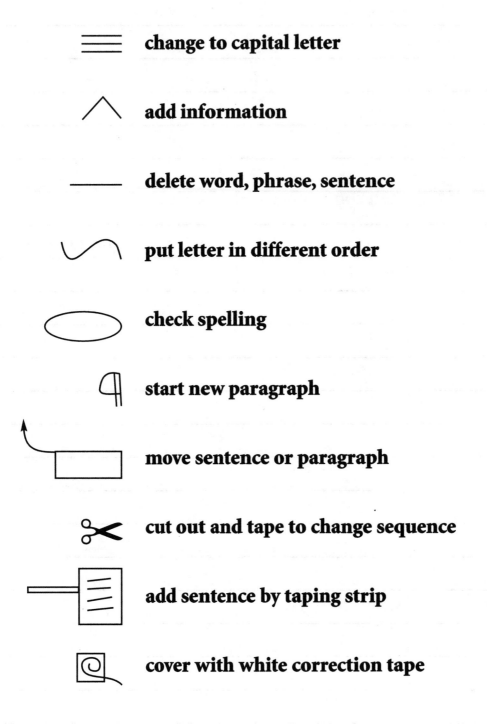

change to capital letter

add information

delete word, phrase, sentence

put letter in different order

check spelling

start new paragraph

move sentence or paragraph

cut out and tape to change sequence

add sentence by taping strip

cover with white correction tape

Guidelines for Writing Workshop

1. You must always be writing or sketching in your writer's notebook or working on a writing project.

2. Put the date in the margin each day as you start writing.

3. You need to work silently so that everyone can do their best thinking.

4. Use a soft voice when conferring with the teacher.

5. When using draft paper, write on every other line and cross out when you make mistakes.

6. Request a teacher conference when you are ready for your final draft.

7. When using final draft paper, use your best handwriting and write on every line.

8. When you complete a writing project, record the information on your Record of Writing. Then record what you learned about being a writer.

9. After you finish a final draft, put your drafts in numerical order. Then staple them together with the final draft on top, and place your project in the hanging file.

10. Place your final draft in the editor's basket when you want the teacher to edit your project for publication.

Conference Record Form

Name	M	T	W	TH	F	Comments

Minilessons:

Reading List

Select a book to read. Enter the title and author on your reading list. When you have completed it, write the genre, and the date. If you abandoned it, write an (**A**) and the date you abandoned it in the date column. Note whether the book was easy (**E**), just right (**JR**) or a challenging (**C**) book for you.

#	Title	Author	Genre	Date Completed	E JR, C

#	Title	Author	Genre	Date Completed	E JR, C

Reading Interests

Topics That Interest Me	Genre/Types of Books That Interest Me	Authors That Interest Me

Books to Read

Title	Author	Check When Completed

Title	Author	Check When Completed

Appendix 14 *(continued)*

Thinkmark

Name _____

Title _____

Author _____

Page

Page

Page

Thinkmark

Name _____

Title _____

Author _____

Page

Page

Page

Thinkmark

Name _____

Title _____

Author _____

Page

Page

Page

Page	Page	Page	Page

Page	Page	Page	Page

Page	Page	Page	Page

Guidelines for Reading Workshop

1. You must always be reading a book or writing your thoughts about your reading.

2. You need to work silently to enable you and your peers to do your best thinking.

3. Use a soft voice when conferring with the teacher.

4. Select books that you think you'll enjoy and abandon books that aren't working for you after you've given them a good chance.

5. List the book information when you begin and record the date when you finish.

6. Always do your best work.

Character Web

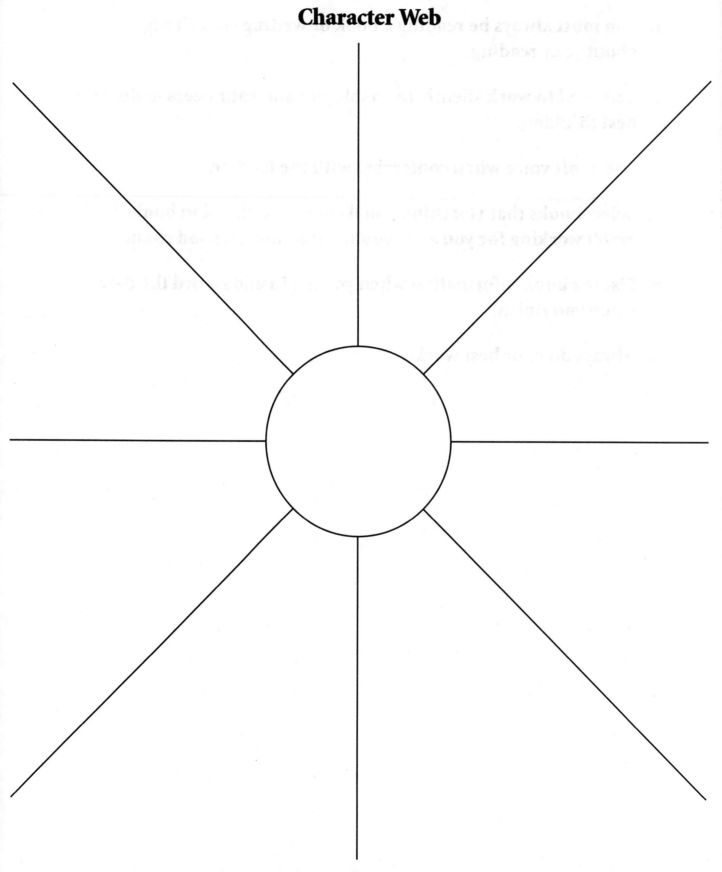

Character Comparison

Character _____

Character _____

Character _____

Similarities

Character Responses to Story Events

Story Title_____

Page	Event	Response

Name/s _____

Character Chart

Title _____   Author _____

Character	Physical Appearance	Personality Traits

Character Sociogram

Name/s _____

Character

Character

Character

Character

Character

Character

Character

Character Grid

Name/s _____

Character:

Says/Thinks	Looks	Does	Others Say/Think

Character:

Says/Thinks	Looks	Does	Others Say/Think

Character Trait and Evidence Analysis

Name/s

Character:

Story Map

Book Title _____ **Author** _____

Setting

Characters

Problem

Goal

| **Event 1** |
| **Event 2** |
| **Event 2** |

Resolution

Story Map
Narrative Text

Title and Author

Setting

Characters
(Main and Supporting)

Problem

Events

Solution

Name/s_____

Title_____

Chapter Grid

In each box, put the chapter number and one or two sentences that summarize the important information.

Chapter Map

Book Title_____

No____ Your Title_____	**No____ Your Title**_____
No____ Your Title_____	**No____ Your Title**_____
No____ Your Title_____	**No____ Your Title**_____

Story Notes

Title

Setting	Character	Character

Character	Character	Character

Problem	Special Language	Interesting Parts

Theme (story message)

Name/s_____

Important Elements

Book Title_____

Setting:

The story takes place_____

_____

_____

Evidence:_____

_____

_____

Characters

An important character is_____

Evidence:_____

_____

Another important character is_____

Evidence:_____

_____

Plot:

The problem begins when:_____

_____

_____

Then _____

_____

After that _____

_____

Finally_____

_____

Book Comparison Chart

Title	Major Character/s	Setting	Problem	Solution	Theme

Name/s _____

Comparison Grid

Title				Similarities	Differences	Conclusions
Setting						
Characters						
Problem						
Events						

Title			Similarities	Differences	Conclusions
Solution/ Ending					
Magic					
Illustrations					
Other					

Biography: Significant Accomplishments

Person_____

1

5

Summary Statement

2

4

3

Name/s_____

Biography:
Important Life Events

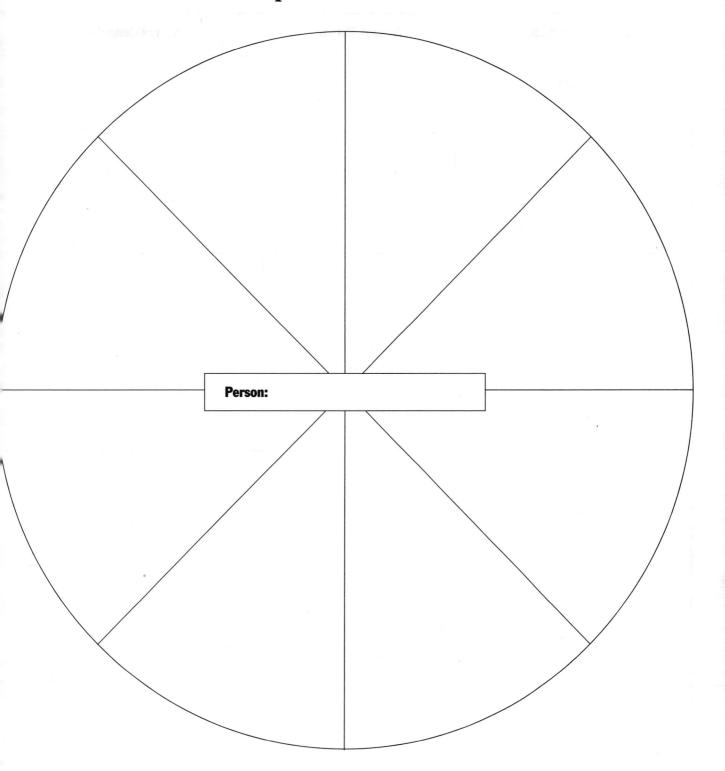

Person:

Biography: Summary and Comparison Chart

Book Title & Author	Famous Person	Accomplishments

Ideas/Details

Important Idea

Details

page____

page____

page____

page____

Information Web

Name/s _____

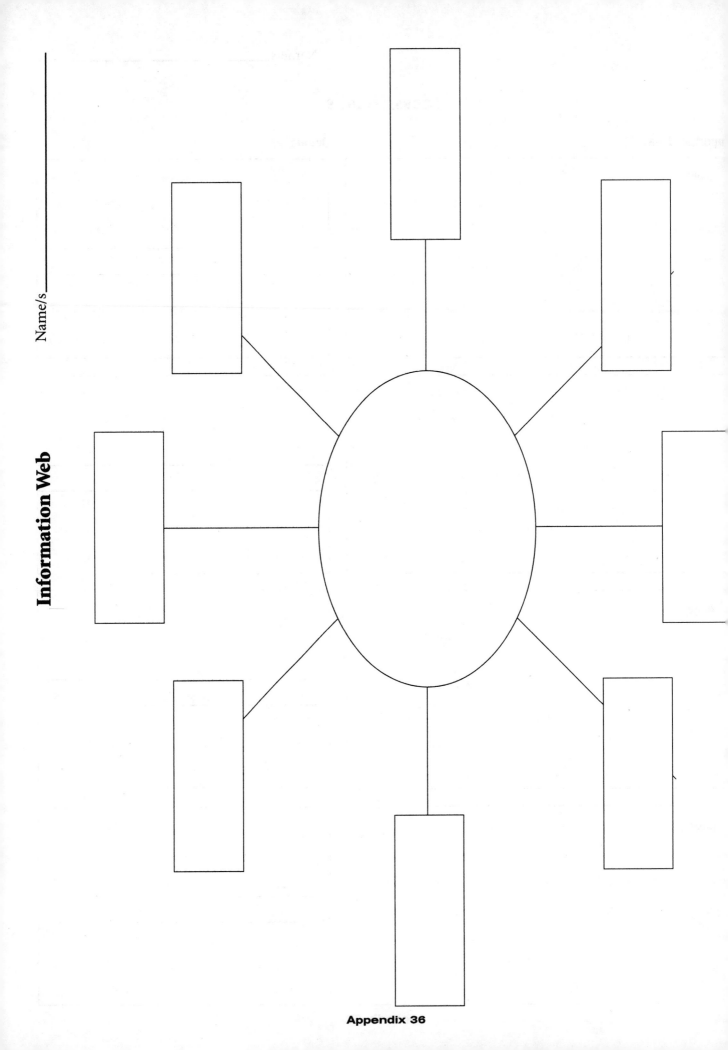

Sequence of Important Events

Name/s _____

Cycle of Events

Name/s _____

Comparison/Contrast Chart

Name/s _____

H-Chart

Both

Cause/Effect

Cause   **Effect**

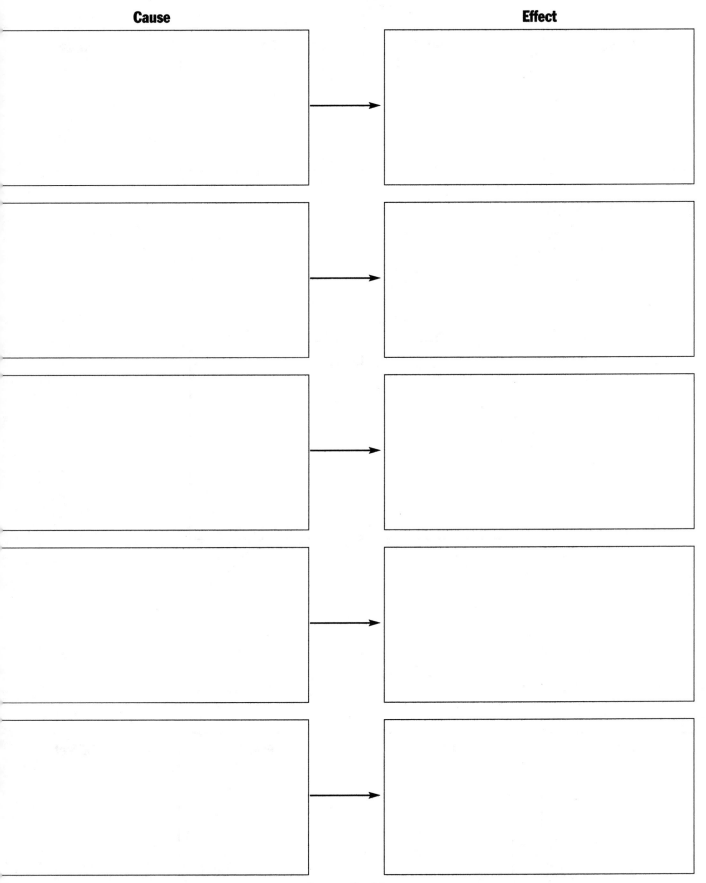

Cause/Effect Chart

Cause	Cause	Cause	Cause

Event

Effect	Effect	Effect	Effect

Name/s _____

Semantic Feature Analysis

Name/s_____

One, Two, Three Analysis

1	2	3

KWL Chart

(K)	(W)	(L)

Name_____

Reading Interview

1. Why do people read? (List as many reasons as you can.) _____

_____

_____

_____

2. Why do you read? (For example, what have you read this week and why?) _____

_____

_____

_____

3. How often do you read when you are not at school? Why? _____

_____

_____

4. How do you decide what to read about? _____

_____

_____

_____

_____

5. How do you feel about the reading that you do at school and at home? _____

_____

_____

_____

6. What is the best thing you have ever read? Why did you like it? _____

_____

_____

_____

7. How did you learn to read? _____

_____

_____

8. What have you learned from reading? _____
_____
_____
_____

9. What kinds of topics do you especially like to read about? _____
_____
_____

10. What kind of reading do you like?

_____ historical fiction   _____ fairy tales/folktales   _____ poetry

_____ realistic fiction   _____ biography and autobiography   _____ science fiction

_____ fantasy   _____ information books

Select one type of book and tell why you like it. _____
_____
_____
_____

11. What advice would you give students in this room to help them read well? _____
_____
_____
_____

12. What would you like to learn how to do better as a reader? _____
_____
_____
_____

13. How can I help you become a better reader? _____
_____
_____

14. Is there anything else you want me to know about you as a reader? _____
_____
_____

Writing Interview

1. Why do people write? (List as many reasons as you can.) _____

_____

_____

_____

2. Why do you write? (For example, what have you written this week and why?) _____

_____

_____

_____

3. How often do you write when you are not at school? Why? _____

_____

_____

4. How do you decide what to write about? _____

_____

_____

_____

_____

5. How do you feel about the writing that you do at school and at home? _____

_____

_____

_____

6. What is the best thing you have ever written? Why do you like it? _____

_____

_____

_____

7. How did you learn to write? _____

_____

_____

8. Have you learned anything about writing from the books someone has read to you or you have read yourself? What have you learned? What is the best book you know that shows kids something about good writing?

_____

_____

_____

9. What kinds of topics do you especially like to write about? _____

_____

_____

10. What kind of writing do you like?

_____letters   _____poetry   _____science fiction/fantasy/fairy tales

_____science reports   _____biography and autobiography   _____realistic story

_____history or social studies reports   _____mystery   _____plays

Select one kind of writing and tell why you like it. _____

_____

_____

_____

11. What advice would you give students in this room to help them write well? _____

_____

_____

_____

12. What would you like to learn how to do better as a writer? _____

_____

_____

_____

13. How can I help you become a better writer? _____

_____

_____

14. Is there anything else you want me to know about you as a writer? _____

_____

_____

Guided Reading Observations

Guided Reading Observations

Names	Title/Level	Comments

Teacher Self-Assessment for Guided Reading

Teacher_____   Date:_____

Grade Level: _____Second _____Third _____Fourth _____Fifth _____Sixth

Assessment: General_____ or 1 Lesson (length of time):_____

Directions: Mark the characteristic within each category that most clearly describes your teaching at this time.

---

1. Materials: My goal is to have all necessary materials organized and accessible for use during the lesson.

☐ My books and other materials are at a beginning point in terms of acquisition and organization. I am just learning about how to keep records of reading behavior and how to use reader's notebooks.	☐ I have a leveled collection of books but it is minimal and not adequate for the needs of my class. I have some other materials but they are not yet organized. I know about record keeping and reader's notebooks but am not yet using them.	☐ I have a leveled set of books and I am using it. I have easel, white board, paper, markers, etc. ready for use. I am just beginning to use some form of reader's notebooks. I am beginning to keep records.	☐ A leveled, well-organized, and tested collection of books exists and is ready for use. I have an area for guided reading with easel, white board, paper, markers, and other materials. My students know how to use notebooks and reading logs. I have a well-organized, usable record keeping system.

---

2. Management: My goal is to engage students in productive reading/writing while I am working with groups and conferring with individuals during the reading block.

☐ I have not yet established a system for independent reading; students need a great deal of attention and I cannot work productively with small groups.	☐ I have begun to teach students how to engage in silent independent reading but the routines are not yet established. I am beginning to establish a schedule that will allow for independent work while I teach small groups and work with individuals.	☐ My system for independent reading is well established and I am conferring with individuals. Students are beginning to use reader's notebooks. I am beginning to work with guided reading groups on a regular basis.	☐ My classroom is well managed during the entire reading block. Students are engaged in silent independent reading and/or writing in reader's notebooks. They work in a completely independent way. I meet with guided reading groups on a regular schedule and have time to confer with individuals.

---

3. Grouping: My goal is to form small groups of students who are similar in their development of a reading process and read the same level of text so that I can teach them in guided reading; I also can identify particular needs and interests for focused guided reading groups.

☐ I am just beginning to observe students' reading behaviors and to think about forming groups based on levels of text; I have not identified any other way of grouping students. Usually I teach the whole class or confer with individuals.	☐ I have formed and met with some needs/interest-based groups when I noticed something that students need to learn. I know how to apply some assessment meacures and have tentatively formed some level-based groups.	☐ I continue to meet with some needs/interest-based groups during the reading block. I have established level-based groups and am keeping regular records of reading behavior; I meet with at least one group each day. I have not yet adjusted my grouping by assessing students.	☐ I use both level-based and needs/interest-based grouping to meet my students' needs. My groups are formed and reformed on the basis of systematic observation. I regularly meet with groups during the reading block. Every student in my class is served in small group instruction.

4. Lesson Management: My goal is to provide a fast-paced, lively, engaging lesson with all components working together effectively.

☐ I have not yet implemented any of the components of guided reading lessons.	☐ I have begun to introduce texts to students and to ask them to read it silently. I am just learning about the procedures for guided reading lessons.	☐ I can introduce texts to students and provide some other components but my lessons do not provide all components and are sometimes too short and sometimes too long.	☐ My lesson is well-timed, smoothly managed and includes an introduction, reading the text [with interaction], discussing/revisiting the text, and teaching for processing strategies. As appropriate, I include an extension and word study component.

5. Text Selection: My goal is to select texts that are appropriate in terms of level for my groups and offer opportunities to extend their processing strategies.

☐ I am just beginning to analyze texts for level of difficulty and opportunities to develop processing strategies.	☐ I am selecting texts with attention to level and text characteristics but often they are not suitable for many of my groups.	☐ Generally, I can select texts that meet the needs of my groups in terms of level, but am just learning to effectively use text characteristics as a way to help students extend their knowledge.	☐ I usually select texts that are appropriate for the level of difficulty for most of my students. I can analyze the text to discern opportunities to learn and use texts effectively to help children extend their strategies.

6. Text Variation: My goal is to provide students with experiences across a wide range of fiction and nonfiction texts.

☐ I am just beginning to learn about genres and how they vary in structure and other characteristics. My book collection does not provide variety to meet my students' needs.	☐ I can identify genres and know about their structure and characteristics. I am just beginning to analyze what my students know and to plan for more variety in my guided reading program.	☐ I have acquired a varied book collection, and I understand and use my knowledge of characteristics of genre in planning for guided reading. My students are provided with fiction and nonfiction texts on a regular basis.	☐ My book collection is rich and varied. I have an in-depth knowledge of the characterstics of different genres. I plan students' guided reading programs carefully so that they are introduced to new genres in guided reading and incorporate them in their independent reading.

7. Text Introduction: My goal is to introduce texts in a way that provides access for students to the meaning, language, and print of fiction and nonfiction texts.

☐ I sometimes introduce texts by reviewing vocabulary words and asking the questions suggested in our reading system. I am just learning how to introduce texts in a way that helps children use processing strategies.	☐ I regularly introduce texts by previewing the meaning and directing children's attention to some features. Sometimes my introductions are too supportive and sometimes they do not seem to provide enough support. I am beginning to plan text introductions based on my observations of student behavior.	☐ I introduce texts in a way that provides students with the support they need to read and comprehend texts at their appropriate reading levels. My introductions are usually well planned and based on students' behaviors. I am working on my introductions to enable students to read with comprehension and other processing strategies.	☐ My text introductions are carefully planned, smooth, and well-paced. They provide students with access to meaning, language, and print features but leave important problem-solving for them to do. My introductions are based on my assessment of students' processing strategies and make it possible for students to learn more from their own reading.

8. **Teaching for Processing Strategies:** My goal is to teach intensively in every part of the guided reading lesson in order to expand my students' ability to use background knowledge, solve words, check on their reading, access and use information, think beyond a text, connect the text to self, world and other texts, maintain phrased, fluent reading, and think about the text in critical ways.

☐ I am just beginning to understand processing strategies and to observe students' behaviors for evidence.	☐ I am able to find evidence of processing strategies as I observe students read. I support their development of strategies by providing texts at appropriate levels but have not yet developed expert teaching skills.	☐ I observe students' behavior continuously and am able to find examples and powerful teaching points to bring to their attention; I am observing the impact of my introduction, interactions, and teaching after the reading.	☐ My decisions and interactions are well-timed and powerful in illustrating processing strategies for students. My decisions allow students to use what they know to process a text. I am aware of and teach for a wide range of processing strategies and I see evidence that students are taking on these strategies for themselves.

Additional goals:

Additional goals:

Additional goals:

School Record of Book Reading Progress

Name_____ Grades_____ 3 _____ 4 _____ 5 _____ 6

Title of Text, Accuracy Rate, SC Rate (○ = above 90%; ● = below 90%)

Book Level																	
Z																	
Y																	
X																	
W																	
V																	
U																	
T																	
S																	
R																	
Q																	
P																	
O																	
N																	
M																	
L																	
K																	
J																	
I																	
H																	
G																	
F																	
E																	
D																	
C																	
B																	
A																	
DATE																	

Self-Assessment: Reading

Name: _____   Date: _____

1. How many books did you read this year? _____

2. What are the different kinds of books you read? (Genres: realistic fiction, fantasy, biography and autobiography, historical fiction, informational books, articles)

   _____   _____   _____

   _____   _____   _____

   _____   _____   _____

3. What are your favorite genres to read?

   _____   _____   _____

4. Which were the best books you read this year? What made these books good?

   _____

   _____

   _____

5. Who are two of your favorite authors and why do you like them? _____

   _____

   _____

6. What is your favorite poem? Why do you like it? _____

   _____

   _____

7. What do you know how to do well as a reader? _____

   _____

   _____

8. What did you learn this year as a reader that you are proud of? _____

   _____

   _____

9. What did you learn about reading fiction this year? _____

   _____

   _____

10. What did you learn about reading nonfiction this year? _____

   _____

   _____

Teacher's Comments: _____

   _____

   _____

Self-Assessment: Writing and Spelling

Name: _____   Date: _____

1. How many writing projects did you finish this year? _____

2. What are the different kinds of writing you completed? (Genres: realistic stories, memoirs, biographies, autobiographies, reports, articles, letters, etc.)

   _____   _____   _____

   _____   _____   _____

   _____   _____   _____

3. What are your favorite genres to write?

   _____   _____   _____

4. What writing projects are the best you have written? What made them good?

   _____

   _____

   _____

5. What can you do well as a writer? _____

   _____

   _____

6. What have you accomplished this year that you are proud of as a writer? _____

   _____

   _____

7. What areas do you want to improve in as a writer? _____

   _____

   _____

8. What did you learn this year as a reader that you are proud of? _____

   _____

   _____

9. What rules and conventions of writing can you use very well? _____

   _____

   _____

10. What did you learnto do as a speller this year? What new knowledge of spelling do you use when you write or **edit** your writing? _____

   _____

   _____

Teacher's Comments: _____

   _____

   _____

Author Websites

Alcott, Louisa May	www.alcottweb.com
Arnold, Caroline	www.geocities.com/Athens/1264
Avi	www.avi-writer.com
Aylesworth, Jim	www.ayles.com
Blume, Judy	www.judyblume.com
Brett, Jan	www.janbrett.com
Brimner, Larry Dane	home.navisoft.com/brimner
Byars, Betsy	www.betsybyars.com
Carle, Eric	www.eric-carle.com
Cobb, Vicki	www.vickicobb.com
Cushman, Karen	www.eduplace.com/rdg/author/cushman/index.html
Dadey, Debbie	www.baileykids.com
Depaola, Tomie	www.tomie.com
Fox, Mem	www.memfox.net
Friedman, Ina	www.tiac.net/users/starobin
George, Jean Craighead	www.jeancraigheadgeorge.com
Gibbons, Gail	www.gailgibbons.com
Gutman, Dan	www.dangutman.com
Hahn, Mary Downing	www.childrensbookguild.org/hahn.html
Halperin, Wendy A.	www.parrett.net/halperin
Hamilton, Virginia	www.virginiahamilton.com
Ketteman, Helen	www.flash.net/~helenket
Leedy, Loreen	www.loreenleedybooks.com
McDaniel, Lurlene	www.eclectics.com/lurlenemcdaniel
Mikaelsen, Ben	www.benmikaelsen.com
Naylor, Phyllis Reynolds	www.simonsays.com/alice
Osborne, Mary Pope	www.randomhouse.com/kids/magictreehouse/
Paterson, Katherine	www.terabithia.com
Paulsen, Gary	www.garypaulsen.com
Pilkey, Dav	www.pilkey.com
Polacco, Patricia	www.patriciapolacco.com
Quackenbush, Robert	www.rquackenbush.com
Redwall (Brian Jacques)	www.redwall.org/dave/jacques.html
Rowling, J.K.	www.scholastic.com/harrypotter/index.htm
Sachar, Louis	www.cbcbooks.org/columns/archives/sachar.htm
Scieszka, Jon and Smith, Lane	www.chucklebait.com
Simon, Seymour	www.users.nyc.pipeline.com:80:/~simonsi/
Smith, Roland	www.rolandsmith.com
Spinelli, Jerry	www.carr.lib.md.us/authco/spinelli-j.htm
Winthrop, Elizabeth	www.absolute-sway.com/winthrop/
Wood, Audrey	www.audreywood.com
The Author Corner	www.carr.lib.md.us/authco
Children's Book Guild	www.childrensbookguild.org
Ask the Author	www.ipl.org/youth/AskAuthor

Sources for Writer Talks

Aardema, Verna. 1992. *A Bookworm Who Hatched*. Katonah, NY: Richard C. Owen.

Adler, David. 1999. *My Writing Day*. Katonah, NY: Richard C. Owen.

Ahrlich, Amy, Ed. 1996. *When I Was Your Age: Original Stories about Growing Up*. Cambridge, MA: Candlewick Press.

Arnosky, Jim. 1988. *Sketching Outdoors in Winter*. New York: Lothrop.

Asch, Frank. 1997. *One Man Show*. Katonah, NY: Richard C. Owen.

Baker, Russell and William Zinsser. 1998. *Inventing the Truth: The Art and Craft of Memoir*. New York: Houghton Mifflin Co.

Blos, Joan. 1994. *The Days Before Now*. New York: Simon & Schuster.

Bomer, Randy. 1995. *Time for Meaning*. Portsmouth, NH: Heinemann.

Bruchac, Joseph. 1999. *Seeing the Circle*. Katonah, NY: Richard C. Owen.

Bunting, Eve. 1995. *Once Upon a Time*. Katonah, NY: Richard C. Owen.

Bulla, Clyde Robert. 1985 *A Grain of Wheat: A Writer Begins*: Boston: David Godine.

Byars, Betsy. 1991. *The Moon and I*. New York: A Beech Tree Paperback.

Cary, Alice. 1996. *Paterson, Katherine*. Santa Barbara, CA: The Learning Works.

Cherry, Lynne. 2000. *Making a Difference in the World*. Katonah, NY: Richard C. Owen.

Cleary, Beverly. 1988. *A Girl from Yamhill*. New York: Avon Books.

Cole, Joanna. 1996. *On the Bus with Joanna Cole: A Creative Autobiography*. Portsmouth, NH: Heinemann.

Cox, Clinton. 1995. *Mark Twain*. New York: Scholastic, Inc.

Dahl, Road. 1986. *Boy: Tales of Childhood*. New York: Puffin Books.

Dahl, Road. 1986. *Going Solo*. New York: Puffin Books.

Dillard, Annie. 1989. *The Writing Life*. New York: HarperCollins.

Dillard, Annie. 1998. *An American Childhood*. New York: HarperCollins.

Ehlert, Lois. 1996. *Under My Nose*. Katonah, NY: Richard C. Owen.

Fiffer, Sharon and Steve. 1995. *Home*. New York: Random House.

Fleischman, Sid. 1996. *The Abracadabra Kid*. New York: Greenwillow.

Fletcher, Ralph. 1996. *Breathing in, Breathing Out*. Portsmouth, NH: Heinemann.

Fritz, Jean 1992. *Surprising Myself*. Katonah, NY: Richard C. Owen.

Gary, Alice. 1996. *Jean Craighead George*. Santa Barbara, CA: The Learning Works.

Goble, Paul. 1994. *Hau Kola: Hello Friend*. Katonah, NY: Richard C. Owen.

Goldberg, Natalie. 1986. *Writing Down the Bones*. Boston: Shambhala Publishing.

Gormley, Beatrice. 1999. *Louisa May Alcott*. New York: Aladdin Paperbacks, Simon & Schuster.

Graham, Paula W. 1999. *Speaking of Journals*. Honesdale, PA: Boyds Mills Press.

Greenfield, Eloise and Lessie Jones Little. 1993. *Childtimes: A Three Generation Memoir* New York: HarperCollins.

Heller, Ruth. 1999. *Fine Lines*. Katonah, NY: Richard C. Owen.

Hinchman, Hannah. 1991. *A Life in Hand*. Salt Lake, UT: Peregrine Smith Books.

Hopkins, Lee Bennett. 1993. *The Writing Bug*. Katonah, NY: Richard C. Owen.

Howe, James. 1994. *Playing with Words*. Katonah, NY: Richard C. Owen.

Hurwitz, Johanna. 1998. *A Dream Come True*. Katonah, NY: Richard C. Owen.

Krementz, Jill. 1992. *A Storyteller's Story*. Katonah, NY: Richard C. Owen.

Kuskin, Karla. 1995. *Thoughts, Pictures, and Words*. Katonah, NY: Richard C. Owen.

Little, Jean 1988. *Little by Little: A Writer's Education*. New York: Viking Press.

Lobel, Anita. 1998. *No Pretty Pictures: A Child of War*. New York: Avon Camelot Books.

Locker, Thomas. 1999. *The Man Who Paints Nature*. Katonah, NY: Richard C. Owen.

London, Jonathan. 1998. *Tell Me a Story*. Katonah, NY: Richard C. Owen.

Lowry, Lois. 1998. *Looking Back: A Book of Memories*. Boston: Houghton Mifflin.

MacNeil, Robert. 1990. *Wordstruck*. New York: Penquin Books.

Mahy, Margaret. 1995. *My Mysterious World*. Katonah, NY: Richard C. Owen.

Marcus, Leonard S. and Judy Blume. 2000. *Author Talk : Conversations With Judy Blume, Bruce Brooks, Karen Cushman, Russell Freedman, Lee Bennett Hopkins, James Howe, Johanna Hurwitz, E. L. Ko*. New York: Simon & Schuster

Markham, Lois. 1995. *Lois Lowry*. Santa Barbara, CA: The Learning Works.

Markham, Lois. 1996. *Avi*. Santa Barbara, CA: The Learning Works.

Martin, Rafe. 1992. *A Storyteller's Story*. Katonah, NY: Richard C. Owen.

McKissack, Patricia. 1997. *Can You Imagine*. Katonah, NY: Richard C. Owen.

McPhail, David. 1996. *In Flight with David McPhail: A Creative Autobiography*. Portsmouth, NH: Heinemann.

Meltzer, Milton. 1991 *Starting From Home: A Writer's Beginnings*. New York: Puffin.

Naylor, Phyllis. 2001. *How I Came to Be a Writer*. New York: Aladdin Paperbacks.

Paulsen, Gary. 1994. *My Life in Dog Years*. New York: Bantam, Doubleday, Dell.

Paulsen, Gary. 1994. *Winterdance: The Fine Madness of Running the Iditarod*. New York: Harcourt Brace and Company.

Peet, William. 1989. *Bill Peet: An Autobiography*. Boston: Houghton Mifflin.

Polacco, Patricia. 1994. *Firetalking*. Katonah, NY: Richard C. Owen.

Pringle, Laurence. 1997. *Nature! Wild and Wonderful*. Katonah, NY: Richard C. Owen.

Ringgold, Faith, Linda Freeman, and Nancy Roucher. 1996. *Talking to Faith Ringgold*. New York: Crown Publishers.

Rylant, Cynthia. 1989. *But I'll Be Back Again*. New York: Orchard Books.

Rylant, Cynthia. 1992. *Best Wishes*. Katonah, NY: Richard C. Owen.

Simon, Seymour. 2000. *From Paper Airplanes to Outer Space*. Katonah, NY: Richard C. Owen.

Spain, Valerie. 1994. *Meet Maya Angelou*. New York: Random House.

Spinelli, Jerry. 1998. *Knots in My Yo-Yo String: The Autobiography of a Kid*. New York: Alfred A. Knopf.

Streissguth, Tom. 1997. *Writer of the Plains: A Story about Willa Cather (Creative Minds)*. Minneapolis, MN: Carolrhoda Books.

Van Leeuwen, Jean. 1998. *Growing Ideas*. Katonah, NY: Richard C. Owen.

Welty, Eudora. 1983. *One Writer's Beginnings*. Cambridge, MA: Harvard University Press.

Yolen, Jane. 1992. *A Letter from Phoenix Farm*. Katonah, NY: Richard C. Owen.

Zinsser, William. 1998. *On Writing Well*. New York: HarperCollins.

Selected Picture Books for Grades 3-6
Fiction and Nonfiction

Fiction Titles:

Bartone, Elisa. 1993. *Peppe the Lamplighter*. New York: Mulberry Book/William Morrow.

Baylor, Byrd. 1983. *The Best Town in the World*. New York: Atheneum.

Bradby, Marie. 1995. *More than Anything Else*. New York: Orchard Books.

Bradby, Marie. 2000. *Momma, Where Are You From?* New York: Orchard Books.

Brooks, Nigel and Abigail Horner. 2000. *Town Mouse House*. New York: Walker & Company.

Bunting, Eve. 1991. *Fly Away Home*. New York: Clarion

Bunting, Eve. 1992. *The Wall*. New York: Houghton Mifflin.

Bunting, Eve. 1993. *Butterfly House*. New York: Scholastic, Inc.

Bunting, Eve. 1996. *A Train to Somewhere*. New York: Clarion Books/Houghton Mifflin Company.

Bunting, Eve. 1999. *A Picnic in October*. New York: Harcourt Brace & Company.

Bunting, Eve. 2000. *The Memory String*. New York: Houghton Mifflin

Cha, Dia. 1996. *Dia's Story Cloth*. New York: Lee & Low Books, Inc.

Chall, Marsha Wilson. 1992. *Up North at the Cabin*. New York: Lothrop, Lee & Shepard Books.

Cherry, Lynne. 1990. *The Great Kapok Tree*. New York: Gulliver Green Book/Harcourt Brace & Company.

Climo, Shirley. 1999. *The Persian Cinderella*. New York: HarperCollins.

Cooney, Barbara. 1982. *Little Brother and Little Sister*. New York: Barnes & Noble, Inc.

Cooney, Barbara. 1982. *Miss Rumphius*. New York: Viking.

Crook, Connie Brummel. 1997. *Maple Moon*. Buffalo, NY: Stoddart Kids.

Diakite, Baba Wague. 1997. *The Hunterman and the Crocodile*. New York: Scholastic, Inc.

Gallaz, Christophe and Roberto Innocenti. 1985. *Rose Blanche*. New York: Harcourt Brace.

Garland, Sherry. 1993. *Lotus Seed*. New York: Harcourt Brace.

George, Jean C. 1999. *Snow Bear*. New York: Hyperion.

Gray, Libba M. 1993. *Dear Willie Rudd*. New York: Simon & Schuster.

Gray, Libba Moore. 1995. *My Mama Had a Dancing Heart*. New York: Orchard Books.

Hamilton, Virginia. 1995. *Her Stories: African American Folktales, and True Tales*. New York: The Blue Sky Press.

High, Linda Oatman. 1999. *Barn Savers*. Honesdale, PA: Boyds Mills Press.

Hest, Amy. 1995. *How to Get Famous in Brooklyn*. New York: Simon & Schuster.

Hoestlandt, Jo. 1993. *Star of Fear, Star of Hope*. New York: Walker & Company.

Hooks, William H. 1996. *Freedom's Fruit*. New York: Alfred A. Knopf.

Houston, Gloria. 1992. *My Great-Aunt Arizona*. New York: HarperCollins.

Johnson, Dinah. 1998. *All Around Town*. New York: Henry Holt & Company, Inc.

Jonas, Ann. 1997. *Watch William Walk*. New York: Greenwillow Books/William Morrow & Company, Inc.

Khalsa, Dayal K. 1986. *Tales of a Gambling Grandma*. New York: Clarkson N. Potter, Inc.

Kirkpatrick, Katherine. 1999. *Redcoats and Petticoats*. New York: Holiday House.

Kroll, Virginia. 1995. *Sweet Magnolia*. Watertown, MA: Charlesbridge Publishing.

Lester, Julius. 1999. *What a Truly Cool World*. New York: Scholastic, Inc.

Lewis, Naomi. 1997. *The Emperor's New Clothes*. Cambridge, MA: Candlewick Press.

Lorbiecki, Marybeth. 1998. *Sister Anne's Hands*. New York: Dial Books for Young Children/Penguin Putnam, Inc.

Martin, Rafe. 1998. *The Rough-Faced Girl*. Paper Star.

McCully, Emily Arnold. 1996. *The Bobbin Girl*. New York: Dial Books/Penguin Putnam.

McDermott, Gerald. 1974. *Arrow to the Sun*. New York: Viking.

McKay, Lawrence. 1998. *Journey Home*. New York: Lee & Low Books.

Miles, Miska. 1985. *Annie and the Old One*. New York: Little, Brown & Company.

Miller, William. 2000. *The Piano*. New York: Lee & Low Books.

Moss, Marissa. 1999. *True Heart*. New York: Harcourt Brace & Company.

Polacco, Patricia. 1994. *Pink and Say*. New York: Philomel Books.

Paulsen, Gary. 1995. *The Tortilla Factory*. San Diego: Harcourt Brace & Company.

Paulsen, Gary. 1999. *Canoe Days*. New York: Bontana Doubleday.

Pinkney, Jerry. 1999. *The Ugly Duckling*. New York: Morrow Junior Books/William Morrow & Company.

Rael, Elsa Okon. 1996. *What Zeesie Saw on Delancey Street*. New York: Simon & Schuster.

Rahaman, Vashanti. 1997. *Read for Me, Mama*. Honesdale, PA: Boyds Mill Press.

Raven, Margot Theis. 1997. *Angels in the Dust*. Mahwah, NJ: Bridgewater Books/Troll.

Ringgold, Faith. 1991. *Tar Beach*. New York: Crown Publications.

Ringgold, Faith. 1992. *Aunt Harriet's Underground Railroad in the Sky*. New York: Crown Publishers/Random House.

Ringgold, Faith. 1993. *Dinner at Aunt Connie's House*. New York: Hyperion Books.

Rylant, Cynthia. 1982. *When I was Young in the Mountains*. New York: Dutton Children's Books/Penguin.

Rylant, Cynthia. 1992. *An Angel for Solomon Singer*. New York: Orchard Books.

Schimmel, Schim. 1994. *Dear Children of the Earth: A Letter from Home*. Minnesota: NorthWord Press.

Sisulu, Elinor Batezat. 1996. *The Day Gogo Went to Vote*. New York: Little, Brown & Company.

Soto, Gary. 1997. *Snapshots from the Wedding*. New York: G.P. Putnam's Sons.

Steig, William. 1971. *Amos and Boris*. New York: Farrar, Straus & Giroux.

Steig, William. 1988. *Brave Irene*. New York: Farrar, Straus & Giroux.

Sturges, Philemon. 1995. *Ten Flashing Fireflies*. New York: North South Books.

Swinburne, Stephen. 1998. *In Good Hands*. San Francisco, CA: Sierra Club Book for Children.

Taulbert, Clifton L. 1999. *Little Cliff and the Porch People*. New York: Dial Books for Young Readers/Penquin Putnam.

Trottier, Maxine. 1998. *Prairie Willow*. New York: Stoddart Kids.

Trottier, Maxine. 1999. *Dreamstones*. New York: Stoddart Kids.

Trottier, Maxine. 2000. *Little Dog Moon*. New York: Stoddart Kids.

Tunnell, Michael O. 1997. *Mailing May*. New York: Greenwillow.

Turner, Ann. 1987. *Nettie's Trip South*. New York: Macmillan.

Turner, Ann. 1992. *Katie's Trunk*. New York: Macmillan Publishing.

Vaughan, Marcia. 1999. *Abbie Against the Storm*. Hillsboro, OR: Beyond Words Publishing, Inc.

Viorst, Judith. 1971. *The Tenth Good Thing About Barney*. New York: Atheneum Books/Simon & Schuster. New York: Dial Books for Young Readers/Penquin Putnam.

Wheatley, Nadia and Donna Rawlins. 1987. *My Place*. Melbourne, Australia: Collins Dove.

Wing, Natasha. 1996. *Jalapeno Bagels*. New York: Atheneum.

Yep, Laurence. 1997. *The Khan's Daughter*. New York: Scholastic, Inc.

Yolen, Jane. 1987. *Owl Moon*. New York: Philomel Books.

Yolen, Jane. 1992. *Encounter*. New York: Harcourt Brace & Company.

Zolotow, Charlotte. 1993. *Snippets*. New York: HarperCollins.

Nonfiction Titles:

Arnosky, Jim. 1988. *Sketching Outdoors in Winter*. New York: Lothrop.

Arnosky, Jim. 1997. *All About Rattlesnakes*. New York: Scholastic Press.

Bachrach, Susan D. 1994. *Tell Them We Remember: The Story of the Holocaust*. New York: Little, Brown & Company.

Baker, Jeannie. 1987. *Where the Forest Meets the Sea*. New York: Greenwillow Books.

Bateman, Robert and Rick Archbold. 1998. *Safari*. New York: Little Brown & Company.

Berger, Melvin. 1999. *Germs Make Me Sick*. New York: Econo-Clad Books.

Bierman, C. and L. McGaw. 1998. *Journey to Ellis Island*. New York: Hyperion Books

Bird, Bettina and Joan Short. 1997. *Insects*. Greenvale, New York: Mondo Books.

Borden, Louise. 1997. *The Little Ships*. New York: Margaret K. McElderrry Books/Simon Schuster.

Brandenburg, Jim. 1995. *An American Safari*. New York: Walker & Company.

Branzei, Sylvia. 1996. *Animal Grossology: The Science of Creatures Gross and Disgusting*. Reading, MA: Planet Dexter/Addison Wesley Longman.

Branzei, Sylvia. 1997. *Virtual Grossology*. Reading, MA: Planet Dexter/Addison Wesley Longman.

Browne, Philippa-Alys. 1995. *African Animals ABC*. San Francisco, CA: Sierra Club Books for Children.

Bruchac, Joseph. 1994. *A Boy Called Slow: The True Story of Sitting Bull*. New York: Philomel Books.

Burleigh, Robert. 1997. *Hoops*. New York: Harcourt Brace & Company.

Burleigh, Robert. 1998. *Home Run*. New York: Harcourt Brace & Company.

Carlson, Laurie. 1998. *Boss of the Plains: The Hat That Won the West*. New York: DK Publishing, Inc.

Cerullo, Mary M. 1996. *Coral Reef: A City that Never Sleeps*. New York: Cobblehill Books/Penquin.

Cisneros, Sandra. 1984, 1994. *Hairs = Pelitos: A Story in English and Spanish from The House on Mango Street*. New York: Alfred A. Knopf, Inc.

Coerr, Eleanor. 1993. *Sadako*. New York: Putnam Publishing.

Cole, Joanna. 1995. *The Magic School Bus: In the Time of the Dinosaurs*. New York: Scholastic, Inc.

Cole, Joanna. 1995. *The Magic School Bus: Inside a Hurricane*. New York: Scholastic, Inc.

Collard, Sneed. 1997. *Animal Dads*. Boston: Houghton Mifflin.

Collard, Sneed. 1999. *1,000 Years Ago on Planet Earth*. Boston: Houghton Mifflin.

Cooney, Barbara. 1996. *Eleanor*. New York: Puffin Books.

Cooper, Floyd. 1996. *Mandela: From the Life of the South African Statesman*. New York: Scholastic, Inc.

Couper, Heather and Nigel Henbest. 1996. *Black Holes: A Journey to the Heart of a Black Hole and Into One of the Greatest Mysteries of the Universe*. New York: DK Publishing, Inc.

Davis, Lucile. 1998. *Cesar Chavez: A Photo-Illustrated Biography*. Mankato, MN: Bridgestone Books/Capstone Press.

Erickson, Paul. 1994. *Daily Life in a Covered Wagon*. Washington, DC: The Preservation Press.

Fanelli, Sara. 1995. *My Map Book*. New York: HarperCollins.

Fritz, Jean. 1993. *Just a Few Words, Mr. Lincoln*. New York: Grosset & Dunlap.

Garza, Carmen Lomas. 1999. *Magic Windows*. San Francisco, CA: Children's Press.

Geisert, Arthur. 1996. *Roman Numerals I to MM*. New York: Houghton Mifflin.

Goodman, Susan. 1998. *Stones, Bones, and Petroglyphs*. Atheneum Books for Young Readers/Simon & Schuster.

Govenar, Alan. 2000. *Memories of a Sharecropper's Daughter*. New York: Hyperion.

Greenaway, Frank. 2000. *The Snake Book*. DK Pub Merchandise.

Hawes, Judy. 1991. *Fireflies in the Night*. New York: TY Corowell Co.

Hearne, Betsy. 1997. *Seven Brave Women*. New York: Greenwillow Books.

Hodge, Deborah. 1997. *Whales: Killer Whales, Blue Whales and More* Buffalo, New York: Kids Can Press.

Jackson, Donna. 1996. *The Bone Detective*. Boston: Little Brown.

King, Casey and Linda B. Osborne. 1997. *Oh, Freedom*. New York: Scholastic, Inc.

Knight, Amelia Stewart. 1993. *The Way West: Journal of a Pioneer Woman*. New York: Simon & Schuster.

Knowlton, Jack. 1988. *Geography from A to Z*. New York: HarperCollins.

Kodama, Tatsuharu. 1995. *Shin's Tricycle*. New York: Walker & Company.

Krull, Kathleen. 1996. *Wilma Unlimited: How Wilma Rudolph Became the World's Fastest Woman*. New York: Harcourt Brace.

Krupp, E.C. 2000. *The Moon and You*. New York: HarperCollins Juvenile Books.

Lasky, Kathryn. 1997. *Marven of the Great North Woods*. New York: Harcourt Brace & Company.

Lasky, Kathryn. 1997. *The Most Beautiful Roof in the World*. New York: Gulliver Green/Harcourt Brace & Company.

Lasky, Kathryn. 2000. *Vision of Beauty: The Story of Sarah Breedlove Walker*. Cambridge, MA: Candlewick Press.

Lauber, Patricia. 1996. *Hurricanes: Earth's Mightiest Storms*. New York: Scholastic Press.

Leigh, Nila K. 1999. *Learning to Swim In Swaziland: A Child's-Eye View of a Southern African County*. New York: Scholastic, Inc.

Loewer, Peter and Joan. 1997. *The Moonflower*. Atlanta, GA: Peachtree Publishers.

Marcus, Leonard S. 1998. *A Caldecott Celebration*. New York: Walker & Company.

Markle, Sandra. 1994. *Outside and Inside Spiders*. New York: Atheneum Books for Young Readers/Simon & Schuster.

Markle, Sandra. 1997. *Bats*. New York: Atheneum Books for Young Readers/ Simon & Schuster.

Martin, Jacqueline B. 1998. *Snowflake Bentley*. Boston: Houghton Mifflin.

McCurdy, Michael. 1995. *The Gettysburg Address*. Boston: Houghton Mifflin.

McGill, Alice. 1999. *Molly Bannaky*. Boston: Houghton Mifflin.

McMillan, Bruce. 1998. *Salmon Summer*. Boston: Houghton Mifflin.

Meltzer, Milton. 1998. *Ten Queens*. New York: Dutton Children's Books/Penguin Putnam.

Mochizuki, Ken. 1993. *Baseball Saved Us*. New York: Lee and Low Books.

Mochizuki, Ken. 1997. *Passage to Freedom: The Sugihara Story*. New York: Lee & Low Books, Inc.

Murphy, Jim. 1995. *The Great Fire*. New York: Scholastic, Inc.

Myers, Walter D. 1998. *Amistad: A Long Road to Freedom*. Dreamworks.

Park, Frances and Ginger Park. 1998. *My Freedom Trip: A Child's Escape From North Korea*. Honesdale, PA: Boyds Mills Press.

Pascoe, Elaine. 1999. *Slime, Molds & Fungi*. CT: Blackbirch Press.

Peacock, Louise. 1998. *Crossing the Delaware: A History in Many Voices*. New York: Atheneum Books for Young Readers/Simon & Schuster.

Pinkney, Andrea D. 1993. *Alvin Ailey*. New York: Hyperion Books for Children.

Pinkney, Andrea D. 1996. *Bill Pickett: Rodeo-Ridin' Cowboy*. New York: Gulliver Books/Harcourt Brace & Company.

Pringle, Laurence. 1995. *Fire in the Forest*. New York: Atheneum Books for Young Readers/ Simon & Schuster.

Quinlan, Susan. 1999. *Puffins*. New York: Carolrhoda Books.

Reiser, Lynn 1996. *Beach Feet*. New York: Greenwillow.

Ringgold, Faith. 1999. *If a Bus Could Talk*. New York: Simon & Schuster.

Ryan, Pam Munoz. 1996. *The Flag We Love*. Watertown, MA: Charlesbridge.

Ryan, Pam Munoz. 1999. *Amelia and Eleanor Go for a Ride*. New York: Scholastic Press.

Rylant, Cynthia. 1991. *Appalachia: The Voices of Sleeping Birds*. New York: Harcourt, Brace & Company.

Sandler, Martin W. 1994. *Cowboys*. New York: HarperCollins.

Simon, Seymour. 1979. *Animal Fact/Animal Fable*. New York: Crown Publishers, Inc.

Simon, Seymour. 1988. *Galaxies*. New York: William Morrow Junior Books.

Simon, Seymour. 1995. *Sharks*. New York: HarperCollins.

Simon, Seymour. 1997. *The Brain*. New York: William Morrow & Company.

Sis, Peter. 1996. *Starry Messenger*. New York: Farrar, Straus, Giroux.

Stanley, Jerry. 1992. *Children of the Dust Bowl:The True Story of the School at Weedpatch Camp*. New York: Crown Publishers.

Stanley, Diane and Peter Vennema. 1988. *Shaka: King of the Zulus*. New York: Mulberry Books.

Stanley, Diane and Peter Vennema. 1992. *Bard of Avon: The Story of William Shakespeare*. New York: Morrow Junior Books.

Stanley, Diane and Peter Vennema. 1993. *Charles Dickens: The Man Who had Great Expectations*. New York: William Morrow and Company.

Stanley, Diane. 2000. *Michaelangelo*. New York: HarperCollins.

Stanley, Fay. 1991. *The Last Princess: The Story of Princess Ka'iulani of Hawai'i*. New York: HarperCollins.

Stanley, Jerry. 1996. *Big Annie of Calumet : A True Story of the Industrial Revolution*. New York: Crown Publishers/Random House.

Sturges, Philemon. 1995. *Ten Flashing Fireflies*. New York: North South Books.

Sturges, Philemon. 1998. *Bridges are to Cross*. New York: G.P. Putnam & Sons.

Sussman, Susan and Robert James. 1987. *Lies People Believe About Animals*. Morton Grove, IL: Albert Whitman & Company.

Swinburne, Stephen. 1998. *In Good Hands*. San Francisco, CA: Sierra Club Book for Children.

Swinburne, Stephen R. 1998. *Lots and Lots of Zebra Stripes*. Honesdale, PA: Caroline House/Boyds Mills Press.

Swineburne, Stephen R. 1999. *Once a Wolf*. Boston: Houghton Mifflin.

Trottier, Maxine. 1998. *Prairie Willow*. New York: Stoddart Kids.

Tsuchiya, Yukio. 1988. *The Faithful Elephants. A True Story of Animals, People and War*. Boston: Houghton Mifflin.

Venezia, Mike. 1990. *Monet*. New York: Children's Press.

Wick, Walter. 1997. *A Drop of Water*. New York: Scholastic, Inc.

Williams, Vera B. 1984. *Three Days on A River in a Red Canoe*. New York: Mulberry Books.

Wilson. 2000. *Imagine That!* New York: Stoddart Publishing.

Woodworth, Deborah. 1998. *Compassion: The Story of Clara Barton*. Chanhassen, MN: The Child's World.

Wu, Norbert. 1996. *A City Under the Sea: Life in a Coral Reef*. New York: Atheneum Books for Young Readers/Simon & Schuster.

Poetry:
Collections, Anthologies, and Picture Books

Abeel, Samantha. 1993. *Reach for the Moon*. Duluth, MN: Pfeifer-Hamilton.

Adedjouma, Davida. 1999. *The Palm of My Heart: Poetry by African American Children*. New York: Econo-Clad Books.

Adoff, Arnold, ed. (1968. *I am the Darker Brother*. New York: Macmillan.

Adoff, Arnold. 1974. *My Black Me*. New York: Dutton Books

Adoff, Arnold. 1979. *Eats*. New York: Lothrop, Lee & Shepard Books.

Adoff, Arnold. 1997. *Love Letters*. Ill. Lisa Desimini. New York: Blue Sky/Scholastic, Inc.

Adoff, Arnold. 1981. *Outside Inside: Poems*. New York: Harcourt Brace & Company.

Adoff, Arnold. 1995. *Street Music: City Poems*. New York: HarperCollins.

Alarcon, Francisco X. 1997. *Laughing Tomatoes and Other Spring Poems*. Ill. Maya Christina Gonzalez. San Francisco: Children's Book Press.

Angelou, Maya. 1986. *Maya Angelou Poems*. New York: Bantam Books.

Asch, Frank. 1998. *Cactus Poems*. Ill. Ted Levin. New York: Harcourt Brace & Co.

Baylor, Byrd. 1978. *The Other Way to Listen*. Ill. Peter Parnall. New York: Atheneum/Simon & Schuster

Baylor, Byrd. 1981. *Desert Voices*. Ill. Peter Parnall. New York: Aladdin Books/Simon & Schuster.

Baylor, Byrd. 1986. *I'm in Charge of Celebrations*. Ill. Peter Parnall. New York: Charles Scribner's Sons.

Baylor, Byrd. 1987. *Everybody Needs a Rock*. Ill. Peter Parnall. New York: Atheneum Books for Young Readers/Simon & Schuster.

Baylor, Byrd. 1991. *Your Own Best Secret Place*. Ill. Peter Parnall. New York: Atheneum.

Begay, Shonto. 1995. *Navajo Visions and Voices Across the Mesa*. New York: Scholastic.

Booth, David, ed. 1990. *Voices in the Wind : Poems for All Seasons*. Ill. Michele Lemieux. New York: Morrow.

Brenner, Barbara, ed. 1994. *The Earth Is Painted Green : A Garden of Poems About Our Planet*. New York: Scholastic.

Bryan, Ashley. 1997. *ABC of African American Poetry*. New York: Atheneum.

Burleigh, Robert. 1997 *Hoops*. New York: Harcourt Brace & Company.

Carlson, Lori M. 1994. *Cool Salsa: Bilingual Poems on Growing Up Latino in the United States*. New York: Henry Holt.

Chandra, Deborah. 1993. *Rich Lizard and Other Poems*. New York: Farrar, Straus & Giroux.

Clements, Andrew. 1999. *Workshop*. Ill. David Wisniewski. New York: Clarion Books/Houghton Mifflin.

Clinton, Catherine. 1998. *I, Too, Sing America*. Ill. Stephen Alcorn. Boston: Houghton Mifflin.

Cullinan, Bernice E. 1996. *A Jar of Tiny Stars : Poems by NCTE Award-Winning Poets*. Honesdale, PA: Wordsong/Boyds Mills.

Dotlich, Rebecca K. 1998. *Lemonade Sun and Other Summer Poems*. Ill. Jan Spivey Gilchrist. Honesdale, PA: Wordsong/Boyds Mills.

Dove, Rita. 1999. *On the Bus with Rosa Parks: Poems*. New York: W.W. Norton.

Dunbar, Lawrence. 1999. *Jump Back, Honey: Poems*. New York: Hyperion Press.

Dunning, S., E. Lueders, and H. Smith, eds. 1966. *Reflections on a Gift of Watermelon Pickle and Other Modern Verse*. Glenview, IL: Scott, Foresman.

Esbenson, Barbara. 1984. *Cold Stars and Fireflies: Poems of the Four Seasons*. Ill. Susan Bonners. New York: Crowell.

Esbenson, Barbara. 1987. *Words with Wrinkled Knees*. New York: HarperCollins.

Esbenson, Barbara. 1992. *Who Shrank My Grandmother's House: Poems of Discovery*. Ill. Eric Beddows. New York: HarperCollins.

Esbensen, Barbara. 1995. *Dance With Me*. New York: HarperCollins.

Esbensen, Barbara. 1996. *Echoes for the Eye: Poems to Celebrate Patterns in Nature*. New York: HarperCollins.

Feelings, Ed. 1994. *Soul Looks Back in Wonder*. New York: Dial Books/ Penguin Books.

Fleischman, Paul. 1985. *I Am Phoenix : Poems for Two Voices*. Ill. Ken Nutt. New York: Harper & Row.

Fleischman, Paul. 1988. *Joyful Noise: Poems for Two Voices*. Ill. Eric Beddows. New York: Charlotte Zolotow Book/HarperCollins.

Fleischman, Paul. 2000. *Big Talk: Poems for Four Voices*. Ill. Beppe Giacobbe. Cambridge, MA: Candlewick Press.

Fletcher, Ralph. 1994. *I Am Wings: Poems About Love*. Ill. Joe Baker. New York: Atheneum Books.

Fletcher, Ralph. 1997. *Ordinary Things: Poems from a Walk in Early Spring*. New York: Atheneum.

Fletcher, Ralph. 1997. *Room Enough for Love: The Complete Poems from I Am Wings and Buried Alive*. New York: Aladdin Paperbacks.

Fletcher, Ralph. 1997. *Twilight Comes Twice*. Ill. Kate Kiesler. New York: Clarion Books.

Fletcher, Ralph. 1999. *Relatively Speaking: Poems About Family*. Ill. Walter Lyon Krudop. New York: Orchard Books.

Florian, David. 1996. *Bing Bang Boing: Poems and Drawings*. New York: Puffin.

Florian, Douglas. 1998. *Beast Feast*. New York: Voyager.

Florian, Douglas. 1998. *Insectlopedia: Poems & Paintings*. New York: Harcourt, Inc.

Florian, Douglas. 1999. *WinterEyes*. New York: Greenwillow.

Florian, Douglas. 2000. *Mammalabilia*. New York: Harcourt, Inc.

Frost, Robert. 1978. *Stopping by Woods on a Snowy Evening*. Ill. Susan Jeffers. New York: E.P. Dutton.

Frost, Robert. 1988. *Birches*. New York: Henry Holt.

George, Kristine O'Connell. 1998. *Old Elm Speaks*. New York: Clarion

Giovanni, Nikki. 1985. *Spin a Soft Black Song*. Ill. George Martins. New York: HarperCollins.

Giovanni, Nikki. 1996. *The Sun Is So Quiet*. Ill. Ashley Bryan. New York: Henry Holt & Company.

Goldstein, Bobbye S. 1992. *Inner Chimes: Poems on Poetry*. Honesdale, PA: Boyds Mills Press.

Gollub, Matthew. 1998. *Cool Melons – Turn to Frogs!* Ill. Kazuko G. Stone. New York: Lee & Low Books.

Graham, Joan B. 1999. *FlickerFlash*. Ill. Nancy Davis. New York: Houghton Mifflin.

Greenfield, Eloise. 1978. *Honey, I Love and Other Love Poems*. New York: Thomas Y. Crowell.

Greenfield, Eloise. 1991. *Under the Sunday Tree*. Ill. Amos Ferguson. New York: Harper & Row.

Grimes, Nikki. 1994. *Meet Danitra Brown*. Ill. Floyd Cooper. New York: Morrow.

Grimes, Nikki. 1999. *Hopscotch Love*. Ill. Melodye Benson Rosales. New York: Lothrop, Lee & Shepard.

Grimes, Nikki. 2000. *Is It Far to Zanzibar?* Ill. Betsy Lewin. New York: Lothrop, Lee & Shepard.

Harrison, M. and C. Stuart-Clark. 1992. *The Oxford Book of Animal Poems*. New York: Oxford: Oxford University Press.

Harrison, Michael and Christopher Stuart-Clark. 1996. *Touching the Distance: A Year Full of Poems*. New York: Oxford University Press.

Heard, Georgia. 1997. *Creatures of Earth, Sea, and Sky*. Honesdale, PA: Boyds Mills Press.

Highwater, Jamake. 1995. *Songs for the Seasons*. Ill. Sandra Speidel. New York: Lothrop, Lee & Shepard Books.

Ho, Minfong. 1996. *Maples in the Mist*. Ill. Jean & Mou-sien Tseng. New York: Lothrop, Lee & Shepard.

Hopkins, Lee Bennett. 1983. *A Song in Stone: City Poems*. New York: Thomas Y. Crowell.

Hopkins, Lee Bennett, ed. 1983. *The Sky is Full of Song*. New York: Harper & Row.

Hopkins, Lee Bennett. 1994. *Hand in Hand: An American History Through Poetry*. New York: Simon & Schuster.

Hopkins, Lee Bennett. 1995. *Been to Yesterdays*. Honesdale, PA: Wordsong/Boyds Mills.

Hopkins, Lee Bennett. 1996. *Opening Days: Sports Poems*. Ill. Scott Medlock. New York: Harcourt Brace.

Hopkins, Lee Bennett. 1996. *School Supplies*. Ill. Renee Flowers. New York: Aladdin Paperbacks/Simon & Schuster.

Hopkins, Lee Bennett. 1999. *L I V E S: Poems About Famous Americans*. Ill. Leslie Staub. New York: Harper Collins.

Hopkins, Lee Bennett, ed. 1999. *Spectacular Science*. Ill. Virginia Halstead. New York: Simon & Schuster.

Hopkins, Lee Bennett. 2000. *My America: A Poetry Atlas of the United States*. Ill. Stephen Alcorn. New York: Simon & Schuster.

Hudson, Wade, ed. 1993. *Pass It on: African-American Poetry for Children*. New York: Scholastic.

Hudson, Wade and Cheryl Willis Hudson. 1997. *In Praise of Our Fathers and Our Mothers*. East Orange, NJ: Just Us Books, Inc.

Hughes, Langston. 1974. *Selected Poems of Langston Hughes*. New York: Random House.

Hughes, Langston. 1994. *The Dream Keeper and Other Poems*. Ill. Brian Pinkney. New York: Alfred A. Knopf.

Hughes, Langston. 1995. *The Block*. Ill. Romare Bearden. New York: Viking Books.

Isaccs, Anne. 1998. *Cat Up a Tree*. Ill. Stephen Mackey. New York: Dutton/Penquin Putnam.

Janeczko, Paul, ed. 1985. *Pocket Poems*. New York: Bradbury.

Janeczko, Paul. 1990. *The Place My Words are Looking for: What Poets Say About and through Their Work*. New York: Simon & Schuster.

Janeczko, Paul, ed. 1993. *Looking for Your Name: A Collection of Contemporary Poems*. New York: Orchard.

Janeczko, Paul. 1994. *Poetry from A to Z*. New York: Simon & Schuster.

Janeczko, Paul. 1998. *That Sweet Diamond*. Ill. Carole Katchen. New York: Atheneum Books.

Jarrell, Randall. 1963. *The Bat Poet*. New York: Macmillan.

Jordan, June, ed. 1969. *Who Look at Me*. New York: Thomas Y. Crowell.

Kennedy, X.J. and D. M. Kennedy. 1999. *Knock at a Star*. Ill. Karen L. Baker. New York: Little, Brown & Company.

Koch, Kenneth & Kate Farrell, eds. 1985. *Talking to the Sun: An Illustrated Anthology of Poems for Young People*. New York: Holt, Rinehart & Winston.

Kuskin, Karla. 1975. *Near the Window Tree*. New York: Harper & Row.

Levin, Jonathan. 1997. *Poetry for Young People, Walt Whitman*. Ill. Jim Burke. New York: Sterling Publishing Company.

Lewin, Betsy. 1995. *Walk a Green Path*. New York: Lothrop, Lee & Shepard.

Lewis, Claudia. 1987. *Long Ago in Oregon*. New York: Harper and Row.

Lewis, J. Patrick. 1991. *Earth Verses and Water Rhymes*. Ill. Robert Sabuda. New York: Atheneum Books.

Lewis, J. Patrick. 1998. *Doodle Dandies: Poems That Take Shape*. Ill. Lisa Desimini. New York: Atheneum Books.

Lewis, J. Patrick. 1999. *The Bookworm's Feast: A Potluck of Poems*. Ill. John O'Brien. New York: Dial Books/Penquin Putnam.

Liatsos, Sandra Olson. 1997. *Bicycle Riding and Other Poems*. Ill. Karen Dugan. Honesdale, PA: Worsong/Boyds Mills.

Livingston, Myra Cohn. 1982. *A Circle of Seasons*. New York: Holiday House.

Livingston, Myra Cohn. 1982. *Earth Songs*. New York: Holiday House.

Livingston, Myra Cohn. 1985. *Celebrations*. New York: Holiday House.

Livingston, Myra Cohn. 1994. *Animal, Vegetable, Mineral: Poems About Small Things*. New York: HarperCollins.

Livingston, Myra Cohn. 1992. *Light and Shadow*. New York: Holiday House.

Lomatewama, Ramson. 1983. *Silent Winds: Poetry of One Hopi*. Hotevilla, AZ: Ramson Lomatewama.

Lomatewama, Ramson. 1993. *Drifting Through Ancestor Dreams*. Flagstaff, AZ: Northland Press.

Longfellow, Henry Wadsworth. 1983. *Hiawatha*. New York: Dial Books for Young Readers.

Longfellow, Henry Wadsworth. 1985. *Paul Revere's Ride*. New York: Greenwillow.

Lynne, Sandford, ed. 1996. *Ten-Second Rain Showers: Poems by Young People*. New York: Simon & Schuster.

Margolis, Richard. 1984. *Secrets of a Small Brother*. New York: Macmillan.

Merriam, Eve. 1986. *Fresh Paint*. Ill. David Frampton. Out of Print.

Merriam, Eve. 1970. *Finding a Poem*. Ill. Seymour Chwast. New York: Atheneum.

Merriam, Eve. 1976. *Rainbow Writing*. New York: Atheneum.

Merriam, Eve. 1985. *Blackberry Ink*. Ill. Hans Wilhelm. New York: Morrow.

Mitchell, Adrian. 1989. *Strawberry Drums*. New York: Delacorte Press.

Mora, Pat. 1998. *The Big Sky*. Ill. Steve Jenkins. New York: Scholastic, Inc.

Moon, Pat. 1996. *Earth Lines: Poems for the Green Age*. New York: Greenwillow.

Moore, Lilian. 1967. *I Feel the Same Way*. New York: Atheneum.

Moore, Lilian. 1969. *I Thought I Heard the City Sing*. New York: Atheneum.

Moore, Lilian. 1997. *Poems Have Roots: New Poems*. Ill. Tad Hills. New York: Atheneum/Simon & Schuster.

Mora, Pat. 1996. *Confetti: Poems for Children*. New York: Lee and Low Books.

Myers, Walter Dean. 1993. *Brown Angels: An Album of Pictures and Verse*. New York: HarperCollins.

Myers, Walter Dean. 1997. *Harlem*. Ill. Christopher Myers. New York: Scholastic, Inc.

Nichols, Grace. 1988. *Come into My Tropical Garden: Children Poems*. Ill. Caroline Binch. New York: J.B. Lippincott.

Nye, Naomi Shihab, ed. 1992. *This Same Sky: A Collection of Poems from Around the World*. New York: Simon & Schuster.

Nye, Naomi Shihab. 1994. *Red Suitcase*. New York: BOA Editions.

Nye, Naomi Shihab. 1995. *The Tree Is Older Than You Are: A Bilingual Gathering of Poems & Stories from Mexico with Paintings by Mexican Artists*. New York: Simon & Schuster.

Nye, Naomi Shihab. 1995. *The Words Under the Words: Selected Poems*. Portland, OR: The Eighth Mountain Press.

Nye, Naomi Shihab, ed. 2000. *Come With Me: Poems for a Journey*. Hong Kong: HarperCollins.

O'Neill, Mary. 1989. *Hailstones and Halibut Bones: Adventures in Color*. Ill. Leonard Weisgard. New York: Doubleday.

Otten, Charlotte F. 1997. *January Rides the Wind*. New York: Lothrop, Lee & Shepard Books

Peacock, M., E. Paschen and N. Neches, eds. 1996. *Poetry in Motion: 100 Poems from the Subways and Buses*. New York: W. W. Norton.

Prelutsky, Jack. 1993. *The Dragons Are Singing Tonight*. Ill. Peter Sis. New York: Mulberry Books/Greenwillow Books.

Prelutsky, Jack. 1997. *The Beauty of the Beast : Poems from the Animal Kingdom*. Ill. Meilo So. New York: Alfred A. Knopf.

Rogasky, Barbara. 1994. *Winter Poems*. Ill. Trina Schart Hyman. New York: Scholastic, Inc.

Rosenberg, Liz, ed. 1996. *The Invisible Ladder: An Anthology of Contemporary American Poems for Young Readers*. New York: Henry Holt.

Ruben, Robert Alden, ed. 1993. *Poetry Out Loud*. New York: Workman Publishing.

Ryder, Joanne. 1985. *Inside Turtle's Shell and Other Poems of the Field*. New York: Macmillan.

Rylant, Cynthia. 1990. *Soda Jerk*. New York: Orchard Books.

Rylant, Cynthia. 1994. *Something Permanent*. Ill. Walker Evans. New York: Orchard Books.

Sandburg, Carl. 1982. *Rainbows are Made*. Sel. by Lee Bennett Hopkins. Orlando, FL: Harcourt Brace and Company.

Schoonmaker, Frances. 1998. *Henry Wadsworth Longfellow*. Ill. Chad Wallace. New York: Sterling Publishing Company.

Simic, Charles. 1974. *Return to a Place Lit by a Glass of Milk: Poems*. New York: Georges Braziller.

Sierra, Judy. 1998. *Anatarctic Antics: A Book of Penguin Poems*. Il. Joe Aruego & Ariane Dewey. New York: Harcourt Brace.

Singer, Marilyn. 2000. *On the Same Day in March: A Tour of the World's Weather*. Ill. Frane Lessac. New York: HarperCollins.

Slier, Deborah. 1991. *Make a Joyful Sound.* Ill. Cornelius Van Wright & Ying-Hwa Hu. New York: Scholastic, Inc.

Soto, Gary. 1990. *A Fire in My Hands.* New York: Scholastic.

Soto, Gary. 1992. *Neighborhood Odes.* Ill. David Diaz. New York: Harcourt Brace & Co.

Soto, Gary. 1995. *Canto Familiar.* New York: Harcourt Brace & Company.

Spooner, Michael. 1993. *A Moon in Your Lunch Box.* Ill. Ib Ohlsson. New York: Henry Holt and Company.

Stevenson, James. 1995. *Sweet Corn: Poems.* New York: Greenwillow.

Stevenson, James. 1998. *Popcorn.* New York: Greenwillow Books/Harper Collins.

Stevenson, James. 1999. *Candy Corn.* New York: Greenwillow Books/Harper Collins.

Stevenson, James. 2000. *Cornflakes.* New York: Greenwillow Books/Harper Collins.

Strickland, Dorothy S. and R. Michael, eds. 1994. *Families: Poems Celebrating the African American Experience.* Ill. John Ward. Honesdale, PA: Wordsong/Boyds Mills.

Sullivan, Charles, ed. 1989. *Imaginary Gardens: American Poetry and Art for Young People.* New York: Abrams.

Sullivan, Charles, ed. 1991. *Children of Promise: African American Literature and Art for Young People.* New York: Abrams.

Swann, Brian. 1998. *The House With No Door: African Riddle-Poems.* Ill. Ashley Bryan. New York: Harcourt Brace & Co.

Swann, Brian. 1998. *Touching the Distance.* Ill. Marvia Rendon. New York: Browndeer Press/Harcourt Brace & Company.

Thomas, Joyce Carol. 1993. *Brown Honey in Broomwheat Tea.* Ill. Floyd Cooper. New York: HarperCollins.

Thurman, Judith. 1976. *Flashlight and Other Poems.* New York: Atheneum.

Turner, Ann. 1997. *Mississippi Mud.* Ill. Robert J. Blake. New York: HarperCollins.

Ward, Leila. 1978. *I Am Eyes: Ni Macho.* New York: Greenwillow Books.

Williams, William Carlos. 1938. *Collected Poems 1909-1939, Vol. 1.* New York: New Directions.

Wong, Janet S. 1996. *A Suitcase of Seaweed and Other Poems.* New York: Simon & Schuster.

Wood, Nancy. 1993. *Spirit Walker.* New York: Doubleday.

Worth, Valerie. 1972. *Small Poems.* Ill. Natalie Babbit. New York: Farrar, Straus and Giroux.

Worth, Valerie. 1976. *More Small Poems.* Ill. Natalie Babbit. New York: Farrar, Straus and Giroux.

Worth, Valerie. 1978. *Still More Small Poems.* Ill. Natalie Babbit. New York: Farrar, Straus and Giroux.

Worth, Valerie. 1994. *All the Small Poems and Fourteen More.* New York: Farrar, Straus and Giroux.

Yolen, Jane. 1993. *Weather Report.* Ill. Annie Gusman. Honesdale, PA: Wordsong/Boyds Mills.

Yolen, Jane. 1996. *Sky Scrape/City Scape : Poems of City Life.* Ill. Ken Condon. Honesdale, PA: Wordsong/Boyds Mills Press.

Yolen, Jane. 1998. *Snow, Snow.* Ill. Jason Stemple. Honesdale, PA: Wordsong/Boyds Mills.

Young, Ed. 1997. *Voices of the Heart.* New York: Scholastic, Inc.

Zolotow, Charlotte. 1993. *Snippets.* Ill. Melissa Sweet. New York: HarperCollinsPublishers.

Zuckerman, Linda, ed. 1998. *Grassroots: Poems by Carl Sandburg.* Ill. Wendell Minor. New York: Harcourt Brace.

Magazines, Themebooks, Newspapers for the Intermediate Grades

Consider the following magazines or themebooks for the classroom library, as sources for short texts for guided reading, or as resources for investigations (see Chapter 25).

Calliope World History for Kids
Cobblestone Publishing, 7 School Rd., Peterborough, NH 03458

Cobblestone The History Magazine for Young People
Cobblestone Publishing, 7 School Rd., Peterborough, NH 03458

Cricket Magazine
Cricket, P.O. Box 7433, Red Oak, IA 51591

Dolphin Log
The Cousteau Log, 870 Greenbrier Circle, Chesapeake, VA 23320

Dragonfly
Dragonfly Magazine, NSTA, 1840 Wilson Blvd., Arlington, VA 22201

Faces: People, Places, and Culture
Cobblestone Publishing, 7 School Rd., Peterborough, NH 03458

Images
Great Source, 181 Ballardvale St., Wilmington, MA 01887

Jr. Scholastic
Scholastic, 555 Broadway, New York, NY 10012

Kids Discover
149 Fifth Ave., 12th floor, New York, NY 10010

Muse
Muse, P.O. Box 7468, Red Oak, IA 51591

National Geographic World
National Geographic Society, Washington, D.C.

Ranger Rick
National Wildlife Federation, 8925 Leesburg Pike, Vienna, VA 22184

Scholastic News
Scholastic, 555 Broadway, New York, NY 10020

Sports Illustrated for Kids
Time, Inc., TIme-Life Building, Rockefeller Center, New York, NY 10020

Stone Soup
Stone Soup Magazine, P.O. Box 83, Santa Cruz, CA 95063

Time for Kids
Time, Inc., Time-Life Building, Rockefeller Center, New York, NY 10020

3-2-1 Contact
Children's Television Workshop, 1 Lincoln Plaza, NY 10023

Tomorrow's Morning
Tomorrow's Morning, Inc., 160 N. Thurston Ave., Los Angeles, CA 90049

U.S. Kids
Children's Better Health, P.O. Box 420235, Palm Coast, FL 32142

Weekly Reader
Scholastic, 555 Broadway, New York, NY 10012

Zillions Consumer Reports for Kids
Consumer Union, 101 Truman Ave., Yonkers, NY 10703

Zoobooks San Diego
Wildlife Education, Ltd., 9820 Willow Creek Rd., San Diego, CA 92131

Books with Memorable Language

Picture Books

All the Places to Love (MacLachlan 1994)
Amos and Boris (Steig 1992)
Appalachia: The Voices of Sleeping Birds (Rylant 1991)
Brave Irene (Steig 1998)
Dreamplace (Lyon 1993)
A Drop of Water (Wick 1997)
Everybody Needs a Rock (Baylor 1987)
Fireflies (Brinckloe 1986)
Home Run (Burleigh 1998)
I'm in Charge of Celebrations (Baylor 1987)
Magic Window / Ventanas Magicas (Garza 1999)
Miz Berlin Walks (Yolen 1997)
My Mama Had a Dancing Heart (Gray 1999)
Owl Moon (Yolen 1987)
A River Ran Wild: An Environmental History (Cherry 1992)
Stones, Bones, and Petroglyphs: Digging into Southwest Archaeology (Goodman 1998)
Tar Beach (Reingold 1991)
The Best Town in the World (Baylor 1983)
The Bone Detectives (Jackson 1996)
The Great Kapok Tree (Cherry 1990)

The Other Way to Listen (Baylor 1997)
Train to Somewhere (Bunting 1996)
Twilight Comes Twice (Fletcher 1997)
What You Know First (MacLachlan 1995)
When I Was Young and in the Mountains (Rylant 1992)
Your Own Best Secret Place (Baylor 1991)

Novels / Short Stories

Abel's Island (Steig 1976)
Baby (MacLachlan 1995)
Dogteam (Paulsen 1999)
Guests (Dorris 1994)
House on Mango Street (Cisneros 1991)
Jip: His Story (Paterson 1998)
J.T. (Wagner 1972)
Missing May (Rylant 1992)
Walk Two Moons (Creech 1994)
The Winter Room (Paulsen 1989)
Woodsong (Paulsen 1990)
Woman Hollering Creek: and Other Short Stories (Cisneros 1991)

Evaluation Response for Text Gradient

Directions: Since any text gradient is always in the process of construction as it is used with varying groups of children, we expect our list to change every year. We encourage you to try the levels with your students and to provide feedback based on your own experiences. Please suggest changes to existing book levels and suggest new books for the list. Please provide the information requested below.

Name: _____   Grade Level You Teach: _____

Telephone: (   ) _____   E-mail address: _____

Address (street, city, state): _____

Book Evaluated:

Book Title: _____

Level: J   K   L   M   N   O   P   Q   R   S   T   U   V   W   X   Y   Z

Author: _____

Publisher: _____

This book is:

_____ A book listed on the gradient that I have evaluated with my class.
(Complete SECTION A and make comments in SECTION C.)

_____ A book listed on the gradient that I am recommending as a benchmark for a level.
(Complete SECTION A and make comments in SECTION C.)

_____ A new book that I suggest adding to the collection.
(Complete SECTION B and make comments in SECTION C.)

SECTION A: (for an evaluation of a book currently included in the list)

Is it appropriately placed on the level (explain)? _____
To what level should the book be moved?
J   K   L   M   N   O   P   Q   R   S   T   U   V   W   X   Y   Z

Are there points of difficulty that make it harder than it seems? _____

_____

Is the text supportive in ways that might not be noticeable when examining the superficial characteristics?

_____

SECTION B: (for the recommendation of a new book) Indicate recommended level:

How does this book support readers at this level? _____

_____

What challenges does it offer? _____

_____

SECTION C: Please place additional comments on the back or on another sheet.

Mail this form to:
Irene Fountas, Lesley University, 1815 Massachusetts Ave., Suite 378, Cambridge, Massachusetts 02140.
Fax: (617) 349-8490   E-mail: ifountas@mail.lesley.edu
Gay Su Pinnell, The Ohio State University, 200 Ramseyer Hall, 29 W. Woodruff Avenue, Columbus, Ohio 43210.
Fax: (614) 292-4260   E-mail: pinnell.1@osu.edu

BOOK LIST
INTRODUCTION

The following is a sampling of books from level J through Z, providing texts of various genres from approximately early grade two through grade six (see chapters 10 and 23 for further information). A level is only an approximation and some levels will be adjusted over time as they are used with students. Please provide your feedback and suggestions for books to be leveled or adjusted on the form in Appendix 60.

A comprehensive list of books for grades kindergarten through three is provided in *Matching Books to Readers (K-3)* (Fountas and Pinnell 1999) and for the intermediate grades in *Leveled Books for Readers, Grades 3-6* (Fountas and Pinnell 2001).

Using the List

The list is sorted in two ways, *by alphabet* and *by level* with five columns on each page. Notice the two dark edged tabs placed alongside the book. These tabs make it possible to quickly turn to the section you want to use.

■ The first column indicates the *title* of the book. The book is placed alphabetically using the first word of the title—unless it is *a* or *the*, in which case the article follows the title.

■ The second column indicates the level of the book, J to Z.

■ The third column provides the type of book, or *genre*. As we explained in Chapter 23, some books might fit more than one genre. The following code is used to indicate the genre:

TL   Traditional Literature
F   Fantasy
RF   Realistic Fiction
HF   Historical Fiction
SF   Science Fiction
I   Information Book
B   Biography (includes autobiography and memoir)

■ The fourth column provides the name of the *author* or *series*.

■ The fifth column indicates the *publisher's or distributor's name*. Addresses and phone numbers for each publisher are provided in Appendix 63. Trade books are available from a variety of general paperback distributors.

Book List
(organized by title)

Title	Level	Genre	Author/Series	Publisher/Distributor
Abel's Island	T	F	Steig, William	Farrar Straus and Giroux
Acid Rain	L	I	Wonder World	Wright Group/McGraw Hill
Across Five Aprils	Z	HF	Hunt, Irene	Follett
Adam Joshua Capers: Halloween Monster	N	RF	Smith, Janice Lee	HarperTrophy
Adam Joshua Capers: Monster in the Third	N	RF	Smith, Janice Lee	HarperTrophy
Adam Joshua Capers: Nelson in Love	N	RF	Smith, Janice Lee	HarperTrophy
Adam Joshua Capers: Superkid!	N	RF	Smith, Janice Lee	HarperTrophy
Adam Joshua Capers: Turkey Trouble	N	RF	Smith, Janice Lee	HarperTrophy
Addie's Bad Day	J	RF	Robins, Joan	HarperTrophy
Addy Saves the Day: A Summer Story	Q	HF	The American Girls Collection	Pleasant Company
Addy's Surprise: A Christmas Story	Q	HF	The American Girls Collection	Pleasant Company
Adventures of Ali Baba Bernstein, The	O	RF	Hurwitz, Johanna	Scholastic
Adventures of Huckleberry Finn, The	Z	HF	Twain, Mark	Scholastic
Adventures of Snail at School	J	F	Stadler, John	HarperTrophy
Adventures of Tom Sawyer, The	Z	HF	Twain, Mark	Scholastic
African-Americans in the Thirteen Colonies	V	I	Cornerstones of Freedom	Children's Press
After the Rain	Z	RF	Mazer, Norma Fox	Avon Books
Afternoon of the Elves	S	F	Lisle, Janet Taylor	Scholastic
Afternoon on the Amazon	M	F	Osborne, Mary Pope	Random House
Ah Liang's Gift	J	RF	Sunshine	Wright Group/McGraw Hill
Ahyoka and the Talking Leaves	S	HF	Roop, Peter and Connie	Beech Tree Books
Ajeemah and his Son	S	HF	Berry, James	HarperTrophy
Aladdin & the Magic Lamp	J	TL	Traditional Tales	Dominie
Aldo Ice Cream	O	RF	Hurwitz, Johanna	The Penguin Group
Aldo Peanut Butter	O	RF	Hurwitz, Johanna	The Penguin Group
Alexander Graham Bell	P	B	Linder, Greg	Capstone Press
Alison's Puppy	K	RF	Bauer, Marion Dane	Hyperion
Alison's Wings	K	RF	Bauer, Marion Dane	Hyperion
All About Bats	J	I	Ready Readers	Modern Curriculum
All About Sam	P	RF	Lowry, Lois	Bantam Doubleday Dell
All For the Better: A Story of El Barrio	R	RF	Mohr, Nicholasa	Steck Vaughn
Allen Jay and the Underground Railroad	O	HF	Brill, Marlene Targ	Carolrhoda Books
Altogether, One at a Time	S	RF	Konigsburg, E.L.	Simon & Schuster
Amalia and the Grasshopper	K	RF	Tello, J. & Krupinski, L.	Scholastic
Amanda Pig and Her Big Brother Oliver	L	F	Van Leeuwen, Jean	Puffin Books
Amazing But True Sports Stories	Q	I	Hollander, Phyllis and Zander	Scholastic
Amazing Eggs	J	I	Discovery World	Rigby
Amber Brown Goes Fourth	N	RF	Danziger, Paula	Scholastic
Amber Brown is Feeling Blue	N	RF	Danziger, Paula	Scholastic
Amber Brown is Not a Crayon	N	RF	Danziger, Paula	Scholastic
Amber Brown Sees Red	N	RF	Danziger, Paula	Scholastic
Amber Brown Wants Extra Credit	N	RF	Danziger, Paula	Scholastic
Amelia Bedelia	L	F	Parish, Peggy	HarperTrophy
Amelia Bedelia and the Baby	L	F	Parish, Peggy	Harper & Row
Amelia Bedelia and the Surprise Shower	L	F	Parish, Peggy	Harper & Row
Amelia Bedelia Goes Camping	L	F	Parish, Peggy	Avon Camelot
Amelia Bedelia Helps Out	L	F	Parish, Peggy	Avon Camelot
Amelia Bedelia's Family Album	L	F	Parish, Peggy	Avon Books
Amelia Earhart	P	B	Parlin, John	Bantam Doubleday Dell
Amelia Earhart	P	B	Rosenthal, M. & Freeman, D.	Capstone Press
Amelia Earhart: Flying for Adventure	S	B	Wade, Mary Dodson	The Millbrook Press
American Alligator, The	R	I	Potts, Steve	Capstone Press
American Revolution, The	V	I	Carter, Alden R.	Franklin Watts
An Early Winter	T	RF	Bauer, Marion Dane	Houghton Mifflin
An Island Far From Home	W	HF	Donahue, John	Carolrhoda Books
An Island Like You: Stories of the Barrio	Z	RF	Cofer, Judith Ortiz	The Penguin Group

Title	Level	Genre	Author/Series	Publisher/Distributor
Anastasia Krupnik	Q	RF	Lowry, Lois	Bantam Doubleday Dell
And I Mean it Stanley	J	RF	Bonsall, Crosby	HarperCollins
And Then What Happened Paul Revere?	R	B	Fritz, Jean	Bantam Doubleday Dell
Animal Dazzlers: The Role of Brilliant Colors in Nature	T	I	Collard, Susan B. III	Franklin Watts
Anne of Green Gables	V	RF	Montgomery, L. M.	Scholastic
Annie's Pet	J	RF	Bank Street	Bantam Doubleday Dell
Arctic Investigations: Exploring the Frozen Ocean	T	I	Young, Karen Romano	Steck Vaughn
Arlington National Cemetery	V	I	Cornerstones of Freedom	Bantam Doubleday Dell
Art Around the World	J	I	Early Connections	Benchmark Education
Arthur Accused!	M	F	Brown, Marc	Little, Brown & Co.
Arthur and the Crunch Cereal Contest	M	F	Brown, Marc	Little, Brown & Co.
Arthur and the Lost Diary	M	F	Brown, Marc	Little, Brown & Co.
Arthur and the Popularity Test	M	F	Brown, Marc	Little, Brown & Co.
Arthur and the Scare-Your-Pants-Off Club	M	F	Brown, Marc	Little, Brown & Co.
Arthur Makes the Team	M	F	Brown, Marc	Little, Brown & Co.
Arthur Rocks with BINKY	M	F	Brown, Marc	Little, Brown & Co.
Arthur's Back to School Day	K	F	Hoban, Lillian	HarperTrophy
Arthur's Camp-Out	K	F	Hoban, Lillian	HarperTrophy
Arthur's Christmas Cookies	K	F	Hoban, Lillian	HarperTrophy
Arthur's Funny Money	K	F	Hoban, Lillian	HarperTrophy
Arthur's Great Big Valentine	K	F	Hoban, Lillian	HarperTrophy
Arthur's Honey Bear	K	F	Hoban, Lillian	Harper Collins
Arthur's Loose Tooth	K	F	Hoban, Lillian	Harper Collins
Arthur's Mystery Envelope	M	F	Brown, Marc	Little, Brown & Co.
Arthur's Pen Pal	K	F	Hoban, Lillian	Harper Collins
Arthur's Prize Reader	K	F	Hoban, Lillian	HarperTrophy
Ask Mr. Bear	J	F	Flack, Marjorie	Macmillan
Attaboy, Sam	P	RF	Lowry, Lois	Bantam Doubleday Dell
Aunt Eater Loves a Mystery	J	F	Cushman, Doug	HarperTrophy
Aunt Eater's Mystery Christmas	J	F	Cushman, Doug	HarperTrophy
Aunt Eater's Mystery Vacation	J	F	Cushman, Doug	HarperTrophy
Autumn Street	V	HF	Lowry, Lois	Bantam Doubleday Dell
Babe the Gallant Pig	R	F	King-Smith, Dick	Random House
Baby	T	RF	MacLachlan, Patricia	Language for Learning Assoc.
Baby Sister for Frances, A	K	F	Hoban, Lillian	Scholastic
Bad Spell for the Worst Witch, A	P	F	Murphy, Jill	Puffin Books
Ballad of the Civil War, A	T	HF	Stolz, Mary	HarperTrophy
Bargain For Frances, A	K	F	Hoban, Russell	HarperTrophy
Baseball in April and Other Stories	U	RF	Soto, Gary	Harcourt Brace
Baseball's Best: Five True Stories	O	B	Step into Reading	Random House
Baseball's Greatest Pitchers	P	B	Kramer, S. A.	Random House
Bat-Poet, The	S	F	Jarrell, Randall	HarperCollins
Bats	O	I	Holmes, Kevin J.	Capstone Press
Beans on the Roof	L	RF	Byars, Betsy	Bantam Doubleday Dell
Bear Called Paddington, A	T	F	Bond, Michael	Bantam Doubleday Dell
Bear Shadow	J	F	Asch, Frank	Simon & Schuster
Bear's Bargain	J	F	Asch, Frank	Scholastic
Bears	O	I	Holmes, Kevin J.	Capstone Press
Beast and the Halloween Horror	M	RF	Giff, Patricia Reilly	Bantam Doubleday Dell
Beast in Ms. Rooney's Room, The	M	RF	Giff, Patricia Reilly	Bantam Doubleday Dell
Beautiful Land: A Story of the Oklahoma Land Rush	S	I	Antle, Nancy	The Penguin Group
Bedtime Story, A	K	RF	Book Shop	Mondo
Bees	O	I	Holmes, Kevin J.	Capstone Press
Beezus & Ramona	O	RF	Cleary, Beverly	Avon
Behind The Bedroom Wall	V	HF	Williams, Laura E.	Milkweed Editions
Benjamin Franklin	U	B	Kent, Deborah	Scholastic

Title	Level	Genre	Author/Series	Publisher/Distributor
Benjamin Franklin: A Man with Many Jobs	O	B	Greene, Carol	Children's Press
Best Enemies	P	RF	Leverich, Kathleen	Beech Tree Books
Best Enemies Again	P	RF	Leverich, Kathleen	Alfred A. Knopf
Best Enemies Forever	P	RF	Leverich, Kathleen	William Morrow
Best Friends for Frances	K	F	Hoban, Russell	HarperTrophy
Best Little Monkeys in the World, The	J	F	Standiford, Natalie	Random House
Best Older Sister, The	L	RF	Choi, Sook Nyul	Bantam Doubleday Dell
Best Teacher in the World, The	K	RF	Chardiet, Bernice	Scholastic
Best Worst Day, The	L	RF	Graves, Bonnie	Hyperion
Best-Loved Doll, The	L	RF	Caudill, Rebecca	Henry Holt & Co.
Better Than TV	J	RF	Miller, Sara Swan	Bantam Doubleday Dell
BFG, The	U	F	Dahl, Roald	The Penguin Group
Big Max	J	F	Platt, Kin	HarperTrophy
Big Wave, The	Q	RF	Buck, Pearl S.	Scholastic
Biggest Klutz in Fifth Grade, The	V	RF	Wallace, Bill	Simon & Schuster
Bill Clinton: Forty-Second President of the U.S.	O	B	Greene, Carol	Children's Press
Bill Gates: Helping People Use Computers	P	B	Community Builders	Children's Press
Billy Magee's New Car	J	RF	Foundations	Wright Group/McGraw Hill
Birds' Nests	J	I	Wonder World	Wright Group/McGraw Hill
Birds of Prey	O	I	Woolley, M. & Pigdon, K.	Mondo
Birthday for Frances, A	K	F	Hoban, Russell	Scholastic
Birthday Room, The	V	RF	Henkes, Kevin	William Morrow
Black Pearl, The	W	RF	O'Dell, Scott	Bantam Doubleday Dell
Black Stallion, The	T	RF	Farley, Walter	Language for Learning Assoc.
Black Star, Bright Dawn	V	RF	O'Dell, Scott	Ballantine Books
Blackberries in the Dark	N	RF	Jukes, Mavis	Alfred A. Knopf
Blackboard Bear	J	F	Alexander, Martha	The Penguin Group
Blubber	T	RF	Blume, Judy	Bantam Doubleday Dell
Blue Door, The	X	HF	Rinaldi, Ann	Scholastic
Blue Ribbon Blues	M	RF	Spinelli, Jerry	Random House
Blue-Eyed Daisy, A	W	RF	Rylant, Cynthia	Simon & Schuster
Bobo's Magic Wishes	L	F	Little Readers	Houghton Mifflin
Boggart, The	U	F	Cooper, Susan	Simon & Schuster
Book of Three, The	U	F	Alexander, Lloyd	Bantam Doubleday Dell
Booker T. Washington	P	B	McLoone, Margo	Capstone Press
Borrowers, The	S	F	Norton, Mary	Harcourt Brace
Boston Tea Party, The	V	I	Cornerstones of Freedom	Children's Press
Boy Called Slow, A	S	B	Bruchac, Joseph	Putnam & Grosset
Boy Who Cried Wolf, The	J	TL	Littledale, Freya	Scholastic
Bracelet, The	R	HF	Uchida, Yoshiko	Philomel Books
Brain	V	I	You And Your Body	Troll
Brave Irene	S	F	Steig, William	Farrar, Straus & Giroux
Bravo Amelia Bedelia!	L	F	Parish, Herman	Avon
Bread and Jam for Frances	K	F	Hoban, Russell	Scholastic
Bridge to Terabithia	S	RF	Paterson, Katherine	HarperTrophy
Brighty of the Grand Canyon	R	RF	Henry, Marguerite	Aladdin
Brigid Beware	L	RF	Leverich, Kathleen	Random House
Brigid Bewitched	L	RF	Leverich, Kathleen	Random House
Brigid the Bad	L	RF	Leverich, Kathleen	Random House
Broccoli Tapes, The	S	RF	Slepian, Jan	Scholastic
Bud, Not Buddy	T	RF	Curtis, Christopher Paul	Random House
Buffalo Gal	U	RF	Wallace, Bill	Simon & Schuster
Building the Capital City	V	I	Cornerstones of Freedom	Bantam Doubleday Dell
Bully for you Teddy Roosevelt!	X	B	Fritz, Jean	Penguin Putnam Books
Bunnicula	Q	F	Howe, James	Avon
Bunnicula Strikes Again!	Q	F	Howe, James	Simon & Schuster
But I'll Be Back Again	V	B	Rylant, Cynthia	Beech Tree Books
Butterflies	O	I	Holmes, Kevin J.	Capstone Press

Title	Level	Genre	Author/Series	Publisher/Distributor
By the Great Horn Spoon!	V	HF	Fleischman, Sid	Little, Brown & Co.
Bye, Bye, Bali Kai	U	RF	Luger, Harriett	Harcourt Brace
Cabin Faced West, The	R	HF	Fritz, Jean	Bantam Doubleday Dell
Caddie Woodlawn	R	HF	Brink, Carol Ryrie	Bantam Doubleday Dell
Caleb's Choice	S	HF	Wisler, Clifton G.	The Penguin Group
Call It Courage	X	RF	Sperry, Armstrong	Aladdin
Call of the Wild	Y	RF	London, Jack	Signet Classics
Cam Jansen and the Chocolate Fudge Mystery	L	RF	Adler, David A.	Puffin Books
Cam Jansen and the Ghostly Mystery	L	RF	Adler, David A.	Puffin Books
Cam Jansen and the Mystery at the Haunted House	L	RF	Adler, David A.	Puffin Books
Cam Jansen and the Mystery at the Monkey House	L	RF	Adler, David A.	Puffin Books
Cam Jansen and the Mystery of Flight 54	L	RF	Adler, David A.	Puffin Books
Cam Jansen and the Mystery of the Babe Ruth Baseball	L	RF	Adler, David A.	Puffin Books
Cam Jansen and the Mystery of the Carnival Prize	L	RF	Adler, David A.	Puffin Books
Cam Jansen and the Mystery of the Circus Clown	L	RF	Adler, David A.	Puffin Books
Cam Jansen and the Mystery of the Dinosaur Bones	L	RF	Adler, David A.	Puffin Books
Cam Jansen and the Mystery of the Gold Coins	L	RF	Adler, David A.	Puffin Books
Cam Jansen and the Mystery of the Monster Movie	L	RF	Adler, David A.	Puffin Books
Cam Jansen and the Mystery of the Stolen Corn Popper	L	RF	Adler, David A.	Puffin Books
Cam Jansen and the Mystery of the Stolen Diamonds	L	RF	Adler, David A.	Puffin Books
Cam Jansen and the Mystery of the Television Dog	L	RF	Adler, David A.	Puffin Books
Cam Jansen and the Mystery of the U.F.O.	L	RF	Adler, David A.	Puffin Books
Cam Jansen and the Triceratops Pops Mystery	L	RF	Adler, David	Puffin Books
Camp Big Paw	J	RF	Cushman, Doug	HarperTrophy
Camp Knock Knock	K	RF	Duffey, Betsy	Bantam Doubleday Dell
Camp Knock Knock Mystery, The	K	RF	Duffey, Betsy	Bantam Doubleday Dell
Can Do, Jenny Archer	M	RF	Conford, Ellen	Random House
Can't You Make Them Behave, King George?	R	I	Fritz, Jean	Putnam & Grossett
Canada Geese Quilt, The	P	RF	Kinsey-Warnock, Natalie	Bantam Doubleday Dell
Candy Corn Contest, The	L	RF	Giff, Patricia Reilly	Bantam Doubleday Dell
Case for Jenny Archer, A	M	RF	Conford, Ellen	Random House
Case of Hermie the Missing Hamster, The	N	RF	Preller, James	Scholastic
Case of the Cat's Meow, The	K	RF	Bonsall, Crosby	HarperTrophy
Case of the Christmas Snowman, The	N	RF	Preller, James	Scholastic
Case of the Cool-Itch Kid, The	L	RF	Giff, Patricia Reilly	Bantam Doubleday Dell
Case of the Double Cross, The	K	RF	Bonsall, Crosby	HarperTrophy
Case of the Dumb Bells, The	K	RF	Bonsall, Crosby	HarperTrophy
Case of the Elevator Duck, The	M	RF	Berends, Polly Berrien	Random House
Case of the Hungry Stranger, The	K	RF	Bonsall, Crosby	HarperTrophy
Case of the Scaredy Cats, The	K	RF	Bonsall, Crosby	HarperTrophy
Case of the Secret Valentine, The	N	RF	Preller, James	Scholastic
Case of the Spooky Sleepover, The	N	RF	Preller, James	Scholastic
Case of the Two Masked Robbers, The	K	F	Hoban, Lillian	HarperTrophy
Castle in the Attic, The	R	F	Winthrop, Elizabeth	Bantam Doubleday Dell
Cat Ate My Gymsuit, The	U	RF	Danziger, Paula	Putnam & Grosset
Cat Who Went To Heaven, The	S	F	Coatsworth, Elizabeth	Aladdin
Cat's Meow, The	O	F	Soto, Gary	Scholastic
Catch That Pass!	M	RF	Christopher, Matt	Little, Brown & Co.
Catcher With a Glass Arm	M	RF	Christopher, Matt	Little, Brown & Co.
Catcher's Mask, The	M	RF	Christopher, Matt	Little, Brown & Co.
Catherine, Called Birdy	U	HF	Cushman, Karen	Clarion
Cats of the Night	K	RF	Book Bank	Wright Group/McGraw Hill
Cay, The	V	HF	Taylor, Theodore	Avon
Cells	J	I	Wonder World	Wright Group/McGraw Hill
Center Court Sting	M	RF	Christopher, Matt	Little, Brown & Co.
Centerfield Ballhawk	M	RF	Christopher, Matt	Little, Brown & Co.

Title	Level	Genre	Author/Series	Publisher/Distributor
Cesar Chavez	Y	B	Rodriguez, Consuelo	Chelsea House
Chalk Box Kid, The	N	RF	Bulla, Clyde Robert	Random House
Chang's Paper Pony	L	RF	Coerr, Eleanor	HarperTrophy
Charley Skedaddle	U	HF	Beatty, Patricia	Troll
Charlie and the Chocolate Factory	R	F	Dahl, Roald	Bantam Doubleday Dell
Charlie and the Great Glass Elevator	R	F	Dahl, Roald	Bantam Doubleday Dell
Charlie Needs a Cloak	J	RF	dePaola, Tomie	Prentice-Hall
Charlotte's Web	R	F	White, E. B.	HarperTrophy
Children of Sierra Leone, The	J	I	Books For Young Learners	Richard C. Owen
Children of the Longhouse	S	HF	Bruchac, Joseph	The Penguin Group
Childtimes: A Three-Generation Memoir	X	B	Greenfield, E. & Little, L. J.	HarperTrophy
Chocolate by Hershey: A Story about Milton S. Hershey	R	B	Burford, Betty	Carolrhoda Books
Circle of Quiet, A	Z	B	L'Engle, Madeleine	Harper Collins
Class Clown	O	RF	Hurwitz, Johanna	Scholastic
Class Play, The	J	RF	Little Readers	Houghton Mifflin
Class President	O	RF	Hurwitz, Johanna	Scholastic
Clouds	J	I	Early Connections	Benchmark Education
Colin Powell: Straight to the Top	S	B	Blue, Rose & Naden, Corinne J.	The Millbrook Press
Colonial Crafts	T	I	Historic Communities	Crabtree
Colonial Town, A: Williamsburg	T	I	Historic Communities	Crabtree
Come Back, Amelia Bedelia	L	F	Parish, Peggy	Harper & Row
Come Sing, Jimmy Jo	V	RF	Patterson, Katherine	The Penguin Group
Commander Toad and the Big Black Hole	K	F	Yolen, Jane	Putnam & Grosset
Commander Toad and the Dis-Asteroid	K	F	Yolen, Jane	Putnam & Grosset
Commander Toad and the Intergalactic Spy	K	F	Yolen, Jane	Putnam & Grosset
Commander Toad and the Planet of the Grapes	K	F	Yolen, Jane	Putnam & Grosset
Commander Toad and the Space Pirates	K	F	Yolen, Jane	Putnam & Grosset
Commander Toad And The Voyage Home	K	F	Yolen, Jane	Putnam & Grosset
Computer Nut, The	R	SF	Byars, Betsy	Bantam Doubleday Dell
Contender, The	Z	RF	Lipsythe, Robert	HarperTrophy
Coral Reef	P	I	Habitats	Children's Press
Count Your Money with the Polk Street School	M	RF	Giff, Patricia Reilly	Bantam Doubleday Dell
Counting Insects	K	I	Early Connections	Benchmark Education
Cracker Jackson	T	RF	Byars, Betsy	Puffin Books
Crazy Fish	T	RF	Mazer, Norma Fox	Avon
Creatures of the Night	M	I	Murdock & Ray	Mondo Publishing
Cricket in Times Square, The	S	F	Selden, George	Bantam Doubleday Dell
Crocodilians	U	I	Short, Joan & Bird, Bettina	Mondo
Cry of the Crow, The	S	RF	George, Jean Craighead	HarperTrophy
Cybil War, The	S	RF	Byars, Betsy	Scholastic
Dancing with Manatees	N	I	McNulty, Faith	Scholastic
Danger Guys	N	RF	Abbott, Tony	HarperTrophy
Daniel's Duck	K	RF	Bulla, Clyde Robert	HarperTrophy
Danny and the Dinosaur	J	F	Hoff, Syd	Scholastic
Danny, Champion of the World	T	RF	Dahl, Roald	Language for Learning Assoc.
Dark Is Rising, The	X	F	Cooper, Susan	Macmillan
Daughter of the Mountains	V	HF	Rankin, Louise	The Penguin Group
Day No Pigs Would Die, A	Z	HF	Peck, Sylvia	Random House
Day of the Dragon King	M	F	Osborne, Mary Pope	Random House
Days With Frog and Toad	K	F	Lobel, Arnold	HarperTrophy
Dear Levi: Letters from the Overland Trail	T	HF	Woodruff, Elvira	Alfred A. Knopf
Dear Mr. Henshaw	Q	RF	Cleary, Beverly	HarperCollins
Definitely Cool	X	RF	Wilkinson, Brenda	Scholastic
Devil's Arithmetic, The	X	F	Yolen, Jane	Puffin Books
Diary of Anne Frank, The	Y	B	Frank, Anne	Pocket Books
Dicey's Song	W	RF	Voigt, Cynthia	Ballantine Books
Different Beat, A	U	RF	Boyd, Candy Dawson	The Penguin Group
Disappearing Cookies and Other Cases, The	O	RF	Simon, Seymour	Avon

Title	Level	Genre	Author/Series	Publisher/Distributor
Disappearing Ice Cream and Other Cases, The	O	RF	Simon, Seymour	Avon
Disappearing Snowball and Other Cases, The	O	RF	Simon, Seymour	Avon
Dog Called Kitty, A	R	RF	Wallace, Bill	Pocket Books
Dog that Pitched a No-Hitter, The	L	F	Christopher, Matt	Little Brown & Co.
Dog that Stole Football Plays, The	M	F	Christopher, Matt	Little, Brown & Co.
Dog that Stole Home, The	L	F	Christopher, Matt	Little, Brown & Co.
Dogs at Work	J	I	Little Readers	Houghton Mifflin
Dogsong	V	RF	Paulsen, Gary	Simon & Schuster
Dolphin	L	I	Morris, Robert A.	HarperTrophy
Dolphin Adventure	P	RF	Grover, Wayne	Beech Tree Books
Dolphin Treasure	P	RF	Grover, Wayne	Beech Tree Books
Dolphins	O	I	Holmes, Kevin J.	Capstone Press
Dominic	R	F	Steig, William	Farrar, Straus and Giroux
Don't Eat Too Much Turkey	J	RF	Cohen, Miriam	Bantam Doubleday Dell
Donavan's Word Jar	N	RF	DeGross, Monalisa	HarperCollins
Donkey's Tale, The	J	TL	Bank Street	Bantam Doubleday Dell
Door in the Wall, The	U	HF	De Angeli, Marguerite	Bantam Doubleday Dell
Doorbell Rang, The	J	RF	Hutchins, Pat	Greenwillow
Double Life of Pocahontas, The	T	B	Fritz, Jean	Language for Learning Assoc.
Dragon Bones	O	F	Hindman, Paul	Random House
Dragon for Sale	Q	F	MacDonald, Marianne	Troll
Dragon in the Family, A	Q	F	Koller, Jackie French	Pocket Books
Dragon Quest	Q	F	Koller, Jackie French	Pocket Books
Dragon Trouble	Q	F	Koller, Jackie French	Pocket Books
Dragon's Gate	W	HF	Yep, Laurence	Harper Collins
Dragonling, The	Q	F	Koller, Jackie French	Pocket Books
Dragons and Kings	Q	F	Koller, Jackie French	Pocket Books
Dragons of Krad	Q	F	Koller, Jackie French	Pocket Books
Dragonsong	V	F	McCaffrey, Anne	Bantam Doubleday Dell
Dragonwings	W	HF	Yep, Lawrence	HarperTrophy
E is for Elisa	N	RF	Hurwitz, Johanna	Puffin Books
Earthquake!: San Francisco, 1906	R	I	Wilson, Kate	Steck-Vaughn
Earthworms	O	I	Holmes, Kevin J.	Capstone Press
Egypt Game, The	U	RF	Snyder, Zilpha Keatley	Bantam Doubleday Dell
Eleanor Roosevelt	P	B	Davis, Lucile	Capstone Press
Eleanor Roosevelt: First Lady of the World	R	B	Faber, Doris	The Penguin Group
Eleven Kids, One Summer	O	RF	Martin, Ann M.	Scholastic
Elisa in the Middle	N	RF	Hurwitz, Johanna	The Penguin Group
Elizabeth Blackwell: First Woman Doctor	O	B	Greene, Carol	Children's Press
Elizabeth Blackwell: Girl Doctor	O	B	Henry, Joanne Landers	Simon & Schuster
Elizabeth Cady Stanton	P	B	Davis, Lucile	Capstone Press
Elizabeth the First: Queen of England	O	B	Greene, Carol	Children's Press
Ella Enchanted	U	F	Carson Levine, Gail	HarperTrophy
Ellen Tebbits	P	RF	Cleary, Beverly	Dell Publishing
Emily Dickinson: American Poet	O	B	Greene, Carol	Children's Press
Encyclopedia Brown Keeps the Peace	P	RF	Sobol, Donald J.	Bantam Doubleday Dell
Encyclopedia Brown Lends a Hand	P	RF	Sobol, Donald J.	Bantam Doubleday Dell
Encyclopedia Brown Saves the Day	P	RF	Sobol, Donald J.	Bantam Doubleday Dell
Encyclopedia Brown Sets the Pace	P	RF	Sobol, Donald J.	Bantam Doubleday Dell
Encyclopedia Brown Shows the Way	P	RF	Sobol, Donald J.	Bantam Doubleday Dell
Encyclopedia Brown Solves Them All	P	RF	Sobol, Donald J.	Bantam Doubleday Dell
Encyclopedia Brown Takes the Cake	P	RF	Sobol, Donald J.	Bantam Doubleday Dell
Encyclopedia Brown Tracks Them Down	P	RF	Sobol, Donald J.	Bantam Doubleday Dell
Encyclopedia Brown's Book of Strange But True Crimes	P	RF	Sobol, Donald J. & Rose Sobol	Scholastic
Enormous Egg, The	R	F	Butterworth, Oliver	Little, Brown & Co.
Every Living Thing	R	RF	Rylant, Cynthia	Aladdin
Exploring Freshwater Habitats	P	I	Snowball, Diane	Mondo

Title	Level	Genre	Author/Series	Publisher/Distributor
Exploring Land Habitats	P	I	Phinney, Margaret Yatsevitch	Mondo
Exploring Saltwater Habitats	P	I	Smith, Sue	Mondo
Exploring Tree Habitats	P	I	Seifert, Patti	Mondo
Face to Face	W	RF	Bauer, Marion Dane	Bantam Doubleday Dell
Facing West: A Story of the Oregon Trail	S	I	Kudlinski, Kathleen V.	The Penguin Group
Fancy Feet	L	RF	Giff, Patricia Reilly	Bantam Doubleday Dell
Fantastic Mr. Fox	P	F	Dahl, Roald	The Penguin Group
Fifth Grade: Here Comes Trouble	S	RF	McKenna, Colleen O'Shaughnessy	Scholastic
Fig Pudding	R	RF	Fletcher, Ralph	Clarion Books
Fighting Ground, The	V	HF	Avi	HarperTrophy
Finding Providence: The Story of Roger Williams	P	B	Avi	HarperTrophy
Fire at the Triangle Factory	P	HF	Littlefield, Holly	Carolrhoda Books
Fire in the Sky	R	HF	Ransom, Candice F.	Carolrhoda Books
Five Brave Explorers	Q	B	Hudson, Wade	Scholastic
Five Notable Inventors	Q	B	Hudson, Wade	Scholastic
Five True Dog Stories	M	I	Davidson, Margaret	Scholastic
Five True Horse Stories	M	I	Davidson, Margaret	Scholastic
Flat Stanley	M	F	Brown, Jeff	HarperTrophy
Fledgling, The	U	F	Langton, Jane	Scholastic
Florence Kelley	P	B	Saller, Carol	Carolrhoda Books
Flossie and the Fox	O	F	McKissack, Patricia	Scholastic
Flower Girls # 1: Violet	L	RF	Leverich, Kathleen	HarperTrophy
Flower Girls # 2: Daisy	L	RF	Leverich, Kathleen	HarperTrophy
Flower Girls # 3: Heather	L	RF	Leverich, Kathleen	HarperTrophy
Flower Girls # 4: Rose	L	RF	Leverich, Kathleen	HarperTrophy
Flowers For Algernon	Z	RF	Keyes, Daniel	Harcourt Brace
Flunking of Joshua T. Bates, The	Q	RF	Shreve, Susan	Alfred A. Knopf
Flying Solo	R	RF	Fletcher, Ralph	Bantam Doubleday Dell
Foolish Gretel	O	TL	Armstrong, Jennifer	Random House
Forever Amber Brown	N	RF	Danziger, Paula	Scholastic
Forgotten Door, The	T	SF	Key, Alexander	Language for Learning Assoc.
Foster's War	V	HF	Reeder, Carolyn	Scholastic
Fourth Grade Celebrity	Q	RF	Giff, Patricia Reilly	Bantam Doubleday Dell
Fox All Week	J	F	Marshall, Edward	Puffin Books
Fox and His Friends	J	F	Marshall, Edward	Puffin Books
Fox at School	J	F	Marshall, Edward	Puffin Books
Fox Be Nimble	J	F	Marshall, James	Puffin Books
Fox In Love	J	F	Marshall, Edward	Puffin Books
Fox on Stage	J	F	Marshall, James	Puffin Books
Fox on the Job	J	F	Marshall, James	Puffin Books
Fox on Wheels	J	F	Marshall, Edward	Puffin Books
Fox Outfoxed	J	F	Marshall, James	Puffin Books
France	O	I	Dahl, Michael	Capstone Press
Freckle Juice	M	RF	Blume, Judy	Bantam Doubleday Dell
Frederick Douglass: Fights For Freedom	M	B	Davidson, Margaret	Language for Learning Assoc.
Freedom Songs	T	HF	Moore, Yvette	Language for Learning Assoc.
Friends, The	Z	RF	Guy, Rosa	Bantam Doubleday Dell
Friendship and the Gold Cadillac, The	S	HF	Taylor, Mildred	Bantam Doubleday Dell
Frightful's Mountain	U	RF	George, Jean	Puffin Books
Frog and Toad All Year	K	F	Little Readers	Houghton Mifflin
Frog and Toad Are Friends	K	F	Lobel, Arnold	Harper & Row
Frog and Toad Together	K	F	Little Readers	Houghton Mifflin
Frog and Toad Together	K	F	Lobel, Arnold	Harper Collins
From the Mixed-up Files of Mrs. Basil E. Frankweiler	S	RF	Konigsburg, E.L.	Bantam Doubleday Dell
From the Notebooks of Melanin Sun	Z	RF	Woodson, Jacqueline	Scholastic
Fudge	O	RF	Graeber, Charlotte Towner	Simon & Schuster
Fudge-a-Mania	Q	RF	Blume, Judy	Bantam Doubleday Dell
Gathering of Days, A: A New England Girl's Journal, 1830-32	U	HF	Blos, Joan	Aladdin

Title	Level	Genre	Author/Series	Publisher/Distributor
Gathering of Flowers, A	Z	RF	Thomas, Joyce Carol	HarperTrophy
George and Martha	L	F	Marshall, James	Houghton Mifflin
George and Martha Back in Town	L	F	Marshall, James	Houghton Mifflin
George and Martha Encore	L	F	Marshall, James	Houghton Mifflin
George and Martha One Fine Day	L	F	Marshall, James	Houghton Mifflin
George and Martha Rise and Shine	L	F	Marshall, James	Houghton Mifflin
George and Martha Round and Round	L	F	Marshall, James	Houghton Mifflin
George Washington	L	B	Pebble Books	Grolier, Capstone
George Washington Carver	P	B	McLoone, Margo	Capstone Press
George Washington Carver: Scientist and Teacher	O	B	Greene, Carol	Children's Press
George Washington: First President of the U.S.	N	B	Rookie Biographies	Children's Press
George Washington's Breakfast	P	B	Fritz, Jean	Putnam & Grosset
George's Marvelous Medicine	P	F	Dahl, Roald	The Penguin Group
Gettysburg Address, The	V	I	Cornerstones of Freedom	Children's Press
Ghost Fox, The	P	F	Yep, Laurence	Scholastic
Ghost On Saturday Night, The	Q	F	Fleischman, Sid	Beech Tree Books
Ghost Town Treasure	M	RF	Bulla, Clyde Robert	The Penguin Group
Ginger Brown: The Nobody Boy	L	RF	Wyeth, Sharon Dennis	Random House
Ginger Brown: Too Many Houses	L	RF	Wyeth, Sharon Dennis	Random House
Ginger Pye	U	RF	Estes, Eleanor	Scholastic
Girl Called Al, A	P	RF	Greene, Constance C.	Puffin Books
Girl From Yamhill, A	W	B	Cleary, Beverly	Bantam Doubleday Dell
Girl In the Window, The	U	RF	Yeo, Wilma	Scholastic
Girl Named Disaster, A	X	RF	Farmer, Nancy	The Penguin Group
Girl Who Chased Away Sorrow, The: The Diary of Sarah Nita, a Navajo Girl	T	HF	Turner, Ann	Scholastic
Girl Who Loved the Wind, The	Q	TL	Yolen, Jane	HarperTrophy
Giver, The	Y	F	Lowry, Lois	Bantam Doubleday Dell
Go Free or Die: A Story About Harriet Tubman	R	B	Ferris, Jeri	Carolrhoda Books
Going Home	T	RF	Mohr, Nicholasa	The Penguin Group
Golden Compass, The	Z	F	Pullman, Philip	Ballantine Books
Golden Goblet, The	V	RF	McGraw, Eloise Jarvis	Scholastic
Golly Sisters Go West, The	K	RF	Byars, Betsy	HarperTrophy
Golly Sisters Ride Again, The	K	RF	Byars, Betsy	HarperTrophy
Good Driving, Amelia Bedelia	L	F	Parish, Peggy	Harper & Row
Good Grief. . . Third Grade	O	RF	McKenna, Colleen	Scholastic
Good Morning Mrs. Martin	K	F	Book Bank	Wright Group/McGraw Hill
Good Night, Mr. Tom	Z	HF	Magorian, Michelle	HarperTrophy
Good Work, Amelia Bedelia	L	F	Parish, Peggy	Avon Camelot
Good-Bye Marianne	T	B	Watts, Irene N.	Tundra Books
Gorillas	T	I	Burgel, Paul H. & Hartwig, M.	Carolrhoda Books
Gorillas	U	I	The Untamed World	Steck-Vaughn
Grain of Rice, A	P	TL	Pittman, Helena Clare	Bantam Doubleday Dell
Grandma Mixup, The	K	RF	Little Readers	Houghton Mifflin
Grandpa's Face	Q	RF	Greenfield, Eloise	Putnam & Grosset
Grasshopper and the Ants	K	TL	Sunshine	Wright Group/McGraw Hill
Great Gilly Hopkins, The	S	RF	Paterson, Katherine	Hearst
Great Whales: The Gentle Giants	W	I	Lauber, Patricia	Henry Holt & Co.
Great Wheel, The	U	RF	Lawson, Robert	Scholastic
Greg's Microscope	K	I	Selsam, Millicent E.	HarperTrophy
Grizzly Bears	N	I	Woolley, M. & Pigdon, K.	Mondo
Guatemala	O	I	Dahl, Michael	Capstone Press
Guide Dog, The	K	I	Foundations	Wright Group/McGraw Hill
Happy Birthday, Dear Duck	K	F	Bunting, Eve	Clarion
Happy Birthday, Martin Luther King	L	B	Marzollo, Jean	Scholastic
Harriet Beecher Stowe and the Beecher Preachers	X	B	Fritz, Jean	The Penguin Group
Harriet the Spy	T	RF	Fitzhugh, Louise	Harper Collins
Harriet Tubman	P	B	McLoone, Margo	Capstone Press
Harry and Chicken	S	F	Sheldon, Dyan	Candlewick Press

Title	Level	Genre	Author/Series	Publisher/Distributor
Harry Houdini: Master of Magic	R	B	Kraske, Robert	Scholastic
Harry On Vacation	S	SF	Sheldon, Dyan	Candlewick Press
Harry Potter and the Chamber of Secrets	V	F	Rowling, J. K.	Scholastic
Harry Potter and the Goblet of Fire	V	F	Rowling, J. K.	Scholastic
Harry Potter and the Prisoner of Azkaban	V	F	Rowling, J.K.	Scholastic
Harry Potter and the Sorcerer's Stone	V	F	Rowling, J. K.	Scholastic
Harry the Explorer	S	F	Sheldon, Dyan	Candlewick Press
Harry's Mad	P	F	King-Smith, Dick	Alfred A. Knopf
Hatchet	R	RF	Paulsen, Gary	Aladdin
Helen Keller	N	B	Davidson, Margaret	Scholastic
Helen Keller: A Light For The Blind	R	B	Kudlinski, Kathleen V.	The Penguin Group
Helen Keller: Crusader for the Blind and Deaf	P	B	Graff, Stewart & Polly Anne	Bantam Doubleday Dell
Helen Keller: From Tragedy to Triumph	O	B	Childhood of Famous Americans	Aladdin
Helen Keller's Teacher	N	B	Davidson, Margaret	Scholastic
Help! I'm a Prisoner in the Library	Q	RF	Clifford, Eth	Scholastic
Help! I'm Trapped in My Teacher's Body	Q	F	Strasser, Todd	Scholastic
Help! I'm Trapped in the First Day of School	Q	F	Strasser, Todd	Scholastic
Henry and Beezus	O	RF	Cleary, Beverly	Avon
Henry and Mudge and the Bedtime Thumps	J	RF	Rylant, Cynthia	Aladdin
Henry and Mudge and the Best Day of All	J	RF	Rylant, Cynthia	Aladdin
Henry and Mudge and the Careful Cousin	J	RF	Rylant, Cynthia	Aladdin
Henry and Mudge and the Forever Sea	J	RF	Rylant, Cynthia	Aladdin
Henry and Mudge and the Happy Cat	J	RF	Rylant, Cynthia	Aladdin
Henry and Mudge and the Long Weekend	J	RF	Rylant, Cynthia	Aladdin
Henry and Mudge and the Wild Wind	J	RF	Rylant, Cynthia	Aladdin
Henry and Mudge Get the Cold Shivers	J	RF	Rylant, Cynthia	Aladdin
Henry and Mudge in Puddle Trouble	J	RF	Rylant, Cynthia	Aladdin
Henry and Mudge in the Family Trees	J	RF	Rylant, Cynthia	Aladdin
Henry and Mudge in the Green Time	J	RF	Rylant, Cynthia	Aladdin
Henry and Mudge in the Sparkle Days	J	RF	Rylant, Cynthia	Aladdin
Henry and Mudge Take the Big Test	J	RF	Rylant, Cynthia	Aladdin
Henry and Mudge: The First Book	J	RF	Rylant, Cynthia	Aladdin
Henry and Mudge Under the Yellow Moon	J	RF	Rylant, Cynthia	Aladdin
Henry and Ribsy	O	RF	Cleary, Beverly	Hearst
Henry and the Clubhouse	O	RF	Cleary, Beverly	Avon
Henry and the Paper Route	O	RF	Cleary, Beverly	Hearst
Henry Huggins	O	RF	Cleary, Beverly	Avon
Here Comes the Strike Out	K	RF	Kessler, Leonard	Harper Trophy
Hey World, Here I Am!	S	RF	Little, Jean	HarperTrophy
Hit-Away Kid, The	M	RF	Christopher, Matt	Little, Brown & Co.
Ho, Ho, Benjamin, Feliz Navidad	N	RF	Giff, Patricia Reilly	Bantam Doubleday Dell
Hobbit, The	Z	F	Tolkien, J.R.R	Ballantine Books
Holes	V	RF	Sachar, Louis	Random House
Homer Price	Q	RF	McCloskey, Robert	Puffin Books
Hooray for the Golly Sisters!	K	RF	Byars, Betsy	HarperTrophy
Hot Fudge Hero	L	RF	Brisson, Pat	Henry Holt & Co.
House on Mango Street, The	W	B	Cisneros, Sandra	Alfred A. Knopf
House with a Clock in its Walls, The	S	F	Bellairs, John	The Penguin Group
How Grandmother Spider Got the Sun	J	TL	Little Readers	Houghton Mifflin
How Many Days to America?: A Thanksgiving Story	S	I	Bunting, Eve	Houghton Mifflin
How Turtle Raced Beaver	J	TL	Literacy 2000	Rigby
Howard Carter: Searching for King Tut	S	B	Ford, Barbara	W. H. Freeman & Co.
Hundred Penny Box, The	P	RF	Mathis, Sharon Bell	Puffin Books
Hungry, Hungry Sharks	L	I	Cole, Joanna	Random House
Hurray For Ali Baba Bernstein	O	RF	Hurwitz, Johanna	Scholastic
Hurricanes & Tornadoes	R	I	The Wonders of our World	Crabtree
I Am A Star: Child of the Holocaust	W	I	Auerbacher, Inge	The Penguin Group
I Am Regina	U	HF	Keehn, Sally	Bantam Doubleday Dell

Title	Level	Genre	Author/Series	Publisher/Distributor
I Am Rosa Parks	O	B	Parks, Rosa	Dial Books
I Have Lived a Thousand Years	Y	B	Bitton-Jackson, Livia	Simon & Schuster
If You Grew Up with George Washington	Q	I	Gross, Ruth Belov	Scholastic
If You Lived at the Time of Martin Luther King	Q	I	Levine, Ellen	Scholastic
If You Lived at the Time of the Civil War	Q	I	Moore, Kay	Scholastic
If You Lived at the Time of the Great San Francisco Earthquake	Q	I	Levine, Ellen	Scholastic
If You Lived in Colonial Times	Q	I	McGovern, Ann	Scholastic
If You Lived with the Sioux Indians	Q	I	McGovern, Ann	Scholastic
If You Sailed on the Mayflower in 1620	Q	I	McGovern, Ann	Scholastic
If You Traveled on the Underground Railroad	Q	I	Levine, Ellen	Scholastic
If You Were There When They Signed the Constitution	Q	I	Levy, Elizabeth	Scholastic
If Your Name was Changed at Ellis Island	Q	I	Levine, Ellen	Scholastic
Immigrants	T	I	Sandler, Martin W.	HarperTrophy
In the Rain Forest	Q	I	Wildcats	Wright Group/McGraw Hill
In the Year of the Boar and Jackie Robinson	S	HF	Lord, Bette Bao	HarperTrophy
Incident at Hawk's Hill	V	F	Eckert, Allen W.	Little, Brown & Co.
Incredible Journey, The	V	F	Burnford, Sheila	Bantam Doubleday Dell
Inn Keepers Apprentice	Z	B	Say, Allen	The Penguin Group
Insects	U	I	Bird, Bettina & Short, Joan	Mondo
Invisible in the Third Grade	M	RF	Cuyler, Margery	Scholastic
Island Keeper	T	RF	Mazer, Harry	Language for Learning Assoc.
Island of the Blue Dolphins	V	HF	O'Dell, Scott	Bantam Doubleday Dell
Italy	O	I	Thoennes, Kristin	Capstone Press
J.T.	Q	RF	Wagner, Jane	Bantam Doubleday Dell
Jack and the Beanstalk	K	TL	Weisner, David	Scholastic
Jackaroo	Y	RF	Voigt, Cynthia	Scholastic
Jackie Robinson: Baseball's First Black Major Leaguer	O	B	Greene, Carol	Children's Press
Jackie Robinson Breaks the Color Line	V	B	Cornerstones of Freedom	Children's Press
Jacob Have I Loved	U	RF	Paterson, Katherine	HarperTrophy
Jacob Two-Two Meets the Hooded Fang	P	F	Richler, Mordecai	Seal Books
James and the Giant Peach	Q	F	Dahl, Roald	The Penguin Group
Jamestown Colony, The	V	I	Cornerstones of Freedom	Children's Press
Japan	M	I	Pair-It Books	Steck-Vaughn
Jazmin's Notebook	Z	RF	Grimes, Nikki	The Penguin Group
Jenny Archer, Author	M	RF	Conford, Ellen	Little, Brown & Co.
Jenny Archer to the Rescue	M	RF	Conford, Ellen	Little, Brown & Co.
Jericho's Journey	U	RF	Wisler, G. Clifton	Penguin Group
Jesse	Y	RF	Soto, Gary	Scholastic
Jesse Jackson	P	B	Simon, Charnan	Children's Press
Jesse Owens: Olympic Hero	P	B	Sabin, Francene	Troll
Jip His Story	V	HF	Paterson, Katherine	The Penguin Group
Job for Jenny Archer, A	M	RF	Conford, Ellen	Random House
Josefina Story Quilt	L	F	Coerr, Eleanor	HarperTrophy
Journey Home	V	RF	Uchida, Yoshika	Aladdin
Journey Home, The	S	RF	Holland, Isabelle	Scholastic
Journey Into Terror	U	RF	Wallace, Bill	Simon & Schuster
Journey Outside	V	F	Steele, Mary Q.	The Penguin Group
Journey to America	U	HF	Levitin, Sonia	Simon & Schuster
Journey to Jo'burg	S	HF	Naidoo, Beverly	HarperTrophy
Journey to Topaz	U	HF	Uchida, Yoshiko	Creative Arts Book Co.
Julian, Dream Doctor	N	RF	Cameron, Ann	Random House
Julian, Secret Agent	N	RF	Cameron, Ann	Random House
Julian's Glorious Summer	N	RF	Cameron, Ann	Random House
Julie of the Wolves	U	RF	George, Jean Craighead	Harper Collins
Julie's Wolf Pack	U	RF	George, Jean Craighead	HarperTrophy
Jump Ship to Freedom	U	HF	Collier, James and Christopher	Bantam Doubleday Dell
Just Juice	Q	RF	Hesse, Karen	Scholastic

Title	Level	Genre	Author/Series	Publisher/Distributor
Justin and the Best Biscuits in the World	P	RF	Pitts, Walter & Mildred	Alfred A. Knopf
Katherine Dunham, Black Dancer	N	B	Rookie Biographies	Children's Press
Keep the Lights Burning Abbie	K	HF	Roop, Peter & Connie	Scholastic
Kenya	O	I	Dahl, Michael	Capstone Press
Kick, Pass, and Run	J	RF	Kessler, Leonard	HarperTrophy
Kid Who Ran For President, The	T	RF	Gutman, Dan	Language for Learning Assoc.
Kind of Thief, A	U	RF	Alcock, Vivien	Bantam Doubleday Dell
King's Equal, The	O	TL	Paterson, Katherine	HarperTrophy
Kiss the Dust	W	RF	Laird, Elizabeth	The Penguin Group
Koya DeLaney and the Good Girl Blues	P	RF	Greenfield, Eloise	Scholastic
Lady Bird Johnson	Q	B	Simon, Charnan	Children's Press
Last Look	P	RF	Bulla, Clyde Robert	Puffin Books
Laura Ingalls Wilder	O	B	Allen, Thomas B.	Putnam
Laura Ingalls Wilder: A Biography	R	B	Anderson, William	HarperTrophy
Laura Ingalls Wilder: An Author's Story	N	B	Glasscock, Sarah	Steck-Vaughn
Laura Ingalls Wilder: Author of the Little House Books	O	B	Greene, Carol	Children's Press
Laura Ingalls Wilder: Growing Up in the Little House	P	B	Giff, Patricia Reilly	Puffin Books
Lazy Lions, Lucky Lambs	M	RF	Giff, Patricia Reilly	Bantam Doubleday Dell
Leftovers, The: Catch Flies!	N	RF	Howard, Tristan	Scholastic
Leftovers, The: Fast Break	N	RF	Howard, Tristan	Scholastic
Leftovers, The: Get Jammed	N	RF	Howard, Tristan	Scholastic
Leftovers, The: Reach Their Goal	N	RF	Howard, Tristan	Scholastic
Leftovers, The: Strike Out!	N	RF	Howard, Tristan	Scholastic
Lemonade Trick, The	Q	RF	Corbett, Scott	Scholastic
Let the Circle Be Unbroken	X	HF	Taylor, Mildred D.	The Penguin Group
Let's Go, Philadelphia!	M	RF	Giff, Patricia Reilly	Bantam Doubleday Dell
Letter, the Witch, and the Ring, The	S	F	Bellairs, John	The Penguin Group
Letters From a Slave Girl: The Story of Harriet Jacobs	X	HF	Lyons, Mary E.	Simon & Schuster
Letters from Rifka	S	HF	Hesse, Karen	Puffin Books
Letters to Julia	W	RF	Holmes, Barbara Ware	HarperTrophy
Lewis and Clark	V	B	Cornerstones of Freedom	Children's Press
Lexington and Concord	V	I	Cornerstones of Freedom	Children's Press
Liberty Bell, The	V	I	Cornerstones of Freedom	Children's Press
Library Card, The	R	RF	Spinelli, Jerry	Scholastic
Life and Words of Martin Luther King, Jr., The	W	B	Peck, Ira	Scholastic
Lightning	L	I	Pebble Books	Grolier, Capstone
Lightweight Rocket and Other Cases, The	O	RF	Simon, Seymour	Avon
Lily and Miss Liberty	N	HF	Stephens, Carla	Scholastic
Lily's Crossing	S	HF	Giff, Patricia Reilly	Delacourte Press
Limestone Caves	N	I	Davis, Gary	Children's Press
Lion and the Mouse, The	J	TL	Sunshine	Wright Group/McGraw Hill
Lion, the Witch and the Wardrobe, The	T	F	Lewis, C. S.	HarperTrophy
Lion to Guard Us, A	P	HF	Bulla, Clyde Robert	HarperTrophy
Lions at Lunchtime	M	F	Osborne, Mary Pope	Random House
Little Bear	J	F	Minarik, E.H.	Harper Collins
Little Bear's Friend	J	F	Minarik, E.H.	HarperTrophy
Little Bear's Visit	J	F	Minarik, E.H.	HarperTrophy
Little House in the Big Woods	Q	HF	Wilder, Laura Ingalls	HarperTrophy
Little House on the Prairie	Q	HF	Wilder, Laura Ingalls	HarperTrophy
Little Lefty	M	RF	Christopher, Matt	Little, Brown & Co.
Little Sea Pony, The	N	F	Cresswell, Helen	HarperTrophy
Littles and the Lost Children, The	M	F	Peterson, John	Scholastic
Littles and the Terrible Tiny Kid, The	M	F	Peterson, John	Scholastic
Littles Go Exploring, The	M	F	Peterson, John	Scholastic
Littles Go to School, The	M	F	Peterson, John	Scholastic
Littles Have a Wedding, The	M	F	Peterson, John	Scholastic
Littles Take a Trip, The	M	F	Peterson, John	Scholastic
Littles, The	M	F	Peterson, John	Scholastic

Title	Level	Genre	Author/Series	Publisher/Distributor
Littles to the Rescue, The	M	F	Peterson, John	Scholastic
Living Up The Street	Y	RF	Soto, Gary	Bantam Doubleday Dell
Locked in the Library!	M	F	Brown, Marc	Little, Brown & Co.
Long Way to Go, A	R	I	O'Neal, Zibby	The Penguin Group
Long Winter, The	Q	HF	Ingalls Wilder, Laura	HarperTrophy
Look Out, Washington D.C.!	O	RF	Giff, Patricia Reilly	Bantam Doubleday Dell
Lost Continent and Other Cases, The	O	RF	Simon, Seymour	Avon
Lost Hikers and Other Cases, The	O	RF	Simon, Seymour	Avon
Lost on a Mountain in Maine	R	RF	Fendler, Donn	Peter Smith Publications
Lost Star: The Story of Amelia Earhart	T	B	Lauber, Patricia	Language for Learning Assoc.
Lucky Stone, The	P	RF	Clifton, Lucille	Bantam Doubleday Dell
Lyddie	U	HF	Paterson, Katherine	The Penguin Group
M.C. Higgins the Great	X	RF	Hamilton, Virginia	Macmillan
M & M and The Bad News Babies	K	RF	Ross, Pat	The Penguin Group
M & M and the Big Bag	K	RF	Ross, Pat	The Penguin Group
M & M and the Halloween Monster	K	RF	Ross, Pat	The Penguin Group.
M & M and the Haunted House Game	K	RF	Ross, Pat	The Penguin Group
M & M and the Mummy Mess	K	RF	Ross, Pat	The Penguin Group
M & M and the Santa Secrets	K	RF	Ross, Pat	The Penguin Group
M & M and the Super Child Afternoon	K	RF	Ross, Pat	The Penguin Group
Magic Fish, The	L	TL	Littledale, Freya	Scholastic
Magician's Nephew, The	T	F	Lewis, C. S.	HarperTrophy
Mama, Let's Dance	W	RF	Hermes, Patricia	Scholastic
Maniac Magee	V	RF	Spinelli, Jerry	Scholastic
Martin and the Teacher's Pets	K	RF	Chardiet, B. & Maccarone, G.	Scholastic
Martin and the Tooth Fairy	K	RF	Chardiet, B. & Maccarone, G.	Scholastic
Martin Luther King Day	L	I	Lowery, Linda	Scholastic
Martin Luther King, Jr.	L	B	Pebble Books	Grolier, Capstone
Martin Luther King, Jr.	O	B	Rookie Biographies	Children's Press
Marvin Redpost: Alone in His Teacher's House	M	RF	Sachar, Louis	Random House
Marvin Redpost: Is He a Girl?	M	RF	Sachar, Louis	Random House
Marvin Redpost: Kidnapped at Birth?	M	RF	Sachar, Louis	Random House
Marvin Redpost: Why Pick on Me?	M	RF	Sachar, Louis	Random House
Mary Marony and the Chocolate Surprise	M	RF	Kline, Suzy	Bantam Doubleday Dell
Mary Marony and the Snake	M	RF	Kline, Suzy	Bantam Doubleday Dell
Mary Marony Hides Out	M	RF	Kline, Suzy	Bantam Doubleday Dell
Mary Marony, Mummy Girl	M	RF	Kline, Suzy	Bantam Doubleday Dell
Mary McLeod Bethune	O	B	Greenfield, Eloise	HarperTrophy
Matilda	S	F	Dahl, Roald	The Penguin Group
Matthew's Meadow	V	RF	Bliss, Corinne Demas	Harcourt Brace
Max Malone and the Great Cereal Rip-off	N	RF	Herman, Charlotte	Henry Holt & Co.
Max Malone Makes a Million	N	RF	Herman, Charlotte	Henry Holt & Co.
Maya Angelou: Greeting the Morning	W	B	King, Sarah E.	The Millbrook Press
Me, Mop, and the Moondance Kid	S	RF	Myers, Walter Dean	Bantam Doubleday Dell
Meet Benjamin Franklin	O	B	Scarf, Maggi	Step-Up Books
Meet M & M	K	RF	Ross, Pat	The Penguin Group
Meg Mackintosh and The Case of the Curious Whale Watch	O	RF	Landon, Lucinda	Secret Passage Press
Meg Mackintosh and The Case of the Missing Babe Ruth Baseball	O	RF	Landon, Lucinda	Secret Passage Press
Meg Mackintosh and The Mystery at Camp Creepy	O	RF	Landon, Lucinda	Secret Passage Press
Meg Mackintosh and The Mystery at the Medieval Castle	O	RF	Landon, Lucinda	Secret Passage Press
Meg Mackintosh and The Mystery at the Soccer Match	O	RF	Landon, Lucinda	Secret Passage Press
Meg Mackintosh and The Mystery in the Locked Library	O	RF	Landon, Lucinda	Secret Passage Press
Mexico	O	I	Dahl, Michael	Capstone Press
Midnight Fox, The	R	RF	Byars, Betsy	Scholastic
Midwife's Apprentice, The	X	HF	Cushman, Karen	HarperTrophy

Title	Level	Genre	Author/Series	Publisher/Distributor
Mieko and the Fifth Treasure	O	HF	Coerr, Eleanor	Bantam Doubleday Dell
Milton Hershey: Chocolate King Town Builder	P	B	Simon, Charnan	Children's Press
Mirandy and Brother Wind	R	F	McKissack, Patricia	Alfred A. Knopf
Missing May	W	RF	Rylant, Cynthia	Bantam Doubleday Dell
Mississippi Bridge	S	HF	Taylor, Mildred	Bantam Doubleday Dell
Misty of Chincoteague	R	RF	Henry, Marguerite	Aladdin
Mixed-up Max	Q	F	King-Smith, Dick	Troll
Moccasin Trail	W	RF	McGraw, Eloise	Scholastic
Moki	Q	HF	Penny, Grace Jackson	Penguin Group
Molly's Pilgrim	M	RF	Cohen, Barbara	Bantam Doubleday Dell
Moon Bridge, The	W	HF	Savin, Marcia	Scholastic
Moon, The	U	I	A First Book	Franklin Watts
More Perfect Union: The Story of Our Constitution	S	I	Maestro, Betsy & Giulio	William Morrow
More Stories Huey Tells	N	RF	Cameron, Ann	Alfred A. Knopf
More Stories Julian Tells	N	RF	Cameron, Ann	Random House
Morning Girl	S	HF	Dorris, Michael	Hyperion
Mouse and the Elephant, The	J	TL	Little Readers	Houghton Mifflin
Mouse and the Motorcycle, The	O	F	Cleary, Beverly	Avon Camelot
Mouse Soup	J	F	Lobel, Arnold	Harper Collins
Mouse Tales	J	F	Lobel, Arnold	Harper Collins
Moving Mama to Town	X	RF	Young, Ronder Thomas	Bantam Doubleday Dell
Mr. Gumpy's Motor Car	L	RF	Burningham, John	Harper Collins
Mr. Lincoln's Drummer	W	HF	Wisler, G. Clifton	The Penguin Group
Mr. Popper's Penguins	Q	F	Atwater, Richard and Florence	Dell
Mr. President: A Book of U.S. Presidents	S	B	Sullivan, George	Scholastic
Mr. Putter and Tabby Bake the Cake	J	RF	Rylant, Cynthia	Harcourt Brace
Mr. Putter and Tabby Fly the Plane	J	RF	Rylant, Cynthia	Harcourt Brace
Mr. Putter and Tabby Pick the Pears	J	RF	Rylant, Cynthia	Harcourt Brace
Mr. Putter and Tabby Pour the Tea	J	RF	Rylant, Cynthia	Harcourt Brace
Mr. Putter and Tabby Walk the Dog	J	RF	Rylant, Cynthia	Harcourt Brace
Much Ado About Aldo	O	RF	Hurwitz, Johanna	The Penguin Group
Music of Dolphins, The	V	RF	Hesse, Karen	Scholastic
My Brother Sam is Dead	Y	HF	Collier, James and Christopher	Scholastic
My Hiroshima	T	HF	Morimoto, Junko	The Penguin Group
My Name is Maria Isabel	N	RF	Ada, Alma Flor	Aladdin
My Name is Not Angelica	V	HF	O'Dell, Scott	Bantam Doubleday Dell
My Side of the Mountain	U	RF	George, Jean Craighead	The Penguin Group
My Sister Annie	S	RF	Dodds, Bill	Boyds Mills Press
My Teacher Fried My Brains	S	F	Coville, Bruce	Pocket Books
My Teacher Is an Alien	S	F	Coville, Bruce	Pocket Books
My Wartime Summers	V	HF	Cutler, Jane	Harper Collins
Mystery in the Night Woods	M	F	Peterson, John	Scholastic
Mystery of the Blue Ring, The	L	RF	Giff, Patricia Reilly	Bantam Doubleday Dell
Nate the Great and Me	K	RF	Sharmat, Marjorie Weinman	Random House
Nate the Great and the Crunchy Christmas	K	RF	Sharmat, Marjorie Weinman	Bantam Doubleday Dell
Nate the Great and the Fishy Prize	K	RF	Sharmat, Marjorie Weinman	Bantam Doubleday Dell
Nate the Great and the Halloween Hunt	K	RF	Sharmat, Marjorie Weinman	Bantam Doubleday Dell
Nate the Great and the Lost List	K	RF	Sharmat, Marjorie Weinman	Bantam Doubleday Dell
Nate the Great and the Missing Key	K	RF	Sharmat, Marjorie Weinman	Bantam Doubleday Dell
Nate the Great and the Mushy Valentine	K	RF	Sharmat, Marjorie Weinman	Bantam Doubleday Dell
Nate the Great and the Musical Note	K	RF	Sharmat, Marjorie Weinman	Bantam Doubleday Dell
Nate the Great and the Phony Clue	K	RF	Sharmat, Marjorie Weinman	Bantam Doubleday Dell
Nate the Great and the Pillowcase	K	RF	Sharmat, Marjorie Weinman	Bantam Doubleday Dell
Nate the Great and the Snowy Trail	K	RF	Sharmat, Marjorie Weinman	Bantam Doubleday Dell
Nate the Great and the Sticky Case	K	RF	Sharmat, Marjorie Weinman	Bantam Doubleday Dell
Nate the Great and the Stolen Base	K	RF	Sharmat, Marjorie Weinman	Bantam Doubleday Dell
Nate the Great and the Tardy Tortoise	K	RF	Sharmat, Marjorie Weinman	Bantam Doubleday Dell
Nate the Great Goes Down in the Dumps	K	RF	Sharmat, Marjorie Weinman	Bantam Doubleday Dell
Nate the Great Goes Undercover	K	RF	Sharmat, Marjorie Weinman	Bantam Doubleday Dell

Title	Level	Genre	Author/Series	Publisher/Distributor
Nate the Great Saves the King of Sweden	K	RF	Sharmat, Marjorie Weinman	Bantam Doubleday Dell
Nate the Great Stalks Stupidweed	K	RF	Sharmat, Marjorie Weinman	Bantam Doubleday Dell
Nigeria	O	I	Thoennes, Kristin	Capstone Press
Nightjohn	W	HF	Paulsen, Gary	Bantam Doubleday Dell
Nine True Dolphin Stories	M	I	Davidson, Margaret	Scholastic
No Dogs Allowed	O	RF	Cutler, Jane	Farrar, Straus and Giroux
Nose for Trouble, A	P	RF	Wilson, Nancy Hope	Avon
Nothing But The Truth	U	RF	Avi	Hearst
Nothing's Fair in Fifth Grade	R	RF	DeClements, Barthe	Scholastic
Novio Boy	X	TL	Soto, Gary	Harcourt Brace
Number the Stars	U	HF	Lowry, Lois	Bantam Doubleday Dell
Ocean Life	Q	I	Weldon Owen	Wright Group/McGraw Hill
Ocean Life: Tide Pool Creatures	Q	I	Leonhardt, Alice	Steck-Vaughn
Octopuses and Squids	O	I	Wonder World	Wright Group/McGraw Hill
Of Mice and Men	Z	RF	Steinbeck, John	The Penguin Group
Oh Boy, Boston!	O	RF	Giff, Patricia Reilly	Bantam Doubleday Dell
Old Yeller	V	RF	Gipson, Fred	Scholastic
On My Honor	S	RF	Bauer, Marion Dane	Bantam Doubleday Dell
One Day in the Tropical Rain Forest	P	I	George, Jean Craighead	HarperTrophy
One Day in the Woods	P	I	George, Jean Craighead	HarperTrophy
One in the Middle Is the Green Kangaroo, The	M	RF	Blume, Judy	Bantam Doubleday Dell
One-Eyed Cat	S	RF	Fox, Paula	Bantam Doubleday Dell
Onion John	U	HF	Krumgold, Joseph	Harper & Row
Onion Tears	Q	RF	Kidd, Diana	William Morrow
Otherwise Known As Sheila the Great	R	RF	Blume, Judy	Bantam Doubleday Dell
Out of the Dust	X	HF	Hesse, Karen	Scholastic
Outsiders, The	Z	RF	Hinton, S.E.	The Penguin Group
Owl At Home	J	F	Lobel, Arnold	Harper Collins
Owls	O	I	Holmes, Kevin J.	Capstone Press
Owls in the Family	P	F	Mowat, Farley	Bantam Doubleday Dell
P.S. Longer Letter Later	U	RF	Danziger, P. & Martin, A.	Scholastic
P.W. Cracker Sees the World	Q	F	Yoshizawa, Linda	Steck-Vaughn
Patrick Doyle is Full of Blarney	O	HF	Armstrong, Jennifer	Random House
Pedro's Journal	Q	HF	Conrad, Pam	Bantam Doubleday Dell
Pee Wee Scouts: The Pooped Troop	L	RF	Delton, Judy	Bantam Doubleday Dell
Perfect Pony, A	O	RF	Szymanski, Lois	Avon Camelot
Pet Parade	O	RF	Giff, Patricia Reilly	Bantam Doubleday Dell
Phantom Tollbooth, The	W	F	Juster, Norton	Bantam Doubleday Dell
Phillis Wheatley: First African-American Poet	N	B	Rookie Biographies	Children's Press
Phoebe The Spy	R	HF	Berry Griffin, Judith	Scholastic
Phoenix Rising	W	RF	Hesse, Karen	Penguin Group
Picking Apples and Pumpkins	L	I	Hutchings, A. & R.	Scholastic
Picture Book of Helen Keller, A	M	B	Adler, David A.	Holiday House
Picture Book of Simon Bolivar, A	Q	B	Adler, David A.	Bantam Doubleday Dell
Pigs Might Fly	R	F	King-Smith, Dick	Scholastic
Pinballs, The	S	RF	Byars, Betsy	HarperTrophy
Pinky and Rex	L	RF	Howe, James	Simon & Schuster
Pinky and Rex and the Bully	L	RF	Howe, James	Simon & Schuster
Pinky and Rex and the Double-Dad Weekend	L	RF	Howe, James	Simon & Schuster
Pinky and Rex and the Mean Old Witch	L	RF	Howe, James	Simon & Schuster
Pinky and Rex and the New Baby	L	RF	Howe, James	Simon & Schuster
Pinky and Rex and the New Neighbors	L	RF	Howe, James	Simon & Schuster
Pinky and Rex and the Perfect Pumpkin	L	RF	Howe, James	Simon & Schuster
Pinky and Rex and the School Play	L	RF	Howe, James	Simon & Schuster
Pioneer Cat	N	HF	Hooks, William H.	Random House
Pioneer Way, The	Q	I	Kummer, Patricia K.	Steck-Vaughn
Place Called Heartbreak, A: A Story of Vietnam	U	I	Myers, Walter Dean	Steck-Vaughn
Plain Girl	Q	RF	Sorensen, Virginia	Harcourt Brace

Title	Level	Genre	Author/Series	Publisher/Distributor
Platypus	P	I	Short, J., Green, J., and Bird, B.	Mondo
Play Ball, Amelia Bedelia	L	F	Parish, Peggy	Harper & Row
Pocket Full of Seeds, A	V	HF	Sachs, Marilyn	Scholastic
Pocketful of Goobers: Story of George Washington Carver	Q	B	Mitchell, Barbara	Carolrhoda Books
Polar Bears Past Bedtime	M	F	Osborne, Mary Pope	Random House
Pony Pals: A Pony for Keeps	O	RF	Betancourt, Jeanne	Scholastic
Pony Pals: A Pony in Trouble	O	RF	Betancourt, Jeanne	Scholastic
Pony Pals: Give Me Back My Pony	O	RF	Betancourt, Jeanne	Scholastic
Pony Pals: I Want a Pony	O	RF	Betancourt, Jeanne	Scholastic
Pony Pals: Runaway Pony	O	RF	Betancourt, Jeanne	Scholastic
Pony Pals: The Wild Pony	O	RF	Betancourt, Jeanne	Scholastic
Pony Trouble	L	RF	Gasque, Dale Blackwell	Hyperion
Poor Girl, Rich Girl	T	RF	Wilson, Johnniece Marshall	Language for Learning Assoc.
Popcorn Shop, The	J	RF	Low, Alice	Scholastic
Poppleton	J	F	Rylant, Cynthia	Scholastic
Poppleton and Friends	J	F	Rylant, Cynthia	Blue Sky Press
Poppleton Everyday	J	F	Rylant, Cynthia	Scholastic
Poppleton Forever	J	F	Rylant, Cynthia	Scholastic
Poppleton in Spring	J	F	Rylant, Cynthia	Scholastic
Poppy	S	F	Avi	Avon
Poppy and Rye	S	F	Avi	Avon
Powder Puff Puzzle, The	L	RF	Giff, Patricia Reilly	Bantam Doubleday Dell
Prairie Songs	Q	HF	Conrad, Pam	HarperTrophy
Preacher's Boy	T	RF	Paterson, Katherine	Houghton Mifflin
Pride of Puerto Rico: The Life of Roberto Clemente	W	B	Walker, Paul Robert	Harcourt Brace
Pushcart War, The	Y	F	Merrill, Jean	Bantam Doubleday Dell
Rain Forest Tree, A	Q	I	Kite, Lorien	Crabtree
Rainbow People, The	V	F	Yep, Lawrence	HarperTrophy
Ralph S. Mouse	O	F	Cleary, Beverly	Harper Trophy
Ramona and Her Father	O	RF	Cleary, Beverly	Avon
Ramona and Her Mother	O	RF	Cleary, Beverly	Avon
Ramona Forever	O	RF	Cleary, Beverly	Hearst
Ramona Quimby, Age 8	O	RF	Cleary, Beverly	Hearst
Ramona the Brave	O	RF	Cleary, Beverly	Hearst
Ramona the Pest	O	RF	Cleary, Beverly	Avon
Rascal	V	HF	North, Sterling	Scholastic
Rats on the Range and Other Stories	O	F	Marshall, James	The Penguin Group
Rats on the Roof and Other Stories	O	F	Marshall, James	The Penguin Group
Real Thief, The	U	F	Steig, William	Farrar, Straus and Giroux
Red Cap	W	HF	Wisler, G. Clifton	The Penguin Group
Red Dog	U	RF	Wallace, Bill	Simon & Schuster
Red Means Good Fortune: A Story of San Francisco's Chinatown	S	I	Goldin, Barbara Diamond	The Penguin Group
Remember Not To Forget: A Memory of the Holocaust	V	I	Finkelstein, Norman H.	William & Morrow
Remember the Ladies: The First Women's Rights Convention	U	I	Johnston, Norma	Scholastic
Rent a Third Grader	O	RF	Hiller, B.B.	Scholastic
Report To the Principal's Office	U	RF	Spinelli, Jerry	Scholastic
Riddle of The Red Purse, The	L	RF	Giff, Patricia Reilly	Bantam Doubleday Dell
Riddle of the Rosetta Stone, The	V	I	Giblin, James Cross	HarperTrophy
Righteous Revenge of Artemis Bonner, The	U	RF	Myers, Walter Dean	HarperTrophy
Road to Memphis, The	X	HF	Taylor, Mildred D.	The Penguin Group
Road to Seneca Falls, The	R	B	Swain, Gwenyth	Carolrhoda Books
Roll of Thunder, Hear My Cry	W	HF	Taylor, Mildred D.	The Penguin Group
Root Cellar, The	V	HF	Lunn, Janet	The Penguin Group
Rosa Parks	P	B	Greenfield, Eloise	HarperTrophy
Rosa Parks: My Story	U	B	Parks, Rosa	Scholastic

Title	Level	Genre	Author/Series	Publisher/Distributor
Runaway Ralph	O	F	Cleary, Beverly	Hearst
Russell and Elisa	M	RF	Hurwitz, Johanna	The Penguin Group
Russell Rides Again	M	RF	Hurwitz, Johanna	The Penguin Group
Russell Sprouts	M	RF	Hurwitz, Johanna	The Penguin Group
Russia	O	I	Thoennes, Kristin	Capstone Press
Sadako and the Thousand Paper Cranes	R	HF	Coerr, Eleanor	Bantam Doubleday Dell
Sadie and the Snowman	L	RF	Morgan, Allen	Scholastic
Salem Days: Life in a Colonial Seaport	T	I	Adventures in Colonial America	Troll
Sam and the Firefly	J	F	Eastman, P.D.	Random House
Samurai's Daughter, The	Q	TL	San Souci, Robert D.	The Penguin Group
San Domingo	R	I	Henry, Marguerite	Scholastic
Sand On The Move: The Story of Dunes	U	I	A First Book	Franklin Watts
Sarah Bishop	X	HF	O'Dell, Scott	Scholastic
Sarah, Plain and Tall	R	HF	MacLachlan, Patricia	HarperTrophy
Sarny: A Life Remembered	W	HF	Paulsen, Gary	Delacorte Press
Saturnalia	W	RF	Fleischman, Paul	Harper Collins
Say "Cheese"	L	RF	Giff, Patricia Reilly	Bantam Doubleday Dell
Say Hola, Sarah	N	RF	Giff, Patricia Reilly	Bantam Doubleday Dell
School's Out	N	RF	Hurwitz, Johanna	Scholastic
Scorpions	Z	RF	Myers, Walter Dean	HarperTrophy
Second Chance	N	RF	Kroll, Stephen	Avon Camelot
Second Mrs. Giaconda, The	T	HF	Konigsburg, E. L.	Language for Learning Assoc.
Secret at the Polk Street School, The	M	RF	Giff, Patricia Reilly	Bantam Doubleday Dell
Secret Garden, The	U	RF	Burnett, Frances H.	Scholastic
Secret Soldier, The: The Story of Deborah Sampson	O	B	McGovern, Ann	Scholastic
Seedfolks	W	RF	Fleishman, Paul	HarperTrophy
Sees Behind Trees	T	HF	Dorris, Michael	Language for Learning Assoc.
Selchie's Seed, The	W	F	Levey Oppenheim, Shulamith	Harcourt Brace
Seven Kisses in a Row	O	RF	MacLachlan, Patricia	Harper Collins
Shadow of a Bull	U	RF	Wojciechowska, Maia	Simon & Schuster
Sheila Rae, the Brave	K	F	Henkes, Kevin	Scholastic
Shh! We're Writing the Constitution	T	I	Fritz, Jean	G.P. Putnam's Sons
Shiloh	R	RF	Naylor, Phyllis Reynolds	Bantam Doubleday Dell
Shoeshine Girl	N	RF	Bulla, Clyde Robert	HarperTrophy
Shorty	M	RF	Literacy 2000	Rigby
Show-and-Tell War, The	N	RF	Smith, Janice Lee	HarperTrophy
Sidewalk Story	N	RF	Mathis, Sharon Bell	The Penguin Group
Sideways Stories from Wayside School	P	F	Sachar, Louis	Hearst
Sign of the Beaver	T	HF	Speare, Elizabeth George	Bantam Doubleday Dell
Sign of the Chrysanthemum, The	U	RF	Paterson, Katherine	HarperTrophy
Silk Route, The	U	HF	Major, John S.	HarperCollins
Silverwing: How One Small Bat Became a Noble Hero	U	F	Oppel, Kenneth	Simon & Schuster
Sing Down the Moon	T	HF	O'Dell, Scott	Language for Learning Assoc.
Sing for Your Father, Su Phan	W	HF	Pevsner, Stella and Tang, Fay	Bantam Doubleday Dell
Sister	W	RF	Greenfield, Eloise	Harper Collins
Sixth Grade Can Really Kill You	S	RF	DeClements, Barthe	Scholastic
Sixth Grade Secrets	S	RF	Sachar, Louis	Scholastic
Sixth-Grade Sleepover	R	RF	Bunting, Eve	Scholastic
Skylark	R	HF	MacLachlan, Patricia	HarperTrophy
Snow Treasure	R	HF	McSwigan, Marie	Scholastic
Snowshoe Thompson	K	HF	Smiler Levinson, N.	HarperTrophy
Sojourner Truth: Ain't I a Woman?	V	B	McKissack, F. and P.	Scholastic
Solo Girl	M	RF	Pinkey, Andrea Davis	Hyperion
Something Queer at the Ball Park	N	RF	Levy, Elizabeth	Bantam Doubleday Dell
Something Queer at the Haunted School	N	RF	Levy, Elizabeth	Bantam Doubleday Dell
Something Queer at the Lemonade Stand	N	RF	Levy, Elizabeth	Bantam Doubleday Dell
Something Upstairs	T	RF	Avi	Language for Learning Assoc.
Song Lee and the Hamster Hunt	L	RF	Kline, Suzy	The Penguin Group

Title	Level	Genre	Author/Series	Publisher/Distributor
Song Lee and the Leech Man	L	RF	Kline, Suzy	The Penguin Group
Song Lee In Room 2B	L	RF	Kline, Suzy	The Penguin Group
Song of the Trees	S	HF	Taylor, Mildred	Bantam Doubleday Dell
Sons of Liberty	Y	RF	Griffin, Adele	Hyperion
Sounder	T	RF	Armstrong, William	Scholastic
Soup	Q	RF	Peck, Robert Newton	Bantam Doubleday Dell
South Korea	O	I	Davis, Lucile	Capstone Press
Speedy Pasta and Other Cases, The	O	RF	Simon, Seymour	Avon
Speedy Snake and Other Cases, The	O	RF	Simon, Seymour	Avon
Speedy Soapbox Car and Other Cases, The	O	RF	Simon, Seymour	Avon
Spider Boy	R	RF	Fletcher, Ralph	Bantam Doubleday Dell
Spiders	O	I	Holmes, Kevin J.	Capstone Press
Squanto: Friend of the Pilgrims	O	B	Bulla, Clyde Robert	Scholastic
Stacy Says Good-Bye	L	RF	Giff, Patricia Reilly	Bantam Doubleday Dell
Star Fisher, The	S	RF	Yep, Lawrence	Scholastic
Starring Rosie	N	RF	Giff, Patricia Reilly	The Penguin Group
Stay Away from Simon!	O	RF	Carrick, Carol	Clarion
Stems	K	I	Pebble Books	Grolier, Capstone
Stone Fox	P	RF	Gardiner, John Reynolds	Harper Trophy
Stone Soup	J	TL	McGovern, Ann	Scholastic
Stories Huey Tells, The	N	RF	Cameron, Ann	Alfred A. Knopf
Stories in Stone: The World of Animal Fossils	U	I	A First Book	Franklin Watts
Stories Julian Tells, The	N	RF	Cameron, Ann	Alfred A. Knopf
Story of Benjamin Franklin, Amazing American	O	B	Davidson, Margaret	Scholastic
Story of George Washington Carver, The	Q	B	Moore, Eva	Bantam Doubleday Dell
Story of Harriet Tubman: Freedom, The	U	B	Sterling, Dorothy	Bantam Doubleday Dell
Story of Harriet Tubman, The: Conductor of the Underground Railroad	S	B	McMullan, Kate	Scholastic
Story of Jackie Robinson, Bravest Man in Baseball	O	B	Davidson, Margaret	Scholastic
Story of Laura Ingalls Wilder, Pioneer Girl, The	Q	B	Stine, Megan	Bantam Doubleday Dell
Story of Muhammad Ali: Heavyweight Champion of the World, The	S	B	Denenberg, Barry	Dell Publishing
Story of Thomas Alva Edison, Inventor, The	R	B	Davidson, Margaret	Scholastic
Story of Walt Disney, Maker of Magical Worlds, The	O	B	Selden, Bernice	Bantam Doubleday Dell
Stranger at the Window	U	RF	Alcock, Vivien	Houghton Mifflin
Stray, The	R	RF	King-Smith, Dick	Alfred A. Knopf
Striped Ice Cream	N	RF	Lexau, Joan M.	Scholastic
Stuart Little	R	F	White, E.B.	HarperTrophy
Sugaring Time	S	I	Lasky, Kathryn	Macmillan
Summer Life, A	Z	RF	Soto, Gary	Bantam Doubleday Dell
Summer of My German Soldier	Z	HF	Greene, Bette	Dell Publishing
Summer of the Swans, The	U	RF	Byars, Betsy	The Penguin Group
Sun & Spoon	R	RF	Henkes, Kevin	The Penguin Group
Super Amos	R	RF	Paulsen, Gary	Bantam Doubleday Dell
Superfudge	Q	RF	Blume, Judy	Bantam Doubleday Dell
Susan B. Anthony	P	B	Davis, Lucile	Capstone Press
Swiftly Tilting Planet, A	V	F	L'Engle, Madeleine	Bantam Doubleday Dell
Taking Sides	S	RF	Soto, Gary	Harcourt Brace
Tale of Peter Rabbit, The	L	TL	Potter, Beatrix	Scholastic
Tales of a Fourth Grade Nothing	Q	RF	Blume, Judy	Bantam Doubleday Dell
Tales of Amanda Pig	L	F	Van Leeuwen, Jean	Puffin Books
Talking Earth, The	U	RF	George, Jean Craighead	HarperTrophy
Tangerine	U	RF	Bloor, Edward	Scholastic
Taste of Blackberries, A	P	RF	Buchanan Smith, Doris	Scholastic
Teach Us, Amelia Bedelia	L	F	Parish, Peggy	Scholastic
Teacher's Pet	O	RF	Hurwitz, Johanna	Scholastic
Tenement Writer, The: An Immigrant's Story	T	I	Sonder, Ben	Steck-Vaughn
Tent, The	V	RF	Paulsen, Gary	Bantam Doubleday Dell

Title	Level	Genre	Author/Series	Publisher/Distributor
Thank You, Amelia Bedelia	L	F	Little Readers	Houghton Mifflin
Thank You, Jackie Robinson	P	B	Cohen, Barbara	Scholastic
Then Again, Maybe I Won't	T	RF	Blume, Judy	Language for Learning Assoc.
There's A Boy In The Girls' Bathroom	Q	RF	Sachar, Louis	Alfred A. Knopf
Third Grade Bullies	N	RF	Levy, Elizabeth	Hyperion
Third Grade Stars	P	RF	Ransom, Candice	Troll
Thomas Alva Edison: Great Inventor	Q	B	Levinson, Nancy Smiler	Scholastic
Thomas Jefferson: Author, Inventor, President	N	B	Rookie Biographies	Children's Press
Thomas Jefferson: Man with a Vision	U	B	Crisman, Ruth	Scholastic
Three Billy Goats Gruff, The	K	TL	Stevens, Janet	Harcourt Brace
Three Days on a River in a Red Canoe	K	I	Williams, Vera B.	Scholastic
Three Lives to Live	T	F	Lindbergh, Anne	Little, Brown and Co.
Three Stories You Can Read to Your Cat	K	F	Miller, Sara Swan	Houghton Mifflin
Throwing Shadows	T	RF	Konigsburg, E. L.	Language for Learning Assoc.
Thunder Rolling in the Mountains	U	HF	O'Dell, Scott & Hall, Elizabeth	Bantam Doubleday Dell
Thunder Valley	T	RF	Paulsen, Gary	Bantam Doubleday Dell
Thurgood Marshall: First Black Supreme Court Justice	N	B	Rookie Biographies	Children's Press
Ties That Bind, Ties That Break	X	HF	Namioka, Lensey	Delacorte Press
Tiger Eyes	W	RF	Blume, Judy	Bantam Doubleday Dell
Tiltawhirl John	U	RF	Paulsen, Gary	The Penguin Group
Time Apart, A	T	RF	Stanley, Diane	William Morrow
Time of Angels, A	W	F	Hesse, Karen	Hyperion
Time Warp Trio: 2095	P	SF	Scieszka, Jon	The Penguin Group
Time Warp Trio: Good, the Bad, and the Goofy, The	P	SF	Scieszka, Jon	The Penguin Group
Time Warp Trio: The Knights of the Kitchen Table	P	F	Scieszka, Jon	The Penguin Group
Time Warp Trio: The Not-So-Jolly Roger	P	F	Scieszka, Jon	The Penguin Group
Time Warp Trio: Tut Tut	P	F	Scieszka, Jon	The Penguin Group
Time Warp Trio: Your Mother Was a Neanderthal	P	F	Scieszka, Jon	The Penguin Group
Titanic, The	V	I	Cornerstones of Freedom	Children's Press
To Kill a Mockingbird	Z	HF	Lee, Harper	Warner Books
Toad for Tuesday, A	O	F	Erickson, Russell E.	Beech Tree Books
Tomorrow's Wizard	R	F	MacLachlan, Patricia	Scholastic
Too Many Babas	K	TL	Croll, Carolyn	HarperTrophy
Too Many Babas	K	TL	Little Readers	Houghton Mifflin
Toothpaste Millionaire, The	T	RF	Merrill, Jean	Houghton Mifflin
Tracker	T	RF	Paulsen, Gary	Scholastic
Transcontinental Railroad, The	V	I	Cornerstones of Freedom	Children's Press
Treasure Island	Z	HF	Stevenson, Robert Lewis	Scholastic
Treasures in the Dust	U	HF	Porter, Tracey	HarperTrophy
Triffic the Extraordinary Pig	R	F	King-Smith, Dick	Bantam Doubleday Dell
Triplet Trouble and the Bicycle Race	L	RF	Dadey, D. & Jones, M. T.	Scholastic
Triplet Trouble and the Class Trip	L	RF	Dadey, D. & Jones, M. T.	Scholastic
Triplet Trouble and the Cookie Contest	L	RF	Dadey, D. & Jones, M. T.	Scholastic
Triplet Trouble and the Field Day Disaster	L	RF	Dadey, D. & Jones, M. T.	Scholastic
Trolls Don't Ride Roller Coasters	M	F	Dadey, D. & Jones, M. T.	Scholastic
Trouble River	S	HF	Byars, Betsy	Scholastic
Trouble with Tuck, The	R	RF	Taylor, Theodore	Avon
Trout Summer	T	RF	Conly, Jane Leslie	Scholastic
True Confessions of Charlotte Doyle, The	V	HF	Avi	Avon
True Story of Balto, The	L	I	Standiford, Natalie	Random House
Trumpet of the Swan, The	R	F	White, E. B.	Scholastic
Tuck Everlasting	U	F	Babbitt, Natalie	Farrar, Straus and Giroux
Tucket's Ride	U	HF	Paulsen, Gary	Bantam Doubleday Dell
Turkey Trouble	M	RF	Giff, Patricia Reilly	Bantam Doubleday Dell
Twenty-One Balloons, The	V	SF	DuBois, William	Scholastic
Twits, The	P	F	Dahl, Roald	The Penguin Group
Tyler Toad and Thunder	M	F	Crowe, Robert	Dutton
Ultimate Field Trip 1: Adventures in the	S	I	Goodman, Susan E.	Simon & Schuster

Title	Level	Genre	Author/Series	Publisher/Distributor
Amazon Rain Forest				
Underground Railroad, The	V	I	Bial, Raymond	Houghton Mifflin
Vacation Journal, A	M	B	Discovery World	Rigby
Vampires Don't Wear Polka Dots	M	F	Dadey, D. & Jones, M. T.	Scholastic
Van Gogh Cafe, The	S	RF	Rylant, Cynthia	Harcourt Brace
Velveteen Rabbit, The	Q	F	Williams, Margery	Hearst
View from Saturday, The	U	F	Konigsburg, E. L.	Atheneum Books
Volcanoes	Q	I	Worldwise	Grolier
Wagon Wheels	K	HF	Brenner, Barbara	HarperTrophy
Wait Till Helen Comes	U	F	Downing Hahn, Mary	Houghton Mifflin
Walking the Road to Freedom:A Story About Sojourner Truth	Q	B	Ferris, Jeri	Dell
Wanted Dead or Alive: The True Story of Harriet Tubman	P	B	McGovern, Ann	Scholastic
War Comes to Willy Freeman	U	HF	Collier, J. L., &Collier, C.	Dell Publishing
War of 1812, The	S	I	A First Book	Franklin Watts
War With Grandpa, The	S	RF	Kimmel Smith, Robert	Bantam Doubleday Dell
Warton and the King of the Skies	O	F	Erickson, Russell E.	Houghton Mifflin
Watcher, The	Z	RF	Howe, James	Simon & Schuster
Watsons Go to Birmingham-1963, The	T	HF	Curtis, Christopher Paul	Bantam Doubleday Dell
Wayside School Gets a Little Stranger	P	F	Sachar, Louis	Avon Camelot
Werewolves Don't Go To Summer Camp	M	F	Dadey, D. & Jones, M. T.	Scholastic
Westing Game, The	V	RF	Raskin, Ellen	The Penguin Group
Whales	O	I	Book Shop	Mondo
Whales	O	I	Holmes, Kevin J.	Capstone Press
What Do Fish Have To Do With Anything?	W	RF	Avi	Candlewick Press
What Jamie Saw	T	RF	Coman, Carolyn	The Penguin Group
What Makes a Bird a Bird?	O	I	Garelick, May	Mondo
What's Cooking, Jenny Archer?	M	RF	Conford, Ellen	Little Brown & Co.
What's It Like to Be a Fish?	L	I	Little Readers	Houghton Mifflin
What's the Big Idea, Ben Franklin?	O	B	Fritz, Jean	Scholastic
Where Do You Think You're Going, Christopher Columbus?	S	B	Fritz, Jean	Putnam & Grosset
Where People Live	J	RF	Early Connections	Benchmark Education
Where the Lilies Bloom	Y	RF	Cleavers, Vera and Bill	HarperTrophy
Where the Red Fern Grows	X	RF	Rawls, Wilson	Bantam Doubleday Dell
Where Was Patrick Henry on the 29th of May?	R	B	Fritz, Jean	Scholastic
Whipping Boy, The	R	F	Fleischman, Sid	Troll
Who Is Carrie?	W	HF	Collier, J. L. and Collier, C.	Bantam Doubleday Dell
Who Shot the President?: The Death of John F. Kennedy	P	I	Donnelly, Judy	Random House
Why Don't You Get a Horse, Sam Adams?	R	B	Fritz, Jean	G.P. Putnam's Sons
Winter Room, The	U	RF	Paulsen, Gary	Bantam Doubleday Dell
Winterdance: The Fine Madness of Running the Iditarod	W	B	Paulsen, Gary	Harcourt Brace
Wish Giver, The	T	F	Brittain, Bill	HarperTrophy
Wish on a Unicorn	T	RF	Hesse, Karen	The Penguin Group
Witch Hunt: It Happened in Salem Village	Q	I	Krensky, Stephen	Random House
Witch of Blackbird Pond, The	W	HF	Speare, Elizabeth George	Bantam Doubleday Dell
Witch of Fourth Street, The	S	HF	Levoy, Myron	Language for Learning Assoc.
Witches, The	R	F	Dahl, Roald	The Penguin Group
Wizard of Earthsea, A	Z	F	LeGuin, Ursula K.	Bantam Doubleday Dell
Wolves of Willoughby Chase, The	V	HF	Aiken, Joan	Bantam Doubleday Dell
Woman Hollering Creek	Z	RF	Cisneros, Sandra	Random House
Women Who Shaped the West	V	B	Cornerstones of Freedom	Children's Press
Women's Voting Rights	V	I	Cornerstones of Freedom	Children's Press
Woodsong	T	B	Paulsen, Gary	Dell
Words of Stone	V	RF	Henkes, Kevin	The Penguin Group
Worst Show-and-Tell Ever, The	J	SF	Walsh, Rita	Troll

Title	Level	Genre	Author/Series	Publisher/Distributor
Worst Witch at Sea, The	P	F	Murphy, Jill	Candlewick Press
Worst Witch Strikes Again, The	P	F	Murphy, Jill	Candlewick Press
Worst Witch, The	P	F	Murphy, Jill	Puffin Books
Wringer	U	RF	Spinelli, Jerry	HarperTrophy
Wrinkle in Time, A	V	F	L'Engle, Madeleine	Bantom Doubleday Dell
Write Up a Storm with the Polk Street School	M	RF	Giff, Patricia Reilly	Bantam Doubleday Dell
Writer of the Plains: A Story about Willa Cather	Q	B	Streissguth, Tom	Carolrhoda Books
Yang the Second and Her Secret Admirer	P	RF	Namioka, Lensey	Bantam Doubleday Dell
Yang the Third & Her Impossible Family	P	RF	Namioka, Lensey	Bantam Doubleday Dell
Yang the Youngest and His Terrible Ear	P	RF	Namioka, Lensey	Bantam Doubleday Dell
Year of Impossible Goodbyes	W	HF	Choi, Sook Nyui	Yearling
Yearling, The	X	RF	Rawlings, Marjorie Kinnan	Simon & Schuster
You Can't Eat Your Chicken Pox, Amber Brown	N	RF	Danziger, Paula	Scholastic
You Want Women to Vote, Lizzie Stanton?	W	B	Fritz, Jean	The Penguin Group
You're Out	N	RF	Kroll, Stephen	Avon Camelot
Young Arthur Ashe: Brave Champion	L	B	First Start Biography	Troll
Young Clara Barton: Battlefield Nurse	L	B	First Start Biography	Troll
Young Jackie Robinson: Baseball Hero	L	B	First Start Biography	Troll
Young Rosa Parks: Civil Rights Heroine	L	B	First Start Biography	Troll
Young Thurgood Marshall: Fighter for Equality	L	B	First Start Biography	Troll
Zack's Alligator	K	F	Mozelle, Shirley	HarperTrophy
Zack's Alligator Goes to School	K	F	Mozelle, Shirley	HarperTrophy
Zeely	R	RF	Hamilton, Virginia	Macmillan

Book List
(organized by level)

Title	Level	Genre	Author/Series	Publisher/Distributor
Addie's Bad Day	J	RF	Robins, Joan	HarperTrophy
Adventures of Snail at School	J	F	Stadler, John	HarperTrophy
Ah Liang's Gift	J	RF	Sunshine	Wright Group/McGraw Hill
Aladdin & the Magic Lamp	J	TL	Traditional Tales	Dominie
All About Bats	J	I	Ready Readers	Modern Curriculum
Amazing Eggs	J	I	Discovery World	Rigby
And I Mean it Stanley	J	RF	Bonsall, Crosby	HarperCollins
Annie's Pet	J	RF	Bank Street	Bantam Doubleday Dell
Art Around the World	J	I	Early Connections	Benchmark Education
Ask Mr. Bear	J	F	Flack, Marjorie	Macmillan
Aunt Eater Loves a Mystery	J	F	Cushman, Doug	HarperTrophy
Aunt Eater's Mystery Christmas	J	F	Cushman, Doug	HarperTrophy
Aunt Eater's Mystery Vacation	J	F	Cushman, Doug	HarperTrophy
Bear Shadow	J	F	Asch, Frank	Simon & Schuster
Bear's Bargain	J	F	Asch, Frank	Scholastic
Best Little Monkeys in the World, The	J	F	Standiford, Natalie	Random House
Better Than TV	J	RF	Miller, Sara Swan	Bantam Doubleday Dell
Big Max	J	F	Platt, Kin	HarperTrophy
Billy Magee's New Car	J	RF	Foundations	Wright Group/McGraw Hill
Birds' Nests	J	I	Wonder World	Wright Group/McGraw Hill
Blackboard Bear	J	F	Alexander, Martha	The Penguin Group
Boy Who Cried Wolf, The	J	TL	Littledale, Freya	Scholastic
Camp Big Paw	J	RF	Cushman, Doug	HarperTrophy
Cells	J	I	Wonder World	Wright Group/McGraw Hill
Charlie Needs a Cloak	J	RF	dePaola, Tomie	Prentice-Hall
Children of Sierra Leone, The	J	I	Books For Young Learners	Richard C. Owen
Class Play, The	J	RF	Little Readers	Houghton Mifflin
Clouds	J	I	Early Connections	Benchmark Education
Danny and the Dinosaur	J	F	Hoff, Syd	Scholastic
Dogs at Work	J	I	Little Readers	Houghton Mifflin
Don't Eat Too Much Turkey	J	RF	Cohen, Miriam	Bantam Doubleday Dell
Donkey's Tale, The	J	TL	Bank Street	Bantam Doubleday Dell
Doorbell Rang, The	J	RF	Hutchins, Pat	Greenwillow
Fox All Week	J	F	Marshall, Edward	Puffin Books
Fox and His Friends	J	F	Marshall, Edward	Puffin Books
Fox at School	J	F	Marshall, Edward	Puffin Books
Fox Be Nimble	J	F	Marshall, James	Puffin Books
Fox In Love	J	F	Marshall, Edward	Puffin Books
Fox on Stage	J	F	Marshall, James	Puffin Books
Fox on the Job	J	F	Marshall, James	Puffin Books
Fox on Wheels	J	F	Marshall, Edward	Puffin Books
Fox Outfoxed	J	F	Marshall, James	Puffin Books
Henry and Mudge and the Bedtime Thumps	J	RF	Rylant, Cynthia	Aladdin
Henry and Mudge and the Best Day of All	J	RF	Rylant, Cynthia	Aladdin
Henry and Mudge and the Careful Cousin	J	RF	Rylant, Cynthia	Aladdin
Henry and Mudge and the Forever Sea	J	RF	Rylant, Cynthia	Aladdin
Henry and Mudge and the Happy Cat	J	RF	Rylant, Cynthia	Aladdin
Henry and Mudge and the Long Weekend	J	RF	Rylant, Cynthia	Aladdin
Henry and Mudge and the Wild Wind	J	RF	Rylant, Cynthia	Aladdin
Henry and Mudge Get the Cold Shivers	J	RF	Rylant, Cynthia	Aladdin
Henry and Mudge in Puddle Trouble	J	RF	Rylant, Cynthia	Aladdin
Henry and Mudge in the Family Trees	J	RF	Rylant, Cynthia	Aladdin
Henry and Mudge in the Green Time	J	RF	Rylant, Cynthia	Aladdin
Henry and Mudge in the Sparkle Days	J	RF	Rylant, Cynthia	Aladdin
Henry and Mudge Take the Big Test	J	RF	Rylant, Cynthia	Aladdin

Title	Level	Genre	Author/Series	Publisher/Distributor
Henry and Mudge: The First Book	J	RF	Rylant, Cynthia	Aladdin
Henry and Mudge Under the Yellow Moon	J	RF	Rylant, Cynthia	Aladdin
How Grandmother Spider Got the Sun	J	TL	Little Readers	Houghton Mifflin
How Turtle Raced Beaver	J	TL	Literacy 2000	Rigby
Kick, Pass, and Run	J	RF	Kessler, Leonard	HarperTrophy
Lion and the Mouse, The	J	TL	Sunshine	Wright Group/McGraw Hill
Little Bear	J	F	Minarik, E.H.	Harper Collins
Little Bear's Friend	J	F	Minarik, E.H.	HarperTrophy
Little Bear's Visit	J	F	Minarik, E.H.	HarperTrophy
Mouse and the Elephant, The	J	TL	Little Readers	Houghton Mifflin
Mouse Soup	J	F	Lobel, Arnold	Harper Collins
Mouse Tales	J	F	Lobel, Arnold	Harper Collins
Mr. Putter and Tabby Bake the Cake	J	RF	Rylant, Cynthia	Harcourt Brace
Mr. Putter and Tabby Fly the Plane	J	RF	Rylant, Cynthia	Harcourt Brace
Mr. Putter and Tabby Pick the Pears	J	RF	Rylant, Cynthia	Harcourt Brace
Mr. Putter and Tabby Pour the Tea	J	RF	Rylant, Cynthia	Harcourt Brace
Mr. Putter and Tabby Walk the Dog	J	RF	Rylant, Cynthia	Harcourt Brace
Owl At Home	J	F	Lobel, Arnold	Harper Collins
Popcorn Shop, The	J	RF	Low, Alice	Scholastic
Poppleton	J	F	Rylant, Cynthia	Scholastic
Poppleton and Friends	J	F	Rylant, Cynthia	Blue Sky Press
Poppleton Everyday	J	F	Rylant, Cynthia	Scholastic
Poppleton Forever	J	F	Rylant, Cynthia	Scholastic
Poppleton in Spring	J	F	Rylant, Cynthia	Scholastic
Sam and the Firefly	J	F	Eastman, P.D.	Random House
Stone Soup	J	TL	McGovern, Ann	Scholastic
Where People Live	J	RF	Early Connections	Benchmark Education
Worst Show-and-Tell Ever, The	J	SF	Walsh, Rita	Troll
Alison's Puppy	K	RF	Bauer, Marion Dane	Hyperion
Alison's Wings	K	RF	Bauer, Marion Dane	Hyperion
Amalia and the Grasshopper	K	RF	Tello, J. & Krupinski, L.	Scholastic
Arthur's Back to School Day	K	F	Hoban, Lillian	HarperTrophy
Arthur's Camp-Out	K	F	Hoban, Lillian	HarperTrophy
Arthur's Christmas Cookies	K	F	Hoban, Lillian	HarperTrophy
Arthur's Funny Money	K	F	Hoban, Lillian	HarperTrophy
Arthur's Great Big Valentine	K	F	Hoban, Lillian	HarperTrophy
Arthur's Honey Bear	K	F	Hoban, Lillian	Harper Collins
Arthur's Loose Tooth	K	F	Hoban, Lillian	Harper Collins
Arthur's Pen Pal	K	F	Hoban, Lillian	Harper Collins
Arthur's Prize Reader	K	TL	Hoban, Lillian	HarperTrophy
Baby Sister for Frances, A	K	F	Hoban, Lillian	Scholastic
Bargain For Frances, A	K	F	Hoban, Russell	HarperTrophy
Bedtime Story, A	K	RF	Book Shop	Mondo
Best Friends for Frances	K	F	Hoban, Russell	HarperTrophy
Best Teacher in the World, The	K	RF	Chardiet, Bernice	Scholastic
Birthday for Frances, A	K	F	Hoban, Russell	Scholastic
Bread and Jam for Frances	K	F	Hoban, Russell	Scholastic
Camp Knock Knock	K	RF	Duffey, Betsy	Bantam Doubleday Dell
Camp Knock Knock Mystery, The	K	RF	Duffey, Betsy	Bantam Doubleday Dell
Case of the Cat's Meow, The	K	RF	Bonsall, Crosby	HarperTrophy
Case of the Double Cross, The	K	RF	Bonsall, Crosby	HarperTrophy
Case of the Dumb Bells, The	K	RF	Bonsall, Crosby	HarperTrophy
Case of the Hungry Stranger, The	K	RF	Bonsall, Crosby	HarperTrophy
Case of the Scaredy Cats, The	K	RF	Bonsall, Crosby	HarperTrophy
Case of the Two Masked Robbers, The	K	F	Hoban, Lillian	HarperTrophy
Cats of the Night	K	RF	Book Bank	Wright Group/McGraw Hill
Commander Toad and the Big Black Hole	K	F	Yolen, Jane	Putnam & Grosset
Commander Toad and the Dis-Asteroid	K	F	Yolen, Jane	Putnam & Grosset
Commander Toad and the Intergalactic Spy	K	F	Yolen, Jane	Putnam & Grosset

Title	Level	Genre	Author/Series	Publisher/Distributor
Commander Toad and the Planet of the Grapes	K	F	Yolen, Jane	Putnam & Grosset
Commander Toad and the Space Pirates	K	F	Yolen, Jane	Putnam & Grosset
Commander Toad And The Voyage Home	K	F	Yolen, Jane	Putnam & Grosset
Counting Insects	K	I	Early Connections	Benchmark Education
Daniel's Duck	K	RF	Bulla, Clyde Robert	HarperTrophy
Days With Frog and Toad	K	F	Lobel, Arnold	HarperTrophy
Frog and Toad All Year	K	F	Little Readers	Houghton Mifflin
Frog and Toad Are Friends	K	F	Lobel, Arnold	Harper & Row
Frog and Toad Together	K	F	Little Readers	Houghton Mifflin
Frog and Toad Together	K	F	Lobel, Arnold	Harper Collins
Golly Sisters Go West, The	K	RF	Byars, Betsy	HarperTrophy
Golly Sisters Ride Again, The	K	RF	Byars, Betsy	HarperTrophy
Good Morning Mrs. Martin	K	F	Book Bank	Wright Group/McGraw Hill
Grandma Mixup, The	K	RF	Little Readers	Houghton Mifflin
Grasshopper and the Ants	K	TL	Sunshine	Wright Group/McGraw Hill
Greg's Microscope	K	I	Selsam, Millicent E.	HarperTrophy
Guide Dog, The	K	I	Foundations	Wright Group/McGraw Hill
Happy Birthday, Dear Duck	K	F	Bunting, Eve	Clarion
Here Comes the Strike Out	K	RF	Kessler, Leonard	Harper Trophy
Hooray for the Golly Sisters!	K	RF	Byars, Betsy	HarperTrophy
Jack and the Beanstalk	K	TL	Weisner, David	Scholastic
Keep the Lights Burning Abbie	K	HF	Roop, Peter & Connie	Scholastic
M & M and The Bad News Babies	K	RF	Ross, Pat	The Penguin Group
M & M and the Big Bag	K	RF	Ross, Pat	The Penguin Group
M & M and the Halloween Monster	K	RF	Ross, Pat	The Penguin Group.
M & M and the Haunted House Game	K	RF	Ross, Pat	The Penguin Group
M & M and the Mummy Mess	K	RF	Ross, Pat	The Penguin Group
M & M and the Santa Secrets	K	RF	Ross, Pat	The Penguin Group
M & M and the Super Child Afternoon	K	RF	Ross, Pat	The Penguin Group
Martin and the Teacher's Pets	K	RF	Chardiet, B. & Maccarone, G.	Scholastic
Martin and the Tooth Fairy	K	RF	Chardiet, B. & Maccarone, G.	Scholastic
Meet M & M	K	RF	Ross, Pat	The Penguin Group
Nate the Great and Me	K	RF	Sharmat, Marjorie Weinman	Random House
Nate the Great and the Crunchy Christmas	K	RF	Sharmat, Marjorie Weinman	Bantam Doubleday Dell
Nate the Great and the Fishy Prize	K	RF	Sharmat, Marjorie Weinman	Bantam Doubleday Dell
Nate the Great and the Halloween Hunt	K	RF	Sharmat, Marjorie Weinman	Bantam Doubleday Dell
Nate the Great and the Lost List	K	RF	Sharmat, Marjorie Weinman	Bantam Doubleday Dell
Nate the Great and the Missing Key	K	RF	Sharmat, Marjorie Weinman	Bantam Doubleday Dell
Nate the Great and the Mushy Valentine	K	RF	Sharmat, Marjorie Weinman	Bantam Doubleday Dell
Nate the Great and the Musical Note	K	RF	Sharmat, Marjorie Weinman	Bantam Doubleday Dell
Nate the Great and the Phony Clue	K	RF	Sharmat, Marjorie Weinman	Bantam Doubleday Dell
Nate the Great and the Pillowcase	K	RF	Sharmat, Marjorie Weinman	Bantam Doubleday Dell
Nate the Great and the Snowy Trail	K	RF	Sharmat, Marjorie Weinman	Bantam Doubleday Dell
Nate the Great and the Sticky Case	K	RF	Sharmat, Marjorie Weinman	Bantam Doubleday Dell
Nate the Great and the Stolen Base	K	RF	Sharmat, Marjorie Weinman	Bantam Doubleday Dell
Nate the Great and the Tardy Tortoise	K	RF	Sharmat, Marjorie Weinman	Bantam Doubleday Dell
Nate the Great Goes Down in the Dumps	K	RF	Sharmat, Marjorie Weinman	Bantam Doubleday Dell
Nate the Great Goes Undercover	K	RF	Sharmat, Marjorie Weinman	Bantam Doubleday Dell
Nate the Great Saves the King of Sweden	K	RF	Sharmat, Marjorie Weinman	Bantam Doubleday Dell
Nate the Great Stalks Stupidweed	K	RF	Sharmat, Marjorie Weinman	Bantam Doubleday Dell
Sheila Rae, the Brave	K	F	Henkes, Kevin	Scholastic
Snowshoe Thompson	K	HF	Smiler Levinson, N.	HarperTrophy
Stems	K	I	Pebble Books	Grolier, Capstone
Three Billy Goats Gruff, The	K	TL	Stevens, Janet	Harcourt Brace
Three Days on a River in a Red Canoe	K	I	Williams, Vera B.	Scholastic
Three Stories You Can Read to Your Cat	K	F	Miller, Sara Swan	Houghton Mifflin
Too Many Babas	K	TL	Croll, Carolyn	HarperTrophy
Too Many Babas	K	TL	Little Readers	Houghton Mifflin

Title	Level	Genre	Author/Series	Publisher/Distributor
Wagon Wheels	K	HF	Brenner, Barbara	HarperTrophy
Zack's Alligator	K	F	Mozelle, Shirley	HarperTrophy
Zack's Alligator Goes to School	K	F	Mozelle, Shirley	HarperTrophy
Acid Rain	L	I	Wonder World	Wright Group/McGraw Hi
Amanda Pig and Her Big Brother Oliver	L	F	Van Leeuwen, Jean	Puffin Books
Amelia Bedelia	L	F	Parish, Peggy	HarperTrophy
Amelia Bedelia and the Baby	L	F	Parish, Peggy	Harper & Row
Amelia Bedelia and the Surprise Shower	L	F	Parish, Peggy	Harper & Row
Amelia Bedelia Goes Camping	L	F	Parish, Peggy	Avon Camelot
Amelia Bedelia Helps Out	L	F	Parish, Peggy	Avon Camelot
Amelia Bedelia's Family Album	L	F	Parish, Peggy	Avon Books
Beans on the Roof	L	RF	Byars, Betsy	Bantam Doubleday Dell
Best Older Sister, The	L	RF	Choi, Sook Nyul	Bantam Doubleday Dell
Best Worst Day, The	L	RF	Graves, Bonnie	Hyperion
Best-Loved Doll, The	L	RF	Caudill, Rebecca	Henry Holt & Co.
Bobo's Magic Wishes	L	F	Little Readers	Houghton Mifflin
Bravo Amelia Bedelia!	L	F	Parish, Herman	Avon
Brigid Beware	L	RF	Leverich, Kathleen	Random House
Brigid Bewitched	L	RF	Leverich, Kathleen	Random House
Brigid the Bad	L	RF	Leverich, Kathleen	Random House
Cam Jansen and the Chocolate Fudge Mystery	L	RF	Adler, David A.	Puffin Books
Cam Jansen and the Ghostly Mystery	L	RF	Adler, David A.	Puffin Books
Cam Jansen and the Mystery at the Haunted House	L	RF	Adler, David A.	Puffin Books
Cam Jansen and the Mystery at the Monkey House	L	RF	Adler, David A.	Puffin Books
Cam Jansen and the Mystery of Flight 54	L	RF	Adler, David A.	Puffin Books
Cam Jansen and the Mystery of the Babe Ruth Baseball	L	RF	Adler, David A.	Puffin Books
Cam Jansen and the Mystery of the Carnival Prize	L	RF	Adler, David A.	Puffin Books
Cam Jansen and the Mystery of the Circus Clown	L	RF	Adler, David A.	Puffin Books
Cam Jansen and the Mystery of the Dinosaur Bones	L	RF	Adler, David A.	Puffin Books
Cam Jansen and the Mystery of the Gold Coins	L	RF	Adler, David A.	Puffin Books
Cam Jansen and the Mystery of the Monster Movie	L	RF	Adler, David A.	Puffin Books
Cam Jansen and the Mystery of the Stolen Corn Popper	L	RF	Adler, David A.	Puffin Books
Cam Jansen and the Mystery of the Stolen Diamonds	L	RF	Adler, David A.	Puffin Books
Cam Jansen and the Mystery of the Television Dog	L	RF	Adler, David A.	Puffin Books
Cam Jansen and the Mystery of the U.F.O.	L	RF	Adler, David A.	Puffin Books
Cam Jansen and the Triceratops Pops Mystery	L	RF	Adler, David	Puffin Books
Candy Corn Contest, The	L	RF	Giff, Patricia Reilly	Bantam Doubleday Dell
Case of the Cool-Itch Kid, The	L	RF	Giff, Patricia Reilly	Bantam Doubleday Dell
Chang's Paper Pony	L	RF	Coerr, Eleanor	HarperTrophy
Come Back, Amelia Bedelia	L	F	Parish, Peggy	Harper & Row
Dog that Pitched a No-Hitter, The	L	F	Christopher, Matt	Little Brown & Co.
Dog that Stole Home, The	L	F	Christopher, Matt	Little, Brown & Co.
Dolphin	L	I	Morris, Robert A.	HarperTrophy
Fancy Feet	L	RF	Giff, Patricia Reilly	Bantam Doubleday Dell
Flower Girls # 1: Violet	L	RF	Leverich, Kathleen	HarperTrophy
Flower Girls # 2: Daisy	L	RF	Leverich, Kathleen	HarperTrophy
Flower Girls # 3: Heather	L	RF	Leverich, Kathleen	HarperTrophy
Flower Girls # 4: Rose	L	RF	Leverich, Kathleen	HarperTrophy
George and Martha	L	F	Marshall, James	Houghton Mifflin
George and Martha Back in Town	L	F	Marshall, James	Houghton Mifflin
George and Martha Encore	L	F	Marshall, James	Houghton Mifflin
George and Martha One Fine Day	L	F	Marshall, James	Houghton Mifflin
George and Martha Rise and Shine	L	F	Marshall, James	Houghton Mifflin
George and Martha Round and Round	L	F	Marshall, James	Houghton Mifflin
George Washington	L	B	Pebble Books	Grolier, Capstone
Ginger Brown: The Nobody Boy	L	RF	Wyeth, Sharon Dennis	Random House

Title	Level	Genre	Author/Series	Publisher/Distributor
Ginger Brown: Too Many Houses	L	RF	Wyeth, Sharon Dennis	Random House
Good Driving, Amelia Bedelia	L	F	Parish, Peggy	Harper & Row
Good Work, Amelia Bedelia	L	F	Parish, Peggy	Avon Camelot
Happy Birthday, Martin Luther King	L	B	Marzollo, Jean	Scholastic
Hot Fudge Hero	L	RF	Brisson, Pat	Henry Holt & Co.
Hungry, Hungry Sharks	L	I	Cole, Joanna	Random House
Josefina Story Quilt	L	F	Coerr, Eleanor	HarperTrophy
Lightning	L	I	Pebble Books	Grolier, Capstone
Magic Fish, The	L	TL	Littledale, Freya	Scholastic
Martin Luther King Day	L	I	Lowery, Linda	Scholastic
Martin Luther King, Jr.	L	B	Pebble Books	Grolier, Capstone
Mr. Gumpy's Motor Car	L	RF	Burningham, John	Harper Collins
Mystery of the Blue Ring, The	L	RF	Giff, Patricia Reilly	Bantam Doubleday Dell
Pee Wee Scouts: The Pooped Troop	L	RF	Delton, Judy	Bantam Doubleday Dell
Picking Apples and Pumpkins	L	I	Hutchings, A. & R.	Scholastic
Pinky and Rex	L	RF	Howe, James	Simon & Schuster
Pinky and Rex and the Bully	L	RF	Howe, James	Simon & Schuster
Pinky and Rex and the Double-Dad Weekend	L	RF	Howe, James	Simon & Schuster
Pinky and Rex and the Mean Old Witch	L	RF	Howe, James	Simon & Schuster
Pinky and Rex and the New Baby	L	RF	Howe, James	Simon & Schuster
Pinky and Rex and the New Neighbors	L	RF	Howe, James	Simon & Schuster
Pinky and Rex and the Perfect Pumpkin	L	RF	Howe, James	Simon & Schuster
Pinky and Rex and the School Play	L	RF	Howe, James	Simon & Schuster
Play Ball, Amelia Bedelia	L	F	Parish, Peggy	Harper & Row
Pony Trouble	L	RF	Gasque, Dale Blackwell	Hyperion
Powder Puff Puzzle, The	L	RF	Giff, Patricia Reilly	Bantam Doubleday Dell
Riddle of The Red Purse, The	L	RF	Giff, Patricia Reilly	Bantam Doubleday Dell
Sadie and the Snowman	L	RF	Morgan, Allen	Scholastic
Say "Cheese"	L	RF	Giff, Patricia Reilly	Bantam Doubleday Dell
Song Lee and the Hamster Hunt	L	RF	Kline, Suzy	The Penguin Group
Song Lee and the Leech Man	L	RF	Kline, Suzy	The Penguin Group
Song Lee In Room 2B	L	RF	Kline, Suzy	The Penguin Group
Stacy Says Good-Bye	L	RF	Giff, Patricia Reilly	Bantam Doubleday Dell
Tale of Peter Rabbit, The	L	TL	Potter, Beatrix	Scholastic
Tales of Amanda Pig	L	F	Van Leeuwen, Jean	Puffin Books
Teach Us, Amelia Bedelia	L	F	Parish, Peggy	Scholastic
Thank You, Amelia Bedelia	L	F	Little Readers	Houghton Mifflin
Triplet Trouble and the Bicycle Race	L	RF	Dadey, D. & Jones, M. T.	Scholastic
Triplet Trouble and the Class Trip	L	RF	Dadey, D. & Jones, M. T.	Scholastic
Triplet Trouble and the Cookie Contest	L	RF	Dadey, D. & Jones, M. T.	Scholastic
Triplet Trouble and the Field Day Disaster	L	RF	Dadey, D. & Jones, M. T.	Scholastic
True Story of Balto, The	L	I	Standiford, Natalie	Random House
What's It Like to Be a Fish?	L	I	Little Readers	Houghton Mifflin
Young Arthur Ashe: Brave Champion	L	B	First Start Biography	Troll
Young Clara Barton: Battlefield Nurse	L	B	First Start Biography	Troll
Young Jackie Robinson: Baseball Hero	L	B	First Start Biography	Troll
Young Rosa Parks: Civil Rights Heroine	L	B	First Start Biography	Troll
Young Thurgood Marshall: Fighter for Equality	L	B	First Start Biography	Troll
Afternoon on the Amazon	M	F	Osborne, Mary Pope	Random House
Arthur Accused!	M	F	Brown, Marc	Little, Brown & Co.
Arthur and the Crunch Cereal Contest	M	F	Brown, Marc	Little, Brown & Co.
Arthur and the Lost Diary	M	F	Brown, Marc	Little, Brown & Co.
Arthur and the Popularity Test	M	F	Brown, Marc	Little, Brown & Co.
Arthur and the Scare-Your-Pants-Off Club	M	F	Brown, Marc	Little, Brown & Co.
Arthur Makes the Team	M	F	Brown, Marc	Little, Brown & Co.
Arthur Rocks with BINKY	M	F	Brown, Marc	Little, Brown & Co.
Arthur's Mystery Envelope	M	F	Brown, Marc	Little, Brown & Co.
Beast and the Halloween Horror	M	RF	Giff, Patricia Reilly	Bantam Doubleday Dell

Title	Level	Genre	Author/Series	Publisher/Distributor
Beast in Ms. Rooney's Room, The	M	RF	Giff, Patricia Reilly	Bantam Doubleday Dell
Blue Ribbon Blues	M	RF	Spinelli, Jerry	Random House
Can Do, Jenny Archer	M	RF	Conford, Ellen	Random House
Case for Jenny Archer, A	M	RF	Conford, Ellen	Random House
Case of the Elevator Duck, The	M	RF	Berends, Polly Berrien	Random House
Catch That Pass!	M	RF	Christopher, Matt	Little, Brown & Co.
Catcher With a Glass Arm	M	RF	Christopher, Matt	Little, Brown & Co.
Catcher's Mask, The	M	RF	Christopher, Matt	Little, Brown & Co.
Center Court Sting	M	RF	Christopher, Matt	Little, Brown & Co.
Centerfield Ballhawk	M	RF	Christopher, Matt	Little, Brown & Co.
Count Your Money with the Polk Street School	M	RF	Giff, Patricia Reilly	Bantam Doubleday Dell
Creatures of the Night	M	I	Murdock & Ray	Mondo Publishing
Day of the Dragon King	M	F	Osborne, Mary Pope	Random House
Dog that Stole Football Plays, The	M	F	Christopher, Matt	Little, Brown & Co.
Five True Dog Stories	M	I	Davidson, Margaret	Scholastic
Five True Horse Stories	M	I	Davidson, Margaret	Scholastic
Flat Stanley	M	F	Brown, Jeff	HarperTrophy
Freckle Juice	M	RF	Blume, Judy	Bantam Doubleday Dell
Frederick Douglass: Fights For Freedom	M	B	Davidson, Margaret	Language for Learning Assoc.
Ghost Town Treasure	M	RF	Bulla, Clyde Robert	The Penguin Group
Hit-Away Kid, The	M	RF	Christopher, Matt	Little, Brown & Co.
Invisible in the Third Grade	M	RF	Cuyler, Margery	Scholastic
Japan	M	I	Pair-It Books	Steck-Vaughn
Jenny Archer, Author	M	RF	Conford, Ellen	Little, Brown & Co.
Jenny Archer to the Rescue	M	RF	Conford, Ellen	Little, Brown & Co.
Job for Jenny Archer, A	M	RF	Conford, Ellen	Random House
Lazy Lions, Lucky Lambs	M	RF	Giff, Patricia Reilly	Bantam Doubleday Dell
Let's Go, Philadelphia!	M	RF	Giff, Patricia Reilly	Bantam Doubleday Dell
Lions at Lunchtime	M	F	Osborne, Mary Pope	Random House
Little Lefty	M	RF	Christopher, Matt	Little, Brown & Co.
Littles and the Lost Children, The	M	F	Peterson, John	Scholastic
Littles and the Terrible Tiny Kid, The	M	F	Peterson, John	Scholastic
Littles Go Exploring, The	M	F	Peterson, John	Scholastic
Littles Go to School, The	M	F	Peterson, John	Scholastic
Littles Have a Wedding, The	M	F	Peterson, John	Scholastic
Littles Take a Trip, The	M	F	Peterson, John	Scholastic
Littles, The	M	F	Peterson, John	Scholastic
Littles to the Rescue, The	M	F	Peterson, John	Scholastic
Locked in the Library!	M	F	Brown, Marc	Little, Brown & Co.
Marvin Redpost: Alone in His Teacher's House	M	RF	Sachar, Louis	Random House
Marvin Redpost: Is He a Girl?	M	RF	Sachar, Louis	Random House
Marvin Redpost: Kidnapped at Birth?	M	RF	Sachar, Louis	Random House
Marvin Redpost: Why Pick on Me?	M	RF	Sachar, Louis	Random House
Mary Marony and the Chocolate Surprise	M	RF	Kline, Suzy	Bantam Doubleday Dell
Mary Marony and the Snake	M	RF	Kline, Suzy	Bantam Doubleday Dell
Mary Marony Hides Out	M	RF	Kline, Suzy	Bantam Doubleday Dell
Mary Marony, Mummy Girl	M	RF	Kline, Suzy	Bantam Doubleday Dell
Molly's Pilgrim	M	RF	Cohen, Barbara	Bantam Doubleday Dell
Mystery in the Night Woods	M	F	Peterson, John	Scholastic
Nine True Dolphin Stories	M	I	Davidson, Margaret	Scholastic
One in the Middle Is the Green Kangaroo, The	M	RF	Blume, Judy	Bantam Doubleday Dell
Picture Book of Helen Keller, A	M	B	Adler, David A.	Holiday House
Polar Bears Past Bedtime	M	F	Osborne, Mary Pope	Random House
Russell and Elisa	M	RF	Hurwitz, Johanna	The Penguin Group
Russell Rides Again	M	RF	Hurwitz, Johanna	The Penguin Group
Russell Sprouts	M	RF	Hurwitz, Johanna	The Penguin Group
Secret at the Polk Street School, The	M	RF	Giff, Patricia Reilly	Bantam Doubleday Dell
Shorty	M	RF	Literacy 2000	Rigby

Title	Level	Genre	Author/Series	Publisher/Distributor
Solo Girl	M	RF	Pinkey, Andrea Davis	Hyperion
Trolls Don't Ride Roller Coasters	M	F	Dadey, D. & Jones, M. T.	Scholastic
Turkey Trouble	M	RF	Giff, Patricia Reilly	Bantam Doubleday Dell
Tyler Toad and Thunder	M	F	Crowe, Robert	Dutton
Vacation Journal, A	M	B	Discovery World	Rigby
Vampires Don't Wear Polka Dots	M	F	Dadey, D. & Jones, M. T.	Scholastic
Werewolves Don't Go To Summer Camp	M	F	Dadey, D. & Jones, M. T.	Scholastic
What's Cooking, Jenny Archer?	M	RF	Conford, Ellen	Little Brown & Co.
Write Up a Storm with the Polk Street School	M	RF	Giff, Patricia Reilly	Bantam Doubleday Dell
Adam Joshua Capers: Halloween Monster	N	RF	Smith, Janice Lee	HarperTrophy
Adam Joshua Capers: Monster in the Third	N	RF	Smith, Janice Lee	HarperTrophy
Adam Joshua Capers: Nelson in Love	N	RF	Smith, Janice Lee	HarperTrophy
Adam Joshua Capers: Superkid!	N	RF	Smith, Janice Lee	HarperTrophy
Adam Joshua Capers: Turkey Trouble	N	RF	Smith, Janice Lee	HarperTrophy
Amber Brown Goes Fourth	N	RF	Danziger, Paula	Scholastic
Amber Brown is Feeling Blue	N	RF	Danziger, Paula	Scholastic
Amber Brown is Not a Crayon	N	RF	Danziger, Paula	Scholastic
Amber Brown Sees Red	N	RF	Danziger, Paula	Scholastic
Amber Brown Wants Extra Credit	N	RF	Danziger, Paula	Scholastic
Blackberries in the Dark	N	RF	Jukes, Mavis	Alfred A. Knopf
Case of Hermie the Missing Hamster, The	N	RF	Preller, James	Scholastic
Case of the Christmas Snowman, The	N	RF	Preller, James	Scholastic
Case of the Secret Valentine, The	N	RF	Preller, James	Scholastic
Case of the Spooky Sleepover, The	N	RF	Preller, James	Scholastic
Chalk Box Kid, The	N	RF	Bulla, Clyde Robert	Random House
Dancing with Manatees	N	I	McNulty, Faith	Scholastic
Danger Guys	N	RF	Abbott, Tony	HarperTrophy
Donavan's Word Jar	N	RF	DeGross, Monalisa	HarperCollins
E is for Elisa	N	RF	Hurwitz, Johanna	Puffin Books
Elisa in the Middle	N	RF	Hurwitz, Johanna	The Penguin Group
Forever Amber Brown	N	RF	Danziger, Paula	Scholastic
George Washington: First President of the U.S.	N	B	Rookie Biographies	Children's Press
Grizzly Bears	N	I	Woolley, M. & Pigdon, K.	Mondo
Helen Keller	N	B	Davidson, Margaret	Scholastic
Helen Keller's Teacher	N	B	Davidson, Margaret	Scholastic
Ho, Ho, Benjamin, Feliz Navidad	N	RF	Giff, Patricia Reilly	Bantam Doubleday Dell
Julian, Dream Doctor	N	RF	Cameron, Ann	Random House
Julian, Secret Agent	N	RF	Cameron, Ann	Random House
Julian's Glorious Summer	N	RF	Cameron, Ann	Random House
Katherine Dunham, Black Dancer	N	B	Rookie Biographies	Children's Press
Laura Ingalls Wilder: An Author's Story	N	B	Glasscock, Sarah	Steck-Vaughn
Leftovers, The: Catch Flies!	N	RF	Howard, Tristan	Scholastic
Leftovers, The: Fast Break	N	RF	Howard, Tristan	Scholastic
Leftovers, The: Get Jammed	N	RF	Howard, Tristan	Scholastic
Leftovers, The: Reach Their Goal	N	RF	Howard, Tristan	Scholastic
Leftovers, The: Strike Out!	N	RF	Howard, Tristan	Scholastic
Lily and Miss Liberty	N	HF	Stephens, Carla	Scholastic
Limestone Caves	N	I	Davis, Gary	Children's Press
Little Sea Pony, The	N	F	Cresswell, Helen	HarperTrophy
Max Malone and the Great Cereal Rip-off	N	RF	Herman, Charlotte	Henry Holt & Co.
Max Malone Makes a Million	N	RF	Herman, Charlotte	Henry Holt & Co.
More Stories Huey Tells	N	RF	Cameron, Ann	Alfred A. Knopf
More Stories Julian Tells	N	RF	Cameron, Ann	Random House
My Name is Maria Isabel	N	RF	Ada, Alma Flor	Aladdin
Phillis Wheatley: First African-American Poet	N	B	Rookie Biographies	Children's Press
Pioneer Cat	N	HF	Hooks, William H.	Random House
Say Hola, Sarah	N	RF	Giff, Patricia Reilly	Bantam Doubleday Dell
School's Out	N	RF	Hurwitz, Johanna	Scholastic
Second Chance	N	RF	Kroll, Stephen	Avon Camelot

Title	Level	Genre	Author/Series	Publisher/Distributor
Shoeshine Girl	N	RF	Bulla, Clyde Robert	HarperTrophy
Show-and-Tell War, The	N	RF	Smith, Janice Lee	HarperTrophy
Sidewalk Story	N	RF	Mathis, Sharon Bell	The Penguin Group
Something Queer at the Ball Park	N	RF	Levy, Elizabeth	Bantam Doubleday Dell
Something Queer at the Haunted School	N	RF	Levy, Elizabeth	Bantam Doubleday Dell
Something Queer at the Lemonade Stand	N	RF	Levy, Elizabeth	Bantam Doubleday Dell
Starring Rosie	N	RF	Giff, Patricia Reilly	The Penguin Group
Stories Huey Tells, The	N	RF	Cameron, Ann	Alfred A. Knopf
Stories Julian Tells, The	N	RF	Cameron, Ann	Alfred A. Knopf
Striped Ice Cream	N	RF	Lexau, Joan M.	Scholastic
Third Grade Bullies	N	RF	Levy, Elizabeth	Hyperion
Thomas Jefferson: Author, Inventor, President	N	B	Rookie Biographies	Children's Press
Thurgood Marshall: First Black Supreme Court Justice	N	B	Rookie Biographies	Children's Press
You Can't Eat Your Chicken Pox, Amber Brown	N	RF	Danziger, Paula	Scholastic
You're Out	N	RF	Kroll, Stephen	Avon Camelot
Adventures of Ali Baba Bernstein, The	O	RF	Hurwitz, Johanna	Scholastic
Aldo Ice Cream	O	RF	Hurwitz, Johanna	The Penguin Group
Aldo Peanut Butter	O	RF	Hurwitz, Johanna	The Penguin Group
Allen Jay and the Underground Railroad	O	HF	Brill, Marlene Targ	Carolrhoda Books
Baseball's Best: Five True Stories	O	B	Step into Reading	Random House
Bats	O	I	Holmes, Kevin J.	Capstone Press
Bears	O	I	Holmes, Kevin J.	Capstone Press
Bees	O	I	Holmes, Kevin J.	Capstone Press
Beezus & Ramona	O	RF	Cleary, Beverly	Avon
Benjamin Franklin: A Man with Many Jobs	O	B	Greene, Carol	Children's Press
Bill Clinton: Forty-Second President of the U.S.	O	B	Greene, Carol	Children's Press
Birds of Prey	O	I	Woolley, M. & Pigdon, K.	Mondo
Butterflies	O	I	Holmes, Kevin J.	Capstone Press
Cat's Meow, The	O	F	Soto, Gary	Scholastic
Class Clown	O	RF	Hurwitz, Johanna	Scholastic
Class President	O	RF	Hurwitz, Johanna	Scholastic
Disappearing Cookies and Other Cases, The	O	RF	Simon, Seymour	Avon
Disappearing Ice Cream and Other Cases, The	O	RF	Simon, Seymour	Avon
Disappearing Snowball and Other Cases, The	O	RF	Simon, Seymour	Avon
Dolphins	O	I	Holmes, Kevin J.	Capstone Press
Dragon Bones	O	F	Hindman, Paul	Random House
Earthworms	O	I	Holmes, Kevin J.	Capstone Press
Eleven Kids, One Summer	O	RF	Martin, Ann M.	Scholastic
Elizabeth Blackwell: First Woman Doctor	O	B	Greene, Carol	Children's Press
Elizabeth Blackwell: Girl Doctor	O	B	Henry, Joanne Landers	Simon & Schuster
Elizabeth the First: Queen of England	O	B	Greene, Carol	Children's Press
Emily Dickinson: American Poet	O	B	Greene, Carol	Children's Press
Flossie and the Fox	O	F	McKissack, Patricia	Scholastic
Foolish Gretel	O	TL	Armstrong, Jennifer	Random House
France	O	I	Dahl, Michael	Capstone Press
Fudge	O	RF	Graeber, Charlotte Towner	Simon & Schuster
George Washington Carver: Scientist and Teacher	O	B	Greene, Carol	Children's Press
Good Grief. . . Third Grade	O	RF	McKenna, Colleen	Scholastic
Guatemala	O	I	Dahl, Michael	Capstone Press
Helen Keller: From Tragedy to Triumph	O	B	Childhood of Famous Americans	Aladdin
Henry and Beezus	O	RF	Cleary, Beverly	Avon
Henry and Ribsy	O	RF	Cleary, Beverly	Hearst
Henry and the Clubhouse	O	RF	Cleary, Beverly	Avon
Henry and the Paper Route	O	RF	Cleary, Beverly	Hearst
Henry Huggins	O	RF	Cleary, Beverly	Avon
Hurray For Ali Baba Bernstein	O	RF	Hurwitz, Johanna	Scholastic
I Am Rosa Parks	O	B	Parks, Rosa	Dial Books

Title	Level	Genre	Author/Series	Publisher/Distributor
Italy	O	I	Thoennes, Kristin	Capstone Press
Jackie Robinson: Baseball's First Black Major Leaguer	O	B	Greene, Carol	Children's Press
Kenya	O	I	Dahl, Michael	Capstone Press
King's Equal, The	O	TL	Paterson, Katherine	HarperTrophy
Laura Ingalls Wilder	O	B	Allen, Thomas B.	Putnam
Laura Ingalls Wilder: Author of the Little House Books	O	B	Greene, Carol	Children's Press
Lightweight Rocket and Other Cases, The	O	RF	Simon, Seymour	Avon
Look Out, Washington D.C.!	O	RF	Giff, Patricia Reilly	Bantam Doubleday Dell
Lost Continent and Other Cases, The	O	RF	Simon, Seymour	Avon
Lost Hikers and Other Cases, The	O	RF	Simon, Seymour	Avon
Martin Luther King, Jr.	O	B	Rookie Biographies	Children's Press
Mary McLeod Bethune	O	B	Greenfield, Eloise	HarperTrophy
Meet Benjamin Franklin	O	B	Scarf, Maggi	Step-Up Books
Meg Mackintosh and The Case of the Curious Whale Watch	O	RF	Landon, Lucinda	Secret Passage Press
Meg Mackintosh and The Case of the Missing Babe Ruth Baseball	O	RF	Landon, Lucinda	Secret Passage Press
Meg Mackintosh and The Mystery at Camp Creepy	O	RF	Landon, Lucinda	Secret Passage Press
Meg Mackintosh and The Mystery at the Medieval Castle	O	RF	Landon, Lucinda	Secret Passage Press
Meg Mackintosh and The Mystery at the Soccer Match	O	RF	Landon, Lucinda	Secret Passage Press
Meg Mackintosh and The Mystery in the Locked Library	O	RF	Landon, Lucinda	Secret Passage Press
Mexico	O	I	Dahl, Michael	Capstone Press
Mieko and the Fifth Treasure	O	HF	Coerr, Eleanor	Bantam Doubleday Dell
Mouse and the Motorcycle, The	O	F	Cleary, Beverly	Avon Camelot
Much Ado About Aldo	O	RF	Hurwitz, Johanna	The Penguin Group
Nigeria	O	I	Thoennes, Kristin	Capstone Press
No Dogs Allowed	O	RF	Cutler, Jane	Farrar, Straus and Giroux
Octopuses and Squids	O	I	Wonder World	Wright Group/McGraw Hill
Oh Boy, Boston!	O	RF	Giff, Patricia Reilly	Bantam Doubleday Dell
Owls	O	I	Holmes, Kevin J.	Capstone Press
Patrick Doyle is Full of Blarney	O	HF	Armstrong, Jennifer	Random House
Perfect Pony, A	O	RF	Szymanski, Lois	Avon Camelot
Pet Parade	O	RF	Giff, Patricia Reilly	Bantam Doubleday Dell
Pony Pals: A Pony for Keeps	O	RF	Betancourt, Jeanne	Scholastic
Pony Pals: A Pony in Trouble	O	RF	Betancourt, Jeanne	Scholastic
Pony Pals: Give Me Back My Pony	O	RF	Betancourt, Jeanne	Scholastic
Pony Pals: I Want a Pony	O	RF	Betancourt, Jeanne	Scholastic
Pony Pals: Runaway Pony	O	RF	Betancourt, Jeanne	Scholastic
Pony Pals: The Wild Pony	O	RF	Betancourt, Jeanne	Scholastic
Ralph S. Mouse	O	F	Cleary, Beverly	Harper Trophy
Ramona and Her Father	O	RF	Cleary, Beverly	Avon
Ramona and Her Mother	O	RF	Cleary, Beverly	Avon
Ramona Forever	O	RF	Cleary, Beverly	Hearst
Ramona Quimby, Age 8	O	RF	Cleary, Beverly	Hearst
Ramona the Brave	O	RF	Cleary, Beverly	Hearst
Ramona the Pest	O	RF	Cleary, Beverly	Avon
Rats on the Range and Other Stories	O	F	Marshall, James	The Penguin Group
Rats on the Roof and Other Stories	O	F	Marshall, James	The Penguin Group
Rent a Third Grader	O	RF	Hiller, B.B.	Scholastic
Runaway Ralph	O	F	Cleary, Beverly	Hearst
Russia	O	I	Thoennes, Kristin	Capstone Press
Secret Soldier, The: The Story of Deborah Sampson	O	B	McGovern, Ann	Scholastic
Seven Kisses in a Row	O	RF	MacLachlan, Patricia	Harper Collins
South Korea	O	I	Davis, Lucile	Capstone Press
Speedy Pasta and Other Cases, The	O	RF	Simon, Seymour	Avon
Speedy Snake and Other Cases, The	O	RF	Simon, Seymour	Avon

Title	Level	Genre	Author/Series	Publisher/Distributor
Speedy Soapbox Car and Other Cases, The	O	RF	Simon, Seymour	Avon
Spiders	O	I	Holmes, Kevin J.	Capstone Press
Squanto: Friend of the Pilgrims	O	B	Bulla, Clyde Robert	Scholastic
Stay Away from Simon!	O	RF	Carrick, Carol	Clarion
Story of Benjamin Franklin, Amazing American	O	B	Davidson, Margaret	Scholastic
Story of Jackie Robinson, Bravest Man in Baseball	O	B	Davidson, Margaret	Scholastic
Story of Walt Disney, Maker of Magical Worlds, The	O	B	Selden, Bernice	Bantam Doubleday Dell
Teacher's Pet	O	RF	Hurwitz, Johanna	Scholastic
Toad for Tuesday, A	O	F	Erickson, Russell E.	Beech Tree Books
Warton and the King of the Skies	O	F	Erickson, Russell E.	Houghton Mifflin
Whales	O	I	Book Shop	Mondo
Whales	O	I	Holmes, Kevin J.	Capstone Press
What Makes a Bird a Bird?	O	I	Garelick, May	Mondo
What's the Big Idea, Ben Franklin?	O	B	Fritz, Jean	Scholastic
Alexander Graham Bell	P	B	Linder, Greg	Capstone Press
All About Sam	P	RF	Lowry, Lois	Bantam Doubleday Dell
Amelia Earhart	P	B	Parlin, John	Bantam Doubleday Dell
Amelia Earhart	P	B	Rosenthal, M. & Freeman, D.	Capstone Press
Attaboy, Sam	P	RF	Lowry, Lois	Bantam Doubleday Dell
Bad Spell for the Worst Witch, A	P	F	Murphy, Jill	Puffin Books
Baseball's Greatest Pitchers	P	B	Kramer, S. A.	Random House
Best Enemies	P	RF	Leverich, Kathleen	Beech Tree Books
Best Enemies Again	P	RF	Leverich, Kathleen	Alfred A. Knopf
Best Enemies Forever	P	RF	Leverich, Kathleen	William Morrow
Bill Gates: Helping People Use Computers	P	B	Community Builders	Children's Press
Booker T. Washington	P	B	McLoone, Margo	Capstone Press
Canada Geese Quilt, The	P	RF	Kinsey-Warnock, Natalie	Bantam Doubleday Dell
Coral Reef	P	I	Habitats	Children's Press
Dolphin Adventure	P	RF	Grover, Wayne	Beech Tree Books
Dolphin Treasure	P	RF	Grover, Wayne	Beech Tree Books
Eleanor Roosevelt	P	B	Davis, Lucile	Capstone Press
Elizabeth Cady Stanton	P	B	Davis, Lucile	Capstone Press
Ellen Tebbits	P	RF	Cleary, Beverly	Dell Publishing
Encyclopedia Brown Keeps the Peace	P	RF	Sobol, Donald J.	Bantam Doubleday Dell
Encyclopedia Brown Lends a Hand	P	RF	Sobol, Donald J.	Bantam Doubleday Dell
Encyclopedia Brown Saves the Day	P	RF	Sobol, Donald J.	Bantam Doubleday Dell
Encyclopedia Brown Sets the Pace	P	RF	Sobol, Donald J.	Bantam Doubleday Dell
Encyclopedia Brown Shows the Way	P	RF	Sobol, Donald J.	Bantam Doubleday Dell
Encyclopedia Brown Solves Them All	P	RF	Sobol, Donald J.	Bantam Doubleday Dell
Encyclopedia Brown Takes the Cake	P	RF	Sobol, Donald J.	Bantam Doubleday Dell
Encyclopedia Brown Tracks Them Down	P	RF	Sobol, Donald J.	Bantam Doubleday Dell
Encyclopedia Brown's Book of Strange But True Crimes	P	RF	Sobol, Donald J. & Rose Sobol	Scholastic
Exploring Freshwater Habitats	P	I	Snowball, Diane	Mondo
Exploring Land Habitats	P	I	Phinney, Margaret Yatsevitch	Mondo
Exploring Saltwater Habitats	P	I	Smith, Sue	Mondo
Exploring Tree Habitats	P	I	Seifert, Patti	Mondo
Fantastic Mr. Fox	P	F	Dahl, Roald	The Penguin Group
Finding Providence: The Story of Roger Williams	P	B	Avi	HarperTrophy
Fire at the Triangle Factory	P	HF	Littlefield, Holly	Carolrhoda Books
Florence Kelley	P	B	Saller, Carol	Carolrhoda Books
George Washington Carver	P	B	McLoone, Margo	Capstone Press
George Washington's Breakfast	P	B	Fritz, Jean	Putnam & Grosset
George's Marvelous Medicine	P	F	Dahl, Roald	The Penguin Group
Ghost Fox, The	P	F	Yep, Laurence	Scholastic
Girl Called Al, A	P	RF	Greene, Constance C.	Puffin Books
Grain of Rice, A	P	TL	Pittman, Helena Clare	Bantam Doubleday Dell
Harriet Tubman	P	B	McLoone, Margo	Capstone Press

Title	Level	Genre	Author/Series	Publisher/Distributor
Harry's Mad	P	F	King-Smith, Dick	Alfred A. Knopf
Helen Keller: Crusader for the Blind and Deaf	P	B	Graff, Stewart & Polly Anne	Bantam Doubleday Dell
Hundred Penny Box, The	P	RF	Mathis, Sharon Bell	Puffin Books
Jacob Two-Two Meets the Hooded Fang	P	F	Richler, Mordecai	Seal Books
Jesse Jackson	P	B	Simon, Charnan	Children's Press
Jesse Owens: Olympic Hero	P	B	Sabin, Francene	Troll
Justin and the Best Biscuits in the World	P	RF	Pitts, Walter & Mildred	Alfred A. Knopf
Koya DeLaney and the Good Girl Blues	P	RF	Greenfield, Eloise	Scholastic
Last Look	P	RF	Bulla, Clyde Robert	Puffin Books
Laura Ingalls Wilder: Growing Up in the Little House	P	B	Giff, Patricia Reilly	Puffin Books
Lion to Guard Us, A	P	HF	Bulla, Clyde Robert	HarperTrophy
Lucky Stone, The	P	RF	Clifton, Lucille	Bantam Doubleday Dell
Milton Hershey: Chocolate King Town Builder	P	B	Simon, Charnan	Children's Press
Nose for Trouble, A	P	RF	Wilson, Nancy Hope	Avon
One Day in the Tropical Rain Forest	P	I	George, Jean Craighead	HarperTrophy
One Day in the Woods	P	I	George, Jean Craighead	HarperTrophy
Owls in the Family	P	F	Mowat, Farley	Bantam Doubleday Dell
Platypus	P	I	Short, J., Green, J., and Bird, B.	Mondo
Rosa Parks	P	B	Greenfield, Eloise	HarperTrophy
Sideways Stories from Wayside School	P	F	Sachar, Louis	Hearst
Stone Fox	P	RF	Gardiner, John Reynolds	Harper Trophy
Susan B. Anthony	P	B	Davis, Lucile	Capstone Press
Taste of Blackberries, A	P	RF	Buchanan Smith, Doris	Scholastic
Thank You, Jackie Robinson	P	B	Cohen, Barbara	Scholastic
Third Grade Stars	P	RF	Ransom, Candice	Troll
Time Warp Trio: 2095	P	SF	Scieszka, Jon	The Penguin Group
Time Warp Trio: Good, the Bad, and the Goofy, The	P	SF	Scieszka, Jon	The Penguin Group
Time Warp Trio: The Knights of the Kitchen Table	P	F	Scieszka, Jon	The Penguin Group
Time Warp Trio: The Not-So-Jolly Roger	P	F	Scieszka, Jon	The Penguin Group
Time Warp Trio: Tut Tut	P	F	Scieszka, Jon	The Penguin Group
Time Warp Trio: Your Mother Was a Neanderthal	P	F	Scieszka, Jon	The Penguin Group
Twits, The	P	F	Dahl, Roald	The Penguin Group
Wanted Dead or Alive: The True Story of Harriet Tubman	P	B	McGovern, Ann	Scholastic
Wayside School Gets a Little Stranger	P	F	Sachar, Louis	Avon Camelot
Who Shot the President?: The Death of John F. Kennedy	P	I	Donnelly, Judy	Random House
Worst Witch at Sea, The	P	F	Murphy, Jill	Candlewick Press
Worst Witch Strikes Again, The	P	F	Murphy, Jill	Candlewick Press
Worst Witch, The	P	F	Murphy, Jill	Puffin Books
Yang the Second and Her Secret Admirer	P	RF	Namioka, Lensey	Bantam Doubleday Dell
Yang the Third & Her Impossible Family	P	RF	Namioka, Lensey	Bantam Doubleday Dell
Yang the Youngest and His Terrible Ear	P	RF	Namioka, Lensey	Bantam Doubleday Dell
Addy Saves the Day: A Summer Story	Q	HF	The American Girls Collection	Pleasant Company
Addy's Surprise: A Christmas Story	Q	HF	The American Girls Collection	Pleasant Company
Amazing But True Sports Stories	Q	I	Hollander, Phyllis and Zander	Scholastic
Anastasia Krupnik	Q	RF	Lowry, Lois	Bantam Doubleday Dell
Big Wave, The	Q	RF	Buck, Pearl S.	Scholastic
Bunnicula	Q	F	Howe, James	Avon
Bunnicula Strikes Again!	Q	F	Howe, James	Simon & Schuster
Dear Mr. Henshaw	Q	RF	Cleary, Beverly	HarperCollins
Dragon for Sale	Q	F	MacDonald, Marianne	Troll
Dragon in the Family, A	Q	F	Koller, Jackie French	Pocket Books
Dragon Quest	Q	F	Koller, Jackie French	Pocket Books
Dragon Trouble	Q	F	Koller, Jackie French	Pocket Books
Dragonling, The	Q	F	Koller, Jackie French	Pocket Books
Dragons and Kings	Q	F	Koller, Jackie French	Pocket Books
Dragons of Krad	Q	F	Koller, Jackie French	Pocket Books

Title	Level	Genre	Author/Series	Publisher/Distributor
Five Brave Explorers	Q	B	Hudson, Wade	Scholastic
Five Notable Inventors	Q	B	Hudson, Wade	Scholastic
Flunking of Joshua T. Bates, The	Q	RF	Shreve, Susan	Alfred A. Knopf
Fourth Grade Celebrity	Q	RF	Giff, Patricia Reilly	Bantam Doubleday Dell
Fudge-a-Mania	Q	RF	Blume, Judy	Bantam Doubleday Dell
Ghost On Saturday Night, The	Q	F	Fleischman, Sid	Beech Tree Books
Girl Who Loved the Wind, The	Q	TL	Yolen, Jane	HarperTrophy
Grandpa's Face	Q	RF	Greenfield, Eloise	Putnam & Grosset
Help! I'm a Prisoner in the Library	Q	RF	Clifford, Eth	Scholastic
Help! I'm Trapped in My Teacher's Body	Q	F	Strasser, Todd	Scholastic
Help! I'm Trapped in the First Day of School	Q	F	Strasser, Todd	Scholastic
Homer Price	Q	RF	McCloskey, Robert	Puffin Books
If You Grew Up with George Washington	Q	I	Gross, Ruth Belov	Scholastic
If You Lived at the Time of Martin Luther King	Q	I	Levine, Ellen	Scholastic
If You Lived at the Time of the Civil War	Q	I	Moore, Kay	Scholastic
If You Lived at the Time of the Great San Francisco Earthquake	Q	I	Levine, Ellen	Scholastic
If You Lived in Colonial Times	Q	I	McGovern, Ann	Scholastic
If You Lived with the Sioux Indians	Q	I	McGovern, Ann	Scholastic
If You Sailed on the Mayflower in 1620	Q	I	McGovern, Ann	Scholastic
If You Traveled on the Underground Railroad	Q	I	Levine, Ellen	Scholastic
If You Were There When They Signed the Constitution	Q	I	Levy, Elizabeth	Scholastic
If Your Name was Changed at Ellis Island	Q	I	Levine, Ellen	Scholastic
In the Rain Forest	Q	I	Wildcats	Wright Group/McGraw Hill
J.T.	Q	RF	Wagner, Jane	Bantam Doubleday Dell
James and the Giant Peach	Q	F	Dahl, Roald	The Penguin Group
Just Juice	Q	RF	Hesse, Karen	Scholastic
Lady Bird Johnson	Q	B	Simon, Charnan	Children's Press
Lemonade Trick, The	Q	RF	Corbett, Scott	Scholastic
Little House in the Big Woods	Q	HF	Wilder, Laura Ingalls	HarperTrophy
Little House on the Prairie	Q	HF	Wilder, Laura Ingalls	HarperTrophy
Long Winter, The	Q	HF	Ingalls Wilder, Laura	HarperTrophy
Mixed-up Max	Q	F	King-Smith, Dick	Troll
Moki	Q	HF	Penny, Grace Jackson	Penguin Group
Mr. Popper's Penguins	Q	F	Atwater, Richard and Florence	Dell
Ocean Life	Q	I	Weldon Owen	Wright Group/McGraw Hill
Ocean Life: Tide Pool Creatures	Q	I	Leonhardt, Alice	Steck-Vaughn
Onion Tears	Q	RF	Kidd, Diana	William Morrow
P.W. Cracker Sees the World	Q	F	Yoshizawa, Linda	Steck-Vaughn
Pedro's Journal	Q	HF	Conrad, Pam	Bantam Doubleday Dell
Picture Book of Simon Bolivar, A	Q	B	Adler, David A.	Bantam Doubleday Dell
Pioneer Way, The	Q	I	Kummer, Patricia K.	Steck-Vaughn
Plain Girl	Q	RF	Sorensen, Virginia	Harcourt Brace
Pocketful of Goobers: Story of George Washington Carver	Q	B	Mitchell, Barbara	Carolrhoda Books
Prairie Songs	Q	HF	Conrad, Pam	HarperTrophy
Rain Forest Tree, A	Q	I	Kite, Lorien	Crabtree
Samurai's Daughter, The	Q	TL	San Souci, Robert D.	The Penguin Group
Soup	Q	RF	Peck, Robert Newton	Bantam Doubleday Dell
Story of George Washington Carver, The	Q	B	Moore, Eva	Bantam Doubleday Dell
Story of Laura Ingalls Wilder, Pioneer Girl, The	Q	B	Stine, Megan	Bantam Doubleday Dell
Superfudge	Q	RF	Blume, Judy	Bantam Doubleday Dell
Tales of a Fourth Grade Nothing	Q	RF	Blume, Judy	Bantam Doubleday Dell
There's A Boy In The Girls' Bathroom	Q	RF	Sachar, Louis	Alfred A. Knopf
Thomas Alva Edison: Great Inventor	Q	B	Levinson, Nancy Smiler	Scholastic
Velveteen Rabbit, The	Q	F	Williams, Margery	Hearst

Title	Level	Genre	Author/Series	Publisher/Distributor
Volcanoes	Q	I	Worldwise	Grolier
Walking the Road to Freedom: A Story About Sojourner Truth	Q	B	Ferris, Jeri	Dell
Witch Hunt: It Happened in Salem Village	Q	I	Krensky, Stephen	Random House
Writer of the Plains: A Story about Willa Cather	Q	B	Streissguth, Tom	Carolrhoda Books
All For the Better: A Story of El Barrio	R	RF	Mohr, Nicholasa	Steck Vaughn
American Alligator, The	R	I	Potts, Steve	Capstone Press
And Then What Happened Paul Revere?	R	B	Fritz, Jean	Bantam Doubleday Dell
Babe the Gallant Pig	R	F	King-Smith, Dick	Random House
Bracelet, The	R	HF	Uchida, Yoshiko	Philomel Books
Brighty of the Grand Canyon	R	RF	Henry, Marguerite	Aladdin
Cabin Faced West, The	R	HF	Fritz, Jean	Bantam Doubleday Dell
Caddie Woodlawn	R	HF	Brink, Carol Ryrie	Bantam Doubleday Dell
Can't You Make Them Behave, King George?	R	I	Fritz, Jean	Putnam & Grossett
Castle in the Attic, The	R	F	Winthrop, Elizabeth	Bantam Doubleday Dell
Charlie and the Chocolate Factory	R	F	Dahl, Roald	Bantam Doubleday Dell
Charlie and the Great Glass Elevator	R	F	Dahl, Roald	Bantam Doubleday Dell
Charlotte's Web	R	F	White, E. B.	HarperTrophy
Chocolate by Hershey: A Story about Milton S. Hershey	R	B	Burford, Betty	Carolrhoda Books
Computer Nut, The	R	SF	Byars, Betsy	Bantam Doubleday Dell
Dog Called Kitty, A	R	RF	Wallace, Bill	Pocket Books
Dominic	R	F	Steig, William	Farrar, Straus and Giroux
Earthquake!: San Francisco, 1906	R	I	Wilson, Kate	Steck-Vaughn
Eleanor Roosevelt: First Lady of the World	R	B	Faber, Doris	The Penguin Group
Enormous Egg, The	R	F	Butterworth, Oliver	Little, Brown & Co.
Every Living Thing	R	RF	Rylant, Cynthia	Aladdin
Fig Pudding	R	RF	Fletcher, Ralph	Clarion Books
Fire in the Sky	R	HF	Ransom, Candice F.	Carolrhoda Books
Flying Solo	R	RF	Fletcher, Ralph	Bantam Doubleday Dell
Go Free or Die: A Story About Harriet Tubman	R	B	Ferris, Jeri	Carolrhoda Books
Harry Houdini: Master of Magic	R	B	Kraske, Robert	Scholastic
Hatchet	R	RF	Paulsen, Gary	Aladdin
Helen Keller: A Light For The Blind	R	B	Kudlinski, Kathleen V.	The Penguin Group
Hurricanes & Tornadoes	R	I	The Wonders of our World	Crabtree
Laura Ingalls Wilder: A Biography	R	B	Anderson, William	HarperTrophy
Library Card, The	R	RF	Spinelli, Jerry	Scholastic
Long Way to Go, A	R	I	O'Neal, Zibby	The Penguin Group
Lost on a Mountain in Maine	R	RF	Fendler, Donn	Peter Smith Publications
Midnight Fox, The	R	RF	Byars, Betsy	Scholastic
Mirandy and Brother Wind	R	F	McKissack, Patricia	Alfred A. Knopf
Misty of Chincoteague	R	RF	Henry, Marguerite	Aladdin
Nothing's Fair in Fifth Grade	R	RF	DeClements, Barthe	Scholastic
Otherwise Known As Sheila the Great	R	RF	Blume, Judy	Bantam Doubleday Dell
Phoebe The Spy	R	HF	Berry Griffin, Judith	Scholastic
Pigs Might Fly	R	F	King-Smith, Dick	Scholastic
Road to Seneca Falls, The	R	B	Swain, Gwenyth	Carolrhoda Books
Sadako and the Thousand Paper Cranes	R	HF	Coerr, Eleanor	Bantam Doubleday Dell
San Domingo	R	I	Henry, Marguerite	Scholastic
Sarah, Plain and Tall	R	HF	MacLachlan, Patricia	HarperTrophy
Shiloh	R	RF	Naylor, Phyllis Reynolds	Bantam Doubleday Dell
Sixth-Grade Sleepover	R	RF	Bunting, Eve	Scholastic
Skylark	R	HF	MacLachlan, Patricia	HarperTrophy
Snow Treasure	R	HF	McSwigan, Marie	Scholastic
Spider Boy	R	RF	Fletcher, Ralph	Bantam Doubleday Dell
Story of Thomas Alva Edison, Inventor, The	R	B	Davidson, Margaret	Scholastic
Stray, The	R	RF	King-Smith, Dick	Alfred A. Knopf
Stuart Little	R	F	White, E.B.	HarperTrophy

Title	Level	Genre	Author/Series	Publisher/Distributor
Sun & Spoon	R	RF	Henkes, Kevin	The Penguin Group
Super Amos	R	RF	Paulsen, Gary	Bantam Doubleday Dell
Tomorrow's Wizard	R	F	MacLachlan, Patricia	Scholastic
Triffic the Extraordinary Pig	R	F	King-Smith, Dick	Bantam Doubleday Dell
Trouble with Tuck, The	R	RF	Taylor, Theodore	Avon
Trumpet of the Swan, The	R	F	White, E. B.	Scholastic
Where Was Patrick Henry on the 29th of May?	R	B	Fritz, Jean	Scholastic
Whipping Boy, The	R	F	Fleischman, Sid	Troll
Why Don't You Get a Horse, Sam Adams?	R	B	Fritz, Jean	G.P. Putnam's Sons
Witches, The	R	F	Dahl, Roald	The Penguin Group
Zeely	R	RF	Hamilton, Virginia	Macmillan
Afternoon of the Elves	S	F	Lisle, Janet Taylor	Scholastic
Ahyoka and the Talking Leaves	S	HF	Roop, Peter and Connie	Beech Tree Books
Ajeemah and his Son	S	HF	Berry, James	HarperTrophy
Altogether, One at a Time	S	RF	Konigsburg, E.L.	Simon & Schuster
Amelia Earhart: Flying for Adventure	S	B	Wade, Mary Dodson	The Millbrook Press
Bat-Poet, The	S	F	Jarrell, Randall	HarperCollins
Beautiful Land: A Story of the Oklahoma Land Rush	S	I	Antle, Nancy	The Penguin Group
Borrowers, The	S	F	Norton, Mary	Harcourt Brace
Boy Called Slow, A	S	B	Bruchac, Joseph	Putnam & Grosset
Brave Irene	S	F	Steig, William	Farrar, Straus & Giroux
Bridge to Terabithia	S	RF	Paterson, Katherine	HarperTrophy
Broccoli Tapes, The	S	RF	Slepian, Jan	Scholastic
Caleb's Choice	S	HF	Wisler, Clifton G.	The Penguin Group
Cat Who Went To Heaven, The	S	F	Coatsworth, Elizabeth	Aladdin
Children of the Longhouse	S	HF	Bruchac, Joseph	The Penguin Group
Colin Powell: Straight to the Top	S	B	Blue, Rose & Naden, Corinne J.	The Millbrook Press
Cricket in Times Square, The	S	F	Selden, George	Bantam Doubleday Dell
Cry of the Crow, The	S	RF	George, Jean Craighead	HarperTrophy
Cybil War, The	S	RF	Byars, Betsy	Scholastic
Facing West: A Story of the Oregon Trail	S	I	Kudlinski, Kathleen V.	The Penguin Group
Fifth Grade: Here Comes Trouble	S	RF	McKenna, Colleen O'Shaughnessy	Scholastic
Friendship and the Gold Cadillac, The	S	HF	Taylor, Mildred	Bantam Doubleday Dell
From the Mixed-up Files of Mrs. Basil E. Frankweiler	S	RF	Konigsburg, E.L.	Bantam Doubleday Dell
Great Gilly Hopkins, The	S	RF	Paterson, Katherine	Hearst
Harry and Chicken	S	F	Sheldon, Dyan	Candlewick Press
Harry On Vacation	S	SF	Sheldon, Dyan	Candlewick Press
Harry the Explorer	S	F	Sheldon, Dyan	Candlewick Press
Hey World, Here I Am!	S	RF	Little, Jean	HarperTrophy
House with a Clock in its Walls, The	S	F	Bellairs, John	The Penguin Group
How Many Days to America?: A Thanksgiving Story	S	I	Bunting, Eve	Houghton Mifflin
Howard Carter: Searching for King Tut	S	B	Ford, Barbara	W. H. Freeman & Co.
In the Year of the Boar and Jackie Robinson	S	HF	Lord, Bette Bao	HarperTrophy
Journey Home, The	S	RF	Holland, Isabelle	Scholastic
Journey to Jo'burg	S	HF	Naidoo, Beverly	HarperTrophy
Letter, the Witch, and the Ring, The	S	F	Bellairs, John	The Penguin Group
Letters from Rifka	S	HF	Hesse, Karen	Puffin Books
Lily's Crossing	S	HF	Giff, Patricia Reilly	Delacourte Press
Matilda	S	F	Dahl, Roald	The Penguin Group
Me, Mop, and the Moondance Kid	S	RF	Myers, Walter Dean	Bantam Doubleday Dell
Mississippi Bridge	S	HF	Taylor, Mildred	Bantam Doubleday Dell
More Perfect Union: The Story of Our Constitution	S	I	Maestro, Betsy & Giulio	William Morrow
Morning Girl	S	HF	Dorris, Michael	Hyperion
Mr. President: A Book of U.S. Presidents	S	B	Sullivan, George	Scholastic
My Sister Annie	S	RF	Dodds, Bill	Boyds Mills Press
My Teacher Fried My Brains	S	F	Coville, Bruce	Pocket Books
My Teacher Is an Alien	S	F	Coville, Bruce	Pocket Books
On My Honor	S	RF	Bauer, Marion Dane	Bantam Doubleday Dell

Title	Level	Genre	Author/Series	Publisher/Distributor
One-Eyed Cat	S	RF	Fox, Paula	Bantam Doubleday Dell
Pinballs, The	S	RF	Byars, Betsy	HarperTrophy
Poppy	S	F	Avi	Avon
Poppy and Rye	S	F	Avi	Avon
Red Means Good Fortune: A Story of San Francisco's Chinatown	S	I	Goldin, Barbara Diamond	The Penguin Group
Sixth Grade Can Really Kill You	S	RF	DeClements, Barthe	Scholastic
Sixth Grade Secrets	S	RF	Sachar, Louis	Scholastic
Song of the Trees	S	HF	Taylor, Mildred	Bantam Doubleday Dell
Star Fisher, The	S	RF	Yep, Lawrence	Scholastic
Story of Harriet Tubman, The: Conductor of the Underground Railroad	S	B	McMullan, Kate	Scholastic
Story of Muhammad Ali: Heavyweight Champion of the World, The	S	B	Denenberg, Barry	Dell Publishing
Sugaring Time	S	I	Lasky, Kathryn	Macmillan
Taking Sides	S	RF	Soto, Gary	Harcourt Brace
Trouble River	S	HF	Byars, Betsy	Scholastic
Ultimate Field Trip 1: Adventures in the Amazon Rain Forest	S	I	Goodman, Susan E.	Simon & Schuster
Van Gogh Cafe, The	S	RF	Rylant, Cynthia	Harcourt Brace
War of 1812, The	S	I	A First Book	Franklin Watts
War With Grandpa, The	S	RF	Kimmel Smith, Robert	Bantam Doubleday Dell
Where Do You Think You're Going, Christopher Columbus?	S	B	Fritz, Jean	Putnam & Grosset
Witch of Fourth Street, The	S	HF	Levoy, Myron	Language for Learning Assoc.
Abel's Island	T	F	Steig, William	Farrar Straus and Giroux
An Early Winter	T	RF	Bauer, Marion Dane	Houghton Mifflin
Animal Dazzlers: The Role of Brilliant Colors in Nature	T	I	Collard, Susan B. III	Franklin Watts
Arctic Investigations: Exploring the Frozen Ocean	T	I	Young, Karen Romano	Steck Vaughn
Baby	T	RF	MacLachlan, Patricia	Language for Learning Assoc.
Ballad of the Civil War, A	T	HF	Stolz, Mary	HarperTrophy
Bear Called Paddington, A	T	F	Bond, Michael	Bantam Doubleday Dell
Black Stallion, The	T	RF	Farley, Walter	Language for Learning Assoc.
Blubber	T	RF	Blume, Judy	Bantam Doubleday Dell
Bud, Not Buddy	T	RF	Curtis, Christopher Paul	Random House
Colonial Crafts	T	I	Historic Communities	Crabtree
Colonial Town, A: Williamsburg	T	I	Historic Communities	Crabtree
Cracker Jackson	T	RF	Byars, Betsy	Puffin Books
Crazy Fish	T	RF	Mazer, Norma Fox	Avon
Danny, Champion of the World	T	RF	Dahl, Roald	Language for Learning Assoc.
Dear Levi: Letters from the Overland Trail	T	HF	Woodruff, Elvira	Alfred A. Knopf
Double Life of Pocahontas, The	T	B	Fritz, Jean	Language for Learning Assoc.
Forgotten Door, The	T	SF	Key, Alexander	Language for Learning Assoc.
Freedom Songs	T	HF	Moore, Yvette	Language for Learning Assoc.
Girl Who Chased Away Sorrow, The: The Diary of Sarah Nita, a Navajo Girl	T	HF	Turner, Ann	Scholastic
Going Home	T	RF	Mohr, Nicholasa	The Penguin Group
Good-Bye Marianne	T	B	Watts, Irene N.	Tundra Books
Gorillas	T	I	Burgel, Paul H. & Hartwig, M.	Carolrhoda Books
Harriet the Spy	T	RF	Fitzhugh, Louise	Harper Collins
Immigrants	T	I	Sandler, Martin W.	HarperTrophy
Island Keeper	T	RF	Mazer, Harry	Language for Learning Assoc.
Kid Who Ran For President, The	T	RF	Gutman, Dan	Language for Learning Assoc.
Lion, the Witch and the Wardrobe, The	T	F	Lewis, C. S.	HarperTrophy
Lost Star: The Story of Amelia Earhart	T	B	Lauber, Patricia	Language for Learning Assoc.
Magician's Nephew, The	T	F	Lewis, C. S.	HarperTrophy
My Hiroshima	T	HF	Morimoto, Junko	The Penguin Group

Title	Level	Genre	Author/Series	Publisher/Distributor
Poor Girl, Rich Girl	T	RF	Wilson, Johnniece Marshall	Language for Learning Assoc.
Preacher's Boy	T	RF	Paterson, Katherine	Houghton Mifflin
Salem Days: Life in a Colonial Seaport	T	I	Adventures in Colonial America	Troll
Second Mrs. Giaconda, The	T	HF	Konigsburg, E. L.	Language for Learning Assoc.
Sees Behind Trees	T	HF	Dorris, Michael	Language for Learning Assoc.
Shh! We're Writing the Constitution	T	I	Fritz, Jean	G.P. Putnam's Sons
Sign of the Beaver	T	HF	Speare, Elizabeth George	Bantam Doubleday Dell
Sing Down the Moon	T	HF	O'Dell, Scott	Language for Learning Assoc.
Something Upstairs	T	RF	Avi	Language for Learning Assoc.
Sounder	T	RF	Armstrong, William	Scholastic
Tenement Writer, The: An Immigrant's Story	T	I	Sonder, Ben	Steck-Vaughn
Then Again, Maybe I Won't	T	RF	Blume, Judy	Language for Learning Assoc.
Three Lives to Live	T	F	Lindbergh, Anne	Little, Brown and Co.
Throwing Shadows	T	RF	Konigsburg, E. L.	Language for Learning Assoc.
Thunder Valley	T	RF	Paulsen, Gary	Bantam Doubleday Dell
Time Apart, A	T	RF	Stanley, Diane	William Morrow
Toothpaste Millionaire, The	T	RF	Merrill, Jean	Houghton Mifflin
Tracker	T	RF	Paulsen, Gary	Scholastic
Trout Summer	T	RF	Conly, Jane Leslie	Scholastic
Watsons Go to Birmingham-1963, The	T	HF	Curtis, Christopher Paul	Bantam Doubleday Dell
What Jamie Saw	T	RF	Coman, Carolyn	The Penguin Group
Wish Giver, The	T	F	Brittain, Bill	HarperTrophy
Wish on a Unicorn	T	RF	Hesse, Karen	The Penguin Group
Woodsong	T	B	Paulsen, Gary	Dell
Baseball in April and Other Stories	U	RF	Soto, Gary	Harcourt Brace
Benjamin Franklin	U	B	Kent, Deborah	Scholastic
BFG, The	U	F	Dahl, Roald	The Penguin Group
Boggart, The	U	F	Cooper, Susan	Simon & Schuster
Book of Three, The	U	F	Alexander, Lloyd	Bantam Doubleday Dell
Buffalo Gal	U	RF	Wallace, Bill	Simon & Schuster
Bye, Bye, Bali Kai	U	RF	Luger, Harriett	Harcourt Brace
Cat Ate My Gymsuit, The	U	RF	Danziger, Paula	Putnam & Grosset
Catherine, Called Birdy	U	HF	Cushman, Karen	Clarion
Charley Skedaddle	U	HF	Beatty, Patricia	Troll
Crocodilians	U	I	Short, Joan & Bird, Bettina	Mondo
Different Beat, A	U	RF	Boyd, Candy Dawson	The Penguin Group
Door in the Wall, The	U	HF	De Angeli, Marguerite	Bantam Doubleday Dell
Egypt Game, The	U	RF	Snyder, Zilpha Keatley	Bantam Doubleday Dell
Ella Enchanted	U	F	Carson Levine, Gail	HarperTrophy
Fledgling, The	U	F	Langton, Jane	Scholastic
Frightful's Mountain	U	RF	George, Jean	Puffin Books
Gathering of Days, A: A New England Girl's Journal, 1830-32	U	HF	Blos, Joan	Aladdin
Ginger Pye	U	RF	Estes, Eleanor	Scholastic
Girl In the Window, The	U	RF	Yeo, Wilma	Scholastic
Gorillas	U	I	The Untamed World	Steck-Vaughn
Great Wheel, The	U	RF	Lawson, Robert	Scholastic
I Am Regina	U	HF	Keehn, Sally	Bantam Doubleday Dell
Insects	U	I	Bird, Bettina & Short, Joan	Mondo
Jacob Have I Loved	U	RF	Paterson, Katherine	HarperTrophy
Jericho's Journey	U	RF	Wisler, G. Clifton	Penguin Group
Journey Into Terror	U	RF	Wallace, Bill	Simon & Schuster
Journey to America	U	HF	Levitin, Sonia	Simon & Schuster
Journey to Topaz	U	HF	Uchida, Yoshiko	Creative Arts Book Co.
Julie of the Wolves	U	RF	George, Jean Craighead	Harper Collins
Julie's Wolf Pack	U	RF	George, Jean Craighead	HarperTrophy
Jump Ship to Freedom	U	HF	Collier, James and Christopher	Bantam Doubleday Dell
Kind of Thief, A	U	RF	Alcock, Vivien	Bantam Doubleday Dell

Title	Level	Genre	Author/Series	Publisher/Distributor
Lyddie	U	HF	Paterson, Katherine	The Penguin Group
Moon, The	U	I	A First Book	Franklin Watts
My Side of the Mountain	U	RF	George, Jean Craighead	The Penguin Group
Nothing But The Truth	U	RF	Avi	Hearst
Number the Stars	U	HF	Lowry, Lois	Bantam Doubleday Dell
Onion John	U	HF	Krumgold, Joseph	Harper & Row
P.S. Longer Letter Later	U	RF	Danziger, P. & Martin, A.	Scholastic
Place Called Heartbreak, A: A Story of Vietnam	U	I	Myers, Walter Dean	Steck-Vaughn
Real Thief, The	U	F	Steig, William	Farrar, Straus and Giroux
Red Dog	U	RF	Wallace, Bill	Simon & Schuster
Remember the Ladies: The First Women's Rights Convention	U	I	Johnston, Norma	Scholastic
Report To the Principal's Office	U	RF	Spinelli, Jerry	Scholastic
Righteous Revenge of Artemis Bonner, The	U	RF	Myers, Walter Dean	HarperTrophy
Rosa Parks: My Story	U	B	Parks, Rosa	Scholastic
Sand On The Move: The Story of Dunes	U	I	A First Book	Franklin Watts
Secret Garden, The	U	RF	Burnett, Frances H.	Scholastic
Shadow of a Bull	U	RF	Wojciechowska, Maia	Simon & Schuster
Sign of the Chrysanthemum, The	U	RF	Paterson, Katherine	HarperTrophy
Silk Route, The	U	HF	Major, John S.	HarperCollins
Silverwing: How One Small Bat Became a Noble Hero	U	F	Oppel, Kenneth	Simon & Schuster
Stories in Stone: The World of Animal Fossils	U	I	A First Book	Franklin Watts
Story of Harriet Tubman: Freedom, The	U	B	Sterling, Dorothy	Bantam Doubleday Dell
Stranger at the Window	U	RF	Alcock, Vivien	Houghton Mifflin
Summer of the Swans, The	U	RF	Byars, Betsy	The Penguin Group
Talking Earth, The	U	RF	George, Jean Craighead	HarperTrophy
Tangerine	U	RF	Bloor, Edward	Scholastic
Thomas Jefferson: Man with a Vision	U	B	Crisman, Ruth	Scholastic
Thunder Rolling in the Mountains	U	HF	O'Dell, Scott & Hall, Elizabeth	Bantam Doubleday Dell
Tiltawhirl John	U	RF	Paulsen, Gary	The Penguin Group
Treasures in the Dust	U	HF	Porter, Tracey	HarperTrophy
Tuck Everlasting	U	F	Babbitt, Natalie	Farrar, Straus and Giroux
Tucket's Ride	U	HF	Paulsen, Gary	Bantam Doubleday Dell
View from Saturday, The	U	F	Konigsburg, E. L.	Atheneum Books
Wait Till Helen Comes	U	F	Downing Hahn, Mary	Houghton Mifflin
War Comes to Willy Freeman	U	HF	Collier, J. L., &Collier, C.	Dell Publishing
Winter Room, The	U	RF	Paulsen, Gary	Bantam Doubleday Dell
Wringer	U	RF	Spinelli, Jerry	HarperTrophy
African-Americans in the Thirteen Colonies	V	I	Cornerstones of Freedom	Children's Press
American Revolution, The	V	I	Carter, Alden R.	Franklin Watts
Anne of Green Gables	V	RF	Montgomery, L. M.	Scholastic
Arlington National Cemetery	V	I	Cornerstones of Freedom	Bantam Doubleday Dell
Autumn Street	V	HF	Lowry, Lois	Bantam Doubleday Dell
Behind The Bedroom Wall	V	HF	Williams, Laura E.	Milkweed Editions
Biggest Klutz in Fifth Grade, The	V	RF	Wallace, Bill	Simon & Schuster
Birthday Room, The	V	RF	Henkes, Kevin	William Morrow
Black Star, Bright Dawn	V	RF	O'Dell, Scott	Ballantine Books
Boston Tea Party, The	V	I	Cornerstones of Freedom	Children's Press
Brain	V	I	You And Your Body	Troll
Building the Capital City	V	I	Cornerstones of Freedom	Bantam Doubleday Dell
But I'll Be Back Again	V	B	Rylant, Cynthia	Beech Tree Books
By the Great Horn Spoon!	V	HF	Fleischman, Sid	Little, Brown & Co.
Cay, The	V	HF	Taylor, Theodore	Avon
Come Sing, Jimmy Jo	V	RF	Patterson, Katherine	The Penguin Group
Daughter of the Mountains	V	HF	Rankin, Louise	The Penguin Group
Dogsong	V	RF	Paulsen, Gary	Simon & Schuster
Dragonsong	V	F	McCaffrey, Anne	Bantam Doubleday Dell
Fighting Ground, The	V	HF	Avi	HarperTrophy

Title	Level	Genre	Author/Series	Publisher/Distributor
Foster's War	V	HF	Reeder, Carolyn	Scholastic
Gettysburg Address, The	V	I	Cornerstones of Freedom	Children's Press
Golden Goblet, The	V	RF	McGraw, Eloise Jarvis	Scholastic
Harry Potter and the Chamber of Secrets	V	F	Rowling, J. K.	Scholastic
Harry Potter and the Goblet of Fire	V	F	Rowling, J. K.	Scholastic
Harry Potter and the Prisoner of Azkaban	V	F	Rowling, J.K.	Scholastic
Harry Potter and the Sorcerer's Stone	V	F	Rowling, J. K.	Scholastic
Holes	V	RF	Sachar, Louis	Random House
Incident at Hawk's Hill	V	F	Eckert, Allen W.	Little, Brown & Co.
Incredible Journey,The	V	F	Burnford, Sheila	Bantam Doubleday Dell
Island of the Blue Dolphins	V	HF	O'Dell, Scott	Bantam Doubleday Dell
Jackie Robinson Breaks the Color Line	V	B	Cornerstones of Freedom	Children's Press
Jamestown Colony, The	V	I	Cornerstones of Freedom	Children's Press
Jip His Story	V	HF	Paterson, Katherine	The Penguin Group
Journey Home	V	RF	Uchida, Yoshika	Aladdin
Journey Outside	V	F	Steele, Mary Q.	The Penguin Group
Lewis and Clark	V	B	Cornerstones of Freedom	Children's Press
Lexington and Concord	V	I	Cornerstones of Freedom	Children's Press
Liberty Bell, The	V	I	Cornerstones of Freedom	Children's Press
Maniac Magee	V	RF	Spinelli, Jerry	Scholastic
Matthew's Meadow	V	RF	Bliss, Corinne Demas	Harcourt Brace
Music of Dolphins, The	V	RF	Hesse, Karen	Scholastic
My Name is Not Angelica	V	HF	O'Dell, Scott	Bantam Doubleday Dell
My Wartime Summers	V	HF	Cutler, Jane	Harper Collins
Old Yeller	V	RF	Gipson, Fred	Scholastic
Pocket Full of Seeds, A	V	HF	Sachs, Marilyn	Scholastic
Rainbow People, The	V	F	Yep, Lawrence	HarperTrophy
Rascal	V	HF	North, Sterling	Scholastic
Remember Not To Forget: A Memory of the Holocaust	V	I	Finkelstein, Norman H.	William & Morrow
Riddle of the Rosetta Stone, The	V	I	Giblin, James Cross	HarperTrophy
Root Cellar, The	V	HF	Lunn, Janet	The Penguin Group
Sojourner Truth: Ain't I a Woman?	V	B	McKissack, F. and P.	Scholastic
Swiftly Tilting Planet, A	V	F	L'Engle, Madeleine	Bantam Doubleday Dell
Tent, The	V	RF	Paulsen, Gary	Bantam Doubleday Dell
Titanic, The	V	I	Cornerstones of Freedom	Children's Press
Transcontinental Railroad, The	V	I	Cornerstones of Freedom	Children's Press
True Confessions of Charlotte Doyle, The	V	HF	Avi	Avon
Twenty-One Balloons, The	V	SF	DuBois, William	Scholastic
Underground Railroad, The	V	I	Bial, Raymond	Houghton Mifflin
Westing Game, The	V	RF	Raskin, Ellen	The Penguin Group
Wolves of Willoughby Chase, The	V	HF	Aiken, Joan	Bantam Doubleday Dell
Women Who Shaped the West	V	B	Cornerstones of Freedom	Children's Press
Women's Voting Rights	V	I	Cornerstones of Freedom	Children's Press
Words of Stone	V	RF	Henkes, Kevin	The Penguin Group
Wrinkle in Time, A	V	F	L'Engle, Madeleine	Bantom Doubleday Dell
An Island Far From Home	W	HF	Donahue, John	Carolrhonda Books
Black Pearl, The	W	RF	O'Dell, Scott	Bantam Doubleday Dell
Blue-Eyed Daisy, A	W	RF	Rylant, Cynthia	Simon & Schuster
Dicey's Song	W	RF	Voigt, Cynthia	Ballantine Books
Dragon's Gate	W	HF	Yep, Laurence	Harper Collins
Dragonwings	W	HF	Yep, Lawrence	HarperTrophy
Face to Face	W	RF	Bauer, Marion Dane	Bantam Doubleday Dell
Girl From Yamhill, A	W	B	Cleary, Beverly	Bantam Doubleday Dell
Great Whales: The Gentle Giants	W	I	Lauber, Patricia	Henry Holt & Co.
House on Mango Street, The	W	B	Cisneros, Sandra	Alfred A. Knopf
I Am A Star: Child of the Holocaust	W	I	Auerbacher, Inge	The Penguin Group
Kiss the Dust	W	RF	Laird, Elizabeth	The Penguin Group

Title	Level	Genre	Author/Series	Publisher/Distributor
Letters to Julia	W	RF	Holmes, Barbara Ware	HarperTrophy
Life and Words of Martin Luther King, Jr., The	W	B	Peck, Ira	Scholastic
Mama, Let's Dance	W	RF	Hermes, Patricia	Scholastic
Maya Angelou: Greeting the Morning	W	B	King, Sarah E.	The Millbrook Press
Missing May	W	RF	Rylant, Cynthia	Bantam Doubleday Dell
Moccasin Trail	W	RF	McGraw, Eloise	Scholastic
Moon Bridge, The	W	HF	Savin, Marcia	Scholastic
Mr. Lincoln's Drummer	W	HF	Wisler, G. Clifton	The Penguin Group
Nightjohn	W	HF	Paulsen, Gary	Bantam Doubleday Dell
Phantom Tollbooth, The	W	F	Juster, Norton	Bantam Doubleday Dell
Phoenix Rising	W	RF	Hesse, Karen	Penguin Group
Pride of Puerto Rico: The Life of Roberto Clemente	W	B	Walker, Paul Robert	Harcourt Brace
Red Cap	W	HF	Wisler, G. Clifton	The Penguin Group
Roll of Thunder, Hear My Cry	W	HF	Taylor, Mildred D.	The Penguin Group
Sarny: A Life Remembered	W	HF	Paulsen, Gary	Delacorte Press
Saturnalia	W	RF	Fleischman, Paul	Harper Collins
Seedfolks	W	RF	Fleishman, Paul	HarperTrophy
Selchie's Seed, The	W	F	Levey Oppenheim, Shulamith	Harcourt Brace
Sing for Your Father, Su Phan	W	HF	Pevsner, Stella and Tang, Fay	Bantam Doubleday Dell
Sister	W	RF	Greenfield, Eloise	Harper Collins
Tiger Eyes	W	RF	Blume, Judy	Bantam Doubleday Dell
Time of Angels, A	W	F	Hesse, Karen	Hyperion
What Do Fish Have To Do With Anything?	W	RF	Avi	Candlewick Press
Who Is Carrie?	W	HF	Collier, J. L. and Collier, C.	Bantam Doubleday Dell
Winterdance: The Fine Madness of Running the Iditarod	W	B	Paulsen, Gary	Harcourt Brace
Witch of Blackbird Pond, The	W	HF	Speare, Elizabeth George	Bantam Doubleday Dell
Year of Impossible Goodbyes	W	HF	Choi, Sook Nyui	Yearling
You Want Women to Vote, Lizzie Stanton?	W	B	Fritz, Jean	The Penguin Group
Blue Door, The	X	HF	Rinaldi, Ann	Scholastic
Bully for you Teddy Roosevelt!	X	B	Fritz, Jean	Penguin Putnam Books
Call It Courage	X	RF	Sperry, Armstrong	Aladdin
Childtimes: A Three-Generation Memoir	X	B	Greenfield, E. & Little, L. J.	HarperTrophy
Dark Is Rising, The	X	F	Cooper, Susan	Macmillan
Definitely Cool	X	RF	Wilkinson, Brenda	Scholastic
Devil's Arithmetic, The	X	F	Yolen, Jane	Puffin Books
Girl Named Disaster, A	X	RF	Farmer, Nancy	The Penguin Group
Harriet Beecher Stowe and the Beecher Preachers	X	B	Fritz, Jean	The Penguin Group
Let the Circle Be Unbroken	X	HF	Taylor, Mildred D.	The Penguin Group
Letters From a Slave Girl: The Story of Harriet Jacobs	X	HF	Lyons, Mary E.	Simon & Schuster
M.C. Higgins the Great	X	RF	Hamilton, Virginia	Macmillan
Midwife's Apprentice, The	X	HF	Cushman, Karen	HarperTrophy
Moving Mama to Town	X	RF	Young, Ronder Thomas	Bantam Doubleday Dell
Novio Boy	X	TL	Soto, Gary	Harcourt Brace
Out of the Dust	X	HF	Hesse, Karen	Scholastic
Road to Memphis, The	X	HF	Taylor, Mildred D.	The Penguin Group
Sarah Bishop	X	HF	O'Dell, Scott	Scholastic
Ties That Bind, Ties That Break	X	HF	Namioka, Lensey	Delacorte Press
Where the Red Fern Grows	X	RF	Rawls, Wilson	Bantam Doubleday Dell
Yearling, The	X	RF	Rawlings, Marjorie Kinnan	Simon & Schuster
Call of the Wild	Y	RF	London, Jack	Signet Classics
Cesar Chavez	Y	B	Rodriguez, Consuelo	Chelsea House
Diary of Anne Frank, The	Y	B	Frank, Anne	Pocket Books
Giver, The	Y	F	Lowry, Lois	Bantam Doubleday Dell
I Have Lived a Thousand Years	Y	B	Bitton-Jackson, Livia	Simon & Schuster
Jackaroo	Y	RF	Voigt, Cynthia	Scholastic
Jesse	Y	RF	Soto, Gary	Scholastic
Living Up The Street	Y	RF	Soto, Gary	Bantam Doubleday Dell

Title	Level	Genre	Author/Series	Publisher/Distributor
My Brother Sam is Dead	Y	HF	Collier, James and Christopher	Scholastic
Pushcart War, The	Y	F	Merrill, Jean	Bantam Doubleday Dell
Sons of Liberty	Y	RF	Griffin, Adele	Hyperion
Where the Lilies Bloom	Y	RF	Cleavers, Vera and Bill	HarperTrophy
Across Five Aprils	Z	HF	Hunt, Irene	Follett
Adventures of Huckleberry Finn, The	Z	HF	Twain, Mark	Scholastic
Adventures of Tom Sawyer, The	Z	HF	Twain, Mark	Scholastic
After the Rain	Z	RF	Mazer, Norma Fox	Avon Books
An Island Like You: Stories of the Barrio	Z	RF	Cofer, Judith Ortiz	The Penguin Group
Circle of Quiet, A	Z	B	L'Engle, Madeleine	Harper Collins
Contender, The	Z	RF	Lipsythe, Robert	HarperTrophy
Day No Pigs Would Die, A	Z	HF	Peck, Sylvia	Random House
Flowers For Algernon	Z	RF	Keyes, Daniel	Harcourt Brace
Friends, The	Z	RF	Guy, Rosa	Bantam Doubleday Dell
From the Notebooks of Melanin Sun	Z	RF	Woodson, Jacqueline	Scholastic
Gathering of Flowers, A	Z	RF	Thomas, Joyce Carol	HarperTrophy
Golden Compass, The	Z	F	Pullman, Philip	Ballantine Books
Good Night, Mr. Tom	Z	HF	Magorian, Michelle	HarperTrophy
Hobbit, The	Z	F	Tolkien, J.R.R	Ballantine Books
Inn Keepers Apprentice	Z	B	Say, Allen	The Penguin Group
Jazmin's Notebook	Z	RF	Grimes, Nikki	The Penguin Group
Of Mice and Men	Z	RF	Steinbeck, John	The Penguin Group
Outsiders, The	Z	RF	Hinton, S.E.	The Penguin Group
Scorpions	Z	RF	Myers, Walter Dean	HarperTrophy
Summer Life, A	Z	RF	Soto, Gary	Bantam Doubleday Dell
Summer of My German Soldier	Z	HF	Greene, Bette	Dell Publishing
To Kill a Mockingbird	Z	HF	Lee, Harper	Warner Books
Treasure Island	Z	HF	Stevenson, Robert Lewis	Scholastic
Watcher, The	Z	RF	Howe, James	Simon & Schuster
Wizard of Earthsea, A	Z	F	LeGuin, Ursula K.	Bantam Doubleday Dell
Woman Hollering Creek	Z	RF	Cisneros, Sandra	Random House

Trade Book Publishers

Aladinn
Albert Whitman & Co.
Alfred A. Knopf
Avon Books
Avon Camelot
Ballantine Books
Bantam Books
Bantam Doubleday Dell
Bantam Skylark
Barron's Educational
Beach Tree Books
Beech Tree
Candlewick Press
Clarion
Crabtree

Creative Arts Book Co.
Delacorte Press
Dell Publishing
Dell Yearling
Dial
Dutton
Farrar, Straus & Giroux
Follett
Franklin Watts
G.P. Putnam Sons
Greenwillow
Harcourt Brace
Harper & Row
HarperCollins
Harpertrophy

Hearst
Henry Holt & Co.
Holiday House
Houghton Mifflin
Hyperion
Ladybird Books
Language for Learning
Association
Little, Brown & Co.
Macmillan
Milkweed
Millbrook Press
Orchard Books
Paper Star
Penguin Group

Pleasant Company
Puffin Books
Random House
Scholastic
Seal Books
Secret Passage Press
Signet Classics
Tundra
Viking
W.H. Freeman & Co.
Warner Books
William Morrow Co.
Yearling

Book Publishers and Distributors

Some companies publish their own titles, while others distribute series books from a variety of sources. Ordering information on series books is available from the following sources. Trade Titles may be ordered form any paperback supplier, many of which offer a flat paperback discount to schools.

Benchmark Education
629 Fifth Avenue
Pelham, NY 10803
Phone 1-877-236-2465
Fax 1-914-738-5063
benchmarkeducation.com

Capstone Press
151 Good Counsel Drive
P.O. Box 669
Mankato, MN 56002-0669
Phone 1-800-747-4992
Fax 1-888-262-0705
www.capstone-press.com

Dominie Press, Inc.
1949 Kellogg Avenue
Carlsbad, CA 92008
Phone 1-800-232-4570
Fax 1-760-431-8777
www.dominie.com
info@dominie.com

Grolier Press
90 Sherman Turnpike
Danbury, CT 06816
Phone 1-800-621-1115
Fax 1-203-797-3197
http://publishing.grolier.com

Houghton Mifflin
1900 South Batavia
Geneva, Ill. 60134
Phone 1-800-733-2828
Fax 1-800-733-2098
www.eduplace.com

Modern Curriculum Press
4350 Equity Drive
P.O. Box 2649
Columbus, OH 43216
Phone 1-800-321-3106
Fax 1-800-393-3156
www.pearsonlearning.com

Mondo Publishing
One Plaza Road
Greenvale, NY 11548
Phone 1-212-268-3560
Fax 1-516-484-7813
www.

Richard C. Owen Publishers
P.O. Box 585
Katonah, NY 10536
Phone 1-800-336-5588
Fax 1-914-232-3977
www.rcowen.com

Rigby
P.O. Box 797
Crystal Lake, IL 60039-0797
Phone 1-800-822-8661
Fax –800-427-4429
www.rigby.com

Shortland Publications
50 South Steele Street, Suite 755
Denver, CO 80209-9927
Phone 1-800-775-9995
Fax 1-800-775-9597
www.shortland.com

Steck Vaughn
P.O. Box 690789
Orlando, FL 32819-0789
Phone 1-800-531-5015
Fax 1-800-699-9459
www.steck-vaughn.com

Troll Publications
100 Corporate Drive
Matwah, NJ 07430
Phone 1-800-526-5289
Fax 1-800-979-8765
www.troll.com

Wright Group
19201 120th Avenue NE
Bothell, WA 98011-9512
Phone 1-800-523-2371
Fax 1-800-543-7323
www.wrightgroup.com

Children's Literature
Chapter Books and Collections Cited in This Book

Adler, David. 1997. *Cam Jansen and the Mystery of the Stolen Diamonds*. New York: Puffin.

Alcott, Louisa May. 1880. *Little Women*. Philadelphia, PA: Courage Books.

Avi.1984. *The Fighting Ground*. Philadelphia: Lippincott.

Babbitt, Natalie. 1975. *Tuck Everlasting*. New York: Farrar, Straus & Giroux.

Babbitt, Natallie. 1991. *The Search for Delicious*. New York: Farrar Straus & Giroux.

Banks, Lynne Reid. 1981. *The Indian in the Cupboard*. New York: Doubleday.

Bauer, Marion Dane. 1986. *On My Honor*. Boston: Houghton Mifflin.

Beatty, Patricia. 1989. *Charley Skedalle*. Mahwah, NJ: Troll Associates.

Bird, Bettina. 1998. *Insects*. New York: Mondo Publishing.

Blair, Gwenda. 1981. *Laura Ingalls Wilder*. Ill. by Thomas B. Allen. New York: G.P. Putnam's Sons.

Blume, Judy. 1976. *Blubber*. New York: Yearling.

Blume, Judy. 1976. *Tales of a Fourth Grade Nothing*. New York: Yearling.

Blume, Judy. 1980. *Superfudge*. New York: Dell.

Blume, Judy. 1985. *The Pain and the Great One*. Ill. Irene Triva. New York: Bantam Doubleday Dell.

Brink, Carol Ryrie. 1936. *Caddie Woodlawn*. New York: Macmillan.

Brittain, Bill. 1990. *The Wish Giver: The Tales of Coven Tree*. New York: HarperCollins.

Brown, M. 1997. *Arthur's Mystery Envelope*. Boston: Little, Brown & Company.

Brown, M. 1998. *Arthur Rocks with Binky*. Boston: Little, Brown & Company.

Burnett, Frances Hodgson. 1989. *The Secret Garden*. Illus. Shirley Hughes. New York: Viking.

Byars, Betsy. 1977. *The Pinballs*. New York: HarperCollins.

Byars, Betsy. 1987. *The Summer of the Swans*. New York: Scholastic, Inc.

Byars, Betsy C. 1990. *Beans on the Roof*. Ill. Melodye Rosales. New York: Yearling.

Carrick, Carol. 1989. *Stay Away from Simon*. New York: Clarion.

Castaneda, Omar S. 1993. *Abuela's Weave*. Ill. Enrique O. Sanchez. New York: Lee and Low Books.

Cleary, Beverly. 1983. *Dear Mr. Henshaw*. Ill. Paul Zelinsky. New York: Dell Publishing.

Cleary, Beverly. 1985. *Henry Huggins*. New York: William Morrow.

Cleary, Beverly. 1993. *Beezus and Ramona*. New York: Camelot.

Coerr, Eleanor. 1977. *Sadako and the Thousand Paper Cranes*. New York: Penguin Putnam.

Collier, J.L. and C. Collier. 1987. *Jump Ship to Freedom*. New York: Yearling.

Collier, James and Christopher Collier. 1974. *My Brother Sam is Dead*. New York: Four Winds.

Conford, Ellen. 1989. *What's Cooking, Jenny Archer?* New York: Little, Brown and Company.

Cooper, Susan. 1973. *The Dark is Rising*. Ill. Alan E. Cober. New York: Artheneum.

Creech, Sharon. 1994. *Walk Two Moons*. New York: HarperCollins.

Creech, Sharon. 1997. *Absolutely Normal Chaos*. New York: HarperCollins.

Curtis, Christopher Paul. 1995. *The Watsons Go to Birmingham -1963*. New York: Bantam Doubleday Dell.

Cushman, Karen. 1996. *The Midwife's Apprentice*. New York: HarperTrophy.

Cutler, Jane. 1992. *No Dogs Allowed*. Ill. Tracy Campbell Pearson. New York: Farrar, Straus & Giroux.

Dahl, Roald. 1998. *Danny, the Champion of the World*. New York: Puffin Books.

Danziger and Martin. 1999. *P.S. Longer A.M.* New York: Econo-Clad.

Danziger, Paula. 1997. *Amber Brown Wants Extra Credit*. New York: Little Apple.

Davis, Lucille and Cesar Chavez. 1998. *Cesar Chavez: A Photo-Illustrated Biography*. New York: Bridgestone Books.

Dorris, Michael. 1992. *Morning Girl*. New York: Hyperion Books.

Dorris, Michael. 1992. *Sees Behind Trees*. New York: Hyperion Books.

Dorris, Michael. 1994. *Guests*. New York: Hyperion Books.

Erickson, Russell E. 1974. *A Toad for Tuesday*. Ill. Lawrence Di Flori. New York: Beach Tree Books.

Ferris, Jeri.1988. *Go Free or Die: A Story About Harriet Tubman*. Minneapolis, MN: Carolrhoda/Lerner.

Fitzhugh, Louise. 1985. *Harriet the Spy*. New York: HarperCollins.

Fleischman, Paul. 1997. *Seedfolks*. Ill. Judy Pedersen. New York: HarperCollins.

Fletcher, Ralph. 1991. *Water Planet*. Paramus, NJ: Arrowbooks.

Fletcher, Ralph. 1995. *Fig Pudding*. New York: Clarion Books.

Fletcher, Ralph. 1997. *Twilight Comes Twice*. Ill. Kate Kiesler. New York: Houghton Mifflin.

Fletcher, Ralph. 1998. *Flying Solo*. New York: Clarion Books.

Fletcher, Ralph. 1998. *Spider Boy*. Des Plaines, IL: Yearling/Bantam Doubleday Books.

Fletcher, Ralph. 2000. *Grandpa Never Lies*. Ill. Harvey Stevenson. New York: Clarion Books.

Fletcher, Ralph. 2000. *Tommy Trouble and the Magic Marble*. Ill. Ben Caldwell. New York: Henry Holt & Company.

Frank, Anne and B.M. Moovaart. 1952. *Anne Frank: A Diary of a Young Girl*. New York: Bantam Books.

Fritz, Jean. 1976. *What's the Big Idea, Ben Franklin?* Ill. Margot Tomes. New York: Coward-McCann.

George, Jean Craighead. 1972. *Julie of the Wolves*. Ill. John Schoenherr. New York: Harper & Row.

Giff, Patricia Reilly. 1997. *Lily's Crossing*. New York: Yearling/Bantam Doubleday Dell Books.

Graves, Bonnie. 1998. *No Copycats Allowed!* New York: Hyperion.

Greene, Carol. 1989. *Martin Luther King, Jr.: A Man Who Changed Things*. Children's Press.

Hall, Donald. 1983. *The Ox-Cart Man*. New York: Puffin Books.

Hesse, Karen. 1997. *A Time of Angels*. New York: Apple

Hesse, Karen. 1998. *Just Juice*. Ill. Robert Andrew Parker. New York: Scholastic, Inc.

Hesse, Karen. 1998. *The Music of Dolphins*. New York: Apple.

Hesse, Karen. 1999. *Out of the Dust*. New York: Scholastic, Inc.

Hinton, S.E. 1997. *The Outsiders*. New York: Puffin/Penguin Putnam.

Hoestlandt, Jo. 1995. *Star of Fear, Star of Hope*. Ill. Johanna Kang and Mark Polizzotti. New York: Walker & Company.

Hudson, Wade. 1995. *Five Brave Explorers*. Ill. Ron Garnett. New York: Scholastic, Inc.

Hurwitz, Johanna. 1987. *Russell Sprouts*. Cincinnati, OH: Beech Tree.

Johnson, Sylvia and Alice Aamodt. 1985. *Wolf Pack: Tracking Wolves in the Wild: Discovery*. Minneapolis, MN: Lerner Publications.

King-Smith, Dick. 1982. *Pigs Might Fly*. Ill. Mary Rayner. New York: Viking.

Kipling, Rudyard. 1990. *Just So Stories*. New York: Penquin.

Konigsburg, Elaine. 1988. *Throwing Shadows*. New York: MacMillan.

Konigsburg, Elaine. 1996. *A View from Saturday*. New York: Atheneum.

L'Engle, Madeleine. 1960. *Meet the Austins*. Boston: Vanguard.

L'Engle, Madeleine. 1980. *A Ring of Endless Light*. New York: Farrar Straus & Giroux.

Lawson, Robert. 1988. *Ben and Me: A New and Astonishing Life of Benjamin Franklin as Written by His Good Mouse, Amos*. Boston: Little, Brown and Company.

Levine, Gail Corson. 1997. *Ella Enchanted*. New York: HarperCollins.

Lipsyte, Robert. 1967. *The Contender*. New York: Harper & Row.

Little, Jean. 1990. *Hey World, Here I Am!* Ill. Sue Fruesdell. New York: HarperTrophy.

Lord, B.B. 1989. *In the Year of the Boar and Jackie Robinson*. New York: HarperCollins.

Lowry, Lois. 1984. *Anastasia Krupnik*. New York: Yearling.

Lowry, Lois. 1989. *Number the Stars*. Boston: Houghton Mifflin.

Lowry, Lois. 1999. *Stay! Keeper's Story*. New York: Yearling.

MacLachlan, Patricia. 1985. *Sarah, Plain and Tall*. New York: Harper & Row.

Magneson, Karen. 1994. *Grandma According to Me*. Ill. Ted Rand. Des Plaines, IL: Yearling/Bantam Doubleday Books.

Namioka, Lensey. 1994. *Yang the Youngest and his Terrible Ear*. Yearling Books.

Naylor, Phyllis R. 1992. *Shiloh*. New York: Yearling.

Neison, Vaunda M. 1988. *Always Gramma*. Ils. Kimanne Uhler. New York: G.P. Putnam's Sons.

Orwell, George. 1940. *Animal Farm*. New York: Harcourt Brace.

Palacco, Patricia. 1994. *Firetalking*. Ill. Laurence Migdale. Katonah, New York: Richard C. Owens.

Parsons, Alexandra. 1990. *Amazing Spiders*. Photos by Jerry Young. New York: Alfred A. Knopf.

Paterson, Katherine. 1976. *The Master Puppeteer*. Ill. Harus Wells. New York: Crowell.

Paterson, Katherine. 1977. *Bridge to Terabithia*. New York: Crowell.

Paterson, Katherine. 1980. *Jacob Have I Loved*. New York: Crowell.

Paterson, Katherine. 1987. *The Great Gilly Hopkins*. New York: HarperTrophy.

Paterson, Katherine. 1992. *Lyddie*. New York: Penguin.

Paterson, Katherine. 1998. *Jip: His Story*. New York: Puffin/Putnam.

Paulsen, G. 1989. *The Winter Room*. New York: Bantam Doubleday Dell.

Paulsen, Gary. 1987. *Hatchet*. New York: Macmillan, Bradbury.

Paulsen, Gary. 1991. *The River*. New York: Delacorte.

Paulsen, Gary. 1999. *Sarny: A Life Remembered*. Des Plaines, IL: Laureleaf/Bantam Doubleday Dell Books.

Peare, Catherine O. Out of print. *The Helen Keller Story*.

Pringle, Laurence. 1995. *Fire in the Forest: A Cycle of Growth and Renewal*. Ill. by Bob Marshall. New York: Atheneum/Simon & Schuster.

Pringle, Laurence. 1997. *Elephant Woman: Cynthia Moss Explores the World of Elephants*. New York: Atheneum.

Roop, Connie. 1985. *Keep the Light Burning, Abbie*. Minneapolis, MN: Carolrhoda.

Ross, Pat. 1980. *Meet M & M*. New York: Econo-Clad.

Rowling, J.K. 1999. *Harry Potter and the Prisons of Azkaban*. New York: Scholastic, Inc.

Roy, Arundhati. 1998. *The God of Small Things*. New York: HarperCollins.

Rylant, Cynthia. 1985. *Every Living Thing*. Ill. S.D. Schindler. New York: Bradbury/Simon & Schuster.

Rylant, Cynthia. 1989. *But I'll Be Back Again*. New York: Orchard Books.

Rylant, Cynthia. 1992. *Missing May*. New York: Orchard Books.

Rylant, Cynthia. 2000. *Mr. Putter & Tabby Paint the Porch*. New York: Harcourt Brace.

Sabin. 1986. *Jesse Owens: Olympic Hero*. New York: Troll.

Sandler, Martin. 2000. *Cowboys*. New York: HarperCollins.

Seidler, T. 1996. *The Wainscott Weasel*. New York: HarperTrophy.

Selden, George. 1960. *The Cricket in Times Square*. New York: Farrar, Straus & Giroux.

Sender, Ruth Minsky. 1980. *The Cage*. New York: Aladdin/Simon & Schuster.

Sharmat, Marjorie W. 1972. *Nate the Great*. New York: Yearling.

Smith, Doris. 1973. *A Taste of Blackberries*. New York: HarperCollins.

Snyder, Zilpha K. 1997. *The Egypt Game*. New York: New York.

Snyder, Zilpha K. 1997. *The Gypsy Game*. New York: Delacorte.

Soto, Gary. 1991. *A Summer Life*. New York: Laurel Leaf.

Soto, Gary. 1991. *Baseball in April*. San Diego: Harcourt.

Soto, Gary. 1992. *Taking Sides*. New York: Harcourt Brace.

Spinelli, Jerry. 1991. *Maniac Magee*. New York: Little, Brown.

Steig, William. 1976. *Abel's Island*. New York: Farrar, Straus, & Giroux.

Streissguth. 1997. *Writer of the Plains: A Story about Willa Cather*. New York: Carolrheda Books.

Stowe, Harriet Beecher. 1861. *Uncle Tom's Cabin*. Cutchogue, New York: Buccaneer Books.

Thomas, Jane. 1988. *Saying Good-by to Grandma*. Ill. Marcia Sewall. New York: Clarion Books.

Trottier, Maxine. 1999. *Dreamstones*. Toronto, Canada: Stoddart.

Turner, Ann. 1985. *Dakota Dugout*. Ill. Ronald Himler. New York: Macmillan.

Viorst, Judith. 1976. *The Tenth Good Thing About Barney*. Ill. Erik Blegvad. New York: Aladdin/Simon & Schuster

Vos, I., T. Edelstein and I. Smidt. 1991. *Hide and Seek*. Boston: Houghton Mifflin.

Wagner, Jane. 1972. *J.T.* New York: Yearling/Bantam Doubleday Books.

White, E.B. 1952. *Charlotte's Web*. New York: Harper & Row.

Wick, Walter. 1997. *A Drop of Water*. New York: Scholastic, Inc.

Wilde, Buck. 1997. *Wolves*. New York: Rigby.

Wilder, Laura Ingalls. 1953, 1932. *Little House in the Big Woods*. New York: Harper & Row.

Woodworth, Deborah. 1997. *Compassion: The Story of Clara Barton*. New York: Childs Wood.

Wyeth, Sharon D. 1996. *Ginger Brown: Too Many Houses*. New York: Random House.

Professional References

Ackert, P. 1999. *Cause and Effect: Intermediate Reading Practice, Third Edition.* Boston: Heinle and Heinle.

Adams, M.J. 1990. *Beginning to Read: Think and Learning About Print.* Cambridge, MA: MIT Press.

Albom, Mitch. 1997. *Tuesdays with Morrie: An Old Man, a Young Man and Life's Great Lesson.* New York: Doubleday.

Alexander, K., D.R. Entwisle, and S. Dauber. 1994. *On the Success of Failure: A Reassessment of the Effects of Retention in the Primary Grades.* New York: Cambridge University Press.

Allen, J. 1999. *Words, Words, Words: Teaching Vocabulary in Grades 4-12.* York, ME: Stenhouse Publishers.

Allington, R.L. 1983. "The Reading Instruction Provided Readers of Differing Reading Ability." *Elementary School Journal,* (83): 548-559.

Allington, R.L. 1994. "The Legacy of 'Slow It Down and Make It More Concrete.'" In J. Zutell and S. McCormick Eds., *Learner Factors/Teacher Factors: Issues in Literacy Research and Instruction.* Chicago: National Reading Conference: 19-30.

Allington, R.L., and A. McGill-Franzen. 1989. "Different Programs, Indifferent Instruction." In D. Lipsky and A. Garther, Eds., *Beyond Special Education*: 3-32. New York: Brookes.

Anderson, Carl. 2000. *How's It Going?: A Practical Guide to Conferring with Student Writers.* Portsmouth, NH: Heinemann.

Anderson, R.C., P.T. Wilson, and L.C. Fielding. 1998. "Growth in Reading and How Children Spend Their Time Outside of School." *Reading Research Quarterly,* XXIII Summer.

Anderson, R.C., R.J. Spiro, and M.C. Anderson. 1978. "Schemata as Scaffolding for the Representation of Information in Connected Discourse." *American Educational Research Journal,* (15): 433-440.

Anthony, H., and T. Raphael. 1989. "Using Questioning Strategies to Promote Students' Active Comprehension of Content Areas Material." In D. Lapp, J. Flood and N. Farnan, Eds., *Content Area Reading and Learning: Instructional Strategies*: 244-257. Englewood Cliffs, NJ: Prentice-Hall.

Armbruster, B.B., T.H. Anderson, and J. Ostertag. 1987. "Does Text Structure/Summarization Instruction Facilitate Learning from Expository Text?" *Reading Research Quarterly,* (22): 331-346.

Atwell, N. 1987. *In the Middle: Writing, Reading and Learning with Adolescents, second edition.* Portsmouth, NH: Heinemann.

Atwell, Nancie. 1998. *In the Middle: New Understandings about Writing, Reading, and Learning.* Portsmouth, NH: Heinemann.

Bakhtin, M.M. 1981. *The Dialogic Imagination.* Austin, TX: The University of Texas Press.

Baldwin, R.S., J.C. Ford, and J.E. Readance. 1981. "Teaching Word Connotations: An Alternative Strategy." *Reading World,* (81): 103-108.

Barnes, D. 1992. *From Communication to Curriculum, second edition.* Portsmouth, NH: Heinemann.

Barr, M.A. 1999. *Assessing Literacy with the Learning Record: A Handbook for Teachers K-6.* Portsmouth, NH: Heinemann.

Barr, R., and R. Dreeben. 1991. "Grouping Students for Reading Instruction." In R. Barr, M. Kamil, P. Mosenthall, and P.D. Pearson, Eds., *Handbook of Reading Research,* (Vol. II): 885-910. New York: Longman.

Barrentine, S.J. 1996. "Engaging with Reading through Interactive Read-Alouds." *The Reading Teacher,* (50): 36-43.

Bear, D.R., M. Invernizze, S. Templeton, and F. Johnston. 2000. *Words Their Way: Word Study for Phonics, Vocabulary, and Spelling Instruction, second edition.* Upper Saddle River, NJ: Merrill.

Beck, I.L., and M. McKeown. 1991. "Conditions of Vocabulary Acquisition." In R. Barr, M.L. Kamil, P. Mosenthal, and P.D. Pearson, Eds., *Handbook of Reading Research* (Vol. II): 789-814. New York: Longman.

Beck, I.L., C.A. Perfetti, and M.G. McKeown. 1982. "The Effects of Long-Term Vocabulary Instruction on Lexical Access and Reading Comprehension." *Journal of Educational Psychology* (74): 506-521.

Beck, I.L., R.C. Omanson, and M.G. McKeown. 1982. "An Instructional Redesign of Reading Lessons: Effects on Comprehension. *Reading Research Quarterly* (17): 462-481.

Berkowitz, S.J. 1986. "Effects of Instruction in Text Organization on Sixth-Grade Students' Memory for Expository Reading. *Reading Research Quarterly* (21): 161-178.

Bigelow, B., L. Christensen, S. Karp, B. Miner, and B. Peterson. 1994. *Rethinking Our Classrooms: Teaching for Quality and Justice.* Milwaukee, WI: Rethinking Schools, Ltd.

Billmeyer, R., and M.L. Barton. 1998. *Teaching Reading in the Content Areas: If Not Me, Then Who? second edition.* Aurora, CO: Mid-continent Regional Educational Laboratory.

Booth, David. 1985. "Imaginary Gardens with Real Toads: Reading and Drama in Education." *Theory Into Practice*: 193-198.

Bransford, John D., and Nancy S. McCarrell. 1974. "A Sketch of a Cognitive Approach to Comprehension: Some Thoughts about Understanding What It Means to Comprehend." In W.B. Wiemer, and D.S. Palermo, Eds.,

Cognition and the Symbolic Processes: 189-229. Hillsdale, NJ: Earlbarum.

Bridges, Lois Bird. 1995. *Creating Your Classroom Community.* York, ME: Stenhouse.

Britton, J., T. Burgess, N. Martin, A. McLeod, and H. Rosen. 1975. *The Development of Writing Abilities 11-18.* Houdmills Basingstoke Hampshire and London: MacMillan Education Ltd. Schools of Council Publications.

Bruner, J. 1990. *Acts of Meaning.* Cambridge, MA: Harvard University Press.

Burke, Jim. 1999. *The English Teacher's Companion: A Complete Guide to Classroom, Curriculum, and the Profession.* Portsmouth, NH: Heinemann.

Burns, Olive Ann. 1984. *Cold Sassy Tree.* New York: Ticknor and Fields.

Calkins, L.M. 1986. *The Art of Teaching Writing 2nd ed..* Portsmouth, NH: Heinemann.

Calkins, L.M., K. Montgomery, and D. Santman. 1998. *A Teacher's Guide to Standardized Reading Tests: Knowledge is Power.* Portsmouth, NH: Heinemann.

Calkins, Lucy M. 1991. *Living Between the Lines.* Portsmouth, NH: Heinemann.

Campbell, L., B. Campbell, and D. Dickinson, 1998. *Teaching and Learning Through Multiple Intelligences.* New York: Allyn and Bacon.

Carlson, G.R. 1974. "Literature is." *English Journal,* 63(2), 23-27.

Carr, E., and D. Ogle. 1987. K-W-L Plus: "A Strategy for Comprehension and Summarization."

Charney, Ruth S. 1992. *Teaching Children to Care: Management in the Responsive Classroom.* Northeast Foundation for Children.

Chatton, Barbara and Lynne D. Collins. 1999. *Blurring the Edges: Integrated Curriculum through Writing and Children's Literature.* Portsmouth, NH: Heinemann.

Chew 1985. In chap. 1, p.3

Clay, M.M. 1993. *An Observation Survey of Early Literacy Achievement.* Portsmouth, NH: Heinemann.

Clay, Marie M. 1993. *Reading Recovery: A Guidebook for Teachers in Training.* Portsmouth, NH: Heinemann.

Conroy, Pat. 1996. *Beach Music.* New York: Bantam Books.

Corson, D. 1988. *Oral Language across the Curriculum.* Philadelphia: Multilingual Matters.

Crowhurst, M. 1991. "Interrelationships Between Reading and Writing Persuasive Discourse." *Research in the Teaching of English* (25): 314-338.

Cunningham, P.M. 1995. *Phonics They Use: Words for Reading and Writing, second edition.* New York: HarperCollins.

Dale, F. and J. O'Rourke. 1976. *The Living Word Vocabulary.* Elgin, IL: Dome.

Damasio, Antonio R. 1999. *The Feeling of What Happens.* New York: Harcourt Brace.

Dillard, Annie. 1998. *The Writing Life.* New York: HarperCollins.

Donne, John, and Charles M. Coffin. 1994. *The Complete Poetry and Selected Prose of John Donne.* New York: Modern Library.

Eckhoff, B. 1983. "How Reading Affects Children's Writing." *Language Arts,* (60): 607-616.

Eder, D. 1982. Differences in Communicative Styles Across Ability Groups." In L.C. Wilkinson, Ed., *Communicating in the Classroom.* 245-264. New York: Academic Press

Edmiston, B. 1993. "Going Up the Beanstalk: Discovering Giant Possibilities for Responding to Literature through Drama." In Holland, K.E., A Hungerford, and S.B Ernst, Eds., *Journeying: Children Responding to Literature.* Portsmouth, NH: Heinemann.

Ehri, L.C. 1998. "Grapheme-Phoneme Knowledge is Necessary for Learning to Read Words in English." In *Word Recognition in Beginning Literacy,* edited by J. Metsala and L.C. Ehri. Hillsdale, NJ: Lawrence Erlbaum.

Enciso, P. (Edmiston). 1990. *The Nature of Engagement in Reading Profiles of Three Fifth Graders Engagement Strategies and Stances.* Doctoral dissertation. Columbus, OH: The Ohio State University.

Englert, C.S., and E.H. Hiebert. 1984. "Children's Developing Awareness of Text Structures in Expository Materials." *Journal of Educational Psychology* (76): 75-74.

Englert, C.S., T.E. Raphael, L.M Anderson, H.M. Anthony, and D.D Stevens. 1991. "Making Strategies and Self-Talk Visible: Writing Instruction in Regular and Special Education Classrooms." *American Educational Research Journal* (28): 337-372.

Fielding, L, P. Wilson, and R. Anderson. 1986. "A New Focus on Free Reading. The Role of Trade Books in Reading Instruction." In T. Raphael and R. Reynolds, Eds., *The Contexts of School-Based Literacy:* 149-160. New York: Random House.

Figuroa, R. 1989. "Psychological Testing of Linguistic Minority Students: Knowledge Gaps and Regulations." *Exceptional Children* (56): 145-52.

Flagg, Fannie. 1992. *Fried Green Tomatoes at the Whistle Stop Café.* New York: Fawcett Books.

Fletcher, R. 1993. *What a Writer Needs.* Portsmouth, NH: Heinemann.

Fletcher, Ralph. 1996. *A Writer's Notebook: Unlocking the Writer Within You.* New York: Avon Camelot Book.

Fletcher, Ralph. 1996. *Breathing In, Breathing Out: Keeping a Writer's Notebook.* Portsmouth, NH: Heinemann.

Fletcher, Ralph. 1999. *Live Writing: Breathing Life in to Your Words.* New York: Avon.

Fountas, I.C., and G.S. Pinnell. 1996. *Guided Reading.* Portsmouth, NH: Heinemann.

Fountas, I.C., and G.S. Pinnell. 1999. *Matching Books to Readers: Using Leveled Books in Guided Reading, K–3.* Portsmouth, NH: Heinemann.

Fountas, I.C., and G.S. Pinnell, Eds. 1999. *Voices on Word Matters: Learning About Phonics and Spelling in the*

Literacy Classroom. Portsmouth, NH: Heinemann.

Freeman, E.B., and Diane Goetz Person. 1998. *Connecting Informational Children's Books with Content Area Learning.* Boston: Allyn and Bacon.

Freire, Paulo. 1973. *Education for Critical Consciousness.* New York: Seabury Press.

Freire, Paulo. 1993. *Pedagogy of the Heart.* Unknown.

Freire, Paulo. 1993. *Pedagogy of the Oppressed.* Unknown.

Ganske, Kathy. 2000. *Word Journeys: Assessment-Guided Phonics, Spelling, and Vocabulary Instruction.* New York: The Guilford Press.

Gardner, Howard. 1993. *Frames of Mind: The Theory of Multiple Intelligences.* Basic Books.

George, P., and G. Lawrence. 1982. *Handbook for Middle School Teaching.* Glenview, IL: Scott, Foresman and Company.

Gillet, Jean W., and Charles A Temple. 1982. *Understanding Reading Problems: Assessment and Instruction.* New York: Addison-Wesley.

Good, T.L., and S. Marshall. 1984. "Do Students Learn More in Heterogeneous or Homogeneous Groups." In P.L. Peterson, L.C. Wilkinson and M. Hallinan, Eds., *The Social Context of Instruction.* New York: Academic Press.

Goodman, K.S. 1982. *Language and Literacy: The Selected Writings of Kenneth S. Goodman* Vol. I: Process, Theory, Research. Frederick V. Gollasch, Ed., Boston: Routledge and Kegan Paul.

Goodman, Y.M., D.J. Watson, and C.L. Burke. 1987. *Reading Miscue Inventory: Alternative Procedures.* Katonah, NY: Richard C. Owens.

Graham, Paula W. 1999. *Speaking of Journals.* Honesdale, PA: Boyds Mills Press.

Grant, J. 1997. *Retention and Its Prevention, Making Informed Decision About Individual Children.* Rosemont, NJ: Modern Learning Press.

Graves, D.H. 1992. *Explore Poetry: The Reading/Writing Teacher's Companion.* Portsmouth, NH: Heinemann.

Graves, Donald H. 1983, 1994. *Writing: Teachers and Children at Work.* Portsmouth, NH: Heinemann.

Graves, M., and B. Graves. 1994. *Scaffolding Reading Experiences: Designs for Student Success.* Norwood, MA: Christopher-Gordon.

Guterson, David. 1995. *Snow Falling on Cedars.* New York: Vintage Books/Alfred A. Knopf.

Halliday, M. A. K. 1975. *Learning How to Mean: Explorations in the Development of Language.* London: Edward Arnold.

Hanff, Helene. 1970. *Charing Cross Road.* New York: Moyer Bell Limited/Viking.

Hansen, J., T. Newkirk, and D. Graves. 1985. *Breaking Ground: Teachers Related Reading and Writing in the Elementary School.* Portsmouth, NH: Heinemann.

Harp, B. 2000. *The Handbook of Literacy Assessment and Evaluation.* Norwood, MA: Christopher-Gordon.

Harvey, Stephanie, and Anne Goudvis. 2000. *Strategies That Work: Teaching Comprehension to Enhance Understanding.* York, ME: Stenhouse.

Harwayne, Shelley. 2000. *Lifetime Guarantees: Toward Ambitious Literacy Teaching.* Portsmouth, NH: Heinemann.

Harwayne, Shelley. 1992. *Lasting Impressions: Weaving Literature into the Writing Workshop.* Portsmouth, NH: Heinemann.

Heard, Georgia. 1998. *Awakening the Heart: Exploring Poetry in Elementary and Middle School.* Portsmouth, NH: Heinemann.

Heard, Georgia, and Lucy Calkins.1998. *For the Good of the Earth and Sun: Teaching Poetry.* Portsmouth, NH: Heinemann.

Heathcote, D. 1983. "Learning, Knowing and Language in Drama." *Language Arts,* (60): 695-701.

Heathcote, D., and Herbert, P. 1985. "A Drama of Learning: Mantle of the Expert." *Theory Into Practice,* (24): 151-157.

Heckleman, R.G. 1966. "Using the Neurological Impress Method of Remedial Reading Instruction. *Academic Therapy Quarterly* (1): 235-239.

Helmes, C.T. 1989. "Grade Level Retention Effects: A Meta-Analysis of Research Studies." In L.A. Shepard and M.I. Smith. Eds. *Flunking Grades: Research and Policies on Retention.* London, England: Falmer Press.

Henderson, E.H. 1990. *Teaching Spelling, second edition.* Boston: Houghton Mifflin Company.

Herber, H.L. 1978. *Teaching Reading in Content Areas, second edition.* Upper Saddle River, NJ: Prentice Hall.

Herman, P.A., and J. Dole. 1988. "Theory and Practice in Vocabulary Learning and Instruction." *The Elementary School Journal,* (89): 41-52.

Hiebert, E.H. 1983. "An Examination of Ability Grouping for Reading Instruction." *Reading Research Quarterly,* (18): 231-255.

Hill, P.W., and C.A.M. Crevola. 1997. *The Literacy Challenge in Australian Primary Schools.* Incorporated Association of Registered Teachers of Victoria: Seminar Series No. 69.

Hindley, Joanne. 1996. *In the Company of Children.* York, ME: Stenhouse.

Hindley, Joanne.1998. *Inside Reading and Writing Workshops* videotape. York, ME: Stenhouse.

Holdaway, D. 1979. *The Foundations of Literacy.* Sydney: Ashton Scholastic, also Portsmouth, NH: Heinemann.

Holt, John 1993. "How Children Learn." Cited in J. Canfield, and M.V. Hansen, *Chicken Soup for the Soul.* Deerfield Beach, FL: Heath Communications.

Huck, C.S., S. Helper, and J. Hickman. 1993. *Children's Literature in the Elementary School.* Forth Worth: Harcourt Brace Jovanovich.

Irwin, J.W., and I. Baker. 1989. *Promoting Active Reading Comprehension Strategies.* Englewood Cliffs, NJ: Prentice-Hall.

Jenkins, J.R., M. Stein, and K. Wysocki. 1984. "Learning Vocabulary through Reading." *American Educational Research Journal*, (21): 767-787.

Jewell, T.A., and, D. Pratt. 1999. "Literature Discussions in the Primary Grades: Children's Thoughtful Discourse about Books and What Teachers Can Do to Make It Happen." *The Reading Teacher*, (52): 842-849.

Johnson, D.D. and P.D. Pearson. 1984. *Teaching Reading Vocabulary, second edition.* New York: Holt, Rinehart and Winston.

Jones, B.F., J. Pierce, and B. Hunter. 1988-1989. "Teaching Students to Construct Graphic Representations." *Educational Leadership*, (46): *4j, 20-25.*

Juel, C. 1988. "Learning to Read and Write: A Longitudinal Study of 54 Children from First through Fourth Grades." *Journal of Educational Psychology,* (80): 437-447.

Juel, C., P.L. Griffith, and P.B. Gough. 1986. "Acquisition of Literacy: A Longitudinal Study of Children in First and Second Grade. *Journal of Educational Psychology,* (78): 243-255.

Keeler, B. and K. Goldner. 1995. "Keeping a River Healthy." *Take Care of Yourself,* (Volume 6, No. 4): 8-15. *Images.* D.C. Heath and Company..

Keneally, Thomas 1993. *Schindler's List.* New York: Touchstone Books.

Kennedy, X.J. 1997. *An Introduction to Poetry.* New York: Addison-Wesley.

Langer, Judith. 1990. "Understanding Literature." *Language Arts,* (Vol. 67): 812-816.

Lapp, D., J. Flood., and N. Farnan. 1996. *Content Area Reading and Learning: Instructional Strategies.* Second Edition. Boston: Allyn and Bacon.

Lehman, B.A., and P.L . Scharer. 1996. "Reading Alone, Talking Together: The Role of Discussion in Developing Literary Awareness," *The Reading Teacher,* (50): 26-35.

Lehr, S., and D.L. Thompson. 2000. "The Dynamic Nature of Response: Children Reading and Responding to Maniac Magee and The Friendship." *The Reading Teacher,* (534): 480-493.

Lesgold, A.M., L.B. Resnick, and K. Hammond. 1985. "Learning to Read: A Longitudinal Study of Word Skill Development in Two Curricula." In G. E. Mackinnon and T.G. Waller, Eds., *Reading Research: Advances in Theory and Practice* (Vol. 4): 107-138. New York: Academic Press.

Lindfors, Judith W. 1999. *Children's Inquiry.* New York: Teachers College Press.

Lowry, Lois. 1998. *Looking Back: A Book of Memories.* Boston: Houghton Mifflin Company.

Lukens, Rebecca J. 1999. *A Critical Handbook of Children's Literature.* New York: Addison-Wesley.

MacLure, M. 1988. "Introduction Oracy: Current Trends, in Context." In M. Mact-Ure, T, Phillips, and A. Wilkinson, Eds., *Oracy Matters.* Philadelphia, PA and Milton Keynes, England: Open University Press.

Marland, M. 1977. *Language across the Curriculum.* London: Heinemann Educational Books.

McCormick, S. 1999. *Instructing Students Who Have Literacy Problems, Third Edition.* Upper Saddle River, NJ: Merrill.

McWhorter, John. 2000. *Spreading the Word: American Language and Dialect.*

Meek, Margaret. 1988. *How Texts Teach What Readers Learn.* London: Thimble Press.

Meyer, B.J.F., and E. Rice. 1984. "The Structure of Text." In P.D. Pearson, Ed., *Handbook of Reading Research* 319-352. New York: Longman.

Meyer, B.J.F., D. Brandt and, G. Bluth. 1980. "Use of Top-Level Structure in Text: Key for Reading Comprehension of Ninth-Grade Students." *Reading Research Quarterly,* (16): 72-103.

Mooney, Margaret. 1988. *Developing Life Long Readers.* Katonah, NY: Richard C. Owen.

Mooney, Margaret. 1990. *Reading to, with, and by Children.* Katonah, NH: Richard C. Owen.

Murray, Donald M. 1968. *A Writer Teaches Writing.* Boston: Houghton Mifflin.

Nagy, W. and R.C. Anderson. 1984. "How Many Words Are There in Printed School English? *Reading Research Quarterly,* (19): 304-330.

Nagy, W., and R.C. Anderson. 1987. "Learning Word Meanings from Context during Normal Reading." *American Educational Research Journal,* (24): *237-270.*

Nagy, W.E. 1988. *Teaching Vocabulary to Improve Reading Comprehension.* Newark, DE: International Reading Association.

Nagy, W.E., and P.A. Herman. 1987. "Depth and Breadth of Vocabulary Knowledge: Implications for Acquisition and Instruction." In M.G. McKeown and M.E. Curtis, Eds., *The Nature of Vocabulary Acquisition.* Hillsdale, NJ: Erlbaum.

New Standards Primary Literacy Committee. 1999. *Reading Grade by Grade Writing: Primary Literacy Standards for Kindergarten through Third Grade.* Washington, DC: National Center on Education and the Economy.

Ogle, D. 1986. "K-W-L: A Teaching Model That Develops Active Reading of Expository Text." *The Reading Teacher,* 39(6), 564-570.

Padgett, Ron. 1987. *The Teachers and Writers Handbook of Poetic Forms.* New York: Teachers and Writers.

Palincsar, A.S., and A.L. Brown. 1984. "Reciprocal Teaching of Comprehension-Fostering and Monitoring Activities." *Cognition and Instruction* (1): 117-175.

Palincsar, A.S., and A.L. Brown. 1986. "Interactive Teaching to Promote Independent Learning from Text." *The Reading Teacher:* 771-777.

Paris, S., M. Lipson, and K. Wixson. 1993. "Becoming a Strategic Reader." *Contemporary Educational Psychology,* (8): 293-316.

Pearson, P., and L. Fielding. 1991. "Comprehension Instruction." In R. Barr, M.L. Kamil, P.B. Mosenthal, and

P.D. Pearson, Eds., *Handbook of Reading Research* (Vol. II): 815-860. New York, Longman.

Performance Standards: English Language of Arts, Mathematics, Science, Applied Learning, Volume 1: Elementary School. 1997. National Center on Education and the Economy and the University of Pittsburgh.

Peterson, R. and M. Eeds. 1990. *Grand Conversations: Literature Groups in Action.* New York: Scholastic, Inc.

Pinnell, G.S. and I.C. Fountas. 2001. *Leveled Books for Readers: Grades 3-6.* Portsmouth, NH: Heinemann.

Pinnell, G.S. and I.C. Fountas. 1998. *Word Matters: Teaching Phonics and Spelling in the Reading/Writing Classroom.* Portsmouth, NH: Heinemann.

Pinnell, G.S., J.J. Pikulski, K.K. Wixson, J.R. Campbell, R.B. Gough, and A.S. Beatty. 1995. *Listening to Children Read Aloud: Data from NAEP's Integrated Reading Performance Record IRPR) at Grade 4.* Report No. 23-FR-04 Prepared by Educational Testing Service under contract with the National Center for Education Statistics, Office of Educational Research and Improvement, U.S. Department of Education. p. 15.

Pittelman, S.D., J.E. Heimlich, R.L. Berglund, and M.P. French. 1991. *Semantic Feature Analysis: Classroom Applications.* Newark, DE: International Reading Association.

Pressley, M. 1998. *Reading Instruction That Works: The Case for Balanced Teaching.* New York: The Guildford Press.

Raban. 1999. "Language and Literacy as Epistemology." In J.S. Gaffney and B.J. Askew, Eds., *Stirring the Waters: The Influence of Marie Clay,* 99-112. Portsmouth, NH: Heinemann.

Raphael, T. 1982. "Question-Answering Strategies for Children." *The Reading Teacher,* (36): 186-190.

Raphael, T.E., and K.H. Au, (Eds.). 1996. *Literature-Based Instruction: Reshaping the Curriculum.* Norwood, MA: Christopher-Gordon.

Reardon, J. 1990. "Putting Reading Tests in Their Place." *The New Advocate,* (3): 29-37.

Reutzel, R., and R.B. Cooter. 1991. "Organizing for Effective Instruction: The Reading Workshop." *The Reading Teacher* (44): 548-554.

Roderick, M. 1994. "Grade Retention and School Dropout: Investigation of the Association." *American Educational Research Journal* (31)(4): 729-759.

Rogers, T., and C. O'Neill. 1993. "Creating Multiple Worlds: Drams, language, and Literary Response." In Newell, G.E., Durst, R.K., Eds., *Exploring Texts: The Role of Discussion and Writing in the Teaching and Learning of Literature.* Norwood, MA: Christopher-Gordon.

Rogoff, B. 1990. *Apprenticeship in Thinking: Cognitive Development in Social Context.* New York: Oxford University Press.

Rosenblatt, Louise M. 1938. *Literature as Exploration.* New York: Noble and Noble Publishers.

Rosenblatt, Louise M. 1978. *The Reader the Text the Poem.* Southern Illinois University Press.

Ross, Elinor Parry. 1996. *The Workshop Approach: A Framework for Literacy.* Norwood, MA: Christopher-Gordon.

Routman, R. 1991. *Invitations.* Portsmouth, NH: Heinemann.

Routman, R. 2000. *Conversations: Strategies for Teaching, Learning, and Evaluating.* Portsmouth, NH: Heinemann.

Ruddell, M.R. 1993. *Teaching Content Reading and Writing.* Boston: Allyn and Bacon.

Rumelhart, D.E. 1977. "Toward an Interactive Model of Reading. In S. Dornio (Ed.), *Attention and Performance* vol. 6. Hillsdale, NJ: Erlbaum.

Rumelhart, D.E. 1982. "Schemata: The Building Blocks of Cognition." In J. Guthrie (Ed.), *Comprehension and Teaching: Research Reviews* 3-26. Newark, DE: International Reading Association.

Rylant, Cynthia. 1989. *But I'll Be Back Again.* New York: Orchard Books.

Sampson, M., M.B. Sampson, and R Van Allen. 1995. *Pathways to Literacy: Process Transactions.* Ft. Worth, TX: Harcourt Brace.

Samuels, S.J. 1979. "The Method of Repeated Readings." *Reading Teacher,* (32): 403-408.

Shepherd, L.A. and M.L. Smith. 1990. "Synthesis of Research on Grad Retention." *Educational Leadership.* London, England: Falmer Press.

Short K.G., J.C. Harste, and C. Burke. 1996. *Creating Classrooms for Authors and Inquirers, second edition.* Edition. Portsmouth, NH: Heinemann.

Shreve, Anita. 1999. *Fortune's Rocks.* New York: Little, Brown, and Company.

Slavin, R.E. 1990. *Cooperative Learning: Theory, Research, and Practice.* Englewood Cliffs, NJ: Prentice-Hall.

Smiley, Jane. 1996. *A Thousand Acres.* Ivy Books.

Smith, Frank. 1978. *Reading without Nonsense.* New York: Holt, Rinehart, and Winston.

Smith, Frank. 1988. *Understanding Reading, fourth edition.* Hillsdale, NJ: Erlbaum.

Snow, C.E., M.S. Burns, and P. Griffin (Eds.). 1998. *Preventing Reading Difficulties in Young Children.* Washington, D.C.: National Academy Press.

Sorenson, A.B., and M.Hallinan. 1984. "Effects of Race on Assignment to Ability Groups." In P.L. Peterson, L.C, Wilkinson, and M. Hallinan, Eds., *The Social Context of Instruction.* New York: Academic Press.

Sorenson, A.B., and M. Hallinan. 1986. "Effects of Ability Grouping on Growth in Academic Achievement." *American Educational Research Journal,* (23): 519-542.

Stanovich K.E. 1985. "Explaining the Variance in Reading Ability in Terms of Psychological Processes: What Have We Learned?" *Annals of Dyslexia,* (35): 67-96.

Stauffer, R.G. 1970. *The Language Experience Approach to the Teaching of Reading.* New York: Harper and Row.

Stauffer, R. 1975. *Directing the Reading-Thinking Process.* New York: Harper and Row.

Stein, N., and C. Glenn. 1979. "An Analysis of Story Comprehension in Elementary School Children." In R. Freedle Ed.), *New Directions in Discourse Processing.* 153-205. Norwood, NJ: Ablex.

Strickland, K., and J. Strickland. 2000. *Making Assessment Elementary.* Portsmouth, NH: Heinemann

Taylor, B.M., and R.W. Beach. 1984. "The Effects of Text Structure Instruction on Middle-Grade Students' Comprehension and Production of Expository Text. *Reading Research Quarterly*, (19): 134-146.

Taylor, K., and S. Walton. 1998. *Children at the Center: A Workshop Approach to Standardized Test Preparation, K-8.* Portsmouth, NH: Heinemann.

Taylor, W.L. 1953. "Cloze Procedure: A New Tool for Measuring Readability. *Journalism Quarterly*, (30): 415-433.

Templeton, S., and D.R. Bear. 1992. *Development of Orthographic Knowledge and the Foundation of Literacy:* A *Memorial Festschrift for Edmund H. Henderson.* Hillsdale, NJ: Lawrence Erlbaum.

Tierney, R.J., J.E. Readence, and E.K. Dishner, 1995. *Reading Strategic and Practices: A Compendium, fourth edition.* Boston: Allyn and Bacon.

Topping K., and G.A. Lindsay. 1992. "The Structure and Development of the Paired Reading Technique." *Journal of Research in Reading* (15): 120-136. A Review of the Literature on Paired Reading.

Topping, K. 1987a. "Paired Reading: A Powerful Technique for Parent Use." *The Reading Teacher* (40): 608-614. A description of the Paired Reading strategy, with the focus on parents working with children.

Tucker, Nicholas. 1981. *The Child and the Book: A Psychological and Literary Exploration.* Cambridge, MA: Cambridge University Press.

Tunnell, Michael, O. and James S. Jacobs. 1989. "Using Real Books: Research Findings on Literature-Based Reading Instruction." *The Reading Teacher*, (Vol. 42.): 470-477.

Vacca, R.T., and J.L. Vacca. 1999. *Content Area Reading: Literacy and Learning across the Curriculum, sixth edition.* New York: Longman.

Vellutino, F.R., and M.B. Denckla. 1991. "Cognitive and Neuropsychological Foundations of Word Identification in Poor and Normally Developing Readers." In R. Barr, M.L. Kamil, P. Mosenthal, and P.D. Pearson, Eds., *Handbook of Reading Research* (Vol. II): 571-608. New York: Longman.

Vellutino, F.R. and D.B. Scanlon. 1987. "Phonolgical Coding, Phonological Awareness, and Reading Ability: Evidence from Longitudinal and Experimental Study." *Merrill Palmer Quarterly*, (33): 321-363.

Vygotsky, L.S. 1978. *Mind in Society: The Development of Higher Psychological Processes.* Cambridge, MA: Harvard University Press.

Vygotsky, L.S. 1986. *Thought and Language.* Cambridge, MA: MIT Press.

Weaver, C. 1994. *Understanding Whole Language: From Principles to Practice, second edition.* Portsmouth, NH: Heinemann.

Wells, R. 1996. *The Divine Secrets of the Ya-Ya Sisterhood.* New York: HarperCollins.

Welty, Eudora, and Peggy Penshaw, Eds. 1984. *Conversations with Eudora Welty.* University Press of Mississippi.

Wertsch. 1985. "Vygotsky and the Social Formation of Mind." Cambridge, MA: Harvard University Press.

White, T.G., M.F. Graves, and W.H. Slater. 1990. "Growth of Reading Vocabulary in Diverse Elementary Schools: Decoding and Word Meaning." *Journal of Educational Psychology*, (82): 281-290.

Wilde, S. 2000. *Miscue Analysis Made Easy: Building on Student Strengths.* Portsmouth, NH: Heinemann.

Wilhelm, J.D., and B. Edmiston. 1998. *Imagining to Learn: Inquiry, Ethics, and Integration through Drama.* Portsmouth, NH: Heinemann.

Wilkinson, A. M., with contributions by A. Davies and D. Atkinson. 1965. *Spoken English.* Birmingham, England: University of Birmingham.

Wilkinson, A. M. 1970. "The Concept of Oracy." *English Journal*, (59): 70-77.

Wilkinson, A. M. 1971. *The Foundations of Language: Talking and Reading in Young Children.* Oxford: Oxford University Press.

Wilkinson, A. M. 1975. *Language and Education.* Oxford: Oxford University Press.

Williams, Miller. 1986. *Patterns of Poetry: An Encyclopedia of Forms.* Baton Rouge: Louisiana State University Press.

Winokur, Jon. 1999. *Advice to Writers: A Compendium of Quotes, Anecdotes, and Writerly Wisdom from a Dazzling Array of Literary Lights.* New York: Pantheon.

Wolf, S. 1993. "What's in a Name?: Labels and Literacy in Readers' Theatre." *The Reading Teacher*, (46 7): 540-545.

Wood, David. 1988. *How Children Think and Learn: The Social Contexts of Cognitive Development.* Cambridge, MA: Basil Blackwell, Inc.

Young, T., and S. Vardell. 1993. "Weaving Readers' Theatre and Nonfiction into the Curriculum." *The Reading Teacher*, (46 5): 396-406.

Zutell, Jerry. 1996. "The Directed Spelling Thinking Activity (DSTA): Providing an Effective Balance in Word Study Instruction." *The Reading Teacher* (50 2): *98-108.*

Zutell, Jerry. 1999. "Sorting It Out through Word Sorts." *Voices on Word Matters: Learning about Phonics and Spelling in the Literacy Classroom.* Portsmouth, NH: Heinemann.

Index